# Michigan Place Names

ST. CLAIR
St. Clair Hardware Store

# GREAT LAKES BOOKS

# Michigan Place Names

## The History of the Founding and the Naming of More Than Five Thousand Past and Present Michigan Communities

Walter Romig, L.H.D.

Foreword by Larry B. Massie

"A People That Take No Pride in the Noble Achievements of Remote Ancestors Will Never Achieve Anything Worthy to be Remembered with Pride by Remote Generations"—Macaulay.

WAYNE STATE UNIVERSITY PRESS DETROIT 1986

Originally published by Walter Romig, 979 Lakepointe Road, Grosse Pointe, Michigan 48230. Great Lakes Books edition 

---

**Library of Congress Cataloging-in-Publication Data**

Romig, Walter, 1905–
Michigan place names.

(Great Lakes books)
Reprint. Originally published: Grosse Pointe, Mich.: W. Romig, 1973.
Bibliography: p.
Includes index.
1. Names, Geographical—Michigan—Dictionaries.
2. Michigan—History, Local—Miscellanea. I. Title.
II. Series.
F564.R6 1986 917.74'003'21 86-15858
ISBN 0-8143-1837-1
ISBN 0-8143-1838-X (pbk.)

---

Illustrations for this edition are taken from F. W. Beers *County Atlas* series, published from 1875–1879; the J. Belden & Co. *Illustrated Historical Atlas* series, published from 1855–1879; the Geo. A. Ogle *Standard Atlas of Macomb County*, published in 1895; and the Everts and Stewart *Combination Atlas* series, published from 1855–1879, all courtesy of the Burton Historical Collection, Detroit Public Library.

CONTENTS

## FOREWORD TO THE GREAT LAKES BOOKS EDITION

Take M 50 east from Tecumseh. Slow down for the villages of Ridgeway and Britton. Admire the old Greek Revival mill at Dundee, and then about halfway to Monroe pass the Ida Maybee Road. You might wonder, as I did, who Ida Maybee was and what she did to get a road named after her. I pictured her as a prim but beloved teacher who had labored in the same one-room school for half a century, a gray-haired pedagogue who wept when the County Road Commissioner honored her long public service before an assemblage of her former students. Alas, a glance at the map dashed my scenario to bits. The little towns of Ida to the south and Maybee to the north are linked, quite naturally, by the Ida Maybee Road. But like Mark Twain's hypnotic "Punch, Brothers, Punch" I could not get the melodious Ida Maybee out of my mind. I had to find out more about those names. There was only one place to go—Walter Romig's *Michigan Place Names.* Ida, I quickly learned, drew its name from Ida M. Taylor and Maybee from Abram Maybee. The discovery of these more forgettable names relieved my Ida Maybee obsession.

If you have ever been perplexed by the origin or meaning of a Michigan place name, confounded by a city's founding date, or confused by an historic reference to a place no longer on the map, you need Romig's indispensable reference tool. Romig spent a decade researching hundreds of printed sources, visiting archives and historical collections, and interviewing scores of knowledgeable authorities in order to compile his concise histories of more than five thousand present and defunct Michigan communities.

*Michigan Place Names* is far more than a compilation of geographical facts, however. The book is a key that unlocks the romantic story of Michigan's geographical origins. Like a gigantic patchwork quilt, bits and snippets of Michigan's colorful heritage adorn the roadsides across the state. From Ahmeek to Zilwaukie, to say nothing of Hell, Hooker, and Home, community names preserve the stories of Indian chiefs, famous statesmen, pioneer settlers, ethnic groups, world events, far-off battlefields, and half-forgotten historical episodes.

Ahmeek, in Keweenaw County, Romig informs us, is Chippewa for "beaver." Zilwaukie was named in 1855 by imaginative, if slightly dishonest, millowners who sought to lure German immigrant workmen bound for Milwaukee. Livingston County's Hell, according to local tradition, earned its title as a result of considerable brawling with the Indians there. Hooker, a defunct Van Buren County post office, to my disappointment simply got its name from the Civil War general Fighting Joe Hooker. And while the Wizard might have taught Dorothy that "there's no place like home," Romig locates Home in three counties.

Romig's research on the derivation of Michigan place names particularly intrigues me. As might be expected, many towns draw their titles from biographical sources. Town founders not only immodestly commemorated their own lives but those of Indian chiefs—Pontiac, Petosky, and Pokagon; explorers—Cadillac, Charlevoix, and Marquette; presidents—Jackson, Buchanan, and Lincoln; and governors—Bagley, Baldwin, and Cass. Washington Irving contributed his cognomen to a tiny settlement in Barry County; Rudyard Kipling's surname survives in a Chippewa County town, although neither ever visited the state.

Other less famous personages also achieved a degree of cartographic immortality. Pickford in Chippewa County honors the name of the community's first settler and postmaster, Canadian Charles W. Pickford, not actress Mary Pickford, as residents are wont to tell inquisitive tourists. Matthew Vassar lent his name to a New York college, and when he loaned money to get a Tuscola County village started, grateful citizens also named it after him.

Current maps have deleted hundreds of Michigan ghost towns, but their apparitions live on in Romig's compendium. The former Sugar Island settlement of Willwalk honored the name of its pioneer storekeeper, William Walker. Midland County's saccharine-sounding Jam, named for the initials of its first postmaster, James A. Murphy, began its short-lived existence in 1894. When village authorities suggested Viola or Olney as a name for their Midland County community in 1880, both were already taken. The post office department, however, took the liberty of amalgamating the two into Volney.

Historic events provided names for other communities. The Alamo is not only remembered in Texas but in a Kalamazoo County township and village. A preponderance of "Black Abolitionist" voters helped an Ingham County Civil War era ghost town earn the appellation Africa. Some Kent County settlers, enthusiastic over Secretary of State William Seward's recent land acquisition, titled their community Alaska in 1868. A tragic shipwreck off the coast of South Haven in 1896 inspired Allegan County residents to enshrine the vessel's name, Chicora, on the Michigan map. Readers will have the adventure of discovering their own favorites—come to think of it, there once was a town named Adventure in Ontonogon County. You will find, as I have, that whether you are doing historical research, tracking down ancestors, or simply driving along past a country crossroad, you will want *Michigan Place Names* within easy reach.

Larry B. Massie

## FOREWORD TO THE FIRST EDITION

As the Documentation section of this volume indicates, the data were principally drawn from state, county, and local histories; diaries, journals, manuscripts (some holograph), and biographies; periodicals and newspapers; postal and census records; correspondence with state, county, and local officials, with editors, historical societies, and historians; genealogies and cemetery records; histories of such community-fostering industries as lumbering, mining, and railroading; maps, land titles, and plat books.

In the post-entry references in the body of the book, pages are not always cited, for (1) in many sources (e.g. The Gazeteer) their contents are entered in one straight alphabetical order and so are simple for anyone to locate, and (2) in others, our data has been brought together from two or more pages in the source; but our references even here are ample whether the reader seeks verification or amplification.

As to scope: this treatise is comprehensive rather than selective. No Michigan community, past or present, has been intentionally omitted.

No introductory essay on any of the factors which were so largely responsible for the full settlement of the state prefaces this volume, such as the ethnic (French, Scandinavian, Polish, German, etc.); or the influx of settlers from other states (New York, via the Erie Canal, in particular); or from the rapid rise and spread of such early industries as lumbering and mining; or from the location of roads, rail or highway, especially when they formed junctions; or from waterways which, besides transportation, first provided the power source for food and shelter in grist mills and sawmills; or communities founded as havens by particular religious groups; or from wars through which veterans were given land grants which in some instances they helped mold into communities, not a few of which remain.

Nor is the work prefaced by an onomastic study dedicated to the fountainheads of the place names, such as the Indian (Alcona, Menominee, Alpena, Tahquamenon, etc.), or on those who influenced such selections (Schoolcraft, Longfellow, etc.); or on the awareness of our pioneers to world events (Emmett, Almont, Ypsilanti, Waterloo, Marengo, Kossuth, Borodino, Austerlitz, etc.); or of their classical interests (Adrian, Athens, Leonidas, Homer, Sparta, Ceresco, etc.); or of their remembrance of their native areas, whether in America (Keene, Clarion, Sidney, Utica, Akron, Augusta, Bainbridge, Brighton, etc.), or abroad, such as Canada (Ayr, Beaverton, Fenwick, etc.), France (Sans Souci, Ecorse, Epoufette, Grand Marais, etc.), Scotland (Argyle, Bruce, Dundee, Montrose, Kinross, etc.), Ireland (Avoca, Boyne City, Grattan, Parnell, etc.), Scandinavia (Wainola, Suomi, Skanee, Askel, Wasas, Toivola, Aura, Tapiola, etc.), Poland (Posen, Cracow, Sobieski, etc.), Germany (Berlin, Westphalia, Hamburg, Frankenmuth, Waldenburg, etc.), England (Bath, Birmingham, Brampton, etc.), Holland (Borculo, Zeeland, Cronje, Nordeloos, etc.), Switzerland (Berne, Engadine, etc.), Balkan (Praha, Traunik, Banat, etc.); or our early settlers' loyalty to their presidents (Washington, Jefferson, Monroe, Buchanan, etc.), their military leaders (Warren, Meade, Grant, Sherman, Wayne, Burnside, etc.), their governors (Cass, Croswell, Luce, Bliss, Pingree, Bagley, Baldwin, Crapo, etc.); their pride in their young nation's history (Alamo, Mt. Vernon, Lexington, Monticello, Perry, Santiago, Shiloh, Sigsbee, etc.); their gratitude to the men who first erected the cross in the wilderness (Allouez, Marquette, Charlevoix, Galien, etc.); their affection for their own wives and children (Clifford, Christiana, Ann Arbor, Lyle, Charlotte, Eloise, Ada, Marysville, etc.); their respect for local Indian chieftains (Petoskey, Tecumseh, Pontiac, Cobmoosa, Mecosta, etc.); their honoring of men of letters (Dryden, Kipling, Carleton, Irving, Hemans, etc.); their salute to their initial industries, such as lumbering (Spalding, Atkinson, Beiter, Stronach, Blendon, Buckley, etc.), and mining (Toltec, Amasa, Bessemer, Pewabic, Vulcan, etc.), and railroading (Agnew, Alden, Annpere, Alanson, Ashley, etc.); their devotion to their religious beliefs (Bethany, Alverno, Olivet, Isadore, Wesley, Brethren, Gilead, Beulah, etc.).

For, from the merely indicated example of just these two aspects, it is evident that many definitive studies in Michigan history can and, hopefully, will be made through the years based largely upon this work.

To the individuals named in the Documentation, as well as to all of the many more, who counseled or otherwise furthered this work, appreciation is here extended.

Nearly ten years were devoted to the researching and the writing of this book, and it is hoped that the reader will consider the decade well spent.

Walter Romig

*The Eighty-Four Counties of Michigan*

Key: *S*, suggested by Schoolcraft; *C*, counties named after members of President Andrew Jackson's Cabinet; *underlined*, original names.

ANN ARBOR

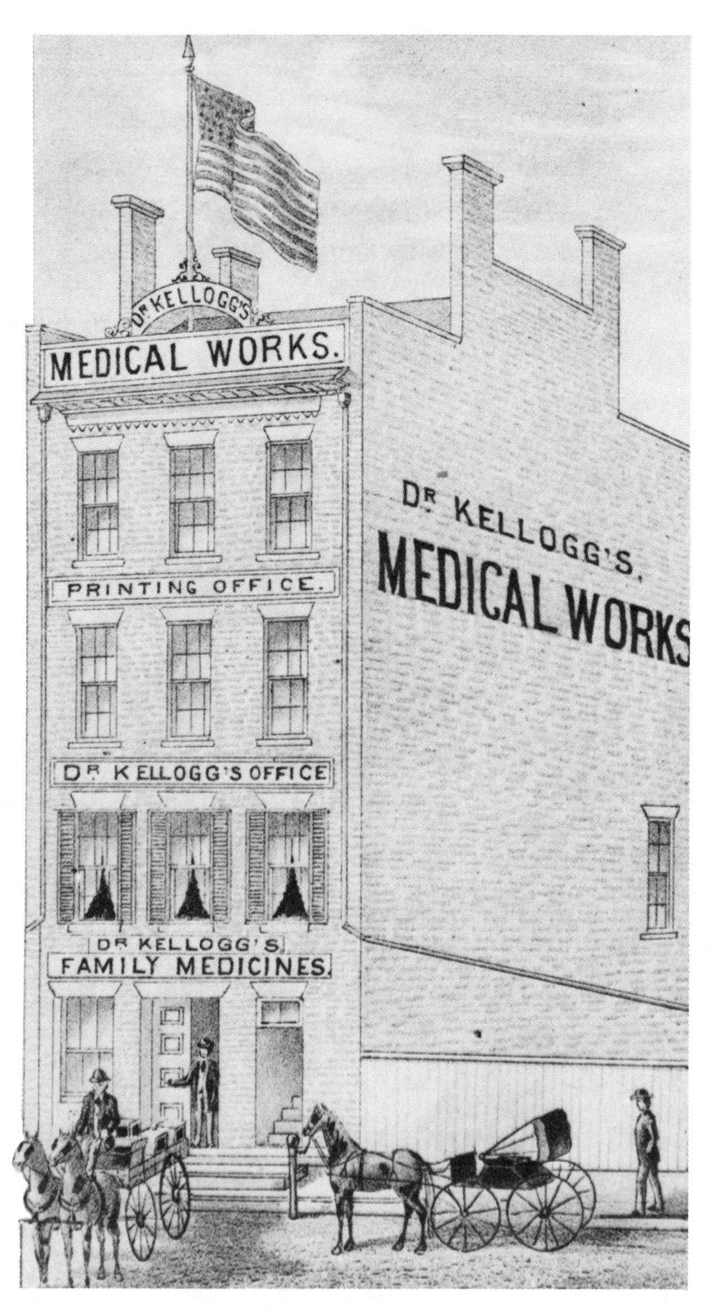
DR KELLOGG'S
MEDICAL WORKS.
PRINTING OFFICE.
DR KELLOGG'S OFFICE
DR KELLOGG'S
FAMILY MEDICINES.
DR KELLOGG'S
MEDICAL WORKS

ANN ARBOR

**AABEC**, Antrim County: Curran Everts became the first postmaster of this rural post office on April 19, 1895, the office operating until May 22, 1896 [GSM 1897; PO Archives].

**AARONVILLE**, Macomb County: a rural post office, opened on March 16, 1858, with Henry Conner as its first postmaster, but the office was closed the following May 29 [PO Archives].

**AARWOOD**, Kalkaska County: a lumber settlement on the Torch River, with a station on the Grand Rapids & Indiana Railroad; storekeeper Allan F. Little became its first postmaster on Sept. 7, 1887, the office operating until Jan. 31, 1901 [GSM 1889; PO Archives].

**ABBOTT**, Mason County: William H. Perring became the first postmaster of this rural post office on Oct. 30, 1884, but the office was closed on Sept. 14, 1892 [GSM 1893; PO Archives].

**ABBOTTSFORD**, St. Clair County: in 1816, Ignace Morass built a sawmill here on Mill Creek; it was bought and rebuilt by James Abbott who also bought the grist mill built by Judge Zephaniah W. Bunce; the settlement around these mills here in Clyde Township was named for Mr. Abbott; Jabin Cronk became its first postmaster on May 21, 1892, the office operating until March 14, 1942 [MPH 6:414 Andreas; PO Archives].

**ABBOTTS MILLS**, Berrien County: although on Farmer's map of 1836, little is known about this settlement, Lucius Abbott (1791-1863), who retired as an army surgeon in 1834, was one of its proprietors [Mich Hist 43:288, 434 1959].

**ABITOSSE**, Gogebic County: a station on the Duluth, South Shore & Atlantic Railroad, four miles from Thomaston, in 1910 [GSM 1911].

**ABRONIA**, Allegan County: Joseph Sawyer became the first postmaster of West Watson, named from its location in Watson Township, on April 14, 1871, with the name changed to Abronia on Oct. 2 of the same year, the office operating until June 30, 1902 [Blinn; PO Archives].

**ABSCOTA**, Calhoun County. See Wet Prairie.

**ACHILL**, Roscommon County: a rural post office in the southeastern part of the county, opened on Dec. 10, 1878, with Charles W. Meyers as its first postmaster, but the office was closed on June 11, 1884 [GSM 1885; PO Archives].

**ACKERSON**, Jackson County: a flag station on the C.N. Railroad, in Napoleon Township; Fayette M. Bromley became its first postmaster on Dec. 9, 1898; the office was closed on Feb. 17, 1899; with tobacconist David E. Gillett as postmaster, it was restored on Nov. 20, 1899, operating until Aug. 30, 1902 [GSM 1901-03; PO Archives].

**ACME**, Grand Traverse County: L. S. Hoxie, a native of Saratoga County, N.Y., came here in 1864, bought land and platted the village; his son, Albertus T. Hoxie, became its first postmaster on June 10, 1869; the office was later closed but has been in operation again since 1951; a station on the Chicago & Western Michigan (now Pere Marquette) Railroad [Traverse].

**ACORN**, Hillsdale County. See Shadyside.

**ACTON**, Iosco County: on April 13, 1880, storekeeper Albert W. Rikely became the first postmaster of this rural post office on Johnson's Creek, in Burleigh Township, the office operating until July 30, 1883 [GSM 1881-85; PO Archives].

**ADA**, Kent County: Rix Robinson (1792-1875), from Massachusetts, built his trading post near here in 1821 and made the first land purchase in 1833; township and town were named for Ada Smith, daughter of Sidney Smith, who became the first postmaster on Jan. 5, 1837; Lucius B. Lyon was called the founder of the village; the Detroit & Milwaukee Railroad came through in 1853 and made it a station; G. A. Dalrymple and H. F. Dunn recorded their plat of the village on Sept. 4, 1857; a bronze tablet erected here by the county refers to Rix Robinson as the Founder of Western Michigan [Chapman; Dillenback; Mich Hist 6:277 1922].

**ADAIR**, St. Clair County: although much of the land here in Casco Township was taken up by 1836, actual settlement did not begin until 1840; a station on the Michigan Central Railroad, it was named by the English contractor who constructed this branch of the line; Albert Blank became its first postmaster on Dec. 7, 1875 [Jenks; PO Archives].

**ADALASKA**, Presque Isle County: hotelman Thomas E. Shaw became the first postmaster of this sawmill settlement on Aug. 18, 1893 [GSM 1895].

**ADAMS**, Calhoun County: a station on a branch of the Michigan Central Railroad, six miles south of Battle Creek, in 1894 [GSM 1895].

**ADAMS**, Hillsdale County: Moscow Township was organized in 1835 and Adams was set off from it in 1836, with Salmon Sharp as its first supervisor, and he became its first postmaster on May 4, 1837; John O. and Julius Swift, as Swift & Company, built the first sawmill in 1837-38; its post office was moved to the larger and lasting village of North Adams on Feb. 28, 1857; named for Henry P. Adams, pioneer settler here [Hogaboam; PO Archives].

**ADAMS**, Houghton County: Myron Tompkins became the first postmaster of this rural post office on Jan. 27, 1870, but the office was closed on July 22 of the same year [PO Archives].

**ADAMS CORNERS**, Huron County. See Ruth.

**ADAMS MILLS**, Branch County: founded about 1831 by Wales Adams where the Chicago Road crossed Prairie River; his settlement never grew to his expectations and he abandoned it for politics, becoming a member of the state legislature of 1844-45 [MPH 7:360 1886].

**ADAMSVILLE**, Cass County: Adamsport was platted by Sterling Adams, of Vermont, in 1832, and Christiana, on the opposite side of the creek, was laid out by merchant and millowner Moses Sage, from New York, in 1834; his site was first called Sage's Mill; since 1838, both have been called Adamsville; Mr. Adams became its first postmaster on Oct. 8, 1831, the office operating until May 31, 1904 [MPH 12:390 1888, 28:162 1897; Glover; Rogers; PO Archives].

**ADDISON**, Lenawee County: John Talbot built a grist mill here in 1835-36, and the settlement was given a post office named Manetau, with Brayton Brown as its first postmaster, on May 11, 1838; the office was renamed Peru on the following Dec. 8 and Brownell's Mills on July 24, 1840; Darius Jackson added a new mill to the settlement and its post office was renamed Jackson's Mills on May 2, 1844; in 1847, a part of the village was platted and called Harrison, but the village never took the name; in 1851, Addison J. Comstock, an Adrian banker, bought extensive land here, platted it and named it Addison, and the post office was renamed Addison on Jan. 15, 1852; incorporated as a village in 1893 [D. Brown, PM; MPH 26:264 1895; PO Archives].

**ADDISON**, Oakland County. See Lakeville.

**ADDISON JUNCTION**, Lenawee County: in 1894, a station at the junction of the Ohio branch of the C., J. & M. Railroad with the main line, a mile east of Addison, which see for the name [GSM 1895].

**ADRIAN**, Lenawee County: Addison J. Comstock (1802-67) came land looking here in 1825; he acquired 1,100 acres in 1826 when he returned from New York State with fellow settlers and a bride; platted as Logan in 1828, she persuaded him to rename it for her hero in history, the Roman emperor Hadrian; Mr. Comstock became the first postmaster on March 20, 1828; incorporated as a village in 1836 and as a city in 1853; the township remained named Logan until March 6, 1838, when the legislature renamed it Adrian [Hudson; GSM 1873].

**ADVANCE**, Charlevoix County: this village on Pine Lake (now Lake Charlevoix), in Eveline Township, was first settled in 1866; Chauncey Baker became its first postmaster on Oct. 20, 1870, the office operating until Oct. 15, 1906 [GSM 1879; Blinn].

**ADVENT CITY**, Allegan County: a village in 1880 [GSM 1881].

**ADVENTURE**, Ontonagon County: the old Adventure Mine was opened in 1850 and its community was given a post office named Adventure on Sept. 26, 1851, with Richard Moyle as its first postmaster, the office operating until Aug. 14, 1860 [Stevens; GSM 1860; PO Archives].

**AETNA**, Mecosta County. See Brady Lake.

**AETNA**, Newaygo County: founded in 1867 by C. A. Bruce, Wesley Young and John Mansfield, sawmill operators here on the White River in Denver Township; Levi W. Simons became its first postmaster on Jan. 14, 1870, the office operating until April 14, 1904; now a hamlet [Harry L. Spooner; PO Archives].

**AFRICA,** Ingham County: in this district in Williamston Township and around its schoolhouse a settlement formed, notably the Webb family consisting of the brothers John, James, George and William, and one sister, Mrs. Winslow; during the Civil War most of the voters here were "black abolitionists," so the district got the name Africa [Adams].

**AFTON,** Charlevoix County: John R. Vance became the first postmaster of this rural post office in Wilson Township on Feb. 28, 1891, the office operating until Oct. 30, 1893 [GSM 1893; PO Archives].

**AFTON,** Cheboygan County: Patrick O'Connor opened the first lumber camp here in Ellis Township in 1887 and it was given a post office named Ellisville on April 22, 1905, with storekeeper Fred Bartholomew as its first postmaster; Mr. MacPherson asked that it be renamed Afton, for he thought that the Pigeon River, flowing nearby, resembled the Afton in Scotland, and its post office was so renamed on Feb. 12, 1906 [Doris Eddy, PM; PO Archives].

**AGATE,** Ontonagon County: also called Agate Siding; founded in a mining district about 1890 as a spur of the Duluth, South Shore & Atlantic Railroad, which named it from the translucent quartz, the agate; John Wakevainen, Jr., became its first postmaster on May 6, 1926 [Charles Willman; PO Archives].

**AGATE HARBOR,** Keweenaw County: René Vion, of France, was the original owner of this site, but title to it was secured by John H. Gatiss, of Eagle Harbor, through purchase at a sheriff's sale in 1900; it was never a producing mine, though prospected to some extent; located on Lake Superior, about ten miles east of Eagle Harbor, its beaches and cliffs are scattered with glazed, varicolored agate stones, hence its name [Stevens; Federal].

**AGNEW,** Ottawa County: first named Johnsville for John Behm who, with his family, first settled here in Grand Haven Township in the early 1860s; John C. A. Bishop became its first postamster, Nov. 8, 1870; the office was closed on Jan. 18, 1875, restored on Jan. 24, 1878, renamed Agnew on Dec. 23, 1887, and closed permanently on June 15, 1911; it was renamed for an executive of the Chicago & Western Michigan Railroad which gave it a station named Agnew, but the successor road, the Pere Marquette, later closed the station; in 1952, the State Highway Dept. deemed it easier to move the 12 remaining buildings of the town than to run a road around it [Page; PO Archives; Escanaba Press Aug. 24, 1968].

**AGNEW,** Saginaw County: A. Davis became the first postmaster of this rural post office on Feb. 18, 1875, but the office was closed on the following Nov. 9 [PO Archives].

**AGRICULTURAL COLLEGE,** Ingham County. See East Lansing.

**AHGOSTATOWN,** Leelanau County: still so called on some old maps; the site was the property of the Ahgosa family till sold to Mr. and Mrs. John N. Clancy in 1932 for their school of speech correction known as Shady Trails [Barnes].

**AHMEEK,** Keweenaw County: a station on the Mineral Range Railroad, in Allouez Township; the village was founded by John Bosch in 1904; lawyer James A. Hamilton became its first postmaster on Feb. 5, 1909, in which year it was incorporated as a village; due to the abundance of beavers in the area, it was named Ahmeek, Chippewa for beaver [Mary Schutte; GSM 1911; PO Archives].

**AINGER,** Eaton County: Carl F. Meads became the first postmaster at this station on the Grand Trunk Railroad, in Walton Township, on March 16, 1882; the name was changed to Thurman on Feb. 13, 1889, then back to Ainger on May 9 of the same year, until it was closed on Feb. 28, 1910; believed to have been named for state official Daniel B. Ainger [GSM 1883; PO Archives].

**AIR LINE JUNCTION,** Jackson County: a station on a branch of the Lake Shore & Michigan Southern Railroad, four miles southwest of Jackson, in 1884; the Air Line was the fast freight division of the road, named as in the phrase, fast as air [GSM 1885; MCRR].

**AITKEN,** Sanilac County: this rural post office was opened on Jan. 26, 1901, with David Parsons as its first postmaster, the office operating until June 30, 1906; named for W. H. Aitken, the county's member of the state Republican executive committee at the time [GSM 1907; PO Archives].

**AKRON,** Tuscola County: Charles H. Beach became the first settler in 1854 and the place became known as Beach's Corners; on July 23, 1857, with Samuel B. Covey as its first postmaster, it was given a post office as Akron, named after its township, which had been named by Mrs. Jane Cook, after Akron, Ohio; a station on the Saginaw, Tuscola & Huron Railroad in 1882; platted by Samuel Lynn in 1882; incorporated as a village in 1910 [Nelson P. Kramer, PM; Page].

**ALABASTER,** Iosco County: the first alabaster rock (gypsum) was bored here in 1841 and the site was known as Alabaster before Alabaster Township was formed in 1866, and thousands of tons of the rock had been shipped from here before that; the first settler in the village was Benjamin F. Smith, Jr., in 1863, and he became its first postmaster on March 14, 1864, the office operating until Aug. 17, 1962 [Lillian W. Polen, PM; GSM 1873].

**ALAIEDON CENTER,** Ingham County: James Phillips became the first settler in the area in 1836; it was also called the German Settlement from the many Germans who came to settle here; given a post office as Alaiedon, with William Lewis as its first postmaster, on Dec. 10, 1838, the office operating until Aug. 22, 1851; the township, formed in 1842, also took the name Alaiedon [Adams; Durant; PO Archives].

**ALAMANDO,** Midland County: the village began as a station named Dorr on a branch of the Pere Marquette Railroad, in Warren Township, in 1822, and formed around the sawmill of Pearsall & Howard; Hager Stevenson became its first postmaster on Feb. 29, 1888, succeeded by L.

Howard in 1890, the office operating until Dec. 31, 1905 [Cole; GSM 1889].

**ALAMO,** Kalamazoo County: John G. Tarbell made the first land purchase here in 1839 and settled on it in 1841; Osmond H. Gregory became the first postmaster on Nov. 16, 1843; the office was closed on July 24, 1855, but was restored from Aug. 8, 1857, to Oct. 5, 1868, and from Dec. 11, 1868, to Jan. 30, 1943; a station on the Michigan Central Railroad in 1882; named after its township which had been organized in 1838 and named for David Crockett and his comrades who "so heroically defended themselves at the famous castle of the Alamo" in the revolt of Texas from Mexico [Mich Hist 43:378 1959; PO Archives; Durant].

**ALANSON,** Emmet County: this village in Littlefield Township was first settled in 1875; it was given a post office named Hinman on Jan. 17, 1877, with Hollis Frayer as its first postmaster; on June 22, 1882, it was renamed Alanson for Alanson Cook, an official of the Grand Rapids & Indiana Railroad which first came through here then; incorporated as a village in 1905 [Frank E. Kroc, PM].

**ALASKA,** Kent County: this village on the Thornapple River, in Caledonia Township, began with the erection of a sawmill here by William H. Brown in 1848; Theodore Nelson became the first postmaster of Brownville on Dec. 13, 1855, changed to North Brownville on Dec. 18, 1855, and to Alaska on Dec. 4, 1868, until the office was closed on Feb. 9, 1906; the 1867 American purchase of Alaska from Russia obviously influenced its renaming [Dillenback; GSM 1860; PO Archives].

**ALBA,** Antrim County: the village began as a flag station named Cascade on the Grand Rapids & Indiana Railroad, in Forest Home Township, in 1876; William J. Barker, who settled here in 1877, became the first postmaster on Dec. 4, 1877, and platted the village in 1878; the post office was named Alba and the depot took the same name in 1884; Alba Haywood, a popular local entertainer, is said to have given his name to the village [Powers; Federal; PO Archives].

**ALBANY,** Isabella County: John Saunders became the first postmaster of this rural post office on Aug. 8, 1857, succeeded by farmer John M. Hursh on Jan. 16, 1860, and Francis G. Babbitt on April 27, 1861; the office was changed to Isabella City on July 9, 1861; in some records as New Albany [Fancher; PO Archives].

**ALBEE,** Saginaw County: named for William C. Albee, from Erie County, N.Y., who became the first permanent settler here in 1855; the township was organized in 1863, with its first meeting held in his home and with James Darling elected its first supervisor [Mills; Leeson].

**ALBERTA,** Baraga County: as a step toward what was believed his intention of building a plant in the region, Henry Ford began his "model" lumber town of Alberta in the spring of 1936, homes, schools, churches, etc., following; when he closed out the operation about 1943, the community dwindled away; it was named after the daughter of one of his top executives, Edward G. Kingsford [Ford Motor Company].

**ALBERTA,** Chippewa County. See Fibre.

**ALBION,** Calhoun County: title to land here was first acquired by speculators in 1830; Tenney Peabody bought their holdings in 1833, and he and his family became the first settlers; in 1835, Jesse Crowell and others joined him in the grist mill business which, at the suggestion of Mrs. Peabody, was named the Albion Company, after Mr. Crowell's home town in New York; Mr. Crowell platted the village in 1836 and became its first postmaster on May 5, 1838; incorporated as a village in 1855 and as a city in 1885 [Everts].

**ALBION MINES,** Marquette County: in 1878 a mining settlement in Marquette Township [GSM 1879].

**ALCONA,** Alcona County: first settled by Canadian-born commercial fisherman William Hill about 1858 and known as The Cove; renamed after the county which Henry Rowe Schoolcraft had named in 1840 from an Indian word meaning the beautiful plain; Bryant S. Lagrange became its first postmaster on Jan. 9, 1867; a fishing town till about 1865, next a lumbering town till about 1880, and now a ghost town; its post office operated until Aug. 15, 1903 [Powers; PO Archives].

**ALDEN,** Antrim County: in 1868, F. J. Lewis built a store here in Helena Township, naming the settlement which formed around it Noble; located at the mouth of Spencer Creek, named for John B. Spencer who operated in the area, the village took the name Spencer Creek and was given a post office of that name on June 15, 1869, with Peter S. Smalley as its first postmaster; after the Pere Marquette Railroad came through in 1891, it was renamed for William Alden Smith, an official of the road, and the post office was renamed Alden on July 18, 1892 [Powers; PO Archives].

**ALDERSON,** Newaygo County: a station on the Pere Marquette Railroad and a settlement around the general store of J. J. Alderson; William L. Walters became its first postmaster on March 6, 1906, succeeded by C. S. Wallace in 1908 [GSM 1909; PO Archives].

**ALDRICH,** Gratiot County: a rural post office in Lafayette Township, with Andrew Schurr as its first and only postmaster, the office operating but from July 29, 1899, to April 30, 1900 [Tucker].

**ALDRICH'S CORNERS,** Calhoun County: among the old settlers who came to Tekonsha Township in 1836-37 were Deacon Nelson Aldrich, and Heman and John Ellis; the vicinity of Aldrich's settlement became known as Aldrich's Corners [Everts].

**ALDRICH'S PRAIRIE,** Kalamazoo County: from about 1831, Isaac Aldrich ran a tavern at the ford of the river where his farm was located, a mile below the present city of Plainwell; a local name, it may have been partly in Allegan County [Mich Hist 31:279 1947].

**ALECTO,** Delta County: a station on a branch of the Chicago & Northwestern Railroad, on the line between Delta and Menominee Counties, in 1844 [GSM 1885].

**ALEMBIC**, Isabella County: Jonathan Foutch became the first postmaster of this rural post office in Chippewa Township on June 23, 1874, the office operating until Dec. 31, 1905 [GSM 1875-1907].

**ALERT**, Oakland County: this rural post office, 17 miles northeast of Pontiac, was opened on Dec. 17, 1894, with William Anderson as its first postmaster, the office operating until Aug. 30, 1902 [GSM 1897; PO Archives].

**ALEXANDER**, Chippewa County: a station on the Minneapolis, St. Paul & Sault Ste. Marie Railroad, six miles south of Sault Ste. Marie, in 1891 [Mich Manual 1899].

**ALEXANDER**, Crawford County: a station on a branch of the Michigan Central Railroad, five miles north of Grayling, in 1889 [GSM 1895].

**ALEXIS**, Monroe County: from 1878 the junction point of two railroads coming into Detroit; this site in Erie Township was also known as Detroit Junction [GSM 1879].

**ALFRED**, Dickinson County: a settlement with a station on the Chicago, Minneapolis & St. Paul Railroad, on the Ford River, in Breen Township; Andrew Kemmeter became its first postmaster on Dec. 8, 1903, the office operating until Nov. 15, 1910 [GSM 1905; PO Archives].

**ALGANSEE**, Branch County: the first land entry in the area was made by Jedehiah Jessup, of Monroe County, N.Y., on Sept. 12, 1835; the first actual settlers were Luther Stiles and Ludovico Robbins; the former, in partnership with Morris Crater, built a sawmill here in the winter of 1836-37; James T. Bailey became its first postmaster on July 19, 1845, the office operating until Jan. 14, 1905; the townspeople had sent in the name of Carlton, but for some unexplained reason the legislature named it Algansee [Johnson].

**ALGER**, Arenac County: the village began as a station at the junction of the Mackinaw division of the Michigan Central and the Detroit, Bay City & Alpena Railroads in 1883; it was given a post office on March 7, 1884, with John Cole as its first postmaster; the village was platted and recorded in 1884 by John S. Newberry, congressman, 1879-80, and Russell A. Alger, governor, 1885-86, and named for the latter [Alfred Campbell; GSM 1885; PO Archives].

**ALGERVILLE**, Oakland County. See Holly.

**ALGODON**, Ionia County: a post office in Odessa Township, opened on Nov. 10, 1864, with Edmond Vandecar as its first postmaster; the office was closed on Feb. 6, 1871, but was restored from April 21, 1871, to June 19, 1899; the place was also called Strothers' Corners for George Strothers, a pioneer settler who became the postmaster about 1880 [Schenck; GSM 1881; PO Archives].

**ALGOMA**, Kent County: first settled by Smith Lapham in 1843 and he became the first supervisor when the township was organized in 1849

Freeman J. Comstock became its first postmaster on Oct. 25, 1856; the office was closed on Aug. 14, 1858, but was restored from Oct. 23, 1858, to May 23, 1860, and from Nov. 14, 1896, to Nov. 30, 1899; named after the steamer Algoma which was then plying on the Grand River, between Grand Rapids and Grand Haven [Dillenback; PO Archives].

**ALGONAC,** St. Clair County: first settled by John Martin in 1805, and called Pointe du Chene (Oak Point), the southern end of the village is still so referred to; on April 5, 1826, with 1816 settler John K. Smith as postmaster, it was given a post office named Plainfield (after its township which Mr. Smith had got named after his old home in Vermont); the township was renamed Clay for statesman Henry Clay in 1828 and its post office was so renamed on Dec. 23, 1835; with Mr. Smith still postmaster, the office was renamed Algonac on Aug. 17, 1843; incorporated as a village by the supervisors in 1867 and by the legislature in 1893; incorp. as a city in 1967; Indian agent Henry Rowe Schoolcraft coined the name from the Algonquin Indian tribe and the suffix ac, meaning place [R. Lee Poole; Jenks; PO Archives].

**ALGONQUIN,** Chippewa County: the settlement took its name from the Algonquin Indian nation; it was known for years as Nieceville, for the owner of a sawmill here [Hamilton].

**ALGONQUIN,** Ontonagon County: the Algonquin Company, organized in 1848, prospected for ten years here in Algonquin (now Bohemia) Township, then in Houghton County; Thomas H. Hogan became the first postmaster of Algonquin on Nov. 1, 1850; the office was closed on Aug. 22, 1851, but was restored on Nov. 3 of the same year; it was transferred to Ontonagon County on Sept. 21, 1860, but was closed permanently on June 7, 1867 [Stevens; Jamison; PO Archives].

**ALICE,** Oceana County: Jason Carpenter became the first postmaster of this rural post office on June 26, 1867, the office operating until July 9, 1873 [PO Archives].

**ALICIA,** Saginaw County. See Prairie Farm.

**ALLEGAN,** Allegan County: in 1833, George Ketchum, of Marshall, and Stephen Vickery and Anthony Cooley, of Kalamazoo, bought from the government the land now covered by the central part of the town; they, and Elisha Ely and his son Alexander, of Rochester, N.Y., projected the village; Samuel Foster became its first postmaster on July 24, 1833; the office was transferred to and renamed Otsego on March 6, 1835, but the Allegan post office was re-established on the sixteenth of the same month, with Alexander L. Ely as its postmaster; first platted in 1837; incorporated as a village in 1838 and as a city in 1907; named by Henry Rowe Schoolcraft after the Allegan or Alleghen Indian tribe [Atwell; PO Archives].

**ALLEN,** Hillsdale County: first settled by War of 1812 veteran, Captain Moses Allen, and his family, in 1827; Richard W. Corbus became the first postmaster of Sylvanus (it was in a wooded area), on July 13,

1830; the office was closed on Sept. 5, 1834, restored on Sept. 9, 1835, and renamed after its first settler on Aug. 17, 1868; a thriving hamlet before it was platted and recorded in 1868; a station on the Lake Shore & Michigan Southern Railway; incorp. as a village in 1950 [Reynolds; Pen Phil 7:3 Jan 1957].

**ALLEN CREEK,** Oceana County: Colfax Township, first settled in 1863, was organized in 1869; its supervisor, Calvin Woodworth, became its first postmaster on July 14, 1871, the office operating until April 14, 1904; John Race operated the Eastman & Bean shingle mill here and the firm opened a store which was managed by F. W. Ratzel [Royal; Mich Hist 30:531 1946; PO Archives].

**ALLENDALE,** Ottawa County: first settled by a Welshman, Richard Roberts, in 1842; the township was organized in his home in 1846, with Jeremy Stubbs as its first supervisor, and named for Captain Hannibal Allen, son of Ethan Allen, of Revolutionary War fame; his widow, Mrs. Agnes B. Allen, was the first person named in the first township roll, and owned 100 acres; Mr. Roberts became the first postmaster on March 24, 1852; the office was closed in 1916, but restored since Nov. 1, 1954 [Frank Sheridan, PM; MPH 9:264 1886; Mich Hist 17:5 1933].

**ALLEN PARK,** Wayne County: Lewis Allen was five years old when his father, Thomas, brought his family from New York State to Detroit in 1819; Lewis became a lawyer and a lumberman whose land holdings included 276½ acres, part of which is in today's Allen Park, and after whom the village was named in 1926; incorporated as a village in 1927 and as a city in 1957; R. Don Pretty became its first postmaster on Sept. 10, 1957; co-pioneer settlers with Allen were Hugert Champagne and Edward Pepper [AP City Directory, 1960-61].

**ALLEN'S,** Eaton County: this village in Chester Township was given a post office from Feb. 7, 1870, to March 13, 1871, and a station on a branch of the Michigan Central Railroad [GSM 1883; PO Archives].

**ALLEN'S PRAIRIE,** Branch County: a village in then Allen Township, named for Mr. Allen who became its first settler in 1837 [MPH 18:610 1891].

**ALLEN'S STATION,** Hillsdale County: a depot on the Lake Shore & Michigan Southern Railroad, a mile north of the village of Allen, which see for the name [GSM 1873].

**ALLENTON,** St. Clair County: this village in Berlin Township was founded about 1844 by Herkimer Smith, an inn keeper who ran a twice-a-week stage coach to Detroit, and it was first called Smith's Corners; it was given a station named Smith's on the Almont branch of the Pere Marquette Railroad and a post office named Smith, with Lenrock P. Lewis as its first postmaster, on April 3, 1883; on March 21, 1910, it was renamed Allenton for Darius and Jesse Allen, the civic and business leaders of the village [Jenks; PO Archives].

**ALLENVILLE,** Mackinac County: a station on the Detroit, Mackinaw & Marquette Railroad; the village was founded by the Martell Furnace Company, charcoal kilns, in 1880-81, and was named by and for its superintendent, Allen P. Hulbert; its post office operated from April 1, 1898, to Sept. 30, 1958 [Robert G. Gille; PO Archives].

**ALLEYTON,** Newaygo County: this village in Everett Township was founded by J. Alley, head of the Alley Lumber Company, in 1873; Charles S. Watson became its first postmaster on Dec. 8, 1873, the office operating until Oct. 1, 1891; the village, also known as Alley's Town, was almost wiped out by fire in 1882 [S. E. Douglass, D. O.; GSM 1875; PO Archives].

**ALLIS,** Presque Isle County: James Sandison became the first postmaster of this rural post office on Dec. 10, 1884, the office operating until July 15, 1907 [PO Archives].

**ALLISON,** Lapeer County. See Burnside.

**ALLOUEZ,** Keweenaw County: founded by the Allouez Mining Company (named for Claude Jean Allouez, early French Jesuit missionary in the area) when they opened a copper mine nearby in 1859; a station on the Hancock and Calumet Railroad; Alex P. Thomas became its first postmaster on Oct. 16, 1873 [Clarence Dolkey, PM].

**ALLYNGTON,** Berrien County: A. C. Penwell became the first postmaster of this rural post office on May 28, 1836, the office operating until June 17, 1837 [PO Archives].

**ALMA,** Gratiot County: first settled in 1853 by General Ralph Ely and three companions; he built a sawmill here in 1855 and platted the village as Elyton in 1856; later an addition was platted by Mr. Gargett and called Alma, the name by which the whole community came to be known and the name, it is believed, of his daughter; General Ely became the first postmaster of Alma on July 7, 1858; incorporated as a village in 1872 and as a city in 1905 [Farmer; Mich Hist 19:129 1935; PO Archives].

**ALMA,** Tuscola County: a village in 1864 [GSM 1865].

**ALMA RIVER,** Schoolcraft County: a station on the Detroit, Mackinaw & Marquette Railroad in 1882 [GSM 1883].

**ALMAR,** Muskegon County: a village in 1878 [GSM 1879].

**ALMENA,** Van Buren County: Jonas Barber became the first actual settler in 1835, building a cabin and a sawmill; when the township was set off in 1842, F. C. Annable, then in the legislature, named it after an Indian princess of whom he had heard; pioneer Samuel B. Fisk operated a grist mill here; from its mills the village was also known as Almena Mills; given a post office as Almena Centre, with John A. Chase as its first postmaster, on April 5, 1848, the office operating until Feb. 8, 1849; on Oct. 26, 1861, the Brewerville post office was transferred to and renamed Almena and it operated until Sept. 14, 1905 [Ellis; PO Archives].

**ALMER,** Muskegon County: on land belonging to J. Scott and A. Cummings a village plat was made here in Egelston Township prior to 1882 [Page].

**ALMER,** Tuscola County: in 1860, this small settlement bid to be designated the county seat, and when Centerville (present-day Caro) was chosen instead, the Universalist church at Almer was moved to Centerville to serve as the courthouse [Schultz].

**ALMIRA,** Benzie County: first settled by John and Alex Heather, Canadian-born brothers, in 1862; named after Almira Burrell, wife of A. J. Burrell, who emigrated here from Steuben County, N.Y., in 1863; Hiram Bowen became its first postmaster on Jan. 18, 1864, the year the town was organized, but the office was closed on Sept. 29, 1893 [MPH 31:102 1901].

**ALMONT,** Lapeer County: first settled by James Deneen in 1828; with Dr. Caleb Carpenter as postmaster; it was given a post office named Bristol on Jan. 29, 1935, for Oliver Bristol, the second permanent settler; the village was platted and recorded as Newburg in 1836; James Thompson, who donated the town clock, had the name changed on Jan. 5, 1846, to honor the Mexican general, Juan N. Almonte; incorporated as a village in 1855 [Nellie Veness; Page].

**ALMONT JUNCTION,** St. Clair County: in 1894, a station on the Almont division of the Pere Marquette Railroad at its junction with the Grand Trunk [GSM 1895].

**ALOHA,** Cheboygan County: the settlement formed around the James B. Patterson sawmill and the F. Hout general store; Mrs. Lillian Hout became the first postmaster on Dec. 17, 1903; this Grant Township village was given a station on the Detroit & Mackinaw Railroad; it was named by Mr. Patterson who had made a trip to Hawaii [Mrs. Elmer Gettinger; GSM 1905].

**ALPENA,** Alpena County: W. F. Cullings, a fisherman, became the first settler about 1835; in 1856, George N. Fletcher and three companions from Detroit laid out the village which they named Fremont for General John C. Fremont; but there was another Fremont in Michigan and so this one was given a post office as Alpena, with Daniel Carter becoming its first postmaster on Dec. 2, 1857; renamed Thunder Bay (it was near Thunder Bay) on Jan. 4, 1859, but changed back to Alpena on Feb. 11, 1859; incorporated as a city in 1871; named after its county which was first named Anamickee after a Chippewa chief, but renamed Alpena, the Indian word for partridge, at the suggestion of Henry Rowe Schoolcraft [Oliver; Dunbar].

**ALPHA,** Iron County: this iron mining settlement with a station on the Chicago & Northwestern Railroad, in Crystal Falls Township, was in Marquette County until Iron was organized in 1885; Alfred Breitung, of Marquette, opened the Mastodon Mine near here in 1881 and the community was given a post office named Mastodon on Oct. 1, 1883, with

Herbert Hughitt as its first postmaster; this post office was closed on Dec. 7, 1888, but the village was given another named Alpha on Dec. 15, 1913, with William H. Peters as its postmaster; incorporated as the village of Alpha in 1914; see Epsilon for its naming [Jack Hill, Sr.; GSM 1885; PO Archives].

**ALPHADELPHIA**, Kalamazoo County: the name, a combined Greek word, reflects the communitarian character of this settlement of some 300 members, founded near Galesburg, about 1842; a German, Dr. H. R. Schetterly, was its leading spirit; internal dissension led to its abandonment in 1848 [Durant; Dunbar].

**ALPINA**, Van Buren County. See Hamilton.

**ALPINE**, Kent County: from Wayne County, N.Y., Solomon Wright, his wife, and their five sons became the first settlers here in 1837; the township was organized in 1847 and named from its then being an area of all pine trees; its village of Alpine was given a station on the Grand Rapids & Newaygo Railroad and, on Jan. 14, 1862, a post office, with Egbert B. Hill as its first postmaster; the office was closed on Feb. 16, 1880, but was restored from May 17, 1880, to Jan. 15, 1937 [Dillenback; PO Archives].

**ALSTON**, Houghton County: the village began with a rural post office named Laird on Aug. 16, 1887, of which Patrick Maloney was the first postmaster; the office was closed on Oct. 26, 1888, but was restored, with Thomas H. Scott as postmaster, on Nov. 12, 1888; when lumberman J. V. Alston became the postmaster on April 16, 1902, the village and its post office were renamed for him, the office operating until June 30, 1957 [GSM 1889-1903; PO Archives].

**ALTO**, Kent County: this village in Bowne Township was founded by David N. Skidmore in 1845; Daniel C. McVean became its first postmaster on Sept. 5, 1851; a station on the Detroit, Grand Rapids & Western Railroad; it was so named by Lucy Skidmore McVean from its being the highest point of land (Latin altus, meaning high) between Grand Rapids and Detroit [PM; Dillenback].

**ALTON**, Kent County: this rural post office in Vergennes Township was opened on Feb. 19, 1851, with Walter White as its first postmaster; the office was closed on Aug. 13, 1868, restored on Feb. 15, 1869, but transferred to and renamed Vergennes on June 11, 1900 [PO Archives; Dillenback].

**ALTON**, Shiawassee County: a village in Bennington Township in 1878 [GSM 1879].

**ALTONA**, Mecosta County: William Seaton and Bartley Davis built a sawmill and Harrison J. Brown a flouring mill, in 1868, on the Little Muskegon River, in Hinton Township, where the village of Altona was later platted; William Judd became its first postmaster on Feb. 5, 1872, the office operating until Nov. 15, 1937 [Chapman; PO Archives].

**ALVAVILLE**, Oceana County. See Hoffman.

**ALVERNO,** Cheboygan County: storekeeper Patrick H. McDonald became the first postmaster here on the Cheboygan River, in Grant Township, on June 21, 1877, with the office named Sova for A. E. Sova, a local merchant and later also the postmaster; on Dec. 7, 1900, the village was renamed to honor the patron of the parish, St. Francis of Assisi, who, while praying at Mount Alverno, received the stigmata [Myrton M. Riggs; GSM 1879-1903].

**ALVERSON,** Ingham County: Stephen D. Alverson was a large landowner here in Williamston Township and he became the first postmaster, with the office in his home, on Sept. 3, 1852; the office was closed on Oct. 31, 1867, but restored, with William D. Alverson as postmaster, on June 19, 1868; it was closed again on Nov. 3, 1874, but restored again from Dec. 16, 1874, to Jan. 3, 1896 [Durant; Foster; PO Archives].

**ALVIN,** Alcona County: Watson F. Bisbee became the first postmaster of this lumber settlement in Mikado Township on Feb. 14, 1906, the office operating until Feb. 15, 1911 [GSM 1907; PO Archives].

**ALWARD,** Clare County: a rural post office opened on June 22, 1898, 14 miles from Clare, with William E. Huball as its first postmaster, the office operating until June 27, 1907 [GSM 1899-1907; PO Archives].

**AMADORE,** Sanilac County: named for pioneer settler Amadore Fuller; surveyor Jefferson W. Galbraith became its first postmaster on June 10, 1868; the office was closed on Oct. 6, 1873, but was restored on Dec. 4, 1873, with Mrs. Adeline Galbraith as postmaster, the office operating until Jan. 1, 1934; this village in Worth Township, with a station on the Pere Marquette Railroad, was also called Galbraith's Corners [GSM 1879; PO Archives].

**AMASA,** Iron County: iron ore croppings were first discovered here along the shore of the Hemlock River by Matthew Gibson and his son J. Thoburn Gibson in 1888; when sufficient ores had been uncovered, the property was taken over by the Hemlock River Mining Company, a subsidiary of the Pickands, Mather Company; the village which they platted in October, 1890, west of the workings, was first named Hemlock, but it was soon renamed for the father-in-law of Col. Henry S. Pickands, Amasa Stone Mather; a station on the Chicago & Northwestern Railroad; Frederick F. Sanford became its first postmaster on March 7, 1891 [Ralph H. Premo, PM; PO Archives].

**AMASA PORTER,** Iron County. See Porter.

**AMBER,** Mason County: the first settlers in the area were Eugene Schreiner in 1861, Charles Hackert and Fred Tetzloff in 1862, and William Carter and Jesse Towns in 1863; Amber Township was formed in 1867; Judge Haight, of Ludington, visited Amber in 1871 and wrote "The railroad grubbed and cleared, a village surveyed and platted, containing a store, post office, hotel, etc.;" but the Amber post office, opened on March 10, 1868, with Henry H. Woods as its first postmaster, was closed on Jan. 23, 1871, restored on Nov. 11, 1872, but closed permanently on March 31, 1908, and the railroad ticket office was closed in 1928; now a hamlet; it is believed to have been named by Charles W. Jones, whose home town was Amber, Indiana; for general storekeeper Silas Slaght the village was also known as Slaghtburg [Percy E. Morse; PO Archives].

**AMBLE,** Montcalm County: this village in the center of Winfield Township, on the Pere Marquette Railroad, was platted and recorded by Parker Merrill for David L. Eaton, Nathan W. Merrill, James T. Hall and Thomas Fisk, proprietors, on July 8, 1886; Samuel M. Crandall became its first postmaster on Feb. 5, 1887, the office operating until Dec. 31, 1953; it was named in honor of Rev. Ole Amble, of the Danish Lutheran Church [Dasef; PO Archives].

**AMBOY,** Hillsdale County: Amboy Township was a part of Rowland until set off from it in 1850; Rowland had been named for Rowland Bird, pioneer settler; given a post office named Rowland on Dec. 12, 1840, with Nathaniel S. Dewey as its first postmaster, the office was renamed Bird on June 10, 1850, and Amboy on Dec. 28, 1855, but it was closed on Dec. 14, 1903; the village was also known as Drake's Corners, with G. Drake as its constable and J. S. Drake as its justice of the peace [Reynolds; Hogaboam; PO Archives].

**AMBOY,** Lapeer County. See Thornville.

**AMELITH,** Bay County: Frederick Koch, a German businessman, was so impressed with the colony his son-in-law, Rev. Ferdinand Sievers, had founded at Frankenlust, that he promoted one of his own in 1851, naming it Amelith after a village in his homeland; cheese-maker John Berger became its first postmaster on March 10, 1894, the office operating until March 15, 1901; now a hamlet [Mich Hist 28:67 Jan 1944; PO Archives].

**AMES,** Menominee County: a station on the Wisconsin & Michigan Railroad, four miles south of Nathan, opened in 1894 [Mich Manual 1899].

**AMITY,** Kalkaska County: George Crawford became the first postmaster of this rural post office in the central part of the county on Dec. 19, 1879, the office operating until Dec. 13, 1880 [GSM 1883; PO Archives].

**AMMON,** Wayne County: the site of the works of the Anchor Manufacturing Company, on the River Rouge, in Ecorse Township, with a station on the Michigan Central and the Lake Shore & Michigan Southern Railroads; Robert S. Osborne became its first postmaster on Sept. 11, 1888, but the office was transferred to and renamed River Rouge on Feb. 19, 1891; when the village of River Rouge was incorporated in 1889, Ammon was included in it [GSM 1889-99; PO Archives].

**AMSDEN,** Montcalm County: founded about 1850 by J. P. Shoemaker, from Herkimer, N.Y.; he and M. P. Follett built a grist mill here in

1859; it was given a post office named Fair Plains (named after the township), on March 20, 1852, with Myron H. Burley as its first postmaster; the office was closed from May 26 to June 23, 1852; with Alexander B. Amsberg as postmaster, it was renamed Amsden on Oct. 24, 1865; the village was platted in 1867; Hiram Amsberg built the dam for the sawmill on Dickerson Creek, and from Amsberg's Dam, the name of the village is believed to have been derived [Wyman C. Bock, J.P.; PO Archives].

**AMY,** Oakland County. See Auburn Heights.

**ANCHORVILLE,** St. Clair County: to serve the French living in the area, then called the Swan Creek Settlement, the Rev. Charles Chambille came here in 1853 and dedicated his church in 1854; that was the nucleus of the village; in 1876, C. A. Calzin renamed it from its location on Anchor Bay; George Augustus Christie served as the first postmaster from Dec. 4, 1885, to 1940 [Mrs. M. Schymanski, 2nd PM].

**ANDERSON,** Livingston County: a station on the Grand Trunk Railroad in 1881; James T. Eaman, farmer and lawyer, became its first postmaster on Aug. 10, 1885; the office was closed on Oct. 31, 1913, but this hamlet in Putnam Township remains [Cole].

**ANDERSON,** Sanilac County: also called Anderson Station on its depot on the Port Huron & Northwestern Railroad; a sawmill was built and a hotel and stores followed [Chapman].

**ANDERSON'S MILLS,** Van Buren County. See Berlamont.

**ANDERSONVILLE,** Cass County: platted in 1871 on the southeast shore of Stone Lake by S. F. Anderson, for whom it was named; now a part of Cassopolis [Fox].

**ANDERSONVILLE,** Oakland County: John Husted settled here in Springfield Township in 1833, followed by Charles and Harry Husted, and it was first known as the Husted Settlement; in 1836, Isaac Anderson and his family arrived from Attica, N.Y., and bought 120 acres, and the neighborhood became known as the Anderson Settlement; given a post office named Andersonville on May 2, 1895, with Elmer E. Cook as its first postmaster, the office operating until Sept. 30, 1912; a station on the Detroit & Milwaukee Railroad [Durant; Seeley; PO Archives].

**ANDOVER,** Calhoun County: Jeremiah Gardner became the first settler here in 1831 and John V. Henry the first postmaster on July 14, 1832, the office operating until April 15, 1846; the townspeople had the legislature change the name of the township to Emmet, after Robert Emmet, the Irish patriot, in 1839 [Gardner; PO Archives].

**ANEEBISH,** Chippewa County. See Neebish.

**ANGELL,** Grand Traverse County: when the Chicago & Western Michigan (now the Pere Marquette) Railroad came through Whitewater Township in 1892, a depot and a post office were opened here; it also had a sawmill and shingle mill; John L. Wealch became its first postmaster on Sept. 7, 1892, the office operating until June 30, 1909 [Sprague; PO Archives].

**ANGELL'S LANDING,** Antrim County: the Angell families were pioneers in the county; this settlement was given a state road in 1869 [Mich Acts].

**ANGLE,** Sanilac County: Henry Perry became the first postmaster of this rural post office in Washington Township on Feb. 15, 1878, the office operating until Feb. 24, 1879 [GSM 1879-81].

**ANGOLA,** Wexford County: Cappitola M. Wait became the first postmaster of this rural post office in Henderson Township on Dec. 20, 1899, the office operating until Feb. 9, 1909 [GSM 1901; PO Archives].

**ANICE,** Mackinac County: in 1838, a Chippewa village, at Oak Point on the Straits of Mackinac [GSM 1839].

**ANN ARBOR,** Washtenaw County: John Allen, of Virginia, and (Elisha) Walker Rumsey, of New York, became the first settlers here in 1823; the area abounded in natural groves or arbors, and they named it for their wives, Ann Allen and Ann Rumsey; platted and recorded as Annarbour on May 25, 1824; John Allen became its first postmaster on Dec. 8, 1824; incorporated as a village in 1833 and as a city in 1851 [MPH 10:130 1886, 12:398 1888, Mich Hist 40:419 1956].

**ANNA RIVER,** Alger County: this rural post office was opened on Oct. 12, 1888, with Neil Steinberg as its first postmaster, but the office was transferred to and renamed Hallston on Dec. 19, 1888 [PO Archives].

**ANNPERE,** Livingston County: the Pere Marquette Railroad came through here in 1871 and the Ann Arbor Railroad, from Howell, in 1888; the crossing with a station was first known as Howell Junction, changed to Annpere, from the names of the two railroads, in 1906 [Ina Hight].

**ANTHONY,** Houghton County: a station on the Duluth, South Shore & Atlantic Railway, opened about 1872 and believed to have been named for Fred Anthony, of Negaunee [Ernest Rankin; Mich Manual 1899].

**ANTLERS,** Marquette County: a station on the M. & S.E. Railroad whose officials named it from its location in the deer country, in 1910 [GSM 1911].

**ANTRIM,** Antrim County: John Otis & Company built a charcoal furnace and sawmill here in 1882; for Mr. Otis, E. K. Robinson platted and recorded the village as Furnaceville in 1883; its station on the Grand Rapids & Indiana Railroad was named Furnace; the village and its depot were renamed Antrim when the Otis interests were bought by the Antrim Iron Company [Traverse; Federal].

**ANTRIM,** Genesee County: a village in 1864 [GSM 1865].

**ANTRIM,** Shiawassee County. See Glass River.

**ANTRIM CITY**, Antrim County: projected as a village in Banks Township, on Lake Michigan, when Wood, Pearl & Company began shipping operations here about 1861; Dexter & Noble, of Elk Rapids, then opened a store here, managed by J. N. Sickles; Richard D. Orr became its first postmaster on July 21, 1862; but the village failed and its projectors move to Norwood [Traverse; GSM 1865; PO Archives].

**ANTWERP**, Van Buren County: first settled by Joel Tomlinson in 1834 and Joseph Woodman in 1835; the township was organized in 1837 and named by its then oldest inhabitant, Harmon Van Antwerp, after Antwerp, Belgium; Reason Holmes, tavern keeper, became its first postmaster on May 23, 1842, but on Jan. 5, 1849, the office was moved to and renamed Mattawan [Ellis; GSM 1860; PO Archives].

**ANVIL LOCATION**, Gogebic County: a station on the Chicago & Northwestern Railroad, in Bessemer Township; the village began as an iron mining location of the Newport Mining Company in 1886; company storekeeper Daniel F. Shea became its first postmaster on Feb. 18, 1918; the name evidently came from the blacksmith's anvil [Victor Lemmer; PO Archives].

**APPENZELL**, Crawford County: a rural post office in Blaine Township with farmer John J. Niederer becoming its first postmaster on Feb. 15, 1886, the office operating until May 10, 1895 [GSM 1887; PO Archives].

**APPIN**, Huron County: this Scottish settlement in Sheridan Township was named after Appin, Scotland; grocer Duncan Paul became its first postmaster on May 3, 1894, the office operating until June 15, 1904 [Hey; GSM 1895-1905].

**APPLE CREEK**, ———— County: if it existed in Michigan at all, it was likely in the southern half of the lower peninsula, but in what present county has not been determined, a post office named Apple Creek, with Isidore Moore as postmaster, was established in the Michigan Territory in March of 1818, the third in Michigan, preceded only by Detroit and Frenchtown (now Monroe) [PO Archives]. Since it is not mentioned in any Michigan map, atlas, county history, etc., it may well have been just a misplaced entry in government records.

**APPLEGATE**, Sanilac County: this village in Washington Township began with George Pack building a sawmill here in 1856; in giving it a post office the department named it for Jesse Applegate (1811-88), leader of the party which opened the southern road into Oregon in 1845; Orrin A. Munn became its first postmaster on June 24, 1880; a station on the Pere Marquette Railroad; incorporated as a village in 1903 [PM; PO Archives].

**APPLETON**, Emmet County: a sawmill settlement at Spring Creek on the Lake Huron shore, in Friendship Township; Harper Talbert became its first postmaster on May 22, 1884, the office operating until Aug. 2, 1889 [GSM 1885; PO Archives].

**ARAL**, Benzie County: this settlement on Otter Creek, at Lake Michigan, in Lake Township, formed around the mill of the Otter Creek

Lumber Company about 1880; the requested post office name of Otter Creek was rejected as there was already one in Michigan; a mill hand suggested the name of his native village in Ireland, Aral; physician S. E. Thurber became its first postmaster in 1884, succeeded by mill superintendent D. W. Goodenough in 1886, the office operating until 1900 [C. Beaver Edwards; GSM 1887].

**ARBELA,** Tuscola County: Milton Whitney lived here for several years before actual settlement began in 1850; the town was organized in 1851, and named for the wife of a pioneer settler; its post office operated from Jan. 16, 1871, to May 31, 1905 [J. A. Gallery; PO Archives].

**ARBRE CROCHE,** Emmet County. See L'Arbre Croche.

**ARBUTUS,** Gladwin County: grocer Hugh L. Oliver became the first postmaster of this village on the eastern shore of Otsego Lake, in Buckeye Township, on June 16, 1904, the office operating until May 31, 1910; there was an Arbutus school, there is still an Arbutus cemetery; so named because the nearby woods were abundant with flowering arbutus [Ritchie; GSM 1905; PO Archives].

**ARBUTUS BEACH,** Otsego County: a small resort colony, named from its location on the eastern shore of Otsego Lake and from the fact that the surrounding woodlands are covered with trailing arbutus [Federal].

**ARCADIA,** Houghton County: the Arcadian Copper Company was formed in 1899, began operations in 1900, and spent some seven million dollars of its investors' money (its Standard Oil backing sold its stock), before it gave up trying to find profitable copper about 1904; its village of Arcadia, on Portage Lake, in Franklin Township, was given a station on the Mineral Range Railroad in 1900; express agent Frank H. Rogers became the first postmaster of Arcadia Mine on March 14, 1899, the office being transferred to and renamed Franklin Mine on Dec. 17, 1904; Arcadia became a ghost town about 1906, and some of its land is in the present village of Paavola [Murdoch; GSM 1901; PO Archives].

**ARCADIA,** Lapeer County: the first settler in the town was Thomas Haskell who came in 1839 and for several years ran a hotel in section 31; the town was organized in 1857, with John B. Wilson as its first supervisor; Major K. Haskell became the first postmaster, in section 30, on July 22, 1857, the office operating until June 26, 1860 [Page; PO Archives].

**ARCADIA,** Manistee County: in 1866, Dr. W. L. Dempster, G. W. Boss and H. Huntington first settled here by Bar Lake (named from the sand bar which crossed the channel opening into Lake Michigan); Arcadia Township was organized in 1870, with W. H. Cotton as its first supervisor; the village was founded in 1880 by Henry Starke, of Milwaukee, who named it Starkeville, but the name was changed by the post office to that of the township when the office was opened on Sept. 19, 1870, with Mrs. Anne M. Dempster as the first postmaster; she was succeeded by Miss Amelia F. Huntington on April 7, 1871; the office was closed on April 22, 1872, but was restored from May 18, 1881, to date [Virginia Stroemel; Page; PO Archives].

**ARCADIAN MINE,** Houghton County. See Arcadia.

**ARCHIE,** Grand Traverse County: Franklin I. Warren became the first postmaster of this rural post office in Peninsula Township on May 25, 1885; the office was closed on Sept. 29, 1900, but was restored from Dec. 3, 1900, to July 31, 1902 [GSM 1887-1903; PO Archives].

**ARDEN,** Berrien County: Wilford Snuff became the first postmaster of this rural post office on April 13, 1896, the office operating until June 30, 1906 [PO Archives].

**ARDIS SIDING,** Missaukee County: the site of a station on the Grand Rapids & Indiana Railroad and of the Gallup & Nowlen general store, four miles south of Star City, in 1918 [GSM 1919].

**ARENAC,** Arenac County: started about 1856, adjacent to the sawmills of Captain J. P. Phillips and John Lentz; Daniel Williams became its first postmaster on May 15, 1858, the office operating until Jan. 31, 1907; took its name from the county which had been named by Henry Rowe Schoolcraft from arena, a sanded area to give gladiators a better footing, and ac, meaning place of,–together, a sandy place [Page; Mich Manual 1859; GSM 1865; PO Archives].

**ARENDAL,** Manistee County: Caroline Oleson became the first postmaster of this rural post office on April 19, 1886, the office operating until Oct. 30, 1909 [GSM 1887-1911].

**ARGENTA,** Allegan County: the Silver Creek area in Gun Plain Township was settled by 1830; it was given a railroad station named Argenta (Latin for silver) in 1907 [Esther W. Hettinger].

**ARGENTA,** Kalamazoo County: a village with a station on the Lake Shore & Michigan Southern Railroad, nine miles south of Kalamazoo, in Cooper Township, in 1878 [GSM 1879].

**ARGENTINE,** Genesee County: James H. Murray and William Lobdell settled here in 1836; Mr. Murray became the first postmaster on Nov. 1, 1837, with the office named Booton; but due to a similarity of names it was changed on March 30, 1842, to Argentine, the name which Mr. Murray had given the township; the village was platted in 1844 by Dr. Isaac Wixom; Lobdell Lake, just to the east of the village, was named for Mr. Lobdell [Ellis].

**ARGYLE,** Sanilac County: the first settlers were mostly Scots from Ontario (McLachlin, McLean, McIntyre, etc.), and that accounts for the Scottish name given Argyle Township when it was organized in 1872 with Alexander McLachlin as its first supervisor, and he became its first postmaster on Feb. 18, 1876; the village is under township government [W. T. Miller; GSM 1877].

**ARKDALE,** Lapeer County: the name of this rural post office was derived from its township of Acradia; Edward P. Stone became its first postmaster on Oct. 30, 1882, the office operating until Oct. 22, 1891 [GSM 1883; PO Archives].

**ARKONA,** Antrim County: farmer John W. Jackson became the first postmaster of this rural post office in Custer Township on July 28, 1879; the office was closed on May 18, 1881, but was restored from May 21, 1883, to May 13, 1886 [GSM 1881; PO Archives].

**ARLAND,** Jackson County: a station on the Jackson & Lansing (now Michigan Central) Railroad, in Tompkins Township; Robert T. Todd became its first postmaster on May 14, 1856; the office was closed on July 20, 1876, but was restored from May 31, 1877, to Oct. 31, 1904 [Pen Phil 14:3 Sept 1963; GSM 1873; PO Archives].

**ARLENE,** Missaukee County: Walter W. Combs became the first postmaster of this rural post office in Caldwell Township on March 18, 1903, succeeded by storekeeper Martin Duffy in 1904 [GSM 1905; PO Archives].

**ARLINGTON,** Van Buren County: William N. Taylor made the first land purchase in the area in 1835, returned to New York to get married and brought his bride back in 1837; Arlington Township was organized in 1842 and named at the suggestion of Revolutionary War veteran James Stevens after his native town in Vermont; a station on the Chicago & Western Michigan Railroad; Calvin C. Biglow became its first postmaster on May 7, 1852; the office was closed on Dec. 27, 1859, but was restored from March 5, 1860, to Feb. 28, 1871 [Ellis; PO Archives].

**ARMADA,** Macomb County: the first town meeting was held in the home of Henry B. Ten Eyck in 1834 and on May 7 of that year he became the first postmaster; the office was closed on Feb. 15, 1837, but was restored in the village on July 2, 1844, with Solomon Lathrop as postmaster; the village was also known as Burk's Corners and as Honeoye, after Honeoye Falls, Monroe County, N.Y., the boyhood home of Elisha D. Andrews who had bought 320 acres in what became Armada Township, in 1831; incorporated as the village of Armada in 1867; named after the township which had been named by Hosea Northrup [Eldredge; PO Archives].

**ARMADA CORNERS,** Macomb County: See Selleck's Corners.

**ARMSTRONG,** Iron County: a station on the Chicago & Northwestern Railroad in 1882; it was in Marquette County until Iron was organized in 1885 [GSM 1887].

**ARN,** Bay County: a sawmill settlement in Merritt Township, with a station on a branch of the Michigan Central Railroad; storekeeper Archibald Meston became its first postmaster on Feb. 28, 1877; the office was closed on May 15, 1886, but was restored from April 20, 1894, to July 30, 1904 [GSM 1887-1901; PO Archives].

**ARN,** Iosco County. See McIvor.

**ARNHEIM,** Baraga County: a station on the Duluth, South Shore & Atlantic Railroad, about midway between L'Anse and Houghton; storekeeper Martin Erickson became its first postmaster on Nov. 13, 1900, the office operating until Sept. 19, 1915; when it was restored on Feb. 13, 1917, William Nettie was appointed its postmaster, but he declined and Jacob B. Wirkkula was appointed on Aug. 15, 1917, the office operating until Sept. 30, 1951 [GSM 1903; PO Archives].

**ARNOLD,** Marquette County: a station on the E. & L. S. Railroad, in Wells Township; the village was named for Ed Arnold, partner in the Mashek Chemical & Iron Company, of Escanaba, which operated in the area; Henry Arnold became its first postmaster on June 21, 1909, the office operating until Jan. 6, 1961 [George Springer; GSM 1911; PO Archives].

**ARNOLD LAKE,** Clare County: a flag station on a branch of the Pere Marquette Railroad, near Arnold Lake, in 1884 [GSM 1885].

**ARNOLD'S CORNERS,** Branch County. See East Gilead.

**ARTHUR,** Saginaw County: this village with a station on a branch of the Michigan Central Railroad was given a post office on Dec. 7, 1880, with Louisa Wells as its first postmaster, the office operating until Oct. 14, 1904 [GSM 1883; PO Archives].

**ARTHUR BAY,** Menominee County: the village developed around the lumber mill of Leathem & Smith on the Arthur Bay shore, in Ingallston Township; John Leathem became the first postmaster, with the office named Leathem, on April 25, 1883; it was renamed Arthur Bay on Nov. 20, 1889, closed on Nov. 1, 1893, but restored from Oct. 20, 1899, to July 31, 1935; named for Arthur Horn by his father, a Chicagoan, who had bought the Leathem mill [Evelyn Bergen; GSM 1885; PO Archives].

**ARTHURSBURG,** Ionia County. See Lyons.

**ARTHURVILLE,** Otsego County: this rural post office operated from Jan. 25 to Nov. 1, 1898, with Antoine Moore as its first and only postmaster [PO Archives].

**ARVA,** Cheboygan County: a rural post office in Waverly Township with town treasurer Charles J. Hutchinson becoming its first postmaster on June 29, 1904, the office operating until July 15, 1907 [GSM 1905; PO Archives].

**ARVON,** Baraga County: began as a slate quarry village, named after its township, in 1872; it was in Houghton County when John Thomas became its first postmaster on June 8, 1874; the office was closed on Nov. 18, 1879, but was restored from May 18, 1882, to Sept. 30, 1893; when Baraga County was organized in 1875, Arvon became a part of it [Andreas; PO Archives].

**ASA,** Lapeer County. See Five Lakes.

**ASH,** Monroe County: a village in 1859 [GSM 1860].

**ASHBED,** Keweenaw County: the lands of this mine, owned by the Copper Falls Company, were set off in 1861 at the suggestion of Captain

William Petherick, agent of the company, and named Petherick in his honor; the Petherick Company failed in 1877 and the Ashbed Mining Company, organized in 1880, purchased its property at receiver's sale; Ashbed ceased operations in 1900 [Stevens].

**ASHLAND,** Newaygo County: a part of Brooks Township until Ashland was organized in 1854; named from the abundance of white ash timber in the area; John Betts became its first postmaster on June 2, 1855, the office operating until Jan. 16, 1871; on Dec. 17, 1894, the Ashland Centre post office was renamed Ashland, but it was closed on April 14, 1904 [Mich Hist 24:450; PO Archives].

**ASHLAND CENTRE,** Newago County: this village was settled in 1850; to distinguish it from Ashland in the same county and township, it was given a post office named Lake, opened on March 19, 1869, with Rensselaer Brace as its first postmaster; the office was closed on Sept. 14, 1870, but restored, again with Mr. Brace as postmaster, on Dec. 7, 1871, and operated until Oct. 31, 1908; since the Ashland post office was now closed, Ashland Centre was given a post office under its own name, with Sullivan Armstrong becoming its first postmaster, on May 6, 1879, but this was changed to Ashland on Dec. 17, 1894, until it was closed on April 14, 1904 [Mich Hist 24:450 1940; PO Archives].

**ASHLEY,** Gratiot County: the village was platted by Ansel H. Phinney, George P. Dudley, and Miles W. Bullock, proprietors, in 1883; Mr. Phinney became its first postmaster on Jan. 14, 1884; incorporated as a village in 1887; named for John M. Ashley, promotor and builder of the Toledo, Saginaw & Muskegon Railroad spur to the town [John Stafford; PO Archives].

**ASHLEY,** Kent County: Patrick M. Tully became its first postmaster on St. Patrick's day, March 17, 1854, succeeded by Sheldon Ashley, pioneer settler, in 1859, the office operating until July 8, 1878, thus allowing for the opening of an office of the same name in Gratiot County in 1884 [GSM 1875; Cole].

**ASHLEY CITY,** Macomb County. See New Baltimore.

**ASHLEY'S MILLS,** Macomb County: Alfred Ashley came here from Mount Clemens in 1821 and, together with Horace Cady, took up lands, erected a dam and built a sawmill; the place has been called Ashley's Mills and, for Lautius Haskin who built a mill here in 1828, Haskin's Mills [Eldredge].

**ASHMORE,** Tuscola County: when storekeeper Charles P. Hill became the first postmaster of this rural post office on April 20, 1899, it was in Brookfield Township, Huron County; it was transferred to Tuscola County on May 31, 1904, operating until Sept. 30, 1911 [PO Archives].

**ASHTON,** Osceola County: this village in Lincoln Township was founded and named by Joseph W. Ash in November, 1868, when the route of the Grand Rapids & Indiana Railroad had been determined through here; given a post office named Bates on Jan. 17, 1870, with Matthias L. Swan as its first postmaster, it was renamed Ashton on Jan. 11, 1872; Mr. Ash platted the village in 1872 [Chapman; GSM 1879; PO Archives].

**ASKEL,** Houghton County: in 1890, five woodcutters who had recently come from Finland, filed their claims and settled here in Portage Township with their families: Peter Tauriainen, John Sotaniemi, Andrew Heikkinen, Sr., Joseph Karky and Enoch Pyykkonen; Leonard Karky became the first postmaster on Feb. 6, 1908, the office operating until June 30, 1943; given the Finnish name for a step, suggested by the topography of the place [Wargelin; Mich Hist 14:381 1930; PO Archives].

**ASSININS,** Baraga County: founded by Rev. Frederic Baraga, an Indian missionary in the area, in 1843, and named for an Assiniboin chief whom he had converted and who remained his devoted friend; in the 1870s, this settlement on Keweenaw Bay was referred to as the Catholic Mission; it was given a post office as Assinins on Dec. 6, 1894, with Simon Denomie as its first postmaster; the office was closed on May 31, 1914, but was restored on Dec. 7, 1916 [Mich Hist 6:315 1922; PO Archives].

**ASSYRIA,** Barry County: first settled by Joseph S. Blaisdell and his family, Vermonters, in 1836; Cleveland Ellis, a New Yorker, came in 1837 and in his house the first town meeting was held in 1844; the name was chosen simply to avoid duplication; Mr. Ellis became the first postmaster on May 23, 1842, the office operating until March 15, 1937 [Johnson; Mich Hist 42:324 1958; PO Archives].

**ASTOR POINT,** Keweenaw County: so named because the brig John J. Astor, a fur trader, went on the shore here, and was a total loss [Mich Hist 9:380 1925].

**ATHENS,** Calhoun County: Isaac Crossett and six others became the first settlers here in 1831; Ephraim Turner became the first postmaster of the settlement on Feb. 15, 1837; the office was closed on Oct. 11, 1859, but was restored on April 3, 1860; the village dates from 1854 when William Simons built the first store; first platted by A. C. Waterman in 1860; incorporated as a village in 1895; named after Athens, N.Y., the region from which many of its first settlers came [Everts; Mich Hist 16:387 1932; PO Archives].

**ATHERTON,** Genesee County: Levi Gilkey made the first land purchase here in 1831; Reuben Tupper became the first actual settler in 1834; the settlement was named for the brothers Shubael and Perus Atherton who, with Pliny A. Skinner, came in 1835; the Atherton schoolhouse was built in 1836 [Wood].

**ATHLONE,** Monroe County: a German Catholic village in Ash Township; Asahel R. Webster became its first postmaster on March 28, 1856; the office was closed on Jan. 30, 1858, but was restored on Dec. 29, 1863, with Conrad M. Berghafer as its postmaster, the office operating until July 18, 1894 [GSM 1875; PO Archives].

**ATKINS,** St. Clair County: this village in Clyde Township was first settled by Allen Atkins in 1837 and William Atkins in 1839; a station on the Pere Marquette Railroad; Jonathan Morden became its first postmaster on April 30, 1873, the office operating until June 29, 1935 [Andreas; GSM 1875; PO Archives].

**ATKINSON,** Iron County: about 1887, the Metropolitan Lumber Company, under the direction of J. K. Stack and Henry M. Atkinson, secured extensive pine holdings along the north and south branches of the Paint River, built a large sawmill and general store and began the village, named for Mr. Atkinson who supervised the firm's operations here; Thomas G. Atkinson, secretary of the company, became the first postmaster on March 12, 1892; the office was closed on Oct. 14, 1905, and the village is now farmland; when the new township was organized in 1892, it was named for the same Mr. Atkinson [Hill; GSM 1893; PO Archives].

**ATKINSON,** Monroe County. See East Raisinville.

**ATLANTA,** Montmorency County: this village on the Thunder Bay River, in Briley Township, was founded by lumberman Alfred J. West, of Capac, in 1881, and he became its first postmaster on Oct. 2, 1882; a Civil War veteran, he named it after the Georgia city [GSM 1883; Claude Sherwood].

**ATLANTIC MINE,** Houghton County: the Atlantic Mining Company, which was controlled by the Copper Range Consolidated Company, was organized in 1872 by consolidating the South Pewabic and the Adams Mining Companies; their stamping works were located here in Adams Township and operated until 1911; their lands and personal property were conveyed to the Copper Range Company in 1925; the settlement became a village and was given a post office on May 8, 1876, with Cornelius D. Murphy as its first postmaster [Florence Gregorich; GSM 1879; PO Archives].

**ATLAS,** Genesee County: the first land purchase in the area was made by Asa Farrar in 1830; the second by Norman Davison in 1831, who built a sawmill in 1833 and a grist mill in 1836; organized in 1836, the village was known as Davisonville and was given a post office with that name on Feb. 14, 1837, with Mr. Davison as its first postmaster; the office was renamed Atlas, after its township, on May 5, 1854, and the village later took the same name; it was originally in Lapeer County [MPH 27:511 1896; Ellis; PO Archives].

**ATTICA,** Lapeer County: William Williams, a native of New York State, built a sawmill here in 1851 and on his land was built the main part of the village; I. N. Jenness, also a New Yorker and a lumberman, is considered the co-founder of the village; given a post office named Mill Station on Oct. 9, 1867, with Oscar A. Williams as its first postmaster, the office was renamed Elk Lake on Sept. 12, 1870, and finally Attica, after its township, on Feb. 1, 1871 [Page; PO Archives].

**ATTICA,** Lenawee County: Charles Perry became the first postmaster of this rural post office in Medina Township on May 1, 1851, the office operating until July 17, 1868 [GSM 1865; PO Archives].

**ATWOOD,** Antrim County: Gilbert Randall became the first postmaster of this lumber settlement in Banks Township on March 20, 1868; it was given permanence by an influx of Dutch settlers in 1882; its post office operated until Jan. 21, 1905 [Mich Hist 31:398 1947; PO Archives].

**ATWOOD'S MILLS,** Clare County: this settlement, formed in 1871 around the Atwood sawmills, was given a station on the Pere Marquette Railroad named Atwood's Siding [GSM 1885-95].

**AU BECS,** Benzie County: a New Map of the Chicago & Northwestern Railway (under patent of Jan. 12, 1875) notes a site north of Frankfort, near the mouth of Otter Creek, named Au Becs; it was not a village or a post office, just a railroad terminus; see Bec Scies for the name [Rand McNally, Pioneer Atlas of the American West, 1856-1956].

**AU BEC SCIES,** Manistee County. See Bec Scies.

**AUBURN,** Bay County: John Gaffney, a native of Ireland, became the first permanent settler here in Williams Township in 1854; the village which followed was given a post office named Skinner on Feb. 26, 1869, with Frederick C. Wolf as its first postmaster; it was renamed Auburn on Nov. 17, 1877; incorporated as a city in 1947; "Sweet Auburn! lovliest village of the plain," so begins The Deserted Village of the Anglo-Irish poet Oliver Goldsmith [Page; GSM 1879; PO Archives].

**AUBURN HEIGHTS,** Oakland County: Elijah Thornton, a Canadian, came here in 1821, but Aaron Webster, who named the town Auburn after Auburn, N.Y., became the first permanent settler later the same year; given a post office as Auburn on July 15, 1825, with Johnson Green as its first postmaster, the office operating until May 10, 1856; platted by Captain Henry Parke in 1826; when it applied for a new post office, H. H. Thatcher proposed the name of Amy, for there was by then another Auburn post office in Michigan; given a office as Amy on Sept. 21, 1880, with John Morris as its first postmaster, and a station on the Grand Trunk Railroad, also named Amy, in 1881; in 1919, the legislature changed the name of the village to Auburn Heights and on Aug. 15 of that year its post office was also renamed Auburn Heights [Durant; Mich Manual; PO Archives].

**AUCHVILLE,** Huron County: for judicial purposes this township was attached to Tuscola County until 1853 when it was transferred to Huron County and organized as Sebewaing Township, with Frederick Schilling as its first supervisor; named for Rev. John F. J. Auch, founder of Sebewaing, q.v. [Gwinn].

**AU GRES,** Arenac County: the early French explorers named Point Au Gres (it is shown on a map of Michigan dated 1828) from the "gritty stone" in the region, and from it were named the Au Gres River and the city of Au Gres; its first settlers were workers on the Saginaw-Au Sable State Road which reached this area about 1862; John Edward Bradley, the first permanent settler, built the Bradley House in 1866; Au Gres was given a post office, with him as its first postmaster, on Aug. 8, 1867; it was then in Bay County; the office was closed on March 2, 1874, but restored on the 30th of the following month; never incorporated as a village but as a city in 1905 [Calvin Ennes; PO Archives].

**AUGUSTA,** Kalamazoo County: Dr. Salmon King (1784-1855) came here with his family in 1832 and built a log cabin and later an inn; in 1836, he sold his holdings to Ezra Convis, Sands McCamly, and Epaphroditus Ransom (governor of Michigan, 1848-50), who platted this village in Ross Township; named by George Rigby after his former home, Augusta, Maine; Mr. Rigby became its first postmaster on March 9, 1838; the office was closed on Jan. 1, 1842, but the Charleston post office was transferred to and renamed Augusta on Dec. 16, 1861; incorporated as a village in 1869 [Mrs. E. L. Townsend; PO Archives].

**AURA,** Baraga County: a station on the Duluth, South Shore & Atlantic Railroad, in L'Anse Township; the village was founded by Tobias Hiltunen in 1914; its first settlers named it Aura, the Finnish word for plow; given a post office in 1921, its first postmaster was Mrs. Hilda Mytly, mother of the present (1963) postmaster, Edna Mytly Lehto [PM; GSM 1923].

**AURELIUS,** Ingham County: first called Howe's Corners after Enoch S. Howe, its first settler; Henry Fiske became its first postmaster on Oct. 7, 1857, with the office named Aurelius but changed to Leslie on Jan. 11, 1841; the Aurelius post office was restored on July 15, 1854, with Mr. Howe as postmaster, the office operating until March 14, 1903; named after its township which had been named by pioneer settler Elijah Woodworth after his old home, Aurelius Township, Cayuga County, N.Y. [Foster, Durant; PO Archives].

**AU SABLE,** Iosco County: Curtis Emerson and James Eldridge bought the site in 1848 and first platted the village in 1849; fisherman Elijah Grandy became the first postmaster on Sept. 23, 1856; Francis B. Smith had the village replatted in 1867; incorporated as a village in 1872 and as a city (the largest in the county) in 1889; wiped out by a forest fire in 1911; its post office was closed on Dec. 15, 1912; it surrendered its city charter in 1931 and is now a township; named from its location on the Au Sable (in French, sandy) River [Powers; PO Archives].

**AUSTA,** Clare County: storekeeper William Dexter became the first postmaster of this rural post office, ten miles from Marion, on April 7, 1902, the office operating until Jan. 15, 1906 [GSM 1903-07].

**AUSTERLITZ,** Kent County: first settled by Andrew Watson in 1837, it was the site of and was known as Imperial Mills, a large flouring mill, located at the junction of the Grand and Rogue Rivers, in Plainfield Township, but the mill burned down in 1876; given a post office as

Austerlitz on Jan. 30, 1841, with Zenas G. Winsor as its first postmaster, renamed Imperial Mills on Nov. 5, 1874, but the Austerlitz post office was re-established on the same day, Nov. 5, 1874, and operated until Sept. 30, 1910; this hamlet was also known as Buena Vista [Dillenback; GSM 1875; PO Archives].

**AUSTIN,** Hillsdale County: first settled by the White family, the place was (and on some maps still is) called Whitetown [Mich Hist 6:578 1922].

**AUSTIN,** Kalamazoo County: named from its location near the north shore of Austin Lake which had been named for Moses Austin who had emigrated here in Portage Township from Genesee County, N.Y., in 1833; it was also known as Austin Lake and was given a post office named Austin's Lake, with Mr. Austin as its first postmaster, on May 18, 1850, the office operating until Aug. 15, 1853; given a station named Austin Lake on the Grand Rapids & Indiana Railroad in 1867 [Durant; PO Archives].

**AUSTIN,** Marquette County: the Austin Mine location of the Cleveland Cliffs Iron Company; developed in 1911 as a residence community for the miners and their families [Sawyer].

**AUSTIN,** Mecosta County: this township was organized in 1869, with Jacob Snyder as its first supervisor [Chapman].

**AUSTIN,** Oakland County: a post office in Groveland Townshsp, named for David Austin Wright, its first postmaster who, with Horatio Wright, secured it on March 2, 1848; the office was changed to Taylorsville on Sept. 5, 1849, then changed back to Austin on May 11, 1853, and closed on April 30, 1901; the place was also called Austin Corners [Durant; Seeley; PO Archives].

**AUSTIN,** Sanilac County: Mr. Watson became the first settler in the area in 1854; he was soon followed by Alexander McRae whose wife taught the first school; a steam sawmill was put up in 1868; the town was named after the township which was organized in 1851 but did not get its final form until 1864 and it had been named for William Austin who settled in the county about 1844 [Chapman].

**AUSTIN'S LAKE,** Kalamazoo County. See Austin.

**AU TRAIN,** Alger County: the river carried so much sand into the lake here as to form a shoal over which the voyageurs would drag (trainerant, in French) their canoes to make a short cut; old maps call it Train River, the Au coming later; William Cameron engaged in hunting and trapping here, 1856-58; then Mr. Whittley operated a sawmill here, 1859-61, followed by Mr. Parmenter who took out Norway piling, from 1869, and C. Doucette, Sr., from 1876; then logging began in earnest and it became a thriving village; given a station on the Detroit, Mackinaw & Marquette Railroad by 1882 and a post office on March 22, 1883, with Edward L. Small as its first postmaster; it was in Schoolcraft County until

Alger was organized in 1885; largely destroyed by fire and only partly rebuilt, it is now a resort village [Gagnieux; GSM 1883; PO Archives].

**AVERILL,** Midland County: this village in Lincoln Township began as a lumbering settlement and after a local saloon was called Red Keg it was popularized in Eugene Thwing's novels The Man from Red Keg, and The Redkeggers; it was given a post office named Averill's Station named for its first postmaster, Averill S. Harrison, on Sept. 30, 1868, with the name shortened to Averill on June 2, 1883; platted in 1870, the year the railroad came through [Mich Hist 20:86 1936, 27:205 1943; Federal; PO Archives].

**AVERY,** Berrien County: named for Gilbert B. Avery who, with Thomas Love, built a sawmill here in Three Oaks Township in 1854; Mr. Avery became its first postmaster on March 3, 1860, succeeded by Mr. Love; also given a station on the Michigan Central Railroad, both depot and post office have since been closed, the latter on Nov. 18, 1890; it was also known as Avery Station and as Avery's Mills [Chauncey; PO Archives].

**AVERYVILLE,** Montcalm County. See Wyman.

**AVIS,** Allegan County: grocer Hiram B. Northrup became the first postmaster of this rural post office in Casco Township on June 30, 1892, the office operating until March 31, 1903 [GSM 1893; PO Archives].

**AVOCA,** St. Clair County: the village was founded about 1884; the Pere Marquette Railroad came through in 1889 and it was given a station; Richard Newkirk became its first postmaster on March 7, 1890; named after the Avoca River and Valley in County Wicklow, Ireland [Francis Fuller; PO Archives].

**AVON,** Ionia County: Asaph C. Smith became the first postmaster of this rural post office in Keene Township on July 11, 1844; the office was closed on July 10, 1862, but was restored from April 2, 1897, to Aug. 30, 1902 [Schenck; PO Archives].

**AVON,** Oakland County: first settled by James Graham, followed by Samuel S. Hubbell, both in 1820; the township was organized and named in 1835; John Miller became its first postmaster on April 13, 1842, the office operating until March 16, 1843 [Seeley; MPH 38:348 1912; PO Archives].

**AVONDALE,** Osceola County: this village serving a wheat growing community in Hartwick Township was settled in 1880 and given a post office on May 22, 1882, with Everett J. Terrell, a storekeeper, as its first postmaster, the office operating until Nov. 30, 1907 [GSM 1885; PO Archives].

**AXIN,** Wexford County: this rural post office, 9½ miles southwest of Cadillac, was named for its first postmaster, J. Axin Morgan, on Aug. 21, 1899, the office operating until Jan. 30, 1943 [GSM 1901; PO Archives].

**AYR,** Emmet County: Patrick J. Burns became the first postmaster of this sawmill settlement in the central part of the county on Dec. 12, 1878; T. B. Snyder operated its general store; homesteaders from Canada named it after Ayr, Ontario [Mrs. Henry Brubacher; PO Archives; GSM 1881].

**AZALIA,** Monroe County: Stephen B. Frink became the first postmaster of East Milan (named from its location in Milan Township) on Aug. 4, 1869; Reeves and son operated the Star Bending Company here and the place was also known as Reeves Station; on Sept. 1, 1887, the post office was renamed Azalia to correspond with its railroad depot which had been named for the daughter of an executive of the road [Wm. L. Noble, PM; PO Archives].

**AZTEC,** Houghton County: a copper mining settlement around the Aztec Mine, opened about 1850 and named in the belief that copper mining in prehistoric times had been done by the Aztecs; its property became part of Adventure Consolidated [Stevens].

**BACH,** Huron County: a station on the Michigan Central Railroad, in Sebewaing Township; the village was founded by Frederick Bach in 1889 and named for him; storekeeper Samuel Sussman became its first postmaster on Nov. 5, 1912 [PM; GSM 1915].

**BACHELOR,** Mason County: storekeeper Robert E. Rogers became the first postmaster here on Feb. 14, 1884; the name was derived from that of the local sawmill firm of Alden A. Batchellor & Company; the sign on the depot of the branch of the Pere Marquette Railroad here was spelled Batchellor [GSM 1885; PO Archives].

**BACKUS,** Livingston County: this rural post office opened 9 miles south of Howell on Dec. 20, 1898, was named for its first postmaster, Frank E. Backus; the office operated until Feb. 14, 1901 [GSM 1901; PO Archives].

**BACON,** Wayne County. See Glenwood.

**BAD AXE,** Huron County: while surveying a road through here in 1861, Captain Rudolph Papst made camp at an old hunter's cabin, finding in it a much-used axe; at the suggestion of Lt. G. W. Pack, Captain Papst used the name Bad Axe Camp in his Minutes of Survey and later on his county map; given a post office named Bad Axe on Nov. 27, 1870, with Charles E. Brown as its first postmaster; on Oct. 15, 1872, the county supervisors voted to make the place the county seat, and the next year they planned and platted the village and moved to it the county seat from Port Austin; incorporated as a village in 1885, with Septimus Irwin, the first settler, as president; incorporated as a city in 1905; the legislature changed its name to Huron in 1909, but the townspeople voted back its original name [Hey; Chapman; PO Archives].

**BADEAUX STATION,** Muskegon County: a depot on the Chicago & Western Michigan Railroad, together with the boarding houses of the

BRIDGEWATER STATION
Store & Res. - H. Guthardt & Sons

BEDFORD TWP.
Farm Res. - W. J. May

workers in the shingle mill built here by George Badeaux in 1878 and the shingle mill of Burrows & Blythe [Page].

**BAD RIVER,** Gratiot County. See Edgewood.

**BAGDAD,** Marquette County: the site of a stone quarry in the 1850s, this settlement, six miles from Marquette, was given a station on the Duluth, South Shore & Atlantic Railroad about 1890; another stop on the line, a mile distant, was named Bagdad Junction; Bagdad is now just a railroad sign [G. Vance Hiney].

**BAGLEY,** Menominee County: founded in 1874 by Fred Wachter, a logging camp operator; he named it for William E. Bagley, builder of many sawmills then going up along the right of way of the Chicago & Northwestern Railroad, including the one here; George H. Paynter became its first postmaster on Dec. 23, 1874, the office operating until Aug. 31, 1933 [Albert Kipfer; PO Archives].

**BAGLEY,** Otsego County: a station in Bagley Township on the Mackinaw division of the Michigan Central Railroad in 1876; named for John J. Bagley, Republican, who had been elected governor of Michigan in 1872; its post office was Mellens, q.v. [GSM 1877].

**BAGLEY'S CORNERS,** Oakland County. See Bloomfield Hills.

**BAGNALL,** Wexford County: this station on the Toledo, Ann Arbor & Northern Michigan Railroad, when opened in 1888, was named Bagnall; its settlement formed around the grist mill and the sawmill of Farnsworth & Chesbrough and was given a post office named Farnsworth on June 20, 1889, with Stephen A. Farnsworth as its first postmaster; the office was renamed Bagnall on Dec. 29, 1902 [GSM 1891-1905; PO Archives].

**BAIE de WASAI,** Chippewa County: Alexander Atkins became the first postmaster of this three sawmill settlement on Sugar Island on Aug. 5, 1908; the office was closed on June 30, 1911, but was restored, with Ambrose E. Thibert as postmaster on Dec. 11, 1915, and operated until Nov. 31, 1933; the name in English is turbot bay, or bay of the bullheads, which still abound here [Hamilton; GSM 1911; PO Archives].

**BAILEY,** Clare County: a railroad station in Surrey Township in 1878 [GSM 1879].

**BAILEY,** Muskegon County: Mr. Bailey cut the first timber here in Casavovia Township in 1865 and named the settlement for himself; given a post office on Oct. 24, 1872, with James I. Walker as its first postmaster; its railroad station was named County Line, being near both the Newaygo and Kent County line [Karl W. Pendell, PM; GSM 1875].

**BAINBRIDGE,** Berrien County: Jehiel Enos, who had the township surveyed in 1830, named it after his native Bainbridge, Chenango County, N.Y.; its first settlers were the Bartholomew Sharrai family, in 1833; John P. David became its first postmaster on Feb. 15, 1836; the town was organized in 1837; its post office was closed on Oct. 29, 1873, but was restored from Aug. 19, 1875, to Jan. 14, 1905 [Fox; GSM 1907; PO Archives].

**BAINTON**, Berrien County: a station on the Milwaukee, Benton Harbor & Columbus Railway in 1898 [Mich Manual 1899].

**BAKER'S**, Hillsdale County: a station on the D., T. & M. Railroad, in Somerset Township; storekeeper Don H. Elliott became its first postmaster on Oct. 20, 1897, the office operating until Dec. 14, 1903 [GSM 1899; PO Archives].

**BAKER'S**, Lenawee County. See Fairfield.

**BAKER'S CORNERS**, St. Clair County. See Berville.

**BAKERSTOWN**, Berrien County: this village in Bertrand Township was named for the Baker brothers who operated a mill here in the 1830s [Fox].

**BALCH**, Kalamazoo County: named for A. R. Balch, pioneer lumberman and political figure, who died in 1872; the Balch family was prominent in Allegan County as well [Fisher; MPH 26:128 1895].

**BALCH**, Lenawee County. See Britton.

**BALDWIN**, Delta County: the township was named for C. S. Baldwin, former superintendent of the Peninsula division of the Chicago & Northwestern Railroad, in 1873 [David S. Coon].

**BALDWIN**, Jackson County. See Horton.

**BALDWIN**, Lake County: first called Hannibal in 1870 for Mr. Hannibal, an early settler in Webber Township, who lived north of the court house where all the locality bore his name; after Isaac Grant built a store here he headed a committee which had its name changed to honor Henry P. Baldwin, then governor of Michigan, in 1872; Colonel F. Basom became the first postmaster of Baldwin City on Dec. 5, 1872, with the name shortened to Baldwin on May 28, 1875; given a station on the Pere Marquette Railroad in 1873; the county seat since 1874; incorporated as a village in 1887 [Judkins; Bessie Duffing; PO Archives].

**BALDWIN LAKE**, Cass County. See Porter.

**BALDWIN'S MILLS**, Jackson County. See Horton.

**BALDWIN'S PRAIRIE**, Cass County: named for John Baldwin who first settled here in 1829, as was its Baldwin Lake; contiguous to the village of Union [Mich Hist 31:281 1947].

**BALL**, Cheboygan County: a rural post office on Mullett Lake, in Grant Township, named after its first postmaster, farmer Nelson H. Ball, on Aug. 21, 1883, the office operating until May 24, 1890 [GSM 1891].

**BALLARDS**, Kent County: also called Ballard's Corners, it was named after a local landowner; Ezra Brown became its first postmaster on Feb. 26, 1889, the office operating until Sept. 30, 1903 [GSM 1891; PO Archives].

**BALL CREEK**, Kent County. See Kent City.

**BALLENTINE**, Ontonagon County. See Lake Gogebic.

**BALL MOUNTAIN**, Oakland County: Platt Johnson became the first postmaster of this hamlet, then five miles northeast of Pontiac, on June 25, 1846, the office operating until Oct. 29, 1869 [GSM 1879; PO Archives].

**BALLOU**, Wexford County: Elmer C. Lewis became the first postmaster of this rural post office in Selma Township on May 16, 1892, the office operating until Sept. 6, 1893 [GSM 1893; PO Archives].

**BALLOU'S SIDING**, Charlevoix County. See Phelps.

**BALSAM**, Iron County: a settlement with a station on the Chicago & Northwestern Railroad, 4 miles southeast of Amasa, in 1884; Frank C. Deming became its first postmaster on Feb. 13, 1909, but the office was closed on Nov. 15 of the same year; named after the tree which dominates the area [Robert Flood; GSM 1895; PO Archives].

**BALTIC**, Houghton County: a station on the Copper Range Railroad, in Adams Township; the village was founded and named by the Baltic Mining Company in 1898, F. W. Denton, superintendent; John Jolly became its first postmaster on Nov. 6, 1902, succeeded by storekeeper John B. Dee in 1903 [GSM 1905; PO Archives].

**BALTIMORE**, Barry County. See Dowling.

**BAMFIELD**, Alcona County: a station on the Au Sable & Northwestern Railroad, near Bamfield Pond; March C. Freeman became its first postmaster on Dec. 11, 1922, the office operating until June 30, 1924 [Mich Manual 1899; PO Archives].

**BANAT**, Menominee County: first settled in 1909 by Austro-Hungarians, mostly from St. Louis, Missouri, and headed by Frank J. Schmidt who became its first postmaster on March 15, 1910; a station on the Wisconsin & Michigan Railroad; named after the district of Banat in Austro-Hungary, from which the settlers originally came [Rev. Thomas Ruppe].

**BANCROFT**, Shiawassee County: founded on land first owned by N. G. Phillips and W. M. Warren; its first plat was not recorded but its second was in 1877, in which year it became a station on the Chicago & Lake Huron Railroad, with H. M. Billings as agent; John L. Simonson became its first postmaster on June 28, 1877; incorporated as a village in 1883 [Ellis].

**BANCROFT**, Marquette County: here on a clearing on the Dead River, 4 miles from Marquette, was located a furnace of the Bancroft Iron Company in 1860; given a station on the Marquette, Houghton & Ontonagon Railroad [Havighurst; GSM 1885].

**BANDOLA**, Wexford County: Herman C. Meyer became the first postmaster of this rural post office in Antioch Township on June 20, 1879, the office operating until Oct. 2, 1890 [Thomas W. Blinn].

**BANFIELD,** Barry County: Harvey F. Bellinger became the first postmaster of this rural post office on April 13, 1880, the office operating until Sept. 15, 1904 [PO Archives].

**BANGOR,** Bay County. See West Bay City.

**BANGOR,** Van Buren County: first settled by Charles U. Cross in 1837, followed by John Smith, John Southard and Caleb Northrop, all later that year; the town was named after the township which was erected in 1853, organized in 1854, and named after Bangor, Maine; Joseph Nyman became its first postmaster on Feb. 9, 1859; the first plat of the village was made by Mr. Nyman, and recorded in 1860, the second by Mr. Cross in 1867; incorporated as a village in 1877 [Ellis; Dunbar; PO Archives].

**BANISTER,** Gratiot County. See Bannister.

**BANKERS,** Hillsdale County: founded by Horace and George Banker who located here in 1838; as a terminus of the Detroit, Hillsdale & Indiana Railroad, this sawmill site was first called Bankers Station; platted in 1869; Charles A. Shattuck became its first postmaster on Jan. 30, 1872, the office operating until Jan. 31, 1909 [Vivian Lyon Moore].

**BANKS,** Bay County. See West Bay City.

**BANKS PARK,** Oakland County. See Huntington Woods.

**BANNER,** Sanilac County: blacksmith Charles J. Burget became the first postmaster of this rural post office in Wheatland Township on Aug. 5, 1891, the office operating until Jan. 14, 1905 [GSM 1893-1907; PO Archives].

**BANNISTER,** Gratiot County: Asahel M. Bannister, of Jackson, bought the land here in 1881; Thomas A. Hanvey, grocery store owner, became the first postmaster on Feb. 23, 1883, with the office spelled Banister, but corrected to Bannister on July 10, 1884; the Ann Arbor Railroad came through in 1884, building a depot here; Messrs. Bannister and Hanvey, together with Benjamin S. Brownell and Ralph Sutfin, platted the village in 1885 [Tucker; PO Archives].

**BARAGA,** Baraga County: in 1843, Rev. Frederic Baraga opened the Holy Name mission for the Indians here and around it the town grew; given a post office named Bristol on June 29, 1869, with Henry Houghton as its first postmaster; the office was renamed Baraga on May 11, 1870, closed on Dec. 18, 1871, but restored from March 26, 1872, to date; it was in Houghton County until Baraga was organized in 1875; incorporated as a village in 1891 [Sawyer; PO Archives].

**BARBEAU,** Chippewa County: Thomas Henderson became the first homesteader here in 1877 and the first postmaster on Nov. 7, 1883; the office was closed on June 15, 1909, but was restored on May 27, 1916; named for pioneer settler Peter B. Barbeau [Bayliss; Hamilton; PO Archives].

**BARCLAY,** Ontonagon County: in 1892, the Chicago & Northwestern Railroad came through the site of the Barclay Lumber Company mill and on Feb. 16 of that year it was given a post office as Barclay, with William H. Clinton as its first postmaster; the office was closed on Sept. 7, 1897, but was restored from May 17, 1898, to May 31, 1904; the last of the pine mills to close, it sawed its last log on July 4, 1901 [Charles Willman; PO Archives].

**BARD,** Gladwin County: pioneer settlers in the area were Celie Nunn and Ed Bennett, both in 1889; the village formed around the sawmill of George Bard; storekeepers John M. Bard became the first postmaster on March 19, 1902, and George Booth, the second, in 1903, but the office was closed on June 15, 1907 [Ritchie; PO Archives].

**BAREFOOT,** Van Buren County. See McDonald.

**BARGER,** Missaukee County: this rural post office, 15 miles east of Lake City, was named for farmer Martin S. Barger who became its first postmaster on April 5, 1902, the office operating until April 29, 1905 [GSM 1903-07; PO Archives].

**BARKER CREEK,** Kalkaska County: William H. Bockes bought land here on Barker Creek in 1866; Norman Ross, who came in 1867, became the first supervisor when Clearwater Township was organized; a station on the Chicago & Western Michigan (now Pere Marquette) Railroad; Mr. Bockes became the first postmaster on Feb. 2, 1874, the office operating until May 19, 1937 [Traverse; GSM 1875; PO Archives].

**BARK RIVER,** Delta County: Captain Charles Pease, the first settler, homesteaded here in 1871; with Luke D. McKenna as its first postmaster, the settlement was given a post office named Barkville on Nov. 30, 1877; with the coming through of the Chicago & Northwestern Railroad in 1882, the village was moved to the north side of the track and renamed Bark River; its post office was renamed on July 11, 1899; located in the birch tree area and near the Bark River, locally the name connotes the area as well as the village [Philip R. Norman, PM; Escanaba Daily Press, Sept. 24, 1965; PO Archives].

**BARK SHANTY,** Sanilac County. See Port Sanilac.

**BARKVILLE,** Delta County. See Bark River.

**BAR LAKE,** Manistee County. See Arcadia.

**BARLOW LAKE,** Barry County: named after Nathan Barlow who with his wife came from Canandaigua, N.Y., to nearby Yankee Springs in 1840 [MPH 36:657 1908].

**BARNARD,** Charlevoix County: this village in Marion Township was settled in 1866 and developed around the sawmill of Barnard Burns for whom it was named and who became its first postmaster on June 29, 1866, the office operating until May 2, 1881; it was in Emmet County until Charlevoix was organized in 1869 [GSM 1873; PO Archives].

**BARNARD**, Newaygo County: this rural post office was named for John W. Barnard who became its first postmaster on May 25, 1883, but the office was closed on Aug. 16 of the same year [PO Archives].

**BARNES**, Midland County: a rural post office named for storekeeper John F. Barnes who became its first postmaster on Jan. 9, 1897, the office operating until Aug. 31, 1903 [GSM 1899-1905; PO Archives].

**BARNES**, Otsego County. See Gaylord.

**BARNETT**, Berrien County: a way station on the Michigan Central Railroad, 3 miles east of Three Oaks, in 1898 [GSM 1899].

**BARNETT**, Oceana County. See Shelby.

**BARNETTSVILLE**, Huron County. See Harbor Beach.

**BARNEYVILLE**, Calhoun County. See Homer.

**BARNUM**, Marquette County: the name of a mine and its community; opened about 1873 by the Iron Cliffs Company and named for its president, William H. Barnum, who was also chairman of the National Democratic Committee [Mich Hist 5:160 1921].

**BARODA**, Berrien County: platted by M. B. Houser who named it Houser, but the post office rejected the name and he then named it after a city in India; a station on the Vandalia Line, express agent Aldis E. Holmes became its first postmaster on Dec. 3, 1890; incorporated as a village in 1907 [Fox; GSM 1891; PO Archives].

**BARRINGTON**, Clinton County. See Eureka.

**BARRON LAKE**, Cass County: this station on the Michigan Central Railroad, near Barron Lake, in Howard Township, was given a post office on July 21, 1885, with Theodore Winchell as its first postmaster; the office was closed on Oct. 29, 1890, but was restored from Dec. 23, 1890, to July 20, 1894; when it was again restored on Oct. 9, 1895, with Frank D. Smith as its postmaster, the office was named simply Barron, but it operated only until Dec. 20, 1899 [GSM 1897; PO Archives].

**BARRY**, Jackson County. See Sandstone.

**BARRY**, Mecosta County: Charles A. Reed became the first postmaster of this rural post office on March 9, 1892, the office operating until Feb. 2, 1893 [PO Archives].

**BARRYTON**, Mecosta County: founded in 1894 by Frank Barry, dealer in groceries, real estate and some drugs (hence nicknamed Doc); given a post office on Oct. 19, 1894, with Edw. R. Sage as its first postmaster; a station on the Detroit, Grand Rapids & Western Railroad; incorporated as a village in 1908 [Beatrice Moorman; PO Archives].

**BARRYVILLE**, Barry County: M. J. Lathrop and his partner, Mr. Corsett, built a grist mill here on Highbank Creek, in Castleton Township, about 1856; the Castleton post office was changed to Barryville on Dec. 22, 1857, but was closed on March 7, 1873 [Johnson; PO Archives].

**BARTLETT**, Grand Traverse County: this rural post office in Mayfield Township was named for Wayland W. Bartlett who became its first postmaster on Dec. 8, 1879, the office operating until April 30, 1903 [Sprague; PO Archives].

**BARTLEY**, Marquette County: Anthony C. Cafferty became the first postmaster of this rural post office on Nov. 27, 1905 [PO Archives].

**BARTON**, Newaygo County: this village, named after its township, was given a post office on May 6, 1869, with Francis H. Hooker as its first postmaster, the office operating until Nov. 6, 1871; it was also given a railroad station [GSM 1873; PO Archives].

**BARTON**, Washtenaw County: an early paper village platted in Ann Arbor Township; by 1881 it comprised one house [Chapman].

**BARTON CITY**, Alcona County: the site of the main branch of the Potts Lumbering Company and the Loud Lumbering Company; it was first called Mud Lake, from its location on Mud Lake, and was given a post office of that name on March 10, 1887, with George W. LaChapelle as its first postmaster; in 1912, two surveyors staying at the home of Frank Barton, a settler here, laid out the town around the lake (on paper), sold lots, and named it for him; the post office took the new name on Feb. 29 of the same year [Blanche Coggan; PO Archives].

**BASE LAKE**, Washtenaw County. See Dover.

**BASE LINE**, Macomb County: this square mile area lies just north of Eight Mile Road, often referred to as Base Line Road since it runs over the approximate location of the surveyors' base line for Michigan; although it was platted and recorded on Nov. 2, 1860, and given a post office on April 25, 1927, with George P. Siagkris as its first postmaster, it was always under township government until annexed by the city of Warren in 1957; its post office was closed on July 31, 1957 [Gerald Neil; County plat liber; PO Archives].

**BASS BEACH**, Montcalm County: platted as a resort village, on Town Line Lake, in Cato Township, and recorded by Mr. and Mrs. George Whitcomb on Aug. 1, 1889 [Dasef].

**BASS LAKE**, Mason County: Miss Hattie L. McKee became the first postmaster of this rural post office (spelled Basslake), in Summit Township, on June 17, 1897, the office operating until Oct. 31, 1902 [GSM 1899-1903; PO Archives].

**BASS LANDING**, Ottawa County: this settlement at a landing on the Grand River, in Allendale Township, was given a post office named North Robinson, on March 23, 1877, with Joseph G. Failing as its first postmaster, the office operating until Aug. 28, 1879 [GSM 1881; PO Archives].

**BASS RIVER**, Ottawa County: this settlement at a landing on the Grand River was given a post office on July 18, 1882, with Andrew J. White as its first postmaster, the office operating until Sept. 30, 1910 [GSM 1883; PO Archives].

**BASSWOOD,** Iron County: a station on a branch of the Chicago & Northwestern Railroad, 12 miles southeast of Watersmeet, in 1894; like several others of these stops, it was named after forest trees [GSM 1895].

**BASSWOOD CORNERS,** Hillsdale County. See Reading.

**BATAVIA,** Branch County: first settled in 1832 by Timothy R. Wallace, from New York State, and named after Batavia, N.Y.; Martin Olds came from Ohio in 1835 and led in organizing the town; given a post office on Aug. 27, 1838, with Lot Whitcomb as its first postmaster, the office operating until Dec. 31, 1954; a station on the Lake Shore & Michigan Southern Railroad [Johnson; PO Archives].

**BATCHELLOR,** Mason County. See Bachelor.

**BATEMAN,** Lenawee County: storekeeper Albert L. Gilhouse became the first postmaster of this rural post office on June 22, 1898, the office operating until June 30, 1903 [GSM 1899; PO Archives].

**BATES,** Grand Traverse County: Thomas T. Bates was secretary of the Traverse City Railroad Company when organized in 1870; because he was believed to have got the road through here in 1891, the village and its post office were named for him; Lyman P. Fox became its first postmaster on Sept. 21, 1891, the office operating until May 31, 1933 [B. McCourtney; PO Archives].

**BATES,** Osceola County. See Ashton.

**BATH,** Clinton County: the first settler in the area was Ira Cushman and his family in 1836; because he came from Canada, it is believed he named the township after Bath, England; the land of the village itself was first entered and settled by a Mexican War veteran, Dustin Marr; he sold out to Charles Thompkins, and when the Michigan Central Railroad came through, Mr. Thompkins gave land for depot and yard purposes, and thus the village began; given a post office on June 7, 1858; platted in 1864 [Lee D. Reasoner; Daboll].

**BATH MILLS,** Jackson County: a station on the Michigan Central Railroad in Concord Township in 1878 [GSM 1879].

**BATTEESE LAKE,** Jackson County. See Henrietta.

**BATTLE CREEK,** Calhoun County: two Indians and two members of John Mullett's surveying party fought it out on the banks of a river here in 1824 and Mr. Mullett dubbed the stream Battle Creek; J. J. Garnsey made the first government land purchase here in 1831; he transferred his claim to Phineas P. Sackett and Ezekiel B. Garnsey; in 1832, Samuel Convis, who had an interest in the Garnsey purchase, built the first house; D. G. Garnsey became the first postmaster in May of 1832, with the office named Garnsey, but changed to Battle Creek on May 8, 1834; surveyed by General Ezra Convis in 1835 and platted by Samuel D. Moore in 1836; incorporated as a village in 1850 and as a city in 1859 [Everts; PO Archives].

**BAUER,** Ottawa County: this village in Georgetown Township was named for pioneer settler N. Bauer; Charles C. Smedley became its first postmaster on March 1, 1880, the office operating until Sept. 30, 1910 [Page; PO Archives].

**BAXTER,** Wexford County: Herman T. Marvin became the first postmaster at this station on the M. & N.E. Railroad on July 30, 1910 [GSM 1911].

**BAY CITY,** Bay County: Joseph and Mader Tromblé (or Trombley), brothers, built a trading post here in 1835 and the first house in 1837; lumberman James Fraser, of Detroit, in 1836, through his Saginaw Bay Company, bought 240 acres of the John Riley Reserve here and platted the village of Lower Saginaw, named from its nearness to the lower shore of Saginaw Bay; given a post office as Hampton, named after its township, with Thomas Rogers becoming its first postmaster on June 4, 1846; the office was renamed Lower Saginaw, but the citizens objected to the word Lower and in 1857 the legislature renamed it Bay City, the post office taking that name on March 22, 1858; incorporated as a village in 1859 and as a city in 1865 [MPH 3:316 1881, 18:441 1891; Mich Hist 15:179 1931; PO Archives].

**BAY De NOC,** Delta County: the bay and the settlement beside it were named after the Noquet Indians on whose tribal lands they were located; given a post office as Bay de Noquet on Nov. 29, 1878, with Robert Peacock as its first postmaster, the spelling was changed to Bay de Noquette on Nov. 8, 1886, but the office was closed on Nov. 5, 1887 [Jean Worth; GSM 1879; PO Archives].

**BAYFIELD,** Emmet County. See Harbor Springs.

**BAY FURNACE,** Alger County: the Bay Furnace Company opened a blast furnace here just west of Munising, on Munising Bay, in 1869; it turned hardwood into charcoal to serve the early iron makers; the settlement was destroyed by fire on May 31, 1877, and the company went out of business about a year later; the area came to be called the Christmas Location [Munising News, March 3, 1935].

**BAY MILLS,** Chippewa County: named from its location on Waiska Bay; James Norris & Company established a lumber business here in 1875; Frank Perry became the first postmaster on May 23, 1879; after fire destroyed the Hall & Munson lumber mills in 1904, the village began to vanish; its post office was closed on Nov. 30, 1909; now an Indian reservation called Bay Mills Community [Bayliss; Dunbar; PO Archives].

**BAY PORT,** this village in Fair Haven Township was founded in 1851 by Carl H. Heisterman; it was first called Geneva, after Geneva, Switzerland, then Wild Fowl Port, from its location on Wild Fowl Bay, and finally Bay Port; the Ora Labora post office was changed to Bay Port on March 19, 1872 [Hey; PO Archives].

**BAY SETTLEMENT,** Monroe County. See Erie.

**BAY SHORE,** Charlevoix County: the land was owned by Eugene R. Sly and Nancy Stauffer; north of the old Gilmartin Road it was known as Bay Side, but both areas came to be called Bay Shore; given a station on the Chicago & Western Michigan (now Pere Marquette) Railroad by 1892 and on July 25, 1892, a post office, with Mr. Sly, then secretary of the Bay Side Resort, as its first postmaster, the office operating until Sept. 30, 1964; surveyed and platted by John Swift in 1896; named from its location on Little Traverse Bay [Lydia C. Stolt, PM].

**BAY SIDE,** Bay County: a coal mining village on Saginaw Bay, in Bangor Township; it has no station but switches from the Detroit & Mackinaw and the Grand Trunk Railroads; Frederick A. Lewis became its first postmaster on Dec. 12, 1899, the office operating until Jan. 15, 1910 [GSM 1901; PO Archives].

**BAY SIDING,** Delta County: in 1874, a station on the Chicago & Northwestern Railroad, five miles north of Escanaba, near Little Bay De Noc [GSM 1875].

**BAY SPRINGS,** Charlevoix County: a resort colony at the head of Pine Lake (now Lake Charlevoix), in 1882; Almond B. Chapman became its first postmaster on Oct. 3, 1884, the office operating until July 15, 1905 [GSM 1883-1907; PO Archives].

**BAY STATE,** Keweenaw County: the settlement around the Bay State Mine which produced its first copper in 1865 and was sold to Phoenix Consolidated in 1868; its mining was financed in Massachusetts, popularly known as the Bay State [Stevens].

**BAY VIEW,** Emmet County: founded by a group of Methodists as the Bay View Association in 1875, for religious purposes; an educational program (lectures and music) was begun in 1886, and the community developed from it; mail was handled in the Association's hotel, Bay View House, but when it burned down a government post office was established; given a station on the Grand Rapids & Indiana Railroad; named from its view of Little Traverse Bay [C. John Wooden; Mich Hist 48:18 Mar 1964].

**BEACH,** Mackinac County: this rural post office near St. Martin Bay was named for John W. Beach who became its first postmaster on July 19, 1912 [GSM 1913; PO Archives].

**BEACH'S CORNERS,** Tuscola County. See Akron.

**BEACON,** Marquette County. See Champion Mine.

**BEACON HILL,** Houghton County: this settlement in Stanton Township was a center of the Trimountain Mining Company, W. J. Uren, superintendent; largely financed by Boston capital, hence its name, Beacon Hill being then a fashionable district in Boston; a station on the Copper Range Railroad; Nathaniel West became its first postmaster on Dec. 11, 1901, the office operating until Aug. 31, 1952 [GSM 1903; PO Archives].

**BEADLE,** Calhoun County: a flag station on the D., T. & M. Railroad, by the Kalamazoo River, in Emmet Township; storekeeper

Charles E. Kistler became its first postmaster on Dec. 3, 1887, the office operating until Nov. 11, 1903 [GSM 1899; PO Archives].

**BEAL CITY,** Isabella County: founded by Mr. Beal who opened a grocery store here in Nottawa Township about 1880; stationer Jacob P. Juncker became its first postmaster on Dec. 19, 1892, the office operating until March 31, 1910 [Fancher; GSM 1895; PO Archives].

**BEAN CREEK,** Lenawee County. See Hudson.

**BEANVILLE,** Oceana County: founded in 1878 by John Bean, Jr., who built a sawmill and general store here in Crystal Township; he sold out to Nickerson & Collister, of Pentwater, in 1880 [Page].

**BEAR CREEK,** Manistee County: a station on the M. & N. Railroad in 1894 [GSM 1895].

**BEAR CREEK,** Schoolcraft County: a station on the B. & S. Railroad, near Bear Creek, in 1912 [GSM 1913].

**BEARDLEY'S PRAIRIE,** Cass County. See Edwardsburg.

**BEAR LAKE,** Charlevoix County. See Walloon Lake.

**BEAR LAKE,** Manistee County: this village on Bear Lake was first settled by Russell F. Smith in 1863 and most of it was platted on land which he sold to the brothers George W. and David H. Hopkins; their business interests developed the village which they platted in 1874; Jerome Hulbert became its first postmaster on April 27, 1865; incorporated as a village in 1893 [Virginia Stroemel; Page; PO Archives].

**BEAR LAKE MILLS,** Van Buren County. See Berlamont.

**BEAR RIVER,** Emmet County. See Petoskey.

**BEASER,** Ontonagon County: a settlement on Lake Superior, at the mouth of the Iron River, it was given a post office as Iron River on Dec. 8, 1875, with Daniel Beaser, supervisor of Carp Lake Township, as its first postmaster, the office operating until April 27, 1882; on Dec. 14, 1885, he was again appointed postmaster, with the office named Beaser, and operating until Sept. 4, 1889 [GSM 1887-89; PO Archives].

**BEATON,** Gogebic County: this settlement began as a siding on the Chicago & Northwestern Railroad and was named for a jobber in the woods [Victor Lemmer].

**BEAUFORT JUNCTION,** Baraga County: a station on the Marquette, Houghton & Ontonagon Railroad in 1884 [GSM 1885].

**BEAUGRAND,** Cheboygan County: Charles Bellant came here about 1852, began in lumbering and then settled on a farm; named for Oliver Beaugrand, another early settler; no village developed from the township [Traverse].

**BEAU RIVER,** Emmet County: in 1878, a hamlet on Little Traverse Bay, in Bear Lake Township [GSM 1879].

**BEAVER**, Delta County: a station on the Chicago & Northwestern Railroad, in Baldwin Township; named by the road because of the many beaver dams on the nearby Days River; the depot, opened in 1873 and closed about 1954, was given a post office named Winde, after Henry Winde, there being already a Beaver post office in Michigan; railroad telegraph operator Joseph M. Richards became its first postmaster on Aug. 30, 1918, the office operating until Feb. 28, 1925 [George T. Springer; GSM 1875; PO Archives].

**BEAVER**, Newaygo County: Albertus M. Andrews became the first postmaster of this hamlet on Aug. 2, 1872, the office operating until Feb. 18, 1874 [GSM 1873; PO Archives].

**BEAVER CREEK**, Gratiot County: located by a stream bearing that name and running from Half Moon Lake into Pine River, in Seville Township; David C. Lamphere became its first postmaster on Dec. 3, 1860, the office operating until June 23, 1875 [Tucker].

**BEAVER DAM**, Ottawa County: general storekeeper Jacob Bardense became the first postmaster here in Zeeland Township on Sept. 3, 1877, the office operating until May 31, 1905 [GSM 1879; PO Archives].

**BEAVER HARBOR**, Charlevoix County. See St. James.

**BEAVER ISLAND**, Charlevoix County: a 14 mile long, 3 to 6 mile wide island (sometimes called Big Beaver), 35 miles west of the city of Charlevoix; named from the many beavers then there, but now nearly exterminated; the early French explorers called it Ile du Castor; Frederick Baraga, who first visited it in 1832, reported an eight-hut Indian village there, which history and tradition now locate as the present Indian Point; the only village now on the Island is St. James, q.v.; Charles W. Wright became the first postmaster of Beaver Island, Michilimackinac County, on Jan. 13, 1849, with the name of the office changed to St. James, Emmet County, on Oct. 10, 1854; the office was closed on March 6, 1868, but was restored from Dec. 19, 1868, to date [Mich Hist 39:385 1955; Pen Phil 7:3 March 1957].

**BEAVER LAKE**, Ogemaw County: this village in Klacking Township was founded in 1872 by George G. Damon of the lumber firm of Cutting & Damon; given a station on the Mackinaw division of the Michigan Central Railroad in 1873; James A. Beerman became its first postmaster on Dec. 29, 1875; the office was closed on Oct. 23, 1895, but was restored by 1898 [GSM 1875; PO Archives].

**BEAVERTON**, Gladwin County: its first settlers, most of them lumbermen, located here about 1863; first known as Grand Forks from its location at the forks of the Tobacco and Cedar Rivers; its continuous settlement dates from 1875; the town was founded in 1890 by Donald Gunn Ross & Sons, lumbermen, from Beaverton, Ontario; Donald Ross became its first postmaster on Feb. 27, 1891; incorporated as a village in 1901 and as a city, with William Ross as mayor, in 1903 [Effa J. Hunter; PO Archives].

**BECKERVILLE**, Ottawa County: a village in 1864 [GSM 1865].

**BECKET**, Sanilac County. See Valley Center.

**BEC SCIES**, Manistee County: this settlement in Springdale Township was given a post office on Aug. 15, 1881, with Cabb Davison as its first postmaster, the office operating until June 8, 1883; named from its location what is now called the Betsie River, originally the Rivière du Père Marquette; the present Otter Creek was originally named the Rivière aux Bec Scies; the French name bec-scie means sawbill, a species of duck which evidently abounded on the stream; on the Nicolas Bellin map of 1744 as Rivière aux Buscies; the name (due to handwriting problems) has also been ill-spelled as Betsies, Bescies, Becscies, etc. [Catherine L. Stebbins, Mich Hist 48:333 Dec 1964; J. Antoine Pelletier; GSM 1883; PO Archives].

**BEDDOW**, Oakland County: this rural post office in Smithfield Township was named for storekeeper John M. Beddow who became its first postmaster on Dec. 15, 1891, the office operating until April 5, 1902 [GSM 1893-1903; PO Archives].

**BEDELL**, Bay County: grocer Frank Goulet became the first postmaster of this rural post office in Kawkawlin Township on April 28, 1884, the office operating until Feb. 28, 1901 [GSM 1885; PO Archives].

**BEDFORD**, Calhoun County: John Bertram entered the first land in the area in 1832, but Roswell Crane became the first actual settler in 1833; Matthias Hutchinson, who had a sawmill built in 1837, began the village in 1838 by platting his land and donating lots to those who would settle permanently thereon; Erastus R. Wattles became the first postmaster on July 5, 1839; the name was suggested by Josiah Gilbert who had come from Bedford, Westchester County, N.Y. [Everts].

**BEDFORD**, Monroe County: a village in 1859 [GSM 1860].

**BEDFORD STATION**, Calhoun County: Henry C. Wilde became its first postmaster on Oct. 17, 1878, the office operating until Sept. 14, 1889; see Bedford for the name [PO Archives].

**BEDWIN**, Charlevoix County: this rural post office was named for storekeeper Robert Bedwin who became its first postmaster on June 24, 1884, the office operating until Jan. 25, 1887 [GSM 1885; PO Archives].

**BEEBE**, Gratiot County: named for Henry L. Beebe who opened a store here in 1883; he soon sold out to Lewis H. Ritchie who became the first postmaster on March 24, 1884, the office operating until Dec. 14, 1904; the place is also called Emerson Center from its location in Emerson Township [Tucker].

**BEEBE'S CORNERS**, Macomb County. See Richmond.

**BEECH**, Wayne County: Albert Fisher ran its general store, and Dunning, Fisher & Rhode operated its sawmill, and the village was known as Fishers while its railroad depot was first called Fishers Station; given a post office named Beech on Dec. 4, 1871, with Albert Fisher as its first postmaster; this Redford Township village was platted in January, 1872; its post office operated until Sept. 17, 1906, when it was absorbed by the city of Detroit; the name is retained locally in Beech Road [GSM 1873; Burton; PO Archives].

**BEECHER**, Benzie County: this settlement was made in 1887 and honored Henry Ward Beecher, famed clergyman and author who had died that year; George W. Sharp was a pioneer settler; nearby Thompsonville was given a depot and a post office and so absorbed whatever potential Beecher may have had [L. H. Maginity; Powers].

**BEECH TREE**, Ottawa County: a station on the Chicago & Western Michigan Railroad, 4 miles south of Grand Haven, in 1882 [GSM 1883].

**BEECHVILLE**, Lapeer County. See North Branch.

**BEECHWOOD**, Iron County: in 1888, the village began by being given a station on the Chicago & Northwestern Railroad and on Nov. 17, 1889, a post office, with Richard M. Dwyer as its first postmaster, succeeded by hotelman J. J. Larsen in 1890; beech trees are said to have been numerous in the area at the time [PM; GSM 1891; PO Archives].

**BEE LINE**, Allegan County: James M. Heath became the first postmaster of this rural post office on May 30, 1951, the office operating until July 29, 1852 [PO Archives].

**BEISEL**, St. Joseph County: platted by C. Barnes for the Proprietors, Peter Beisel and George Mathews; while a mill, a store and a cabin or two were erected, it remained a paper village [Mich Hist 4:589 1920].

**BEITNER**, Grand Traverse County: William Beitner built a lumber mill here by the Boardman River, in Blair Township, in 1878 and it was in operation until 1904; given a station on the Grand Rapids & Indiana Railroad as Beitner's in 1878 and a post office as Beitner on Aug. 5, 1880, with Benjamin Hunter as its first postmaster; the office was transferred to and renamed Keystone on Oct. 9, 1883, but on Feb. 1, 1893, the Beitner post office was re-established with Elsie Beitner as its postmaster, the office operating until March 26, 1895 [Barnes; GSM 1879; PO Archives].

**BELDEN**, Wayne County: platted and recorded by Francis J. Belden in 1871; given a post office on Sept. 27, 1873 [Burton; County plat liber].

**BELDING**, Ionia County: Charles Broas, from Broome County, N.Y., became the first settler here in 1839 and the settlement became known as Broas Rapids; Lucius Patterson bought an interest in the Broas mill property in 1842 and the town was given a post office as Patterson's Mills on Feb. 23, 1857, with Andrew C. Reynolds as its first postmaster; Hiram Belding bought the land of Levi Broas in 1855 and to help pay for it, sold silk goods on commission, thus beginning the Belding brothers silk making business here, which led to the renaming of the town and its post office for them on Sept. 18, 1871; incorporated as a city in 1893 [Richard Bivins].

**BELFORD**, Oakland County: a station on the Pere Marquette Railroad, 11 miles south of Flint, in 1894 [GSM 1895].

**BELGRADE**, Wayne County. See Delray.

**BELKNAP**, Allegan County: John McDonald became the first postmaster of this rural post office on May 24, 1889, the office operating until July 31, 1901 [PO Archives].

**BELL**, Keweenaw County: the Bell Mine was just south of Lake Fanny Hooe; a little exploratory work was done on its property in 1850 [Stevens].

**BELL**, Presque Isle County: this village which developed around the Presque Isle Brick & Lumber Company was also called False Presque Isle Harbor; Odell W. Smith became its first postmaster on May 9, 1884, the office operating until Feb. 28, 1911 [GSM 1885; PO Archives].

**BELLAIRE**, Antrim County: the supervisors wanted a more centrally located county seat than Elk Rapids, and chose to move it to a site on the property of Ambrose E. Palmer; thus Bellaire was founded in 1879; named by Mr. Palmer for its pure air; given a post office named Keno, with Rufus Hall as its postmaster, on June 20, 1879; it was renamed Bellaire on May 26, 1880; given a station on the Chicago & Western Michigan (now Pere Marquette) Railroad in 1891; incorporated as a village in 1891 [Harry T. Cook; PO Archives].

**BELL BRANCH**, Wayne County: also called Redford Center, from its location in Redford Township; Charles A. Pierce became the first postmaster of Bell Branch on June 6, 1877, but the office was closed on Feb. 27, 1907, when the village was absorbed by the city of Detroit [Mich Hist 33:352 1949; PO Archives].

**BELL CROSSING**, Mecosta County. See Borland.

**BELLE HARBOR**, Keweenaw County: a summer resort on Isle Royale; Fred Schofield became its first postmaster on May 28, 1917, the office operating until June 30, 1939 [GSM 1919; PO Archives].

**BELLE ISLE**, Wayne County: first called Rattlesnake Island; after hogs were put here to kill off the snakes, it was called Hog Island (Isle aux Cochons); Cadillac granted it to his settlers as a public common; owned by individuals from 1768 to 1879 (George McDougall, William Macomb, Barnabas Campau, et al.); its name was changed from Hog Island, July 4, 1845, in honor of Belle (Isabelle) Cass, daughter of General Lewis Cass, governor of the Michigan Territory; Detroit purchased it for a park for $200,000 in 1879 [MPH 9:352, 422, 463].

**BELLE RIVER**, St. Clair County: Samuel Ward became the first postmaster of present-day Marine City, with the office named Belle River, on Dec. 27, 1831, and renamed Marine City on May 20, 1865; in the same county, on the Belle River, in Berlin Township, was the village of Belle River (also called Lesterville); it was given a post office as Belle River, with

Ginley Lester as its first postmaster, on March 28, 1867, with the spelling changed to Belleriver on Jan. 9, 1895; the office operated until Jan. 30, 1904 [PO Archives].

**BELLEVILLE**, Eaton County. See Bellevue.

**BELLEVILLE**, Wayne County: Archibald Fleming, Samuel McNath and his two sons settled here in 1826; Lorton Holden became its first postmaster on March 13, 1844; George D. Hill, Daniel L. Quirk and R. P. Clark platted and recorded the village in 1848; incorporated as a village in 1905 and as a city in 1946; named from the French, belle ville, beautiful town [Burton; PO Archives].

**BELLEVUE**, Eaton County: in 1832, Luther Lincoln made the first government land purchase here; he sold to Isaac E. Crary, of Marshall, who platted the village in 1835; Reuben Fitzgerald became the first actual settler in 1833; given a post office spelled Bellvue, on May 2, 1835, with John T. Hoyt as its first postmaster; it was in Calhoun County until Eaton was organized in 1837; the county seat from 1838 to 1840; with J. P. Woodbury as postmaster, it was renamed Bellevue on Jan. 8, 1841; incorporated as a village in 1867; named from its pleasant location [MPH 3:386 1881; Mich Hist 42:414 1958; PO Archives].

**BELL OAK**, Ingham County: first settled by James L. Nichols in 1842; but the actual village was due to George Fisher, Jr., who, with his brother-in-law, Truman Spencer, built a sawmill here about 1855; the bell in the solid oak school gave it the name Bell Oak School, and the village took the name Bell Oak; the names Bell Oak and Locke (many settlers came here from Locke Township, Cayuga County, N.Y.) were used interchangeably for years, but now it is Bell Oak; its post office, named Locke, was opened on Oct. 30, 1861, with Moses P. Crowell as its first postmaster; the office was closed on April 10, 1873, but was restored from May 13, 1873, to June 29, 1901 [Foster; GSM 1860; PO Archives].

**BELL'S CROSSING**, Mecosta County: a station on the Detroit, Lansing & Northern Railroad, opened in 1870, and named for John A. Bell, local landowner [Chapman].

**BELLTOWN**, Gratiot County. See Sumner.

**BELLVUE**, Eaton County. See Bellevue.

**BELMONT**, Kent County: here in Plainfield Township, Truman H. Burch became the first postmaster on Nov. 11, 1869, and George N. Reynolds the first railroad agent in 1870; the village was platted and recorded by A. B. Coffinberry, for Garret A. Clement, on June 29, 1874 [Meta W. Huff, PM; PO Archives].

**BELSAY**, Genesee County: this hamlet had a station on the Grand Trunk Railroad by 1882; Arthur Oliver became its first postmaster on March 3, 1893; the office was closed on Feb. 21, 1898, but was restored from Sept. 23, 1898, with Mr. Oliver again its postmaster, to April 15, 1901 [GSM 1883-1903; PO Archives].

**BELT**, Ontonagon County. See Lake Mine.

**BELVEDERE**, Charlevoix County: a station on the Chicago & Western Michigan (now Pere Marquette) Railroad, a mile south of Charlevoix, in 1893; Gilbert E. Dunbar became its first postmaster on June 20, 1893, with the office first spelled Belvidere, but changed to Belvedere on July 11, 1893, until it was closed on Dec. 21, 1893 [Mich Manual 1899; PO Archives].

**BELVIDERE**, Macomb County: in 1835, David and James L. Conger, of Cleveland, bought land at the mouth of the Clinton River where it enters into Lake St. Clair and had Abel Dickerson plat the village; the next year, Edward R. Blackwell made a larger and more accurate plat; it was given a post office in 1837; lots were sold and businesses begun, but high waters so flooded the area that the project was abandoned in 1838; the site was first called Huron Point [Eldredge].

**BELVIDERE**, Montcalm County: first settled by William Goodwater in the winter of 1855-56; Belvidere Township was erected in 1866-67; J. C. Richards became its first postmaster on Jan. 27, 1880, the office operating until April 14, 1887 [Schenck; PO Archives].

**BENDON**, Benzie County: this sawmill settlement in Inland Township was first named Kentville for farmer Albert Kent who became its first postmaster on April 24, 1888; given a station on the Chicago & Western Michigan (now Pere Marquette) Railroad and renamed Bendon on June 30, 1892, the office operating until March 31, 1954 [GSM 1889-93; MPH 31:145 1901; PO Archives].

**BENGAL**, Clinton County: first settled in 1837 by newly-weds from New York, Cortland and Luncida Hill, and he became the first postmaster of Bengal (it was by then in Bengal Township) on Aug. 5, 1850, the office operating until Feb. 10, 1888 [Ellis; PO Archives].

**BENNETT**, Lake County: this post office at a logging siding on a branch of the Pere Marquette Railroad was opened on April 28, 1887, with Justus S. Stearns as its first postmaster, the office operating until Sept. 29, 1900 [GSM 1893; PO Archives].

**BENNETT'S CORNERS**, Jackson County: Barnabas C. Hatch became the first postmaster here on May 1, 1843, the office operating until Feb. 3, 1859 [PO Archives].

**BENNINGTON**, Shiawassee County: three New Yorkers, Samuel Nichols, Israel Parsons and Benjamin L. Powers, made the first government land purchases here in 1835, and Mr. Nichols became the first actual settler; when organized in 1838, with Lemuel Castle as its first supervisor, the township was named after Bennington, Vermont, whence some of the early settlers had come; its village was given a railroad depot and on Dec. 13, 1848, a post office, with Benjamin Davis as its first postmaster, the office operating until Feb. 28, 1958 [Ellis; Campbell; PO Archives].

**BENONA**, Oceana County: connecting Stony Lake with Lake Michigan is Stony Creek; here Rev. William F. Ferry and his son, Thomas W. Ferry, built a sawmill in 1849; they sold it to Campbell & Wheeler in 1853, and on March 17, 1855, Amos R. Wheeler became the first postmaster of New Stony Creek (there was already a Stony Creek post office in Michigan at the time); as supervisor, Mr. Wheeler had the legislature renamed the town Benona and its post office was also so renamed on June 10, 1857; the village was platted and was developing until floods took away the dam; its post office was closed on Sept. 30, 1901; it is believed that Benona was the name of a maiden in an Indian legend [Royal; PO Archives].

**BENSON**, Wexford County: this rural post office was named for farmer Swan Benson who became its first postmaster on Nov. 17, 1884, the office operating until April 30, 1911 [Thomas Blinn].

**BENTHEIM**, Allegan County: John Rulst became the first postmaster of this rural post office, 12 miles from Zeeland, on Feb. 17, 1899, the office operating until Sept. 30, 1905 [GSM 1901-07; PO Archives].

**BENTLEY**, Bay County: founded by Oscar F. Bentley who was born in Monroe County, N.Y., in 1833; he had served three years in the Minnesota Volunteer Cavalry in the Civil War before coming here and building a sawmill in 1886, in which business he was succeeded by his son, Frank E. Bentley, who became the first postmaster of Bently on Feb. 26, 1887, with the spelling corrected to Bentley on June 16, 1909 [M.S. Causley, Jr.; PO Archives].

**BENTLEY**, Gladwin County. See Estey.

**BENTLEY CORNERS**, Midland County: Lyman E. Pratt became its first postmaster on Oct. 20, 1879, the office operating until June 17, 1880 [PO Archives].

**BENTON**, Berrien County: a village in present Niles Township, mentioned in Lanman's History of Michigan, 1839, appearing on Farmer's Map of Michigan, 1853, and described as a village in the Gazeteer, 1865; said to have been located opposite the mouth of McCoy's Creek (named for Rev. Isaac McCoy, founder of the Carey Mission, q.v.) and to have been platted [Fox].

**BENTON**, Eaton County: Bennett I. Claflin, from New York State, became the first settler in 1837; the legislature created the town in 1843 and named it Tom Benton, but the people in 1845 effected a legal change to Benton; named for Thomas Hart Benton [MPH 6:271 1883, 39:353 1899].

**BENTON**, Livingston County: founded about 1836; with the building of a sawmill and a grist mill here on Ore Creek in the southeastern part of the county, it was given a stage coach post office in 1837 [GSM 1838].

**BENTON**, Washtenaw County: a village on the Detroit-Chicago pike, in Saline Township; Joseph Tuttle became its first postmaster on May 8,

1834; the office was closed on May 21, 1883, but was restored from Sept. 13, 1883, to Jan. 5, 1885 [GSM 1863-85; PO Archives].

**BENTON HARBOR,** Berrien County: in 1860, Sterne Brunson, Henry C. Morton and Charles Hull developed the site by having a canal built from it to the harbor and in 1863 they platted the village; first named Brunson Harbor, for Sterne Brunson, it was renamed for Thomas Hart Benton, a Missouri senator who had fostered Michigan's plea for statehood; Mr. Morton became its first postmaster on Feb. 14, 1865; incorporated as a village by the supervisors in 1866 and by the legislature in 1869; incorporated as a city in 1891 [Chauncey; Earl L. Tidey].

**BENTON HEIGHTS,** Berrien County: first known as Euclid Center, it was renamed by popular vote in 1957; named from its location in relation to Benton Harbor [Cunningham].

**BENZONIA,** Benzie County: founded by Rev. Charles E. Bailey as the site of a proposed Christian college in 1858, while it was still a woodland wilderness; the Herring Creek post office was moved here in 1859; incorporated as a village in 1891; the French called the local river Aux Bec Scies (bec-scie meaning sawbill, a species of duck, evidently abounding on the stream then), which the American sailors corrupted into the Betsie River, and that in turn was refined into Benzie when the county was organized in 1869 [MPH 1:118 1874; Mich Hist 48:333 Dec 1964].

**BERGLAND,** Ontonagon County: a station on the Duluth, South Shore & Atlantic Railroad, on the Lake Gogebic shore, in Matchwood Township; the village was founded and named by Gunlak A. Bergland, of Milwaukee, who built a sawmill here in 1900; storekeeper Peter A. Johnson became its first postmaster on April 20, 1903 [Jamison; GSM 1905].

**BERGLAND'S MILL TRACK,** Houghton County: this spur on the Chicago, Milwaukee & St. Paul Railroad, a mile from Sidnaw, serviced one of the sawmills operated by Gunlak A. Bergland in 1898 [Mich Manual 1899].

**BERKLEY,** Oakland County: located at Woodward and 12 Mile Road; first settled largely by Detroiters to escape the higher cost of living there; incorporated as a village in 1923 and as a city in 1932; Elmer Cromie named the road that ran through his farm Berkley and the Berkley School was then under construction, so Berkley was selected from the names proposed [Viola E. Toben].

**BERKSHIRE,** Sanilac County: a rural post office at the Sanilac Stock Farm with James L. Balmer becoming its first postmaster on Aug. 29, 1890, succeeded by farm manager Alexander Mann in 1892, the office operating until March 31, 1914; Berkshire is the name of a breed of swine [GSM 1893-1915; PO Archives].

**BERLAMONT,** Van Buren County: formerly known as Bear Lake Mills and also as Anderson's Mills; in 1857, Dr. H. Anderson and Amos S. Brown built a sawmill here at Bear Lake in Columbia Township and in

1862 they bought Heath's grist mill, at the outlet of the same lake; Mr. Brown sold his interest to Dr. Anderson in 1868; a station on the Kalamazoo & South Haven Railroad; given a post office named Bear Lake Mills on Feb. 26, 1868, with James M. Alden as its first postmaster; the office was renamed Berlamont on Dec. 21, 1877, and operated until Sept. 30, 1953; the name would seem to have been derived from Bear Lake Mills [Ellis; GSM 1875; PO Archives].

**BERLIN**, Ionia County: the first land entry here was made by the first settler, John E. Morrison, in July, 1833; Alonzo Sessions settled here in October of the same year; Berlin Township was organized in 1839, with Mr. Sessions as its first supervisor; given a post office named Cass, after Governor Lewis Cass, on Feb. 8, 1840, with Levi Taylor as its first postmaster; the office was renamed Berlin on April 13, 1842, but was closed on Sept. 28 of the same year; given a post office as New Berlin (there was by then another Berlin post office in Michigan), with Mr. Sessions again the postmaster, on March 17, 1855, the office operating until March 5, 1858 [Schenck; Branch; PO Archives].

**BERLIN**, Ottawa County. See Marne.

**BERNE**, Huron County: this village in Caseville Township was also known as Berne Corners; it was founded about 1878, and was named after Berne, Switzerland; Joseph Schluchter became its first postmaster on May 29, 1882; the office was closed on Oct. 2, 1896, but was restored from May 3, 1897, to April 30, 1904; when the Saginaw, Huron & Tuscola Railroad was built and crossed the Pontiac, Oxford & Port Austin Railroad (the former now Pere Marquette, the latter now Grand Trunk), at Pigeon, about 1884, the village of Berne was gradually but literally moved a mile south to Pigeon [Otto Woelke; Gwinn; PO Archives].

**BERRIEN CENTER**, Berrien County: Dr. L. A. Barnard, from Sandusky, Ohio, became one of the first settlers in the area in 1828; the town was named after the township, which had been named after the county, which had in turn been named after John M. Berrien, attorney general under President Andrew Jackson; Zera F. Wright became its first postmaster on April 28, 1857 [Fox; PO Archives].

**BERRIEN SPRINGS**, Berrien County: the John Pike family settled here in 1829; George Kimmel, who also came in 1829, bought out Mr. Pike but did not settle here with his family until 1831; first called Wolf's Prairie as it had been the village of an Indian chief named Wolf; platted by Samuel Marrs for the proprietors, Pitt Brown, Horace Godfrey and Francis B. Murdock, in 1831; tavern keeper Pitt Brown became the first postmaster, with the office named simply Berrien, on Dec. 4, 1832; named for President Andrew Jackson's attorney general John M. Berrien; because of the many springs in the area, merchant R. E. Ward got it renamed Berrien Springs on April 18, 1836; it became the county seat in 1837; incorporated as a village by the supervisors in 1863 and by the legislature in 1867 [Ellis; PO Archives].

**BERRY**, Muskegon County: a settlement around a branch of the Belle Isle Creamery, of Detroit, in 1924 [GSM 1925].

**BERRYVILLE**, Otsego County: the first lumber mill in the county was built here in Corwith Township by John G. Berry in 1877 and he became the first postmaster of the village on Jan. 16, 1878; it was then in Charlevoix County; the post office was closed on Nov. 30, 1907 [MPH 28:113 1897; GSM 1879; PO Archives].

**BERTIE**, Bay County: storekeeper Lucius Fogelsanger became the first postmaster of this rural post office in Mount Forest Township on June 21, 1899, the office operating until Oct. 31, 1904 [GSM 1901-05; PO Archives].

**BERTRAND**, Berrien County: Joseph Bertrand, a French-Canadian, had a trading post here by 1812; after the Pottawattomi ceded their lands to the government in 1833, his Indian wife became a large landowner here under an Indian title; Daniel G. Garnsey secured President Andrew Jackson's permission and Mrs. Bertrand's consent to locate a village here; Alonzo Bennett platted it in 1833 and became its first postmaster on June 9, 1834; the project suffered from a fever of speculation but its post office operated until April 15, 1901 [Paré; PO Archives].

**BERVILLE**, St. Clair County: named to contain the first syllable of the name of its township, Berlin; speculators began buying its land by 1835 and actual settlement began by 1840, with Lewis Smith, John A. Warner, and Townsend Lockwood being among the pioneers; William F. Hewett became its first postmaster on Feb. 5, 1862, the office operating until July 31, 1962; also known locally as Baker's Corners [Blinn; Jenks].

**BESSEMER**, Gogebic County: the discovery of iron ore near the site of the (Charles L.) Colby Mine, in what is now Bessemer, was claimed by Richard Langford, a trapper and hunter from Rockland, in 1880; in October, 1884, the Milwaukee, Lake Shore & Western Railroad reached the vicinity of the mine and platted the village; its president, F. H. Rhinelander, named it for Sir Henry Bessemer (1813-1898), who discovered the smelting process which bears his name; merchant Frank F. Jeffres became the first postmaster on Dec. 10, 1884; it was in Ontonagon County until Gogebic was organized in 1887; incorporated as a village in 1887 and as a city in 1889 [Victor F. Lemmer].

**BETE GRISE**, Keweenaw County: the name is French for grey beast and is believed to have been so named by some one who saw one on the shore, though some hold that the name is derived from the outline of the bay, or the shore, or the crest of the hills along it; still a village [Madeleine Gibson].

**BETHANY**, Gratiot County: the Rev. Edward R. Baierlein founded a Lutheran mission to the Indians here in 1847, called Bethanien; later called Indiantown and still later, the Indian Mission; the government gave the Indians a tract of land in Isabelle County for a reservation and the mission here was closed in 1857; only its cemetery remains, but when the township was organized in 1858, with W. J. Partello as its first supervisor, it was given the name of Bethany, and still retains it; Bethany was the home of Mary, Martha and Lazarus, where Christ often visited and worked some of His greatest miracles [Florer; Chapman].

**BETHEL**, Branch County: Eleazer Snow, who became the first settler in the area in 1830, sold out to Moses Olmstead in 1831; the town was first called Elizabeth, probably by Mr. Olmstead and after Elizabeth, N.J., but the legislature, for reasons unknown, changed the name to Bethel in 1838-39 (the word is Old Testament Hebrew for House of the Lord); William T. Ammerman became the first postmaster on April 30, 1857, with the office in his home, the office operating until Nov. 30, 1905 [Johnson; PO Archives].

**BETHEL CENTRE**, Branch County. See Snow Prairie.

**BETSEY LAKE**, Grand Traverse County: this hamlet was given a post office on Jan. 27, 1868; the office was closed on Aug. 3, 1868, but was restored on Aug. 24, 1868, with Kendall Kennett as the postmaster, the office operating until Aug. 9, 1872 [PO Archives].

**BETSIE POINT**, Benzie County. See Bec Scies.

**BETZER**, Hillsdale County: the name of this hamlet in Wright Township was derived from the name of Daniel Colbetzer who became its first postmaster on Nov. 15, 1886, the office operating until Dec. 31, 1901 [GSM 1889; PO Archives].

**BEULAH**, Benzie County: founded about 1880 by Rev. Charles E. Bailey and named by him from Isaiah 62:4 "You shall no more be termed Forsaken and your land shall no more be termed Desolate; but you shall be called My Delight is in Her, and your land Beulah, that is Married"; detached from the village of Benzonia and given a post office on Feb. 8, 1892, with Charles S. Merritt as its first postmaster; incorporated as a village in 1932 [Leonard L. Case, J. P.; PO Archives].

**BEULAH**, Grand Traverse County. See Mayfield.

**BEVERLY HILLS**, Oakland County: several subdivision associations proposed a village government for this part of Southfield Township; the boundaries were established and in 1958 it was incorporated as the village of Westwood, so named because the area was west of Woodward Avenue; in 1959, it was renamed, the area having been known for years as the Beverly Hills Subdivisions [Fannie Adams].

**BIDDLE CITY**, Ingham County: the name of a proposed village platted in 1836 by Jerry and William Ford, named for Major John Biddle of Detroit, and now within the city of Lansing [Darling; Foster].

**BIG BAY**, Marquette County: founded by lumbermen about 1875 and named from its location on Big Bay, by Lake Superior; the village was given a post office on Feb. 10, 1902, with Andrew McAfee as its first postmaster [Ernest Rankin; PO Archives].

**BIG BEAVER**, Oakland County: Ira Smith, a New Yorker, built the first house here in Troy Township in 1826 and in it opened the first tavern about 1828; he also became the first postmaster on July 11, 1844; the office operated until Feb. 3, 1914; the place was also called the Beaver; named from a large dam built by a colony of beavers, across the nearby brook called Beaver Creek [Durant; PO Archives].

**BIG CREEK**, Mecosta County: the first post office in Deerfield Township opened here on Jan. 5, 1867, with Lyman Nethaway as its postmaster; the office was moved to and renamed Stanwood on Oct. 17, 1870 [PO Archives].

**BIGGS**, Oscoda County: Jacob H. Frank became the first postmaster of this sawmill settlement in Elmer Township on Dec. 12, 1891, succeeded by Mattie Scholtke in 1892, the office operating until Sept. 30, 1912 [GSM 1893; PO Archives].

**BIG PRAIRIE**, Newaygo County: the township was organized in 1852, and likely named by Ephraim H. Utley, township leader; then prairie land, it has since been planted to pine trees; Mr. Utley became the first postmaster on Feb. 4, 1852, the office operating until Sept. 30, 1909; the village was named after its township [Harry L. Spooner; PO Archives].

**BIG RAPIDS**, Mecosta County: Robert P. Mitchell and John Parish made the first land entries here in 1853; the brothers Zera and George French became the first permanent settlers in 1855; when made the first county seat in February, 1859, it was called Leonard for Dr. F. B. Leonard who owned much of its land; he sold out to George P. Warren and Chauncey P. Ives who platted the village and recorded it as Big Rapids in November, 1859; Zera French platted and recorded adjacent land as Glen Elm in 1860, but within a month renamed it French's Addition to Big Rapids; Jesse C. Shaw became the first postmaster of Leonard on Jan. 24, 1857, with the named changed on Sept. 29, 1859, to what the lumbermen had called it from its being beside the biggest of the many rapids on the Muskegon River; given a station on the Grand Rapids & Indiana Railroad; incorporated as a city in 1869 [MPH 30:28 1905; Chapman; PO Archives].

**BIG RAPIDS**, Shiawassee County. See Owosso.

**BIG RAPIDS JUNCTION**, Muskegon County: first settled by W. A. Hanchett in 1865; here in southern Dalton Township was the junction of the Chicago & Western Michigan Railroad with its Big Rapids branch [Page].

**BIG RIVER**, Delta County: storekeeper Peter J. Jordan became the first postmaster of this rural post office on March 11, 1890, the office operating until Sept. 15, 1893 [GSM 1891-95; PO Archives].

**BIG ROCK**, Montmorency County: grocer Seth Gillett became the first postmaster of this village in Briley Township on March 24, 1882, but the office was transferred to and renamed Atlanta on October 2 of the same year; William H. Remington, owner of the general store here, secured a post office named Remington on May 26, 1884, and it was renamed Big Rock on Dec. 14, 1885 [GSM 1883; PO Archives].

**BIG SALT LICK,** Shiawassee County. See Knaggs Place.

**BIG SAUBLE,** Mason County. See Lincoln.

**BIG SPRING,** Ottawa County: this village in Wright Township was given a post office on May 18, 1850, with John S. McClain as its first postmaster, the office operating until Nov. 19, 1891 [GSM 1875; PO Archives].

**BILLINGS,** Gladwin County: this village, named after its township, was settled in 1875; storekeeper M. L. Kent became its first postmaster on April 14, 1902 [Ritchie; GSM 1905].

**BIMO,** Lenawee County: a station on the Lake Shore & Michigan Southern Railroad; Frazey S. Johnson became its first postmaster on Nov. 23, 1896, the office operating until Dec. 31, 1903 [GSM 1899; PO Archives].

**BINGEN,** Mecosta County. See Remus.

**BINGHAM,** Clinton County: first settled by Stephen W. Downer, from Vermont, in 1841; George W. Estes became the first postmaster of Bingham, named for Governor Kingsley S. Bingham, on June 19, 1851, taking the office with him when he moved to the site chosen for the village of Saint Johns in 1854, and it was given that name on Feb. 6, 1855 [MPH 26:88 1895; Ellis; PO Archives].

**BINGHAM,** Huron County: James R. Frank, Joseph Frantz and Joseph Deachin became the first settlers here in 1856; organized in 1863, with Robert Scott as its first supervisor, the township was named for then Governor Kingsley S. Bingham; Edward O'Connor became its first postmaster on Oct. 6, 1862, but the office was closed the following Nov. 18 [Gwinn; Chapman; PO Archives].

**BINGHAM,** Leelanau County: William Core became its first postmaster on Nov. 26, 1878; development of the village began with a sawmill owned by C. S. Darrow and built by Boone and Johnson in 1881; town and township were named for Kingsley B. Bingham, governor of Michigan, 1855-58, U.S. senator, 1859-61, when he died in office; its post office was closed on May 31, 1908; now a cross-roads store and school [Laura Lindley; PO Archives].

**BINGHAM FARMS,** Oakland County: founded in 1955 by a group of residents who elected William King as the first president of the village; named after its main thoroughfare (Bingham Road) which was taken from the family name of the original owners of the farm; incorporated as a village in 1955 [Mich Manual].

**BIRCH,** Marquette County: a station on the M. & S.E. Railroad, in Powell Township; the settlement formed around the Northern Lumber Company mill and general store; L. Frank McKnight became its first postmaster on Nov. 21, 1905, succeeded by W. H. Elliott in 1906; named from the birch trees in the area [Rankin; GSM 1907; PO Archives].

**BIRCH BEACH**, Sanilac County: this village on Lake Huron in Worth Township was first called Stevens' Landing and was given a post office of that name on Jan. 10, 1856, with David Johnson as its first postmaster; the office was closed on Jan. 20, 1860, but was restored from Feb. 21, 1863, to Aug. 11, 1868; the village was renamed Birch Beach, with Mrs. Nellie Emigh as postmaster, on May 18, 1927, the office operating until Sept. 29, 1934; now chiefly a resort [DuMonde; GSM 1860; PO Archives].

**BIRCH CREEK**, Menominee County: founded in 1855, its first settlers were Henry Blade, Sr., William Hackeman, and the Siemen brothers; this station on the Chicago & Northwestern Railroad was named after its township [Evelyn Bergen].

**BIRCH RUN**, Saginaw County: founded as a station on the Pere Marquette Railroad, in the birch region, in 1852, and named after its creek; John Moore became its first postmaster on June 15, 1854; the office was changed to Deer Lick on April 13, 1863, but the Birch Run post office was re-established on the same day, April 13, 1863; the office was closed on July 15, 1865, but the Deer Lick post office was changed back to Birch Run since May 29, 1868; incorporated as a village in 1954 [Verne M. Geiger; PO Archives].

**BIRD**, Hillsdale County. See Amboy.

**BIRD**, Oceana County: this village in Leavitt Township was first settled in 1866; Rufus J. Carpenter became its first postmaster on Aug. 8, 1872, the office operating until Aug. 1, 1890 [GSM 1873; PO Archives].

**BIRDSALL**, Lenawee County: Darius Comstock, fruit grower and brother of Addison Comstock, founder of Adrian, settled here in 1827; in 1831, he gave the land and promoted the building of a Quaker Meeting House and in 1848 he did the same for a Quaker school or seminary, which operated from 1850 to 1908; until 1897, the hamlet was just a part of Adrian Township; in that year, it was given a station on the Detroit & Lima Northern Railroad; named for its first and only postmaster, Daniel B. Birdsall; but though the office, opened on July 15, 1897, was closed on Oct. 15, 1901, the hamlet and its Quaker church remain [Edith Haviland; GSM 1899-1903].

**BIRKETT**, Washtenaw County. See Dover.

**BIRMINGHAM**, Oakland County: John W. Hunter, from Auburn, N.Y., made the first land entry here in 1818 and with his father, Elisha, and brother, Daniel, made the first actual settlement in 1819; about the same time, John Hamilton and Elijah Willets settled nearby, and the settlement was variously known as Hunter's, or Hamilton's, or Willets'; later called Piety Hill, after a Methodist preacher, in his fervid zeal, prayed that this might become "a hill of piety"; given a post office named Bloomfield, after its township, on March 24, 1821, with Sidney Dole as its first postmaster; first platted in 1836 and recorded by Roswell T. Merrill who, believing in its industrial future, named it after Birmingham, England; its post office was renamed Birmingham on April 5, 1838; incorporated as a village in 1864 and as a city in 1932 [Charles L. Lyle; Seeley; PO Archives].

**BISHOP**, Newaygo County: this village in Garfield Township was founded in 1898 by Gerrit Dobben, a storekeeper and first postmaster, who named it for the congressman from the district, Roswell P. Bishop; its post office opened on March 3, 1898, operated until Oct. 31, 1901 [Harry L. Spooner; PO Archives].

**BISMARK**, Alger County. See Onota.

**BISMARK**, Eaton County: the brothers Silas P. and J. Hatch Loomis emigrated here in southwestern Sunfield Township in 1853 and the area was given a post office named Bismark on Jan. 26, 1871, with J. Hatch Loomis as its first postmaster, the office operating until June 30, 1904 [Durant; PO Archives].

**BITELY**, Newaygo County: a station on the Chicago & Western Michigan (now Pere Marquette) Railroad in 1884, this village was founded by Steven and Jerome Bitely in 1889, and given a post office on Sept. 19, 1889, with Archer D. Martin as its first postmaster; named for Steven Bitely, who built a sawmill here, but the post office has always spelled the name Biteley [Raymond F. Michalski, PM; GSM 1891].

**BIXBY**, Muskegon County: John H. Pickle became the first postmaster of this rural post office on May 28, 1900, the office operating until Oct. 31, 1901 [PO Archives].

**BLACKBERRY RIDGE**, Oceana County. See Peach Ridge.

**BLACK CREEK**, Mason County. See Lincoln.

**BLACK LAKE**, Muskegon County: a railroad station and sawmill village in Norton Township, at the head of Black Lake; first settled in 1855; Fletcher Fowler became its first postmaster on April 10, 1866, the office operating until June 22, 1894; in 1880, the lake was renamed Mona Lake after Mona May, daughter of the superintendent of the Grand Haven Railroad, Colonel May; but the name survives in Little Black Lake, just to the south of it [GSM 1873-93; PO Archives].

**BLACKMAN**, Jackson County: first settled by Lyman Pease and A. W. Daniels in 1830; when the first board of county supervisors met in the home of Lemuel Blackman in 1857, the township was named for Horace Blackman who had become the first white settler in the county in 1829 [DeLand; Interstate; MPH 9:464 1886].

**BLACKMAR**, Saginaw County: this village in Taymouth Township formed around the sawmill of A. T. Blackmar and was named for him; a station on the Pere Marquette Railroad; Levi Bronson became its first postmaster on Jan. 28, 1874, the office operating until Oct. 14, 1904 [GSM 1875; PO Archives].

**BLACK RIVER**, Alcona County: the settlement was named from the stream flowing through it into Lake Huron; a fishing station, first occupied by William Cullings in 1849; settled by French trappers and fishermen, it is still French; seat of the lumbering operations of Alger, Smith & Company (A. A. Alger, M. S. Smith), 1876-1880 (then the largest pine timber producers in the world); it is now a fishing village again; Edgar O. Cheney became its first postmaster on Feb. 9, 1877, the spelling was changed to Blackriver on May 16, 1894, and then back to Black River in 1958 [Mrs. Arthur LeClair, PM; Page].

**BLACK RIVER,** Ottawa County. See Holland.

**BLACK RIVER,** Sanilac County. See Croswell.

**BLACK RIVER STATION,** Allegan County: George Kraal built a sawmill here in 1871; he sold it to William Ferguson who discontinued it about 1874, but David J. Dorkey built another one in 1875, and he became the first postmaster on Aug. 20, 1877, with the office named Lee after the township; named from its being a railroad station near the middle branch of the Black River [Johnson; PO Archives].

**BLACK'S CORNERS,** Lapeer County: Abel H. Smith became its first postmaster on Dec. 24, 1866, but the office was changed to Imlay on April 10, 1869 [PO Archives].

**BLACKWOOD,** Grand Traverse County. See Grawn.

**BLAINE,** Benzie County: Harrison Averill operated a mill here near Herring Lake for Loyed & Thomas, of Chicago, from about 1851 until high water swept its dam away about 1862; the town was organized in 1867 as a part of Gilmore and set off from Gilmore in 1876, John Hunt being chosen supervisor in both elections [MPH 28:118 1897].

**BLAINE,** St. Clair County: the first land purchase here was made by Thomas S. Knapp, of Detroit, in 1828; on his land he built a sawmill which Judge Zephaniah W. Bunce operated for a while; the township was organized in 1866 and named for General (later President) U.S. Grant; from its location in it, the village took the name Grant Center; but there was another Michigan post office with that name and so Frank Brothwell and others here got one named for Republican U.S. Senator James G. Blaine in 1879, with John T. Dawson becoming its first postmaster on Nov. 28, 1879, the office operating until Dec. 31, 1960 [Roy Brothwell; Jenks; PO Archives].

**BLAIR,** Barry County: this post office, named for Austin Blair, governor of Michigan, was opened on June 10, 1862, with James M. Cole as its first postmaster; the office was moved to Castleton, then back to Woodland Township, and finally closed on Dec. 20, 1876 [Johnson; Dunbar; PO Archives].

**BLAIRVILLE,** Chippewa County: founded in 1880 by William H. Wise who named it for his father-in-law, George Blair, who came here in 1881 and around whose homestead the settlement developed; the Blairs were of Irish descent and emigrated to Canada and thence to Michigan; it is still a farming community [William LeBlanc].

**BLAKE**, Jackson County: John O'Bryan became the first postmaster of this rural post office on Aug. 8, 1881 [PO Archives].

**BLAKE'S CORNERS**, Presque Isle County: Julius Dramburg built a grist mill here and Wilson Pines a sawmill in 1883 [Advance].

**BLANC**, Lenawee County: James McCrillen became the first postmaster of this rural post office on Feb. 24, 1843, the office operating until July 29, 1845 [PO Archives].

**BLANCHARD**, Isabella County: Peter G. Blanchard lumbered the land and founded the village on the Pine River, in Rolland Township, which was named for Herbert P. Blanchard who became its first postmaster on Sept. 13, 1878; incorporated as a village in 1879; most of its business district was destroyed by fire in August, 1884 [Retta Munger; GSM 1885].

**BLANCHARD'S**, Montcalm County: a railroad station in Home Township in 1878 [GSM 1879].

**BLANCH LAKE**, Newaygo County: a summer resort colony in Ashland Township in 1878 [GSM 1879].

**BLANEY PARK**, Schoolcraft County: Captain Neil Blaney was commodore of the lake fleet of the William Mueller Company, of Chicago; for it, he located and acquired a tract of timberland on which the company set up logging headquarters, with cottages, stores, post office, etc., in 1902, and named it Blaney; Charles E. Ebert became its first postmaster on Dec. 5, 1902; the venture failed and the entire property was sold in 1909 to the Wisconsin Land & Mining Company, of which G. Harold Earle was president; logging continued until 1927 when Mr. Earle began to convert the town into a resort operation named Blaney Park; on Feb. 1, 1936, its post office was also named Blaney Park [G. Harold Earle].

**BLEMER'S**, Gogebic County: a station on the Chicago & Northwestern Railroad, 7 miles west of Watersmeet, in 1894 [GSM 1895].

**BLENDON**, Ottawa County: John Ball became the first settler in the area in 1836; Booth Kinney came in 1845 and the first town meeting was held in his home in 1854; the Blendon Lumber Company owned most of the land here and it was named for them; Alfred H. Vredenburg was the first supervisor; given a post office on May 22, 1860, with Milton N. Woodruff as its first postmaster, the office operating until Oct. 31, 1899; later town settlements were named North Blendon and South Blendon [Page; MPH 9:255 1886; PO Archives].

**BLISS**, Emmet County: Charles S. Barton became its first postmaster on Dec. 20, 1878; named after its township which had been named for Aaron T. Bliss, wealthy lumberman and later governor of Michigan [Dunbar; PO Archives].

**BLISSFIELD**, Lenawee County: William Kedzie, of Delhi, N.Y., made the first government land purchase here in May, 1824, but he did not settle on it until October, 1826; Hervey Bliss, from Monroe County, bought his land in June, 1824, and moved on it the December following; Blissfield Township was organized in 1827 and he became the first postmaster of its village on March 28, 1838; a station on the Lake Shore & Michigan Southern Railroad; incorporated as a village in 1875 [Hogaboam].

**BLISSFIELD JUNCTION**, Lenawee County. See Grosvenor.

**BLOM**, Menominee County: a district rather than a village; A. W. Blom was president of the Peninsular Paper Company, Menominee, and a large landowner in the area [Mrs. Ethyl Schuyler].

**BLOODY CORNERS**, Van Buren County. See Hartford.

**BLOOMER**, Montcalm County: Jonathan Cole and Sylvester Pennington became the first permanent settlers here in 1851; named from the fact that at a local dance several ladies appeared in bloomers, shocking the deacons but making the term a by-word in the infant colony, and when the township was organized in 1852 and a name was needed, this one was adopted; given a post office as Bloomer Centre on Jan. 21, 1858, with Ariel K. Richardson as its first postmaster; the name was shortened to Bloomer on June 6, 1883, but the office was closed on July 28, 1886 [Schenck; PO Archives].

**BLOOMFIELD**, Oakland County. See Birmingham.

**BLOOMFIELD CENTER**, Oakland County. See Bloomfield Hills.

**BLOOMFIELD HEIGHTS**, Huron County. See Smith's Corners.

**BLOOMFIELD HILLS**, Oakland County: the first land entry in Bloomfield Township was made on Jan. 28, 1819, by Colonel Benjamin H. Pierce, brother of Franklin Pierce, afterwards President of the U.S.; later that year, Judge Amasa Bagley became the first actual settler at what came to be known as Bagley's Corners, later as Bloomfield Center, and now as Bloomfield Hills; in the tavern which he and his son-in-law, William Morris, operated, the township meetings were held for many years; Eugene Walton became its first postmaster on Feb. 26, 1929; incorporated as a village in 1927 and as a city in 1932 [Robert J. Stadler; Seeley].

**BLOOMINGDALE**, Van Buren County: founded by Davis Haven and Henry Killefer, both from Ohio, in 1855; given a post office on Jan. 17, 1856; the office was closed on April 4, 1856, but restored, with Rufus M. Brown as postmaster, on May 24, 1856; platted by William Killefer and George W. Haven in 1870, the year the Michigan Central Railroad came through; incorporated as a village in 1881; so named by Davis Haven because it was a blooming valley [Ellis; PO Archives].

**BLOOMINGROVE**, Berrien County. See Liverpool.

**BLOOMINGTON**, Huron County: this village in Bingham Township was given a post office on Feb. 8, 1882, with William Reimann as its first postmaster; the office operated until April 8, 1884; the village, also called Bloomington Heights, is now a part of Verona Hills [Hey; GSM 1883; PO Archives].

**BLOOMINGTON**, Sanilac County: William Thurtle became the first postmaster of this rural post office in the south east corner of the county on June 24, 1874, the office operating until April 20, 1881 [GSM 1879; PO Archives].

**BLOOMING VALLEY**, Oceana County: Benjamin Moore became the first postmaster of this rural post office in Shelby Township on Dec. 8, 1873, the office operating until Feb. 15, 1878 [Royal; PO Archives].

**BLOUNT**, Menominee County: this rural post office in Nadeau Township was named for storekeeper Charles H. Blount who became its first postmaster on Jan. 12, 1900, the office operating until Jan. 31, 1911 [GSM 1901; PO Archives].

**BLUE BILL**, Gogebic County: a station on the Chicago, Milwaukee & St. Paul Railroad; Paul V. Rowlands became its first postmaster on March 4, 1914, with the office moved to Boulder Junction on July 31, 1917 [GSM 1919; PO Archives].

**BLUE JACKET**, Gogebic County: an iron mining location and settlement, between Ironwood and Bessemer, founded about 1870 [Havighurst].

**BLUE LAKE**, Muskegon County: Austin P. Ware came here from New York State in 1864 and was the first supervisor of the township from the year it was organized in 1865 until 1869; a station on the Chicago & Western Michigan Railroad; Elmore E. Burlingham became its first postmaster on April 15, 1868, the office operating until Sept. 9, 1872; named from its having Big Blue Lake in the north and Little Blue Lake in the south [Page; PO Archives].

**BLUFF**, Keweenaw County: a mining settlement; Bluff Mine was opened in 1852 but abandoned in 1855 [Stevens].

**BLUFFTON**, Muskegon County: this lumbering village at the mouth of the Muskegon River, in Laketon Township, was first settled in 1862; given a post office named Millville on Feb. 3, 1868, with Theodore B. Wilcox as its first postmaster; the office was renamed Bluffton on March 16, 1868, but was closed on July 22, 1892; absorbed by the city of Muskegon in 1889 [GSM 1873; Mich Hist 5:519 1921; PO Archives].

**BLUMFIELD CORNERS**, Saginaw County, the township was first settled by emigrants who had fled from Germany to escape persecution, and was named Blumfield for Robert Blum, a political offender who was shot in 1848 by the King's soldiers; the chief pioneer of the settlement was George F. Veenvliet, whose son Frederick (later to fall in battle in our Civil War) was an elector when the township was organized in 1853; given a post office named Blumfield on April 26, 1866, with George F. Veenvliet as its first postmaster; the office was closed on July 24, 1879, but was restored from Sept. 22, 1879, to June 15, 1901; located on Cheboyganing Creek, its station on the Pere Marquette Railroad was named Cheboyganing [Mills; MPH 28:495 1898; GSM 1879; PO Archives].

**BLUMFIELD JUNCTION,** Saginaw County: settled in 1856 and given a post office on May 31, 1862, with Emerson Marsh as its first postmaster, the office operating until Oct. 20, 1880; see Blumfield Corners for the name [GSM 1879; PO Archives].

**BLUNT COURT HOUSE,** Isabella County: Langdon Bentley became the first postmaster on March 6, 1863, with the office named Blunt, but transferred to Isabelle on Aug. 17, 1865 [Fancher; PO Archives].

**BOARDMAN,** Kalkaska County. See South Boardman.

**BOARDMAN JUNCTION,** Grand Traverse County: a station on the Chicago & Western Michigan Railroad, a mile west of Traverse City, which see for the name [Sprague; Mich Manual 1899].

**BODUS,** Leelanau County: Theodore Thompson was appointed the first postmaster here on May 4, 1904, but it was rescinded on the 18th of the same month [PO Archives].

**BOGARTUS,** Delta County: the Bogartus sawmill and hamlet beside the stream entering Little Bay de Noc; shown on William A. Burt's original government survey of 1844 [Jean Worth].

**BOGUE MILLS,** Livingston County. See Oak Grove.

**BOHEMIAN,** Ontonagon County: the Bohemian Mining Company was organized in 1848, bought the Piscatauqua Mine in 1853, renaming it the Bohemian; the company was reorganized in 1863, closed its mine in 1866, reopened it in 1870, and again closed it in 1871; its settlement was given a post office named Bohemian on March 13, 1883, the office operating until Dec. 14, 1885 [Stevens; GSM 1884; PO Archives].

**BOHEMIAN SETTLEMENT,** Antrim County. See Praha.

**BOHEMIAN SETTLEMENT,** Leelanau County: first settled by Joseph Krubner, Frank Kraitz and Vachaw Musil, from Chicago, in 1855; the name is popular rather than official, though used in the records of its mission church; its post office was North Unity [Rev. S.A. Bur].

**BOIS BLANC ISLAND,** Mackinac County: its Indian name was Mikobiminiss, meaning white wood, birch being prevalent, and the French merely translated the Indian name; it was an extra and voluntary gift of the Chippewa nation when Mackinac Island was ceded to the U.S. by the treaty of Greenville in 1795; Michael Dousman's land claim here was surveyed in 1827 but until 1844 he was unable to obtain a patent for it; given a post office as Bois Blanc on Dec. 12, 1884, with James Vosper as its first postmaster; the office was closed on June 19, 1886, but was restored, with Thomas Green as postmaster, on June 15, 1888, with its spelling changed to Boisblanc on Oct. 19, 1895; now a part of the Federal forest reserve and a summer resort colony [MPH 27:569 1896; Mich Hist 12:513 1928; PO Archives].

**BOLLES HARBOR,** Monroe County: platted, recorded and subdivided in 1921 by William Watson Bolles, of Toledo; he had the E. H. Close

Realty Company, of Toledo, sell the lots for year 'round homes here on the shores of Lake Erie [Mrs. Matthew Urban].

**BOLSTER,** Ionia County: a rural post office in the general store of E. T. Bolster & Son, with Harris M. Bolster becoming its first postmaster on Dec. 28, 1896; they sold out to the White Brothers, and G. N. White became its postmaster in 1900, but the office was closed on Sept. 13, 1902 [GSM 1899-1903; PO Archives].

**BOLTON,** Alpena County: a village in Maple Ridge Township, with a station on the Detroit & Mackinaw Railroad; named for Henry Bolton who, with Donald McRae, opened a general store in Alpena in 1866, and from 1871, as Bolton & McRae, operated one of the leading cedar lumbering firms in the area; Francis G. Dowling became its first postmaster on Oct. 18, 1880, the office operating until March 15, 1955 [Page; PO Archives].

**BOMANVILLE,** Gladwin County: George W. Boman, a founder of the Bowman Lumber Company, came up the Tittawabassee River in 1868, had 11 children, bought and cleared three farms here; it became the site of a sawmill, shingle mill and stave mill, with all lumber shipped by train on the Bowmanville line; Mrs. Florence Swanton became its first postmaster on April 5, 1906; the lumber game broke up in 1910 and the train pulled out the same year [Ritchie; PO Archives].

**BOMBAY MILLS,** Midland County: tradition has it that the place began as a hangout for railroad and logging camp drifters, and was referred to as Bum's Bay; later settlers euphemized it to Bombay and added Mills, now a hamlet [Mich State Lib].

**BONANZA,** Ionia County: the Russell brothers, Wellington, Emory, Esteven, Sumner and J. Ashley Russell, began settling here in 1839, and it became known as the Russell Settlement; given a post office named Bonanza, with Horace F. Miner becoming its first postmaster on May 17, 1880; the office was moved to and renamed Lake Odessa on Aug. 10, 1880 [Schenck; PO Archives].

**BOND'S MILLS,** Wexford County: along the shores of Clam (now Cadillac) Lake, in Haring Township, in 1872 were the lumber mills of William W. Mitchell and Jonathan W. Cobbs, as Cobbs & Mitchell, and of Bond & Kyser; its post office was named for Myron H. Bond who became its first postmaster on Oct. 30, 1872, succeeded by Frank Kyser, the office operating until Nov. 30, 1883 [Mich Hist 25:238 1941; GSM 1873; PO Archives].

**BONIFAS,** Gogebic County: founded in 1910 by the Kimberly-Clark Corporation as their pulpwood center and named for William Bonifas, one of the directors; Edward L. Neman became its first postmaster on July 6, 1910, the office operating until 1930 [Victor F. Lemmer].

**BONINE'S CORNERS,** Cass County: a settlement in Penn Township made before 1845 and named for a local landowner [Mich Hist 44:379 1960].

**BONNEY,** Lenawee County: storekeeper Hermon W. Gillett became the first postmaster of this rural post office in Rome Township on Dec. 15, 1891, the office operating until April 30, 1902 [GSM 1893-1903; PO Archives].

**BOON,** Wexford County: a station on the Toledo, Ann Arbor & Northern Michigan Railroad in 1888; the village was platted in 1889 and given a post office on Dec. 19, 1899, with Joseph Matveia as its first postmaster [Powers; PO Archives].

**BOOTON,** Genesee County. See Argentine.

**BORCULO,** Ottawa County: a Dutch settlement in Blendon Township, founded by Jackus Klamderman in 1867 who named it after his native village (Borkulo) in the Netherlands; Herman A. Wiegmink became its first postmaster on March 29, 1882, the office operating until Dec. 31, 1913 [Harris Nieusma; PO Archives].

**BORLAND,** Mecosta County: this hamlet in Deerfield Township was founded by John A. Bell about 1869, and was first called Bell Crossing; when the Grand Rapids & Indiana Railroad came through, it was renamed Bell Siding; Daniel Borland (1836-93) opened a general store with a post office in it and the place was renamed Borland with him becoming its first postmaster on Dec. 26, 1884; the office was closed on April 17, 1886, but restored, with lumberman Fred S. Nichols as postmaster, on April 19, 1886, and operated until April 11, 1887; with Mr. Borland again its postmaster, it was restored again on Aug. 7, 1889, and operated until May 15, 1905 [Lola M. Adkins; PO Archives].

**BORODINO,** Wayne County: Roswell Root became the first postmaster of this village on June 29, 1826; the office was closed on April 4, 1855, but was restored, with Henry B. Root as its postmaster, on March 12, 1856, and operated until June 20, 1863; Napoleon won the Battle of Borodino against the Russians on Sept. 7, 1812 [GSM 1860; PO Archives].

**BOSTON,** Houghton County: the Albany & Boston Mining Company, organized in 1860, sold its property to the Peninsula Company in 1882, which in turn sold it to the Franklin Mining Company in 1905; a station on the Mineral Range Railroad; Jemima White became the first postmaster of Boston on Jan. 26, 1900, with the office renamed Demmon, for Daniel L. Demmon, secretary and treasurer of the Franklin Mining Company, on April 2, 1906; the office was closed on Nov. 30, 1933, but the hamlet of Boston remains [Sawyer; Stevens; PO Archives].

**BOSTON,** Ionia County: first settled by Jacob Francisco and his son-in-law, Ira A. Dane, in 1836; but they moved away in 1837, the year the first permanent settler, Worcester (or Worster) English, came, and the town was also known as the English Settlement; on Dec. 30, 1840, Timothy White became the first postmaster of Boston (named after the township, which had been named by the early settlers, many of whom came from New England); the office was transferred to and renamed Saranac on Feb. 12, 1859 [Schenck; Branch; PO Archives].

**BOSTON JUNCTION**, Marquette County: a station on the Marquette, Houghton & Ontonagon Railroad in 1884 [GSM 1885].

**BOSTWICK**, Kent County: Marquis L. Jackson became the first postmaster of this rural post office in Cannon Township on Oct. 27, 1884, the office operating until Feb. 15, 1901; see Bostwick Lake for the names Cannon and Bostwick [GSM 1887; PO Archives].

**BOSTWICK LAKE**, Kent County: in the 1840s, E. B. Bostwick acted as business agent for LeGrand Cannon, an eastern capitalist with large land holdings here in what is now Cannon Township and this large lake was named for him as well as the township; its settlement was given a station on the Grand Rapids & Indiana Railroad and, on Aug. 31, 1861, a post office, with Nathaniel Steele as its first postmaster, the office operating until March 27, 1874 [Dillenback; PO Archives].

**BOULDER JUNCTION**, Gogebic County. See Blue Bill.

**BOVEE**, Mackinac County: the settlement around the lumber mill operated by John V. Bovee and F. W. Robinson, as Bovee, Robinson & Company, was given a station on the Minneapolis, St. Paul & Sault Ste. Marie Railroad in 1891; Mr. Bovee became its first postmaster on Dec. 14, 1897, the office operating until April 30, 1901 [GSM 1899-1903].

**BOWEN STATION**, Kent County. See Crosby.

**BOWEN'S MILLS**, Barry County: Nathan Barlow built a sawmill here in 1840 and he became the first postmaster, with the office named Gun Lake (which see for the name), on June 21, 1850; in 1864, the mill became the property of E. H. Bowen who, in 1871, also built a grist mill, and who in 1865 became the postmaster of Gun Lake, having the office renamed Bowen's Mills on Feb. 7, 1870; the office operated until April 2, 1906 [Johnson; PO Archives].

**BOWERS HARBOR**, Grand Traverse County: S. E. Whittier Wait taught the first school in this region, during the winter of 1851, aboard the schooner Madeline, anchored off this point [Mich Hist 15:213 1931].

**BOWNE**, Kent County: this hamlet, named after its township, was two miles from the village of Bowne Center; Justus G. Beach became its first postmaster on Sept. 16, 1850; the office was closed on Aug. 19, 1868, but was restored from Oct. 5, 1868, to April 30, 1904 [Chapman; PO Archives].

**BOWNE CENTER**, Kent County: in 1837, Jonathan Thomas, from Ovid, N.Y., became the first settler in Bowne Township, named, it is believed, for civic leader, John Bowne; Roswell C. Tyler, Norman Foster and Justus G. Beach founded the village of Bowne Center in 1838 [Chapman].

**BOYCES**, Roscommon County: a lumbermill settlement to which a branch of the Mackinac division of the Michigan Central Railroad ran a line about 1874; it never became a village.

**BOYDEN,** Isabella County: this post office in Deerfield Township was named for the Boyden family in whose farmhouse it was opened on Oct. 22, 1892, with Lucy Boyden as its first postmaster, the office operating until Nov. 30, 1906 [GSM 1895-1907; PO Archives].

**BOYDEN'S PLAINS,** Washtenaw County: named for Luther Boyden who, with his wife and three children, emigrated here from Conway, Mass., in 1826 [Beakes; MPH 28:393, 564 1897].

**BOYD'S,** Houghton County: a station on the Chicago, Minneapolis & St. Paul Railroad, 9 miles northwest of Sidnaw, in 1894 [GSM 1895].

**BOYNE CITY,** Charlevoix County: first settled in 1856 by the John Dixon and the John Miller families; Mr. Miller named it Boyne, for it was near the mouth of the Boyne River, which had been named after a river in Ireland; given a post office as Boyne on Sept. 20, 1869, with Mr. Miller as its first postmaster; the village as such began with the building of an inn, the Pine Lake House, by A. J. Hall in 1879; incorporated as the village of Boyne in 1885; renamed Boyne City in 1904; incorporated as city in 1907 [Phyllis Clark; GSM 1879; Page; PO Archives].

**BOYNE FALLS,** Charlevoix County: the village was brought into existence by the coming through of the Grand Rapids & Indiana Railroad in 1874; in that year, A. D. Carpenter built a store and on Sept. 5, William Nelson became the first postmaster; incorporated as a village in 1893; named for the falls on nearby Boyne River, which had been named after a river in Ireland [Powers; Mich Hist 37:174 1953].

**BOYNTON VILLAGE,** St. Clair County: a hamlet three miles west of Port Huron in 1878 [GSM 1879].

**BRACEVILLE,** Kent County: this rural post office, opened on March 16, 1858, was named for Elisha Brace, its first postmaster, the office operating until Oct. 13, 1859 [PO Archives].

**BRADFORD,** Midland County. See Gordonville.

**BRADFORD LAKE,** Otsego County. See Waters.

**BRADLEY,** Allegan County: on May 10, 1844, David Bradley was appointed postmaster of the Bradley post office on an old mail route, prior to the building of the plankroad; on the completion of that road in 1854, several families settled near it on the present site of the village, formed a town, and got the post office moved there; on Feb. 7, 1854, Uriah Gregory got it transferred to his store and renamed Wayland Centre (see Wayland for the name), with himself as postmaster; but on the following April 29, the first settler, Joel Bronson, became postmaster at Bradley with the name Bradley restored; the office operated until June 2, 1855, but the village of Bradley remains [Johnson; PO Archives].

**BRADLEY,** Otsego County. See Salling.

**BRADLEY,** Saginaw County: a flag station on the Saginaw division of the Michigan Central Railroad in 1878 [GSM 1879].

**BRADY**, Cass County: located on the south shore of Eagle Lake; platted and recorded by John M. Brady in 1895; chiefly a summer resort [Glover].

**BRADY**, Kalamazoo County. See Vicksburg.

**BRADY**, Saginaw County: while land purchases were made here from 1836, tavern-leeper Philip Mickles became the first permanent settler in 1842; farms were carved out of the wilderness by Richard Walsh, Frank O'Connor, John Healy, and others; the township was organized in 1856 and named for General Hugh Brady, of Detroit; Mortimer W. Owen became its first postmaster on April 24, 1891; the office was closed on March 1, 1895, but was restored from May 23, 1895, to Feb. 28, 1903 [Blinn; Mills].

**BRADY LAKE**, Mecosta County: named by George Brady for himself; he came from Ohio and is believed to have been the first settler in the township which he named Aetna when it was organized in 1865 [Chapman; Mich Hist 21:163 1937].

**BRADYVILLE**, Oceana County: named for the four Norwegian-born brothers, Halver, Andrew, Tolif, and Otto Brady, who first settled here in Benona Township in 1850; Charles S. Heeg became its first postmaster on May 18, 1899, the office operating until Aug. 31, 1901 [MPH 35:702 1907: GSM 1900; PO Archives].

**BRAIDWOOD**, Sanilac County: this rural post office was named for John M. Braidwood who became its first postmaster on March 15, 1900, the office operating until May 14, 1906 [PO Archives].

**BRAKEMAN'S CREEK**, Huron County. See Huron City.

**BRAMPTON**, Delta County: when first settled in 1864, it was called Day's River from the stream beside it, and which had been named for John Day, an early trapper and hunter; it was renamed after the city in England by the Chicago & Northwestern Railroad whose promotors were selling issues of their securities to investors in the British Isles; William H. Wellsteed became its first postmaster on June 23, 1874 [George T. Springer; Federal; PO Archives].

**BRANAGAN'S CORNERS**, Sanilac County. See Roseburg.

**BRANCH**, Branch County: named after the county which, when organized in 1833, was named for John Branch, secretary of the Navy under President Andrew Jackson; first settled by Elisha Warren, Seth Dunham and Harvey Warner who bought from a Dr. Hill the Black Hawk mill (named after an Indian chief who lived in the Gilead Lake region); they platted the village which became the county seat, 1831-1840; but they put too high a price on their lots and thus discouraged its formation as a business center; Harvey Warner became its first postmaster on May 2, 1835, the office operating until Jan. 29, 1864; gradually the last vestiges of this once-promising village were removed, only the old mill remaining [Mich Hist 25:244 1941; PO Archives].

**BRANCH,** Lake County: this village on the Mason-Lake county line was founded about 1873 by Benjamin F. Barnett who built a lumbermen's hotel past which the Pere Marquette Railroad later ran and made it a station; he became the first postmaster of Branch, Mason County, on Feb. 1, 1876, named after its township through which ran the north branch of the Pere Marquette River; on Oct. 1, 1962, the post office was transferred to Lake County [Ellen Stevensen; GSM 1879; PO Archives].

**BRANCHVILLE,** Calhoun County: John Wilson, a carpenter, settled here in 1834; Mr. Farmer opened the first hostelry in 1836 and Mr. Underdonk the first store in 1838; the latter was its postmaster until April 3, 1860, when the office was moved to Athens; the village, about a mile east of Athens, had ceased to exist by 1876 [Everts].

**BRANDON,** Oakland County: while the first land purchase was made in 1831, John G. Perry became the first actual settler in 1835; the township, from which the town was named, was erected in 1837; Jonathan Selden became its first postmaster on Sept. 13, 1843, the office operating until July 24, 1885; located on the line between Brandon and Oxford Townships [Mrs. Donald E. Adams; PO Archives].

**BRANT,** Saginaw County: named after the township which had been established in 1858; its first settlers included Alpheus Oliver, Ezra T. Cogswell, and Benjamin Colville; George Ward, Jr., became its first postmaster on March 17, 1884 [Mills; PO Archives].

**BRASSAR,** Chippewa County: this village on Sugar Island carries the name of a pioneer French family here; Urban Nightingale became its first postmaster on March 18, 1911, the office operating until Nov. 30, 1939 [Hamilton; PO Archives].

**BRAVO,** Allegan County: Ezra L. Davis and Alonzo Sherman came here in Clyde Township in 1867 and set up a sawmill and opened a general store; the community became known as Sherman, named for General William T. Sherman; but there was another Sherman post office in Michigan and this one was given a post office named Bravo, a name indicating the spirit of these pioneers in starting a village in the woods, and gradually the village took the same name; Royal Chandler Eaton became its first postmaster on April 10, 1872, the office operating until July 31, 1950 [Esther W. Hettinger; Ensign; PO Archives].

**BRAZIL,** Osceola County: this station on the Pere Marquette Railroad was given a post office on June 30, 1892, with Charles Allen as its first postmaster, the office operating until Jan. 17, 1894 [GSM 1895; PO Archives].

**BRECKENRIDGE,** Gratiot County: Charles H. Howd located the land here in Wheeler Township in 1860 and settled on it in 1872 when the Pere Marquette Railroad came through; he became the first postmaster on May 19, 1873; incorporated as a village in 1908; named for early mill-owners Daniel W. and Justin A. Breckenridge [Tucker].

**BRECKENRIDGE**, Newaygo County: believed to have been named for presidential candidate John C. Breckenridge; Nathaniel J. Russell became its first postmaster on Aug. 23, 1856, the office operating until Jan. 27, 1857 [GSM 1860; PO Archives].

**BREEDSVILLE**, Van Buren County: here in Columbia Township by the Black River in May, 1835, Jonathan Hinkley and Barnard M. Howard came seeking lumbering prospects; late that year, they returned from Monroe County, N.Y., with a party of 25; one of them, Silas Breed, built a sawmill and the village that followed was named for him; another, Amos S. Brown, became its first postmaster on Sept. 25, 1837; the office was closed on Jan. 13, 1841, but was restored on May 7, 1852; incorporated as a village in 1883 [Doris Farley; Rowland; PO Archives].

**BREEN**, Dickinson County. See Waucedah.

**BREESE**, Allegan County: laid out on land owned by Mrs. Breese, 1835-38; but its lots did not sell, and it never became more than a village on paper [Johnson].

**BRENT**, Genesee County: after twenty years in the U.S. diplomatic service in Spain and Portugal, Virginia-born Thomas Ludwell Lee Brent bought a large tract of land here and settled on it; in 1837, his workers built a mill on Charlotte Creek, named for his daughter, but later renamed Brent Creek; given a post office named Brent Creek on Nov. 2, 1888, with Frank J. Browne as its first postmaster; its spelling was changed to Brentcreek on June 25, 1894 [Doris Hidde; PO Archives].

**BREST**, Monroe County: settled by the French about 1810 and named after one of their great seaports; American promotors organized the Gibralter & Flat Rock Company in 1836 to develop Gibralter into a city and Brest into its lake port, but the venture failed; Joseph Metcalf became the first postmaster of Brest on July 15, 1836; the office was closed on July 8, 1863, but was restored from Feb. 28, 1890, to Aug. 15, 1903 [Burton; PO Archives].

**BRETHREN**, Manistee County: founded in 1900 by Samuel S. Thorpe as a colony of the Brethren (the German Baptist Brethren Church); he became its first postmaster on Aug. 5, 1901, and it was given a station on the Pere Marquette Railroad [Lillian Payne; PO Archives].

**BREVORT**, Mackinac County: in 1845, a surveyor, Henry Brevort (or Brevoort), was assigned to subdivide the area; for him the settlers named a lake, a township, a river, and this village; Peter Hombach acquired three lots here in 1867, but Charles Gustafson is considered the original pioneer; he was followed by so many more Swedes that it became a Swedish colony; when the Mackinac Lumber Company built a supply depot here in 1875 it was called The Warehouse; given a post office named Brevort on June 25, 1890, with Hattie C. Vought as its first postmaster, the office operating until Dec. 30, 1864 [Edith M. Gustafson; Emerson Smith].

**BREWERVILLE**, Van Buren County: named for Lawrence Brewer, mill owner and storekeeper, who became its first postmaster on Aug. 24, 1857; the office was transferred to and renamed Almena on Oct. 26, 1861 [Ellis; PO Archives].

**BRIAR HILL**, Monroe County, a station on the Detroit & Lima Northern Railroad, between Flat Rock and Carleton, in 1897 [Mich Manual 1899].

**BRICE**, Gratiot County: began as a trading point in North Shade Township; named for William Brice, township supervisor, 1872-1884; Justus B. Gardner became the first postmaster on June 16, 1882, succeeded by Richard W. Brice in 1895, the office operating until Dec. 14, 1904 [Tucker; Chapman; PO Archives].

**BRICKERSVILLE**, Antrim County: a rural post office in the Bricker & Company general store, with Samuel Bricker becoming its first postmaster on April 20, 1902, the office operating until Feb. 28, 1905 [GSM 1907; PO Archives].

**BRICK TAVERN**, Kent County: a post office in Alpine Township, housed in the Brick Tavern, with its proprietor, Edward P. Camp, becoming its first postmaster on June 26, 1874, the office operating until June 24, 1878 [GSM 1879; Chapman; PO Archives].

**BRIDGEHAMPTON**, Sanilac County: this village, named after its township, was given a post office on Aug. 19, 1868, with Samuel Bice as its first postmaster; the office was closed on Jan. 3, 1870, but was restored from June 17, 1880, to Oct. 31, 1901; the village was platted and recorded on June 14, 1880 [GSM 1881; PO Archives].

**BRIDGEPORT**, Saginaw County: the settlement was first known as Cass Bend, due to the sharp bend of the Cass River here; Sidney S. Campbell became the first postmaster of Bridgeport on Oct. 12, 1836; the name was changed to Cass Bridge on Jan. 30, 1864, but the office was closed on Jan. 30, 1904; meanwhile in the same township there had been a post office opened as Bridgeport Centre, with Samuel C. Munson becoming its first postmaster on Aug. 1, 1851, but, with Charles D. Pattee as postmaster, its name was changed permanently to Bridgeport in 1880; named for the numerous bridges that cross the river here [Emmett Robinson; Federal; PO Archives].

**BRIDGETON**, Newaygo County: first settled in 1849, Bridgeton Township was organized in 1852, and its village began with the sawmill of Isaac D. Merrill (for whom Merrill Township, north of here, was named), in 1854; both the town and the township were named from the bridge crossing the Muskegon River here; Amos Slater became its first postmaster on July 29, 1857; the office was closed on May 21, 1860, but was restored from June 27, 1861, to Dec. 31, 1913 [Harry L. Spooner; PO Archives].

**BRIDGEVILLE**, Gratiot County: located in Washington Township where the Maple River is spanned by the state road bridge; John Hicks had some of his land here platted in 1864; William P. Bolds became the first postmaster on Aug. 10, 1865, the office operating until Jan. 28, 1896 [Tucker; PO Archives].

**BRIDGEWATER**, Washtenaw County: first settled in 1829 by Colonel Daniel Hixon after whom the township was first named Hixon in 1832; George Howe, in whose home the town organization took place in 1833, became the first supervisor and had it renamed after Bridgewater, Oneida County, N.Y.; given a post office named Columbia Lake on April 3, 1833, with John Poucher as its first postmaster; the office was also renamed Bridgewater, on May 8, 1843; the office was closed on March 1, 1869, but was restored on Jan. 19, 1871 [Chapman; PO Archives].

**BRIDGMAN**, Berrien County: the settlement was known as Plummer's Pier before Charlotteville was founded by a lumbering company in 1856 and named for Charlotte Howe, wife of one of the owners; in 1870, another owner, George C. Bridgman, platted a village a half mile east, on the railroad, where a station was opened that year, and both the station and the village were named Bridgman; later it came to include both plats; given a post office named Laketon (it is in Lake Township), with Elijah Cowles as its first postmaster, on Nov. 11, 1862, with Mr. Bridgman succeeding him, 1863-1870; through the efforts of the fifth postmaster, William A. Babcock, the name of the office was changed to Bridgman on April 9, 1874; incorporated as a village in 1927 and as a city in 1949 [Ester Leskey; GSM 1873; PO Archives].

**BRIER**, Midland County: John Falls became the first postmaster of this rural post office in Mills Township on Oct. 19, 1898 [GSM 1899; PO Archives].

**BRIER HILL**, Dickinson County: the location of the Brier Hill Mine of the Penn Iron Company; the town was annexed by the city of Norway in 1891 [Sawyer].

**BRIGHTMOOR**, Wayne County: in 1921, B. E. Taylor, a realtor and builder, of Detroit, bought 160 acres out Grand River Avenue, a mile from Detroit, and in 1922 opened the Brightmoor Subdivision; the village grew so rapidly that he added 2913 acres in 1923-24; the village was annexed by the city of Detroit in 1926 and is now a postal station of that city [GSM 1925-27].

**BRIGHTON**, Lenawee County. See Morenci.

**BRIGHTON**, Livingston County: founded in 1832 by Maynard Maltby who named it Ore Creek from the stream which runs through the town and at that time showed mineral deposits; Wilber Fisher became its first postmaster on Nov. 5, 1836; by popular approval it was renamed on Feb. 13, 1838, after Brighton, N.Y. from which area many of the settlers had come; incorporated as a village in 1867 and as a city in 1928 [Mrs. Carol Hills].

**BRIGHTON**, Monroe County: a hamlet in 1830 [MPH 27:26 1896].

**BRILEY**, Montmorency County. See Hetherton.

**BRIMLEY**, Chippewa County: this village on the Waska River in Superior Township was given a station on the Duluth, South Shore & Atlantic Railroad in 1872; it was platted in 1887 and given a post office named Superior, after its township, on May 2, 1888, with George Hodge as its first postmaster; for an official of the postal department it was renamed Brimley on March 6, 1896 [Hamilton; GSM 1897; PO Archives].

**BRINTON**, Isabella County: settled in 1862 and named Letson for its storekeeper, Samuel A. Letson, who became its first postmaster on April 20, 1886; on April 17, 1888, this village in Coldwater Township was renamed Brinton for Oscar T. Brinton; its post office operated until Nov. 30, 1906 [John Cumming; GSM 1887; PO Archives].

**BRISTOL**, Houghton County. See Baraga.

**BRISTOL**, Iosco County: a flag station on the Detroit, Bay City & Alpena Railroad in 1884 [GSM 1885].

**BRISTOL**, Isabella County: this hamlet on the Pine River, in Fremont Township, was first settled in 1866; William K. Gibbs became its first and only postmaster on Feb. 19, 1872, the office operating until Nov. 21, 1873 [Chapman; PO Archives].

**BRISTOL**, Lake County: Bertram D. Payne became the first postmaster of this rural post office on Feb. 16, 1887, the office operating until April 14, 1904 [PO Archives].

**BRISTOL**, Lapeer County. See Almont.

**BRISTOLVILLE**, Barry County: named for W. P. Bristol, local landowner and realtor; Solomon H. Hess became its first postmaster on May 1, 1851, but the office was transferred to and renamed Johnstown on Jan. 9, 1865 [GSM 1860; PO Archives].

**BRITTON**, Lenawee County: when the Wabash Railroad came through here in 1881, they named the station Balch; storekeeper John Britton, who became its first postmaster on Aug. 13, 1881, after several trips to Detroit and the payment of $500, finally got the railroad to rename it Britton and its post office was renamed Britton on April 13, 1888 [Ronald P. Cheever, PM; PO Archives].

**BROAS RAPIDS**, Ionia County. See Belding.

**BROCKTON**, Sanilac County: settled around the Lamotte Farmers Elevator Company; a station on the Detroit, Bay City & Western Railroad in 1920 [GSM 1921].

**BROCKWAY**, St. Clair County: grist mill and sawmill owner Lewis Brockway settled here in 1840, and the township, when organized in 1848, was named for him; this lumbering village took the name of its township; John Grinnell became its first postmaster on June 23, 1852, the office operating until Jan. 2, 1907; when by-passed by a branch of the Pere

Marquette Railroad in favor of Brockway Center (now Yale), most of its houses were moved there on skids over an old corduroy road that is now State 19 [Jenks; Federal; PO Archives].

**BROCKWAY CENTER**, St. Clair County. See Yale.

**BROHMAN**, Newaygo County: this village with a station on the Chicago & Western Michigan Railroad, in Monroe Township, was founded by hotelman Otia Dingman; with Jarred Dingman as its first postmaster it was given a post office named Otia on June 20, 1882, with the name changed to Dingman on Sept. 28, 1883, back to Otia on Jan. 20, 1885, and finally to Brohman on May 5, 1920 [Morris D. Olsson, PM; GSM 1885; PO Archives].

**BRONSON**, Branch County: Jabez B. Bronson, of Ohio, became the first white settler in the county in 1828; the township of Prairie River and its village of York were both renamed for him by the state legislature in 1837; given a post office named Bronson's Prairie, with him as its first postmaster, on Jan. 21, 1830, shortened to Bronson on June 5, 1871; a station on the Lake Shore & Michigan Southern Railroad; incorporated as a village, 1866, and as a city, 1934 [MPH 10:67 1886, 12:400 1888; PO Archives].

**BRONSON**, Kalamazoo County. See Kalamazoo.

**BROOKFIELD**, Eaton County: Peter Moe, with his sons Ezra and Henry, became the first settlers here in 1837, and for years this settlement was known as Moetown; later in the same year, Jesse Hart and his bride Rachel settled here; Brookfield Township was organized in 1841 and the village was named after it; Thomas D. Bryan became its first postmaster on July 13, 1858; the office was closed on Dec. 13, 1865, but was restored from July 8, 1867, to July 30, 1904 [MPH 22:502 1893; 39:355 1899; PO Archives].

**BROOKFIELD**, Huron County: A. H. Burton became its first settler in 1865; the first township election was held in his home in 1868 and he named it after his old home in New York State; he was the first township clerk, with Elijah Thompson the first supervisor [Gwinn].

**BROOKINGS**, Newaygo County: this settlement around a mill of the Brookings Lumber Company, after which it was named, was given a station on the Chicago & Western Michigan (now Pere Marquette) Railroad in 1884 and on Feb. 7, 1889, a post office, with Corrain S. Udell as its first postmaster; the office was closed on April 29, 1892, but was restored from Jan. 28, 1895, to June 8, 1895 [GSM 1893; PO Archives].

**BROOKLANDS**, Oakland County: a rural station of the Rochester post office, opened in 1948, with P. T. Smith in charge [D. C. Colyer].

**BROOKLYN**, Jackson County: Calvin H. Swaine, a Baptist minister from Washington County, N.Y., made the first land claim here in 1832, built a sawmill in 1833, and became the first postmaster of Swainesville on July 28, 1834; co-settlers were Calvin H. Swaine, Jr., Chauncey Hawley,

Lewis Cass and Israel Love; by popular vote the name was changed to Brooklyn, after Brooklyn, N.Y., on Oct. 25, 1836; incorporated as a village in 1879 [MPH 26:256 1895; Mich Hist 33:47 1949; Pen Phil 8:6 1958].

**BROOKLYN**, Macomb County. See Davis.

**BROOKLYN**, St. Joseph County: a hamlet in 1864 [GSM 1865].

**BROOKS**, Bay County: a station on the Cincinnati, Saginaw & Mackinaw Railroad, some two miles west of Bay City, in 1894 [Mich Manual 1899].

**BROOKS**, Menominee County: this rural post office was named for Howard S. Brooks who became its first postmaster on Jan. 12, 1900, the office operating until Nov. 30, 1903 [PO Archives].

**BROOKS**, Newaygo County: this village, founded in 1860 and named for John A. Brooks, early Newaygo lumberman, was given a post office on May 3, 1881, with Lucius B. Mills as its first postmaster, the office operating until May 3, 1890 [GSM 1891; PO Archives].

**BROOKSIDE**, Newaygo County: this village at the center of Sheridan Township was named by pioneer settler William E. Gould from its nearness to Brooks Creek, which had been named for John A. Brooks, early Newaygo lumberman; storekeeper John Pikaart became its first postmaster on April 11, 1890, the office operating until Oct. 31, 1901 [Harry L. Spooner; GSM 1891; PO Archives].

**BROOKSIDE**, Osceola County: George W. Lemon became the first postmaster of this rural post office on May 25, 1868, the office operating until March 1, 1872 [PO Archives].

**BROOMFIELD**, Isabella County: first settled by Doraville Whitney in 1860; the township was organized in 1866 and named for pioneer settler William Broomfield, its supervisor, 1868-76, and later twice again; the Broomfield post office was opened on Feb. 24, 1871, with George L. Hitchcock as its first postmaster; the office was closed on Oct. 31, 1879, but was restored from June 15, 1899, to Jan. 2, 1907 [Fancher; Chapman; PO Archives].

**BROTHERTON**, Houghton County: a station on the O. & B. Railroad; storekeeper Jesse B. Moore became its first postmaster on Dec. 7, 1889, the office operating until March 27, 1896 [GSM 1891-97; PO Archives].

**BROUARD**, Barry County. See Doster.

**BROWN**, Manistee County: first settled by Henry L. Brown in 1853; the township was named for him when organized in 1855; its village on the Manistee River was given a post office named Up River on July 3, 1872, with Samuel Potter as its first postmaster, but the office was renamed Brown on the 16th of the following month, and operated until April 29, 1874 [Page; GSM 1873; PO Archives].

**BROWN CITY**, Sanilac County: this village in Maple Valley Township began as a station on the Port Huron & Northwestern Railroad; founded in 1879 by Robert G. and John M. Brown, a part of the village having been built on the former's farm and he became the first postmaster, with the office named Errol, on Jan. 27, 1880; it was renamed Brown City on May 17, 1881; incorporated as a village in 1887 and as a city in 1907 [Chapman; PO Archives].

**BROWNELL**, Kalamazoo County: named for Thomas C. Brownell who emigrated here from New York State in the 1830s and became for more than 20 years superintendent of the county poor; given a station as Brownell's on the Michigan Central Railroad in 1882 [Fisher].

**BROWNELL'S MILLS**, Lenawee County. See Addison.

**BROWN'S CORNERS**, Wayne County. See Yew.

**BROWN'S DALE**, Otsego County: storekeeper David Brown was the first and only postmaster here at the Cheboygan River, in Dover Township, from Feb. 27, 1880, to June 9, 1882 [GSM 1883; PO Archives].

**BROWN'S MILLS**, Muskegon County: Henry L. Brown became the first postmaster of this sawmill settlement on May 10, 1870, the office operating until only Oct. 10 of the same year [GSM 1871; PO Archives].

**BROWN'S MILLS**, Van Buren County: this station on the Michigan Central Railroad, opened at the Allegan County line in 1882, served a sawmill settlement [Mich Manual 1899].

**BROWN'S SIDING**, Marquette County: a station on the Dulth, South Shore & Atlantic Railroad, opened about 1890 [Mich Manual 1899].

**BROWNSTOWN**, Antrim County. See Torch Lake.

**BROWN'S TOWN**, Wayne County: legend has it that the village was named for Adam Brown who, as a boy of eight in 1764, was captured by Indians in Virginia who adopted him into their tribe, which later migrated to Michigan, and he became a chief; he was still living during the War of 1812, in which Brown's Town was the scene of a battle; John Sturgis became the first postmaster of Brownstown on Aug. 15, 1825; the office was closed on Feb. 20, 1830, restored on March 16, 1830, but transferred to and renamed Flat Rock on May 20, 1872; his name survives in Brownstown Township in which his village, at the junction of the Huron and the Detroit Rivers, near Gibraltar, was located [Burton; PO Archives].

**BROWNSVILLE**, Cass County: Pleasant Grubb built a gristmill here in Calvin Township, at the outlet of Diamond Lake, in 1831; it passed into the possession of William and David Brown, brothers and native Scotsmen, from whom the ensuing village derived its name; Jonathan C. Robinson became its first postmaster on Oct. 6, 1854, the office operating until Sept. 30, 1901 [Mathews; Glover; PO Archives].

**BROWNTOWN**, Berrien County: Oliver R. Brown built a sawmill here in Lake Township in 1861 and platted the village; its Pere Marquette

Railroad depot was named Brown's Station; village and depot are now gone [Fox].

**BROWNVILLE**, Kent County. See Alaska.

**BROWNVILLE**, Lenawee County: the first land bought of the government here was in 1823 when Austin Wing entered two lots, covering the Brownville mill privilege; located on Evans Creek, both settlement and stream were named for the founders of Tecumseh, Musgrove Evans and Joseph W. Brown; less than a mile north of Tecumseh, it was annexed by the village in 1838; the Gazeteer 1838 spells its name Brownsville [Hogaboam; Clara Waldron].

**BRUCE**, Chippewa County: named after the township which in turn had been named at the suggestion of a pioneer settler, Andrew J. Smith, for Lord Bruce, of the Shetland Islands, who had befriended the Smith family when they were tenants on his estate [Bayliss].

**BRUCE**, Macomb County: surveyed by Joseph Wampler in 1817; David Hill made the first government land purchase in 1821, followed by Ashel Bailey in 1822; when the settlers met in 1832 to organize the town, Neil Gray suggested it be named after the great Scottish chieftain Robert Bruce; Nes. Palmerlee became its first postmaster on Jan. 29, 1835; the office was closed on April 19, 1847, but was restored from Oct. 20, 1851, to Aug. 22, 1853 [MPH 28:422 1898; PO Archives].

**BRUCE**, Marquette County: a station on the Marquette, Houghton & Ontonagon Railroad, six miles from the city of Marquette, in 1878 [GSM 1879].

**BRUCE**, Ontonagon County: on Military Road, built north and south through the center of the county, and opened for public use about 1865, relay stations for mail were set up 10 to 12 miles apart; one of these, in present Haight Township, was named Bruce, for Alfred L. Bruce, of Rockland, and was located about a mile north of present Bruce Crossing [Charles Willman].

**BRUCE**, Tuscola County. See Deford.

**BRUCE CROSSING**, Ontonagon County: August Neuman built a sawmill here and a town formed around it; Donald M. Bruce had a store near where the Duluth, South Shore & Atlantic Railroad crossed the old Military Road, and when he was named the first postmaster on March 5, 1888, it was called Bruce's Crossing; since Aug. 13, 1891, the name has been Bruce Crossing [Albert E. Holmes, PM].

**BRUNSON HARBOR**, Berrien County. See Benton Harbor.

**BRUNSWICK**, Newaygo County: this village on the line between Newaygo and Muskegon Counties was founded about 1873 as the point where the stage met the Muskegon to White Cloud train and mail and passengers were taken to Hesperia, and was first called County Line; it was later called Marionville after its first postmaster, Isaac Marion, appointed on

May 31, 1881, but the name of the post office was Dash; the post office was renamed Brunswick, Muskegon County, on Sept. 15, 1897, and was transferred to Newaygo County on April 1, 1943 [Mrs. Anne M. Drake, PM; Page; PO Archives].

**BRUSH CREEK,** Van Buren County. See Lawrence.

**BRUTUS,** Emmet County: as a stage coach stop in Maple River Township, Abner S. Lee built an inn, the Brutus House, in 1874, and was named the first postmaster of Brutus on Nov. 10 of the same year; D. R. Sherman was his business associate; on Sept. 1, 1882, the post office was moved two miles west to a station on the Grand Rapids & Indiana Railroad, and the village soon developed [Traverse; GSM 1883].

**BRUTUS,** Ingham County: in 1837, the legislature organized Ingham Township; in 1839, it set off the north half of it as Brutus, the name chosen by Ephraim Meech, the first settler, who had come here from Brutus, Cayuga County, N.Y.; the first town meeting was held in his home in 1840; later that year, the eastern half of Brutus was organized as Leroy and in 1841 the remaining half was renamed Wheatfield [Durant].

**BRYAN,** Mackinac County: founded in 1905-1906 as a railroad headquarters of the Escanaba Lumber Company (owned and operated by the John K. Stack interests), who named it for William P. Bryan, a logging foreman, who in turn laid out and built this village in Newton Township; Cassius W. McEwen became its first postmaster on June 19, 1906, to 1912, succeeded by Richard B. Stack, 1912 to 1918 (with the office renamed Pike Lake on Nov. 17, 1914), George Fearnley from Dec. 5, 1918, to Aug. 31, 1920, when the office was closed; by this time, the forest products were well cut out, and by 1930 the buildings had been wrecked or removed, and the site is now grown over with brush [Cassius W. McEwen].

**BRYANT'S,** Cheboygan County: this rural post office, 4 miles from Pellston, was named for John Bryant who became its first postmaster on July 16, 1898, the office operating until Nov. 14, 1903 [GSM 1899; PO Archives].

**BRYAR HILL,** Wayne County: a station on the Chicago & Canada Southern Railroad, in Brownstown Township, in 1874 [GSM 1875].

**BRYDEN,** Dickinson County. See Ralph.

**BUCHANAN,** Berrien County: the first white settler, Charles Cowles, came here from Vermont in 1833, followed by John Hatfield and Russell McCoy in 1834; it was first called McCoy's Creek; platted and recorded as Buchanan by flour-mill owner John Hamilton in 1842; John D. Ross became its first postmaster on March 2, 1848; incorporated as a village in 1858 and as a city in 1929; named for U.S. Senator (later President) James Buchanan [Betty Hamilton; Coolidge; PO Archives].

**BUCHTEL,** Isabella County. See Loomis.

**BUCK CREEK,** Kent County: this village in Byron Township was given a post office on Feb. 6, 1856, with George S. Tuttle as its first postmaster; the office was closed on April 8, 1869, restored on April 12, 1869, but changed to Byron Centre on Oct. 15, 1869 [GSM 1860; PO Archives].

**BUCKEYE**, Hillsdale County: Joseph H. Edinger became the first postmaster of this rural post office, 18 miles south of Hillsdale, near the line of Ohio, the Buckeye State, on May 22, 1898, the office operating until May 31, 1902 [GSM 1903; PO Archives].

**BUCKEYE LANDING**, Alger County. See Traunik.

**BUCKHORN**, Berrien County: when the village was first platted, no lots were sold or buildings erected, but nearly a century later, about 1926, the village was revived [Mich Hist 12:322 1928].

**BUCKHORN**, Cheboygan County: a rural post office in Monroe Township, with hotelman Stillman Wixson becoming its first postmaster on Jan. 21, 1885, the office operating until May 31, 1893; so named from its being in deer country [GSM 1887; PO Archives].

**BUCKHORN**, Oakland County. See Rose Center.

**BUCKLEY**, Wexford County: a station on the M. & N.E. Railroad, in Hanover Township; the village was founded by G.A. Brigham in 1905 and named for the locally operating Buckley & Douglas Lumber Company; merchant Frank Wightman became its first postmaster on March 31, 1906; incorporated as a village in 1907 [Mrs. D.M. Slack; GSM 1907].

**BUCKLIN**, Wayne County: named for Timothy Bucklin who became its first postmaster on Jan. 8, 1833; the office was renamed Centre Port, with Abel Perrin as postmaster, on Feb. 1, 1838, closed on March 14, 1838, restored, with Andrew L. Stevens as postmaster, on Feb. 17, 1841, and then closed permanently on Dec. 3, 1845 [PO Archives].

**BUCKROE**, Marquette County: a station on the M. & S.E. Railroad whose officials named it from its location in the deer country, about 1910; its cedar log depot has since been razed; it is worth noting that while many of the early railroad stations in the north country served mining camps and lumber settlements, not a few were just unsheltered stops for the convenience of fishermen and hunters [GSM 1911; Ernest H. Rankin].

**BUCKS**, Crawford County: the Holloway Buck family settled on what came to be called Buck's Hill in 1870; a branch of the Michigan Central Railroad came through near their farm and on the land of Gilbert and Nina (Buck) Valad in 1889; they furnished board and room for the railroad builders, and the place was called Buck's Crossing, later just Bucks [Minnie M. Hartley].

**BUCKS**, St. Joseph County: the township was erected in 1829 and named for pioneer settler George Buck; in 1840, the legislature renamed it Fabius; the post office at present-day Three Rivers was named Bucks for the same man from 1831 to 1837 [Cutler].

**BUEL**, Sanilac County: first settled by Ezra Van Camp in 1852; James L. McGrath became the first postmaster on Jan. 10, 1856, succeeded by Ezra Van Camp on Feb. 11, 1860, and James Van Camp on Aug. 17, 1865; the office was closed on May 9, 1871, but restored on Nov. 26, 1877, with James L. Van Camp as its postmaster, the office operating until July 15, 1901; named after its township, which had been named for a pioneer settler in the county [Chapman; PO Archives].

**BUENA VISTA**, Kent County. See Austerlitz.

**BUENA VISTA**, Saginaw County: Justin Smith made the first land purchase here in 1823; Gardner D. Williams bought land and made the first clearing in 1832; Curtis Emerson bought a disused mill here in 1846; he built up a settlement around it and gave the place its name in honor of General Zachary Taylor's then recent victory over Santa Ana, in the Mexican War; Michael Ludlein became the first postmaster on Sept. 28, 1868; the office was closed on Jan. 31, 1894, but was restored from July 7, 1898, to June 15, 1901; a station on a branch of the Michigan Central Railroad [Blinn; Mills].

**BULLIS**, Livingston County: George W. Mower became the first postmaster of this rural post office on March 7, 1884, the office operating until Aug. 11, 1885 [PO Archives].

**BULLOCK'S CORNERS**, Washtenaw County: Jacob E. Bullock located here in 1827 and the settlement was named for him; the first Salem Township meeting was held in the schoolhouse near the home of Mr. Bullock in 1833 [Chapman].

**BULL'S CROSSING**, Barry County: also called Bull's Cut and Bull's Prairie; site of the trading post of Louis Moreau, 1827-1836; surveyor Albert E. Bull became the first permanent settler in 1836; a settlement, never a village [Mich Hist 15:178 1931, 31:285 1947].

**BUNCEVILLE**, St. Clair County: Zephaniah W. Bunce sailed up the St. Clair River in 1817 and located at the mouth of Baby's Creek (named for Duperon Baby who had a mill a short distance up the stream); there he held forth for 65 years as Indian trader, postmaster, lumberman, and judge; the place where he and his sons, Mumford and Lefferts, operated a water-power mill from 1820 to about 1870 was called Bunceville; a member of the first Michigan Legislature in 1824, he died in 1889 at the age of 102 [H.A. Hopkins].

**BUNDY**, Isabella County: the Bundy Company bought the timber-land here in Bloomfield Township from Edmond Hall about 1870, built a sawmill and began the village; a station on the Detroit, Grand Rapids & Western Railroad; Andrew J. Acker became its first postmaster on Aug. 20, 1894, the office operating until Dec. 30, 1897 [Fancher; GSM 1895; PO Archives].

**BUNKER HILL**, Ingham County: the township was organized in 1839; the first house in it was built by Adam Bunker after whom some say the township was named; older maps call its village Bunker Hill Center, present day ones Bunker Hill or Bunkerhill; Harvey Taylor became its first postmaster on Feb. 12, 1841; the office was closed on Feb. 5, 1842, but was restored from Dec. 21, 1848, to March 14, 1903 [Adams; Foster; PO Archives].

**BUNYEA**, Wexford County: this settlement, with a station on the Ann Arbor Railroad, formed around the Sturtevant & Bunyea sawmill; David Davidson was appointed its first postmaster on Sept. 8, 1903, but declined and Drayton Seaman took the office on Nov. 5, 1903, with it operating until Dec. 15, 1913 [GSM 1905; PO Archives].

**BURCHVILLE**, Kent County: this village in Algoma Township, with a station on the Grand Rapids & Indiana Railroad, was platted in 1868 by John S. Weller, of Ann Arbor, and named for his partner, Jefferson Burch, who had built the first steam sawmill here in 1866; its post office, named Burch's, was opened on Nov. 20, 1868, with Earl K. Childs as its first postmaster, the office operating until Sept. 8, 1879; its depot was named Burch [Dillenback; GSM 1881; PO Archives].

**BURDEN**, Sanilac County: a rural post office in Custer Township with storekeeper James C. McMahon becoming its first postmaster on June 14, 1897, the office operating until April 14, 1904 [GSM 1899; PO Archives].

**BURDICK SETTLEMENT**, Kalamazoo County: in 1833, Robert and Caroline Burdick; and their sons, Lankford, Alvan and Charles, with their young families, emigrated from Otsego County, N.Y.; the father and sons each locating separate lands in Charleston Township formed the nucleus of a colony that was long and widely known as the Burdick Settlement [MPH 10:189 1886].

**BURDICKVILLE**, Leelanau County: here in Empire Township, on the east shore of Glen Lake, William D. Burdick built a sawmill and a grist mill in 1864; John Helm came in 1867 and opened a general store which also housed the post office of which he became the first postmaster on Jan. 13, 1868; a lumbering village until its mills burned in 1870 and were not rebuilt; it became a ghost town about 1912 and is now the site of a public park [Dickinson; Barnes; GSM 1873; PO Archives].

**BURGESS**, Charlevoix County: this sawmill settlement in Hayes Township was named for mill owner E. H. Burgess in 1877; resident farmer Elizabeth W. Mandaville became its first postmaster on Feb. 28, 1877, the office operating until July14, 1904 [GSM 1879-1905; PO Archives].

**BURKE'S CORNERS**, Macomb County. See Armada.

**BURLINGTON**, Calhoun County: founded by William and Ansel Adams in 1833; several men in the settlement had served in the War of 1812 before they migrated to Michigan and the town was named after the gunboat Burlington which had engaged in that conflict on the Great Lakes; Levi Houghtaling became its first postmaster on April 5, 1838; incorporated as a village in 1869 [Mrs. William Heal; PO Archives].

**BURNEY**, Houghton County: Kate Brigham became the first postmaster of this rural post office on Nov. 13, 1889, the office operating until May 25, 1895 [PO Archives].

**BURNHAMVILLE,** Manistee County: this village on Bar Lake at Lake Michigan, in Arcadia Township, developed around the mill of the Burnham Wood & Pier Company, and was named after it; given a post office named Burnham on April 17, 1882, with Dean A Hull as its first postmaster, the office operating until April 22, 1895 [Page; GSM 1887; PO Archives].

**BURNIPS,** Allegan County: first known as Salem Center from its location in Salem Township; James Burnip owned land here and built the first store in 1856; he began selling lots for building purposes in 1858; it was given a post office named Burnip's Corners on April 10, 1868, with John S. Warner as its first postmaster; the name was changed to Burnips on June 7, 1915 [Naomi Moomey, PM].

**BURNS,** St. Clair County: a station on a branch of the Port Huron & Northwestern Railroad in 1886; given a post office on Dec. 6, 1893, with George Ryan as its first postmaster [GSM 1887-95; PO Archives].

**BURNS,** Shiawassee County: although Whitmore Knaggs opened a trading post here as early as 1820, actual settlement did not begin until Dyer Rathburn and his family came in 1835; town government began that year and the village, named after its township, was given a post office on May 31, 1848, with Ebenezer F. Wade as its first postmaster, the office operating until Nov. 21, 1881; the village was platted in 1872 [Ellis; GSM 1873; PO Archives].

**BURNSIDE,** Lapeer County: the first settlers in the area William Brown in 1854 and Franklin Keeler in 1855; Allison Township was organized in 1855 and its village was given a post office named Allison, with Simeon P. Gates becoming its first postmaster on Aug. 24, 1857, renamed on Aug. 7, 1866, to honor Ambrose E. Burnside, a Union general in the Civil War; the office operated until Oct. 30, 1913 [Page; PO Archives].

**BURNSIDE,** Tuscola County. See Richland.

**BURNT BLUFF,** Menominee County: a station on a branch of the Chicago & Northwestern Railroad in 1884 [GSM 1885].

**BURR OAK,** St. Joseph County: settled in 1835; the township was given a post office named Burr Oaks, with Julius A. Thompson becoming its first postmaster on May 10, 1837, but the office was closed on July 24, 1855; the village was platted and recorded in 1851 by William Lock and Henry Weaver, its chief landowners; the railroad was projected in 1850 and Mr. Lock gave it land for a depot if it would be named Lock's Station; it was, as was its post office, opened on Feb. 16, 1852, with John E. Clewes as its first postmaster; on Oct. 1, 1857, the post office and the village were renamed Burr Oak; incorporated as a village in 1859; named from the many burr oaks in the area [Genera M. Smith; PO Archives].

**BURROWS**, Branch County: Nicolas Y. Mast became the first postmaster of this rural post office in Noble Township on June 13, 1892, the office operating until Nov. 30, 1901; named for Julius C. Burrows, then a congressman from this district [GSM 1893; PO Archives].

**BURROWS CORNER**, Lapeer County: a hamlet in 1864 [GSM 1865].

**BURSAW**, Chippewa County: Donald McFarlane became the first postmaster of this rural post office on April 28, 1896, the office operating only until the following Aug. 27 [PO Archives].

**BURT**, Cheboygan County: John Heaphy became the first postmaster of this rural post office on Oct. 19, 1860, the office operating until Oct. 29, 1867; see Burt Lake for the name [PO Archives].

**BURT**, Saginaw County: a station on the Cincinnati, Saginaw & Mackinaw Railroad; DeWitt C. Ashman became its first postmaster on Feb. 9, 1889 [Thomas Blinn].

**BURTCHVILLE**, St. Clair County: lumberman Jonathan Burtch settled here in 1840 and became the first supervisor when the township was organized in 1862 and was named for him; this former village in it, on the Black River, was given a post office on Jan. 20, 1846, with Hannibal Hollister as its first postmaster, but the office was transferred to Lake Port on June 19, 1857 [Jenks; Andreas; PO Archives].

**BURTIS**, Lapeer County: Isaac P. Roberts became the first postmaster of this rural post office on May 1, 1863, but the office was closed on Sept. 19 of the same year [PO Archives].

**BURT LAKE**, Cheboygan County: settled in 1875 and known as the Ohio Settlement, and then as Tuscarora, it being in Tuscarora Township; on Jan. 14, 1878, Warren Finn became the first postmaster of Burt Lake, the village being renamed after the lake beside it; it was also called Sager's Landing for storekeeper Edwin H. Sager who was its postmaster in 1882; Burt Lake was named for William A. Burt (1792-1858), who had surveyed the area in 1840; Burt Township, organized in 1860, was also named for him [L.J. Waldron, PM; GSM 1883].

**BURTON**, Genesee County: Horace L. Donelson became the first postmaster of this rural post office on Dec. 13, 1861, the office operating until Aug. 6, 1862 [PO Archives].

**BURTON**, Shiawassee County: on Jan. 22, 1864, Philander Munger became the first postmaster of Mungerville, a station on the Detroit & Milwaukee Railroad, on the west border of Owosso Township; on Feb. 4, 1878, its name was changed to Burton; its post office operated until Jan. 31, 1936 [Ellis; PO Archives].

**BURTON HEIGHTS**, Kent County: Barney Burton came here in 1833; he built the first log cabin in Paris Township and the first barn in Kent County; the village was absorbed by the city of Grand Rapids by

1910, its name being retained by a postal station in that city [Buena Bailey].

**BUSH**, Midland County: this rural post office, 20 miles southeast of Midland, was opened on July 7, 1897, with Alanson Gould as its first postmaster, the office operating until Oct. 15, 1901 [GSM 1899; PO Archives].

**BUSHKILL**, Ottawa County: a station on a branch of the Chicago & Western Michigan Railroad in 1884 [GSM 1885].

**BUSHNELL**, Montcalm County: the township was organized in 1850 and named for Daniel P. Bushnell, then clerk of the state legislature; the first permanent settler in the area was John J. Hammel in 1851; a post office named Bushnell Centre was opened in the home of William C. Griffin on Nov. 28, 1857, but it was transferred to and renamed Dean's Mills on Jan. 10, 1872; the Bushnell Centre post office was restored on May 8, 1872, with Jedediah W. Lane as its postmaster, but it was closed on Aug. 8, 1878; it was restored again from March 6, 1879, to June 5, 1882; on March 25, 1892, with William H. Mills as postmaster, it was given a post office named Bushnell, and the office operated until July 30, 1910 [Schenck; PO Archives].

**BUSHVILLE**, Cheboygan County: a way station on a branch of the Michigan Central Railroad in 1882 [GSM 1883].

**BUSS**, Leelanau County. See Manitou.

**BUTLER**, Berrien County: Abraham Ogden became the first postmaster of this rural post office on May 28, 1836, the office operating until Aug. 23, 1841 [PO Archives].

**BUTLER**, Branch County: Jonathan Hart, from Washington County, N.Y., entered the first government land purchase in the area on July 25, 1835, and Caleb Wilcox became the first actual settler in 1836; nearby, a few days later, Jacob Shook and Robert Wood took up land they had bought in 1835; the first settlement was called Shook's Prairie; the township was erected in 1838 and so named because the majority of the voters here at the time had come from Butler, Wayne County, N.Y.; it was the county seat and on Sept. 23, 1853, it was given a post office, with John Hager as its first postmaster [Johnson; PO Archives].

**BUTMAN**, Gladwin County: the Lovell P. Sherman family came here from Providence, R.I., in 1878, and were the first permanent settlers; he built a log house and the first store; Butman Township was organized in 1883 and he was elected its first supervisor, but the Butman School had been built in 1881; Joseph Cunningham became the first postmaster on Aug. 11, 1884; named for Myron Butman, of Saginaw, whose business interests here dated from 1868 [Ritchie; PO Archives].

**BUTTE des HORT**, Brown County: Nathaniel Perry became the first postmaster of this rural post office on Sept. 10, 1835; it was then in Michigan Territory, but now in Wisconsin [PO Archives].

CHINA TWP.
Res.- F. Layle

CANNON TWP.
Farm Res.-W. Hartwell

**BUTTERFIELD**, Missaukee County: a rural post office, 17 miles southeast of Lake City, opened on Oct. 30, 1895, with Henry J. Coopman as its first postmaster [GSM 1897[.

**BUTTERFIELD CORNERS**, Eaton County: named for Hiram Butterfield who located his farm here in 1837, and lived to be 96 [MPH 32:588 1902].

**BUTTERNUT**, Montcalm County: A station on the Toledo, Saginaw & Muskegon (now Grand Trunk) Railroad, in Bloomer Township, in 1888; storekeeper Jesse S. Dennis became its first postmaster on April 19, 1888, the office operating until Aug. 31, 1955; so named from its being the site of a butternut cheese factory [Dasef; PO Archives].

**BUTTERSVILLE**, Mason County: Burr Caswell became its first white settler in 1847; in 1880, the Horace U. Butters family, in particular his son Marshall F. Butters, founded the village; the narrow gauge Mason & Oceana Railroad came through in 1886 and the station was given a post office on July 7, 1887, with Edward L. Waldwin as its first postmaster, the office operating until Jan. 2, 1907 [Rose D. Hawley; Mich Hist 24:385 1940; PO Archives].

**BUTTONVILLE**, Midland County. See North Bradley.

**BYERS**, Mecosta County: the village began as a shingle mill settlement, with a depot on the Grand Rapids & Indiana Railroad, in Colfax Township, in 1870, and was first called Byers Station; given a post office named Byers on May 11, 1877, with Benjamin Smith as its first postmaster, the office operating until May 15, 1902 [Chapman; GSM 1879; PO Archives].

**BYRD'S CREEK**, Huron County. See Port Austin.

**BYRON**, Shiawassee County: founded by Judge Samuel W. Dexter in 1824; he transferred his lands in 1836 to Major Francis J. Prevost who became the first postmaster on Aug. 12, 1837; he was succeeded in 1842 by Holden White who had opened the first store here; incorporated as a village in 1873, with Charles H. Lemmon as president; a station on the Ann Arbor Railroad; named after its township [L.W. Van Alstine; Campbell].

**BYRON CENTER**, Kent County: Nathan Boynton became the first settler in the area in 1836, the year that Byron Township was organized; this village, named from its location in it, was given a railroad station and, on Oct. 15, 1869, a post office; it was platted and recorded for Augustine Godwin, by Samuel S. Towner, on Aug. 6, 1872 [Dillenback; Chapman].

**CABERFAE**, Wexford County: named by Kenneth MacKenzie, of Chicago, the name being derived from Cabar Feiah (in Gaelic, stag's head), a symbol on the MacKenzie crest dating from 1225; begun as the Caberfae Ranch, it was hit by the Depression and sold to the U.S., and became part of the Manistee National Forest; it is now a ski resort with the ski area on government land and the club house on private property [Catherine Herby].

**CADE'S LAKE,** St. Joseph County: named for Thomas Cade who built a brewery on its shores in 1836 [Cutler].

**CADILLAC,** Wexford County: the land comprising the original village site was bought from the government by L. J. Clark and I. H. Maqueston in 1871; they sold out to lumberman George A. Mitchell who platted the village of Clam Lake in 1872 (it was at the eastern end of Clam Lake, since renamed Lake Cadillac); John S. McClain became its first postmaster on Jan. 3, 1872; incorporated as the village of Clam Lake in 1875 and as the city of Cadillac, with Mr. Mitchell as mayor, in 1877; its post office was renamed Cadillac on June 15, 1877; named for Antoine de la Mothe Cadillac, founder of Detroit [Powers; Wheeler; Mich Hist 25:238 1941; PO Archives].

**CADIZ,** Iron County: the take-off point of a spur track of the Chicago & Northwestern Railroad leading to the early Chicago Lake Mine in Sec. 26 T 43 R 34 [Jack Hill, Sr.].

**CADMUS,** Lenawee County: a station in Dover Township on the Lake Shore & Michigan Southern Railroad; Frank Potts began the village by building a store here in 1887; Peter W. Gander became its first postmaster on Oct. 2, 1888; named by W. H. Shaw after Cadmus, Kansas [Iva Cleveland, PM; GSM 1889].

**CADY,** Macomb County: also called Cady's Corners; first settled by Chauncey G. Cady in 1833; he held the offices of supervisor, town clerk, and, in 1849, was a member of the state legislature; the village was given a post office on July 15, 1864, with George A. Page as its first postmaster, the office operating until July 31, 1906 [MPH 26:162 1895; PO Archives].

**CADYVILLE,** Lapeer County: in 1838, a log schoolhouse was built in Hadley Township, with Nelson Cady as schoolmaster; in 1842, a school district was formed in the southwestern part of the town and named for him; but it was absorbed by other organizations after several years [Page].

**CAFFEY,** Mackinac County: began as a lumber settlement with a station on the Minneapolis, St. Paul & Sault Ste. Marie Railroad named Lewis in 1891; but there was another Lewis post office in Michigan and this one was given a post office named for Pennsylvania-born Civil War veteran William N. Caffey who became its first postmaster on Nov. 23, 1899; the office was closed on Sept. 30, 1909, but was restored, with Mr. Caffey again its postmaster, on June 9, 1913; the office has since been closed permanently and the place now consists of the old Caffey Cemetery and a railroad siding marked Caffey [Ted S. Caffey, g.s. of Wm. N.].

**CAHOON,** Isabella County: this rural post office was named for Morris B. Cahoon who became its first postmaster on Nov. 24, 1891, the office operating until Jan. 9, 1892 [PO Archives].

**CAIRNS,** Clare County: a station on the Toledo, Ann Arbor & Northern Michigan Railroad; named for shingle mill owner Cairns E. Smith who became its first postmaster on Mar. 11, 1890, the office operating until April 1, 1891 [GSM 1891-1903; PO Archives].

**CALDERWOOD**, Ontonagon County: in the pine era of the 1880s, a group of Minnesota men organized a company for logging and sawmill operation, naming it the Calderwood Lumber Company; it was succeeded by the Mercer-de-Laittre Company mill here in Interior Township, but when the settlement was given a post office on Feb. 5, 1908, with Glen McClatchie as its first postmaster, it was called Calderwood [Charles Willman; GSM 1909; PO Archives].

**CALDWELL**, Isabella County. See Two Rivers.

**CALDWELL**, Missaukee County: Thomas T. Caldwell was on the county ticket in the first election of 1871; Quilna Township was renamed Caldwell for him in 1873 and James C. Caldwell became its first postmaster on Aug. 26, 1884, the office operating until Nov. 30, 1906 [Stout; PO Archives].

**CALEDONIA**, Kent County: first settled by Asahel Kent, from Ohio, in 1838; he died in 1840 and his widow married tavern-keeper Peter D. McNaughton who became the first postmaster on Aug. 15, 1843; the office was closed on April 30, 1877, but on July 20, 1894, the Caledonia Station post office was changed to Caledonia; incorporated as a village in 1888; named after Caledonia, N.Y. [MPH 6:399 1883, 27:429 1896; PO Archives].

**CALEDONIA CENTER**, Kent County. See Labarge.

**CALEDONIA STATION**, Kent County: a depot with the coming through of the Grand River Valley Railroad in 1870; given a post office, with Adam B. Sheek as its first postmaster, on April 4, 1870, but the office was changed to Caledonia on July 20, 1894; the village was platted and recorded by R.S. Jackson for David Kinsey on Aug. 20, 1870; named after its township which had been named after Caledonia, N.Y. [Dillenback; Chapman; PO Archives].

**CALIFF STATION**, Muskegon County: in 1874, a depot on the Chicago & Western Michigan Railroad, named for O.W. Califf who was elected constable when its township of Dalton was organized in 1859 [Page].

**CALIFORNIA**, Branch County: Israel R. Hall, of Ontario County, N.Y., located 640 acres of government land here in 1835 and settled on it with his family in 1836; also in 1836, came Samuel Beach from Saline; the settlement was called Hall's Corners after Joseph Hall who had a general store here, with the name, for reasons unknown, later changed to California; the town was organized in 1846; Israel R. Hall became its first postmaster on Jan. 17, 1850, the office operating until Nov. 30, 1905; the railroad came through in 1872 and the village was given a station [MPH 2:188 1877, 18:359 1891; PO Archives].

**CALKINSVILLE**, Isabella County. See Rosebush.

**CALOS**, Calhoun County: a station on the Grand Trunk Railroad, opened in 1882 and named Ransom; given a post office as Calos on Oct. 3, 1882, with John A. Shannon as its first postmaster; the office was closed on Aug. 6, 1883, but was restored from Aug. 21, 1886, to Aug. 8, 1887 [GSM 1887; PO Archives].

**CALSPAR**, Schoolcraft County: Vera J. Rodgers became the first postmaster of this rural post office on Sept. 1, 1927, the office operating until June 29, 1936 [PO Archives].

**CALUMET**, Houghton County: given a post office on Dec. 24, 1866, with Edmund F. Krellwitz as its first postmaster; beginning as a civil township in 1866, the village developed around the mines of the Calumet & Hecla Mining Company and was then composed mainly of the officers and employees thereof; gradually it encompassed the separate communities of Laurium, Hecla, and South Hecla, and in 1929, united with the incorporated village of Red Jacket under the name Calumet; a calumet was the clay stone bowl of the Indian peace pipe [Hudson; Andreas].

**CALVIN**, Cass County: Elijah Osborn was the first postmaster of this rural post office, opened on July 5, 1867 on the west side of Shavehead Lake, in Calvin Township, named for Calvin Britain, territorial representative for the county when the township was organized in 1835; the post office operated until July 25, 1896 [Fox; PO Archives].

**CALVIN CENTER**, Cass County. See Day.

**CAMBRIA**, Hillsdale County: John and Andrew McDermid built a grist mill and a sawmill here in 1835; the Willits brothers, Moses, Barron, and Jonathan, came in 1837, and in 1841 they named the newly formed township after their native Cambria, Niagara County, N.Y.; given a post office as Woodbridge, named for Michigan governor William Woodbridge, on Dec. 14, 1840, with James (Jacob) S. Hancock as its first postmaster; the office was renamed Cambria on June 1, 1841, but was closed on Aug. 22, 1853; Albert Dresser became the first postmaster of nearby Cambria Mills on April 17, 1848, renamed Cambria on Nov. 28, 1882, though the postmaster continued to use the Cambria Mills canceller until at least 1888; the office was closed on Sept. 17, 1906; the village was platted in 1878 [Vivian L. Moore; M.F. Cole; PO Archives].

**CAMBRIDGE JUNCTION**, Lenawee County: Norman Geddes, from western New York, bought the first government land here in 1833 and settled on it in 1835; in 1838, Sylvester Walker, later a state senator, built a tavern at the crossroads of the Chicago turnpike and LaPlaisance Bay Road and the place became known as Walker's Junction; Cambridge Township was organized and named in 1835, and the settlement took its name; given a post office as Cambridge on Feb. 5, 1840, with Mr. Walker as its first postmaster, the office operating until Jan. 14, 1904; Walker's Tavern still stands and is a tourist attraction [Whitney; Dowling; Bonner; PO Archives].

**CAMDEN**, Hillsdale County: founded by its landowners: Easton T. Chester, his son, Orson D. Chester, and Nathan Alward; given a post office named Cranbrook, with James Fowle as its first postmaster, on Aug. 10, 1837, changed to Camden on Sept. 7, 1840; the village grew up around the sawmills built by Frederick Perring in 1838 and Easton T. Chester in 1839; platted in 1867; incorporated as a village in 1899; the name was the one drawn from a hat by its founders, being the one proposed by Easton T. Chester (who became the second postmaster), who had come from Camden, Oneida County, N.Y. [Earl T. Clark].

**CAMPANIA,** Allegan County: this post office by the Boston Rope Company plant was opened about 1900 and closed by 1920 [GSM 1921].

**CAMPAU,** Macomb County: a rural post office, near Mount Clemens, opened on April 29, 1899, with Frank A. Campau as its first postmaster, the office operating until May 31, 1900 [GSM 1901; PO Archives].

**CAMPBELL,** Delta County: a station on the Chicago & Northwestern Railroad in 1878; named by the road whose promotors were selling issues of their securities to investors in the British Isles [GSM 1879].

**CAMPBELL,** Ionia County: Jeremiah and Martin Campbell, brothers and recent immigrants from Ireland, became the first settlers here, in 1840, as squatters until they later bought the land; when the township was organized in 1849, it was named for them; Richard D. Hudson became the first postmaster on Aug. 1, 1854, the office operating until Sept. 15, 1902 [Schenck; Branch; PO Archives].

**CAMPBELL CITY,** Clare County. See Temple.

**CAMPBELL'S CORNERS,** Oakland County. See Oakwood.

**CAMPBELL'S CORNERS,** Ogemaw County: this hamlet, with a railroad station, in Klacking Township, was founded by and named for James Campbell; Henry Phillips became its first postmaster on Dec. 27, 1877, the office operating until Sept. 30, 1911 [GSM 1879; PO Archives].

**CAMPBELLTON,** St. Clair County: this village on the Belle River was given a post office on Aug. 14, 1854, with Cortland Lindsay as its first postmaster, the office operating until Oct. 30, 1863 [GSM 1860; PO Archives].

**CAMP CREEK,** Eaton County: Silas E. Millett became the first postmaster of this rural post office on May 14, 1856, the office operating until Feb. 21, 1862 [PO Archives].

**CAMP CUSTER,** Calhoun County: established in 1917, this World War I training camp of the U.S. Army was given a post office as Custer in 1918; after the war (1920) the office became a branch of the Battle Creek post office; named for Michigan-born General George A. Custer, of Custer's Last Stand fame; it was closed as a military district, June 14, 1968 [GSM 1922].

**CAMP DOUGLAS,** Manistee County: this lumber camp settlement in Brown Township was composed chiefly of employees of the Buckley & Douglas Logging Railroad which put logs into the Manistee River here; Bamlet W. Clark became its first postmaster on June 2, 1884, the office operating until March 1, 1888 [GSM 1885; PO Archives].

**CAMP GRAYLING**, Crawford County. See Rasmus.

**CAMP HANSON**, Crawford County. See Rasmus.

**CAMP PORI**, Houghton County. See Pori.

**CAMP SAINT LOUIS**, Kalamazoo County: a station on the Detroit, Toledo & Milwaukee Railroad in 1898 [Mich Manual 1899].

**CAMP SKEEL**, Iosco County. See Wurtsmith AFB.

**CAN**, Huron County. See Canboro.

**CANAAN**, Hillsdale County. See Waldron.

**CANADA**, St. Joseph County: a hamlet in Lockport Township in 1864 [GSM 1865].

**CANADA CORNERS**, Muskegon County: three Canadians, from Ontario, were pioneer settlers here in central Casnovia Township: Alexander McInnis in 1866, D. Bartram in 1867, and Charles Fraleigh in 1868; James E. Goodman became the first postmaster of the settlement on March 5, 1880, the office operating until Nov. 30, 1905 [Page; GSM 1881; PO Archives].

**CANADA CREEK**, Montmorency County: Hazel L. Smith became the first postmaster of this rural post office on July 8, 1939, the office operating until May 31, 1941 [PO Archives].

**CANADA SETTLEMENT**, Eaton County: in the southeast corner of Oneida Township in 1836-37, six young men (Martin, Jason and J. H. Nichols, and James, Robert and Samuel Nixon) and their families, from London, Ontario, Canada, settled; followed soon by others from the same area, the place came to be called the Canada Settlement [MPH 39:377 1899; Williams].

**CANADIAN SETTLEMENT**, Ionia County. See Keene.

**CANANDAIGUA**, Lenawee County: the Indians had a village here on Bean (now Tiffin) Creek; Samuel Gregg became the first white settler in 1824; most of the early settlers here were from New York and they named it after Canandaigua, N.Y.; platted by Ira White in 1835; give a stage coach post office in 1837 [Hogaboam; Dowling].

**CANANDAIGUA CITY**, Oakland County. See Lake Orion.

**CANBORO**, Huron County: first settled by Levi Williamson in 1863 and he became the first supervisor when the township (Grant, for General U.S. Grant) was organized in 1867; Columbus G.W. Parker became the first postmaster of this village on the Pigeon River on May 27, 1870, with the office named Can, but renamed Canboro on Nov. 3, 1879; the office operated until Aug. 14, 1905 [Gwinn; GSM 1881; PO Archives].

**CANBY**, Emmet County: this village in Bliss Township was given a post office on April 28, 1884, with Edwin D. Matthews as its first postmaster, the office operating until June 29, 1907 [GSM 1885; PO Archives].

**CANFIELD**, Ogemaw County: a rural post office in Hill Township, near the shingle mill of C. Corgan; farmer George L. Miller became its first postmaster on April 4, 1900, the office operating until Sept. 15, 1913 [GSM 1901; PO Archives].

**CANFIELD MILL SETTLEMENT**, Manistee County: on the south bank of the Manistee River, near Lake Michigan; in 1849, John Cantield took over the mill and properties from his father, Roswell Canfield; the Canfield & (E.D.) Wheeler Company built the village; when Poles began moving in about 1881, it became known as the Polish Settlement; the mill quite operating about 1900 and the settlement dwindled away, its last house being torn down in 1923 [Russell].

**CANNONSBURG**, Kent County: the first settler was Andrew Watson in 1837; the town came into being in 1844 with the separation of Cannon from Plainwell Township; named for LeGrand Cannon, a New York financier who, through his agent, E.B. Bostwick, bought land here, had the village platted in 1848, and gave away 25 fine lots; Mr. Bostwick applied for a post office in 1844 and it was given on May 7 of that year as Cannonsburgh, with Sidney S. Haskins as its first postmaster; the office was closed on Aug. 19, 1847, but was restored on Sept. 22, 1847; on Feb. 5, 1894, its spelling was changed to Cannonsburg [Elizabeth H. Belke, PM; MPH 27:573 1896; PO Archives].

**CANOVA**, St. Clair County: this lumber town in Brockway Township was settled in 1866 and given a post office on March 10, 1876, with Justin L. Paldi as its first postmaster; the office was closed on Dec. 15, 1879, but was restored from March 1, 1880, to Dec. 14, 1883 [Andreas; PO Archives].

**CANTON**, Wayne County. See Sheldon.

**CAPAC**, St. Clair County: founded and platted by a group from Romeo, headed by George R. Funstan and Hon. DeWitt C. Walker in 1857; the Judge named it after Huayna Ccapac (d. 1527), head of a Peruvian line of Ynca Indian emperors; a nearby rural post office named Pinery was transferred to and renamed Capac, with William B. Preston as postmaster, on Jan. 5, 1858; the Grand Trunk Railroad opened a station here in 1866; incorporated as a village in 1873 [Jenks; MPH 39:183; Andreas].

**CARBON**, Saginaw County: Feldy George Ruby became the first postmaster of this village in Albee Township on April 5, 1899, the office operating until Sept. 30, 1903; named from its being in a coal mining region [GSM 1901-05; PO Archives].

**CARBONDALE**, Menominee County: this settlement began with the charcoal kilns (hence its name) of the Menominee Furnace Company and the sawmills of E.P. Sherlock, in 1881; James Osborne, agent for Mr. Sherlock, became its first postmaster on Dec. 21, 1881, the office operating until April 14, 1904; still a definite locality, with its name also retained in Carbondale Road [Mrs. Ethel Schuyler; GSM 1883; PO Archives].

**CARETON**, Muskegon County: Henry Dodge became the first postmaster of this rural post office on May 16, 1870, the office operating until July 11, 1871 [PO Archives].

**CAREY**, Lake County: a station on a branch of the Chicago & Northwestern Railroad, 3 miles from Luther, in 1884 [GSM 1885].

**CAREY MISSION**, Berrien County: Governor Lewis Cass invited Isaac McCoy, a Baptist minister, to build an Indian mission here in 1822; due to the government removal of the Indians to the west, in closed in 1830; named for Rev. William Carey, noted English Baptist missionary [Rogers].

**CARL**, Berrien County: a station on the Milwaukee, Benton Harbor & Columbus Railroad, in Royalton Township; named for grocer Carlton L. Bunker who became its first postmaster on March 21, 1898, the office operating until May 10, 1911 [GSM 1899; PO Archives].

**CARLAND**, Shiawassee County: the village began as a station on the Toledo, Ann Arbor & Northern Michigan Railroad in 1884, and was named after one of its officials; given a post office on Dec. 3, 1884, with Ezra Lattimer as its first postmaster [Clara Horn, PM].

**CARLETON**, Monroe County: the village was laid out in 1872 by Daniel A. Matthews (who helped select the site of the state capital at Lansing) and Charles A. Kent on a plat of 80 acres, to which Mr. Matthews and William Hickok later added 80 more; the Matthews House, an inn, was the first building erected; Mr. Matthews became the first postmaster on Feb. 24, 1874; a station on the Pere Marquette Railroad; incorporated as a village in 1911; named for Will Carleton (1845-1912), popular Michigan poet [Wing; MPH 39:191 1915].

**CARLETONVILLE**, Chippewa County: founded in 1853 by Guy H. Carleton who built several houses and operated a sawmill here; but the venture failed and it is now a ghost town [Bayliss].

**CARLISLE**, Eaton County: Charles T. Moffit (or Moffat) settled here in 1836 and built a sawmill in 1837; when it passed into the hands of Oliver A. Hyde, the locality became known as Hyde's Mills; given a post office as Carlisle, with Edward D. Lacy as its first postmaster, on Aug. 15, 1843, the office operating until May 30, 1903 [Durant; PO Archives].

**CARLISLE**, Kent County. See West Carlisle.

**CARLSHEND**, Marquette County: founded about 1893 by Karl Petros Janssen; he was known as Carl Peter Johnson, but he was appointed postmaster on Dec. 7, 1894, as Charles Peter Johnson; he sent in the name Carlslund (Carl's land) but it came back Carlshend, and has so remained; Johnsons continued as postmasters until 1931, Charles P. being followed by Henry D. and he by Gilbert A. [PM; Ernest Rankin; PO Archives].

**CARLSON**, Baraga County: a farming community, first settled by Nicholas Alfred Carlson in 1875, and followed soon after by other Swedish farmers, among them Anders Erickson, Johannes Anderson, August Arvidson and Anders Hansen [Ralph Soli].

**CARLSON,** Gogebic County: the village began as a lumbering site with a station on the Chicago & Northwestern Railroad; Joseph J. Benik became its first postmaster on Jan. 29, 1921, the office operating until Sept. 30, 1924; named for Conrad Carlson, county register of deeds in 1889-90 [Victor F. Lemmer].

**CARLTON CENTRE,** Barry County: named from its location in Carlton Township which was first settled by Samuel Wickham and his family and George Fuller, his son-in-law, from Carlton Township, in western New York, in 1836; Jared S. Rogers became the first postmaster of Carlton on Aug. 28, 1849; the office was closed on Sept. 26, 1859, but was restored from Oct. 7, 1862, to June 7, 1866; the office was re-established as Carlton Centre, with James N. Covert as postmaster, on Sept. 26, 1874, the office operating until April 15, 1903 [Johnson; PO Archives].

**CARMEL,** Eaton County. See Charlotte.

**CARNEY,** Menominee County: when opened about 1879, this station on the Chicago & Northwestern Railroad was named for Fred Carney, of Marinette, Wisconsin, who had timber and land interests in this area, Nadeau Township; Charles A. Brown became the first postmaster on Nov. 14, 1882 [Evelyn Bergen; GSM 1885; PO Archives].

**CARO,** Tuscola County: Curtis Emerson built his logging camp here along the Cass River in 1847; the village which ensued was first called Centerville and was given a post office named Tuscola Center on April 25, 1866; to get rid of this confusion, the founding fathers met in 1868 and, at the suggestion of one of them, William E. Sherman, the name Caro (a shortened form of Egypt's Cairo) was chosen; in 1869, both the state legislature and the post office department accepted the change of name; the post office change was made on June 15, 1969; incorporated as a village in 1871 [Schultz; John M. Duncan; PO Archives].

**CARP,** Marquette County. See Carp River.

**CARP LAKE,** Emmet County: the village was founded by Octave Terrian; given a station on the Grand Rapids & Indiana Railroad and on Jan. 27, 1880, a post office, with Alpheus B. Hendricks as its first postmaster; named from a kind of fish still abounding in nearby Carp Lake [PM; PO Archives].

**CARP LAKE,** Ontonagon County: a copper mining community near the Porcupine Mountains, a half mile south of Lake Superior; the company was organized by Cleveland men in 1858; from lack of funds they closed the mine in 1862, but they were able to reopen it in 1897 [Stevens].

**CARP RIVER,** Marquette County: the site of the Carp River Forge, erected by the Jackson Iron Company in 1847, first produced iron in 1848, but was closed in 1856; given a post office on Jan. 12, 1847, as

Carp River (the settlement was known as the Jackson Location), with William B. McNair as its first postmaster until he was succeeded by Philo Marshall Everett, of Jackson, who had organized the Jackson Iron Company; the office was closed on April 2, 1851; its station on the Duluth, South Shore & Atlantic Railroad was named Carp; named from its location on Carp River which, like its outlet Carp Lake, was incorrectly named after a species of fish therein abounding [Mich Hist 15:292 1931, 29:263 1945; PO Archives].

**CARPENTER**, Emmet County: Jacob Lehmer became the first postmaster of this rural post office in Bear Creek Township, in the southwest corner of the county, on Nov. 23, 1881, the office operating until Oct. 21, 1897 [GSM 1883; PO Archives].

**CARPENTER**, Lenawee County. See Ogden.

**CARPENTER'S**, Washtenaw County: in 1878, a hamlet 3 miles west of Ypsilanti [GSM 1879].

**CARPENTER'S CORNERS**, Kalamazoo County: named for Ezra Carpenter who first settled in the area in 1849 and later ran a blacksmith shop here [Durant].

**CARPENTER'S STATION**, Lapeer County. See Oregon.

**CARROLL**, Calhoun County: Heman Cowles became the first postmaster of this rural post office on Aug. 30, 1839, the office operating until Nov. 11, 1850 [PO Archives].

**CARROLLTON**, Macomb County: Wallace C. Everts became the first postmaster of this rural post office on July 9, 1842, the office operating until Oct. 24, 1843 [PO Archives].

**CARROLLTON**, Saginaw County: Dr. Carroll made land entries here in 1835 and the village which was named for him was given a post office on Feb. 6, 1864, with township supervisor Charles E. Gillett as its first postmaster; a station on the Cincinnati, Saginaw & Mackinaw Railroad [Helen Daly, PM].

**CARRS**, Mason County: this rural post office was in Lake County when Romanzo E. Smart became its first postmaster on June 5, 1900, the office operating until Feb. 15, 1907 [GSM 1901; PO Archives].

**CARR SETTLEMENT**, Lake County: in 1867, some 12 Union Army veterans from the same cavalry regiment took out timber claims here; they were from St. Lawrence County, N.Y., and they named the place after their leader, Charles Carr [Judkins].

**CARR'S CORNERS**, Tuscola County: Henry F. Carr and family had settled here in eastern Denmark Township in 1854, and he became the first postmpaster, with the office named Denmark, on May 31, 1862, the office operating until Oct. 31, 1900 [Page; PO Archives].

**CARSON CITY**, Montcalm County: its land was first entered in part by Joseph Throop in 1850; platted on land owned by R.M. Abbott, Delia Miner and Hiram T. Sherman in 1866 and recorded in 1871; the first lot was sold in 1867 to Thomas Scott and his two nephews, John and Thomas LaDue who, under the firm name of Scott & LaDue, built a sawmill in 1868 and a grist mill in 1870; the North Shade post office in Gratiot County was transferred here on Aug. 3, 1868, with Hiram T. Sherman becoming the first postmaster of Carson City, named by Mr. Scott who had been in Carson City, Nevada, in its boom days; incorporated as a village in 1887 and as a city in 1960 [City Charter]. The Nevada town, founded in 1858, was named for Christopher ('Kit') Carson, western U.S. frontiersman (1809-1868) [New Amer. Ency.]

**CARSONVILLE**, Sanilac County: the village began with a log store built in 1853; the place was called Hall's Corners, after Silas C. Hall, the storekeeper, and he became its first postmaster on Aug. 17, 1857, with the office named Farmers; Arthur Carson built a store here in 1864, a larger one in 1872, and a grain elevator in 1880, and on Nov. 14, 1884, the post office and the village were renamed for him; a station on the Pere Marquette Railroad; incorporated as a village in 1887 [Bonnie Backus; PO Archives].

**CASCADE**, Antrim County. See Alba.

**CASCADE**, Kent County: the first owner of the site was Joel Guild; in 1845, D.S.T. Weller bought it and platted the village, named from "the fine fall of water," which he hoped would lead to the erection of water-power mills; Dr. Melancthon W. Alfred became the first postmaster on March 7, 1854, the office operating until Sept. 30, 1910 [Dillenback; PO Archives].

**CASCADE**, Marquette County: ore was located here in 1878, and the settlement developed from the mining operations of the Cascade Iron Company; its station at the intersection of the Chicago & Northwestern with the Marquette, Houghton & Ontonagon Railroad was called Cascade Junction [Hatcher; GSM 1885].

**CASCO**, Allegan County: John Thayer and his two sons bought and cleared the first land in the area in 1845 and built the first home in 1846; when the township was set off from Ganges in 1854, L.D. Cook wanted it named for General Lewis Cass, but political feeling forced him to compromise and accept Casco; its post office, West Casco, located in the western part of the township, was opened on April 7, 1863, with Timothy McDowell as its first postmaster, the office operating until Jan. 31, 1902 [Johnson; Ensign; PO Archives].

**CASCO**, St. Clair County: William Fenton, Dennis Bates, and James Reynolds were among those who settled here before 1840; when the township was organized in 1849, it is believed to have been named by Captain John Clarke after Casco, Maine, he being a native of that state; Stephen A. Fenton became the first postmaster on Aug. 14, 1854, the office operating until Jan. 31, 1907 [Jenks; PO Archives].

**CASE**, Presque Isle County: the village was named after its township which had been named for Charles E. Case who became its supervisor; a station on the Detroit & Mackinaw Railroad; Christopher C. Smith became the first postmaster on March 10, 1899, the office operating until Oct. 15, 1907 [Advance; GSM 1901; PO Archives].

**CASEVILLE**, Huron County: Ruben Dodge, a hunter and trapper from Maine, settled here with his family in 1836; it first became known as the Pigeon River Settlement; it was renamed Port Elizabeth or Elizabethtown for the wife of William Rattle who represented the interests here of large landowner Leonard Case; it was renamed Caseville in 1856 when Francis Crawford bought 20,000 acres in and around the village from Mr. Case; Mr. Crawford became the first postmaster on Jan. 28, 1863; incorporated as a village in 1896 [F. William Nienstedt, PM; MPH 39:353 1915].

**CASH**, Sanilac County: named for Edward Cash who became the first settler here in 1851 and in whose home the Watertown Township organizational meeting was held in 1868; David Fowles built a sawmill in 1882 and moved it to the village; given a post office on June 6, 1883, with William M. Tomlinson as its first postmaster, the office operating until Feb. 28, 1905 [Chapman; PO Archives].

**CASNOVIA**, Muskegon County: when founded by tavern-keeper Lot Fulkerson in 1850, it was in Kent County; Daniel David Bennett became its first postmaster on Oct. 9, 1851; platted and recorded by J.H. Sanford for R.H. Merritt, John More, R.H. and S. Topping, Richard Hawkins and Harmon Hamilton, on July 13, 1862; pioneer merchant Milton L. Squier served as postmaster from July 5, 1867, to 1886; incorporated as a village in 1875; the name is from the Latin (casa, home, and nova, new), our new home; in some records it was also spelled Casinova and Cazenovia [Chapman; Charlotte Hervey, g.d. of Lot Julkerson].

**CASPIAN**, Iron County: a station on a branch of the Chicago & Northwestern Railroad in 1884; a village was platted and recorded as Palatka in 1901 and given a post office of that name on April 12, 1906, with William G. Hanson as its first postmaster; it was the headquarters of the Veroner Mining Company, which operated the Caspian, Baltic, and Fogarty mines; to provide for more housing facilities, an adjacent village named Caspian was platted in 1908, and the Palatka post office was moved to it; the venture failed because the location was poor, and at a better one nearby the village of New Caspian was platted in 1909; the Palatka post office was moved to it in 1915 and renamed Caspian in 1918; incorporated as a village in 1919; the place was also known locally as Spring Valley and as Newtown, but now only as Caspian [Sawyer; Hill; PO Archives].

**CASS**, Hillsdale County. See Prattville.

**CASS**, Ionia County. See Berlin.

**CASSANDRA**, Wayne County: Benjamin F.H. Witherell, a Detroit judge, platted the village and recorded it on March 9, 1836, naming it after his third wife, Cassandra Brady Witherell; on the original plat it is misspelled Cassandia; in Greenfield Township, on Woodward Avenue, north of Detroit, the site is now covered by the city of Highland Park [Catlin].

**CASS BRIDGE,** Saginaw County. See Bridgeport.

**CASS CITY,** Tuscola County: land entries, probably for lumbering rights in the area, were recorded in 1851, and Messrs. Cooper and Wright, of Saginaw, began operating their mill here soon after; the first permanent settlers were Hugh Seed, Andrew Walmsley and John H. Bird, all coming in 1855; the post office, opened in a rural section of Elkland Township in 1960, was transferred to and renamed Cass City on July 6, 1868, with John C. Laing as its first postmaster; incorporated as a village in 1883; being located near the forks of the Cass River, the village was named after the river, which in turn had been named for General Lewis Cass, territorial governor of Michigan, 1813-1831 [Frederick H. Pinney; PO Archives].

**CASS LAKE,** Oakland County: a settlement on Cass Lake, 2 miles from Pontiac, in 1922 [GSM 1923].

**CASSOPOLIS,** Cass County: Abram Tietsort, Jr., and his family, from Ohio, became the first settlers here in 1829; in that year, both the county and the county seat were organized by legislative act and named for territorial governor Lewis Cass; platted in 1831 and recorded by its proprietors, Elias B. Sherman, Alexander H. Redfield, Abram Tietsort, Oliver Johnson and Ephraim McCleary; Mr. Redfield became its first postmaster on Aug. 17, 1832; incorporated as a village in 1863; first spelled Cassapolis, its first newspaper, the National Democrat, changed it to Cassopolis in 1865 [Glover; Rogers; MPH 1:132 1874].

**CASSVILLE,** Crawford County: this post office, named for territorial governor Lewis Cass, was in Michigan Territory when Allen Hill became its first postmaster on April 28, 1828; it is now in Iowa County, Wisconsin [PO Archives].

**CASTLE PARK,** Allegan County: John H. Parr became the first postmaster of this rural post office on May 15, 1903, the office operating until Dec. 31, 1953 [PO Archives].

**CASTLETON,** Barry County: a post office, named after its township, with Seth Davis becoming its first postmaster on July 4, 1842; the office was changed to Barryville on Dec. 22, 1857, but was closed on March 7, 1873 [GSM 1860; PO Archives].

**CAT HEAD,** Leelanau County: a hamelt on Keweenaw Bay at the extreme north end of the county in 1878, but now simply Cat Head Point [GSM 1879].

**CATHOLIC MISSION,** Baraga County. See Assinins.

**CATHOLIC POINT,** St. Clair County: this designation on early county maps referred to a strip of land created by the parallel courses of the Belle and the St. Clair Rivers, just north of their confluence; the site, some two miles below present-day Marine City, was bought for a mission location by Rev. Gabriel Richard, of Detroit, in June, 1824; Rev. Pierre Déjean built the first Catholic church in the county here in 1826, naming it St. Félicite [Paré; Federal].

**CATHRO**, Alpena County: a station on the Detroit & Mackinaw Railroad; the village was named for George Cathro, a prominent farmer in the area; Elspeth Cathro became its first postmaster on Nov. 5, 1894, the office operating until March 15, 1955 [Fred R. Trelfa; PO Archives].

**CATO**, Montcalm County: Edmond Smith became the first settler in the area in 1855; Cato Township was erected in 1957 and named by Westbrook B. Divine after his native town of Cato, N.Y.; Edwin French became its first postmaster on Dec. 2, 1857, the office operating until July 30, 1892 [Schenck; PO Archives].

**CATO**, Sanilac County. See Charleston.

**CATVILLE**, Wayne County. See New Boston.

**CAYTON**, Grand Traverse County. See Wormwood.

**CAYUGA**, Jackson County: Michael S. Brown became the first postmaster of this rural post office in Springport Township on Feb. 12, 1839, the office operating until Feb. 5, 1861 [DeLand; PO Archives].

**CAZENOVIA**, Muskegon County. See Casnovia.

**CECELIA**, Calhoun County: a post office in Athens Township, kept in the Pine Creek House, with Smoles Wood becoming its first postmaster in 1860, the office operating until 1875 [Everts].

**CECIL**, Emmet County: a sawmill settlement named for its storekeeper, Mr. Cecil; Palmer V. Clark became its first postmaster on Jan. 31, 1901 [GSM 1903; PO Archives].

**CEDAR**, Gladwin County. See Gladwin.

**CEDAR**, Ingham County. See Williamston.

**CEDAR**, Leelanau County: founded by Benjamin Boughey about 1885, who moved here to go into the lumbering business; he named it Cedar City because it was located in a cedar forest, and its depot is still so named; its name on maps and its post office is Cedar; Frederick McFall became its first postmaster on Aug. 15, 1893 [Helen M. Kucera, PM; Dickinson; PO Archives].

**CEDAR**, Livingston County. See Fowlerville.

**CEDAR**, Menominee County: a station on a branch of the Chicago & Northwestern Railroad in 1886 [GSM 1887].

**CEDAR**, Osceola County: G.S. Slaybough was the first settler and he became the first supervisor when Cedar Township was organized in 1871 [Chapman].

**CEDAR BANK,** Jackson County: grocer Charles J. Van Schoick became the first postmaster of this rural post office in Liberty Township on April 23, 1889, the office operating until March 31, 1902 [GSM 1895; PO Archives].

**CEDAR CITY,** Leelanau County. See Cedar.

**CEDAR CREEK,** Barry County: in 1849, Isaac LaGrange built a sawmill on Cedar Creek, so named because the stream had a cedar swamp at its source; Mr. LaGrange became the first postmaster of the village on Feb. 27, 1850; the office was closed on Sept. 3, 1866, but was restored from Dec. 9, 1868, and from Jan. 12, 1877, to Dec. 31, 1904 [Johnson; PO Archives].

**CEDAR CREEK,** Wexford County. See Manton.

**CEDARDALE,** Danilac County: this flag station on the Port Huron & Northwestern Railroad, in the cedar timber region, was given a post office as Cedar Dale on Sept. 14, 1868, with Nelson O. Thayer as its first postmaster; the spelling was changed to Cedardale on Jan. 9, 1895, but the office was closed on March 15, 1904 [GSM 1873; PO Archives].

**CEDAR FORKS,** Menominee County: first settled in 1850; named from its being located at the point where the Cedar River empties into Green Bay; in Cedarville Township, it was also known as Cedarville; it was in Delta County when its post office was opened on Feb. 27, 1852, with Edwin S. Briggs as its first postmaster; the office was closed on Oct. 14, 1859, restored on Feb. 17, 1860, but changed to Cedar River on May 9, 1883 [GSM 1877; PO Archives].

**CEDAR LAKE,** Calhoun County: this rural post office at Cedar Lake was opened on May 4, 1839, with David Aldrich as its first postmaster, the office operating until Sept. 25, 1863 [GSM 1860-65; PO Archives].

**CEDAR LAKE,** Montcalm County: the village developed around a railroad station in Home Township; Frederick H. Harlin became its first postmaster on July 26, 1876, the year the village was platted; named from its location in an area of cedar trees and at the edge of a lake [Schenck; PO Archives].

**CEDARMERE,** Iosco County: this station on the Detroit & Mackinaw Railway was given a post office named Serradella on Nov. 26, 1912, with Nathan H. Chandler as its first postmaster, the office being renamed Cedarmere on March 7, 1913 [GSM 1915; PO Archives].

**CEDAR RIVER,** Menominee County: the oldest settlement on the Green Bay shore, it began with the Hackbone & Boyden water-powered sawmill in 1854; it was given a post office on May 9, 1883; on the Big Cedar River whose valley was the great white cedar country [Jean Worth].

**CEDAR RUN,** Benzie County: this post office in the cedar timber region of Long Lake Township was in Grand Traverse County when Mrs. Eliza Willobee became its first postmaster on Jan. 27, 1868, but it was transferred to Benzie County on Jan. 18, 1892, the office operating until Oct. 31, 1934; its station on the Manistee & Northwestern Railroad was first called Ruthardt's Siding [Sprague; GSM 1873; PO Archives].

**CEDAR SPRINGS**, Kent County: first settled by Robbins Hicks in 1855; Nicholas Hill became its first postmaster on Feb. 4, 1857; the village was platted in 1859 and he recorded it in 1860; the Grand Rapids & Indiana Railroad came through in 1868; incorporated as a village in 1871 and as a city in 1960; so named because the area was then covered with a dense growth of cedar and abounding in springs, two being in the creek at the site of the town [Dillenback; Mrs. Verne Mabie; PO Archives].

**CEDAR SWAMP**, Ottawa County: the village was platted and recorded in 1848, with Albertus C. Van Raalte, founder of nearby Holland, as proprietor [Lillie].

**CEDARVILLE**, Mackinac County: the village began as a lumber settlement on the Lake Huron shore in 1884; William Clarke became its first postmaster on July 14, 1888; named from its trade in cedar poles, posts and ties [GSM 1889; PM].

**CEDARVILLE**, Menominee County. See Cedar Forks.

**CEDARVILLE**, Sanilac County: a station on the Pere Marquette Railroad, in Marion Township, in 1912 [GSM 1913].

**CELERON ISLAND**, Wayne County: in the Detroit River near its entrance into Lake Erie; named for Celeron de Blainville whom the French sent to protect their claims in the Ohio Valley in 1749 and who became the commander of their fort at Detroit; in some sources spelled Celoron [Eleanor Trizisky; Mich Hist 22:282 1938; Dunbar].

**CELSUS**, Kent County: Shepard B. Cowles became the first postmaster of this rural post office in Spencer Township on Feb. 17, 1866, the office operating until May 21, 1868 [PO Archives; GSM 1867].

**CEMENT CITY**, Lenawee County: Almer Smith became the first postmaster of Woodstock (named after its township, which Charles M. McKenzie had named after his native Woodstock, Vermont), on Jan. 3, 1838; the office was closed on Oct. 13, 1859, but was restored from Dec. 3, 1859, to May 5, 1871, and from Jan. 27, 1881, to May 21, 1887; the Kelly's Corners post office, named for pioneer local landowner Orson Kelly, was opened on Feb. 17, 1868, with John E. Turk as its first postmaster; the office was changed to Woodstock on Dec. 6, 1886, to Cement on Feb. 21, 1901, and finally to Cement City on March 5, 1901; the founder of the new village, William Cowhan, renamed it in 1900 with the coming in of a cement company; incorporated as a village in 1953 [Owen D. Sprunger; GSM 1860; PO Archives].

**CENTENNIAL HEIGHTS**, Houghton County: the Schoolcraft Mining Company was organized in 1863, shut down in 1873, and became bankrupt in 1876; its properties were bought by a company organized for that purpose, the Centennial Mining Company, which took the name Centennial from the date of its organization, 1876, the year being the hundredth anniversary of the independence of the U.S.; renamed the Centennial Copper Mining Company in 1896; the company platted and sold the lots of the village of Centennial Heights on part of its highland in 1900 [Sawyer; Stevens].

**CENTER**, Eaton County. See Hoytville.

**CENTER HARBOR**, Huron County: after Jeremiah Ludington built a sawmill here in 1856, the place became known as Jerry's Hill; he sold it in 1864 and it became known as Center Harbor from its location on Saginaw Bay; it was wiped out by the forest fire of October, 1871 [Gwinn].

**CENTER LINE**, Macomb County: named by the French from its having been the middle one of three Indian trails from the fort at Detroit to the trading posts of the north; Joseph Buechel built the first general store here in 1863; Hieronymous Engelmann became the first postmaster on July 19, 1878, succeeded by Sophia Buechel in 1885; this post office, spelled Centre Line, was closed on July 31, 1906, but was later restored as Center Line; incorporated as a village in 1925 and as a city in 1936 [Paul Van Den Branden; PO Archives].

**CENTER PLAINS**, Crawford County. See Pere Cheney.

**CENTERVILLE**, Benzie County. See Homestead.

**CENTERVILLE**, Delta County. See Lathrop.

**CENTERVILLE**, Tuscola County. See Caro.

**CENTRAL**, Keweenaw County: this settlement in Sherman Township developed from the very successful Central Mine nearby, which was opened in 1854 and closed in 1898; with William Cox as its first postmaster; it was given a post office named Central Mine, on Dec. 8, 1871, with its spelling changed to Centralmine on June 30, 1894; the office operated until Sept. 15, 1906; the village comprised mostly Methodist Cornishmen, and though it is now a ghost town, many of their descendants still keep up the church here to which they make an annual pilgrimage [Murdoch; GSM 1857-1907; PO Archives].

**CENTRAL CITY**, Midland County: platted and advertised by a group of men from Ohio about 1870; it was in the center of Greendale Township, half way between the cities of Midland and Mount Pleasant, and exactly in the center of the southern peninsula; it failed to develop [Chapman].

**CENTRAL LAKE**, Antrim County: Stephen B. Davis became its first postmaster on April 26, 1869; James M. Wadsworth (son of Abram S. Wadsworth, founder of Elk Rapids) opened the first store here in 1872; the village was platted in 1883; the Chicago & Western Michigan (now Pere Marquette) Railroad came through in 1892; incorporated as a village in 1895; the lake on which it was located was then called Intermediate or Central Lake, being in the center of a chain of lakes from Ellsworth to Bellaire [Franklin L. Erickson, PM; GSM 1873].

**CENTRAL MINE**, Keweenaw County. See Central.

**CENTRE**, Eaton County. See Hoytville.

**CENTRE PORT**, Wayne County. See Bucklin.

**CENTREVILLE**, St. Joseph County: Thomas W. Langley became the first settler, building a tavern here in 1831, and he became the first postmaster on March 2, 1833; platted and recorded by the proprietors, Electra W. Deane, Daniel B. Miller, Charles Noble and Robert Clark, Jr., a government surveyor who acted as attorney in fact for his coadjutors; Columbia Lancaster built the first home on land which the proprietors had given him for services rendered; its plat was recorded on Nov. 17, 1831, and 15 days later it was made the county seat and has been so since; first incorporated as a village in 1837; named from its location in the county [Everts].

**CERESCO**, Calhoun County: first settled in 1830, the village dates from 1838 with the building of a sawmill and a stone flour mill on the Kalamazoo River here; Isaac Crary and John D. Pierce founded the village and the latter named it by combining the name of the Greek goddess of growing grail (Ceres) with that of the first two letters of the word company,–she to provide the harvest for the millers to prepare for use; Winslow S. Hale became its first postmaster on Dec. 30, 1843 [Sylvia Metzger].

**CEYLON**, Barry County: grocer Herman C. Hagerman became the first postmaster of this rural post office in Assyria Township on March 9, 1888, the office operating until March 31, 1903 [GSM 1889-1905; PO Archives].

**CHADWICK**, Ionia County: Charles Chadwick settled here in Orleans Township in 1856; when the Detroit, Lansing & Northern Railroad came through, he got a depot built here, with himself as station agent and he got a post office opened on April 10, 1872, with himself as its first postmaster; the office operated until Jan. 15, 1907; also known as Chadwick's Corners [Schenck; PO Archives].

**CHAISON**, Delta County: application for the erection of Baldwin Ridge Township in 1873 was made by 17 settlers including Daniel Chaison after whom this hamlet was named [David Coon; GSM 1875].

**CHAMBERLAIN**, St. Joseph County: first settled in 1842; named for Francis J. Chamberlain who became its first postmaster on March 4, 1872, the office operating until only Dec. 23 of the same year [GSM 1873; PO Archives].

**CHAMBERLAIN'S**, Kalamazoo County: a station on a branch of the Grand Trunk Railroad in 1886 [GSM 1887].

**CHAMBERS CORNERS**, Allegan County. See Wayland.

**CHAMPION**, Marquette County: the village was named from its proximity to the Champion Mine which opened in 1867; John R. Case became its first postmaster on Dec. 29, 1869; a station on the Duluth, South Shore & Atlantic Railroad; the mine was closed in 1910, but the village and its post office remain [G. Vance Hiney; Andreas; PO Archives].

**CHAMPION HILL,** Benzie County: E. Wellman became the first permanent settler here in 1862, followed by the Isaac Maxfield and George Sinclair families in 1863; for Kent Anderson, pioneer settler, the name of Andersonville was suggested for the settlement, but rejected as too suggestive of the southern Civil War prison; as the place was put on the Methodist circuit, a decision had to be made, and Champion Hill was adopted, which seemed very appropriate, as all would agree who have ever mounted the highest hills [MPH 28:115 1897].

**CHAMPION JUNCTION,** Marquette County: a station on the Marquette, Houghton & Ontonagon Railroad, 15 miles west of Ishpeming, in 1886; name derived from the Champion Mine [GSM 1887].

**CHAMPION MINE,** Marquette County: this mine of the Champion Iron Company opened in 1867 and closed in 1910; from its location below a hill it was given a post office named Beacon on June 8, 1877, with Robert T. McKay as its first postmaster, the office operating until Feb. 27, 1957 [GSM 1883; PO Archives].

**CHANDLER,** Clinton County: this station on the Michigan Central Railroad, then 8 miles north of Lansing, was named Chandler's in 1882, later just Chandler [GSM 1883-1907].

**CHANDLER,** Delta County: founded about 1898 and named for Alden Chandler, a pioneer lumberman in the region [David S. Coon].

**CHANDLER,** Huron County: first settled by Thomas Edwards in 1860, the township was organized in 1880, with William Smith as its first supervisor; named for Zachariah Chandler, U.S. senator from Michigan [Chapman].

**CHANDLER,** Ionia County: Dayton M. Church became the first postmaster of this rural post office in Boston Township on Sept. 22, 1879, succeeded by Eustace E. Church on Dec. 27, 1879, the office operating until Oct. 30, 1902 [Schenck; Branch].

**CHANDLER,** Wayne County: a station on the Lake Shore & Michigan Southern Railroad, in Brownstown Township, in 1882 [GSM 1883].

**CHANNING,** Dickinson County: this village in Sagola Township began as a railroad junction called Ford Siding, with Michael Aylward as its first railroad agent; given a post office as Channing, for John Parke Channing, a mining engineer surveying the area; Horace W. Bent became its first postmaster on Dec. 7, 1892 [Harry T. Dransfield, PM].

**CHAPEL,** Kent County: farmer Dougald J. McNaughton became the first postmaster of this rural post office in Ada Township on Feb. 1, 1884, the office operating until Sept. 30, 1903; the place was also called Egypt [GSM 1885; PO Archives].

**CHAPIN**, Menominee County: a station on the Minneapolis, St. Paul & Sault Ste. Marie Railroad in 1894 [GSM 1895].

**CHAPIN**, Saginaw County: first settled by Joseph G. Taylor in 1855; named for Austin Chapin, an organizer of the township in 1867; John W. Everett became its first postmaster on June 6, 1876, the office operating until Oct. 31, 1933 [Mills; PO Archives].

**CHAPIN LAKE**, St. Joseph County: a settlement in Sherman Township, on Chapin Lake, named for David Chapin who had settled on its banks about 1840 [Cutler].

**CHAPIN MINE**, Dickinson County. See Iron Mountain.

**CHAPIN'S STATION**, Ingham County. See Eden.

**CHAPMAN LAKE**, Ogemaw County. See Walker's Corners.

**CHAPPLE CORNERS**, Mason County: this village on the Big Sable River, in Victory Township, was first settled in 1864; Edmund C. Chambers became the first postmaster on Jan. 27, 1874, the office operating until Sept. 27, 1881 [Page; GSM 1883; PO Archives].

**CHARLES**, Mackinac County: a settlement around the mill and railroad siding of the Sterling Lumber Company, in St. Ignace Township; Cassius J. Galbreath became its first postmaster on May 24, 1905, succeeded by lumberman Charles F. Read, after whom it was named, in 1906 [Emerson Smith; GSM 1907; PO Archives].

**CHARLESTON**, Cass County: a village in Volinia Township, platted in 1836 by Jacob Morlan, Samuel Fulton, and Jacob Charles, for whom it was named; Elijah Goble built a tavern here in 1837; it was an important stop on the Kalamazoo-Niles Stage Line in the early 1840s, but the building of the Michigan Central Railroad was its death blow [Fox; Glover].

**CHARLESTON**, Kalamazoo County: William Harrison, a son of Judge Bazel Harrison, became the first settler, building his log cabin here beside the Kalamazoo River in 1829; the town was named for another early settler, Charles M. Nichols, who became its first postmaster on May 2, 1836; the office was transferred to and renamed Augusta on Dec. 16, 1861 [MPH 7:483 1886; PO Archives].

**CHARLESTON**, Ottawa County: in 1810, Pierre Constant built a trading post here on Trader's Creek; in 1836 the village of Charleston was platted and recorded; when the mill machinery of Richard Roberts' sawmill was removed in 1872, the village began to fade away [Lillie; Page].

**CHARLESTON**, Sanilac County: this village in Delaware Township was first settled about 1864 and first called Cato; it was given a post office as Charleston on Dec. 17, 1872, with Thomas L. Ward as its first postmaster; its entire 21 buildings were wiped out by fire in September, 1881, after which the village was begun again [GSM 1883; PO Archives].

**CHARLESTON,** Van Buren County: an extinct village, its history is in Decatur Republican, July 24, 1843 [Mich Hist 27:185 1943].

**CHARLESWORTH,** Eaton County: first settled in 1863, this village was given a railroad station and on Feb. 16, 1874, a post office, with John W. Loomis as its first postmaster, the office operating until March 15, 1907 [GSM 1879; PO Archives].

**CHARLEVOIX,** Charlevoix County: a colony of fishermen by 1852; John S. Dixon bought land here in 1854 and in 1864 had a large dock built; in 1878, resort associations began to plan and settle the site, leading to its incorporation as a village, with Mr. Dixon as president, in 1879, and as a city in 1905; in the early days it was also known as Pine River, its permanent name honors the Jesuit missionary, Pierre F. X. Charlevoix [Powers; PO Archives].

**CHARLOTTE,** Eaton County: the site was government land bought by George Barnes in 1832; he sold it to Edmond Bostwick, of New York City, in 1835; he in turn sold part of it to H. I. Lawrence, Townsend Harris, and Francis Cochran, and the four developed the village which they named after Mr. Bostwick's wife; Jonathan Searles became its first postmaster on March 17, 1838; incorporated as a village in 1863 and as a city in 1871; at various times it was also known as Eaton Centre and as Carmel, but never officially [Hazel Murray Sleater; PO Archives].

**CHARLOTTEVILLE,** Berrien County. See Bridgman.

**CHASE,** Lake County: Lorenzo Conklin became the first settler in 1862; this settlement, first called Grendale, by clerical error appeared in the act as Green Dell; Charles Joiner located here in 1869 and built a sawmill, a broom handle factory, and a shingle mill; given a post office as Chase, with Alvin Joiner as its first postmaster, on March 29, 1872; this village on the Marquette River served as the county seat until 1874; named by homesteader John Bigbee for Salmon Portland Chase, governor of Ohio [Judkins; PO Archives].

**CHASE'S,** Lenawee County. See Raisin Center.

**CHASE'S CORNERS,** Oakland County: given a post office in 1826, with local landowner Joseph Chase as its first postmaster [Mich Hist 18:496 1929].

**CHASSELL,** Houghton County: founded in 1887 by John Chassell, a French farmer; first named Pike's Bay, and later, Robinson for Orrin Robinson, manager of the Sturgeon River Lumber Company and later lieutenant governor of Michigan; given a station on the Duluth, South Shore & Atlantic Railroad in 1888; William Johnson became the first postmaster of Chassell, named after its founder, on Feb. 2, 1888 [H. Kenneth Hamar; GSM 1889; PO Archives].

**CHATHAM**, Alger County: founded by James Finn who built a lumber camp here in 1896 and named it after Chatham, Ontario; John H. Gatiss, Jr., became its first postmaster on Jan. 19, 1897; a station on the Munising Railway, in Rock River Township; only the remnants of the camp remained when in 1899 it was made the location of a State Agricultural Experiment Station; the village was then developed under the direction of W. G. Mather, president of the Cleveland Cliffs Iron Company [Sawyer; PO Archives].

**CHAUNCEY**, Kent County: founded about 1882, and named for its chief landowner, Chauncey Porter, who became its first postmaster on Dec. 1, 1882, the office operating until Sept. 30, 1903 [John B. Martin; PO Archives].

**CHAUVIN**, Wayne County: a small village, then a mile east of Detroit, in Grosse Pointe Township; on Aug. 21, 1897, grocer Peter Defer became its first postmaster, the office operating until April 30, 1908, when the area was absorbed by the city of Detroit, being now in the Hilger Avenue district; named for Charles Chauvin on whose farmland it was largely located [Fintan L. Henk; GSM 1899-1909; PO Archives].

**CHEBOWGAN**, Brown County: when William Payne became the first postmaster of this rural post office on April 18, 1836, it was in Michigan Territory; it is now the city of Sheboygan, Wisconsin [PO Archives].

**CHEBOYGAN**, Cheboygan County: in 1844, Jacob Sammons (1804-1859), a cooper from Fort Mackinac, set out in his scow to seek his fortune on a site of his own; he chose this old Indian camping ground (Shabwegan, they had called it), built his cabin, plied his trade, and recruited other settlers and craftsmen; given a post office as Duncan in 1846, changed to Cheboygan in 1870; incorporated as a village in 1871 and as a city in 1889; the Chippewas were also called Cehboys and the term gan meant water; so Cheboygan may mean Chippewa Water, namely the river which now bears that name, and from which the county and the city took their name [Mich Hist 25:243 1941; Hudson].

**CHEBOYGANING**, Saginaw County. See Blumfield Corners.

**CHELSEA**, Wayne County: Jedeiah Hunt became the first postmaster of this rural post office on March 16, 1835, but the office was closed the following Sept. 9 [PO Archives].

**CHELSEA**, Washtenaw County: in 1820, Cyrus Beckwith became the first settler in what was to become Sylvan Township in 1834; for land concessions, the Congdon brothers, Elisha and James, got the Michigan Central Railroad to build a station here in 1848; on Jan. 4, 1849, Elisha Congdon became the first postmaster of Kedron (a nearby hamlet, named after Kedron, N.Y.) changed to Chelsea on July 19, 1850, when the depot was actually built and the village platted; the records burned in 1870, and the village was reincorporated in 1889; named by Elisha Congdon after his old home across the river from Chelsea, Mass. [Chapman; Beakes; PO Archives].

**CHEMUNGVILLE,** Livingston County. See Oak Grove.

**CHENEAUX,** Mackinac County. See Les Cheneaux.

**CHENEY,** Crawford County. See Pere Cheney.

**CHERRIE,** Charlevoix County: a station on the Chicago & Western Michigan (now Pere Marquette) Railroad in 1892 [GSM 1895].

**CHERRY CREEK,** Sanilac County: Adolphus B. Christian became the first postmaster of this rural post office on March 31, 1856, the office operating until March 27, 1858 [PO Archives].

**CHERRY GROVE,** Wexford County: Sven A. Benson became the first postmaster of this rural post office on Feb. 7, 1879, but the office was closed on the 3rd of the following month [PO Archives].

**CHERRY HILL,** Wayne County: Canton Township was first settled in 1825 and erected in 1835; this hamlet in it was given a post office on May 22, 1867, with Abner Hitchcock as its first postmaster; the office was closed on Nov. 1, 1867, but was restored from Feb. 5, 1897, to Sept. 15, 1908 [Burton; PO Archives].

**CHERRY HOME,** Leelanau County: this area in Leelanau Township was the largest cherry orchard in the world; Gilman M. Dame, president of the Francis H. Haserot Company, canners, became its first postmaster on June 12, 1919, the office operating until Dec. 31, 1931 [GSM 1921; PO Archives].

**CHESANING,** Saginaw County: Thomas W. Wright and his family became the first settlers here in 1839; the first five settlers organized Northampton Township in 1846; Mr. Wright became the first postmaster of Northampton on Jan. 28, 1846; on Aug. 8, 1853, the post office, village and township were all renamed Chesaning (Chessening, Indian for big rock); incorporated as a village in 1869 [Chesaning Hist. Comm.; PO Archives].

**CHESHIRE,** Allegan County: Simeon Pike, from Monroe County, N.Y., became the first white settler here in 1839; the township was organized in 1851 and this sawmill village (it had four of them) was named after it; Jonathan Howard became its first postmaster on March 8, 1856; the office was renamed Lake on april 10, 1858, then back to Cheshire on Feb. 18, 1863, until it was closed on March 6, 1879; the office was restored from June 20, 1879, to July 31, 1905 [Johnson; Rowland; PO Archives].

**CHESHIRE JUNCTION,** Marquette County. See Forsyth.

**CHESTER,** Eaton County: the first permanent settlers were Harvey, Isaac and Orton Williams, in 1836; the first town meeting was held in the home of Harvey Williams in 1839; it was given a post office on Jan. 29, 1842; the office was transferred to Allen's on Feb. 7, 1870, but the Chester post office was re-established the following day; a station on the Grand Rapids division of the Michigan Central Railroad; it was first platted as Chester Station by Jesse Betz in 1870, with an addition by George

Brenner later the same year; its post office was closed on Oct. 13, 1873, but was restored from May 7, 1874, to Oct. 31, 1913; named after its township [Durant; PO Archives].

**CHESTERFIELD**, Macomb County: a hamlet in Chesterfield Township; first settled in 1830, but not until the Grand Trunk Railroad came through in 1865 was there any business development; given a post office on March 10, 1875, with James C. Patton as its first postmaster, the office operating until July 15, 1907 [Leeson; PO Archives].

**CHESTONIA**, Antrim County: Thomas R. Van Wert and his family became the first settlers in May, 1874; the township was organized later that year and he became the first supervisor as well as the first postmaster when the post office was opened on Nov. 28, 1876 [Traverse; PO Archives].

**CHEVINGSTON**, Sanilac County: a settlement in Wheatland Township around the sawmill of Charles Reinelt; storekeeper Fred Fair became the first postmaster on Dec. 21, 1893, the office operating until June 30, 1906 [GSM 1895-1907; PO Archives].

**CHICAGO**, Keweenaw County: a 520-acre mining property; the Chicago Mine became inactive by 1900 [Stevens].

**CHICAGO & GRAND TRUNK JUNCTION**, St. Clair County: a station 4 miles west of Port Huron in 1886 [GSM 1887].

**CHICAGO JUNCTION**, Ingham County. See Trowbridge.

**CHICAGON LAKE**, Iton County: Andrew J. Blackbird's Ottawa grammar gives She-gog for skunk and She-gog-ong, also She-kaw-gong, for Chicago, i.e., skunk place; written in French orthography, the final g was dropped; Joutel's spelling of the name survives here in Chicagon Lake [Mid-America 40:164 July 1958].

**CHICKAMING**, Berrien County: Luman Northrop became the first settler in the area about 1840, and built a cabin and a sawmill; the township was formed in 1856, with Silas Sawyer as its first supervisor; John C. Miller became its first postmaster on Nov. 11, 1862, the office operating until July 21, 1879; named from an Indian word meaning lake [Ellis; PO Archives].

**CHICORA**, Allegan County: Herman D. Clark became the first postmaster of this village in Cheshire Township on Jan. 10, 1896, the office operating until May 31, 1904; named after a boat which sank in Lake Michigan [Esther W. Hettinger; PO Archives].

**CHIEF**, Manistee County: a village in Brown Township with a post office since Dec. 20, 1881, when Jacob Laisy became its first postmaster; its station on the M. & N.E. Railroad was named Chief Lake; the village is just east of Chief Lake [GSM 1895; PO Archives].

**CHIGAUMISHKENE**, Ionia County. See Lyons.

**CHILDSDALE**, Kent County: the village began with the building of a sawmill by Zenas G. Winsor in 1848 and was first called Gibraltar; bought by H.B. Childs, who added the Childsdale Paper Mills in 1866; its depot on the Grand Rapids & Indiana Railroad was renamed Childs Mills Station; its post office, opened on Sept. 15, 1900, with Claire C. B. Kutts as its first postmaster, was named Childsdale [Dillenback; GSM 1895-1901; PO Archives].

**CHILDS MILLS STATION**, Kent County. See Childsdale.

**CHILSON**, Livingston County: this settlement in Genoa Township, with a station on the Toledo & Ann Arbor Railroad, formed about 1878 around the sawmill and the flour mill of the firm of Chilson & Joslin, and Avery J. Chilson became its first postmaster on March 16, 1887 [GSM 1889; PO Archives].

**CHINA**, St. Clair County: Samuel Ward and William Gallagher built a dam and a grist mill here in 1825; named by an early resident, Captain John Clarke, who had lived in China Township, Kennebec County, Maine, and be became the first postmaster on March 23, 1835; the office was closed on Sept. 25, 1876. but was restored from March 10, 1886, to Jan. 25, 1887, and from Jan. 19, 1889, to Jan. 9, 1894 [Jenks; PO Archives].

**CHIP VILL**, Iosco County: designated as a settlement at the mouth of the Au Sable River on a map engraved by Rawdon Clark & Company, of Albany, N.Y., in 1829, and included in John Farmer's Emigrant's Guide or Pocket Gazeteer of the Surveyed Part of Michigan, printed by B.D. Packard & Company, Albany, 1831 [MPH 22:457 1893].

**CHIPPEWA**, Ontonagon County: a copper mine property of 160 acres in Bohemia Township; exploratory work was done on it about 1850 [Stevens].

**CHIPPEWA LAKE**, Mecosta County: Chippewa Lake, named after the Chippewa Indians, is the largest body of water in the county; the village was platted by the Chippewa Lake Lumber Company; Solomon V. Tice became its first postmaster on Feb. 10, 1870; a station on the Detroit, Grand Rapids & Western Railroad [Hazel Rowlin, PM; Chapman; PO Archives].

**CHIPPEWA STATION**, Osceola County: the post office at this depot opened on April 25, 1878, with Frank Twiss as its first postmaster [GSM 1901; PO Archives].

**CHITTENDENS**, Oakland County: Asa Castle, a farmer, was the first settler; in 1826; Ralph Chittenden built and operated a distillery here and Mr. Barmore a pottery; but the future of the village was doomed by its failure to get Washington to put it on a mail route [MPH 18:662 1891].

**CHOATE**, Ontonagon County: a station on the L., M.S. & W. Railroad, in McMillan Township; Mary J. Forcier became the first postmaster of Sucker Creek on Jan. 8, 1892, with the name changed to Choate for the Choate Lumber Company which operated here, on April 14, 1893, but the office was closed on Jan. 14, 1904 [Charles Willman; GSM 1893; PO Archives].

**CHOCOLAY**, Marquette County: a station on the Duluth, South Shore & Atlantic Railroad, four miles from Marquette, in 1898, as well as the name of a township and a creek in the county; the name dates from the missionary era and was derived from that of a Fench fur trader (M. Choquette) in the area; the village of Harvey, in the same county, was also referred to as Chocolay [GSM 1899; Marquette Co. Hist. Soc.].

**CHRISTIANA**, Cass County: platted by Moses Sage in 1834 on the west side of Christiana (now spelled Christiann) Creek, opposite Adamsport (now Adamsville), of which it became a part; named for Christiana McCoy, wife of Rev. Isaac McCoy, of Carey Mission [Fox].

**CHRISTMAS**, Alger County: a swamp area when Julius Thorson, of Munising, bought the land here in 1938; he built a factory to make gift articles, and with the holiday trade in mind, he named the place Christmas; a fire in June, 1940, wiped out the place and ended the endeavor, but the area still retains the name [Charles A. Symon].

**CHRISTY**, Delta County: Lyman Feltus became the first postmaster of this rural post office on April 20, 1886 [PO Archives].

**CHUBB'S CORNERS**, Livingston County: this hamlet on the line between Marion and Putnam Townships was given a post office on Feb. 15, 1849, with Alva H. Mead as its first postmaster; the office was changed to East Marion on July 5, 1849, but was restored on Sept. 26, 1865; it was closed again on Oct. 29, 1866, but was restored again from Oct. 19, 1877, to Sept. 24, 1894 [GSM 1879; PO Archives].

**CHURCH**, Hillsdale County: farmer Francis G. Church, clerk of Wheatland Township, became the first postmaster of Church's Corners on June 27, 1870, with the name of the village and its post office changed to Church on May 28, 1894, the office operating until June 15, 1901 [GSM 1895; PO Archives].

**CHURCHILL**, Ogemaw County. See Rose City.

**CHURCHILL'S**, Manistee County. See Harlan.

**CHURCHILL'S CORNERS**, Oceans County. See Shelby.

**CHURCH'S CORNERS**, Hillsdale County. See Church.

**CHURCH'S LANDING**, Chippewa County: Philetus Church came from New York State to north Michigan in 1845 and to Sugar Island in 1846; here he established a post for Indian trade and for supplying wood to Lake Superior vessels and he became the township supervisor [Hamilton].

**CIRCLE**, Oakland County: George H. Mitchell became the first postmaster of this rural post office in Bloomfield Township on Oct. 27, 1894, succeeded by Fenn Weston on Oct. 28, 1897, the office operating until April 30, 1902 [PO Archives].

**CISCO LAKE,** Gogebic County: a railroad siding by Cisco Lake; cisco is a fish, the speckled trout [Victor Lemmer].

**CLAGGETTVILLE,** Wexford County: in 1897, the people of Sherman Township built and gave to the Ann Arbor Railroad a spur which came within a mile of the village of Sherman to the west; a hamlet resulted, which was sometimes called West Sherman, sometimes Claggetville, after Mr. Claggett, in whose interests the spur was built, he having built a large mill here, most of its workers living in Sherman [Wheeler].

**CLAIREVIEW,** Wayne County. See Grosse Pointe Shores.

**CLAM LAKE,** Antrim County. See Clam River.

**CLAM RIVER,** Antrim County: from its proximity to Clam Lake, this village in Forest Home Township was given a post office named Clam Lake, with Solomon M. Dewey as its first postmaster; the office was renamed Helena, after its then township, on Sept. 17, 1911; with Mrs. Alma Miller as postmaster, it was changed to Clam River on Dec. 5, 1925, the office operating until Sept. 30, 1944 [GSM 1931; PO Archives].

**CLARE,** Clare County: the county, when established in 1840, was named Kaykakee (Pigeon Hawk) after a chief who had signed the Treaty of 1826; it was renamed Clare, after a county in Ireland, in 1843; this settlement, named after it, was founded with the coming through of the Pere Marquette Railroad in 1870-71; Chester L. Harrington became its first postmaster on Jan. 20, 1871; incorporated as a village in 1879 and as a city in 1891 [Powers].

**CLARENCE,** Calhoun County: Benjamin P. Gillette and his family became the first settlers in 1836; Clarence Township was organized in 1838; John B. Snyder became its first postmaster on Feb. 3, 1841, the office operating until Dec. 15, 1871 [Everts; PO Archives].

**CLARENCE,** Clare County: this settlement in Redding Township, with a station on the Toledo & Ann Arbor Railroad, formed about 1888 around the mill of the Clarence Lumber Company, and lumberman Frederick Church became its first postmaster on Jan. 12, 1893 [GSM 1895; PO Archives].

**CLARENCEVILLE,** Oakland County: this village on the line between Wayne and Oakland Counties began with the building of a tavern by Stephen Jennings in 1836; on May 20, 1851, the Livonia post office was changed to Plank Road, named from its location on a road made of planks, which ran between Detroit and Pontiac; the office was closed on Jan. 20, 1860, but was restored, with Milton C. Botsford as postmaster; it was renamed Clarenceville on Dec. 23, 1897, but was closed on Sept. 14, 1907; the settlement began to fade with the closing of the stage lines, but the name Clarenceville remains as a school district [GSM 1860-73; Burton; Durant; PO Archives].

**CLARENDON CENTRE,** Calhoun County: Anthony Doolittle and Deacon Henry Cook, with from New York State, settled here in 1832, and the settlement became known as Cook's Prairie; given a post office named

Clarendon on July 25, 1840, with Lewis Benham as its first postmaster, but the office was closed on Aug. 24, 1858; the Clarendon Centre post office was opened on June 14, 1854, with Warren L. Deming as its first postmaster; the office was moved some two miles north to Clarendon Station on the Michigan Central Railroad and renamed Clarendon on May 11, 1871; the office was closed on Nov. 16, 1877, but was restored from Oct. 4, 1883, to April 30, 1910; so named because many settlers in the area had come from Clarendon, Orleans County, N.Y. [Everts; Pen Phil 8:3 1958; PO Archives].

**CLARION**, Charlevoix County: in the fall of 1874; John E. Darrah came here from Kent County and the next spring his wife and family joined him; his homestead in Melrose Township covered the site of the present village of which he became the first postmaster on Dec. 8, 1879, the office operating until Oct. 31, 1945; a station on the Grand Rapids & Indiana Railroad; he named it after Clarion, Pa. [Mildred Burns; GSM 1883; PO Archives].

**CLARK**, Lake County: this rural post office, opened on Aug. 6, 1887, was named for George H. Clark who became its first postmaster, the office operating until Jan. 3, 1899 [PO Archives].

**CLARK CITY**, Monroe County: John W. Clark built a stave mill here on Swan Creek in Ash Township; Justus Clark became the first postmaster of the settlement which grew up around it, on Jan. 25, 1855, the office operating until Dec. 19, 1866 [GSM 1860; PO Archives].

**CLARKLAKE**, Jackson County: the lake (Clark Lake) was named by Robert Clark, of Monroe, a government Surveyor in this area, in 1824; in 1833, George Stranahan settled on the north side, west end of the lake, and the village which developed was called Clarklake; a station on the C., J. & M. Railroad; Jay D. Reed became its first postmaster on April 25, 1896; in Columbia Township [Viola Moon, PM; DeLand; PO Archives].

**CLARK'S**, Huron County: this station on the Pere Marquette Railroad, 6 miles north of Bad Axe, was opened by 1894, and was named for the local storekeeper [Hey; GSM 1895].

**CLARKSBURG**, Marquette County: this village on a branch of the Escanaba River, in Ely Township, with a station on a branch of the Pere Marquette Railroad, was first settled in 1862; the Michigan Iron Company had its blast furnace here and Henry J. Colwell, the company superintendent, became the first postmaster of Clarksburgh on Nov. 27, 1871; the village was platted in 1881 by George P. Cummings for William Ward, of Pittsburgh, Pa.; its post office was closed on June 22, 1876, but was restored from Jan. 3, 1881, to Dec. 2, 1887, and from Jan. 5, 1888, to May 28, 1894; its spelling had been changed to Clarksburg on May 14, 1891 [Andreas; GSM 1883; PO Archives].

**CLARK'S CORNERS**, Mason County. See Sugar Grove.

**CLARK'S MILL**, Osceola County: C. Clark operated a lumber mill here in Marion Township in 1880, and a settlement formed around it [Chapman].

**CLARKSTON,** Oakland County: in 1830, Linus Jacox, a squatter from New York State, built the first home within the present town, a cedar-pole shanty; in 1832, Butler Holcomb built the second house and a sawmill; the Clark brothers, Jeremiah, Nelson W., and Milton H., platted and named the village in 1840; the Independence post office was transferred to and renamed Clarkston on Dec. 12, 1840; incorporated as a village in 1884 [Durant; PO Archives].

**CLARKSTON STATION,** Oakland County: in 1864, a depot on the Detroit & Milwaukee Railroad, 2½ miles from the village of Clarkston, which see for the name [GSM 1865].

**CLARKSVILLE,** Ionia County: the first settlers in the area were Jeremiah and Martin Campbell, brothers and recent immigrants from Ireland, in 1840, and the township, organized in 1849, was named for them; after the owners of a local cheese factory, this village in Campbell Township was called Skipperville; Clark L. Howard opened a store in 1875 and secured a post office named Clarksville on May 12, 1875, with him as its first postmaster; a station on the Detroit, Grand Rapids & Western Railroad; incorporated as a village in 1925 [Ruth Darby].

**CLAUSDALE,** Saginaw County. See Prairie Farm.

**CLAWSON,** Oakland County: the first resident of the area was David Williams who bought 160 acres of wooded land for $50 in 1822; Joshua Fay bought 160 acres, in which was part of the present town site, in 1826, and built his house on the property in 1829; the settlement which followed was called Pumachug or The Corners; grocer John Lawson applied for a post office named Lawson, but it came back Clawson, on Aug. 16, 1880, and no one ever bothered to correct it; Andrew A. Bean was the first postmaster; incorporated as the village of Clawson in 1921 and as a city in 1940 [Mildred B. Parady; Mich Manual; PO Archives].

**CLAY,** St. Clair County. See Algonac.

**CLAYBANKS,** Oceana County: the first settlement in the area was made by C.B. Clements, Asa C. Haggarty and Alex. Pelett, in 1849; Alexander S. Anderson became the first supervisor when the town was organized in 1855; John Barr became the first postmaster of Clay Banks on March 17, 1855, the office operating until Aug. 31, 1901; named from the large clay banks which rose 360 feet above the level of Lake Michigan near Whiskey Creek [MPH 35:702 1907; Hartwock; PO Archives].

**CLAY HILL,** Wexford County. See Hoxeyville.

**CLAYTON,** Genesee County: a hamelt, 10 miles east of Flint, in 1859 [GSM 1860].

**CLAYTON,** Lenawee County: first settled in 1836; given a post office as East Dover, from its location in Dover Township, with Levi H.

Soper as its first postmaster, on March 8, 1837; platted by Reuben E. Bird in 1843, and he had the village and its post office renamed Clayton on July 17, 1849, for a friend in New York State, Rev. Clayton, a Presbyterian minister; a station on the Lake Shore & Michigan Southern Railroad; incorporated as a village in 1870 [Hogaboam; Dowling; PO Archives].

**CLEAR LAKE**, Montcalm County: Selah Lake became the first postmaster of this rural post office on Jan. 12 1859, the office operating until June 15, 1869 [Schenck].

**CLEARWATER**, Kalkaska County: Mr. and Mrs. William Copeland became the first white settlers here in present White Water Township in 1855, and they remained the only permanent settlers in the county for 12 years; it was in Antrim County when grocer Albert T. Kellogg became its first postmaster on May 21, 1869, with the office spelled Clear Water, but changed to Clearwater on Dec. 12, 1893; the office was closed on Nov. 18, 1898, but was restored from Feb. 15, 1899, to Feb. 28, 1905 [PO Archives; Powers].

**CLEMENT**, Gladwin County: Joseph Fournier became the first postmaster on this rural post office on Feb. 11, 1891, the office operating until Jan. 31, 1894 [PO Archives].

**CLEON**, Manistee County: this village on the Manistee River was first settled in 1865 and was named after its township; Joseph Seamons became its first postmaster on Oct. 11, 1871, the office operating until Jan. 31, 1902 [GSM 1873; PO Archives].

**CLEVELAND MINE**, Marquette County: a mining settlement, a mile west of Ishpeming, founded by the Cleveland Iron Mining Company, of Cleveland, Ohio, in 1866 [GSM 1879; Havighurst].

**CLEW**, Genesee County: storekeeper Melissa Elliott became the first postmaster of this rural post office in Forest Township on June 2, 1882, the office operating until Nov. 28, 1884 [GSM 1883-85; PO Archives].

**CLIFF**, Keweenaw County: the village grew up around the Cliff Mine founded by the Pittsburgh & Boston Company in 1844; named by John Hayes, a Pittsburgh pharmacist turned prospector, from its location below a high bluff; one of the most profitable of copper mines, it was sold to the Cliff Mining Company in 1871, who in turn sold it to the Tamarack Mining Company in 1880; now the mine is a ruin and its village a ghost town [Murdoch].

**CLIFFORD**, Lapeer County: this village on Indian Creek, in Burlington Township, was founded about 1862 by Arden W. Lyman; he built its first building, occupying it as a home, store, and post office, of which he became the first postmaster on April 23, 1864; the office was closed on July 1, 1867, but was restored from Oct. 31, 1867, to July 9, 1877, and from Feb. 27, 1878, to date; incorporated as a village in 1891; the founder named it for his son, Clifford Lyman [Helen P. Gleason, PM; Page; PO Archives].

**CLIFFORD LAKE**, Montcalm County. See Point Richards.

**CLIFFS**, Baraga County: a station on the Marquette, Houghton & Ontonagon Railroad in 1884 [GSM 1885].

**CLIFTON**, Jackson County: H.S. Platt became the first postmaster of this rural post office on Nov. 10, 1897 [PO Archives].

**CLIFTON**, Keweenaw County: the Clifton Mine (copper) was opened in 1852; the North American Mine post office was transferred to and renamed Clifton on Feb. 24, 1853; the office was closed on July 8, 1870, but was restored, with Daniel C. Brockway as postmaster, on May 27, 1872; the Clifton Mine was closed in 1855 but the Clifton post office operated until Dec. 3, 1884 [Stevens; PO Archives].

**CLIFTON**, Macomb County: the site of a mill which had burned down at least as early as 1840; about 1855, Neil and Hugh Gray, brothers, founded Gray's Mills on the site and around them gathered quite a little settlement; it was platted as a village [Eldredge].

**CLIMAX**, Kalamazoo County: the area was first settled in 1835 and the town site in 1838; they named it Climax Prairie because it climaxed the end of their search for a place to settle; given a post office as Climax Prairie, with Daniel B. Eldred, who had led in the townsite settlement, as its first postmaster on Jan. 15, 1836, the office being renamed Climax on April 9, 1874; to its post office the first R.F.D. mail service in Michigan began on Nov. 1, 1896; incorporated as a village in 1899 [Richard Puffer; PO Archives].

**CLINCH**, Iron County: Emily V. Leece became the first postmaster of this rural post office on Oct. 20, 1899, the office operating until June 30, 1900 [PO Archives].

**CLINCH**, Van Buren County: when the township was organized in 1837, I.W. Clary, a member of the state legislature, had it named for Judge Clinch, of Georgia, whom he admired; but the name was dropped in 1842, when the township was divided into Waverly and Almena, both parts newly named at the suggestion of F.C. Annable, then in the legislature too [Ellis].

**CLINTON**, Lenawee County: John Terrill looked at land here in 1825 and returned from the east with Thaddeus Clark, in 1830; Horatio N. Baldwin became its first postmaster on Oct. 8, 1831; he took the first census here in 1836, the count being 925; incorporated as a village in 1838; given a station when the Lake Shore & Michigan Southern Railroad came through in 1878; named for DeWitt Clinton, father of New York State's Erie Canal, on which so many early settlers came to Michigan [Whitney; PO Archives].

**CLINTON JUNCTION**, Eaton County: this sawmill settlement in Sunfield Township was given a post office on Feb. 3, 1871, with William Kilpatrick as its first postmaster, the office operating until Nov. 30, 1874 [GSM 1873; PO Archives].

**CLINTON SALT WORKS**, Clinton County: in 1838, a company incorporated for the purpose of boring for salt water and manufacturing salt and a settlement grew around its plant here on the Maple River [GSM 1838].

**CLINTONVILLE**, Oakland County: the first settler here in Waterford Township was Samuel C. Munson in 1830, and he built a grist mill and a sawmill; Israel Osmun came in 1835 and his brother John in 1836, and in 1847 they uniformly platted the village; flour mill owner John R. Welsh became its first postmaster on Sept. 26, 1898, the office operating until Jan. 15, 1902; named from its location on the Clinton River; incorporated as a city in 1968 [Durant; Ripley; PO Archives].

**CLIO**, Genesee County: Theodore P. Dean built a sawmill here in 1837, but the development of the village came with the Pere Marquette Railroad in 1861; its station was on the Varna family farm and was called Varna; the name was changed to Clio when David A. Huyck became the first postmaster on June 4, 1866; incorporated as a village in 1873 and as a city in 1928 [Elizabeth C. Ronan].

**CLOUD**, Kent County: grocer Andrew McDonald became the first postmaster of this rural post office on april 23, 1894, the office operating until July 31, 1900 [PO Archives].

**CLOVERDALE**, Barry County: about 1885, the village of Hope Center was moved here to be beside the Chicago, Kalamazoo & Saginaw Railroad; Mr. Bab Payne renamed it, it is believed because it lay in a valley of clover; Howard Mosher became its first postmaster on May 20, 1887, and retained the office until 1891 [R.M. Reed, PM].

**CLOVERDALE**, Muskegon County: a station on the Grand Rapids & Indiana Railroad, six miles south of Muskegon, in 1866 [GSM 1895].

**CLOWRY**, Marquette County: this station on the Chicago & Northwestern Railroad, 12 miles east of Ishpeming, was on part of the land of the Clowry homestead; William F. Tobin became its first postmaster on Dec. 22, 1892, the office operating until May 4, 1894 [GSM 1895-1911; PO Archives].

**CLYDE**, Oakland County: a village in Highland Township, with a station on the Pere Marquette Railroad; first settled by Morris Wheeler; John Wendell built the first house in 1836 and Isaac Wheeler became the first postmaster on May 2, 1872; platted by Julian Bishop, county surveyor, for Lyman Johnson in 1875 [Durant; Seeley].

**CLYDE CENTRE**, Allegan County: the village began with the Eggleston & Hazleton sawmill and general store in 1872; Brooks B. Hazleton became its first postmaster on Feb. 27, 1873, and he was still postmaster when the office was closed on May 31, 1877; the local timber supply became exhausted in that year and the village began to revert to farmland; named from its location in Clyde Township which, when organized in 1859, was named by the first supervisor, Ralph Parish, who had come from Clyde, N.Y. [Ensign; Johnson; PO Archives].

**CLYDE MILLS**, St. Clair County. See Wadhams.

**COALWOOD**, Alger County: a station, opened in 1901, on the Munising Railroad, 11 miles from Munising, with two general stores; Isadore Cyr became its first postmaster on Sept. 21, 1906, the office operating until July 15, 1910 [GSM 1907; PO Archives].

**COATS' GROVE**, Barry County: a station on the Chicago, Kalamazoo & Saginaw Railroad; named for storekeeper George W. Coats who became its first postmaster on Sept. 22, 1879 [Johnson; GSM 1881].

**COATS POINT**, Mackinac County: named for Captain L.B. Coats [Emerson Smith].

**COBMOOSA**, Oceana County: in 1855, the federal government and 54 Indian chiefs, including Cobmoosa (1768-1866), signed a treaty by which the Indians gave up their lands near Grand Rapids and Ionia for new lands here and $540,000 in money and goods; in 1857, some 750, and in 1858, some 550 more were transported here by boat, and a log cabin for the chief (still standing on the Neil Weirich farm) and schools were built; about three miles east, in a store operated by (I.M.) Cook and Wessel, was the Cobmoosa post office, opened on Dec. 10, 1866, with Daniel W. Crosby as its first postmaster; the office was closed on Feb. 7, 1878, but was restored from March 22, 1878, to June 13, 1916; when the store burned down in June, 1916, the post office was not re-opened, but the area and its lake are still known as Cobmoosa [Lee Evans; GSM 1885-1917; PO Archives].

**COBURNTOWN**, Houghton County: a station and hamlet on the Mineral Range Railroad, 1½ miles from Hancock, named for Henry W. Coburn, iron furnace operator [GSM 1923].

**COCOOSH PRAIRIE**, Branch County. See Hodunk.

**CODY**, Genesee County: a station of the Flint post office, named for Alvin Cody, former superintendent of Flint public schools [Elizabeth C. Ronan].

**CODY'S MILLS**, Kent County. See Corinth.

**COE**, Isabella County: Perry H. Estee made the first land entry in the area in 1854, and later that year, James Woolsey, Daniel Brickley and John Steward, and their families, became the first settlers; the township was organized in 1855 and named for Lt. Governor George A. Coe, with William P. Bowen as its first supervisor; storekeeper Archibald Leonard became its first postmaster on Aug. 17, 1891, the office operating until Dec. 14, 1904 [Chapman; GSM 1907; PO Archives].

**COE**, Mecosta County. See Marshfield.

**COHOCTAH**, Livingston County: when the Ann Arbor Railroad came through here in 1886, Richard and his son Frank Wrigglesworth built a grain elevator, thus starting the town; with William B. Owens as postmaster, it was given a post office on Oct. 15, 1887, under the name of East

Cohoctah, for there was a post office named Cohoctah two miles to the west (it was closed and became a rural route and East Cohoctah became just Cohoctah on Jan. 13, 1908); Cohoctah, an Indian word of unknown meaning, was taken from the township [John Wrigglesworth, 92, son and brother of the founders and 3rd PM in the 1890s].

**COHOCTAH CENTER,** Livingston County: the first land entries in the area were made by Lyman Boughton and Gilbert W. Prentiss, both in April, 1833, and the latter became the first actual settler later than year; the town was also called Sprungtown, for Isaac Sprung, one of its leading citizens; when organized in 1838, the township was named Tuscola, renamed Bristol in 1857, and Cohoctah in 1867; given a post office as Tuscola, with Hiram Stoddard becoming its first postmaster on July 15, 1840, and renamed Cohoctah on April 20, 1858; the office was closed on Sept. 30, 1902, and the post office at East Cohoctah took the name Cohoctah on Jan. 13, 1908; the old village of Cohoctah is now Cohoctah Center [Ellis; PO Archives].

**COLBY,** Montcalm County: the site of the Colby Brothers sawmill, then one of the largest in the county; given a station as Colby's on the Stanton branch of the Detroit, Lansing & Northern Railroad in 1878, and a post office as Colby, with Humphrey R. Wagar as its first postmaster, on May 14, 1879; the office was closed on July 13, 1894, but was restored on Aug. 17 of the same year [Schenck; Dasef; GSM 1879; PO Archives].

**COLBY MINE,** Gogebic County. See Bessemer.

**COLDEN,** Bay County: a crossroads center just inside Midland County, on the Bay City-Midland Railroad line, when given a post office on April 22, 1891, with storekeeper Myron T. Johnson as its first postmaster; in 1902, the office was moved a half mile east on the rail line into Bay County, where it remained until closed on Jan. 2, 1907 [Pen Phil 10:4 Feb 1960].

**COLD SPRING,** Kalkaska County: farmer William Campbell (father of James A. Campbell, the first postmaster of Darragh) became the first postmaster of this rural post office, named after its township, on Oct. 3, 1879, succeeded by Joseph W. Chase on July 7, 1882, the office operating until Nov. 19, 1883 [D.C. Colyer].

**COLDWATER,** Branch County: Allen Tibbits and Joseph Hanchett purchased land here in 1830, laid out a village in 1832, naming it Lyons after Mr. Tibbits' native town; William H. and Robert Cross, brothers, also settled here in 1830; in what is now the western part of the city, James B. Stewart bought land and platted a village (on paper) and called it Masonville, after Governor Stephens T. Mason; renamed in 1833 after the township which had been named after the Coldwater River which runs through it; Harvey Warner became its first postmaster on Sept. 22, 1838; the county seat since 1842; incorporated as a village in 1837 and as a city in 1861 [MPH 6:219 1883, 27:284 1896; GSM 1873; PO Archives].

**COLD WATER,** Genesee County: a settlement in Genesee Township, first made by Luman Beach and Addison Stewart in 1833; all the early settlers here were total abstainers and the name was given in jest by their neighbors; it had the first school in the township, 1835, and the first organized religious society, 1836 [Wood].

**COLD WATER**, St. Joseph County: Abraham F. Bolton became the first postmaster of this rural post office on Aug. 17, 1830 [PO Archives].

**COLDWATER LAKE**, Branch County: a settlement on Coldwater Lake, 10 miles from the city of Coldwater, in 1922 [GSM 1923].

**COLE**, Oakland County: a station on the Pontiac, Oxford & Northern Railroad, in Orion Township; Erastus T. Cole became its first postmaster on Dec. 23, 1884, the office operating until July 15, 1907 [Mrs. Donald E. Adams; Seeley; PO Archives].

**COLEBECK**, Gladwin County: storekeeper Emory Wells became the first postmaster of this rural post office, 10 miles from Beaverton, on March 18, 1902, but the office was transferred to and renamed Billings on the 14th of the following month [GSM 1903; PO Archives].

**COLE CREEK**, Newaygo County: farmer David Maynard became the first postmaster of this rural post office in Beaver Township on April 27, 1904, the office operating until Feb. 28, 1907 [GSM 1905; PO Archives].

**COLEMAN**, Midland County: Ammi W. Wright bought government land here in present Warren Township for speculation, but it was not rapidly settled and after several years he sold 1000 acres of it to Seymour Coleman who had 160 acres surveyed and platted and gave land to the Pere Marquette Railroad in return for a depot here; the road reached the town in 1871; the first actual settler was Jonathan Pierce who built a sawmill here in 1870 and became the first postmaster on May 15, 1871; incorporated as a village in 1887 and as a city in 1905 [Fred Wardent].

**COLEMAN'S CORNERS**, Clinton County. See Keystone.

**COLERAIN**, Oakland County: a station on the Detroit, Grand Haven & Milwaukee Railroad; Albert C. Jennings became its first postmaster on April 29, 1890, the office operating until Oct. 31, 1902 [GSM 1891; PO Archives].

**COLFAX**, Bay County: John S. Wuepper became the first postmaster of this rural post office on Jan. 16, 1897; the office was closed on May 15, 1900, but was restored, with Joseph Fournier as its postmaster, on May 29, 1900, operating until May 15, 1901 [PO Archives].

**COLFAX**, Mason County: this rural post office was named Greenwood when opened on Feb. 6, 1868, with George W. Annis as its first postmaster; it was renamed Colfax, for Vice President Schuyler Colfax on June 22, 1868; the office operated until Feb. 7, 1871 [Blinn; PO Archives].

**COLFAX**, Mecosta County: the township, organized in 1869, with

Sidney L. Rood as its first supervisor, was named for Vice President Schuyler Colfax [Chapman].

**COLFAX**, Oceana County: Anson Freeman became the first settler here in 1863; the township was organized in 1869 and named for Vice President Schuyler Colfax [Hartwick].

**COLFAX**, Wexford County: J. Faust operated the general store here in Colfax Township, which had been named for Vice President Schuyler Colfax; Joseph V. Richardson became the first postmaster on Oct. 20, 1877, the office operating until Oct. 12, 1889 [Traverse; PO Archives].

**COLINE**, Wexford County: this settlement in Springville Township formed around the plant and general store of Consumers Power Company, from which its name was derived; Frank G. Hamilton became its first postmaster on Oct. 1, 1924, the office operating until Oct. 31, 1925 [GSM 1925; PO Archives].

**COLLEGEVILLE**, Ingham County: a plat recorded in 1887 for a development bordering Michigan State College (now University) on the north; now East Lansing, which see.

**COLLING**, Tuscola County: named for William Colling who came here from Canada in 1880 and secured 180 acres of land; this village in Columbia Township was given a station on the Michigan Central Railroad; lumberman Clarence B. Mansfield became its first postmaster on Jan. 30, 1903, the office operating until Oct. 31, 1936; now reduced to a grain elevator and a few houses [J.A. Gallery; GSM 1905; PO Archives].

**COLLINS**, Ionia County: platted by Josephus Stebbins, who settled here in Portland Township about 1850, and first called Stebbinsville; when William A. Staley became its first postmaster on April 11, 1871, he had the office named, and the Detroit, Grand Rapids & Western Railroad station renamed, to honor his father-in-law, Alfred Collins, a large landowner in the area; the post office operated until Dec. 15, 1911 [Schenck; Branch; PO Archives].

**COLLINS PLAINS**, Washtenaw County: this settlement in Lyndon Township was named for B., Josiah H. and Harrison W. Collins, brothers, who had settled here in 1833 [Beakes].

**COLLINSVILLE**, Marquette County: a hamlet near the Lake Superior shore, just north of Marquette; it was the site of the forge of the Collins Iron Company, built about 1856, and named for company president, Edward K. Collins [Havighurst; GSM 1879].

**COLLINSVILLE**, Oceana County: this settlement around the Kerswell & Davis sawmill, in Golden Township, was named for Kins R. Collins who became its first postmaster on April 10, 1872, with the office changed to East Golden on May 1, 1874 [Royal; PO Archives; GSM 1873].

**COLLISON**, Benzie County: this rural post office, 7 miles northeast of Benzonia, was named for William E. Collison who became its first postmaster on March 11, 1891, the office operating until Nov. 30, 1895 [GSM 1893; PO Archives].

**COLOMA**, Berrien County: the first house was built here in 1834 by Stephen R. Gilson, a shingle maker, from Chataqua, N.Y.; the village was first called Dickerville, said to have been given because money was scarce here and most businesses were conducted by bartering or dickering; Mr. Gilson platted the village in 1855 and had its name changed to that of a town in which he had once lived in California (coloma is a Pacific coast wild flower); Dr. Henry M. Marvin became its first postmaster on Aug. 23, 1856; incorporated as a village in 1893 and as a city in 1941 [Mrs. Harold Warriner].

**COLON**, St. Joseph County: platted but not recorded by George Schellhouse and an Indian trader named Hatch in 1832; platted and recorded by John H. and William F. Bowman in 1844; Lorensie Schellhouse became its first postmaster on Jan. 15, 1836; incorporated as a village in 1904; when the founders were seeking a name, Lorensie Schellhouse opened a dictionary at random and saw the word colon; he said "We will call it Colon, for the lake and the river correspond exactly to the shape of a colon," and it was so named [Calvin Wagner; PO Archives].

**COLONIE SAXONIA**, Sanilac County. See Germania.

**COLONVILLE**, Clare County: storekeeper Curtis Palmer became the first postmaster of this rural post office in Sheridan Township on Dec. 4, 1894, the office operating until Jan. 15, 1904 [GSM 1895; PO Archives].

**COLUMBIA**, Ingham County: platted in 1836-37, but not recorded; 13 families lived here in 1838; also known as Columbiaville; believed to have been named for Columbia County, N.Y., when some of the local settlers had come; Foster says another village, Norton, succeeded to the site, but the Gazeteer of 1865 still described it as a village [Foster; GSM 1865].

**COLUMBIA**, Jackson County. See Jefferson.

**COLUMBIA**, Tuscola County. See Columbia Corners.

**COLUMBIA**, Van Buren County: settled by 1864; platted in 1870 by A.J. Pierce, county surveyor, on land owned by William Dickinson and Samuel Rogers, and recorded in 1871; named after its township; it remained only a hamlet by a station of the Michigan Central Railroad [Ellis; GSM 1865].

**COLUMBIA CORNERS**, Tuscola County: the first settlers in the area were Horace C. Marvin and Andrew Marshall in 1854; the township of Columbia was erected and named in 1855, and the village took its name; Rudolph Nemode became the first postmaster, with the office named Columbia, on June 18, 1879, the office operating until March 31, 1903 [PO Archives; Page].

**COLUMBIA LAKE**, Washtenaw County. See Bridgewater.

**COLUMBIAVILLE**, Lapeer County: Levi D. Cutting became the first permanent resident on the village site in 1847; George and Henry Niver built a sawmill here in 1848, and the place became known as Niverville; their old neighbor in Columbia County, N.Y., William Peter, came to work for them here; he came into possession of their entire property here and his business interests largely built up the village; given a post office as Columbiaville, the name suggested by the Nivers, on April 25, 1857, with Peter Van Dyke as its first postmaster; incorporated as a village in 1879 [Hilton Burgess; Page; PO Archives].

**COLUMBUS**, Hillsdale County. See Litchfield.

**COLUMBUS**, St. Clair County: its settlement followed the cutting through of the Fort Gratiot turnpike in 1832; its first settlers included Peter Kilroy, James Mallory, George Bathey and Benjamin Weeks; the township was organized in 1837 and named for Christopher Columbus; its village was given a station on the Grand Trunk Railroad; John S. Parker became its first postmaster on March 14, 1839; the office was closed on July 14, 1876, but was restored from July 31, 1876, to July 18, 1892, and from Jan. 31, 1894, to Feb. 15, 1904; the Hickey post office was changed to Columbus on Aug. 19, 1909, until it was closed on July 15, 1940 [Jenks; PO Archives].

**COLWELL**, Montcalm County: a station, in Maple Village Township, on the Detroit, Lansing & Northern Railroad; Glenn H. Barnard became its first postmaster on Sept. 22, 1879, the office operating until June 28, 1882 [Schenck; GSM 1881; PO Archives].

**COLWOOD**, Tuscola County: named from its township (Columbia) and its principal product (lumber); storekeeper Charles A. Post became its first postmaster on Feb. 27, 1884, the office operating until May 31, 1905 [GSM 1885-1907; PO Archives].

**COMFORT**, Antrim County: a station on the Pere Marquette Railroad, in Helena Township; railroad agent Frank H. Lyon became its first postmaster on Jan. 28, 1913 [GSM 1915].

**COMINS**, Oscoda County: soon after the H.M. Loud & Sons Lumber Company, of Oscoda and Au Sable, acquired the lumbering interests of the Potts Lumber Company in 1885, they also began to carry mail and passengers on their narrow gauge railroad; after the depot was moved from McKinley to Comins, a post office was opened, with Joseph W. Salt becoming its first postmaster on Nov. 15, 1900; the office was closed on Feb. 28, 1913, but was restored on March 11, 1914 [Northern Light; GSM 1889; PO Archives].

**COMMERCE**, Oakland County: the first settler here, Abram Walrod, came from New York State in 1825; the first permanent settler, Reuben Wright, came from Orleans, N.Y., in 1832; Sylvester Stoddard became the first postmaster on June 17, 1833; Jones Hibley arrived in 1835 and acquired most of the village site; Amasa Andrews and Joseph G. Farr purchased his property and platted to town in 1836; so named because they hoped it would become a business center; it reached its peak in that respect in 1877; its post office was closed on Nov. 30, 1911, and it is now a small residential village [Durant; PO Archives].

**COMSTOCK**, Kalamazoo County: Judge Caleb Eldred located the first land here in 1830; General Horace H. Comstock, from Cooperstown, Otsego County, N.Y. (his wife was a niece of the novelist, James Fennimore Cooper), had it surveyed in 1831 and labored in vain to have his village named the county seat instead of Kalamazoo; its first grist mill was opened in 1832; Lyman J. Daniel became its first postmaster on Feb. 28, 1832, with the office in his general store [MPH 5:359 1884; PO Archives].

**COMSTOCK PARK**, Kent County: Daniel North built a sawmill here on Mill Creek, in Plainfield Township, 5 miles north of Grand Rapids, in 1838, and the place became known as North Park; it was given a station named Mill Creek on both the Grand Rapids & Indiana and the Chicago & Western Michigan Railroads, and on Dec. 28, 1848, a post office, also named Mill Creek, with John Colton as its first postmaster; the office was closed on Aug. 12, 1851, but was restored on Oct. 28, 1868; the North mill was bought by Eli Plumb who added a flouring mill in 1866; Charles C. Comstock represented this district in Congress, 1885-86, and on June 8, 1906, the village and its post office were renamed for him; some early train schedules referred to it as North Mills Station [Paul F. Kempter; Dillenback; PO Archives].

**COMUS**, Menominee County: a station on a branch of the Chicago & Northwestern Railroad in 1884; see Dryads for the name [GSM 1885].

**CONCORD**, Jackson County: in 1832, William Van Fossen became the first settler to take up land and build a home within the present village limits; the town was first known as Van Fossenville; when they were applying for a post office, Thomas McGee suggested that since all the settlers were living in such harmony it should be named Concord and they were given a post office as Concord on Jan. 15, 1836, with Isaac Van Fossen as its first postmaster; incorporated as a village in 1871 [Robert D. Aldrich; MPH 21:418 1892].

**CONCORD CITY**, Houghton County. See Paavola.

**CONDIT**, Calhoun County: a station on the Lake Shore & Michigan Southern Railroad, in Albion Township, in 1876 [GSM 1877].

**CONE**, Monroe County: lumberman John C. Cone became the first postmaster of West Milan (named from its location in Milan Township) on Aug. 4, 1869; in 1880, the Wabash Railroad opened a station here calling it Cone and on Jan. 27, 1882, the name of the post office was changed to correspond [Buckley; Wing; PO Archives].

**CONGER**, Manistee County: Colin Leitch became the first postmaster of Sweet's Bridge, in Brown Township, on Nov. 14, 1876, with the name changed to Conger on Feb. 2, 1881; the office was closed on June 23, 1884, but was restored from Nov. 20, 1884, to June 14, 1889; believed to have been named for Omar D. Conger, U.S. senator from Michigan, 1881-87 [GSM 1883; PO Archives].

**CONGER**, Montcalm County: this village in Reynolds Township, with a station on the Grand Rapids & Indiana Railroad, was platted, recorded and named for John Conger, its proprietor, on March 5, 1872; Benjamin B. Powell became its first postmaster on Aug. 29, 1872, the office operating until Jan. 25, 1876; it went the way of most exclusively sawmill towns [Schenck; Dasef; PO Archives].

**CONGER**, Ottawa County: Garrett H. Woodbrink became the first postmaster of this rural post office in Allendale Township on April 5, 1899, the office operating until Feb. 28, 1907 [GSM 1901; PO Archives].

**CONGLOMERATE BAY**, Keweenaw County: this settlement on Conglomerate Bay in the southeastern part of Isle Royale, when the island was a separate county, was given a post office on July 12, 1878, with James Cruso as its first and only postmaster, for the office was closed on the 22nd of the following month [PO Archives].

**CONKLIN**, Ottawa County: this station on the Grand Rapids & Indiana Railroad was opened in 1886 in Chester Township; merchant Henry Miller became its first postmaster on June 2, 1887; Oscar Conklin had it named for him [GSM 1889].

**CONNER'S CREEK**, Wayne County: the stream was first called Tremble's Creek for Gazet Tremble whose sister Therese married Richard Conner, for whom it was renamed; where Mr. Conner, paymaster to the Indians, built his home was in Macomb County and some 20 miles north of what became in 1832 the village of Conner's Creek, which was platted and recorded for the heirs of H. Connor (so spelt on the plat), on Sept. 13, 1853; on Nov. 20, 1855, Thomas McMannon became its first postmaster; the office was closed on April 26, 1856; with J.B. Gravier as postmaster, it was restored on Nov. 15, 1856, but was closed again on July 20, 1857; with Nicholas Greiner as postmaster, it was restored again on July 19, 1858, and on Nov. 4, 1893, the office was renamed Greiner; but on Sept. 15, 1899, the name of Conner's Creek was restored and was retained until the office was closed permanently on March 30, 1907; located in the present Gratiot Avenue-City Airport area of Detroit, it was absorbed by that city in 1907 [Eldredge; County plat liber; PO Archives].

**CONNERS POINT**, Mackinac County: this site in Clark Township was named for lumberman Charles Conner [Emerson Smith].

**CONNORVILLE**, Gogebic County: W.D. Connor, Sr., president pf the Connor Land & Lumber Company, of Wisconsin, built a logging camp here in 1925, and a mill in 1935; the mill is still in operation [Victor Lemmer].

**CONSTANTINE**, St. Joseph County: Judge William Meek came here from Wayne County, Ohio, in 1828, built a sawmill in 1830, and later a grist mill, and the settlement was known as Meek's Mills; Niles F. Smith, businessman and lawyer, had the name changed in honor of Constantine the Great, in 1835; John S. Barry, who later served as governor of Michigan for three terms, opened a store here in 1834 and became the first postmaster of the village on Jan. 15, 1836; incorporated as a village in 1837 [A.V. Whittington; PO Archives].

**CONVIS**, Calhoun County: Convis Township, organized in 1837, was named for General Ezra Convis; Elisha Brace became its first postmaster on Feb. 15, 1840; the office was later closed but was restored, with William C. Wilbitts as its postmaster, on July 15, 1899, the new office operating until March 31, 1903 [GSM 1860-1905; PO Archives].

**CONVIS CENTRE**, Calhoun County: Sanford Chaffee became the first settler in the area in 1835; James Lane, William Newman, and Paul Moss came here directly from England later the same year; John W. Sammons became the first postmaster on June 13, 1856, the office operating until Nov. 25, 1878; the town was organized in 1837 and named for General Ezra Convis, then a member of the state legislature [Everts; PO Archives].

**CONWAY**, Emmet County: this settlement on the west shore of Crooked Lake, in Little Traverse Township was named Crooked Lake in 1878; it was renamed Dodge's Landing in 1881, honoring the Dodge family who gave the church and school; on May 18, 1882, with Horace C. Miller as its first postmaster, it was given a post office named Conway, in honor of Conway Dodge; also in 1882, it was given a station on the Grand Rapids & Indiana Railroad [GSM 1883; PO Archives].

**CONWAY**, Livingston County: this village in Conway Township was given a post office on May 10, 1842, with Warren G. Grant as its first postmaster; the office was closed on Feb. 26, 1869, but was restored from June 17, 1869, to Sept. 6, 1870 [GSM 1860-71; PO Archives].

**COOKS**, Schoolcraft County: John C. Cook built a sawmill here in Thompson Township about 1883, and the place became known as Cook's Mills; on June 28, 1888, it was given a post office named Cooks, with Norman McDonald as its first postmaster; its station the Minneapolis, St. Paul & Sault Ste. Marie Railroad was named Cooks Mill; platted by David Spielmacher and recorded as Durham, which name still stands at the court house, though both the village and its post office are called Cooks [P.V. Thelander, PM].

**COOKS CORNERS**, Ionia County: Rufus R. Cook led a prospecting group here from New York State in 1829; the hamlet became known as Corners in 1837 and Mr. Cook became its first postmaster in 1838, built a tavern in it in 1846 and a general store in 1850; he platted and on May 1, 1856, recorded this village in Otisco Township as Cooks Corners [Schenck].

**COOKS MILL**, Schoolcraft County. See Cooks.

**COOKS PRAIRIE**, Calhoun County. See Clarendon Centre.

**COOK'S STATION**, Newaygo County: Erastus Downing became its first postmaster on Feb. 27, 1868, the office operating until April 30, 1874 [PO Archives].

**COOLEY**, Huron County: named for the Cooley family, pioneer settlers here, 16 Cooley being listed on abstracts by the time John H. Newcombe became the first postmaster on April 2, 1883; the office operated until Nov. 28, 1884 [GSM 1885; Hey; PO Archives].

**COOLEY ROAD**, Sanilac County: a station on a branch of the Port Huron & Northwestern Railroad in 1884 [GSM 1885].

**COOLEY'S CORNERS**, Macomb County: first settled by Samuel Cooley in 1831; widely known as the home of the botanist, Dr. Dennis Cooley, another early settler [MPH 26:547 1895].

**COOMER**, Isabella County: this rural post office in Deerfield Township was named for Noah V. Coomer who became its first postmaster on Dec. 22, 1892, the office operating until Nov. 30, 1906 [GSM 1895; PO Archives].

**COON TOWN**, Lenawee County: during the political campaign of 1840, because nearly every voter in the village was a Whig, and coon skins (one of the Whig campaign emblems) were displayed at nearly every door, Thomas McCourtney gave present-day Addison the nickname of Coon Town, an appelation it took nearly a half a century to outgrow [Hogaboam].

**COOPER CENTER**, Kalamazoo County: David E. and Cyrus P. Deming, brothers from Vermont, became the first settlers here in 1834; the township, organized in 1836, was named by Horace H. Comstock, member of the legislature, for his wife, niece of James Fennimore Cooper, who wrote his novel of Michigan frontier life, Oak Openings, in this locality; Barney Earl, who came here from New York City in 1835, became the first postmaster, with the office named Cooper, on July 24, 1837, the office operating until Feb. 28, 1902; its station on the Grand Rapids & Indiana Railroad, opened in 1878, was also named Cooper [MPH 5:403 1884; PO Archives].

**COOPER'S CROSSING**, Iosco County: a station on a branch of the Detroit & Mackinaw Railroa,d 16 miles from Tawas City, in 1894 [GSM 1895].

**COOPERSVILLE**, Ottawa County: Benajmin F. Cooper, of Utica, N.Y., bought 640 acres here in 1845, and he and his two sons built a sawmill; Dr. Timothy Eastman, an organizer of the township in 1845 named it Polkton, for the then President James Knox Polk; with Dr: Eastman as its first postmaster, it was given a post office named Polkton on May 28, 1846; when the railroad came through in 1858, Mr. Cooper offered it all the land it needed if the station would be named after him, and it was; and on Jan. 22, 1859, the post office too was renamed Coopersville; incorporated as a village in 1871 [Marion E. Lillie; MPH 39:420 1915; PO Archives].

**COPEMISH,** Manistee County: the Buckley Douglass Lumber Company, of Manistee, set up camp here about 1883; platted in 1889 when the first trains came through; Frank W. Clark became its first postmaster on Jan. 11, 1890; incorporated as a village in 1891; the name means big beech, and the belief is that the Indians held councils under a large beech tree here [Almira B. Digby; PO Archives].

**COPLEY,** Lake County: this village in Ellsworth Township developed around the sawmill and general store of E.J. Copley; James A. Panting became its first postmaster on Feb. 4, 1884, the office operating until April 14, 1890 [GSM 1885-93; PO Archives].

**COPPER CITY,** Houghton County: a station on the K.C. Railroad, in Calumet Township, in the copper mining region; storekeeper John R. Bennetts became its first postmaster on Dec. 10, 1910; incorporated as a village in 1917 [GSM 1913-19; PO Archives].

**COPPER CROWN,** Ontonagon County: Enoch Henderson became the first postmaster of this copper mining settlement on Nov. 27, 1906 [PO Archives].

**COPPER FALLS,** Keweenaw County: a copper boom town; the Copper Falls Mine, owned by William Petherick, opened in 1846; the Arnold Mine was set off from it in 1863, and the Arnold Mining Company absorbed it in 1898; it was in Houghton County when given a post office as Copper Falls Mine on Sept. 10, 1860, with Samuel G. Benjamin as its first postmaster; the office was transferred to Keweenaw County on Sept. 16, 1861, but was closed on Feb. 15, 1916 [Stevens; GSM 1873; PO Archives].

**COPPER HARBOR,** Keweenaw County: Governor Stevens T. Mason named Douglass Houghton state geologist and the references in his reports on 1840 to copper deposits in the county stimulated a rush of prospectors; in 1843, Copper Harbor was named headquarters of a special government agent, Walter Cunningham, for permits to locate copper mines; Daniel D. Brockway built the first log structure here, a hotel called Brockway House, in 1846, and on May 4, 1860, he became the first postmaster [Serene D. Westcoat, PM].

**CORAL,** Montcalm County: Stump and Morris had a sawmill here in Maple Valley Township, and the place was called Stumptown; in 1862, Charles Parker recorded the plat of forty acres and named it Coral "because it was easy to spell"; a station on the Detroit, Lansing & Northern Railroad; John Holcomb became its first postmaster on March 22, 1869 [Carl Greenwood, PM; PO Archives].

**CORBIN'S MILL,** Oceana County: this settlement, also called Corbinville, in Hart Township, became the county seat in Jan., 1865, and a post office for it was immediately requested [Royal].

**CORBUS,** Lenawee County: a station on a branch of the Lake Shore & Michigan Southern Railroad in 1884 [GSM 1885].

**COREY**, Cass County: this village in Newberg Township was platted in 1872 by Amanda Weatherwax and named from its nearness to Corey Lake (just over the line in St. Joseph County), which had been named for Joshua B. Corey who had settled beside it about 1840; Hazen W. Brown became its first postmaster on May 20, 1872; its station on the Michigan Central Railroad was called Corey's and was opened in 1871 [Rogers; Cutler].

**CORFU**, Manistee County. See High Bridge.

**CORINNE**, Mackinac County: this lumber settlement in Newton Township was given a station on the Minneapolis, St. Paul & Sault Ste. Marie Railroad named Corinne; but to avoid confusion with Corunna, it was given a post office named Viola, with John S. Craig becoming its first postmaster on July 22, 1889, the office operating until April 15, 1842 [Cole; GSM 1891; PO Archives].

**CORINTH**, Kent County: in 1866, three brothers named Cody built a steam grist mill and sawmills here in Gaines Township, and the place became known as Cody's Mills; it was given a post office of that name on May 22, 1867, with Nathan K. Evarts as its first postmaster; the office was renamed Corinth on March 6, 1871, and operated until Dec. 15, 1899; the village was platted and recorded as Corinth for Jacob and David Rosenberg, by Robert S. Jackson, on Sept. 14, 1871 [Chapman; PO Archives].

**CORKIN**, Clinton County: this rural post office was named for Joshua Corkin who became its first postmaster on June 15, 1883, the office operating until Nov. 17, 1884 [PO Archives].

**CORNELL**, Delta County: first settled by Marcell Adhland and Edward Hollywood, both farmers, in 1886; the town was founded by George H. Mashek, an Escanaba Lumberman, and Edward Arnold, about 1887, and named for the University which Mr. Mashek had attended; Mr. Arnold became its first postmaster on April 12, 1899 [PM; PO Archives].

**CORNELL**, Ionia County. See Sebewa.

**CORNELL**, St. Clair County: a station on the Grand Trunk Railroad, six miles west of Port Huron, in 1866 [Mich Manual 1899].

**CORNING**, Allegan County: this settlement in Leighton Township was given a post office on March 8, 1882, with grocer Eli Runnels as its first postmaster, the office operating until Feb. 28, 1902 [GSM 1883; PO Archives].

**CORNWELL**, Cheboygan County: a settlement around the L. Cornwell sawmill; it was in Otsego County when Charles E. Cornwell became its first postmaster on June 29, 1905, the office operating until Dec. 30, 1916 [GSM 1907; PO Archives].

**CORNWELL**, Washtenaw County: began about 1877 as the site of the Cornwell Mills, in Ann Arbor Township; the place was also known as Foster's or Foster's Station, for pioneer settler Samuel W. Foster, and as Newport [Beakes; GSM 1879].

**CORRIGAN**, Ogemaw County: this lumber settlement in Logan Township was named for a local lumberman, Michael Corrigan; farmer George S. Thompson became its first postmaster on Aug. 18, 1891, the office operating until Aug. 6, 1897 [GSM 1893-99; PO Archives].

**CORUNNA**, Shiawassee County: Jonathan Kearsley made the first government land purchase here in 1832; John Davids and family, from New York, became the first settlers in 1836; the Shiawassee County Seat Company (Alexander McArthur, Andrew Mack, Horace H. Comstock, et al.) platted the village in 1837; Joel K. Ankrim became its first postmaster on July 24, 1838; the county seat since 1840; incorporated as a village in 1858 and as a city in 1869; believed to have been named by Mr. Mack after Corunna, Spain, where he had embarked with sheep which he drove over the Cumberlands to Cincinnati at the age of 24 [Homer J. Bush, J.P.].

**CORWIN**, Van Buren County: this rural post office was opened on June 19, 1890, with Almon I. Jenkins as its first postmaster, the office operating until Oct. 31, 1902 [PO Archives].

**CORYELL ISLANDS**, Mackinac County: given a post office as Coryell, with John Coryell as its first postmaster, on Aug. 25, 1908; the office was closed on Jan. 15, 1913, but was restored, with Eva D. McBain as postmaster, on June 11, 1915, the office operating until April 30, 1958 [PO Archives].

**COTES CREEK**, Houghton County: here was built in 1903 the great reduction plant, shops, offices, etc., of the Michigan Smelting Company, at which the mineral product of the Altlantic, Baltic, Champion, Mohawk, Wolverine, and other mines were refined and prepared for the market [Sawyer].

**COTTAGE GROVE**, Wayne County. See Grosse Pointe City.

**COTTAGEVILLE**, Macomb County. See Warren.

**COTTRELLVILLE**, St. Clair County: this township was set off in 1822 and named for George Cottrell, then county commissioner; its village was given a post office, with Seth Taft as its first postmaster, on Dec. 18, 1827; the office was closed on Dec. 28, 1831, but was restored, with Lambert Gauchois as postmaster, on July 8, 1834, and operated until Oct. 16, 1838; it was restored again, with Stephen B. Grummond as postmaster, on May 30, 1850, and operated until Oct. 8, 1863 [GSM 1838; PO Archives].

**COUNCIL CORNERS**, Oakland County: a hamlet 2½ miles from Clawson in 1920 [GSM 1921].

**COUNTY LINE**, Eaton County: Andrew Haupt became the first postmaster of this rural post office on March 19, 1869, the office operating until Dec. 20, 1870 [PO Archives].

**COUNTY LINE**, Muskegon County. See Bailey.

**COUNTY LINE**, Newaygo County. See Brunswick.

**COUNTY LINE**, Saginaw County: this village began as a sawmill settlement in 1862; with John Hughes as its first postmaster, it was given a post office as Hughesville on July 7, 1870; located on the line between Saginaw and Genesee Counties, its post office was renamed County Line on Feb. 17, 1875, the office operating until Oct. 14, 1904; a station on the Pere Marquette Railroad [GSM 1883-1905; PO Archives].

**COURTLAND CENTER**, Kent County: first settled by Barton Johnson in 1838 and Alexander Dean in 1839; Courtland Township was organized in 1839 and the village was named after it; given a post office as Courtland on Jan. 30, 1841, with Philo Beers as its first postmaster, the office operating until Nov. 10, 1860; the Courtland Center post office was opened on Oct. 24, 1856, with John Woodruff as its first postmaster, the office operating until Feb. 15, 1901 [Dillenback; PO Archives].

**COVERT**, Genesee County: a township post office opened on the farm of Bergan C. Covert on Oct. 4, 1852, and called Gaines; the township had been named for General E.P. Gaines; the office was renamed Covert on Jan. 2, 1863, and operated until April 13, 1865 [Thomas Blinn].

**COVERT**, Van Buren County: first settled by Benoni Young in 1845; the development of the village dates from 1866 when Hawks & Lambert, of Niles, bought timberlands and built mills here; in 1868, Alfred H. Packard, Jr., as Packard & Company, bought their mills and additional lands; Thomas Hawks became the first postmaster on March 24, 1868; a station on the South Haven & Eastern Railroad; named after the township, first called Deerfield but renamed Covert, both names recalling the days when deer roamed its forests [Ellis; PO Archives].

**COVEY HILL**, Van Buren County: named for Almon and Amon Covey, pioneer settlers; in 1843 a Free Will Baptist church was built here on the Almena Township side of the site, followed soon by a grange hall [Rowland].

**COVINGTON**, Baraga County: first settled in 1885 by French Canadians; when John Lyons became its first postmaster on Oct. 17, 1895, he had it named after Covington, Kentucky, whence he had come in 1886; he was succeeded in office by Richard J. Howes on Oct. 23, 1901; now a Finnish village [Gerald Nopola, PM].

**COWEN'S MILLS**, St. Joseph County: James and Robert Cowen built their mill here on Nottawa Creek, in Lionides Township, in 1832; Isaac G. Bailey became the first postmaster, 1834-39, when he died; he was also a member of the state legislature, 1838-39 [Cutler].

**COW PENS**, Berrien County. See Parc aux Vaches.

**COY**, Crawford County: this rural post office was opened on Oct. 27, 1910, in the home of its first postmaster, Harry Coy Newton, and was given his middle name; it was located on the northern edge of Roscommon County, but the second and last postmaster, Oliver B. Scott, lived on the southern edge of Crawford County and the office moved there with him in 1912 [Grace L. Funsch].

**COYVILLE**, Allegan County: this rural post office in Wayland Township was named for Harlow F. Coy who became its first postmaster on March 3, 1857, the office operating until Dec. 29, 1859; Jacob Coyman was a pioneer settler in the township [GSM 1860; PO Archives].

**CRACKER HILL**, Jackson County. See Parma.

**CRACOW**, Huron County: a village in Paris Township, settled by Poles in 1862 and named by them after the Polish city; Frank Buchkowski became its first postmaster on June 8, 1869, the office operating until April 10, 1874 [GSM 1873; PO Archives].

**CRAIG**, Houghton County: named for George Craig who first settled here in 1883; Francis Jackson became the first postmaster on April 19, 1884, the office operating until May 1, 1896 [GSM 1889; PO Archives].

**CRAIG ROY**, Houghton County: this proposed village in Stanton Township was platted by A.W. Bates for W. J. Uren, W.G. Rice and G.A. Sherman, owners of the land, and recorded on Jan. 2, 1903; but the village did not develop [County plat liber].

**CRAIGSMERE**, Ontonagon County: a sawmill town named after the Craig Lumber Company which began operations here about 1885; a station on a branch of the Chicago & Northwestern Railroad in 1892 [Charles Willman].

**CRAMPTON**, Tuscola County: a way station on a branch of the Michigan Central Railroad in 1888 [GSM 1889].

**CRANBROOK**, Hillsdale County. See Camden.

**CRANBROOK**, Oakland County: in 1904, Ellen Scripps Booth and George G. Booth, president of the Detroit News, bought 300 acres of farmland here, naming it Cranbrook after the village in Kent, England, where Mr. Booth's father was born; since then, they have turned the estate into a complex of buildings, called the Cranbrook Foundation,–a vast cultural and educational project; its post office is Bloomfield Hills [Robert J. Stadler; Federal].

**CRANE**, Midland County: storekeeper Louis J. Maus became the first postmaster of this rural post office, 4 miles southwest of Midland, on Oct. 15, 1901, the office operating until Aug. 31, 1903 [GSM 1903-05; PO Archives].

**CRANSTON**, Oceans County: farmer Hiram Myers became the first postmaster of this rural post office in Grant Township on June 19, 1886, the office operating until Aug. 31, 1901 [GSM 1887; PO Archives].

**CRAPO**, Mecosta County: this lumber settlement was originally in Richmond Township, Osceola County; a station on the Grand Rapids & Indiana Railroad; Franklin S. Robbins became its first postmaster on June 24, 1868, the office operating until Aug. 30, 1902; named for Henry H. Crapo (1804-69) who, having invested in Michigan pine lands, settled in the state in 1856 and became its governor in 1865 [Mich Hist 19:459 1935; PO Archives].

**CRAPO FARM**, Genesee County: a hamlet and a station (the depot was called Crapo) on the Grand Trunk Railroad; named after the 1,100 acre swamp-reclaimed farm of former governor Henry H. Crapo; an early employee here was Henry M. Flagler, later a millionaire east coast hotel chain owner [Wood].

**CRARY**, Calhoun County: Sidney Sweet became the first postmaster of this rural post office on July 24, 1837, the office operating until Feb. 1, 1840; named for Isaac E. Crary, a pioneer settler in the county and a father of the Michigan public school system [Federal; PO Archives].

**CRAVENS' MILLS**, Clinton County: in 1845, Joseph, Thomas and Robert Craven, brothers and early settlers in Duplain Township, built a sawmill on the Maple River; they platted the village (but did not record it), and Alpheus Bebee built a store, a wagonship and in 1856 a tavern; he sold out to Job D., Aaron, and William Sickles, but when in 1857 these brothers moved their interests and started the village of Elsie a mile east, the Cravens' project collapsed [Ellis; Daboll].

**CRAWFORD**, Crawford County: a station on the Saginaw dividion of the Michigan Central Railroad in 1876 [GSM 1877].

**CRAWFORD**, Isabella County: a village with a railroad station, in Lincoln Township; John W. Barnes became its first postmaster on Aug. 4, 1863, the office operating until Sept. 15, 1904 [GSM 1877; PO Archives].

**CRAWFORD SETTLEMENT**, Macomb County. See Meade.

**CRAWFORD'S CORNERS**, Oakland County. See Southfield.

**CRAWFORD'S QUARRY**, Presque Isle County: this settlement was named for Francis Crawford, Jr., who became its first postmaster on March 14, 1864; the office was closed on March 6, 1867, but was restored, with Leonard Crawford as postmaster, on Jan. 30, 1872; the office was renamed Crawford Quarry on May 23, 1894, but was closed on July 23, 1894; with Emma Crawford as postmaster, it was restored as Quarry on Feb. 15, 1895, and operated until April 30, 1900; it became a ghost town but came to life again in 1910 when the property was bought by the Michigan Limestone & Chemical Company (since 1920, the Michigan Limestone Division of the U.S. Steel Corp.), and renamed Calcite; it is now within the city limits of Rogers City [W.H. Whiteley; PO Archives].

**CRAWLEY**, Chippewa County: William C. Williams became the first postmaster of this rural post office on April 30, 1890, but the office was never in operation, and was officially closed on June 27, 1895 [PO Archives].

**CRAWVILLE**, Muskegon County. See Fruitport.

**CRAW WINGLE**, Mason County: this Dutch settlement flourished from about 1860 to 1880 [Page].

**CREEL**, Huron County: this village in Brookfield Township was founded by Mr. Montague; Joseph H. Cross became its first postmaster on

July 13, 1886; the office was transferred to and renamed Owendale on June 4, 1889; the word creel means fish-basket [GSM 1887; Hey; PO Archives].

**CREENS**, Tuscola County: a station on the Saginaw, Tuscola & Huron Railroad in 1884 [GSM 1885].

**CREEVY**, Huron County: this station, adjacent to Filion, on the Port Huron & Northwestern Railroad, was first called Creevy Siding; named for Mr. Creevy who operated a salt block in the area [GSM 1887].

**CREIGHTON**, Schoolcraft County: a station on the Detroit, Mackinaw & Marquette Railroad in 1882; the Creighton brothers were midwestern railroad pioneers [GSM 1883].

**CRESCENT**, Leelanau County: on North Manitou Island, which was first settled by the brothers Nicholas and Simon Pickard who started a lumbering business here in 1846 to supply propeller wood for the boats sailing Lake Michigan; the village was named from its location on the crescent-shaped lowland; Frank A. Dean became its first postmaster on Sept. 21, 1908; the lumber business closed down in 1917 and most of the island is now devoted to fruit production [Dickinson; PO Archives].

**CRESSEY'S CORNERS**, Barry County: John Q. Cressey and his wife Dorcas settled on a farm in Prairieville Township in 1854; the post office of Cressey's Corners was located in his home, with him becoming its first postmaster on March 24, 1873, shortened to Cressey on Aug. 22, 1888, and closed on Sept. 30, 1954; but the name survived in the station of Cressey on the Chicago, Kalamazoo & Saginaw Railroad [MPH 37:684 1909; PO Archives].

**CRESWELL**, Antrim County: first settled in 1852, this village in Milton Township was given a post office on June 15, 1869, with Archibald Cameron as its first postmaster, the office operating until July 14, 1904 [GSM 1873-1905; PO Archives].

**CRESTVIEW**, Keweenaw County: began as a recreation resort, owned by the Keweenaw Central Railroad, which ran a spur here.

**CREW**, Huron County: storekeeper Randolph Ducolon became the first postmaster of this rural post office in Brookfield Township on Aug. 19, 1904, the office operating until June 2, 1907 [GSM 1905; PO Archives].

**CRIMEA**, Muskegon County: it was in Ottawa County when George A. Read became its first postmaster on March 17, 1855, the office operating until Dec. 24, 1864; the Crimean War, 1854-56, was headline news at the time [Page; PO Archives].

**CRISP**, Ottawa County' Wybe Nienhuis became the first postmaster of this Dutch settlement in Olive Township on Nov. 20, 1893, the office operating until Dec. 31, 1904 [PO Archives; GSM 1895].

**CRISP POINT**, Chippewa County: named for Captain Christopher Crisp, first commander of the U.S. Coast Guard here [Hamilton].

**CROCKERSVILLE,** Genesee County: named for George Crocker who became the first postmaster of this rural post office on Aug. 21, 1843, the office operating until Jan. 9, 1862 [PO Archives].

**CROCKERY CREEK,** Ottawa County. See Nunica.

**CROFTON,** Kalkaska County: this village in Boardman Township was founded and platted by Peter Duthie, David E. and his wife Anna Meek, and John S. and his wife Sarah Harper; they named it for E. Crofton Fox, from whom they had bought the land; John F. Hiatt became its first postmaster on Oct. 25, 1875; the office was closed on Nov. 26, 1884, but was restored from March 24, 1886, to Jan. 15, 1909; a station on the Grand Rapids & Indiana Railroad [Elmer C. Sherwood; GSM 1877; PO Archives].

**CRONJE,** Ottawa County: the Dutch settlement at Holland in 1847 soon overflowed into others, of which this was one [Page].

**CRONK,** Genesee County: a settlement in Flint Township, founded by James W. Cronk in 1837 [Wood].

**CROOKED LAKE,** Barry County. See Milo.

**CROOKED LAKE,** Clare County. See Lake.

**CROOKED LAKE,** Emmet County. See Conway.

**CROSBY,** Kent County: the depot here in Paris Township on the Michigan Central Railroad was first called Bowen Station and it was given a post office of that name on Dec. 16, 1870, with Frederick S. Clark as its first postmaster; on Sept. 18, 1883, the post office was renamed Crosby [GSM 1875; PO Archives].

**CROSBY'S MILLS,** Montcalm County: a mill village in 1878, named for the mill owner [GSM 1879].

**CROSSING,** Manistee County. See Kaleva.

**CROSSMAN,** Tuscola County: a sawmill settlement and general store around a station on a branch of the Michigan Central Railroad in 1880; George H. Clark became its first postmaster on Sept. 11, 1882, the office operating until Feb. 14, 1901 [GSM 1887-1903; PO Archives].

**CROSSMAN LAKE,** St. Joseph County: a settlement in Sherman Township, on Crossman Lake, named for Abel Crossman who had settled on its banks about 1840 [Cutler].

**CROSS VILLAGE,** Emmet County: the Ottawas called the area, from Cross Village to Harbor Springs, Waganakisi (Crooked Tree), while the white traders called just this village L'Arbre Croche (Crooked Tree); when the Jesuit missionaries erected a large cross on the bluff at Cross Village (Rev. Gabriel Richard mentions seeing it on his tour of the missions in 1799), the Indians called the village Anamiewatigoing (At the Tree of Prayer, or Cross); it was called Old L'Arbre Croche to distinguish it from New L'Arbre Croche which the missionaries built at Harbor Springs about

1830; the name La Croix (The Cross) was used from 1847 to 1875 when it was changed to Cross Village; Amos T. Burnett became the first postmaster of Cross Village on Oct. 31, 1870 [Mary Belle Shurtleff, whose grandmother became PM here in 1873].

**CROSWELL**, Sanilac County: from 1845, when Ephraim Pierce built his sawmill here on the banks of the Black River, until 1861, the settlement was called Black River; in 1861, it was renamed Davisville for Randall E. Davis who completed Mr. Pierce's mill and became his partner; given a post office on Sept. 12, 1857, with Mr. Davis as its first postmaster (the residents on the west side of the river separated from Davisville, formed the village of Falcon, and were given a post office of that name on Oct. 3, 1882, with Cephes W. Arnot as its first postmaster, the office operating until May 11, 1898); on May 9, 1877, Davisville was renamed for Charles M. Croswell, who had become governor of Michigan that year; incorporated as a village in 1881 and as a city in 1905; Thomas L. McKenney in his Sketches of a Tour of the Lakes (1826) says the Black River was "so called on account of the colour of the water, which is as black as ink, occasioned, doubtless, by a vegetable deposit" [Ray Hurley; PO Archives].

**CROTON**, Newaygo County: first settled in 1840 by Louis Bohne and John F. Stearns who built a sawmill here; unofficially called Muskegon Forks, when Mr. Stearns bought out his partner, it became known as Stearns Mills and was given a post office of that name on Dec. 30, 1847, with him as its first postmaster; on Sept. 25, 1850, he had it renamed Croton, after the Croton Water Works, in New York, of which the topography reminded him; the village was platted in 1854 and incorporated in 1870; its post office operated until Jan. 31, 1908 [Harry L. Spooner; GSM 1873; PO Archives].

**CROW ISLAND**, Saginaw County: this settlement on the west bank of the Saginaw River, in Buena Vista Township, was given a spur on the Pere Marquette Railroad; Charles Colpean became the first postmaster on Feb. 6, 1882; the office was closed on March 13, 1883, but was restored, with Fred B. Tyler as postmaster, on May 3, 1883, the office operating until Aug. 31, 1894; it was again restored from Sept. 18, 1894, to March 1, 1895 [GSM 1883-95; PO Archives].

**CROWN**, Huron County: storekeeper Lewis A. Mosey became the first postmaster of this rural post office in Meade Township on May 20, 1899, the office operating until Oct. 14, 1904 [GSM 1901-05; PO Archives].

**CROZIER'S MILL**, Gogebic County: a station on a branch of the Chicago & Northwestern Railroad, 4 miles northeast of Watersmeet, in 1888 [GSM 1895].

**CRUMP**, Bay County: grocer William R. Stevens became the first postmaster of this sawmill settlement in Garfield Township on Aug. 30, 1898, the office operating until March 31, 1954; named for Rousseau O.

Crump, a congressman from this district, 1895-1902 [Gansser; GSM 1899; PO Archives].

**CRYSTAL**, Montcalm County: the first settlers in the area were John W. Smith and his brother Humphrey, lumbermen, in 1853; Enos P. Drake first settled in the present village in 1857, and built a sawmill; on land owned by him and Samuel Burtch, Asa Ward platted the village; Alfred A. Proctor became its first postmaster on March 2, 1857; named from its location by Crystal Lake [Schenck].

**CRYSTAL CITY**, Benzie County: a station on the Ann Arbor Railroad in 1893; named from its location at the head of Crystal Lake; platted by 1908 as Crystal City and Beulah View Resort, but then familiarly and now only as Beulah [MPH 9:217 1925; GSM 1899].

**CRYSTAL FALLS**, Iron County: it was in Marquette County when founded in 1880 by George Runkel, Samuel D. Hollister and William Morrison; platted for Mr. Runkel and James H. Howe by John Pumpelly in 1881; named by Mr. Runkel from the crystal beauty of the valls (Crystal Falls) on the Paint River running by it; his daugher, Julia Runkel, became the first postmaster on Sept. 28, 1881; Iron County was set off in 1884 (but not organized until 1885) and Henry C. Kimball became the first postmaster with the office in Iron County on July 1, 1884; the county seat; incorporated as a village in 1889 and as a city in 1899 [William P. Bradish; PO Archives].

**CRYSTAL LAKE**, Houghton County: John Robertson became the first postmaster of this rural post office on July 30, 1890, the office operating until Sept. 29, 1897 [PO Archives].

**CRYSTAL LAKE**, Oceana County: William F. Lake became the first postmaster of this rural post office on Nov. 2, 1865, the office operating until Oct. 29, 1866 [PO Archives].

**CRYSTAL VALLEY**, Oceana County: Jared H. Gay, as blacksmith to the Indians, became the first settler here in 1861; he led in organizing Crystal Township and its first meeting was held in his home in 1866; Dr. J.J. Kittredge, who had settled here in 1863, became the first supervisor; Hart & Maxwell built a large sawmill and stores here about 1866; James Corsant became the first postmaster on July 14, 1871, with the spelling of the office changed to Crystalvalley on Sept. 17, 1879; named by Mrs. Gay from the beautiful streams of water for which the area is noted [Hartwick; PO Archives; Royal].

**CRYSTALLIA**, Benzie County: the resort, owned by a corporation, was platted in 1895, and was built on a narrow strip of land, between Crystal Lake and Lake Michigan, known as the Crystal Lake Bar [Federal].

**CUBA**, Kent County: Andrew Mesnard became the first postmaster of this hamlet on May 10, 1844, the office operating until Jan. 16, 1868 [PO Archives].

**CUBE'S POINT**, Mackinac County: the corruption of the name of an old Indian, Animikiwab; the name became Kiob for short, and finally Cube [Gagnieur].

**CUCUSH PRAIRIE,** Branch County. See Hodunk.

**CULVER,** Arenac County: this village in Austin Township was founded in 1872 by J.W. and Alvin N. Culver, brothers and lumbermen; the latter became its first postmaster on Jan. 6, 1873; its depot on the Mackinac division of the Michigan Central Railroad was named Culver Station; on Sept. 29, 1881, its post office was transferred ten miles south, to Wells, another station on the same road [Page; GSM 1879; PO Archives].

**CULVER,** Calhoun County: this rural post office was named for David S. Culver who became its first postmaster on June 26, 1852; on Dec. 8, 1855, the office was changed to Newton Centre [GSM 1860; PO Archives].

**CULVER,** Kalkaska County: Lewis Myers became the first postmaster of this rural post office on Dec. 16, 1908 [PO Archives].

**CUMBER,** Sanilac County: T.M. Bradshaw opened a blacksmith shop here in Austin Township in 1869 and other businesses followed; William Jordan became the first postmaster on June 24, 1874 [Chapman].

**CUMMINGS,** Bay County: grocer Harmon Lapan became the first postmaster of this rural post office on Sept. 19, 1895, the office operating until Aug. 31, 1903 [PO Archives].

**CUNARD,** Menominee County: about 1880, John H. Cunard, a lumber camp foreman, sold cut over land here to Swedish farmers, keeping 260 acres; it was first called Cedar, then Camp Four, then Vesper, and finally Cunard; Mr. Cunard became the first and only postmaster of Cunard, Jan. 11, 1895, to Dec. 20, 1897 [Mrs. Minnette Cunard Froberg; PO Archives].

**CURRAN,** Alcona County: Philip Curran built a lumber camp here about 1875; the village began about 1886; the Loud & Sons Lumber Company built a narrow gauge railroad through the area in 1890; Edward Cunning became the first postmaster on April 28, 1890, the office operating only until Sept. 12, 1890; it was restored, with John S. Fullerton as its postmaster, on Oct. 10, 1890 [J.B. Wilcox; PO Archives].

**CURTICE,** Midland County: a settlement around the mill of J.E. Curtice & Company; Joshua E. Curtice became its first postmaster on March 2, 1895, the office operating until July 15, 1901 [GSM 1897-1901; PO Archives].

**CURTIS,** Alcona County. See Curtisville.

**CURTIS,** Mackinac County: the settlement was first called Portage from the Indian name for the place; in 1905, at the suggestion of U.S. senator Julius C. Burroughs, it was renamed in honor of state senator William L. Curtis, of Petoskey; Mark Howard Miller became its first postmaster on Nov. 15, 1905; a station on the Manistique Railroad; the village was platted in 1906; it was also known as Sawaquato Beach [Clara S. Moore, PM].

**CURTISVILLE**, Alcona County: Curtis Township was organized in 1881 and named for its first settler, Mr. E.D. Curtis; James Simons became the first postmaster of Curtis on June 14, 1881, the office operating only until Aug. 23, 1881; the office was restored as Curtisville on Dec. 29, 1897, with cattle dealer Joseph Bell as its postmaster, and operated until Feb. 15, 1955 [Page; GSM 1899; PO Archives].

**CUSHING**, Cass County: from 1874, it was called Stark's Corners; given a post office as Cushing, named for pioneer settler Dexter Cushing, on Jan. 27, 1880, with Eli G.D. Ridenour as its first postmaster, the office operating until May 31, 1904; this village in Silver Creek Township was also known as Cushing's Corners and as Hardscrabble [Mathews; Fox; GSM 1875; PO Archives].

**CUSINO**, Alger County: a station on the Munising Railway; storekeeper John G. Gauthier became the first postmaster of this lumber settlement on April 21, 1906, the office operating until Dec. 15, 1912 [GSM 1907; PO Archives].

**CUSTER**, Calhoun County. See Camp Custer.

**CUSTER**, Mason County: founded in 1876 and platted in 1878 by Charles E. Roussegui, of Ludington, at a station on the Pere Marquette Railroad, and station agent L.T. Southworth became its first postmaster on Dec. 23, 1878; incorporated as a village in 1895; named for General George A. Custer (1839-76), of Custer's Last Stand fame [Rose D. Hawley; GSM 1881; PO Archives].

**CUSTER**, Montcalm County. See McBride.

**CUTCHEON**, Missaukee County: Chauncey L. Bishop became the first postmaster of this rural post office on June 23, 1884; named for Byron M. Cutheon, congressman from this district, 1883-86 [GSM 1885; PO Archives].

**CUTLER'S CORNERS**, Hillsdale County. See North Adams.

**CUTLERVILLE**, Kent County: in 1853, John Cutler and his wife and ten children came from New York State and settled here in Gaines Township, bought 312 acres and built his log cabin; in 1891, his son John I. Cutler, built the Cutler mansion which in 1910 became the nucleus of the Pine Rest Christian Hospital; as early as 1906, the road from this village, going six miles north into Grand Rapids, has been called the Cutlerville Road [Louise Downs; GSM 1923].

**CUT RIVER**, Mackinac County: a small summer resort on the Cut River [Federal].

**CYR**, Marquette County: founded by Dr. Louis D. Cyr (1823-1904), who built a hunting camp here; given a station on the Chicago & Northwestern Railroad about 1883 [Rankin].

DETROIT
Res.-T.Berry

DEXTER
Res. & Store - W.F. Schlander

**DAFOE**, Alpena County: began as a sawmill settlement, in Wilson Township, with a station on the Hillman branch of the Detroit & Mackinaw Railroad, about 1865; storekeeper Samuel Daggett became its first postmaster on Aug. 5, 1899 [Powers; GSM 1901; PO Archives].

**DAFTER**, Chippewa County: this lumber settlement was given a post office as Stevensburgh on Jan. 27, 1879, with George Stevens as its first postmaster, changed to Dafter, after its township, on July 19, 1893; a station on the Minneapolis, St. Paul & Sault Ste. Marie Railroad [Hamilton; GSM 1895; PO Archives].

**DAGGETT**, Menominee County: this village in Stephenson Township was founded in 1876 by Thomas Faulkner who was in charge of a farm for the Holmes & Son Lumber Company; he married Clara Daggett, who kept the first post office for him in their kitchen (opened on May 17, 1880), and the village was named for her father, who lived in Elmira, N.Y.; a station on the Chicago & Northwestern Railroad in 1880; incorporated as a village in 1902 [Rev. Thomas Ruppe; GSM 1881; PO Archives].

**DAILEY**, Cass County: this village in Jefferson Township was first named Itaska, by Israel A. Shingledecker, a name formed by Henry Rowe Schoolcraft from the Latin, veritas (true) and caput (head); Jesse D. Blood became its first postmaster on March 4, 1872, with the office renamed Dailey on the 18th of the same month; the office was closed on Oct. 6, 1873, but was restored on Nov. 3, 1873, with Matthew T. Garvey as its postmaster; the new name honored A. H. Dailey, roadmaster of the Michigan Central Railroad which came through here in 1871 and gave it a station; Levi M. Vail recorded the first plat of the village in 1880 [Mathews; Mich Hist 23:151 1938; Glover; PO Archives].

**DALE**, Gladwin County: on March 1, 1895, June B. Miller became the first postmaster of Tobacco, named after its township; the office was renamed Dale on July 14, 1898, and operated until July 15, 1904; the office was conducted in the general store run by David and June B. Miller; one of the first settlers, Claude Fairchild bought the store in 1904 [GSM 1895-1905; PO Archives].

**DALLAS**, Allegan County: James K. Searls became the first postmaster of this rural post office on March 17, 1900, the office operating until March 31, 1903 [PO Archives].

**DALLAS**, Clinton County. See Fowler.

**DALTON**, Muskegon County: Dalton Township was organized in 1859 and named for Peter Dalton who became its first supervisor; the village began as a sawmill settlement and was given a post office named Dalton's Mills on March 24, 1857, with lumberman Peter Dalton as its first postmaster, the office operating until July 21, 1863; its depot on the Chicago & Western Michigan Railroad was named Dalton Station; the post office was restored, with its name simply Dalton, on Oct. 11, 1871, with Leander A. Richards as its postmaster, the new office operating until March 31, 1904 [Bryndene Frederickson; GSM 1860-75; Page; PO Archives].

**DALTON'S CORNERS**, Wayne County. See North Detroit.

**DALTON'S MILLS**, Muskegon County. See Dalton.

**DALTON SUMMIT**, Muskegon County: George H. Scoles became the first postmaster of this rural post office on May 15, 1866, the office operating until Sept. 3, 1867 [PO Archives].

**DALTONVILLE**, Eaton County: a hamlet, 7 miles west of Charlotte, in 1878 [GSM 1879].

**DAMON**, Ogemaw County: this lumber town in Foster Township was first settled in 1878 and was named for George G. Damon, of the firm of Cutting & Damon, which operated in the area; Frank W. Davison became its first postmaster on Jan. 27, 1880; the office was closed on Oct. 31, 1907, but was restored from Nov. 16, 1907, to April 11, 1911; the town site was abandoned in 1915 [Pen Phil 6:3 Oct 1955; PO Archives].

**DANA**, Crawford County: a station on a branch of the Michigan Central Railroad, six miles southeast of Lovells, in 1889 [GSM 1895].

**DANBY**, Ionia County: first settled by Chancellor Barringer in 1835 on land owned by A. S. Wadsworth; John Compton and his family came in 1838; a flag station on the Detroit, Lansing & Northern Railroad; named by Charles B. Brooks after his native Danby, Conn., when the township was organized in 1845; John Compton was the first postmaster, Sept. 16, 1850, to 1868, while Samuel F. Davis became the last in 1879, the office being closed on April 21, 1900 [Schenck; Branch; Dillenback; PO Archives].

**DANFORTH**, Delta County: first settled by Civil War veteran David Danforth and other farmers about 1885 [David S. Coon].

**DANIEL'S STATION**, Clinton County. See Ingersoll.

**DANSVILLE**, Ingham County: in 1844, Samuel Crossman came from Cahuga County, N.Y., and settled at Ingham Center, named from its location in Ingham Township; he opened the first store in 1847 but sold out to his son, Daniel C. Crossman who, in 1857, platted the village and recorded it as Dansville; Dr. Daniel T. Weston became its first postmaster on May 14, 1857; incorporated as a village in 1867, with Daniel T. Crossman as president [MPH 31:51 1901].

**DANSVILLE**, Kent County. See Lowell.

**DANSVILLE**, Tuscola County: a hamlet in 1878 [GSM 1879].

**DARRAGH**, Kalkaska County: storekeeper James A. Campbell became the first postmaster of this rural post office in Cold Springs Township on March 11, 1902; Archibald B. Darragh was the congressman from this district, 1901-08 [GSM 1903; PO Archives].

**DASH**, Muskegon County. See Brunswick.

**DAVIDSON STATION**, Washtenaw County: named for Hugh Davidson, who owned an adjacent farm; with the burning down of the depot in 1848, the station and its business moved to Chelsea [Chapman].

**DAVIS**, Macomb County: first called Brooklyn; but there was another Brooklyn in Michigan and when this one was given a post office on March 9, 1876, with Bela R. Davis as its first postmaster, it was renamed for Rev. Jonathan E. Davis, a pioneer settler in Ray Township; the office operated until Aug. 31, 1910 [Eldredge; PO Archives].

**DAVISBURG**, Oakland County: first settled by, founded by and named for Cornelius Davis, from Ulster County, N.Y., in 1836; he and his two sons, John C. and James H., platted the village in 1857; John C. Davis became its first postmaster on March 4, 1855, with the office spelled Davisburgh, but changed to Davisburg on May 26, 1894; a station on the Detroit & Milwaukee Railroad [Durant; PO Archives].

**DAVIS CORNERS**, Sanilac County. See Urban.

**DAVISON**, Genesee County: Eleazer Thurston became its first settler in 1842; given a post office as Davison Centre on April 19, 1850, with Goodenough Townsend as its first postmaster, the office was renamed Davison on April 28, 1864, but closed on May 24, 1873; E. W. Rising came in 1872, helped plat the village, acquired most of it, and was its chief promotor until his death in 1893; the Davison Station post office was changed to Davison on June 30, 1893; incorporated as a village in 1889 and as a city in 1938; as the name proposed (Middlebury) was already taken, the legislature named it for Norman Davison whose village of Davisonville had been changed to Atlas [MPH 22:85 1893; PO Archives].

**DAVISON STATION**, Genesee County: a depot on the Port Huron & Lake Michigan Railroad; its village was platted in 1871; its post office, opened on April 10, 1872, with Daman Stewart as its first postmaster, was changed to Davison on June 30, 1893; annexed by the city of Davison from which it was a mile to the north [GSM 1873; PO Archives].

**DAVISONVILLE**, Genesee County. See Atlas.

**DAVISVILLE**, Ottawa County. See Ventura.

**DAVISVILLE**, Sanilac County. See Croswell.

**DAWSON**, Genesee County: a station on the Chicago & Northwestern Railroad in 1878 [GSM 1879].

**DAY**, Cass County: the unplatted village of Calvin Center was named from its location in Calvin Township which had been named for Calvin Britain, territorial representative of the county when the township was organized in 1835; the village formed around the Chain Lakes First Baptist Church, the oldest Negro church (1837) in Michigan, and the township is still 75% Negro; given a post office named Day on March 29, 1875, with William Lawson as its first postmaster; the office was closed on July 9, 1895, but was restored from Jan. 22, 1896, to Sept. 30, 1901 [Mrs. L. L. Vanderburg; Federal; Fox; PO Archives].

**DAY**, Muskegon County: this hamlet on Black Creek, 8 miles from Muskegon, was given a post office on Nov. 12, 1856, with Adna Eggleston as its first postmaster, the office operating until July 27, 1860 [GSM 1860; PO Archives].

**DAYBURG**, Branch County: a little settlement, in Butler Township, when Hiram H. Bennett and his wife moved there in 1845 [MPH 28:309 1898].

**DAYHUFF LAKE**, Wexford County. See Meauwataka.

**DAY'S RIVER**, Delta County. See Brampton.

**DAYTON**, Berrien County: founded in 1830 by Benjamin Redding and given a post office named Redding's Mills on June 17, 1850, with Mr. Redding as its first postmaster; designated on Burr's Map of Michigan, 1839, as Terré Coupe; when the Michigan Central Railroad came through about 1848, its depot here was named Terre Coupe (also spelled Terra Coupée), but it too was changed to Dayton when the post office was renamed Dayton on April 11, 1851; named after Dayton, Ohio, whence many of its early settlers had come; never rebuilt after its second fire, it now comprises a store with a post office in it [Jane F. Schau, PM; Fox; MPH 22:488 1893].

**DAYTON**, Tuscola County: the first settlers in the township were George W. Spencer and Joseph Crawford in 1856; it was organized in 1857 and named for William Lewis Dayton, vice-presidential candidate on the Free Soil ticket in 1856 [Page].

**DEAD RIVER**, Marquette County: to the Indians, the mists arising at the foot of the falls conveyed the souls of the departed into the unknown, and so they named the stream Djibis-manitou-sibi, or the river of the spirits of the dead; the early French here retained the name in Rivière de Mort, which the Americans translated into Dead River; the adjacent Lake Superior & Ishpeming Railroad station named Dead River was opened by 1910 [GSM 1911; Ernest H. Rankin].

**DEAN'S MILLS**, Montcalm County: George L. Dean built the first sawmill in Bushnell Township in 1865; John Hitchcock built a dry-goods store near the mill in 1868; the store was bought by William M. Thomas in 1869 and he became the first postmaster on Jan. 10, 1872; the office operated until June 6, 1877 [Schenck].

**DEANVILLE**, Lapeer County: this village in southeastern Burnside Township took its name from John C. Dean who built a steam mill here about 1870; James Black became the first postmaster on June 23, 1874, the office operating until April 30, 1903 [Page; PO Archives].

**DEARBORN**, Wayne County: first settled by James Cisne in 1795; Conrad Ten Eyck built his tavern in 1826 and the place was called Ten Eyck; later until 1829 it was called Bucklin for pioneer A. J. Bucklin; its town of Pekin was renamed for General Henry Dearborn, American commander in the War of 1812, and incorporated as Dearbonville; platted by Paul D. Anderson in 1833; given a post office as Dearbonville on March 7, 1833, with Thornby N. Schoolar as its first postmaster, with the office renamed Dearborn on May 28, 1875; incorporated as the village of Dearborn in 1893 and as a city in 1927; in 1928, it absorbed Fordson which had already absorbed Springwells [Mich Hist 5:536 1921, 10:303 1926; Burton; PO Archives].

**DEARBORN COLONY,** Otsego County: this settlement was formed by a back to the land movement begun during the Depression (1932), by six families from Dearborn, with aid from that city [Federal].

**DEARBORN HEIGHTS,** Wayne County: carved out of Dearborn and Inkster, it was incorporated as a city in 1960; its formation was approved by the courts in April, 1961.

**De BEQUE,** Delta County: Hannah R. D. Hay became the first postmaster of this rural post office on July 31, 1876, the office operating until Jan. 28, 1879; named for a local landowner [PO Archives].

**DEBRI,** Ottawa County: storekeeper William D. Struik became the first postmaster of this rural post office on Nov. 16, 1893, the office operating until Oct. 31, 1901 [PO Archives].

**DECATUR,** Van Buren County: founded in 1847 by Joseph D. Beers and Samuel Sherwood, both of New York City; they gave land for the depot built in 1848; George B. Sherwood became the first postmaster of Decatur Depot, on Oct. 5, 1848, with the name shortened to Decatur on Sept. 20, 1849; incorporated as a village by the supervisors in 1859 and by the legislature in 1861; both town and township were named for the naval hero, Stephen Decatur [Ellis; PO Archives].

**DECATUR BRIDGE,** Gladwin County: a hamlet, 4 miles southeast of Gladwin, in 1878 [GSM 1879].

**DECATUR DEPOT,** Van Buren County. See Decatur.

**DECIPLE,** Mecosta County: this shingle mill settlement in Fork Township was given a post office on June 23, 1884, with Marvin Rogers as its first postmaster, the office operating until Oct. 12, 1894 [GSM 1891-95; PO Archives].

**DECKER,** Sanilac County: storekeeper Clinton J. Beers became the first postmaster of this village in Lamotte Township on Jan. 4, 1899; the office was closed on June 30, 1906, but was restored, with Otto W. Nigue as postmaster, on March 10, 1914; the Deckers were local pioneers and large landowners [GSM 1900-19; PO Archives].

**DECKERVILLE,** Sanilac County: in 1865, Charles Decker began his lumber business in Marion Township where in 1870, the village named for him was platted; his son Martin became its first postmaster on Jan. 3, 1870; a station on the Pere Marquette Railroad; incorporated as a village in 1893 [Chapman].

**DECORA,** Montcalm County: this village in Winfield Township was given a post office on Sept. 22, 1879, with John Gaffield as its first postmaster, the office operating until Sept. 14, 1880; in some records as Decorah [Schenck].

**DEEP RIVER,** Arenac County: founded in 1870 by A. Stevens & Company as their lumber camp; named by its tavern-keeper, Mr. Kellogg, after Deep River, Conn.; a station on the Mackinaw division of the Michigan Central Railroad in 1872; Alex C. Rorison became its first postmaster on June 13, 1872, the office operating until March 15, 1900; in Bay County until Arenac was organized in 1883 [Page; GSM 1873; PO Archives].

**DEER CREEK,** Livingston County. See Deerfield Centre.

**DEERFIELD,** Lapeer County: this village on the Flint River, in Deerfield Township, was first settled by Lorenzo Merrill and family, natives of New York, in 1853; the town was organized in 1855; since there was already a Deerfield post office in Michigan, this one was given a post office named Drake, with Abner C. Folson as its first postmaster, on Nov. 26, 1877, the office operating until June 30, 1905 [Page; PO Archives].

**DEERFIELD,** Lenawee County: William Kedzie, of Delhi, N. Y., made the first land purchase here in 1824 and became the first settler in 1826; he became the first postmaster of Kedzie's Grove on March 20, 1828, with the office renamed, from the numerous deer in the area, on Aug. 29, 1837; incorporated as a village in 1873 [Laura J. Diver, PM; MPH 17:528 1890].

**DEERFIELD,** Mecosta County: the township was organized in 1861, with Samuel S. Chipman as its first supervisor [Chapman].

**DEERFIELD,** Van Buren County. See McDonald.

**DEERFIELD CENTER,** Isabella County: first settled in 1876 and so named because it was a great runway for deer [John Cumming].

**DEERFIELD CENTRE,** Livingston County: John How, a native of England, became the first settler here in 1834; named from its location in Deerfield Township; because there was already a Deerfield post office in Michigan, this one was given a post office as Deer Creek on May 15, 1838, with Alfred Holmes as its first postmaster, John How as the second, 1843-48, and his son, William How, as the third, 1848-64, succeeded for some months by William's widow; the office operated until May 15, 1903 [Ellis; PO Archives].

**DEER LAKE,** Lake County: a lumber settlement in Pinora Township, with a station on the Grand Rapids & Indiana Railroad; Edwin P. Hayes became its first postmaster on Feb. 14, 1881, the office operating until Sept. 15, 1893 [GSM 1883; PO Archives].

**DEER LAKE,** Marquette County: the Deer Lake Furnace Company, of Norwich, Conn., began iron ore operations here on Carp River, near Deer Lake, in 1867, with E. C. Hungerford and E. C. Ward in charge [Andreas].

**DEER LICK,** Saginaw County. See Birch Run.

**DEER PARK,** Luce County: a station in McMillan Township on the Duluth, South Shore & Atlantic Railroad; the settlement formed around the Cook & Wilson sawmill; W. L. M. Powell became its first postmaster on July 12, 1888, the office operating until Jan. 15, 1900; named from the numerous deer in the area [GSM 1889; PO Archives].

**DEERTON,** Alger County: the village began as a station on the Detroit, Mackinaw & Marquette Railroad in 1882; Dora H. Gogain became its first postmaster on July 11, 1922; it was in Schoolcraft County until Alger was organized in 1885; named from its location in deer country [GSM 1885; PO Archives].

**DEFIANCE,** Delta County: a station on the Chicago & Northwestern Railroad, in Maple Ridge Township; farmer Joseph Lusardi became its first postmaster on April 17, 1888 [GSM 1889; PO Archives].

**DEFORD,** Tuscola County: here in Novesta Township the Grand Trunk Railroad came through in 1883, naming the station Bruce, for local landowner Elmer Bruce; Arthur Newton founded the village in 1884, naming it for his friend, Mr. Deford; Theron Spencer became its first postmaster on Jan. 21, 1884 [PM; GSM 1887].

**DELANO,** Arenac County: in 1886, Ezra Delano, a land agent, originally from Maine, cleared a couple of acres here, built a house and a stable; in Feb., 1887, he brought his household goods and settled here along with M. J. Whitman [Zella Whitman Pendred].

**DELAWARE,** Keweenaw County: mining company president Horace Greeley got a post office opened here, named Penn Mine, on Nov. 18, 1862, with Perkins Duraham as its first postmaster; the Delaware Mining Company was organized in 1863 and merged with the Pennsylvania Mining Company in 1876 as the Delaware Copper Mining Company, and the post office was renamed Delaware Mine on April 19, 1876; what remains of the village is called Delaware [Andreas; GSM 1877; PO Archives].

**DELAWARE SETTLEMENT,** Cass County. See Milton.

**DELHI,** Ingham County: Frederick Luther, of Lenawee County, settled here in Jan., 1837; the town took the name of the township which had been named by Roswell Everett, probably after Delhi, N.Y., since many of the early settlers came from that region; George Phillips became the first postmaster of Delhi Center on Feb. 3, 1848; to avoid confusion with Delhi Mills, the name was changed on Feb. 10, 1860, to Holt, honoring Joseph Holt, postmaster general; the village was platted at the railroad station by Matthew King and was also known as Delhi Station [Durant; Adams].

**DELHI,** Washtenaw County: platted in 1836 by Jacob Doremus as Michigan Village, but soon renamed Delhi; in 1842, all the unsold lots came into the hands of Norman C. Goodale, founder of Delhi Mills; the Scio post office was transferred to and renamed Delhi Mills, with Frank W.

Goodale as postmaster, on Feb. 3, 1871, the office operating until Sept. 30, 1903 [Chapman; PO Archives].

**DELIN**, Van Buren County: founded by Hank & Lambert, of Niles, who gave it nearly that place name spelled backwards [Rowland; Madalyn Bradford].

**DELL**, Chippewa County: named for John W. Dell who became the first postmaster of this rural post office on June 8, 1909, the office operating until Aug. 31, 1913 [PO Archives].

**DELLWOOD**, Eaton County. See Delwood.

**DeLOUGHORY**, Menominee County. See Harris.

**DELRAY**, Wayne County: first platted and recorded as Belgrade on Sept. 10, 1836; replatted and recorded as Delray, Oct. 14, 1851; additional plat by Elisha and Caroline Chase on Sept. 8, 1856, but not recorded until Feb. 24, 1860; Frederick F. Englington became the first postmaster of Delray on Feb. 8, 1870; incorporated as a village in 1897; annexed by the city of Detroit in 1906, and its post office made a station of the Detroit post office on May 31, 1906; Augustus D. Burdeno, a pioneer resident, after soldiering in the Mexican War, got the townspeople to rename it after the Mexican village of Del Rey (Of the King, or the King's), later Americanized as Delray (in 1895 its depot sign was Del Rey) [Arthur Burdeno, About Old Delray. 1906 Burton HC-DPL; County plat liber; PO Archives].

**DELTA**, Delta County: Donald A. Wells became the first postmaster of this rural post office on June 25, 1866, the office operating until Jan. 10, 1868 [PO Archives].

**DELTA**, Eaton County: also called Delta Mills, named after its township which had been named from the bend of the river here which resembled the fourth letter of the Greek alphabet, delta; when its village was first platted it was called Grand River City; given a post office as Delta, with Whitney Jones as its first postmaster, on Sept. 6, 1842; the office was closed on Sept. 16, 1865, but was restored from Nov. 4, 1865, to Nov. 15, 1910; a station on the Detroit, Grand Rapids & Western Railroad [MPH 1:157 1874; PO Archives].

**DELTA JUNCTION**, Schoolcraft County: a station on the Minneapolis, St. Paul & Sault Ste. Marie Railroad, 6 miles southwest of Manistique, in 1889 [GSM 1895].

**DELTA MILLS**, Eaton County. See Delta.

**DELTON**, Barry County: Josiah Hine bought the first government land here in 1839; Adelbert E. Monroe (known as Dell Monroe), bought the corner lot, built a store, and was named the first postmaster on May 22, 1877; Mrs. Thursa Bush sent in the name Dellstown, but it came back Delton, and has remained that; a station on the Chicago, Kalamazoo & Saginaw Railroad [H. D. Burpee].

**DELWIN**, Isabella County: the village began as a station on the Pere Marquette Railroad; James Small became its first postmaster on April 27, 1880, the office operating until Nov. 15, 1906; platted on a small scale (5 blocks and 54 lots) in 1888 [Fancher; PO Archives].

**DELWOOD**, Eaton County: the village in Sunfield Township was given a post office on April 17, 1882, with DeWitt I. Loomis as its first postmaster, the office operating until March 14, 1903; in some records spelled Dellwood [GSM 1883; PO Archives].

**DEMINGSBURGH**, Oakland County. See Oxford.

**DEMMON**, Houghton County. See Boston.

**DEMPSEY**, Missaukee County: a station on the Chicago & Western Michigan (now Pere Marquette) Railroad, in 1898 [Mich Manual 1899].

**DENIS**, Menominee County: this rural post office was named for Paul Denis who became its first postmaster on June 22, 1883, the office operating until Jan. 5, 1885 [PO Archives].

**DENMARK**, Montcalm County: a station on the Detroit, Lansing & Northern Railroad in 1878 [GSM 1879].

**DENMARK**, Tuscola County. See Carr's Corners.

**DENMARK JUNCTION**, Tuscola County: named after its township (Denmark), which was organized in 1853, and so named only to avoid duplication, by Joseph Selden and his son, Charles R., the county treasurer; the hamlet was at the junction of the Saginaw, Tuscola & Huron and the Detroit & Bay City Railroads; here the charcoal kilns of the Detroit Iron Company were located; given a post office named Jenney on Jan. 17, 1881, with Frank Calkins as its first postmaster, the office operating until July 26, 1894 [Page; GSM 1883].

**DENNISON**, Ottawa County: named for T. D. Dennison who had settled in Mill Point, Polk Township, in 1850. Washington W. Worden became the first postmaster, with the office named Polkten, on Feb. 16, 1866, but on the following April 9, it was renamed Dennison to avoid confusion with the but recently renamed post office of Polkton in the same township; a station on the Detroit, Grand Haven & Milwaukee Railroad [Lillie; GSM 1873; PO Archives].

**DENT**, Allegan County: Benjamin F. Maud became the first postmaster of this rural post office, two miles from Otsego, on Sept. 29, 1899, the office operating until April 30, 1901 [GSM 1901; PO Archives].

**DENTON**, Roscommon County: this town was the site of the Denton & Rowe sawmill; of its post office, named Edna, Clara Denton was the postmaster in 1876 and J. W. Denton in 1878 [GSM 1877-79].

**DENTON**, Wayne County: adjacent to the station here which had been opened by the Michigan Central Railroad in 1864, landowner Samuel T. Denton platted the village in 1866; the South Plymouth post office, which had been opened on April 22, 1830, with Timothy F. Sheldon as its first postmaster, was changed to Denton on Feb. 28, 1870, the office operating until Oct. 14, 1933 [Carlisle; GSM 1860-65; PO Archives].

**DENVER**, Isabella County: first settled by Lewis Hawkins, John Collins and Julius C. Jordan, 1875-76; the township was organized in 1876, with Robert Pearson as its first supervisor, succeeded by Mr. Hawkins, 1878-80; a station on the Mt. Pleasant & Saginaw Railroad [Chapman].

**DENVER**, Newaygo County: Lewis Martin became the first postmaster of this post office, named after its township, on Aug. 3, 1866; the office was closed on July 12, 1870, but on the same day, the Martinsburgh post office was transferred to and renamed Denver; this Denver office was closed on Jan. 12, 1882, but was restored from March 15, 1882, to Nov. 14, 1891 [Cole; PO Archives].

**DEPEW'S**, Macomb County: a station on a branch of the M. O. Railroad in 1884 [GSM 1885].

**DEPOT**, Monroe County. See Port Lawrence.

**DERBY**, Berrien County: a station on the St. Joseph-Galien branch of the Michigan Central Railroad, in Lincoln Township; named by the builders of the road; James Morrow became its first postmaster on Dec. 31, 1890 [Fox; GSM 1893; PO Archives].

**DERBY'S CORNERS**, Wayne County. See Wayne.

**DESMOND**, Houghton County: Grace Van Patten became the first postmaster of this rural post office on Feb. 16, 1901, the office operating only until Sept. 14, 1901 [PO Archives].

**DESMOND**, St. Clair County. See Port Huron.

**DeTOUR**, Chippewa County: an early French Canadian settlement; Warren Township; organized in 1850, was named for Ebenezer Warren, its first postmaster; an 1848 map calls the place Warrenville; its name was changed to Detour on July 25, 1856, when Henry A. Williams became its first postmaster; the office was closed on Aug. 10, 1857, but was restored from Sept. 21, 1869, to July 9, 1877, and from Aug. 16, 1877, to date; incorporated as a village in 1899; its spelling was changed to DeTour on July 1, 1953, and its post office name to DeTour Village on May 1, 1961; the French name, and the original Indian one, had the same significance, to go around, for it is here that the navigator turns the point for Mackinac Island and the Straits [Bayliss; GSM 1865; PO Archives].

**DETROIT**, Wayne County: the site of a succession of Indian villages, their recorded names including Yondotiga, Waweatunong, Tsychsardonia, and Teuchsa Grondie; the present city was founded in July, 1701, by Antoine de La Mothe, Sieur de Cadillac; named after the French word for strait (détroit) from its location on the river connecting Lakes Erie and St. Clair; among the early French settlers, these later had (and still have) streets named for them: Beaubien, Rivard, Dequindre, Chene, Dubois, and

Joseph Campau; the settlement was first called Fort Pontchartrain du Détroit after Jerome Phelypeaux, Count de Pontchartrain who, as minister of marine, decided Cadillac's proposal for the settlement; shortened to Detroit in 1751; a British possession, 1763-1783, when the U.S. gained jurisdiction (but did not occupy it until 1796); Frederick Bates became its first postmaster on Jan. 1, 1803 (the first post office in Michigan); incorporated as a town on Jan. 17, 1802, and as a city on Oct. 24, 1815; first platted in 1806 by Augustus B. Woodward, after whom its main thoroughfare, Woodward Avenue, was named; the Territorial capital, 1805-1837, the State capital, 1837-1847 [Burton; Farmer; Inside 3:42 Dec 1953; PO Archives].

**DETROIT BEACH,** Monroe County: founded by the Industrial Development Company in 1923 and named by them because of its proximity to Detroit and to attract Detroit lot buyers [Rev. A. A. Madeja].

**DETROIT JUNCTION,** Monroe County. See Alexis.

**DETROIT JUNCTION,** Wayne County. See West Detroit.

**DEVEREAUX,** Jackson County: this village in Parma Township was settled in 1872; it was given a post office on March 18, 1873, with Lewis H. King as its first postmaster; when the Lake Shore & Michigan Southern Railroad came through in 1876, it was given a station [GSM 1877; PO Archives].

**DEVIL RIVER,** Alpena County. See Ossineke.

**DEVIL'S LAKE,** Lenawee County: said to have been named by Pottawattomi chief Meteau (or Mitteau), whose tribe had inhabited the area, and so named because his daughter, a fine swimmer, was drowned here and her body never recovered; he believed her to have been taken away by evil spirits; the first white settlers were Mr. Lapham and Levi Thompson in 1833; John B. Allen became its first postmaster on Oct. 19, 1885, the office operating until Oct. 31, 1936 [Adrian Telegram, July 20, 1959; PO Archives].

**DEVIL'S LAKE,** Newaygo County: a three sawmill settlement, 3 miles north of Fremont, in 1884 [GSM 1885].

**DEWARD,** Crawford County: named by his heirs for D(avid) Ward whose estate was a vast pine tract; he died in 1900 and they liquidated the estate by exhausting the wood; the town started with their mill in 1901 and ended with it in 1912, though the last resident did not leave until 1932; George K. Root had become its first postmaster on June 3, 1901 [Mich Hist 28:5 1944].

**DEWEY'S CORNERS,** Luce County: the crossroads of M-28 and M-117, with a schoolhouse, called the Dewey School; the record of its naming goes back to at least 1933, and it was named for the man who owned the land here at the time [Thomas Tobey].

**DEWEYVILLE**, Livingston County: Milford Milem became the first postmaster of this rural post office in Iosco Township on Jan. 13, 1899, the office operating until Feb. 14, 1901 [GSM 1901; PO Archives].

**DEWING'S**, Osceola County: on this spur of the Grand Rapids & Indiana Railroad, in LeRoy Township, from 1871, the Ashton Lumber Company operated its mill and general store, and the place was called Dewing's Siding; the members of the firm were Messrs. Dewing, Halladay and Watson, and its storekeeper, John A. Erickson, became its first postmaster, with the office named Dewing's, on April 7, 1900, the office operating until April 30, 1907 [Chapman; PO Archives].

**DeWITT**, Clinton County: the land on the south side of the Looking Glass River, in DeWitt Township (named for DeWitt Clinton, then governor of New York), was owned by Frederick A. Boles, for whom it was platted and recorded Dr. Bennett and J. M. Wilcox on Jan. 2, 1837; but the village became the property of the state of Michigan for the taxes of 1842, and so passed out of existence; the land on the north side of the river was first settled by Captain David Scott and his family, from Ann Arbor, in 1833; Ephraim H. Utley became the first postmaster on March 2, 1837; Captain Scott platted the village in 1841; incorporated as a village in 1928 [MPH 26:396 1895; Daboll; PO Archives].

**DEXTER**, Marquette County: a station on the Marquette, Houghton & Ontonagon Railroad, 7 miles west of Ishpeming, in 1884 [GSM 1885].

**DEXTER**, Washtenaw County: Judge Samuel W. Dexter, who bought the first land here in 1824, was soon followed by Dr. Cyril Nichols and Samuel W. Foster; Judge Dexter became the first postmaster on April 24, 1826; platted in 1830, the year that Charles P. Cowden opened the first store; incorporated as a village in 1855 [Chapman; PO Archives].

**DIAMONDALE**, Eaton County. See Dimondale.

**DIAMOND LAKE**, Cass County: a summer resort on the west shore of Diamond Lake, with a station on a branch of the Michigan Central Railroad in 1884; platted and recorded as Diamond Lake Park in 1891 by its proprietors, C. S. Jones, Henly Lamb and LeRoy Osborn [Glover].

**DIAMOND LAKE**, Newaygo County. See Ramona.

**DIAMONDLOCH**, Newaygo County. See Ramona.

**DIAMOND SPRINGS**, Allegan County: this village in southwestern Salem Township, on the Rabbit River, was first settled in 1867; Charles K. Calkins became its first postmaster on Oct. 11, 1871; the office was closed on April 5, 1875, but was restored from Aug. 5, 1875, to Nov. 14, 1905 [Ester W. Hettinger; PO Archives].

**DIBBLEVILLE**, Genesee County. See Fenton.

**DICE**, Saginaw County: storekeeper Frank P. Winslow became the first postmaster of this hamlet in Thomaston Township on May 28, 1894, the office operating until Oct. 14, 1904 [GSM 1895-1905; PO Archives].

**DICK**, Chippewa County: a lumber settlement with a station on the Minneapolis, St. Paul & Sault Ste. Marie Railroad; Lemuel E. Green became its first postmaster on Dec. 15, 1904, succeeded by lumberman E. G. Person in 1906 [GSM 1907; PO Archives].

**DICKERTOWN**, Ionia County: the first settlers here in Keene Township included Robert Taylor, James Crysler, John Follett, and Cyrus Rose; the settlement was named from the penchant its pioneers had for trading or dickering [Branch].

**DICKERVILLE**, Berrien County. See Coloma.

**DICKINSON**, Newaygo County: a station on the Chicago & Northwestern Railroad, in Ashland Township; lumberman William Reiley became its first postmaster on May 31, 1888, the office operating until Jan. 29, 1901; named for Don M. Dickinson, a prominent Michigan Democrat, who had been a member of the cabinet of President Grover Cleveland [Blinn; GSM 1889; PO Archives].

**DICKINSONVILLE**, Ionia County. See Kiddville.

**DICKSON**, Kent County: a station on the Detroit, Lansing & Northern Railroad; its post office was opened on March 4, 1879, with George H. Hazelwood as its first postmaster, succeeded by William H. Graham, Jr., on March 2, 1880, the office operating until Jan. 23, 1882 [GSM 1883; PO Archives].

**DICKSON'S CORNERS**, Berrien County: this hamlet, on Titus' Map of Michigan, 1873, was named for E. E. Dickson, a farmer here in Berrien Township [Fox].

**DIGHTON**, Osceola County: this village in Sherman Township is located at the highest point on the Lower Peninsula; Harvey Iler became its first postmaster on June 23, 1884, the office operating until June 30, 1955 [Blinn; PO Archives].

**DILDINE**, Ionia County: storekeeper Manly B. Lansing became the first postmaster of this hamlet in Easton Township on May 24, 1899, the office operating until Sept. 13, 1902 [GSM 1901; PO Archives].

**DILLER**, Mackinac County: Asher Sheppard became the first postmaster of this rural post office on May 17, 1907, the office operating only until Dec. 31, 1907 [PO Archives].

**DIMONDALE**, Eaton County: in 1840, Isaac M. Dimond began to build a dam and a sawmill on the Grand River here and in 1856 he built a grist mill; he had the village platted by Hosey Harvey in 1856, and named it for himself; Bradley Sloan became its first postmaster on July 3, 1872; when the Lake Shore & Michigan Southern Railroad came through in 1878 it was given a station as Diamondale; incorporated as a village in 1906 [Reo A. Goff, PM].

**DINCA**, Missaukee County: storekeeper John Spoelma became the first postmaster of this rural post office in Aetna Township on Oct. 20, 1906, the office operating until May 31, 1914 [GSM 1909; PO Archives].

**DINGMAN**, Newaygo County. See Brohman.

**DINGMAN**, St. Clair County: this rural post office, 5 miles north of Memphis, was named for George Dingman who became its first postmaster on Nov. 3, 1897, the office operating until Aug. 24, 1900 [GSM 1901; PO Archives].

**DIORITE**, Marquette County: a station on the Chicago & Northwestern Railroad in 1883; the site of the American Boston Mine, it was given the name of the geological word for igneous rock; Frank Platto became its first postmaster on Oct. 20, 1908, the office operating until Jan. 15, 1940 [GSM 1911; PO Archives].

**DISCO**, Macomb County: Isaac Monfore, John Noyes and Chauncey Church owned the land on which the village was platted in 1849; the townspeople employed Alonzo M. Keeler to supervise their high school, the Disco Academy, named from the Latin word for to learn, and the village and its post office took the same name; Henry F. Keeler became its first postmaster on May 5, 1854, the office operating until July 31, 1906 [Leeson; PO Archives].

**DISHNO**, Marquette County: a station on the Chicago & Northwestern Railroad, 4 miles east of Michigamme, in 1894 [GSM 1895].

**DIVER**, Cheboygan County: a hamlet with a station on a branch of the Michigan Central Railroad; Wilford P. West became its first postmaster on Feb. 15, 1881, the office operating until Jan. 12, 1882 [GSM 1883; PO Archives].

**DIXBORO**, Washtenaw County: founded by sea-captain John Dix in 1825 and platted for him by A. B. Rowe in 1826 and recorded in 1828; it was in Wayne County until Washtenaw was organized in 1829; given a post office as Dixborough, with Mr. Dix as its first postmaster, on Dec. 6, 1825; the office was closed on Sept. 25, 1850, but was restored, with Nelson Townsend as postmaster, on July 11, 1861, operating until Jan. 20, 1863, and then was restored again from May 26, 1890, to June 15, 1905 [Wendell W. Hobbs; PO Archives].

**DIXON**, Alger County. See Forest Lake.

**DODGE**, Clare County: a station on the Pere Marquette Railroad; the settlement formed around the mill of the Lansing Lumber Company; named for William H. Dodge who became its first postmaster on June 17, 1889; the office was closed on Sept. 16, 1895, but was restored from Dec. 12, 1895, to Dec. 19, 1898, and from May 18, 1899, to June 30, 1911 [GSM 1891; PO Archives].

**DODGE MUNUSCONG STATE PARK**, Chippewa County: once privately owned, now a game refuge under the supervision of the state department of conservation; elaborate lodge buildings, erected by the

Dodge brothers, Horace and John, then Detroit motor magnates, are used by state research workers; near Munuscong Bay, Indian for bay of the rushes [Federal].

**DODGE'S LANDING**, Emmet County. See Conway.

**DODGE'S POINT**, Cheboygan County. See Mullett Lake.

**DODGEVILLE**, Houghton County: its settlement began with the opening of the Dodge Copper Mine in 1901; given a post office on Jan. 15, 1912, with Agnes C. Glavin as its first postmaster [PM; PO Archives].

**DODGEVILLE**, Ionia County: Francis Gihon became the first postmaster of this rural post office on Jan. 9, 1833; the office was closed on July 24, 1833, but was restored on May 24, 1834, with William Henry as its postmaster [PO Archives].

**DOLLAR BAY**, Houghton County: this village in Osceola Township began as a lumbering settlement; when the timber in the area had been cut, it was maintained by its Portage Lake harbor; a station on the Hancock & Calumet Railroad; Frank Naun became its first postmaster on Feb. 2, 1888; named from the shape of the bay by which it was begun [Federal; PO Archives].

**DOLLARVILLE**, Luce County: this village in McMillan Township formed around the mill and general store of the American Lumber Company in 1882, and was named for Robert Dollar, its general manager (who later went on to a fortune in shipping); a station on the Detroit, Mackinaw & Marquette Railroad; George W. Rule became its first postmaster on Aug. 13, 1883; the office was closed on Oct. 14, 1903, but was restored on June 3, 1904 [Martin; GSM 1885; PO Archives].

**DOLPH**, Missaukee County: named for storekeeper Charles L. Dolph who became its first postmaster on April 13, 1898 [GSM 1899; PO Archives].

**DOLPH'S MILLS**, Gladwin County: a settlement around the lumber mill and general store of L. H. Dolph, begun about 1884 [Chapman].

**DONALD**, Mackinac County: this rural post office was named for farmer Donald A. McDonald who became its first postmaster on April 24, 1900, the office operating until Oct. 31, 1912 [PO Archives].

**DONALDSON**, Chippewa County: this village was named for Rev. Matthew Donaldson, a Methodist preacher, who arrived here in 1878, built a log church in 1879, and a parsonage in 1882; farmer David Lyall became the first postmaster on May 2, 1881, the office operating until Dec. 31, 1913 [Bayliss; GSM 1883; PO Archives].

**DONKEN**, Houghton County: a station on the Copper Range Railroad, in Elm River Township; settled around the Case Lumber Company mill and general store, Earl J. Case, proprietor, and he became its first postmaster on April 7, 1919 [GSM 1921; PO Archives].

**DORIS**, Ionia County: grocer Milton J. Lambert became the first postmaster of this rural post office in Berlin Township on Sept. 6, 1899, the office operating until Nov. 30, 1901 [GSM 1901; PO Archives].

**DORR**, Allegan County: the first land purchases in this area were made by Hull Sherwood and Almerin L. Cotton, in 1835, and the first settlement by Nathaniel Goodspeed and his son Orrin, in 1845; the first settler in the village itself was German-born Frank Neuman, in 1856; he built a wagon shop and, as proprietor, had the village platted in 1869; William H. Ewing became its first postmaster on Jan. 3, 1870; believed to have been named for Thomas Wilson Dorr, principal in Dorr's Rebellion (this Rhode Islander took up arms against his State to force repeal of its law refusing the franchise to all who did not own $134 worth of real estate); first called Dorr Centre [Johnson; Ensign].

**DORR**, Midland County. See Alamando.

**DORRANCE**, Branch County: Miss Melinda A. Mallison became the first postmaster of this rural post office in Quincy Township on Nov. 22, 1892, the office operating until Nov. 29, 1902 [GSM 1895; PO Archives].

**DORSEY**, Alger County. See Sundell.

**DOSTER**, Allegan County: this village on the line between Barry and Allegan Counties was founded by and named for Stephen Doster; it was given a station on the M. & O. Railroad in 1884; William H. Brouard, the railroad agent, became the first postmaster, with the office named Brouard, on March 7, 1884, but renamed Doster on March 3, 1900; Burchett Doster became its postmaster on Jan. 30, 1928, but the office was closed on July 21, 1961 [PM; GSM 1885-1901; PO Archives].

**DOT**, Charlevoix County: Thomas J. Stradling became the first postmaster of this rural post office in Springvale Township on May 17, 1880, the office operating until June 15, 1901 [GSM 1881; PO Archives].

**DOTY**, Alger County: in 1901, the Superior Veneer & Cooperage Company, of Munising, built a spur from the Marquette & Eastern Railway easterly into some forest land which they owned, and named it after their general manager, Marcus A. Doty; while its crossing with the Duluth, South Shore & Atlantic (now the Soo Line) Railroad is known as Doty on the M. & E. (now L.S. & I.), it is called Evelyn by the Soo Line; on some maps Doty appears as a village [Ernest H. Rankin].

**DOTY**, Allegan County: Lucinda Wells became the first postmaster of this rural post office on Aug. 5, 1891, the office operating until Nov. 2, 1892 [PO Archives].

**DOUBLING**, Manistee County: this station on the Chicago & Western Michigan Railroad was given a post office on July 16, 1892, with Melvin H. Beveridge as its first postmaster, the office operating only until Dec. 9, 1892 [GSM 1893; PO Archives].

**DOUGLAS**, Allegan County: in 1851, Jonathan Wade bought land, built a house, and laid out a village south of present Center Street, naming it Dudleyville for his brother, Dudley Wade, of Canada; soon after, William Dutcher bought and platted the land north of Center Street, naming it Dutcherville; in 1861, he bought the north half of Mr. Wade's land and, putting the two parcels together, platted the village; at the suggestion of his son-in-law, Colonel Fred May, he named it after the town of Douglas, on the Isle of Man, whence came the ancestors of the Mays; contrary to this, Fred Wade, nephew of Jonathan Wade, stated he was at a meeting where it was named for the American statesman, Stephen A. Douglas; Dyer C. Putnam became its first postmaster on March 27, 1866; incorporated as a village in 1870 [Howard C. Schultz; PO Archives].

**DOUGLAS**, Gratiot County. See North Star.

**DOUGLAS**, St. Joseph County. See Klinger.

**DOUGLASS**, Houghton County: a copper mining location, organized in 1863, and named for Columbus C. Douglass, agent of the Ohio & Isle Royale Company [Stevens].

**DOUGLASS**, Montcalm County. See Westville.

**DOUGLASS HOUGHTON**, Ontonagon County. See Henwood.

**DOVER**, Cass County: Talmon Skinner became the first postmaster of this rural post office on May 28, 1836, the office operating until Oct. 26, 1841 [PO Archives].

**DOVER**, Clare County: William Crawford and his family became the first settlers in the county in 1866; they located near present-day Dover, in the northeast corner of Grant Township; Charles Waggoner became the first postmaster on April 24, 1882, the office operating until Feb. 15, 1905 [Louis J. Becker; J. C. McNamara; PO Archives].

**DOVER**, Genesee County. See Mount Morris.

**DOVER**, Lenawee County: given a post office as Unionville on Jan. 5, 1836, with James Phillips as its first postmaster; the office was renamed Dover, after its township, on April 22, 1842, but was closed on Nov. 29, 1867 [Cole].

**DOVER**, Washtenaw County: this village on the Huron River, in Dexter Township, was settled in 1833; given a post office as Base Lake on Aug. 30, 1849, with Moses Y. Hood as its first postmaster; the place was also known as Dover Mills; in 1882, Thomas Birkett made it the site of his Birkett Manufacturing Company and the post office was renamed Birkett, with him as its first postmaster, on March 29, 1882, the office operating until Oct. 14, 1893 [Beakes; GSM 1883; PO Archives].

**DOW**, Cheboygan County: grocer George Delamarter became the first postmaster of this rural post office in Hebron Township on July 16, 1904 [GSM 1905; PO Archives].

**DOWAGIAC**, Cass County: in 1847, Nicholas Chesbrough, a right of way buyer for the Michigan Central Railroad, and Jacob Beeson, of Niles, bought of Patrick Hamilton 80 acres and first platted the village, recording the plat on Feb. 16, 1848; named after the river which on early maps is spelt Dowagiake, but when the railroad came through late in 1848, they gave it its present spelling; according to Michael B. Williams, of Niles, titular head of all the Pottawattomi Indians in the U.S., the original word was Ndowagayuk or foraging ground, meaning that in this area the Indian could fill all his needs for food, clothing and shelter; Arad C. Balch became its first postmaster on Oct. 9, 1848; incorporated as a village in 1863 and as a city in 1877 [Glover; Beth Ward; PO Archives; Everett Claspy. Dowagiac. 1970].

**DOWEN**, Kalkaska County: Frank Dempsey became the first postmaster of this rural post office, 12 miles east of Kalkaska, on Oct. 22, 1901, the office operating until Aug. 30, 1904 [GSM 1905; PO Archives].

**DOWLING**, Barry County: built on land first owned by John Stall; Baltimore Township "was informally christened as early as 1842 by the foremost settlers within its boundaries, who thus perpetuated the memory of their former home"; given a post office as Baltimore on May 30, 1850, with John Baker as its first postmaster; the name was changed to Dowling on March 16, 1880 [Johnson; PO Archives].

**DOWNINGTON**, Sanilac County: William Bancroft, of Port Huron, built the first building, a store, on the present site of the village in 1862; named for Alonzo Downing, another businessman, who served as supervisor of its township (Marion), 1873-76; it was given a station as Downing on the Port Huron & Northwestern Railroad in 1880 and a post office as Downington on April 6, 1883, with John Southworth as its first postmaster [Chapman; PO Archives].

**DOYLE**, St. Clair County: when the Port Huron & Northwestern Railroad came through here about 1885, this station was named for its local agent, Charles P. Doyle; Andrew Martin became the first postmaster here on the Belle River, in Riley Township, on Sept. 23, 1885, the office operating until Nov. 30, 1913 [GSM 1887; PO Archives].

**DOYLE'S SIDING**, Charlevoix County: a station on the Boyne City & Southeastern Railroad, 2 miles southeast of Boyne City, in 1894 [GSM 1895].

**DRAKE**, Lapeer County. See Deerfield.

**DRAKE'S CORNERS**, Hillsdale County. See Amboy.

**DRAYTON PLAINS**, Oakland County: the first permanent settler was Daniel Windiate who came here from England in 1835; he and his son-in-law, Thomas Whitfield, built a grist mill in 1836 and Drayton Plains Hotel in 1838 (in England, Windiate had called his mill the Drayton Mill); given a post office on Aug. 24, 1858; platted by Lewis L. Dunlap in 1860 [Mrs. Donald E. Adams; Seeley].

**DRENTHE**, Ottawa County: the first settler here in Zeeland township was Jan Hulst in 1847; John D. Everhard became the first postmaster on Nov. 21, 1877, the office operating until Jan. 2, 1907; named after a province in the Netherlands whence many of the early settlers had emigrated [Willard C. Winchers; PO Archives].

**DREW,** Isabella County: storekeeper Edward W. Benn became the first postmaster at this station on the Pere Marquette Railroad, in Sherman Township, on Jan. 24, 1899, the office operating until Nov. 15, 1904 [GSM 1901-1905; PO Archives].

**DRIGGS,** Schoolcraft County: several railroad houses and a station, 8 miles west of Seney, on the Detroit, Mackinaw & Marquette Railroad; named for Frederick E. Driggs (1838-1919) who came from New York City to Detroit in 1859; a lawyer, he helped finance and build the railroad of which he was also a director, as well as a manager of the Peninsula Land Co.; a logging area until 1889, its station operated from at least 1882 to 1896; a lake as well as a river flowing from it, in the same county, were also named for him [GSM 1883-1895; Escanaba Press Dec. 27, 1967; H. R. Driggs, Driggs Family History].

**DRISKEL LAKE,** Cass County. See Jones.

**DRISSEL,** Saginaw County: a station on a branch of the Pere Marquette Railroad in 1882 [GSM 1883].

**DRUMMOND ISLAND,** Chippewa County: named for Sir Gordon Drummond, British commander of the lake district; he built Fort Drummond here after the War of 1812, but when it was found to be on American territory it was abandoned in 1822; Daniel Murray Seaman came as a Mormon missionary to the Indians and settled here in 1853, followed soon by other Mormons, and he became the first postmaster, with the office named Drummond and located on the west side of the island, on Feb. 9, 1881; the office was renamed Drummond Island on July 1, 1953 [Bayliss; Mich Hist 15:150 1941; PO Archives].

**DRYADS,** Menominee County: a station on a branch of the Chicago & Northwestern Railroad in 1884; within a dozen miles, the road gave mythological names to four of its stations: Dryads, Faunus, Comus, and Hylas [GSM 1885].

**DRYBURG,** Chippewa County: a station on the Minneapolis, St. Paul & Sault Ste. Marie Railroad, in Rudyard Township; John Elfendink became its first postmaster on Oct. 31, 1903, the office operating until Jan. 30, 1943; named by local residents who agreed to banish strong drink from the community [Hamilton; GSM 1905; PO Archives].

**DRYDEN,** Lapeer County: in 1840, Jonathan Sweet built a store here; about 1846, he sold it to John M. Lamb and the place became known as Lamb's Corners; Sanford Kendrick had the name of the township changed from Lomond to Dryden, honoring the English poet, John Dryden, and when the Look's Corners post office was transferred here on Feb. 16, 1846, it took the same name; incorporated as a village in 1887 [Page; Pearl Millikin; PO Archives].

**DRY PRAIRIE**, Calhoun County: Lot Whitcomb, from Vermont, put up a shanty here and Alfred Holcomb and his family moved into it in 1831; a log schoolhouse was built that year; Mr. Whitcomb became the first postmaster in 1835 [MPH 2:212 1877].

**DUBLIN**, Manistee County: a station on the Chicago & Western Michigan (now Pere Marquette) Railroad; the Wellston post office was changed to Dublin on April 18, 1898, with J. R. Willett as its first postmaster here, the office operating until Aug. 15, 1933 [GSM 1899; PO Archives].

**DUBOISVILLE**, Wayne County: named for James Dubois, who projected the village on his land in Redford Township in 1878; absorbed by the city of Detroit in 1925 [Burton].

**DUCK LAKE**, Calhoun County: Walter F. Hale became the first postmaster of this rural post office on May 5, 1875, with the spelling of the office changed to Ducklake on June 10, 1893, but the office was closed on Sept. 14, 1901 [PO Archives].

**DUCK LAKE**, Muskegon County: Charles Mears became the first settler here, building his sawmill on Duck Lake in 1840; when Edward H. Townsend became the first postmaster of the village which developed it was in Ottawa County; the post office, opened on March 24, 1856, was closed on July 24, 1858, and the village faded into a hamlet [Page; PO Archives].

**DUDLEYVILLE**, Allegan County. See Douglas.

**DUEL**, Bay County: the village was named for its storekeeper, Luther L. Duel, who became its first postmaster on Nov. 30, 1892, the office operating until March 31, 1908 [GSM 1895; PO Archives].

**DUFFIELD**, Genesee County: a station on the Grand Trunk Railroad in 1882; Charles A. Hurd became its first postmaster on June 13, 1884 [GSM 1883; PO Archives].

**DUKE**, Gogebic County: a lumbering settlement with a station on the Duluth, South Shore & Atlantic Railroad, in Wakefield Township; Andrew Emerson became its first postmaster on April 24, 1901, the office operating until Oct. 31, 1906; named after the owner of the mill [Victor Lemmer].

**DUKES**, Marquette County: a station on the L.S. & I. Railroad, in Skandia Township, opened in 1926 and called Lawson; the Skandinavian settlers here called their settlement Lehtola, the name of a number of villages in Finland, the word meaning a copse or grove; given a post office as Dukes with merchant Axel G. Laxo as its first postmaster, on June 3, 1929; the office was closed later but was restored from June 21, 1935, to Nov. 22, 1963 [Kenyon Boyer; GSM 1931; PO Archives].

**DUNBAR**, Grand Traverse County. See Williamsburg.

**DUNBAR'S**, Berrien County: a flag station on the St. Joseph Valley Railroad in 1884 [GSM 1885].

**DUNCAN,** Cheboygan County: also called Duncan City; here on Duncan Bay, Alexander and R. McLeod and J. W. Duncan built sawmills; given a post office as Duncan, with Alexander McLeod as its first postmaster, on Dec. 16, 1850, the office was changed to Cheboygan, Feb. 14, 1870; the village became the county seat in 1853 and the government land office in 1855; the Duncan post office was re-established on Oct. 27, 1888, but closed permanently on Sept. 7, 1894; now a part of the city of Cheboygan [Powers; Page; PO Archives].

**DUNCAN,** Marquette County: a station on the M. & S.E. Railroad in 1910 [GSM 1911].

**DUNDEE,** Monroe County: in 1823, William Remington made the first land entry here and in 1824, Riley Ingersoll, from New York State, became the first settler; S. Van Ness founded and laid out the village in the early 1830s, and it was called Van Ness's Mills; on May 2, 1834, a post office named Winfield was opened in the home of John H. Montgomery; on Jan. 11, 1836, he was succeeded by Alonzo Curtis, the office was moved to the village two miles west, and its name changed to Dundee after the township which Mr. Curtis had named after the city of his forebears in Scotland; incorporated as a village in 1855 [Wing; Whitney; PO Archives].

**DUNHAM,** Arenac County: when this station on the Mackinaw division of the Michigan Central Railroad was opened in 1872 it was in Bay county [GSM 1879].

**DUNHAM,** Gogebic County: a station on the Chicago & Northwestern Railroad, in Bessemer Township; the settlement formed around the Ashland Iron & Steel Company plant, with company manager Frank L. Scott becoming its first postmaster on Oct. 6, 1902; the office was closed on June 15, 1911, and it is now a ghost town [Victor Lemmer].

**DUNN,** Iron County: a settlement around the Dunn Iron Mining Company, with a station on the Menominee River branch of the Chicago & Northwestern Railroad in 1884; the depot was named Dunn Mine, as was its post office, opened on April 11, 1890, with Nelson J. Webb as its first postmaster; the name of the office was shortened to Dunn on Oct. 31, 1894, but closed on Nov. 30, 1900 [GSM 1897; PO Archives].

**DUNNINGVILLE,** Allegan County: the first settler, Andrew Whistler, built a sawmill here in 1855; Messrs. D. Dunning and Hopkins, from Saugatuck, operated it; around it the village arose; its station on the Chicago & Western Michigan (now Pere Marquette) Railroad was named simply Dunning, but its post office, opened on Feb. 23, 1870, with Isaiah Williston as its first postmaster, was named Dunningville; the office operated until July 31, 1937 [Margaret Lovett; MPH 17:563 1890; PO Archives].

**DUNN MINE,** Iron County. See Dunn.

**DUPLAIN,** Clinton County: the Maple River, known early by the French name, Rivière du Plain, winds from south to north through the township which was called Sena when erected in 1840, but changed to Du

Plain in 1841; first settled by an organized group from Rochester, N.Y., in 1836, and known as the Rochester Colony; platted as Mapleton by Edward R. Everest, for the Colony, in 1837; given a post office as Mapleton, with Mr. Everest as its first postmaster, on Jan. 29, 1844, changed to Duplain on Dec. 12, 1844, the office operated until March 14, 1903 [Ellis; Daboll; PO Archives].

**DURAND**, Shiawassee County: built on land owned by Mary Miller, William Young and Dr. L. D. Jones in 1836; William H. Putnam acquired some of it and had James C. Brand plat and record the village as Vernon Center, named from its location in Vernon Township; given a post office as Durand, named for George H. Durand, congressman from the 6th district, 1875-76, with Mr. Putnam as its first postmaster, on May 8, 1876; incorporated as a village in 1887 and as a city in 1932 [PM; Campbell].

**DURHAM**, Branch County. See Sherwood.

**DURHAM**, Schoolcraft County. See Cooks.

**DURKEE**, Presque Isle County: this rural post office was named for its first postmaster, Walter Durkee; it was established on Jan. 13, 1896, but was never in operation, and was discontinued on Jan. 4, 1897 [PO Archives].

**DUSHVILLE**, Isabella County. See Winn.

**DUTCHERVILLE**, Allegan County. See Douglas.

**DUTTON**, Kent County: the village began in 1870 on the farmland of Stephen A. Hammond when the Grand River Valley Railroad came through and built a depot here named Hammond Station; given a post office as Hammond on Jan. 27, 1870, with George W. Woodward as its first postmaster; platted and recorded as Hammond for Mr. Hammond, by Robert S. Jackson, on Dec. 29, 1875; it is still carried on the Gaines Township records as Hammond Station although renamed Dutton for one of their officials after the Michigan Central took over the Grand River Valley Railroad; its post office was renamed Dutton on Dec. 6, 1882, the office operating until Feb. 10, 1966 [Myrtle E. Leatherman, ex-PM; Chapman; Dillenback].

**DUVAL**, Delta County: William Rowe was appointed its first postmaster on Dec. 16, 1892, but it was rescinded on Jan. 11, 1893 [PO Archives].

**DWIGHT**, Allegan County: in 1837, a village at the point where Gun Creek empties into the Kalamazoo River [GSM 1838].

**DWIGHT**, Charlevoix County: storekeeper DeGrove Haight became the first postmaster of this rural post office in South Arm Township on May 28, 1866, the office operating until July 19, 1898 [GSM 1887-99; PO Archives].

**DWIGHT**, Huron County: first settled by Henry B. Hellems in 1856 and he became the first supervisor when the township was organized (record of date lost in county fire), and was returned to office in 1866, 1868, and 1877; named for Alfred Dwight of the local lumbering firm of Smith, Austin & Dwight [Chapman].

**DWIGHTVILLE,** Huron County. See Port Austin.

**DYE,** Genesee County: a settlement in Flint Township, founded by Ruben Dye in 1843 [Wood].

**DYER,** Cass County: a station on the Air Line (now Michigan Central) Railroad, in Newberg Township, opened in 1871 [Rogers].

**DYERSBURG,** Livingston County. See Plainfield.

**EAGLE,** Clinton County: first settled by Anthony Niles and Stephen B. Groger in 1834, and they named it after the township; William Fletcher Jenison became its first postmaster on Feb. 15, 1841, with the office named Waverly, but changed to that of the town on Feb. 4, 1842; the village was moved a half mile east with the donation of land, a depot, and a Methodist church by George W. McCrumb in 1872, and he is considered its founder; platted and recorded in 1873; incorporated as a village in 1873 [Mrs. Charles Westfall; MPH 28:324 1898; Daboll; PO Archives].

**EAGLE BAY,** Huron County: a station on the Pere Marquette Railroad, a mile from Grindstone City, in 1894 [GSM 1895].

**EAGLE HARBOR,** Keweenaw County: Edward Taylor, the first settler, built a log warehouse here in 1844; the Eagle Harbor Mining Company located here in 1845; the village was platted by Mr. Slaughter; Hiram Joy became its first postmaster on May 11, 1847, the office operating until July 31, 1959; it was in Houghton County until Keweenaw was organized in 1861 [Mich Hist 34:309 1950; PO Archives].

**EAGLE LAKE,** Oakland County: Asabel Kent became the first postmaster of this hamlet on the shores of Eagle Lake on Sept. 13, 1843, the office operating until May 5, 1856 [GSM 1860; PO Archives].

**EAGLE MILLS,** Kent County: a sawmill settlement with a station on the Lake Shore & Michigan Southern Railway in 1878; then 3 miles south of Grand Rapids [GSM 1879].

**EAGLE MILLS,** Marquette County: the Iron Mountain Railroad from Marquette to the Eagle Mills was surveyed in 1852, began operations in 1855, and was relocated in 1873; the F. W. Read & Company sawmill opened here about 1873; Ford W. Read became the first postmaster of this village in Negaunee Township on Aug. 22, 1877; the office was closed on July 30, 1908, but was restored from June 26, 1911, to April 15, 1912 [Andreas; Mich Hist 5:152 1921; PO Archives].

**EAGLE POINTE,** Macomb County: this settlement, platted and recorded by Edward J. and Louise M. Hickey, proprietors, on May 23, 1916, was absorbed by the village of St. Clair Shores in 1925; it was located on a point of land projecting into Lake St. Clair, in Lake Township [Rt. Rev. Msgr. Edward J. Hickey].

**EAGLE RIVER,** Keweenaw County: the Keweenaw Copper Company obtained several leases in 1843, including the land later laid out by the Phoenix Company and sold as lots, which began the village; Columbus C. Douglas became its first postmaster on Oct. 24, 1845; named, the same as the river which divides it, from the many eagles then in the area; it was in Houghton County until Keweenaw was organized in 1861 and is now the county seat [Bessie Phillips; Ernest Rankin; PO Archives].

**EAGLETOWN,** Leelanau County. See Peshawbestown.

**EAMES,** Oakland County: a flag station on the P., O. & P.A. Railroad, in Orion Township, in 1874; given a post office on Nov. 15, 1883, with Charles A. Carpenter as its first postmaster [GSM 1885; PO Archives].

**EARDLY,** Kent County: a station on the Detroit, Lansing & Northern Railroad; its post office was opened on Aug. 28, 1891, and was named for its first postmaster, James H. Eardley, the office operating until July 31, 1902 [GSM 1893-1903; PO Archives].

**EARL,** Osceola County: farmer Stuart Allan became the first postmaster of this rural post office in Sylvan Township on June 15, 1892, the office operating until May 26, 1894 [GSM 1893; PO Archives].

**EARLE,** Iron County: with the development of the Rogers Mine, Dr. George Washington Earle, director the Wisconsin Land & Lumber Company, from 1889, platted and recorded the village of Earle on his lands in Bates Township in Sept., 1913, but the project failed and was abandoned [Hill].

**EAST ANN ARBOR,** Washtenaw County: incorporated as a city in 1947; annexed by Ann Arbor in 1957.

**EAST BAY,** Grand Traverse County: the township, when organized in 1867, was named from its location on the east arm of Grand Traverse Bay; J. B. Haviland was elected its first supervisor; a sawmill settlement in it was given a post office on Feb. 3, 1868, as East Traverse Bay, with Morris Mahan as its first postmaster; the office was renamed Traverse Bay on Dec. 22, 1873, and East Bay on Jan. 9, 1874, and operated until March 24, 1879 [Sprague; GSM 1875; PO Archives].

**EAST BELLEVUE,** Eaton County. See Walton.

**EAST BERLIN,** St. Clair County: a post office named from its location in Berlin Township, with William H. Baker becoming its first postmaster on March 15, 1851, the office operating until Dec. 5, 1856 [GSM 1860; PO Archives].

**EAST BRANCH,** Chippewa County: a station on the Detroit, Mackinaw & Marquette Railroad in 1886 [GSM 1887].

**EAST BRANCH,** Ontonagon County: a rural post office near the east branch of the Ontonagaon River; John A. Niemela became its first postmaster on July 12, 1912 [GSM 1913; PO Archives].

**EAST CHINA,** St. Clair County: a hamlet in eastern China Township in 1878 [GSM 1879].

**EAST COHOCTAH,** Livingston County. See Cohoctah.

**EAST COOPER,** Kalamazoo County: a station on the Chicago, Kalamazoo & Saginaw Railroad, 4 miles north of Kalamazoo in 1894; see Cooper Center for the name [GSM 1895].

**EAST DAYTON,** Tuscola County: George Sorter began the village with his general store in 1856; he was succeeded in business by Lorenzo Hurd, and the place became known as Hurd's Corners; on Aug. 8, 1857, with Mr. Hurd as its first postmaster, it was given a post office named East Dayton, from its location in Dayton Township, named for William Lewis Dayton, vice-presidential candidate on the Free Soil ticket in 1856; the village today is equally referred to as Hurd's Corners or as East Dayton; its post office was closed on May 31, 1905 [J. A. Gallery; Page; PO Archives].

**EAST DETROIT,** Macomb County: first settled in 1831 by Irish and German homesteaders; on Oct. 13, 1897, it was given a post office named Halfway (it was equidistant between downtown Detroit and Mount Clemens), with grocer Herman Hummrich as its first postmaster; this community in Erin Township was incorporated as a village in 1925 and as a city in 1928; the Detroit P.O. bundled mail for this area as going to "East Detroit" and, with Otto C. Miller as postmaster, the Halfway post office was officially renamed East Detroit on Dec. 11, 1926; in an election on Jan. 7, 1929, the townspeople voted to take that name [Mich Hist 46:371 1962; Christenson; PO Archives].

**EAST DOVER,** Lenawee County. See Clayton.

**EAST ESSEX,** Clinton County: a post office, named from its location in Essex Township, opened on May 14, 1856, with Israel Coats as its first postmaster, the office operating until June 30, 1858 [GSM 1860; PO Archives].

**EAST EXETER,** Monroe County: this post office in Exeter Township was opened on March 14, 1850, with Peter Partlan as its first postmaster, the office operating until only Oct. 2, 1851 [GSM 1860; PO Archives].

**EAST FARMINGTON,** Oakland County: this post office, named from its location in Farmington Township, was opened on April 16, 1839, with George Brownell as its first postmaster, the office operating until May 10, 1842 [PO Archives].

**EAST FREMONT,** Sanilac County: a rural post office in eastern Fremont Township, which had been named for Civil War general, John C. Fremont; Stephen O. Coon became its first postmaster on Oct. 27, 1874, the office operating until June 30, 1906 [GSM .1879; PO Archives].

**EAST GILEAD,** Branch County: Samuel Arnold bought government land here in 1837 and the place became known as Arnold's Corners; on April 30, 1857, he became the first postmaster of East Gilead; the office was closed on Oct. 22, 1859, but was restored from May 14, 1867, to Nov. 30, 1905; see Gilead for the name [Johnson; PO Archives].

**EAST GOLDEN**, Oceana County. See Golden.

**EAST GRAND RAPIDS**, Kent County: founded by Lew and Ezra Reed in 1832; incorporated as a village in 1891 and as a city in 1926; named from its location in relation to Grand Rapids [Louis F. Battjes].

**EAST GREENWOOD**, St. Clair County: this rural post office in eastern Greenwood Township, was opened on Oct. 8, 1874, with George Todd as its first postmaster, the office operating until Nov. 30, 1905 [GSM 1879-1907; PO Archives].

**EAST HOLLAND**, Ottawa County: Henry Schepers became its first postmaster on July 24, 1886, succeeded by P. Van Geldere in 1887, the office operating until Nov. 14, 1902; named from its location, then some three miles east of Holland [GSM 1891; PO Archives].

**EAST JORDAN**, Charlevoix County: William F. Empey, a Canadian, became the first settler at this point on the east side of the Jordan River in 1873, built the first store in 1874, and became the first postmaster on May 31, 1878; it absorbed the adjacent village of South Arm; incorporated as a village in 1887 and as a city in 1911 [William W. Bennett, PM; East Jordan by Barb Christiensen. 1970].

**EAST KINGSFORD**, Dickinson County: an unincorp. village between Kingsford and Iron Mountain [Columbia Ency.].

**EASTLAKE**, Manistee County: in 1870, Louis Sands built a mill here which was bought by Richard G. Peters in 1879; he was evidently the founder of the village, for in an 1881 record he is referred to as "the proprietor of the village of Eastlake"; Henry W. Magoon became its first postmaster on May 21, 1883; a station on the Pere Marquette Railroad; incorporated as a village in 1912; named from its location on the east shore of Manistee Lake [Virginia S. Stroemel; PO Archives].

**EAST LANSING**, Ingham County: D. Robert Burcham became the first settler here in 1849; here in 1855, the world's first agricultural college was founded and named Michigan Agricultural College (renamed Michigan State College in 1925 and Michigan State University in 1955); Rev. Robert G. Baird, secretary of the college, became the first postmaster, with the post office named Agricultural College, on June 30, 1884; the community which grew up around the college was known as Collegeville, and its plat was so recorded in 1887; on Aug. 26, 1907, college and community were renamed East Lansing, it being located east of Lansing; incorporated as a city in 1907 [Federal; Cole; PO Archives].

**EAST LEROY**, Calhoun County: Ira Case bought the first land here in 1835, but David C. Fish became the first permanent settler in 1836; his wife suggested the name in honor of their first-born son, LeRoy Fish, when the township was set off in 1837; a marsh through it caused the two sections to be called East Leroy and West Leroy; a post office in East

Leroy was opened under the name Secillia, with William H. Gilles as its first postmaster, on June 28, 1852; Jeremiah Drake became the first postmaster of East Leroy on Dec. 24, 1855; the office was closed on Nov. 6, 1871, but was restored from Jan. 6, 1872, to Nov. 25, 1872; the Secillia post office was renamed East Leroy in 1874 [Everts; PO Archives].

**EASTMANVILLE,** Ottawa County: first settled by Dr. George W. Scranton in 1835; in that year, Dr. Timothy Eastman came from Maine to Grand Haven and located near Dr. Scranton in 1842; some improvements had been made here and the place was called Scranton as was its post office which was opened on July 11, 1838, with Dr. Scranton as its first postmaster, but the office was closed on March 18, 1842; in 1845, Dr. Eastman organized the town of Polkton, naming it for the then president, James K. Polk; he became the first postmaster of Polkton on May 28, 1846; together with his sons, Galen and Mason, he platted the village in 1855, naming it Eastmanville, and on March 8, 1856, the Polkton post office was changed to Eastmanville [MPH 39:420 1915; PO Archives].

**EAST MARION,** Livingston County: this post office in eastern Marion Township was opened on July 5, 1849, and operated until Nov. 12, 1856 [PO Archives].

**EAST MILAN,** Monroe County. See Azalia.

**EAST MUNISING,** Alger County. See Munising.

**EAST MUSKEGON,** Muskegon County: David W. Squier became its first postmaster on July 27, 1857, with the office in Ottawa County until Muskegon County was organized in 1859; the office operated until May 21, 1860 [GSM 1865; PO Archives].

**EAST NANKIN,** Wayne County: a sawmill settlement in eastern Nankin Township; general storekeeper Francis Stringer became its first postmaster on Oct. 1, 1857; the office was closed on Jan. 9, 1858, but was restored on Jan. 23, 1858 [GSM 1860; PO Archives].

**EAST OGDEN,** Lenawee County: John P. Hubbard became the first postmaster of this rural post office in eastern Ogden Township on Oct. 10, 1843, the office operating until May 22, 1867 [PO Archives].

**EASTON,** Ionia County: first settled in 1833 by Alfred Cornell, Sr., and his family; Thomas Cornell, son of Alfred, was elected supervisor when Easton Township was organized in 1843; William Dildine arrived from Elmira, N.Y., in 1843 and became the first postmaster on May 21, 1862; the office was closed on Nov. 8, 1871, but was restored from Jan. 30, 1872, to Sept. 4, 1872 [Schenck; PO Archives].

**EASTON,** Siawassee County: Milford A. Taylor became the first postmaster of this rural post office on Feb. 17, 1887, the office operating until April 30, 1903 [PO Archives].

**EAST ONONDAGA,** Ingham County: Buell Buckland became the first postmaster of this rural post office in eastern Onondaga Township in

1838; in the early 1840s, ownership of much of the land passed from the federal government to the Farmers' Loan & Trust Company, of New York City, which resold it to speculators and homesteaders, among the latter, Adney Hunt in 1845 [Adams].

**EAST PARIS**, Kent County: the first settlers in the area were Barney Burton, James Vanderpool, and the Guild brothers, Edward, Joel and Daniel, all in 1833; Paris Township was organized in 1839 and this village was named from its location in it; Abraham C. Barclay became its first postmaster on June 4, 1875, the office operating until March 15, 1914 [Paul Kempter; Dillenback; PO Archives].

**EASTPORT**, Antrim County: woodsman Murdock Andress became the first settler here in 1863; Mr. Phillips followed with a hotel in 1869; given a post office named Wilson on March 29, 1872, it was renamed Eastport on Sept. 8, 1873, with Andrew Mudge as postmaster; Cicero Newell and L. G. Wilcox built a mill and a dock directly east across Grand Traverse Bay from Northport, hence the name Eastport; this bay shore project was abandoned and the village began at the head of Torch Lake, but retained the name of Eastport [PO Archives; Powers].

**EAST PORTAGE**, Jackson County. See Waterloo.

**EAST RAISIN**, Lenawee County: Noah Norton became the first settler in the area in 1825; emigration flowed into eastern Raisin Township in 1831 and the village of East Raisin developed; see Raisinville for the name [Whitney].

**EAST RAISINVILLE**, Monroe County: here in Raisinville Township, Samuel Atkinson became the first postmaster of a post office named Atkinson after him on May 22, 1829; the office was renamed East Raisinville on Jan. 20, 1838, but was closed on Nov. 24, 1868; a station on the Lake Shore & Michigan Southern Railroad; see Raisinville for the name [GSM 1860-70; PO Archives].

**EAST RIVERTON**, Mason County: settled in 1863; given a post office named Indiantown on Aug. 25, 1865, with Samuel Hull as its first postmaster, renamed from its location in Riverton Township, on Aug. 16, 1875, but closed on Jan. 27, 1888 [GSM 1879; PO Archives].

**EAST SAGINAW**, Saginaw County. See Saginaw.

**EAST SAINT JOSEPH**, St. Joseph County: H. Adams platted and recorded this village on the banks of the St. Joseph River in 1835; it was declared vacant by a special Act of the legislature in 1850 [Mich Hist 4:589 1920].

**EAST SAUGATUCK**, Allegan County: this village on the Chicago & Northwestern (now Pere Marquette) Railroad was first settled about 1859, and from 1867, almost exclusively by Hollanders; storekeeper Warner C. Semple became its first postmaster on Feb. 24, 1874, the office operating until Dec. 30, 1965; named from its being east of the village of Saugatuck [Johnson; Thomas; PO Archives].

**EAST SIDE**, Alpena County: Mrs. Ellen Roberts became its first postmaster on Jan. 6, 1875, the office operating until Jan. 24, 1881; named from its being to the east of the city of Alpena [MPH 6:200 1883; PO Archives].

**EAST SPRINGPORT**, Jackson County: this rural post office in eastern Springport Township was opened on Jan. 26, 1874, with John A. Fish as its first postmaster, the office operating until June 2, 1900 [GSM 1875; PO Archives].

**EAST TAWAS**, Iosco County: a western New York firm, Smith, Van Valkenburg & Company, was interested in Michigan pine; Henry Perkins Smith, senior member of the firm, sent his son George P. here in 1862, and he became the father of the town; Christopher C. Parker was appointed its first postmaster on April 15, 1867; given a station on the Detroit & Mackinaw Railroad; incorporated as a village in 1887 and as a city in 1895; it absorbed Tawas Beach in 1922; named from its being east of older Tawas City [Richard L. Price, PM].

**EAST THETFORD**, Genesee County. See Thetford.

**EAST TRAVERSE BAY**, Grand Traverse County. See East Bay.

**EAST UNADILLA**, Livingston County: this village, named from its location in Unadilla Township, was platted by Richard Peterson, Jr., in 1837, and recorded in 1840 by Robert Glenn and Thomas G. Sill, the latter the administrator of the estate of John Drake [Ellis].

**EAST UNION**, Macomb County: Daniel Shattuck became the first postmaster of this rural post office on Jan. 10, 1856, the office operating until Nov. 4, 1864 [PO Archives].

**EAST WALTON**, Eaton County: this rural post office, named from its location in Walton Township, was opened on April 3, 1866, with Gabriel D. Wickham as its first postmaster, the office operating until Jan. 27, 1870 [Durant; PO Archives].

**EAST WHITE LAKE**, Oakland County: Charles Smith became the first postmaster of this rural post office in eastern White Lake Township, on July 29, 1846, the office operating until March 11, 1850 [PO Archives].

**EAST WINDSOR**, Eaton County: George Cheney and Rev. McCarty, a Baptist minister, were among the first postmasters of this rural post office opened about 1860 in eastern Windsor Township; the office was transferred to Dimondale on July 3, 1872 [Reo A. Goff].

**EASTWOOD**, Saginaw County: named for farmer Edward A. Eastwood who became the first postmaster of this coal mining settlement in Swan Creek Township on July 19, 1881, the office operating until Feb. 15, 1914 [GSM 1883; Federal; PO Archives].

**EAST YPSILANTI**, Washtenaw County: in 1841, the village of Ypsilanti was divided into two wards; in 1844, in a dispute over the distribution of taxes for improvements, the ward comprising that part of the village east of the Huron River set itself off from the village and soon afterward was organized into a village called East Ypsilanti; but when the city of Ypsilanti was incorporated in 1858, East Ypsilanti became a part of it [Beakes].

**EASY**, Tuscola County. See Silverwood.

**EATON**, Eaton County: William Southworth became the first postmaster of this rural post office on Feb. 27, 1839, the office operating until Nov. 12, 1856 [PO Archives].

**EATON**, Otsego County. See Elmira.

**EATON CENTRE**, Eaton County. See Charlotte.

**EATON MILLS**, Washtenaw County: this lumber settlement in Augusta Township was given a post office on June 24, 1878, with James H. Sherman as its first postmaster, the office operating until Sept. 30, 1879 [GSM 1881; PO Archives].

**EATON RAPIDS**, Eaton County: platted in 1838 by Amos and Pierpont E. Spicer, Benjamin Knight, Samuel Hamlin and C. C. Darling, all from Ohio; Mr. Knight became the first postmaster on Sept. 27, 1838; incorporated as a village by the supervisors in 1859 and by the legislature in 1871; incorporated as a city in 1881; named from the rapids of the nearby Grand River and from the county, which had been named for John H. Eaton, secretary of war in Andrew Jackson's cabinet [Strange; MPH 22:505 1893].

**EATON RAPIDS JUNCTION**, Jackson County. See Rives Junction.

**EAU CLAIRE**, Berrien County: Martin Reese migrated here from New England about 1850, homesteading on virgin forest; in 1861, William Smyth Farmer and R. J. Tulle, supervisor, applied for a post office which Mr. Farmer named for a sparkling creek nearby (French for clear water); Henry Buch became its first postmaster on Nov. 7, 1861; incorporated as a village in 1891 [PM; PO Archives].

**EBEN JUNCTION**, Alger County: a station at the junction of the Minneapolis, St. Paul & Sault Ste. Marie and the Munising Railway; Emil Hoppe became the first postmaster of this Finnish village in Rock River Township on Aug. 1, 1908; on some maps simply as Eben [Federal; GSM 1911].

**ECHO**, Antrim County: Hilam C. Scofield, a Baptist minister, became the first postmaster of this rural post office, named after its township, on May 10, 1877; the office was closed on Jan. 7, 1879, but was restored from March 4, 1879, to July 31, 1905 [Blinn; PO Archives].

**ECKERMAN**, Chippewa County: founded and named by Mr. Eckerman, a timber jobber, in 1889; Carlos D. Lincoln became its first postmaster on Sept. of that year, succeeded by Luther Rogers in 1892; a station on the Duluth, South Shore & Atlantic Railway [PM].

**ECKERT**, Washtenaw County: this rural post office in Freedom Township was named for grocer Frederick Eckert who became its first postmaster on Oct. 7, 1893, the office operating until Aug. 31, 1901 [GSM 1895; PO Archives].

**ECKFORD**, Calhoun County: first settled by Oshea Wilder, a surveyor from Rochester, N.Y., in 1832; he named it for Henry Eckford, a friend who had met while traveling in England; Mr. Wilder platted the village, first called Lower Eckford, in 1834, and he became the first postmaster, with the office named Eckford, on May 7, 1834; the office was closed on Jan. 11, 1859, but was restored from Nov. 20, 1884, to June 15, 1934; nearby Wilder Creek was named for him as was Wilder's Prairie [Everts; Mich Hist 33:229 1949; PO Archives].

**ECO CITY**, Oakland County: a settlement located at Woodward Avenue and 14 Mile Road, in Bloomfield Township, in 1922 [GSM 1923].

**ECORSE**, Wayne County: about 1795, the French made a settlement here on the Rivière aux Ecorces (Bark Creek: the Indians procured birch bark along its banks to make their wigwams and canoes); its post office, always named Ecorse, was opened on Oct. 29, 1827, with Daniel Goodell as its first postmaster; the office was closed on July 28, 1842, but was restored, with David LeBlanc as postmaster, on June 21, 1850; it was closed again on Feb. 21, 1857, but was restored permanently on Sept. 26, 1863, with Alexis M. Salliotte as the new postmaster; the village was first platted for Alexis Labadie, Simeon Rousseau, L. Bourassau, and P. White, in 1836, and recorded as Grandport; incorporated as the village of Ecorse in 1903 and as a city in 1941; some early maps and records spell it Ecorce [Burton; PO Archives].

**EDDYS**, Arenac County: this flag station on the Michigan Central Railroad, two miles from Standish, was in Bay County until Arenac was organized in 1883; named for Mr. Eddy, of Maine, a lumberman who made a fortune in timber in this area [GSM 1883].

**EDEN**, Ingham County: Almon M. Chapin settled here in Vevay Township in 1843 and when the railroad came through in 1874, the depot carried the name Chapin's Station; but since Judson W. Hopkins became its first postmaster on June 7, 1843, the post office has been named Eden, and the Michigan Central depot was renamed Eden; named from the fertility of the soil in the area [Foster; PO Archives].

**EDEN**, Lake County. See Willville.

**EDENVILLE**, Midland County: Jacob Bailey, of New York, and Charles Taylor, of Chicago, had first titles to the land, though they never lived here in what was then known as The Forks; at that time, transient workers in nearby lumber camps lived here; its early settlers are considered its founders (Sylvester Erivay came in 1854, Aaron Havens, David Burton and Daniel Bowman in 1855, and Alvin Marsh in 1859); the village was then called Sixteen from its location (Sec. 1, township 16 range 1 west); when given a post office on March 16, 1668, Henry Church, the first postmaster, named it Edenville because of its natural beauty; he also platted the village in 1878 [Harry R. Stone, PM; Chapman].

**EDGEL,** Van Buren County: this rural post office was named for storekeeper George Edgel who became its first postmaster on Jan. 3, 1881, the office operating until Feb. 19, 1884 [GSM 1883; PO Archives].

**EDGEMERE,** Houghton County: the stamp mill of the Adventure Consolidated Mining Company opened here in 1902; located on Lake Superior, the name means by the sea [Sawyer].

**EDGERTON,** Kent County: Andrew House platted this village in Algoma Township when the Grand Rapids & Indiana Railroad came through and built a station here, and he became its first postmaster on Jan. 25, 1869, the office operating until April 15, 1937; poetess Julia A. Moore, "the sweet singer of Michigan," was a pioneer storekeeper here; the Edgertons were early settlers and landowners in the area; the place was also called Port Hollow [Dillenback; Chapman; PO Archives].

**EDGETTS,** Lake County: this lumber settlement in Ellsworth Township was given a station on the Manistee & Grand Rapids Railroad; storekeeper Lewis Wenzel became its first postmaster on July 22, 1902 [GSM 1903].

**EDGEWATER,** Benzie County: a settlement around the mill and general store of the Platte Lumber Company; its manager, Alex M. Richey, became its first postmaster on Feb. 23, 1888, succeeded by John Little, on Sept. 17, 1891, the office operating until March 15, 1910; named from its location by the Platte River [GSM 1889-1910; PO Archives].

**EDGEWOOD,** Gratiot County: this village in Hamilton Township is believed to have been founded by Philander Sisson who built and ran a general store here in 1867; its post office, opened on Dec. 23, 1867, with William Barton as its first postmaster, was named Bad River, but was changed to Edgewood on Jan. 26, 1874, the office operating until Dec. 14, 1904 [Mrs. Carew S. LeBlanc; PO Archives].

**EDINBURGH,** Hillsdale County. See Perrinburgh.

**EDMORE,** Montcalm County: this village in Home Township was founded and platted by a real estate man, Edwin B. Moore, in 1878, and given a contraction of his name; Abraham West became its first postmaster on July 22, 1878; its station on the Detroit, Lansing & Northern Railroad was called Edmore Junction; incorporated as a village in 1879, with Mr. Moore as its first president [Clio M. Stinson].

**EDNA,** Montcalm County. See Hiram.

**EDNA,** Roscommon County. See Prudenville.

**EDSON,** Iosco County: this rural post office was named for Edson M. Raymond who became its first postmaster on July 20, 1897, the office operating until May 31, 1905 [PO Archives].

**EDSON CORNERS**, Missaukee County: this hamlet on the Big Muskegon River in Reeder Township was named for Edson Witherell who became its first postmaster on Aug. 21, 1878, the office operating until March 15, 1900 [GSM 1879-1901; PO Archives].

**EDWARD**, Ogemaw County: Richard M. Moore became the first postmaster of this rural post office on Feb. 7, 1895, the office operating until Jan. 30, 1904 [PO Archives].

**EDWARDS**, Delta County: platted in 1900; the Escanaba & Lake Superior Railroad ran through it and the Wolverine Cedar & Lumber Company had their headquarters here [David S. Coon].

**EDWARDSBURG**, Cass County: first settled by Ezra Beardsley and called Beardsley's Prairie; founded and named by the county's first merchant, Thomas H. Edwards, in 1828, Mr. Edwards became the first postmaster of Saint Joseph's on Dec. 4, 1828, with the office renamed Edwardsburgh, on Feb. 1, 1830; it was later closed and then restored on Aug. 23, 1841, with Henry A. Chapin as postmaster; the spelling was changed to Edwardsburg on Dec. 29, 1845; platted by Alexander H. Edwards in 1831; incorporated as a village in 1911 [MPH 18:610 1891; Mich Hist 31:282 1947; PO Archives].

**EDWIN**, Delta County: Isaac Papineau became the first postmaster of this rural post office on May 7, 1894, the office operating until Jan. 31, 1901 [PO Archives].

**EGBERT**, Midland County: Elizabeth Gingrich became the first postmaster of this rural post office, 5 miles north of Sanford, on Feb. 8, 1900, the office operating until June 30, 1908 [PO Archives; GSM 1901].

**EGGLESTON**, Muskegon County: the township was organized in the home of William Sturdefant, one of the petitioners, in 1859; Adna Eggleston (in some sources Egelston), for whom it was named, was elected supervisor annually from 1859 to 1873 [Page; GSM 1865].

**EGLESTON**, Emmet County. See Van.

**EGYPT**, Kent County. See Chapel.

**EGYPT**, Mason County: Frederick King became the first postmaster of this rural post office on Dec. 20, 1882, the office operating until June 16, 1884 [PO Archives].

**EIGHT FOOT GRADE**, St. Clair County: a station on the Port Huron & Northwestern Railroad in 1886 [GSM 1887].

**EKLUND**, Schoolcraft County. See Walsh.

**ELBA**, Gratiot County: first settled by William and Daniel Call; when organized in 1856, the township was named by its first supervisor, Hanson Sinclair [Chapman].

**ELBA**, Lapeer County: Hozial Howland and his son Ira, natives of Rhode Island, became the first settlers in the area in 1835; Elba Township was organized in 1838 and this village, founded in 1871, was named after it; storekeeper John Winship became its first postmaster on Dec. 26, 1871, the office operating until Sept. 30, 1941; a station on the Grand Trunk Railroad [Margaret Caffall; Page; GSM 1879; PO Archives].

**ELBA**, Washtenaw County: Alanson H. Squire became the first postmaster of this hamlet in Manchester Township on May 7, 1834, the office operating until Feb. 15, 1853 [Cole].

**ELBERTA**, Benzie County: the first white settler here, John Greenwood, came in 1855; George M. Cartwright recorded the first plat in 1866 as Frankfort City, and it was given a post office as South Frankfort on April 10, 1872, with George A. Douglass as its first postmaster; the name Frankfort was applied to the general harbor area; later, the present city of Frankfort occupied the north half, while Elberta occupied the south half; incorporated as the village of South Frankfort in 1894; on June 1, 1911, the name was changed to that of the locally popular and plentiful Elberta peach [Allen Babcock; PO Archives].

**ELBRIDGE**, Oceana County: part of the Indian Reservation under the Treaty of 1855; Elbridge Township was cut off from Benona in 1858 and named for Elbridge R. Farmer; J. R. Mooney built the first frame building in the town in 1860; the village was given a post office on Nov. 2, 1883, with William J. Tennant as its first postmaster, the office operating until March 31, 1905; site of the Cobmoosa Monument [Royal; PO Archives].

**ELDORADO**, Crawford County: to serve a scattered settlement here, a post office named Jack Pine was opened, 1885-1898, with William Edwards as postmaster, then re-opened as Jackpine, 1898-1908, with George Hartman as postmaster, and finally, by petition of its patrons, as Eldorado, with Ivory R. Gale as postmaster, 1908-1911, James F. Crane, 1911-1923, and Grace L. Funsch, 1923-1952, when she retired and the office was closed; pioneer settlers were George and Henry Hartman, William Edwards, George Funsch; El Dorado means place of wealth, here lumber; jack pine was a smaller and scrubbier variety of pine than white pine or Norway (sometimes called red) pine [Grace L. Funsch].

**ELDRED**, Jackson County: this village in Napoleon Township began with a station on the Lake Shore & Michigan Southern Railroad in 1878; Grace V. Chapman became its first postmaster on Oct. 9, 1889, the office operating until June 30, 1902; believed to have been named for Andrew Eldred, Michigan congressman, 1879-80 [Dunbar; GSM 1879; PO Archives].

**ELGIN**, Antrim County: George H. Wealch became the first postmaster of this rural post office in Milton Township on Sept. 1, 1875, the office operating until Dec. 15, 1881 [GSM 1877-83; PO Archives].

**ELGIN**, Genesee County: William Moore became the first postmaster of this, the first post office established in Mundy Township, on March 9, 1855, the office operating until April 12, 1871 [Ellis; PO Archives].

**ELGIN**, Ottawa County: John Rose became the first postmaster of this rural post office on Aug. 20, 1886, succeeded by Clarence E. Dudley on Sept. 7, 1893, the office operating until May 31, 1902 [PO Archives].

**ELIZABETH LAKE**, Oakland County: a resort community beside the lake named for the wife of Governor Lewis Cass, after he made a tour of inspection of the area in 1818; the first post office in the township (Waterford) was opened here, under the name Lake Elizabeth, on May 2, 1835, with William Terry as its first postmaster; the office was transferred to Waterford Centre on July 13, 1841 [Seeley; Ripley; PO Archives].

**ELIZABETH PARK**, Wayne County. See Slocum's Island.

**ELIZABETHTOWN**, Huron County. See Caseville.

**ELK**, Genesee County: Horatio W. Felt became the first postmaster of this rural post office on July 2, 1857, the office operating until Oct. 14, 1903; it operated for a time in Maple Grove Township, Saginaw County [PO Archives].

**ELK GROVE**, Iowa County: when Justus DeSeelhorst became the first postmaster of this rural post office on Sept. 17, 1831, it was in Michigan Territory; now in Wisconsin [PO Archives].

**ELK LAKE**, Lapeer County. See Attica.

**ELKLAND**, Tuscola County: a post office in deer country, named after its township, with John Anyon becoming its first postmaster on May 31, 1862 [GSM 1860-77; PO Archives].

**ELK RAPIDS**, Antrim County: in 1848, Connecticut-born Abram S. Wadsworth built his cabin here, the first white man's home in the county; he platted the village in 1852 and named it Stevens; in 1858, he renamed it from his having found a pair of elk horns in the sand at the mouth of the river; Theron Bostwick became the first postmaster of Stevens on March 31, 1854, renamed Elk Rapids on Aug. 30, 1858; a station on the Chicago & Western Michigan (now Pere Marquette) Railroad; incorporated as a village in 1900 [Powers; PO Archives].

**ELKTON**, Huron County: first known as Oliver Center, from its location in Oliver Township (named for pioneer settler John Oliver) when organized in 1877; the village was founded in 1886 by W. J. McGillivray, a blacksmith, who built the first house here; he named it to commemorate his killing a huge elk entangled in his wife's clothesline; Simon Hoffman became the first postmaster on Nov. 24, 1886; a station on the Saginaw, Tuscola & Huron Railroad; incorporated as a village in 1897 [Edward A. Bumhoffer; PO Archives; Chapman].

**ELLAKE**, Iosco County. See Long Lake.

**ELLAVILLE**, Isabella County: hotel proprietor Alexander R. Bush became the first postmaster of this rural post office in Vernon Township on April 16, 1878, with its name evidently derived from its county, the office operating until Feb. 24, 1879 [GSM 1879; PO Archives].

**ELLINGTON**, Tuscola County: when the township was being organized in 1855, Simeon Botsford was chosen to present the name of Eden, with Paradise as second choice, to the supervisors, but they rejected both and, for no known reason, named it Ellington; Inman J. B. McKenney became its first postmaster on May 31, 1862, the office operating until May 31, 1905 [J. A. Gallery].

**ELLIOTT**, St. Clair County: Conrad Feiger became the first postmaster of this rural post office on Feb. 25, 1889, the office operating until Sept. 30, 1903 [PO Archives].

**ELLIS**, Calhoun County: Lafayette C. Williams became the first postmaster of this rural post office in Fredonia Township on March 31, 1882, the office operating until July 31, 1901 [GSM 1883; PO Archives].

**ELLISVILLE**, Cheboygan County. See Afton.

**ELLISVILLE**, Wayne County: a hamlet in Sumpter Township, six miles west of Waltz, in 1878 [GSM 1879].

**ELLSWORTH**, Antrim County: founded in 1881 by Erwin A. Dean and his nephew, August Davis; Lewis A. DeLine became its first postmaster on Feb. 1, 1884, serving until 1891 (the new village and post office included the small settlements of Needmore and Ox Bow); named by Mr. DeLine who had served under Colonel Ephraim Elmer Ellsworth, the first Union officer killed in the Civil War; incorporated as a village in 1938 [Mrs. John Timmer].

**ELLSWORTH**, Lake County: this village, named after its township, was first settled in 1867; Samuel Balzell became its first postmaster on May 2, 1872, the office operating until Dec. 5, 1876; the township was named for Ephraim Elmer Ellsworth, commander of the New York Zouaves, killed while they served with the First Michigan Infantry Regiment at Alexandria in 1862 [GSM 1875; PO Archives].

**ELM**, Wayne County. See Elmwood.

**ELM CREEK**, Lapeer County: Elias B. Van Marter became the first postmaster of this rural post office in Deerfield Township on Nov. 7, 1873, the office operating until Feb. 12, 1875 [GSM 1879; PO Archives].

**ELMDALE**, Ionia County: this village at the Kent County line was given a station on the Detroit, Grand Rapids & Western Railroad and, on Jan. 28, 1889, a post office, with Leonard E. Lott as its first postmaster, the office operating until May 15, 1940 [Mich Manual 1899; PO Archives].

**ELMER**, Sanilac County: the first settler in the area, Walter Hyslop, came in January, 1866, and that year and the next there was quite an immigration; given a schoolhouse in 1869; the village was named after the township which had been organized in 1870 and of which S. P. Davis became the first supervisor, 1870-71, and Mr. Hyslop the second, 1872-75; William Essery became its first postmaster on Jan. 31, 1876, the office operating until June 30, 1906 [Chapman; PO Archives].

**ELM GROVE,** Isabella County: platted across the tracks from the Rosebush depot in 1894; it is what its name indicates, elm bottom lands [Fancher].

**ELM HALL,** Gratiot County: the first settlers here in Sumner Township were three brothers, Michael, Nathaniel and Jacob Strayer, and their wives, and Mr. and Mrs. Baron Blanchard, all coming in 1855; the Strayers lived in a long building or hall made of elm logs, and hence the name of the village; Baron Blanchard became its first postmaster on Aug. 18, 1857; the village was platted and recorded in 1863 [Mrs. Winnie Story, ret. PM].

**ELMIRA,** Eaton County: Joseph Norstraut became the first postmaster of this rural post office on Feb. 14, 1855, the office operating until May 1, 1871 [PO Archives].

**ELMIRA,** Otsego County: when the Grand Rapids & Indiana Railroad came through in 1877 the station here was called Eaton; the village was platted and recorded as Windsor on Sept. 4, 1880; hotelman William S. Hartwell became the first postmaster on Sept. 3, 1877, with the office named Elmira, after its township [GSM 1883; PO Archives].

**ELM RIVER,** Houghton County: the Elm River Copper Company was organized in 1899 and began work on its 2,360 acres immediately; feed waters for its boilers came from a dam across the head waters of the Elm River; in 1900, it was given a station on the Copper Range Railroad, and on March 8, 1900, a post office spelled Elmriver, with Dominic W. Sutter as its first postmaster, the office operating until Sept. 14, 1907 [Stevens; GSM 1901; PO Archives].

**ELM ROCK,** Leelanau County: storekeeper Mrs. Eliza Willobee became the first postmaster of this rural post office in Elmwood Township on Jan. 17, 1879, the office operating until Sept. 20, 1883 [GSM 1881; PO Archives].

**ELMWOOD,** Iron County: when opened in 1887, this depot on the Chicago & Northwestern Railroad was named Paint River, it being near the Paint River; given a post office as Paint River on Nov. 15, 1887, with John F. Brenvel as its first postmaster; the spelling was changed to Paintriver on Feb. 8, 1895, but the office was closed on July 31, 1901; the station was renamed Elmwood by 1898 [GSM 1889; PO Archives].

**ELMWOOD,** Oceana County: Charles Willett and his family became the first settlers here in eastern Crystal Township in 1873 and around his shingle mill the settlement formed; he and A. O. Aldrich built the first school in 1876; named from its location [Royal].

**ELMWOOD,** Tuscola County: Elijah S. White became its first settler in 1855; the township was organized as Waterloo in 1860 and renamed Elmwood by the legislature in 1863; John C. Laing became the first postmaster on May 31, 1862; the office was closed on June 1, 1868, but was restored from Dec. 18, 1871, to June 23, 1873, and from Feb. 25, 1874, to May 31, 1905 [Page; PO Archives].

**ELMWOOD**, Wayne County: the Detroit, Lansing & Northern Railroad depot here in Livonia Township was called McKinney's Station, and its post office was named Elm; Henry Battenburg became its first postmaster on June 30, 1858, the office operating until Sept. 17, 1906 [GSM 1879; PO Archives].

**ELMWOOD VILLAGE**, Leelanau County: a settlement around the Elmwood Manufacturing Company lumber mill, 1½ miles from Traverse City, in 1890 [GSM 1891].

**ELO**, Houghton County: this village in Portage Township was settled in 1900; Albert Karry became its first postmaster on Dec. 23, 1908, succeeded by storekeeper Samuel J. Mattila in 1910, the office operating until Oct. 31, 1957 [GSM 1913; PO Archives].

**ELOISE**, Wayne County: the home for the poor for which the county voted in 1832 was moved from Gratiot Road to Nankin Township in 1839; it was known as the Wayne County Almshouse until given a post office on July 9, 1894, as Eloise after the little daughter of Freeman B. Dickerson, chairman of the board; the bookkeeper of the institution, Stanislaus M. Keenan, was its first postmaster; a station on the Michigan Central Railroad; its legal name is Eloise Infirmary, Sanitorium and Hospital, and comprises 435 acres and more than 50 buildings; it was renamed Wayne County General Hospital in 1945 but its post office is still Eloise [Burton; PO Archives].

**ELSIE**, Clinton County: Job Durkee Sickles, from Palmyra, N.Y., founded the village and recorded its plat in 1857; it was named for the first child born in it, the daughter of Frank Tillotson, who became the first postmaster on May 14, 1857; incorporated as a village in 1885 [Neva Keys; Daboll].

**ELTON**, Wexford County: James L. Falton became the first postmaster of this rural post office, 8 miles from Cadillac, on July 6, 1897, the office operating until Sept. 30, 1907; it would seem to have been derived from the first postmaster's name [GSM 1899-1907; PO Archives].

**ELVA**, Tuscola County: Horace H. Crosby became the first postmaster of this rural post office in Arbela Township on Jan. 3, 1873, the office operating until Sept. 30, 1903 [Pen Phil 6:3 Oct 1955].

**ELWELL**, Gratiot County: founded about 1877; George O. Adams became its first postmaster on April 15, 1880; platted and recorded by order of the Seville Township board in 1911; named for Colonel John A. Elwell, of St. Louis, Michigan, who was instrumental in getting the Detroit, Lansing & Northern (now Pere Marquette) Railroad through it [Tucker].

**ELWOOD**, Oceana County: storekeeper Mrs. Dorothy A. Brown became its first postmaster on April 7, 1898, the office operating until May 31, 1901; its name was derived from its township of Elbridge and its principal product, it being a lumber settlement [GSM 1899; PO Archives].

**ELY**, Emmet County: this village in Center Township was settled in 1876 and named for state representative Heman D. Ely; Charles Cook became its first postmaster on Jan. 2, 1879, the office operating until May 31, 1908 [Mich Hist 13:7 1929].

**ELYTON**, Gratiot County. See Alma.

**EMBO**, Charlevoix County: this village was given a railroad station and on April 3, 1873, a post office, with Alexander Ross as its first postmaster, the office operating until Oct. 27, 1875 [GSM 185; PO Archives].

**EMERALD**, Mecosta County: storekeeper William Wilson became the first postmaster of this rural post office, 7½ miles from Evart, on April 15, 1898, the office operating until April 14, 1904 [GSM 1899; PO Archives].

**EMERSON**, Chippewa County: the settlement formed around the sawmill built of the Chesbrough Brothers, of Detroit, here on the Lake Superior shore in 1880; Fremont B. Chesbrough became its first postmaster on April 15, 1884; the mill closed in 1912, its post office on Feb. 15, 1914, but the town lingered on until 1915, and is now a fishing hamlet; named for a relative of the Chesbrough family [Wm. J. Chesbrough; GSM 1885; PO Archives].

**EMERSON**, Gratiot County: first settled by Isaiah Allen and his five sons, John Knight, Alanson Bailey, Melancthon Pettit, and others, in 1855; Mr. Pettit became the first supervisor when the township was organized in 1855; its name was derived, by accidental corruption, from William Imisson, an English-born pioneer settler [Chapman].

**EMERSON CENTER**, Gratiot County. See Beebe.

**EMERY**, Washtenaw County: first settled by Joshua G. Leland who came here from Madison County, N.Y., in 1831; named for his son, Emery Leland, who became supervisor of its township (Northfield) in 1875 and later the probate judge of its county; its station the Toledo, Ann Arbor & Northern Michigan Railroad was named Leland in 1884, but its post office, opened on Feb. 20, 1884, with David F. Barritt as its first postmaster, was named Emery; the office operated until March 31, 1903 [Beakes; GSM 1885; PO Archives].

**EMERY JUNCTION**, Iosco County. See National City.

**EMMETT**, Calhoun County: in 1839, the people of this township had the legislature change its name from Andover to Emmett, honoring Robert Emmett, the Irish patriot; Howell Sanford became its first postmaster on Aug. 15, 1846, the office operating until March 12, 1859 [Gardner; PO Archives].

**EMMETT**, St. Clair County: the township, named for Robert Emmett, the Irish patriot, was organized in 1850; its pioneers included Patrick Kennedy, Dennis Gleason, Patrick Fitzgerald, James Cogley, David Donahue, Henry P. McCabe; in 1856, Thomas Crowley platted part of his land as the village of Mount Crowley, though the area was very level; on

Dec. 13, 1869, Oel N. Sage became the first postmaster of Emmett, with the village soon afterward taking the same name; incorporated as a village in 1883 [Jenks; GSM 1865; PO Archives].

**EMPIRE**, Leelanau County: first settled by John LaRue and his family in 1851, and he became its first postmaster on Nov. 10, 1864; named after the schooner Empire which became icebound in its harbor in the winter of 1863; the vessel was then used as a schoolhouse; Empire developed into a lumber town and E. R. Dailey, manager of the Empire Lumber Company, became its first president when it was incorporated as a village in 1895 [Dickinson; Powers].

**ENGADINE**, Mackinac County: the village began as a lumber settlement called Kennedy Siding and was given a post office named Kennedy on Aug. 25, 1889, with Richard D. Conway as its first postmaster; the first railroad agent here was Sam Peterson, a native of Switzerland, and he had the name changed to Engadine, after a scenic Swiss valley, on Dec. 2, 1893 [Rita C. Fandrick, PM].

**ENGLE**, Huron County: this rural post office in Sigel Township was named for Theodore Engle who became its first postmaster on June 6, 1879, the office operating until May 2, 1887 [GSM 1879; PO Archives].

**ENGLISH**, Menominee County: settled in 1872 around the charcoal kilns of Robert O'Neil; its depot on the Chicago & Northwestern Railroad was first called Kloman; Henry H. Sterling became its first postmaster, with the office named English, on Feb. 18, 1875, and the office operated until May 23, 1895 [GSM 1879; PO Archives].

**ENGLISHVILLE**, Kent County: first settled in 1845 and named for Joseph S. English, landowner here in Alpine Township; its schoolhouse was built in 1852; given a post office on July 29, 1856; Richard S. English became its postmaster in 1876 [Dillenback; PO Archives].

**ENNIS**, Luce County: Robert Bryers became the first postmaster of this rural post office in Mackinac County when opened on Dec. 15, 1886; it was transferred to Luce in 1887 and closed on Aug. 4, 1888 [GSM 1889; PO Archives].

**ENSIGN**, Delta County: this village in Masonville Township was first settled by Edward P. Bennett about 1880 and named by him for the national emblem; given a station on the Minneapolis, St. Paul & Sault Ste. Marie Railroad in 1888; Cyrus Dunbar became its first postmaster on Sept. 18, 1890; the office was closed on May 9, 1894, but was later restored and has been operating since [Mrs. Blanche C. Papineau, PM; PO Archives].

**ENSLEY**, Montcalm County: it was in Newaygo County when Asa C. McConnell became the first postmaster of this rural post office on April 15, 1867; the office was closed on Sept. 11, 1867, but was restored from Dec. 30, 1867, to April 27, 1869, and from June 10, 1869; it was changed into Montcalm County on Feb. 14, 1898, but was closed on Sept. 14, 1903; see Ensley Center for the name [PO Archives].

**ENSLEY CENTER**, Newaygo County: Benjamin Ensley came in 1854 and opened a half-way house here on the state road between Grand Rapids and Grand Traverse; the township, organized in 1858, was named for him; storekeeper George F. Cook became the first postmaster of Ensley Center in 1882; also known as Ensley's Corners [Harry L. Spooner; GSM 1873].

**ENTERPRISE**, Shiawassee County: Otis Hicks became the first postmaster of this hamlet on Aug. 11, 1843, the office operating until Oct. 22, 1864 [PO Archives].

**ENTRICAN**, Montcalm County: named for George W. Entrican, among the first in the area to enlist in the Union Army; he was clerk of Douglass Township, 1879-80; Albert L. Entrican became the first postmaster on Nov. 12, 1887; the office was closed on Jan. 31, 1908, but was restored on Feb. 6, 1908 [Clio M. Stinson; PO Archives].

**EPOUFETTE**, Mackinac County: John R. McLeod, a government surveyor, found an Indian village here about 1848; Amable Goudreau began a commercial fishing business here in 1859, but it was not given a post office until lumbering operations started; Mr. McLeod became its first postmaster on Dec. 19, 1879; named by the early French settlers Epoufette, place of rest; some say it was because they believed that Father Jacques Marquette used its harbor as the first step on his trip down Lake Michigan from St. Ignace [Belle L. Bigelow, PM; Federal].

**EPSILON**, Emmet County: the village began with the Purchis family, from New York State, who built a grist mill here; William D. Purchis became the first postmaster on Oct. 5, 1882, the office operating until May 31, 1914; letters of the Greek alphabet were given as names to several Michigan post offices: Alpha, Delta, Sigma, Epsilon, etc. [Allen F. Purchis; PO Archives].

**EPSPORT**, Schoolcraft County. See Manistique.

**EPWORTH HEIGHTS**, Mason County: founded by the Epworth League of the Methodist Episcopal Church of Michigan in 1894; primarily for chatauqua programs and cultural art classes [Rose D. Hawley].

**ERIE**, Kent County: a village founded in 1836 at the confluence of the Thorn Apple and the Grand Rivers; given a stage coach post office in 1837 [GSM 1838].

**ERIE**, Monroe County: about 1790, French settlers moving south from Frenchtown (now Monroe) made clearings in the walnut stands behind the shores of Maumee Bay; the log church of the settlement was named St. Joseph sur la Baie Miami by Rev. Gabriel Richard who often used it between 1798 and 1820; the village, formed further inland, was given a post office as Bay Settlement on April 18, 1827, with Benoni M. Newkirk as its first postmaster; on March 5, 1835, his successor, Salmon Keeney, had the name changed to that of the township, which had been so named because it borders on Lake Erie [Wing; Mich Hist 39:499 1955; PO Archives].

**ERIN**, Kent County: Richard Giles became the first postmaster of this rural post office on Nov. 22, 1854 [PO Archives].

**ERIN**, Macomb County: the township was organized in 1837 as Orange, but there was soon afterward a large influx of Irish Catholic settlers and they had the name changed to Erin in 1843; with Leon Vernier as its first postmaster, the settlement was given a post office on Oct. 14, 1899, located in the Frazho store at Gratiot and 10½ (now Frazho) Roads, the office operating until only Jan. 31, 1900 [Leeson; PO Archives].

**ERROL**, Sanilac County. See Brown City.

**ESCANABA**, Delta County: the settlement was first called Sandy Point from its location on a sandy point jutting out into Little Bay de Noc; given a post office as Esconawba, with Alden Chandler as postmaster, on Dec. 7, 1853, changed to Flat Rock on June 28, 1864, restored to Esconawba on the same day, until changed to Escanaba on June 1, 1875; it was named the county seat in 1861; the Chicago & Northwestern Railroad began operations here in 1863 and built the first ore dock; the dock builder, R. A. Connolly, came later that year and built the first frame house, a hotel; the railroad was completed in 1865 and the first lighthouse in 1867; incorporated as a village in 1866 and as a city in 1883; named from the Chippewa word for flat rock, first given to the river which flows over a bed of flat rock and is the "rushing Esconawba" of Henry Longfellow's Hiawatha legend [Sawyer; PO Archives].

**ESCHOL**, St. Joseph County: Benjamin N. King and his wife Martha became the first settlers in 1832; platted by Charles B. Fitch and Asa Wetherbee in 1833, from a survey by John S. Barry; located on the east bank of the St. Joseph River, two miles south of Three Rivers, in Constantine Township; when its dam went out in 1840, and was not rebuilt, it became a ghost town [MPH 10:183 1886; Mich Hist 4:591 1920; Silliman].

**ESCONAWBA**, Delta County. See Escanaba.

**ESMOND**, Iosco County: this rural post office in Plainfield Township was named for Edward V. Esmond who became its first postmaster on July 14, 1886, the office operating until Jan. 17, 1889 [GSM 1887-91; PO Archives].

**ESMONDS CORNERS**, Calhoun County: this rural post office was named for Wright J. Esmond who became its first postmaster on July 27, 1839, the office operating until May 25, 1852 [PO Archives].

**ESSEX**, Antrim County: Henry Chamberlain became the first postmaster of this lumber settlement in Banks Township on May 23, 1900, the office operating until Sept. 14, 1904 [GSM 1901; PO Archives].

**ESSEX**, Clinton County: Timothy H. Pettit became the first postmaster of this rural post office in Essex Township on Jan. 29, 1844; the office was changed to Maple Rapids on Feb. 24, 1857, but the Essex post office was restored on June 30, 1858; the office was closed on May 29,

1865, but was restored again from June 22, 1869, to June 23, 1875 [PO Archives].

**ESSEXVILLE,** Bay County: first settled by Ransom P. Essex and his brother-in-law, Joseph Hudson in 1850; Mr. Essex first platted the village in 1867, and named it Essex; but the early settlers called it Essexville and it was given a post office with that name on Feb. 27, 1871, with William L. Ames as its first postmaster; he was soon succeeded by Mr. Essex who held the office until his death in 1874; the office was closed on Jan. 20, 1879, but was restored from Feb. 24, 1879, to date; incorporated as a village in 1883 and as a city in 1934 [Rita Ratajczak; Butterfield; PO Archives].

**ESTELLA,** Gratiot County. See Sumner.

**ESTEY,** Gladwin County: the Estey, Calkins & Oliver Lumber Mill was built here by 1891; Estey school was organized in 1891; Lafayette Denton became the first postmaster on March 5, 1894; but the village was discontinued in 1920 and again became a part of the township of Bentley, named for storekeeper and first (1892) supervisor, Murray Bentley [Ritchie; PO Archives].

**ESTHER,** Allegan County: Adam Reid became the first postmaster of this rural post office in Ganges Township on July 23, 1894, the office operating until Feb. 28, 1901 [PO Archives; GSM 1895].

**ESTRAL BEACH,** Monroe County: this resort settlement, near Newport, was incorporated as a village in 1925; estral is Spanish for star [Mich Manual 1959-60].

**ETNA,** Lapeer County: Harry F. Perkins became the first postmaster of this rural post office on Oct. 4, 1841, but the office was changed to Metamora on June 6, 1854 [PO Archives].

**EUCLID CENTER,** Berrien County. See Benton Heights.

**EUGENE,** Gratiot County: Eugene M. Terpening operated a four-corners store here in Arcada Township and became the first postmaster of the post office named for him on April 25, 1894, the office operating until April 30, 1902 [Tucker].

**EUREKA,** Clinton County: first settled by John Ferdon in 1836; he was a member of the Rochester Colony which founded Duplain, his land lying in both Duplain and Greenbush Townships; before platting, the place was known as Williamsport (for pioneer settler Clark Williams), Barrington (for another pioneer settler, J. A. Barrington), and Swizzletown (which suggests the inhabitants were bibulous); platted in 1857 by Isaac Eagles and Mr. Barrington who named it Greenbush after the township which had been given a post office of that name on Jan. 29, 1844, with Lyman M. Richmond as its first postmaster; on May 9, 1867, both post office and village were renamed Eureka, Greek for I have found it; Edward Stark gave it the new name as a place where he had found and others would find a fine place for doing business [Ellis; Daboll; PO Archives].

**EUREKA**, Montcalm County: the first settlers in the area were Stephen H. Warren and R. K. Divine, both New Yorkers, in 1843; Eureka Township was organized in 1850, and named by state representative A. L. Roof from the Greek for I have found it; Orpheus T. Nelson became the first postmaster on Nov. 22, 1854, the office operating until Sept. 18, 1858 [Schenck; PO Archives].

**EUREKA PLACE**, Montcalm County: a station on the Toledo, Saginaw & Muskegon Railroad, two miles east of Greenville, in 1894 [GSM 1895].

**EUSTIS**, Menominee County: a station on the Minneapolis, St. Paul & Sault Ste. Marie Railroad, in Spalding Township; August School became its first postmaster on Dec. 18, 1891, succeeded by storekeeper George W. DeLoughory in 1892; the office was closed on Nov. 16, 1896, but was restored from May 12, 1902, to July 15, 1912; now a hamlet [George Springer; GSM 1893; PO Archives].

**EVANS**, Kent County: the first settler in the area, now Courtland Township, was Barton Johnson in 1838; a station on the Toledo, Saginaw & Muskegon Railroad; George W. Morris became its first postmaster on May 3, 1888 [Paul F. Kempter; PO Archives].

**EVANS LAKE**, Lenawee County: storekeeper Edward L. Clapp became the first postmaster of this rural post office in Franklin Township on Aug. 23, 1890, the office operating until Sept. 15, 1900 [GSM 1893; PO Archives].

**EVART**, Osceola County: after serving in the Union Army in the Civil War, Perry Oliver Everts (commonly called Frank Everts) bought 80 acres and settled in the area; when the village came into being it was named for him (the secretary of the founding fathers' meeting misspelled his name and the misspelling was allowed to stand); Orlando R. Windsor became its first postmaster on Aug. 16, 1870; platted by James Kennedy and Delos A. Blodgett in 1872; incorporated as a village in 1872 and as a city in 1938 [Glen Hammond].

**EVELINE**, Charlevoix County: Harry Hammond became the first postmaster of this rural post office, named after its township, on Feb. 28, 1877 [GSM 1877; PO Archives].

**EVELYN**, Alger County. See Doty.

**EVENWOOD**, Muskegon County: a station on a branch of the Chicago & Western Michigan Railroad in 1886 [GSM 1887].

**EVERGREEN**, Montcalm County: settlement of the area began in 1848 with the sawmill of Fite Rossman; the township was erected in 1856 and named after the prevailing kinds of timber found in it [Dasef].

**EVERGREEN**, St. Clair County: Lewis A. Mosey became the first postmaster of this rural post office in Burtchville Township on April 14, 1884, the office operating until Feb. 26, 1886 [GSM 1885; PO Archives].

ERIE
Flour Mill – W. Delphey

FLAT ROCK
Res., Store & Hall - W.S. Morey

**EVERGREEN CENTER**, Sanilac County. See Shabonna.

**EWEN**, Ontonagon County: a logging camp in 1888; given a depot named Ewen Station, in 1889, on the Duluth, South Shore & Atlantic Railroad, and named for W. A. Ewen, treasurer of the road; given a post office named Ewen Station on Oct. 5, 1889, with Oscar H. Carus as its first postmaster; the name was shortened to Ewen on Sept. 19, 1894 [PM; GSM 1891; PO Archives].

**EXCELSIOR**, Kalkaska County: the first settlers were William H. Eckler, a farmer, and Harvey Wright, both in 1879, and the latter became the first postmaster on Nov. 20, 1879, with the office named after its township; he was succeeded by Lemings J. Eckler on Aug. 3, 1883, and William H. Eckler on Sept. 27, 1883, the office operating until Feb. 28, 1902 [Traverse; PO Archives].

**EXETER**, Monroe County: Henry Palmer became the first postmaster of this hamlet, named after its township, on July 6, 1840; the office was closed on June 28, 1842, but was restored from March 14, 1850, to Sept. 14, 1903 [GSM 1860; PO Archives].

**FABIUS**, St. Joseph County: Garrett Sickles and his family became the first permanent settlers in 1830; originally a part of White Pigeon Township, in 1832-33, the legislature set off what are now Fabius and Lockport into a separate township and named it Bucks after George Bucks, a pioneer Lockport settler; in 1840, Bucks was divided into Bucks and Lockport, and in 1841, the name of the former was changed to Fabius, and its first town government was formed; Thomas H. Boles became the first postmaster of Fabius on May 19, 1890, the office operating until Jan. 31, 1902 [Everts; PO Archives].

**FACTORYVILLE**, St. Joseph County: in 1839, Theodore Robinson and James Bishop built a sawmill here on Nottawa Creek in Leonidas Township; in 1842-43, William, Charles and Nathan Schofield built a woolen factory at the same place; the hamlet that gathered around these enterprises was called Factoryville; cabinet maker Henry Fredenburg became its first postmaster on Jan. 31, 1888, the office operating until April 30, 1907 [Everts; PO Archives].

**FAIRBANKS**, Oakland County. See Rice's.

**FAIRCHILD**, Macomb County: a station on the Rapid Railway System, in Chesterfield Township, 4½ miles north of Mount Clemens; storekeeper John Van Farowe became its first postmaster in 1906 [GSM 1907].

**FAIRDALE**, Lenawee County: Cornelius Milspaw became the first postmaster of this rural post office on Jan. 15, 1836, the office operating until only Dec. 29, 1836 [PO Archives].

**FAIRFAX**, St. Joseph County: this rural post office was opened on March 27, 1891, and named for its first postmaster, Robert W. Fair [PO Archives].

**FAIRFIELD,** Lenawee County: Moses, Orin, and Jacob Baker bought land here in 1831-32, and the settlement became known as Bakers' Corners; given a post office as Bakers on Jan. 29, 1835, with Orin Baker as its first postmaster, the office was renamed after its township on April 13, 1842 [Jeannette Roberts; Bonner; PO Archives].

**FAIRFIELD,** Oakland County. See Groveland.

**FAIRGROVE,** Tuscola County: the first settler in the area was Amasa Clay in 1852; he became the first postmaster of Fair Grove, located at Fair Grove Center, on June 29, 1857; when the railroad came through Fair Grove village in 1881, the office was moved to it, and was renamed Fairgrove on Jan. 10, 1894; incorporated as a village in 1901; named from a grove of trees that stood just west of the present village [Beatrice C. Wright, PM; Page; PO Archives].

**FAIR HAVEN,** St. Clair County: a French settlement, made before 1837, and named first after the stream beside it, the Rivière des Cygnes; American settlers translated the name, calling it Swan Creek, and it was given a post office named Swan Creek on Oct. 17, 1857, with Thomas C. DeLano as its first postmaster; on Feb. 11, 1862, it was renamed Fair Haven, a descriptive name, given it by Mr. Hathway, an original proprietor [Jenks; PO Archives].

**FAIRLAND,** Berrien County: a station on the Chicago & Western Michigan Railroad, in Berrien Township; Mrs. Leah Matthews became its first postmaster on July 21, 1885, the office operating until Jan. 20, 1906 [GSM 1887; PO Archives].

**FAIR PLAIN,** Berrien County: first called Heath Corners, after a local landowner; given a post office as Fairplain on April 14, 1898, with T. A. Young as its first postmaster, but it was rescinded on Sept. 26 of the same year; locally it is spelled Fairplain, but on most maps and records Fair Plain [Cunningham; PO Archives].

**FAIR PLAINS,** Montcalm County. See Amsden.

**FAIRPORT,** Delta County: began as a commercial fishing port in 1886 when a group of fishermen from St. Martin's Island settled here [David S. Coon].

**FAIRPORT,** Lenawee County: Alvin D. Rice became the first postmaster of this rural post office on Jan. 12, 1891, the office operating until April 10, 1912 [PO Archives].

**FAIRVIEW,** Mason County: this village in Summit Township was given a post office on Oct. 12, 1860, with William Quevillon as its first postmaster; the office was closed on June 11, 1874, but was restored from Dec. 15, 1875, to May 2, 1876 [Cole; PO Archives].

**FAIRVIEW,** Muskegon County: this district became part of the city of Muskegon in 1917 [Mich Hist 5:524 1921].

**FAIRVIEW,** Oscoda County: a station on the Au Sable & Northwestern Railroad; the village was founded by W. L. Bond; Alex Scott became its first postmaster on Aug. 24, 1883 [PM].

**FAIRVIEW,** Wayne County. See Grosse Pointe Park.

**FAITH,** Crawford County: Samuel H. Miller became the first postmaster of this rural post office on May 3, 1882, the office operating until May 3, 1883 [PO Archives].

**FAITHORN,** Menominee County: first settled in succession by four lumber firms: the Fence River Company, the Kirby, Carpenter Company, Ludington, Wells & Van Shaick, and Hamilton & Merriman; the town was named for J. Nathan Faithorn, an official of the Wisconsin & Michigan Railroad which came through here in 1894; its station, named Faithorn Junction, was the crossing point of the W. & M. and the Minneapolis, St. Paul & Sault Ste. Marie Railroads; its post office, named Faithorn, operated from March, 1905, to March 31, 1955 [Evelyn Bergen; PO Archives].

**FALCON,** Sanilac County. See Croswell.

**FALLASBURG,** Kent County: J. Wesley Fallas settled here in 1839 and built a grist mill in 1840; John M. Waters became the first postmaster of Fallasburgh, on Jan. 21, 1851, with the spelling changed to Fallasburg on July 29, 1893; the office was closed on Sept. 29, 1900, but was restored from Dec. 24, 1900, to April 30, 1901 [PO Archives; Dillenback; Mich Hist 15:267 1931].

**FALLS,** Ontonagon County: this rural post office was established on Dec. 2, 1895, but was never in operation, and was discontinued the following June 15 [PO Archives].

**FALMOUTH,** Missaukee County: this old lumbering settlement in Clam Union Township was first called Pen Hook; Eugene W. Watson became its first postmaster, with the office named Falmouth, on Dec. 18, 1871; it lost to Reeder (now Lake City) by one vote from being chosen the county seat in 1873; John Koopman built a store here in 1879, and in 1881, he bought the village plat along with its saw, shingle, and grist mill [Stout; PO Archives].

**FALSE PRESQUE ISLE,** Presque Isle County: a sparsely settled peninsula jutting into Lake Huron; Presque Isle is French for almost an island, namely, a peninsula [GSM 1879].

**FALSE PRESQUE ISLE HARBOR,** Presque Isle County. See Bell.

**FARGO,** St. Clair County: a station on the Port Huron & Northwestern Railroad, in Greenwood Township; named for local sawmill and grist mill owners, A. Farr & Sons; Charles P. Farr became its first postmaster on March 28, 1881, the office operating until March 31, 1959; the village was also known as Farrs [GSM 1885; PO Archives].

**FARLEIGH,** Bay County: the Farleigh family operated the grocery in this hamlet near Essexville [GSM 1919].

**FARLEY'S**, Berrien County: a flag station on the St. Joseph Valley Railroad in 1884 [GSM 1885].

**FARM**, Jackson County. See Portage Lake.

**FARMERS**, Sanilac County. See Carsonville.

**FARMERS CREEK**, Lapeer County: this village on the borderline between Hadley and Metamora Townships was named from the stream by which it is located; John L. Morse located land here in 1833, settling on it in 1834; John Look and his family also became settlers in 1834; Mr. Morse became the first postmaster on Jan. 3, 1836, the office operating until Sept. 30, 1903 [Page; PO Archives].

**FARMERSVILLE**, Washtenaw County. See Milan.

**FARMINGTON**, Oakland County: Arthur Power, with his son John, and David Smith, became the first settlers in 1824; they were Quakers and the settlement came to be called Quakertown; they were from Farmington, N.Y., and it was given a post office named Farmington, on Jan. 7, 1826, with Ezekiel Webb as its first postmaster; Elkanah Comstock who in 1824 became the first Baptist minister to settle and labor as a pastor in Michigan, organized the church here in 1826; Mr. Power built the first sawmill in 1825; incorporated as a village in 1867 and as a city in 1926 [MPH 4:419 1881; Mich Hist 30:750 1946; Seeley].

**FARNHAM**, Houghton County. See Withey.

**FARNHAM**, Menominee County: a station on the Minneapolis, St. Paul & Sault Ste. Marie Railroad, 7 miles east of Hermansville, in 1887 [GSM 1895].

**FARNSWORTH**, Wexford County. See Bagnall.

**FARO**, Houghton County. See Nisula.

**FAROWE**, Ottawa County: this rural post office, 3 miles from Hudsonville, was opened on March 9, 1892, and named for John Van Farowe who became its first postmaster, the office operating until Aug. 31, 1905 [GSM 1893-1907; PO Archives].

**FARRANDVILLE**, Genesee County: named for Ira T. Farrand, first known by tax records of 1844; consists of a Methodist church and some 15 other buildings [John K. McEvoy].

**FARRS**, St. Clair County. See Fargo.

**FARWELL**, Clare County: founded in 1870 by Edmund Hall, John Van Riper and George L. Hitchcock; platted on paper in 1871; platted and recorded by Josiah L. Littlefield, of Ann Arbor, in 1872; the Pere Marquette Railroad from Saginaw to Ludington was coming through here at the time and the town was named for Samuel Farwell who had an interest in the road and was the father-in-law of Mr. Potter, superintendent of the road; given a post office on Jan. 20, 1871, with Mr. Hitchcock as its first postmaster; the first county seat, 1871 to 1879; incorporated as a village in 1879; Littlefield Park is within the village and Littlefield Lake is ten miles southwest of it [Federal; Donald E. Smith].

**FAWN RIVER,** St. Joseph County: named after its township which was named from the stream meandering across its southern area; Captain Philip R. Toll located the first land here in 1836, built a sawmill that year and a grist mill the next, and had the village platted by John Kromer in 1837, but the plat was not recorded until 1852; Isaac D. Toll became the first postmaster on June 24, 1844, the office operating until Sept. 14, 1905; a station on the Lake Shore & Michigan Southern Railroad [Everts; PO Archives].

**FAUNUS,** Menominee County: a station on a branch of the Chicago & Northwestern Railroad in 1884; Charles W. Zastrow became its first postmaster on May 14, 1896, the office operating until Jan. 31, 1908; see Dryads for the name [GSM 1885; PO Archives].

**FAXON,** Branch County: Jennie David became the first postmaster of this rural post office in Butler Township on Feb. 20, 1893, the office operating until Dec. 31, 1900 [GSM 1895; PO Archives].

**FAY,** Saginaw County: James H. Waltermire became the first postmaster of this rural post office on Feb. 20, 1891, but the office was closed the following Aug. 10 [PO Archives].

**FAYETTE,** Delta County: named for Fayette Brown, of the Jackson Iron Company, which created this village in Fairbanks Township in 1867 while building a charcoal iron smelter; Marvin H. Brown became its first postmaster on Sept. 13, 1870; the furnace was dismantled in 1891; now a ghost town within Fayette State Park [Mich Hist 41:204 1957; Havighurst; Jean Worth].

**FAYMOUTH,** Saginaw County. See Taymouth.

**FAYVILLE,** Genesee County. See Thetford.

**FEATHER SETTLEMENT,** Berrien County: begun by a group of families from Pennsylvania in the 1830s, led by Joshua Feather, spelled Vedder until he settled here in Oronoko Township [Chauncey].

**FEDERMAN,** Monroe County: this village began as a station at the crossing of a branch of the Lake Shore & Michigan Southern and the Toledo, Ann Arbor & Northern Michigan Railroads in 1884; Jay Bates became its first postmaster on June 22, 1899, the office operating until Aug. 31, 1906 [GSM 1885-1907; PO Archives].

**FELCH,** Dickinson County: a station on the Chicago & Northwestern Railroad, in Felch Township, which had been named for Alpheus Felch, governor of Michigan in 1846; storekeeper Andrew Rian became its first postmaster on March 13, 1906 [GSM 1907; PO Archives].

**FELCH MOUNTAIN,** Dickinson County. See Metropolitan.

**FELT'S,** Ingham County: the area was first called Felt's Plains, the post office, Felt's; named for Dorman Felt who settled here in 1847; Alba Blake became the first postmaster on Sept. 19, 1851, the office operating until March 10, 1875 [Foster; PO Archives].

**FENMORE**, Saginaw County: Oliver D. Miller became the first postmaster of this rural post office in Chapin Township on April 11, 1899, the office operating until Oct. 14, 1904 [GSM 1901; PO Archives].

**FENNVILLE**, Allegan County: this, the first village in Clyde Township (named after Clyde, N.Y.), was settled in 1860 by Henry Blakslee who joined the Union Army in 1861 and was killed in action; Elam A. Fenn, in company with Levi Loomis, built a sawmill here in 1862; given a post office as Fenn's Mills, on Feb. 27, 1868, with Mr. Fenn as its first postmaster; the village was platted in 1871 by Emerson & Company who owned much of the land here, and its post office was renamed Fennville on Sept. 27 of the same year; later that year, the village burned down; it was restored on adjacent land platted by M. C. Wilson; incorporated as a village in 1889 and as a city in 1961 [Barbara Comeau; Ensign; PO Archives].

**FENTON**, Genesee County: first settled in 1834 by Clark Dibble and the Dustin Cheney family, and called Dibbleville; in 1837, lawyer William M. Fenton (who became lieutenant-governor of Michigan in 1847) and Robert LeRoy bought a large part of the townsite and platted the village as Fentonville; Mr. LeRoy built the first hotel in 1837 and became the first postmaster of Fentonville, on June 26, 1837, with the office renamed Fenton on Feb. 25, 1886; incorporated as the village of Fenton in 1863 [Ellis; PO Archives].

**FENWICK**, Montcalm County: this village in Fair Plain Township was founded in 1872 by B. C. Loree, who named it after his home town in Canada; James R. Hall became its first postmaster on April 28, 1873; platted and recorded by S. C. Aderman for Simon M., Sarah, and David Griswold, proprietors, on May 22, 1874 [PM; Dasef].

**FERGUS**, Saginaw County: this station on the Michigan Central Railroad, 3 miles south of Saint Charles, was given a post office on Dec. 28, 1882, with John A. Spencer as its first postmaster, the office operating until Aug. 15, 1933 [GSM 1883; PO Archives].

**FERN**, Mason County: this settlement around the sawmill of J. S. Adams, in Eden Township, was given a station on the Mason & Oceana Railroad in 1886 and a post office on Sept. 28, 1888, with Carrie S. Adams as its first postmaster, the office operating until Feb. 28, 1907 [GSM 1889; PO Archives].

**FERNDALE**, Lake County: Jennie Simonds became the first postmaster of this rural post office in Eden Township on March 18, 1884, the office operating until Oct. 29, 1885 [GSM 1885-87; PO Archives].

**FERNDALE**, Oakland County: founded in 1917 by Lovell G. Turnbull who named it from the many ferns in the area; it became a classified branch of the Detroit post office in 1924, with John W. Allison as superintendent; incorporated as a village in 1918 and as a city in 1927 [Lawrence P. Kress].

**FERRIS,** Montcalm County: Elijah Ferris and his family came here from Geauga County, Ohio, in 1854; the township, named for him, was organized in 1857; Nathan B. Scott, who had come here in 1855 and made one of the first clearings, became the first postmaster on Nov. 20, 1858, the office operating until July 31, 1907 [Schenck; PO Archives].

**FERRISBURG,** Ottawa County. See Ferrysburg.

**FERRY,** Delta County: a station on the Chicago & Northwestern Railroad in 1878; Thomas W. Ferry, a wealthy Grand Haven lumberman, represented Michigan in the U.S. Senate, 1871-1883 [GSM 1879].

**FERRY,** Oceana County: the township, when organized in 1869, was named Reed, with B. F. and Theodore F. Reed as supervisors, 1869-72; the legislature renamed the township after Thomas W. Ferry, U.S. Senator, 1871-83, and his father, Rev. William M. Ferry, who was responsible for the building of the first sawmill in the county; the Reed post office was changed to Ferry on Feb. 8, 1871 [Royal; PO Archives].

**FERRYSBURG,** Ottawa County: the place was referred to as Ottawa Point in 1850 and as Ferry Point in 1855; Ferrysburg was founded, platted and recorded by Colonel William Montague Ferry, Jr., and Thomas White Ferry, in 1857, and named for their father, Rev. William M. Ferry (founder of Grand Haven); carpenter Uzell B. Eames became its first postmaster on Aug. 20, 1859; the office was closed on May 6, 1863, but was restored on Dec. 17, 1866, renamed Ferrisburg on Aug. 17, 1894, but changed back to Ferrysburg on the 27th of the following month [A. L. Strevy, PM; PO Archives].

**FERRY SWITCH,** Menominee County. See Wilson.

**FERRYVILLE,** Mason County: this village in Eden Township was settled in 1875, and given a post office on Sept. 1, 1875, with Edwin M. Comstock as its first postmaster; the office was transferred to and renamed Custer on Dec. 23, 1878 [GSM 1879; PO Archives].

**FEWSVILLE,** Baraga County: this village in Baraga Township was settled in 1872 and named for the Few family, pioneer settlers; Gershom B. Few operated a distillery here and George W. Few became the first postmaster on Sept. 22, 1875, the office operating until Jan. 18, 1877 [Andreas; GSM 1873-79; PO Archives].

**FIBORN JUNCTION,** Chippewa County: compounds the names of W. F. Fitch and Chase S. Osborn, promotors of the Fiborn limestone quarry to which this was a spur from the South Shore's main line [Hamilton].

**FIBORN QUARRY,** Mackinac County: a station on the Duluth, South Shore & Atlantic Railroad, in Hendrie Township; about 1900, W. F. Fitch and Chase S. Osborn (later governor of Michigan) promoted a limestone quarry here, and the village compounds their names; by 1906, it was operated by S. B. Martin & Company, and Samuel B. Martin became the first postmaster on Jan. 31, 1907, the office operating until Jan. 31, 1936 [Prentiss M. Brown; GSM 1909; PO Archives].

**FIBRE**, Chippewa County: in 1891, a station on the Minneapolis, St. Paul & Sault Ste. Marie Railroad named Alberta; it was given a post office of the same name on July 10, 1895, with John B. Wilson as its first postmaster; it was renamed Fibre on Jan. 20, 1896 [GSM 1897; PO Archives].

**FIELDS**, Newaygo County: a station on a branch of the Chicago & Western Michigan Railroad in 1886; lumberman John J. Williams became the first postmaster of this sawmill settlement on June 17, 1889, the office operating until Nov. 15, 1900 [GSM 1887-1903; PO Archives].

**FIFE LAKE**, Grand Traverse County: L. L. Shaw, and others, from Grand Rapids, platted a village as Fyfe Lake, and Thomas T. Bates platted another as North Fife Lake, both in 1872; Richard P. Thurber became the first postmaster of Fyfe Lake on Dec. 12, 1872, with the spelling corrected to Fife Lake on Dec. 1, 1875, for they had been named after the lake they border, which in turn had been named for William H. Fife, of Acme, a state highway commissioner; the two towns were incorporated as the village of Fife Lake in 1889 [Powers; Page; PO Archives].

**FIFIELD**, Saginaw County: a station on the Pere Marquette Railroad, in Buena Vista Township, serving a sawmill settlement of which Harry M. Hammond became the first postmaster on Aug. 19, 1898, the office operating until Feb. 15, 1900; named for Eugene Fifield [GSM 1899-1901; PO Archives].

**FILER CITY**, Manistee County: Delos L. Filer built the D. L. Filer & Sons mill here in 1867; Elihu G. Filer became the first postmaster on March 10, 1868; the village was platted the same year; its post office was closed on April 12, 1871, but was restored from July 13, 1883, to date; its station on the M. & N.E. Railroad was called Filer's Switch [Virginia S. Stroemel; PO Archives].

**FILION**, Huron County: named for Desire Filion who located here in 1861, opened a store some two years later, and became the first postmaster on Feb. 18, 1876, serving some thirty years; its township of Meade was organized in 1869 and named for General George G. Meade, Union commander, with Spencer A. Case as its first supervisor [Gwinn; PO Archives].

**FILLMORE**, Allegan County: a depot (also called Fillmore Station) on a branch of the Michigan Central Railroad, a mile from Fillmore Centre, in 1894; see Fillmore Centre for the name [GSM 1895].

**FILLMORE**, Barry County: David D. Darling became the first postmaster of this rural post office, named for President Millard Fillmore, on Oct. 11, 1866, the office operating until Aug. 27, 1887 [Johnson; PO Archives].

**FILLMORE**, Macomb County: William F. Myers became the first postmaster of this rural post office on July 22, 1851, the office operating until March 17, 1859; named for Millard Fillmore who had become President on July 10, 1850 [GSM 1861; PO Archives].

**FILLMORE CENTRE**, Allegan County: named after the township, which had been set off in 1849, with Isaac Fairbanks as its first supervisor, and named for the then vice-president of the U.S., Millard Fillmore; shortly after the Grand Haven Railroad came through, Telman, Hoffman & Wagenaar's sawmill was built here in 1870; Gerrit Wagenaar became the first postmaster on March 17, 1873 [Johnson].

**FINDLEY**, St. Joseph County: given a station on the Lake Shore & Michigan and the Michigan Central Railroads; William Reiterman became the first postmaster on Feb. 27, 1889, succeeded by storekeeper F. E. Luton in 1890, the office operating until March 31, 1908 [GSM 1891; PO Archives].

**FINDLEY JUNCTION**, Houghton County: a station on the Chicago, Milwaukee & St. Paul Railroad in 1898; Peter Diefenbach became its first postmaster on June 13, 1903, but it was rescinded on April 15, 1904; in some records as Finley Junction [Mich Manual 1899; PO Archives].

**FINGER BOARD**, Huron County. See Popple.

**FINKTON**, Antrim County: storekeeper German Button became the first postmaster of this rural post office on June 13, 1882, the office operating until Jan. 31, 1908 [GSM 1883; PO Archives].

**FINLEY JUNCTION**, Houghton County. See Findley Junction.

**FINNASEY**, Ottawa County: Erastus Fisher became the first postmaster of this rural post office in Tallmadge Township on April 21, 1882, the office operating until Oct. 18, 1883 [GSM 1883; PO Archives].

**FINN DAM**, Delta County: a Finnish co-operative worked a sawmill here [David Coon].

**FISHER**, Kent County: a station on the Grand Rapids & Indiana Railroad, six miles south of Grand Rapids, in 1880 [GSM 1895].

**FISHER**, Menominee County. See Koss.

**FISHER**, Presque Isle County: this lumber settlement on Lake Huron was named for lumberman Edward Fisher who became its first postmaster on April 28, 1887; the office was closed on Oct. 31, 1899, but was restored from March 5, 1901, to Sept. 14, 1901 [GSM 1889; PO Archives].

**FISHERS**, Wayne County. See Beech.

**FISHER'S LAKE**, St. Joseph County: this settlement in Park Township was begun in 1834 by Harvey Kinney who was assisted in building his cabin by George Leland and by Jonas and Leonard Fisher, after whom the lake was named [Cutler].

**FISHER'S STATION**, Kent County: a settlement around the depot of the Grand Rapids & Indiana Railroad here in Wyoming Township in 1870; J. E. Virgil became its first postmaster on Feb. 28, 1871; the village was platted and recorded by R. S. Jackson for David Fisher and Warren S. Crippen, on Dec. 26, 1873; its post office operated until Dec. 31, 1903 [Chapman; GSM 1873; PO Archives].

**FISHERVILLE**, Bay County: in 1866, when Mr. Spicer built his sawmill here in Williams Township the place became known as Spicer's Corners; about 1875, it was renamed for Spencer O. Fisher who had lumbering operations in the area and who became the congressman from this district, 1885-88; Collingwood Campbell became the first postmaster on Aug. 19, 1892, with the office named Laredo; the office was closed on Jan. 11, 1898, but was restored from Feb. 8, 1899, to April 30, 1906; a station on a branch of the Michigan Central Railroad [Gansser; PO Archives].

**FISH LAKE**, Lapeer County. See Stephens.

**FISHVILLE**, Montcalm County: this settlement in Evergreen Township began with a sawmill and a general store in 1879; storekeeper Robert Evans became its first postmaster on Nov. 9, 1886, the office operating until July 31, 1905; named from its location on Fish Creek [GSM 1889; PO Archives].

**FISK**, Allegan County. See Watson.

**FITCHBURG**, Ingham County: Ferris S. Fitch, from Livingston County, N.Y., became its first settler in 1848, followed later that year by his brother, Selah B. Fitch; Hubbard Fitch became the first postmaster of the settlement on March 8, 1856, the office operating until March 14, 1903 [Durant; Foster; PO Archives].

**FITCHVILLE**, Antrim County: named for John H. Fitch who became the first postmaster of this rural post office on May 5, 1880, but the office was never in operation [PO Archives].

**FITZGERALD**, Montcalm County. See Maple Valley.

**FIVE CHANNELS**, Iosco County: William A. Freeman became the first postmaster of this rural post office on the Au Sable River on July 27, 1912, the office operating until Oct. 15, 1913 [GSM 1913; PO Archives].

**FIVE CORNERS**, Ingham County: named from the junction of the roads here; also called North Holt, and now a part of the village of Holt [Durant; Foster].

**FIVE LAKES**, Lapeer County: first settled in 1855; Piper & Thompson built the first sawmill here in Mayfield Township, followed by Sage, Ferry & Lee, and A. B. Royce; inn-keeper William G. Stone became its first postmaster on May 28, 1869, with the office renamed Asa on April 6, 1874, but changed back to Five Lakes on April 29, 1878; named from its nearby lakes; denuded of its neighboring pine, the village faded out [Page; GSM 1879; PO Archives].

**FIVE POINTS,** Wayne County: this rural post office in Redford Township, on Five Points Road, between 6 and 7 Mile Roads, operated only in 1918 [GSM 1919].

**FLANDERS,** Alpena County: began as a sawmill settlement in Green Township in 1869; named for local lumber merchant S. W. Flanders; lumberman Arthur B. Richardson became its first postmaster on Dec. 7, 1885, the office operating until Feb. 15, 1914 [GSM 1887; PO Archives].

**FLAT RIVER,** Kent County: Rodney Robinson became the first postmaster of this rural post office on the Flat River, a branch of the Grand River, on Oct. 16, 1838, the office operating until May 15, 1865 [GSM 1860-65; PO Archives].

**FLAT ROCK,** Delta County: there were some settlers in the area when Joseph Smith started his sawmill here in 1844; a settlement formed and was given a post office on Feb. 19, 1852, named Flat Rock, with Jefferson S. Bagley as its first postmaster; the office was closed on Sept. 24, 1852, but on June 28, 1864, the Esconawba post office was changed to Flat Rock, with sawmill owner David Langley, Jr., as its postmaster; named from its location on the Escanaba (in Chippewa, flat rock) River, which flows over a bed of flat rock [David S. Coon; PO Archives].

**FLAT ROCK,** Wayne County: first settled in 1821 by Michael Vreelandt and family from New York State; it was platted and recorded as Vreelandt in 1834; from the smooth rock bed of the Huron River running through it, it was renamed Smooth Rock; in 1838, the Gibralter & Flat Rock Company laid out and platted additional area under the name of City of Flat Rock; it was given a post office as Flat Rock on May 20, 1872; incorporated as a village in 1923 [Ruth Rhody; PO Archives].

**FLEMING,** Livingston County: a village with a railroad station, in Howell Township; John W. Smith became the first postmaster on Aug. 22, 1842; the office was closed on March 21, 1863, but was restored from April 13, 1863, to Jan. 13, 1864, and from Jan. 27, 1865, to Dec. 31, 1902 [Ellis; PO Archives].

**FLETCHER,** Kalkaska County: a post office in the home of farmer Oscar L. Giddings, in Glade Township, opened on Aug. 21, 1883, and operating until May 31, 1912 [GSM 1885; PO Archives].

**FLETCHER'S CORNERS,** Genesee County: Ephraim Fletcher, from Orleans County, N.Y., bought land and settled here in 1836; the meeting to organize Gaines Township was held in his house and he was elected treasurer, both in 1842 [Ellis].

**FLINT,** Genesee County: Jacob Smith, a Canadian-born German, and his Chippewa wife opened a trading post here in 1819 and the site was called Grand Traverse or the great crossing; Jacob Stevens, a farmer from New York State, became the first settler in what was then called Flint River, in 1825; John Todd, of Pontiac, bought 785 acres from Francis Campau in 1830 for $800, and the place became known as Todd's Crossing; the first village plat was entered by A. E. Wathares in 1830 and recorded as Sidney; it was included in the 1833 plat of John Clifford and renamed Flint River; Wait Beach platted the village of Flint in 1836; Chauncey S. Payne platted Grand Traverse on the north side of the river in 1837; Lyman Stowe became the first postmaster of Flint River on Aug. 5, 1834, with the name shortened to Flint on Sept. 1, 1836; in 1855, these plats (they were never incorporated villages), were incorporated as the city of Flint; named from the river running through it, which the Indians called Pawanunking, or the river of flint, from its rocky bed [MPH 35:359 1907; PO Archives; Wood].

**FLINT RIVER JUNCTION,** Genesee County: the post office at this railroad station was opened on July 12, 1887, with David W. Savory as its first postmaster, the office operating until Dec. 28, 1891 [GSM 1895; PO Archives].

**FLINTSTEEL,** Ontonagon County: a mining settlement post office, near the Flint Steel River, 8 miles east of Ontonagon, with Peter Hazzy becoming its first postmaster on March 7, 1898, the office operating until April 14, 1906 [GSM 1899-1907; PO Archives].

**FLOETER,** Alger County. See Wetmore.

**FLOODWOOD,** Dickinson County: the village began as a lumber settlement on the Milwaukee & Northern Railroad, in Humboldt Township; when station agent Thom E. Timlin became its first postmaster on Nov. 21, 1887, it was in Marquette County; the office was transferred to Dickinson County on Jan. 23, 1892, and operated until March 31, 1905 [GSM 1889; PO Archives].

**FLORENCE,** Manistee County: a station on the Chicago & Western Michigan (now Pere Marquette) Railroad in 1885 [Mich Manual 1899].

**FLORENCE,** Marquette County: a mining boom town in 1881; its hostel was the Florence House.

**FLORENCE,** Saginaw County: in 1864, a sawmill settlement on the west bank of the Saginaw River, opposite the city of Saginaw, and since absorbed by it [GSM 1865].

**FLORENCE,** St. Joseph County: a post office opened on July 29, 1837, in the tavern of Lyman Bean, who had come here from Maine in 1834; named after the township which had been named in 1837 by St. Joseph County territorial representative Neal McGaffey after Florence, Italy; the post office operated until May 31, 1902 [PO Archives; Everts].

**FLORENCE,** Shiawassee County. See Fremont.

**FLORIDA,** Hillsdale County: the legislature set off Florida Township in 1837, renaming it Jefferson in 1849; Warren Thompson became the first postmaster of Florida on July 23, 1839, with the office changed to Ossea on Dec. 14, 1861 [Hogaboam; GSM 1865; PO Archives].

**FLOWER CREEK,** Oceana County: J. Collins built a sawmill here in Claybanks Township in 1863 and A. A. Lillie built another in 1867; Adam

Huston became the first postmaster on April 11, 1863, resigning in 1879; the spelling of the name of the office was changed to Flowercreek on Nov. 19, 1895, but the office was closed on Aug. 31, 1906; named from its location on a stream of the same name [Royal; PO Archives].

**FLOWERFIELD**, St. Joseph County: Mishael Beadle and his family, from Ohio, became the first permanent settlers near the present village site in 1829; he built a sawmill in 1830 and a grist mill in 1831; the village was platted in 1833 by Dr. David E. Brown on land then owned by storekeeper Challenge S. Wheeler who had become the first postmaster on Dec. 13, 1832; the office operated until Dec. 31, 1936; Flowerfield was so named because "it oftentimes, in the days of its earlier settlement, presented a lovely appearance" [Everts; Silliman; PO Archives].

**FLOYD**, Isabella County: blacksmith Edward Y. Kelley became the first postmaster of this rural post office in Chippewa Township on June 3, 1891, the office operating until Nov. 13, 1895 [GSM 1893; PO Archives].

**FLOYD**, Midland County: farmer John A. Mallory became the first postmaster of this rural post office on Nov. 24, 1899, the office operating until Nov. 30, 1907 [GSM 1901; PO Archives].

**FLOYD**, St. Clair County: Lester Gross became the first postmaster of this rural post office on Dec. 18, 1855, the office operating until July 21, 1857 [PO Archives].

**FLUSHING**, Genesee County: Charles Seymour bought land here in 1835 and Horace Jerome water-power in 1836, and they ran a sawmill in partnership; Mr. Seymour made the first plat of the village in 1840, and his brother James, to whom he had sold out in 1843, made the second in 1847; Ezekiel Ewing became the first postmaster on May 9, 1839; incorporated as a village in 1877; named after its township, which had been named by the legislature when the name sent in (Dover) was found to be already in such use [Ellis; Wood].

**FLYNN**, Sanilac County: the township was organized in 1869 and named for Thomas Flynn, its first supervisor; Charles A. Hagle became its first postmaster on Oct. 30, 1895, the office operating until March 15, 1904 [Chapman; PO Archives].

**FOGO**, Allegan County: James Redpath became the first postmaster of this rural post office on June 19, 1851, the office operating until Oct. 1, 1855 [PO Archives].

**FORD CITY**, Wayne County: named for John B. Ford, president of the Michigan Alkali Company; incorporated as a village in 1902; Mr. Ford, who wanted the tax relief for his firm that a larger community could give, promised to build a public hospital if Ford City would merge with Wyandotte; it did, in 1922, and he deeded the completed Wyandotte General Hospital to the city in 1926; the place was also known as Ford and as Ford Village [Burton].

**FORD ISLAND**, Grand Traverse County. See Marion Island.

**FORD REPUBLIC**, Wayne County: planned as early as 1890 by Mrs. Agnes d'Arcambal, this training school for delinquent boys was established in 1907; a large bequest was made by the Emory L. Ford family, for whom it was named, as well as from the fact that it is student-governed [Federal].

**FORD RIVER**, Delta County: named for Thomas Ford, a governor of Illinois, who had explored part of the Upper Peninsula in 1842-46, and mentioned the river in his history of Illinois; in 1845, Silas Billings, George Richards, and David Bliss built a mill up the river, and when they sold out in 1857, the mill moved to the site of the village; George Ligare became the first postmaster on May 3, 1860; the office was closed on July 2, 1870, but was restored from Jan. 23, 1872, to March 15, 1914 [David S. Coon; PO Archives].

**FORDNEY**, Saginaw County: George H. Woolston became the first postmaster of this rural post office on Oct. 23, 1899, the office operating until Feb. 28, 1903; named for Joseph W. Fordney, congressman from this district in 1899-1900 [GSM 1901-05; PO Archives].

**FORDSON**, Wayne County. See Springwells.

**FOREST**, Crawford County. See Frederic.

**FOREST**, Genesee County: James Seymour made the first land entry in the town in March, 1836, and Henry Heister and his family, from Livingston County, N.Y., became the first settlers in 1837; the next settler, Nathaniel Smith, became the first supervisor when the township was organized in 1843; John Crawford became the first postmaster on Feb. 14, 1855, with the office changed to Otisville on April 5, 1861; its name was derived from its heavy growth of timber [Wood; PO Archives].

**FOREST BAY**, Huron County: it was in Sanilac County when William D. Ludington became the first postmaster of this rural post office on Nov. 1, 1856, but in Huron County by the time the office was closed on Sept. 20, 1870 [GSM 1881; PO Archives].

**FOREST CITY**, Oceana County: this part of Greenwood Township was first settled in 1855; it was in Ottawa County when Norman Cunningham became its first postmaster on Jan. 13, 1859; the office was closed on July 21, 1875; the village was also given a railroad station [GSM 1877; PO Archives].

**FORESTER**, Sanilac County: Alanson Goodrich became the first settler in 1849; Jacob Sharp came in 1851 and lived in the first house built here; F. T. Smith & Company built the general store in 1852; James B. Kelley became the first postmaster of Forrester on April 20, 1858, with the name officially shortened to Forester on Feb. 9, 1883, though the latter spelling came into use, even by the local post office, before that; its post office operated until Jan. 31, 1907; named from its having been a lumbering center [Chapman; PO Archives].

**FOREST GROVE**, Ottawa County: a Dutch settlement in Jamestown

Township; they built a church here in 1869 and were given a post office on June 23, 1874, with John Tiesinga as its first postmaster; its spelling was changed to Forestgrove on Feb. 11, 1895, but the office was closed on May 14, 1904 [Page; PO Archives].

**FOREST HALL,** Cass County: the Air Line division of the Michigan Central Railroad came through here at the north shore of Diamond Lake, in Penn Township, in 1871; the next year, Nathan Corwith and J. P. Smith, Chicago businessmen laid out the grounds and built a large club house; in 1898, the site was platted and recorded as Forest Hall Park, by Barak L. Rudd, its proprietor [Glover; Schoetzow].

**FOREST HILL,** Gratiot County: platted in 1857, partly on the Moody homestead, the Hon. Silas Moody is regarded as the father of the village; Rev. Elisha H. Brooks, pastor of the Christian Church, became the first postmaster on Feb. 24, 1857; so named because the area was heavily forested and on higher ground than that around it, but when an improved roadway crossed a site four miles away, the village was moved to it, retaining the name though there was here neither forest or hill; its post office operated until Jan. 31, 1957 [Federal Tucker].

**FOREST HOME,** Antrim County: James A. Cummings became the first postmaster of this rural post office on July 12, 1875, the office operating until Feb. 10, 1876 [PO Archives].

**FOREST HOME,** Van Buren County: Fitz E. Adams became the first postmaster of this rural post office on Sept. 16, 1867, the office operating until Sept. 20, 1869 [PO Archives].

**FOREST LAKE,** Alger County: a station on the M.M. & S. Railroad; the village was founded by the Cleveland Cliffs Company in 1890 and first called Dixon; storekeeper William J. Roberge became its first postmaster on May 8, 1915, with the office renamed Forest Lake on Nov. 25, 1921, from its lumber industry and nearby lake [Kenyon Boyer; GSM 1917; PO Archives].

**FORESTVILLE,** Sanilac County: so named because the area was heavily timbered; Alva Kelley took up the first land here in 1853; Captain E. B. Ward built the first sawmill in 1854; Isaac Green, who became the first postmaster on Jan. 17, 1856, was elected the first supervisor when Delaware Township was organized in 1858, and in the later year, built the first hotel; its post office, closed on Oct. 2, 1872, was restored from Jan. 20, 1873, to date; incorporated as a village in 1895 [Chapman; PO Archives].

**FORGINSON LAKE,** Roscommon County. See Higgins Lake.

**FORK,** Mecosta County: Marvin A. Rogers became the first settler in the area in the winter of 1865-66; Fork Township was organized in 1867, with William Creery as its first supervisor, and he became its first postmaster on Feb. 11, 1870; the office was closed on Oct. 26, 1880, but was restored from Feb. 14, 1881, to May 25, 1882, and from Feb. 16, 1887, to March 22, 1904 [Chapman; PO Archives].

**FORK'S SWITCH**, Monroe County: a station on the Lake Shore & Michigan Southern Railroad in 1864 [GSM 1865].

**FORMAN**, Lake County: C. H. Forman built a lumber mill and general store here in Pleasant Plains Township in 1873, and the village formed around them; given a station on the Pere Marquette Railroad and on Feb. 24, 1875, a post office, with William Forman as its first postmaster [GSM 1877; PO Archives].

**FORRESTER**, Sanilac County. See Forester.

**FORSYTH**, Marquette County. See Little Lake.

**FORT BRADY**, Chippewa County: erected by Colonel Hugh Brady, July, 1822, to protect Sault Ste. Marie from the Indians [GSM 1838].

**FORT CHEVALIER de REPENTIGNY**, Chippewa County: built by the French in 1750, surrendered to the British, 1762, burned by the Indians, Dec. 28, 1862; Chevalier de Repentigny, a French officer, was an ally of the U.S. during the Revolution; now within the city limits of Sault Ste. Marie [Mich Hist 15:204 1931].

**FORT de BAUDE**, Mackinac County: built at St. Ignace by Louis de La Porte, Sieur de Louvigny, in 1681, and named for Louis de Baude, Count Frontenac; closed by royal order about 1697, with Antoine Cadillac as commanding officer; Frontenac then sent him to France to point out the need for a western fort to protect trade against the British, and the result was Fort Pontchartrain du Detroit in 1701.

**FORT DETROIT**, Wayne County. See Fort Shelby.

**FORT DRUMMOND**, Chippewa County. See Drummond Island.

**FORT GEORGE**, Mackinac County. See Fort Holmes.

**FORT GRATIOT**, St. Clair County: it was first the site of Fort St. Joseph (q.v.); in 1814, to protect naviagtion, the U.S. built this fort, named for the engineer in charge, Captain (later Colonel) Charles Gratiot; the Huron Light House post office was changed to Fort Gratiot in Dec., 1826, and was closed and restored as the fort was abandoned and re-garrisoned, the fort and its post office operating from Dec., 1826, to Nov. 22, 1837, from July 11, 1838, to Nov. 19, 1845, and from March 18, 1870, to June 13, 1895, when both were permanently discontinued; in the meantime, in the 1870s, the village of Fort Gratiot began to occupy its site; a station on the Grand Trunk Railroad in 1865; the village has been a part of the city of Port Huron since 1895; the name is retained by the township of Fort Gratiot which was organized in 1867 [MPH 18:667 1891; GSM 1877; PO Archives].

**FORT HOLMES**, Mackinac County: built by the British after their capture of Fort Mackinac in 1812 and named Fort George for their king, George III; renamed by the Americans after Major Andrew Hunter Holmes, who was killed in the Battle of Mackinac Island, in 1814; destroyed by fire in 1933; restored by the Mackinac Island State Park Commission in 1936 [Mich Hist 20:295 1936, 26:236 1942].

**FORT IGNATIUS**, Mackinac County: the French Jesuit, Jacques Marquette, established a mission here on Mackinac Island in 1669, naming it after the founder of the Jesuits, St. Ignatius Loyola; some French soldiers followed and built Fort Ignatius; the next year the mission was abandoned and the fort soon fell in ruin [Mich Hist 15:130 1931].

**FORT LERNOULT**, Wayne County. See Fort Shelby.

**FORT MACKINAC**, Mackinac County. See Fort Michilimackinac.

**FORT MIAMI**, Berrien County. See St. Joseph.

**FORT MICHILIMACKINAC**, Mackinac County: the first French fort on the Straits of Mackinac was Forte de Buade built at St. Ignace in 1681, closed on order of Antoine Cadillac in 1701, rebuilt at Mackinaw City as Fort Michilimackinac, under Commander Lignery, in 1712; taken over by the British in 1761; its garrison massacred by the Indians in 1763; the fort was re-occupied by the British, 1764-1781, when they withdrew to Mackinac Island, taking the fort with them; hence, in records and writings the name Michilimackinac is found applied indiscriminately to forts at St. Ignace, Mackinaw City, and Mackinac Island; Michilimackinac in Indian meant great turtle, for they fancied that Mackinac Island resembled a turtle in shape [MPH 38:89 1912].

**FORT PLEASANT**, St. Joseph County. See Leonidas.

**FORT PONTCHARTRAIN**, Wayne County. See Detroit.

**FORT SAGINAW**, Saginaw County. See Saginaw.

**FORT SAINT JOSEPH**, Berrien County. See Niles.

**FORT SAINT JOSEPH**, St. Clair County: the visit of Joliet in 1669 and of Louis Hennepin and Rene-Robert LaSalle in 1679 resulted in the first white settlement here when Daniel DeLuth, under orders of Louis XIV of France, built this fort and trading post in 1686; it was a French strategic stronghold when France and England were contesting for the Great Lakes region; more than a century later it became the site of Fort Gratiot [Ann W. McLay; MPH 11:249 1887].

**FORT SHELBY**, Wayne County: preceded by Fort Pontchartrain built by Cadillac in 1701 and Fort Lernoult, built by British Captain Richard B. Lernoult in 1778; here in 1796, the American flag was raised over Michigan soil for the first time, and it was called Fort Detroit; renamed Fort Shelby in 1814 for Governor Isaac Shelby, of Kentucky, who fought the British and Indians in Michigan in the War of 1812; occupied until 1826, when it was razed; these forts were within the present city limits of Detroit; Fort Shelby is now the name of a station of the Detroit post office [Mich Hist 26:238 1942].

**FORT SINCLAIR**, St. Clair County: in the Gazeteer 1838 as Fort St. Clair; built in 1764 by Lieutenant Patrick Sinclair, of the British Army, at the mouth of the Pine River, at its confluence with the St. Clair Strait, opposite the village of Palmer, now Saint Clair; erected to facilitate the transporting of supplies between Detroit and Michilimackinac [Mich Hist 15:332 1931].

**FORT SUMTER,** Berrien County: a local name for a settlement in Buchanan Township, on the south side of the St. Joseph River near the mouth of McCoy's Creek (named for Rev. Isaac McCoy, founder of the Carey Mission); named during the Civil War and after the South Carolina fort [Fox].

**FORT WAYNE,** Wayne County: the original grant of the land was made by the Pottowattomie Indians to Robische Navarre in 1770; French boatmen had called the site Place aux Fontaines, because of its numerous springs, and under British occupation it was called Springwells; the Army bought the 90 acres for $150,000 from two French farmers in 1842, built the fort and named it for General Anthony Wayne in 1843, enlarged it in 1844, and completed it in 1851, but did not garrison it with regular troops until 1861; though the original fortifications were transferred in 1949 to the city of Detroit (which restored and refurnished them as an historical museum), the fort was continuously occupied until July 1, 1965, when declared surplus by the Army; when built it was five miles southwest of Detroit, but is now well within the city [Mich Hist 26:242 1942, 30:5 1946; Detroit News, Pictorial, July 4 1965].

**FORT WILKINS,** Keweenaw County: built to protect local governments interests in the early mining period, 1844-46; given a post office, with Charles R. Bush as its first postmaster, on June 4, 1845; the office was closed on March 19, 1850, but was restored on July 30, 1851, with Daniel D. Brockway as postmaster; on May 4, 1860, the office was transferred to Copper Harbor; the fort was alternately abandoned and used several times until 1870, when it was discontinued; it was in Houghton County until Keweenaw was organized in 1861; bought by both counties in 1921 to preserve and restore it; this was done by WPA labor in 1939-40, and it was converted into a state park; named for the secretary of war under President John Tyler, William Wilkins [Mich Hist 29:155 1945; Federal; PO Archives].

**FORTUNA,** Monroe County: a settlement in the southeast corner of the county, near Toledo, in 1918 [GSM 1919].

**FORTUNE LAKE,** Iron County: although the mine property here had been explored in 1915 and again in 1920, and a shaft sunk, no ore was produced until Pickands took it over in 1952; the railroad and highway were relocated, and mining began, the first ore coming up in 1953; now a developed recreation area [Havighurst; Jack Hill, Sr.].

**FORTUNEVILLE,** Oakland County: a hamlet in 1864 [GSM 1865].

**FORWARD,** Missaukee County: Joseph Nederhoed became the first postmaster of this rural post office in Riverside Township on Oct. 10, 1903, the office operating until Jan. 15, 1908 [GSM 1907; PO Archives].

**FOSS,** Missaukee County: W. A. Pickerd became the first postmaster of this rural post office on Oct. 9, 1905, but it was rescinded on June 12, 1906 [PO Archives].

**FOSTER CITY,** Dickinson County: a station on a branch of the Chicago & Northwestern Railroad, in Breen Township, in 1884; the village was founded and named by Alonzo L. Foster in 1884, and he became its first postmaster on Feb. 5, 1886; this lumberman disposed of his holdings here in 1895; it was in Menominee County until Dickinson was organized in 1891 [B. Milligan, PM; GSM 1887].

**FOSTERS,** Saginaw County: Gardner W. Foster was the first male child born in the county, in 1831, and his numerous descendants became large landowners in the area; Almond Hastings became the first postmaster here on Aug. 14, 1889, the office operating until Aug. 24, 1956; a station on the Cincinnati, Saginaw & Mackinaw Railroad [Mills; PO Archives].

**FOSTERS,** Washtenaw County. See Cornwell.

**FOSTORIA,** Tuscola County: Governor Henry H. Crapo, who owned most of the pine land in the area, had the Pere Marquette Railroad from Flint run through his headquarters here, and named the place for his foreman, Thomas Foster, in 1881; given a post office from July 24, 1882, to May 11, 1883 [Page; PO Archives].

**FOUCH,** Leelanau County: in 1866, at the age of 21, John R. Fouch came from Ohio and settled here at the head of Carp Lake, in Solon Township; in 1893, he built a hotel for fishermen and when the Michigan & Northwestern Railroad came through, he gave his name to the station built on his land, and he became the first postmaster of Fouch on March 3, 1893; the office was closed on Nov. 13, 1895, but was restored, with Mrs. Kate V. Herbert as its postmaster, on May 20, 1905; with the death of Mr. Fouch, his land was acquired in 1927 by Daniel Perrin who developed it into a summer colony, and the place is now also called Perrin's Landing [Edmund M. Littell; Dickinson; PO Archives].

**FOUNTAIN,** Mason County: founded in 1882 by Nicholas J. Bockstanz who so named it because of a local spring; he became its first postmaster on Sept. 12, 1882; a station on the Pere Marquette Railroad; incorporated as a village in 1913 [Helvi Wright; PO Archives].

**FOUR MILE CORNER,** Luce County: a hamlet named from its being four miles north of Newberry [Newberry News].

**FOUR TOWNS,** Oakland County: named from its being the corner of the four townships of White Lake, Waterford, Commerce, and West Bloomfield; John Solon Cooley became its first postmaster on May 14, 1856, the office operating until Dec. 31, 1902 [GSM 1873-1905; Ripley; PO Archives].

**FOWLER,** Clinton County: John Parks became the first postmaster of a rural post office named Dallas, after its township, on Jan. 18, 1849; Robert Higham, chief engineer of the Detroit & Milwaukee Railroad, chose the site for a village in 1856; he and E. A. Wales, of Detroit, bought 160 acres and platted the village in 1857; surrounded by swamps, the venture was doomed, and in 1867 it was moved to land owned by J. N. Fowler, of Detroit, about a mile to the west, and the village (but not its post office) was renamed Isabella (Mr. Fowler also owned land in Isabella County); at the villagers' request, Mr. Fowler changed the name to his own in 1869; its post office was renamed Fowler on July 17, 1871; incorporated as a village in 1885 [Ernest Halfman, PM; PO Archives].

**FOWLERVILLE**, Livingston County: Chilson Sanford, of Washtenaw County, made land entries here in 1834, but the first permanent settler was Ralph Fowler in 1836, and it was he who instructed Amos Adams to plat the village in 1849; given a post office named Cedar on April 5, 1838, with Elijah Gaston as its first postmaster, the office was renamed Fowlerville on May 10, 1853, with tavern-keeper David Lewis as postmaster; first incorporated as a village in 1871 [Mrs. Bernard Hamlin Glenn; PO Archives].

**FOX**, Menominee County: a small community on Green Bay, 5 miles north of Cedar River; Henry Harkins became its first postmaster on May 21, 1902, the office operating until Aug. 31, 1951 [Mrs. Ethel Schuyler; PO Archives].

**FOXBORO**, St. Joseph County: Joseph W. Bryant became the first postmaster of this rural post office on Nov. 19, 1889, the office operating until May 25, 1895 [PO Archives].

**FOX ISLANDS**, Leelanau County: South Fox Island, in Lake Michigan, was given a post office named Leelanau on March 17, 1905, with storekeeper John O. Plank, Jr., as its first postmaster; on March 11, 1909, the office was renamed Fox Islands [GSM 1911; PO Archives].

**FOX'S CORNERS**, Kent County: named for James S. Fox who first settled here in Vergennes Township in 1836; its schoolhouse was built in 1870 [Dillenback].

**FOXVILLE**, Lake County: Edward W. Stiles became the first postmaster of this rural post office on March 18, 1884, the office operating until June 19, 1886 [PO Archives].

**FRANCE**, Kalkaska County. See French Landing.

**FRANCIS**, Ontonagon County: Jacob H. Brown was appointed the first postmaster of this rural post office on March 9, 1906, but it was rescinded on the following May 11 [PO Archives].

**FRANCISCO**, Jackson County: first settled in 1834, it was named for associate circuit judge Henry A. Francisco who became the first postmaster of Franciscoville on Oct. 4, 1843, with the office renamed Francisco on June 16, 1877; the office operated until Jan. 31, 1914 [John Daball; PO Archives].

**FRANKENHILF**, Tuscola County. See Richville.

**FRANKENLUST**, Bay County: founded in 1848 by a Lutheran community from Germany under Rev. Ferdinand Sievers; it was in

Kochville Township, Saginaw County, when that township was organized in 1856; the township was renamed Frankenlust and annexed to Bay County in 1880; John Schmidt became its first postmaster on Sept. 23, 1852; the office was closed on July 19, 1882, but was restored from April 1, 1890, with Walhem Schmidt as postmaster, to Nov. 28, 1892; its name combines Franconia, a district in Bavaria, with lust, the German for pleasure [Page; PO Archives].

**FRANKENMUTH,** Saginaw County: founded in 1845 by a Lutheran community from Bavaria, Germany, under Rev. Friedrich August Craemer, on a site previously selected and named by Rev. Johann Wilhelm Loehe; John G. Hubinger built a sawmill here in 1847 and the first store in 1849; George A. Ranzenberger became the first postmaster on Sept. 26, 1851; the settlement was designed also to do missionary work among the Indians; incorporated as a village in 1904; its name combined Franconia, a district of Bavaria, and muth, the German for courage [Florer; Mills; PO Archives; Herman F. Zehnder, Teach My People the Truth. 1970].

**FRANKENMUTH STATION,** Saginaw County. See Gera.

**FRANKENTROST,** Saginaw County: founded in 1847 by a Lutheran community from Bavaria, Germany, under Rev. Philip Graebner; given a post office as Trostville, by which name the village was also known, on May 7, 1868, with John G. Schnell as its first postmaster, the office operating until March 9, 1881; its name combined Franconia, a district of Bavaria, with trost, the German for comfort or consolation [Florer; GSM 1873; PO Archives].

**FRANKFORT,** Benzie County: first settled by Joseph Oliver in 1850; a Detroit colony, organized by George S. Frost, Ransom Gardner, and others, began developing the town in 1859; William H. Coggashall became its first postmaster on June 30, 1860; the office was closed on Sept. 1, 1865, but was restored, with Nathaniel W. Nelson as postmaster, on Feb. 17, 1868; it was originally in Leelanau County; it is said that a former resident remarked that the area so reminded him of Frankfort, Germany, that he suggested the name for the new town; incorporated as a village in 1874 [Powers; PO Archives].

**FRANKFORT,** Macomb County: laid out in 1837; its 400 lots were platted along broad streets about a center marked "extensive salt spring," but there was no salt and it became no village; from the influx of German settlers in the area it was named after Frankford, Germany [Eldredge].

**FRANKFORT CITY,** Benzie County. See Elberta.

**FRANKLIN,** Houghton County. See Franklin Mine.

**FRANKLIN,** Oakland County: the land on the east side of the site was bought by Dilucena Stoughton in 1824, and on the west side by Elijah Bullock in 1825; it became known as the Stoughton Bullock Settlement; it was renamed by Dr. Ebenezer Raynale when he was made the first postmaster on Sept. 19, 1828, and since he and his bride came from

Pennsylvania, it was evidently named for Benjamin Franklin; incorporated as a village in 1953 [Bert D. Wood; Seeley].

**FRANKLIN CENTER**, Lenawee County. See Tipton.

**FRANKLIN MINE**, Houghton County: the village began with the Franklin Mining Company opening in 1857, with Charles H. Palmer as agent; by 1861, it employed 250 men, but the venture was failing when, in 1874, Johnson Vivian, as local manager, restored its copper yield to a profit; a station on the Mineral Range Railroad named Franklin; on Dec. 17, 1904, the Arcadian Mine post office was transferred to and renamed Franklin Mine, the office operating until May 3, 1957 [Andreas; PO Archives].

**FRANKS**, Muskegon County: James L. Franks was appointed the first postmaster of this rural post office, named for him, on April 13, 1899, but it was rescinded on Jan. 4, 1900 [PO Archives].

**FRASER**, Macomb County: the village was founded in 1857 by Alex Fraser (or Frazer) and was given a post office on June 14, 1860, as Fraser, with Leonard Scott as its first postmaster; the office was closed on Sept. 13, 1860, but was restored, with Mr. Scott again its postmaster, on Sept. 22, 1860; for pioneer settler William McPherson, the post office was renamed McPhersonville, on Oct. 15, 1860, but it was changed back to Fraser on Jan. 13, 1863; when the Grand Trunk Railroad came through a quarter of a mile from the post office in 1865, its station was named Fraser; incorporated as the village of Frazer in 1895, the name was legally changed to Fraser in 1928; incorporated as a city in 1956 [Judge Walter O. Steffens; Leeson; PO Archives].

**FRED**, Montcalm County. See Stanton.

**FREDA**, Houghton County: William Paine, of Boston, controlled the Copper Range Company which obtained the land and built a mill here in Stanton Township to concentrate copper ore from 1899 to 1901; the village which grew up around it was given a station on the Copper Range Railroad and on July 12, 1907, a post office, with Norman Burkman as its first postmaster, the office operating until March 13, 1864; named for Freda Paine, daughter of William Paine [PM; GSM 1909; PO Archives].

**FREDERIC**, Crawford County: the village began about 1874 as a wooding-up stop on the Mackinaw division of the Michigan Central Railroad, and was called Forest, it being in Maple Forest Township; when Collins W. Wight became its first postmaster on Dec. 17, 1877, the office was named Fredericville for pioneer settler Frederic Barker; with William Putnam as postmaster, on Aug. 4, 1886, the name was shortened to Frederic [Mich Hist 32:321 1948; Grace L. Funsch].

**FREDERICK**, Macomb County: this site, just southwest of present Mount Clemens was originally the location of the Gnadenhuetten (q.v.) mission; Mr. Tremble built a sawmill here before the War of 1812 and Job C. Smith built another in 1826; in 1836, Horace Stephens, of Detroit, bought land here and laid out the village which he named in honor of his brother; it prospered about a decade but is now a ghost town [Eldredge; MPH 28:135 1897].

**FREDERICKTON**, Dickinson County: annexed by the city of Norway in 1891 [Sawyer].

**FREDONIA**, Calhoun County: Thomas Burland, with his wife and three daughters, left Yorkshire, England, in 1831, and became the first settlers here in 1833; John B. Fredenburg brought his family from Orleans County, N.Y., in 1836, and after the township was organized he became its supervisor three times [Gardner].

**FREDONIA**, Washtenaw County: Levi Rogers became the first postmaster of this rural post office on July 11, 1838, the office operating until July 31, 1901 [PO Archives].

**FREEDOM**, Cheboygan County: Charles R. Kniffin became the first settler here in Beaugrand Township in 1875 and the first postmaster on July 26, 1876, the office operating until May 5, 1884; a station on the Mackinaw division of the Michigan Central Railroad by 1882 [Blinn; PO Archives].

**FREEDOM**, St. Joseph County: Freeman A. Tisdell built a tavern here in Fawn River Township, on the Chicago road, in 1836, had the village platted by D. M. Cook, a civil engineer, in the same year, and became its first postmaster on May 18, 1838; when by-passed by the railroad, the village declined, and on June 24, 1844, its post office was transferred to and renamed Fawn River [MPH 27:585 1896; PO Archives].

**FREEDOM**, Washtenaw County: James W. Hill became the first settler here in 1831; the first town meeting was held in 1834, with Henry M. Griffin elected supervisor; Henry J. Davidter became the first postmaster on May 21, 1867, the office operating until March 27, 1869 [MPH 4:395 1881; GSM 1860; PO Archives].

**FREELAND**, Saginaw County: the Jay post office, named for Jefferson Jaqruth, its first postmaster, was opened on April 23, 1856, and was in the settlement of Loretta; in 1867, George Truesdale was chiefly instrumental in having it moved to the settlement of Tittabawassee (named from the river running beside it; the tavern here was run by "Mammy Freeland," and the lumber jacks and river men who frequented it named the village Freeland; the post office changed the name from Jay to Freeland on Jan. 16, 1879; a station on the Pere Marquette Railroad [Alfreda E. Swanson, PM].

**FREEMAN'S MILLS**, Mason County: the settlement grew around a steam sawmill here on Freesoil Creek; given a post office on March 17, 1855, with Charles Freeman as its first postmaster, the office operating until May 7, 1860 [GSM 1860; PO Archives].

**FREENEY'S MILL**, Isabella County. See Wise.

**FREEPORT**, Barry County: founded by Michael S. and Samuel Roush, brothers, who owned the land and who named it after their former home of Freeport, Ohio; platted in 1874; a station on the Lowell & Hastings Railroad; Samuel Roush became the first postmaster on Jan. 2, 1878; incorporated as a village in 1907 [Mrs. Allen B. Fish; Potter].

**FREE SOIL**, Mason County: the Free Soil or anti-slavery party was organized in Buffalo, N.Y., in 1848; at a lumber settlement, named Free Soil Mills after it, the first township meeting was held in the home of Charles Freeman in 1855, the township and later its village taking the same name; Alva L. Freeman became its first postmaster on Feb. 10, 1862; the office was closed on Oct. 17, 1865, but was restored from Jan. 29, 1873, to date; a station on the Pere Marquette Railroad; incorporated as a village in 1915 [Clare E. Tubbs; PO Archives].

**FREIBURGERS**, Sanilac County: Archibald C. Graham became the first postmaster of this village, five miles south of Ubly, on July 3, 1888, the office operating until June 30, 1906; on some maps as Freidberger [GSM 1889-1907; PO Archives].

**FREMONT**, Alpena County. See Alpena.

**FREMONT**, Newaygo County: in 1854, Daniel R. Joslin built his log cabin near the site, called from early days Elm Corners; in 1855, Wilkes Stuart and Daniel Weaver arrived; given a post office as Weaversville, named after Daniel Weaver, and with him as its first postmaster, on Aug. 23, 1856, changed to Fremont Center on Oct. 18, 1862, and to Fremont on Dec. 20, 1882; incorporated as the village of Fremont Center in 1875 and as the city of Fremont in 1911; named by Samuel Shupe for John C. Fremont, Civil War general [Fred Dawe, Jr.; Mich Hist 25:56 1941; PO Archives].

**FREMONT**, Saginaw County: Thomas P. Hynes was elected supervisor when this township was organized in 1867, and named for Civil War general, John C. Fremont [Mills].

**FREMONT**, Shiawassee County: platted in 1841 and recorded in 1842 as the village of Florence by Nelson Ferry for John W. Gilbert and Isaac M. Banks; given a post office as Fremont, with Alonzo Howard as its first postmaster, on Nov. 2, 1847; the village flourished until 1856 when the new railroad by-passed it and diverted its business; its post office was closed on Aug. 2, 1881 [Ellis; PO Archives].

**FREMONT**, Tuscola County: William Turner became the first settler in the area in 1856; Fremont Township was organized in 1857; Ezra Tripp, the second settler, became the first postmaster on Oct. 16, 1860, with the office named May, but in 1865, it was moved to and renamed Mayville; the town was named for John C. Fremont, presidential candidate on the Free Soil ticket in 1856 [Page; PO Archives].

**FREMONT LAKE**, Newaygo County: a railroad flag station, near the lake of the same name, in Sheridan Township, in 1878 [GSM 1879].

**FRENCH LANDING,** Kalkaska County: first called France; Mr. McNulty, of Chicago, built the first home here; later, Link Simmons built a sawmill nearby; around 1900, the French Lumber Company, of Battle Creek, built a steam-powered sawmill, giving the settlement its new name, though it was known in the region as France; with the removal of the French mill the village faded away [Barnes].

**FRENCH LANDING,** Wayne County: a station on the Wabash Railroad, in southwest Van Buren Township; Stephen E. Wilson became its first postmaster on Feb. 25, 1896, succeeded by storekeeper Franklin L. Robb; its post office name was spelt as one word, Frenchlanding [Burton; PO Archives].

**FRENCHTOWN,** Monroe County: in 1780, Francois Navarre left Detroit and built his cabin on land deeded him here on the north side of the Rivière aux Raisins by the Indians; by 1784, a hundred French families from Canada had joined him, and Frenchtown became the third permanent community in Michigan, and on Nov. 21, 1815, its second post office, with Laurent Durocher as its first postmaster; the village became a district of the city of Monroe, but the name is retained by the township [Paré; Wing; PO Archives].

**FREY,** Missaukee County: this station on the Grand Rapids & Indiana Railroad, six miles east of Lake City, was given a post office on March 23, 1900, with Edd J. Johnson as its first postmaster, the office operating until June 15, 1903 [GSM 1901; PO Archives].

**FRIDAY,** Delta County: a station on the Whitefish branch of the Chicago & Northwestern Railroad; named for pioneer George Friday [George T. Springer].

**FRIELINGVILLE,** Osceola County: Jacobus Van den Berge became the first postmaster of this rural post office in Highland Township on April 10, 1883, the office operating until March 4, 1887 [GSM 1889; PO Archives].

**FRIEND,** Grand Traverse County: this rural post office, 7½ miles west of Traverse City, was opened on June 29, 1881, with Mrs. Mary Whitesell as its first postmaster, the office operating until July 31, 1882 [GSM 1883; PO Archives].

**FRIESLAND,** Ottawa County. See Vriesland.

**FRITCH,** Sanilac County. See Grange.

**FRITZ CORNERS,** Wayne County: a settlement in Taylor Township, 4 miles southwest of Dearborn, in 1880 [GSM 1881].

**FRONTDALE,** Charlevoix County: Cornelius A. Burnan became the first postmaster of this rural post office on Sept. 11, 1879, the office operating until Aug. 17, 1881 [PO Archives].

**FRONTIER,** Hillsdale County: the first settlers in the area were the William Saxton family in 1834; this village in Woodbridge Township was organized in 1851 and named from its being then the last Michigan settlement before reaching the Ohio line; Benjamin Duealer became its first postmaster on Jan. 30, 1857; the office was closed on Aug. 6, 1858, but was restored from Nov. 9, 1861, to date [Marcine M. Vallieu, PM; Reynolds; PO Archives].

**FROST**, Saginaw County: storekeeper John Shepherd became the first postmaster of this rural post office in Thomaston Township on April 13, 1880; the office was closed on Dec. 8, 1887, but was restored from Jan. 24, 1888, to Sept. 30, 1907 [GSM 1881; PO Archives].

**FROST JUNCTION**, Houghton County. See Withey.

**FRUE**, Houghton County: a copper mining location; organized about 1860 and incorporated in the Miners Copper Company in 1899; named for Captain William Frue, a veteran mine shaft sinker in the area [Stevens].

**FRUITLAND**, Muskegon County: the township, organized in 1869, was so named because it was a land of fruit, chiefly grapes and peaches; on the south shore of White Lake, George Rodgers built a sawmill, which James Dalton bought in 1879, and the village around it was called Mar and its station on the Chicago & Western Michigan (now Pere Marquette) Railroad was named Sweets or Sweets Station; given a post office as Fruitland on May 12, 1871, with Hiram B. Bennett as its first postmaster, the office was renamed Sweet's Station on Oct. 17, 1874, but was closed on Aug. 11, 1876 [Page; PO Archives].

**FRUITPORT**, Muskegon County: founded by Edward L. Craw in 1868 and platted by him for the public use as Crawville; it was renamed Fruitport (it is in a fruit growing area and is a lake port) in 1869; its station on a branch of the Pere Marquette Railroad was named Fruitport Junction; given a post office as Fruitport on April 8, 1869, with Jacob Chapman as its first postmaster; incorporated as a village in 1891 [Charles E. Kinney; PO Archives].

**FRUIT RIDGE**, Lenawee County: this village in Fairfield Township was given a post office named Granger, with storekeeper J. B. Horton as its first postmaster on Feb. 20, 1882; the office was renamed Fruit Ridge on Aug. 28, 1883, and operated until June 15, 1932 [GSM 1885; PO Archives].

**FULLER**, Gogebic County: a railroad siding on the Chicago & Northwestern; named for a jobber in the woods [Victor Lemmer].

**FULLER'S**, Washtenaw County: this rural post office was named for Ormon Fuller who became its first postmaster in March, 1832, but the office was closed on May 8, 1832 [PO Archives].

**FULTON**, Barry County. See Prairieville.

**FULTON**, Gratiot County: first settled in 1846 by Robert Fulton, Arnold Payne, and James Fulton; the township was organized in 1855, with William Norton as its first supervisor [Chapman; MPH 39:68 1899].

**FULTON**, Kalamazoo County: founded in 1843 by Jacob Gardner as Gardner's Corners, about a mile north of the present village; about 1860, its buildings were removed here, and the place was named Wakeshma Centre, from its location in Wakeshma Township; William H. Selkrig became its first postmaster on July 30, 1868; at the request of Justice John Codman, the committee of the townspeople renamed it Fulton after his native county in New York State; its post office was so renamed on Nov. 1, 1869 [Lillian E. Kersten, PM; PO Archives].

**FULTON**, Keweenaw County: a mining location; the Forsyth Mine had been worked here until 1847; it was re-opened by the Fulton Mining Company in 1853; in 1898, the Mohawk Mining Company took over the lands of the Fulton firm, but the name Fulton remained and remains on maps; a station on the Hancock & Calumet Railroad [Madeleine Gibson].

**FUMEE**, Menominee County: a station on a branch of the Chicago & Northwestern Railroad, near the Wisconsin line, in 1884 [GSM 1885].

**FURNACEVILLE**, Antrim County. See Antrim.

**FYFE LAKE**, Grand Traverse County: the Grand Rapids & Indiana Railroad officials made an error when they spelled it Fyfe Lake; see Fife Lake.

**GAASTRA**, Iron County: the tract upon which the city is located was selected by Alfred Kidder, of Marquette, in 1879, and he received his patent to it in 1881; he conveyed it to Andrew Young in 1884; Edwin H. Piper owned it in 1902, and in Oct., 1908, Douwe Gaastra, a building contractor and real estate speculator, bought it and platted the village named for him; merchant Olaf A. Olson became its first postmaster on Sept. 26, 1914, serving until he retired in 1953; incorporated as a village in 1919 and as a city in 1949 [Hill].

**GAGETOWN**, Tuscola County: in 1869, Joseph Gage built a mill and a store on his land here, and in 1871, platted the village; James Gage became its first postmaster on May 24, 1870; incorporated as a village in 1887 [J. A. Gallery; PO Archives].

**GAINES**, Genesee County: the first settler in the area was Hartford Cargill in 1836; Joshua Dart came in 1839, and, when the township was organized in 1842, he had it named for his friend, General E. P. Gaines; in 1856, the first passenger train came through the forest here, and its depot was the first building in the future town; a post office just east of here was opened on the Bergan C. Covert farm on Oct. 4, 1852, and was moved to Gaines with the coming of the railroad; the office was named Gaines (after the township), but was renamed Covert on Jan. 2, 1863; the Gaines Station post office was renamed Gaines on Sept. 25, 1902 [Ruth Barton: Wood; PO Archives].

**GAINES CENTER**, Kent County: this village in Gaines Township was given a post office on June 6, 1854, with Peter Van Lew as its first postmaster, the office operating until Nov. 15, 1856 [GSM 1860; PO Archives].

**GAINES STATION,** Genesee County: on Dec. 22, 1856, George B. Runyan became the first postmaster at this station on the Detroit & Milwaukee Railroad; the office was renamed Gaines on Sept. 25, 1902, and the Station is now a part of the village of Gaines [GSM 1860; PO Archives].

**GAINESVILLE,** Kent County: Gaines Township was first settled by Alexander Clark in 1837 and Alexander L. Bouck later that year; the township was organized in 1848; its village was given a station on the Grand Rapids & Indiana Railroad and on Sept. 29, 1856, a post office, with Peter Van Lew as its first postmaster, the office operating until Oct. 25, 1871 [Dillenback; PO Archives].

**GALBRAITH'S CORNERS,** Sanilac County. See Amadore.

**GALE,** Oceana County: farmer James W. Hibbard became the first postmaster of this rural post office in Newfield Township on Oct. 14, 1899, the office operating until Sept. 15, 1906 [GSM 1901-07; PO Archives].

**GALESBURG,** Kalamazoo County: founded in 1835 by George L. Gale who named it Morton, believed to have been given in honor of John Morton, a signer of the Declaration of Independence; Nathaniel Cothren became the first postmaster on Jan. 15, 1836; platted by F. J. Littlejohn in 1837; in that year a citizens' committee voted to change the name to that of the founder, and on May 2, 1838, its post office was changed to Galesburg (first spelled Galesburgh); incorporated as a village in 1861 and as a city in 1931 [Winifred M. Buss, PM].

**GALIEN,** Berrien County: locally pronounced Galeen; in 1853, George A. Blakeslee bought the mill here and the future village site; in 1854, he built the first store, in which was the first post office, with him becoming its first postmaster on June 9, 1856; platted in 1861; incorporated as a village in 1879; named from the nearby river which had been named for René Brehant de Galinée, a Sulpician priest who was a map maker for the missionaries in the state as early as 1670; by legislative action, the name of the river was altered to Galien in 1829 and of the township in 1844 [Noggle; PO Archives].

**GALILEE,** Emmet County: a hamlet in 1859 [GSM 1860].

**GALLOWAY,** Gratiot County: when Richard Galloway became the first postmaster of this rural post office, named for him, on Feb. 16, 1883, it was in Saginaw County; the office was closed on Jan. 19, 1885, but was restored on July 16, 1889; on Jan. 15, 1896, the postmaster moved across the Gratiot County line and took the office with him where it remained until it was closed on Oct. 31, 1902 [Tucker; PO Archives].

**GALT,** Missaukee County: William McBain became the first postmaster of this village in Riverside Township on June 23, 1874; the office was closed on Jan. 20, 1879, but was restored from March 28, 1879, to Sept. 15, 1908; it was also known locally as Galt Farm [Thomas Blinn; PO Archives].

**GAMBLEVILLE,** Hillsdale County. See Somerset.

**GANGES,** Allegan County: Harrison Hutchins, from Vermont, became the first settler in the area in 1838; besides farming, the first business here was the blacksmith shop of C. O. Hamlin who arrived in 1846; Ganges Township was organized in 1847, and was named by Dr. Joseph Coates, a member of the legislature from Otsego, after the holy river of India, for reasons unknown; the town took the name of the township; Samuel M. Thompson became its first postmaster on June 15, 1854, the office operating until Nov. 12, 1954 [Johnson; MPH 26:23 1895; PO Archives].

**GARDEN,** Delta County: from the fertility of the soil the township was named Garden, the adjoining bay Garden Bay, and the village which followed, Garden; Philomen Thompson, the first settler, built his cabin here in 1850; most of the early settlers were of French origin; the settlement was also known as Haley's Bay, or as Garden Bay; given a post office as Garden on Sept. 7, 1865, with Asel Y. Bailey as its first postmaster; the office was closed on Jan. 30, 1871, but was restored from Sept. 20, 1872, to April 27, 1874; incorporated as a village in 1886 [David S. Coon; PO Archives].

**GARDEN CITY,** Keweenaw County: a copper mining location; the Garden City Mine opened in 1859 and was closed in 1868, after which it became the property of Phoenix Consolidated [Stevens].

**GARDEN CITY,** Wayne County: founded and platted as subdivisions in Nankin Township by Arnold F. Folker in 1921 and when the village was incorporated in 1927 he became its first president; Glenn O. Donner became its first postmaster on April 28, 1931; incorporated as a city in 1933; so named because it was platted into large enough lots for their owners, when unemployed, to cultivate vegetable gardens [L. Clarke Oldenburg; PO Archives].

**GARDENDALE,** St. Clair County: a station on the Pere Marquette Railroad; Thomas S. Skinner became its first postmaster on March 28, 1891, the office operating until March 24, 1906 [Mich Manual 1899; PO Archives].

**GARDENVILLE,** Gratiot County: lumberman Robert McFarland became the first postmaster of this rural post office in western New Haven Township on March 28, 1895, the office operating until Dec. 31, 1902 [Tucker].

**GARDNER,** Menominee County: began as a logging spur, about 1894; named for Auti Gardner, a lumberman, in 1934; now a farming community with a general store [Mrs. Daniel Deacon].

**GARDNER'S CORNERS,** Clinton County: Samuel Gardner located land here in 1839 and built a widely-known tavern in 1840; after his death in 1867, his widow ran the tavern until it burned down in 1872; he was also the first postmaster here from Nov. 16, 1855, until the office was closed on June 30, 1858 [Ellis; PO Archives].

**GARDNER'S CORNERS,** Kalamazoo County. See Fulton.

**GARD'S PRAIRIE,** Cass County: the camping ground of Chief Weesaw and his Pottawattomis; named for Jonathan Gard, pioneer settler in 1829, in what became Volinia Township [Mich Hist 32:25 1948].

**GARFIELD,** Bay County: named after its township, which was organized in 1887, and named for the late President James A. Garfield, with Elof Johnson as its first supervisor; Clara E. Johnson became its first postmaster on May 13, 1897, the office operating until April 30, 1904 [Gansser; PO Archives].

**GARFIELD,** Grand Traverse County: the township was organized in 1882, with H. E. Steward as its first supervisor; named for General (later President) James A. Garfield [Sprague].

**GARFIELD,** Missaukee County: farmer William N. Taylor became the first postmaster of this rural post office in Richland Township on July 12, 1880, the office operating until June 15, 1882; named for President James A. Garfield [GSM 1883; PO Archives].

**GARFIELD,** Saginaw County: began as a lumbering town about 1870, with the mills of L. Pennoyer and R. H. Nason; the latter, with Helen B. Allen and W. Husen, also built a salt block here in 1879; a station on the Michigan Central Railroad; named after the nearby Garfield coal mine; its post office was Eastwood [Mills; Federal].

**GARFIELD HARBOR,** Mackinac County: here on the northern shore of Lake Michigan, Hall, Thompson & Company built a large steam sawmill in 1882, and it was soon followed by stores and homes [Andreas].

**GARLICK,** Ontonagon County: Daniel Beaser became the first postmaster of this rural post office on Feb. 4, 1860, the office operating until April 12, 1865 [PO Archives].

**GARNET,** Mackinac County: a station named Welch on the Minneapolis, St. Paul & Sault Ste. Marie Railroad, in Hendricks Township, in 1891; the settlement formed around the sawmill and general store of Hudson & Donaldson in 1897; George A. Donaldson became its first postmaster on Nov. 4, 1898, and was still serving when the name was changed to Garnet on Dec. 31, 1904 [GSM 1899-1905; PO Archives].

**GARNSEY,** Calhoun County. See Battle Creek.

**GARTH,** Delta County: first known as Whitefish Point and as Peacock Point for Robert Peacock who built a sawmill here in 1872; he sold it to Jacob Martin, of Chicago, who in turn sold it to the Garth Lumber Company, of Wisconsin, in 1893, when it was renamed Garth; Omer G. Lindsay became its first postmaster on May 7, 1894; the office was closed on Oct. 31, 1903, but was restored from May 10, 1906, to Nov. 30, 1907; now just the site of summer homes along Little Bay de Noc [Gertrude Henderson; PO Archives].

**GARWOOD LAKE,** Berrien County: named for the first white settler in Galien Township, Samuel H. Garwood, who in 1834 selected his land and built his cabin by this body of water [Noggle].

**GASKILL,** Barry County: a rural post office named for nursery agent Stephen Gaskill, who became its first postmaster on Dec. 21, 1889, the office operating until Oct. 15, 1903 [GSM 1891; PO Archives].

**GASTON,** Wexford County. See Harrietta.

**GATES,** Tuscola County. See Reese.

**GATES CORNERS,** Barry County: Benjamin S. Dibble became its first postmaster on May 6, 1839; the office was moved some three miles to Middleville on May 18, 1843; in 1848, the legislature changed the name of the township from Gates to Yankee Springs [Potter].

**GATESVILLE,** Chippewa County. See Goetzville.

**GAY,** Keweenaw County: the Mohawk Mining Company, organized in 1898, had a stamping mill here on the Lake Superior shore; Barnett Shearer, superintendent of the firm, became the first postmaster on Aug. 11, 1904, with the office still operating though the village is now a hamlet; named for Joseph E. Gay, long identified with copper mining in the area [PM; GSM 1903; PO Archives].

**GAYLORD,** Otsego County: the settlement was first called Barnes; early settlers included Dr. N. L. Parmater, C. C. Mitchell and William H. Smith; when the Jackson, Lansing & Saginaw Railroad came through in 1874, the village was renamed for A. S. Gaylord, an attorney for the road; William H. Smith became its first postmaster on June 23, 1874; made the county seat in 1878; incorporated as a village in 1881 and as a city in 1922 [Herbert A. Hutchins].

**GEARY,** Clinton County: John Miller became the first postmaster at this railroad station in Victor Township on June 5, 1857, the office operating until May 15, 1903; named by a local admirer of General John White Geary, then governor of Kansas [Ellis; PO Archives].

**GEDDES,** Washtenaw County: Orrin White and his family became the first settlers in 1824, followed by George Rush and his family later that year; Robert Geddes came in 1825, and it was on his farm that the village was located; John Geddes became its first postmaster on July 21, 1875; the office was closed on Sept. 21, 1875, but was restored from May 3, 1894, to July 31, 1901; a station on the Michigan Central Railroad in 1878; its first industry was the pulp mill of the Ypsilanti Paper Company [Chapman; PO Archives].

**GEELS,** Roscommon County: believed to have been named for the lumberman who used its Michigan Central Railroad siding; had a general store, a school and a post office of which Henry Traubenkraut became the first postmaster on May 18, 1914; it was about midway between Roscommon and St. Helen [Co. Bd. of Ed.; PO Archives].

**GEER,** Washtenaw County: a rural post office named for William

Geer who became its first postmaster on June 13, 1890, the office operating until Aug. 31, 1900 [GSM 1891-1901; PO Archives].

**GELOSTER**, Kalamazoo County. See Richland.

**GEM**, Ontonagon County: founded in a mining district about 1890 as a spur of the Duluth, South Shore & Atlantic Railroad, which also named it [Charles Willman].

**GENA**, Delta County: Franklin E. Lowell became its first postmaster on Aug. 12, 1861, the office operating until May 7, 1866; the name is believed to have been a corruption of Jena, probably after Oliver Newberry's Great Lakes supply ship, Jena [David S. Coon; PO Archives].

**GENEREAUVILLE**, Ionia County: about 1830, Louis Genereau and his son began an Indian trading post here on the Grand River, about a mile west of Lyons; the Campaus, who came into possession after the departure of the Genereaus, tried in vain to make a village of it [Schenck].

**GENESEE**, Genesee County: the first settlers in the area were Luman Beach and Addison Stewart in 1833; Ruben McCrury and Simon King platted the village as Geneseeville in 1858; Genesee (village, township, and county) were so named because many of the early settlers had come from Genesee (Jenishiyeh, Seneca for beautiful valley) County, N.Y.; the Mount Morris post office was changed to Genesee on Jan. 19, 1839, but back to Mount Morris on April 25, 1857, but on the same day, Geneseeville was given a post office as Genesee Village, with Martin W. Lake as postmaster; the name was shortened to Genesee on May 21, 1892 [Wood; PO Archives].

**GENESEE PRAIRIE**, Kalamazoo County: Enoch Harris became the first settler here in 1829; Anthony Cooley and Edward Smith, pioneer settlers, named after the town they had come from, Genesee, N.Y. [MPH 18:598 1891].

**GENEVA**, Cass County: here in Penn Township, on the north shore of Deadwood (now Diamond) Lake, John Agard opened a general store in 1830; the village was platted in 1831 and recorded in 1832 by Colonel E. S. Sibley, H. L. and A. C. Stewart, Abner Kelsey, and Dr. Henry H. Fowler; Dr. Fowler named it after Geneva, N.Y.; the first (1830) county seat for about a year; now a ghost town; the village site and vicinity becoming known as Shore Acres [Fox; Glover; Rogers].

**GENEVA**, Huron County. See Bay Port.

**GENEVA**, Lenawee County: William Town became the first postmaster of this rural post office in Rollin Township on July 7, 1854, the office operating until Jan. 15, 1908 [PO Archives].

**GENOA**, Livingston County: the first land entries in the area were made by Almon Maltby and John White, both in 1833; the first actual settlement was made by Pardon and Eli Barnard, brothers, and Thomas Pinckney, in 1835; the township was organized in 1837, and the town was named after it; Charles P. Bush became its first postmaster on May 29, 1839; the office was changed to South Genoa on March 13, 1863, but the Genoa post office was re-established on June 12, 1863, and operated until Jan. 31, 1882 [Ellis; PO Archives].

**GENOA**, Macomb County: in 1837, John N. Draper platted and named this village in Armada Township, laying out 192 lots of 50 by 100 feet; but why it was conceived and why it never existed, except on paper, is not known [Eldredge].

**GEORGETOWN**, Cass County. See Nicholsville.

**GEORGETOWN**, Ottawa County: named after its township which was first settled in 1834 by Hiram and Samuel Jenison; Stephen L. Lowing became its first postmaster on March 24, 1852, succeeded by Isaac Lowing on July 15, 1858, the office operating until Aug. 31, 1901 [Lillie; PO Archives].

**GERA**, Saginaw County: the village began as a depot on the Michigan Central Railroad and was first named Frankenmuth Station (it is in Frankenmuth Township; see Frankenmuth for the name); on April 23, 1894, it was renamed Gera, after a town in Germany, and given a post office with George F. McNeal as its first postmaster, the office operating until 1902 [Blinn; GSM 1895].

**GERKEY**, Barry County: Dennis Haskell became the first postmaster of this small settlement in Carlton Township on Jan. 4, 1884, the office operating until June 17, 1902 [GSM 1895-1903; PO Archives].

**GERMAN**, Ingham County: also called the German Settlement; this community in Alaiedon Township got its name from the large number of Germans who settled in the area [Foster].

**GERMAN SETTLEMENT**, Huron County. See Ruth.

**GERMAN SETTLEMENT**, Ionia County. See Miriam.

**GERMANIA**, Sanilac County: in 1872, Julius Davis, acting for the Bay Furnace Company and the Munising Iron Company, went to Saxony, Germany, to induce fifty miners and their families to mine in Michigan; in 1873, he brought back some 250, and since these were more than the mines needed, some bought land here in Marlette Township, produced farms and formed a community; Henry Planz became its first postmaster on Feb. 19, 1878, the office operating until July 15, 1911 [Jenks; PO Archives].

**GERMFASK**, Schoolcraft County: the town was named from the township which had been named by Dr. W. W. French from a word formed from the surname initials of the eight founding settlers of 1881: John Grant, Matthew Edge, George Robinson, Thaddeus Mead, Dr. W. W. French, Ezekiel Ackley, Oscar Shepard, Hezekiah Knaggs; the village was started in 1890 and was given a post office on Feb. 26, 1890, with Janet E. Robinson as its first postmaster; a station on the Manistique Railway [Leonard England, PM].

**GERT**, Monroe County: John Gilhousen became the first postmaster of this rural post office on Feb. 16, 1895, the office operating until March 31, 1904 [PO Archives].

**GEYERSVILLE**, Cheboygan County: this rural post office in Inverness Township was named for Chalres H. Geyer who became its first postmaster on Nov. 12, 1877, the office operating until June 7, 1878 [GSM 1879; PO Archives].

**GIBBS**, Alger County: a station on the Detroit, Mackinaw & Marquette Railroad in 1886 [GSM 1887].

**GIBBS**, Ionia County: a hamlet in 1878 [GSM 1879].

**GIBBS CITY**, Iron County: a sawmill settlement on the Paint River; named for R. F. Gibbs, a hardwood lumberman, who operated here from 1913 to 1921; Ame E. Raidle became its first postmaster on May 24, 1917, the office operating until Oct. 31, 1952; now a ghost town [Jack Hill, Sr.; PO Archives].

**GIBRALTAR**, Kent County. See Childsdale.

**GIBRALTAR**, Wayne County: first settled in 1811, it was platted and recorded on March 14, 1837, by Peter Godfroy, Benjamin B. Kerchival and Joshua Howard, trustees of the Gibralter & Flat Rock Company; Amos Dunbar became the first postmaster of Gibralter on Oct. 2, 1837; the office was renamed Woodbury on Dec. 8, 1838, but back to Gibralter on May 13, 1839, with the spelling changed to Gibraltar on Dec. 19, 1900, until it was closed on Jan. 31, 1910; the village did not prosper until revived by the suburban boom; incorporated as a village in 1954 and as a city in 1961 [Burton; County plat liber; PO Archives].

**GIBSON**, Allegan County: fruit grower Harvey Doane became the first postmaster of this rural post office on Feb. 8, 1878, the office ope ating until Jan. 14, 1905 [GSM 1879; PO Archives].

**GIBSONVILLE**, Genesee County: also known as Whigville; here was built the first sawmill in the county, by Rowland B. Perry, in 1828; during the lifetime of Charles D. W. Gibson, considerable business was done in this village named for him, but when in 1864 the railroad by-passed it, its trade was transferred to Grand Blanc, and it reverted to hamlet status by 1877 [Ellis].

**GIDDINGS**, Baraga County: this settlement around the Giddings sawmill, 3 miles west of Baraga, was given a post office on Aug. 1, 1888, with Luther W. Giddings as its first postmaster, the office operating until May 31, 1889 [GSM 1889; PO Archives; George Springer].

**GIDLEY'S STATION**, Jackson County: the first railroad station on the Michigan Central in Parma Township, named for local landowner Townsend E. Gidley, in 1845; Cornelius Coolbaugh became its first postmaster on Feb. 11, 1845, but the office was transferred to Parma on Jan. 27, 1862 [DeLand; MPH 27:593 1896; PO Archives].

**GIFFORD**, Ingham County: this hamlet was given a post office named for Daniel Gifford who became its first postmaster on Feb. 8, 1871, the office operating until Dec. 23, 1872 [GSM 1873; PO Archives].

**GILBERT**, Oakland County: Lester Sowles became the first postmaster of this rural post office on Feb. 20, 1857, the office operating until Dec. 19, 1862 [PO Archives].

**GILBERT**, Wexford County: a lumber settlement with a station on a branch of the Grand Rapids & Indiana Railroad, in Cedar Creek Township; storekeeper Andrew Carlson became its first postmaster on Nov. 1, 1883 [GSM 1889; PO Archives].

**GILCHRIST**, Allegan County: a hamlet with a station on the Chicago & Western Michigan (now Pere Marquette) Railroad in 1878 [GSM 1879].

**GILCHRIST**, Mackinac County: a lumber settlement with a station on the Minneapolis, St. Paul & Sault Ste. Marie Railroad, in Garfield Township; Walter Burton became its first postmaster on Sept. 26, 1879; the office was closed on June 25, 1883, but was restored from June 12, 1888, to Oct. 3, 1891, and from Nov. 26, 1906; named for John Gilchrist, a local landowner [Emerson Smith; GSM 1889; PO Archives].

**GILEAD**, Branch County: the first settler in the town was John Croy in 1831; later the same year, Bishop Philander Chase, who had come from Mount Gilead, Ohio, intending to found an Episcopalian community and college, began by building the first frame house here, named the place, and became its first postmaster on March 2, 1833; but his plans failed and he soon left for other parts, but its post office operated until Jan. 31, 1906 [Johnson; PO Archives].

**GILFORD**, Tuscola County: named for the Gilford family who lived on the northeast corner of the crossroads here; James A. Black became the first postmaster on June 8, 1869; the office was closed on July 12, 1875, but was restored on Aug. 5, 1878, with furniture manufacturer Solon E. Stanton as postmaster, and has been operating since [Claudie R. Horne, PM].

**GILL'S PIER**, Leelanau County: a settlement around the William Gill & Son lumber mill on the Lake Michigan shore between Leland and the tip of the peninsula in 1875; the son's name was Wilbur, and he became the first postmaster on Jan. 22, 1883, the office operating until Jan. 15, 1908 [Dickinson; GSM 1885; PO Archives].

**GILMORE**, Benzie County: Joseph Robar and John B. Dory settled here in Blaine Township, on the Lake Michigan shore, in 1855; Benjamin Farley became the first postmaster on Dec. 19, 1870, the office operating until Aug. 11, 1884; L. W. Crane, veteran lumberman, built a sawmill here in 1872; James Gilmore was the pioneer newspaper publisher in the county [MPH 31:125 1901; PO Archives].

**GILMORE**, Isabella County: the township was organized in 1870 and named for General Gilmore by Rufus F. Glass, who was elected the first supervisor; Jesse H. Wood became its first postmaster on Nov. 30, 1891, the office operating until Nov. 30, 1906 [Fancher; PO Archives].

**GILTEDGE**, Wayne County: Asa B. Smith was appointed the first postmaster of this rural post office in Livonia Township on Nov. 19, 1898, but declined, and Frank E. Bradley became the first postmaster on Feb. 10, 1899, the office operating until July 31, 1902 [GSM 1903; PO Archives].

**GINGELLVILLE**, Oakland County: in 1927, Frank Gingell bought 18 acres on Baldwin Road, in Orion Township; he platted it and called it Gingellmont Subdivision, and as business and homes were built, it took the name of Gingellville [Mrs. Ella Gingell].

**GIRARD**, Branch County: founded by Richard W. Corbus in 1829; John Parkinson became its first postmaster on May 2, 1835; named for Stephen Girard, American philanthropist; the village is governed by its township [Oscar F. Renshaw; PO Archives].

**GITCHEL**, Ottawa County: John Danistra became the first postmaster of this Dutch settlement in Jamestown Township on Dec. 4, 1886, the office operating until Oct. 31, 1902 [GSM 1887-1903; PO Archives].

**GLADSTONE**, Delta County: the townsite was carved from the Township of Minnewasca (Sioux for white water); in 1887, when the plat was about to be recorded, William D. Washburn, flour miller and projector of the Minneapolis, St. Paul & Sault Ste. Marie Railroad (completed with British capital), got its name changed from Minnewasca to that of the British prime minister, William Ewart Gladstone; Richard Mertz became the first postmaster on May 24, 1887; incorporated as a village in 1887 and as a city in 1889 [George T. Springer; Mich Hist 30:380 1946].

**GLADWIN**, Gladwin County: the village was first platted in 1875 and named Cedar from its location on the Cedar River; but there was another Cedar post office in Michigan and when this village was given one on Sept. 8, 1875, with Elias Steele as its first postmaster, it took the name of its county which had been named in 1831 for Major Henry Gladwin, British commander at Detroit, hero in Pontiac's assaults; incorporated as a village in 1885 and as a city in 1893 [Emma Clamer; PO Archives].

**GLADYS**, Chippewa County: it began as a railroad station where the products of the area were picked up; Mr. Sykes built the first home here and when Judge Colwell bought it from him he named the place for his daughter, Gladys Colwell [Lillian M. Wylie].

**GLASS CREEK**, Barry County: a post office was opened on Dec. 10, 1849, as Glass Creek, in the home of the first postmaster, Chauncey H. Brewer, who lived on Glass Creek, in Rutland Township, the office operating until Sept. 17, 1864 [Johnson; PO Archives].

**GLASS RIVER**, Shiawassee County: the first land entries here were made by Allen Beard and Lyman Melvin, New Yorkers, in 1836, Antrim Township was organized in 1838, with Thomas B. Flint as its first supervisor; also in 1838, John Stiles conducted the first school, in a cabin, the former home of Horace R. Flint; the first post office was opened in the home of the postmaster, John Sear, on May 1, 1851, and was named Antrim after its township; on March 17, 1868, it was renamed after the Looking Glass River which runs the length of the township; the office operated until Sept. 13, 1888 [Ellis; MPH 26:478 1895; Campbell; PO Archives].

**GLEASON'S**, Marquette County: a railroad station in 1878 [GSM 1879].

**GLEN ARBOR**, Leelanau County: John LaRue, from Chicago, took up residence here in 1848; he was joined by John E. Fisher and John Dorsey about 1854; the village was named by Mrs. Fisher who, observing a dense mass of wild grapes entwined in the tree tops, said it was a glen arbor created by nature, and the name stood and still stands; it had a hollow-tree post office before being given an official one by the federal government on July 6, 1857, with Mr. George Ray as its first postmaster [Barnes].

**GLENCOE**, Bay County: it began as a lumber settlement around the mill of George Campbell & Company in 1873, and he became its first postmaster on Aug. 18, 1876, the office operating until May 28, 1878 [GSM 1875-79; PO Archives].

**GLENCOE**, Huron County: Thompson Shepherd became the first postmaster of this rural post office on Feb. 15, 1901, the office operating until July 14, 1914 [PO Archives].

**GLENDALE**, Van Buren County: storekeeper William D. Lane became the first postmaster of Lemont, in Waverly Township, on Jan. 2, 1868; the office was named by Bailey Stanley after one of his favorite hymn-book tunes; but the name was so often confused with Lamont, a post office in Ottawa County, that on Nov. 11, 1868, it was changed to Glendale until it was closed on March 15, 1904 [Ellis; PO Archives].

**GLENDORA**, Berrien County: the village began in 1890 as a station on the St. Joseph-Galien branch of the Michigan Central Railroad; named by the officials of the Vandalia Company which built the road; storekeeper H. H. Hutchinson became its first postmaster on Jan. 2, 1891, the office operating until March 17, 1966 [Fox; GSM 1893; PO Archives].

**GLEN ELM**, Mecosta County. See Big Rapids.

**GLENGARRY**, Wexford County: a settlement near Sherman in 1910 [GSM 1911].

**GLEN HAVEN**, Leelanau County: its hotel, Sleeping Bear House, was built in 1857, and a dock for steamers to wood about 1859, then a sawmill, a store, a lighthouse and a coast guard station were added; given a post office on Oct. 28, 1869, with Enos R. Matthews as its first postmaster; the office was closed on May 5, 1879; but was restored from June 24, 1879, to Dec. 31, 1936 [Sprague; Federal; PO Archives].

**GLENLORD**, Berrien County: the Titus Atlas of Berrien County, 1873, shows the station as Lincoln (after its township); Monroe N. Lord donated the land for the right of way to the Chicago & Western Michigan (now Pere Marquette) Railroad, and Mr. Morrison, who constructed the road, named it for him; given a post office as Glen Lord, with Mr. Lord as its first postmaster, on March 28, 1879, the office operating until Oct. 31, 1905 [Fox; PO Archives].

**GLENMERE**, Leelanau County: Richard Tobin became the first postmaster of this rural post office, 8 miles from Cedar, on Jan. 31, 1905 [GSM 1907; PO Archives].

**GLENN**, Allegan County: on Dec. 8, 1856, with Lawrence Heydt as its first postmaster, the New Casco post office was opened in Casco Township; during the tenure of the third postmaster, William O. Packard, the office was moved to Packard Corners in Ganges Township, and on May 15, 1876, the name of the office was changed to Glenn [Donald Hutchins, PM; GSM 1860; PO Archives].

**GLENNIE**, Alcona County: given a depot on the Detroit & Mackinaw Railroad as Glennie Station and a post office of the same name on Oct. 5, 1889, with Ella Deacon as its first postmaster; the name was shortened to Glennie on Oct. 2, 1894; the village plat was not recorded until 1940 [Blinn; PO Archives].

**GLENWOOD**, Cass County: it was first called Tietsort's Crossing after Abram "Big Abe" Tietsort (cousin of the Ambram Tietsort, the first settler in Cassopolis); he had a store here in Wayne Township and the Michigan Central Railroad named its station here Tietsort's; on Aug. 1, 1865, with Amasa H. Wordan as its first postmaster, it was given a post office named Model City, but the office was renamed Glenwood on Dec. 10, 1873; platted by Craigie Sharp in 1874 [Mrs. L. L. Vanderburg; Rogers; PO Archives].

**GLENWOOD**, Wayne County: a station on the Lake Shore & Michigan Southern Railroad, in Ecorse Township; first called New Jerusalem, due to the polyglot makeup of its citizenry; incorporated as the village of Glenwood in 1900; storekeeper Herman G. Turske became its first postmaster on Oct. 21, 1901, with the office named Bacon, after a prominent local family (there was already a Glenwood post office in Michigan); an additional plat of the village was made by J. S. Johnson and recorded on May 26, 1903; annexed by the city of Wyandotte in 1905; its post office was closed on April 30, 1906 [GSM 1903-05; County plat liber; PO Archives].

**GLOVER**, Bay County: Matthew P. Umphrey became the first postmaster of this rural post office, 8 miles from Sterling, on March 15, 1900, the office operating until March 15, 1905 [GSM 1901-07; PO Archives].

**GNADENHUETTEN**, Macomb County: a Moravian Indian mission founded by Rev. David Zeisberger in 1782, but closed in 1786 due largely to the increasing hostility of the Chippewas; the name means tents of grace; it is called New Gnadenhuetten in Moravian history to distinguish it from other places which the sect had called Gnadenhuetten; sometimes referred to as Moravian Village; its site is marked by a small monument on Moravian Drive, just west of Mount Clemens [Mich Hist 23:367 1939].

**GOBLES**, Van Buren County: John Goble built the first building here, a hotel, in 1864-65; platted as Gobleville by Hiram E. Goble in 1870, with an addition by Warren Goble in 1872; Hiram E. Goble became the first postmaster of Gobleville on April 16, 1872; incorporated as a village in 1893; renamed Gobles on April 10, 1922; incorporated as a city in 1957 [Donna Curtiss; PO Archives].

**GODFREY**, Montmorency County: a rural post office in Long Rapids Township, named for Henry C. Godfrey who became its first postmaster on Aug. 23, 1883; the office, then in Alpena County, was changed to Montmorency on March 4, 1887, and operated until Oct. 31, 1912 [GSM 1885; PO Archives].

**GOETZVILLE**, Chippewa County: the Goetz family, Joseph, Alois, Matthew, Paul, and Alexander, settled here in Detour Township and opened business in 1882; Joseph Goetz became the first postmaster on Oct. 24, 1882, with the office spelled Gatesville, but changed to Goetzville on Feb. 13, 1917 [GSM 1885; PO Archives].

**GOGARNVILLE**, Alger County: on Oct. 23, 1889, the Munising post office was moved to the Gogarn farm and named Gogarnville, with German-born, American Civil War veteran, and first Munising Township supervisor Julius Gogarn as its postmaster, the office operating until July 7, 1893 [PO Archives; Munising News, March 3, 1935].

**GOGEBIC**, Gogebic County: a station on the M., L.S. & W. Railroad; Louis F. Bourquin became its first postmaster on March 3, 1885, the office operating until Nov. 11, 1886; it was in Ontonagon County until Gogebic was organized in 1887; the Gogebic Station post office was opened on June 4, 1886, with Frank Crowe as its first postmaster; this office was closed on April 20, 1888, but was restored on May 12, 1888, and was renamed simply Gogebic, on May 25, 1894; the office was closed on Sept. 15, 1900, but was restored from March 4, 1902, to March 31, 1908, and from June 25, 1908, to Jan. 31, 1914; Gogebic was derived from the Indian word agogebic, of disputed meaning, Havighurst says it meant trembling ground [PO Archives; Victor Lemmer].

**GOGOMAIN**, Chippewa County: this village was given the Indian name for porcupine [Hamilton].

**GOGUAC**, Calhoun County: also called Goguac Prairie; first settled by the man who first surveyed it, Dorrance Williams; Isaac Thomas came in 1830; the name (also spelled Coguaiack, Goguagick, etc.), is Indian for pleasant water; the name is retained in Goguac Lake [MPH 5:256 1884; Mich Hist 32:27 1948].

**GOLDEN**, Oceana County: Golden Township was formed in 1864 and the town on the Chicago & Western Michigan (now Pere Marquette) Railroad was named after it; given a post office as East Golden, from its location in the township, on May 1, 1874, with Henry Howarth as its first postmaster; the office was closed on March 21, 1881, but was restored from May 2, 1881, to Nov. 2, 1883; pioneer settler William J. Haughey had recommended his mother's maiden name of (Maria) Golding, but through a clerical error it became Golden and remained so in the records [Royal; Hartwick; PO Archives].

**GOLDING**, Oceana County: Henry Bosworth became the first postmaster of this rural post office on March 12, 1866, the office operating until Feb. 6, 1877; for the name see Golden [GSM 1879; PO Archives].

**GOODAR**, Ogemaw County: Samuel A. Robinson became the first postmaster of this rural post office on Sept. 4, 1909 [PO Archives].

**GOODELLS**, St. Clair County: about half of the land in the area was bought by speculators, and as late as 1840, there were but three resident property owners; Clark S. Cusick, Joseph H. Dutton and Joshua Tompkins; the village was founded in 1866 when the Grand Trunk Railroad came through and opened a station here; John C. Johnstone became its first postmaster on Nov. 7, 1870; named for John Goodell [PM; Jenks].

**GOOD HARBOR**, Leelanau County: first settled by lake-man, H. D. Pheatt in 1863; he built a dock and later a sawmill here, but he moved away and the brothers Richard, Otto and Henry Schomberg moved in and developed the village; August Bartling became its first postmaster on June 27, 1866; when the mill burned down in 1906, the village lost its heart, and the inhabitants began to move away; its post office was closed on July 31, 1907; named from its being on a good harbor [Dickinson; Kropp; PO Archives].

**GOOD HART**, Emmet County: the site was part of the Indian settlement of L'Arbre Croche; Joseph Black Hawk was one of its chiefs, and his brother was named Great Heart or Good Heart; Silas W. McNeil became the first postmaster of Good Hart (which the Indian agent misspelled for Good Heart, and the error still stands), on Dec. 17, 1874; now mostly a summer resort, with few Indians left [Clifford Powers, PM].

**GOODING**, Ottawa County: it was in Kent County when given a station on the Toledo, Saginaw & Muskegon Railroad and a post office, with storekeeper Richard J. Gooding becoming its first postmaster, with the office named for him, on Nov. 19, 1888; the office was transferred to Ottawa County on June 5, 1918, and operated until Jan. 31, 1923 [GSM 1889; PO Archives].

**GOODISON**, Oakland County: among the first settlers in the area, Jonathan Carpenter, of Dutchess County, N.Y., took up land here about 1834; Needham Hemingway built a dam across the Paint Creek for his grist mill in 1835; William Goodison bought and enlarged the mill and the settlement around it was named for him; Lemuel P. Tower became its first postmaster on Dec. 12, 1872; the office was closed on Jan. 26, 1873, but was restored on Jan. 20, 1874 [Mrs. C. G. Lorion; Seeley; PO Archives].

**GOODLAND,** Lapeer County: James Hills became the first actual settler here in 1851; although he did not remain, he is said to have recommended the name given to the township when it was organized in 1855; John C. Marris became its first postmaster on July 11, 1856, the office operating until April 15, 1901 [Page; PO Archives].

**GOODMAN,** Huron County: a station on the M., T. & H. Railroad; Mrs. Alice M. Robinson became its first postmaster on June 26, 1889; the office was transferred to and renamed Grassmere on Aug. 7, 1891 [GSM 1891; PO Archives].

**GOODRICH,** Genesee County: in 1835, the Goodrich brothers, Enos, Moses and Levi, bought 1000 acres here and built a cabin; next year, they brought their families and settled; Enos Goodrich became the first postmaster of Atlas (named after the township), on Jan. 13, 1846; on March 1, 1849, when Reuben Goodrich became the postmaster, the name of the office was changed to Goodrich; incorporated as a village in 1957 [R. M'ellon; Wood; PO Archives].

**GOODRICH,** Marquette County: a railroad station, 19 miles from Marquette, in 1878 [GSM 1879].

**GOODRICH PRAIRIE,** St. Joseph County. See Prairie Corners.

**GOODRICH'S,** Manistee County: a station on the Manistee & Northwestern Railroad in 1888 [Mich Manual 1899].

**GOODWELL,** Newaygo County: Mary Jane Seward became the first postmaster of this farmhouse post office, named after its township, on July 25, 1898, the office operating until Dec. 15, 1905, 9½ miles from White Cloud [GSM 1899; PO Archives].

**GOODWINVILLE,** Branch County. See Union City.

**GOODYEAR,** Gogebic County: a lumbering town, named after the sawmill owner; John S. Brown became its first postmaster on May 5, 1910, the office operating until Nov. 30, 1912 [Victor Lemmer].

**GOOSE LAKE,** Marquette County: a station on the Chicago & Northwestern Railroad in 1878 [GSM 1879].

**GORDON,** Marquette County: a station on the Duluth, South Shore & Atlantic Railroad in 1898 [GSM 1911].

**GORDONVILLE,** Midland County: a settlement around a shingle mill on the Pine River, in Mount Haley Township; its post office, named Headache, was opened on Aug. 10, 1875, with Charles J. Bradford as its first postmaster; the office was renamed Bradford, after the postmaster, on Sept. 1, 1875, and then renamed Gordonville from March 16, 1906, until it was closed in July, 1910 [GSM 1879-1907; PO Archives].

**GORE,** Huron County: when this township was organized in 1862, with John H. Tucker as its first supervisor, it was named from its triangular shape [Gwinn].

**GORMAN**, Lenawee County: Timothy E. Bentley became the first postmaster of this village in Madison Township on March 3, 1893, the office operating until Oct. 31, 1902 [GSM 1895; PO Archives].

**GORMER**, Osceola County: Jane V. Underwood became the first postmaster of this rural post office on May 25, 1893, the office operating until Feb. 14, 1906 [PO Archives].

**GORTON**, Branch County: Duty Gorton was the storekeeper in the village and when he was appointed its first postmaster on July 16, 1889, the office was named for him; it operated until Sept. 14, 1901 [GSM 1891-1903; PO Archives].

**GOSS**, Clinton County: this rural post office was named for David Goss, Jr., who became its first postmaster on Feb. 2, 1857, the office operating until Nov. 7, 1861 [GSM 1860; PO Archives].

**GOTTS CORNERS**, Huron County: this settlement in Lake Township was founded by Robert Gotts, a homesteader, and he became its first postmaster, with the office named Gotts, on Oct. 5, 1895, the office operating until Aug. 14, 1905 [GSM 1897-1907; PO Archives].

**GOUGEBURG**, Kent County: the name given by Henry Helsel to a sawmill settlement in Algoma Township; this mill on the Rouge River was built by C. C. Comstock, of Grand Rapids, in 1856 [Chapman].

**GOUGH**, Isabella County: John D. Gulick became the first postmaster of this rural post office on Jan. 24, 1882, the office operating until only June 28, 1882 [PO Archives].

**GOULD CITY**, Mackinac County: Sam Stiles, grocery storekeeper and lumberman, founded this village in 1886 and named it for another lumberman; Adolph Highstone became its first postmaster on Sept. 26, 1888; a station on the Minneapolis, St. Paul & Sault Ste. Marie Railroad [PM].

**GOULD'S CORNERS**, Tuscola County: the settlement was named for general storekeeper, H. D. Gould and hotel proprietor, S. H. Gould, in 1878 [GSM 1879].

**GOULD'S MILLS**, Kent County: in 1878, a mill settlement named for J. E. Gould, pioneer lumberman [Chapman].

**GOURDNECK PRAIRIE**, Kalamazoo County: first settled by John McComsey on bounty lands he received as a veteran of the War of 1812; named from its gourd-shape with the neck of the gourd pointing south; the name is retained in Gourdneck Lake [Mich Hist 32:28 1948].

**GOURLEY**, Menominee County: in 1905, Arthur Gourley and his partner, Samuel L. Hall, bought the Jasper and Blahnik mill and founded the village; Mr. Hall became its first postmaster on Oct. 21, 1905, succeeded by John A. Loudeville in 1906; the township, a part of Cedarville Township from 1863, was divided in 1920, and the new one was also named for him, Gourley Township [Evelyn Bergen; PO Archives].

**GOWEN,** Montcalm County: it began as a lumbering center about 1847 and was first called Gregor's Mills, and later, Kaywood; the present village was founded by Colonel James Gowen, a native of Lancaster County, Pa.; he platted it in 1871; Samuel N. Peck became its first postmaster on March 4, 1872; a station on the Detroit, Grand Rapids & Western Railroad [Iva C. Larsen, PM].

**GRAAFSCHAP,** Allegan County: in 1848, a group of members of the Dutch Reformed Church organized, incorporated, and bought 81 acres of land here, and laid out the village; they had come from the region between Hanover and the Netherlands where small principalities were ruled by graafs or counts, whose districts were called graafschaps, and they gave that name to their new home; Abel H. Brink became the first postmaster on Feb. 17, 1866, the office operating until Nov. 15, 1909 [Esther W. Hettinger; PO Archives].

**GRACE,** Benzie County: first settled in 1878; Charles Ehman became the first postmaster on April 14, 1880, but this office on the Aux Bec Scies River, in Gilmore Township, was closed on Aug. 19, 1884 [GSM 1885; PO Archives].

**GRACE,** Presque Isle County: this village on the shore of Hammond Bay, Lake Huron, in Bearinger Township, was also known as Grace Harbor; it was founded by the Grace Lumber Company, of Detroit, in 1893; Rawson Wager became its first postmaster on Dec. 26, 1894, the office operating until April 30, 1942 [W. H. Whiteley; GSM 1895; PO Archives].

**GRAFFVILLE,** Montcalm County: a station on the Detroit, Lansing & Northern Railroad in 1878 [GSM 1879].

**GRAFTON,** Monroe County: this Pere Marquette Railroad station, by the Swan Creek, in Ash Township, was given a post office on March 14, 1850, with Josiah Littlefield as its first postmaster, the office operating until April 30, 1903 [Wing; GSM 1875; PO Archives].

**GRAHAM STATION,** Saginaw County. See Ward.

**GRAHAMVILLE,** Kent County: this rural post office in Spencer Township was named for Philander Graham who became its first postmaster on Jan. 29, 1857, the office operating until March 16, 1865 [GSM 1860; PO Archives].

**GRAND BEACH,** Berrien County: a resort on the Lake Michigan shore, in New Buffalo Township; Philip Hesse became its first postmaster on May 10, 1912, the office operating until June 30, 1957; a station on the Michigan Central Railroad; incorporated as a village in 1934 [D. C. Colyer; PO Archives].

**GRAND BLANC,** Genesee County: first called Grumlaw, this early

Indian camping ground was settled by the first white family to locate in the county when Jacob Stevens and his family, New Yorkers, settled here in 1823; his son Rufus opened a trading post in 1826; Elijah Davenport became the first postmaster on May 7, 1834; its growth dates from the coming through of the railroad in 1864; incorporated as a city in 1930; named after a husky trader named Fisher whom the Indians called Grand Blanc, or Big White [Ellis; Wood; MPH 17:449 1890; PO Archives].

**GRAND FORKS**, Gladwin County. See Beaverton.

**GRAND HAVEN**, Ottawa County: Rix Robinson built a trading post here in 1833; in 1834, he, together with Rev. William M. Ferry, Robert Stuart and Nathan M. White, formed the New Haven Company to develop the area; Mr. Robinson had C. Burns plat and record the village of Grand Haven (named from its location at the mouth of the Grand River, near Lake Michigan), in April, 1835; Rev. Ferry became the first postmaster on May 2, 1835, with the office named Stuart, for his friend Robert Stuart, with the name of the office changed to Grand Haven on Aug. 12, 1835; incorporated as a city in 1867 [Atwell; Lillie; PO Archives].

**GRAND ISLAND**, Alger County: this heavily forested, sparsely settled, 13,000 acre island in Lake Superior, opposite Munising, is nearly all owned by the Cleveland-Cliffs Iron Company, which logs it periodically; trapper Trueman W. Powell settled here in 1845, as did John Murray, who became the first supervisor of Schoolcraft County (it was in that county until Alger was organized in 1885); the island had a post office from 1851 to 1854; its lighthouse, on the northwest tip of the island, built in 1856 to aid copper and iron ore ships to navigate the lake, is 817 feet above sea level [Munising News, March 3, 1935; GSM 1885].

**GRAND JUNCTION**, Van Buren County: because of the townsite value of this junction of two railroads, the lumbering firm of William F. Dickinson and Samuel Rogers gave 40 acres for platting by A. J. Pierce, county surveyor; its proprietors were Marvin Hannahs, Samuel Rogers, Conrad Crouse and George W. Crouch; David Young bought six lots in 1869, built an inn and became the first settler; Mr. Crouch became the first postmaster on March 4, 1872 [Ellis; PO Archives].

**GRAND LEDGE**, Eaton County: H. Mason, a speculator, made the first land entry here in 1831, but it was sold for taxes four years later; Edmund L. Lamson made the first permanent settlement in 1848, for Henry A. Trench, whom he found living here, later moved away; in 1850, Mrs. Lamson suggested the name after the Grand River running past and the great ledge of rocks nearby; Mr. Trench became the first postmaster on July 20, 1850; incorporated as a village in 1871 and as a city in 1893 [Grace P. Pierce; Mich Hist 7:13 1923].

**GRAND MARAIS**, Alger County: the visit of Radisson and Grossilliers to the site and the harbor in 1660 was recorded in the writings of the former and on the map of Charlevoix and Bellin, as "le Grand Marais," dated Paris, 1745; permanent settlement began soon after the Civl War with the (E. G.) Endress Fish Company its first business, founded in 1872; Charles A. Loughlin became its first postmaster on Nov. 21, 1882; platted in 1884; it was in Schoolcraft County until Alger was organized in 1885, and it was the county seat until 1902; literally translated, Grand Marais means great marsh, but in voyageur French it signified a sheltered inlet or small harbor, whether marshy in origin or not [James Carter].

**GRANDON**, Clare County: Mrs. Christiana Howard became the first postmaster of this rural post office in Winterfield Township on March 15, 1895, the office operating until Jan. 15, 1906 [GSM 1897; PO Archives].

**GRAND POINTE**, St. Clair County: a resort colony on Harsen's Island, founded in 1888 by the Grand Pointe Improvement Company, of Detroit; Oscar F. Morse became its first and only postmaster, Oct. 16, 1889, to Jan. 5, 1892 [GSM 1891-93; PO Archives].

**GRANDPORT**, Wayne County. See Ecorse.

**GRAND PORTAGE**, Houghton County: a copper mining community near Portage Lake; the Grand Portage Mine was organized in 1852, reorganized in 1860, sold in 1879, reorganized anew in 1880, and sold in 1897 to the Isle Royale Consolidated [Stevens].

**GRAND RAPIDS**, Kent County: here trader McKenzie located in 1820 and McCoy's unsuccessful Baptist Indian mission in 1823; trader Louis Campau opened a post here in 1826, and in 1831, he bought the city's present business district for $90; Leonard Slater became the first postmaster of Grand Rapids on Dec. 22, 1832; Lucius Lyon bought some of Campau's land in 1835, and on Sept. 1, 1836, got the post office renamed Kent, after a New York State chancellor; the village was named Grand Rapids (from its location on the Grand River, near the rapids), but its post office remained Kent until Feb. 6, 1844, when Campau got it changed back to Grand Rapids; incorporated as a village in 1838 and as a city in 1850 [MPH 17:351 1890, 27:494, 567 1896; Mich Hist 10:477 1926; PO Archives].

**GRAND RIVER**, Eaton County: Erastus S. Ingersoll became the first postmaster of this rural post office on Sept. 13, 1837, the office operating until July 25, 1839 [PO Archives].

**GRAND RIVER CITY**, Clinton County: in 1834, Erastus Ingersoll bought land in northern Delta Township, Eaton County, and in 1836, added 80 acres in southern Watertown Township, Clinton County: Elihu P. Ingersoll also bought 80 adjoining acres in 1836, built a log house, had a dam and a mill built, and employed John Thayer to plat the prospective village, named from its location between the Grand River turnpike and the Grand River; but Michigan's wildcat banking system collapsed and with it, in 1839, all the hopes for the future of Grand River City; the site became that of Delta Mills [Ellis; Daboll].

**GRAND SALINE**, Shiawassee County. See Knaggs Place.

**GRAND TRAVERSE**, Genesee County. See Flint.

**GRAND TRAVERSE,** Grand Traverse County. See Old Mission.

**GRAND TRUNK JUNCTION,** St. Clair County: a station on the Grand Trunk Railroad, four miles from Port Huron, in 1888 [GSM 1889].

**GRAND TRUNK JUNCTION,** Wayne County. See Detroit Junction.

**GRAND VIEW,** Oceana County: Harvey Tower became the first postmaster of this rural post office in Grant Township on June 20, 1879, the office operating until Nov. 2, 1893 [Page; PO Archives].

**GRANDVILLE,** Kent County: in 1832, Luther Lincoln and companions came down the Grand River looking for a favorable site and spent the winter here; the next spring, he purchased the site from the land office in White Pigeon; the settlement was given a post office on May 24, 1834, with William B. Godwin as its first postmaster; it was first platted and recorded by Elijah Smith for Charles Oates, Benjamin Slater, Levi White, and John Boynton, on April 13, 1835; given a station on the Chicago & Western Michigan (now Pere Marquette) Railroad in 1872; incorporated as a village in 1887 and as a city in 1933; named from its location on the Grand River [Howard Nyenhuis; PO Archives].

**GRANGE,** Sanilac County: this rural post office was first named Fritch, for storekeeper James A. Fritch, who became its first postmaster on July 7, 1897; the office was renamed Grange on March 29, 1901, and operated until Aug. 30, 1902 [GSM 1899; PO Archives].

**GRANGER,** Lenawee County. See Fruit Ridge.

**GRANITE,** Marquette County: a station on the Chicago & Northwestern Railroad, five miles north of Republic, in 1894 [GSM 1895].

**GRANITE BLUFF,** Dickinson County: the village began as a sawmill settlement with a station on the M. & N. Railroad; when lumberman Fred H. Strup became its first postmaster on Feb. 18, 1890, it was in Menominee County; the office was transferred to Dickinson County on Oct. 1, 1891; it was closed on Sept. 19, 1895, but was restored from Dec. 22, 1895, to June 15, 1900, and from May 7, 1904, to June 29, 1918 [GSM 1891; PO Archives].

**GRANT,** Grand Traverse County: the township was organized in 1866, and named for General Ulysses S. Grant, with P. C. Hopkins as its first supervisor [Sprague].

**GRANT,** Huron County: first settled by Levi Williamson in 1863 and he became the first supervisor when the township was organized in 1867; named for General U.S. Grant [Chapman].

**GRANT,** Kent County. See Slayton.

**GRANT,** Mason County: this township, organized in 1867, was named for General U.S. Grant, with William Freeman as its first supervisor [Page].

**GRANT,** Newaygo County: this station on a branch of the Chicago &

Western Michigan (now Pere Marquette) Railroad was named Grant Station by Andrew J. Squier who had built a sawmill here in 1882; Grant Station was given a post office on May 14, 1892, with the name shortened to Grant on Jan. 10, 1899; also called Grant Center from its location in the township; incorporated as the village of Grant in 1893; named for General U.S. Grant [Mich Hist 24:450 1940; Harry L. Spooner; PO Archives].

**GRANT**, Oceana County: the first settler in the area was Fernando Seaver, in 1851; the township was organized in 1866 and named for General U.S. Grant [Hartwick].

**GRANT CENTER**, Mecosta County: the first settler in the area was Sylvanus Ford, a single man, who came in 1863; later that year, Charles L. Tuttle came with his family; he was elected the first supervisor when Grant Township, named after General U.S. Grant, was organized in 1865; the village was named from its location in the township [Chapman].

**GRANT CENTER**, St. Clair County. See Blaine.

**GRANT HOUSE**, Benzie County. See Homestead.

**GRANTON**, Arenac County. See Standish.

**GRANT'S CORNER**, Luce County. See Newberry.

**GRANT STATION**, Newaygo County. See Grant.

**GRAPE**, Monroe County: Hannah W. Atkinson became the first postmaster of this rural post office in Raisinville Township on June 1, 1887, the office operating until Oct. 15, 1906; named after its township, raisin being French for grape [GSM 1889-1907; PO Archives].

**GRASS LAKE**, Jackson County: David Sterling and his family were squatters here when a party from Niagara County, N.Y., to wit: George C. Pease, his son, William H. Pease, and William's cousin, David Keyes, came in 1829; Daniel Walker came in 1830; Lorenzo D. Hale became the first postmaster on Dec. 30, 1839; the village developed with the coming through of the railroad in 1842; incorporated as a village in 1871; named after the lake lying just north of the village, said to have been named from the exclamation of a girl who on seeing it said: O what a grassy lake! [MPH 5:347 1884].

**GRASSMERE**, Huron County: a station on the Saginaw, Tuscola & Huron Railroad, in both Colfax and Oliver Townships; storekeeper M. A. Vogel became its first postmaster on Aug. 7, 1891, the office operating until Dec. 31, 1909 [GSM 1893; PO Archives].

**GRATIOT BEACH**, St. Clair County: a summer resort on the Lake Huron shore, in Fort Gratiot Township, founded in 1892; Captain Charles Gratiot, an officer in General Harrison's army in the War of 1812, built Fort Gratiot at Port Huron in 1814 [GSM 1893].

**GRATIOT CENTER**, Gratiot County. See Ithaca.

**GRATIOT CENTRE**, St. Clair County: a station on a branch of the Port Huron & Northwestern Railroad in 1884 [GSM 1885].

**GRATTAN**, Kent County: the town began as an Irish Catholic settlement in 1844 and had a church in 1845; it was also called Grattan Center, but was given a post office as Grattan on Jan. 18, 1849, with Edward S. Bellamy as its first postmaster; he and his brother-in-law, Nathan Holmes, began the village by building a grist mill here on Seeley Creek, at Wolf Lake, in 1850; platted and recorded as Grattan Center by Henry M. Caulkin for Nathan Holmes and Alvin Stocking on Jan. 29, 1857; its post office was closed on Feb. 14, 1906, but the village of Grattan remains; named after its township which early Celtic settlers had named for Henry Grattan, Irish statesman and orator [Dillenback; PO Archives].

**GRAVEL PIT**, Menominee County: a station on the Chicago & Northwestern Railroad in 1878 [GSM 1879].

**GRAVEL RUN**, Washtenaw County: this village in Northfield Township was founded by Roswell Curtis in 1842 and he became its first postmaster on May 18, 1850, holding the office until his death in 1870; the office had been renamed Northfield on Oct. 2, 1860, then back to Gravel Run on Oct. 22, 1860, closed on Nov. 19, 1875, restored on Nov. 12, 1877, and then closed permanently on July 19, 1878; Gravel Run was named after the stream beside it [GSM 1879; PO Archives].

**GRAWN**, Grand Traverse County: this village was platted and recorded as Blackwood for James R. Blackwood who owned a majority of lots in the original plat; when the Pere Marquette Railroad came through they named it Grawn Station; it was given a post office as Grawn on Oct. 19, 1890, with William H. Gibbs as its first postmaster [PO Archives; Traverse].

**GRAY**, Midland County: this rural post office, ten miles north of Midland, was opened on Nov. 1, 1902, and named for grocer Orson Gray who became its first postmaster, the office operating until Jan. 15, 1907 [GSM 1905; PO Archives].

**GRAYLING**, Crawford County: the village was platted by the Saginaw & Jackson Railroad in 1874 and given a post office on Jan. 19 of that year, with John E. Corbet as its first postmaster, succeeded by Leonard M. Simons on Feb. 2, 1874; incorporated as a village in 1903 and as a city in 1935; named after the grayling trout, once so plentiful in the Au Sable River; the fish was identified by Martin Metcalf in 1861 and named by Prof. Jean Agassiz, of Harvard [Mich Hist 45:135 1961; Russell Carlson; PO Archives].

**GRAYLOCK**, Mackinac County: a station on the Minneapolis, St. Paul & Sault Ste. Marie Railroad, two miles east of Engadine, in 1891 [Mich Manual 1899].

**GRAY'S**, Berrien County: a station on the St. Joseph Valley Railroad in 1890 [GSM 1891].

**GREAT LAKES BEACH**, Sanilac County: a summer resort on Lake Huron and on M-29, 4 miles south of Lexington, in 1930 [GSM 1931].

**GREAT WESTERN,** Iron County: a mine was discovered and opened here by Solomon D. Hollister and George Runkle in 1881; it was operated by the Great Western Mining Company, but is now inactive and reportedly a reserve holding; its settlement was given a station on the Chicago & Northwestern Railroad in 1884 [Jack Hill, Sr.].

**GREEN,** Mecosta County: the James Montague family became the first settlers here in 1854; the first frame building was erected by Andrew and Lewis H. Green in 1857, and the township was named for them when it was organized in 1858; Jesse A. Barker became the first supervisor in 1859 [Chapman].

**GREEN,** Ontonagon County. See Green City.

**GREEN BAY,** Brown County: John Deane became the first postmaster of this settlement on Dec. 16, 1821, with the office renamed Greenbay, later changed to Menominie, then on April 3, 1833, to Navarine, and finally to Green Bay on July 30, 1834; it was then in Michigan Territory but is now in Wisconsin [PO Archives].

**GREENBUSH,** Alcona County: in 1848-49, Crosier Davison, of Detroit, built a fishery and cooperage here; Morris & McDougal, of New York State, bought government pine land and set up lumber operations here in 1862; the site of these two enterprises became known as McDougal's Landing; later, William Conklin owned the largest of the lumbering companies and built the first sawmill here; about 1867, at the suggestion of a Conklin employee, who had come from Greenbush, Rensselaer County, N.Y., the name was changed; given a post office as Greenbush on May 16, 1870, with James Burton as its first postmaster, with the office being renamed Perfection on May 18, 1917 [Mrs. H. G. Carow, Sr.; PO Archives].

**GREENBUSH,** Berrien County. See Harbert.

**GREENBUSH,** Clinton County. See Eureka.

**GREENBUSH,** Sanilac County. See Lexington.

**GREEN CITY,** Ontonagon County: given a post office as Green on July 12, 1904, with Mary Hannah as its first postmaster [PO Archives].

**GREEN CREEK,** Muskegon County: William F. Rogers became the first postmaster of this rural post office on April 18, 1883, the office operating until July 25, 1892 [PO Archives].

**GREENDALE,** Midland County: storekeeper Mrs. Elizabeth A. Gould became the first postmaster of this rural post office, 16 miles from Midland, on June 21, 1902, the office operating until March 15, 1911 [GSM 1903; PO Archives].

**GREEN DELL,** Lake County. See Chase.

**GREENE,** Saginaw County. See Merrill.

**GREENE'S CORNERS**, Lapeer County: first settled by the Greene family from northern New York State in 1840; known as Greene's Corners since 1860 [C. L. Greene, Life at Greene's Corners. 1956 Boston].

**GREENFIELD**, Wayne County: as this township, when erected in 1833, had such fine farms it was named for its green fields; first settled by John Strong in 1826, followed during the next three years by other Americans, and in 1842 by a group of immigrants from near Coblenz, Germany; John Kennedy became the first postmaster on Dec. 8, 1937; the office was closed on Oct. 12, 1838, but was restored from June 30, 1839, to Jan. 30, 1841, and from Dec. 15, 1841, to May 23, 1842, and from Sept. 23, 1852, to April 4, 1857; the village was first platted and recorded on Feb. 17, 1872; once an active business center, but through separate annexations between 1875 and 1926, both the township and its village became a part of the city of Detroit [Burton; County plat liber; PO Archives].

**GREENFIELD VILLAGE**, Wayne County: reproduction of an early New England village, complete with a church, a town hall, an inn, a school, a court house, a general store, mills and craft shops, established by Henry Ford at Dearborn in 1933 as part of the Edison Institute [Columbia Ency.].

**GREENGARDEN**, Marquette County: the settlement was given a post office with farmer William F. Koepp as its first postmaster on Dec. 4, 1894, the office operating until 1911; of this community there remains only its church atop a steep hill and its graveyard; in some sources the name is spelled as two words [Ernest Rankin; GSM 1895; PO Archives].

**GREENING**, Monroe County: a settlement two miles southeast of Monroe in 1898; named for the Greening brothers, George A. and Charles E., nurserymen; the latter became its first postmaster on March 3, 1898, the office operating until only Aug. 6, 1898 [GSM 1899; PO Archives].

**GREENLAKE**, Allegan County: a summer resort on Green Lake, in Leighton Township, with storekeeper Arthur M. Hooker becoming its first postmaster on Feb. 17, 1899, the office operating until Nov. 30, 1901 [GSM 1901; PO Archives].

**GREENLAND**, Ontonagon County: William W. Spalding moved from Ontonagon with his family to his mining claim here on the mineral range in 1858; the settlement which formed was given a post office on June 26, 1858, with John Brady as its first postmaster; a station on the Chicago, Milwaukee & St. Paul Railroad; named after the township which had been named after Greenland, New Hampshire, the boyhood home of Clement March, a capitalist interested in the development of the mineral lands of this area [Spalding's Diary and J. K. Jamison].

**GREENLEAF**, Sanilac County. See New Greenleaf.

**GREEN OAK**, Livingston County: the Stephen Lee family, from western New York, became the first settlers in the area in 1830; William H. Weatherhead owned the first local grist mill and sawmill; Kingsley S.

Bingham became the first postmaster on June 9, 1834, the office operating until Aug. 12, 1852; the Warnerville post office was changed to Green Oak on May 5, 1854, but it was changed back to Warnerville on Oct. 13, 1854, however, on the same day, the Green Oak post office was re-established, and operated until Jan. 24, 1881; on March 14, 1887, the Green Oak Station post office was re-opened as Green Oak, this time operating until July 16, 1906; a station on the Detroit, Grand Rapids & Western Railroad; named after its township which then consisted largely of oak openings; it was also known as Green Oak Mills [Ellis; PO Archives].

**GREEN OAK CENTRE,** Livingston County: a post office opened on Sept. 9, 1850, with Ambrose S. Warner as its first postmaster; it was renamed Warnerville for him on Dec. 23, 1850, changed to Green Oak on May 5, 1854, back to Warnerville on Oct. 15, 1854, until it was closed on Nov. 2, 1857 [PO Archives].

**GREEN OAK STATION,** Livingston County: a depot on the Detroit, Lansing & Northern Railroad, in Green Oak Township; the Green Oak Station post office was opened on Nov. 13, 1871, with Robert W. Olds as its first postmaster, but it was changed to Green Oak on March 14, 1887 [GSM 1875; PO Archives].

**GREEN RIVER,** Antrim County: a station on the D. & C. Railroad, in Chestonia Township; Solomon C. Miller became its first postmaster on Dec. 3, 1902, succeeded by grocer H. L. Dunson in 1904, the office operating until Aug. 31, 1906 [GSM 1905; PO Archives].

**GREEN'S CORNERS,** St. Clair County. See Hartsuff.

**GREENSKY HILL,** Charlevoix County: an Indian mission founded in 1844 by Peter (Shagasokicki) Greensky, an Indian preacher; from its beginning it was under the control of the Methodist Episcopal Church [Mich Hist 20:247 1936].

**GREENVILLE,** Montcalm County: first settled and founded by John Green, from Fulton County, N.Y., in 1844; Abel French became the first postmaster on Jan. 20, 1848; Mr. Green first platted the village in 1853; a station on the Detroit, Grand Rapids & Western Railroad; incorporated as a village in 1867 and as a city in 1871 [Schenck; PO Archives].

**GREENWOOD,** Marquette County: a station on the Duluth, South Shore & Atlantic Railroad, in Ely Township; the village was first platted in 1865; it was the site of the blast furnaces of the Michigan Iron Company and was first known as Greenwood Furnace; Walter N. Colburn became the first postmaster of Greenwood on March 8, 1867, the office operating until Oct. 27, 1875, the year the furnaces were closed [Mich Hist 15:284 1931; PO Archives; Andreas].

**GREENWOOD,** Mason County. See Colfax.

**GREENWOOD,** Oceana County: Greenwood Township was first settled in 1855 by Henry D. Clark, organized in 1858, and named from the appearance of its forests; its post office, located on the Oceana-Newaygo

County line, was opened on Dec. 1, 1858, with Oliver Swain as its first postmaster, but on Aug. 2, 1867, the office was transferred to Hesperia [Hartwick; PO Archives].

**GREENWOOD**, Ogemaw County: between 1870 and 1895, some 2000 men were employed in nearly fifty camps in the area during the lumbering season; hence the name of its post office, of which George W. Hotchkiss, of the lumber firm of Hotchkiss & Codding, became the first postmaster, on Jan. 13, 1873; a station on the Mackinaw division of the Michigan Central Railroad by 1878; the post office was closed on Feb. 14, 1901, but this village in Horton Township remains [Pen Phil 6:3 Oct 1955; PO Archives].

**GREENWOOD CENTRE**, St. Clair County: Greenwood Township was organized in 1855, with Lincoln Small as its first postmaster; this village in it was given a railroad station and, on Oct. 8, 1874, a post office, with Jotham A. Vincent as its first postmaster, the office operating until Nov. 9, 1885; its first general store was run by Charles Fuller [GSM 1889; Andreas; PO Archives].

**GREENWOOD FURNACE**, Marquette County. See Greenwood.

**GREENWOOD STATION**, Oceana County. See Rothbury.

**GREGOR'S MILLS**, Montcalm County. See Gowen.

**GREGORY**, Livingston County: a branch of the Grand Trunk Railroad came through the Halstead Gregory farm here in Unadilla Township in 1884 and near its depot he built a store in which there was a post office with him becoming its first postmaster on March 14, 1884 [GSM 1885; PO Archives].

**GREILICKVILLE**, Leelanau County: founded about 1875 and given a post office named Norrisville after Seth H. and Albert Norris, brothers, who built and operated a grist mill, a tannery, a brick yard, and a pottery factory here; Ebenezer Cobb became its first postmaster on Sept. 7, 1881; the office was closed on June 13, 1882, but was restored from May 7, 1884, to July 31, 1902; Godfrey Greilick and his sons, John, Anthony and Edward, emigrated from Austria in 1848, came to Michigan in 1856, where they built and operated several sawmills, one of them here; when the Manistee & Northwestern Railroad came through about 1893, its station here was named Greilickville, and gradually the village took the name [Dickinson; Traverse; PO Archives].

**GREINER**, Wayne County. See Conner's Creek.

**GRESHAM**, Eaton County: this village in Chester Township was settled in 1883 and given a post office on Oct. 30 of that year, with Syrenus P. Roller as its first postmaster, the office operating until March 31, 1903 [GSM 1887; PO Archives].

**GRIDLEY**, Ionia County: Oscar E. Jennings became the first postmaster of this rural post office in Berlin Township on Feb. 6, 1900, the office operating until Nov. 15, 1901 [GSM 1901; PO Archives].

**GRIFFITH,** Lenawee County. See North Morenci.

**GRIND STONE CITY,** Huron County: founded by Captain Aaron G. Peer and James Dufty in 1834, when they came to open its grindstone quarries (the village receded when carborundum took the place of grindstone); a station on the Port Huron & Northwestern Railroad; James Green became its first postmaster on Feb. 5, 1872, the office operating until Aug. 9, 1962; now a small fishing village [Wanda Rothgarber; MPH 39:353 1915; PO Archives].

**GRINDSTONE CREEK,** Eaton County: a mill settlement in 1837, on a stream which took its name from a sand-stone ledge, through which it runs [GSM 1838].

**GRISWOLD,** Kent County: a small lumber and shingle mill village on the Grand Rapids & Indiana Railroad, in Spencer Township, founded before 1877 by lumberman J. W. Griswold and farmers Alonzo and John Griswold; Ebenezer D. Boynton became its first postmaster on March 13, 1877, the office operating until Aug. 31, 1900; it was also called Griswoldburg [GSM 1879; PO Archives].

**GROESBECK,** Ontonagon County: a station on the Duluth, South Shore & Atlantic Railroad, 3 miles east of Matchwood, in 1894 [GSM 1895].

**GRONINGEN,** Ottawa County. See New Groningen.

**GROOS,** Delta County: a rural post office in Wells Township, named for Jacob A. Groos who became its first postmaster on March 15, 1900, the office operating until Nov. 30, 1913 [GSM 1901; PO Archives].

**GROS CAP,** Mackinac County: on a map dated about 1750, this area was called St. Helena, the same as the offshore island which now bears the name; named by the French, big cape, from its location on land jutting into the Straits of Mackinaw; the name of this village is also spelled Groscap; first settled in 1855 by Mr. Cheeseman, a Mormon refugee from Beaver Island; grocer James B. Blanchard became the first postmaster here in Moran Township on Dec. 1, 1892 [Federal; Emerson Smith; PO Archives].

**GROSSE ILE,** Wayne County: Kitche-minishen was the Pottawattomi name for the island, and it was so called in the deed from that Indian tribe to the brothers Alexander and William Macomb in 1776; this island in the Detroit River was first surveyed in 1808 by Adam Greely and its major cross-roads laid out in 1824-25 by Abram C. Truax and Artemas Hosmer; given a post office named Grosse Isle on March 14, 1851, with Charles Fox as its first postmaster; the office was closed on June 21, 1862, but was restored on June 9, 1873, and given its present spelling of Grosse Ile on Aug. 18, 1890 [MPH 35:559 1907; PO Archives].

**GROSSE POINTE,** Wayne County: comprises five separate communities (which see, below); together they extend from the Detroit city limits north just over the Wayne-Macomb County line, and form most of the present Grosse Point Township, which was separated from Hamtramck

Township in 1848; Grosse Pointe was named from the point of land projecting into Lake St. Clair, which forms the eastern boundary of the township; first settled by the French, some of whom were descendants of those who had come to Detroit with Cadillac in 1701; by 1834, they were numerous enough here to build St. Paul's church, of which Belgian-born Rev. Ghislemus Bohema was named first pastor that year; the first Grosse Pointe post office was opened on Nov. 3, 1870, with Joseph Yates as its first postmaster, the office operating until Nov. 14, 1903 [Burton; Kerby; PO Archives].

**GROSSE POINTE CITY,** Wayne County: incorporated as a village in 1880; grocer Matthias Lodewyk became its first postmaster, with the office named Cottage Grove, on May 28, 1888; divided on the liquor issue in 1893, the northern section became Grosse Pointe Farms; re-incorporated as a village in 1893; incorporated as a city in 1934 [Burton; GSM 1889; PO Archives].

**GROSSE POINTE FARMS,** Wayne County: the present Grosse Pointe City and Grosse Pointe Farms comprised one village, so incorporated in 1880; the City broke off on the liquor issue in 1893, and the Farms was incorporated as a village in 1893 and as a city in 1949; given a post office as Grosse Pointe Farms on Dec. 28, 1898, with Frank R. Cadieux as its first postmaster [GSM 1901; Burton; PO Archives].

**GROSSE POINTE PARK,** Wayne County: the village of Fairview extended from Bewick to Cadieux Road; in 1907, the area from Bewick to Alter Road was absorbed by the city of Detroit, while that from Alter to Cadieux was incorporated as the village of Grosse Pointe Park, with Thomas W. Corby as its first president; incorporated as a village in 1907 and as a city in 1950 [Fintan L. Henk; GSM 1907].

**GROSSE POINTE SHORES,** Wayne County: within its corporate limits (which extend into Macomb County) there was a post office named Claireview, named from its location on Lake St. Clair, with Henry C. Wann, manager of the Claireview Stock Farm, becoming its first postmaster on Jan. 14, 1889, the office operating until April 30, 1904; Grosse Pointe Shores was incorporated as a village in 1911 [GSM 1891; PO Archives].

**GROSSE POINTE WOODS,** Wayne County: the original plat, since enlarged, was incorporated in 1926 as the village of Lochmoor; the name being derived from the Scottish words for a lake and a level area, it being flat land near Lake St. Clair; the new plat was renamed Grosse Pointe Woods in 1939; incorporated as a city in 1950.

**GROSVENOR,** Lenawee County: this station at the crossing of the Lake Shore & Michigan Southern and the Chicago & Canada Southern Railroads, 2 miles west of Blissfield, was opened in 1874, and named Blissfield Junction; with George Sparrow as its first postmaster it was given a post office named Grosvenor on Jan. 26, 1874, and the station took the same name; the post office operated until Jan. 9, 1880 [GSM 1875; PO Archives].

**GROULEAU**, Alcona County: this rural post office was named for storekeeper Alfred Grouleau who became its first postmaster on May 14, 1890; the office was closed on June 10, 1892, but was restored from March 3, 1893, to June 18, 1895 [GSM 1891-93; PO Archives].

**GROUT**, Gladwin County: Willard Grout took the first homestead here, but Benjamin Teeple became the first to bring his family to live in the township in 1863; Mr. Grout became the first postmaster in Grout Township, with the office named Grout, on Dec. 16, 1874, with Marvin N. Sackett appointed in 1878; the office operated until 1880 [Ritchie; PO Archives].

**GROVE**, Mecosta County: John Moore became the first postmaster of this rural post office on July 22, 1857, the office operating until May 11, 1865 [PO Archives].

**GROVE**, Newaygo County: George F. Cook became the first postmaster of this village in Ensley Township on Nov. 6, 1883, the office operating until Sept. 14, 1903 [PO Archives].

**GROVELAND**, Jackson County. See Parma.

**GROVELAND**, Oakland County: William Roberts made the first land purchase in the area in 1829; given a post office as Fairfield on May 2, 1834, with Philip H. McOmber as its first postmaster; the office was renamed Groveland on June 2, 1835, the year that township organization began; the office was closed on Dec. 3, 1852, but was restored from June 1, 1853, to April 15, 1874, from Oct. 6, 1874, to Feb. 3, 1881, and from June 7, 1881, to April 30, 1901 [Durant; PO Archives].

**GROVENBURG**, Ingham County: land purchases from the federal government were made here in Delhi Township by Henry Grovenburgh (so spelled in the records) on Sept. 4, 1847, by Benjamin F. Grovenburgh on Oct. 17, 1847, and by Samuel Grovenburgh on Aug. 24, 1853; it was also called the Grovenburg Settlement [Esther Loughlin].

**GROVER**, Calhoun County. See Groverville.

**GROVERTON**, Houghton County: a rural post office in then Fortis Lake Township, with Martin Dee becoming its first postmaster on Nov. 13, 1886, with the office transferred to South Lake Linden on Aug. 21, 1889 [GSM 1887-91; PO Archives].

**GROVERVILLE**, Calhoun County: given a station on the C., J. & M. Railroad as Grover and a post office on Dec. 11, 1888, as Groverville, with William J. Folk as its first postmaster, the office operating until June 15, 1900 [GSM 1891; PO Archives].

**GROVETON**, Saginaw County: a station on the Michigan Central Railroad in 1882 [GSM 1883].

**GRUMLAW**, Genesee County. See Grand Blanc.

**GULL CORNERS**, Kalamazoo County. See Richland.

**GULLIVER**, Schoolcraft County: this village was named from its location near Gulliver Lake; Alba R. Monroe became its first postmaster on Dec. 21, 1889; its mile distant station on the Minneapolis, St. Paul & Sault Ste. Marie Railroad was named Whitedale after him, alba being Latin for white; its track into the village was called Gulliver Spur [Federal; PO Archives].

**GULL LAKE**, Barry County: Wesley P. Andrus became its first postmaster on March 23, 1867, succeeded by George Thomas on Dec. 20, 1870, the office operating until Dec. 31, 1904; named from its location near the northern end of Gull Lake, which lies mostly in Kalamazoo County [Blinn; PO Archives].

**GULL PRAIRIE**, Barry County: a settlement in 1837, it never became a village [GSM 1838].

**GULL PRAIRIE**, Kalamazoo County. See Richland.

**GUN LAKE**, Allegan County: it was in Barry County when Nathan Barlow built his sawmill here in 1840 and when he became the first postmaster of Gun Lake on June 21, 1850; the post office was changed to Bowen's Mills on Feb. 7, 1870, but the Gun Lake post office was re-established on Oct. 1, 1890; transferred to Allegan County on May 5, 1892, it was renamed Gunlake on Jan. 12, 1895, and closed on Oct. 31, 1905 [Johnson; PO Archives].

**GUN LAKE**, Barry County: Nathan Barlow, who settled near Barlow Lake, named for him, in 1837, built a sawmill in 1840, and became the first postmaster of Gun Lake on June 21, 1850; in 1865, E. H. Bowen became the postmaster and on Feb. 7, 1870, he had the name of the office changed to Bowen's Mills; in the treaty of March 28, 1836, between the U.S., represented by Henry Schoolcraft, and the Ottawa and Chippewa chiefs regarding the ceding of lands in this part of Michigan, is included promise of payment to a chief named "Penasee, or Gun Lake," which indicated that Gun Lake is the English translation of Penasee [Johnson; Indian Affairs, Laws and Treaties, v2].

**GUN MARSH**, Allegan County: this post office in Gun Plain Township was opened on May 18, 1854, with Joshua R. Goldsmith as its first postmaster; the office was closed on Feb. 29, 1876, but was restored on March 13, 1876; on Jan. 21, 1899, it was transferred to and renamed Hooper [GSM 1860-1900; PO Archives].

**GUNNELL**, Tuscola County: Leslie N. York became the first postmaster of this rural post office on June 21, 1894, the office operating until only Oct. 25, 1894 [PO Archives].

**GUNNISONVILLE**, Clinton County: storekeeper Boyden F. Hubbard became the first postmaster of this rural post office on Jan. 8, 1891, the office operating until April 15, 1901 [GSM 1893; PO Archives].

**GUN PLAINS**, Allegan County: so named because it lay in an angle made by a junction of the Gun and the Kalamazoo Rivers and because of

GEORGETOWN TWP.
Res.– J. Haire

HAMTRAMCK
Res. & Green Houses - J. Breitmeyer

its prairie-like appearance; Sylvester Sibley, who ran its section lines in 1831, made the first land purchase here that year, but Dr. Cyrenius Thompson, a native of Ohio, made the first settlement in 1832 and became the first postmaster in 1833 [Thomas].

**GURNEE,** Mason County: Horace Buttels became the first postmaster of this rural post office in the northwest corner of the county on May 9, 1873, the office operating until Dec. 20, 1875 [GSM 1875; PO Archives].

**GUSTIN,** Alcona County: a station on the Detroit, Bay City & Alpena Railroad in 1886; Adelbert J. Wood became its first postmaster on June 6, 1891, the office operating until Oct. 15, 1910; named after its township [Blinn; PO Archives].

**GWINN,** Marquette County: the Cleveland-Cliffs Iron Company acquired the site in 1902, opened the Gwinn Mine in 1905, and had Warren H. Manning plat a model village in 1907, named by William Gwinn Mather, president of the company, for his mother whose maiden name was Elizabeth Lucy Gwinn; Winfield S. Nelson became its first postmaster on Nov. 19, 1908 [Mich Hist 5:164 1921; Hatcher; PO Archives].

**HAAKWOOD,** Cheboygan County: this settlement in Mentor Township formed around the mill of the Haakwood Lumber Company, with its secretary-treasurer, Charles E. Haak, becoming its first postmaster on Aug. 5, 1901; the office operated until Jan. 31, 1908 [GSM 1903; PO Archives].

**HACKETT'S SETTLEMENT,** Ionia County: founded by Peter and Bernard Hackett, in the southeast corner of Orange Township, in 1837; Irish and Catholic [Paré].

**HACKLEY,** Muskegon County: a summer resort on Lake Michigan and Mona Lake, in Norton Township, named Hackley Park in 1894, but shortened to Hackley when given a post office on Feb. 26, 1895; George L. Erwin was its first postmaster; the office operated until Nov. 17, 1897; Charles H. Hackley was Muskegon's leading citizen and benefactor [GSM 1895; PO Archives].

**HADLEY,** Lapeer County: first settled by the brothers John and H. M. Look in 1834; the settlement came to be known as Farmers Creek; in 1835, William Hart, Abraham Tunison and Charles Campbell located here and became community leaders; John Mills, Jr., became the first postmaster on May 7, 1838; about 1907, Franklin Hadley became postmaster and for fifty years some member of the Hadley family held the office; the village was named for the Rev. Hadley [J. A. Mitchell, PM].

**HAFF,** Chippewa County: a station on the Minneapolis, St. Paul & Sault Ste. Marie Railroad, in Trout Lake Township; the settlement formed around the Manistique Iron Company, with company store manager Henry Lilliquist becoming its first postmaster on Sept. 11, 1903, the office operating until Aug. 31, 1913 [GSM 1905; PO Archives].

**HAGAR,** Berrien County: Aaron H. Smith became its first postmaster on March 1, 1872, but as it was a railroad shipping point rather than a village and Benton Harbor was only four miles distant, the office was closed on Dec. 17, 1898; named after the township which had been named for William S. Hagar by his son-in-law, John N. Rogers, who was privileged to name it because of services he had rendered in its organization [Fox; GSM 1860; PO Archives].

**HAGAR SHORES,** Berrien County: it began as a subdivision called Lake Michigan Beach in 1922; from a summer resort it has developed into a village of 1,200 permanent residents; the post office in 1958 rejected the name Lake Michigan Beach and, by vote of the residents, the name was changed to Hagar Shores, for it is located on Hagar Road and has shore boundaries on Lake Michigan, Harris Lake and Hibbing Lake; see Hagar for the name [Ruth H. Joyce].

**HAGEMAN,** Hillsdale County: a cross-roads post office in Amboy Township, named for storekeeper Isaac C. Hageman who became its first postmaster on June 19, 1890, the office operating until Dec. 31, 1900; the place was also known as Hageman Corners [GSM 1891; PO Archives].

**HAGENSVILLE,** Presque Isle County: a settlement in Belknap Township around the sawmill of Hagen & Pines (William Hagen and Wilson Pines), with Mr. Hagen becoming its first postmaster on March 12, 1886, the office operating until March 31, 1912 [GSM 1887; PO Archives].

**HAIGHT,** Ontonagon County: named for Joseph Haight, of Ontonagon, chairman of the board of supervisors when this township was organized in 1899 [Jamison].

**HAIRE,** Wexford County: a station on the Grand Rapids & Indiana Railroad serving a lumber settlement in Liberty Township; Samuel R. Hepburn became its first postmaster on Aug. 21, 1883, the office operating until Dec. 15, 1908 [GSM 1885; PO Archives].

**HALE,** Iosco County: C. D. Hale came from New York State and began lumbering in the northwest part of Iosco County about 1880; his camps were located at the lake there, and the lake and the creek, as well as this village were named for him; a flag station on the Detroit, Bay City & Alpena Railroad; Furman N. Dean became its first postmaster on Jan. 17, 1889 [Edna M. Otis; PO Archives].

**HALE,** Shiawassee County. See Maple Valley.

**HALE'S BAY,** Delta County. See Garden.

**HALFWAY,** Macomb County. See East Detroit.

**HALLERS,** Livingston County: this rural post office in Hartland Township was named for storekeeper Paul H. Haller who became its first postmaster on March 4, 1899, the office operating until April 30, 1902 [GSM 1901-03; PO Archives].

**HALLOCK,** Otsego County: founded in 1906 and named for Benjamin Hallock, a farmer, on whose land the B.C., G. & A. Railroad crossed here in Elmira Township; storekeeper Arthur L. Bruce became its first postmaster on June 27, 1906, the office operating until April 15, 1914 [William H. Granlund; GSM 1907; PO Archives].

**HALL'S,** Mason County: a station on the T.S. & M. Railroad, 12 miles east of Muskegon, in 1894 [GSM 1895].

**HALL'S CORNERS,** Branch County. See California.

**HALL'S CORNERS,** Sanilac County. See Carsonville.

**HALL'S LAKE,** Isabella County: a lumber settlement, in Broomfield Township, on Hall's Lake, named for lumberman E. Hall in 1865 [Chapman].

**HALLSTON,** Alger County: a station on the Duluth, South Shore & Atlantic Railroad, in Au Train Township; railroad agent Julius W. Gogarn became its first postmaster on Dec. 19, 1888, the office operating until July 24, 1897; Nathaniel Lobb ran a brick yard here [GSM 1891; PO Archives].

**HALSEY,** Oakland County: a hamlet, four miles from Royal Oak, in 1922 [GSM 1923].

**HAMBLEN,** Bay County: a rural post office, its name derived from that of storekeeper Noah Hembling who became its first postmaster on March 1, 1888, the office operating until Aug. 30, 1902 [GSM 1889-1903; PO Archives].

**HAMBLIN,** Shiawassee County: Philip Schanable became the first postmaster of this rural post office in Rush Township on March 7, 1884, the office operating until Nov. 15, 1886 [GSM 1887; PO Archives].

**HAMBURG,** Livingston County: in 1835, E. F. Gay, an Ann Arbor merchant, bought 30 acres here from Jesse Hall and built a dam and a sawmill; in 1837, he sold out to the Messrs. Grisson who added a grist mill, a store and a hotel; the village plat was laid out and recorded in 1837; 19 men holding a meeting to name the town deadlocked 8 and 8 over naming it Steuben or Knox, the three Germans (the Messrs. Grisson) having no choice; finally the 18 agreed to let the Grissons name it and they chose the name of their native city, Hamburg, Germany; Reuben H. Bennett became the first postmaster of Hamburgh on March 8, 1837, changed to North Hamburgh on Nov. 10, 1852; the Livingston post office (named for Edward Livingston, President Andrew Jackson's secretary of war) was opened on July 25, 1840, with William Grisson as its first postmaster, but it was changed to Hamburgh on Nov. 10, 1852, and to its present spelling of Hamburg in 1894 [Charles N. Davis, PM; PO Archives].

**HAMILTON,** Allegan County: in 1835, Charles Butler entered the entire section of the present village; it was first called Rabbit River, from its location on the Rabbit River, and Simon Howe became its first postmaster on May 30, 1851, but the office was closed on Sept. 13, 1852; Aaron Willyards platted the village in 1862; the next Rabbit River post office was opened on July 9, 1864, with J. W. Purdy as its postmaster, and he kept the office at nearby Purdy Lake; when David Burch became the postmaster about 1865, he moved the office into the village; Charles A. Field became the postmaster on May 19, 1870, and the name was changed to Hamilton [Benjamin Rankens; PO Archives].

**HAMILTON**, Clare County: W. W. Weatherwax was chairman of the board of supervisors of Hayes Township when this township was subdivided from it in 1885; the attempt to have it named for him was out-voted by those who favored naming it Hamilton [J. C. McNamara].

**HAMILTON**, Genesee County. See Swartz Creek.

**HAMILTON**, Gratiot County: first settled by Elijah Curtis (and named for a relative of his, Frank Hamilton), William Barton, Dr. John R. Cheesman, and others in 1854 [Chapman].

**HAMILTON**, Ingham County. See Okemos.

**HAMILTON**, Van Buren County: the first structure in the area was a hunter's cabin, put up in 1833, by Benjamin Reynolds and Joel Clark, of Kalamazoo; Robert Nesbitt made the first land entry and became the first settler in 1835; the township, organized in 1839, was first named Alpina, and renamed in 1840 in honor of American statesman Alexander Hamilton; given a post office as Alpina on July 25, 1840, with Henry Coleman as its first postmaster, the office was renamed Hamilton on Dec. 15, 1841, but was closed on Jan. 31, 1862 [Ellis; PO Archives].

**HAMILTON'S**, Oakland County. See Birmingham.

**HAMLIN**, Eaton County: Colonel John Montgomery first settled here in 1836; originally a part of Bellevue Township, later of Eaton, still later of Tyler in 1841; the townships of Tyler and Eaton Rapids were united in 1850 and in 1869, Hamlin was set off from Eaton Rapids by the legislature; named for Samuel Hamlin who for the government had cut a road through from Clinton to the Thornapple River in the northwestern part of the county [Durant; MPH 22:518 1893].

**HAMLIN**, Mason County. See Lincoln.

**HAMLIN**, Monroe County: this railroad station in Raisinville Township was given a post office on March 28, 1862, with Calvin Clark as its first postmaster, but the office was transferred to Raisinville on Oct. 2, 1876; named for Hannibal Hamlin, vice-president of the U.S., 1861-65 [GSM 1865-75; PO Archives].

**HAMMER'S**, Charlevoix County: a flag station on the Grand Rapids & Indiana Railroad in 1876 [GSM 1877].

**HAMMOND**, Kent County. See Dutton.

**HAMMOND**, Presque Isle County: the village began with a sawmill in 1870; the Hammond Coast Guard Station opened here in 1878; it was given a post office as Hammond's Bay (it is on Hammond Bay) on April 17, 1891, with storekeeper Francis W. Corcoran as its first postmaster; the name was shortened to Hammond on April 25, 1894 [Federal; GSM 1893; PO Archives].

**HAMPTON,** Bay County: this hamlet was in Saginaw County when Thomas Rogers became its first postmaster on June 4, 1846; the office was changed to Bay City on March 22, 1858 [GSM 1925; PO Archives].

**HAMTRAMCK,** Wayne County: Colonel John Francis Hamtramck, under General Anthony Wayne, commanded the troops which took possession of Detroit upon the evacuation of the British in 1796, and this township, when erected in 1798, was named for him; it then started at the Detroit River and most of its first settlers were French families spreading out from Detroit (Antoine Reneau, James and Louis Allard, Francois Thibaut, Leon and Charles Varnier, Joseph Renaud, Joseph Furton, et al.); the township was organized on April 12, 1827, and its village, southeast of present-day Hamtramck Township, was given a post office on Oct. 3, 1828, with Thomas Noxon as its first postmaster, but the office was closed on March 2, 1836; the village was platted largely on the land of J. Godfrey and recorded on Jan. 12, 1847; on April 5, 1899, present-day Hamtramck was given a post office named Kraft, for Christopher Kraft, the first postmaster, with the name of the office being changed to Hamtramck on Oct. 15, 1905, with Arthur P. Schroeder as postmaster; incorporated as a village in 1901 and as a city in 1921; it lies entirely within the city of Detroit, but is politically independent [Burton; Farmer; County plat liber; PO Archives].

**HANCOCK,** Houghton County: in 1846, a log cabin was built here to hold the Ruggles mineral claim; Christopher C. Douglas owned the land and came to live on it in 1852; he sold it to the Quincy Mining Company, of which he was agent; in 1859, Samuel W. Hill, then agent of the company, platted the town; Lewis F. Leopold became its first postmaster on Jan. 10, 1860; incorporated as a village in 1875 and as a city in 1903; named for John Hancock, a signer of the Declaration of Independence [Sawyer].

**HAND,** Wayne County: a station, also known as Hand Station, on the Wabash Railroad, named for railroad agent, S. S. Hand; Charles H. Purdy became the first postmaster here in northern Taylor Township on Oct. 10, 1882, succeeded by storekeeper George Lapham; it was then 12 miles southwest of Detroit [Farmer; GSM 1887; PO Archives].

**HANDY,** Alcona County. See Roy.

**HANDY,** Livingston County: John T. Watson became the first postmaster of this rural post office on Feb. 21, 1850, the office operating until March 22, 1855 [PO Archives].

**HANLEY,** Alger County: the Cleveland Cliffs Iron Company operated this cordwood settlement, with a station on the East Branch of the Munising Railroad, in 1885; Isadore Sears ran its general store [Munising News, March 3, 1935].

**HANLEY,** Ottawa County: this village in Jamestown Township was given a post office on Sept. 21, 1869, with Daniel E. Yarrington as its first postmaster, the office operating until Jan. 30, 1904 [Page; PO Archives].

**HANNAH,** Grand Traverse County: landowner Lorenzo M. Tompkins became the first postmaster of this rural post office in Mayfield Township on Aug. 15, 1881, the office operating until Jan. 14, 1904; the place was also called Tompkins Corners [Sprague; PO Archives].

**HANNAHVILLE,** Menominee County: it began as a Pottawattomi settlement on land reserved for them by the federal government in 1870; named for the wife of Rev. Peter Marksman, the first Methodist missionary in the area [David S. Coon].

**HANNIBAL,** Lake County. See Baldwin.

**HANOVER,** Jackson County: named for Henry Wickman, who came here from Hanover, Germany, in 1836; John Cruttenden became the first postmaster on Dec. 13, 1837; George O. Bibbins, a pioneer settler, platted the village when the railroad came through in 1870; incorporated as a village in 1885 [Esther Parish; DeLand; PO Archives].

**HANOVER,** Keweenaw County: a copper mining location; the Hanover Mine was organized in 1860, opened two fissure veins, spent $20,000, and quit [Stevens].

**HANOVER,** Wexford County. See Wexford.

**HANSEN,** Oceana County: James Harvey Rathbone became the first postmaster of this rural post office in Ferry Township on April 13, 1869, the office operating until July 25, 1878 [Blinn; PO Archives].

**HANSON STATE MILITARY RESERVATION,** Crawford County. See Rasmus.

**HARBEC,** Bay County: a hamlet, 8 miles west of Pinconning, in 1878 [GSM 1879].

**HARBERT,** Berrien County: this region was barren and sandy, but a small swamp kept vegetation green all season, and it was first called Greenbush; it was renamed Harbert for a Chicago capitalist by the officials of the Chicago & Western Michigan (now Pere Marquette) Railroad when they built a station here in 1889; Wilson Collins became its first postmaster on May 13, 1889, succeeded by storekeeper G. B. Sheler in 1890 [Fox; GSM 1891; PO Archives].

**HARBOR BEACH,** Huron County: founded by John Allen and Alanson Daggett in 1837; with John Hunting as its first postmaster, it was given a post office named Barnettsville on March 31, 1856, changed to Sand Beach on Dec. 18, 1861; a station on the Pere Marquette Railroad in 1880; incorporated as a village in 1882, with Jeremiah Jenks, builder of the community, as its first president; with lumberman Mark Harrington as postmaster, the village and its post office were renamed Harbor Beach on April 18, 1889, the change being made to rid outsiders of the impression that the place was nothing but sand; incorporated as a city in 1910 [Hey; GSM 1860; PO Archives].

**HARBOR POINT**, Emmet County: in 1878, a party of Lansing people camped on this peninsula on Little Traverse Bay and were so impressed by the site that they organized and bought the land from its owner, Rev. John Weitkamp, of Cross Village; they then platted and built the Lansing Resort, as it was first called; given a post office as Harbor Point on June 28, 1917, with Clio I. Wright as its first postmaster [PO Archives; Powers].

**HARBOR SPRINGS**, Emmet County: the Ottawa village here was built on an eminence, near a large crooked tree, under which they held their councils, and whence the mission established by the Jesuits in 1742 took its name, L'Arbre Croche, or the crooked tree; in 1827, Rev. Pierre Dejean moved the mission to and built a log church at adjacent Little Traverse; French voyageurs had found two deep indentations on Michigan's west coast; the smaller one they called La Petite Traverse, or the little crossing; in 1853, Richard Cooper opened a general store for Captain Kirtland and began the modern development of the village; given a post office as Little Traverse on March 27, 1862, with William H. Fife as its first postmaster, the office was renamed Harbor Springs on March 17, 1881; the village was sometimes called Bayfield; incorporated as the village of Harbor Springs in 1881 and as a city in 1932; named from its natural harbor and the many springs in the area [Powers; GSM 1879; MPH 39:229 1915; Mich Hist 4:596 1920, 10:471 1926; PO Archives; U.P. Hedrick, Land of the Crooked Tree].

**HARDGROVE**, Crawford County: Esther Kent became the first postmaster of this rural post office, 7 miles from Frederic, on July 25, 1900 [GSM 1901; PO Archives].

**HARDLUCK**, Gladwin County: a station on the Michigan Central Railroad, in Barrett Township; Sidney A. Swanton became its first postmaster on April 24, 1904, the office operating until Aug. 31, 1906 [GSM 1905-07; PO Archives].

**HARDSCRABBLE**, Cass County. See Cushing.

**HARDWOOD**, Dickinson County: a station on the Chicago & Northwestern Railroad, in Breen Township; named by its principal proprietors, the Menominee Hardwood & Shingle Company, in 1884; company manager James H. Walton became its first postmaster on July 23, 1891; it was in Menominee County until Dickinson was organized in 1891, its post office being transferred on Oct. 1, 1891 [GSM 1893; PO Archives].

**HARDWOOD LAKE**, Ogemaw County: a settlement around the William D. Brinkman sawmill, on Hardwood Lake, in Logan Township; Mr. Brinkman became its first postmaster on May 4, 1908 [GSM 1911; PO Archives].

**HARDY**, Alcona County: this station on a branch of the Detroit & Mackinaw Railroad was given a post office on Sept. 7, 1909, with Cyrus T. Bickle as its first postmaster, succeeded by S. J. Evans in 1912 [GSM 1911; PO Archives].

**HARING**, Wexford County: a lumber settlement along the shores of Clam (now Cadillac) Lake; it formed around the mill of William M. Mitchell and Jonathan W. Cobbs, operating as Cobbs & Mitchell, in 1872; its railroad station was named Linden; its post office, opened on Dec. 18, 1872, with Hiram B. Wilcox as its first postmaster, was named Haring after its township; the office operated until Nov. 14, 1891 [Mich Hist 25:238 1941; GSM 1873; PO Archives].

**HARLAN**, Manistee County: the station here on the Toledo, Ann Arbor & Northern Railroad, on the line between Wexford and Manistee Counties, was opened in 1888, and was named Churchills; in state matters, the village is in Cleon Township, Manistee County; it was given a post office as Harlan, Wexford County, on March 31, 1890, with Byron L. Deen as its first postmaster; the office was closed on Jan. 15, 1906, but was restored on Feb. 12, 1906, and operated until July 15, 1935 [GSM 1891; PO Archives].

**HARLEM**, Ottawa County: the Dutch settlement at Holland in 1847 soon overflowed into others, of which this was one, named for Haarlem, a city in the mother-country [Page].

**HARLEY'S**, Mason County. See Riverton.

**HARLOW**, Macomb County. See Utica.

**HARLOW'S**, Marquette County: in 1878, a hamlet two miles west of Marquette, which see for the name [GSM 1879].

**HARMAN**, Bay County: Alpha W. Crowl became the first postmaster of this rural post office on May 29, 1878, the office operating until Oct. 20, 1879 [PO Archives].

**HARMON**, Oscoda County. See Ryno.

**HARMON**, Oakland County: this rural post office was named for William A. Harmon who became its first postmaster on June 14, 1897, the office operating until June 30, 1902 [PO Archives].

**HARMON**, St. Clair County: James Ogden became the first postmaster of this rural post office on March 26, 1836, the office operating until Nov. 22, 1841 [PO Archives].

**HARMONIA**, Calhoun County: in 1850, Reynolds Cornell and his wife, Deborah, from Battle Creek, platted the village in southwestern Bedford Township; they had been identified with the Quakers, after becoming Spiritualists, and they planned the village as the site of the Bedford Harmonial Seminary; some school buildings were erected and a few families followed, but the project failed and the site is now farmland [Everts].

**HARPERVILLE**, Marquette County: this rural post office, near Ishpeming, was named for Jacob Harper who became its first postmaster on Feb. 20, 1893, the office operating until May 3, 1897 [GSM 1895-99; PO Archives].

**HARPER WOODS**, Wayne County: first settled by Caspar Salter in 1850; the first plat was recorded in 1920 and was called Manchester Park; other subdivisions followed, but the 1929 Depression brought the area back to virtual wilderness; but in 1934, the subdividers began again, and a solid, home-owning community developed; in 1949, it was renamed from its being in a heavily wooded area and from its then main thoroughfare, Harper Avenue, which begins in Detroit and was named in 1874 for Walter Harper, founder of Harper Hospital, in Detroit; incorporated as a city in 1951 [Noreen Woodworth].

**HARRICKSVILLE**, Branch County. See Butler.

**HARRIETTA**, Wexford County: a post office in the home of Andrew J. Green, some two miles north, was opened as Springdale on July 17, 1874; the Ashleys, father and two sons, built the Ann Arbor Railroad through here, and in 1889, James M. Ashley platted and recorded the village as Harriette, formed by combining his father's name, Harry, with that of his fiancee, Henriette Burt; the post office was moved here but still càlled Springdale; in 1890, Mr. P. D. Gaston and Mr. W. W. Campbell platted the Gaston and Campbell additions to the village; in 1891, it was incorporated as the village of Gaston; the railroad officials threatened to close the station unless the old name was restored, and it was renamed Harriette on May 18, 1892, with the spelling changed to Harrietta on May 7, 1923 [Wretha Bastrom, PM; Wheeler; PO Archives].

**HARRIS**, Ingham County: named for George H. and J. N. Harris who migrated here from New York State; Tyrannus C. Crysler became its first postmaster on July 24, 1889, the office operating until April 10, 1894 [Foster; PO Archives].

**HARRIS**, Menominee County: lumberman Michael B. Harris, later a member of the legislature from this district, settled here in 1875; it was given a post office named DeLoughory, for farmer George W. DeLoughory, who became its first postmaster on July 8, 1880; he resigned and the office was closed on May 4, 1883; the office was restored on July 13, 1883, with Mr. Harris as its postmaster, and on Sept. 6, 1900, the office was renamed for him; a station on the Chicago & Northwestern Railroad [Sawyer; PO Archives].

**HARRISBURG**, Ottawa County: a station on the Toledo, Saginaw & Muskegon Railroad; William H. Harrison became its first postmaster on Dec. 8, 1888, with the office named for him; it operated until Feb. 28, 1907 [GSM 1891; PO Archives].

**HARRIS CREEK**, Clare County: a hamlet at the junction of the Little Thornapple and Coldwater Rivers, in Hayes Township in 1882 [GSM 1883].

**HARRIS CREEK**, Kent County: a settlement in Bowne Township, on Harris Creek, named for John Harris, son-in-law of the first settler, Jonathan Thomas, who came here from Ovid, N.Y., in 1837; Wilber L.

March became its first postmaster on Jan. 29, 1869, the office operating until Jan. 23, 1882 [Dillenback; PO Archives].

**HARRISON,** Clare County: the board of supervisors sent a committee to locate a county seat in 1877; it reported its selection of this site on Jan. 8, 1878; the Flint & Pere Marquette Railroad platted the village in 1879, presenting a block to the county for a county seat; John Hatfield built the first house in 1879; given a post office on Jan. 27, 1880, with Reuben Smith as its first postmaster; incorporated as a village in 1885 and as a city in 1891; named for President William Henry Harrison [Robert E. Roth; J. C. McNamara; PO Archives].

**HARRISON,** Kalamazoo County. See Harrison Lake.

**HARRISON,** Lenawee County: in 1837, a village on the Raisin River, in Blissfield Township, called Harrisonville, but renamed Harrison by 1859 [GSM 1838, 1865].

**HARRISON,** Macomb County: a hamlet in Harrison Township in 1859 [GSM 1860].

**HARRISON,** Washtenaw County: its station on the D.H. & S.W. Railroad was named Harrison's, but its post office, opened on Oct. 23, 1841, with James M. Hallock as its first postmaster, was named Harrison; the post office was closed on April 24, 1851 [GSM 1860; PO Archives].

**HARRISON JUNCTION,** Clare County: in 1888, the southern terminus of the H division of the Flint & Pere Marquette Railroad; see Harrison, Clare County, for the name [GSM 1889].

**HARRISON LAKE,** Kalamazoo County: named for Bazel Harrison (1774-1874), who became the first permanent settler in the county in the winter of 1827-28; he was immortalized by James Fennimore Cooper as Bee Hunter in the novel Oak Openings; given a station named Harrison on the Michigan Central Railroad in 1870 [Mich Hist 15:254 1931].

**HARRISON'S,** Washtenaw County: a station on the Lake Shore & Michigan Southern Railroad, five miles south of Ypsilanti, in 1888 [GSM 1889].

**HARRISONVILLE,** Lenawee County. See Harrison.

**HARRISVILLE,** Alcona County: in 1854, two fishermen, Simeon Holden and Crosier Davison, in partnership, first purchased pine lands and water power privilege here, and the place became known as Davison's Mill; they sold out to Benjamin Harris and his sons, Levi O. and Henry H. Harris, of West Bloomfield, N.Y.; when the township was organized in 1860, it was named Harris for them; it was given a post office named Harrisville on Sept. 16, 1857, with Levi O. Harris as its first postmaster; the Harris brothers sold out to Weston, (George L.) Colwell & Company, and they founded the village in 1866; they had it platted by H. G. Rothwell in 1870; incorporated as a village in 1887 and as a city in 1905 [Stannard; Powers; PO Archives].

**HARRISVILLE,** Menominee County. See Harris.

**HARSENS ISLAND,** St. Clair County: James Harsen, and his son-in-law, Isaac Graveraet (or Graveret), from Albany, N.Y., were the first white settlers on the island, coming here about 1779; Mr. Harsen bought the island from the Indians about 1783; it was also called Jacob Island (James or Jacobus) as late as 1809; the post office of Sans Souci, on the island, was changed to Harsens Island on Dec. 31, 1960 [Evelyn Harm, PM; Mich Hist 22:301 1938, 30:381 1946; PO Archives].

**HART,** Oceana County: Nelson Glover became the first settler in the area in 1856; Hart Township was organized in 1858 and named for a pioneer, Wellington Hart; Lyman Corbin completed his sawmill in 1862 and then built the county's first grist mill, and around these the town formed; the village was platted in 1864 to become the county seat on Jan. 2, 1865, with Mr. Corbin erecting the buildings; William M. Leach became its first postmaster on Feb. 6, 1865; incorporated as a village in 1885 and as a city in 1946 [Eva Hanson-Osborn].

**HARTFORD,** Van Buren County: Ferdino Olds became the first settler in the township in 1837 and when it was organized in 1840 he named it Hartland after his native town in New York; but there was another Hartland in Michigan and, at the suggestion of another 1837 settler, Burrill A. Olney, it was renamed Hartford; its hamlet, first called Bloody Corners, due to its early unsavory reputation for liquor, was given a post office as Hartford on March 31, 1856, with James E. Griffin as its first postmaster; first platted by Truman Stratton, W. W. Shepard, and others, in 1859; given a station on the Pere Marquette Railroad in 1870; incorporated as a village in 1877 [Ellis; Rowland; PO Archives].

**HARTLAND,** Livingston County: the first settler in the area was Colonel Samuel Mapes in 1831, and in the town itself, Rufus Tenney; Isaac Parshall became the first postmaster of Hartland, named after its township, on June 19, 1837; the first store was opened by George J. Griffin in 1839 [Ellis; PO Archives].

**HARTLEY'S,** Gogebic County: a station on the Chicago & Northwestern Railroad, 7 miles northwest of Marenisco, in 1894 [GSM 1895].

**HARTMAN,** Berrien County: a depot on the Chicago & Western Michigan Railroad named Pipestone Station, in Pipestone Township, a mile southwest of Pipestone village; it was given a post office on Feb. 14, 1888, with Charles K. Farmer as its first postmaster, but on March 15, 1889, the name was changed, due to confusion with the post office at Pipestone; it was renamed Hartman for F. Hartman, a farmer who had given the railroad an acre of land for its depot; the office operated until Aug. 31, 1913 [Amos R. Green; PO Archives].

**HART STATION,** Oceana County: when the Chicago & Michigan Lake Shore Railroad came through, its station nearest to (4½ miles west of) the village of Hart was named Hart Station; see Hart for the name [GSM 1873].

**HARTSUFF**, St. Clair County: William Green became the first postmaster on Aug. 30, 1881, the office operating until March 4, 1895; named for General William Hartsuff, a former commander of nearby Fort Gratiot and in 1887 mayor of Port Huron; it is in Greenwood Township and its railroad station was named Green's Corners [GSM 1883; Cole].

**HARTWELLVILLE**, Shiawassee County: Giles Tucker opened the first store here in Bennington Township, succeeded by Jonathan M. Hartwell, from Norwich, N.Y., in 1838, and he became the first postmaster on Feb. 11, 1841, with the office named for him; members of his family held the position until the office was closed on Jan. 15, 1901 [Ellis; Campbell; MPH 39:103 1899; PO Archives].

**HARTWICK**, Osceola County: Smith Hawking became the first settler in the area in 1866 and the first supervisor when the township was organized in 1870; general storekeeper Alfred Davis became the first postmaster on Dec. 13, 1881, the office operating until March 31, 1911 [Chapman; PO Archives].

**HARTWICK PINES STATE PARK**, Crawford County: in 1927, Mrs. Karen B. Hartwick donated 8,320 acres for this park, named for lumberman Colonel Edward E. Hartwick; it includes a logging exhibit and a museum [Mich Hist 36:414 1952].

**HARVARD**, Kent County: a station on the Toledo, Saginaw & Muskegon Railroad in 1888; Freeman Addis became its first postmaster on Aug. 22, 1888, the office operating until May 5, 1934 [GSM 1889; PO Archives].

**HARVEY**, Marquette County: this village began as the site of the blast furnace of the Northern Iron Company in 1860; it was founded by Charles T. Harvey (1829-1912) and named for him; George P. Cummings became its first postmaster on Oct. 16, 1860; a station on the Chicago & Northwestern Railroad; from its location on Chocolay Creek in Chocolay Township, it was also known as Chocolay [Andreas; PO Archives].

**HARWOOD**, Muskegon County: Joseph A. Stocking became the first postmaster of this rural post office on March 19, 1869, but the office was transferred to and renamed Lake Harbor on March 2, 1871 [PO Archives].

**HASKIN'S MILLS**, Macomb County. See Ashley's Mills.

**HASLER**, Lapeer County: Alanson Hammond became the first postmaster of this rural post office on June 7, 1866, but the office was transferred to and renamed Elba on Dec. 26, 1871 [PO Archives].

**HASLETT**, Ingham County: it was given a post office named Pine Lake, from its location on Pine Lake, with Edward Elliott as its first postmaster, on May 14, 1879; by legislative action, it was renamed Haslett Park on Sept. 19, 1890, and Haslett on June 28, 1895, for James Haslett; he began it as a summer camp for Spiritualists and hoped to make it their national headquarters, but that program ended with his death [Foster; Mich Hist 43:377 1959; PO Archives].

**HASTINGS,** Barry County: in 1836, Eurotas P. Hastings, president of the Bank of Michigan, sold his holdings here to a Marshall firm of promotors on the strength of the promise of the county commissioners to make his site the county seat; that fall, the company built a sawmill and a grist mill to attract settlers; Slocum H. Bunker, the first settler, built the first house in 1836; Willard Hays became the first postmaster on March 14, 1839; the village became the county seat about 1841; incorporated as a village in 1855 and as a city in 1871 [Atwell; MPH 26:235 1895; Mich Hist 15:176 1931].

**HASTINGS,** Oakland County. See Troy.

**HASTY,** Gratiot County: this settlement in southeastern Hamilton Township began in 1870 around the sawmill and general store of Potter, Beattie & Company; Ezra A. Cole became its first postmaster on June 7, 1878, succeeded by the foreman of the mill, E. M. Potter, in 1888, but the office was closed on Nov. 3, 1891; the place was also called Potter's Mill [Tucker; GSM 1889].

**HATCH'S CROSSING,** Leelanau County: in 1894, the main line of the Manistee & Northwestern Railroad, which ran from Manistee to Traverse City, built a branch line from here to Provemont (now Lake Leelanau), and soon after, another connecting line, the Traverse City, Leelanau & Manistique Railroad was built from here to Northport; but it never became a village, just a station; it had an agent-telegrapher up till about 1925; the crossing got its name from the Hatch family who owned the adjoining farm; it was six miles north of Traverse City [Conrad Gronseth].

**HATMAKER,** Branch County: this village in Bethel Township was named for the pioneer Hatmaker family: Aaron the cider-maker, and Peter the grocer, who became its first postmaster on May 23, 1887; the office was closed on Aug. 14, 1894, but was restored from Jan. 5, 1899, to May 25, 1900 [GSM 1889; PO Archives].

**HATTON,** Clare County: this settlement around the station of the Pere Marquette Railroad was begun in 1881; given a post office on May 18, 1882, with James G. Landry as its first postmaster; a fire in 1910 all but obliterated the town [GSM 1885; PO Archives].

**HAVANA,** Kalkaska County. See Westwood.

**HAVANA,** Saginaw County. See Oakley.

**HAVRE,** Monroe County: this village in Erie Township was named from its location at the junction of the Havre, Bay, and Ottawa Rivers, on the north shore of Maumee Bay, a mile and a half north of the Ohio border; Joshua B. Van Deusen became its first postmaster on June 19, 1837, the office operating until only Dec. 15, 1837 [GSM 1838; PO Archives].

**HAVRE,** Wexford County: Samuel R. Hepburn became the first postmaster of this rural post office on Aug. 21, 1883 [PO Archives].

**HAWES**, Alcona County: a station on the Detroit & Mackinaw Railroad, in Hawes Township; Alexander Savage became its first postmaster on March 13, 1899, the office operating until March 31, 1908 [GSM 1901; PO Archives].

**HAWE'S BRIDGE**, Gladwin County: a sawmill settlement on the Tittabawassee River, in Buckeye Township, with a station on the S. B. & N.W. Railroad; the village which developed was on the hill above it and away from the river, and was given a post office as Highwood on Feb. 9, 1892 [GSM 1893; PO Archives].

**HAWKHEAD**, Allegan County: the settlement grew up around the sawmill and the flour mill of William Hawkhead and was given a post office on March 22, 1882, with Sylvester Munger as its first postmaster; Theron and Adelbert Johnston, brothers, acquired the general store here in Casco Township in 1893, and it was while Theron was postmaster that the office was closed on Jan. 31, 1902 [Thomas; GSM 1883; PO Archives].

**HAWKINS**, Newaygo County: this rural post office was named for storekeeper George D. Hawkins who became its first postmaster on Nov. 13, 1889, the office operating until April 16, 1906 [Harry L. Spooner; PO Archives].

**HAWKS**, Presque Isle County: when the Detroit & Mackinaw Railroad came through here in Bismarck Township in 1895, they named the station for James Dudley Hawks, president of the road; Harris Harvey Horwitz became its first postmaster on Aug. 26, 1896 [M. M. Prell, PM].

**HAWTHORN**, Monroe County: a station on the Toledo & Ann Arbor Railroad in 1878 [GSM 1879].

**HAYES**, Huron County: storekeeper Charles F. Leippraudt became the first postmaster of this rural post office on Nov. 21, 1876, the office operating until Oct. 31, 1903; Rutherford B. Hayes was elected President of the U.S. in 1876 [GSM 1879-1905; PO Archives].

**HAYES POINT**, Keweenaw County: named for John Hayes who opened the first copper pit at Copper Harbor, and the first on the lake in 1844; site of a lighthouse [Mich Hist 9:379 1925].

**HAYMARSH**, Missaukee County: Berlie Dorr became the first postmaster of this rural post office, 20 miles northeast of Lake City, on May 16, 1903; the office was closed on Oct. 13, 1912, but was restored, with Berlie Dorr again its postmaster, on April 11, 1913 [GSM 1905; PO Archives].

**HAYNES CORNERS**, Ingham County: a post office moved here from Ingham about 1851, with Thomas Densmore as its first postmaster here; on May 14, 1857, it was moved to and renamed Dansville [Cole].

**HAY'S CORNERS**, St. Clair County. See Merrillsville.

**HAYTOWN**, Keweenaw County: a former mining settlement on Isle Royale, at the foot of Pickett Bay; named for Alexander H. Hay, then secretary of the Isle Royale Land Corporation [Dustin].

**HAYWOOD VALE,** Huron County: a hamlet in 1880, named for the Haywood family, pioneer settlers [GSM 1881; Hey].

**HAZEL,** Iron County: a spur take-off from the Chicago & Northwestern Railroad to the lumber communities in the area in the 1880s; like several others of these stops, it was named after forest trees; its post office was Beechwood [Jack Hill, Sr.].

**HAZEL GREEN,** Shiawassee County. See Henderson.

**HAZEL GROVE,** Oceana County: this village on Hazel Creek, in Greenwood Township, was first settled in 1868, Rufus Skeels became its first postmaster on March 29, 1872, the office operating until Jan. 20, 1875 [GSM 1875; Royal; PO Archives].

**HAZEL PARK,** Oakland County: it dates to a purchase in 1869 by Anthony Neusius who had the original 80 acres; it was first called Hazel Slump because of a profusion of hazelnut bushes and water; it was a part of Royal Oak Township until it was incorporated as the city of Hazel Park on Jan. 5, 1842; Percy T. Morden became its first postmaster on July 1, 1946 [Durant; Seeley; PO Archives].

**HAZELTON,** Shiawassee County: the first land entry here was made by General James Wadsworth, of Geneseo, N.Y., in 1836, but when the village was formed it was named for Porter Hazelton who, for building a bridge across the Flint River, was given much of the land here by the state in 1849; John D. Newell became its first postmaster on July 7, 1857; the office was closed on Jan. 6, 1873, but was restored from Feb. 25, 1873, to April 30, 1902; the village was "vulgarly known as Ratville" [Ellis; GSM 1875; PO Archives].

**HAZENVILLE,** Branch County. See Sherwood.

**HEADACHE,** Midland County. See Gordonville.

**HEADLAND,** Osceola County: this station on the Pere Marquette Railroad was given a post office on March 1, 1880, with John Parkinson as its first postmaster, the office operating until May 21, 1881 [GSM 1885; PO Archives].

**HEART,** Macomb County: Jenison F. Glazier became the first postmaster of this rural post office on March 21, 1837, the office operating until Sept. 22, 1838 [PO Archives].

**HEARTTS,** Tuscola County: in 1860, this small settlement sought to be designated the county seat [Schultz].

**HEATH,** Allegan County: Simeon Howe and John Saddler became the first settlers here in 1850; when the town was organized in 1851, it was named for James M. Heath, the first supervisor [MPH 17:563 1890; Thomas].

**HEATH,** Ottawa County: John Lahuis became the first postmaster of this rural post office, 7 miles from Hudsonville, on June 21, 1897, the office operating until Oct. 31, 1902 [GSM 1899-1905; PO Archives].

**HEATH CORNERS**, Berrien County. See Fair Plain.

**HEBARD**, Keweenaw County: a station on the Mineral Range Railroad; its post office was opened on June 30, 1903, in the Wetton & Wyckoff general store, with Annie Wetton as its first postmaster; named for Charles and Edward Hebard, two English-born lumbermen who operated large sawmills on Keweenaw Bay [GSM 1905; Havighurst; PO Archives].

**HEBRON**, Cheboygan County: storekeeper Joseph H. Borrowcliff became the first postmaster of this rural post office on July 18, 1900, the office operating until Oct. 31, 1906 [GSM 1901-07; PO Archives].

**HECLA**, Houghton County. See Calumet.

**HEIGHTS (THE)**, Roscommon County. See Houghton Lake Heights.

**HEISTERMAN ISLAND**, Huron County: Carl H. Heisterman bought its 400 acres from the federal government in 1851; he and his wife lived here alone, except for a few friendly Indians, for more than 30 years; now a duck hunting and small game refuge; the Indian name for it was Chinquaka or Stony Island, and on some current maps it is called Stony Island [Hey].

**HELENA**, Antrim County. See Clam River.

**HELENA**, Huron County: founded by Alex Snetzinger about 1870, who named it for his wife; he became its first postmaster on Dec. 6, 1887, the office operating until Aug. 14, 1905; a station on the Pere Marquette Railroad since 1887; now a hamlet [Thomas R. McAllister; PO Archives].

**HELENA**, Marquette County: this village, with a station on the Chicago & Northwestern Railroad, was first settled in 1878 [GSM 1879; Andreas].

**HELL**, Livingston County: the community dates from 1841 when New Yorkers, migrating westward via the Erie Canal, took over a sawmill, adding a flour mill and a distillery; local tradition attributes the name to brawling by and with drunken Indians; a May 1-Sept. 30 rural postal station of Pinckney since July, 1961 [L. A. Baughn, PM].

**HELLEMS**, Huron County: Enoch Pleski became the first postmaster of this hamlet, some 5 miles northeast of Kinde, on Feb. 18, 1895, the office operating until only April 29, 1895; named for Henry B. Hellems who served in Company C, 15th Michigan Infantry, in the Civil War [Chet Hey; PO Archives].

**HELLTOWN**, Keweenaw County. See Wyoming.

**HELMER**, Luce County: Rev. Mills built a mission building here in Lakefield Township about 1880; when he left, the building was bought by Mr. and Mrs. Gaylord Helmer, who used it for a store with a post office in it, he becoming the first postmaster of Helmer on March 19, 1894; their store and resort were purchased by Mr. and Mrs. Charles L. Fyvie; some 20 years later, the post office was closed and it became an RFD station;

present-day Helmer is owned by Dr. James H. Fyvie, of Manistique [Mrs. James Fyvie Goldthorpe].

**HELMER'S**, Calhoun County: this hamlet, then 3 miles southwest of Battle Creek, dates from 1878; it was named for Andrew Helmer, local landowner and for six terms supervisor of Battle Creek Township [Gardner; GSM 1879].

**HEMANS**, Sanilac County: a station on the Detroit, Bay City & Western Railroad, in Lamotte Township; first called Poverty Nook, it was renamed for Lawton T. Hemans, Michigan historian, in 1914; storekeeper Austin G. Wentworth became its first postmaster on March 6, 1916, the office operating until June 30, 1933 [Gerard Schultz; GSM 1917; PO Archives].

**HEMLICK SETTLEMENT**, Berrien County: begun by Jesse Hemlick who came here in Oronoko Township on horseback from Ohio in 1835 [Chauncey].

**HEMLOCK**, Iron County. See Amasa.

**HEMLOCK**, Saginaw County: Philo Thomas became the first settler here in 1865, followed by John Codd in 1866; W. S. Gillespie built a sawmill here in 1868, and soon after, the Saginaw Valley & St. Louis Railroad came through from Saginaw, bringing an influx of settlers; given a post office as Hemlock City on May 24, 1869, with Jacob King as its first postmaster, the name being shortened to Hemlock on March 27, 1895; named from the vast number of hemlock trees which covered the area [Mary C. Rauchholz; Mills; PO Archives].

**HENDERSON**, Dickinson County: this hamlet is believed to have been named for R. C. Henderson, former prosecuting attorney for the county [Victor Lemmer].

**HENDERSON**, Shiawassee County: Gideon Lee, of New York City, entered the first land here in Rush Township in 1836; he sold it to Josiah Isham who in turn sold it to Andrew Henderson, of Ohio, in 1858, his son, John Henderson, for whom the village was first named, as Hendersonville, built the first store in 1868 and the first hotel in 1875; given a post office as Hazel Green on May 14, 1868, with William Cook as its first postmaster, but the office was renamed Henderson on Oct. 16, 1876; the village was platted by Ezra Mason for Andrew Henderson in 1879; its station on a branch of the Michigan Central Railroad was first named Henderson's [Ellis; Campbell; PO Archives].

**HENDERSON**, Wexford County: a hamlet in the southeast part of the county in 1882 [GSM 1883].

**HENDRICKS**, Delta County: a small settlement around a loading station on the Escanaba & Lake Superior Railroad, formed about 1902, to haul logs, lumber and iron ore; Peter Lemmer (d. 1915), who owned 320 acres here, named it after William (Billy) Hendricks, a local shacker; now a ghost town [Victor Lemmer].

**HENDRICK'S QUARRY,** Mackinac County: a station on the Soo Line at the site of the Union Carbide quarry, William Hanson, superintendent, and of two sawmills; given a post office named Naveaux on June 12, 1916, with storekeeper Frederick J. Graunstadt as its first postmaster; the office was renamed Hendrick's Quarry on Jan. 15, 1921, but was closed on June 30, 1922 [GSM 1917; PO Archives].

**HENDRIE,** Mackinac County: George Hendrie, a Detroit lumberman, helped finance the Detroit, Mackinaw & Marquette Railroad, and the station here was named for him in 1882 [Mich Hist 46:167 1962].

**HENPECK,** Genesee County. See Thetford.

**HENRIETTA,** Jackson County: Jean Baptiste Berard (or Boreaux, as his descendants have it), established his trading post here in 1831, and said he had settled here in 1816; his name was commonly written Battise by the early settlers, and nearby Batteese Lake was named for him; the township, organized in 1837, was first named West Portage, but renamed in 1839 by Henry Hurd after his native town of Henrietta, N.Y.; John Davidson became the first postmaster of Portage on May 21, 1838, with the office changed to West Portage on Dec. 14, 1838, and then to Henrietta on May 13, 1840, but being closed on Dec. 14, 1903 [John Daball; MPH 27:571 1896; Mich Hist 12:338 1928; PO Archives].

**HENRY,** Alcona County: a station on the Detroit, Bay City & Alpena Railroad in 1886 [GSM 1887].

**HENRY,** Manistee County: a station on the A. & B.R. and the Pere Marquette Railroads, in Springdale Township; railroad agent David R. Rensberger became the first postmaster on Feb. 12, 1902; named for Henry Starke, of Arcadia, who owned the Arcadia & Betsie River Railroad, as well as a sawmill in the area [Virginia S. Stroemel; GSM 1905; PO Archives].

**HENRY'S,** Ingham County: a hamlet in 1878 [GSM 1879].

**HENWOOD,** Ontonagon County: a copper mining location; opened in 1853 as the Douglass Houghton Mine, named after the pioneer state geologist; later renamed the Henwood for Edwin Henwood, of Hancock, a pioneer mining executive in the area [Stevens].

**HERBERT,** Roscommon County: lumberman James Nolan became the first postmaster of this sawmill settlement in Richfield Township on May 22, 1902, and named the office after his son; on Sept. 13, 1910, it was transferred to and renamed Keno [Co. Bd. of Ed.; PO Archives].

**HERMAN,** Baraga County: this village was founded by Herman Keranen in 1901 and was named for him by Nels Majhannu; Edward Herkoner became its first postmaster on Jan. 13, 1902 [Martha Dantes, PM].

**HERMANSVILLE,** Menominee County: in 1878, Charles J. L. Meyer, a Wisconsin lumberman, bought land here, built a mill and began a town which he named for his younger son, Herman; it became the headquarters of the Wisconsin Land & Lumber Company which he organized in 1883; it is in Meyer Township, which had been named for him; Herman P. Meyer became the first postmaster on Dec. 9, 1878; given a station on the Chicago & Northwestern Railroad in 1880 [Sawyer; PO Archives].

**HERPS**, Allegan County: a hamlet near North Dorr, in 1918 [GSM 1919].

**HERRICK**, Isabella County: a station on the Pere Marquette Railroad; Robert Maxwell became its first postmaster on Dec. 10, 1895, the office operating until Sept. 15, 1908 [GSM 1897; PO Archives].

**HERRICKVILLE**, Branch County: a hamlet near Butler in 1853 [GSM 1895].

**HERRING CREEK**, Benzie County: when Harrison Averill became the first postmaster of this rural post office on Sept. 12, 1857, it was in Leelanau County, but it was moved to Benzonia, Benzie County, on July 16, 1859 [Traverse].

**HERRING LAKE**, Benzie County. See Watervale.

**HERRINGTON**, Ottawa County: this station on the Grand Rapids & Indiana Railroad was given a post office on April 13, 1888, with George W. Sovey as its first postmaster [GSM 1903; PO Archives].

**HERRON**, Alpena County: founded in 1920 by Fred Herron, and named for him; Alexander Martin became its first postmaster on Oct. 5, 1920 [PM; PO Archives].

**HERSEY**, Osceola County: Nathan Hersey, a trapper, is believed to have been the first white man in the county, coming in 1843; Delos A. Blodgett became the first settler in this area in 1851 and the first postmaster of Hersey, the first post office in the county, on May 21, 1868; he platted the village on part of his farm in 1869; a station on the Pere Marquette Railroad; incorporated as a village in 1875 [Chapman; PO Archives].

**HERSEY'S MILLS**, Oakland County: here on Stony Creek in Avon Township John Hersey built a sawmill in 1824 [GSM 1839].

**HESPERIA**, Oceana County: Booth Perry became the first settler in the area in 1856-57; he induced Patrick McFarland and Alexander McLaren to settle nearby, which they did in February, 1858; after the latter was named McLaren Lake; the first resident of the village itself was Joseph W. Sweet, who employed Jeryma Streeter to clear his land and build his home, into which he and his family moved in the spring of 1859; the village was platted in 1866 by John P. Cook who, with his partner, Daniel Weaver, built a sawmill and a general store and promoted the village; given a post office on Aug. 2, 1867; incorporated as a village in 1883; named by Mary, daughter of Mr. Cook, from its resemblance to a garden [MPH 7:553 1886; PO Archives].

**HESSEL**, Mackinac County: founded on the Lake Huron shore in Cedar Township in 1885 by two Swedes and a Norwegian, John and Carley Hessel and John A. Johnson; storekeeper John Hessel became its first postmaster on Sept. 13, 1888 [M. J. Mortinsen].

**HETHERTON**, Montmorency County: Allen Briley became the fist postmaster of Briley, Montmorency County, in 1881; the site was moved across the line into Otsego County and the name changed to Heatherton on Nov. 2, 1885; the name remained Hetherton when it was changed back to Montmorency County on Oct. 28, 1903; the hamlet straddles the line between the two counties [PO Archives].

**HEWLETTON**, Huron County: named for Rev. Francis Hewlett, first resident pastor of St. Felix Catholic Church here, in July 1899; then he built a new church, selling the old one to Joseph R. Foy, who used it for a general store; besides the store, a church, rectory, blacksmith shop, and a few homes comprised the hamlet; now only the church, rectory and parish hall (the rebought general store) remain [Rev. Joseph A. Schabel].

**HIAWATHA**, Schoolcraft County: a co-operative colony, founded in 1893 by Thomas Mills, an American Socialist, on 240 acres donated by Abe Byers, the Populist leader; John D. Kelper became its first postmaster on April 14, 1894; dissention split this colony, located 13 miles north of Manistique, and it was abandoned in 1896, but its post office operated until Jan. 31, 1941; it was Michigan Indian agent, Henry Rowe Schoolcraft, who in "The Myth of Hiawatha," in his book Algic Researches (1839), probably first introduced the name immortalized in 1855 in Henry Longfellow's poem [Federal; Ency. Brit.; PO Archives].

**HICKEY**, St. Clair County: grocer John H. Rector became the first postmaster of this rural post office in Columbus Township on March 8, 1895, but the office was transferred to and renamed Columbus on Aug. 19, 1909 [GSM 1897; PO Archives].

**HICKORY CORNERS**, Barry County: the first settler, a half mile from the present town, was Rev. Moses Lawrence who built his home on the shore of present Lake Lawrence in 1834; surveyors in 1837 found a large hickory tree in the center of Section 28 and with the building of a schoolhouse here that year it took the name of Hickory Corners; Solomon C. Hall built the first home in 1839 and was named the first postmaster on July 11, 1844 [Mrs. Roger E. Davis, wife of PM].

**HICKORY CORNERS**, Branch County. See Noble.

**HICKORY GROVE**, Jackson County: John Mott became the first postmaster of this rural post office on March 14, 1839, the office operating until Oct. 6, 1855 [GSM 1860; PO Archives].

**HICKORY RIDGE**, Oakland County: a Highland Township settlement, with a stone schoolhouse, "built at an early date," about 1860 [Seeley].

**HICKOX**, Wayne County: the log meeting house on the Huron circuit of Protestant preachers in 1828, named for Rev. Joseph Hickox, who was sent to Detroit by the Genesee conference in 1816; the locality was later known as the Wallace Place, after its owner, John Wallace [MPH 28:152 1897].

**HICKS**, Sanilac County: this rural post office in Buel Township was named for farmer George W. Hicks who became its first postmaster on Sept. 6, 1893, the office operating until Jan. 9, 1895 [GSM 1895; PO Archives].

**HICKVILLE**, Oakland County. See West Novi.

**HIGBEE**, Mecosta County: named for Nelson Higbee who operated its general store and who became its first postmaster on March 12, 1898; the office was closed on Sept. 30, 1901 [GSM 1899-1903; PO Archives].

**HIGGINS**, Roscommon County. See Higgins Lake.

**HIGGINS LAKE**, Roscommon County: Charles Lyon, a local resort hotelman, subdivided this property on Higgins Lake, in Gerrish Township, in 1902, and began the village; a post office named Higgins was opened on June 17, 1902, with John W. Derby as its first postmaster, the office operating until only Aug. 30, 1902; the Higgins Lake post office was opened on May 3, 1909, with Otto J. Willer as its first postmaster; the lake had been named for Sylvester Higgins, an early (1837) topographer; it was first called Forginson Lake in the 1839 survey of John Brink, but was renamed Higgins Lake in the 1852 survey of William A. Burt [Mich Hist 16:364 1932; Ruth L. Buck; GSM 1911-21; PO Archives].

**HIGHBANK**, Barry County: Frank A. Wilcox became the first postmaster of this rural post office, 9 miles southeast of Hastings, on Sept. 6, 1894, the office operating until April 15, 1903 [GSM 1895-1905; PO Archives].

**HIGH RIDGE**, Manistee County: this station on the Chicago & Western Michigan Railroad, in Brown Township, was first named Corfu, the name of a Grecian island in the Adriatic; given a post office as High Ridge on Oct. 24, 1890, with James Silverly as its first postmaster; the office was closed on Jan. 31, 1903, but was restored on Oct. 18, 1911 [GSM 1893; PO Archives].

**HIGH ISLAND**, Charlevoix County: Gladys Hill became the first postmaster of this rural post office on Beaver Island on June 5, 1913 [GSM 1915; PO Archives].

**HIGHLAND**, Oakland County: named after the township which was so named because of its elevation; among the first settlers were Zenas Phelps and George Lee, about 1835; Jonathan F. Stratton became its first postmaster on March 16, 1835; upon completion of the Flint & Pere Marquette Railroad in 1871, the village was platted by Germain St. John and Almon Ruggles; on Dec. 23, 1873, the Spring Mills post office was moved here and renamed Highland Station; it was renamed Highland on

March 26, 1903, and West Highland on Feb. 2, 1906, but operated until only Oct. 13, 1906 [Seeley; Durant; PO Archives].

**HIGHLAND BEACH,** Cass County: a resort on the north shore of Indian Lake, in Silver Creek Township; platted and recorded in 1905 by Talmadge Tice, proprietor [Glover].

**HIGHLAND CORNERS,** Oakland County. See West Highland.

**HIGHLAND PARK,** Wayne County: the first known settler was Richard Ford who built his cabin upon the highland for which the town was eventually named, a ridge later leveled when Woodward Avenue was put through from Detroit (it was then some six miles northwest of that city, but is now completely surrounded by it); Judge Augustus B. Woodward bought the ridge in 1818 and platted the village of Woodwardville in 1825; his plans failed as did those of Judge Benjamin F. Witherell who attempted to found a village on the site in 1836; the settlement was given a post office as Whitewood on Feb. 12, 1873, with Adolphus Trombley as its first postmaster; the office was closed on Oct. 20, 1875, but was restored on Jan. 25, 1876, with John T. Mott, Jr., as its postmaster; the office was renamed Highland Park on June 27, 1889, but was closed on April 30, 1909, when it became a branch of the Detroit post office; the successful promotion of the town is credited to William H. Stevens and Henry Ford's building a factory here in 1909; incorporated as a village in 1889 and as a city in 1917 [Burton; Federal; PO Archives].

**HIGHLAND STATION,** Oakland County. See Highland.

**HIGHWAY,** Houghton County: a station on the Mineral Range Railroad in 1882 [GSM 1883].

**HIGHWOOD,** Gladwin County: it began as a lumber town; George I. and Ellen Jane Sprowl came here from Pinconning in 1887; next year he built a new house up on the hill close to the railroad as a boarding house for section hands and lumber jacks; he applied for a post office as Highwood (due to its high surroundings from the river), received the commission on Feb. 9, 1892, and operated it until, kicked by a horse, he died in 1900, when he was succeeded by Julia A. (Mrs. Henry) Robbins; the office operated until Dec. 14, 1936 [A. N. Sprowl; PO Archives].

**HILL,** Mecosta County: this rural post office was named for lumberman Andrew Hill who became its first postmaster on June 27, 1901, the office operating until March 22, 1904 [GSM 1903-05; PO Archives].

**HILLIARDS,** Allegan County: Lonson Hilliard, a Canadian lumberman, bought large timber acreage here in Hopkins Township about 1860; it was given a railroad station and on Oct. 26, 1869, a post office, with Wallace B. Smith as its first postmaster, the office operating until Oct. 31, 1953 [Esther W. Hettinger; GSM 1875; PO Archives].

**HILLMAN,** Montmorency County: founded in 1880 by John Hillman Stevens who gave the land he had platted; Selah Arms became its first postmaster on April 4, 1882; incorporated as a village in 1891 [PM; PO Archives].

**HILL'S CORNERS**, Berrien County: named for Alpheus Hill who settled here in 1846; Aaron E. Gardner became its first postmaster on March 29, 1878; on Jan. 2, 1891, the office was changed to Glendora, of which it is now a part [Fox; PO Archives].

**HILLSDALE**, Hillsdale County: first settled by Jeremiah Arnold who came from DePeyster, N.Y., in 1834; platted in 1835; got its first store and inn in 1838; John Potter Cook became its first postmaster on Feb. 2, 1839; incorporated as a village in 1847 and as a city in 1869; in the early days it was also called Hillsdale Center from its location in the county, which had been named from its topography of hills and dales [Vivian Lyon Moore].

**HILLTOP**, Berrien County: a station on the Pere Marquette Railroad, so named from its location at the top of a hill en route from St. Joseph [Fox].

**HILLTOWN**, Keweenaw County. See Wyoming.

**HINCHMAN**, Berrien County: a station on the Milwaukee, Benton Harbor & Columbus Railway; grocer Jacob Richards became its first postmaster on Aug. 18, 1888, the office operating until April 15, 1908 [GSM 1889; PO Archives].

**HINES CROSSING**, Muskegon County: a station on the Toledo, Saginaw & Muskegon Railroad, 17 miles east of Muskegon, in 1888 [GSM 1895].

**HINKLEVILLE**, Clare County: Henry Hinkle built a sawmill here in 1868; it was the impromptu county seat even before the county was organized in 1871; now a ghost town [J. C. McNamara].

**HINMAN**, Emmet County. See Alanson.

**HINTON**, Mecosta County: John Hinton became the first settler here in 1855 and the township was named for him when organized in 1860; R. Van Dewater was its first supervisor; William Brockway became its first postmaster on July 17, 1862, the office operating until Oct. 16, 1863 [Chapman; PO Archives].

**HIRAM**, Montcalm County: the settlement grew around the sawmill of Taylor & McMullen in 1868; given a post office named Edna on July 31, 1868, with Daniel L. Shook as its first postmaster; its station on the Grand Rapids & Indiana Railroad was renamed Wood Lake, as was its post office on Nov. 19, 1869; it was beside that body of water which had been named for pioneer settlers Ransom E. and George Wood; the village was platted and recorded by Edward H. Jones for Henry M. Carpenter, proprietor, on March 21, 1870; its post office was closed on May 24, 1893, restored as Woodlake on May 17, 1898, and then closed permanently on Dec. 30, 1899; what remains of the village has since been renamed Hiram [Schenck; Dasef; PO Archives].

**HITCHCOCK**, Antrim County: this station on the Pere Marquette Railroad, 6 miles northeast of Bellaire, was given a post office on Nov. 13,

1900, named for Harvey R. Hitchcock, its first postmaster; the office operated until Oct. 15, 1910 [GSM 1903; PO Archives].

**HOBART**, Wexford County: it began as a lumber settlement in Clam Lake Township in 1871; given a station on the Grand Rapids & Indiana Railroad the same year; John Copper became its first postmaster on July 7, 1876, the office operating until Jan. 30, 1932 [Pen Phil 8:3 April 1958; PO Archives].

**HOBSON**, Alpena County: Mrs. Kate Turner became the first postmaster of this rural post office in Wilson Township on April 26, 1899, the office operating until Dec. 31, 1909 [GSM 1901; PO Archives].

**HOCKADAY**, Gladwin County: Mr. and Mrs. John Yeager, Sr., came here in 1881; like others who came soon after, they were from Sanilac County, and the settlement was first called New Sanilac; Mr. and Mrs. Robert Hockaday ran a grocery store here and in it a post office was opened on April 22, 1902, with Mr. Hockaday as the first postmaster, the office operating until Jan. 31, 1913; both the village and its post office were named for him [Ritchie; PO Archives].

**HODENPYL WOODS**, Kent County: named for Anton G. Hodenpyl who in 1912 gave these 40 acres near Reed's Lake to the people of his native Grand Rapids as a forest park [Mich Hist 15:264 1931].

**HODGE**, Grand Traverse County: the name of this lumber settlement in Fife Township was derived from that of a local lumberman, Giles Hodges; storekeeper Benjamin C. Mills became its first postmaster on June 25, 1891, the office operating until Jan. 30, 1904 [GSM 1893-1905; PO Archives].

**HODGEBURG**, Livingston County. See Tyrone.

**HODUNK**, Branch County: Abram Aldrich, a Quaker, from Wayne County, N.Y., became the first settler here in 1833; he built a mill known as Cocoosh Mill, named from its location on Cocoosh Prairie, an Indian word meaning pork or hog (in some sources spelled Cucush and Kookush); Alexander C. Carr became the first postmaster of Orangeville on Jan. 23, 1866, with the name changed to Hodunk on May 16, 1882, the office operating until Sept. 30, 1904 [Mich Hist 32:20 1948; PO Archives].

**HOFFMAN**, Oceana County: this post office in the farm home of Alva E. Hoffman was opened on Jan. 6, 1892, and was first named Alvaville; it was renamed Hoffman on March 11, 1892, and operated until Aug. 31, 1901 [PO Archives].

**HOFFMAN**, Presque Isle County: a flag station on the Alpena & Northern Railroad, 25 miles north of Alpena, in 1894 [GSM 1895].

**HOFFMAN**, Wayne County: a hamlet three miles west of Wayne, in Canton Township, in 1880 [GSM 1881].

**HOGSTROM**, Marquette County: a station on the M.M. & S.E. Railroad, in Skandia Township; Louis Hogstrom kept its general store and

Lydia Hogstrom became its first postmaster on Aug. 16, 1920, the office operating until May 28, 1937 [GSM 1921; PO Archives].

**HOLBROOK,** Sanilac County: John T. Barnes became the first postmaster of this rural post office on July 17, 1888, the office operating until Oct. 31, 1905 [PO Archives].

**HOLLAND,** Kalamazoo County: Russell Brown became the first postmaster of this rural post office on Gourd Neck Prairie on June 2, 1843; on Jan. 27, 1849, the office was moved to and renamed Brady, present-day Vicksburg [Durant; PO Archives].

**HOLLAND,** Ottawa County: Rev. Albertus C. Van Raalte, with his family and 53 others, sailed from Rotterdam in September, 1846, arrived in New York seven weeks later, made their way to Detroit, and thence to land they had bought from the government for their proposed settlement, which they began in February, 1847; platted and recorded in 1848, and named for their fatherland; given a post office as Black River (it was by that stream), on Feb. 9, 1848, with Henry D. Post as its first postmaster; the office was renamed Holland on May 11, 1851; incorporated as a city in 1867 [MPH 569 1895; PO Archives].

**HOLLISTER,** Livingston County: this rural post office was named for Anna Hollister who became its first postmaster on March 22, 1858, the office operating until Oct. 21, 1862 [PO Archives].

**HOLLISTER,** Oakland County: this rural post office in Waterford Township was named for Linda D. Hollister who became its first postmaster on June 20, 1899, the office operating until Nov. 15, 1900 [GSM 1901; PO Archives].

**HOLLOWAY,** Lenawee County: founded when the Wabash Railroad was put through here in Raisin Township in 1881; the townspeople called it Butler for Butler Holloway who sold the lots for the first homes; but there was already a Butler post office in Michigan and this one was given the name Holloway on July 19, 1881, with Homer E. Wilson as its first postmaster; the office operated until May 25, 1962 [Stanley Doty; PO Archives].

**HOLLOWAY'S CORNERS,** Lenawee County: Dr. William Holloway, the first physician to locate in Raisin Township, settled here with his four sons, Edwin, William, Silas and Butler, about 1833; a log schoolhouse was built here in 1835 [Bonner; Whitney].

**HOLLY,** Oakland County: Nathan Herrick made the first land entry here in 1830. Ira C. Alger built a sawmill in 1843 and a grist mill; he became the first station-agent of Algerville when the Detroit & Milwaukee Railroad came through in 1855; Peter Fagan secured a post office named Holly Mills, with Marcus L. Young becoming its first postmaster on July 3, 1851; first platted by James G. Mitchell in 1855; renamed Holly on Dec. 7, 1861, doubtless from the beautiful holly which grew and still grows in the area as well as from the fact that 1835 settler Jonathan T. Allen came from Mount Holly, N.J.; incorporated as a village in 1865 [Durant; Cole; Seeley].

**HOLLYWOOD**, Berrien County: this cross-roads in Royalton Township, then 8 miles from St. Joseph, was given a post office on Nov. 20, 1888, with Thaddeus J. Sherman as its first postmaster, the office operating until July 31, 1902 [GSM 1891-1903; PO Archives].

**HOLMDALE**, Newaygo County: the name of this rural post office, opened on April 24, 1901, was derived from that of its first postmaster, Jennie Holman; the office operated until June 14, 1902 [GSM 1903; PO Archives].

**HOLMES**, Menominee County: this settlement around the iron mine of the Iron Cliffs Company was given a post office on March 14, 1884, with Nels G. Nickelson as its first postmaster, the office operating until June 19, 1886 [Hatcher; PO Archives].

**HOLMESVILLE**, Gogebic County: a lumbering town, named after the mill owner; Jerry Holland became its first postmaster on Oct. 26, 1888; the office was not officially closed until March 31, 1890, but it is believed that it never actually operated [Lemmer; Priestly].

**HOLSTEIN**, Oceana County: a rural post office in Claybanks Township, opened on Jan. 5, 1887, with Joseph Baker as its first postmaster, succeeded by grocer Frank L. Baker in 1888; the office operated until Aug. 31, 1901 [GSM 1889-1903; PO Archives].

**HOLT**, Ingham County: while several land purchases were made here in 1836, the first actual settlement was made by Frederick R. Luther and John Norris in 1837; first known as Delhi, Delhi Center, or Delhi Station (it is in Delhi Township), even for a while after it was renamed by the post office after John Holt, postmaster general, on Feb. 10, 1860; now the Delhis, North Holt, and Five Corners are considered extinct and are all known as Holt [Durant; Foster; PO Archives].

**HOLTON**, Muskegon County: platted by Blodgett & Byrne in 1871 and named for Henry H. Holt, Muskegon County delegate to the State Convention of 1867 (and later lieutenant governor of Michigan, 1873-76); he donated the (still used) bell to the local Methodist Church; given a post office on Feb. 21, 1872, with Merrit White as its first postmaster [Dorathea S. Parmenter, PM].

**HOLY ISLAND**, Charlevoix County: an eleven acre island in the south arm of Pine Lake (now Lake Charlevoix), which Mormon king James J. Strang set apart in 1855 as a place for holding the Feast of First Fruits; some years after his death in 1856, it began to be converted into a popular summer resort [Powers].

**HOME**, Keweenaw County: a 240-acre, non-producing copper mine location, organized in 1863 [Stevens].

**HOME**, Montcalm County: the first settler in the area was Edward

Wolbert about 1860; Home Township was erected in 1864; given a post office as New Home on Feb. 26, 1868, with Thomas Forquer as its first postmaster, the office operating until Sept. 16, 1872 [Schenck; Dasef; PO Archives].

**HOME**, Newaygo County: Edwin Pettibone became the first postmaster of this rural post office on Oct. 7, 1867; on April 20, 1874, the office was transferred to and renamed Woodville; but the Home post office was re-established on Feb. 18, 1875, and operated until Nov. 13, 1882 [PO Archives].

**HOMER**, Calhoun County: founded by Milton Barney who built a sawmill and a grist mill here in 1832, a store in 1834, and an inn in 1835; the township, when organized in 1834, was named after Homer, Cortland County, N.Y., at the request of James Hopkins and other early settlers who had come from that area; its village, first called Barneyville, was given a post office as Homer on May 7, 1834, with Mr. Barney as its first postmaster; incorporated as a village in 1871 [GSM 1873; Everts; PO Archives].

**HOMER LAKE**, Oceana County: a small lumbermill settlement by 1873 [Royal].

**HOMESTEAD**, Benzie County: first settled in 1862 by E. E. Kirkland and given a post office on June 8, 1864, with David B. Spencer as its first postmaster; Timothy M. Walker came in 1866 and opened the first hotel; this village on the Platte River was named after its township; it was also known as Centerville, from its location in the county, and as Grant House; its post office operated until Sept. 30, 1903 [Traverse; PO Archives].

**HOMESTEAD**, Chippewa County: Captain Samuel Ward had a wood dock here on Sugar Island in the 1850s; named by Charles Schulz who became the first keeper of the lighthouse and supply depot here about 1894; Mrs. Gesina Schulz became its first postmaster on May 23, 1906, the office operating until Jan. 31, 1946 [Hamilton; PO Archives].

**HANEOYE**, Macomb County. See Armada.

**HONKY TOWN**, Lenawee County: this settlement, two miles from Blissfield, was named from its first having been occupied by a colony of Hungarians; in 1940, it became a colony of Mexican migrant workers from Texas [Mich Hist 42:343 1958].

**HONOR**, Benzie County: this village on the Platte River, in Homestead Township, was founded in 1895 by the building of the Guelph Patent Cask Company and was named for the baby daughter of its general manager, J. A. Gifford; a station on a branch of the Chicago & Western Michigan (now Pere Marquette) Railroad; lawyer Leslie C. Hart became its first postmaster on July 16, 1895; incorporated as a village in 1914 [Powers; GSM 1897; PO Archives].

**HOOKER**, Van Buren County: a post office in Geneva Township, opened on Jan. 5, 1864, and operating until April 4, 1873; named for Civil War general Joseph "Fighting Joe" Hooker [GSM 1879; PO Archives].

**HOOPER**, Allegan County: this village in Martin Township was founded by William H. Hooper in 1890; a station on the C., J. & M. Railroad in 1894; the Gun Marsh post office was transferred to and renamed Hooper on Jan. 21, 1899, and operated here until Oct. 31, 1913 [Esther W. Hettinger; GSM 1895; PO Archives].

**HOPE**, Keweenaw County: a copper mining location; the Hope Mine was organized in 1864 [Stevens].

**HOPE**, Midland County: the first settlers, Orrin Maltby and Joseph Rooker, located here in 1856; the first township meeting was held in 1871; its village was given a post office on May 19, 1871, with Marshall Carr as its first postmaster; named by its citizens [Chapman; John S. Elmore].

**HOPE CENTER**, Barry County. See Cloverdale.

**HOPKINS**, Allegan County: when the railroad came through here, three miles west of Hopkinsburg, in 1874, its depot was named Hopkins Station; John Hoffmaster, who had settled here in 1854, became the stationmaster, and he also platted the village; given a post office as Hopkins, with Erastus Congdon as its first postmaster, on May 20, 1854, the office operating until May 31, 1904; but on June 6, 1906, the Hopkins Station post office, which had been opened on March 28, 1870, with Henry F. Guyot as its first postmaster, was changed to Hopkins; Claude B. Hoffmaster became its postmaster on Jan. 31, 1929; incorporated as a village in 1920 [Thomas; PO Archives].

**HOPKINSBURG**, Allegan County: first settled by R. C. Round in 1837, and his brother-in-law, Erastus Congdon, in 1838; Mr. Round was the great grandson of Martha Hopkins Round, who was a sister of Stephen Hopkins, a signer of the Declaration of Independence, and thus the ensuing village came to be named Hopkinsburg [Thomas].

**HOPKINS MILL**, Ottawa County. See Spring Lake.

**HOPKINS' ROAD**, St. Clair County: a station on a branch of the Port Huron & Northwestern Railroad in 1888 [GSM 1889].

**HOPKINS STATION**, Allegan County. See Hopkins.

**HOPKINSVILLE**, Grand Traverse County: this rural post office, opened on Sept. 11, 1867, was named for Peleg C. Hopkins who became its first postmaster, the office operating until Oct. 5, 1868 [PO Archives].

**HOPPERTOWN**, Allegan County. See Pullman.

**HORICON**, Grand Traverse County. See Karlin.

**HORJU**, Houghton County: a station on the Mineral Range Railroad, in Osceola Township; mining agent Joseph Hocking became its first postmaster on April 9, 1919, the office operating until Jan. 15, 1921 [GSM 1921; PO Archives].

**HORR**, Arenac County. See Pine River.

**HORR**, Isabella County: named for Roswell G. Horr, congressman from this district, 1879-1880; farmer William F. Sherman became its first postmaster on April 8, 1884; the grist mill and the sawmill of Henry Woodin were located here in Sherman Township and the post office was renamed Woodin's Mills on Dec. 15, 1886; but it was changed back to Horr on March 15, 1890, until it was closed on Nov. 15, 1904 [GSM 1887; PO Archives].

**HORSE SHOE**, Allegan County: William P. Hall became the first postmaster of this rural post office in Lee Township on May 26, 1890, succeeded by farmer George Hildebrand, the office operating until Sept. 14, 1903 [GSM 1891-1905; PO Archives].

**HORTON**, Jackson County: Abiel Tripp, from Vermont, became the first settler here in Hanover Township in 1832; in 1842, George A. Baldwin built a flour mill and deeded the land to the public for a village which was named Baldwin for him; the village was platted in 1844; it was given a post office as Baldwin's Mills on Aug. 21, 1854, with James C. Bell as its first postmaster, the name being shortened to Baldwin's on Dec. 28, 1871; but since there was already a Baldwin post office in Michigan, Mrs. Horace Gifford, whose mother's maiden name was Horton, proposed that name; it was accepted and the post office was renamed Horton on Feb. 19, 1874 [Mrs. Velma Strait, ret. PM; DeLand].

**HORTON BAY**, Charlevoix County: this village on the north central shore of Pine Lake (now Lake Charlevoix) was given a post office as Horton's Bay on Feb. 27, 1879, with Alonzo J. Stroud as its first postmaster; the name was shortened to Horton Bay on Oct. 12, 1894, but the office was closed on Jan. 15, 1910 [GSM 1881; PO Archives].

**HORTON'S CORNERS**, Ingham County: this settlement in Vevay Township was named for landowner William H. Horton; its tavern, operated by a family named Briggs, burned down about 1865 [Adams].

**HOSNER**, Macomb County: this rural post office, 7 miles from Romeo, was named for James M. Hosner who became its first postmaster on Feb. 3, 1899, the office operating until Dec. 31, 1900 [GSM 1901; PO Archives].

**HOUGHTON**, Houghton County: Ransom Sheldon bought land here around Portage Lake, and in 1852, opened a store on the south side; William W. Henderson became the first postmaster on May 22, 1852; first platted by Ernest F. Pletschke in 1854; incorporated as a village in 1867; named after the county which had been named for pioneer state geologist Douglass Houghton [Sawyer; PO Archives].

**HOUGHTON**, Marquette County: Douglas D Meniclier became the first postmaster of this rural post office on March 24, 1846; the office was changed to Keweenaw Bay, Houghton County, on Nov. 2, 1846 [PO Archives].

**HOUGHTON LAKE**, Roscommon County: in his survey of 1849, William A. Burt called it Muskegon Lake, and in his of 1908, John Brink called it Red Lake; but since about 1852, it has carried the name of pioneer state geologist Douglass Houghton; the settlement here began as the center of the lumber operations of S. C. Hall in 1873; Henry H. Woodruff became its first postmaster on Nov. 8, 1875; since the decline of lumbering operations, it has become a resort community [MPH 39:127 1915; Mich Hist 16:364 1932; PO Archives].

**HOUGHTON LAKE HEIGHTS**, Roscommon County: the S. C. Hall Lumber Company began operations here about 1883; because of its elevation, the place was called The Heights and was given a post office of that name on Nov. 24, 1923, with William H. Parks as its first postmaster; the office was renamed Houghton Lake Heights in 1956; Douglass Houghton was a pioneer state geologist [Pauline Wood, PM].

**HOUGHTON POINT**, Roscommon County: founded about 1945 by Jack H. Howe and he became its first postmaster on Nov. 1, 1949; named from its location on northern Houghton Lake, which had been named for pioneer state geologist Douglass Houghton [Co. Bd. of Ed.; PO Archives].

**HOUSEMAN**, Oceana County: storekeeper Mary A. McLouth became the first postmaster of this rural post office in Elbridge township on April 12, 1886, the office operating until Aug. 31, 1909 [GSM 1887-1911; PO Archives].

**HOUSE OF DAVID**, Berrien County: a religious colony with an Old Testament name, founded in 1903 by Benjamin and Mary Purnell; in Benton Township, on the outskirts of Benton Harbor; members hold their property in common, consisting of nearly 1000 acres of fruit and grain farms, amusement park, trade shops, etc.; with King Ben's death in 1927, the colony was split, Judge Dewhirst ruling the original foundation, while Ben's widow set up the rival Israel, its City of David adjacent to it [Federal].

**HOWARD**, Cass County. See Howardville.

**HOWARD**, Muskegon County: a sawmill community on the north shore of Muskegon Lake, opposite the city of Muskegon; Thomas E. Rand became its first postmaster on Dec. 4, 1866; the office was closed on Jan. 31, 1868, but was restored from Dec. 16, 1868, to Feb. 17, 1873 [GSM 1873; PO Archives].

**HOWARD CITY**, Montcalm County: Benjamin Ensley owned the land on which he, E. W. Muenscher and Mr. Shaw began the village which Mr. Muenscher platted in 1868; the Detroit, Grand Rapids & Western Railroad depot opened here in 1869; John B. Spencer became the first postmaster on Jan. 12, 1870; named for William A. Howard, Detroit railroad attorney; incorporated as a village in 1873; its post office name was shortened to Howard on Feb. 2, 1895, but was changed back to Howard City on Jan. 19, 1899 [Cole; PO Archives; James B. Haskins].

**HOWARDSVILLE**, St. Joseph County: Robert Gill built the first house here in 1833; he sold out to the Morse brothers who ran a sawmill on the property until 1836 when Franklin Howard bought it and ran it until his death in 1845; the village was first called Tinker Town or Tinkerville, after Chauncey Tinker, a pioneer settler, but when he became its first postmaster on Sept. 22, 1858, it was named for Mr. Howard; its post office was closed on Jan. 29, 1873, but was restored from Feb. 24, 1874, to May 31, 1904 [Everts; Mich Hist 5:315 1921; PO Archives].

**HOWARDVILLE**, Cass County: platted and recorded in 1835 by George Fosdick; named after its township which, when organized in 1834, is said to have been named by the territorial representative for Cass County, C. K. Green, for a Miss Howard, of Detroit; located on the north bank of Lake Alone, so named from its remoteness from any other body of water, and its absence of surface outlets; the lake was renamed Barron Lake when the Michigan Central Railroad came through here and named its station Barron Lake [Fox; Glover].

**HOWELL**, Livingston County: the first settlements within the present city were made by George T. and James Sage, John D. Pinckney and David Austin, in 1834; the settlement was first known as Livingston Centre, from its location in the county; platted in 1835 by Flavius J. B. Crane and Edward Brooks, who named it for Thomas Howell, a friend of Mr. Crane, and a son of Judge Howell, of Canandaigua, N.Y.; Mr. Crane became the first postmaster on Jan. 15, 1836; incorporated as a village in 1863 and as a city in 1914 [Ellis; MPH 38:176 1912].

**HOWELL JUNCTION**, Livingston County. See Annpere.

**HOWE'S CORNERS**, Ingham County. See Aurelius.

**HOWLANDSBURG**, Kalamazoo County: this village in Ross Township was founded by Edward K. Howland in 1834 [Durant].

**HOWLETT**, Wayne County: a station on the Detroit & Northwestern Electric Railway, in Greenfield Township, then 5 miles from Detroit; named for storekeeper James Howlett who became its first postmaster on July 26, 1899 [GSM 1901; PO Archives].

**HOWRY'S**, Gladwin County: a station on a branch of the Michigan Central Railroad, 3 miles southeast of Gladwin, in 1888 [GSM 1895].

**HOXEYVILLE**, Wexford County: this village in Henderson Township began as a lumbering center; given a post office as Clay Hill on July 20, 1870, with Thomas S. Henderson as its first postmaster; on April 25, 1891, the name was changed to that of the first settler, Jobe Hoxie [Catherine Herby, PM].

**HOXIE**, Hillsdale County: this hamlet near North Adams was given a post office on Jan. 8, 1896, with Charles M. Chapman as its first postmaster, the office operating until Oct. 31, 1901 [GSM 1919; PO Archives].

**HOXIE SETTLEMENT**, Macomb County. See Romeo.

**HOYTVILLE,** Eaton County: named for Dr. Henry A. Hoyt, of New Haven, Conn., who opened a store here in 1869; M. D. Halladay moved his sawmill here in 1872; given a post office as Centre on June 10, 1856, with Gardner S. Allen as its first postmaster; the office was later moved a mile south to the Centre (named from its location in Roxand Township), but in 1876, it was returned to Hoytville and renamed Hoytville on March 3, 1880, with Dr. Hoyt as postmaster; the office was closed on June 15, 1905; it was also known as Hoyt's Corners [Durant; PO Archives].

**HUBBARD,** Midland County: Isaac M. Barr became the first postmaster of this rural post office in Larkin Township on Nov. 21, 1892, succeeded by H. G. Spring in 1894, the office operating until Aug. 21, 1895 [GSM 1893; Blinn].

**HUBBARD LAKE,** Alpena County: the lake, which is entirely within Alcona County, was named for Bela Hubbard, a pioneer state surveyor; the village is a mile and a half north of the lake; an early settler here, John Ellsworth, began farming in 1878, and as the village formed, he became its first postmaster on June 21, 1883 [Lora Shunk; PO Archives].

**HUBBARDSTON,** Ionia county: in 1836, James R. Langdon, of Montpelier, Vermont, bought 2000 acres which included most of the present town; from him in 1852, Joseph Brown, of Kalamazoo, bought 240 acres, which included the Fish Creek water power, and built a dam and a sawmill; in 1853, he was bought out by Thomas Hubbard, Wilson Homer, Noah Hitchcock and Newton W. Taylor, and in 1865, they platted the village; given a post office as Plains on Sept. 13, 1858, with Linus Van Alstine as its first postmaster, it was renamed for Thomas Hubbard on Dec. 27, 1859; incorporated as a village in 1867 [Harvey G. Allen, PM].

**HUBBARDVILLE,** Barry County. See Irving.

**HUBBELL,** Houghton County: the settlement around the Hubbell sawmill was given a station on the Chicago, Milwaukee & St. Paul Railroad, named Hubbell's Mill, about 1894; on Nov. 19, 1903, the South Lake Linden post office was changed to Hubbell [Sawyer; PO Archives; GSM 1891; Hubbell by Donald Chaput].

**HUBBELL,** Mackinac County: Simon Dumond was appointed the first postmaster of this rural post office on June 30, 1892, but the office was never in operation and was discontinued on June 18, 1895 [PO Archives].

**HUBBELL JUNCTION,** Mackinac County: a station on the Minneapolis, St. Paul & Sault Ste. Marie Railroad in 1894 [GSM 1895].

**HUBER,** Newaygo County: John H. Koopman operated a county store here in Denver Township; when he became the postmaster on March 23, 1901, he named the office for Huber Hilton, son of state representative George Hilton, of Fremont, who helped him get the post office; it operated until Feb. 28, 1907 [Harry L. Spooner; PO Archives].

**HUBINGER,** Saginaw County: a hamlet by 1878 [GSM 1879].

**HUDSON,** Lenawee County: with his wife and family, Hiram Kidder, from Yates County, N.Y., became the first settler here in 1833; it was called Bean Creek from its location by a stream which had been so named from the quality of bean timber that grew on its banks; with the appointment of principal landowner Beriah H. Lane as postmaster on April 19, 1836, the settlement was renamed Lanesville; in 1840, by common consent, it took the name of its township which Mr. Kidder had named for Dr. Daniel Hudson, from Geneva, N.Y., one of the first landowners in the town; its post office was renamed Hudson on April 27, 1840; a station on the Lake Shore & Michigan Southern Railroad; incorporated as a village in 1853 and as a city in 1893 [Bonner; Whitney].

**HUDSON,** Washtenaw County: it began as a mill settlement on the Huron River, in Dexter Township, given a post office as Base Lake on Aug. 30, 1849, with Moses Y. Hood as its first postmaster, the office being changed to Birkett on March 29, 1882; its station on the Michigan Central Railroad was called Hudson's Mills [Beakes; GSM 1885].

**HUDSONVILLE,** Ottawa County: Homer E. Hudson became the first postmaster of South Georgetown, named from its location in Georgetown Township, on April 30, 1868; the office was renamed Hudsonville for him on Jan. 22, 1872, with him holding the post until 1881; given a station on the Chicago & Western Michigan (now Pere Marquette) Railroad in 1874, with storekeeper Horace A. Hudson as the first station agent; incorporated as a village in 1826 and as a city in 1857 [Henry Van Noord; Page; PO Archives].

**HUFF,** Marquette County: this farmhouse post office in Skandia Township was named for James W. Huff who became its first postmaster on July 21, 1894, the office operating until May 23, 1895 [GSM 1895; PO Archives].

**HUGHART,** Emmet County: Caleb N. Teeters became the first postmaster of this rural post office on Jan. 24, 1881, the office operating until Jan. 16, 1882 [PO Archives].

**HUGHESVILLE,** Saginaw County. See County Line.

**HULBERT,** Chippewa County: while cruising for timber for himself, Francis R. Hulbert discovered this high area in 1872; he died in 1896, before he could develop the village; this was done by his son, Richard C. Hulbert; the families of Andrew J. DeWitt and Lee DeWitt became the first permanent settlers; Elmer M. Holley became the first postmaster on Jan. 23, 1892, succeeded by Andrew J. DeWitt on Dec. 1, 1906, the office operating until only March 31, 1908; it was becoming a ghost town when saved by a wooden ware plant built by James Shepherd Parrish in 1919; given a post office as Taquaminon on March 28, 1919, with Eda B. Dillingham as its first postmaster, with the office renamed Hulbert on July 30, 1920; J. E. Campbell was the first railroad agent of its station on the Duluth, South Shore & Atlantic Railroad [Irene M. Reed, PM; Mich Hist 31:174 1947; PO Archives].

**HUMBOLDT**, Marquette County: this village on the Escanaba River, in Ely Township, was named from its proximity to the Humboldt Range; it was first settled in 1865 with the opening of the Edwards Mine, located on land owned by J. H. Edwards; a station on the Duluth, South Shore & Atlantic Railroad; Joel Francis Allen became the first postmaster on May 11, 1870, the office operating until Jan. 15, 1936 [Andreas; PO Archives].

**HUMBUG ISLAND**, Wayne County: just south of Slocum's Island and like it owned by Giles Bryan Slocum, but unlike it, not an island, and hence its name [Farmer].

**HUME**, Calhoun County: this rural post office in Bedford Township was named for stock buyer Lafayette Hume who became its first postmaster on Feb. 11, 1899, the office operating until Dec. 30, 1905 [GSM 1901-07; PO Archives].

**HUME**, Huron County: John A. Stockman made the first land purchase here, but Walter Hume, a Canadian, became the first settler in 1844; the township was named for him when organized at a meeting in his store in 1860 and he was elected its first treasurer [Chapman; Gwinn; MPH 39:355 1915].

**HUMPHREY**, Manistee County: a station on the Arcadia & Betsey River Railroad, in Springdale Township; named for farmer Ellis Humphrey who became its first postmaster on July 20, 1897, the office operating until Sept. 30, 1909 [GSM 1899; PO Archives].

**HUNGERFORD**, Newaygo County: it began as a lumber settlement in Norwich Township in 1872; a station on the Chicago & Northwestern Railroad; George French became its first postmaster on March 3, 1876, the office operating until May 14, 1906; named from its location near Hungerford Lake [GSM 1877; PO Archives].

**HUNT**, Ogemaw County. See South Branch.

**HUNTER**, Van Buren County: in 1847, Marvin Hannah (who later spelled it Hannahs) built a sawmill and a boarding house here in Geneva Township; he added a tannery the next year and later a school; he never lived here, Eri Bennett, later supervisor of the town, represented him; Mr. Hannah named the settlement Hunter but his employees named it Jericho, by which name the locality is still known, though nothing remains of its business activities; it was given a post office as Hunter on May 7, 1852, with the office being changed to Hooker on Jan. 5, 1864; Mr. Bennett was its first postmaster [Rowland; PO Archives].

**HUNTERS**, Oakland County. See Birmingham.

**HUNTER'S CREEK**, Lapeer County: this settlement, named from the stream beside it, dates from about 1836; Harris M. Tripp became its first postmaster on Oct. 30, 1857; the Detroit & Bay City Railroad came through in 1872, making it a station; John Clark built a sawmill and a shingle mill here in 1873 [Page; PO Archives].

**HUNTER'S MILL,** Luce County: this site between Soo Junction and Newberry was the location of a lumber camp, since abandoned [Federal].

**HUNTINGTON WOODS,** Oakland County: J. Lockwood, a War of 1812 veteran, received the first land grant here, signed by President James Monroe, in 1824; the area comprised some nine farms until 1916 when Fred Remole, owner, platted and recorded a part of the site as Banks Park; other parts were the subdivisions of Huntington Woods, Manor, Bronx, and Huntington Park, and the unplatted fifty acre tract called Hannan's West; they were a part of Royal Oak Township until incorporated as the village of Huntington Woods in 1926; incorporated as a city in 1932; the fact that much of the area was wooded and used for small game hunting seems to have suggested the name [H. W. Study Club].

**HUNTON MILL,** Genesee County: the mill built by Francis Otis in 1853, at what is now Otisville, was bought by Weeks, Hunton & Company in 1866; in 1867, A. K. Hunton moved it a mile and a quarter north to be on Butternut Creek; a sizeable settlement with a schoolhouse grew up east of the mill, and it was called Hunton Hill; its post office was Otisville [Paul L. Laing].

**HUNTS SPUR,** Mackinac County: a station on the Minneapolis, St. Paul & Sault Ste. Marie Railroad, at the Michigan Cedar Company mill; Henry O. Rindy became its first postmaster on Oct. 9, 1889, succeeded by railroad agent C. E. Riddle in 1890; its post office, which for a period was spelled Huntspur, operated until Oct. 30, 1937 [GSM 1891; PO Archives].

**HURD'S CORNERS,** Tuscola County. See East Dayton.

**HURD'S MILL,** Sanilac County: this sawmill settlement at Lake Huron, on Cherry Creek, dates from 1836; when Oliver Hazard Perry visited it in 1850, Mr. Buel was in charge of the mill [Schultz].

**HURON,** Huron County. See Bad Axe.

**HURON,** Wayne County: a rural post office, near the Huron River, in Romulus Township, opened on May 11, 1833, with John F. Smith as its first postmaster; the office was transferred to and renamed Romulus on Jan. 15, 1836, but the Huron post office was re-established on the same day, and it operated until Oct. 11, 1859 [GSM 1860; PO Archives].

**HURON BAY,** Baraga County: this rural post office, near Huron Bay, was opened on July 29, 1892, with Azade V. Bourret as its first postmaster, the office operating until Jan. 18, 1894 [GSM 1895; PO Archives].

**HURON CITY,** Huron County: Theodore Luce built a water-powered sawmill here on Willow Creek in 1837; he sold out to Mr. Brakeman who came here from Port Huron in 1852, and the place became known as Brakeman's Creek; Langdon Hubbard bought the property in 1856 and through his lumbering operations for forty years developed the village (his daughter Annabel wed Yale English literature lecturer William Lyon Phelps, and they made Huron City their summer home); given a post office as

Willow Creek on Feb. 14, 1856, with Joshua S. Sadler as its first postmaster; the office was closed on Nov. 12, 1856, but was restored on Jan. 27, 1857; it was renamed Huron City on Nov. 14, 1861, shortened to Huron on Feb. 21, 1883, and closed on Aug. 14, 1905; but the village of Huron City remains [MPH 39:353 1915; Hey; PO Archives].

**HURONIA BEACH,** St. Clair County: a private resort on the west shore of Lake Huron, founded in 1882 by Marcus Young, and he became its first postmaster on Dec. 27, 1886, the office operating until June 14, 1901 [GSM 1887; PO Archives].

**HURON LIGHT HOUSE,** St. Clair County: George McDougall became the first postmaster of this post office opened in January, 1826, on the west side of the St. Clair River as it enters Lake Huron; the office was changed to Fort Gratiot in December, 1826 [Cole].

**HURON MOUNTAIN,** Marquette County: founded as a club on the Pine River, in Powell Township, by J. M. Longyear, and others, about 1896; Herbert E. Perkins became its first postmaster on Sept. 16, 1914, the office operating until May 31, 1957; named from its location at the northern edge of the Huron Mountains [Ernest Rankin; PO Archives].

**HURON POINT,** Macomb County. See Belvidere.

**HURON STATION,** Wayne County. See Rockwood.

**HURONTOWN,** Houghton County: this settlement in Portage Township began with the Huron Copper Company opening in 1855; it was reorganized as the Houghton Mining Company in 1871 and as the Huron Mining Company in 1880; it was finally made productive when Johnson Vivian became its local manager [Andreas].

**HURST,** Presque Isle County: a station on the Alpena & Northern (now Detroit & Mackinaw) Railroad, 34 miles north of Alpena, in 1894 [GSM 1895].

**HUSTED SETTLEMENT,** Oakland County. See Anderson Settlement.

**HUYCKSTOWN,** Cass County: platted about a store in 1836 and named for John Huyck; it was first called Volinia (after its township) and, about 1859, Little Prairie Ronde (after the prairie on whose edge it stood); Richard J. Huyck became the first postmaster of its post office, named Little Prairie Ronde, on Nov. 1, 1837, but the office and what was left of the village were later moved to Nicholsville, a half mile south [Fox; PO Archives].

**HYDE,** Delta County: Alexander Morin became the first postmaster of this hamlet, seven miles west of Escanaba, on Dec. 13, 1890, but the office was closed in 1913 [Blinn; PO Archives].

**HYDE'S MILLS,** Eaton County. See Carlisle.

**HYLAS,** Menominee County: a station on a branch of the Chicago &

Northwestern Railroad, four miles east of Hardwood, in 1884; see Dryads for the name [GSM 1885].

**ICEBURG,** U.S.A., Bay County: the name given a transient fishing community of some 350 on an average which each year from December to March is located on Saginaw Bay from 3 to 30 miles north of Bay City [Gansser].

**IDA,** Monroe County: Ida Township was organized in 1837 and named for Ida M. Taylor, a civic leader; William L. Riggs became the first postmaster of its village on July 11, 1844; the office was closed on July 29, 1852, but was restored from June 11, 1853, to date; the village was platted in 1868 [PM; GSM 1860; PO Archives].

**IDLEWILD,** Genesee County: Philip H. McOmber built a resort hotel here on Long (now Fenton) Lake in 1834, and for some fifty years the place was an excursion point; the area is now occupied by year around and summer homes [Mrs. Georgia McKinley].

**IDLEWILD,** Lake County: named after one of its five nearby lakes; the village dates its founding as 1912, when it had two year-round residents; in 1915, the real estate firm of Branch, Anderson & Tyrrell purchased and platted the site, and sold its lots to Negroes; a station on a branch of the Pere Marquette Railroad; Abraham L. Jones was appointed its first postmaster on Aug. 18, 1923, but he declined and Susie J. Bantom took the office on Sept. 26, 1923 [Judkins; Mrs. Julia Thomas, PM; PO Archives].

**IDLEWILD,** Montmorency County: a special supply post office in Albert Township, with Michael M. McCormack becoming its first postmaster on June 12, 1884, the office operating until Aug. 18, 1887 [PO Archives].

**ILE de MICHILIMACKINAC,** Mackinac County: Jesuit missionary Claude Dablon found that his Indian charges were drifting to the Straits area and he followed them there, conducting a mission in the winter of 1670-71, at a site he called the Ile de Michilimackinac; presumably this meant Mackinac Island (which see), but since the term Michilimackinac was commonly used by the French to describe the entire Straits area, it is uncertain whether Dablon was referring to the island or to the mainland [Paré; Dunbar].

**IMLAY,** Lapeer County: this settlement in northwestern Imlay Township was named for William H. Imlay, pioneer pine forest owner in the area; John N. Deneen became its first postmaster on May 14, 1857; the office was closed on Dec. 14, 1868, but on April 10, 1869, the Black's Corners post office was changed to Imlay, operating until Nov. 10, 1897 [Page; PO Archives].

**IMLAY CITY,** Lapeer County: William H. Imlay, a Connecticut capitalist, began buying pine forests in the area in 1836, and when the township was organized in 1850, it was named Imlay for him; when the

Port Huron & Lake Michigan Railroad first came through here on July 28, 1870, it was nothing but forest, but Charles Palmer, chief engineer for the road, saw the need for a market place here, purchased the land that year and built a hotel; Edward E. Palmer became the first postmaster on Dec. 12, 1870; by August, 1872, it had 15 stores, a grain elevator, a sawmill, a grist mill and a shingle mill; incorporated as a village in 1873 [Clifford Dorow; Page; PO Archives].

**IMPERIAL MILLS,** Kent County. See Austerlitz.

**INA,** Osceola County: storekeeper Adelbert Kanouse became the first postmaster of this rural post office in Highland Township on March 8, 1899, the office operating until Dec. 14, 1907 [GSM 1901; PO Archives].

**INDEPENDENCE,** Oakland County: in 1819, A. Phillips made the first land claim here, but relinquished it; Alpheus Williams made the next claim in 1823; John Beardslee, whose entry was of 1826, became the first actual settler in 1831; the township was organized in 1837 and named at the suggestion of Joseph Van Syckle who had come here from Independence, N.J., in 1833; Thomas Johnson became its first postmaster on May 27, 1837, but the office was transferred to and renamed Clarkston on Dec. 12, 1840 [MPH 7:560 1886; Seeley; PO Archives].

**INDEX,** Lapeer County: a station on the Port Huron & Northwestern Railroad; Robert Hillis became its first postmaster on Sept. 2, 1881, succeeded by storekeeper Frederick A. Jones in 1884; the office was closed on Oct. 14, 1895, but was restored from Nov. 13, 1895, to Feb. 26, 1896 [GSM 1885; PO Archives].

**INDIAN CREEK,** Kent County. See Walker.

**INDIAN FIELDS,** Kalamazoo County: originally the site of a large Pottawattomi village; here during the War of 1812, while the warriors were fighting with the British, against the Americans, their families were concentrated, and captured U.S. soldiers were held captive; the Grand Rapids & Indiana Railroad station, five miles south of Kalamazoo, was named Indian Fields in 1867 [Mich Hist 15:249].

**INDIAN FIELDS,** Tuscola County: on the south bank of the Cass River, across from present-day Caro, was an Indian village, and in that vicinity they raised corn and potatoes; this ground came to be known as the Indian Fields, and when the township was erected in 1852, it was given that name; Charles Stuck and Daniel Dopking had become its first white settlers in 1851 and their settlement was visited by Oliver Hazard Perry in 1852 [Mich Hist 33:170 1949; Page].

**INDIAN LAKE,** Cass County. See Silver Creek.

**INDIAN LAKE,** Kalamazoo County: a railroad station in 1878 [GSM 1879].

**INDIAN LAKE,** Oscoda County: when John Moody became the first postmaster of this rural post office on Sept. 11, 1879, it was in Alcona

County; the office was transferred to Oscoda County on April 18, 1881, until it was closed on Dec. 24, 1898 [PO Archives].

**INDIAN RESERVE,** Alpena County: originally reserved for the Indians in the region (now Wilson Township), it is now a farming district, comprising mostly French settlers [Fred R. Trelfa].

**INDIAN RIVER,** Cheboygan County: this part of Tuscarora Township was first settled in 1876 by David Smith, Jackson Corey, S. P. Hayes, M. A. McHenry and John B. Clark; the village was founded by Floyd E. Martin who bought his land here in 1878, had it surveyed by Oliver S. Hayden in 1879 (the plat was recorded in 1880), and named it after the river which runs through it; Mr. Heyden became the first postmaster on Sept. 22, 1879 [Helen B. Martin, ret. PM; Page].

**INDIAN TOWN,** Antrim County. See Kewadin.

**INDIANTOWN,** Calhoun County: about 1850, a committee of Athens townspeople collected $3,000 that the Government owed a group of Pottawattomi who had refused to go westward with their tribe; with it they established a settlement, buying land and building log cabins, a barn and a schoolhouse; now only 60 Indians remain here [Federal; Dunbar].

**INDIANTOWN,** Mason County. See East Riverton.

**INDIAN TOWN,** Menominee County: named for Mrs. Simons, an Indian woman who served the area as a midwife and also prescribed herb remedies for the sick; it was an important junction for the Chicago & Northwestern Railroad which came through here in 1882 and served the lumber and shingle mills in the area [Evelyn Bergen].

**INDIAN VILLAGE,** Gogebic County: a Chippewa village (never a reservation) at Lac Vieux Desert (Lake of the Sand Plains); the French Jesuit missionary, René Ménard, was here in 1661; the original deeds given to these Indians by Presidents Lincoln and Grant are in the Archives of the Michigan Historical Collection at the University of Michigan; its Chippewa name was Katikitegon [Mich Hist 32:120 1948; Victor Lemmer].

**INDIAN VILLAGE,** Macomb County. See Romeo.

**INEZ,** Kent County: Fred W. Harrison became the first postmaster of this rural post office on July 13, 1889, the office operating until July 9, 1890 [PO Archives].

**INGALLS,** Menominee County: homesteader Thomas Caldwell made the first clearing here in 1858; named for Judge Eleazer S. Ingalls who led in organizing the county in 1863; given a station on the Chicago & Northwestern Railroad in 1872; Louis Dobeas became its first postmaster on June 20, 1879, the office operating until Aug. 31, 1951 [Sawyer; PO Archives].

**INGALLSTON,** Menominee County: the township, and later the town, was named for Eleazer S. and Charles B. Ingalls, brothers, who built a sawmill here in 1866 (they had led in organizing the township in 1863);

Frank Grabowski became the first postmaster on Oct. 14, 1899, the office operating until Aug. 31, 1951 [Sawyer; PO Archives].

**INGERSOLL**, Clinton County: this village in Watertown Township was first settled in 1870 and was given a post office on Oct. 13, 1873, with Barthold Wagner as its first postmaster, the office operating until July 15, 1901; its depot on the Detroit, Lansing & Northern Railroad was first called Daniel's Station [GSM 1879; PO Archives].

**INGHAM**, Ingham County: Caleb Carr, owner of the first sawmill here, became the first postmaster on Nov. 24, 1837, with the office changed to Haynes Corners about 1851, and transferred to Dansville on May 14, 1857; named after its county and township which had been named for Samuel D. Ingham, secretary of the treasury under Andrew Jackson [Cole; PO Archives].

**INGHAM CENTER**, Ingham County. See Dansville.

**INGLESIDE**, Cheboygan County: a summer resort with a station on the Grand Rapids & Indiana Railroad, in Monroe Township; storekeeper Lambert Wilson became its first postmaster on July 23, 1904; the office was closed on Oct. 31, 1906, but was restored, with Mr. Wilson again its postmaster, on June 17, 1907 [GSM 1905; PO Archives].

**INGOLSDORF**, Menominee County. See Norway.

**INKSTER**, Wayne County: the area was first settled in 1825 and was given a post office as Moulin Rouge on Dec. 31, 1857, with Josiah Dort as its first postmaster; Robert Inkster, a Scot, operated a steam sawmill on present-day Inkster Road, near Michigan Avenue, in the early 1860s, and the post office was renamed Inkster on July 11, 1863; given a station on the Michigan Central Railroad by 1878; incorporated as a village in 1926 and as a city in 1964 [Burton; GSM 1873; PO Archives].

**INLAND**, Benzie County: first settled by Daniel Sherman, from New York State, in 1863; the town was organized as North Climax in 1867, with the name changed to Inland in 1869; Nathaniel Borrows became its first postmaster on Feb. 17, 1866, the office operating until Oct. 31, 1903 [MPH 31:134 1901; PO Archives].

**INTERIOR**, Ontonagon County: the Milwaukee, Lake Shore & Western Railroad came through here in 1888; the Interior Lumber Company began operations that year, and a village of 41 buildings (including a church, school, and town hall) developed; Finley Morrison became its first postmaster on Dec. 11, 1888; Interior sawed its last log in 1895, but lumber dressing operations were carried on for two more years; its post office was closed on May 17, 1897; its cemetery sign, put up by someone from Paulding, says it is "Forgotten by everyone but God" [Charles Willman; PO Archives].

**INTERLOCHEN**, Grand Traverse County: named from its location between two lakes, to which their Indian names have been restored: Lake Wahbekaness (Water Lingers), formerly Duck Lake, and Lake Wahbekanetta

(Water Lingers Again), formerly Green Lake; partly the site of the ghost town of Wylie (which see); a station on the M. & N.E. and the C. & N.M. Railroads; storekeeper James R. Lee became its first postmaster on July 26, 1890; Willis Pennington, a Quaker, came here about 1900; he opened a drug store, and later a children's camp; in 1927, he induced Prof. Joseph Edgar Maddy, head of the Music Education Department at the University of Michigan, to locate his National High School Orchestra Camp Association (now the National Music Camp) here; the Interlochen Arts Academy followed in 1962 [Barnes; GSM 1891; PO Archives].

**INTERMEDIATE**, Charlevoix County: on March 2, 1874, Eugene A. H. Cole became the first postmaster at this point midway between the north and south ends of the south arm of Pine Lake (now Lake Charlevoix), the office operating until Nov. 30, 1892 [Traverse; PO Archives].

**INVERNESS**, Cheboygan County: a hamlet in the northern part of the county in 1878 [GSM 1879].

**INWOOD**, Charlevoix County: this settlement in Norwood Township was given a post office on Sept. 11, 1879, with Jason Belton as its first postmaster, the office operating until June 30, 1904 [GSM 1881-1905; PO Archives].

**IONIA**, Ionia County: when established in 1831, the county was named after the ancient Greek province; in 1833, a party of sixty-three, from Herkimer County, N.Y., led by Samuel Dexter (1787-1856), who had prospected the site the fall before, settled here; Erastus Yeomans became its first postmaster of Ionia, the first post office in the county, on Aug. 29, 1835; Mr. Dexter had the first plat of the village made and recorded in 1841; incorporated as a village in 1865 and as a city in 1873 [Schenck; Branch; PO Archives].

**IOSCO**, Iosco County: when organized in 1857, the county was named with an often-used word in the published works of Henry Rowe Schoolcraft, Iosco, said to mean water of light; first settled in 1849, it developed as a great lumbering area and became the site of the Lumberman's Memorial; the Iosco post office operated until Jan. 30, 1932 [Mich Manual; PO Archives].

**IOSCO**, Livingston County. See Parker's Corners.

**IRA**, St. Clair County: the township was created in 1837 and was named for Ira Marks, one of its prominent early settlers; its village, on the north shore of Lake St. Clair, was given a post office on May 13, 1851, with Mr. Marks as its first postmaster, the office operating until June 23, 1854 [Jenks; PO Archives].

**IRISH HILLS**, Lenawee County: in 1831, a small colony of English and Irish settled in this area; the rolling green hills and some 62 nearby lakes reminded them of the Emerald Isle, and the locality came to be known as the Irish Hills [Gierut; Mich Hist 19:187 1935].

**IRISHTOWN,** Gratiot County: the first homesteaders settled here in 1855, among them Fergus Connelly, Patrick and Michael Murray, Michael and Susan Egan, and Timothy Battle; this rural community, which spreads over into Isabella County, has a history, a tradition, and a mission church, St. Patrick's [Rev. Joseph O. Bauer].

**IRON BAY,** Marquette County. See Marquette.

**IRON CITY,** Keweenaw County: a mining location near Mosquito Lake; Iron City Mine opened in 1853, but proved barren [Stevens].

**IRON CITY,** Marquette County. See Republic.

**IRON CREEK,** Washtenaw County: this rural post office in the northwestern part of the county was opened on Feb. 8, 1840, with Fordyee Foster as its first postmaster, the office operating until June 25, 1859 [GSM 1860; PO Archives].

**IRONDALE,** Gogebic County. See Ramsay.

**IRON MOUNTAIN,** Dickinson County: after the Civil War, the Chapin brothers went north from Lower Michigan and bought a forty-acres tract which included the site of the present city which was founded by Dr. Nelson P. Hulst and laid out in 1879 with the opening of the nearby Chapin Mine; except for 1932-1933, this mine produced iron ore continuously from 1880 till its closing in 1934; the settlement was in Menominee County when Renel O. Philbrook became its first postmaster on May 17, 1880, being transferred to Dickinson on Oct. 1, 1891; incorporated as a village in 1887, with Dr. A. E. Anderson as its first mayor; incorporated as a city in 1889 [Fred Gianunzio; Havighurst; PO Archives].

**IRON RIVER,** Iron County: from its being the location of the profitable Nanaimo Mine, this area, then in Marquette County, and its post office, opened on April 21, 1882, with John McDonald as its first postmaster, were first called Nanaimo; influenced by the rapid flow of miners and homesteaders to the area, the bachelor brothers, Donald C. and Alexander MacKinnon, acquired land here about 1878, and in 1881 had J. A. Van Cleve plat the village as Iron River; James Innis built an inn in 1881, the first permanent structure; given a station on the Chicago & Northwestern Railroad; its post office was renamed Iron River on Sept. 8, 1882; with Albert E. Steller as postmaster, it was transferred to Iron County on June 16, 1884; incorporated as a village in 1885 and as a city in 1926; named from its location in an iron ore region [Hill; Sawyer; PO Archives].

**IRON RIVER,** Ontonagon County. See Beaser.

**IRON RIVER JUNCTION,** Iron County. See Stager.

**IRONS,** Lake County: a station on the Chicago & Western Michigan (now Pere Marquette) Railroad in 1894; this village in Eden Township was founded about 1909 by A. Glenn Haslett and G. E. Hilderbrand who built a general store here and platted the village; named for the Irons family, early settlers; Mr. Haslett became its first postmaster on July 27, 1910 [Joseph T. Kaderabek, PM].

**IRONTON**, Charlevoix County: here in Eveline Township, on Pine Lake (now Lake Charlevoix), in 1879, Robert Cherry, of the Pine Lake Iron Company, of Chicago, began a plant which, from 1881, converted into pig iron the ore brought in barges from the Upper Peninsula; Leslie E. Hildreth became its first postmaster on Jan. 31, 1881; the village was platted in 1884; the operation failed in 1893, but the village remained; its post office operated until Dec. 30, 1965 [Roy E. Meyers, ex-PM; PO Archives].

**IRONWOOD**, Gogebic County: first settled in 1885 as the commercial center of the Gogebic iron mining district and platted that year by the Milwaukee, Lake Shore & Western (now the Chicago & Northwestern) Railway; named for a man prominent in early mining deals, James R. Wood, known as "Iron" Wood; George E. Kelly became its first postmaster on Jan. 22, 1886; it was in Ontonagon County until Gogebic was organized in 1887; incorporated as a village in 1887 and as a city in 1889 [Victor Lemmer].

**IROQUOIS**, Chippewa County: Mary F. Gowan became the first postmaster of this rural post office in Superior Township on July 3, 1882; the office was closed on July 6, 1883, but was restored from Dec. 1, 1884, to Nov. 15, 1905 [GSM 1887; PO Archives].

**IRVING**, Barry County: the water power of the Thornapple River here induced L. B. Hills to buy 480 acres in 1849; he let the contract for building the dam that year and built a sawmill in 1851; Asahel Hubbard joined him in 1854 as Hills & Hubbard; when the business passed into the control of Mr. Hubbard, the town became known as Hubbardville; its post office, named Irving after the township, was opened on March 2, 1848, in the home of Albert W. Bull, its first postmaster; in 1865, with Mr. Hubbard as postmaster, it was removed to Irving village; named for the American writer, Washington Irving [Johnson; PO Archives].

**IRVINGTON**, Van Buren County. See Lacota.

**ISABELLA**, Clinton County. See Fowler.

**ISABELLA**, Delta County: this village on the shore of Big Bay de Noc began as a station on the Minneapolis, St. Paul & Sault Ste. Marie Railroad, and was first called New Minneapolis; it was given a post office as Isabella on Dec. 20, 1887, with Joseph A. Henderson as its first postmaster, the office operating until May 31, 1941; named in memory of the little daughter of Peter Mallman, pioneer logger and kiln operator in the area [David S. Coon; PO Archives].

**ISABELLA**, Isabella County: a station on the Pere Marquette Railroad; the Blunt post office was transferred here and renamed Isabella on Aug. 17, 1865; it was transferred in turn to Mount Pleasant on Feb. 23, 1869 [PO Archives].

**ISABELLA CENTRE,** Isabella County: Nelson Mosher became the first postmaster of this rural post office on Jan. 19, 1860, the office operating until June 25, 1863 [PO Archives].

**ISABELLA CITY,** Isabella County: A. M. Fitch, then Indian agent, with Francis C. Babbitt and John S. Eastman, platted the village and recorded it in 1861, the first recorded plat in the county; Mr. Babbitt became its first postmaster on July 19, 1861; the office was closed on July 3, 1866, restored on Feb. 4, 1870, but changed to Longwood on Sept. 7, 1871; named after the county which had been named at the suggestion of Henry R. Schoolcraft for Queen Isabella, of Spain, patron of Columbus [Fancher; PO Archives].

**ISABELLA RESERVATION,** Isabella County: its lands are held in trust by the federal government for the benefit of the Indians; the reservation has a tribal organization with a written constitution approved under the provisions of the Indian Re-organization Act [Dunbar].

**ISADORE,** Leelanau County: founded about 1870 when some Polish settlers came from Milwaukee to homestead land in the area; Jacob Rosinski became its first postmaster on July 27, 1892, the office operating until May 15, 1912; named for St. Isadore, the patron saint of farmers [Dickinson; PO Archives].

**ISHPEMING,** Marquette County: the site was known in the early mining days as the Lake Superior Location, taking its name from its parent, the Lake Superior Mine; first settled in 1856, it took the name of Ishpeming (Chippewa for heaven or high place) in 1862; Captain Gilbert D. Johnson became its first postmaster on Feb. 17, 1863; incorporated as a village in 1871 and as a city in 1873 [Andreas; PO Archives].

**ISLAND LAKE,** Livingston County: this resort settlement, three miles southeast of Brighton, was given a station on the Detroit, Lansing & Northern (later the Detroit, Grand Rapids & Western) Railroad in 1888 [GSM 1889].

**ISLAND MINE,** Keweenaw County: the Island Copper Mining Company was organized in 1873, and operated on Isle Royale; its village was the county seat when the island was a separate county; Hiram K. Cole became its first postmaster on Dec. 3, 1874, the office operating until Oct. 7, 1878 [MPH 1:519 1874; Stevens; PO Archives].

**ISLE AUX COCHONS,** Wayne County. See Belle Isle.

**ISLE ROYALE,** Keweenaw County: the first white man to visit it was Etienne Brulé in 1622; old maps call it Minong, Chippewa for a good high place; named Isle Royale by the French Jesuit missionaries, in honor of their royal patrons, about 1670; the American Fur Company established a fishing station here in 1837; the island was bought from the Chippewas in 1842, attached to Ontonagon County in 1843, to Houghton County in 1845, and to Keweenaw County in 1861; it was a separate county from 1861 to 1897, when it was reunited to Keweenaw; it became a part of the national park system in 1931; it was given a post office named Isle Royal National Park on June 15, 1959 [Mich Hist 22:281 1938, 25:331 1941; PO Archives].

**ISLINGTON**, Mackinac County. See Les Cheneaux.

**ITASKA**, Cass County. See Dailey.

**ITHACA**, Gratiot County: James J. Bush came here from Howell in 1850; John Jeffrey, from New York State, located land here in 1853, and came to live on it permanently in 1855; from its location in the county, it was given a post office named Gratiot Center on Nov. 16, 1855, with John Knight as its first postmaster; first platted for Mr. Jeffrey by Sidney S. Hastings in 1856; on April 13, 1857, it was renamed after Ithaca, N.Y.; incorporated as a village in 1869 and as a city in 1961 [Frederick Howes; PO Archives].

**ITTNER'S CORNERS**, Bay County: a hamlet near Bay City in 1918 [GSM 1921].

**IVA**, Saginaw County: this rural post office, 5½ miles from Hemlock, was opened on Dec. 7, 1894, with John F. Shovan as its first postmaster, the office operating until Oct. 14, 1904 [GSM 1895-1905; PO Archives].

**IVAN**, Kalkaska County: John M. Calkins became the first postmaster of this rural post office in Garfield Township on June 6, 1881, the office operating until April 30, 1911 [PO Archives].

**IVANHOE**, Huron County: Mathew Ternes became the first postmaster of this rural post office on June 29, 1899, the office operating until Aug. 14, 1905 [PO Archives].

**IVANHOE**, St. Joseph County. See Sturgis.

**JACK PINE**, Crawford County. See Eldorado.

**JACKSON**, Jackson County: in July, 1827, Horace Blackman built his log cabin here; while he was back in New York State that winter, to get his relatives, surveyors laying out a territorial road (now US-12), stayed at his cabin and recorded the location as Jacksonburgh, for President Andrew Jackson; first platted by Jonathan F. Stratton in 1830; Isaiah W. Bennett became the first postmaster of Jacksonburgh in 1830, changed to Jacksonopolis on Aug. 6, 1835, with Daniel Coleman as postmaster, and to Jackson on Dec. 8, 1838; it became the county seat in 1833; incorporated as a village in 1843 and as a city in 1857 [DeLand; Pen Phil 8:6 April 1958; PO Archives].

**JACKSON JUNCTION**, Jackson County: a station on the Michigan Central Railroad, at the intersection of the Jackson branch of the Lake Shore & Michigan Southern Railroad, a mile east of Jackson, in 1886 [GSM 1887].

**JACKSON LAKE**, Montmorency County: a station on the Alpena & Northern Railroad, 5 miles north of Atlanta, in 1894 [GSM 1895].

**JACKSON LOCATION**, Marquette County. See Carp River.

**JACKSON'S MILLS**, Lenawee County. See Addison.

**JACOB CITY**, Mackinac County. See Moran.

**JACOB ISLAND**, St. Clair County. See Harsens Island.

**JACOBSVILLE**, Houghton County: founded about 1885 by John Henry Jacobs and named for him; Andrew Hendrickson became its first postmaster on Nov. 29, 1887, the office operating until Dec. 30, 1964 [Jean M. Tomlinson, ex-PM].

**JACWAC**, Roscommon County: Albert A. Thomas became the first postmaster of this rural post office on Dec. 18, 1909, the office operating until May 31, 1910 [PO Archives].

**JAM**, Midland County: this rural post office was named from the initials of storekeeper James A. Murphy who became its first postmaster on July 11, 1894, the office operating until Sept. 30, 1903 [GSM 1895-1909; PO Archives].

**JAMES**, Saginaw County: James Murphy came here in 1865 and engaged in brick-making until 1874 when he bought 168 acres and turned to farming; James Township, better known locally as Jimtown, was organized in 1875 [Mills].

**JAMESTOWN**, Cass County. See Penn.

**JAMESTOWN**, Ottawa County: first settled by James Conkright in 1843; the town was organized in 1849 and was so named because a third of the original twelve voters had the first name of James (their family names were Cronkright, Sr. and Jr., Skeels, and Brown); Squier L. Gutchel became the first postmaster on July 29, 1857 [H. Van Regenmorter, PM].

**JAMESTOWN**, Schoolcraft County: also called Jamestown Slough; in 1875, the partners Eben James and Cornelius Ruggles, of Oshkosh, Wis., bought government land here about a mile east of Manistique, near the Manistique River, and built a sawmill and a boarding house for their workers; the area was low land, with a creek running through it, and was named after Mr. James and the terrain; it became the site of the Manistique Pulp & Paper Company [Harvey C. Saunders].

**JASPER**, Lenawee County: Andrew Millett first settled here in Fairfield Township in 1824; Henry Ferguson became the first postmaster of the ensuing settlement on June 18, 1874; its railroad station was first called Fairfield [Naomi Dowling; GSM 1875].

**JAY**, Saginaw County. See Freeland.

**JEAN**, Marquette County: a station on the M. & S.E. Railroad in 1910 [GSM 1911].

**JEDDO**, St. Clair County: A. S. Potter had settled here in Burtchville Township by 1840 and the settlement which followed became known as

Potter's Corners; given a post office as Pottersburg on Feb. 12, 1859, with Nelson Potter as its first postmaster; simply to avoid confusion with the Petersburg post office, it was renamed Jeddo on July 6, 1864 [GSM 1867; Jenks; PO Archives].

**JEFFERSON**, Eaton County: Peter De Riemer became the first postmaster of this rural post office on Oct. 5, 1837, but on Jan. 29, 1842, the office was transferred to and renamed Chester [PO Archives].

**JEFFERSON**, Hillsdale County: it was a part of Moscow Township until 1837 when the legislature set it off and named it Florida; Henry P. Adams was elected its first supervisor; in 1849, the name of the township was changed to Jefferson; David Wines became its first postmaster on April 4, 1856, the office operating until Feb. 28, 1902 [Hoganboam; PO Archives].

**JEFFERSON**, Jackson County: Anson H. DeLamatter became the first settler here in 1834; John H. and Broadhead DuBois are considered the founders of the village for, after settling here in 1835, they had it surveyed and platted by Mr. DeLamatter in 1836; given a post office named Columbia, after its township, on June 27, 1839, with DeWitt C. DeLamatter as its first postmaster, the office operating until June 15, 1875; named for Thomas Jefferson [John Deball; DeLand; PO Archives].

**JEFFERSON**, Ingham County: Josiah Sabin bought the entire section in 1836; George Howe bought a quarter from him, formed a company, and they platted the village (also called Jefferson City), in 1838; Nichols Lewis built a sawmill here in 1837; William Lewis became the first postmaster in 1839, but this village, named for Thomas Jefferson, did not flourish [Adams; Durant].

**JEFFERSONVILLE**, Cass County: the settlement was given a post office as Liberty Church on March 16, 1858, with Robert Shidler as its first postmaster; on May 17, 1862, it was renamed Jeffersonville, after its township of Jefferson, which had been named after Jefferson Township, Logan County, Ohio, by the families of Moses and William Reames, Abner Tharp and Nathan Norton, who had come from there and who had become the first settlers in this area; its post office operated until May 16, 1873; it is also to be found in some early records as Jefferson [Fox; GSM 1863; PO Archives].

**JEFFERY**, Ionia County: storekeeper Lyman J. Clark became the first postmaster of this rural post office in Danby Township on Oct. 11, 1899, the office operating until Nov. 15, 1902 [GSM 1901; PO Archives].

**JENISON**, Ottawa County: founded by the twin brothers Luman and Lucius Jenison who built a large grist mill here in Georgetown Township in 1864; George Weatherwax became the first postmaster of Jenisonville on Jan. 29, 1872, with the name changed to Jenison on Oct. 14, 1887 [Harold C. Lowing, PM; Page].

**JENNEY**, Alger County: a station on the M.M. & N. Railroad, 19 miles from Munising; Napoleon L. Nevans became its first postmaster on Aug. 8, 1903, the office operating until Nov. 30, 1905 [GSM 1905; PO Archives].

**JENNEY**, Tuscola County. See Denmark Junction.

**JENNINGS**, Missaukee County: this lumbering center in Lake Township was founded by Austin and William Mitchell who named it from their admiration for William Jennings Bryan; J. Frank Schryer became its first postmaster on March 18, 1883, the office operating until July 31, 1956; it was made the terminus of the Missaukee branch of the Grand Rapids & Indiana Railroad with its station named Round Lake; now a ghost town [Milton Molitor; PO Archives].

**JENNISONVILLE**, Ottawa County: named for local lumberman Hiram Jennison; its station on the Chicago & Western Michigan (now Pere Marquette) Railroad was opened in 1872 and was first named Jennison's [GSM 1873].

**JENSON**, Newaygo County: James F. Barnes became the first postmaster of this rural post office on Oct. 31, 1882, the office operating until Sept. 6, 1883 [PO Archives].

**JERICHO**, Newaygo County: Edward A. Darby became the first postmaster of this rural post office in Ashland Township on Aug. 13, 1881, the office operating until Sept. 22, 1882 [PO Archives].

**JERICHO**, Van Buren County. See Hunter.

**JEROME**, Hillsdale County: when the D.H. & I. Railroad came through the forest here in 1871, Jerome Smith platted a village and gave it his name; he was the first station agent and he became the first postmaster on April 26, 1871 [Vivian Lyon Moore].

**JEROME ISLAND**, Huron County. See Mai Sou Island.

**JEROMEVILLE**, Alger County. See Shingleton.

**JERRY'S MILL**, Huron County. See Center Harbor.

**JERSEY**, Oakland County: many of the early settlers here in western Orion Township were from New Jersey; William Kile became the first postmaster of the settlement on July 22, 1847, the office operating until Aug. 18, 1887 [Mrs. Donald E. Adams].

**JERSEY CITY**, St. Joseph County: a hamlet in 1874 [GSM 1865].

**JERSEYVILLE**, Isabella County: James A. Hunt became the first postmaster of this rural post office on May 12, 1892, the office operating until Nov. 30, 1906 [PO Archives].

**JERUSALEM**, Huron County. See Palestine Colony.

**JERUSALEM**, Washtenaw County: platted and named New Jerusalem by John K. Bingham who had built a sawmill here in Lima Township on the south branch of Mill Creek in 1832; the New was dropped and the hamlet became known simply as Jerusalem [Chapman; Beakes].

**JESSE**, Menominee County: Jessie L. Hamilton became the first postmaster of this rural post office on March 4, 1884, the office operating until June 19, 1886 [PO Archives].

**JESSIE**, Clinton County: storekeeper Perry J. St. Clair became the first postmaster of this rural post office on April 3, 1894, the office operating until Jan. 31, 1902 [PO Archives].

**JESSIEVILLE**, Gogebic County: a mining location in Ironwood Township, with a station on the M., L.S. & W. Railroad; Mary L. Downs became its first postmaster on Jan. 26, 1887, the office operating until June 12, 1891; named for the girl friend of one of the miners [Victor Lemmer; PO Archives].

**JEWELL**, Newaygo County: a station on the Pere Marquette Railroad; Oscar L. Heath became its first postmaster on June 8, 1901, the office operating until Aug. 14, 1906 [PO Archives].

**JEWELL LAKE**, Alcona County: renamed from Mud Lake, by the State, about 1929, for Jewell Freer whose father was then the owner of this island in the lake and supervisor of Millen Township [Mich Hist 15:697 1931].

**JOE B'S**, Gratiot County. See Pompeii.

**JOHANNESBURG**, Otsego County: a station on the Michigan Central Railroad, in Charlton Township; the settlement formed around the sawmill of the Johannesburg Manufacturing Company; Thorwald W. Hanson became its first postmaster on Jan. 7, 1901 [GSM 1903; PO Archives].

**JOHNNYCAKE PRAIRIE**, St. Joseph County: johnnycake, comprising the pioneer schoolboy's lunch, resulted in the school here being called Johnnycake, after which the plate-like terrain about it became Johnnycake Prairie; to this day the name survives in both prairie and school [Mich Hist 32:34 1948].

**JOHNS**, Keweenaw County: this summer resort on Isle Royale was given a post office on April 5, 1902, named for Will T. Johns, its first postmaster; the office operated until Dec. 15, 1909; the place was also known as Washington Harbor [GSM 1903; PO Archives].

**JOHNSON**, Calhoun County: David Aldrich became the first postmaster of this rural post office on Feb. 15, 1837, the office operating until only Sept. 4, 1837 [PO Archives].

**JOHNSON**, Huron County: a station on the Port Huron & Northwestern Railroad, four miles south of Port Austin, in 1884 [GSM 1895].

**JOHNSON**, Jackson County: this settlement on the west branch of the River Raisin, in Columbia Township, was named for the head of the Daniel W. Johnson Company, local sorghum plant; grocer William A. Clark became its first postmaster on May 21, 1888, the office operating until April 30, 1901 [GSM 1889-1903; PO Archives].

**JOHNSON**, Mackinac County: a station on the Detroit, Mackinaw & Marquette Railroad; named for Otis R. Johnson, chief operator and part owner of the Mackinaw Lumber Company, which operated in the area [GSM 1883].

**JOHNSTOWN**, Barry County: John Mott, a Quaker preacher, bought a large tract of land in the area, intending to found a Quaker colony; he was commonly called John by his brethren, and early settlers and land-seekers referred to this locality as John's Town; so, with the creation of the township in 1838, it was named Johnstown; but he did not go through with his plan, and the first actual settlement was made by Harlow Merrill who purchased his land in 1835-36; the village which developed was given a post office as Johnstown on Feb. 12, 1839, with Stephen V. R. York as its first postmaster, succeeded by Emory Cherry on April 13, 1842, the office operating until July 25, 1864; the Bristolville post office was transferred to Johnstown on Jan. 9, 1865, but was closed on May 25, 1874; it was restored from May 18, 1875, to April 6, 1887 [Johnson; MPH 26:221 1895; PO Archives].

**JOHNSTOWN**, Ionia County: storekeeper Frank L. Keech became the first postmaster of this rural post office on April 16, 1898, the office, which was 3 miles from Orleans, operating until Sept. 15, 1903 [GSM 1899; PO Archives].

**JOHNSVILLE**, Ottawa County. See Agnew.

**JOHNSVILLE**, Tuscola County: a hamlet in the northern part of the county in 1878 [GSM 1879].

**JOHNS WOOD**, Chippewa County: this village on Drummond Island began as a sawmill site and was called Scammon's Cove; the Kreetan Company, of Tonawanda, N.Y., took over the mill and the place was given a post office named Kreetan on Sept. 7, 1905, with Maggie J. Walz as its first postmaster; with lumberman Harold C. Johnson as postmaster, the name was changed to Johns Wood on March 19, 1914, the office operating until 1927 [Hamilton; Mich Hist 22:288 1938; PO Archives].

**JOLIET**, Midland County: Timothy Keely became the first postmaster of this rural post office on Dec. 6, 1895, the office operating until Oct. 19, 1896 [PO Archives].

**JONES**, Cass County: it was first settled in 1831 and 1833 by John Blair and Daniel Driskel and their families, respectively; it is on Driskel Lake, named for the latter man; the first business structure was built by H. Meskell on land owned by William D. Jones, in 1870; Mr. Jones platted the village named for him, in 1875, the plat being recorded by Alonzo P. Beeman in 1897; the Newberg post office was changed to Jones on Dec. 19, 1881, with E. H. (son of William) Jones as its first postmaster; in its early days, the place was also known as Jones' Crossing [Pearl Taylor; Rogers; PO Archives].

**JONESFIELD**, Saginaw County: the area was a wilderness until the Saginaw Valley & St. Louis Railroad came through in 1872; the township was organized in 1873 by pioneers William Jones, Joel Nevins, Alexander Fales and Arnold J. West [Mills].

**JONES' MILL,** Cass County: Jones & Langston built a sawmill here in LaGrange Township in 1830, later adding a cording mill and a furniture factory; while no village developed, the area is still known as Jones' Mill [Schoetzow].

**JONESVILLE,** Hillsdale County: Benaiah Jones, from Painesville, Ohio, land-looked here in 1828, with his brother, Edmund, bought the land in 1829, surveyed it in 1830, and platted the village named for him in 1831; the first platted village in the county and the first county seat; Elisha P. Champlin became its first postmaster on Jan. 21, 1841; a station on the Lake Shore & Michigan Southern Railroad; incorporated as a village in 1855 [Vivian Lyon Moore; Mich Hist 32:78 1948].

**JOPPA,** Calhoun County: a station on the Michigan Central Railroad; John A. Frey became its first postmaster on Jan. 11, 1890, the office operating until July 15, 1909 [Cole].

**JORDAN,** Antrim County: this village on the Jordan River was settled in 1874 and given a post office on July 12, 1875, with Gilbert E. Green as its first postmaster; the office was closed on June 20, 1879, but was restored on Nov. 6, 1901 [GSM 1879; PO Archives].

**JORDAN,** Isabella County: a flag station on the Pere Marquette Railroad in 1884 [GSM 1889].

**JORDAN'S CORNERS,** Eaton County: this hamlet in Chester Township was named for its first settler, Amasa L. Jordan, who came here from Vermont about 1840; John Williams built the first sawmill about 1856 and Shaw & Bottomly the first store about 1866 [Durant].

**JOSCO,** Livingston County. See Parker's Corners.

**JOY,** Emmet County: when grocer Joseph K. Feick became the first postmaster of this rural post office on May 5, 1884, it was in Charlevoix County; the office was closed on July 9, 1890; it was restored on Feb. 26, 1891, changed into Emmet County on Nov. 20, 1895, but closed permanently on Oct. 31, 1899 [PO Archives; GSM 1885-91].

**JOYFIELD,** Benzie County: the first homestead entry here was made on July 11, 1863, by Rev. Amariah Joy, a Baptist minister and native of Putney, Vermont; he secured its first post office and became its first postmaster on Feb. 15, 1864, serving until 1883; it was the second post office opened in the county; he was succeeded in office by William A. Joy; the office was given the name of Joyfield at the suggestion of Rev. Charles E. Bailey; when the town was organized in 1868, it took the name of its post office; the office operated until Sept. 30, 1903 [MPH 31:146 1901; PO Archives].

**JUDAH LAKE,** Oakland County. See Lake Orion.

**JUDDVILLE,** Shiawassee County: John and Matilda Judd obtained

400 acres here in Hazelton Township in 1853 (their descendents still own 100 acres of it); in 1854, they cleared the land, built a log house and a log school in which their daughter Jane was the first teacher; given a post office as Judd's Corners on June 20, 1879, with blacksmith Eri D. Babcock as its first postmaster; the office was closed on Sept. 30, 1902, but the village of Juddville remains [Mrs. Vera Judd Jacobs; Pen Phil 6:3 Oct 1955].

**JUDGE,** Crawford County: a station on a branch of the Michigan Central Railroad in 1889; George F. Owen became its first postmaster on Feb. 10, 1892, the office being changed to Lovells on Feb. 8, 1909 [Grace L. Funsch].

**JUHL,** Sanilac County: this village in Elmer Township was founded in 1882 by Jens C. Juhl who, with his wife and six children, had come directly from Denmark; storekeeper Niels M. Smith became the first postmaster on Feb. 25, 1889, the office operating until June 30, 1906; it became a Danish community with as many as a hundred families living there at a time [Edward P. Dougherty; PO Archives].

**JUNCTION,** Genesee County: a station at the intersection of the Flint River division and the main line of the Pere Marquette Railroad, four miles above Flint, in 1886 [GSM 1887].

**JUNET,** Gogebic County: a siding on the Duluth, South Shore & Atlantic Railroad, named for an early family in the area, about 1871 [Victor Lemmer].

**JUNIATA,** Tuscola County: Rogers Township, named for Levi Rogers, in whose home the first town meeting was held, began organization in 1851; the name of the town was changed to Juniata by legislative act in 1857; its village was given a station on the Port Huron & Northwestern Railroad in 1882 and a post office on Dec. 11, 1882, with storekeeper Richard H. Williams as its first postmaster, the office operating until Feb. 28, 1907 [J. A. Gallery; GSM 1883 [PO Archives].

**JUSTUS,** Macomb County: Frank J. Schulz became the first postmaster of this rural post office, 2½ miles from Utica, on March 11, 1898, the office operating until only Oct. 27, 1898 [GSM 1899; PO Archives].

**K. I. SAWYER AIR FORCE BASE,** Marquette County: in 1941, Kenneth I. Sawyer, Marquette County road commissioner, presented plans to the county board for a county airport here; it was named for him after his death in 1944; negotiations by the federal government were begun in 1954 and completed on Jan. 24, 1955, for leasing the field to the Air Force, this link in the Air Defense Command chain of installations guarding the frontiers of America is located 23 miles southeast of Marquette [Leroy S. Ray, SSgt., USAF].

**KAISERVILLE,** Bay County: in 1873, the lumber firm of Van Etten, Kaiser & Company built the Pinconning & Kaiserville Railroad from their mill in Pinconning to their new mill here, both villages arising from their enterprises; the former prospered, the latter did not [Page].

IDA TWP.
Res.—S. McFetridge

JAMES TWP.
Farm Res.—T. Blower

KENT CO.
Manufacturer & Dealer in Boots & Shoes - G. Weitz

LIMA TWP.
Res. - R. Goodwin

**KALAMAZOO,** Allegan County. See Saugatuck.

**KALAMAZOO,** Calhoun County. See Sheridan.

**KALAMAZOO,** Kalamazoo County: Titus Bronson, of Connecticut, built his log cabin here in 1829 and platted the village of Bronson in 1831; in that year, came General Justus Burdick and other pioneers; Smith L. Wood built the first frame house in 1832; Dr. Jonathan G. Abbott became the first postmaster of Bronson on July 14, 1832, with the office renamed Kalamazoo on April 20, 1836; the U.S. Land Office was moved here in 1834; the legislature renamed the village Kalamazoo in 1836, the name under which the county had been organized in 1830, from the original Indian name of Kikalamazoo, said to mean the mirage or reflecting river; incorporated as a village in 1838 and as a city in 1883 [GSM 1873; MPH 18:570 1891; PO Archives].

**KALAMAZOO HARBOR,** Allegan County: the village was laid out at the mouth of the Kalamazoo River in 1835-38; but its lots did not sell and it never became more than a village on paper [Johnson].

**KALAMO,** Eaton County: the first land was located here by N. and H. Weed and Martin Leach about the same time in 1835; the township was organized in 1838 and the village named after it; Alexander Merritt became its first postmaster on March 5, 1842, the office operating until Aug. 31, 1903 [MPH 3:403 1881; Williams; Durant; PO Archives].

**KALEVA,** Manistee County: in 1894, Jacob Saari, of Brooklyn, N.Y., and John Haksluto moved here in Maple Grove Township; the former had been employed by the Michigan Land Society to found a Finnish settlement at this junction of the Pere Marquette and the Manistee & Northeastern Railroads; the station here was named Manistee Crossing; the Society had the village platted by J. E. Merritt, of Manistee, in 1894, and on Feb. 6, 1895, Frank Schimmel became its first postmaster, with the office named Crossing, from its being a railroad junction; on Jan. 20, 1900, Mr. Saari had it renamed Kaleva, a name derived from that of the national Finnish epic, Kalevala; incorporated as a village in 1948 [John Rengo, ret. PM; GSM 1895; PO Archives].

**KALKASKA,** Kalkaska County: in 1872, Albert A. Abbott came here from Decatur, Michigan, bought 1000 acres and built a sawmill; he platted the village and on May 12, 1873, became its first postmaster; a station on the Chicago & Western Michigan (now Pere Marquette) Railroad; incorporated as a village in 1887; Kalkaska is a Chippewa word of uncertain meaning [Powers; PO Archives].

**KARLIN,** Grand Traverse County: this village in Grant Township began with a station on the Manistee & Northeastern Railroad; sawmill owner Edward Wilson became its first postmaster on July 12, 1897; both the depot and the post office were named Horicon but were renamed Karlin on April 6, 1903, after a town in Czechoslovakia whence a number of the settlers had come [A. Hantak, PM; GSM 1899-1905; PO Archives].

**KARR**, Tuscola County: a station on the Michigan Central Railroad and a general store, five miles from Gagetown, in 1910 [GSM 1911].

**KASKA**, Kalkaska County: Abram West became the first postmaster of this rural post office on May 17, 1880, the office operating until Nov. 22, 1880 [PO Archives].

**KASSON**, Leelanau County: Jonathan Dewing, a Vermonter, was the first settler in the area, about 1863, and he became the first supervisor when Kasson Township was organized in 1865; named for Kasson Freeman, first county surveyor from 1863 to 1865; its post office operated from March 14, 1871, to June 12, 1894; the town did not become a village [Traverse; GSM 1873; PO Archives].

**KATES**, Dickinson County: a station on the E. & L.S. Railroad; Charles K. Verity became its first postmaster on April 16, 1906, the office operating until Dec. 31, 1907 [GSM 1907; PO Archives].

**KATES**, Marquette County: Claude C. Carlisle became the first postmaster of this rural post office on April 25, 1908 [PO Archives].

**KATE'S BAY**, Delta County: named for an old Indian woman who engaged in commercial fishing here; first settled in 1849; a priest from France failed in his attempt to found French colony here and only a few families stayed on [Estella Bergeron].

**KATIKITEGON**, Gogebic County. See Indian Village.

**KAVANAUGH LAKE**, Washtenaw County: Adney A. Hall became the first postmaster of this rural post office on Feb. 13, 1893, the office operating until Jan. 6, 1894 [GSM 1895; PO Archives].

**KAWKAWLIN**, Bay County: by 1855, settlers had clustered around the water powered mill of James Fraser (later operated by O. A. Ballou) and the steam powered mill of Frederick A. Kaiser; the village was organized by O. A. Ballou, John Sutherland, Dennis Stanton, and others, in 1868; Mr. Stanton became its first postmaster on March 6, 1868; named from its location by the Kawkawlin River, which the Indians called Oganconning, or place of the pike fish [Gansser].

**KAYWOOD**, Montcalm County. See Gowen.

**KEARNEY**, Antrim County: George Palmer became the first postmaster of this rural post office, named after its township, Jan. 17, 1876, the office operating until March 30, 1883 [GSM 1879; PO Archives].

**KEARSLEY**, Genesee County: Ogden Clarke became the first postmaster of this rural post office on Aug. 25, 1841, the office operating until Jan. 11, 1867 [PO Archives].

**KEARSARGE**, Houghton County: first settled in 1867; the master amygdaloid lode was mined by various companies successively from 1882 to 1925, when closed due to depletion; Barnett S. Shearer became the first postmaster on Nov. 20, 1893, the office operating until March 11, 1966;

named for the U.S.S. Kearsarge by a former naval officer who became an employee of the Calumet & Hecla Consolidated Copper Company; a station on the Hancock & Calumet Railroad [Lembi Timonen, PM; Federal; PO Archives].

**KEATINGTON**, Oakland County: the Howard T. Keating Company, realtors, of Birmingham, began to develop this 3,200 acre tract in Orion Township into a village in 1865 [Detroit Free Press, July 23, 1966].

**KEDRON**, Washtenaw County. See Chelsea.

**KEDZIE'S GROVE**, Lenawee County. See Deerfield.

**KEEGO HARBOR**, Oakland County: J. E. Sawyer settled here in West Bloomfield Township in 1902; he built three cottages on Willow Beach, developed the present Cass Lake Subdivision (he called it The Park), converted Dollar Lake into a harbor by building a canal connecting it with Cass Lake, and named it Keego Harbor; Neil McMillan became its first postmaster on Jan. 16, 1920; incorporated as a village in 1954; keego is the name of a slender fish [Eileen B. Van Horn; PO Archives].

**KEELER**, Van Buren County: John and James Nesbitt, natives of Ireland, bought 120 acres of government land in the area in 1834; they sold out in 1835 to Eleazer H. Keeler, and the first township election was held in his tavern; he became the first post master of Keelersville on Nov. 11, 1835, with the office moved to the village of Keeler in 1856 and renamed Keeler on May 26, 1892; it operated until June 30, 1911 [Ellis; PO Archives].

**KEENAN**, Lake County: Quincy K. Bridge became the first postmaster of this rural post office on Dec. 19, 1900, the office operating until Nov. 15, 1901 [PO Archives].

**KEENE**, Hillsdale County: entirely on his farm in Pittsford Township, Charles Ames, from Keene, N.H., platted the village in 1836; its post office, which was opened on Sept. 27, 1841, was changed to Pittsford on Jan. 30, 1846 [Hogaboam; PO Archives].

**KEENE**, Ionia County: the first actual settlers were Edward Butterfield and Cyrus Rose who cleared some land here in 1837 and settled in 1838; later in 1838, James Monk, from Canada, founded the Canadian Settlement; the township was organized in 1842, and the town was named after it; Wallace Davenport became its first postmaster on June 22, 1868; the office was closed on March 28, 1884, but was restored from Aug. 7, 1884, to May 11, 1886; Mr. Butterfield had the township named after his native Keene, N.H. [Schenck; Dillenback; PO Archives].

**KEEWAHDIN BEACH**, St. Clair County: a resort developed by the Keewahdin Park Association, on Lake Huron, near Port Huron, in 1914; the name was likely derived from that of the famous Michigan Indian chief Kewadin [GSM 1915].

**KEGOMIC**, Emmet County: a station on the Grand Rapids & Indiana

Railroad, 2 miles east of Petoskey, in 1886; it became a small village with the coming of the W. W. Rice Leather Company tannery and general store [GSM 1887].

**KELDEN**, Chippewa County: Walter Todd became the first postmaster of this village in Pickford Township on May 24, 1896 [GSM 1895-1925; PO Archives].

**KELLER**, Kent County. See Logan.

**KELLOGG**, Allegan County: a station on the Michigan & Ohio Railroad; this settlement in Watson Township formed around the Charles Miner sawmill and the McClelland & Miner general store; Finley C. McClelland became its first postmaster on Jan. 4, 1884, the office operating until Jan. 31, 1906 [GSM 1885-1907; PO Archives].

**KELLOGGVILLE**, Kent County: named for Francis W. Kellogg who located here the headquarters of his lumbering firm of Kellogg, White & Company about 1845; he was elected to the state legislature from Grand Rapids in 1857, followed by three terms in congress; George W. Kellogg became the first postmaster on June 4, 1856, the office being changed to Fisher's Station on Feb. 28, 1871; it was given a depot on the Grand Rapids & Indiana Railroad [MPH 35:510 1907; PO Archives].

**KELLS**, Menominee County: a station on the Wisconsin & Michigan Railroad in 1894; George P. Gunderson became its first postmaster on March 1, 1895, the office operating until only Oct. 30, 1895 [GSM 1897; PO Archives].

**KELLY**, Eaton County: a post office in the (M. K.) Bosworth, Kelly & Son general store, with Cornelius S. Jackson becoming its first postmaster on Oct. 4, 1895, the office operating until March 31, 1903 [GSM 1895-1905; PO Archives].

**KELLY**, Roscommon County: this rural post office was named for James M. Kelly who became its first postmaster on Sept. 26, 1895, the office operating until Jan. 3, 1895 [PO Archives].

**KELLY'S CORNERS**, Lenawee County. See Cement City.

**KELSO JUNCTION**, Iron County: believed to have been named for C. E. Kelso, of Manistique, a lumber and railroad company executive [Victor Lemmer].

**KENDALL**, Van Buren County: this station on a branch of the Michigan Central Railroad was named Kendall's; given a post office named Kendall on March 11, 1836, with John D. Freeman as its first postmaster, the office operating until March 10, 1842; in 1864, Lucius B. Kendall bought of Judge E. B. Dyckman 160 acres of timberland here, and with James Thistle and Albert Arms, built a sawmill; Mr. Kendall and his associates platted the village and recorded it in 1870; its post office was re-opened on Jan. 6, 1870, with Albert Arms as its postmaster [Ellis; PO Archives].

**KENDALL MILLS,** Montcalm County. See Maple Valley.

**KENDALLVILLE,** Montcalm County: in 1865, the firm of Price & Kendall built a sawmill in the northern part of Pine Township and a settlement, called Kendallville, developed; but it was never platted and with the exhaustion of the timber it faded out [Dasef].

**KENNEDY,** Mackinac County. See Engadine.

**KENNETH,** Mackinac County: a station on the Duluth, South Shore & Atlantic Railroad; named for the son of William J. Ross who began lumbering in the area about 1900; William J. Ross became its first postmaster on Aug. 21, 1903 [Emerson Smith; GSM 1905; PO Archives].

**KENNEY'S,** Shiawassee County: this rural post office was named for James Kenney who became its first postmaster on April 9, 1850, the office operating until Jan. 6, 1851 [PO Archives].

**KENO,** Antrim County. See Bellaire.

**KENO,** Newaygo County: William H. Horning became the first postmaster of this rural post office on June 17, 1889, the office operating until May 21, 1897 [PO Archives].

**KENO,** Roscommon County: the area was first known as Hard Scrabble; through the efforts of the Hyde family, early settlers from Virginia, it was renamed Keno; Sarah O. Wheeler became its first postmaster on Sept. 13, 1910 [Co. Bd. of Ed.; PO Archives].

**KENOCKEE,** St. Clair County: James O'Leary became the first settler here in 1837; when the township was organized in 1855, it was given the Chippewa name for long-legged; Abel Stockwell was the first supervisor and he became the first postmaster on Jan. 2, 1856; the office was closed on Aug. 19, 1878, but was restored from March 1, 1880, to June 30, 1903 [MPH 28:371 1898; Jenks; PO Archives].

**KENSINGTON,** Oakland County: first settled in 1832; Joel Redway built the first house and the first sawmill in 1834; platted by Alfred A. Dwight in 1836; given a post office named Lyon on June 9, 1834, after its township, which the legislature had named for Lucius Lyon; the office was renamed Kensington on Sept. 6, 1836, and operated until July 31, 1902; the village, familiarly called Kent, is now farmland [Durant; Seeley; PO Archives].

**KENT,** Kent County. See Grand Rapids.

**KENT,** Oakland County. See Kensington.

**KENT CITY,** Kent County: although this village in Tyrone Township was platted for John W. Thompson in 1870, it was not founded until 1873; Charles H. Barrett became its first postmaster on Feb. 11, 1873, with the post office named Ball Creek; the office was closed on Sept. 25, 1873, but was restored on Nov. 12, 1873, and renamed Kent City on Oct. 5, 1876; incorporated as a village in 1908; named after its county which had been named for James Kent (1763-1847), a noted New York jurist [Ann Noonan; GSM 1879; PO Archives].

**KENTON,** Houghton County: a station on the Duluth, South Shore & Atlantic Railroad; George C. Townsend became its first postmaster on Feb. 18, 1889; when the stand of white pine in the area was exhausted, the community turned to farming [Federal; PO Archives].

**KENTVILLE,** Benzie County. See Bendon.

**KENTWOOD,** Kent County: a branch post office out of Grand Rapids and a geographic expression referring to this area in southeast Kent County; the county was named by Lucius Lyon for eminent New York jurist James Kent [Paul F. Kempter].

**KERBY,** Shiawassee County: the first settler here in Caledonia Township was Samuel W. Kerby in 1885; a station on the D., G.H. & M. Railroad; storekeeper Joseph Leavitt became its first postmaster on Aug. 1, 1888, the office operating until Feb. 13, 1904 [Ellis J. Bowler; GSM 1889; PO Archives].

**KESSINGTON,** Cass County: Moses McKessick came here from Toledo, Ohio, in 1863; in 1872, he platted the village and named it for himself; given a post office named Sailor on June 30, 1892, named for its first postmaster, Benjamin F. Sailor; the office operated until May 31, 1904 [Bernice L. Vanderburg; Glover; PO Archives].

**KESWICK,** Leelanau County: farmer William Mebert became the first postmaster of this rural post office in Bingham Township on Sept. 17, 1889, the office operating until Nov. 15, 1910 [GSM 1891; PO Archives].

**KETCHAM,** Midland County: this lumber settlement in Lincoln Township was named for James G. Ketcham who became its first postmaster on Sept. 18, 1883, the office operating until April 6, 1888 [GSM 1885; PO Archives].

**KEW,** Menominee County: a station on the Chicago & Northwestern Railroad, opened in 1872; named after a town in England by the road whose promotors were selling issues of their securities to investors in the British Isles [George Springer; Mich Manual 1899].

**KEWADIN,** Antrim County: Charles Avery acquired patents on property here in 1856, but it was occupied only by Indians until 1876 and was known as Indian Town; when the white settlement formed, George D. Wyckoff became its first postmaster on June 4, 1883, with the office named Kewadin after a local Indian chief [Leon R. Barnes, PM; GSM 1887; PO Archives].

**KEWAWENON,** Baraga County: the Rev. John Clark opened a Methodist mission here for the Indians in 1834, with their cabins lining the shore of L'Anse Bay [Sawyer].

**KEWEENAW BAY,** Baraga County: a land patent was issued to Frank Laffrenire by President U. S. Grant on May 10, 1875, and the town was called Leffrenire until 1898; Annie La Fernier became the first postmaster on March 26, 1898, with the office named La Fernier, but she had it changed on June 1, 1901, to that of the bay by which the village was located; she was succeeded in office in 1902 by Thomas D. Tracy, clerk of the Mass Consolidated Mining Company, whose stamp mill was the chief business of the village; a station on the Duluth, South Shore & Atlantic Railroad; Keweenaw (Kewawenon) was the Indian word for portage [Hazel D. Froberg, PM; GSM 1899; PO Archives].

**KEWEENAW BAY,** Houghton County: the Houghton, Marquette County, post office was opened on March 24, 1846; it was changed to Keweenaw Bay, Houghton County, Nov. 2, 1846, and to L'Ance on Feb. 16, 1865 [PO Archives].

**KEWEENAW BAY COMMUNITY,** Baraga County: it began as an Indian mission in 1660, and is now the largest Indian reservation in Michigan (15,738 acres); its land is held in trust by the federal government for the benefit of the Indians; the reservation has a tribal organization with a written constitution approved under the provisions of the Indian Reorganization Act; it was the first site of L'Anse [Sawyer; Dunbar].

**KEYSTONE,** Clinton County: this post office, with Horace Caster as its first postmaster, was opened at Coleman's Corners, in Greenbush Township, on Jan. 13, 1857, and named presumably by an admirer of Pennsylvania or of then President James Buchanan; the office operated until May 30, 1866 [Ellis; PO Archives].

**KEYSTONE,** Grand Traverse County: a station on the Grand Rapids & Indiana Railroad in 1874; the Beitner post office was changed to Keystone on Oct. 9, 1883, the office operating until June 2, 1894; the Slights post office was changed to Keystone on Dec. 21, 1898; this office was closed on April 15, 1901, but was restored from May 8, 1901, to April 15, 1908; it was located six miles south of Traverse City [GSM 1875; PO Archives].

**KIBBIE,** Van Buren County: it is on the line between Van Buren and Allegan Counties, in the former's Geneva Township; it was organized when the Kalamazoo & South Haven Railroad came through in 1870; grocer Fred Dawson became its first postmaster on Aug. 8, 1872, the office operating until Feb. 28, 1945 [Rowland; GSM 1873; PO Archives].

**KIDDVILLE,** Ionia County: George W. Dickinson, a New Yorker, built a sawmill here in 1836, and the settlement which followed became known as Dickinsonville, but its post office, opened on June 20, 1838, with Dr. Dickinson as its first postmaster, was named Otisco, after its township, which had been named after Otisco, Oswego County, N.Y.; Mr. Dickinson sold his mill to James M. Kidd, of Ionia, in 1845; Mr. Kidd platted the village and on Aug. 20, 1855, became the first postmaster of Kiddville; William E. Kidd became its last postmaster in 1878, the office being closed on June 26, 1894 [Dillenback; Schenck; PO Archives].

**KILKENNY,** Huron County. See Linkville.

**KILLMASTER**, Alcona County: this rural post office in Harrisville Township was named for lumberman John H. Killmaster who became its first postmaster on Dec. 15, 1885, the office operating until Feb. 28, 1911 [GSM 1887; PO Archives].

**KILMANAGH**, Huron County: it was first called Thompson's Corners, for Francis Thompson, a homesteader, who came here from Ireland in 1861; Kilmanagh, an Irish name, was first used here to describe Shebeon Creek which overflowed each spring; Mr. Thompson became the first postmaster of Kilmanagh on Feb. 11, 1873, holding the office until at least 1884, while the office itself operated until June 15, 1904 [Hey; Gwinn; PO Archives].

**KILNS**, Marquette County: a station on the Detroit, Mackinaw & Marquette Railroad, in the charcoal kiln region, in 1884 [GSM 1885].

**KILTON**, Gogebic County: August Bye was the first railroad agent of this station on the Duluth, South Shore & Atlantic Railroad, in Wakefield Township; Lyle J. Murdoch became its first postmaster on March 2, 1920, the office being moved to Lake Gogebic on June 15, 1929 [Victor Lemmer; GSM 1921; PO Archives].

**KIMBALL**, St. Clair County: land purchases were made here by 1825, but actual settlement did not begin until about 1840 when Barzillai Wheeler and John S. Kimball arrived; the township, when organized in 1855, was named for the latter, with William B.Verity as its first supervisor, succeeded by Mr. Kimball; a station on the Port Huron & Northwestern Railroad in 1882; given a post office as Kimbal on Dec. 21, 1882, with David Pace as its first postmaster; the spelling was corrected to Kimball on Jan. 31, 1889, but the office was closed in June, 1908 [Jenks; Andreas; PO Archives].

**KIMBALL POINT**, Huron County: a room in the Kimball home here was used for school purposes in 1854, making it one of the first schools in the county [Hey].

**KINCHELOE AIR FORCE BASE**, Chippewa County: it was founded by the U.S. Army Air Force in 1941 as Kinross Auxiliary Field; in 1947, the Air Force became a separate branch of the services and it became Kinross Air Force Base; in 1959, it was renamed in honor of Captain Iven C. Kincheloe; a native of Cassopolis, Michigan, he was a jet ace in the Korean conflict and later a test pilot for the X-2 experimental rocket-powered aircraft; he died in July, 1958, in attempting to eject from a F-104, and was buried in Arlington National Cemetery [Richard A. Silva, USAF].

**KINDE**, Huron County: the village began with a station on the Port Huron & Northwestern Railroad in 1884 and was named for storekeeper John Kinde who became its first postmaster on Dec. 7, 1885; incorporated as a village in 1903 [Hey; PO Archives].

**KINDERHOOK**, Branch County: the first land purchases in the area were made by John Shaft, Joshua Baker, and Alma H. White, all in 1836; the coming of John Waterhouse and his family formed the nucleus around which the village of Waterhouse Corners grew; John Waterhouse, Jr., became its first postmaster on April 1, 1837, with the office and village renamed Kinderhook on June 7, 1843, honoring President Martin Van Buren, who had been born in Kinderhook, Columbia County, N.Y.; the post office was closed on Jan. 5, 1862, but was restored on Jan. 26, 1863 [Johnson; PO Archives].

**KINGSFORD**, Dickinson County: the community was planned by the Ford Motor Company around its plant here and was named for Edward G. Kingsford, of Iron Mountain, a local Ford executive; incorporated as a village on Jan. 24, 1924, with J. Arthur Minnear as its first president; incorporated as a city in 1947 [Henry L. Wagner].

**KINGSLAND**, Eaton County: a station on the Muskegon Central Railroad, in Eaton Rapids Township; William Drake became its first postmaster on May 31, 1882; the office was closed on April 24, 1896, but was restored, with Sarah Drake as postmaster, on Jan. 19, 1898, the office operating until Aug. 31, 1903 [GSM 1895; PO Archives].

**KING'S LANDING**, Baraga County. See Pelkie.

**KINGSLEY**, Grand Traverse County: the village was first platted by Judson W. Kingsley on a part of his homestead, and its depot on the Grand Rapids & Indiana Railroad was first named Kingsley Station in 1874; Dr. Myron S. Brownson, a native of Steuben County, N.Y., laid out lots on property adjoining on the west, which he recorded in 1876 as the village of Paradise, named after its township; Mr. Kingsley became the first postmaster of Paradise on Feb. 14, 1873, with the office renamed Kingsley on Dec. 5, 1882; Mr. Kingsley was succeeded in office by his son, C. W. Kingsley, in 1883; in 1890, both plats were incorporated as the village of Kingsley [Traverse; Sprague; GSM 1877; PO Archives].

**KING'S MILL**, Lapeer County: this village in Arcadia Township formed around the grist mill and the sawmill of Harvey King; a station on the P., O. & P.A. Prailroad; its post office operated from Dec. 4, 1883, to Feb. 15, 1934 [GSM 1885; PO Archives].

**KINGSTON**, Tuscola County: this village in Koylton Township was first settled by Alanson K. King in 1857; it was given a post office as Newbury on May 28, 1867, changed to Kingston, after its first settler, on Feb. 16, 1871; incorporated as a village in 1893 [Mich Hist 42:109 1958; Mrs. Vernon Everett; PO Archives].

**KINNEY**, Kent County: a station on the Grand Rapids & Indiana Railroad, in Walker Township; Joseph L. Manley became its first postmaster on May 14, 1887, succeeded by John Kinney, the pioneer settler after whom it was named, in 1888 [GSM 1889; PO Archives].

**KINNEY SETTLEMENT**, Van Buren County: founded in 1835 by Elijah Kinney who came here in Porter Township from Milan, Ohio, with his wife, seven unmarried children, his son Luther and family, and his son-in-law, Samuel Corey [Ellis].

**KINNEYVILLE**, Ingham County: the plat of the village that Stephen Van Kinney recorded in 1849 called it Nova Scotia, whence he had migrated; it was given a post office as Winfield on April 29, 1862, with William Earll as its first postmaster, the office operating until March 14, 1903; but the village was best known locally as Kinneyville, after its founder, but spelled on some maps as Kinnieville and on others as Kinneville [Foster; Durant; PO Archives].

**KINROSS**, Chippewa County: a station on the Minneapolis, St. Paul & Sault Ste. Marie Railroad in 1891; John W. Wallis became its first postmaster on June 30, 1892; the office was closed on Dec. 10, 1894, but was restored from March 8, 1898, to date; it was named after Kinross, Scotland, by the Scottish-Irish settlers who had emigrated here by way of Canada [Hamilton; GSM 1895; PO Archives].

**KINTNER**, Tuscola County: a station on the S.T. & H. Railroad, in Fair Grove Township; Lyndon L. Whipper became its first postmaster on July 24, 1882, the office operating until Oct. 28, 1898 [GSM 1883-99; PO Archives].

**KIPLING**, Delta County: the Cleveland Cliffs Iron Company built a charcoal iron furnace and a village here on Bay de Noc about 1885; when the Soo Line came through in 1887, Fred D. Underwood, its general manager, named the station for the English poet, Rudyard Kipling; Orville A. Norton became its first postmaster on May 16, 1903, the office operating until Sept. 30, 1935 [Mich Hist 12:590 1928; PO Archives].

**KIPP'S CORNERS**, Genesee County: this village in the southeast corner of the county was named for a local landowner; David Vantine became its first postmaster on Oct. 9, 1862, the office operating until Nov. 6, 1871 [GSM 1879; PO Archives].

**KIRK**, Newaygo County: Albertus Andrus became the first postmaster of this rural post office on July 24, 1889, the office operating until April 14, 1904 [PO Archives].

**KIRKLAND**, Roscommon County: this rural post office in Denton Township was named for township supervisor Frank Kirkland; the township clerk, Lawrence W. Finley, became its first postmaster on Sept. 27, 1907, the office operating until Sept. 29, 1934 [PO Archives; Co. Bd. of Ed.; GSM 1909].

**KIRK'S JUNCTION**, Ottawa County: a station, a mile north of Ferrysburg, on the Chicago & Western Michigan (now Pere Marquette) Railroad in 1884 [GSM 1885].

**KIRKTOWN**, Berrien County: this sawmill settlement was named for mill owner Dexter Curtis, who was nicknamed Kirk [Fox].

**KIRTLAND**, Washtenaw County: this hamlet had a bank by 1837 [MPH 2:73 1877].

**KISSIPEE**, Montmorency County: grocer Minnie O. Wilder became the first postmaster of this rural post office in Vienna Township on July 19, 1918; the office was intermittently opened and closed until it was discontinued permanently on Oct. 31, 1928 [GSM 1919; PO Archives].

**KITCHI**, Houghton County: the station on the Duluth, South Shore & Atlantic Railroad here was opened in 1888 and was named Kitchi; it was given a post office named Vanzile on Oct. 31, 1888, named for Marshall Vanzile, its first postmaster; but the post office also took the name of Kitchie on Aug. 3, 1889; it operated until March 15, 1901 [GSM 1889; PO Archives].

**KIVA**, Alger County: the Huber family in 1880 became the first white settlers in the area, then known as Whitefish from its being by the Whitefish River, and later as West Limestone from its location in Limestone Township; but when given a post office on Dec. 11, 1915, it was named Kiva, a shortened form of the name of Sigrid Kivimaki, the first postmaster, and her husband, Anselmi Kivimaki, assistant postmaster [Anna K. Heeti, PM].

**KLACKING CREEK**, Ogemaw County: John Klacking became the first homesteader here in 1871; a creek ran through his property; together they gave the name to the settlement [Rev. Edward Trombley].

**KLEIN**, Montmorency County: this rural post office, 11 miles southeast of Atlanta, was named for William Klein, who became its first postmaster on April 21, 1903, the office operating until April 30, 1908 [GSM 1905; PO Archives].

**KLINE**, Genesee County: storekeeper George E. Hill became the first postmaster of this rural post office in Mundy Township on May 3, 1892, the office operating until Dec. 13, 1895 [GSM 1893-95; PO Archives].

**KLINGENSMITH**, Otsego County: this rural post office in Charlton Township was named for Sarah A. Klingensmith who became its first postmaster on Nov. 12, 1885, the office operating until Oct. 31, 1900 [GSM 1887; PO Archives].

**KLINGER**, St. Joseph County: the village began as a station named Douglas on the Lake Shore & Michigan Southern Railroad in 1878; with Erastus P. Moon as its first postmaster, it was given a post office as Klinger's Lake on Sept. 26, 1879, and its depot was also so renamed; its name was changed to Klingers on Oct. 5, 1895, the office operating until April 30, 1937; it was named from its location on Klinger Lake, named for Peter Klinger who had settled beside it in 1827; on various maps it is to be found as Klinger, Klingers, or Klinger's Lake [John L. Holmes; GSM 1895; PO Archives].

**KLINK**, Ingham County: this now extinct hamlet in Aurelius Township was named for storekeeper John W. Klink who became its first postmaster on Jan. 11, 1895, the office operating until Sept. 29, 1900 [Foster; PO Archives].

**KLOMAN**, Menominee County. See English.

**KLONDIKE**, Oceana County: storekeeper Enoch M. Mugford became the first postmaster of this settlement in Leavitt Township on July 29, 1898; the office was closed and then restored; the Klondike region in Alaska was in the news then for there in 1897 prospectors had mined two million dollars in gold [Rex Royal; PO Archives].

**KNAGGS PLACE**, Shiawassee County: on this important ford on the Shiawassee River was located Kitchewandanguonink, the best known Indian village in the county; white settlers called it Big Salt Lick or Grand Saline; Henry Bolieu, a French guide, built his log house here about 1817; the widely-known trading post which Whitmore Knaggs established here in 1820 was continued by his son John until 1839; the name still clings to the place and the modern iron bridge which spans the Shiawassee at the Old Indian Crossing in present Burns Township is called Knaggs Bridge [MPH 32:247 1902; Mich Hist 47:141 1963; Ball].

**KNEELAND**, Oscoda County: Enos R. Frame became the first postmaster of this rural post office on Dec. 22, 1905, the office operating until Sept. 30, 1912 [PO Archives].

**KNEELAND'S**, Crawford County: a station on a branch of the Michigan Central Railroad, 8 miles northwest of Grayling, in 1889 [GSM 1895].

**KNIGHT'S STATION**, Lenawee County. See Riga.

**KNOT MAUL**, Montcalm County: in 1855, James Taylor became the first settler here in Cato Township; during the presidential campaign of 1860, Abraham Lincoln was extolled as a rail-splitter and his followers here severed a tree trunk just above a huge knot in it, and to make the contrast more striking, they took the bark from the handle of what was intended to represent a large maul; when completed, it was exhibited here, and some referred to it as the Knot, others as the Maul, and from the union of the two words, the settlement became known as Knot Maul; storekeeper Mary Blumberg became its first postmaster on March 3, 1898, with the name of the office spelled Knotmaul; postal records say the office was closed on April 1, 1898, but it was still listed as a rural post office in the 1899 editions of both the Michigan Manual and the Michigan State Gazeteer [Dasef; PO Archives].

**KNOX CORNERS**, Mason County: this settlement in Amber Township had a post office in 1881, with Joseph Dart as postmaster [Page].

**KOCHVILLE**, Saginaw County: land purchases were made here by 1836, but permanent settlement did not begin until 1849; German-born Frederick Charles Koch came in 1849 and the township, when organized in 1856, was named for him; its village was given a post office named Phillips on May 15, 1890, for David Phillips, its first postmaster; the office was renamed Kochville, for Mr. Koch, on May 23, 1892, and operated until Jan. 31, 1901 [MPH 28:83, 495 1897; Mills; PO Archives].

**KOEHLER**, Cheboygan County: this settlement on Mullett Lake, in Burt Township, was named for hotelman Herman L. Koehler who became its first postmaster on June 8, 1881; the office was closed on Feb. 29, 1888, but, with Mr. Koehler again its postmaster, it was restored on April 4, 1888 [GSM 1883-89; PO Archives].

**KORELOCK**, Ontonagon County. See Lake Gogebic.

**KORTH STATION**, Lenawee County: a hamlet near Riga in 1910 [GSM 1919].

**KOSS**, Menominee County: after John Bagley made a survey from Peshtigo, Wisconsin, to Faithorn, Michigan, a standard gauge railroad, called the Wisconsin & Michigan, was built in 1894; Messrs. Bagley, Fisher, Keough and Nathan built a lumber and shingle mill on the Michigan side of the Menominee River here near its station in Stephenson Township, and started the village of Fisher; there was another Fisher post office in Michigan this one was given a post office named Koss, named for O. A. Koss, auditor of the railroad; storekeeper George P. Gunderson became its first postmaster on March 26, 1896; the village was devastated by a forest fire on May 14, 1900; its post office was closed on March 31, 1913; now a ghost town [John Hallfrisch; PO Archives].

**KOSSUTH**, Ionia County: this rural post office was named for the Hungarian patriot Lajos (Louis) Kossuth, who visited the U.S. in 1851; George W. Dickinson became its first postmaster on Dec. 6, 1855, the office operating until 1868 [Schenck; PO Archives].

**KOYLTON**, Tuscola County: Peter Koyl settled here in 1856, Orville Koyle and Levy Koyl in 1857; when the township was organized in 1859 it was named for them, freeholders who signed the application; Leander Moyer became its first postmaster on Nov. 28, 1863, with the office transferred to Newbury on May 28, 1867 [Page; PO Archives].

**KRAFT**, Wayne County. See Hamtramck.

**KREETAN**, Chippewa County. See Johnswood.

**KULMBACH**, Saginaw County: a settlement in Brumfield Township with a station on the Michigan Central Railroad; George Wissmiller became its first postmaster on Feb. 27, 1891, the office operating until April 30, 1901 [GSM 1893; PO Archives].

**KURTZ**, Alcona County: this logging camp by a railroad siding in Mikado Township was founded by and named for Hugo Kurtz about 1900; storekeeper Samuel P. Hertzler became its first postmaster on July 31, 1909, the office operating until March 31, 1911; now farmland [Gus Holm; PO Archives].

**LABARGE**, Kent County: this village was first called Caledonia Centre from its location in Caledonia Township; it was given a post office as Labarge on Dec. 11, 1876, with Alexander Kilgore as its first postmaster, the office operating until Nov. 30, 1901; in some records it is spelled La Barge [GSM 1895; PO Archives].

**LA BRANCHE**, Menominee County: a station on a branch of the Chicago & Northwestern Railroad, in Spalding Township, opened in 1882 and named for a pioneer settler, Israel La Branche; the settlement formed around the sawmill of the William Mueller Company; Louis La Branche became its first postmaster on Dec. 5, 1902, the office operating until May 15, 1948 [Ethel Schuyler; PO Archives].

**LA CARP**, Mason County: William Barnhart became the first postmaster of this rural post office on Dec. 31, 1873, the office operating until Jan. 6, 1875 [PO Archives].

**LACEY**, Barry County: Levi N. Mosher ran a general store here in Johnstown Township and he became the first postmaster of Lacey on Aug. 11, 1881, the office operating until June 15, 1905; probably named for Edward S. Lacey, congressman from this district from 1881 [Cole; PO Archives].

**LACHINE**, Alpena County: founded as a station by the Detroit & Mackinaw Railway in 1909 and named by a railroad conductor who came from Lachine, Quebec; Jennie Moore became its first postmaster on March 28, 1910 [Kathleen I. Adams, PM; W. T. Yake].

**LAC LaBELLE**, Keweenaw County: the settlement arose from the operations of the Mendota Mining Company operations here; named from the lake it borders on; now a resort community [Andreas; Federal].

**LACOTA**, Van Buren County: Clark Pierce became the first settler here in 1837; for his son Irving (the first white child born in the township), the platted part of the original village was named Irvington; it was platted by Enoch M. Pease in 1870; from its location in Geneva Township, it was given a post office as West Geneva on May 20, 1864, with Jerome B. Watson as its first postmaster, changed to Irvington on June 2, 1874, and to Lacota on Dec. 22, 1884; the Michigan Central Railroad had a town of Irving on its lines and they requested the change of name here; the new name was suggested by V. D. Dilley whose father, Varnum M. Dilley, was reading a novel whose chief character was an Indian maiden named Lacota [C. E. Dilley; PO Archives].

**LA CROIX**, Emmet County. See Cross Village.

**LA CROSSE**, Emmet County: the name some early sources, for example, the Gazeteer 1865, used for Cross Village.

**LAC VIEU**, Gogebic County. See Indian Village.

**LADOGA**, Alger County: the settlement began with a lumber camp of the Wisconsin Land & Lumber Company, on a branch of the Chicago & Northwestern Railroad.

**LAFAYETTE**, Gratiot County: Eber M. Monroe became the first postmaster of this rural post office in southwestern Lafayette Township on Sept. 18, 1857; the office was closed on April 14, 1860, but was restored from Sept. 27, 1860, to March 13, 1896, and from April 23, 1896, to April 30, 1902 [Tucker; PO Archives].

**LAFAYETTE**, Iowa County: Aaron F. Boyce became its first postmaster on Jan. 19, 1835, when it was in Michigan Territory; it is now in Wisconsin [PO Archives].

**LAFAYETTE**, Van Buren County: in 1835, the legislature of the Territory of Michigan erected Lafayette Township, naming it for the patriot Marquis de La Fayette; a settlement of that name was on Farmer's map of 1836; described in the Gazeteer 1838 as a village on the east branch of the Paw Paw River; the township was renamed Paw Paw in 1867 [Mich Hist 43:283 1959; Rowland].

**LA FERNIER**, Baraga County. See Keweenaw Bay.

**LAFFRENIRE**, Baraga County. See Keweenaw Bay.

**LA GRANGE**, Cass County: Job Davis built the first sawmill here in 1829; in 1831, he sold it to Martin C. Whitman who added a grist mill in 1832; Mr. Whitman platted and recorded the village as Whitmanville in 1834; in 1836, Erastus H. Spalding platted an adjoining village which he called LaGrange after the township (which had been organized in 1829, and named by its first settler, Abram Townsend, after General La Fayette's home in France); Mr. Whitman became the first postmaster of LaGrange on Dec. 22, 1832, with the office renamed Whitmanville on Feb. 11, 1835, and back to LaGrange on April 18, 1838, for in that year the legislature named the united plats LaGrange, but locally it is still often referred to as Whit or Whit's; its post office operated until Jan. 31, 1902 [Glover; Fox; PO Archives].

**LAING**, Sanilac County: this rural post office was named for Herman Laing who became its first postmaster on Jan. 11, 1896, the office operating until June 30, 1906 [PO Archives].

**LAINGSBURG**, Shiawassee County: founded by tavern-keeper Dr. Peter Laing in 1836; Henry Smith became its first postmaster on Nov. 22, 1841, with the office being renamed Nebraska on July 8, 1854, but changed back to Laingsburg on Feb. 4, 1862; the village was not platted until 1860 when the Jackson, Lansing & Northern (now Michigan Central) Railroad came through; incorporated as a village in 1871 and as a city in 1951 [Eleanor L. Allen; Campbell; Daboll; PO Archives].

**LAIRD**, Houghton County. See Alston.

**LAKE**, Allegan County: the Cheshire post office was transferred to this hamlet on April 10, 1858, but was changed back to Cheshire on Feb. 18, 1863 [GSM 1860; PO Archives].

**LAKE**, Clare County: the village began as a depot on the Pere Marquette Railroad, named Lake Station, in 1877; Charles Howard Bates, the railroad agent, became the first postmaster on Feb. 28, 1877, with the office named Crooked Lake, after the lake it lay beside; on March 11, 1909, the name of this village in Surrey Township was shortened to just Lake [W. T. McLane, PM; PO Archives; GSM 1883].

**LAKE**, Kent County: John Farnham became the first postmaster of this hamlet on March 24, 1857, the office operating until only Jan. 22, 1858 [GSM 1860; PO Archives].

**LAKE**, Newaygo County: this sawmill settlement, known also as Shantyville and as Ashland, was given a post office named Lake on March 19, 1869, with Rensselaer Brace as its first postmaster; the office was closed on Sept. 14, 1870, but was restored from Dec. 7, 1871, to Oct. 31, 1908 [GSM 1879; PO Archives].

**LAKE ALONE**, Cass County. See Howardville.

**LAKE ANGELUS**, Oakland County: the village was founded by a group of men including Elmer E. Gallogly, Charles Staff, Fenn J. Holden, Charles Roehm, Neil C. McMath and Hiram L. Walton; in the 1920s, for reasons thought to have been religious, Mrs. Sollace B. Collidge was chiefly instrumental in having the name changed from Three Mile Lake (no combination of its dimensions totaled three miles and it was not three miles from any particular place); incorporated as a village in 1929 [Robert W. Hodge, Short History of Lake Angelus, 1958].

**LAKE ANN**, Benzie County: in 1862, A. P. Wheelock became the first settler here beside the lake which was named after his wife, the lake giving its name to the village; a station on the M. & N.E. Railroad in 1888; Elijah Ransom became its first postmaster on Jan. 30, 1891; incorporated as a village in 1892; nearly burned out in 1897, rebuilt, but nearly burned out again in 1914 [PM; MPH 31:102 1901].

**LAKE BREWSTER**, Grand Traverse County: this lake and post office in Mayfield Township were named for Charles E. Brewster who built his store beside the one and became the first postmaster of the other on Sept. 9, 1887, the office operating until Sept. 21, 1893 [GSM 1889-95; PO Archives].

**LAKE CITY**, Bay County. See West Bay City.

**LAKE CITY**, Ionia County. See Richmond's Corners.

**LAKE CITY**, Missaukee County: Daniel Reeder built the first log cabin beside Muskrat (now Missaukee) Lake in 1868, and he became the first postmaster of Reeder on Jan. 22, 1872; by a one vote margin it was chosen the site of the county seat in 1873; a station on the Grand Rapids & Indiana Railroad; it was renamed Lake City on Jan. 25, 1877; platted and incorporated as a village in 1889 and as a city in 1932 [PO Archives; Harvey E. Bouwknegt].

**LAKE CORA**, Van Buren County: a station on the T. & S.H. Railroad; Charles O. Scovill became the first postmaster of this resort village on June 2, 1887, succeeded by railroad superintendent John Ihling in 1888; the post office was closed on Dec. 31, 1903, but was restored from May 18, 1908, to Aug. 31, 1913 [GSM 1889; PO Archives].

**LAKE ELIZABETH**, Oakland County. See Elizabeth Lake.

**LAKEFIELD**, Saginaw County: pioneer settler Herbert C. Fessenden was elected the first supervisor when Lakefield Township was organized in 1875; storekeeper Henry Hintermann became its first postmaster on July 15, 1892, the office operating until Sept. 14, 1903 [Mills; PO Archives].

**LAKE GEORGE**, Clare County: a station on the Toledo, Ann Arbor & Northern Michigan Railroad; the village began as a lumber settlement; it was founded by George Lake in 1880 and named for him; lumberman Edward J. Roys became its first postmaster on Dec. 8, 1999 [Lula Seats, PM].

**LAKE GOGEBIC**, Ontonagon County: the lands of the Gogebic Mining Company, organized in 1853, were near here; this village beside Lake Gogebic was given a station on the Duluth, South Shore & Atlantic Railroad; its first post office, opened on Nov. 19, 1891, was named Ballentine after its first postmaster, Harvey H. Ballentine; when storekeeper Alfred C. Hargrave became the postmaster on Jan. 13, 1911, the office was renamed Korelock, and with him still the postmaster, it was renamed Lake Gogebic on Oct. 11, 1918; Gogebic (accented on its middle syllable) was derived from the Indian word agogebic, of disputed meaning [Stevens; GSM 1893-1919; PO Archives].

**LAKE GROVE**, Emmet County: Edwin A. Morford became the first postmaster of this summer resort on Bear Lake, 7 miles from Petoskey, on May 11, 1896; the post office spelling was Lakegrove, and the office operated until only Sept. 25, 1897 [GSM 1895; PO Archives].

**LAKE HARBOR**, Muskegon County: this village in Norton Township was first called Black Lake when settled about 1856; when the mouth of Black Lake was widened and renamed Lake Harbor, the village took the name too; Daniel Upton became the first postmaster of Lake Harbor on March 2, 1871; the office was closed on July 31, 1882, but was restored on July 1, 1899; a station on the Chicago & Western Michigan (now Pere Marquette) Railroad by 1884; Black Lake is now Mona Lake and Lake Harbor a resort community [GSM 1873; Page; PO Archives].

**LAKE JUNCTION**, Lake County: a station on the Grand Rapids & Indiana Railroad, 9 miles north of Reed City, in 1894 [GSM 1965].

**LAKE LaGRANGE**, Cass County. See LaGrange.

**LAKELAND**, Livingston County: named from its location in a land of lakes; Louis A. Saunders became its first postmaster on May 28, 1903 [Blinn; PO Archives].

**LAKE LEELANAU**, Leelanau County: in 1867, Mr. A. DeBelloy sunk a well here, hoping to strike oil, but secured a flow of artesian water instead; located at the narrows of Carp Lake, it was first called Le Naro; given a post office as Provement on May 10, 1871, with William Horton as its first postmaster; the name is said to have been derived from improvement; the village and its post office, with Paul Plamondon as postmaster, were renamed Lake Leelanau on March 31, 1924; Leelanau was Indian for delight of life [Dickinson; Sprague; GSM 1873; PO Archives].

**LAKE LINDEN,** Houghton County: first settled in 1851; the Beasley brothers, Alfred and James, opened a public house here in 1853; the village was the outgrowth of the Calumet & Hecla mining interests, their stamp mills locating here in 1867; Prosper Robert became the first postmaster of Lake Linden on June 23, 1868; a station on the Hancock & Calumet Railroad; first called Torch Lake from its location near the head of Torch Lake, it was renamed from the linden trees lining the lake; incorporated as a village in 1885 [Ethel K. Turner; PO Archives].

**LAKE MARGRETHE,** Crawford County. See Rasmus.

**LAKE MICHIGAN BEACH,** Berrien County. See Hager Shores.

**LAKE MILLS,** Van Buren County: this rural post office in Bloomingdale Township was named from its location in a region of lakes (more than 20) and sawmills; Nathan Baker became its first postmaster on Dec. 8, 1855; on April 16, 1872, the office was moved to and renamed Gobleville, now Gobles [Ellis; PO Archives].

**LAKE MINE,** Ontonagon County: here in Greenland Township the Belt Mine, opened in 1848, was taken over by the Belt Mines Company in 1882; it failed, and a part of its land was bought by the Lake Copper Company in 1905; the settlement was given a post office named Belt on Feb. 8, 1908, with Henry O. Flint as its first postmaster; with Mrs. Louise H. Mack as postmaster, the office was renamed Lake Mine on March 15, 1910, and operated until Aug. 31, 1939; C. H. Mack was the railroad agent at its station on the Copper Range Railroad [Jamison; Sawyer; GSM 1911; PO Archives].

**LAKE ODESSA,** Ionia County: Humphrey R. Wager, a capitalist from Ionia and Stanton, developed the Russell Settlement into the village of Bonanza, which he so named because he saw great promise for it; Horace F. Miner became its first postmaster on May 17, 1880; when the Pere Marquette (now C. & O.) Railroad came through, the village was moved about a mile southwest and renamed Lake Odessa, as was its post office on Aug. 10, 1880; incorporated as a village in 1889; named after Odessa Township and its three lakes, Jordan, Tupper, and August, all named for early settlers [Marjorie Hershiser; Schenck; PO Archives].

**LAKE ORION,** Oakland County: John Wetmore and Judah Church (nearby Judah Lake was named for him) made the first land entries in the area in 1819; a power dam, built in 1828, united several small lakes and formed the present mile-wide lake; the settlement was first called Canandaigua for and by the settlers who had come here from the Canandaigua, N.Y., area; the village was first platted as Canandaigua City by James Stillson in 1836; but when it was given a post office the townspeople chose Orion "because it was short, handy to write, and altogether lovely"; James Decker became its first postmaster on June 30, 1834; the office was renamed Oakland on May 11, 1842, but was later closed; on June 28, 1854, the New Canandaigua post office was transferred here and renamed Orion; incorporated as the village of Orion in 1859; its post office was renamed Lake Orion on March 25, 1926, and by popular vote the village took the same name in 1929 [Grace Wilson; Seeley; GSM 1838; PO Archives].

**LAKE ORION HEIGHTS**, Oakland County: unincorp. village, suburb of Lake Orion, q.v. [Columbia Ency.].

**LAKE POINT**, Berrien County: a summer resort with a station on the St. Joseph and Paw Paw Lake Electric Railway; Alice M. Baker became its first postmaster on July 26, 1909 [GSM 1911; PO Archives].

**LAKEPORT**, St. Clair County: in 1837, Jonas H. Titus platted Milwaukie City at the mouth of a small stream which he named Milwaukie Creek; the plat was not recorded, and it remained a paper city until lumberman B. C. Farrand had the village replatted by David Ward in August, 1853, and recorded it as Lakeport on Aug. 30, 1858; this village in Burtchville Township was given a post office on June 19, 1857, the office operating until April 30, 1911; Mr. Farrand named it from its nearness to Lake Huron [Jenks; Andreas; PO Archives].

**LAKE RIDGE**, Lenawee County: Henry Darling became the first postmaster of this hamlet in Macon Township on Sept. 5, 1851, the office operating until April 25, 1898 [GSM 1860-99; PO Archives].

**LAKE ROLAND**, Houghton County. See Twin Lakes.

**LAKE SHORE**, Antrim County: Calvin C. Cutler became the first postmaster of this rural post office on Feb. 7, 1876, the office operating until May 17, 1881 [PO Archives].

**LAKE SHORE**, Macomb County: formerly a hamlet on the shores of Lake St. Clair, in Erin Township; Henry Vernier became its first postmaster on March 30, 1899, succeeded by storekeeper Frank G. Defer in 1900, the office operating until May 31, 1904; the site was a part of the Vernier farm and the name is still retained locally in Vernier (Eight Mile) Road; when St. Clair Shores was incorporated as a village in 1925, Lake Shore became a part of it [GSM 1901; Mich Manual; PO Archives].

**LAKESIDE**, Berrien County: John W., James, and Joseph Wilkinson, brothers and natives of Virginia, built a pier and a sawmill here in 1854; when the Chicago & Western Michigan (now Pere Marquette) Railroad came through in 1858, the place was given a station named Wilkinson; because of the alleged southern sympathies of the Wilkinsons in the Civil War, it is said that the post office department frowned on the name for its post office and the name Lake Side was adopted from its location on Lake Michigan; John S. Gibson became its first postmaster on June 23, 1874, with the spelling changed to Lakeside since June 11, 1894 [Fox; Chauncey; PO Archives].

**LAKESIDE**, Macomb County: projected about 1900, chiefly by Pittsburgh capitalists who anticipated making it a lake port for Mount Clemens on L'Anse Creuse Bay; it did not achieve much more than an electric interurban connection with that city [Eldredge].

**LAKESIDE,** Muskegon County: in 1867, the firm of Shupe, Haines & Weymouth built a mill here on Muskegon Lake; in 1868, John W. Moon (who was elected to congress in 1892) and Alexander V. Mann, as A. V. Mann & Company, bought the mill and operated it until 1889; the village of Lakeside, which grew up around it, was absorbed by the city of Muskegon in 1889; its post office had been named Ryerson for Martin Ryerson, a distinguished pioneer in the area (there was at the time another Lakeside post office in Michigan); Albert W. Fowler became its first postmaster on May 10, 1881, the office operating until Jan. 28, 1890 [MPH 28:359; Page; PO Archives].

**LAKESIDE FARM,** Antrim County. See Snowflake.

**LAKE STATION,** Clare County. See Lake.

**LAKE SUPERIOR LOCATION,** Marquette County. See Ishpeming.

**LAKETON,** Luce County: a whistle stop on the Duluth, South Shore & Atlantic Railroad, some two miles west of McMillan, in a lake region, in Columbus Township; storekeeper John M. Carr became its first postmaster on March 11, 1902, the office operating until May 15, 1913 [Newberry News; PO Archives].

**LAKETON,** Muskegon County: this township was set off from Muskegon Township in 1865, with S. A. Brown as its first supervisor; it is surrounded by lakes on all but its north side and has a three-mile lake within its borders; Clark W. Storrs became its first postmaster on Jan. 3, 1879; the office was transferred to and renamed North Muskegon on April 20, 1881; the Laketon post office was re-established on April 6, 1883, but operated until only April 18, 1883 [Page; PO Archives].

**LAKETOWN,** Allegan County: Aaron Neerken and James Rutgers, with their families, became the first settlers here in 1847; the town was organized in 1859 and named from its location in a lake district [MPH 17:562 1890].

**LAKE VALE,** Alpena County: a farming settlement in Long Rapids Township in 1879 [GSM 1881].

**LAKEVIEW,** Montcalm County: the village was first settled in 1858, and platted in 1867 by Albert S. French, a New Yorker; originally an Indian camp site, he named it from its location on the west bank of Tamarack Lake; Hiram S. Barton became its first postmaster on Oct. 7, 1867; a station on the Chicago, Saginaw & Canada Railroad in 1879; incorporated as a village in 1881 [Dallas Lincoln; PO Archives].

**LAKE VIEW PARK,** Cass County: located on the northwest shore of Eagle Lake; platted and recorded by Cora M. Stryker in 1899; chiefly a summer resort [Glover].

**LAKEVILLE,** Oakland County: founded and named by Sherman Hopkins in 1830; he found here the location for water-power which he sought; it was the first white settlement in Addison Township, which had been named for pioneer settler Addison Chamberlain; Mr. Chamberlain became its first postmaster on Nov. 15, 1836, succeeded by George Larzelier in 1838; the village was platted in 1840 [Mrs. Dan Haddrill, PM; PO Archives].

**LAKEWOOD**, Alpena County: founded as a summer resort subdivision on East Long Lake, about 1912 [Fred R. Trelfa].

**LAKEWOOD**, Emmet County: John R. Neilan became the first postmaster of this rural post office on April 8, 1903, the office operating until May 31, 1910 [PO Archives].

**LAKEWOOD**, Monroe County: an unincorporated village, named from its location on Lake Erie [Columbia Ency.].

**LAKEWOOD CLUB**, Muskegon County: founded by the Mayo brothers in 1912; the lot owners association named it from its location amid lakes (it is on Fox Lake) and woods; W. Laddyslaw Sajowski became its first postmaster on Aug. 1, 1914, with the office open only in the summer, but during World War II, it was made an all-year post office, until it was closed on Oct. 25, 1963; its depot, Lakewood Station, on the Pere Marquette Railroad, is three miles distant [Sophia Vejr, PM; PO Archives].

**LAMB**, St. Clair County: a station on a branch of the Port Huron & Northwestern Railroad, in Wales Township, in 1883; the settlement formed around the lumber mill and the flour mill of J. A. Lamb, and was named for him; Byron M. Jenne became its first postmaster on March 3, 1884, the office operating until April 30, 1942 [GSM 1889; PO Archives].

**LAMBERTVILLE**, Monroe County: this village in Bedford Township was founded by John Lambert in 1832, and named for him; given a post office named West Erie (from its location in Erie Township) on June 13, 1834, with William Dunbar as its first postmaster; the office was renamed Lambertville on Jan. 15, 1836; it was closed on March 25, 1865, but was restored from Dec. 4, 1865, to date [Wing; PO Archives].

**LAMB'S CORNERS**, Lapeer County. See Dryden.

**LAMONT**, Ottawa County: in 1833, Harry and Zine Steele settled here on the banks of the Grand River, in Tallmadge Township; it became known as Steele's Landing and was given a post office of that name on Jan. 9, 1851, with Reuben Reynolds as its first postmaster; in 1851, the Steeles platted the village as Middleville, from its location midway between Grand Rapids and Grand Haven, but its post office remained Steele's Landing; in 1855, the offer of Lamont Chubb, of Grand Rapids, of a road scraper in exchange for renaming the village for him was accepted, and the village and its post office were renamed Lamont on July 2, 1856 [Henry C. Slaughter; Page; PO Archives].

**LAMOTTE**, Sanilac County: Enos Johnson became the first settler in the area about 1858, followed soon by James Moore; the settlement was given a post office named Newman, after Alexander Newman who became its first postmaster on July 19, 1860; the office was closed on Dec. 16,

1864, but was restored on Jan. 9, 1866; Lamotte Township was organized in 1870, and the Newman post office was renamed Lamotte on Sept. 7, 1870; the office was closed on July 8, 1886, but was restored from July 28, 1866, to June 30, 1906 [Chapman; PO Archives].

**L'ANCE**, Houghton County. See Keweenaw Bay.

**LANE**, Ogemaw County. See Lupton.

**LANESVILLE**, Lenawee County. See Hudson.

**LANESVILLE**, Tuscola County. See Millington.

**LANGPORT**, Gratiot County: farmer Frederick G. Biddlecom became the first postmaster of this rural post office in the northeast corner of Lafayette Township on March 1, 1899, the office operating until Oct. 31, 1902 [Tucker; PO Archives].

**LANGSTON**, Montcalm County: the John Green Company built the first sawmill here in 1851-52; it failed, and one of the buyers of the property was Edwin Breese; when he in turn failed, his foreman, Daniel Lang, went into the hotel business here which so prospered that when Henry M. Caukins platted the village it was named for Mr. Lang; Mr. Caukins became its first postmaster on Sept. 10, 1868, the office operating until Aug. 15, 1907 [Schenck; PO Archives].

**L'ANSE**, Baraga County: what began as an Indian mission, founded by the French Jesuit René Ménard, in 1660, later became the site of the Methodist mission; Peter Crebassa opened a trading post here in 1837 and became the first postmaster on July 2, 1866; in 1871, on the completion of the Marquette, Houghton & Ontonagon Railroad, the office was removed to the new village site, which still retained the name L'Anse; the village was platted by S. L. Smith, Charles H. Palmer and James Bendry in 1871; incorporated as a village in 1873; from its location it had been given the French name for the bay [Sawyer; PO Archives].

**L'ANSE CREUSE**, Macomb County. See St. Clair Shores.

**LANSING**, Ingham County: government land purchases were made in the area from 1835 by James Seymour, Frederick Bushnell, and Isaac and William H. Townsend; within the present city limits, Jerry and William Ford platted and recorded Biddle City in 1836, a paper city; Jacob F. Cooley purchased land here on Nov. 2, 1837, and built the first permanent dwelling; the township, formed in 1841, was named by Joseph H. North, Jr., after his native Lansing, Tompkins County, N.Y., which in turn had been named for John Lansing, New York Revolutionary War hero and legal light; in 1847, the legislature voted to locate the state capitol in this township and to name the site Michigan; thus, from April 27, 1847, to April 20, 1848, its name and post office were Michigan, Mich.; George W. Peck was its first postmaster; the legislature renamed the village Lansing, after its township, in 1848; incorporated as a city in 1859 [Darling; Foster; Cowles; PO Archives].

**LANSING RESORT**, Emmet County. See Harbor Point.

**LAPEER**, Lapeer County: early French traders in the area noted the rocky bed of its river, and thus the village which developed around the site where Alvin N. Hart and his family settled on Nov. 11, 1831, came to be known as the stone (in French, La Pierre; in American adoption, Lapeer); the Pontiac Mill Company built a sawmill here on Farmers Creek also in 1831; Jonathan R. White, who came in 1833, platted and recorded the village as Whitesville in 1834, but it was replatted and renamed Lapeer in 1836; it was given a post office named Lapeer on July 3, 1833, with Dr. Minor Y. Turrill as its first postmaster; the office was renamed Whitesville on Jan. 11, 1834, but was changed back to Lapeer on May 3, 1836; incorporated as a village in 1858 and as a city in 1869 [Page; GSM 1860; PO Archives].

**LAPHAM'S CORNERS** Washtenaw County: Joseph Lapham settled here in Salem Township in 1828 and this hamlet was located on his land [Beakes; Chapman].

**LAPHAMVILLE**, Kent County. See Rockford.

**LAPORTE**, Midland County: this village on Swan Creek, in Ingersoll Township, was given a post office as Lee's Corner, after a local landowner, on Jan. 26, 1874, with Curtis J. Winslow as its first postmaster; the office was renamed Laporte on April 6, 1895, and operated until Jan. 31, 1910 [Blinn; PO Archives].

**LARAMIE**, Chippewa County: this rural post office, 7 miles southeast of Sault Ste. Marie, was named for Albert Laramie, who was appointed its first postmaster on Oct. 18, 1906, but he declined and Mrs. Delia Laramie accepted the office on Nov. 20, 1906 [GSM 1909-19; PO Archives].

**L'ARBOR CROCHE**, Emmet County. See Harbor Springs.

**LARCH**, Chippewa County: Henry Guest became the first postmaster of this rural post office, 14 miles west of Sault Ste. Marie, on July 1, 1902, the office operating until Jan. 31, 1911 [GSM 1903; PO Archives].

**LAREDO**, Bay County. See Fisherville.

**LARKIN**, Midland County: first settled in 1876 and named for John Larkin, landowner and lumber camp operator, who petitioned the supervisors to establish the township, which they did in 1879; storekeeper Frank E. Burton became its first postmaster on Aug. 14, 1900, the office operating until Jan. 15, 1907 [Kathryn Cummins; PO Archives].

**LARKS LAKE**, Emmet County: the first settlers, Nicholas and Peter Goldsmith, John Gales and Nicholas Dusseldorf, came here about 1890, and called it Round Lake; but due to the superfluidity of Round Lakes, it was renamed Larks Lake, for Alexander Lark, a pioneer landowner, and he became its first postmaster on Oct. 27, 1900, with the office named Larks; the office operated until Oct. 31, 1905 [Bruno Zulkiewski; PO Archives].

**LARKTON**, Emmet County: this rural post office was named for B.

C. Lark who became its first postmaster on July 3, 1888, the office operating until July 9, 1890 [PO Archives].

**La ROCQUE**, Presque Isle County: when the Detroit & Mackinaw Railroad came through here in 1895, this was a flag station, named for the boss of the working crew, Mr. R. La Rocque; a depot was built in 1908; the station was closed and the depot torn down in 1959, but it remains a flag stop [W. T. Yake].

**LA SALLE**, Monroe County: founded by Mr. Vallequette in 1831; named for two brothers named LeSelle; given a post office as LaSalle in April, 1832, with Martin V. Withington as its first postmaster; the office was closed on Dec. 5, 1833, but has been restored since May 21, 1834 [Melvin E. Lietzke, PM; PO Archives].

**LATHROP**, Delta County: when the Chicago & Northwestern Railroad line from Escanaba to Negaunee was completed in 1865, some of the construction workers remained here and formed a settlement which was first called Centerville; on Dec. 16, 1873, it was given a post office and renamed for Azel Lathrop, the local agent of the railroad and the first supervisor when the township of Maple Ridge was organized earlier the same year; Daniel M. Sheldon was its first postmaster and the office operated until Aug. 10, 1945 [Delta Reporter, Sept. 1, 1965; L. S. Altobello; PO Archives].

**LATHRUP VILLAGE**, Oakland County: although her parents owned most of the property originally, Louise Lathrup, a successful real estate developer, is credited with being the founder of Lathrup Village in 1926; she wed Charles D. Kelley, real estate editor of the Detroit News, in 1929, and together they developed the village; incorporated as a city in 1953; Veld E. Blue became its first postmaster on April 20, 1856, the office operating until March 13, 1964 [Frank C. Derby; PO Archives].

**LATTIN**, Oceana County: this village in Elbridge Township was named for storekeeper Horace E. Lattin who became its first postmaster on Oct. 28, 1897, the office operating until Sept. 30, 1910 [GSM 1899; PO Archives].

**L'AUNCE**, Alger County: a depot and settlement of the American Fur Company, on Grand Island, in 1838 [GSM 1839].

**LAUREL**, Sanilac County: storekeeper Lester J. Billings became the first postmaster of this rural post office on March 3, 1891, the office operating until Aug. 31, 1905 [PO Archives; GSM 1893-1907].

**LAURIUM**, Houghton County: the original village was platted by the Laurium Mining Company (Laureium, in Attica, a district of ancient Greece, was a famed mining site,–there silver, here copper); incorporated by the supervisors as Calumet in 1889; reincorporated and renamed Laurium in 1895; Thomas Buzzo became its first postmaster on Feb. 28, 1895, the office operating until Dec. 31, 1935, when it became a branch of the Calumet post office [PM; PO Archives].

**LAWNDALE**, Saginaw County: a station on the Pere Marquette Railroad, in Kochville Township; on Dec. 15, 1891, it was given a post office as Ohman, named after its first postmaster, William Ohman; the office was renamed Lawndale on Jan. 20, 1892, and operated until April 30, 1903 [GSM 1893-1905; PO Archives].

**LAWRENCE**, Van Buren County: founded in 1835 by John Allen who named it Mason after Governor Stevens T. Mason; Mr. Allen did not record his plat of the village and by 1843, it had become known as Brush Creek from the stream running through it; in 1844, by foreclosing on the mortgage given by Mr. Allen, John R. Baker owned most of the village; he replatted it, had his plat recorded, and renamed it Lawrence after the township; the Weston post office was transferred here and renamed Lawrence on April 17, 1844; incorporated as a village in 1869, and re-incorporated in 1879 [Mrs. Louis Longcore; Rowland; GSM 1860; PO Archives].

**LAWSON**, Marquette County. See Dukes.

**LAWTON**, Van Buren County: to get the Michigan Central Railroad to put a station on his land, Nathan Lawton gave it ten acres for a depot in 1848 and had the village platted in 1849. It was called Paw Paw Station or South Paw Paw (it was four miles south of the village of Paw Paw), but when Andrew Longstreet became its first postmaster on March 15, 1851, he had it named after Mr. Lawton, and the depot and the village also took the name; incorporated as a village in 1858 [Mich Hist 39:130 1955; Ellis; PO Archives].

**LAWTONVILLE**, Branch County: platted as a village in the late 1830s and named for the man who owned the land; it was poorly located and never became more than a paper town; its lots were sold sight unseen to easterners who, when they came to get what they had bought, realized that they had been duped [Johnson].

**LAYTON CORNERS**, Saginaw County: this, the village of Maple Grove Township, was also called Layton's Corners; it was first settled by Joseph Voith in 1854 and was named for a local landowner; Albert Kless became its first postmaster on May 16, 1878, the office operating until Aug. 31, 1907 [Mills; PO Archives].

**LAYTON'S CORNERS**, Jackson County: L. J. Layton built the first store here in 1868 and another in 1877, and the hamlet took his name [John Deball].

**LEATHEM**, Menominee County. See Arthur Bay.

**LEATON**, Isabella County: attorney John C. Leaton settled in Mount Pleasant in 1871 and also engaged in real estate and lumbering operations throughout the county; this village, named for him, was given a post office on March 1, 1880, with William Allenbaugh as its first postmaster; a station on the Pere Marquette Railroad; the village was platted by the firm of Leaton & Upton (J. C. Leaton and A. B. Upton) in 1886 [PO Archives; Fancher].

**LEAVITT**, Oceana County: the first settler in the area was Hazen Leavitt in 1864, followed by David Lampson and John Henning in 1865; Leavitt Township was formed from the east half of Elbridge Township in December, 1866 [Royal].

**LEBANON**, Clinton County: Norton H. Beckwith became the first postmaster of this rural post office, named after its township, on July 11, 1844; the office was closed on Oct. 16, 1845, later restored, but closed again on Jan. 10, 1881 [GSM 1883; PO Archives].

**LE BARON**, Genesee County: this rural post office was named for Charlie L. LeBaron who became its first postmaster on June 30, 1900, the office operating until April 30, 1902 [PO Archives].

**LEE**, Allegan County: Thomas Scott came in as a hunter in 1844 but remained until 1858; Thomas Raplee came as a settler in 1858 and when the town was organized in 1859, it was evidently named for him, its first supervisor; David J. Dorkey, sawmill owner at Black River Station, became its first postmaster on Aug. 20, 1877 [MPH 17:563 1890].

**LEE CENTER**, Calhoun County: in 1835, Amos Hadden and Nicholas Stanley became the first settlers here; Lee Township was organized in 1840, and the town took its name from it [Gardner].

**LEELANAU**, Leelanau County: storekeeper John O. Plank, Jr., became the first postmaster of this rural post office on South Fox Island, in Lake Michigan, on March 17, 1905; the office was renamed Fox Islands on March 11, 1909; Leelanau was so named at the suggestion of Henry R. Schoolcraft and was Indian for delight of life [GSM 1907; Dunbar; PO Archives].

**LEER**, Alpena County: this rural settlement in Long Rapids Township was named after Leer, Norway, by its Norwegian settlers; John Carl Alfsen became its first postmaster on March 27, 1901, the office operating until April 10, 1935 [George R. Trelfa; PO Archives].

**LEESBURG**, St. Joseph County: this rural post office was named for Joel L. Lee who became its first postmaster on June 23, 1876, the office operating until Jan. 30, 1904 [PO Archives].

**LEE'S CORNER**, Midland County. See Laporte.

**LEESVILLE**, Wayne County: English-born John and Esther Aspinwall Cooper settled here in 1853; he opened a brickyard on his farm in 1854 and supplied the material for the building of much of the early village; Thomas G. Scott became its first postmaster on May 2, 1872; the office was closed on Jan. 4, 1876, but was restored from Aug. 2, 1876, to Feb. 2, 1885, and from Jan. 12, 1886, to April 8, 1896, when the village was absorbed by the city of Detroit; it was located in the present Gratiot-Conner area; in some records as Leeville [Burton; PO Archives].

**LEETSVILLE**, Kalkaska County: when the Grand Rapids & Indiana Railroad was coming through here in Rapid River Township, A. B. Leet, general passenger agent, bought land for resale to start the village named for him; David Nimmo became its first postmaster on April 30, 1875, the office operating until Dec. 31, 1954 [Traverse; PO Archives].

**LEGARE,** Cass County: this the first post office in Mason Township was located on the farm of Moses McKessick; Ezra Hatch became its first postmaster on March 8, 1844, the office operating until Dec. 16, 1847 [Mathews; PO Archives].

**LEGRAND,** Cheboygan County: a station on the Detroit & Mackinaw Railroad, in Koehler Township; Leslie Wright became its first postmaster on Aug. 5, 1901, succeeded by W. Johnston in 1902 [GSM 1903; PO Archives].

**Le GRAPH,** Wayne County: a substation of the Dearborn post office; named from a contraction of its location, the intersection of Lehigh Street and Telegraph Road.

**LEHTOLA,** Marquette County. See Dukes.

**LEIGHTON,** Allegan County: it was first settled by tavern-keeper and merchant Lucius A. Barnes in 1837; George W. Barnes and William Logan engaged in lumbering here in 1839; the town was organized in 1848, with George Lewis as its first supervisor; Charles Furber became its first postmaster on July 29, 1854; the office was closed on May 16, 1859, but was restored from Oct. 12, 1861, to Feb. 8, 1869 [MPH 17:562 1890; PO Archives].

**LEISURE,** Allegan County: Henry Overhiser first settled here in Casco Township in 1861 and with his sons, Charles Henry, Lonson Marion, and William Albert, were among its foremost developers; this hamlet, named for the Leisure family, pioneer settlers, included a general store and a United Brethren church; Samuel M. Leisure became its first postmaster on April 29, 1892, the office operating until March 31, 1903 [Thomas; GSM 1893; PO Archives].

**LEITCH,** Sanilac County: John T. West became the first postmaster of this rural post office on May 5, 1886, the office operating until March 31, 1903 [PO Archives].

**LELAND,** Leelanau County: it lies just south of an old Indian village called Shemacopink; the first white settler, Antoine Manseau, from Manistee, built his home here in 1853; lumberman John I. Weber became the first postmaster on Sept. 7, 1857, holding the office until June, 1861; the count seat since 1882; the name lee land (from stormy seas,–the quarter toward which the wind blows,–it is quite exposed to winds from the north) became Leland [Amalia M. Kropp; Sprague; PO Archives].

**LELAND,** Washtenaw County. See Emery.

**LEMON LAKE,** Manistee County: a station on the Manistee & Northwestern Railroad, near Lemon Lake, in Marilla Township, in 1884; the Yates post office was transferred to and renamed Lemon Lake on April

21, 1902, the office operating until Feb. 29, 1904 [GSM 1895-1905; PO Archives].

**LEMONT,** Van Buren County. See Glendale.

**LE NARO,** Leelanau County. See Lake Leelanau.

**LENAWEE,** Hillsdale County: Hillsdale County was a part of Lenawee County when mill owner Hiram Kidder platted this village in 1834; Dudley Worden became its first postmaster on April 18, 1836; the office was changed to Osceola, Hillsdale County, on Dec. 5, 1838, moved to its twin village of Keene on Sept. 27, 1841, and then changed to Pittsford on Jan. 30, 1846 [Vivian Lyon Moore; Pen Phil 7:3 Jan 1957; Hogaboam; PO Archives].

**LENAWEE JUNCTION,** Lenawee County: Lenawee is said to have been the Shawnee word for Indian; others say the French coined the word, it meaning sluggish, referring to the River Raisin running through the area; Lenawee Junction was named by 1864 from its being the crossing point of the Jackson branch and the main line of the Lake Shore & Michigan Southern Railroad; Thomas Bennett became its first postmaster on Oct. 22, 1877 [Whitney; GSM 1873; PO Archives].

**LENGSVILLE,** Bay County: a station on the Michigan Central Railroad, in Fraser Township; the settlement formed around the lumber mill of the P. L. Sherman & Company; Henry C. Mansfield became its first postmaster on March 25, 1892, the office operating until March 31, 1911 [GSM 1893; PO Archives].

**LENNON,** Shiawassee County: the village was founded by Peter Lennon, Sr., who got the Grand Trunk Railroad through here and its depot built here; he built a grain elevator, and other businesses followed; it was in Clayton Township, Genesee County, when he became its first postmaster on July 6, 1880, but was transferred to Shiawassee County on Feb. 2, 1889 [Elizabeth M. Smith; GSM 1881; PO Archives].

**LENOX,** Macomb County. See Richmond.

**LEO,** Baraga County: a station on the Duluth, South Shore & Atlantic Railroad, 12 miles south of L'Anse, in 1918 [GSM 1919].

**LEON,** Gratiot County: a post office opened on April 14, 1879, to accomodate the lumber interests here in eastern Elba Township at the time; Horatio G. Tyler became its first postmaster; the office was closed on Feb. 8, 1883, but was restored, with Mrs. Ira Marriott as postmaster, on Aug. 3, 1883, and operated until Feb. 18, 1887 [Tucker; PO Archives].

**LEONARD,** Mecosta County. See Big Rapids.

**LEONARD,** Oakland County: founded by Leonard Rowland in 1882 and named for him who donated the Rowland Hall to the community; the Pontiac, Oxford & Northern Railroad came through here in Addison Township in 1882, and the Trombley post office was moved a mile and a half north to the station here and renamed Leonard on Dec. 22, 1884; incorporated as a village in 1887 [Seeley; GSM 1887; PO Archives].

**LEONI**, Jackson County: in 1830, Joseph H. Otis, from Vermont, settled on the village site with his two step-sons, Zimri and Isaac Barber; on June 26, 1837, a post office was opened in the home of Moses P. Crowell, a mile east of the village; J. H. Goodale platted the village in 1834; its post office operated until April 15, 1908 [DeLand; Eunice Ballard; PO Archives].

**LEONIDAS**, St. Joseph County: first settled by George Mathews and family, from New York City, in 1831; the settlement located on Nottawa Creek was given a post office as Fort Pleasant (ancient fortifications were unearthed in the township), with Connecticut-born Isaac G. Bailey as its first postmaster, on April 20, 1836; the office was moved to the village site, first platted by E. G. Terry in 1946, and renamed Leonidas on Feb. 21, 1850; named by lawyer Niles F. Smith after an ancient king of Sparta; Leonidas Center, a village without a post office, was located in the same township [Everts; Cole; GSM 1860; PO Archives].

**LEOTA**, Clare County: Arthur E. Rhoden became the first postmaster of this rural post office, 12 miles northwest of Harrison, on June 15, 1899 [GSM 1901; PO Archives].

**LeROY**, Calhoun County. See East LeRoy.

**LEROY**, Genesee County: a village from 1837 to at least 1860, on the Thread River, then a mile and a half from Flint, and now within its city limits [GSM 1838, 1860].

**LeROY**, Ingham County. See Webberville.

**LEROY**, Lenawee County: a hamlet of Palmyra Township in 1837 [GSM 1838].

**LeROY**, Osceola County: when the Grand Rapids & Indiana (now the Pennsylvania) Railroad was being built through here in 1871, James E. Bevins, W. W. and Charles G. Westfall, Samuel L. Kimball, James M. Brown and H. C. Booth chose this site for engaging in business; the village was platted by James E. Bevins, its founder, in 1872; Samuel L. Kimball became its first postmaster on Jan. 3, 1872; incorporated as a village in 1883; named after its township which had been named for LeRoy Carr, a land agent representing the federal government in the area [Neil Lindquist; Chapman; PO Archives].

**LES CHENEAUX ISLANDS**, Mackinac County: les cheneaux, in French the channels, has been corrupted locally as the Snows; on some maps it appears as Chenos, Chenoux, etc.; their Indian name, Shebawononing, also means channels; Rev. D. J. Piret established a mission here in 1850; given a post office as Cheneaux, with Frank J. Haynes becoming its first postmaster on Jan. 26, 1885, the office operating until March 16, 1888; on June 26, 1899, they were given a post office as Les Cheneaux, with Milo Melchers as the postmaster, succeeded by Rose S. Melchers on

July 7, 1903; the office was changed to Islington on April 30, 1927, and operated until Oct. 30, 1951 [Mich Hist 22:289 1938; Federal; PO Archives].

**LESLIE**, Ingham County: Elijah Woodworth built his log cabin here in 1836; the place was first called Meekersville for pioneer settler Benjamin Meeker; the name was changed to Leslie by Dr. A. J. Cornell for a Leslie family in his native eastern New York; Henry Fiske became its first postmaster on Jan. 11, 1841; incorporated as a village in 1869 [Mich Hist 15:230 1931; Foster; PO Archives].

**LESTER**, Branch County: Aaron C. Hall became the first postmaster of this rural post office in Algansee Township on March 6, 1879, the office operating until March 31, 1903 [PO Archives].

**LESTERVILLE**, St. Clair County: it began as a mill settlement about 1866 and was first called Lester's Mills; from its location on the Belle River it was also known as Belle River and was given a post office of that name on March 28, 1867, with Ginley Lester as its first postmaster, the spelling being changed to Belleriver on Jan. 9, 1895, and the office closed on Jan. 30, 1904, but the village of Lesterville remains [GSM 1879-1905; PO Archives].

**LETSON**, Isabella County. See Brinton.

**LEUTZ**, Saginaw County: Francis M. Cobb became the first postmaster of this sawmill settlement in Brant Township on Nov. 28, 1879, the office operating until June 30, 1903 [GSM 1881; PO Archives].

**LEVEL PARK**, Calhoun County: unincorp. village (including Oak Park), a suburb of Battle Creek [Columbia Ency.].

**LEVERING**, Emmet County: this village in then Egleston Township was founded in 1882 as a way station on the Grand Rapids & Indiana Railroad and first named Leverington after Joshua Levering; the name was shortened to Levering and it was given a post office on Feb. 15, 1883, with James Heany as its first postmaster [PM; PO Archives].

**LEVINGTON**, Clare County: a way station on a branch of the Pere Marquette Railroad in 1884; it was also called Levington Siding [GSM 1885].

**LEWIS**, Calhoun County: Samuel Ribbet became the first postmaster of this rural post office on April 19, 1836, the office operating until only July 11, 1837 [PO Archives].

**LEWIS**, Genesee County: a settlement on the Flint River around the flour mill and general store of Frank G. Lewis who became its first postmaster on May 17, 1899, the office operating until April 20, 1902 [GSM 1901-03; PO Archives].

**LEWIS**, Mackinac County. See Caffey.

**LEWISTON**, Montmorency County: a station on the Michigan Central

Railroad; this settlement on the east shore of East Twin Lake, in Albert Township, formed around the mill and general store of the Michelson & Hanson Lumber Company; druggist Frederick L. Barker became its first postmaster on April 25, 1892; named after Lewiston, N.Y. [Mich Hist 16:387 1932; Powers; GSM 1893].

**LEXINGTON,** Sanilac County: the first actual settler was John Beebe; he sold out to Reuben Simons in 1838; the settlement which formed was first called Greenbush; in 1842, Samuel W. and William Monroe bought and platted a part of it as Monrovia; the two parts were given a post office as Lexington on Jan. 20, 1846, with Mark Carrington as its first postmaster; it was in St. Clair County until Sanilac was organized in 1848; incorporated as a village in 1855; named by Reuben Diamond whose wife was a cousin of Ethan Allen who had fought at Lexington [Chapman; PO Archives].

**LIBERTY,** Jackson County: in 1835, Moses Tuthill became the first settler in the township which was organized in 1837; Jesse Bivins proposed the unanimously adopted name, believed to have been prompted by Patrick Henry's "Give me liberty or give me death"; given a post office named Montgomery on April 13, 1837, with Franklin Pierce as its first postmaster; the office was renamed Liberty on Jan. 19, 1839, and operated until March 31, 1903 [John Deball; DeLand; Interstate; PO Archives].

**LIBERTY CHURCH,** Cass County. See Jeffersonville.

**LIBERTY MILLS,** Jackson County: this settlement in Liberty Township was made about 1864; see Liberty for the name [Interstate].

**LICKLEY'S CORNERS,** Hillsdale County: this village in Wright Township was first called Wood's Corners for pioneer settler David Wood who became its first postmaster on April 17, 1848, the office operating until Aug. 2, 1862; the village was renamed for the Lickley family, early settlers, in 1873, and given a post office as Lickley's Corners on June 23, 1874, with Henry A. Camp as its postmaster; the office was closed on Sept. 22, 1883, but was restored from Oct. 28, 1884, to Feb. 28, 1901; not now a village, just four corners [Vivian Lyon Moore; GSM 1867; PO Archives].

**LIGHTON,** Berrien County: a station on the Milwaukee, Benton Harbor & Columbus Railway; this settlement on the St. Joseph River, in Oronoko Township, formed around the saw mill of William Light who became its first postmaster on April 2, 1900, the office operating until Feb. 15, 1902 [GSM 1901-03; PO Archives].

**LILLEY,** Newaygo County: the village was founded in 1844 as a station on the Chicago & Western Michigan (now Pere Marquette) Railroad, by the Sisson & Lilley Lumber Company (George E. Sisson and Francis Lilley), of Grand Haven; Edward Keets became its first postmaster on May 22, 1884 [Harry L. Spooner; PO Archives].

**LIMA,** Wayne County. See Nankin Mills.

**LIMA CENTER**, Washtenaw County: William C. Lemmon made the first land purchase here in 1825 but did not settle on it until 1830; Samuel Clements bought his land later in 1825 and settled on it at once; on Feb. 12, 1833, Asa Williams became the first postmaster of Mill Creek, the name by which the village was known until it was platted in 1838; the office was renamed Lima on May 2, 1834; the Mill Creek post office was restored as a private office on Sept. 29, 1834, and operated until April 28, 1836; the Lima post office operated until Aug. 15, 1901; Lima Center was named from its location in the township, which had been named by Oliver L. Cooper [Chapman; PO Archives].

**LIME CREEK**, Lenawee County: Calvin L. Rogers became the first postmaster of this rural post office on April 11, 1840, the office operating until Nov. 6, 1843; when it was restored on March 25, 1986, with Roy Gallup as its postmaster, the office name was spelled Limecreek, and it operated until Aug. 15, 1903 [PO Archives].

**LIME ISLAND**, Chippewa County: early French maps call this island in the St. Mary's River Isle de Platre (Plaster Island); the first settler of record was Joseph Kemp, who arrived about 1848, and engaged in the lime business; Francis O. Davenport became its first postmaster on Oct. 6, 1891; the office was closed on Sept. 12, 1892, but was restored from Nov. 4, 1913, to Nov. 15, 1939 [Mich Hist 22:285 1938; PO Archives].

**LIMESTONE**, Alger County: first settled in 1889; John H. Johnson became its first postmaster on Oct. 12, 1892; named from the limestone bed of Johnson Creek which runs through it [PM].

**LIMINGA**, Houghton County: this hamlet, 7 miles northwest of Houghton, was given a post office on Dec. 26, 1908, with Abel Johnson as its first postmaster [GSM 1911; PO Archives].

**LINCOLN**, Alcona County: the village was first settled as a lumber mill site in 1885 and from its location 7½ miles west of Harrisville it was named West Harrisville; given a station on the Detroit, Bay City & Alpena Railroad in 1886; platted in 1886 and recorded in 1887; William C. Reynolds became its first postmaster on April 28, 1887, with the office renamed Lincoln on June 24, 1899; incorporated as a village in 1907 [Powers; GSM 1901; PO Archives].

**LINCOLN**, Berrien County. See Glenlord.

**LINCOLN**, Huron County: first settled by John H. Prevorse in 1865; the township was organized in 1877, in the home of George Collins, with Desire Filion as its first supervisor; named for Abraham Lincoln [Gwinn].

**LINCOLN**, Kalamazoo County. See Vicksburg.

**LINCOLN**, Mason County: when Charles Mears built a dam and a mill here about 1850, it was called Black Creek; by 1854, the lake and the settlement were known as Little Sauble (with Mr. Mears becoming its first postmaster on March 17, 1855), and the larger lake, five miles south, where he had also begun developments, as Big Sauble; by 1861, both were thriving villages; when Mr. Mears, an admirer of Abraham Lincoln, was a Michigan state senator in 1861, he had the name Little Sauble changed to Lincoln, on March 23, 1861, and the name Big Sauble changed to Hamlin, for Hannibal Hamlin, Lincoln's vice president; Lincoln was the county seat until it was moved to Ludington in 1872; its post office was closed on April 16, 1891, for the clearing off of the timber and the collapse of the dam were making Lincoln a ghost town [C. E. Mears; Mich Hist 28:498 1944; PO Archives].

**LINCOLN LAKE,** Kent County: a flag station on the Toledo, Saginaw & Muskegon Railroad, in Oakfield Township, by 1898; given a post office on July 16, 1901 [GSM 1903; PO Archives].

**LINCOLN PARK,** Wayne County: although this area in Ecorse Township was settled by small farms from before the Civil War, it was not laid out until 1906; from its first subdivision names of Lincoln Park Subdivision, Lincoln Park Estates, Lincolnmoor, Lincolnshire, etc., the area became generally known as Lincoln Park, and that name was adopted when it was incorporated as a village in 1921 and as a city in 1925 [Lawrence M. Bailey].

**LINDEN,** Genesee County: first settled in 1835 by Richard and Perry Lamb; first platted in 1840 by Consider Warner and Eben Harris, partners in the sawmill and grist mill business; Claudius W. Thompson became the first postmaster on Sept. 23, 1851; incorporated as a village in 1871; named after the linden tree [Ellis].

**LINDEN,** Wexford County. See Haring.

**LINDERMAN'S SIDING,** Muskegon County: a small settlement around a shingle mill in Cedar Creek Township, built by W. C. Dunning & Company in 1879, and purchased by A. T. Linderman in 1880 [Page].

**LINKVILLE,** Huron County: this hamlet on the Pigeon River, in Grant Township, was founded in 1870, and was first called Kilkenny; it was given a post office of that name on Dec. 19, 1879, with Henry D. Hyser as its first postmaster, the office operating until Jan. 9, 1883; the office was restored on Jan. 31, 1887, and renamed Linkville, for Mr. Link, a homesteader, on Sept. 16, 1893; this office was closed on April 30, 1906, but was restored again from Sept. 5, 1907, to Nov. 15, 1913 [Hey; GSM 1885; PO Archives].

**LINNVILLE,** Presque Isle County: William Sims became the first postmaster of this rural post office on May 25, 1895, the office operating until only Aug. 16, 1895 [PO Archives].

**LINWOOD,** Bay County: the village began in 1872 as a depot called Terry's or Terry's Station on the Mackinaw division of the Michigan Central Railroad, and was named for James G. Terry, head of the local lumber firm of Terry, Seely & Company; he became the first postmaster of Terry Station on Feb. 21, 1872, succeeded by E. Mahlow Parsons on July 10, 1873; the office was closed on Feb. 16, 1874, but was restored on July

6, 1877; at the suggestion of James Tyne, a village leader, the name was changed on June 28, 1882, to Linwood, from a combination of the words line and wood: it lay on the dividing line between Kawkawlin and Fraser Townships, and it was heavily wooded; its railroad station was renamed Linwood Park [Marguerite Moore; GSM 1873-83; PO Archives].

**LISBON**, Kent County: first settled by John Pintler, who came here from New York State in 1846, and he became the first postmaster, with the office named Pintler's Corners, Ottawa County, on Dec. 30, 1847; the office was changed to Lisbon, Kent County, on Oct. 21, 1859, and operated until Oct. 15, 1912; incorporated as a village in 1869 [Dillenback; PO Archives].

**LISBON**, Monroe County: in 1837, a village on the Saline River, in London Township [GSM 1838].

**LISKE**, Presque Isle County: founded about 1880 and named for Joseph Liske, a prominent pioneer settler in Pulawski Township; on some early maps as Liske Station [Advance].

**LITCHFIELD**, Hillsdale County: first settled by Samuel Riblet and Henry Stevens in 1834; platted by Hervey Smith and his son David Lewis Smith, and recorded as Smithville, in 1836; Hervey Smith became its first postmaster on Feb. 3, 1837, with the office named Columbus, and it was renamed Litchfield on Aug. 12, 1837; Mr. Stevens had it renamed after Litchfield, Conn., whence some of the early settlers had come; incorporated as a village in 1877 [Vivian Lyon Moore; MPH 33:736 1903 PO Archives].

**LITTLEFIELD**, Emmet County: it was first settled by Civil War veterans and their families, and was named after its township; Joel E. Gray became its first postmaster on Dec. 10, 1878, the office operating until Sept. 30, 1909 [Mrs. Frank Blanchard; PO Archives].

**LITTLEFIELD LAKE**, Isabella County. See Farwell.

**LITTLE GIRL'S POINT**, Gogebic County: the site of an old Indian village, its white settlement began with Elias Fink in 1889; the various Indian legends accounting for its naming are recounted by Norman Bunker and Victor Lemmer in Mich Hist 38:169-73 1954.

**LITTLE HARBOR**, Schoolcraft County: this sawmill settlement on Lake Michigan, in Thompson Township, was given a post office on Feb. 18, 1888, with Alfred A. Tracy as its first postmaster; the office was closed on Oct. 31, 1888, but was restored from June 9, 1906, to May 14, 1910 [GSM 1889-1911; PO Archives].

**LITTLE LAKE**, Marquette County: the village was first settled in 1863 around the mill and general store of the Cheshire Iron Manufacturing Company, and its station on the Chicago & Northwestern Railroad was first called Cheshire Junction; the village, from its nearness to Little Lake was first called Little Lake, but it was given a post office named Forsyth, after its township, with Ira Clark as its first postmaster, on Oct. 20, 1877, but on March 1, 1966, the post office name too was changed to Little Lake; the township had been named for O. F. Forsyth, general agent for the pioneer mining firm in the area [Sawyer; PO Archives].

**LITTLE LAKE**, Monroe County: William S. Tuttle became the first postmaster of this hamlet in Bedford Township on Aug. 11, 1873, the office operating until Dec. 30, 1879 [GSM 1875; PO Archives].

**LITTLE POINT SABLE**, Oceana County: Joseph M. Sammons settled here in Benona Township on the Lake Michigan shore in 1869, built a pier for the transport of his own and other mills' products, and the place became known as Sammons' Landing, with him becoming its first postmaster on Feb. 13, 1879; the office operated here until Jan. 16, 1896; Mr. Newton built the Little Sable Point Lighthouse here in 1876, and gradually the place became known as Little Point Sable and was given a post office under that name on July 25, 1914, with Adolph Heeg as its first postmaster; it is on some maps as Little Sable Point [Royal; GSM 1881; PO Archives].

**LITTLE RIVER**, Menominee County: John P. Miller became the first postmaster of this rural post office in the southern corner of the county on March 4, 1884, the office operating until April 15, 1902 [PO Archives].

**LITTLE SABLE POINT**, Oceana County. See Little Point Sable.

**LITTLE SAUBLE**, Mason County. See Lincoln.

**LITTLE TRAVERSE**, Emmet County. See Harbor Springs.

**LIVERPOOL**, Berrien County: platted in 1836 by Major Timothy Smith, Robert Richards, E. P. Deacon and Hiram Brown; the venture failed, as did a later attempt to revive it under the name of Blooming Grove (Bloomingdale, Bloomington, on various maps); Farmer's Map of Michigan, 1853, shows it as a village; the Gazeteer of 1865 calls it the village of Blooming Grove [Fox].

**LIVERPOOL**, Macomb County: in 1856, Edgar H. Shook platted the village on L'Anse Creuse Bay, hoping to make it a port comparable to Liverpool, England; he built a dock and a hotel, but the project failed [Eldredge].

**LIVINGSTON**, Berrien County: in 1837, a village of 80 blocks was platted in Lake Township, 12 miles north of St. Joseph, on Lake Michigan, but nothing further was done to develop it, and it reverted to farmland; named for Edward Livingston, U.S. secretary of state, 1831-33; another village of the same name, some 8 miles south of St. Joseph, was given a post office on Aug. 25, 1890, with William N. Blakeman as its first postmaster, the office operating until July 31, 1912 [GSM 1838; Ellis; PO Archives].

**LIVINGSTON**, Livingston County. See Hamburg.

**LIVINGSTON CENTRE**, Livingston County. See Howell.

**LIVONIA**, Wayne County: one of its first settlers was Daniel Blue, from Oneida, N.Y., who located his claim here in 1832; Livonia Township was erected in 1834, and was named for other early settlers who came here from the Livonia, N.Y., area (the name originated as a province in western Russia); given a post office as Livonia on May 7, 1834, with James Gunning as its first postmaster; the office was transferred to and renamed Plank Road on May 20, 1851; the village was platted and recorded as Livonia City on May 20, 1836; the Livonia post office was re-established on Jan. 30, 1872, closed on Sept. 16, 1906, restored as a branch of the Detroit post office in 1952, and was made an independent office again on April 1, 1954; its 36 square miles were incorporated as the city of Livonia in 1950 [Maria W. Clark; County plat liber; GSM 1875-1907; PO Archives].

**LIVONIA CENTRE**, Wayne County: this post office in Livonia Township was opened on Aug. 28, 1849, with Daniel P. Hinson as its first postmaster; the office was closed on March 14, 1864, but was restored from April 2, 1864, to May 25, 1865; see Livonia for the name [PO Archives].

**LIVONIA STATION**, Wayne County. See Stark.

**LOBDELL LAKE**, Genesee County. See Argentine.

**LOCHMOOR**, Wayne County. See Grosse Pointe Woods.

**LOCKE**, Ingham County. See Bell Oak.

**LOCKPORT**, St. Joseph County. See Three Rivers.

**LOCK'S STATION**, St. Joseph County. See Burr Oak.

**LOCKWOOD**, Branch County: storekeeper Charles Carroll became the first postmaster of this hamlet, 5½ miles south of Coldwater, on Jan. 26, 1900, the office operating until Nov. 30, 1905 [GSM 1901-07; PO Archives].

**LOCKWOOD**, Kent County: a station on the Grand Rapids & Indiana Railroad; the census of 1870 showed that James A. Lockwood owned a mill here; Lyman H. Austin became the first postmaster on Dec. 4, 1871, the office operating until April 16, 1892 [Beuna Bailey; PO Archives].

**LOCUST**, Hillsdale County: Parmenus Cunningham became the first postmaster of this rural post office in Pittsford Township on May 23, 1892, the office operating until June 15, 1901 [GSM 1893-1903; PO Archives].

**LOCUST CORNERS**, Hillsdale County. See Pittsford.

**LODGE**, Alcona County: John Newell became the first postmaster of this rural post office on April 5, 1895; the office was closed on March 20, 1896, but was restored from May 28, 1900, to April 30, 1903 [PO Archives].

**LODI**, Kalkaska County: Orange Township was first settled by

Orange A. Row, A. P. Wheeler and Lewis Deuel, in 1871, and organized in 1872; the town was given a post office named Lodi on March 28, 1879, with Mr. Row as its first postmaster, the office operating until April 15, 1905 [Traverse; PO Archives].

**LODI**, Washtenaw County: Hugh Crestie made the first land purchase in the area in 1824, but he never became a resident; Allen Williams built the first log house here and became the first settler in 1825; Orrin Howe became the first postmaster on Aug. 29, 1827, the office operating until Feb. 3, 1856; the village (now extinct) was also known as Lodi Plains; named after Lodi in the Finger Lakes region of New York, whence many of the early settlers had come [Frances L. Pyle; PO Archives].

**LOEHNE**, Bay County: named for storekeeper Edwin Loehne who became the first postmaster of this rural post office in Beaver Township on April 20, 1894, the office operating until July 20, 1904 [GSM 1895; PO Archives].

**LOGAN**, Kent County: on March 8, 1881, this settlement in Bowne Township was given a post office named Keller for its storekeeper and first postmaster, Christian Keller; with him still in office, it was renamed Logan on Sept. 17, 1884; the office was closed on Oct. 3, 1888, but was restored from Nov. 6, 1999, to Jan. 15, 1906 [GSM 1885-1907; PO Archives].

**LOGAN**, Lenawee County. See Adrian.

**LOGAN**, Otsego County: this settlement, six miles north of Gaylord, formed around the sawmill and general store of the Yuill Brothers, John and Thomas; a station on the Mackinaw division of the Michigan Central Railroad; Joshua Lantz became its first postmaster on May 31, 1880; the office was closed on Aug. 1, 1883, and on Sept. 17, 1884, its name was given to the former Keller post office [GSM 1881-1913; PO Archives].

**LOGANSPORT**, Washtenaw County: a hamlet, two miles southwest of Saline, in 1882 [GSM 1883].

**LOMAX CITY**, Allegan County. See Wayland.

**LONDON**, Monroe County: Henry Post became the first postmaster of this rural post office on Dec. 22, 1832; London Township was organized in 1833 in the home of Abraham Hayck, with Cyrus Everett as supervisor from then until 1837; its post office operated until Feb. 15, 1905 [Wing; PO Archives].

**LONG LAKE**, Clare County: James H. Norman became the first postmaster of this rural post office, 8 miles north of Harrison, near Long Lake, on June 20, 1899; the office (spelled Longlake) operated until May 15, 1912 [GSM 1901; PO Archives].

**LONG LAKE**, Genesee County: John and Solomon Cook were probably the first settlers in this village which was platted by the former as Mount Pleasant in 1840, with an added plat by him in 1845; its name was changed to Long Lake in 1850; its post office, opened on March 6, 1851, and also named Long Lake, was transferred on March 24, 1852; the lake, after which it was named, has since been renamed Lake Fenton, and the village is extinct [Mrs. Georgia McKinley; Wood; PO Archives].

**LONG LAKE**, Grand Traverse County: Hannah, Lay & Company located the land here on the north shore of Long Lake in 1866 and built their sawmill in 1871; Benjamin H. Durga became the first supervisor when the township, also named Long Lake, was organized in 1867; its village was given a post office on Dec. 8, 1873, with Lorenzo F. Green as its first postmaster; the office was closed on Jan. 22, 1878, but was restored from March 4, 1884, to March 22, 1887 [Sprague; Page; PO Archives].

**LONG LAKE**, Iosco County: this station on a branch of the Detroit & Mackinaw Railroad was named Long Lake in 1894; but it was given a post office as Ellake, from the shape of the lake, on March 5, 1902, with Craig H. Flitecroft as its first postmaster; the office was renamed Long Lake on March 17, 1916 [GSM 1895; PO Archives].

**LONG LAKE**, Wexford County: the site of a lumber mill of William W. Mitchell and Jonathan W. Cobbs, as Cobbs & Mitchell, about 1873, on the shores of Long Lake [Mich Hist 25:238 1941].

**LONGPOINT**, Cheboygan County: a summer resort on Mullet Lake, in Burt Township, with a station on the Michigan Central Railroad; Clyde M. Aldrich became its first postmaster on April 5, 1912 [GSM 1913].

**LONG RAPIDS**, Alpena County: the township, organized in 1871, was named from the long rapids of the Thunder Bay River which runs through it; its village began around the sawmill of Albert Merrill and was also known as Merrillsville; it was given a post office as Long Rapids on Oct. 27, 1873, with John Louden as its first postmaster, the office operating until Aug. 31, 1933 [Fred R. Trelfa; GSM 1879; PO Archives].

**LONGRIE**, Monominee County: a rural settlement in Lake Township.

**LONGWOOD**, Isabella County: the village was founded in 1871 by Major James W. Long and John P. Hawkins, and named for the former; it was given a post office on Sept. 7, 1871, the office operating until Aug. 27, 1878; the Major built a small factory here in Union Township, but his village did not prosper and he moved to Mount Pleasant [Fancher; PO Archives].

**LONGSDALE**, Emmet County: Martin Cosmer became the first postmaster of this rural post office on Jan. 25, 1881, the office operating until June 1, 1883 [PO Archives].

**LOOK'S CORNERS**, Lapeer County: this hamlet in Dryden Township was named for Deacon Elijah Look who settled here in 1836 and became its first postmaster on Feb. 24, 1841; the office was changed to Dryden on Feb. 16, 1846 [Page; PO Archives].

**LOOMIS**, Isabella County: in 1871, Erastus G. Loomis, George W. Wise and E. F. Gould built a sawmill and a general store here and platted the village; a station on the Pere Marquette Railroad; its post office, named Buchtel, was opened on May 1, 1871, with Mr. Wise as its first postmaster; the village and its post office were renamed Loomis on Dec. 8, 1871; the township, organized on Jan. 24, 1872, was named Wise for its co-founder, George W. Wise [Chapman; Fancher; PO Archives].

**LOOMISVILLE**, Kent County: Andrew Loomis was a carriage maker in this village in Walker Township and he became its first postmaster on Feb. 9, 1848, the office operating until July 10, 1862 [GSM 1865; PO Archives].

**LORANGER**, Monroe County: the Loranger grist mill (now removed to Greenfield Village, Dearborn) was built on Stony Creek, near Monroe, in 1832; the scattered settlement was given a post office on Jan. 16, 1865, with Joel J. Dussean as its first postmaster, the office operating until April 26, 1869 [Bulkley; PO Archives].

**LORENZO**, Montcalm County: this rural post office was named for farmer Lorenzo D. Thomas who became its first postmaster on April 13, 1888; the office was transferred to and renamed Lincoln Lake, Kent County, on July 16, 1901 [GSM 1889; PO Archives].

**LORETTA**, Saginaw County. See Freeland.

**LORETTO**, Dickinson County: a station on the Chicago & Northwestern Railroad; the village was founded and platted by the Appleton Mining Company in 1892; Mathew E. Gleason became its first postmaster on Nov. 18, 1895, the office operating until March 31, 1964 [PM; PO Archives].

**LOTHROP**, Shiawassee County. See New Lothrop.

**LOTT**, Alcona County: a station on the Au Sable & Northwestern Railroad; farmer Eli M. Barker became its first postmaster on June 22, 1899 [GSM 1901; PO Archives].

**LOUD'S SPUR**, Alger County: a general store and a railroad siding serving the Loud-Brewster Lumber Company here in Rock River Township in 1918 [GSM 1919].

**LOUISEVILLE**, Washtenaw County. See North Lake.

**LOUISVILLE**, Leelanau County: it began as a pagan Indian settlement (most Ottawas believed in the Great Spirit; those here did not); it took the name Louisville about 1860 after a resident, Louis Kookosh (Louis the Pig); now the site of Petersen Park [Barnes].

**LOVELLS**, Crawford County: this village on the Au Sable River, in Maple Forest Township, was given a station on a branch of the Michigan Central Railroad in 1889; Mary A. B. Simms became its first postmaster on Feb. 8, 1909, the office operating until Sept. 15, 1936 [Grace L. Funsch].

**LOWE**, Clinton County: Lorenzo D. Wilson was appointed the first postmaster of this rural post office on June 1, 1895, but the office was never in operation and was discontinued on Oct. 4, 1895 [PO Archives].

**LOWELL**, Kent County: Daniel Marsac, from Detroit, built a trading post on the south bank of the Grand River in 1831; in 1847, he bought land on the north bank, platted it and named it Dansville; it was given a post office as Lowell, after its township, on June 17, 1851, with George K. White as its first postmaster; the village was replatted by Richards and Wickham in 1854 and renamed after its post office; incorporated as a village in 1861; believed to have been named after Lowell, Mass. [Dillenback; MPH 38:60 1912; PO Archives].

**LOWELL**, Lenawee County: a hamlet in Blissfield Township in 1837; it had a stage coach post office [GSM 1838].

**LOWELL**, Washtenaw County: a hamlet with a depot on the Michigan Central Railroad in 1859 [GSM 1860].

**LOWER ECKFORD**, Calhoun County. See Eckford.

**LOWER SAGINAW**, Bay County. See Bay City.

**LOXLEY**, Roscommon County: a mill and lumber camp settlement, founded by the John R. Bowman family, who named it after Loxley, England; Frank H. Kirkland became its first postmaster on Jan. 29, 1904, the office operating until about 1917 [Co. Bd. of Ed.; PO Archives].

**LUCAS**, Missaukee County: founded in 1878 by William Taylor; Harm Lucas and his five sons, together with other Dutch settlers, came in 1882, and when given a post office on Feb. 23, 1883, this village in Richland Township was named for him; Abraham Lucas was its first postmaster; the office was closed on Feb. 16, 1885, but was restored, with Peter Van den Bosch as postmaster, on Sept. 7, 1886 [William Schaaf, PM; Mich Hist 31:397 1947; PO Archives].

**LUCE**, Saginaw County: William Craig became the first postmaster of this rural post office in St. Charles Township on March 31, 1890, the office operating until Jan. 15, 1914; named for Cyrus G. Luce, governor of Michigan, 1887-90 [GSM 1891; PO Archives].

**LUCERNE**, Washtenaw County: John Renwick became the first postmaster of this rural post office on May 10, 1837, the office operating until July 6, 1853 [PO Archives].

**LUDINGTON**, Mason County: settlement of the area dates from 1847; John P. Sedam was its pioneer general merchant; David A. Melendy became its first postmaster on June 1, 1864; named for James Ludington who had large timber investments in the region; its plat was recorded in 1867; incorporated as a city in 1873; Charles Mears and Eber B. Ward were leaders in its early development [Mich Hist 25:406 1941, 35:406 1951; PO Archives].

**LULL**, Antrim County: a flag station on the Pere Marquette Railroad, in Helena Township, in 1891; Andrew Stebbins became its first postmaster on Jan. 20, 1900; the office was closed on May 15, 1901, but was restored, with Mr. Stebbins again its postmaster, on June 12, 1901, and operated until Aug. 30, 1902 [GSM 1903; PO Archives].

**LULU**, Monroe County: Ida Township was organized in 1837; Henry Y. West came to Ida in 1853, and took up forty acres of wild land at what became the village of Lulu; storekeeper Paul Nill became its first postmaster on June 29, 1880, the office operating until July 15, 1941; a station on the Toledo & Ann Arbor Railroad; believed to have been named for the daughter of an early settler [Buckley; Wing; PO Archives].

**LUM**, Lapeer County: a station on the Pontiac, Oxford & Northern Railroad; the village was founded in 1884; Elijah Vincent became its first postmaster on March 24, 1884, the office operating until Aug. 28, 1864; named by Wallace Huntley for Colonel Lum under whom he had served in the Civil War [Cora Vincent, PM].

**LUMAN**, Midland County: a rural post office at the shingle mill of Luman A. Bliss who became its first postmaster on March 27, 1896, the office operating until April 14, 1904 [GSM 1897-1905; PO Archives].

**LUMBERTON**, Newaygo County: a lumber settlement in Norwich Township, with a station on a branch of the Chicago & Northwestern Railroad; Daniel J. Reichert became its first postmaster on May 17, 1880, the office operating until Nov. 19, 1886 [GSM 1881; PO Archives].

**LUMBERTOWN**, Allegan County: this settlement in Wayland Township, founded by the Isaac Barnes family in 1841, is now farmland [Durant].

**LUNA**, Gratiot County: William V. Carothers became the first postmaster of this rural post office in Washington Township on March 2, 1858, the office operating until only June 22, 1858; Luna is Latin for moon, and the same county had a post office opened on the same day named Stella, Latin for star [Tucker; PO Archives].

**LUNA PIER**, Monroe County: this settlement on Lake Erie was given a post office on Oct. 31, 1929, with Mrs. Grace Baker as its first postmaster; incorporated as a city in 1963 [Mich Manual; PO Archives].

**LUPTON**, Ogemaw County: this village in Rose Township was first settled by several Quaker families from Ohio, including Emmor Lupton, his wife and three sons, in 1880; it was first known as Lane Heights and was given a post office as Lane on April 11, 1881, with Levi R. Lupton as its first postmaster; its depot on the Detroit, Bay City & Alpena Railroad was opened on Jan. 1, 1893; the village and its post office, located about a mile north of the original settlement, were renamed Lupton on June 8, 1893 [Mich Heritage 4:110 1962; PO Archives].

**LUTHER**, Lake County: the village was first settled and called Wilson in 1880; it was platted and renamed for B. T. Luther, the other member of the local sawmill firm of Luther & Wilson, in 1881; a station on the Grand Rapids & Indiana Railroad; Thomas Crebbin became its first postmaster on

Jan. 4, 1882; incorporated as a village in 1893 [Gary Burnett; Judkins; GSM 1883; PO Archives].

**LUZERNE,** Oscoda County: Myron B. Hagaman and his family moved here in Bay Creek Township from Luzerne, Pennsylvania, in 1881, and he became the first postmaster on Nov. 4, 1881 [Leone Sprague Whitlock, PM].

**LYLE,** Gladwin County: the first land deed recorded for this community is dated 1855 to the St. Mary's Ship Canal Company from the State of Michigan which paid for the canal partly with land; the Flint & Pere Marquette Railroad obtained its right of way here in 1888; Aaron T. Bliss, of Saginaw (and governor of Michigan, 1900-1904), built a sawmill and lumber camp here in 1891; in 1903, he sold part of the land to Fred Drake who built a house in a part of which was a store and a post office, of which he became the first postmaster on Nov. 5, 1903; the lumber camp was called Halfway (it was about midway between Beaverton and the railroad); but there was then another Halfway post office in Michigan, so this one was named Lyle by Mr. Drake after his daughter [Ritchie; PO Archives].

**LYMAN,** Kent County: Anna Scott became the first postmaster of this rural post office, four miles north of McCords, on Jan. 17, 1900, the office operating until Sept. 30, 1902 [GSM 1903; PO Archives].

**LYMBURN,** Oscoda County: a station on the Au Sable and Northwestern Railroad in 1888 [Mich Manual 1899].

**LYNDON,** Washtenaw County: it was first settled by S. B. Collins and his brother in 1833; the township was set off in 1836 and organized in 1837, with Horace Leek as its first supervisor [MPH 17:452 1890].

**LYNN,** St. Clair County: it was first settled by Daniel Alverson who had a sawmill here in 1840; lumberman Alfred A. Dwight, who became the first supervisor when the township was organized in 1850, had it named after his foreman, Edward J. Lynn; Rollin A. Smith became its first postmaster on Dec. 21, 1852, the office operating until Jan. 31, 1901 [Jenks; Andreas; PO Archives].

**LYON,** Oakland County: in 1832, the legislature named the township for Lucius Lyon, a member; Hiram Goodspeed became its first postmaster on June 9, 1834; the office was renamed Kensington on Sept. 5, 1836, and operated until July 31, 1902 [Seeley; PO Archives].

**LYON LAKE,** Calhoun County: Chauncey Sibley became the first postmaster of this rural post office on April 29, 1857, the office operating until Oct. 22, 1859 [PO Archives].

**LYON MANOR,** Roscommon County: named for Charles Lyon, a local hotel proprietor and property developer; Anton W. Elgas became its first postmaster on Aug. 12, 1910. the office operating until Jan. 1, 1960 [GSM 1911; PO Archives].

MONROE
Young Ladies Seminary & Collegiate Institute

MONROE CO.
Star Bending Factory

**LYON TOWN HALL,** Roscommon County: Charles Lyon, a local resort hotel man, subdivided the property in 1902, and began the village [Ruth L. Buck].

**LYONS,** Branch County. See Coldwater.

**LYONS,** Ionia County: it was originally the site of the Indian village of Chigaumishkene; the first white settlers were H. V. Libhart and family, from Naples, N.Y., in 1833; on Feb. 24, 1836, Lucius Lyon wrote Edward Lyon: "The place is called Arthursburg . . . but we will change the name . . . I own the whole town site . . . It will become one of the most important towns in Michigan"; platted on both sides of the Grand River and recorded as Lyons by Lucius Lyon on Nov. 26, 1836; Truman H. Lyon became its first postmaster on Dec. 31, 1836; incorporated as a village in 1859; its township was organized as Maple in 1837, but was renamed Lyons in 1840 [MPH 27:481 1896; GSM 1839; Dillenback; PO Archives].

**LYONS,** Lenawee County: the land here on the east side of the River Raisin, in Blissfield Township, was located by George Giles in 1826; after opening an inn, he platted a village and named it Lyons [Bonner].

**LYON'S LAKE,** Calhoun County: Solomon Platner became the first postmaster of this rural post office near Lyon Lake on Feb. 15, 1836, succeeded by Caleb Hanchett on Nov. 13, 1841 [GSM 1838; PO Archives].

**LYON'S MILLS,** Clinton County: this settlement in Bengal Township formed around the sawmill of Charles W. Lyon and he became its first postmaster on June 27, 1867, the office operating until Feb. 23, 1882 [Ellis; PO Archives].

**McBAIN,** Missaukee County: this sawmill settlement in Riverside Township was founded in 1887 by Gillis McBain; its station on the Toledo, Ann Arbor & Northern Michigan Railroad and its post office, opened on Aug. 27, 1888, with storekeeper George W. Hughston (or Heughston) as its first postmaster, were both named Owens; but they were renamed McBain for the founder on Sept. 17, 1889; incorporated as a village in 1893 and as a city in 1907 [Stout; GSM 1889; PO Archives].

**McBRIDES,** Montcalm County: named for Alexander B. McBride, a native of Wayne County, N.Y., who built a sawmill here in Day Township in 1874; the railroad station was named McBride's Mill, while the post office, opened on March 26, 1878, with Mr. McBride as its first postmaster, was named McBrides; platted by D. L. Jacobs in 1877; Phipps Waldo platted the adjacent village of Custer on April 2, 1878, but it became a part of McBrides when that village was incorporated in 1883 [Schenck; PO Archives].

**McCAMLY PRAIRIE,** Calhoun County: named for the first settler here in Burlington Township, Eleazer McCamly, who came with his large family from New York in 1832 [Mich Hist 33:117 1949].

**McCARGO'S COVE,** Keweenaw County. See Minong.

**McCARRON,** Chippewa County: named for David McCarron, an early homesteader; John McCarron became its first postmaster on Dec. 19, 1892 [Hamilton; PO Archives].

**McCASKILL,** Bay County: this rural post office was named for Thomas McCaskill who became its first postmaster on June 13, 1900, the office operating until March 15, 1901 [PO Archives].

**McCLURE,** Gladwin County: a lumber town, named for William C. McClure, a large landowner in the township; it dates from about 1883 and had a post office in its general store, with James H. Campbell becoming its first postmaster on Feb. 18, 1883; few of its buildings still stand [Ritchie; PO Archives].

**McCLURE'S,** Saginaw County: a station on the Cincinnati, Saginaw & Mackinaw Railroad, six miles south of Saginaw, in 1894 [GSM 1895].

**McCOLLUM'S,** Berrien County: a flag sation on the St. Joseph Valley Railroad in 1884 [GSM 1885].

**McCORDS,** Kent County: this settlement in Cascade Township was founded on the stage line between Hastings and Ada in the 1850s; it was given a station when the Detroit, Lansing & Northern Railroad came through in 1888; Charles Freyermuth became its first postmaster on Oct. 26, 1888, the office operating until Oct. 31, 1947; originally called McCord, its depot and post office were named McCords [Mich Hist 17:147 1933; PO Archives].

**McCOY'S CREEK,** Berrien County. See Buchanan.

**McCOY'S MISSION,** Kent County: the succeeding city of Grand Rapids is designated as McCoy's Mission on Young's Map of Michigan, 1835, though this Baptist Indian mission, opened by Rev. Isaac McCoy in 1823, was short lived [MPH 22:484 1893].

**McCOY'S SIDING,** Wexford County: the site of a lumber mill of William W. Mitchell and Jonathan W. Cobbs, as Cobbs & Mitchell, about 1873, along the shores of Clam (now Cadillac) Lake [Mich Hist 25:238 1941].

**McDONALD,** Alger County. See Youngs.

**McDONALD,** Delta County: a hamlet in 1872 [GSM 1873].

**McDONALD,** Van Buren County: the village was platted and recorded as Deerfield by Henry Goss and James J. Clark in 1871; but there was then another Deerfield post office in Michigan and this one was given a post office as McDonald on Feb. 28, 1872, with Mr. Goss as its first postmaster; in 1874, he gave the Chicago & Western Michigan (now Pere Marquette) Railroad right of way if they would build a depot and make a daily stop here; he was said to have been a farmer who wore no shoes from spring till fall and local tradition says the railroad first named the station Barefoot; its post office was closed on Dec. 31, 1954, and the depot was torn down about 1958, but the village remains, in the county records as

Deerfield, on most maps as McDonald [Glenn W. Smiley; Rowland; PO Archives].

**McDONALD'S SIDING**, Osceola County. See Orono.

**McDONOUGH**, Saginaw County: William L. Crofoot became the first postmaster of this rural post office, nine miles from Chesaning, on Aug. 8, 1892, the office operating until June 30, 1903 [GSM 1893-1907; PO Archives].

**McDOUGAL'S LANDING**, Alcona County. See Greenbush.

**MacDOUGALVILLE**, Macomb County. See Utica.

**MacFARLAND**, Marquette County. See Turin.

**McGEE**, Kalkaska County: named for Thomas McGee, a walking boss for the Mitchell Lumber Company when the Manistee & North Eastern Railroad laid their line through here in 1900-01; except for two potato warehouses, it was and is only a railroad crossing [T. J. Fisher].

**McGINN**, Alcona County: this village in Mitchell Township was founded by the Crowell brothers in 1915; with Mrs. Celia Crowell as its first postmaster, a post office was opened on their farm on McGinn Creek (from which the village was named); the office was opened on Dec. 14, 1922, and operated until June 30, 1939 [Dorothea Galbreath; PO Archives].

**McGLONE CORNERS**, Tuscola County. See Watrousville.

**McGRAW'S**, Bay County: a station on the Bay City division of the Pere Marquette Railroad in 1878 [GSM 1879].

**McGREGOR**, Sanilac County: the village was founded by Adam McGregor in 1859, and named for him; a station on the Pere Marquette Railroad; storekeeper James Powers became its first postmaster on Sept. 19, 1894, the office operating until April 30, 1958 [PM; GSM 1895; PO Archives].

**McGULPIN POINT**, Emmet County: this site at the northern tip of the county was named for Alexander McGulpin, a widely known fisherman in the area from 1855 [Mich Hist 10:87 1926].

**McIVOR**, Iosco County: the Detroit, Bay City & Alpena Railroad station here in Sherman Township was named Arn, after John Arn, the local grocer; but its post office, opened on Sept. 11, 1882, was named for its first postmaster, James McIvor; the office operated until April 15, 1955 [GSM 1883; PO Archives].

**McKAINS CORNERS**, Kalamazoo County: this hamlet, on some maps as McKain Corners, was named for Martin McKain who had bought most of the land in the area in 1835, including that of the adjacent hamlet of Pavilion [Gardner; Durant].

**McKEE'S CORNERS**, Kalamazoo County: the site was named for

David McKee, pioneer farmer and nurseryman, here on Indian Fields in Portage Township [Durant].

**McKEEVER**, Ontonagon County: named for R. T. McKeever, general manager of the Copper Range Railroad Company in 1899, which, as a subsidiary of the Copper Range Company, helped promote and develop the local copper industry [Stevens].

**McKENNEY'S PRAIRIE**, Cass County: named for pioneer settler here in LaGrange Township, Thomas McKenney, spelled McKinney in Blois Gazeteer, 1838-40 [Mich Hist 33:118 1949].

**McKENZIE'S PORT**, Lenawee County: a settlement on the west shore of Devil's Lake, named for original landowner Charles M. McKenzie, from Vermont, in 1834 [Bonner].

**McKESSON**, Mackinac County: Ruth Simons became the first postmaster of this rural post office in Marquette Township on April 5, 1916 [GSM 1917; PO Archives].

**McKINLEY**, Oscoda County: the settlement formed around the works of the J. E. Potts Salt & Lumber Company and was given a post office as Potts on June 3, 1886, with Jeremiah D. Hunt as its first postmaster, succeeded by the president of the company, Albert J. Potts, in 1888, the H. M. Loud & Sons Lumber Company bought the mill machinery, railroad equipment, timber and lands of the defunct Potts firm in 1891 and developed the Potts headquarters into a thriving lumber town; the Potts post office was renamed McKinley on Jan. 28, 1892; soon after 1900, the railroad repair shops burned, and lack of timber did not warrant their rebuilding; the post office was closed on Sept. 30, 1913, and McKinley became a ghost town [Otis; GSM 1889-93; PO Archives].

**McKINNEY'S PRAIRIE**, Cass County. See McKenney's Prairie.

**McKINNEY'S STATION**, Wayne County. See Elmwood.

**McLANE**, Newaygo County: a lumber settlement with a station on a branch of the Chicago & Western Michigan (now Pere Marquette) Railroad; lumberman Alexander Reid became its first postmaster on Sept. 11, 1882, the office operating until Aug. 17, 1886 [GSM 1883-87; PO Archives].

**McLAREN LAKE**, Oceana County. See Hesperia.

**McLEAN'S**, Newaygo County: this settlement in Bridgeton Township was named for John W. McLean who became its first postmaster on May 3, 1898, the office operating until May 31, 1909 [GSM 1899; PO Archives].

**McLEOD'S CORNER**, Luce County: born in Canada in 1859, Daniel N. McLeod came to the Upper Peninsula pine forest in 1885 and became both a lumberman and a hotel-keeper for lumbermen [Mich Hist 30:59 1946].

**McMASTER'S CORNERS**, Clinton County. See Union Home.

**McMILLAN**, Luce County: the village was founded with the coming through here of the Duluth, South Shore & Atlantic Railroad in 1881, and was named for James Stoughton McMillan, an executive of the road, and later a U.S. senator; storekeeper Lewis Pearl became its first postmaster on April 21, 1882; it was then in Chippewa County and was transferred to Luce in 1887 [Roby Brown, PM].

**McPHEE**, Montmorency County: a station on the Alpena & Northern (now Detroit & Mackinaw) Railroad, 50 miles west of Alpena, in 1894 [GSM 1895].

**McPHERSONVILLE**, Macomb County. See Fraser.

**McSORLEY**, Alpena County: this rural post office, 13 miles southwest of Alpena, was named for John McSorley who became its first postmaster on Oct. 31, 1891, the office operating until Nov. 6, 1893 [GSM 1893; PO Archives].

**McVILLE**, Chippewa County. See Mackville.

**MABLE**, Grand Traverse County: a lumber settlement at a station on the Chicago & Western Michigan (now Pere Marquette) Railroad; Adelbert Fairbanks became its first postmaster on Aug. 25, 1892; named for the daughter of Thomas T. Bates, pioneer newspaper publisher [Barnes; GSM 1893; PO Archives].

**MACATAWA**, Ottawa County: Macatawa was the Ottawa word for black, and the water of nearby Lake Macatawa was very dark before the government cut the canal to Lake Michigan; in some records Macatawa Lake is called Black Lake, and on the village plat, which was recorded in 1836, it is referred to as Black River Lake; the village did not develop, and about 1850, it became a settlement for religious purposes fostered by Protestant missionaries; its station on the Chicago & Western Michigan (now Pere Marquette) Railroad is named Macatawa Junction; in 1885, more than 200 cottages were built here and it is now a non-religious resort; stationer William Van Regenmorter became its first postmaster on May 9, 1896 [A. J. Tazelaar, PM; Lillie; PO Archives].

**MACEDAY LAKE**, Oakland County: it is believed to have been named for pioneer hunter and fisherman Mason Day; it was first referred to as Mase Day's Lake, and later shortened to Maceday Lake [Ripley].

**MACK CITY**, Oscoda County: this rural post office in Long Lake Township was named for storekeeper Harrison Mack who became its first postmaster on Jan. 16, 1884, the office operating until April 5, 1892 [GSM 1885-93; PO Archives].

**MACKINAC ISLAND**, Mackinac County: from its Indian name, the French called it Michilimackinac; the claim that it was explored by Jean Nicolet in 1634 and visited by the Jesuits Claude Dablon in 1670 and Jacques Marquette in 1671 is disputed; the first permanent white settlement was made in 1780; French control passed to the English who, contrary to the Treaty of 1773, did not give it up to the U.S. until 1795; lost in the War of 1812, it was regained in 1815; with the appointment of

Adam B. Stewart as its first postmaster on April 14, 1819, it became the fourth post office in Michigan, preceded only by Detroit, Frenchtown (now Monroe), and Apple Creek; it became the county seat of Michilimackinac County in 1822; its post office was renamed Mackinac Island on May 12, 1884; the island was ceded to the State for park purposes in 1895 [Mich Hist 12:513 1928; Robinson; PO Archives].

**MACKINAW CITY,** Cheboygan County: here Jean Nicolet was sent in 1634 by Samuel Champlain to explore the country and to make peace with the Indians; it became a fur-trading post in 1673 and one of the sites of Fort Michilimackinac, 1712-1781; in 1857, Edgar Conkling and Asbury M. Searles, as trustees of the proprietors of Mackinaw lands, had the village platted by R. C. Phillips; George W. Stimson is credited with founding the present village in 1870, general storekeeper Louis J. Willets became its first postmaster on April 25, 1871; its name was shortened to Mackinaw on Nov. 22, 1894, but was restored to Mackinaw City on Dec. 19, 1935; the coming through of the Grand Rapids & Indiana Railroad in 1881 guaranteed the success of the community; incorporated as a village in 1882 [Powers; Page; PO Archives].

**MACK'S PLACE,** St. Clair County: named for Andrew Mack (1780-1854), successively deep sea captain, colonel in the War of 1812, and in 1834, mayor of Detroit; in 1792, Meldrum and Park built a sawmill here on what was called Meldrum's Creek; in 1849, Mack bought the mill, and the creek became Mack's Creek; finally, George W. Carleton bought the home of Andrew and Amelia Mack and the creek became (and still is) Carleton Creek; Mack was postmaster of Mack's Place from its founding on Jan. 5, 1849, until his death on July 19, 1854; the office was re-opened on July 28, 1854, transferred to Vicksburgh on April 24, 1855, and renamed Marysville on Dec. 28, 1858 [H. A. Hopkins; PO Archives].

**MACKVILLE,** Chippewa County: it was first settled by the McDowell and the McDonald families; it was on Pealine Road, so named because for the first few years the farmers in the area grew mostly peas; given a post office as McVille, of which William J. Scott became the first postmaster, Jan. 22, 1898, to 1911, and Robert Anderson became the second, 1911 to 1913, when the office was closed; and gone, too, its church and its school, but the McDowells and the McDonalds remain [Verna Brood, g.d. of William Scott].

**MACOMB,** Macomb County: it was founded by Daniel Kniffin, Calvin Davis, Daniel Miller and Lester Giddings; Mr. Davis became its first postmaster on March 16, 1835; the office was moved to Waldenburgh on March 29, 1860, but the Macomb post office was re-established on Dec. 19, 1860, and operated until June 15, 1904; named after the township and county which had been named for Revolutionary War General, Alexander Macomb [Leeson; PO Archives].

**MACON,** Lenawee County: in 1824, William C. Kendell, of Tompkins County, N.Y., became the first to buy government land here, followed by John Pennington in 1829; but the first actual settler was Samuel Klee in

1830; Peter Sones, another 1830 settler, built its first schoolhouse in 1832; the settlement was first called Pennington's Corners; it was given a post office as Macon on June 17, 1837, with Mr. Pennington as its first postmaster; Israel Pennington said the town took its name from the creek running through it, which had been named after an Indian chief who had lived on its banks [MPH 13:590 1888; GSM 1881; PO Archives].

**MADISON,** Lenawee County: the first settlers in Lenawee Township, Nelson and Curran Bradish, came here from New York State in 1827; the township was renamed Madison in 1838, to avoid confusion with the name of the county; while it has some industries, it is primarily rural, and is under township government [Donald L. Frazier].

**MADISON,** Livingston County: Darius Lewis became the first postmaster of this rural post office in Deerfield Township on Sept. 7, 1844, the office operating until May 5, 1903; the office "without doubt" was named in honor of ex-president James Madison [Ellis; PO Archives].

**MADISON HEIGHTS,** Oakland County: it was formed from Royal Oak Township and was named by John B. Michrina; incorporated as a city in 1955 and given a post office in 1959 [Dorothy McGuire Lents].

**MAGICIAN BEACH,** Cass County: located on the north shore of Magician Lake; it was a summer resort only until it was platted and recorded by Mr. and Mrs. Albert E. Gregory in 1901 [Glover].

**MAHOPAC,** Oakland County: located here by Mill Lake on the stage line were a steam operated mill and a general store; given a post office as Steam Mill on July 22, 1847, with Daniel T. Pierce as its first postmaster, it was renamed Mahopac on April 9, 1850; the office was closed on Aug. 25, 1860, but was restored from Aug. 15, 1861, to Dec. 18, 1871; the name, meaning pine forest, is said to have been that of an Indian chief buried on the west shore of the lake; the little plat named Mahopac was south of the lake [Lake Orion Review; PO Archives].

**MAI SOU ISLAND,** Huron County: the claim that it was named after its first settlers, the massasauga rattlesnakes, is disputed; Henry Lambly bought it from the federal government in 1868; he sold it to Joseph Chape in 1870; he in turn sold it to Adelia Jerome, and early settlers in the county called it Jerome Island; New York millionaire Herbert H. Walker bought it in 1884 and his Chinese cook named it Kate Chai; but since 1933, its only official name has been Mai Sou [Hey].

**MAIN STREET,** Berrien County: a hamlet due south of Niles in 1878 [GSM 1879].

**MALACCA,** Menominee County: the name refers to a species of tree and this was a lumbering station on the Minneapolis, St. Paul & Sault Ste. Marie Railroad in 1887 [Mich Manual 1899].

**MALCOLM,** Manistee County: a station on the Arcadia & Betsey River Railroad, in Pleasanton Township; Henry C. Johnson became its first postmaster on July 20, 1897, succeeded by storekeeper H. D. Farnsworth in 1898 [GSM 1899; PO Archives].

**MALLETT'S CREEK,** Washtenaw County: this settlement in Pitt Township was named after a nearby stream; it was given a post office named Mallett's on June 4, 1834, with Nehemiah P. Parsons as its first postmaster, succeeded by Benjamin Woodruff on June 28, 1839, the office operating until Jan. 23, 1840 [GSM 1838; PO Archives].

**MALLORY,** Hillsdale County: schoolmaster Benjamin W. Ware became the first postmaster of this rural post office in Pittsford Township on Feb. 3, 1899, the office operating until June 15, 1901 [GSM 1901-03; PO Archives].

**MALTA,** Oceana County. See Rothbury.

**MALTBYS,** Ogemaw County: the village was founded about 1888 by Alvin and Alzina Maltby who bought land here in Goodar Township and formed the Maltby Lumber Company; the town clerk, who was also secretary and general manager of the Goodar Lumber Company, Fred G. Wood, became the first postmaster on Feb. 13, 1900; a station on the Detroit & Mackinaw Railroad [Fred Litzner; GSM 1901; PO Archives].

**MALTON,** Delta County. See Rock.

**MALT'S,** Saginaw County: this village in Saginaw Township, nine miles north of the city of Saginaw, was named for the local brick maker, Solomon Malt; grocer Charles W. Spencer became its first postmaster on Dec. 10, 1897, the office operating until June 15, 1901 [GSM 1899; PO Archives].

**MANCELONA,** Antrim County: the first settler, Perry Andress, homesteaded here with his family in 1869; Leander C. Handy and A. D. Carpenter opened the first store in 1872; Mr. Handy, who bought the first lot, built the first frame building, and otherwise promoted the village, is considered its founder; a station on the Grand Rapids & Indiana Railroad; Mr. Andress became the first postmaster on March 10, 1874, and the village, which was incorporated in 1889, was named for his youngest daughter [Powers].

**MANCHESTER,** Washtenaw County: in 1833, Major John Gilbert received a grant of 400 acres and had it surveyed and platted, but did not settle on it; however, in that year, James Harvey Fargo, and his uncle, Steven Fargo, built and operated a sawmill and a grist mill here as the Manchester Mill Company; Harry H. Gilbert became the first postmaster on May 8, 1834; incorporated as a village in 1867; so named because most of its early settlers came from Manchester Township, Ontario County, N.Y. [Jane Palmer; Beakes].

**MANCHESTER PARK,** Wayne County. See Harper Woods.

**MANDAN,** Keweenaw County: in 1905, the Keweenaw Copper Company began exploring property here in Grant Township with diamond drill, followed by shaft sinking; the mine location was called Mandan (one account says for "that man Dan," Daniel Spencer, a Scottish-Irish miner from Canada); the Keweenaw Railroad ran trains from Calumet in 1907; company superintendent Arthur H. Sawyer became the first postmaster on Feb. 29, 1908; there were 12 double houses and the mine office here, but only it and one or two houses still stand [Edith Yokie].

**MANETAU**, Lenawee County. See Addison.

**MANGUM**, Marquette County: a station on the M. & S.E. Railroad; the settlement formed around the Joseph Dupra & Brothers sawmill; Lars Olson became its first postmaster on Oct. 31, 1903 [GSM 1905].

**MANHATTAN**, Keweenaw County: a copper mining location; the company was organized in 1856 and took over the old Albion property; it stopped work in 1857, resumed in 1862, and stopped permanently in 1865; its property later became a portion of the Cliff Mine [Stevens].

**MANHATTAN**, Monroe County: Daniel Chase became its first postmaster on Feb. 8, 1836; after the Michigan-Ohio boundary dispute, it was ceded to Ohio, made a part of Lucas County, and is now within the city limits of Toledo; see under Vistula for the terms of the settlement [Bulkley].

**MANISTEE**, Manistee County: the county was formed in 1840 and given the Indian name of its chief river, the name of which the Historical Society of Manistee says means spirit of the woods, referring to the sound of the winds through the forests (for other explanations of the meaning of the name, see Mich Hist 48:365-366 Dec 1964); the town was named after the county; deciding upon the site in 1840, John, Joseph and Adam Stronach built the first permanent sawmill here in 1841, thus laying the foundations of the village; Stephen Batchelder became the first postmaster on Jan. 31, 1850; the office was closed on July 23, 1851, but was restored from July 24, 1854, to date; incorporated as a city in 1869; the fire of 1871 nearly wiped it out, but another lumberman, Charles Rietz, led to its rejuvenation by successfully drilling for salt here in 1880-81 [Mich Hist 26:92 1942, 48:333 1964; Russell; PO Archives].

**MANISTEE BRIDGE**, Wexford County. See Sherman.

**MANISTEE CROSSING**, Manistee County. See Kaleva.

**MANISTEE JUNCTION**, Mason County. See Walhalla.

**MANISTIQUE**, Schoolcraft County: the village was founded in 1871 by Henry Schoolcraft who named it after the Ojibawa name for the Monistique (meaning vermillion) River, but when registered with the state, an error in spelling was made, and let stand; William M. Colwell became the first postmaster on March 17, 1873, with the office named Epsport, but changed to Manistique on Jan. 27, 1879; a station on the Minneapolis, St. Paul & Sault Ste. Marie Railroad; incorporated as a village in 1885 and as a city in 1901 [Carl R. Graves; PO Archives].

**MANITOU**, Leelanau County: North and South Manitou Islands, together with Beaver Island, formed Manitou County from 1855 to 1895, when the first two were transferred to Leelanau County and the third to Charlevoix County; there were wooding stations on North Manitou before 1843; Nicholas Pickard came in 1846 and built Pickard's Wharf in 1854; in Manitou County, Richard Kitchen became the first postmaster of South Manitou on Sept. 26, 1879, with the office transferred to Leelanau County on May 27, 1895, and closed on April 31, 1943; Daniel L. Buss became the first postmaster of the office named Buss for him on June 21, 1880, the office operating until only Nov. 8, 1881; and Miss Stella J. Platt became the first postmaster of North Manitou Island on June 15, 1888, with the office transferred to Leelanau County on May 27, 1895, and closed on Sept. 30, 1950; Manitou is the Indian for Great Spirit [Mich Hist 11:342 1927; Colyer; PO Archives].

**MANITOU BEACH,** Lenawee County: located on Devil's Lake; Manitou was the Indian word for great spirit, good or evil, and, given here, the name is believed to bear out the reason given for the naming of Devil's Lake (which see under Devil's Lake); the Pottawattomi were driven out in 1834; as the white settlement formed here in Rollin Township it was given a post office on March 20, 1889, with Columbus F. Beckey as its first postmaster; a station on the C., J. & M. Railroad [PM; GSM 1891; PO Archives].

**MANLIUS,** Allegan County: Ralph R. Mann built a sawmill here in 1844, and settlers followed, early among them Jonathan Wade in 1844, and Asa Bowker in 1845; Randall Curtis, who had a tannery here, became the first postmaster on July 22, 1846; the Chicago & Northwestern Railroad built a station here; but the post office was moved to New Richmond on Oct. 3, 1872, the mill was abandoned in 1874, and the depot was closed in 1879; believed to have been named after the town of Manlius, N.Y. [PO Archives; Johnson].

**MANNING,** Cheboygan County: this rural post office in Grant Township was named for Daniel A. W. Manning who became its first postmaster on March 19, 1884, the office operating until July 15, 1911 [GSM 1885; PO Archives].

**MANN'S,** Clare County: a station on a branch of the Pere Marquette Railroad, also called Mann's Siding, five miles south of Harrison, in 1884 [GSM 1885].

**MANSFIELD,** Iron County: the adjacent mine was developed by the Mansfield Mining Company; the village was platted in 1889 by W. S. Calhoune who had discovered ore in profitable quantities here; the railroad was extended to the site in 1890; John Erikson became the first postmaster on July 23, 1891; the waters of the Michigamme River seeped into the mine workings in September, 1893, and brought death to 27 miners; by providing a new channel for the river, the mine was later redeemed and was operated for some years by the Oliver Iron Mining Company; the post office was closed on May 15, 1913 [Jack Hill, Sr.; Stevens; PO Archives].

**MANTON,** Wexford County: the first three settlers in the area (then known as Cedar Creek) were George Manton, Ezra Harger and William Meares in 1872; Mr. Manton became the first postmaster on Jan. 3, 1873; the first plat was recorded in 1874; a station on the Grand Rapids & Indiana Railroad; incorporated as a village in 1877 and as a city in 1923; George Manton was the largest property owner and the town was named for him [Erna McBrian].

**MAPLE**, Ionia County: it was first settled by Robert Toan, with his sons, Robert, Jr., William, and Thomas, in 1837; the Maple post office was first opened in Lyons Township on July 11, 1838, with Zena Lloyd as its first postmaster, and when he moved his home here in Portland Township, he carried the office with him; the office was closed on Sept. 14, 1868, but was restored from Sept. 28, 1868, to Nov. 30, 1901; named from its location on the Maple River, it was also known as Maple Corners [Schenck; PO Archives; Branch].

**MAPLE CITY**, Leelanau County: the township was surveyed by Kasson Freeman and when it was organized in 1865, it was named Kasson for him; in the town, in 1867, a wooden shoe-peg factory was built by William Parks and J. T. Sturtevant, of Ohio, and the settlement was called Peg Town; but when they applied for a post office another name was desired and they chose Maple, for maple timber abounded here and was used to make the shoe-pegs in their factory, and thus it was given a post office as Maple City on March 9, 1875, with William H. Crowell as its first postmaster [G. K. Dechow, PM].

**MAPLE GROVE**, Barry County: the first settler in the area was Eli Lapham in 1837; the township was formed in 1846, and named by the wife of one of the early settlers from the richness of its maple groves; its village was given a post office on Feb. 19, 1851, with Joel Hyde as its first postmaster, the office operating until Nov. 30, 1910; from its location in the township, the village was also known as Maple Grove Center [Johnson; PO Archives].

**MAPLE GROVE**, Ontonagon County: the village began as an outgrowth of the mining interests surrounding it; Daniel Cavina built the first log house in it in 1850; James Burdenshaw kept the first store, platted the village, and recorded it in 1858 [Andreas].

**MAPLE GROVE**, Oscoda County: a station on the Au Sable & Northwestern Railroad in 1888 [Mich Manual 1899].

**MAPLE GROVE**, Saginaw County: first settled by Joseph Voith in 1854, Maple Grove Township was organized in 1857 [Mills].

**MAPLE GROVE**, Van Buren County. See Toquin.

**MAPLE HILL**, Montcalm County: in 1862, Dr. Daniel L. Shook, a native of Dutchess County, N.Y., settled here in Pierson Township (named for the Stephen Pierson family, pioneer settlers in the area), and became the first postmaster on April 29, 1870; the village was platted and recorded by Edward H. Jones and Caleb B. and William Price, proprietors, on Oct.

22, 1870; its post office was closed on May 24, 1893, but was restored, with its spelling changed to Maplehill, on Jan. 25, 1898, and operated until Oct. 31, 1907 [Schenck; Dasef; PO Archives].

**MAPLE ISLAND**, Cass County: this island in Magician Lake was platted and recorded in 1896 by W. F. Hoyt as president of the Maple Island Resort Association [Glover].

**MAPLE RANGE**, Oceana County: this village in Ferry Township was settled in 1858 and was given a station when the railroad came through; Mrs. Sophronia J. Mallison became its first postmaster on Sept. 14, 1874, the office operating until Sept. 5, 1878 [PO Archives; GSM 1873].

**MAPLE RAPIDS**, Clinton County: George (brother of Louis) Campau came here from Grand Rapids, began a trading post in 1826, bought land in 1832, built his home in 1835 near the rapids on the Maple River, calling the place Maple Rapids; in 1852, William A. Hewett bought the land from Solomon Moss and others; in 1853, he built a dam, a sawmill and a store, and platted the village; the plat was not recorded until the village was replatted in 1867; Mr. Hewett became the first postmaster on Feb. 24, 1857, when the Essex post office was transferred here; incorporated as a village in 1881 [Carl Bates; Daboll; PO Archives].

**MAPLE RIDGE**, Arenac County: this village on the Rifle River, in Clayton Township, was founded by Stillman Smith who came here in 1869 and owned three of the four corners at which it began; it was in Bay County when he became its first postmaster on Dec. 4, 1873; named by Mr. Smith who had lived seven years in Vermont, which leads the nation in the production of maple syrup and maple sugar [Page; PO Archives].

**MAPLE RIDGE**, Delta County. See Rock.

**MAPLETON**, Clinton County. See Duplain.

**MAPLETON**, Grand Traverse County: the Ogdens family came here from New York State about 1855 and first settled at what is now the hamlet of Ogdensburg; later, they moved some four miles south and founded Mapleton, named from the many maple trees in the area; John Garland became the first postmaster on Jan. 14, 1859, the office operating until Jan. 30, 1904 [Rev. Patrick Barrett; PO Archives].

**MAPLETON**, Iron County: located in an area of dense maple forests; a farming community and the seat of Bates Township government; storekeeper Michael Krick became its first postmaster on July 26, 1910 [Jack Hill, Sr.; PO Archives].

**MAPLE VALLEY**, Montcalm County: located on land owned by William Fitzgerald, the place was also known as Fitzgerald; he sold 80 acres to R. Kearney, who platted the village in 1872; Ambrose Atwood became the first postmaster of Maple Valley, named after its township, on March 4, 1872, the office operating until Dec. 13, 1893; for local lumberman Lucius B. Kendall, the place was also known as Kendall Mills; the village did not prosper and is now farmland [Dasef; GSM 1883; PO Archives].

**MAPLE VALLEY,** Roscommon County: the settlement here began about 1907 in the valley between two branches of Cameron Creek [Co. Bd. of Ed.].

**MAPLE VALLEY,** Shiawassee County: a rural post office in Middlebury Township was opened on Aug. 5, 1852, in the home of Ira Stimson, under the name of Hale; it was renamed Maple Valley on Dec. 11, 1855, and operated until Oct. 18, 1860 [Ellis; PO Archives].

**MAPLEWOOD,** Allegan County: Addie E. Foster became the first postmaster of this rural post office opened on the Maplewood Stock Farm, in Allegan Township, on July 17, 1899, the office operating until March 31, 1903 [GSM 1901; PO Archives].

**MAPLEWOOD,** Emmet County: Lorenzo D. French became the first postmaster of this rural post office in Bear Creek Township, opened on July 29, 1878, the office operating until Sept. 2, 1880 [GSM 1879; PO Archives].

**MAR,** Muskegon County. See Fruitland.

**MARATHON,** Lapeer County: Marathon Township was organized in 1839; about 1848, Rufus Pierson began his pine lumbering operations at what was known as the village of Marathon; it was given a post office on May 5, 1852, with Samuel H. Miller as its first postmaster, the office operating until Oct. 29, 1873; the village faded when by-passed by the railroad, and the place became known as Piersonville [Page; GSM 1860; PO Archives].

**MARBLE,** Mason County: John B. Marsh became the first postmaster of this rural post office in Eden Township on March 1, 1880, the office operating until Sept. 13, 1890 [GSM 1881; PO Archives].

**MARCELLUS,** Cass County: Harrison Dykeman became the first postmaster here on Dec. 30, 1856; the village was platted in 1870 by George W. Jones, Leander Bridge, Maria Snyder and George R. Roach who, by purchase of stock and granting of right of way, got the Peninsular Railroad to come through the middle of their plat; Flavius J. Littlejohn, then a state senator, gave the name Marcellus and, judging from his own first name, probably after the great Roman general; incorporated as a village in 1879 [Rogers; Glover; GSM 1860; PO Archives].

**MARCELLUS,** Macomb County: the site was part of the farm located in Clinton Township by Joseph Hayes in 1819; the village was platted by Green Freeman in 1838; it had a sawmill, a store, a blacksmith shop, and a few homes, but it did not prosper and became extinct by 1890 [Eldredge; GSM 1891].

**MARCELLUS CENTER,** Cass County: this hamlet was named from its location in its township; see Marcellus for the name [Rogers].

**MARENGO,** Calhoun County: the first land entries here were made by Seeley Neal, Asahel Warner, Elijah Crane, and A. Dustin, all in 1831;

the first town meeting was held in the house of Mr. Neal in 1833 and he was elected the first supervisor; they consulted on their choice of a name and came up with that of Napoleon's horse at the battle of Waterloo; James Winters became the first postmaster on June 23, 1842 [PO Archives; Everts].

**MARENISCO,** Gogebic County: this village was in Ontonagon County when founded by Alfred L. Corry, of Milwaukee, in 1886; it was platted by Edward H. Rummele, of Sheboygan, also in Wisconsin, and also in 1886; a station on the Chicago & Northwestern Railroad; Robert Fair became its first postmaster on June 4, 1886; named for the wife of E. H. Scott, a timber producer, Mary Enid Scott, taking the first three letters of her name: Mar-eni-sco [Victor F. Lemmer].

**MARILLA,** Manistee County: C. Churchill became its first settler in 1866; Marilla Township was formed in 1869 and named for the sister of one of the members of the original township board; John Brimmer became its first postmaster on Oct. 11, 1871, the office operating until June 29, 1935; a station on the Manistee & Northwestern Railroad; now more a farming community than a village [Virginia S. Stroemel; PO Archives].

**MARINE CITY,** St. Clair County: the area at the mouth of the Belle River was first called Yankee Point, having been first settled by eastern Yankees; with his wife and son, lake captain Samuel Ward came here in 1820 and built his log house on what is now the main street; the town was set off in 1822 and named Cottrellville, for county commissioner George Cottrell; it was given a post office as Belle River on Dec. 27, 1831, with Captain Ward as its first postmaster; in 1835-37, General Duthan Northrup, as agent for Ohio speculators, bought much of Belle River land and platted the village, naming it Newport; but its post office remained Belle River as there was then another Newport post office in Michigan; the legislature named it Marine in 1865, and on May 20, 1865, its post office was renamed Marine City; the legislature renamed it Marine City in 1867; incorporated as a city in 1887 [James R. Ticknor; MPH 21:336 1892; PO Archives].

**MARION,** Livingston County: although the name was suggested by Hiram Wing who had come from Marion, N.Y., it was by that town derived from General Francis Marion of Revolutionary War fame; Sardis Davis became the first resident of the area in 1834; George W. Lee became the first postmaster on March 8, 1837, with Hiram Wing succeeding him; the office was closed on Jan. 13, 1863, but was restored from June 27, 1867, to May 12, 1875; the town, which took the name of the township, remained under township government [Ellis; PO Archives].

**MARION,** Oakland County. See West Bloomfield.

**MARION,** Osceola County: this village was founded at a station of the Pere Marquette Railroad by Christopher Clarke and John Chadwick, and was named for the former's wife, Maryann Clarke; Mr. Clarke, a storekeeper, became the first postmaster on Jan. 27, 1880; incorporated as a village in 1889 [Mrs. Lon Turner; GSM 1885; PO Archives].

**MARION,** Sanilac County: a hamlet in Marion Township in 1864 [GSM 1865].

**MARION ISLAND,** Grand Traverse County: this island lies in the western arm of Grand Traverse Bay; known first as Island No. 10, one-third of it was patented to Archibald Buttars in 1864 and the rest to Daniel C. Benton in 1866; they conveyed it to Albert Bacon, from him to Walter Bacon, then to William Thomas, then in 1872 to Frederick Hall, of Ionia, who renamed it in honor of his daughter, Marion Hall (later Mrs. Fowler); she sold it in 1922 to Henry Ford and it became generally known as Ford Island [Mich Hist 11:363 July 1927].

**MARION SPRINGS,** Saginaw County: the town was named after its township of Marion, which was organized in 1880, with pioneer settler Daniel Paul as its first supervisor; sawmill owner Edward W. Fowler became its first postmaster on July 13, 1892, the office operating until Aug. 31, 1907 [Mills; PO Archives].

**MARIONVILLE,** Newaygo County. See Brunswick.

**MARK,** Clare County: Milo T. Dean became the first postmaster of this rural post office in Greenwood Township on May 31, 1877, the office operating until Aug. 29, 1887 [GSM 1879; PO Archives].

**MARKELL,** Tuscola County: it was first settled by Calvin C. Waller in December, 1836, followed by Alva Bishop in January, 1837; Franklin W. Wright became the first postmaster of Watertown, named after its township, on Oct. 20, 1860; a station on a branch of the Pere Marquette Railroad in 1883; on April 23, 1883, John H. Markell became the postmaster, and the village was renamed for him on May 11, 1883; the office operated until June 30, 1902 [MPH 10:115 1886; GSM 1883-1903; PO Archives].

**MARKEY,** Roscommon County: founded as a sawmill settlement by William Markey; Benjamin F. Robbins became its first postmaster on Aug. 22, 1905, succeeded by grocer J. K. Carrick in 1906, and later by Ida DeWit, the office operating until about 1933 [Co. Bd. of Ed.; GSM 1907; PO Archives].

**MARKS,** Iosco County: a station on the Detroit & Mackinaw Railroad, six miles southwest of Tawas City, in 1894 [GSM 1895].

**MARLBOROUGH,** Lake County: the village was founded by the Great Northern Portland Cement Company in 1902; Frederick T. Houk became its first postmaster on June 19, 1903; named from the marl, a clay and calcium carbonate, which the company took out of the lake here to make its product; but the supply of marl soon petered out, the company failed and the village vanished; its post office was closed on Aug. 31, 1907 [Mrs. L. J. Moothart; Judkins; PO Archives].

**MARLETTE,** Sanilac County: Robert Stinson became the first settler in the area in 1854; the land on which the village was built was originally owned by Benjamin Hobson, John McGill, Charles Harwack, and Robert

Wilson; Robert and John Wilson built the first grist mill in 1866 and John McGill the first sawmill in 1867; Gordon W. Rudd became the first postmaster on Nov. 3, 1866, with the office first located south of the village; in 1869, it was moved into the village with John McGill as postmaster; incorporated as a village in 1881; the maiden name of two early Irish settlers in the area was Marlett; they carved the name on a log and later an "e" was added by Mr. Rudd when he suggested the name for the town [Chapman; PO Archives].

**MARNE**, Ottawa County: Justin Walker became the first settler in Wright Township in 1839; its village of Berlin was given a post office on Sept. 23, 1852, with George W. Woodward as its first postmaster; the village was platted and recorded in 1857; it was so named because of the many German settlers in the area; but due to conflicting emotions arising during World War I, the name was changed on June 5, 1919, commemorating the Battle of the Marne, in which so many American soldiers participated; but their annual fair continued to be called the Berlin Fair [Clyle Ryan, PM; Lillie; Page; PO Archives].

**MARQUETTE**, Marquette County: located on the shore of Iron Bay (now Lower Harbor), it was popularly called Iron Bay; the village began in 1849 when Robert J. Graveraet, who had prospected the region for ore, Edward Clark, agent for Waterman A. Fisher, of Worcester, Mass., who financed it, and Amos Rogers Harlow, organized the Marquette Iron Company; on Sept. 14, 1849, Mr. Harlow became the first postmaster of Worcester, with the name changed on Aug. 21, 1850, to honor Jacques Marquette, a French Jesuit missionary; this post office was closed on Aug. 16, 1852; the Marquette firm failed, and was succeeded by the Cleveland (later Cleveland-Cliffs) Company who had the village platted in 1854; it was recorded by Peter White, who at 18 had come with Graveraet, and in time became one of the chief promotors and benefactors of the town; what is called the second Carp River post office (there was already one operating at the Jackson Location) was opened here by Mr. White, in competition with Mr. Harlow, on Oct. 13, 1851; Mr. Harlow withdrew from the field on Aug. 16, 1852, and on April 17, 1856, the Carp River post office of Mr. White was renamed (as Mr. Harlow's Worcester post office had been renamed) Marquette; incorporated as a village in 1859 and as a city in 1871 [Hatcher; Sawyer; Rankin; PO Archives].

**MARR**, Muskegon County: Governeur B. Rathbun built a sawmill here on White Lake and the settlement which developed around it was given a post office as Marr on Oct. 5, 1858, with him as its first postmaster, and he was also the township supervisor; it was then in Oceana County; the post office was closed on Dec. 8, 1862, but was restored from May 9, 1863, to April 3, 1867; named for Charles S. Marr, Muskegon political leader [GSM 1860; PO Archives].

**MARSH**, Menominee County: Mary A. Boland became the first postmaster of this rural post office on Jan. 26, 1896, the office operating until Jan. 22, 1897 [PO Archives].

**MARSHALL**, Calhoun County: settled in 1830, the village was first platted in 1831 by Sidney Ketchum, from Clinton County, N.Y.; George Ketchum became its first postmaster on Oct. 10, 1831; two of its pioneer settlers were John D. Pierce (who became its second postmaster on Aug. 5, 1833) and Isaac Crary, the fathers of the Michigan public school system; incorporated as a village in 1836 and as a city in 1859; named for U.S. Chief Justice, John Marshall [Everts; Federal; PO Archives].

**MARSHFIELD**, Mecosta County: this station in Colfax Township on the Stanton branch of the Detroit, Lansing and Northern Railroad was first named Coe, for Lt. Governor George A. Coe; on June 24, 1880, William McNaughton became the first postmaster of Coe, with the office renamed Marshfield on Feb. 13, 1882 [GSM 1883; PO Archives].

**MARSHONA**, Gogebic County: Joshua D. Veale became the first postmaster of this mining location on May 21, 1917, but there is no evidence that the office actually operated [Kenneth Priestley].

**MARSH'S CORNERS**, Jackson County: this hamlet was named after its general storekeeper, William H. Marsh [GSM 1877].

**MARSHVILLE**, Oceana County: Henry J. Marsh built a sawmill here on Stony Creek in Benona Township in 1862 and a grist mill in 1863; George M. Marsh became the first postmaster of the settlement on April 13, 1869, the office operating until Jan. 15, 1901 [Royal; GSM 1877; PO Archives].

**MARTIN**, Allegan County: the village was founded by Mumford Eldred in 1836; it was named by George Barnes, state representative from this district, for President Martin Van Buren; Abraham Shellman became its first postmaster on May 11, 1844; given a station on the Grand Rapids & Indiana Railroad; incorporated as a village in 1946 [Myron L. Newman, PM; PO Archives].

**MARTINEY**, Mecosta County. See Martiny.

**MARTINEZ**, Mecosta County. See Martiny.

**MARTINSBURGH**, Newaygo County: George H. Hubbard became the first postmaster of this rural post office on May 16, 1870; the office was transferred to and renamed Denver on July 12, 1870 [PO Archives].

**MARTINSVILLE**, Wayne County: Van Buren Township was erected in 1835 and this community was founded about 1840 to be its metropolis; Stephen Randall became its first postmaster on April 7, 1868, the office operating until Sept. 16, 1906; the town and township were named for President Martin Van Buren; the name is retained locally in Martinsville Road [Burton; PO Archives].

**MARTINY**, Mecosta County: the first settler, John Martiny, came in 1868, and the township, when organized in 1875, was named for him; Nicholas Thieson was its first supervisor; its village, a sawmill settlement on the west branch of the Little Muskegon River, had a siding on the Detroit,

Lansing & Northern Railroad; given a post office spelled Martinez, with George Shields becoming its first postmaster on Oct. 6, 1875, the office operating until March 17, 1880, and another, spelled Martiney, with William T. Brink becoming its first postmaster on May 26, 1888, this office operating until July 19, 1893 [Chapman; PO Archives].

**MARVIN**, Lenawee County: a station on the D. & L.N. Railroad; with Lowell H. Mason as its first postmaster, it was given a post office as Packard on Feb. 5, 1898, named for a pioneer settler and storekeeper in its township of Seneca, Marvin A. Packard; with Mr. Packard as postmaster, the office was renamed Marvin on June 24, 1901, the office operating until April 15, 1908 [Chapman; GSM 1899-1903; PO Archives].

**MARYSVILLE**, St. Clair County: in 1843, Edward P. Vickery bought land from Cummings Sanborn here and built a sawmill; the place became known as Vickery's Landing and later as Vicksburgh; the post office was moved here from Mack's Place on April 24, 1855, with Mr. Vickery as the first postmaster; but there was another Vicksburgh post office in Michigan, so while Timothy Barron was postmaster, on Dec. 28, 1858, the name of the office was changed to honor Mary Mills, wife of local sawmill owner Nelson Mills; incorporated as a village in 1921 and as a city in 1924 [H. A. Hopkins; PO Archives].

**MASHEK**, Marquette County: this hamlet in Wells Township was named for George Mashek, of the Mashek Chemical & Iron Company, of Escanaba, who operated in the area and had a general store here [George T. Springer].

**MASON**, Cass County: first settled by Elam Beardsley in 1830; the township, when organized in 1836, was named for Governor Stevens T. Mason [Mathews].

**MASON**, Houghton County: the village began as the Torch Lake location of the Quincy Mine and was named for its president, Thomas F. Mason; a station on the Hancock & Calumet Railroad [Mich Hist 24:96 1940].

**MASON**, Ingham County: the first settler, Lewis Lacey, came here in 1836 to build a sawmill for (Charles) Noble & Company, of Monroe; Ephraim B. Danforth, a member of the firm, located here in 1837 and became its first postmaster on May 5, 1838; Mr. Noble made and recorded the first plat of the village in 1838; it became the county seat in 1840; its name was changed from Mason Center to Mason on Nov. 10, 1842; incorporated as a village in 1865 and as a city in 1875; named for Governor Stevens T. Mason [Foster; Durant].

**MASON**, Van Buren County. See Lawrence.

**MASON CENTER**, Ingham County. See Mason.

**MASON CENTER**, Mason County. See Scottville.

**MASONVILLE**, Branch County. See Coldwater.

**MASONVILLE**, Delta County: Ferguson & Williamson, the pioneers of the town, built a sawmill here in 1850; in 1852, it passed into the hands of Richard Mason & Son, of Chicago; given a post office as Masonville on March 25, 1857, with Richard Mason as its first postmaster; the office was closed on April 17, 1858, but was restored from April 12, 1872, to Aug. 12, 1880, and from March 24, 1886, to March 31, 1858; it was the county seat from 1860 to 1864; given a station when the Soo Line came through in 1887 [David S. Coon; PO Archives].

**MASS**, Ontonagon County: in 1848, Noel Johnson, a Negro slave escaped from Missouri, discovered copper deposits here which he later sold to the Mass Mining Company; organized in 1855, the name was due to the mass copper produced by the mines in this area; the original townsite of Mass City, located about two miles west, was abandoned when Abram Mathews and his wife Nellie platted Mass in 1899; given a post office on June 15, 1899, with Christ P. Anderson as its first postmaster [Charles Willman; PO Archives].

**MASTODON**, Iron County. See Alpha.

**MASTODON MINE**, Iron County: Alfred Breitung, of Marquette, opened the Mastodon Mine in 1881; Louis Newman became the first postmaster of its settlement on Jan. 21, 1884; the office was closed on Nov. 12, 1887, but was restored from April 3, 1888, to Feb. 13, 1896; after the village of Mastodon took the name Alpha, the village of Mastodon Mine became known as Mastodon; it was in Marquette County until Iron was organized in 1885; the mastodon was a huge mammal, now extinct [Jack Hill, Sr.; PO Archives; GSM 1885].

**MATCHWOOD**, Ontonagon County: the Diamond Match Company, which owned most of the pine in the area, founded this village in 1888 to accommodate and supply their logging camps; Fred J. Hargrave became its first postmaster on April 23, 1889; a thriving village when nearly wiped out by a forest fire in 1893; rebuilt, it suffered another such conflagration in 1906 [Rudolph Stindt; PO Archives].

**MATHERTON**, Ionia County: Asaph L. Mather, Dr. Norton Beckwith and James R. Langdon built the first sawmill in North Plains Township here on Fish Creek in 1843; Asaph L. Mather platted the village in 1851, and named it for himself; his brother, Dr. William Mather, became its first postmaster on March 2, 1848, while Asaph was appointed the second in 1850, the office operating until Dec. 3, 1965 [Schenck; Branch; PO Archives].

**MATLOCK**, Midland County: Albert E. Cary became the first postmaster of this sawmill settlement on Feb. 24, 1898, the office operating until only Dec. 3, 1898 [PO Archives].

**MATTAWAN**, Van Buren County: about 1845, while the Michigan Central Railroad was being built through here, Nathaniel Chesbrough, an attorney for the road, bought 40 acres and made the first plat of the village, which he named after a village on the Hudson River, in New York; Rev. J. J. Bliss became the first postmaster on Jan. 5, 1849; the first recorded plat was made by Lyman Lawrence in 1850; Charles W. Scott made two additional plats, donated land for the depot, and otherwise developed the village [Bliss; Rowland; PO Archives].

**MATTHEWS PRAIRIE**, Kalamazoo County. See Tolland's Prairie.

**MATTISON**, Arenac County: a settlement on Saginaw Bay, 9 miles northwest of Au Gres, in 1888 [GSM 1889].

**MATTISON**, Branch County: the first land entry here was made by Robert Watson in 1834; Amos Mattison and his family came in 1836, and the town, which was organized in 1838, was named for him; Edwin S. Faxon became its first postmaster on April 17, 1848, the office was closed on June 12, 1874, but was restored from May 7, 1875, to Jan. 31, 1901 [Johnson; PO Archives].

**MAXFIELD**, Genesee County. See Richfield Center.

**MAXSON'S CORNERS**, Eaton County: this hamlet was named for Roswell R. Maxson who bought the land here in Chester Township in 1837 and settled on it with his family in 1840 [Durant].

**MAXTON**, Chippewa County: this village on Drummond Island came into existence when the Cleveland Cedar Company built a mill here; Ernest A. Sims became the first postmaster on March 9, 1900, the office operating until 1950 [Mich Hist 22:288 1938, GSM 1901; PO Archives].

**MAXWELL**, Bay County: a station opened in 1870 on the Mackinaw division of the Michigan Central Railroad, in Fraser Township; William Michie became its first postmaster on June 24, 1875; lawyer Andrew C. Maxwell was an organizer of Bay County in 1857 and a state representative from Bay City in 1865 [Page; PO Archives].

**MAXWELL**, Iosco County: Robert G. Allan became the first postmaster of this rural post office on June 27, 1884, the office operating until Jan. 5, 1885 [PO Archives].

**MAXWELL TOWN**, Manistee County: a suburb of Manistee in 1884 [GSM 1885].

**MAY**, Allegan County: a station on the Chicago & Michigan Lake Shore Railroad, five miles southeast of Holland, in 1876; Laurence Dykhuis became its first postmaster on Sept. 25, 1895, the office operating until Nov. 14, 1902 [GSM 1877-1907; PO Archives].

**MAY**, Tuscola County. See Mayville.

**MAYBEE**, Monroe County: an outgrowth of the building of the Canadian Southern Railway in 1873; the large amount of timber adjacent to the site developed the manufacture of charcoal, and the village sprang up around the kilns and side track; its original site was around the grist mill and sawmill of Abram Maybee, and the place was named after him;

Charles S. Cook became its first postmaster on Feb. 24, 1874; incorporated as a village in 1899 [Bulkley; Wing; PO Archives].

**MAYBURY,** Wayne County: a station on the Michigan Central Railroad, in Hamtramck Township, then 7 miles northwest of Detroit; storekeeper John Milns became its first postmaster on Oct. 17, 1888, the office operating until May 10, 1892; named for Congressman William Maybury who inherited lands in the county [GSM 1893; PO Archives].

**MAYFIELD,** Grand Traverse County: Messrs. Neal, Gibbs and Knight built a sawmill here in Paradise Township in 1868, and later a grist mill; first called Beulah, it was given a post office as Mayfield on July 20, 1869, with Charles A. Denniston as its first postmaster; the Traverse City Railroad gave it a station in 1872 [Traverse; PO Archives].

**MAYFLOWER,** Houghton County: the Mayflower Mining Company, organized and named in Boston in 1899, owned and operated an 840-acre copper mining tract here [Stevens].

**MAY LAKE JUNCTION,** Presque Isle County: a station on the Alpena & Northern (now Detroit & Mackinaw) Railroad, 14 miles south of Rogers City, in 1894 [GSM 1895].

**MAYVILLE,** Tuscola County: two miles southwest of here a post office was opened on Oct. 16, 1860, and named May, with Ezra Tripp as its first postmaster; in 1865, Dexter Choat founded and named Mayville and the post office was moved here, but it kept the name of May until July 30, 1890, when like the town it was named Mayville; a station on the Pere Marquette Railroad; incorporated as a village in 1887 [Donald Plain, PM; PO Archives].

**MAYWOOD,** Iron County: a station on the Chicago & Northwestern Railroad; Charles Shaw became its first postmaster on Aug. 22, 1900, the office operating until Dec. 14, 1903 [GSM 1901-03; PO Archives].

**MEADE,** Huron County. See Filion.

**MEADE,** Macomb County: on April 5, 1838, Stewart Taylor became the first postmaster of a rural post office named Vienna; the office was renamed for Civil War general, George Gordon Meade, on Nov. 28, 1863, and operated until July 31, 1906; in the 1870s, the place was known locally as the Crawford Settlement [Leeson; GSM 1873; PO Archives].

**MEAD'S MILLS,** Wayne County: midway between Plymouth and Northville, Amos and Jabesh M. Mead, brothers, built a dam and a sawmill; their settlement was given a post office on Sept. 10, 1850, with Jabesh M. Mead as its first postmaster, the office operating until Feb. 20, 1884; when their mill burned down for the second time, they did not rebuild, and the settlement dwindled away [Mich Hist 26:319 1942; PO Archives].

**MEADVILLE,** Barry County: this village in Castleton Township was platted in 1867; it was given a railroad station and on June 15, 1869, a post office, with Miner Mead as its first postmaster; the office was renamed

Thorn Apple Lake on June 22, 1875, but back to Meadville on July 16, 1875, until it was transferred to and renamed Morgan on Dec. 16, 1878; named for local pioneers R. B. and Kenyon Mead [GSM 1873-81; PO Archives].

**MEADVILLE**, Ingham County: named for William S. Mead who ran an inn here in southeastern Ingham Township in 1850; but his attempt to develop the place into a village failed [Durant].

**MEARS**, Muskegon County. See Whitehall.

**MEARS**, Oceana County: this village in Golden Township was founded and named by mill-owner Charles Mears in 1873; Albert G. Avery, store manager for Mr. Mears, became its first postmaster on May 14, 1873 [Mich Hist 30:534 1946; Royal].

**MEAUWATAKA**, Wexford County: this village in Colfax Township, with the Indian name for half-way, was settled in 1867, near Lake Meauwataka; it was first called Dayhuff Lake, and Enos C. Dayhuff became its first postmaster of Meauwataka on May 2, 1872, the office operating until April 30, 1952 [GSM 1877; PO Archives].

**MECHANICSBURG**, Cass County: this village in LaGrange Township was platted by and named by Revolutionary War veteran John E. Pettigrew in 1837; three buildings were erected; now only a schoolhouse, marking the site, retains the name [Rogers; Fox].

**MECOSTA**, Mecosta County: John Davis, the first settler in the county, located in 1851; the county was organized in 1859 and named for a Pottawattomi chief, whose name means Big Bear, and who signed the Treaty of Washington in 1836; the township of Mecosta was organized in 1861, with R. A. Moon as its first supervisor; it was given a rural post office on Jan. 5, 1867, with Henry E. Clark as its first postmaster, the office operating until June 9, 1873; the present village of Mecosta, in Morton Township, owes its existence to the Detroit, Lansing & Northern Railroad, which came through in 1879; in that year, Edwin B. Moore, of Edmore, and Giles Gilbert, of Stanton, platted and recorded the village, and John Van Vleck became the first postmaster of its re-established post office; incorporated as a village in 1883 [MPH 30:29 1905; Chapman; PO Archives].

**MEDINA**, Lenawee County: the first settler in the present township was Daniel W. Upton, from Peterboro, N.H., in 1812; the village was platted in 1837 by Cook Hotchkiss, A. Finch, and Artemus Allen; Mr. Allen became the first postmaster on Sept. 20, 1837 (the office was moved to Canandaigua on Feb. 28, 1850, but re-established at Medina in 1851); named after its township, which, since many of its early settlers were from New York State, was probably named after Medina, N.Y. [MPH 17:508 1890; PO Archives].

**MEEKERSVILLE**, Ingham County. See Leslie.

**MEEK'S MILLS**, St. Joseph County. See Constantine.

**MELBOURNE,** Saginaw County: a station on the Cincinnati, Saginaw & Mackinaw Railroad, 7 miles north of Saginaw, in 1894 [GSM 1895].

**MELITA,** Arenac County: this lumbermill settlement was in Bay County until Arenac was organized in 1883; George M. Winnie kept its store and L. S. Marson became its first postmaster on Nov. 15, 1880, the office operating until July 15, 1905 [Page; GSM 1881; PO Archives].

**MELLEN,** Menominee County. See Wallace.

**MELLENS,** Otsego County: the settlement formed around the lumber mill of Mellen Harvey and was named for him; Emma J. Dickinson became its first postmaster on June 8, 1880, the office operating until April 18, 1883; its station on the Mackinaw division of the Michigan Central Railroad was named Bagley [GSM 1881; PO Archives].

**MELROSE,** Charlevoix County. See Walloon Lake.

**MELSTRAND,** Alger County: a station on the M.M. & S.E. Railroad, in Munising Township; Frank C. Sorenson became its first postmaster of this sawmill village on July 11, 1917, the office operating until Feb. 16, 1926 [GSM 1919; PO Archives].

**MELVA,** Benzie County: a station on the M. & N.E. Railroad, in Almita Township; Jesse B. Grant became its first postmaster on Dec. 7, 1901, succeeded by railroad agent J. F. Jenks in 1902 [GSM 1903; PO Archives].

**MELVILLE,** Leelanau County: Austin B. Burdick became the first postmaster of this rural post office on Feb. 3, 1862, but the office was transferred to Kasson on March 14, 1871 [PO Archives].

**MELVIN,** Sanilac County: the first building here in Speaker Township was put up for a saloon in 1862; given a station on the Port Huron & Northwestern Railroad; Charles Dewey became its first postmaster on Nov. 7, 1874; incorporated as a village in 1907 [Chapman].

**MELVINDALE,** Wayne County: settled in 1870, the place was first called Oakwood Heights; Melvin Wilkinson and others platted the village to provide homes for nearby Ford Rouge workers; he died during the development and it was named in his memory; incorporated as a village in 1925 and as a city in 1932 [Thomas J. Anderson].

**MEMPHIS,** Macomb County: the site straddles the Macomb-St. Clair County Line; it was first settled by Anthony Wells in 1834 and James Wells in 1835; Oel Rix built a sawmill; it was known as the Wells' Settlement until Dec. 8, 1848, when, with Henry Rix as its first postmaster, it was given a post office named Memphis, after the Egyptian city and meaning place of good abode; incorporated as a village in 1865 and as a city in 1953 [R. B. Doig, M.D.; Jenks].

**MENCKAUNEE,** Chippewa County: a fishing point on Lake Superior between Sault Ste. Marie and White Fish Point [GSM 1879].

**MENDON**, Lenawee County: Mathew Bennett became the first postmaster of this hamlet on March 27, 1838, the office operating until July 1, 1854 [PO Archives].

**MENDON**, St. Joseph County: the first settlers in the area were traders: Gabriel Godfroy in 1829 and Francois Moutan in 1831; Moses Taft, who came here from Mendon, Mass., in 1835, and Benjamin P. House, who came here from Mendon, N.Y., in 1837, named it in 1844; Leander Meatha (or Metty) became the first settler on the village site in 1834, and he and Patrick Marantette platted it in 1845; William Pollett became its first postmaster on Dec. 17, 1858; a station on the Grand Rapids & Indiana Railroad; incorporated as a village in 1875 [MPH 30:401 1912; Silliman; Everts; PO Archives].

**MENDOTA**, Keweenaw County: the village was laid out by the Mendota Mining Company adjacent to its copper mine in 1866; when this expensive mine, largely promoted by Horace Greeley, did not produce, the village failed too [Edith Yokie].

**MENOMINEE**, Menominee County: Farnsworth & Brush built the first sawmill in the area in 1836, soon followed by others; the settlement was given a post office on May 23, 1863, with Norman Soule as its first postmaster; the Chicago & Northwestern Railroad reached here in 1871; incorporated as a city in 1883; named after the Indian tribe from whom the federal government obtained the remainder of the Upper Peninsula by treaty in 1836 [Andreas].

**MENOMINEE JUNCTION**, Menominee County. See Spalding.

**MENONAQUA BEACH**, Emmet County: this resort community on Little Traverse Bay was given a station on the Grand Rapids & Indiana Railroad about 1882 [Mich Manual 1899].

**MENTHA**, Van Buren County: A. M. Todd, of Kalamazoo, turned the swamp here in Pine Grove Township into a great peppermint producing center; hence the name of the village, for mentha is mint in Latin; organized in 1870 when the Kalamazoo & South Haven Railroad came through; John H. Shirley became its first postmaster on Oct. 18, 1906, the office operating until March 31, 1954 [Madalyn Bradford; Rowland].

**MENTOR**, Cheboygan County. See Wildwood.

**MERE**, Macomb County: Isaac Brabb became the first postmaster of this rural post office on March 11, 1852, the office operating until Sept. 6, 1864 [PO Archives].

**MEREDITH**, Clare County: in its lumber boom days a village of 1,800; Chauncey C. Sears became its first postmaster on Jan. 14, 1884, the office operating until Oct. 14, 1895; now only its cemetery remains [Federal; Blinn].

**MERIDIAN**, Ingham County: named after its township which had been so named because the principal meridian forms its eastern boundary;

Abner Bartlett became its first postmaster on Sept. 4, 1841, the office operating until Dec. 3, 1845; across the Red Cedar River here was a red bridge, a toll gate on the Detroit, Howell & Lansing Plank Road, and the place was given a post office as Red Bridge on July 25, 1854, with Samuel Doyle as its first postmaster; the office was renamed Meridian on Oct. 9, 1871, and operated until Oct. 31, 1933 [Foster; PO Archives].

**MERIDIAN**, Saginaw County. See West's Mills.

**MERLE BEACH**, Clinton County: Mrs. Kittie E. Moore, proprietor of this summer resort on Muskrat Lake, in Olive Township, became its first postmaster on May 24, 1898; the office was closed on Oct. 31, 1900, but was restored, with Theodore Loomis as its postmaster, from Sept. 19, 1903, to Dec. 15, 1922 [GSM 1899; PO Archives].

**MERRILL**, Saginaw County: a wilderness until 1872 when the Saginaw Valley & St. Louis Railroad came through; Mr. Greene built a sawmill here and the settlement around it was given a post office as Greene on May 21, 1875, with William P. Stacy as its first postmaster; A. C. Melze and another merchant moved their stores to a cross-roads a short distance away and the site became the village of Merrill in 1881; the Greene post office was renamed Merrill on Nov. 2, 1881; named for N. W. Merrill, a railroadman who had befriended the villagers when the area was swept by a forest fire in 1881; incorporated as a village in 1889 [Mills; PO Archives].

**MERRILL PARK**, Calhoun County. See Springfield.

**MERRILLSVILLE**, Alpena County. See Long Rapids.

**MERRILLSVILLE**, St. Clair County: this village in Brockway Township, with a station on a branch of the Port Huron & Northwestern Railroad, was given a post office on June 2, 1852, with John D. Jones as its first postmaster, the office operating until Nov. 17, 1876; the place was also known as Hays Corners [Andreas; GSM 1879; PO Archives].

**MERRIMAN**, Dickinson County: a station on the Chicago & Milwaukee & St. Paul Railroad in 1894, and around it the village developed [GSM 1895].

**MERRITT**, Barry County: David W. Smith became the first postmaster of this rural post office on July 22, 1851, the office operating until June 3, 1868 [PO Archives].

**MERRITT**, Missaukee County: this village in Butterfield Township was founded by Charles Bert Merritt in 1908, and named for him by the railroad surveyors; merchant Charles P. Sherman became its first postmaster on Nov. 22, 1910 [Evelyn Bowman, PM; PO Archives].

**MERRIWEATHER**, Ontonagon County: this site on the Lake Gogebic shore, in Bergland Township, first belonged to Jeremiah Robinson, of New York; he sold it to Algernon Merriweather, of Ontonagon, Michigan, in 1858; the village was founded by the Haskins brothers, John and James, in 1916-17, and John became its first postmaster on Feb. 27, 1925; a station on the Duluth, Shore & Atlantic Railroad; the village was platted in 1924; the same Merriweather has a mine (now inactive), and a river, west of the town, named for him [Gordon Thomasini, PM; PO Archives].

**MERRY**, Chippewa County: named for Captain Merry, the first mining superintendent in the iron region of the county, who opened the Jackson Mine in 1846 [Myrtle Elliott].

**MERSHON**, Saginaw County: this village in Carrollton Township was named for William B. Mershon who built a sawmill here in 1871, later adding to his enterprises the making of band resaws and portable houses; the Pere Marquette Railroad came through in 1871 and gave it a station; then a mile south of Saginaw, it has since been absorbed by that city [Mills; GSM 1895].

**MERSON**, Allegan County: storekeeper William Harvey became the first postmaster of this rural post office in Trowbridge Township on April 1, 1898, the office operating until April 30, 1908 [GSM 1899-1903; PO Archives].

**MESICK**, Wexford County: a station on the Toledo, Ann Arbor & Northern Michigan Railroad, in Springville Township; founded and platted by sawmill owner Howard Mesick in 1890; Henry N. Brooks became its first postmaster on Jan. 9, 1881, the office operating until April 15, 1966; incorporated as a village in 1901 [Powers; PO Archives].

**METAMORA**, Lapeer County: Eber Barrows took up land and built an inn here in 1843; the first store was built in 1850; Price B. Webster became its first postmaster on Jan. 23, 1850; the office was closed on April 29, 1854, but the Etna post office was changed to Metamora on June 26, 1854; a station on the Detroit & Bay City Railroad; incorporated as a village in 1885; an Indian name meaning among the hills, or, in another version, the name of an Indian hero, son of Massasoit, in a play popular in the east in the 1840s [Grove C. Morse; GSM 1860; Mich Hist 28:319 1944; PO Archives].

**METHODIST MISSION**, Baraga County: located on Keweenaw Bay, near L'Anse, in 1878 [GSM 1879].

**METROPOLITAN**, Dickinson County: a station on a branch of the Chicago & Northwestern Railroad in 1880; the village was platted by the Metropolitan Mining Company in 1881; it was in Marquette County when Louis A. Fredericks (Friederichs) became its first postmaster on Aug. 31, 1881; it was transferred to Iron County in 1885 and to Dickinson in 1891; its post office operated until Dec. 30, 1963; because of its proximity to the Felch Mountains, the village was also known as Felch Mountain [Andreas; GSM 1883; PO Archives].

**METZ**, Presque Isle County: the first settlers here came from Metz, Germany, about 1879, and named the township and then the town, Metz; Robert Hoffman became the first postmaster on June 20, 1895; the office was closed on Sept. 26, 1896, but was restored, with Mr. Hoffman again its postmaster, on Jan. 19, 1901, and it operated until April 22, 1966; the Detroit & Mackinaw Railroad came through in 1895 and gave Metz a station; the village was burned out by a forest fire in 1908, and then rebuilt [Carl W. Dramburg; PO Archives].

**MEYER**, Mackinac County: this summer resort on Lake Huron, in Cedar Township, was named for soda manufacturer and first postmaster, Frederick W. Meyer, May 20, 1910 [GSM 1911].

**MEYER**, Menominee County. See Hermansville.

**MEYERS**, Monroe County: a station on the Michigan Central and the Lake Shore & Michigan Southern Railroads; it was named for storekeeper Charles J. Meyers who became its first postmaster on May 20, 1898, the office operating until Sept. 30, 1903 [PO Archives; GSM 1901].

**MEYER'S SPUR**, Menominee County: in 1878, Charles J. L. Meyer, a Wisconsin lumberman, bought timberland in this area, organizing the Wisconsin Land & Lumber Company in 1883, and when the Soo Line came through here in 1886, this siding, serving largely his interests, was named for him [Sawyer].

**MICHAM**, Leelanau County: this settlement on Grand Traverse Bay was given a post office on Dec. 13, 1865, with Heman F. Hurlbut as its first postmaster, the office operating until June 3, 1872 [GSM 1879; PO Archives].

**MICHELSON**, Roscommon County: a station on the Grand Rapids & Indiana Railroad; the settlement formed around the mills of the N. Michelson Lumber Company, a shingle mill about 1904, and a sawmill in 1908; company superintendent Alex E. Michelson became its first postmaster on June 1, 1909 [GSM 1911; PO Archives].

**MICHIANA**, Berrien County: the area was partly in Indiana and partly in Michigan, and its developers called it Michigan Shores; the Michigan side being the first to incorporate (1945) and unwilling to lose area identity, chose the name Michiana [Rita A. Cole].

**MICHIE**, Bay County: this village in Fraser Township was named for William Michie, who became a pioneer settler in the area in 1870; he also became the first township supervisor in 1875 and the first postmaster on Dec. 20, 1880; located at the junction of the state road and the Detroit & Mackinaw Railroad; its post office operated until Oct. 15, 1904 [GSM 1877; Page; PO Archives].

**MICHIGAMME**, Marquette County: here Jacob Houghton discovered the Michigamme Mine in 1872; the town's first building was a log cabin built on the shore of Lake Michigamme (Great Lake) for the mining engineers; the Michigamme Mining Company platted the village in 1872 and settlement began immediately; John C. Powle became its first postmaster on Jan. 20, 1873; incorporated as a village in 1873; after the mine was exhausted in 1905, the town began to dwindle [Martin; Andreas; PO Archives].

**MICHIGAN**, Houghton County: the Michigan Copper Mining Company was organized by E. F. Conely and others, of Detroit, in 1898; its combined mineral and surface rights totaled nearly 5,000 acres [Stevens].

**MICHIGAN**, Ingham County: from April 27, 1848, to April 3, 1848, the official name of Lansing was Michigan, Mich.; the name Michigan was derived from two Indian words, michi (great or large) and gama (lake); the territory and then the state were named from Lake Michigan which was discovered by Jean Nicolet in 1634; the name went through changes (Michigama, Michiguma, Michigamaw, etc.) until by 1750 the name Michigan was firmly established; in 1805, Congress established the Territory of Michigan consisting of the present lower peninsula and a small eastern portion of the upper peninsula [Mich Hist Commission; PO Archives].

**MICHIGAN AIR LINE CROSSING**, Macomb County: a station at the junction of the M.A.L. division and the Saginaw branch of the Michigan Central Railroad, 7 miles southeast of Utica, in 1894 [GSM 1895].

**MICHIGAN CENTER**, Jackson County: in 1834, Martin Schumacker, Abel F. Fitch and John Allendorf began the settlement; Mr. Fitch became the first postmaster on Feb. 1, 1838; the office was closed on Nov. 12, 1856, but was restored from Aug. 28, 1857, to Nov. 9, 1860, and from Dec. 3, 1860, to June 30, 1908, and then to date; it was named from its location as the east-west center of the state [Audrey Huston, PM; DeLand; PO Archives].

**MICHIGAN CITY**, Wayne County. See Rawsonville.

**MICHIGAN VILLAGE**, Washtenaw County. See Delhi.

**MICHILIMACKINAC**, Mackinac County: the name has been given, and shown on maps, for the general area of the strait; a settlement (Fort de Baude at a spot earlier called St. Ignace) was generally referred to as Michilimackinac; it was terminated by royal order about 1697 (Antoine Cadillac was commanding officer at the time); Michilimackinac next appeared as a community name on the tip of the lower peninsula about 1715; in 1780 the community name (corrupted as Mackinac) moved to the island, and has remained; for meaning and pronunciation of the name see Mich Hist 42:385-413 1958.

**MICHILLINDA**, Muskegon County: this resort settlement on White Lake, in Fruitland Township, dates from 1896; Fred H. Mason became its first postmaster on June 4, 1896; the office was closed on Sept. 30, 1901; but with hotelman John R. Austin as its postmaster, it was restored on April 29, 1903, and operated until Feb. 28, 1954; David Forbes, Sr., of Grand Rapids, named it from the fact that its resorters came from MICHigan, ILLinois, and INDiana [Arthur H. Ruggles, ret. PM; PO Archives].

**MICKLEVILLE**, Saginaw County. See Oakley.

**MIDDLEBURY**, Livingston County. See Middletown, Ingham County.

**MIDDLEBURY,** Shiawassee County: Obed Hathaway bought the first land here in 1836 and he and his family became the first settlers in 1837; John and William Palmer came in 1838 and named the town after their native Middlebury, N.Y. (which their father had named after his native Middlebury, Vt.); George W. Slocum became the first postmaster of Middleburgh (there was another Middlebury post office in Michigan then), on July 13, 1848, the office operating until Sept. 25, 1862 [Ellis; PO Archives].

**MIDDLESEX,** Keweenaw County: an 800-acre mining location on which no mining was ever done, though a company was organized for it in 1864 [Stevens].

**MIDDLESEX,** Oceana County: named, platted and recorded by Charles Mears, a Chicago capitalist, who organized the Middlesex Brick & Tile Company to utilize the clay banks on the north shore of nearby Pentwater Lake; in 1865, Middlesex failed by one vote to become the county seat; now a part of the village of Pentwater [Hartwick; Royal].

**MIDDLETON,** Clinton County: the proprietors of this tract, platted and recorded in 1836, were Sebastian Beckwith, Joel Wickes and George J. Goodhue; the place was also known as Middletown [Daboll].

**MIDDLETON,** Gratiot County: founded by George Middleton in 1885; given a station on the Toledo, Saginaw & Muskegon (now Grand Trunk) Railroad in 1886; Michael S. Howell became its first postmaster on Nov. 26, 1887; the village was first platted by Mr. Howell, George Flanks, John B. Resseguie, and George S. and William T. Naldrett, and recorded in 1887 [Tucker; PO Archives].

**MIDDLETOWN,** Clinton County. See Middleton.

**MIDDLETOWN,** Ingham County: named from its location half-way between Iosco and White Oak; the town straddles the county line, and its post office opened on May 31, 1848, with Luther Palmer as its first postmaster, was Middlebury, Livingston County, but the office was renamed Middletown, Ingham County, on May 23, 1850; it operated until May 12, 1875 [Foster; PO Archives].

**MIDDLETOWN,** Van Buren County: first settled by John Allen, a native of Vermont, in 1835; he platted the village, naming it from its location as the middle town on the stage route he projected from Paw Paw to St. Joseph in 1836; but both ventures failed, and he lost his land by foreclosure of his mortgage [Ellis].

**MIDDLE VILLAGE,** Emmet County: in some records as Middletown; named from its location midway between Cross Village and L'Arbre Croche; it was an Indian mission founded by Rev. Frederic Baraga in 1832 [MPH 38:229 1912; Mich Hist 25:177 1941].

**MIDDLEVILLE,** Barry County: in 1834, Calvin G. Hill, a native of New York, bought from the government 400 acres lying on both sides of the Thornapple River, within the present limits of the village; it was known as Thornapple until the Middleville post office (established on May 6, 1839, and kept in the home of its first postmaster, Benjamin S. Dibble) was moved here on May 18, 1843, and the village took the name of its post office, with Calvin G. Hill as its postmaster; incorporated as a village in 1867; Thornapple Township was named from the river which in turn had been so named because of the abundance of thornapple trees upon its banks; Middleville was so named because of its proximity to Middle Village [Ivan J. Payne, PM; Johnson].

**MIDDLEVILLE,** Ottawa County. See Lamont.

**MIDLAND,** Midland County: it was named after its county which is located in about the middle of the state; John A. Whitman, the first white settler, made a clearing for his farm here in 1836; John Larkin, who pioneered in developing the village, became its first postmaster on March 6, 1856; the village developed from lumbering, the city from the brine and salt works (now the Dow Chemical Company) of Herbert H. Dow (1866-1930); incorporated as a village in 1869 and as a city in 1887 [Mich Hist 11:177 1927; Pen Phil 10:6 April 1960].

**MIDWAY,** Cheboygan County: Lebbens B. Curtis became the first postmaster of this rural post office in Forest Township on June 22, 1897, the office operating until March 31, 1901 [PO Archives].

**MIDWAY,** Marquette County: this station on a branch of the Marquette, Houghton & Ontonagon Railroad was midway between Ishpeming and Michigamme in 1884 [GSM 1885].

**MIKADO,** Alcona County: the village was founded by Daniel Bruce who built a hotel for lumbermen here in 1886 and persudaded the Detroit & Mackinaw Railroad officials to make it a station; Philip O. Partridge became its first postmaster on May 11, 1886, the post office department naming it Mikado after rejecting the locally requested name of Bruceville; incorporated as a village in 1906 [Powers].

**MILAN,** Washtenaw County: the village was first called Tolanville for Henry Tolan (brother-in-law of William Marvin, son of John Marvin, who became the first settler in the area in 1830), who built a potash factory, a drug store and a hotel; it was still in Monroe County when Bethuel Hack became its first postmaster on March 27, 1833, with the office named Farmersville; it was renamed Milan on April 21, 1836; up to 1859, it was popularly but not officially known as Woodward's Mills for mill-owner David A. Woodward who became its second postmaster in 1834; incorporated as a village in 1885 [Bulkley; Wing; Pen Phil 14:3 Sept 1963].

**MILBURN,** Osceola County: Guy W. Disbrow became the first postmaster of this rural post office in Highland Township on Aug. 2, 1881, the office operating until Jan. 15, 1890 [PO Archives].

**MILE CREEK,** Muskegon County: Ornan Brunson became the first postmaster of this rural post office on May 16, 1870, the office operating until Sept. 2, 1872 [PO Archives].

**MILESBOROUGH,** Van Buren County: this rural post office, opened on Aug. 22, 1865, was named for Fabius Miles who became its first postmaster, the office operating until March 13, 1867 [PO Archives].

**MILFORD,** Oakland County: Levi Pettibone became the first settler in present Milford Township in 1827; among those who came in before 1836 were Jabesh M. Mead, Aaron Phelps and Lumen Fuller; Mr. Mead made and recorded the first plat of the village and built the first store, and Mr. Phelps became the first postmaster, all in 1836; its post office dates from May 28, 1836; incorporated as a village in 1869; the Huron River and Pettibone Creek were the means of furnishing such valuable water power as to give the village and the township their name [Durant; Seeley; PO Archives].

**MILLBROOK,** Mecosta County: Hazen Aldrich built the first log dwelling on the village site in 1863 and the first water-power sawmill in 1864; the business gave the name to the township when it was organized in 1865 and to the village when it was given a post office on Jan. 10, 1867, with Orsen N. Earll as its first postmaster [Chapman; PO Archives].

**MILLBURG,** Berrien County: the village was platted by Jehiel Enos and Amos S. Amsden in 1835; Enos Fenton became its first postmaster on March 19, 1852, the office operating until April 15, 1907; named from its being the site of both lumber mills and grist mills; on some records and maps it is spelled Milburg and Millburgh [Fox; PO Archives].

**MILL CREEK,** Grand Traverse County. See Williamsburg.

**MILL CREEK,** Kent County. See Comstock Park.

**MILL CREEK,** St. Joseph County: Ulrich Wolf became the first postmaster of this rural post office on Aug. 14, 1858, the office operating until July 16, 1863 [PO Archives].

**MILL CREEK,** Washtenaw County. See Lima Center.

**MILLECOQUINS,** Mackinac County: this is the name of a river, a large lake, and a village near its southern shore; pronounced Milikoki and meaning in French a thousand thieves; derived from the Indian Manana koking, or Minakoking, meaning a place where the hardwood is plentiful [Gagnieur].

**MILLER,** Montcalm County: a depot on the Grand Trunk Railroad, in Fair Plain Township, and named Miller's Station; given a post office as Miller on Aug. 14, 1889, with John K. Rasmussen as its first postmaster, succeeded by Alfred Stone in 1890 [GSM 1891; PO Archives].

**MILLER HILL,** Leelanau County: Ellen Brotherton became the first postmaster of this rural post office on Feb. 20, 1891, the office operating until March 24, 1892 [PO Archives].

**MILLERSBURG,** Presque Isle County: a station on the Detroit & Mackinaw Railroad, in Case Township; C. R. Miller, of Adrian, founded the village in 1897, and had it named for him; John D. Walker became its first postmaster on Feb. 14, 1898; Gardner & Peterman built a sawmill here in 1899; incorporated as a village in 1901 [Mrs. Lucy Mills; Advance; PO Archives].

**MILLER SETTLEMENT**, Genesee County. See Swartz Creek.

**MILLER'S STATION**, Montcalm County. See Miller.

**MILLERSVILLE**, Wexford County: this station on the Toledo, Ann Arbor & Northern Railroad was opened about 1888 and was named for storekeeper Humphrey W. Miller who became its first postmaster on March 8, 1890, the office operating until March 30, 1895 [GSM 1891; PO Archives].

**MILLERTON**, Mason County: the site was secured by Dodge Squire who moved his shingle mill here on the Au Sable River, in Sheridan Township, built a general store, and became the first postmaster on April 28, 1898, and the first railroad agent at the local station of the Manistee & Grand Rapids Railroad, also in 1898; it was named for John Miller who claimed to be the oldest resident in this part of the township [Elsworth; PO Archives].

**MILLETT**: Eaton County: this village in Delta Township formed around the coal and clay beds of S. E. Millett, for whom it was named; it was given a station named Milletts on the C. & L.H. (now Grand Trunk) Railroad in 1877, and on May 14, 1877, a post office named Millett, with Franklin P. Wells as its first postmaster, the office operating until July 30, 1910 [GSM 1879; PO Archives].

**MILLEVILLE**, Presque Isle County: John D. Walker was appointed the first postmaster of this rural post office on Jan. 10, 1898, but the office was never in operation [PO Archives].

**MILL GROVE**, Allegan County: the founder and first settler was Levi M. Comstock, about 1850; his sawmill failed but others succeeded and it became a mill town with a school and a post office; the latter opening on Dec. 22, 1873, with Edgar E. Brownson as its first postmaster, the office operating until Sept. 30, 1905; a station on the Chicago & Western Michigan (now Pere Marquette) Railroad [Johnson; PO Archives].

**MILLIKEN**, Cheboygan County. See Paradise.

**MILLINGTON**, Tuscola County: from the early mills along it, the government survey of 1822 named the stream which flows past here Millington Creek; Amos Wolverton became the first postmaster of Millington on June 29, 1857; (David) Lane & Wolfe built a sawmill in 1859, and the village was platted in 1860 and named Lanesville; since about 1866, the village has again been called Millington, and in 1872, it was replatted and renamed as such officially by D. M. Blocher, then its principal owner, and Samuel Atwood and Joel Beckwith; incorporated as a village in 1877 [Alice Cutlar; Page; PO Archives].

**MILL POINT**, Ottawa County. See Spring Lake.

**MILLPORT**, Kalamazoo County: a mill settlement in Richland Township in 1837 [GSM 1838].

**MILLS**, Houghton County. See Point Mills.

**MILLS**, Iosco County: a station on the Detroit & Mackinaw Railroad, 3 miles northwest of Whittemore, in 1894 [GSM 1895].

**MILLS**, Sanilac County: this rural post office in Marion Township was named for Thomas A. Mills who became its first postmaster on March 13, 1884, the office operating until Dec. 31, 1904 [PO Archives].

**MILLSPAW'S**, Lenawee County: it was named for Cornelius Millspaw who, with Jesse Osborn, made the first land purchase and settled here in 1833; the settlement, which grew rapidly, was organized as Woodstock Township in 1836, with Nahum Lamb, who had come here in 1834, as its first supervisor [Hogaboam].

**MILL STATION**, Lapeer County. See Attica.

**MILLSVILLE**, Gladwin County: William Bowers was 16 when he came here from Defiance, Ohio, in 1901; he became a lumberjack and later a telephone lineman; he built the store here for Mr. and Mrs. Mills, for whom the town was named; it was also called New Headquarters from its being the location of a lumber company warehouse [Ritchie].

**MILLVILLE**, Ingham County: the land on which this village is located was first owned by James Reeves, in whose name it was entered in 1836; he sold it to Nelson F. Osborn who in turn sold in part to Elias S. Clark; Mr. Clark built a sawmill on it, this giving the village its name; its post office was at White Oak, a half mile south [Foster; Durant].

**MILLVILLE**, Lapeer County: in 1837, Horace N. Lathrop, a native of Connecticut, built a sawmill and a grist mill where the village now stands, and thus gave it its name; he became the supervisor of Marathon Township in 1839 (the site is now in Oregon Township); its post office was opened on Jan. 17, 1877, with Stephen E. Dickens as its first postmaster [Page; PO Archives].

**MILLVILLE**, Muskegon County. See Bluffton.

**MILLVILLE**, St. Joseph County. See White Pigeon.

**MILNES**, Hillsdale County: Wilson Houseknecht became the first postmaster of this rural post office, 5 miles from Jonesville, on Jan. 17, 1896, the office operating until June 15, 1901 [GSM 1897-1903; PO Archives].

**MILO**, Barry County: Archibald S. Allen became the first postmaster of Prairieville (not the present Prairieville, also in Barry County), on May 13, 1851; the office was renamed Crooked Lake (it is just south of that body of water), on Dec. 8, 1855, and then changed to Milo, on June 14, 1856; the office was closed on Oct. 6, 1873, but was restored from May 3, 1875, to May 5, 1881, and from Nov. 21, 1887, until it was closed permanently; but the village remains [Cole; PO Archives].

**MILTON,** Cass County: Cannon Smith, a native of Delaware, bought land here in 1829, and settled on it in 1831; he was followed by so many from that State that the area became known as the Delaware Settlement, and when the township was organized in 1838, Peter Truitt named it Milton, after a Delaware township; an agricultural community with no post office, but the Gazeteer 1860 lists it as a village [Mathews; Rogers].

**MILTON,** Macomb County: a station on the Grand Trunk Railroad, in Chesterfield Township; Edmund Matthews became its first postmaster on Jan. 10, 1856, the office operating until July 15, 1904 [Leeson; PO Archives].

**MILTON,** Ontonagon County: an 880-acre copper mining location; organized in 1864, it was sold at receiver's sale in 1900 to Byron N. White, of Spokane, Wash. [Stevens].

**MILTON JUNCTION,** Osceola County: in 1871, the Grand Rapids & Indiana Railroad built its line north and south through Lincoln Township, with a branch line running northwest; at this junction was a depot, general store and hamlet, named Milton Junction [Chapman].

**MILWAUKEE,** Brown County: given a post office as Melwaukee, with Solomon Juneau, as its first postmaster, on March 16, 1835; it was then in Michigan Territory, but now in Wisconsin [PO Archives].

**MILWAUKEE CITY,** St. Clair County. See Lakeport.

**MINARD,** Jackson County: George Minard settled here in Tompkins Township late in 1834 and built a sawmill in 1835; the place became known as Minard Mills but was given a post office as Minard on Nov. 24, 1888, with storekeeper Henry T. Whitmore as its first postmaster, the office operating until Aug. 30, 1902 [DeLand; PO Archives].

**MINDEN CITY,** Sanilac County: the village was founded in 1855 by Philip Link, who named it after his native Minden, Germany; Alfred Gunning opened the first store in 1859; he sold it in 1861 to William Donner who became the first postmaster of Minden on Oct. 10, 1862; given a station on the Pere Marquette Railroad in 1880; incorporated as a village in 1882; on June 15, 1883, the village was renamed Minden City [Chapman; Pen Phil 13:3 May 1963; PO Archives].

**MINER,** Saginaw County: this rural post office in Brant Township was named for storekeeper Plum P. Miner who became its first postmaster on April 4, 1896, the office operating until Aug. 15, 1902 [GSM 1897-1903; PO Archives].

**MINERAL BRANCH,** Marquette County: a station on the Chicago & Northwestern Railroad, serving a mining region, in 1886 [GSM 1887].

**MINERAL HILLS,** Iron County: named from the very productive iron bearing hills in the area; incorporated as a village in 1918 [Jack Hill, Sr.].

**MINERAL SPRINGS,** Newaygo County: Ranson E. French became the first postmaster of this rural post office in Ensley Township on Feb. 10, 1873, the office operating until Nov. 17, 1876 [GSM 1875; PO Archives].

**MINER LAKE,** Allegan County: this settlement on Miner Lake, 4 miles northeast of Allegan, was given a post office spelled Minerlake on Oct. 27, 1897, with George Miller as its first postmaster, the office operating until Aug. 15, 1935 [GSM 1899; PO Archives].

**MINESOTA MINE,** Ontonagon County: organized as the Minnesota Mining Company, an error in spelling was made in the state charter, and it was never corrected; the village was platted by the company as Rosendale, but was given a post office as Minesota Mine on May 7, 1857, with William Peck as its first postmaster; for the National Mining Company (which after costly litigation had won this land from the Minnesota in 1860), the post office was renamed National on March 16, 1861, with storekeeper Benjamin T. Rogers as its postmaster; when the town was consolidated into the village of Rockland on Dec. 7, 1863, the post office was renamed Rockland [Andreas; Jamison; Stevens; PO Archives].

**MINONG,** Keweenaw County: this copper mining settlement on Isle Royale took the Chippewa name of the island; the Minong Mining Company was organized in 1874 and closed its mine in 1883; Alonzo G. Davis became the first postmaster on Aug. 16, 1876; the office was closed on June 7, 1880, but was restored on Nov. 8, 1880; it was the county seat when Isle Royale was a county; the place was known locally as McCargo's Cove, named for John McCargo, a widely-known lake captain in his day; the settlement is gone but the landmark remains on maps variously as McCarga, McCargoe, or McCargo Cove [Stevens; Mich Hist 30:680 1946; PO Archives].

**MINT,** St. Joseph County: Abner P. Yorton became the first postmaster of this rural post office in Park Township on June 30, 1890, the office operating until April 30, 1903 [GSM 1891-1905; PO Archives].

**MIO,** Oscoda County: the village was founded by Coolige Comins, John Randall, Henry Deyarmond and Reirlo Fosdick in 1881; John Randall became its first postmaster on May 3, 1882, with the office named Mioe, for Henry Deyarmond's wife, but it was renamed Mio on Nov. 21, 1883 [David Colyer; PO Archives].

**MIRACLE MILE,** Oakland County: founded and named by Donald M. Casto, owner of this shopping center in which a branch of the Pontiac post office has been operating since 1959 [Marie E. Marinick].

**MIRIAM,** Ionia County: here in Otisco Township a small Catholic settlement was founded in 1841 by John Albert, an itinerant German clock peddler, a native of Baden, who now became a farmer; it was soon given a church which became a schoolhouse when a second church was erected in 1871; when given a post office on Oct. 10, 1882, with Adam Hehl as its first postmaster, it was named after their parish church, St. Mary's; the office operated until April 30, 1902; it was also known as the German Settlement [Paré; Branch; PO Archives].

**MISHAQUAKA**, Berrien County: also spelled Misaquakee; a Pottawattomi Indian village of some 25 families found here when the first white settlers came in 1833; it was located on the eastern part of the present village of Buchanan [Ellis].

**MISSAUKEE**, Missaukee County: the county was organized in 1871 and named for a local Indian chief who was better known as Nesaukee; this rural post office, 8 miles northeast of Lake City, was opened on June 6, 1901, with Burt W. Forquer as its first postmaster [Mich Manual 1959-60; PO Archives].

**MISSAUKEE JUNCTION**, Wexford County: this village, four miles north of Cadillac, began as a station on the Grand Rapids & Indiana Railroad about 1876; named after an Ottawa chief, who was better known as Nesaukee [Mich Manual 1899].

**MISSION**, Baraga County: a station on the Marquette, Houghton & Ontonagon Railroad, named from its nearness to Methodist Mission [GSM 1885].

**MISSION HARBOR**, Grand Traverse County. See Old Mission.

**MITCHELL**, Antrim County: this flourishing mill village in Banks Township was settled in 1868; John McNeill became its first postmaster on Apr. 26, 1869, the office operating until Oct. 31, 1902; it was on Wiltse Creek, named for pioneer settler E. Wiltse, who was the postmaster in 1876 [GSM 1871-75; PO Archives].

**MITCHELL**, Missaukee County: a station on a branch of the Grand Rapids & Indiana Railroad in 1888 [GSM 1889].

**MITCHELL**, Tuscola County: a settlement around the Cass City Grain Company elevator, near Fairgrove, in 1918 [GSM 1919].

**MITCHELL STATE PARK**, Wexford County. See William Mitchell State Park.

**MITCHELL'S PRAIRIE**, Newaygo County: this rural post office was named for Samuel S. Mitchell who became its first postmaster on Feb. 6, 1868, the office operating until March 1, 1870 [PO Archives].

**MOAB**, St. Joseph County. See Three Rivers.

**MOCCASIN**, Berrien County: an Indian village when the first white settlers came here in 1833; located in present Buchanan Township, on the west side of the St. Joseph River; named for its chief; Moccasin Shoals and Moccasin Bluff were named from their proximity to it [Ellis].

**MODDERSVILLE**, Missaukee County: the first settlers, Mr. White and his family, came in 1875, but later moved away; Wynand Modders and his family came in 1878, followed by others, chiefly, like the Modders, from the Netherlands; they stayed and raised their families here, and when given a post office on Aug. 6, 1890, they named it for Mr. and Mrs. Modders; he was the first postmaster, and the office operated until Oct. 31, 1934 [Cornelius Mendendorp; Mich Hist 31:396 1947; PO Archives].

**MODEL CITY,** Cass County. See Glenwood.

**MOFFAT,** Arenac County: a flag station on the Detroit, Bay City & Alpena Railroad in 1888 [GSM 1889].

**MOFFATT,** Alcona County: Asahel Atherton became the first postmaster of this rural post office on Oct. 31, 1903, the office operating until Feb. 28, 1907 [PO Archives].

**MOFFATT,** Grand Traverse County: Charles Howard became the first postmaster of this rural post office on July 18, 1881, the office operating until Sept. 25, 1882 [PO Archives].

**MOHAWK,** Keweenaw County: in 1896, Ernest Koch, a lumberman, chanced to find some native copper here in Allouez Township; explorations by Joseph E. Gay proved the value of the find, and in 1898, the Mohawk Mining Company was formed and began operations; the village developed with the mine and was named from it; storekeeper George H. Petermann became its first postmaster on March 1, 1901; Mohawk was the name of an Indian tribe [PM; Stevens; PO Archives].

**MOLINE,** Allegan County: this village in Dorr Township was first settled in 1840 and was given a post office on Jan. 2, 1863, with Charles A. Orton as its first postmaster; the village developed with the coming through of the Grand Rapids & Indiana Railroad in 1870; platted by Alfred Chapple in 1872; other pioneers included John L. Shaw and Edward P. Vining [GSM 1865; Thomas; Johnson; PO Archives].

**MOLTKE,** Presque Isle County: Anton Dullack became the first postmaster of this rural post office, 3 miles from Rogers City, on June 22, 1910, the office operating until May 31, 1912 [GSM 1911; PO Archives].

**MONA LAKE,** Muskegon County: a resort and station, founded in 1880, and named for Mona May, daughter of the superintendent of the Grand Haven Railroad, Colonel May; the Muskegon County Pioneer and Historical Society held their annual meetings here for many years, beginning in 1882; the name is also retained in Mona Shores [MPH 21:640 1892; GSM 1881].

**MONGUAGO,** Wayne County. See Trenton.

**MONGUAGON,** Wayne County: quarries were worked here by the French before 1749; American troops defeated English and Indian forces in the Battle of Monguagan in the War of 1812; an American settlement was made here by 1818; named after a local Indian chief; Monguagon Township was created in 1827; the site was incorporated into the city of Riverview in 1958 [MPH 1:501 1874, 2:102 1877; Mich Hist 46:355 1962].

**MONISTIQUE,** Schoolcraft County: John H. Whitbeck became the first postmaster of this rural post office on June 15, 1865, the office operating until Aug. 20, 1869; this post office was not connected with the present city of Manistique, but see it for the origin of the name [PO Archives].

**MONITOR,** Bay County: William Hemingway became the first settler here in 1858, followed by Joseph Dell in 1859; the town was named after its township which was created in 1869, with William H. Needham as its first supervisor; grocer Moritz Uhlmann became its first postmaster on April 20, 1894, the office operating until March 14, 1903; its station, also named Monitor, on the Michigan Central Railroad, was three miles north of the village [Gansser; GSM 1895; PO Archives].

**MONONGAHELA,** Iron County: a mining location, its name reflecting the interests of Pittsburgh iron industrialists in the area [Jack Hill, Sr.].

**MONROE,** Monroe County: in 1780, Francois Navarre left Detroit and built his cabin on land deeded him here on the north side of the Rivière aux Raisins by the Indians; by 1784, a hundred French families from Canada had joined him, and Frenchtown became the third permanent community in Michigan and on Nov. 21, 1815, its second post office (after only Detroit); on lands belonging to Joseph Loranger and others, who ceded lots for public use, an American settlement was platted on the south side of the river in 1817, and named for newly elected President James Monroe; Laurent Durocher was the first postmaster of Frenchtown, and with Charles Noble as postmaster, the office was renamed Monroe on July 24, 1824; incorporated as a village in 1827 and as a city in 1837; Frenchtown is now a district in Monroe and the name of one of the two townships in which the city is located [Paré; Wing; PO Archives].

**MONROE CENTER,** Grand Traverse County: it was named for pioneer settler William Monroe who came here in 1859 and bought 400 acres of farmland; it was given the first post office in Green Lake Township on Feb. 28, 1866, with Mrs. Pauline Monroe as its first postmaster, the office operating until Aug. 30, 1910 [Traverse; PO Archives].

**MONROVIA,** Sanilac County. See Lexington.

**MONTAGUE,** Muskegon County: in 1855, Mr. Rogers and Nat Sargent owned the site of the present city and in that year the latter built the first house; given a post office on March 21, 1867, with Ophir R. Goodno as its first postmaster; the town was founded in 1874 by George E. Dowling, Joseph Heald, Peter Dalton, and William Montague Ferry, and named for the last mentioned; incorporated as a village in 1883 and as a city in 1935 [Edna Medbery; PO Archives].

**MONTCALM,** Montcalm County: Luther Lincoln was the first settler in the area, followed in 1844 by Lyman H. Pratt and his brother-in-law, S. D. Barr; Montcalm Township was organized in 1845; it was named after the county which in turn had been named for the Marquis Louis de Montcalm, when organized in 1835; Lyman H. Pratt became the first postmaster on Jan. 31, 1846; the office was closed on June 24, 1863, restored, with John Mills as postmaster, on July 31, 1868, and transferred to Coral on March 22, 1869 [Schenck; PO Archives].

**MONTEITH STATION,** Allegan County: it was named for the Monteith family, Thomas, Sr., and Jr., William, and Walter, who bought land and settled in the area in 1836-37; it was the crossing point of the Grand Rapids & Indiana, and the Allegan & Southeastern Railroads; but it never became a village; John James Neelley became its first postmaster on Oct. 9, 1871, the office operating until March 15, 1907; it was, unlike the town, named simply Monteith [Johnson; PO Archives].

**MONTEREY CENTRE,** Allegan County: it was first settled by Horace Wilson in 1835; other pioneers here included Samuel A. Hewitt, storekeeper Frank Hewitt, and the three Granger brothers; named from its location in Monterey Township; given a post office as Monterey on Dec. 16, 1851, with Eli D. Granger as its first postmaster, the office operating until Sept. 30, 1905 [PO Archives; Johnson].

**MONTEZUMA,** Houghton County. See West Houghton.

**MONTGOMERY,** Hillsdale County: in 1870, Joshua Dobbs, Israel Sheppard, Enoch P. Teachout, and George Hewitt took up farms here; when the railroad came through, it was called The Station; in 1871, when the men who platted the village went to Hillsdale to record it, the county clerk, William R. Montgomery, said he would record it gratis if they would name it after him, and they agreed; Benjamin Hagerman became its first postmaster when the post office was moved here from Edinbrugh (known locally as The Berg), on Dec. 20, 1871; incorporated as a village in 1906 [Myrta Null; PO Archives].

**MONTGOMERY,** Jackson County. See Liberty.

**MONTGOMERY,** Muskegon County: this village in Casnovia Township was first settled in 1872; on Sept. 2, 1874, it was given a post office named Moon (there was at the time another post office in Michigan named Montgomery), with Charles L. Ballard as its first postmaster, the office operating until June 6, 1896 [Page; GSM 1879; PO Archives].

**MONTGOMERY PLAINS,** Eaton County: it was named for John Montgomery who first settled here in Hamlin Township in 1836; he was a brigadier-general and in 1849 was elected to the state legislature [Strange].

**MONTICELLO,** Gratiot County: located in New Haven Township, its second supervisor, Henry P. Clark, became the first postmaster of this rural post office named after the Virginia home of Thomas Jefferson, on Nov. 2, 1857; the office operated until March 23, 1863 [Tucker; PO Archives].

**MONT LAKE,** Livingston County: William A. Clark became the first postmaster of this rural post office on Nov. 20, 1838, the office operating until Oct. 26, 1851 [PO Archives].

**MONTREAL,** Gogebic County: the Montreal Mine operated on both sides of the Montreal River, in Wisconsin and in Michigan; the Montreal in

Ironwood Township, Michigan, was given a station on the Duluth, South Shore & Atlantic Railroad, and on Aug. 4, 1903, a post office, with Ella Stage as its first postmaster; the office was closed in 1915, as was the mine; but on the Wisconsin side, both mine and village still flourish [Victor Lemmer].

**MONTREAL,** Keweenaw County: a pioneer copper mining property which later became part of the Clark Mine [Stevens].

**MONTROSE,** Genesee County: it was originally Pewonagowink, and part of Vienna Township; Daniel Pifford made the first land purchase here in 1835; in 1842, Seymour W. Ensign bought the land of the present village from Thomas L. L. Brent, for whom Brent Creek and the village of Brent were named; when the township was organized in 1848, John Farquharson, a Scot, had the name changed to Montrose to impress his Scottish friends; the town, named after the township, was given a post office on March 8, 1856, with William Streeter as its first postmaster, succeeded by Seymour W. Ensign; incorporated as a village in 1899 [Elizabeth C. Ronan; PO Archives].

**MONTROSE STATION,** Ionia County. See Muir.

**MONUSCONG,** Chippewa County. See Munuscong.

**MOON,** Muskegon County. See Montgomery.

**MOONSHINE,** Tuscola County: in 1860, this small settlement, located between Cass City and the Cass River, began to build a courthouse in its unsuccessful attempt to be designated the county seat [Schultz].

**MOORE,** Roscommon County: believed to have been named for the lumberman who first used it, the site began as a siding on the Mackinaw division of the Michigan Central Railroad, 8 miles northwest of St. Helen, about 1890 [Co. Bd. of Ed.].

**MOORE,** Sanilac County: the first permanent settler in the area was James Minard in 1860; he was followed in 1864 by Martin Moore, who became the first supervisor when Moore Township was organized in 1865; Samuel Moore, who became the supervisor in 1875, built the first frame house in 1876 [Chapman].

**MOOREPARK,** St. Joseph County: Edward S. Moore bought 450 acres here in 1834, and he became the first supervisor when Park Township was organized in 1838; the Lake Shore & Michigan Southern Railroad built a station here and named it Moorepark in 1871; given a post office on Feb. 19, 1872, with David P. Smith as its first postmaster, the office operating until Feb. 29, 1960 [W. P. Schoppe, PM; Cutler; PO Archives].

**MOORE'S,** Clare County: this station on a branch of the Pere Marquette Railroad, 4 miles north of Clare, in 1888, was also called Moore's Siding [GSM 1889].

**MOORE'S,** Eaton County: a station on the C. & L.H. Railroad, just north of Olivet, in 1876 [GSM 1877].

**MOORE'S CORNERS**, Sanilac County. See Speaker.

**MOORE'S JUNCTION**, Arenac County: the village began as a lumber settlement on a logging branch of the Michigan Central Railroad, in Adams Township; Joseph Price became its first postmaster on Dec. 19, 1889, the office operating until Sept. 14, 1907; named for a lumberman [Alfred Campbell; GSM 1891; PO Archives].

**MOORESTOWN**, Missaukee County: the village was founded in 1881 by J(ames) Henry Moores, an Ohioan who became a wealthy Michigan lumberman; he recorded his plat in 1882 and became the first postmaster on Sept. 5, 1882, the office operating until June 30, 1957 [Fred C. Hirzel; PO Archives].

**MOOREVILLE**, Allegan County: its settlement began as the seat of the lumbering operations of Horace D. Moore, of Vermont, in 1856; it became a western suburb of the village of Saugatuck [MPH 3:309 1881].

**MOOREVILLE**, Washtenaw County: the village was named for its founder, John L. Moore, who came from New York and settled here by the Saline River about 1830 and was appointed the first postmaster on Jan. 5, 1833; the post office was renamed York, after its township, from May 2, 1834, until it was closed on April 30, 1907, but the village of Mooreville (in some records as Mooresville) remains [Chapman; PO Archives].

**MOORLAND**, Muskegon County: so named because it was originally swampland; first settled in 1857 by Peter Conklin, John W. Tibbets, and John F. Chichester; the town was organized in 1860, with O. F. Conklin as its first supervisor; its village, a sawmill settlement, was given a station on the Toledo, Saginaw & Muskegon Railroad in 1888; Charles W. Beers became its first postmaster on Feb. 14, 1888, the office operating until Nov. 5, 1913 [Page; GSM 1880; PO Archives].

**MORAN**, Mackinac County: this village in Brevort Township was first called Jacob City for the president of the German Land Company, of Detroit, a colonization scheme by which land was sold to 27 of its members in 1881 and to the rest in 1882-1883; Mr. Jacob was accused of fraud in 1883 and ousted from the organization which then proceeded to borrow from one of its members, William B. Moran, to buy more land; they renamed the village after him in 1883; Frank J. Becker became the first postmaster of Jacob City on Feb. 23, 1882, with the office renamed Moran on Jan. 24, 1883; it was transferred to and renamed Allenville on April 1, 1898, but the Moran post office was re-established on May 14, 1910; Moran Bay at St. Igance, West Moran Bay on Lake Michigan, Moran Township, and Moran River, all have a different origin from the village of Moran: their name was originally French: Morin [Emerson Smith; A. J. Roggenbuck, PM; Mich Hist 46:167 1962; PO Archives].

**MORAVIAN VILLAGE**, Macomb County. See Gnadenhuetten.

**MORENCI**, Lenawee County: it was the site of a sawmill in 1835, and of the tavern of William Sutton and of the general store of Japheth

Whitman, both in 1836; Franklin Cawley, who also came in 1836, bought his land of James Armitage, of Monroe, and on it he made the first plat of the village, which he named Brighton, in 1852; but there was another Brighton in Michigan, and this village retained the name of Morenci which had been given it by Simon D. Wilson and Japheth Whitman when it had been given a post office on Oct. 12, 1838, with Mr. Whitman as its first postmaster; a station on the Lake Shore & Michigan Southern Railroad; incorporated as a village in 1871 and as a city in 1934 [Hogaboam; Bonner; PO Archives].

**MOREY,** Missaukee County: this village was named for pioneer settler William J. Morey; Thomas McManus became its first postmaster on Dec. 17, 1887 [Blinn; PO Archives].

**MOREY'S,** Missaukee County. See Pioneer.

**MORGAN,** Barry County: E. E. Cook bought 80 acres of land here in Castleton Township in 1866 and built a sawmill; Z. B. Wilson built the first store in 1869, but sold it to Horace Hall in 1873; a station on a branch of the Michigan Central Railroad in 1878; first called Sheridan, the hamlet was renamed Morgan when given a post office on Dec. 16, 1878, for there was then another Sheridan post office in Michigan; the office here operated until Sept. 15, 1933 [Johnson; PO Archives].

**MORGAN,** Marquette County: a station on the Iron Mountain Railroad, about midway between Marquette and Negaunee; the blast furnase of the Morgan Iron Company opened here in 1863, and the settlement was named for Lewis H. Morgan, of Rochester, N.Y., president of the company; Byron M. Colwell became its first postmaster on June 25, 1866, the office operating until July 24, 1877 [Andreas; GSM 1879; PO Archives].

**MORGANDALE,** Hillsdale County: this settlement in the southwestern part of the county was given a post office as Morganville on Dec. 11, 1851, with Nile J. Parrish as its first postmaster; after the office was closed on April 24, 1874, the place became known as Morgandale [GSM 1860, 1889; PO Archives].

**MORGAN STATION,** Newaygo County. See White Cloud.

**MORGANVILLE,** Hillsdale County. See Morgandale.

**MORIN,** Mackinac County. See Moran.

**MORLEY,** Mecosta County: Charles Lawson, Nelson Pike and George H. Ward were among the first settlers here in 1869; the Grand Rapids & Indiana Railroad came through that year, and it was its first station master here who became its first postmaster on Sept. 30, 1869; incorporated as a village in 1870 [Champan; MPH 30:29 1905; Mich Hist 21:169 1937].

**MOROCCO,** Monroe County: John Griner became the first postmaster of this rural post office on Oct. 30, 1884, the office operating until Oct. 15, 1906 [PO Archives].

**MORRELL,** Eaton County: a hamlet in 1912 [GSM 1913].

**MORRICE,** Shiawassee County: Joshua Purdy became the first settler here in Perry Township in 1836; William Morrice, for whom the village was named, came in 1837, followed by his brothers, John, George, and Alexander, in 1838; the Morrices were natives of Aberdeenshire, Scotland; a station on the Grand Trunk Railroad; Charles Tyler became its first postmaster on May 14, 1877, the year the village was platted and recorded by Isaac Gale; incorporated as a village in 1884 [Betty A. Hayes; Campbell; PO Archives].

**MORRIS,** Berrien County: a station on the Chicago & Western Michigan (now Pere Marquette) Railroad in 1878 [GSM 1879].

**MORRIS' MILLS,** Oakland County: this village in the southern part of the county, on the River Rouge, began with a grist mill and a sawmill built by William Morris in 1828 [GSM 1839].

**MORRISON,** Jackson County: this rural post office in Summit Township was named for William F. Morrison who became its first postmaster on June 20, 1899, the office operating until June 14, 1902 [GSM 1901-03; PO Archives].

**MORTON,** Kalamazoo County. See Galesburg.

**MOSCOW,** Hillsdale County: Peter Benson became the first settler here in 1831, with Judge Lyman Blackmar the second in 1832; Lewis T. Miller became its first postmaster on May 7, 1834; the village was named by Alonzo Kies who came here from Moscow, Cayuga County, N.Y. [Hogaboam; Reynolds; Pen Phil 7:3 Jan 1957].

**MOSHERVILLE,** Hillsdale County: the village was named for the Mosher brothers, David, Charles, James, and Giles, who settled here in 1838, 1842, 1843, and 1848, respectively; David returned to New York State but his brothers stayed and built a sawmill and a grist mill; they platted the village in 1852, and Giles platted an addition in 1856; given a post office as Scipio, named after its township, on July 2, 1849, with Samuel E. Smith as its first postmaster; the office was renamed Tylerville, after the then-living ex-president John Tyler, on March 9, 1857, and finally on April 20, 1858, it was renamed Mosherville, with John Cross as its postmaster; David Mosher held the office in 1866, he having returned to join his brothers [Vivian L. Moore; GSM 1860; PO Archives].

**MOSSBACK,** Kalkaska County. See Rugg.

**MOSSLAKE,** Delta County: this settlement on Moss Lake, near Nahma Junction, was made in 1924 [GSM 1931].

**MOSSVILLE,** Emmet County: Squire Phillips became the first postmaster of this rural post office on July 26, 1876, the office operating until March 4, 1878 [PO Archives].

**MOSTELLER,** Clare County: this rural post office, 5 miles east of Harrison, was named for William H. Mosteller who became its first postmaster on Jan. 24, 1888, the office operating until only Dec. 7, 1888 [GSM 1891; PO Archives].

**MOTTVILLE,** St. Joseph County: the first settler here was Joseph Quimby in 1828; the village was platted by George Risdon and John R. Williams in 1830; Hart L. Stewart became its first postmaster in June, 1830, the office operating until June 15, 1908; Mottville Township, a part of White Pigeon Township until 1837, was named after the village, which was named for Alva Mott; his grave in the Mottville Cemetery bears only the inscription "Alva Mott, Died 1879" [Edward B. Buckley; Cutler; PO Archives].

**MOULIN ROUGE,** Wayne County. See Inkster.

**MOUNT BLISS,** Antrim County: Robert M. Webster became the first postmaster of this village in Jordan Township on Nov. 8, 1877, the office operating until Feb. 14, 1887 [Mich Hist 42:169 1958; PO Archives].

**MOUNT CLEMENS,** Macomb County: Christian Clemens was so impressed with the site when he surveyed it in 1795 that he returned in 1799, bought John Brooks' distillery here, and helped to plat the village which was named for him in 1818; Governor Lewis Cass made it the county seat that year; John Stockton became its first postmaster on Jan. 12, 1821; the act to incorporate it as a village was approved in 1837 but, due to the panic of that year, was not acted on; incorporated as a village in 1851 and as a city in 1879 [Eldredge].

**MOUNT CROWLEY,** Emmet County. See Emmett.

**MOUNT FOREST,** Bay County: a sawmill settlement in Mount Forest Township, with a station on the Michigan Central Railroad in 1888; hotelman Clarence A. Fairchild became its first postmaster on Oct. 12, 1888; the spelling was changed to Mountforest on Sept. 7, 1894, but the office was closed on March 31, 1855; now nearly deserted [Gansser; GSM 1889; PO Archives].

**MOUNT HALLEY,** Midland County: the village began as an Irish settlement; Joseph Barton, the first to arrive, came in 1865, followed by Michael Doyle in 1868; the township, when organized in 1871, was named Mount Halley for pioneer settler John Halley, with P. H. Murphy as its first supervisor; Anthony Dean became its first postmaster on April 1, 1879, but the office operated until only Oct. 20, 1879; in some records as Haley, for example, the Michigan Manual 1899 it is Mount Haley, but in the 1859 edition, Mount Halley [Chapman; PO Archives].

**MOUNT MORRIS,** Genesee County: Benjamin Pearson became the first settler in the area in 1833; Frederick Walker became the first settler on the village site in 1836; Charles N. Beecher became the first postmaster of Mount Morris on July 11, 1837, with the name of the office changed to Genesee on Jan. 19, 1839, back to Mount Morris on April 25, 1857, then to Mount Morris Station on April 17, 1865, and finally back to Mount Morris again on March 9, 1874; impetus was given village development by the projection of the Pere Marquette Railroad in 1857; platted in 1862 as

Dover; incorporated as the village of Mount Morris in 1867 and as a city in 1929; so named because many of its early settlers had come from Mount Morris, Livingston County, N.Y. [James L. Kidman; Wood; PO Archives].

**MOUNT PLEASANT,** Genesee County. See Long Lake.

**MOUNT PLEASANT,** Isabella County: when the county was organized in 1859, a central but uninhabited site was chosen as the county seat; agitation for a better location was begun when David Ward, owner of 120 acres here, offered to give five of them for county purposes; the location was ideal and in 1860 the voters accepted it; the land which Harvey and George Morton, of New York, bought from him in 1863, they platted and recorded in 1864; a station on the Pere Marquette Railroad; Milton Bradley became the first postmaster on Feb. 23, 1869; incorporated as a village in 1875 and as a city in 1889 [Fancher; PO Archives].

**MOUNT PLEASANT,** Oakland County: this settlement in the western part of the county was given a post office as Salome on Aug. 10, 1833, with Richard H. Benedict as its first postmaster; the office was renamed Mount Pleasant on April 4, 1837, and operated until July 6, 1868 [Ellis; PO Archives].

**MOUNT PLEASANT,** Wayne County: this village in Romulus Township, platted and recorded by Zachariah E. Adams in 1836, did not prosper [County plat liber].

**MOUNT SALEM,** St. Clair County: grocer John Lothian became the first postmaster of this rural post office in Emmet Township on July 23, 1884, the office operating until Nov. 14, 1903 [GSM 1885-1905; PO Archives].

**MOUNT VERNON,** Ionia County. See Smyrna.

**MOUNT VERNON,** Macomb County: named after the Virginia estate of our first President; its most prominent citizen, William A. Burt, surveyor, became its first postmaster on Dec. 19, 1832; the office, renamed Mountvernon on April 8, 1894, operated until July 15, 1905; it is in Washington Township and was given a railroad station [Lesson; PO Archives].

**MOUTH (THE),** Muskegon County: in 1850, William M. Ferry built a steam sawmill at the mouth of the White River; it developed into a thriving community, but the opening of the channel to Lake Michigan in 1870 meant the death knell of The Mouth; its business gone, in less than a decade it dwindled away [Page].

**MOWERS,** Benzie County: Ray S. Drew became the first postmaster of this rural post office on Oct. 17, 1902, the office operating until March 31, 1904 [PO Archives].

**MUD CREEK,** Eaton County: Joel Bailey became the first postmaster of this rural post office on Mud Creek, in Oneida Township, on Sept. 5, 1851, the office operating until Nov. 9, 1870 [GSM 1860; PO Archives].

**MUD LAKE**, Alcona County. See Barton City.

**MUD LAKE JUNCTION**, Alcona County: a station on the Detroit & Mackinaw Railroad, 33 miles south of Alpena and some 30 miles from Mud Lake, in 1894 [GSM 1895].

**MUGFORD**, Oceana County: Abe W. Corliss was appointed the first postmaster of this rural post office on April 9, 1895, but the office was never in operation and was discontinued on July 13, 1895 [PO Archives].

**MUIR**, Ionia County: the village began in 1854 with the lumber mill of Soule, Robinson & Company (Ambrose L. Soule, Andrew Byron Robinson, and Rev. Isaac Errett); it was platted in 1857; on Sept. 12, 1857, Mr. Robinson became the first postmaster of Montrose Station, so named because some of the early settlers had come from Montrose, N.Y.; railroad superintendent, H. K. Muir, was instrumental in having the Detroit, Muskegon & Western (now Grand Trunk) Railroad come through the village and they renamed it for him on Feb. 15, 1859; incorporated as a village in 1871, with Mr. Robinson as its first president [L. L. Swanson, PM; GSM 1873].

**MULBERRY**, Lenawee County: storekeeper George A. Pifer became the first postmaster of this rural post office in Ogden Township on May 17, 1897, the office operating until Nov. 30, 1904 [GSM 1899-1907; PO Archives].

**MULLET LAKE**, Cheboygan County: in 1849, Donald McDougal made the first settlement here on Mullett Lake, named for the original surveyor of the county; L. P. Riggs followed in 1850; first known as Dodge's Point after Anson R. Dodge, a homesteader, it was given a post office as Mullet (single t ending, and never corrected) Lake on March 11, 1873, with Mr. Dodge as its first postmaster; its local government is invested in its township of Inverness [R. E. Lewis, PM; Federal; PO Archives].

**MULLIKEN**, Eaton County: the village was founded in 1888 by Theodore E. Potter; Albert Lawrence became its first postmaster on Sept. 20, 1888; incorporated as a village in 1903; named for Mr. Mulliken, the contractor who built what is now the Chesapeake & Ohio Railroad that runs through the village [Clayton R. Ramsay, PM; PO Archives].

**MUNDAY**, Delta County: the settlement was named for a pioneer family here [Jean Worth].

**MUNDY**, Genesee County: it was first settled by Daniel Williams, Morgan Baldwin, and Volney Stiles, successively, but all in 1833; the township was named Independence, but owing to duplication, it was renamed for Lieutenant-Governor Edward S. Mundy; John C. Griswold became the first postmaster of Mundy on May 1, 1848, with the name changed to Long Lake, with George Judson as postmaster, on March 6, 1851, and then back to Mundy on March 24, 1852; the office operated until Dec. 31, 1900 [Ellis; PO Archives].

**MUNGER**, Bay County: this village in Merritt Township was first settled in 1874 and named for Curtis and Algernon S. Munger, of Bay City, who owned the land around its Detroit & Bay City Railroad station; Horace D. Blodgett became its first postmaster on June 6, 1876 [Gansser; GSM 1877; PO Archives].

**MUNGERVILLE**, Shiawassee County. See Burton.

**MUNISING**, Alger County: the town on the east shore of Munising Bay began in 1850 when the Munising Iron Company bought the land and platted the village, known as Old Munising and later as East Munising; William A. Cox became the first postmaster of Munising on Dec. 22, 1868; the office was closed on April 10, 1873, as the Munising Iron Company failed, and the office was alternately opened and closed as other iron firms continued the enterprise; in 1894, Timothy Nester and his associates began building the present city at the foot of the harbor where it was platted in 1895; Arthur S. Nester became the postmaster of its permanent post office on Jan. 4, 1896; incorporated as a village in 1897 and as a city in 1915; the county seat since 1902; it was in Schoolcraft County until Alger was organized in 1885; Munising, a change from Minissing, was Indian for island in a lake, or near the island, and was so called after Grand Island opposite [Sawyer; Hatcher; Gagnieur; PO Archives].

**MUNITH**, Jackson County: a Grand Trunk Railroad depot was built here on Hiram Sutton's farm and the place was first called Sutton's Crossing; the post office of West Portage was moved here from Nelson Hoyt's home and, at the suggestion of Charles H. Smith, was renamed after Munich, Germany; Mr. Hoyt became the first postmaster of Munith on April 28, 1880; when Mr. Sutton platted the village he also recorded it as Munith [Mich Hist 5:46 1921; GSM 1883; PO Archives].

**MUNSON**, Lenawee County: the Blanchard family came to this area about 1838; Levi Blanchard platted and named the village in 1881 and he became its first postmaster on Nov. 23, 1881; so named (with a one letter change) because the family came from Monson, Mass. [G. B. Britsch, PM].

**MUNUSCONG**, Chippewa County: John C. Blanchard became the first postmaster of this village on the St. Mary's River, at Munuscong Bay, in Bruce Township, on March 20, 1884, but the office was closed on June 28, 1886; the Thorice post office was changed to Munoscong on Dec. 16, 1926, with the spelling changed to Munuscong on July 1, 1937, the office operating until May 31, 1958; named from its location by Munuscong Bay, the bay of the rushes, where the Indians still make their mats [Hamilton; GSM 1907-27; PO Archives].

**MURPHY**, Baraga County: this settlement formed around the mill of the Murphy Lumber Company; after being given a station on the Duluth, South Shore & Atlantic Railroad, James F. Baker, the railroad agent, became its first postmaster on Aug. 19, 1890, the office operating until March 27, 1894 [GSM 1891-95; PO Archives].

**MURRAY**, Sanilac County: William White became the first postmaster of this rural post office on Feb. 4, 1886, the office operating until April 30, 1900 [PO Archives].

**MUSCOWAUBIC**, Ontonagon County: a 1000-acre copper mining location; a very limited amount of exploring work was done on it; see Pewabic for the derivation of the name [Stevens].

**MUSKEGON**, Muskegon County: Lewis B. Baddeau opened a trading post here in 1834, followed by Joseph Troutier in 1835; it is located near a river the French called Masquignon, from the Indian word for marshy river; Muskego Township was formed in 1837 and renamed Muskegon in 1838; Henry Pennoyer became the first postmaster on Jan. 3, 1838; the office was closed on Feb. 11, 1847, but has been restored since March 2, 1848; sawmill owner Theodore Newell made the first village plat in 1849; incorporated as a village in 1861 and as a city in 1869 [MPH 1:286 1874; PO Archives].

**MUSKEGON HEIGHTS**, Muskegon County: with the lumbering era gone, the area needed new business; its leaders formed the Muskegon Improvement Company in 1890, bought some 1000 acres of land, platted it, and sold the lots in lottery fashion; the profits were used chiefly to subsidize new industries; the plan succeeded and the town was incorporated as a village in 1891 and as a city in 1903; given a station on the Chicago & Western Michigan (now Pere Marquette) Railroad; William Charles Hopper became its first postmaster on July 25, 1891, the office becoming a branch of the Muskegon post office on May 14, 1896 [C. D. McNamee; PO Archives].

**MUSSEY**, St. Clair County: when the township was organized in 1855 it was named for Dexter Mussey, a member of the state legislature from Macomb County [Jenks].

**MUTTONVILLE**, Macomb County: by 1882, this had become a predominately sheep raising area, and Muttonville was founded at the junction of U.S. 25 and State Highway 19 as a sheep slaughtering center, chiefly for the Detroit market [Miriam Altman].

**MYNNINGS**, Missaukee County: this lumber settlement, 9 miles east of Lake City, was named for lumberman Christen F. Mynning who became its first postmaster on Jan. 15, 1900, the office operating until Dec. 31, 1907 [GSM 1901; PO Archives].

**MYRA**, Menominee County. See Wilson.

**MYRTLE**, Oakland County: Thomas Browning became the first postmaster of this rural post office on Oct. 28, 1899, the office operating until Oct. 15, 1900 [PO Archives].

**MYSTIC**, St. Clair County: a hamlet in 1878 [GSM 1879].

**MYSTIC**, Wexford County: David B. Vox became the first postmaster of this rural post office on March 3, 1900, the office operating until Aug. 31, 1901 [PO Archives].

**NADEAU**, Menominee County: the site was first the farm of Barney Nadeau and was called the Nadeau Section; the Chicago & Northwestern Railroad built a station on it in 1878, Mr. Nadeau became the first postmaster, with the office spelled Nadean and not corrected to Nadeau until Feb. 20, 1890 [Bernice S. Bickel, PM].

**NAGEL**, Presque Isle County: this rural post office was named for Julius Nagel who became its first postmaster on June 11, 1904, the office operating until Jan. 14, 1906 [PO Archives].

**NAHMA**, Delta County: it was a flourishing mill town when Joseph F. Merrill became its first postmaster on Feb. 21, 1856; the office was closed on March 25, 1859, but was restored from Sept. 7, 1865, to Dec. 23, 1867, and from Feb. 28, 1868, to May 22, 1873, and finally from Feb. 20, 1882, to date; the first county board meeting was held here in 1862; nahma was the Indian word for sturgeon: Henry Longfellow's Hiawaths "saw the sturgeon, Nahma, leaping, scattering drops like beads of wampum" [David S. Coon; Jean Worth; G. SM 1860; PO Archives].

**NAHMA INDIAN SETTLEMENT**, Delta County: the site is west of the village of Nahma, directly across the Sturgeon River; here some 100 remnants of the Chippewa, Ottawa, and Pottawattomi tribes live on land owned by the Bay de Nocquette Company, paying rent of one dollar a year so that they may not claim squatters' rights; see Nahma for the name [Federal].

**NANAIMO**, Iron County. See Iron River.

**NANKIN CENTER**, Wayne County. See Swift.

**NANKIN MILLS**, Wayne County: the first land purchase in the area was made by Dennison Palmer in 1818, followed in 1819 by William Woodbridge (later governor of Michigan), James H. Parmalee, and Henry J. Hunt; but Marenus Harrison and his family became the first actual settlers in 1825; on Jan. 9, 1828, the settlement was given a post office named Lima, with Henry Wells as its first postmaster; in 1829, the township of Bucklin (which had been named for its clerk, William Bucklin) was divided into Pekin and Nankin (both names chosen simply to avoid duplication), and the post office was renamed Nankin on April 2, 1830; in 1834, the north half of the township was given the name Livonia, the south half remaining Nankin; the first of the mills here was built by Noah Hull in 1835, and the place became known as Nankin Mills; the Nankin post office operated until 1902 [MPH 14:431 1889; GSM 1860; PO Archives].

**NAOMI**, Berrien County: a station on the Chicago & Western Michigan (now Pere Marquette) Railroad when James F. Haskins applied for a post office here; the department asked that the name be short and unlike any other in the state; storekeeper D. M. Hartwell suggested Naomi; Chester M. Broth became the first postmaster on March 7, 1884, the office operating until March 31, 1903; now a hamlet [Amos R. Green; GSM 1887; PO Archives].

**NAPIER**, Berrien County: a station on the Milwaukee, Benton

Harbor & Columbus Railroad, 3 miles south of Benton Harbor, in 1898 [GSM 1899].

**NAPLES**, Allegan County: the village was laid out by the Kalamazoo River in 1835-38, but its lots did not sell and it never became more than a paper town [Johnson].

**NAPLES**, Missaukee County: a station on the Pere Marquette Railroad, in Springfield Township; the settlement formed around the mill of the Thayer Lumber Company; Lennie Twining became its first postmaster on Nov. 13, 1900, the office operating until Dec. 31, 1904 [GSM 1903-07; PO Archives].

**NAPOLEON**, Jackson County: the village was founded in 1830 by General Abram F. Bolton, Charles Blackmer and Aaron B. Goodwin; Mr. Goodwin, an admirer of Napoleon Bonaparte, named the village and became its first postmaster on Jan. 5, 1833; when the Lake Shore & Michigan Southern Railroad came through in 1878 it was given a station [E. B. Sulski, PM; DeLand].

**NARENTA**, Delta County: a junction of two lines of the Chicago & Northwestern Railroad, nine miles west of Escanaba, in 1884 [GSM 1885].

**NASHVILLE**, Barry County: the village was founded by George and Robert Gregg, father and son, and platted on their farmland in 1865; named by Robert Gregg for George Nash, engineer in charge of construction of the Michigan Central Railroad, who in turn drew all the plats; John H. Palmer became its first postmaster on June 29, 1866; the first train came through in 1869, in which year it was incorporated as a village [Mrs. Stanzell; PO Archives].

**NASHVILLE**, Genesee County: Philander McLane became the first postmaster of this rural post office on Feb. 19, 1840, the office operating until only Dec. 23, 1840 [PO Archives].

**NASHVILLE**, Kalamazoo County: this hamlet was named for its general storekeeper, T. H. Nash, before 1874 [GSM 1875].

**NASHVILLE**, Kent County. See Sparta.

**NATHAN**, Menominee County: this village in Holmes Township began as a logging center and was given a post office as Wittmund on March 1, 1895, with Henry Moreen as its first postmaster; Charles W. Wilkins, Eugene Houte and Paul Brunette were the first settlers; in 1894, the Wisconsin & Michigan Railroad enlarged from a narrow gauge (which had moved the timber) to standard; then the road was bought by the Chicago dry goods firm of Kuhn, Nathan & Fischer, and the post office was renamed Nathan on April 3, 1895, with storekeeper Charles W. Wilkins as postmaster, the office operating until Dec. 31, 1940; the railroad has been torn up and Nathan is now a farming community with a general store [Charles W. Wilkins; PO Archives].

**NATIONAL**, Ontonagon County. See Minesota Mine.

**NATIONAL CITY**, Iosco County: the village began as a flag station on the Detroit, Bay City & Alpena Railroad in 1884; it was called Emery Junction and was given a post office of that name on March 21, 1904, with Quincy Martin as its first postmaster; the National Gypsum Company opened a quarry here in 1925 and the name of the village was changed to National City in 1926 [Lawrence H. Jordan, PM; GSM 1885; PO Archvies].

**NATIONAL MINE**, Marquette County: the village was founded in 1878 as part of the estate of the Lake Superior Iron Company, in the Winthrop Range; it was given a post office on Dec. 5, 1879, with Richard F. Ellis as its first postmaster [Andreas; PO Archvies].

**NAUBINWAY**, Mackinac County: the Indian name of this lumbering town on the north shore of Lake Michigan means place of echoes; Benjamin B. C. Perkins became its first postmaster on Nov. 28, 1879 [Emerson R. Smith; PO Archives].

**NAVAN**, Genesee County: this Irish settlement in Montrose Township was named after a town in Ireland; Simon Moran became its first postmaster on June 29, 1886, the office operating until June 30, 1902 [GSM 1887-1903; PO Archives].

**NAVARRE**, Wayne County: this salt block village on the River Rouge, in Ecorse Township, was named for an early French settler, Robert Navarre; William Wiegert became its first postmaster on Dec. 11, 1899; incorporated as a village in 1910; it was renamed Oakwood on Nov. 25, 1918, but its post office was closed on Dec. 31, 1918, and the village was annexed by the city of Detroit in 1922 [Burton; GSM 1901; PO Archives].

**NAVEAUX**, Mackinac County. See Hendrick's Quarry.

**NAZARETH**, Kalamazoo County: this community, then three miles from Kalamazoo, was founded in 1897 by Rt. Rev. Msgr. Francis A. O'Brien; it was given a post office on Feb. 27, 1899, with Sister Mary Anthony Nolan, S.S.J., as its first postmaster; it was named Nazareth because it was the motherhouse (as well as the college and academy) of the Sisters of St. Joseph, and St. Joseph was the head of the Holy Family at Nazareth, in Galilee [Sister Catherine Siena, S.S.J.].

**NEAHTAWANTA**, Grand Traverse County: a resort colony, with a hotel, ten miles north of Traverse City; founded by the Neahtawanta Association about 1890; a station on the Chicago & Western Michigan (now Pere Marquette) Railroad; Miss Mary Kroupa became its first postmaster on Aug. 1, 1907, the office operating until May 31, 1914; the name is Indian for placid waters, and here the waters deepen very gradually [Sprague; PO Archives].

**NEAL**, Grand Traverse County: this village in Long Lake Township was named for township clerk Warren Neal, and he became its first postmaster on Sept. 11, 1890, the office operating until Sept. 14, 1903 [GSM 1891-1905; PO Archives].

**NEBOSHONE**, Lake County: Henry Allen, from Pennsylvania, homesteaded here beside the Pine River and later was joined by other Civil War veterans who helped form the settlement which they named after the Indian word for a bend in the river; their holdings came into the possession of Ohio industrialists who made it their exclusive resort [Judkins].

**NEBRASKA**, Shiawassee County. See Laingsburg.

**NEBRASKA**, Washtenaw County: in 1878 a hamlet six miles east of Saline [GSM 1879].

**NEEBISH**, Chippewa County: the name of an island and since 1885 the name of a settlement on it; on some maps as Aneebish, Nibish, or Neebeesh; its Indian name is said by some to refer to the grand foliage that marks the island, by others that it meant where the water boils, referring to the rapids in the St. Mary's River here; in 1908, the government cut through these rapids to make a channel; farmer George Lawrence became the first postmaster of the settlement on July 21, 1885 [Gagnieur; Federal; PO Archives].

**NEEDMORE**, Eaton County. See Roxand.

**NEGAUNEE**, Marquette County: it was first settled by the Jackson Iron Company in 1846; the Pioneer Furnace opened here in 1857; the settlement was given a post office as Neganee on Jan. 21, 1858, with Edward C. Hungerford as its first postmaster; the spelling was changed to Negaunee on Feb. 11, 1858; in 1865, J. P. Pendill and the Pioneer Company had two plats made, that of the former called Iron and of the latter Negaunee; on these two plats, together with some of the Jackson land, the present city stands; incorporated as a village in 1865 and as a city in 1873; the name is Chippewa for pioneer [Mich Hist 28:199 1944; Andreas; PO Archives].

**NIEKERK**, Ottawa County: kerk is Dutch for church, and this hamlet had a Dutch Reformed church and a general store in 1876 [GSM 1877].

**NELLSVILLE**, Roscommon County: the village was founded by and named for Roscommon Township supervisor Edward Nelson, and he became its first postmaster on Aug. 20, 1906, the office operating until about 1927 [Co. Bd. of Ed.; GSM 1907].

**NELSON**, Kent County: Nelson Township was first settled by William H. Bailey in 1851, followed by John S. Jones later that year; the township was organized and named by the supervisors in 1854; Miles B. Dean became its first postmaster on Nov. 26, 1856 [Dillenback; PO Archives].

**NELSON**, Saginaw County: pioneer settlers who organized Fremont Township in 1867 included Nathan Herrick, Thomas Guilford and Joel Draper; they elected Thomas P. Hynes as the first supervisor and he named its village for his wife whose maiden name was Nancy Nelson; Eliza Montieth became its first postmaster on June 4, 1883, the office operating until May 31, 1912 [Mills; PO Archives].

**NELSONVILLE**, Charlevoix County: this village in South Arm Township was first settled in 1865; Nelson, Reddington & Company was the first lumbering firm in the area; it was in Antrim County until Charlevoix was organized in 1869; David C. Nettleton became its first postmaster on April 26, 1869; on Nov. 23, 1874, the office was transferred to and renamed South Arm [Traverse; GSM 1879; PO Archives].

**NELSONVILLE**, Monroe County. See Oakville.

**NEMOKA**, Ingham County: the plat of the village was recorded in 1882; the name is apparently a variant of the Indian term Nameoke, or Nameaug, meaning a place to fish; an unverified local tradition names it for a Chief Nemoka [Foster].

**NERO**, Isabella County: Martin M. Ryerson became the first postmaster of this rural post office in Coldwater Township on Feb. 24, 1871, the office operating until Nov. 30, 1877 [GSM 1873; PO Archives].

**NESSEN CITY**, Benzie County: a station on the Manistee & Northwestern Railroad; the village was founded and platted by John O. and Edith L. Nessen, of Manistee, in 1889; he built the first sawmill here, opened the first store, and on Dec. 5, 1889, became the first postmaster [Linda Potts; GSM 1891].

**NESTER**, Ogemaw County: this lumber settlement was named for Thomas Nester who had large lumber operations in the area; Dell Rose became its first postmaster on Sept. 6, 1901, the office operating until June 30, 1911 [Fred Litzner; PO Archives].

**NESTORIA**, Baraga County: the Nester Lumber Company was logging here when the Duluth, South Shore & Atlantic Railroad in 1871, and its name was given to the depot and to the village which followed; Albert Heath became the first postmaster of Nestonia on May 11, 1887, with the spelling changed to Nestoria on June 4, 1887; the office was closed on April 30, 1892, but has been restored since May 7, 1895 [Mrs. Joseph Heikkinen, PM; PO Archives].

**NET RIVER**, Iron County. See Parks Siding.

**NEW ALBANY**, Clinton County: Hiram F. Sheldon, of Cleveland, owned the land on which he platted the village in 1833; he sold it to George F. Clark, of Albany, N.Y., in 1836; many lots were sold but the village did not develop and they went for unpaid taxes, 1840-1848 [Ellis; Daboll].

**NEW ALBANY**, Isabella County. See Albany.

**NEWARK**, Allegan County. See Saugatuck.

**NEWARK**, Gratiot County: John H. Shafer became the first postmaster of this rural post office, named after its township, on Aug. 28, 1857; the office was closed on May 21, 1860, but was restored, with Abraham M. Butterfield as postmaster, on Dec. 8, 1863, and operated until April 30, 1902 [Tucker; PO Archives].

**NEWARK**, Oakland County: it was in Genesee County when farmer William H. Butts became its first postmaster on Sept. 10, 1873, with the office named South Grand Blanc; the office was renamed Newark on May 8, 1909, and operated until 1925; its station on the Pere Marquette Railroad was named Stony Run Siding [GSM 1879; PO Archives].

**NEWAYGO**, Newaygo County: Jack McBride and his employer, lumbermen, established the first claims here; Mr. McBride sold his claim to George W. Walton who in turn sold to John A. Brooks, who came here in 1836, and is considered the founder of the village; he became its first postmaster on Dec. 30, 1847; the office was closed on Nov. 17, 1851, but was restored from Jan. 8, 1852, to date; incorporated as a village in 1867; believed to have been named for Chippewa chief Naw-wa-goo, who signed the Treaty of Saginaw in 1812 [Allen F. Smith; Mich Hist 20:259 1936; PO Archives].

**NEW BALTIMORE**, Macomb County: it was first settled by Pierre Yax in 1796; Fabian Robertjean made the first government land purchase here in 1820; Alfred Ashley came here from Mount Clemens in 1845, built the first sawmill and the first dock, and in 1851, he platted the village as Ashley; with him as its first postmaster, it was given a post office as Ashleyville on Sept. 20, 1851, renamed New Baltimore on March 7, 1855; incorporated as a village in 1867 and as a city in 1931 [Eldredge; PO Archives].

**NEWBERG**, Cass County: platted in 1836 by Spencer Nicholson; named by John C. Saxon after Newburgh, N.Y.; but when Horace Nicholson was appointed its first postmaster on Aug. 4, 1837, he had the spelling changed to Newberg, "just to spell it different"; the office was closed on Oct. 4, 1859, and when it was restored on Oct. 24, 1861, with Henry Crego as postmaster, the spelling was changed to Newburgh, but the office was transferred to and renamed Jones on Dec. 19, 1881 [Fox; PO Archives].

**NEW BERLIN**, Ionia County. See Berlin.

**NEWBERRY**, Luce County: founded in 1882 as the logging headquarters of the Vulcan Furnace Company, and first called Grant's Corner; it was renamed for Detroit industrialist Truman H. Newberry and given a post office as Newberry on June 21, 1882, with Richard H. Weller as its first postmaster; incorporated as a village in 1885; platted under the supervision of W. O. Strong and the land commissioner of the Detroit, Mackinaw & Marquette Railroad in 1887, in which year it became the county seat; it had been in Chippewa County until Luce was organized in 1887 [N.K. Zeigler; PO Archives].

**NEWBERRY**, Wayne County: George S. Comer became the first postmaster of this rural post office named for Detroit industrialist Truman H. Newberry; the office was closed on March 15, 1882, to allow the name to be used by the village of Newberry, also named for him, and now in Luce County, on June 21, 1882 [Burton; Farmer; PO Archives].

**NEW BOSTON**, Wayne County: when first settled about 1820, the village was called Catville from the initials of its proprietor, C. A. Trowbridge, and was given a post office of that name on April 3, 1860, with Moses R. Nowland as its first postmaster; on March 20, 1868, it was renamed New Boston after the Massachusetts city, which had been named after Boston, England, a contraction of the original name of St. Botolph's Town [Burton; GSM 1865; PO Archives].

**NEWBRE**, Van Buren County: a station on the Michigan Central Railroad, opened about 1846, and also called Newbre Crossing [Mich Hist 39:181 1955].

**NEW BUFFALO**, Berrien County: the land here was located by Captain Wessel Whitaker in 1834, and he named it after his home port of Buffalo, N.Y.; he, along with Henry Bishop, Freeman A. Clough, and William Hammond became the first settlers in 1835; Alonzo Bennett platted the village in 1835, became its first president when it was incorporated as a village in 1836, and its first postmaster on July 29, 1837 [MPH 1:125 1874].

**NEWBURG**, Lapeer County. See Almont.

**NEWBURG**, Ottawa County: platted and recorded in 1857, Jacob V. DeMunn, proprietor [Lillie].

**NEWBURG**, Shiawassee County: Hosea Baker came here in 1835 and bought so much of the land that he is regarded as the founder of the village; he built a sawmill here on the Shiawassee River in 1836; it was named by another 1836 settler, Dr. Nicholas P. Harder who had formerly lived near Newburgh-on-Hudson, N.Y.; John Grumley became the first postmaster, with the office named North Newburg, on Aug. 4, 1863, and it operated until Aug. 26, 1893 [Ellis; Campbell; PO Archives].

**NEWBURG**, Wayne County: Asa G. Johns, a merchant and later the postmaster, became its first settler, in 1819; Anthony Paddack, who emigrated here from Newburgh, N.Y., supposedly named the village, but he said it was so named only because it was a "new burg"; now a part of the city of Livonia, but its name is retained in Newburg Road, Lake, and School; its post office operated in 1882 [Mich Hist 39:345 1955; PO Archives].

**NEWBURGH**, Cass County. See Newberg.

**NEWBURGH**, Lenawee County: Helen L. McNeil became the first postmaster of this rural post office on April 29, 1891, the office operating until Oct. 15, 1909 [PO Archives].

**NEWBURY**, Tuscola County. See Kingston.

**NEWBURYPORT**, Berrien County. See St. Joseph.

**NEW CANANDAIGUA**, Oakland County: Robert Jarvis became the first postmaster of this rural post office on Sept. 10, 1839; the office was changed to Orion (now Lake Orion) on June 28, 1854; named after

Canandaigua, N.Y., from where many of its early settlers had come [Seeley; PO Archives].

**NEW CASCO**, Allegan County. See Glenn.

**NEW CASPIAN**, Iron County. See Caspian.

**NEW COLOMA**, Berrien County: in 1869, pending completion of the railroad to this point in Watervliet Township, speculators bought land here, platted the village, and sold lots; some stores and homes were built, but the loyalty of the residents of the region to the businesses of the old Coloma bankrupted the new one and it reverted to farmland; see Coloma for the name [Ellis].

**NEWCOMB**, Washtenaw County. See Willis.

**NEW DALTON**, Marquette County: this settlement in Skandia Township formed around the sawmill of the Cleveland Cliffs Iron Company; Edwin S. Harris became its first postmaster on March 6, 1911 [GSM 1921; PO Archives].

**NEW DUBLIN**, Monroe County: named from the fact that most of the laborers on the excavation of the government canal to improve the harbor of Monroe were Irishmen; their settlement is now in the southwest part of the city, in the first ward [Bulkley].

**NEW ERA**, Oceana County: this village in Carleton Creek, in Shelby Township, was founded in 1870 by Gilbert B. Goble and Dr. Spaulding and named by the latter, who had come here from Erie, Pa.; Mr. Goble became the first postmaster on May 15, 1872, with the office in the depot of the Chicago & Western Michigan (now Pere Marquette) Railroad; he was succeeded in office by Joseph Zeck on Nov. 6, 1877; incorporated as a village in 1948 [Edmund Schiller; PO Archives].

**NEWFIELD**, Oceana County: when the township was shortly to be organized in 1866, pioneer settlers Joseph W. Sweet, Alexander McLaren, Elbridge Green and (the first settler) Booth Perry met and chose the name of Newfield [Hartwick].

**NEW GNADENHUETTEN**, Macomb County. See Gnadenhuetten.

**NEW GREENLEAF**, Sanilac County: James McNeil became the first postmaster of Greenleaf, named after its township, on March 6, 1886; the office was closed on June 30, 1906, and the hamlet is now known as New Greenleaf [Chapman; PO Archives].

**NEW GRONINGEN**, Ottawa County: the village was founded in 1858 and platted by Albert Borgers and H. ten Have; other pioneers were J. van Eenenaan, William Huizenga, and the man who named the village when it was given a post office and who became its first postmaster on March 4, 1872, Annius J. Hillebrands; the office operated until June 29, 1901; named after Groningen, a province in the Netherlands [Willard C. Wichers; PO Archives].

**NEWHALL**, Delta County: this village, 3 miles north of Hyde, began as a station on the Minneapolis, St. Paul & Sault Ste. Marie Railroad in 1887; Hans T. Hanson became its first postmaster on Jan. 14, 1894, the office operating until July 31, 1913 [GSM 1895; PO Archives].

**NEW HAVEN**, Macomb County: settlers first purchased land here in 1835 and the settlement became known as the new Baltimore Station; it was organized and given a post office as New Haven on Jan. 6, 1838, with Charles B. Matthews as its first postmaster; Adam A. Bennett was one of the organizers; the Grand Trunk Railroad opened a station here in 1865; incorporated as a village in 1869 [Nathan Whitford; GSM 1860; PO Archives].

**NEW HAVEN**, Shiawassee County: a hamlet in 1859 [GSM 1960].

**NEW HAVEN CENTER**, Gratiot County: Joseph Wiles, Jr. became its first postmaster on Sept. 26, 1863, the office operating until Dec. 14, 1904; it was located in the center of New Haven Township and was the site of its town hall [Tucker; PO Archives].

**NEW HOLLAND**, Ottawa County: the village was first settled in 1847 by Jan Vantongeren and Jan Van Dyke, at the suggestion of Rev. Albertus Van Raalte, the founder of Holland, and it was located five miles north of that village; its station on the Chicago & Western Michigan (now Pere Marquette) Railroad was named North Holland; given a post office as New Holland on April 10, 1872, with Adrian Wagenaar as its first postmaster, the office operating until Oct. 15, 1906 [Page; PO Archives].

**NEW HOME**, Houghton County: a station on the M. & M. Railroad; Retta B. Wadsworth became its first postmaster on Feb. 6, 1891, the office operating until Jan. 25, 1893 [PO Archives].

**NEW HOME**, Montcalm County. See Home.

**NEW HUDSON**, Oakland County: in 1830, Russell Alvord and Daniel Richards came from New York State and obtained 40 acres of land with the deed signed by President Andrew Jackson; in 1831, they opened an inn, the Old Tavern, a changing point for the stage line, known as the New Hudson Station. Dr. John Curtis became the first postmaster in 1834 (this was a stage postal service; the first government post office on record was established on June 2, 1852, with Alanson Smith as its first postmaster); the village was platted by Mr. Alvord in 1837 [Harold T. Hass, PM; Seeley; PO Archives].

**NEW JERUSALEM**, Washtenaw County. See Jerusalem.

**NEWLAND**, Manistee County: a station on the Manistee & Northwestern Railroad, six miles north of Manistee, in 1894 [GSM 1895].

**NEW LOTHROP**, Shiawassee County: the first land entry here was made by James Butler, of New York, in 1836; the village was later formed by the men who owned the four corners: Gideon Silverthorn, A. W. Gillett, Warren Williams, and Nathan Colby; it was first named Lothrop for William Lothrop who gave the bells for the Methodist church; to avoid confusion with the Lathrop post office, it was given a post office as New

Lothrop, with Carlton K. Runnels becoming its first postmaster on May 20, 1878; incorporated as a village in 1957 [Grace Streng; PO Archives].

**NEWMAN**, Sanilac County. See Lamotte.

**NEW MISSION**, Leelanau County. See Omena.

**NEW PLAINS**, Clinton County: a hamlet in 1864 [GSM 1865].

**NEWPORT**, Monroe County: it was first settled by the French who called it Rivière aux Signes (Cygnes), or Swan Creek (the village still has a Swan Creek Road), in 1830; it was boomed by American promotors in 1836; William White built a sawmill here in 1836; Safford Hopkins became the first postmaster of Newport on Aug. 16, 1836; the office was closed on July 1, 1841, but was restored on Aug. 16, 1842, with William White as its postmaster; named from its location on Swan Creek near Lake Erie [GSM 1860; Bulkley; PO Archives].

**NEWPORT**, St. Clair County. See Marine City.

**NEWPORT**, Washtenaw County. See Cornwell.

**NEWPORT MINE**, Gogebic County: first called the Iron King, it was discovered by geologist Raphael Rumpelly, of Newport, Rhode Island, and later named the Newport Mine; it was opened in 1886, and became owned successively by Ferdinand Schlesinger, Harrison Williams, the Steel & Tube Company of America, the Youngstown Sheet & Tube Company in 1923, and Pickands Mather in 1924 [Havighurst].

**NEW RICHMOND**, Allegan County: three eastern capitalists owned large tracts of land in the area and John Allen, of Ann Arbor, arranged with them for him to found a city here; he came and platted it in 1836, naming it after Richmond, Virginia, whence he had come to Michigan; he and Ralph R. Mann cleared some land, built a store and some houses; Jonathan F. Stratton became the first postmaster of Richmond on Nov. 4, 1837, and Mr. Mann succeeded him from 1838 to Oct. 19, 1839, when the office was closed, because Mr. Allen had failed in 1838, and the prospects of a city had faded out; but in 1871, when the Chicago & Northwestern Railroad came through, H. F. Marsh laid out a new village of Richmond; he built a sawmill and a store, and others built homes; another store and a large tavern were built by Gilbert Lamoreaux who, on Oct. 3, 1872, became the first postmaster of New Richmond (for there was by then another Richmond post office in Michigan); and now both the village and its post office bear the name of New Richmond [Johnson; PO Archives].

**NEW RIVER**, Huron County: J. Spikerman and Walter Hume became its first settlers in 1845; John Ginn built a sawmill here in 1853 and Thomas S. Donahue built both a sawmill and a gristmill in 1856; Mr. Donahue became the first postmaster on March 26, 1866, but the office was transferred to Grind Stone City on Feb. 5, 1872; it became the site of the W. H. Cooper & Company steam salt block in 1874, but it was only about a mile north of Huron City, and it receded to a hamlet by 1880, and is now a ghost town [Hey; PO Archives].

**NEW ROCHESTER**, Allegan County. See Pine Creek.

**NEW SALEM**, Allegan County: it began with a rural post office on Sept. 8, 1857, with Isaiah Nanes as its first postmaster; the office was closed on March 19, 1859, but was restored from April 19, 1860, to Jan. 15, 1861, and from Jan. 21, 1863, to Dec. 6, 1864, and finally from March 27, 1865, to Sept. 30, 1905; Peter Castor owned 120 acres here; in 1865, his brother Theodore bought five acres of it and began the town, which was named after its township [Johnson; PO Archives].

**NEW SANILAC**, Gladwin County. See Hockaday.

**NEWSTEAD**, Branch County: Ryon Williams became the first postmaster of this rural post office on Feb. 13, 1867; the office was transferred to and renamed Sherwood on April 16, 1868 [PO Archives].

**NEW STONY CREEK**, Oceana County. See Benona.

**NEW SWANZY**, Marquette County: this village in Forsyth Township began as a mining enterprise, a leasehold of which J. J. Pierce and others were the leasees; they formed the Swanzy Iron Company in 1883 [Andreas].

**NEWTON**, Calhoun County: it was first settled by Granville Beardslee and his family, from Rochester, N.Y., in 1834; when the township was set off in 1838, Benjamin Chamberlin, who had come here in 1836, had it named after Newton, Mass., he having been born in that state; Moses S. Gleason became its first postmaster on Aug. 1, 1839; the office was closed on June 7, 1866, but was restored from June 26, 1866, to April 18, 1881 [Everts; PO Archives].

**NEWTON**, Mackinac County: this township was named for Nelson Newton, one of the firm of Newton Brothers who developed the St. Helena Island fishery about 1765; it was organized in 1878 [Emerson Smith].

**NEWTON**, Mecosta County: this rural post office was opened on July 30, 1897 and was named for Newton L. Stafford who became its first postmaster, the office operating until Aug. 30, 1902 [PO Archives].

**NEWTON CENTER**, Calhoun County: this rural post office in Newton Township operated from Dec. 8, 1855, to Nov. 2, 1956; see Newton, Calhoun County, for the name [PO Archives].

**NEWTONVILLE**, Baraga County: this settlement on the shore of Keweenaw Bay was given a station on the Marquette, Houghton & Ontonagon Railroad named Newton's; it developed around the sawmill of Erastmos D. Newton and he became its first postmaster on Feb. 6, 1884; the office was named Newtonville and it operated until May 26, 1897 [GSM 1885-00; PO Archives].

**NEWTOWN**, Iron County. See Caspian.

**NEW TROY**, Berrien County: it was first settled by Solomon and Hiram Gould, brothers, who built a sawmill here in 1836; it was platted in

1837 and called Troy, probably by Joseph G. Ames; it was given a post office named Weesaw, after its township, which had been named after a sub-chief of the Pottawattomi Indians, and meant He, the Torchbearer; Charles Beard became its first postmaster on June 23, 1852; the office was closed on Sept. 24, 1852, but was restored from Jan. 5, 1854, to Sept. 20, 1872; the Chicago & Western Michigan (now Pere Marquette) Railroad station two miles west was called Troy (it is now Sawyer), and Troy took the name New Troy and was given a post office of that name on Sept. 21, 1865, with Charles H. Bostick as its first postmaster [Fox; PO Archives].

**NEW YORK MINE**, Marquette County: a station on the Chicago & Northwestern Railroad, a mile above Ishpeming, in 1878 [GSM 1879].

**NEY**, Calhoun County: this rural post office was in Ross Township, Kalamazoo County, when it was opened on May 28, 1898, with farmer Isabelle Travis as its first postmaster; it was transferred to Calhoun County on Nov. 6, 1901, and operated until Sept. 30, 1903 [GSM 1899-1905; PO Archives].

**NICHOLS**, Calhoun County: a station on the C. & L.H. (now Grand Trunk) Railroad, a mile from Battle Creek, in 1878 [GSM 1879].

**NICHOLSON**, Shiawassee County: this rural post office was named for Joseph C. Nicholson who became its first postmaster on July 18, 1896, the office operating until Jan. 31, 1901 [GSM 1897; PO Archives].

**NICHOLSON HILL**, Alpena County: it became the site of the Nicholson Lumber Company mill about 1860; the settlement around this hill (there are several in the area) became known as Nicholson Hill; it also has a church and some homes, but its post office and shopping center is Ossineke [Rev. Robert Pelletier].

**NICHOLSVILLE**, Cass County: the first sawmill in the county was built here in 1835 by Alexander Copley; Henry George built his grist mill here in 1851, and the place was called Georgetown after him; he sold out to the Nichols brothers for whom Nelson Copley renamed the village in 1855; Jonathan Nichols conducted the first hotel here [Fox; Glover; Rogers].

**NICKELPLATE**, Ionia County: Julia A. Jones became the first postmaster of this rural post office, six miles north of Ionia, on Nov. 20, 1897, the office operating until Sept. 13, 1902 [GSM 1899-1903; PO Archives].

**NIECEVILLE**, Chippewa County. See Algonquin.

**NILES**, Berrien County: the Indian mission which Claude Aveneau, a French Jesuit, founded on this site in 1690 was given a land concession by Governor Jacques Denonville of New France, at Quebec, in 1694, and the protection of a detatchment of soldiers in 1695; but it was not until 1697 that a military post was established here, from which date it became known in history as Fort St. Joseph; the fort fell to the British in 1761, to the Indians (Pontiac's Rebellion) in 1763, and to the Spanish and Indians in 1780, 1781, and was abandoned in 1781; permanent settlement of the site began in 1828 when Eli P. Bunnell and Abram Tietsort, both from Ohio, built their cabins here; later that year they sold out to Samuel B. Walling and Obed P. Lacey; the settlement was first called Pogwatigue (running water); Mr. Lacey first platted and recorded the village in 1829, naming it for Hezekiah Niles, publisher of the Niles Register, a Whig paper in Baltimore; it had been given a post office as Carey (it was adjacent to the Carey Mission, q.v.), on Dec. 4, 1828, with Samuel B. Walling as its first postmaster; the name of the office was changed to Pogwatigue on Feb. 27, 1829; Isaac Gray became the postmaster in 1830, but he soon died and was succeeded by Mr. Lacey in 1831; the post office was renamed Niles on Aug. 21, 1841, with Joseph G. Larimore as its postmaster; incorporated as a village in 1835 and as a city, with Elijah Lacey as its first mayor, in 1859; it was in Lenawee County until Berrien was organized in 1831; Niles is the only community in Michigan to have been under four flags: French, English, Spanish, and American [MPH 35:545 1907; Mich Hist 15:182 1931; Lewis; GSM 1860; PO Archives].

**NILES**, Oakland County: in 1837 a hamlet in Troy Township [GSM 1838].

**NINE MILE**, Bay County: a station on the Michigan Central Railroad, in Mount Forest Township, in 1894, and still a hamlet [GSM 1895].

**NIPPESING**, Isabella County: a hamlet in 1878 [GSM 1879].

**NIRVANA**, Lake County: Darwin Knight registered the plat of the village in 1874 and became its first postmaster on March 4, 1874; it lay in Yates Township, just south of the Flint & Pere Marquette (now Chesapeake & Ohio) Railroad, and in an area of a fine stand of white pine; there were eleven sawmills near the town, and when the pine slaughter was done, so was the town, and it is now a hamlet; Nirvana is Buddhist for highest heaven, and the town's best hotel was named the Indra House, after Indra, the principal god of the Ayran-Vedic religion, so Mr. Knight was evidently an admirer of Oriental religions [Harry B. Loree; PO Archives].

**NISULA** Houghton County: it was first settled by homesteaders and called Faro; Finnish settlers from Baraga began arriving in 1894 and one of the earliest, August Nisula, became the first postmaster on July 7, 1903, and the department named the village for him; it was also given a station on the Michigan Central Railroad in 1903 [Alina A. Keranen, PM].

**NIVERVILLE**, Lapeer County. See Columbiaville.

**NIXON**, Missaukee County: George E. Brainard became the first postmaster of this rural post office on Feb. 14, 1876, the office operating until July 11, 1882 [PO Archives].

**NOBLE**, Antrim County. See Alden.

**NOBLE**, Branch County: the first land entries here on the north side of Fawn River were made by William Robinson and Mr. Dusenberry in 1835; the first settlers, William Rippey, John Grove and William Butts, came in 1836; several hickory trees stood at its cross-roads and the place was first known as Hickory Corners; the town was organized in 1845 and was probably named at the suggestion of James Anderson who had worked in Noble County, Indiana; William Butts became the first postmaster of Noble Centre on Aug. 28, 1849, with the name shortened to Noble on March 25, 1884; the office operated until Jan. 31, 1903 [Johnson; PO Archives].

**NOBLE**, Washtenaw County: the first post office in Manchester Township was opened in this hamlet in 1833, with Harvey Squires as its first postmaster [Beakes].

**NOBLE CENTRE**, Branch County. See Noble.

**NOGI**, Mackinac County: this settlement was founded by Willis E. Johnson, forester for the Central Paper Company, of Muskegon, in 1905; a pulpwood logging camp and sawmill on the Carp River and the Duluth, South Shore & Atlantic Railroad, it flourished for some twenty years until destroyed by forest fires; it was named for Count Maresuke Nogi, Japanese hero in the Russo-Japanese War [Ernestine G. Johnson].

**NOKO**, Sanilac County: storekeeper Clinton J. Beers became the first postmaster of this hamlet in Lamotte Township on Jan. 6, 1896, the office operating until Sept. 15, 1904 [GSM 1897-1905; PO Archives].

**NOLAN**, Roscommon County: this lumber mill settlement in Nester Township was founded in 1890 by James Nolan, and named for him; William Finley became its first postmaster on June 12, 1891, the office operating until July 30, 1909; now a ghost town [Co. Bd. of Ed.].

**NOMAD**, Charlevoix County: a settlement on Beaver Island formed around the Nomad Shingle Company mill, Evart Cole, president; Mrs. Julia Cole became its first postmaster on March 10, 1917, the office operating until Oct. 31, 1933 [GSM 1919; PO Archives].

**NONESUCH**, Ontonagon County: the Nonesuch Mine was discovered in 1865 and opened in 1867; Thomas Hooper was the leasee of the Nonesuch Mining Company; Miss Addie Dickins became the first postmaster of its settlement on July 3, 1876; a station on the Toledo, Ann Arbor & Northern Michigan Railroad; this village in Carp Lake Township grew and dwindled with the fortunes of the mine; its post office was closed on March 16, 1887; the village site is now within the Porcupine Mountains State Park [Jamison; Stevens; PO Archives].

**NOORDELOOS**, Ottawa County: this Dutch settlement was made by members of the Holland Christian Reformed Church about 1863; Kerst O. Van Dyke became its first postmaster on April 13, 1880, the office operating until Dec. 31. 1904; it was named after a village in the west central part of the Netherlands [MPH 9:307 1886; PO Archives].

**NORA**, Washtenaw County: this station on the Toledo & Ann Arbor Railroad was given a post office on Jan. 28, 1879, with Peter C. Lowe as its first postmaster, the office operating until March 19, 1887 [GSM 1879; PO Archives].

**NORRIE MINE,** Gogebic County: this mine was discovered by Canadian-born Captain James R. Wood, prospector agent for English-born A. Lanfear Norrie; its settlement was a mining camp rather than a village, due to its nearness to Ironwood [Havighurst].

**NORRIS,** Wayne County. See North Detroit.

**NORRISVILLE,** Leelanau County. See Greilickville.

**NORTH ADAMS,** Hillsdale County: William Cutler came here from Niagara County, N.Y., and opened a tavern in 1835; the place became known as Cutler's Corners and was given a post office of that name on June 27, 1848, with Nicholas G. Vreeland as its first postmaster; the office was renamed North Adams on May 1, 1850; when the Adams post office was closed on Feb. 28, 1857, its mail went to North Adams, which eventually became the name of the village too; it was platted and recorded in 1871; incorporated as a village in 1881; named from its location in Adams Township [Vivian L. Moore; Reynolds; PO Archives].

**NORTH ADRIAN,** Lenawee County: this rural post office, north of the city of Adrian (which see for the name), was opened on May 13, 1839, with Asahel B. Treat as its first postmaster, the office operating until April 14, 1860 [GSM 1860; PO Archives].

**NORTH AMERICAN MINE,** Houghton County: Marquis W. Kelsey became the first postmaster of this mining settlement on Oct. 21, 1852; the office was transferred to and renamed Clifton, Keweenaw County, on Feb. 24, 1853 [PO Archives].

**NORTH AURELIUS,** Ingham County: this rural post office in the northern part of Aurelius Township was opened on Sept. 6, 1858, with Hirus I. Smith as its first postmaster; the office was closed on Oct. 16, 1860, but was restored from Feb. 10, 1888, to March 14, 1903 [Durant; PO Archives].

**NORTH BATAVIA,** Branch County. See Olds.

**NORTH BLENDON,** Ottawa County. See Blendon.

**NORTH BRADLEY,** Midland County: William A. Babcock became its first postmaster on Nov. 5, 1873, and supervisor of its township of Geneva in 1879; it was called North Bradley for there was already a post office named Bradley in the southern part of the state; the village was also called Buttonville or Button, for William R. Button who was closely connected with its early development [Mich Hist 46:375 1962; Chapman; PO Archives].

**NORTH BRANCH,** Lapeer County: the village was founded by the brothers John and Richard Beech in 1856 and was first called Beechville; in less than a year it was renamed from its location on the north branch of the Flint River; Richard Beech became the first postmaster on June 4, 1856; incorporated as a village in 1881 [Clare Keeler; PO Archives].

**NORTH BRIGHTON,** Livingston County: this rural post office, north of the village of Brighton, was opened on Sept. 5, 1851, with Guy C. Fond as its first postmaster, the office operating until Oct. 16, 1863; see Brighton for the name [GSM 1860; PO Archives].

**NORTH BROWNVILLE**, Kent County. See Alaska.

**NORTH BURNS**, Huron County: it was a lumbering community in Sheridan Township until the forest fires of 1871 when the land was cleared for farming; Donald McTaggart became its first postmaster on Feb. 20, 1871; the spelling was changed to Northburns on Nov. 14, 1894, but the office was closed on March 31, 1903 [GSM 1873-1905; PO Archives].

**NORTH BYRON**, Kent County. See Scudderville.

**NORTH CANNON**, Kent County: James W. Weed became the first postmaster of this hamlet on Jan. 9, 1851, the office operating until May 13, 1852; see Cannonsburg for the name [GSM 1860; PO Archives].

**NORTH DETROIT**, Wayne County: the place was first called Dalton's Corners for Lawrence Dalton who became its first postmaster on March 11, 1868, and a representative from the second district of Wayne County in 1871-72; although a federal survey had classified the site as "worthless," Colonel Philetus W. Norris, who had come to Michigan in 1821, purchased it and platted it as a village in 1873; he wanted to name it Prairie Mound in honor of an Indian burial ground here (the name is retained locally in Mound Road), but the Detroit & Bay City Railroad, whom he persuaded to run a tract through the area, posted the name Norris on its depot, and on March 5, 1873, the name of its post office was also changed to Norris; on Feb. 10, 1891, the village and its post office were renamed North Detroit; eventually it became just an area in the city of Detroit now bounded by Six (McNicholas) and Seven Mile Roads, Van Dyke (M-53) and Mound Roads [Sugars; Burton; PO Archives].

**NORTH DORR**, Allegan County: it began as a farming community about 1865; named from its being on the northern edge of Dorr Township (see Dorr for the name); Philipp Endres became its first postmaster on March 19, 1874, the office operating until Sept. 30, 1905 [Rev. E. G. Walters; PO Archives].

**NORTH EAGLE**, Clinton County: this rural post office, in northern Eagle Township, was opened on June 21, 1857, with George R. Stark as its first postmaster, the office operating until May 14, 1879 [GSM 1881; PO Archives].

**NORTH ESCANABA**, Delta County: in 1890, George T. Burns, manager of the I. Stephenson Company, platted a village, sometimes referred to as Parnell, but generally known as North Escanaba, and they sold 400 lots the first day; a station on the Minneapolis, St. Paul & Sault Ste. Marie Railroad; located just north of the city of Escanaba, it was made a station of the post office of that city in 1908 [David S. Coon; GSM 1895; PO Archives].

**NORTH FARMINGTON**, Oakland County: the rural post office of

North Farmington, in northern Farmington Township, was first opened a mile south, at Wolcott's Corners, with Ezra C. Hatten becoming its first postmaster on Feb. 11, 1847; John H. Button, the last resident postmaster, located his lands here in 1828 and settled on them in 1831; the post office operated until Sept. 15, 1902 [Durant; PO Archives].

**NORTHFIELD,** Washtenaw County: on June 9, 1834, George W. Dexter became the first postmaster of this village which had been named after its township; the office was transferred to and renamed Whitmore Lake on Dec. 27, 1854, but the Northfield post office was re-established from Feb. 16, 1855, to Jan. 3, 1856; then the Gravel Run post office was transferred to Northfield on Oct. 2, 1860, only to be transferred back to Gravel Run on Oct. 22, 1860 [GSM 1879; PO Archives].

**NORTH FIFE LAKE,** Grand Traverse County. See Fife Lake.

**NORTH GRAND RAPIDS,** Kent County. See Walker.

**NORTHGROVE,** Tuscola County: Ernest Kinney became the first postmaster of this rural post office on Feb. 21, 1899, the office operating until March 15, 1901 [PO Archives].

**NORTH HAMBURGH,** Livingston County. See Hamburg.

**NORTHAMPTON,** Saginaw County. See Chesaning.

**NORTHAMPTON JUNCTION,** Marquette County: a station on the Toledo, Ann Arbor & Northern Michigan Railroad, 7 miles from Michigamme, in 1888 [GSM 1889].

**NORTH HOLLAND,** Ottawa County. See New Holland.

**NORTH HOLT,** Ingham County. See Holt.

**NORTH IRVING,** Barry County: Peter Cobb became the first postmaster of this rural post office in the northern part of Irving Township on Feb. 6, 1858; the office was closed on Jan. 5, 1885, but was restored from Feb. 12, 1885, to Dec. 31, 1901 [Johnson; PO Archives].

**NORTH LAKE,** Lapeer County: a settlement in Marathon Township, near Otter Lake, in 1920 [GSM 1921].

**NORTH LAKE,** Marquette County: a former mining location and suburb of Ishpeming [Ernest H. Rankin].

**NORTH LAKE,** Washtenaw County: May Stevenson became the first postmaster of the rural post office of Louiseville on Jan. 21, 1835, with the office renamed North Lake on April 18, 1836, but closed on May 26, 1847 [PO Archives].

**NORTHLAND,** Marquette County: a station on the E. & L.S. Railroad; the village was founded and platted by the Wolverine Lumber Company and formed around its mill and general store, in 1900; John M. Thompson became its first postmaster on Dec. 24, 1900 [Louis Bertils, PM; GSM 1903].

**NORTH LANSING**, Ingham County: John Burchard began to build a mill and dam across the Grand River here in 1842; he drowned soon after and both were completed by Joab Page in 1843; the settlement was later named from its location, a mile above Lansing; a station on the Pere Marquette Railroad [Adams].

**NORTH LESLIE**, Ingham County: William Haynes became the first postmaster of this rural post office on Feb. 11, 1862, the office operating until Feb. 10, 1866; now a part of the village of Leslie, which see for the name [Federal; PO Archives].

**NORTH MANITOU**, Leelanau County. See Manitou.

**NORTH MARSHALL**, Calhoun County: Jacob King became the first postmaster of this rural post office on April 19, 1836, the office operating until April 24, 1855; see Marshall for the name [PO Archives].

**NORTH MILLS STATION**, Kent County. See Comstock Park.

**NORTH MORENCI**, Lenawee County: Orson D. Griffith platted the village in 1881 and named it Griffith; but, from its location due north of Morenci, it was given a post office as North Morenci on Feb. 12, 1883, with Nathan Justice as its first postmaster [Elizabeth Thompson; PO Archives].

**NORTH MUSKEGON**, Muskegon County: an old lumber boom town; Archibald Reed platted its eastern end as Reedsville; in 1872, Messrs. Phillips and Brown unofficially named the settlement around their mill North Muskegon, from its location north of that city; given a post office on April 20, 1881 as North Muskegon, the office operating until Dec. 31, 1907, when it was made a branch of the Muskegon post office; incorporated as a village in 1881, with E. C. Misner as its first president, and as a city in 1891 [Page; Anna M. Kueny; PO Archives].

**NORTH NEWBURG**, Shiawassee County; See Newburg.

**NORTH OXFORD**, Oakland County: John Rossman became the first postmaster of this rural post office in northern Oxford Township on July 19, 1854, the office operating until Feb. 23, 1869 [Durant; PO Archives].

**NORTH PARK**, Kent County. See Comstock Park.

**NORTH PEKIN**, Wayne County. See Redford.

**NORTH PLAINS**, Ionia County: it was first settled by Hector Hayes and Hiram Brown in 1836, the latter becoming the first postmaster on March 31, 1846; the town was named after its township, which was organized in 1844, with Nathaniel Sessions as its first supervisor, and named at the suggestion of H. B. Libhard from its occupying a broad stretch of level land north of the Maple River; its post office operated until Nov. 11, 1878 [Schenck; Branch; PO Archives].

**NORTHPORT**, Leelanau County: Deacon Joseph Dame founded and platted the village in 1852, naming it from its location; later that year, it annexed nearby Waukazooville, which had been named for Chief

Waukazoo; Aaron B. Page became its first postmaster on June 13, 1856; William Voice built the first sawmill in 1856; it was the first county seat, 1863 to 1883; incorporated as a village in 1903 [MPH 32:80 1902; Dickinson; PO Archives].

**NORTHPORT POINT**, Leelanau County: George Winans, of Kalamazoo, and Orin A. Ward, of Grand Rapids, bought the site in 1899; it had been called Carion Point, because the Indians carried their canoes across the narrows here; the new owners so renamed it because it lay across the Grand Traverse Bay from Northport; Mr. Ward became its first postmaster on July 28, 1911 [Mrs. Orin A. Ward].

**NORTH PORTER**, Cass County: John White became the first settler here in 1831; it was named from its location in Porter Township which had been named for Governor George B. Porter [Rogers; PO Archives].

**NORTH RAISINVILLE**, Monroe County: Amos P. Taylor became the first postmaster of the rural post office named Taylorsville for him on March 6, 1833; with Elephalet Clark as postmaster, the office was renamed North Raisinville on Jan. 20, 1838, the office operating until March 19, 1879; see Raisinville for the name [GSM 1889; PO Archives].

**NORTH RILEY**, Clinton County. See Riley.

**NORTH ROBINSON**, Ottawa County. See Bass Landing.

**NORTH ROCK**, Delta County: it was first settled by the Englund and the Smedberg families in 1876, and so named because it was north of the village of Rock.

**NORTH ROWLAND**, Hillsdale County. See Ransom.

**NORTH SHADE**, Gratiot County: when a rural post office was opened here on Aug. 3, 1854, with Joseph Comstock as its first postmaster, Mrs. Lane, mother of Henry Lane, suggested the name for it, and the name was also adopted by the township when it was organized in 1855, with Henry Lane as its first supervisor; on Aug. 3, 1868, the post office was transferred across the Montcalm County line to Carson City, but the town of North Shade remains [Tucker; Chapman; PO Archives].

**NORTH STAR**, Gratiot County: the Ann Arbor Railroad station here was named Douglas, but it was given a post office named North Star, after its township, on Oct. 20, 1857, with James M. Luther as its first postmaster; T. H. Harrod platted a village, a mile and a half southwest, for James Anderson, Marshall A. Coss and Marshall Iles, in 1884; the North Star post office was moved here and the village was renamed North Star; the post office was closed on Oct. 16, 1874, but was restored on Oct. 28, 1874, with its spelling changed to Northstar on March 31, 1894 [Tucker; PO Archives].

**NORTH STREET**, St. Clair County: a station on the Pere Marquette Railroad; Charles G. Townsend became its first postmaster on April 7, 1879; the office was closed on May 22, 1879, but was restored from June 11, 1884, to date; it was so named because its main road is North Street, which runs north out of Port Huron [Phyllis E. Simpson, PM; PO Archives].

**NORTH UNITY,** Leelanau County: this village in Cleveland Township, on Lake Michigan, at Pyramid Point, was first settled by Joseph Shalda and others in 1855; John Hartung became its first postmaster on July 27, 1859; the village was destroyed by fire in 1871 and its post office was closed on Dec. 10, 1875; but the office was restored from Aug. 21, 1876, to Nov. 30, 1892, and from Feb. 23, 1894, to Feb. 14, 1905 [Dickinson; GSM 1895-1907; PO Archives].

**NORTH VERNON,** Shiawassee County: this rural post office in northern Vernon Township was opened on Aug. 21, 1843, with Samuel W. Whitcomb as its first postmaster, the office operating until Jan. 2, 1873 [PO Archives].

**NORTHVILLE,** Wayne County: settlers from New York State came into the area in 1825; Abraham B. Markham built a grist mill here in 1826; Northville Township was separated from Plymouth Township in 1831, and being north of it was called Northville; J. M. Mead became the first postmaster of Northville on Oct. 10, 1831; the village was platted and recorded by William Dunlap and D. L. Cady in 1840; incorporated as a village in 1867 and as a city in 1955 [Mich Hist 34:203 1950; PO Archives].

**NORTHWEST MINE,** Houghton County: the Northwest Copper Association was organized in 1847 and re-organized as the Northwest Mining Company in 1849; its settlement here was given a post office on Nov. 19, 1849, with Daniel D. Brockway as its first postmaster, the office operating until Feb. 1, 1960; the firm was re-organized as the Pennsylvania Mining Company in 1861 and as the Delaware Copper Mining Company in 1876 [Stevens; PO Archives].

**NORTH WHEELER,** Gratiot County: a station on a branch of the Detroit, Lansing & Northern Railroad in 1894; on March 6, 1894, Lawrence J. Hoyt became its first postmaster, the office operating until May 14, 1904; named from its location in the township; see Wheeler for the name [Tucker; PO Archives].

**NORTH WILLIAMS,** Bay County: William W. Skelton bought land and became the first settler here in northern Williams Township in 1854; Armus H. Buzzard became the first postmaster on March 20, 1891, the office operating until May 15, 1903 [Page; PO Archives].

**NORTON,** Ingham County: on the site of the old village of Columbia, Hiram Norton built a mill, and the settlement which formed around it was given a post office as Norton, with him becoming its first postmaster on May 2, 1857; the office operated until Oct. 19, 1860 [Foster; PO Archives].

**NORTONVILLE,** Ottawa County: Colonel Amos N. Norton built a sawmill here, four miles up from the mouth of the Grand River, in 1837, and on Jan. 5, 1846, became the first postmaster of the settlement which formed around it; the office was closed on March 22, 1859, but was restored from April 22, 1872, to July 31, 1876; its station on the Chicago & Western Michigan (now Pere Marquette) Railroad was named Norton [Lillie; MPH 9:268 1886, 27:585 1896; PO Archives].

**NORVELL**, Jackson County: William Hunt became the first settler in the area in 1831; the village which followed was given a post office on March 17, 1838, with Harvey Austin as its first postmaster; it was given a station when the Lake Shore & Michigan Southern Railroad came through in 1878; in exchange for a large tract of land, it was named for John Norvell, U.S. senator from Michigan, 1836-41 [Mana Frieske, PM; LeLand; PO Archives].

**NORVESCO**, Chippewa County: Alvin P. Goodreau became the first postmaster of this rural post office, near Fibre, on July 20, 1928, the office operating until Feb. 15, 1932 [PO Archives].

**NORWALK**, Manistee County: this hamlet in Bear Lake Township was given a post office from Jan. 21, 1863, to Feb. 15, 1954 [GSM 1873; PO Archives].

**NORWAY**, Dickinson County: the village was born with the sinking of the first test pit of the old Norway Mine by Anton Odell, a Norwegian, in 1877, and the platting of the original town by him in 1879; George and James O'Callaghan built a sawmill here in 1878; the village was given a post office as Ingolsdorf on Sept. 11, 1879, with Charles E. Knowlton as its first postmaster, but was renamed Norway on Dec. 8, 1879; incorporated as a city in 1891; a station on the Chicago & Northwestern Railroad; it was in Menominee County until Dickinson was organized in 1891 [Sawyer; PO Archives].

**NORWAY HALL**, Lake County: Seymour Fowler became the first postmaster of this rural post office in Chase Township on April 8, 1875, the office operating until June 3, 1878 [GSM 1877; PO Archives].

**NORWICH**, Missaukee County. See Stittsville.

**NORWICH**, Ontonagon County: the settlement began with the Norwich Mine in 1850 and was also known as Norwich Gap and the Norwich Location; in 1853, the superintendent of mine was elected supervisor of the township (Pewabic); it became "quite a little village" until the nearby stamp mill ran out of business in 1865 [Jamison; Rudolph Stindt].

**NORWOOD**, Charlevoix County: it was in Emmet County when Orvis Wood, Lucius Pearl and Orin Adams built a dock and a sawmill here in 1867; William Harris built its hotel in 1868, and the settlement became an important shipping point; Mr. Harris became its first postmaster on Feb. 1, 1868, the office operating until April 30, 1913; it was named from its location in the northern woods [Charles A. Robinson. GSM 1873; PO Archives].

**NOTTAWA**, Isabella County: its first white settler was Michael

McGeehan who became the first supervisor when the township was organized in 1875; he was succeeded by state senator Alonzo T. Frisbee in 1877; it was named for a local Chippewa chief who lived from 1781 to 1881 [Chapman].

**NOTTAWA,** St. Joseph County: the village began as a rural post office opened on Jan. 15, 1836, with William Nottram as its first postmaster; the office was closed on Jan. 4, 1844, but was restored from Feb. 6, 1844, to May 23, 1859; the village developed with the coming through of the Grand Rapids & Indiana Railroad in 1867, and the Oporto post office was changed to Nottawa on Dec. 19, 1870, with Charles E. Sabin as its postmaster; its name was derived from a St. Joseph band of Indians known as the Nottawa-Seepes [Rachel Harbeson, PM; PO Archives].

**NOTTAWA PRAIRIE,** St. Joseph County: a post office in an inn, both operated by Captain Henry Powers; the post office was opened about 1830 but was transferred to Mendon on Dec. 17, 1858; see Nottawa for the name [Everts; PO Archives].

**NOVA SCOTIA,** Ingham County. See Kinneyville.

**NOVESTA,** Tuscola County: when it was being separated from Elkland Township in 1869, it is said that some of the freeholders were in Frawley Craw's store at Centerville (now Caro) discussing a name for it when Mr. Craw pointed to a stove the name on which was Vesta. No.—, and suggested that the name be reversed to Novesta; be that as it may, the new township was actually named Novesta; W. B. Brooks built its first store in 1871; Jefferson Green became the first postmaster on Aug. 24, 1874, the office operating until July 31, 1905; the village straddles the line between Tuscola and Sanilac Counties, and in some records it is listed as in the latter [PO Archives; Page; J. A. Gallery; Chapman].

**NOVI,** Oakland County: Erastus Ingersoll and family, from Ontario County, N.Y., became the first settlers in the area in 1825; Dr. J. C. Emery, at his wife's suggestion, proposed the name Novi when the township was organized in 1832; the first settler in Novi Corners was John Elmore, who came before 1830; with the office named Novi, Gideon W. Smith became its first postmaster on Jan. 5, 1833; some say the name was derived from No. VI, it being the sixth terminus on the plank road from Detroit, while others hold it was derived from the Latin word for new, implying that here was to be had a fresh start in life; incorporated as a village in 1958 [Atwell; Seeley; PO Archives].

**NUNICA,** Ottawa County: the first white settlers here were Manley Patchin in 1836, and William Hathaway, Jr., in 1839; Mr. Hathaway became the first postmaster of Crockery Creek on Feb. 7, 1848, with the name of the office changed to Nunica on Jan. 8, 1859; Henry Ernst made the first plat of the village in 1865; the word Nunica is derived from the Indian menonica, meaning clay earth, from which they made pottery; this was also the reason for the earlier name of Crockery Creek [Bernath S. Ernst, PM, g.s. of Henry Ernst; PO Archives].

NEW BOSTON
Thayer House

OTTAWA CO.
Res. & Restaurant - T. Hardy

**OAK,** Wayne County: this station on the Detroit, Grand Rapids & Western Railroad, then 12 miles northwest of Detroit, in Redford Township, was given a post office on June 30, 1858, with Salem T. Philips as its first postmaster, the office operating until Sept. 17, 1906; now within the city limits of Detroit [Burton; PO Archives].

**OAK BEACH,** Cass County: chiefly a summer resort, this site on Eagle Lake was platted and recorded by Henry J. French in 1906 [Glover].

**OAKDALE PARK,** Kent County: a station on the Detroit, Lansing & Northern Railroad; lawyer Charles L. Wilson became its first postmaster on Sept. 18, 1888; the office operated until Aug. 29, 1894, when it became Station F of the Grand Rapids post office [GSM 1889-95; PO Archives].

**OAKFIELD,** Kent County: present Oakfield Township was first settled by William R. Davis in 1838 and organized and named, through the influence of Sheldon Ashley, in 1849; William Horton became its first postmaster on Oct. 4, 1850, the office operating until March 19, 1877; the place was also known as Oak Center and as Podunk [PO Archives; Dillenback].

**OAKFIELD CENTRE,** Kent County: this village, settled in 1874, was named from its location in the township; Nathan H. Gould became its first postmaster on Jan. 18, 1875, the office operating until Oct. 31, 1906 [Chapman; PO Archives].

**OAKFORD,** Lenawee County. See Weston.

**OAK GROVE,** Livingston County: two brothers, Guy N. and Abner Roberts, from Chemung County, N.Y., bought 40 acres here in 1849; intending to found a village, the first built a grist mill; it was known as Bogue Mills while the village came to be known as Chemungville; the Oak Grove post office, opened on March 6, 1839, with Roswell Barns as its first postmaster, was two miles away; it was transferred to Chemungville, which was renamed Oak Grove in 1859; a station on the Ann Arbor Railroad [Ivan H. Taber, PM; PO Archives].

**OAK GROVE,** Otsego County: Oris W. Farrar developed the land; named after a grove of oak trees [Neil Hercules].

**OAK HILL,** Manistee County: it was named from its location on a hill dotted with large oaks; Charles Rietz and his brother built a lumber mill here under the hill and beside Manistee Lake about 1869; Charles Rietz built a fine home on the brow of the hill about 1875, and this section came to be known as Rietz Hill, while the remainder was known as the village of Oak Hill and was given a post office of that name on June 11, 1886, with Edward B. Eaton as its first postmaster; the office was closed on April 6, 1888, but was restored from May 5, 1888, to June 15, 1911 [Virginia S. Stroemel; PO Archives].

**OAK HILL,** Oakland County: Guy W. Selden became the first postmaster of this rural post office on Oct. 7, 1862, the office operating until May 18, 1877 [PO Archives].

**OAKLAND,** Allegan County: Matthew Heyboer became the first postmaster of this rural post office on May 24, 1889, the office operating until Sept. 30, 1905 [PO Archives].

**OAKLAND,** Berrien County: a station on the Milwaukee, Benton Harbor & Columbus Railroad in 1898 [Mich Manual 1899].

**OAKLAND,** Oakland County: Cyrus Chipman became the first postmaster of this rural post office on Jan. 13, 1823; the office was closed on May 27, 1835; the Orion post office was changed to Oakland on May 11, 1842; it was closed on Oct. 25, 1862, but was restored on Jan. 20, 1864, and operated here until it was transferred to and renamed Goodison on Dec. 12, 1872 [PO Archives].

**OAKLET,** Lapeer County: a station on a branch of the Grand Trunk Railroad in 1882 [GSM 1883].

**OAKLEY,** Saginaw County: Philip Mickle opened a tavern here in 1842 and was named the first postmaster of Mickleville on March 12, 1856; on April 18, 1860, this post office was changed to Havana, but on June 12, 1868, the post office was moved from the hamlet of Havana, two miles northeast, to Oakley and renamed Oakley; in 1868, Andrew Huggins platted and recorded the village as Oakley, for its landowners, Mr. Mickle, Isaac S. Bockee, and Henry Parshall; it was named for Judge Oakley, of Dutchess County, N.Y., an uncle of one of the proprietors; incorporated as a village in 1887 [Mills; PO Archives].

**OAK PARK,** Calhoun County. See Level Park.

**OAK PARK,** Oakland County: it was developed from the Oak Park Subdivision, recorded by the county register of deeds in 1914; community organization began in 1921; incorporated as a village in 1927 and as a city in 1945; given a sub-station post office in 1952 [Louise Shaw].

**OAK PLAINS,** Livingston County: James M. Holden became the first postmaster of this rural post office on Sept. 9, 1850, the office operating until March 22, 1858 [PO Archives].

**OAK RIDGE PARK,** Chippewa County: Stuart Ten Eyck became its first postmaster on April 6, 1911, succeeded by storekeeper John R. Barry in 1912, the office operating until Aug. 31, 1942; the name is descriptive of the height of the land here on Neebish Island, bordering upon the St. Mary's River, and of the trees growing upon it [Hamilton; PO Archives].

**OAKVIEW,** Oakland County: in 1902, the Ferry Seed Company, of Detroit, bought a half section of land (south half of 36) for $50,000, which it developed into its seed farm [Seeley].

**OAKVILLE,** Monroe County: Cyrus Everett built the first home in the area in 1831, the same year that Asa H. Reading and David Hardy built their water-powered sawmill; Ichabod S. Nelson became the first postmaster on May 7, 1834; the office was closed on Nov. 24, 1834, but was restored, with Mr. Nelson again its postmaster, on Jan. 21, 1835; with Asa H.

Reading as postmaster, the office was renamed Readingville on May 2, 1835; with Mr. Nelson again the postmaster, the office was renamed Nelsonville on June 18, 1836; it was again renamed Oakville on Jan. 3, 1837, and remained so until it was closed permanently on Feb. 29, 1904; it was in the records of Washtenaw County as Readingville, the village being near the Monroe-Washtenaw County line [GSM 1838; Pageant of Monroe History; PO Archives].

**OAKWOOD,** Oakland County: it was first settled by Hosea, Welcome and William Campbell, and Alexander Huff, in 1839, and first called Campbell's Corners; it was given a post office of that name on July 22, 1847, with David W. Fitch as its first postmaster; the office was renamed Oakwood on April 14, 1856, and operated until Jan. 21, 1913 [Mrs. Donald E. Adams; PO Archives].

**OAKWOOD,** Wayne County. See Navarre.

**OAKWOOD PARK,** Wayne County: Solon E. Spurr became the first postmaster of this rural post office on Aug. 13, 1891, the office operating until June 23, 1892 [PO Archives].

**OBERLIN,** Gladwin County: this hamlet, 7½ miles from Gladwin, was named by a Baptist minister for a clergyman friend; Frederick J. Reithel, Sr., became its first postmaster, with the office in his store, on May 27, 1902; the office was closed on March 31, 1948, and there is now also no store [Ritchie; PO Archives].

**O'BRIEN,** Ontonagon County: a Thomas Nester lumber camp on the Duluth, South Shore & Atlantic Railroad, with its express agent, David B. Henley, as its first postmaster, on Oct. 26, 1888, the office operating until July 10, 1893 [GSM 1889; PO Archives].

**OCEANA,** Muskegon County: Israel E. Carleton became the first postmaster of this rural post office on July 21, 1863, the office operating until Sept. 17, 1867 [PO Archives].

**OCEANA,** Oceana County: this county, organized in 1855, was named from its long shoreline on Lake Michigan; the Oceana post office was opened on Nov. 4, 1881, with Roena Powers as its first postmaster, the office operating until Sept. 25, 1882 [Blinn; PO Archives].

**OCEOLA,** Livingston County: H. H. Graves became the first settler in the area on August 31, 1834; the township, when organized in 1837, was called Byron, but was renamed Oceola in 1838; its town was given a post office as Oceola Centre on June 27, 1839, with Hiram Goodrich as its first postmaster; the office was closed on Nov. 2, 1856, but was restored from Dec. 19, 1856, to Feb. 24, 1899 [Ellis; PO Archives].

**OCINA,** Gratiot County: Abraham Fredenburgh became the first postmaster of this rural post office in southern New Haven Township on March 8, 1881, the office operating until only Sept. 7, 1881 [Tucker; PO Archives].

**OCONTO**, Ottawa County: a station on the Chicago & Michigan Lake Shore Railroad in 1876 [GSM 1877].

**OCQUEOC**, Presque Isle County: an Indian word for crooked waters, this village in Case Township was named after the winding Ocqueoc River; it has had a post office since Jan. 28, 1885, when Alexander Jarvin became its first postmaster [PM; PO Archives].

**ODEN**, Emmet County: this village on the north shore of Crooked Lake was given a station on the Grand Rapids & Indiana Railroad in 1882; storekeeper Joseph M. Luce became its first postmaster on Sept. 13, 1882 [GSM 1883; PO Archives].

**ODESSA**, Ionia County: it was named after its township which had been named after the Russian city; Myron Tupper, of Monroe County, N.Y., entered the first land here in 1839; he became the first postmaster on Dec. 30, 1840, with the office named South Cass, for Odessa was then a part of Cass Township, named for Governor Lewis Cass; the post office operated until March 7, 1899 [Schenck; PO Archives].

**ODESSA**, Oscoda County: Arthurbert H. Lawrence became the first postmaster of this lumber settlement in Big Creek Township on Oct. 18, 1882, the office operating until Dec. 27, 1898 [GSM 1883-99; PO Archives].

**ODLAM**, Sanilac County: a station on the Port Huron & Northwestern Railroad in 1886 [GSM 1887].

**O'DONNELL**, Barry County: storekeeper John E. Edwards became the first postmaster of this rural post office on Feb. 16, 1887, serving the office during most, if not all, of its existence until it was closed on Dec. 6, 1902 [Cole].

**OGDEN**, Marquette County: an iron mine and its community, named for William B. Ogden, of Chicago, who, with Samuel J. Tilden, of New York, had organized the Iron Cliffs Company in 1864 [Hatcher; Dunbar].

**OGDEN**, Lenawee County: a station on the Lake Shore & Michigan Southern Railroad; the settlement, named after its township, was given a post office on Nov. 24, 1874, with Russell B. French as its first postmaster, the office operating until July 30, 1932; the place was also known as Carpenter [GSM 1879; PO Archives].

**OGDEN CENTER**, Lenawee County: the first settler in the area was Moses Valentine, from New York State, who built his home here in 1826; the township was organized in 1837, and the town was named from its location in it; James Robertson became its first postmaster on Dec. 29, 1869, the office operating until Jan. 2, 1907 [MPH 7:519 1886; Bonner; PO Archives].

**OGDENSBURG**, Grand Traverse County. See Mapleton.

**OGDEN STATION**, Lenawee County: when the railroad came through it was some three miles from the village of Ogden Center, so the settlement around the depot took the name Ogden Station; named Ogden after its township [Naomi Bowling].

**OGEMAW,** Iosco County: this hamlet, 8 miles west of Tawas City, was given a post office on Nov. 2, 1868, with Elias Marsh as its first postmaster, the office operating until Feb. 6, 1875; Ogemaw was the Chippewa word for chief [GSM 1888; PO Archives].

**OGEMAW SPRINGS,** Ogemaw County: the oldest settlement in the county, it followed the building of a mill here on the Rifle River by the Ogemaw Lumber Company in 1871; a station on a branch of the Michigan Central Railroad; Case L. Nauman became its first postmaster on Jan. 23, 1873; the village was successful until hit by the panic of 1873; when the county was organized in 1875, it made an unsuccessful bid for the county seat, and that decided its fate; its post office was closed on April 17, 1893; Ogemaw was the Chippewa word for chief [GSM 1875-85; Powers; PO Archives].

**OGIMA,** Ontonagon County: a copper mining settlement; the Ogima Mine operated from 1862 to 1867, and later became part of the Mass Consolidated [Stevens].

**OGONTZ,** Delta County: a settlement around the George W. Slauson lumber mill, on the shore of Big Bay de Noc, in Nahma Township; he became its first postmaster on April 4, 1882; the office was closed on Sept. 2, 1882, but was restored, with Emily Slauson as postmaster, on Aug. 4, 1884, and it operated until July 31, 1913 [GSM 1885; PO Archives].

**OHIO MILL,** Ottawa County. See South Blendon.

**OHIO SETTLEMENT,** Cheboygan County. See Burt Lake.

**OHMAN,** Saginaw County. See Lawndale.

**OIL CITY,** Midland County: the discovery well was drilled in 1928 on the Walter Root property, a half mile south of the corner that is known as Oil City; by 1929, the oil boom was in full swing in the area; the Pure Oil Company built the first field camp, called the Porter Camp, under the direction of C. E. Dougherty [Betty Cochran].

**OJIBWAY,** Keweenaw County: a station on the K. C. Railroad, at the Gratiot River, in Allouez Township; the settlement formed around the location of the Ojibway Mining Company, and its supply clerk, John Sullivan, became the first postmaster on Feb. 15, 1908, the office operating until July 31, 1913; the Ojibway or Chippewa Indians were native to this area [GSM 1909-15; PO Archives].

**OKEMOS,** Ingham County: the first settler on the site was Sanford Marsh in 1839 and it was given a post office named Sanford on April 8, 1840, with Joseph H. Kilborn as its first postmaster; in 1840-41, Freeman Bray platted the village as Hamilton, after Alexander Hamilton; so for a time, the village was Hamilton and its post office was Sanford; residents began to call the town Okemos after the Indian chief whose tribe had often camped in the vicinity, and on May 26, 1862, both the village and its post office became officially known as Okemos [Jessie Turner; PO Archives].

**OLA**, Gratiot County: it began in 1887 as a station on the Toledo, Saginaw & Muskegon (now a division of the Grand Trunk) Railroad, in Washington Township; Alvin Shaver became its first postmaster on May 26, 1887, the office operating until Dec. 31, 1904; a small tract was platted and recorded by Mr. Shaver in 1888 [Tucker; PO Archives].

**OLD COLONY**, Houghton County: the Old Colony Mining Company was organized and named in Boston in 1898, and began work immediately on its copper property here [Stevens].

**OLD MISSION**, Grand Traverse County: this mission, then in Michilimackinac County, was founded by Rev. Peter Dougherty, a Presbyterian minister who built a log cabin and a mission church here in 1839; the settlement was called Grand Traverse and was given a post office of that name on April 26, 1850, with Robert Campbell as its first postmaster; when the Indians were moved to Omena in 1852, it was called the New Mission and Grand Traverse became the Old Mission; the Grand Traverse post office was renamed Old Mission on Feb. 1, 1869 [Grace K. Pratt; PO Archives].

**OLD MISSION HARBOR**, Grand Traverse County: platted in 1879-80 by L. N. Beers, it became a summer resort community [Traverse].

**OLD MUNISING**, Alger County. See Munising.

**OLD PORT**, Monroe County: it was first called Newport, but when a railroad was run a mile west of the settlement, the station was called Newport, and so to avoid confusion, the older settlement took the name Old Port, about 1836; named from its nearness to Lake Erie [Bulkley].

**OLDS**, Branch County: on Oct. 9, 1874, Gideon D. Baggerly became the first postmaster of the rural post office of North Batavia, named from its location in Batavia Township; the office was renamed Olds on Aug. 6, 1883, and operated until Jan. 31, 1901 [Pen Phil 10:4 Dec 1959].

**OLIVE**, Clinton County: Peter Merrihew and his sons made the first land purchase in the area in 1836 and the first settlement in 1837; when the township was organized in 1841, they named it Olive, after the place in New York whence they had come to Michigan; it was given a post office on July 13, 1848, with Perryn Armstrong as its first postmaster, the office operating until June 18, 1875 [Ellis; PO Archives].

**OLIVE**, Ottawa County. See South Olive.

**OLIVE BRANCH**, Oakland County: a hamlet in 1864 [GSM 1865].

**OLIVE CENTER**, Ottawa County: a hamlet named from its location in Olive Township, which was organized in 1857; M. R. Merritt first settled here in 1864; its large sawmill was owned and operated by James H. Carey; Henry D. Jones became its first postmaster on Dec. 20, 1875, the office operating until Nov. 30, 1906 [Page; PO Archives].

**OLIVER,** Lake County: this station on the Pere Marquette Railroad, in Chase Township, was named Olivers; it was given a post office as Oliver on Nov. 23, 1898, with farmer Alexander Walcott as its first postmaster, the office operating until July 31, 1902 [GSM 1899-1903; PO Archives].

**OLIVER CENTER,** Huron County. See Elkton.

**OLIVET,** Eaton County: Rev. John Shipherd, founder of Oberlin College in Ohio, led a colony of 39 here in 1844, to found a Congregational college and community; he had planned to go to the Delta valley, but lost his way in the wilderness and landed here; believing it was providential, he remained and named it after Mount Olivet of the Bible; Albertus L. Green, as a college student, conducted the first post office; Prof. O. Hosford became the first government appointed postmaster on Aug. 17, 1849; the village was first platted by Carlo Reed and William Hosford in 1848; incorporated as a village by the supervisors in 1865 and by the legislature in 1867; incorporated as a city in 1958 [Mich Hist 28:397 1944; Durant; PO Archives].

**OLNEY,** Shiawassee County: Albert St. Clair became the first postmaster of this rural post office on Dec. 7, 1883, the office operating until June 30, 1902 [PO Archives].

**OLSON,** Midland County: John B. Moore became the first postmaster of this rural post office on April 5, 1899, succeeded by storekeeper L. P. Larsen in 1904, the office operating until Jan. 15, 1913 [PO Archives].

**OMARD,** Sanilac County: its first building was a schoolhouse, built in 1869, and until at least 1884, the rest of the settlement consisted of its post office which was opened on April 25, 1871, with Richard J. Nicholl as its first postmaster; the schoolhouse also served as the church; it was located in Flynn Township, named for Thomas Flynn who became its first supervisor in 1869; its post office operated until March 15, 1904 [Chapman; PO Archives].

**OMENA,** Leelanau County: in 1852, Rev. Peter Dougherty, a Presbyterian minister, moved his Indian mission from Old Mission to New Mission (across the Grand Traverse Bay); it was given a post office as Omena on Feb. 9, 1858, with him as its first postmaster; tradition has it that the place acquired its name from his habitual response to any statement made by an Indian: Omena? (Is it so?); services have been held in its church each Sunday since its dedication in 1858; it was in Grand Traverse County until Leelanau was organized in 1863 [Horace P. Wheeler, PM; Federal; PO Archives].

**OMER,** Arenac County: it was founded by George Carscallen and George L. Gorie who built a large sawmill here on the Rifle River about 1866, and was first called Rifle River Mills; Mr. Carscallen, who became the first postmaster on Sept. 19, 1872, wanted to name it Homer, but there was then another Homer post office in Michigan, so he shortened it to Omer; a station on the Detroit & Mackinaw Railroad; the village was platted in 1872; incorporated as a city in 1903; it was in Bay County until Arenac was organized in 1883 [Page; PO Archives].

**OMO**, Macomb County: storekeeper Frank Will became the first postmaster of this hamlet in Lenox Township on Oct. 16, 1897, the office operating until Jan. 14, 1905 [GSM 1899-1907; PO Archives].

**ONAWAY**, Presque Isle County: civil engineer Thomas E. Shaw became the first postmaster of this farming community in Allis Township on Oct. 23, 1882, with the office named Shaw, after himself; Marritt Chandler arrived in 1886, platted the village, and called it Onaway (said to be the name of an Indian maiden), and the post office was renamed Onaway on March 29, 1890, with him as its postmaster; Mr. Shaw got the post office back from Mr. Chandler and had it renamed Adalaska on Aug. 18, 1893; but it was changed back to Onaway on Nov. 15, 1897, and the village was incorporated as Onaway in 1899; incorporated as a city in 1903 [Mich Hist 53:292-306 Winter 1969; GSM 1883-99; PO Archives].

**ONEIDA**, Eaton County: Solomon Russell, from Orleans County, N.Y., became the first settler in 1836, followed by Samuel Preston, from Cayuga County, N.Y., in 1837; the legislature created and named the town in 1838; Mr. Preston became its first postmaster on Jan. 19, 1839; the office was closed on Aug. 6, 1852, but was restored from June 3, 1854, to Aug. 3, 1866 [MPH 28:40 1897, 39:339 1899; Mich Hist 11:498 1927; Durant; PO Archives].

**ONEIDA**, Lenawee County: George H. Deline became the first postmaster of this rural post office, 3½ miles from Clayton, on Oct. 30, 1897, the office operating until April 10, 1902; named after Oneida, N.Y., many of the settlers having come from that area [GSM 1899-1903; PO Archives].

**ONEKAMA**, Manistee County: the village that developed from the mill which Adam Stronach built here on the creek between Lakes Portage and Michigan in 1845 was called Portage; but there was another Portage post office in Michigan at the time and this one was given a post office as Onekama on May 8, 1871; the lake, as early as 1840, had been called Oneka-ma-engk or Portage Lake, so Onekama was chosen; Augustine W. Farr, the town's leading citizen, became its first postmaster from 1871 to 1876; a station on the Manistee & Northwestern Railroad in 1888; incorporated as a village in 1891 [Elsket Chaney; PO Archives].

**ONEKAMA JUNCTION**, Manistee County: a station on the Manistee & Northwestern Railroad, built in 1888, ten miles northeast of Manistee; see Onekama for the name [GSM 1895].

**ONNELA**, Houghton County: Arthur Henry Lampinen became the first postmaster of this rural post office in Stanton Township on July 6, 1909 [GSM 1911; PO Archives].

**ONONDAGA**, Ingham County: Oliver Booth entered the first land here in 1834; Warren B. Buckland became the first postmaster on Oct. 16, 1838; John Howland, who acquired land here in 1837, with others, platted the village in 1870; named after its township which had been named by Orange Phelps after his old home, Onondaga County, N.Y. [Foster; PO Archives].

**ONOTA**, Alger County: originally an Indian fishing site, it was given the name Onota, the place where the fishermen lived; when the white man came and built sawmills here, it became known as Bismark and later as Wayne's Mill; as Onota, it became the first county seat when Schoolcraft County was established in 1848; Charles H. Schaffer, who named his daughter Onota (Mrs. Onota Schaffer Koch, at whose Pasadena home he died at 99 in 1945), operated charcoal kilns here from 1869; it was given a post office on May 16, 1870, with Robert A. White as its first postmaster; the village was wiped out by fire in 1877, and not rebuilt; its post office was closed on Aug. 14, 1879, but was restored and transferred to Alger County on May 18, 1881; the Cleveland Cliffs Iron Company gave its 54 acres here to the U.S. Forest Service for historical and recreational use in 1948 [Escanaba Press; GSM 1873; Ernest Rankin; PO Archives].

**ONSTED**, Lenawee County: it was founded by William Onsted in 1884 when the Michigan & Ohio Railroad came through here; James E. Gibbs became its first postmaster on Feb. 28, 1884; incorporated as a village in 1907; it was named for the founder's father, John Onsted, whose land, which he bought from the government, became the site of the village [Luella Reynolds; PO Archives].

**ONTARIO**, Lenawee County: a railroad station in the southwest corner of the county; Edwin Ash became its first postmaster on June 28, 1881, the office operating until Jan. 31, 1902 [GSM 1883-1903; PO Archives].

**ONTONAGON**, Ontonagon County: its site lays in the claim pre-empted by prospector James Kirk Paul in 1843; he built his log cabin here and began to plat the town, recording his plat in 1854; Daniel S. Cash became the first postmaster on Sept. 28, 1846; incorporated as a village in 1885; it was in Houghton County until Ontonagon was organized in 1853; the name Ontonagon was first found on a Jesuit map of 1672, identifying the river which flows through the area and taken from the Chippewa word Nan-ton-a-gon, meaning bowl, from the shape of the river's mouth [Jamison; Andreas; PO Archives].

**ONTWA**, Cass County: it was first settled by Ezra Beardsley and family in 1829; the township, when organized in 1829, comprised nearly half of the county, and was named after an Indian girl employed by Thomas H. Edwards, the first township clerk [Rogers].

**ONUMENESEVILLE**, Leelanau County: a hamlet in 1878 [GSM 1879].

**OPECHEE**, Houghton County: this station on the Mineral Range Railroad was given a post office on July 10, 1882, with Frank Haun as its first postmaster, but the office was changed to Osceola on Feb. 18, 1909 [Mich Hist 17:192 1933; PO Archives].

**OPORTO**, St. Joseph County: this settlement on Sand Lake was given a post office on April 6, 1837, with Levi E. Thompson as its first postmaster; the office was changed to Nottawa on Dec. 19, 1870; it was platted by Mr. Whitney, an early settler [GSM 1875-77; PO Archives].

**ORAL**, Benzie County: Frank E. Thurber became the first postmaster of this rural post office on June 15, 1883; the office was closed on Oct. 30, 1891, but was restored from March 14, 1892, to Aug. 15, 1900, and from Dec. 9, 1902, to July 15, 1904 [PO Archives].

**ORAL**, Clinton County: Hulse L. Pruden became the first postmaster of this rural post office on Feb. 12, 1891, succeeded by William P. Wandell on Nov. 24, 1891, the office operating until April 30, 1902 [PO Archives].

**ORA LABORA**, Huron County: in December, 1862, Rev. Emil Gottlob Baur led fifty families, members of the (Methodist) Christian German Agricultural and Benevolent Society, in founding a religious-socialistic colony called Ora et Labora (Latin for pray and work); its secretary, Louis Faul became the first postmaster of Ora Labora on May 15, 1863; the office was closed on Feb. 10, 1866, but was restored with schoolteacher Herman Roedel as postmaster, on April 2, 1866; most of the members were from the urban working classes, lacking the knowledge and hardihood needed by pioneer backwoodsmen, and many gave up and left, and the venture failed; its post office was moved to Bay Port, about a mile southwest, on March 19, 1872 [Schultz; PO Archives].

**ORANGE**, Branch County: William Aldrich, a Quaker from Wayne County, N.Y., who settled here about 1833, became the first postmaster of this rural post office on July 13, 1838, the office operating until June 2, 1851 [PO Archives].

**ORANGE**, Ionia County: Selah Arms became the first settler here in 1835; the township was organized in the home of Dean M. Tyler in 1845, with him as moderator, and he so named it simply because of its pleasant sound; Alexander K. Hall was elected its first supervisor; Lewis Priest became its first postmaster on Nov. 20, 1858, the office operating until April 30, 1904 [Schenck; Branch; PO Archives].

**ORANGE**, Kalkaska County. See Lodi.

**ORANGEVILLE**, Barry County: when the township was organized in 1847, Peter Falk wanted it named Orange, after an Ohio township, but there was already one in Michigan, and so a compromise was made on Orangeville; E. G. Salisbury and his brother-in-law bought a mill site and water power here in 1850 and completed their mill in 1851; the village, named after the township, was given a post office on June 8, 1854, with Hiram Tillotson as its first postmaster, with the office named Orangeville Mills, for there was then an Orangeville post office in Michigan, but after it was renamed in 1882, this one was changed to Orangeville on June 13, 1894 [PO Archives; Johnson].

**ORANGEVILLE**, Branch County. See Hodunk.

**ORANGEVILLE MILLS**, Barry County. See Orangeville.

**ORAY**, Sanilac County: Isaac Losie became the first postmaster of this rural post office on June 1, 1891, the office operating until Jan. 18, 1892 [PO Archives].

**ORCHARD HILL,** Alpena County: this lumber settlement was given a post office on Feb. 16, 1883, with James W. Farrier as its first postmaster, succeeded by farmer Joseph Bryan in 1884, the office operating until Jan. 31, 1909 [GSM 1885; PO Archives].

**ORCHARD LAKE,** Oakland County: the Orchard Lake Hotel opened in 1872 and was given a post office on March 18, 1873, as Orchard Lake, through the efforts of General Joseph Copeland, who became its first postmaster; the Indians had called the lake beside it Menahsagorning, or Apple Place, because of the many apple trees and orchards nearby; thus the lake came to be called Orchard Lake as was the village by it, which was founded in 1927 by local residents, William H. Morley, Frederick S. Strong, Jr., William H. Bouma, Edward M. Horton, and Loren C. Row; incorporated as a village in 1927 [Yvonne Coates; PO Archives].

**ORE CREEK,** Livingston County. See Brighton.

**OREGON,** Lapeer County: in 1836, Richard Bronson settled near a lake which was later named Lake Bronson for him; Oregon Township was organized in 1846; Sarah A. Carpenter became the first postmaster of this settlement near Lake Bronson on Oct. 13, 1873, with the office named Oregon; the Detroit & Bay City Railroad depot, also built in 1873, housed the office but was named Carpenter's Station for Samuel Carpenter, who owned the land; the post office operated until June 30, 1905 [Page; PO Archives].

**ORE SIDING,** Delta County: a station on the Chicago & Northwestern Railroad, a mile north of Escanaba, in 1878 [GSM 1879].

**ORIENT,** Osceola County: Robert S. Covert became the first postmaster of this rural post office, named after its township, on Jan. 15, 1900, the office operating until June 27, 1911 [PO Archives].

**ORION,** Oakland County. See Lake Orion.

**ORLEANS,** Ionia County: the first settler here was Guy Webster, from Lorain County, Ohio, in 1837; it was in a wheat-growing region and was given a post office as Wheatland on Sept. 7, 1844, with Joel C. Green as its first postmaster; many of its settlers came from Orleans County, N.Y., and the name was changed to Orleans on June 22, 1868; in 1870, Asa Palmer gave land to the Detroit, Lansing & Northern Railroad in return for a depot on his land here; in 1871, he had the village platted and named Palmer; but the post office remained Orleans and the village is now also known as Orleans [Leo F. Leiter; Branch; PO Archives].

**ORONO,** Osceola County: this station on the Grand Rapids & Indiana Railroad was named McDonald's Siding; but the hamlet beside it, in southern Lincoln Township, was given a post office as Orono on Nov. 5, 1875, with James M. Hawkins as its first postmaster [Pen Phil 12:3 Sept 1961; Chapman; PO Archives].

**ORONOKO,** Berrien County: the township was set off in 1837 and named by Governor Stevens T. Mason, doubtless in honor of Oronoko, the

Indian chief; the first township meeting was held in the home of William F. St. John who was elected clerk and justice of the peace, with Edward Ballengee as supervisor [Ellis].

**ORR,** Saginaw County. See Orville.

**ORRVILLE,** Mackinac County. See Scott's Point.

**ORTONVILLE,** Oakland County: the village was founded by Amos Orton who built a dam across Kearsley Creek here to furnish water power for his sawmill in 1848; he became the first postmaster on Aug. 18, 1857; platted by Hiram Ball, Charles Herrington, and others, in 1866; incorporated as a village in 1902 [Mrs. John Waltz; Seeley; PO Archives].

**ORVILLE,** Saginaw County: this station on the Cincinnati, Saginaw & Mackinaw Railroad was given a post office as Orr on July 7, 1896, with storekeeper Hector S. Smith as its first postmaster, the office operating until Oct. 14, 1904 [GSM 1897-1905; PO Archives].

**OSBORN,** Benzie County: storekeeper Frank Berry became the first postmaster of this rural post office in Platte Township on April 23, 1887, the office operating until Feb. 15, 1911 [GSM 1889; PO Archives].

**OSBORNE'S,** Calhoun County: a flag station on a branch of the Michigan Central Railroad, six miles east of Union City, in 1884 [GSM 1885].

**OSCEOLA,** Houghton County: the Osceola copper mine was discovered by Edward H. Hurlbut who, in 1875, organized the Osceola Consolidated Mining Company; its successive local agents were John R. Ryan, Hon. Frank G. White, and, in 1878, Captain John Daniel; the company immediately began to plat and build the village; its post office was Opechee, a mile to the south, opened in 1882, and changed to Osceola on Feb. 18, 1909; a station on the Hancock & Calumet Railroad [Mich Hist 17:192 1933; Andreas; PO Archives].

**OSCEOLA,** Osceola County: Samuel Fitzgerald, one of the first settlers in the township, was elected its first supervisor in 1869; named after its county which had been named for an Indian chief who led the second war between the Seminoles and the U.S. [Chapman].

**OSCEOLA JUNCTION,** Osceola County: a station on the Grand Rapids & Indiana Railroad, 8 miles south of Cadillac, in 1894; see Osceola for the name [GSM 1895].

**OSCODA,** Iosco County: in 1867, the firm of Smith, Kelley & Dwight purchased the land and platted and named the village; Edward Smith is considered the father of Oscoda; George P. Warner continued to be the postmaster when the location and the name of the Au Sable post office were changed to Oscoda in 1874 and on July 1, 1875, respectively; incorporated as a village in 1885; nearly wiped out by a forest fire in 1911, it vacated its village charter in 1919 and reverted to township government; Henry Rowe Schoolcraft created the name, a shortened form of ossin and muscoda, meaning pebbly prairie [Powers; Page; PO Archives].

**OSEOLA**, Hillsdale County. See Lenawee.

**OSEOLA CENTRE**, Livingston County: Hiram Goodrich became the first postmaster of this rural post office, named after its township, on June 27, 1839; the office was closed on Nov. 2, 1856, but was restored from Dec. 19, 1856, to Feb. 24, 1899 [PO Archives].

**OSHTEMO**, Kalamazoo County: the first land purchase here was made by Reason Holmes; later, Mortimer Fuller bought 60 acres and platted the village; Daniel Divers kept the first dry goods store here and William Drummonds became the first postmaster on March 2, 1857, named from its township which had been erected in 1838-39; Oshtemo is an Indian word meaning head waters [Gardner; Durant; Kalamazoo County Directory, 1868-70; PO Archives].

**OSIER**, Delta County: French Canadians began homesteading here about 1880; the Chicago & Northwestern Railroad built its Whitefish branch through here in 1898 and this village in Masonville Township boomed during the logging heyday; it was named for Onesime James Osier, an early settler who became its first postmaster on June 28, 1898; the office was closed on Jan. 31, 1901, but was restored, with Walter W. Thompson as its postmaster, on Feb. 5, 1910 [Delta Reporter, Sept. 1, 1965; Jean Worth; GSM 1899; PO Archives].

**OSKAR**, Houghton County: Oskar Eliasson (or Eliasen), a Finn, first came here in Hancock Township about 1870 and became a charcoal tycoon; he was appointed the first postmaster of this settlement on Feb. 2, 1888 [GSM 1889; PO Archives].

**OSSAWA**, Clinton County: William H. H. Culver became the first postmaster of this rural post office on Sept. 6, 1842, but the office was changed to Bath on June 7, 1858 [PO Archives].

**OSSEO**, Hillsdale County: this village in Jefferson Township was named for an Indian chief; it was the legal but never used county seat from about 1840 to 1843, while Jonesville and Hillsdale were contending for the honor, which Hillsdale won in 1843; the Florida post office was changed to Osseo on Dec. 14, 1861; a station on the Lake Shore & Michigan Southern Railroad in 1864 [Vivian L. Moore; GSM 1873; PO Archives].

**OSSINEKE**, Alpena County: in 1844, Jonathan Burtch and Anson Eldred made the first government land purchase here at the mouth of the Devil River (so named by the Indians, not because it was a bad river but because it kept bad company, flowing between two large swamps); David O. Oliver, who had surveyed the area in 1840, bought the mill property of Mr. Burtch in 1847; in 1848, Lee R. Sanborn bought much of Mr. Oliver's land, and platted and recorded the village; George B. Melville became its first postmaster on Feb. 13, 1867; a station on the Detroit & Mackinaw Railroad; the Indian name for the site was Wawsineke, which the white man changed to Ossineke [James A. Gonyea, PM; PO Archives].

**OTIA**, Newaygo County. See Brohman.

**OTISCO,** Ionia County. See Kiddville.

**OTISVILLE,** Genesee County: Stephen and Amos Biegel and Matthew McCormick had built their homes here when, in 1851, John Hayes came with men and machinery and built a sawmill; in 1852, Francis Otis who, with his two brothers, owned 5000 acres of pineland in the township, bought out Mr. Hayes; the settlement was given a post office on April 5, 1861; the first plat of the village was made and recorded by William F. Otis and T. D. Crocker in 1863; given a station on the Pere Marquette Railroad in 1874; incorporated as a village in 1877; named for Francis Otis [Paul L. Laing; PO Archives].

**OTSEGO,** Allegan County: Samuel Foster and his family became the first settlers on the village site in 1831; by an understanding with Mr. Foster, who pre-empted it, Horace H. Comstock purchased the land from the government in 1832; Mr. Comstock secured a post office, with him as its first postmaster, on March 16, 1835, having the office named after his native county of Otsego in New York; in 1836, a dam, mill-race, and sawmill were built, and he had the village platted by O. J. Wilder; incorporated as a village in 1865 and as a city in 1918 [Blaine E. Bacon; PO Archives].

**OTSEGO LAKE,** Otsego County: families were invited to settle here in 1872 while the Jackson, Lansing & Saginaw Railroad was under construction; George A. Finch and Adam Assal came in late 1872, and Blackford Smalley in the following spring; Jacob M. Great became its first postmaster on July 23, 1873; named after the lake it borders on [PO Archives; Powers].

**OTTAWA,** Ottawa County: the plat of this village on the Grand River near Ottawa Creek was recorded in 1835, but it never became more than a paper city [Lillie].

**OTTAWA BEACH,** Ottawa County: the West Michigan Association (A. B. Watson, J. B. Mullikin, I. K. Agnes, George N. Davis, and others) was organized in 1886 to acquire land here on Lake Michigan and build a resort hotel; a station on the Chicago & Western Michigan (now Pere Marquette) Railroad; Joseph H. Spires became the first postmaster on Aug. 12, 1886; the office was closed on Oct. 12, 1886, but was restored from May 24, 1887, to Oct. 12, 1889, and from June 16, 1890, to Aug. 5, 1891; as a summer office only it was restored again in 1892 [George Cook; PO Archives].

**OTTAWA CENTRE,** Ottawa County: Benjamin Smith became its first postmaster on July 11, 1853; it was platted and recorded in 1855; from its central location in the county it not only received its name but was considered by the supervisors as the county seat in 1856 [Lillie; PO Archives].

**OTTAWA LAKE,** Monroe County: John Wilder became the first postmaster of this settlement in Whiteford Township, near the Ohio line, on June 12, 1846; a station on the Lake Shore & Michigan Southern Railroad [Blinn; PO Archives].

**OTTAWA STATION,** Ottawa County: this village in Olive Township was named after its depot on the Chicago & Western Michigan (now Pere Marquette) Railroad; Joel M. Fellows became its first postmaster on Oct. 11, 1871; the village was platted by James Sawyer in 1872; its post office operated until Dec. 31, 1904 [Page; PO Archives].

**OTTERBURN,** Genesee County: a station on the Grand Trunk Railroad, in Flint Township, in 1882; Charles F. Shumway became its first postmaster on Aug. 27, 1887, the office operating until Oct. 31, 1913; named from the many otters on the nearby small burn or creek [Elizabeth C. Ronan; PO Archives].

**OTTER CREEK,** Jackson County: Daniel Griffith became the first postmaster of this rural post office in Springport Township on June 23, 1842, the office operating until June 2, 1900 [DeLand; PO Archives].

**OTTER CREEK,** Monroe County. See LaSalle.

**OTTER LAKE,** Houghton County. See Tapiola.

**OTTER LAKE,** Lapeer County: it was first settled by Andrew McArthur in 1838; John M. McDonald became its first postmaster on Feb. 12, 1873; the pine lumber firm of Page & Benson platted and recorded the village in 1874 when the Pere Marquette Railroad came through; incorporated as a village in 1883; named after the body of water near it, once abounding in otters [Elvin Ruby; Page; PO Archives].

**OTTO,** Oceana County: Norwegian-born Otto Brady settled here with his three brothers in 1850; the town was organized in 1860 and got a tannery in 1863; Elnathan J. Reed became its first postmaster on May 22, 1864; the office was renamed Reed for him on Dec. 9, 1868, but was transferred to and renamed Ferry on Feb. 8, 1871 [MPH 35:702 1907; Royal; PO Archives].

**OTTO,** Sanilac County: Malinda J. Van Camp became the first postmaster of this rural post office, five miles from Croswell, on April 18, 1898, the office operating until Jan. 15, 1903 [GSM 1899-1905; PO Archives].

**OVERISEL,** Allegan County: in 1848, Rev. Seine Bolks settled here with his colony from the province of Overisel, Holland; the town was organized in 1857, with C. J. Voorhorst as its first supervisor; Lucas Dangremond became its first postmaster on Sept. 8, 1857 [MPH 17:562 1890; PO Archives].

**OVIATT,** Leelanau County: this settlement in Kasson Township developed around the sawmill of M. C. Oviatt; Levi B. Carr became its first postmaster on April 10, 1878, the office operating until Aug. 31, 1909 [GSM 1881; PO Archives].

**OVID,** Branch County: it was first settled by Howard Bradley and Richard and Nelson Salsberry in 1834; the first government land purchase was entered by William D. Popple on May 4, 1836; Parley Stockwell came in 1842 and the area was known for a time as Parley's Corners; Mr.

Stockwell became the first postmaster of Ovid, named after Ovid, N.Y., on June 7, 1843, the office operating until Jan. 7, 1856 [Johnson; Mich Hist 16:387 1932 PO Archives].

**OVID**, Clinton County: the first settler in the area was Samuel Barker in 1836; B. I. Udell opened the first store here in 1856; Josiah B. Park, manager of the Park House, became the first postmaster on Feb. 25, 1857; the chief landowners were B. O. Williams, Amos Gould, and H. G. Higham, chief engineer of the Detroit & Milwaukee Railroad, and Mr. Higham got the railroad to build a station here; Mr. Williams' plat of the village was recorded in 1858; incorporated as a village in 1869; named after its township which was organized in 1840 and named by William Swarthout who had come here from Ovid, N.Y. [PM; Daboll; PO Archives].

**OVID CENTRE**, Clinton County. See Shepardsville.

**OWASIPPE**, Muskegon County: a scout reservation founded by the Boy Scouts of America, Chicago council, in 1911, and named for a local Indian chief; given a post office spelled Owasippi on Aug. 1, 1924, with Herman Mahew as its first postmaster; with Craig Atkinson as postmaster, the spelling was changed to Owasippe on May 22, 1929 [Marjorie Teall; PO Archives].

**OWASSO**, Shiawassee County. See Owosso.

**OWENDALE**, Huron County: the village was named for John G. Owen and his cousin, John S. Owen, who operated a large sawmill here; James and Edward Erskine bought land here in Brookfiled Township in 1877; a station on the Pontiac, Oxford & Northern Railroad in 1888; given a post office on June 4, 1889; incorporated as a village in 1905 [Hey; PO Archives].

**OWENS**, Missaukee County. See McBain.

**OWOSSO**, Shiawassee County: on August 2, 1833, Benjamin O. and Alfred L. Williams, brothers, made the first land purchase in the area; the first actual settlement in the township was made in 1835 by Elias Comstock, Lewis Findley, and the latter's son-in-law, Kilburn Bedell; in 1836, John D. Overton and David Van Wormer, employees of Mr. Comstock, erected a double log house near the river, the first building erected within the limits of the city proper; the settlement was first known as Big Rapids; it was given a post office as Owasso, with Daniel Ball as its first postmaster, on Nov. 4, 1838; its name was not officially changed to Owosso until June 8, 1875, though the latter spelling came into use at least by 1844; first platted for the proprietors, the Messrs. Williams, by Daniel Gould in 1838; incorporated as a city in 1859; named for Chief Wasso whose tribe the U.S., by the treaty of 1836, moved from this area to a reservation [Mich Hist 47:134 1963; Ball; Ellis; PO Archives].

**OXBOW LAKE**, Oakland County: it was founded by Erastus Hopkins, from Steuben County, N.Y., in 1833; it was named from the lake it borders on which was so named from its shape; it was given a post office as White Lake Centre, from its location in White Lake Township, on June

11, 1873, with Ralph W. Hopkins as its first postmaster; the office was renamed Ox Bow on March 10, 1875, and operated until June 29, 1901 [Durant; PO Archives].

**OXFORD**, Oakland County: Elbridge G. Deming made the first land entry here in 1823, and with his family, settled on his land in 1832; he became the first postmaster of Demingsburgh on May 2, 1834; Oxford Corners was founded in 1836 and the post office was moved there on Jan. 15, 1839, and renamed Oxford; the village was first platted by George Loucks in 1845; incorporated as a village in 1876; it was named after its township which had been so named by Otis C. Thompson, "since nearly all the settlers had ox-teams and probably would hold on to them for some years to come" [MPH 22:421 1893; Mich Hist 16:387 1932; Seeley; PO Archives].

**OYER'S CORNERS**, Jackson County. See Springport.

**OZARK**, Mackinac County: it was the site of the charcoal kilns of the Martel Furnace Company and a flag stop called Johnson's on the Duluth, South Shore & Atlantic Railroad in 1882; storekeeper George R. Phillips became the first postmaster, with the office named Ozark, on June 18, 1884; the name was derived from the early French name for the place, Aux Arc (pronounced Ozark), meaning at the bend; its post office operated until Aug. 12, 1966 [Emerson Smith; Mich Hist 45:259 1961; PO Archives].

**PAAVOLA**, Houghton County: the village was platted in 1895 as Concord City by John Paavola and his wife Kaisa; the mining companies left the area about 1906 and Finnish farmers came in; when Mr. Paavola became the first postmaster on June 8, 1909, the village was renamed for him [Jennie G. Kesti, PM].

**PABAMA LAKE**, Oceana County: Joseph Pabama was an Indian chief whose tribe came here from the Grand River valley under the Treaty of 1855; he became a Catholic and a lay reader; for many years he was treasurer of Elbridge Township, one of the few Indians ever elected to public office in Michigan; the lake and the school district were named after him [Royal].

**PACKARD**, Ingham County: a hamlet with a station on the Lake Shore & Michigan Southern Railroad in 1878 [GSM 1879].

**PACKARD**, Lenawee County. See Marvin.

**PACKARD**, Van Buren County: a station on the South Haven & Eastern Railroad, five miles south of South Haven, in 1890; David Leslie became its first postmaster on July 13, 1901, the office operating until Sept. 14, 1905 [Mich Manual 1899; PO Archives].

**PACKARD CORNERS**, Allegan County. See Glenn.

**PACK SIDING**, Presque Isle County: a station on the Alpena & Northern (now Detroit & Mackinaw) Railroad, 40 miles northwest of Alpena, in 1894 [GSM 1895].

**PACK'S MILLS**, Sanilac County: this sawmill settlement in Washington Township was named for George Pack, local mill owner, and he became its first postmaster July 6, 1868, the office operating until Feb. 18, 1876 [GSM 1873; PO Archives].

**PAGE**, Emmet County: a station on a branch of the Grand Rapids & Indiana Railroad in 1884 [GSM 1885].

**PAGETT'S CORNERS**, Huron County. See Ubly.

**PAGGEOTVILLE**, Manistee County. See Stronach.

**PAINES**, Saginaw County: it was first settled in 1871 and named for A. B. Paine, local brick manufacturer; a station at the junction of the Michigan Central and the Pere Marquette Railroads, in James Township; with Albert T. Putnam as its first postmaster, it was given a post office as Painesville on Oct. 10, 1873; the office was closed on May 29, 1876, but was restored on July 14, 1876, renamed Paines on Oct. 19, 1880, and operated until June 30, 1904 [Mills; GSM 1877; PO Archives].

**PAINESDALE**, Houghton County: the Champion Copper Company was organized in 1899 and this mining village was named for its president, William A. Paine; John Polglase became its first postmaster on March 6, 1901 [Stevens; PO Archives].

**PAINESVILLE**, Saginaw County. See Paines.

**PAINT CREEK**, Washtenaw County: the first post office in present Augusta Township was located at Wejinigan-sibi, or Paint Creek, which runs through the township; the office was opened on Jan. 15, 1833, with David Hardy as its first postmaster, but was transferred to Newcomb on Sept. 27, 1881 [Chapman; Beakes; PO Archives].

**PAINTER'S LAKE**, Cass County: named for Robert Painter who built a four mill on its shore in 1835 [Schoetzow].

**PAINTERVILLE**, Berrien County: about 1863, John Painter built a pier and a sawmill around which were the employee shacks and the company store; the place, now extinct, was known as Painterville [Chauncey].

**PAINT RIVER**, Iron County. See Elmwood.

**PALATKA**, Iron County. See Caspian.

**PALESTINE COLONY**, Huron County: a part of the Baron Maurice de Hirsch plan, this Jewish colony of 21 families totaling 75 persons was established on 1200 acres of land some five miles northeast of Bad Axe in 1891; this farming settlement failed within ten years; the present Verona School No. 3 is called the Jew School from its having been built on the site of the colony's synagogue and then the area became popularly known as Jerusalem [Hey].

**PALISADES PARK**, Van Buren County: this settlement on the Lake Michigan shore, in Covert Township, was first called Paulville; it was renamed about 1906 by Arthur C. Quick, a naturalist, who made it a wild flower sanctuary; later, as a summer resort, it was given a post office, with Mrs. Grace A. Ballou becoming its first postmaster on July 12, 1910, the office operating until June 30, 1957; it is now a private club [Madalyn Bradford; GSM 1911; PO Archives].

**PALM STATION**, Sanilac County. See Palms.

**PALMER**, Ionia County. See Orleans.

**PALMER**, Marquette County: this station on the Chicago & Northwestern Railroad was named for L. C. Palmer, mining executive, of Marquette; Robert M. Gilleland became its first postmaster on May 23, 1873; its Volunteer Mine was leased by the Cleveland-Cliffs Iron Company in 1899 [Mich Hist 5:163 1921; Stevens; PO Archives].

**PALMER**, St. Clair County. See St. Clair.

**PALMER'S PLAINS**, Calhoun County: named for Charles K. Palmer, who in 1832 came from Rochester, N.Y., and settled here in Eckford Township [Gardner].

**PALMERVILLE**, Newaygo County: this rural post office in the northeast corner of the county was named for Luke Palmer who became its first postmaster on May 25, 1883, the office operating until July 21, 1884 [GSM 1885; PO Archives].

**PALMS**, Mackinac County: Francis Palms, a Detroit lumberman, helped finance the Detroit, Mackinaw & Marquette Railroad, and the station here was named for him when opened in 1882; the settlement beside it was given a post office as Pines on June 2, 1884, with Charles E. Switzer as its first postmaster; the office was closed on May 17, 1897, and it is now a ghost town [Mich Hist 46:167 1962; PO Archives].

**PALMS**, Sanilac County: founded by Mr. Palm about 1859; given a station on the Port Huron & Northwestern Railroad in 1880 and a post office named Palm Station on Oct. 27, 1882, with Leander W. Thompson as its first postmaster; with Mary McCafferty as the postmaster, it was renamed Palms on April 18, 1896 [E. Meyer, PM].

**PALMYRA**, Lenawee County: the village was founded in 1827 by Timothy B. Goff, who named it after his home town in New York; Alexander R. Tiffany became its first postmaster on March 27, 1833; a station on the Lake Shore & Michigan Southern Railroad in 1874 [Donald Bowen, PM; GSM 1838].

**PALO**, Ionia County: the village began on land owned by Matthew and John Van Vleck; the latter suggested the name of the town in honor of General Zachary Taylor's victory at Palo Alto in the first battle of the Mexican War on May 8, 1846; Doctor Orla H. Tyler became the first postmaster on July 14, 1857; the village was first platted and recorded by William H. Freeman on March 12, 1867 [Schenck; Branch].

**PANAMA**, Newaygo County: a settlement five miles north of Fremont in 1888 [GSM 1889].

**PANGBORN**, Kent County: this rural post office was named for Elisha Pangborn who became its first and only postmaster on Aug. 21, 1883, the office operating until only Sept. 17, 1883 [PO Archives].

**PANOLA**, Iron County: a spur take-off from the Chicago & Northwestern Railroad in 1884; the pine and blueberry plains lying east of here are known as Panola Plains [Jack Hill, Sr.].

**PANSY**, Midland County: John W. Crawford became the first postmaster of this rural post office on Jan. 11, 1897, succeeded by William Dundas in 1899; the office was closed on March 30, 1901, but was restored from July 14, 1906, to Jan. 15, 1907 [PO Archives].

**PAPAME**, Oceana County: this hamlet was given a post office on Feb. 7, 1867, with Henry S. Sayles as its first postmaster, the office operating until Sept. 6, 1871; in some records it is spelled Pa Pa Me [GSM 1879; PO Archives].

**PARADISE**, Cheboygan County: this settlement in Forest Township formed around the L. C. Clark sawmill; it was given a post office as Milliken, named for William Milliken, who became its first postmaster on June 17, 1907; he was succeeded by J. A. Clark in 1908; the office was renamed Paradise on Dec. 21, 1909, and operated until Nov. 30, 1910 [GSM 1909; PO Archives].

**PARADISE**, Chippewa County: the village was founded by Ed. LeDuc in 1925, and named by Leon McGregor, of Bay City, resorting promotor, from the abundance of fish and game and the beautiful country and shoreline; Roy W. Monk became its first postmaster on May 1, 1947 [W. F. Jacques, PM; Hamilton; PO Archives].

**PARADISE**, Grand Traverse County. See Kingsley.

**PARC AUX VACHES**, Berrien County: M. LaClare settled here about 1760 to trade with the Indians; Joseph Bertrand opened a trading post near him in 1775; by 1781, the place was called Parc aux Vaches (by the Americans cow pasture or pens) and was designated as a trading post on the 1824 government survey map of John Tipton, Indian Agent; it was on or near the site of the future village of Bertrand; the word cow in the name referred to buffalo [MPH 1:124 1874, et al.].

**PARCHMENT**, Kalamazoo County: it was founded when Jacob Kindleberger built the Kalamazoo Vegetable Parchment Company, a paper mill, here in 1909; incorporated as a village in 1931 and as a city in 1938; given a branch post office in 1958 [Carolyn Vander Weele].

**PARIS**, Kent County: Jonathan H. Gray became the first postmaster of this rural post office, named after its township, on May 10, 1844, succeeded by John Davison on May 18, 1850, and Harley F. Barstow on Dec. 12, 1856, the office operating until Aug. 15, 1857 [PO Archives].

**PARIS**, Mecosta County: John Parish, a fisherman and hunter, became the first white settler in the county, building his hut here in present Green Township in 1851; he bought the land in 1853 and founded the village in 1865; it was first named Parish for him, but was later changed to Paris; given a railroad station and on March 16, 1866, a post office named Paris, with him as its first postmaster [MPH 30:27 1905; PO Archives].

**PARISVILLE**, Huron County: in 1954, three Polish immigrants, John Wojtalewicz, Ambrose Ciechanowski and Anthony Slawik, came here with their families by way of Canada; Stephen Pawlowski and John Poynk joined them in 1955, and from then on the settlement grew rapidly; James Erskine became its first postmaster on March 12, 1873, the office operating until Aug. 14, 1905; it was named after its township, which was organized in 1861, and named by another pioneer settler in the county, Gregoire Des Jardins, who had been born near Paris, France [Hey; PO Archives].

**PARK**, St. Joseph County: Charles M. Moore became the first postmaster of this rural post office in Mendon Township on July 11, 1838; the office was closed on Aug. 25, 1841, but was restored from April 9, 1850, to May 20, 1865, and from May 10, 1866, to March 3, 1873 [PO Archives].

**PARK CITY**, Newaygo County: a station on a branch of the Chicago & Western Michigan (now Pere Marquette) Railroad in 1884 [GSM 1885].

**PARKDALE**, Manistee County: Frank E. Taber became the first postmaster of this rural post office, 3 miles from Manistee, on April 30, 1897; the office was closed on Sept. 30, 1898, but was restored on Oct. 4, 1898, with Georgia L. Cranmer as its postmaster, the office operating until April 30, 1900 [PO Archives; GSM 1901].

**PARKEDALE**, Oakland County: in 1908, Parke, Davis & Company, manufacturing chemists, of Detroit, bought 750 acres, adjacent to Rochester, for biological research [Federal; Seeley].

**PARKERS CORNERS**, Livingston County: the first land entry here was made by Alonzo Platt on Aug. 12, 1835, and the second by Elbert Parker on Oct. 29, 1835; George C. Wood became the first resident in May, 1836; on May 27, 1838, his father, John Wood, became the first postmaster, with the office named Woodbridge after Michigan's second governor, William Woodbridge; the office was renamed Josco on Dec. 8, 1838, and Iosco, after its township, on June 21, 1880, until it was closed on Oct. 31, 1907; but since about 1870, the village has been called Parkers Corners after Hiram Parker who owned the general store and who became the postmaster in 1875 [Ellis; GSM 1865; PO Archives].

**PARKERVILLE**, Chippewa County: Simon Parker, a Canadian, homesteaded here with his family in 1875, and the place was named for him [Myrtle Elliott].

**PARKINSON**, Gratiot County: the settlement formed around the sawmill of Thomas & Parkinson (Edgar Thomas and Jehu E. Parkinson), and was named for the latter; his son, Henry J. Parkinson, became the first postmaster on Sept. 30, 1887; the office was closed on July 15, 1889, but was restored from April 4, 1890, to June 17, 1895 [GSM 1889-97; Tucker; PO Archives].

**PARKINGTON**, Schoolcraft County: a station on the Minneapolis, St. Paul & Sault Ste. Marie Railroad, in Doyle Township, in 1889; the settlement formed around the sawmill and general store of the Peninsular Cedar Company (Donald and G. F. Ross); Donald Ross became its first postmaster on Nov. 17, 1798, the office operating until July 15, 1905 [GSM 1899; PO Archives].

**PARK LAKE**, Osceola County: this sawmill settlement in Highland Township was given a station on the Toledo, Ann Arbor & Northern Michigan Railroad and on Dec. 3, 1888, a post office, with Guy W. Disbrow as its first postmaster [GSM 1891; PO Archives].

**PARKS**, Newaygo County: John A. Bartman became the first postmaster of this rural post office on Jan. 4, 1892, the office operating until May 31, 1912 [PO Archives].

**PARK'S CORNERS**, Washtenaw County: a hamlet, four miles above Manchester, in 1878 [GSM 1879].

**PARKS SIDING**, Iron County: this lumber settlement on a siding of the Chicago, Milwuakee, St. Paul & Pacific Railroad, was founded by and named for John Parks, a local lumberman; from its location just west of the Net River, it was given a post office as Net River on Dec. 9, 1907, with Herbert E. Hessetine as its first postmaster; the office operated until May 31, 1910 [Jack Hill, Sr.; PO Archives].

**PARKVILLE**, St. Joseph County: the village was named from its township which had been so named "from its park-like appearance, when it was visited by the settlers"; platted in 1851 by James Hutchinson on land bought by Luther Carlton from N. H. Taylor; Schellhouse & Carlton built a woolen mill here in 1851 and Reed & Huffman followed with a grist mill in 1853; Lorensie Schellhouse became the first postmaster on June 8, 1854 [Everts; Cutler; PO Archives].

**PARLEY'S CORNERS**, Branch County. See Ovid.

**PARMA**, Jackson County: Eli Gould first settled here in 1833; James M. Gould platted the village, recording his plat on April 5, 1848, and naming it Groveland; when given a post office on Jan. 28, 1862, it was renamed after Parma, N.Y., whence some of its pioneers had come; incorporated as a village in 1864; in its early days, the settlement was nicknamed Cracker Hill, and so appears on some old maps [MPH 31:188 1901; Cowles; PO Archives].

**PARMELEE**, Barry County: this hamlet was named for Erastus K. Parmelee who, after pioneering in Lenawee and Hillsdale Counties from 1836 to 1860, came here to Thornappie Township in 1860; in 1874, the

Michigan Central Railroad built Parmelee Station on land he had given for that purpose, and he was made the station agent; on April 19, 1878, he became the first postmaster, with the office spelled Parmalee, but corrected to Parmelee on Aug. 5, 1878; the office operated until July 31, 1913 [Johnson; PO Archives].

**PARNELL,** Kent County: it was named by its Irish immigrants for Charles Stewart Parnell, Irish political leader; under the leadership of Father Rivers, they built St. Patrick's church here in 1848, and around it their community life developed; James T. Sullivan became the first postmaster on Jan. 4, 1889, the office operating until Sept. 30, 1903 [Dillenback; GSM 1889; PO Archives].

**PARSHALLBURG,** Shiawassee County: the village began with a grist mill built here on the Shiawassee River to 1887 [GSM 1889].

**PARSHALLVILLE,** Livingston County: Isaac Parshall entered 400 acres of land here in present Hartland Township in 1834, but he did not actually settle and become the founder of the village until 1837; Jacob S. Griswold became the first postmaster on May 11, 1857, the office operating until Dec. 15, 1905 [Ellis; PO Archives].

**PARSON'S CORNERS,** Kalamazoo County. See Texas.

**PARTELLO,** Calhoun County: Colonel Charles Dickey located six lots here in 1836; G. W. Dryer and others formed the Dover Company in 1844, bought land and began a mill; their property was bought by J. R. Partello and the village, named for him, developed; Jepthah T. Scarlett became its first postmaster on April 23, 1856, the office operating until June 15, 1905 [Everts; PO Archives].

**PARTRIDGE,** Marquette County: a station on the Chicago & Northwestern Railroad, three miles east of Negaunee, in 1878 [GSM 1879].

**PATTERSON'S MILLS,** Ionia County. See Belding.

**PATTERSON'S POINT,** Mackinac County. See Point Patterson.

**PAUL,** Kent County: Charles H. Lewis became the first postmaster of this rural post office, then four miles from Grand Rapids, on Nov. 12, 1892, the office operating until Aug. 14, 1900 [PO Archives].

**PAULDING,** Ontonagon County: the Paulding Lumber Company set up camp here in 1891; it was given a station on the Chicago & Northwestern Railroad in 1892; a post office named Roselawn, a few miles north, was transferred here and renamed Paulding on Aug. 19, 1893, with Fred Barnett as its first postmaster; the office was closed on April 30, 1904, but was restored from May 1, 1936, to date [Alfred A. Hopp, PM; GSM 1903; PO Archives].

**PAULVILLE,** Van Buren County. See Palisades Park.

**PAVILION,** Kalamazoo County: the town was named after Pavilion, Genesee County, N.Y., from which the first settler here, Ruel Starr, had emigrated in 1831; Friend Clark Bird became the first postmaster on July 11, 1838 [Gardner; Durant; PO Archives].

**PAWLOWSKI**, Huron County: this Polish settlement, then four miles from Ruth, was named for Joseph Pawlowski who became its first postmaster on Nov. 30, 1892; the office was closed on March 2, 1894, but was restored on April 13, 1894, with Ignatz Buchkowski as its postmaster, the office operating until Nov. 15, 1904 [GSM 1893-1905; PO Archives].

**PAW PAW**, Van Buren County: Rodney Hinckley located his farm here in 1832, the year that Pierce Barber built his sawmill; in 1833, Mr. Barber sold out to Peter Gremps and Lyman J. Daniels; Mr. Gremps built the first store, became the first merchant, and on May 7, 1834, the first postmaster; it became the county seat in 1838; incorporated as a village in 1859 and re-incorporated in 1867; it was named after the nearby Paw Paw River which the Indians had named from the paw paw fruit, growing thickly upon its banks; the township, formed in 1835 and organized in 1836, with Mr. Gremps as its first supervisor, was first called Lafayette, but in 1867 it too took the name of Paw Paw [Ellis; PO Archives].

**PAW PAW LAKE**, Berrien County: this summer resort on Paw Paw Lake was opened by the 1850s; it was given a station on the Benton Harbor, Coloma & Paw Paw Railroad; hotelman William A. Baker became its first postmaster on Aug. 14, 1901, the office operating until Sept. 30, 1907; see Paw Paw for the name [GSM 1903; PO Archives].

**PAYE**, Wayne County: it was a station on the electric Detroit United Railway, in Grosse Pointe Township, 8 miles from Detroit, in 1908; named for grocer Horace E. Paye who became its first postmaster on July 13, 1909, the office operating until March 31, 1914 [GSM 1911; PO Archives].

**PAYMENT**, Chippewa County: Canadian-born Roger G. Payment, the first permanent white settler here on Sugar Island, arrived from Detroit about 1842, established a trading post and platted the town site; given a post office on Dec. 19, 1892, with James S. Shields as its first postmaster [Bayliss; PO Archives].

**PAYNESVILLE**, Ontonagon County: this village in McMillan Township was founded by the Payne family (Willis, Henry, Sidney and Etta), all of whom acquired homesteads in the area; a station on the Duluth, South Shore & Atlantic Railroad; storekeeper Charles T. Andrews became its first postmaster on March 5, 1890 [Charles Willman; GSM 1891; PO Archives].

**PEACH BELT**, Allegan County: Walter Billings became the first postmaster of this rural post office on the northern line of Ganges Township on Jan. 10, 1879; the office was closed on Oct. 27, 1879, but was restored from Dec. 19, 1879, to Oct. 31, 1905; the land in the area was devoted chiefly to the growing of peaches [Johnson; PO Archives].

**PEACH RIDGE**, Oceana County: one of the first settlers here in Benona Township was James Gibbs, Jr., who came in 1857, and because of the many wild blackberry patches on it, the ridge was called Blackberry Ridge; it was given a post office of that name on April 9, 1866, with him as its first postmaster, the office operating here until it was transferred to Sammon's Landing on Feb. 13, 1879; but when the orchards were planted here, an apple tree and a peach tree were set alternately in each row; since peach trees grow and mature more quickly, it was primarily a peach growing place; it was renamed Peach Ridge and a post office of that name (but spelled Peachridge) on Jan. 16, 1896, the office operating until Aug. 31, 1901; now all the peach trees have passed their productive years and have been removed, and it is now an apple-growing community, though it still retains the name of Peach Ridge [Royal; PO Archives].

**PEACHVILLE**, Oceana County: Charles S. Sidler became the first postmaster of this rural post office, in a fruit growing region, on May 20, 1895, the office operating until Sept. 26, 1906 [GSM 1897-1907; PO Archives].

**PEACOCK**, Lake County: a station on the Chicago & Western Michigan (now Pere Marquette) Railroad, 11 miles north of Baldwin; it was named for David J. Peacock who became its first postmaster on April 15, 1897 [GSM 1899; PO Archives].

**PEACOCK POINT**, Delta County. See Garth.

**PEARL**, Allegan County: the village began with a sawmill built by Eggleston & Hazleton in 1872; it was first called Clyde Center from its location in Clyde Township; it was renamed for Simeon O. Pearl in 1881, and was given a post office named Pearl on April 15, 1881, with George H. Smith as its first postmaster; a station on the Chicago & Western Michigan (now Pere Marquette) Railroad [Esther W. Hettinger; PO Archives].

**PEARL BEACH**, St. Clair County: a Clay Township village on the north side of the channel connecting Anchor Bay with the St. Clair River; first settled by the French, 12 private claims were listed here in 1796; Harry E. Bryant became its first postmaster, with the name of the office first spelled Pearlbeach, on Aug. 2, 1898, and he was the agent at its station on the Detroit and River St. Clair Railroad [Federal; PO Archives].

**PEARLINE**, Ottawa County: fruit grower John W. Everhart became the first postmaster of this rural post office in Allendale Township, a fruit growing district, on April 29, 1891, the office operating until May 31, 1908 [GSM 1893; PO Archives].

**PEARL SETTLEMENT**, Berrien County: Phineas Pearl, father of one of the country's most prominent families, came here in present Benton Township, from New York State, in 1840; he became the supervisor of the township [Chauncey].

**PEARL SHANTY**, Ingham County: it was a log building where Abner D. Felton, a War of 1812 veteran, kept a tavern; the community was given a post office named Pearl Shantee on March 6, 1860, with Henry D.

Wilcox as its first postmaster, the office operating until June 15, 1861; now extinct [Foster; PO Archives].

**PEBBLE RUN**, Oakland County: George B. Daniels became the first postmaster of this rural post office in Holly Township on April 13, 1880, the office operating until June 6, 1881 [GSM 1883; PO Archives].

**PECK**, Sanilac County: Nathaniel Vannest became the first settler here in Elk Township in 1852, built the first building, the Globe Hotel, in 1859, and the first store in 1868; Ransom R. Pearce became the first postmaster on Nov. 9, 1858; incorporated as a village in 1903 [Chapman; PO Archives].

**PECKTOWN**, Van Buren County: in 1838, Joseph S. Peck located in the northwest corner of Bloomingdale Township and as the locality became settled it became known as Pecktown, but it never became a village [Ellis].

**PEEBLES CORNERS**, Washtenaw County. See Worden.

**PEKIN**, Ingham County. See Stockbridge.

**PEKIN**, Wayne County. See Dearborn.

**PELHAM'S CORNERS**, Jackson County: a hamlet 4 miles southwest of Brooklyn in 1878 [GSM 1879].

**PELKIE**, Baraga County: it was first settled by French Canadian woodsmen about 1885; first known as King's Landing, it was soon renamed Pelkie, after an early settler; a station on the Michigan Central Railroad; Theodore Duquette became its first postmaster on April 30, 1903 [Ralph H. Jakipu, PM; PO Archives].

**PELLSTON**, Emmet County: William H. Pells, a native of Poughkeepsie, N.Y., came to Michigan from Illinois where he had founded the village of Paxton in 1872; he bought 1300 acres in Emmet County in 1876, began re-selling it to settlers, built a store and a hotel, and in 1882 platted the village named for him; Henry Park became its first postmaster on Sept. 20, 1882, and in that year it was given a station on the Grand Rapids & Indiana (now Pennsylvania) Railroad; incorporated as a village in 1907 [Traverse; PO Archives].

**PEMBINA**, Menominee County: this lumber settlement formed around the mill of Harter & LaCroix, with Mary E. Harter becoming its first postmaster on March 4, 1884; the office was transferred to and renamed Faithhorn on March 9, 1905 [GSM 1885-1907; PO Archives].

**PENASA**, Osecola County: Arthur H. Smith became the first postmaster of this rural post office on April 13, 1880, the office operating until July 10, 1895 [PO Archives].

**PENFIELD**, Calhoun County: the first land entry here was made by Albert H. Smith in 1831, but the first actual settler was Estes Rich, who broke ground for crops in 1835; this land was owned and occupied from 1836 until his death by Samuel Convis; the township was organized in

1838 when, on motion of Joseph P. Markham, who had come here in 1836, it was named to honor William Penn, founder of Pennsylvania; a station on the Grand Trunk Railroad; Henry Parsons became its first postmaster on Dec. 18, 1849; the office was closed on Jan. 8, 1864, but was restored on June 9, 1897 [Everts; PO Archives].

**PEN HOOK**, Missaukee County. See Falmouth.

**PENINSULA**, Ontonagon County: S. O. Knapp became the first postmaster of this rural post office in the upper peninsula on Aug. 21, 1850, the office operating until July 23, 1851 [PO Archives].

**PENN**, Cass County: the village was founded and platted in 1869 by Isaac P. James who named it Jamestown; but there was then a Jamestown post office in Michigan and this one was named Penn after its township which had been so named when organized in 1829 by its first settlers, Pennsylvania Quakers, who named it for William Penn; Lewis Cowgill became the first postmaster on Oct. 24, 1871, the office operating until July 15, 1935; a station on the Grand Trunk Railroad [Rogers; Fox; PO Archives].

**PENN**, Keweenaw County. See Delaware.

**PENNINGTON'S CORNERS**, Lenawee County. See Macon.

**PENN MINE**, Keweenaw County. See Delaware.

**PENNOCK**, Clare County: this station, opened about 1888, on the Ann Arbor Railroad, five miles north of Marion, was named Pennock's; it was given a post office as Pennock on Feb. 7, 1892, with Thomas J. Flevens as its first postmaster, the office operating until Nov. 30, 1907 [GSM 1899; PO Archives].

**PENN YANN**, Berrien County: this settlement in southwestern Bainbridge Township was first made by Simeon Brant and his family in 1836; Jediah Safford became its first postmaster on Jan. 14, 1898, with the office spelled Penyann, and it operated until Dec. 14, 1905; first settled by Pennsylvanians and New Englanders, Isaac Youngs chose a name which gave both recognition by combining Pennsylvania and Yankee [Fox; GSM 1899; PO Archives].

**PENNOYER CREEK**, Newaygo County: lumbermen Augustus and Frederick Pennoyer built the first sawmill in the area here in 1836-37; the brothers operated the mill until their death by drowning in 1841, when it was continued by their associates, Samuel Rose and Hannibal Hyde [MPH 21:646 1892; Mich Hist 20: 258 1936].

**PENTECOST**, Lenawee County: George W. Fuller became the first postmaster at this station on the C., J. & M. Railroad, in Franklin Township, ten miles northwest of Adrian, on May 26, 1887 [GSM 1889; PO Archives].

**PENTOGA**, Iron County: in 1896, Herman Velguth secured a large tract of timberlands southwest of Chicaugon Lake and built a sawmill on the south shore of Indian Lake; this mill site became known as Pentoga; but before milling operations began, he sold out to the Hood & Mahoney Lumber Company who moved the mill 2½ miles south to a site near the railroad and the river; they retained the mill site name and their operations begun the village of Pentoga in 1900; on March 27, 1900, Francis G. Hood became its first postmaster and it was given a station on the Chicago & Western Michigan Railroad; its post office operated until Jan. 30, 1937; named for Pentoga Edwards, wife of John Edwards, chief of the local Chippewas; it is now a ghost town, but a county park on Chicaugon Lake retains her name [Hill; PO Archives].

**PENTWATER,** Oceana County: Edwin R. Cobb and Andrew Rector bought the first government land here in 1849 and built their sawmill in 1853; Charles Mears came in 1856, built a sawmill and a boarding house, and called his part of the village Middlesex; Mr. Cobb became the first postmaster of Pent Water on March 17, 1855, and the first supervisor when the township was organized in 1856; it was platted in 1862 and incorporated as the village of Pent Water in 1867; the spelling was changed to Pentwater on May 23, 1894; some take the name from the smallness of the outlet of Pentwater Lake, hence pent-up water, others say it was a corruption of paint water, a name originally given from the dark color of the lake beside which the village was built [GSM 1873; MPH 35:691 1907; Yvonne Maynard; PO Archives].

**PENYANN,** Berrien County. See Penn Yann.

**PEPPERGRASS,** Washtenaw County. See Sharon.

**PEQUAMING,** Baraga County: it was originally the Indian village of Pequaquawaming (Point Village or Cape Point); it was named from its location at a point on Keweenaw Bay; the Indians had left by the time Peter Crebassa, a trader, came in 1836; the Hebard & Thurber Lumber Company (Charles and Edward W. Hebard and H. C. Thurber) began building mills, homes and stores here in 1878, and Charles Hebard platted the village in 1879; Edward W. Hebard became its first postmaster on May 17, 1880, the office operating until Jan. 31, 1944 [Andreas; PO Archives].

**PERCH,** Baraga County: a station on the Duluth, South Shore & Atlantic Railroad, three miles west of Sidnaw, opened in 1871 [GSM 1895].

**PERE CHENEY,** Crawford County: this village developed around the sawmill of G. M. Cheney in 1874; it was given a station on the Michigan Central Railroad and a post office, with storekeeper Stewart Hutt becoming its first postmaster on Dec. 1, 1874, the office operating until 1912; the village was also called Center Plains after its township (the township has since been renamed); its depot was called Cheney; now a ghost town [Grace L. Funsch; GSM 1881; PO Archives].

**PERE MARQUETTE,** Mason County: Burr Caswell and his family became the first white settlers here at the mouth of the Pere Marquette River in 1847; a sawmill was built in 1849 and the settlement which followed was given a post office as Pere Marquette on March 17, 1855, with George W. Ford as its first postmaster, the office operating until July 25, 1864 [Mich Hist 25: 406 1941, 35:401 1951; PO Archives].

**PERFECTION**, Alcona County. See Greenbush.

**PERKINS**, Arenac County. See Sterling.

**PERKINS**, Delta County: the village was founded on the Whitefish branch of the Chicago & Northwestern Railroad about 1872 by the Cascade Company, later known as the Escanaba Furnace Company, which built charcoal kilms here and employed a force of men to cut wood; it was given a post office on May 7, 1894, with John Fuhriman as its first postmaster [David Coon; PO Archives].

**PERRINBURGH**, Hillsdale County: James Fowle located here in 1835, bringing in his family in 1836; Timothy T. Wilkinson became the second settler, joined in 1837 by Frederick and Stephen C. Perring; the community became known as Perrinburgh, later as Edinburgh, and still later as the Burgh or the Berg; it was given a post office as Edinburgh on Sept. 6, 1843, with Murray Knowles as its first postmaster, but the office was transferred to Montgomery on Dec. 20, 1871 [Reynolds; PO Archives].

**PERRINS**, Kent County: John Landheer became the first postmaster of this rural post office on March 11, 1899, the office operating until Jan. 31, 1903 [PO Archives].

**PERRIN'S LANDING**, Leelanau County. See Fouch.

**PERRINSVILLE**, Wayne County: it was first settled by Thomas Dickerson in 1831; the brothers Abraham and Isaac F. Perrin built their sawmill here on the Middle Rouge in 1832; Isaac F. Perrin platted the village in 1834; James A. Peck became its first postmaster on Oct. 11, 1861, with the name changed to Pike's Peak on Dec. 21, 1887, the office operating until Aug. 30, 1902 [Burton; PO Archives].

**PERRINTON**, Gratiot County: the village began with the coming through of the Toledo, Saginaw & Muskegon Railroad in 1886; it was first named Perrin for the head of a St. Johns law firm with large interests here in Fulton Township, but was given a post office as Perrinton on May 9, 1887, with Thompson Kirby as its first postmaster; it was first platted by Ansel H. Phinney and Warren W. Baker in 1887; incorporated as a village in 1891 [Tucker; PO Archives].

**PERRONVILLE**, Menominee County: the railroad came through here in 1873, first hauling ore and later, logs; in 1883, Manazipe Perron built a dam and a sawmill here and he became the first postmaster on Sept. 11, 1897, of the settlement which followed; when the woods were cleared, many Poles came here to farm, with Henry Gasman as their guiding spirit [David S. Coon; PO Archives].

**PERRY**, Shiawassee County: it was located on land owned by Horace

Green and Dr. Joseph P. Roberts; William P. Laing founded the village, opening its first store in 1850 and becoming its first postmaster on Jan. 17, 1850; the Grand Trunk Railroad came through in 1876 and the village, then called Perry Center, from its location in Perry Township (though its post office was always named simply Perry), moved a mile south to be on the line; incorporated as the village of Perry in 1893; named after the American naval hero, Oliver Hazard Perry [Lucille M. Griffith; Campbell; PO Archives].

**PERRY'S GROVE**, Monroe County: this rural post office was named for Warren Perry who became its first postmaster on May 2, 1834, the office operating until May 17, 1838 [PO Archives].

**PERRY'S PIER**, Manistee County. See Pierport.

**PERU**, Lenawee County. See Addison.

**PESHAWBESTOWN**, Leelanau County: it was begun by Rev. Angelus Van Praemel as a Catholic mission to the Ottawa Indians in 1852; the future bishop of Marquette, Rev. Ignatius Mrak, who succeeded him in 1855, refers to the settlement as Eagletown; in 1883, his successor, Rev. Philip Zorn, calls it Peshaube, after its then ruling chief Peshaba; from 1895 on, Rev. Bruno Torka, O.F.M., who was next in charge, calls it Peshawbestown; the Grand Rapids diocesan clergy took it over from the Franciscans in 1948; it is now an Indian village with a church and a school; the 1965 Catholic Directory calls it Peshabetown, and in other sources it is also referred to as Pshawbatown, Preshabestown, etc. [Barnes, Sprague, Paré].

**PETERS**, Lake County: a station on the Chicago & Western Michigan (now Pere Marquette) Railroad, 11 miles north of Baldwin, in 1894 [GSM 1895].

**PETERS**, St. Clair County: the village, founded about 1864, was first called Petersburg for pioneer settler John Peters; but there was another Petersburg post office in Michigan and this one was given a post office named Peters, with Mr. Peters becoming its first postmaster on Nov. 25, 1891, the office operating until Sept. 14, 1905 [GSM 1865; PO Archives].

**PETERSBURG**, Monroe County: it was originally the site of the farm of Richard Peters who came to this region in 1824; he became the first postmaster in April, 1831, with the office named Summerfield, but changed to Petersburgh on Jan. 24, 1863, and to Petersburg, on Dec. 18, 1893; Thomas G. Cole and Austin E. Wing, of Monroe, founded the village on land acquired from Mr. Peters in 1836; incorporated as a village in 1869 and as a city in 1967 [Bulkley; Cole; PO Archives].

**PETHERICK**, Keweenaw County. See Ashbed.

**PETOSKEY**, Emmet County: a Presbyterian Indian mission was founded here in Bear Creek Township in 1852 by Rev. Andrew Porter and, with him as its first postmaster, it was given a post office as Bear River, on Dec. 2, 1857, and for him the place was also known as Porter's Village; the first permanent white settler, Hazen Ingalls, came in 1865 and, for the community which developed, the post office was renamed Petoskey on Dec. 5, 1873, with the coming through of the railroad; incorporated as a village in 1879 and as a city in 1896; Chippewa Chief Petoskey (said to be a corruption of Petosega, meaning the rising sun) had owned much of the land of the city named for him and in which he died [Virginia Hubbard; GSM 1873; PO Archives].

**PETREL**, Alger County: a station on the Duluth, South Shore & Atlantic Railroad, in Munising Township; the settlement formed around the C. H. Worcester Company, loggers; E. V. McGregor was appointed its first postmaster on Sept. 2, 1903, but declined, and Marcel A. Nadeau was appointed on Nov. 2, 1903, and accepted; the office operated until June 29, 1907 [GSM 1905; PO Archives].

**PETREVILLE**, Eaton County: this village in Eaton Rapids Township was first settled in 1880; Alice E. Jenks became its first postmaster on April 8, 1898, the office operating until Jan. 31, 1901; the townspeople voted on consolidation with Eaton Rapids in 1956 [GSM 1881; PO Archives].

**PETTEYSVILLE**, Livingston County: Seth A. Petteys, a native of New York State, came here in 1843, when he built a fulling mill which he later converted into a grist mill, and then added to his interests a cider mill and a blacksmith shop; Valentine Wiegand became the first postmaster on July 12, 1870, the office operating until June 29, 1901 [Mich Hist 30:605 1946; Ellis; PO Archives].

**PEWABEE**, Ontonagon County: Thomas Palmer became the first postmaster of this rural post office on Feb. 11, 1847, the office operating until Oct. 25, 1848; it was in a mining region, and its name was evidently derived from the Ojibway word pewabic, meaning any mineralized formation [Sawyer; PO Archives].

**PEWABIC**, Dickinson County: a now-deserted mining location; see Pewabee for the name [Sawyer].

**PEWABIC**, Ontonagon County: this township was erected in 1848; it was dissolved in 1866 and its area was absorbed by Carp Lake and Ontonagon Townships; the Pewabic Mine operated from 1852 to 1884, and its community had a post office as Pewabic, opened on Aug. 12, 1854, with Charles B. Hawley as its first postmaster; the office was closed on May 21, 1862, but was restored from Jan. 25, 1864, to July 10, 1865 [PO Archives; GSM 1860; Jamison].

**PEWAMO**, Ionia County: the Detroit & Milwaukee Railroad built a station here in 1857; it was surveyed by a local landowner, A. F. Bell, in 1857, but not recorded until 1859 (officially the village takes 1859 as its founding year); it was named at the suggestion of another pioneer resident, J. C. Blanchard, for an Indian chief with whom he had hunted along the Grand River; Hiram W. Blanchard, the first postmaster, served from July 14, 1857, to 1870; incorporated as a village in 1871 [John Cotter, PM].

**PHELIPEAUX ISLAND**, Keweenaw County: it would now be attached to Keweenaw County if it existed where the map of Bellin in 1874 and the map of Mitchell, used in the peace negotiations of 1783, placed it; but the island does not exist, the error being due, perhaps, to an incorrect translation of the Chippewa name for Isle Royale [Dunbar].

**PHELPS**, Charlevoix County: it began with a sawmill built by Mr. Olmstead, and was first called Ballou's Siding; it was given a post office as Phelps on April 30, 1900, with Alexander Paton as its first postmaster [C. A. Robinson; PO Archives].

**PHELPSTOWN**, Ingham County. See Webberville.

**PHILLIPS**, Saginaw County. See Kochville.

**PHOENIX**, Keweenaw County: the Lake Superior Copper Association was begun in 1842 by Charles H. Gratiot and Jacob Bernard (another member was David Henshaw who became secretary of the navy under President John Tyler); they chose sites along Lake Superior in 1843 and organized in Boston in 1844; since they had no capital, they sold some of their 15 leases to the Copper Falls, the North Western, and the Central Mine; but in 1849, they went broke, and the Phoenix Copper Company was organized in Boston to buy their remaining properties; this village developed around their Phoenix Mine and was given a post office named Phoenix on Sept. 1, 1865, with Joseph Paull as its first postmaster; the office operated until June 30, 1954 [Madeleine Gibson; GSM 1873; PO Archives].

**PHOENIX**, Wayne County: this settlement in Northville Township began with a dam and a mill in the 1830s; it was platted and recorded as Phoenix Mill by J. A. Austin on Jan. 19, 1857; now only an artificial lake (called Phoenix Lake) and a Ford precision parts plant remain [Mich Hist 26:319 1942; County plat liber].

**PICKANDS' JUNCTION**, Muskegon County: this junction of the M. & L.S. with the Chicago & Western Michigan Railroad, in Fruitport Township, provided a track to the Spring Lake Iron Works, after whose general manager, Major Henry S. Pickands, it was named when built in 1880 [Page; Hill].

**PICKERAL LAKE**, Kalamazoo County: Caleb Lammon became the first postmaster of this rural post office on Feb. 17, 1857, the office operating until only May 11, 1857 [PO Archives].

**PICKEREL LAKE**, Marquette County: a station on the M. & S.E. Railroad in 1910 [GSM 1911].

**PICKETT'S CORNERS**, Cass County: Selah Pickett kept a tavern on the Kalamazoo-Niles Stage Line and in it a post office from Dec. 11, 1851, to July 11, 1862; the once prosperous inn failed with the coming through of the railroad [Fox; PO Archives].

**PICKFORD**, Chippewa County: this village on the Moneskong River, in Sault Ste. Marie Township, was first settled by Charles W. Pickford, from Ontario, Canada, in 1877, and he became its first postmaster on Feb. 16, 1880 [GSM 1881; PO Archives].

**PIERCEVILLE**, Washtenaw County: Alfred C. Holt, who settled here in 1834, became the first postmaster on May 2, 1835; the office operating until Jan. 8, 1841; it was named for Nathan Pierce who had become the supervisor of Sylvan Township in 1834; by-passed by the railroad, it became a ghost town [Chapman; PO Archives].

**PIER COVE**, Allegan County: Deacon Sutherland located here in 1849 and laid out the village in 1851; into the lake, he built a large lumber shipping pier, from which the town got its name; Samuel W. Thompson became its first postmaster in 1853; it was a flourishing village until the lumber supply became exhausted in 1867, when it became a hamlet [Johnson].

**PIERPORT**, Manistee County: in 1866, the Turnersport Pier Company built a pier here on the Lake Michigan shore, in Onekama Township, to ship wood. the place was first called Turnersport and was given a post office of that name on Aug. 1, 1868, with Charles Eckel as its first postmaster; in that year, Charles W. Perry bought the property and developed the village which was renamed Pierport as was its post office on June 13, 1872; the place was also known as Perry's Pier; its post office operated until Dec. 30, 1933 [GSM 1873-75; PO Archives; Page].

**PIERSON**, Montcalm County: forty acres were acquired here by David S. Pierson in 1856 and he and Dexter Clark and John L. Shar founded the village, then in Mecosta County; Mr. Pierson opened the first post office in his home on Jan. 29, 1857; the village was platted in 1870 and incorporated in 1873 [Gladys Rubingh; PO Archives].

**PIERSONVILLE**, Lapeer County. See Marathon.

**PIETY HILL**, Oakland County. See Birmingham.

**PIEGON**, Huron County: the village was founded by John Nitz and C. A. Applegate in 1888; Albert Kleinschmidt became its first postmaster on April 20, 1890; incorporated as a village in 1902; named from its proximity to the Pigeon River which was so named because of the large number of wild pigeons in the area [Otto Woelke; PO Archives].

**PIGEON LAKE**, Mackinac County: a station on the Minneapolis, St. Paul & Sault Ste. Marie Railroad, 26 miles east of Manistique, in 1894 [GSM 1895].

**PIGEON RIVER**, Ottawa County. in 1876, a station on the Chicago & Michigan Lake Shore Railroad at the crossing of the Pigeon River in Olive Township [GSM 1877].

**PIKE BAY**, Houghton County. See Chassell.

**PIKE LAKE**, Mackinac County. See Bryan.

**PIKE'S PEAK**, Wayne County. See Perrinville.

**PIKE'S PIER**, Berrien County: this shipping point on Lake Michigan had a station on the Chicago & Western Michigan Railroad in 1878 [GSM 1879].

**PILGRIM**, Benzie County: a station on the Ann Arbor Railroad, in Crystal Lake Township; the village was founded by the Congregational Summer Assembly about 1909; Leslie W. Chatham became its first postmaster on June 7, 1923; the post office was changed to Pilgrim Rural Station, Frankfort, on June 16, 1956; it was named from the fact that the Congregational Church traces its history back to the Pilgrim Fathers [Walter S. Pope, PM].

**PINCKNEY**, Livingston County: in 1827, William Kirkland wed Caroline Stansbury (pen name, Mary Clavers); in 1835, he bought the holdings of the Sanford Marble Company and part of Colonel Peterson's land in Livingston County; with his brother-in-law, James W. Stansbury, of New York, as business manager, he organized the William Kirkland Company and began the village which he named for his brother, Charles Pinckney Kirkland, a New York lawyer; the first settler arrived on April 18, 1836; Mr. Stansbury became the first postmaster on Feb. 25, 1837; the village was platted and recorded on Aug. 9, 1837; incorporated as a village in 1883 [Mildred Ackley; MPH 18:451 1891].

**PINCONNING**, Bay County: it was founded in 1872 by George H. Van Etten, of Van Etten, Kaiser & Company; they built a sawmill and platted some 100 acres, lying on both sides of the Detroit & Mackinaw Railroad tracks; Edward B. Knight became its first postmaster on Jan. 29, 1873; incorporated as a village in 1887 and as a city in 1931; it was named from its proximity to the Pinconning River, originally O-pin-cin-conning, Indian for potato place [Sr. M. Yolanda; Butterfield; PO Archives].

**PINE CREEK**, Allegan County: the first settlers in this the first settlement in the county were Uri Baker and Turner Aldrich in 1828, and it was laid out as New Rochester; Eber Sherwood and his wife Alvira came in 1831; from the first sawmill in this present township of Otsego, Oka Town and Abijah Chichester floated the first lumber down the Kalamazoo River from here in 1834 [MPH 27:23, 36, 292 1896].

**PINE CREEK**, Calhoun County: this hamlet, also called Riley's Corners, in Athens Township, was given a post office on Jan. 28, 1851, with Captain James Winters as its first postmaster, the office operating until Nov. 14, 1903 [Everts; PO Archives].

**PINE GROVE**, Saginaw County: a station on the J., L. & S. Railroad, in St. Charles Township, in 1880 [Leeson].

**PINE GROVE**, Tuscola County: Samuel Evans became the first postmaster of this lumber settlement on June 2, 1858, with the office changed to Arbela on Jan. 16, 1871 [GSM 1865; PO Archives].

**PINE GROVE MILLS**, Van Buren County: David D. Wise and his partner, D. O. Everest, both from New York State, began lumbering in this region in 1852; a settlement formed here and Mr. Wise became its first postmaster on Feb. 9, 1859, the office operating until March 31, 1932; when a branch of the Michigan Central Railroad came through here in 1870, Mr. Wise and Benjamin De Puy platted the village; Mr. Wise and Mr. Everest built a grist mill and a planing mill in 1872; it was named after its township of Pine Grove [Ellis; PO Archives].

**PINE HILL**, Sanilac County. See Sanilac Mills.

**PINE LAKE**, Ingham County. See Haslett.

**PINE LAKE**, Mackinac County. See Bryan.

**PINE LAKE**, Oakland County: John Ellenwood was justice of the peace of West Bloomfield Township from 1836 to 1856, and he became its first post master, with the office named Pine Lake, on May 29, 1832, serving until his death, July 28, 1856 [Durant; PO Archives].

**PINE PLAINS**, Allegan County: it was first settled by T. M. West and Daniel Ammerman in 1838; Levi Loomis had built a sawmill on Swan Creek for David B. Stout in 1837, and when the town was organized in 1850, it was named from its chief timber; Timothy S. Coates was the first supervisor, and on May 26, 1851, he became the first postmaster of "Pine Plain, late Montcalm County"; the office was closed on Sept. 27, 1867, but was restored from Oct. 15, 1867, to Oct. 2, 1868 [MPH 17:561 1890; PO Archives].

**PINE RIDGE**, Delta County: a station on the Chicago & Northwestern Railroad in 1888; a settlement formed around it [GSM 1889].

**PINE RIVER**, Arenac County: here at the mouth of the Pine River, on the west shore of Saginaw Bay, in Standish Township, German-born John Lentz built a sawmill in 1854 and a larger one in 1882; the settlement was given a post office named Horr (after Roswell G. Horr, congressman from this district, 1879-80), with grocer Wallace W. Alexander becoming its first postmaster on Sept. 22, 1879, the office operating until July 22, 1881; it was given a station on the Detroit & Mackinaw Railroad as Pine River, with James J. Mahony becoming its first postmaster on June 22, 1899; the office operated until Sept. 30, 1913; it was in Bay County until Arenac was formed in 1883 [Page; PO Archives].

**PINE RIVER**, Charlevoix County. See Charlevoix.

**PINE RIVER**, Chippewa County. See Rudyard.

**PINE RIVER**, Gratiot County. See St. Louis.

**PINE RIVER**, Lake County: Horatio W. Johnson became the first postmaster of this rural post office on Sept. 30, 1869; the office was closed on March 9, 1871, but was restored from June 12, 1871, to April 10, 1873 [PO Archives].

**PINE ROAD**, Midland County: this lumber settlement on the Pine River was given a post office on July 26, 1876, with John W. Bailey as its first postmaster, the office operating until Jan. 9, 1877 [GSM 1877; PO Archives].

**PINE RUN**, Genesee County: Charles McLean and Sylvester Hubbard became the first settlers here in 1833; located near the Pine Run River, in a pine forest region, it was given a post office as Pine Run on Jan. 15, 1836, with Mr. McLean as its first postmaster; platted and recorded as Vienna, but when the township took that name in 1837, the village took the name Pine Run; the post office was changed to Thetford on Dec. 26, 1844, but was restored as Pine Run from 1852 to 1867, and from 1898 to 1905, when it was closed permanently [Elizabeth C. Ronan; PO Archives].

**PINERY**, St. Clair County: Daniel Alverson became the first postmaster of this rural post office, named from its being in a pine forest region, on May 15, 1852; the office was closed on Sept. 24, 1852, but was restored on Aug. 8, 1853, with William B. Preston as postmaster; he was still in office when it was transferred to and renamed Capac on Jan. 5, 1858 [Jenks; Andreas; PO Archives].

**PINES**, Mackinac County. See Palms.

**PINES, THE**, Schoolcraft County: a bustling village during the lumbering years, about 1880 to 1895, and still a railroad loading station [Federal].

**PINE STUMP JUNCTION**, Luce County: the first cuts of big timber were made in this area in the 1860s; there was a main logging road running from Grand Marais east to Paradise, nearly 100 miles, and all along it were logging camps; the mail came up from Newberry by logging road, and the two roads junctioned here; right at the junction was a huge pine stump and the mailman attached a big iron mailbox to it, and left the mail there for the camps along the Grand Marais-Paradise road, and some one from each camp would pick it up from there and deliver it; the RFD ended with the timber operations, but the pine stump, nearly five feet across the butt, still stands at the junction; the place was named on county maps in the 1860s and 1870s, and is still a hamlet [R. J. Fair].

**PINEX**, Ontonagon County: John Saam became the first postmaster of this rural post office in a pine forest region on May 1, 1916 [PO Archives].

**PINGREE**, Livingston County: James S. Smith became the first postmaster of this rural post office in Marion Township on Dec. 12, 1898, the office operating until Feb. 14, 1901; Hazen S. Pingree took office as the governor of Michigan on Jan. 1, 1897 [GSM 1899; PO Archives].

**PINGREE**, Sanilac County: Philip Mark became the first postmaster of this rural post office, named for Michigan governor Hazen S. Pingree, on Dec. 26, 1896; the office was closed on March 28, 1898 [GSM 1899; PO Archives].

**PINGREE'S DAM**, Newaygo County: a station on the Chicago & Michigan Lake Shore Railroad in 1876 [GSM 1877].

**PINNEBOG**, Huron County: Walter Hume, "the Daniel Boone of Hume Township," became the first settler in the area in 1844; this settlement was first called Pinnepog (Chippewa for partridge drum); but there was another Pinnepog five miles north on Saginaw Bay, so this one changed to Pinnebog ("a high sounding and dignified way of saying pine bog"), while the other one changed to Port Crescent; Arthur Heminger became the first postmaster of Pinnebog on April 15, 1863; the office was closed on Jan. 2, 1872, but was restored on Dec. 19, 1879; it was named from its location near the Pinnebog River [Mich Hist 25:235 1941, 46:303 1962; PO Archives].

**PINTLER'S CORNERS**, Ottawa County. See Lisbon.

**PIONEER**, Mecosta County: Isaac Griffin became the first postmaster of this rural post office on Oct. 10, 1862, the office operating until July 30, 1863 [PO Archives].

**PIONEER**, Missaukee County: a hamlet with a general store and the Pioneer Township hall in 1876; it was also known as Morey's after William J. Morey who became its first postmaster, with the office named Pioneer, on Feb. 14, 1876 [GSM 1879; PO Archives].

**PIPER**, Ogemaw County: Frank M. Thompson became the first postmaster of this early and now vanished lumbering town on April 6, 1882, the office operating until March 8, 1892; it was also known as Sunken Lake and was on the southeast shore of Beaver (now Piper) Lake [Pen Phil 6:3 Oct 1955].

**PIPESTONE**, Berrien County: it was first platted and recorded in 1836 by Daniel Wilson, William McKaleb, Theodore R. Phelps, and Jehiel and Joab Enos; but the lots were not sold and the plat was vacated; in 1837, a brother and a brother-in-law of Jehiel and Joab Enos, Dr. Morgan Enos and William Boughton, settled on the plat; the latter became the first postmaster on Sept. 25, 1850; the place was also known as Shanghai Corners after a breed of chickens Dr. Enos imported and raised; but the post office was named Pipestone after the township, a name believed to have come from the fact that Indians found in this region the best clay for making their stone pipes; its post office operated until March 31, 1903 [C. Larsen; PO Archives].

**PIPESTONE STATION**, Berrien County. See Hartman.

**PITCARNIA**, Saginaw County. See Prairie Farm.

**PITT**, Washtenaw County. See Pittsfield.

**PITTSBURG**, Shiawassee County: Moses Pitts and his wife Sally, from Vermont, took land here from the government in 1836 and settled on it in 1838; he died in 1850, and his eldest son, Safford Pitts, developed part of his farm on Grand River Road, where it is intersected by the Owosso & Perry Road, into a village with a church, school, businesses and homes; it was called Pittsburg and was given a post office of that name on Nov. 5, 1856, with resident farmer Henry Ruthruff as its first pastmaster,

Safford Pitts serving after him; the office operated until Jan. 15, 1901 [MPH 22:165 1893; PO Archives].

**PITTSBURGH LANDING,** Chippewa County: this coal dock settlement fueled the boats carring ore from the western upper peninsula mines to the Pittsburgh mills; James H. M. Florey became its first postmaster on Oct. 9, 1906, the office operating until Dec. 31, 1908 [Havighurst; PO Archives].

**PITTSFIELD,** Washtenaw County: George W. Noyes made the first government land purchase here in 1824; the McCracken School, the first in the county, was built here in 1825; the first town meeting was held in the home of John Gilbert in 1831; on the motion of Ezra Carpenter, the town was named Pitt, honoring William Pitt, the English prime minister; George N. Beckwith became the first postmaster on Jan. 21, 1835, the office operating until Sept. 14, 1836; the village was renamed Pittsfield in 1840; with the coming of the Toledo & Ann Arbor Railroad in 1878, its post office was restored in Sept., 1879, and operated until Dec. 31, 1907 [MPH 4:396 1881; Beakes; PO Archives].

**PITTSFORD,** Hillsdale County: it was founded by Hiram Kidder in 1833 and was first called Locust Corners; but Alpheus Pratt, who had come here in Pittsford, N.Y., had it named Pittsford, and it was given a post office of that name on Sept. 19, 1840, with Elijah B. Seelye as its first postmaster; the office was closed on Sept. 12, 1845, but was restored on Dec. 3, 1845; the office was moved to the west part of the township and renamed Sparta on Jan. 4, 1846, but the Keene post office was changed to Pittsford on Jan. 30, 1846; a station on the Lake Shore & Michigan Southern Railroad [Reynolds; PO Archives].

**PLAINFIELD,** Allegan County: surveyor William Forbes attempted to found the first village in Gun Plains Township; in 1837, he platted it, named it, and built a sawmill on the site, but it was removed in the 1840s, and the village failed, though several of its lots had been sold [GSM 1838; Thomas].

**PLAINFIELD,** Kent County: it began as a ferrying post across the Grand River; first settled in 1837 by George Miller and James Clark, the township was organized in 1838 and named from the many plains within its borders [Dillenback].

**PLAINFIELD,** Livingston County: Jacob Dunn, from Newton, N.J., became the first settler in 1835 and opened a tavern here in 1836; the town was first called Dyersburg, for Philip Dyer who had been the second settler; when given a post office on April 14, 1837, it was renamed by Mr. Dunn after Plainfield, N.J.; Emery Beal, the first postmaster, kept the office in his home; it was in operation until Oct. 30, 1913 [PO Archives; Ellis].

**PLAINFIELD,** St. Clair County. See Algonac.

**PLAINS,** Ionia County. See Hubbardston.

**PLAINS**, Marquette County: a station on the Chicago & Northwestern Railroad in 1878; a settlement formed around it [Andreas].

**PLAINVILLE**, Oakland County: Embrie Ferguson became its first postmaster on July 11, 1838; the village was named from the lovely plain on which it was located; its post office was moved to White Lake on May 29, 1841 [Durant; Seeley].

**PLAINWELL**, Allegan County: Sylvester Sibley bought his land here on June 15, 1831, thus becoming the first private owner of lands in the county; he was followed later that year by Samuel C. Wells and Hull Sherwood; but the first actual settler was Dr. Cyrenius Thompson and he became the first postmaster of Plainwell on April 10, 1833; it was also called the Junction when Henry Wellever built his tavern here in 1853; the village was platted and recorded as Plainwell by Ira Chichester for the proprietors on April 8, 1863; incorporated as a village in 1869 and as a city in 1934; it was named after the original name of its township, which was renamed Gun Plain in 1845 [Fannie M. Pell; Ensign; PO Archives].

**PLANK ROAD**, Wayne County. See Clarenceville.

**PLANTERS**, Gogebic County: this settlement, near Bessemer, was made in 1922 [GSM 1931].

**PLATO**, Houghton County: a station on the Chicago, Minneapolis & St. Paul Railroad; the settlement formed around the mill of the Northern Lumber Company; storekeeper Charles Van Oss became its first postmaster on Oct. 13, 1910, the office operating until Feb. 28, 1933 [GSM 1913; PO Archives].

**PLATTE**, Benzie County: pioneer settlers in Platte Township included F. B. Van Platten, and its first supervisor, V. F. Thurston. Abel Briggs became the town's first postmaster on June 22, 1868, the office operating until Sept. 14, 1905 [Graverse].

**PLATTEVILLE**, Iowa County: John H. Rountree became the first postmaster of this settlement on July 25, 1833; it was then in Michigan Territory, but is not in Wisconsin [PO Archives].

**PLEASANT**, Kent County: "Every acre added to the cleared space adds more than its proportionate amount of pleasure to the soul of the laborer," and so the settlers of this hamlet in Alpine township named it Pleasant; John Coffee became its first postmaster on Dec. 30, 1847, the office operating until July 13, 1889 [Dillenback; PO Archives].

**PLEASANT CITY**, Leelanau County. See Suttons Bay.

**PLEASANT LAKE**, Jackson County: it was called Spring Lake until John Wenstren acquired 1800 acres of government land adjoining the lake in 1836 and renamed it Pleasant Lake; the village was platted in 1868; Leo E. Osterberg became its first postmaster on Oct. 13, 1961 [John Deball; Interstate; PO Archvies].

**PLEASANTON**, Manistee County: it was first settled by Rev. George

B. Pierce, a retired clergyman, and B. Sibly, about 1864; Rev. Pierce became its first postmaster on Sept. 24, 1864; the office was closed on June 9, 1882, but was restored from Dec. 17, 1884, to Nov. 21, 1892, and from Nov. 5, 1897, to April 30, 1909 [GSM 1873-93; Page; PO Archives].

**PLEASANT RIDGE**, Oakland County: it was begun when Burt Taylor subdivided the Mayday farm in 1913; incorporated as a village in 1921 and as a city in 1927; believed to have been named from a local thoroughfare, Ridge Road [Ashton Berst].

**PLEASANT VALLEY**, Berrien County: Charles W. Bakeman became the first postmaster of this rural post office in Pipestone Township on May 11, 1870; when Charles Hartlerode, Sr., resigned as postmaster on Sept. 18, 1874, the office was discontinued [PO Archives].

**PLEASANT VALLEY**, Livingston County: Elijah March became the first postmaster of this rural post office on July 24, 1837, the office operating until July 29, 1852 [PO Archives].

**PLEASANT VALLEY**, Midland County: Edgar M. Smith became the first postmaster of this rural post office in the south west corner of the county on March 6, 1876, the office operating until Oct. 15, 1910 [GSM 1881; PO Archives].

**PLEASANT VIEW**, Emmet County: Pleasant View Township was organized in 1876, and George W. Law became the first postmaster of this hamlet in it on Jan. 14, 1878, the office operating until July 31, 1907 [GSM 1879; PO Archives].

**PLUMB BROOK**, Macomb County: John S. St. John became the first postmaster of this rural post office near Plumb Brook on July 21, 1840, the office operating until July 6, 1863 [GSM 1860-63; PO Archives].

**PLUMB CREEK**, Monroe County: a hamlet in 1880 [GSM 1881].

**PLUMMER'S PIER**, Berrien County. See Bridgman.

**PLUMMERVILLE**, Allegan County: it was founded in 1846 by Benjamin Plummer and Orlando Weed, who set up a sawmill on the creek nearby; later, it had a store, a tannery, and a lake pier, but "it has ceased to show any of the characteristics of a village" [Johnson].

**PLUMVILLE**, Newaygo County: a settlement around the grist mill and sawmills of John Frey; apiarist S. Wilbur Frey became its first postmaster on Dec. 6, 1892, the office operating until Sept. 14, 1903 [GSM 1893-1905; PO Archives].

**PLYMOUTH**, Wayne County: William Starkweather built his log cabin here in 1825; it was first called Plymouth Corners, some of its early settlers having been descendants of the Pilgrim Fathers; Gideon P. Benton became the first postmaster on Dec. 27, 1828, with the office named simply Plymouth; the village was platted and recorded on June 12, 1837, by Henry B. Holbrooks and Mr. Bradner; incorporated as a village in 1867 and as a city in 1932 [Burton; County plat liber].

**POCAGON**, Cass County. See Summerville.

**PODUNK**, Ingham County: originally a mill built in 1815 in Leroy Township, the name was applied to the community of Phelpstown; it was also called Shacksboro; Podunk is said to have been named after a town of that name in New York State [Foster].

**PODUNK**, Kent County. See Oakfield.

**POGWATIGUE**, Barrien County. See Niles.

**POGY**, Mecosta County: Lansing F. Corey kept the first general store in this hamlet in Grant Township and Orville L. Smith became its first postmaster on Jan. 19, 1901, the office operating until June 30, 1905; named after nearby Pogy (on some maps as Pogie) Creek [Chapman; GSM 1903-07; PO Archives].

**POINTE AUX BARQUES**, Huron County: the name, meaning point of ships, was given it by French sailors about 1760 because the ragged rock formation jutting into Lake Huron here look like boats moored along the shore. its settlement was given a post office on June 12, 1897, with George T. Miller as its first postmaster, the office operating until June 20, 1957; a station on the Pere Marquette Railroad; F. Demarest became the first township supervisor in 1903; now a resort community [Schultz; PO Archives].

**POINT AU FRENE**, Chippewa County: a settlement on the St. Mary's River, in Detour Township; Charles E. Robinson became its first postmaster on March 12, 1888, but the office was transferred to and renamed Raber on Sept. 19, 1889; frene is French for ash-tree which grow in the area [GSM 1891; PO Archives].

**POINTE AUX PINS**, Mackinac County: this resort village on the south side of Bois Blanc Island was platted and recorded by the Bois Blanc Island Land Company, of Jackson, proprietors, in 1888; Julia A. Webb became its first postmaster on May 15, 1889; the office was closed on Oct. 25, 1889, but was restored, with Mrs. Webb again the postmaster, on May 29, 1890; it was named from its location in a pine forest area [GSM 1889; PO Archives].

**POINTE AUX TREMBLE**, St. Clair County: a station on the Rapid Railway system, in Clay Township, at a hamlet three miles from Algonac, in 1904 [GSM 1905].

**POINT BRULÉ**, Mackinac County: it juts into St. Martin Bay, west of Hessel, and was named for the first white man to visit the Straits of Mackinac, Etienne Brulé, in 1621 or 1622; Samuel Champlain had received a gift of pure copper, which he was told came from this region, and he commissioned Brulé to find the source of it; on his way back to Quebec, Brulé told the story of his journey to Recollect missionary Gabriel Sagard who mentioned it in his Histoire de Canada (Paris, 1636); the Indians were forced out of this area in 1870; John Chadester, wanting its cedar, made the first land claim here in 1892 [Paré; Federal; Russell].

**POINT CATOSH**, Mackinac County: Charles Wehner became the first postmaster of this rural post office on Nov. 1, 1904, the office operating until Nov. 15, 1905 [PO Archives].

**POINTE du CHENE**, St. Clair County. See Algonac.

**POINT MILLS**, Houghton County: this settlement seven miles east of Houghton, on a point of land extending into Torch Lake, formed around the iron ore and stamp mills of the Arcadian and the Franklin Mining Companies; James O. Baudin became its first postmaster on March 14, 1899, succeeded by the manager of the company store, Joseph Gibson, in 1900; it is still on some maps as Mills and that was the name of its station on the Hancock & Calumet Railroad [Glinn; GSM 1901; PO Archives].

**POINT PATTERSON**, Mackinac County: this site, also known as Patterson's Point, was named from the fact that Charles Patterson, one of the chief members of the Northwest Fur Company, was drowned here with all his crew about 1788 [MPH 6:350 1883].

**POINT RICHARDS**, Montcalm County: this village in Douglass Township, on the west side of Clifford Lake, was given a post office on Feb. 21, 1881, with William B. Mason as its first postmaster, the office operating until July 3, 1883; it was platted and recorded by F. A. Palmer for James Will Richards on June 11, 1881; the site became the location of the Clifford Lake summer resort, owned and operated by Ulysses G. Hayden; Clifford Lake was named for Mr. Clifford who had settled near it [Dasef; PO Archives].

**POINT SABLE**, Mason County: William Willer became the first postmaster of this rural post office on May 22, 1878, the office operating until May 16, 1887 [PO Archives].

**POINT SAINT IGNACE**, Mackinac County. See St. Ignace.

**POKAGON**, Cass County: in 1838, Pottawattomi chief Pokagon bought some 900 acres here in Silver Creek Township, which he parceled out to his people; a Catholic, he built a log chapel; the first parish priest to live beside it, Father Theophilus Marivault, C.S.C., began a set of parish records on Jan. 4, 1845, styling himself Pastor of Pokagon or Silver Creek; the settlement was gradually inhabited by whites and it was platted by William Baldwin in 1858 and on June 26 of the same year was given a post office, with Garrett Stansel as its first postmaster [Paré; Fox; PO Archives].

**POLASKI**, Presque Isle County: when the Detroit & Mackinaw Railroad came through in 1894, its depot here was named Polaski Station, the name derived from its township of Pulawski, so named by its early settlers who were mostly Poles; in some records it is spelled Pulaski [W. H. Whiteley].

**POLISH SETTLEMENT**, Manistee County. See Canfield Mill Settlement.

**POLKTEN**, Ottawa County. See Dennison.

**POLKTON**, Ottawa County. See Coopersville.

**POLLOCK**, Ingham County: named for pioneer settlers, the Pollock family; M. J. Pollock came to Michigan from Sodus Point, N.Y., and was a justice of the peace at Pollock in 1852; Judson H. Phelps became its first postmaster on March 14, 1899, the office operating until Aug. 31, 1900 [Foster; PO Archives].

**POMONA**, Manistee County: a station on the Toledo, Ann Arbor & Northern Michigan Railroad, in Cleon Township; its settlement formed around the sawmill of S. & E. Crooks; John E. Stiver became its first postmaster on Dec. 7, 1889 [GSM 1891; PO Archives].

**POMPEII**, Gratiot County: it was first settled in 1854 by Joseph B. Smith and was called Joe B's; he became the first postmaster on May 14, 1856, with the office named Pompei (the spelling was changed to Pompeii on Oct. 20, 1897); the village was torn down in 1886-87 and moved a mile and a half south to be on the Toledo, Saginaw & Muskegon (now Grand Trunk) Railroad; it was first platted by Joseph Foster and Burton P. Bradley in 1887; named after Pompeii, Italy [Tucker; PO Archives].

**PONAMA**, Newaygo County: Lewis Martin became the first postmaster of this rural post office on June 9, 1860, succeeded by Ebenezer Dobson on Aug. 18, 1863, and William Rogers on Nov. 29, 1869, the office operating until Jan. 15, 1872 [PO Archives].

**PONCA**, Alcona County: a rural post office in Mitchell Township, conducted in the home of Ralph Jacobs, with Mary E. Jacobs becoming its first postmaster on July 19, 1915 [GSM 1919; PO Archives].

**PONTIAC**, Oakland County: it was founded by promoters from Detroit,–Colonel Stephen Mack who, with Major Joseph Todd, William Lester and Orison Allen, became the first settlers in 1818; it was developed by the Pontiac Company, of which Colonel Mack was manager; given a post office on May 1, 1822, with Olmstead Chamberlin as its first postmaster; platted by H. J. Goodale in 1841; incorporated as a village in 1837 and as a city in 1861; named for a local Ottawa chief [Mich Hist 25:248 1941; Durant; PO Archives].

**POOL**, Lapeer County: Lyman Russell became the first postmaster of this settlement in Attica Township on May 27, 1856, the office operating until Aug. 27, 1887 [GSM 1889; PO Archives].

**POPLAR GROVE**, Huron County: Samuel H. Wright became the first postmaster of this rural post office in Colfax Township on Sept. 26, 1874, the office operating until April 14, 1879 [GSM 1877; PO Archives].

**POPPLE**, Huron County: this village in Sheridan Township was first called Finger Board when founded in 1870; when given a post office on Jan. 19, 1882, with storekeeper Loren D. Dann as its first postmaster, the name was changed to that of the popple trees; its post office was closed on Jan. 5, 1883, but was restored from Oct. 30, 1883, to Aug. 14, 1905 [Hey; PO Archives].

**PORI**, Houghton County: this hamlet in Laird Township was named after a city in Finland; storekeeper Benze G. Rosted became its first postmaster on Dec. 12, 1889, the office operating until Jan. 14, 1904; its station on the Chicago, Milwaukee & St. Paul Railroad was first called Pori and now Pori Siding; Camp Pori, three miles east, was a Civilian Conservation Corps camp during the Depression of the 1930s, and a German prisoner of war camp from 1943 to 1945, when it became a field training camp for Michigan Tech forestry students; it was abandoned in 1953 and razed in 1955 [Eric A. Burdo, Jr.; GSM 1905; PO Archives].

**PORTAGE**, Jackson County. See Henrietta.

**PORTAGE**, Kalamazoo County: the first white settler in the area was Mr. Herring who built his cabin in 1830; the settlement was given a post office as Sweetland on May 28, 1836, with John E. Howard as its first postmaster; Moses Austin helped organize and name Portage Township in 1838, and with Henry M. Tuttle as postmaster, the office was renamed Portage on June 26, 1839; the office was closed on Dec. 21, 1846, but was restored from Feb. 12, 1851, to July 31, 1906, and since Feb. 26, 1907; it was named from its chief stream, Portage Creek [Ray Dirksen; PO Archives].

**PORTAGE**, Mackinac County. See Curtis.

**PORTAGE**, Manistee County. See Onekama.

**PORTAGE CREEK**, Manistee County: Hiram Sawyer became the first postmaster of this rural post office on Oct. 5, 1858; the office was closed on Jan. 28, 1861, but was restored on Feb. 3, 1862, and changed to Norwalk on Jan. 21, 1863 [PO Archives].

**PORTAGE ENTRY**, Houghton County: it was so named because it was the point where Portage Lake entered through Portage River, which connected it and Lake Superior; storekeeper Ransom Sheldon was the first and only postmaster of this hamlet, the office operating from Oct. 10, 1851, to Aug. 8, 1853 [Andreas; PO Archives].

**PORTAGE FORK**, Jackson County: William C. Balch became the first postmaster of this rural post office on Sept. 21, 1875, the office operating until May 16, 1876 [PO Archives].

**PORTAGE LAKE**, Jackson County: Benoni Pixley became the first postmaster of this rural post office on July 18, 1844; the office was renamed Farm on Jan. 26, 1863, but was closed on June 16, 1864; it was restored from July 22, 1864, to Sept. 16, 1867 [PO Archives].

**PORTAGE LAKE**, Keweenaw County: it was part of an old portage route for Indians and voyageurs; later it was a name given by men going to the Civil War to the villages of Houghton and Hancock before they were incorporated; thus the first newspaper in the area came to be named the Portage Lake Mining Gazette [Mich Hist 38:54 1954; Nute; Gibson].

**PORTAGE LAKE**, St. Joseph County: a station on the Grand Rapids & Indiana Railroad in 1868 [GSM 1889].

**PORTAGE POINT,** Manistee County: this summer resort on a narrow strip of land between Portage Lake and Lake Michigan, in Onekama Township, was developed by the Portage Point Association, Harry D. Jewell, of Grand Rapids, president; Roger A. Jewell became its first postmaster on Aug. 6, 1917, the office operating until Sept. 30, 1921 [GSM 1919; PO Archives].

**PORT AUSTIN,** Huron County: it was first called Byrd's Creek for Jeduthan Byrd who built a sawmill here in 1839; he sold out to the lumbering firm of Smith, Austin & Dwight, and the name was changed to Dwightville in 1854 for firm-member Alfred Dwight; firm-member P. C. Austin built a boat dock for himself, enlarged it for the use of others, and put a street light on a pole for a lighthouse; thus it became known as Austin's Dock, later as Austin Port, and finally as Port Austin; Rollin C. Smith became its first postmaster on Jan. 19, 1856; for some time the east side of the town retained the name Dwightville, but eventually as the result of a compromise, the entire village was named Port Austin and the township Dwight; it was the county seat from 1865 to 1875; incorporated as a village in 1887 [Willet H. Schmidt, PM; PO Archives].

**PORT CRESCENT,** Huron County: Walter Hume, the first settler, built a trading post and an inn here in 1844, and the place became known as Pinnepog (Chippewa for partridge drum), from the river running by it; later, five miles inland, on a branch of the same river, a new settlement also took the name of Pinnepog; the original town asked the later one to change its name, and it did to Pinnebog; that helped so little that Pinnepog took the name of Port Crescent, from the crescent-shaped contour of its shore line; Jonas B. Learned became its first postmaster on May 8, 1868, the office operating until April 8, 1902; in 1936, its last business moved away and it became a ghost town; in 1962, it began to be developed as Port Crescent State Park [Mich Hist 25:234 1941; 46:303 1962; Chapman; PO Archives].

**PORT ELIZABETH,** Huron County. See Caseville.

**PORTER,** Cass County: it was first settled by John Baldwin, a Southerner, in the winter of 1828-29, and nearby Baldwin Lake was named for him; it was given a post office as Union, with Jacob Charles as its first postmaster, in 1831; when the township was organized in 1833, it was named for George B. Porter, then governor of Michigan[Schoetzow; Mathews].

**PORTER,** Iron County: it was also called Amasa Porter; the Nevada Mining Company developed a mine here in 1914; a sand cave resulted in the death of 16 miners on Feb. 21, 1918; it was five miles south of Amasa and was probably named for industrialist H. H. Porter [Jack Hill, Sr.].

**PORTER,** Midland County: among the residents and free-holders who potitioned for the organization of Porter Township was Lewis K. Brewer; it was organized in 1868, with the first election held in his home in 1869, and on June 5, 1869, he became its first postmaster, the office operating until May 15, 1907 [Chapman; PO Archives].

**PORTER**, Van Buren County: Abner Mack became the first settler here in 1833, locating the land and building his cabin upon it; when the township was organized in 1845, Harriet, daughter of Nathan Cook, suggested the name of an American naval hero, Commodore David Porter (1780-1843); it was given a post office as Decatur, named after its township (which had been named after another American naval hero, Stephen Decatur), with George S. Freese becoming its first post master on July 11, 1838, with the office being renamed Porter on Sept. 20, 1849 [Ellis; PO Archives].

**PORTER'S ISLAND,** Keweenaw County: it was named for Joseph Porter, who was the land commissioner in the 1840s, and whose office was on the island, near the Gap; now a summer colony [Mich Hist 9:380 1925].

**PORTER'S STATION,** Saginaw County. See Randall,

**PORTER'S VILLAGE,** Emmet County. See Petoskey.

**PORT HOLLOW,** Kent County. See Edgerton.

**PORT HOPE,** Huron County: in 1855, Dr. DiMond took out patents on the timberland here; Diamond Creek was named for him; Mr. Southard and Mr. Witcher, while drifting in a small skiff in 1857, succeeded in making land and they named the place Port Hope; William R. Stafford bought the DiMond and Southerd claims, built a lumber mill in 1858, and around it the town grew; the lumber firm of Stafford & Haywood were its principal proprietors, and the place was also called Stafford; it was given a post office as Port Hope, with Mr. Stafford becoming its first postmaster on Jan. 6, 1860; incorporated as a village in 1887 [Hey; PO Archives; GSM 1873].

**PORT HURON,** St. Clair County: to protect their fur trade against English aggression, the French built Fort St. Joseph here in 1686; when it burned in 1688, its garrison was transferred to Mackinac; the first permanent settlement here was made by Anselm Petit in 1790; in 1814, it became the site of Fort Gratiot (q.v.); the town was organized in 1828 and given a post office as Desmond on April 30, 1833, with Jonathan Burtch as its first postmaster; by Circuit court permission, the Desmond and Gratiot plats were renamed Port Huron, as was the Desmond post office, both in 1837, the post office being so renamed on May 4; incorporated as a village in 1849 and as a city in 1857 [Schultz; Federal; PO Archives].

**PORT INLAND,** Schoolcraft County: it was the headquarters, completed in 1930, of the Inland Lime & Stone Company, and their shipping point on Lake Michigan [Federal].

**PORTLAND,** Ionia County: the first government land purchase here was made by Elisha Newman in 1833, but before he took possession in 1836, other settlers had arrived; Joshua Boyer became its first postmaster on March 11, 1837; platted by A. S. Wadsworth in 1838; incorporated as a village in 1869; located at the mouth of the Looking Glass River, it was named from its fine loading for boats [Malcolm B. Robertson; PO Archives].

**PORT LAWRENCE**, Monroe County: this settlement was given a post office as Depot, with Benjamin F. Stickney becoming its first postmaster on Dec. 1, 1823, renamed Port Lawrence on Oct. 7, 1825; it was named after a vessle, Lawrence, which Commodore Oliver Hazard Perry commanded in the Battle of Lake Erie in the War of 1812; it was changed to Tremainville on Jan. 7, 1834, but the Lawrence post office was reestablished the following day, with Stephen B. Comstock as its postmaster; in the Michigan-Ohio boundary dispute (called the Toledo War), it was transferred to Lucas County, Ohio, on March 23, 1835, and is now within the city limits of Toledo; see under Vistula for the terms of the agreement [Buckley; Wing; PO Archives].

**PORT ONEIDA**, Leelanau County: a rural community in Glen Arbor Township on the shores of Lake Michigan in the Pyramid Point region; it was first settled in 1853 by Carson Burfield; Thomas Kelderhouse completed his dock here in 1862 and it is said that the first steamer to stop at it was named the Oneida, and that was how the settlement was named; lumberman William Kelderhouse became its first postmaster on June 3, 1886, the office operating until April 15, 1905 [Dickinson; PO Archives].

**PORT SANILAC**, Sanilac County: about 1840, some Detroiters came here to make tan-bark and built a bark shanty; passing sailors gave the place the name of Bark Shanty Point; William Austin and others took up claims on the site about 1844; Anthony Oldfield and the Thompsons, William, Hugh and Quintin, built their sawmill in 1848; William Van Camp became the first postmaster of Bark Shanty on Dec. 30, 1854, with the office renamed Port Sanilac, after the county, on Aug. 4, 1857; incorporated as a village in 1877 [Chapman; PO Archives].

**PORT SHELDON**, Ottawa County: in 1837, Alex H. Joudon (or Jaudon), of Philadelphia, and other eastern capitalists, formed the Port Sheldon Land Company and spent a fortune laying out and building a boom city here in Olive Township, near Pigeon Creek; Edmund R. Badger became its first postmaster on Feb. 13, 1838; the office was closed on June 7, 1845, but was restored from July 1, 1867, to July 15, 1872; the original venture failed and the site became a resort colony which was given a post office on April 23, 1894, with Christian J. Cook as its first postmaster, the office operating until Oct. 15, 1906; all its post offices were named Port Sheldon, but the site has become known as Pigeon Creek [MPH 28:527 1898; Mich Hist 35:226 1951; PO Archives].

**PORT SHERMAN**, Muskegon County: this village became part of the city of Muskegon in 1889 [Mich Hist 5:519 1921].

**PORTSMOUTH**, Bay County: in 1836, probate judge Albert Miller bought a tract of land here from Joseph and Mader Trombley, built a sawmill and platted a village, naming it from its location near the mouth of the Saginaw River; he became its first postmaster on Dec. 3, 1836; the office was closed on July 3, 1840, but was restored from May 31, 1856, to Feb. 20, 1985, when the gradual annexation of the village by Bay City was completed [Page; Butterfield; PO Archives].

**POSEN**, Presque Isle County: a group of Poles, the first being Lawrence Kowalski, settled here in 1870; they named the township and thence the town Posen, after the province of Poznan in Poland; it was given a post office on Feb. 24, 1875, with Frank Roshek as its first postmaster; the office was closed on Jan. 16, 1877, but has been restored since Oct. 14, 1881; its station on the Alpena & Northern Railroad was called Vincent; incorporated as a village in 1907 [Robert Polski; PO Archives].

**POSEYVILLE**, Midland County: town clerk Patrick Nagle became the first postmaster of this rural post office in Ingersoll Township on July 12, 1898, the office operating until Jan. 15, 1907 [GSM 1899-1909; PO Archives].

**POST**, Tuscola County: Julius J. Haske became the first postmaster of this rural post office, six miles from Reese, on May 9, 1898, the office operating until Oct. 31, 1900 [PO Archives].

**POTTAMIE**, Ottawa County: Alonzo Carter became the first postmaster of this rural post office on the south bank of the Grand River on Jan. 28, 1870, the office operating until April 10, 1873 [GSM 1875; PO Archives].

**POTTER**, Washtenaw County. See Willis.

**POTTERSBURG**, St. Clair County. See Jeddo.

**POTTER'S CORNERS**, St. Clair County. See Jeddo.

**POTTER'S MILL**, Gratiot County. See Hasty.

**POTTERSVILLE**, Sanilac County: a hamlet in 1880 [GSM 1881].

**POTTERVILLE**, Eaton County: it was first settled by Linus Potter with his wife and seven children in 1844; within two years he died, but his family cleared the land and carried on; in 1868, his eldest son, George N. Potter, built a sawmill and a boarding house for the hands, the latter becoming a hotel; James W. Potter became the first postmaster (at $12 a year) on March 15, 1870; it was platted and recorded in 1868 by R. D. Phelps and Charles H. Brown; incorporated as a village in 1881 and as a city in 1962 [Hal O. Fry, PM; Durant].

**POTTS**, Oscoda County. See McKinley.

**POTTS' POINT**, Iosco County: the Buckus Brothers, Absolom and Albert S., built a sawmill here in 1865; they sold out to J. E. Potts, of Simcoe, Canada, in 1875, and the mill of J. E. Potts Salt & Lumber Company became one of the largest in the world until it failed in 1890 [Otis].

**POULSON**, Mason County: this hamlet in Victory Township was first settled in 1877; Rasmus Lykkeby became its first postmaster on June 29, 1886, the office operating until Jan. 14, 1902; in some records as Poulsen [GSM 1887; PO Archives].

**POVERTY NOOK,** Sanilac County. See Hemans.

**POWELL,** Marquette County: a station on the M. & N.E. Railroad, near Birch, in 1910 [GSM 1911].

**POWERS,** Barry County: it was named for pioneer settler L. K. Powers; in Johnson as having a post office from 1855 to 1865, but there is no official record of it [PO Archives; Johnson].

**POWERS,** Menominee county: in 1872, Edward Powers, a civil engineer for the Chicago & Northwestern Railroad, began to acquire land here in Spalding Township, platted it, named it, and for many years was associated with its development; Carrie Brooks became its first postmaster on June 29, 1877; incorporated as a village in 1915 [Escanaba Daily Press, Aug. 26, 1965; Evelyn Bergen; PO Archives].

**PRAHA,** Antrim County: its postal name was Praha, its political name is Jordan Township, its ecclesiastical name is Praga, its popular name if Bohemian Settlement; it was first settled by Bohemian farmers who acquired government land here by homesteading from about 1871; its post office was opened on Dec. 5, 1876, with Frank Votruba as its first postmaster, the office operating until only Sept. 9, 1878; its name was derived from Prague or Praha, the capital of old Bohemia, now Czechoslovakia; the community is dying out due to marriages with non-Czechs [GSM 1881; Rev. C. G. Klimowicz; PO Archives].

**PRAIRIE CORNERS,** St. Joseph County: pioneer settler Byron Q. Goodrich is believed to have given his name to Goodrich Prairie, the site of this community in Colon Township [Mich Hist 32:28 1948].

**PRAIRIE CREEK,** Ionia County: it was named after the stream beside it; the land was bought by Nathaniel Brown in 1835, and he platted it; John P. Place, of Chicago, bought a half interest and built a sawmill and the first store in the township in 1836; though a few lots were sold, their attempts to make it a village were given up in 1837; in 1872, Laura Place replatted Prairie Creek as an addition to the village of Ionia [Schenck; Branch].

**PRAIRIE du CHIEN,** Crawford County: James H. Lockwood became the first postmaster of this settlement on Dec. 6, 1824; it was then in Michigan Territory but is now in Wisconsin [PO Archives].

**PRAIRIE FARM,** Saginaw County: a group from Saginaw in the 1880s found the cost of draining the marshland here so great that they sold out to the Saginaw Realty Company which in 1903 sold it to John Pitcairn, of Pittsburgh, president of the Pittsburgh Plate Glass Company and the Owosso Sugar Company; he wanted to make it a great center for beet, sheep, and peppermint growing; his dream continued to take shape as his heirs, Raymond, Theodore, and Harold Pitcairn, took title in 1929; but with the Depression, they sold out in 1933 to a New York-Chicago combine which operated it as the Sunrise Co-operative Farm Community; they failed, and in 1936, sold it to the U.S. Resettlement Administration which, about 1945, sold it to the Saginaw Valley Co-operative Farms who split its 10,000 acres up among its members; while it lasted, Prairie Farm included three small settlements for its managers and workers, and they have appeared on maps and in records and writings as villages, to wit, Pitcarnia named for John Pitcairn, Clausdale named for William Lewis Clause, chairman of the board of PPG, and Alicia named for his eldest daughter Alice Clause Campbell; the village of Alicia was given a post office on Jan. 26, 1904, with Harry W. Kline as its first postmaster, the office operating until May 31, 1947 [Robert T. McMillen; PPG; PO Archives].

**PRAIRIE RIVER**, Branch County: William S. Kent became the first postmaster of this settlement on May 17, 1834; the office was closed on Aug. 2, 1845, but was restored from Feb. 19, 1851, to Aug. 22, 1853 [PO Archives; GSM 1860].

**PRAIRIE RONDE**, Cass County: Richard J. Huyck became the first postmaster of the rural post office of Little Prairie Ronde on Nov. 1, 1837; the Westfield post office was changed to Prairie Ronde on Jan. 31, 1846, and operated until June 17, 1862; the Little Prairie Ronde post office was changed to Prairie Ronde on Aug. 6, 1901, and operated until Dec. 14, 1913 [PO Archives].

**PRAIRIE RONDE**, Kalamazoo County. See Schoolcraft.

**PRAIRIE RONDE VILLAGE**, Cass County: this tract of six square miles was reserved by the Pottawattomi Indians in the Treaty of Chicago, 1821, but their claim to the land was exhausted in 1836 [Fox].

**PRAIRIEVILLE**, Barry County: Amasa Parker, the first settler in the county, entered land here in 1831; Charles W. Spalding came in 1834, and the township when organized in 1841, was named Spalding for him, but renamed Prairieville in 1843; he became the first postmaster, with the office named Fulton, on March 8, 1837; the office was renamed Prairieville on Dec. 8, 1855, and operated until Jan. 15, 1934; Hiram Lucas came in 1837 and his tavern formed the nucleus of the village; in 1836-37, Leonard Slater, a Baptist minister, brought a band of 300 Indians, bought land and began a school; hence the village was sometimes referred to as Slater or the Slater Mission, but the mission land is now a privately owned farm [Charles A. Weissert; MPH 35:142 1907; PO Archives].

**PRATT LAKE**, Kent County: a station on the Lowell & Hastings Railroad, near Pratt Lake, 3 miles south of Lowell, in 1898 [Mich Manual 1899].

**PRATTS**, Benzie County: this rural post office was named for Mary A. Pratt who became its first postmaster on May 16, 1899, the office operating until July 15, 1908 [PO Archives].

**PRATT'S HILL**, Hillsdale County: the settlement was named for lawyer Daniel L. Pratt who first settled here in 1845; it is now within the west city limits of Hillsdale [Mich Hist 6:577 1922].

**PRATTVILLE**, Hillsdale County: Wellington and Henry Pratt, brothers, came here in Wright Township, from Farmingham, Mass., in 1866, and built a mill and a store; a rural post office named Cass, which had been opened on Aug. 3, 1848, with Timothy Johnson as its first postmaster, was renamed for them on Jan. 26, 1872 [Pen Phil 9:2 June 1958; Vivian L. Moore].

**PRENTICE**, Monroe County: Joseph M. Bale became the first postmaster of this rural post office on Feb. 26, 1873, the office operating until March 23, 1874 [PO Archives].

**PRENTIS BAY**, Mackinac County: this settlement in Holmes Township, on the north shore of Lake Huron, formed around the sawmill of George H. Prentis in 1872; storekeeper Edgar J. Swart became its first postmaster on Jan. 22, 1879, the office operating until July 24, 1895 [GSM 1881; PO Archives].

**PRESBYTERY POINT**, Marquette County: the site of a summer institute for young Presbyterians, established in 1937 [Federal].

**PRESCOTT**, Ogemaw County: C. H. Prescott bought the Lake Huron & Southwestern Railroad in 1879 and renamed it the Tawas & Bay County Railroad; the settlement was known as Prescott's Camp Six, shortened to Prescott on Oct. 27, 1882, when given a post office, with Mrs. Julia A. Davison as its first postmaster; incorporated as a village in 1947 [Willis O. Best; PO Archives].

**PRESQUE ISLE**, Presque Isle County: the village was named from the county which had been established in 1840; the name (French for almost an island) was given by the French canoers because the land here formed a narrow peninsula jotting out into Lake Huron; the first settler, Frederick G. Burnham, came here about 1860 to engage in the cordwood business and built a dock and boat landing in Presque Isle Harbor; it was given a post office on April 7, 1884, with Mr. Burnham as its first postmaster; the office was closed on Nov. 12, 1892, but has been restored since April 6, 1899 [F. J. Doyle, PM; PO Archives].

**PRESTEL**, Clare County: this settlement around the sawmill of Neff & Prestel was given a post office on Nov. 11, 1891, with Charles L. Dolph as its first postmaster, succeeded by L. G. Prestel in 1892 [GSM 1893; PO Archives].

**PRESTON**, Wayne County: this station on the Wabash Railroad is believed to have been named for David Preston, banker and landowner; storekeeper Albert Bull became its first postmaster on March 6, 1899, the office operating until Sept. 17, 1906 [GSM 1901; PO Archives].

**PRESTON CORNERS**, Macomb County: in 1826, Ira and Deborah Preston bought 400 acres of government land here in Shelby Township and settled on it in 1827; they built a sawmill and later a picket fence factory; in 1926, a bronze plate was erected in their memory and marking Preston Corners [Mich Hist 35:94 1951].

**PRICE**, Clinton County: Ezra Lattimer became the first postmaster of this rural post office on April 17, 1888, the office operating until April 30, 1901 [PO Archives].

**PRINCETON**, Marquette County: this village on the Escanaba River, in Forsyth Township, was founded in 1896 by John Stambaugh and Mr. Todd, representing the Princeton Mining Company, which had been named by a mining engineer who had attended Princeton University; George J. Sarasin became its first postmaster on Dec. 27, 1898, and served continuously for 43 years; the nine mines which operated in the area are all closed now [Carl A. Sather, PM; PO Archives].

**PRINT**, Benzie County: John Griner became the first postmaster of this rural post office in the southeast corner of the county on June 20, 1879; the office was transferred to and renamed Nessen City on Dec. 5, 1889 [GSM 1881; PO Archives].

**PRISON SIDING**, Ionia County: a station on the Detroit, Grand Haven & Milwaukee Railroad, near the Ionia House of Correction, in 1856 [GSM 1895].

**PRISON SIDE TRACK**, Jackson County: a station built in 1878 on the Michigan Central Railroad, for the convenience of those going to and from the state prison, about a mile from the city of Jackson [GSM 1879].

**PRITCHARDVILLE**, Barry County: Daniel S. Chase bought 120 acres here in Baltimore Township, built a sawmill in 1853, and a grist mill in 1855; the village was named for George Pritchard who, with his brother, operated a foundry and a grist mill here in 1878; George H. Risbridger became its first postmaster on June 20, 1879, the office operating until Nov. 30, 1903 [Johnson; GSM 1881; PO Archives].

**PROCTOR**, Allegan County: William S. Miner, from Rochester, N.Y., bought land and built his log house here in 1836, and he became the first postmaster on Sept. 9, 1850, the office operating until July 8, 1868 [Johnson; PO Archives].

**PROSPECT LAKE**, Van Buren County: Hiram Jacobs became the first postmaster of this rural post office near Prospect (formerly Crystal) Lake, in Lawrence Township, on Aug. 1, 1851, the office operating until July 30, 1900 [Ellis; PO Archives].

**PROSPER**, Missaukee County: John R. Meyering became the first postmaster of this settlement in Clam Union Township on July 5, 1901, the office operating until May 31, 1914 [GSM 1903; PO Archives].

**PROVEMONT**, Leelanau County. See Lake Leelanau.

**PROVIDENCE**, Presque Isle County: lumberman Reuben Mitchell became the first postmaster of this lumber settlement on the Ocqueoc

River, in Case Township, on April 25, 1899, the office operating until April 14, 1904 [GSM 1901-05; PO Archives].

**PRUDENVILLE**, Roscommon County: the village was founded by John Pruden in 1875 and was given a post office on Sept. 6, 1875, with Mrs. Clara J. Denton as its first postmaster; its name was changed to Edna on Jan. 10, 1876, but back to Prudenville on Jan. 14, 1886; the office was closed on Aug. 15, 1911, but has been operating again since 1921 [PM; PO Archives].

**PSHAWBATOWN**, Leelanau County. See Peshawbestown.

**PUDDLEFORD**, Jackson County: by puddling, cast iron is converted into wrought iron, and hence the name of this coal and iron mining settlement in Blackman Township; George H. Fry became its first postmaster on April 24, 1895, the office operating until Feb. 14, 1901 [Interstate; GSM 1897-1903; PO Archives].

**PUDDLEFORD**, St. Joseph County: the popular name of a settlement before it was platted and recorded as Constantine [Mich Hist 4:590 1920].

**PULASKI**, Jackson County: it was first settled by John Howard in 1834; the township was organized in 1838, and named by Colonel Luther L. Ward for Count Casimir Pulaski, Polish hero in the American Revolution. Byron L. Harlow became the first postmaster on Oct. 15, 1840, the office operating until Feb. 16, 1945 [John Deball; DeLand; PO Archives].

**PULASKI**, Presque Isle County. See Polaski.

**PULLEN'S CORNERS**, Wayne County: the first settler in the area was Samuel Poyne in 1787; Jenks Pullen and his six sons came here from New York State in 1831; it was named in 1835 when Romulus Township was organized in the home of Joseph Y. Pullen, with D. J. Pullen as the first supervisor [Burton].

**PULLMAN**, Allegan County: two brothers named Clement built a sawmill here in Lee Township in 1870; in 1871, the Chicago & Western Michigan (now Pere Marquette) Railroad came through and built a station on land owned by Messrs. Hopper and Bennett; the place became known as Hoppertown and was given a post office of that name on Dec. 8, 1875, with Ranson Shell as its first postmaster; the office was closed on July 19, 1880, but was restored on Feb. 4, 1891, and on July 15, 1901, it was renamed Pullman, evidently for George Pullman (1831-1897), of sleeping car fame [Edward Hutchinson; PO Archives].

**PURCHASE**, Hillsdale County: a station on the Lake Shore & Michigan Southern Railroad; its settlement was named for storekeeper Wilson W. Purchase who became its first postmaster on Oct. 16, 1891, the office operating until June 29, 1901 [GSM 1893; PO Archives].

**PURITAN**, Gogebic County: it was founded in 1886 by the Oliver Iron Mining Company (U.S. Steel) as an iron ore mining location, and was named for our nation's pioneers; storekeeper Richard F. Harris became its first postmaster on May 7, 1910, the office operating until Aug. 5, 1953 [Victor Lemmer].

**PUTNAM,** Lenawee County: this rural post office was named for Elmer E. Putnam who became its first postmaster on April 18, 1898 [PO Archives].

**PUTNAM,** Livingston County: a hamlet in Putnam Township in 1859 [GSM 1860].

**PUTNAM,** Missaukee County. See Star City.

**PUTNAM STATION,** Cass County: this railway stop in Pokagon Township was named for the first settler in the county, Uzziel Putnam, Sr., who lived less than a mile from the depot [Fox].

**PUTNEY'S CORNERS,** Benzie County: in 1884, O. E. Putney built a mill on land leased from Willis Osgood, and began to manufacture hardwood lumber; in 1894, a letter was granted to 25 members to organize a Disciples' church here in Blaine Township [MPH 28:121 1897].

**QUAKER,** Lenawee County: this Quaker settlement in Rollin Township was given a post office on June 3, 1886, with Solomon B. Hughes as its first postmaster, the office operating until June 30, 1906 [GSM 1887-1907; PO Archives].

**QUAKERTOWN,** Oakland County: Farmington was first called Quakertown; present-day Quakertown began with a subdivision called Quaker Valley Farms; incorporated as the village of Quakertown in 1959 [Isabel Haynes].

**QUANICASSE,** Tuscola County: being on the edge of the lake, it drew white men here for fishing just as it had the Indians in the past, so it is impossible to state that the village which formed here in Wisner Township was founded by any one person in any one year; it was given a post office as Quanicasse City on June 11, 1886, with Horace G. Webster as its first postmaster, the office operating until March 31, 1902; it has retained its Indian name, meaning lone tree [Leland Service; GSM 1887; PO Archives].

**QUEEN MINE,** Marquette County: a station on the Duluth, South Shore & Atlantic Railroad, some ten miles west of Marquette, opened about 1890 [Mich Manual 1899].

**QUARRY,** Presque Isle County. See Crawford's Quarry.

**QUICK,** Otsego County: this rural post office, nine miles east of Gaylord, was opened on April 8, 1899, and was named for James A. Quick who became its first postmaster [GSM 1901; PO Archives].

**QUICK'S CORNERS,** Calhoun County. See Steamburg.

**QUIMBY,** Barry County: H. L. Quimby came here in Hastings Township, from Grand Rapids, in 1870, built a large sawmill, homes for his

PITTSFIELD TWP.
Washtenaw Co. Poor House & Insane Asylum

RAISIN TWP.
Raisin Union Cheese Factory

workmen, a store, and secured a post office which opened on June 9, 1871, with George Quimby as its first postmaster; the office was closed on June 27, 1876, but was restored from March 6, 1890, to Sept. 30, 1932; the progress of this village on the Thornapple River was halted permanently by the burning down of the mill [Johnson; PO Archives].

**QUINCY**, Branch County: the first settler in the township, Horace Wilson, Sr., bought 320 acres of government land and built his log cabin in 1830; John Cornish built the first house in the present village in 1833; when this township was separated from Coldwater in 1836, the suggestion of Dr. Hiram Allen, a recent settler from Quincy, Mass., for the new name was accepted; Enos G. Berry's log cabin home became the first post office on Dec. 16, 1836; a station on the Lake Shore & Michigan Southern Railroad; incorporated as a village in 1858 [Genevieve Ludlow].

**QUINN**, Macomb County: Theodore Kath became the first postmaster of this rural post office in Clinton Township on Dec. 10, 1869, the office operating until Sept. 15, 1873 [PO Archives; GSM 1879].

**QUINNESEC**, Dickinson County: John L. Bell discovered the Quinnesec Mine in 1871 and successfully developed it; he founded this village which followed from it and which was platted in 1876; Roscoe G. Brown became its first postmaster on Sept. 25, 1877; a station on the Chicago & Northwestern Railroad; then in Menominee County, it was transferred to Dickinson on Oct. 1, 1871; the name is Indian for smokey waters, referring to the mist hanging over the nearby Menominee River [PM; Havinghurst; PO Archives].

**RABBIT RIVER**, Allegan County. See Hamilton.

**RABER**, Chippewa County: John Stevenson, born in Scotland, emigrated here in 1878 and is said to have been the first white settler; it was named for Mueller M. Raber, a pioneer lumberman in the area; George Raber became its first postmaster on Sept. 19, 1889, the office operating until Dec. 31, 1954 [Bayliss; PO Archives].

**RACO**, Chippewa County: the village was named from the initials of the Richardson & Avery Company which began building a sawmill here in 1913; by the next summer it was in full swing and a town had developed from it; the founders were Lloyd M. Richardson, of Saginaw, Mich., and Sewell L. Avery, of Evanston, Ill.; the latter was then president of U.S. Gypsum and later became president of Montgomery Ward; Raco was given a post office on Jan. 20, 1915, with James A. Lillie as its first postmaster; a station on the Duluth, South Shore & Atlantic Railroad [N. K. Zeigler; GSM 1915; PO Archives].

**RACY'S CORNERS**, Saginaw County: this hamlet in Brady Township was named for a local landowner and was first settled in 1842; it was given a post office as Racy on Sept. 5, 1894, with Alonzo M. Brown as its first postmaster, the office operating until March 31, 1905 [Mills; PO Archives].

**RAIGUEL**, Lake County: a station on the Grand Rapids & Indiana

Railroad, serving a sawmill settlement in Cherry Valley Township; Eugene A. Jones became its first postmaster on Dec. 11, 1888, succeeded by town clerk Milo Reynolds in 1890, the office operating until Dec. 16, 1892 [GSM 1891-92; PO Archives].

**RAINS' LANDING**, Chippewa County: this settlement was named for Allen Rains whose large home stood here on Sugar Island until it burned down in 1937 [Hamilton].

**RAINY LAKE**, Presque Isle County: a station on the Alpena & Northern (now Detroit & Mackinaw) Railroad, 42 miles northwest of Alpena, in 1894 [GSM 1895].

**RAISIN**, Lenawee County: Darius G. Jackson became the first postmaster of this settlement in Raisin Township, on Sept. 9, 1835, the office operating until March 22, 1855; see Raisinville for the name [GSM 1838; PO Archives].

**RAISIN CENTRE**, Lenawee County: emigration flowed into Raisin Township in 1831; the Friends (Quakers) built a meeting house here in 1834; Stephen Galloway became the first postmaster on June 9, 1868, and the Lake Shore & Michigan Southern Railroad gave it a station named Chase's when it came through here in 1878; its post office operated until Nov. 29, 1902; see Raisinville for the name [Whitney; PO Archives].

**RAISIN RIVER**, Monroe County: Monroe County was organized in 1822 and this post office on the River Raisin when opened in 1807 was named Raisin River, Miami County, with Moses Morse as its first postmaster, succeeded by Colonel John Anderson in 1808 (the records on this territorial settlement are questionable; it may have had a stage coach postal service rather than a government post office); see Raisinville for the name [Mich Hist 32:151 1948; Pen Phil 12:5 Feb 1962; PO Archives].

**RAISINVILLE**, Monroe County: Colonel John Anderson entered the first land in the area in 1822; he sold it to Mr. Blanchard who became the first settler in 1823; in that year, Raisinville Township was organized, with Riley Ingersoll as its first supervisor; its village, 2½ miles east of Dundee, was given a post office as Raisinville, with Thomas B. Benjamin as its first postmaster, in June, 1825, the office operating until March 20, 1828; the West Raisinville post office, opened on Nov. 28, 1832, with W. H. Montgomery as its first postmaster, was changed to Raisinville on July 24, 1833, but back to West Raisinville on Jan. 20, 1838, until it was closed on Feb. 17, 1842; the Hamlin post office was changed to Raisinville on Oct. 2, 1876, until it was closed permanently on Oct. 15, 1906; the village was bisected by the River Raisin, so named because wild grapes (in French, raisin) grew on its banks [Wing; GSM 1838; MPH 4:318 1881; PO Archives].

**RALPH**, Dickinson County: it was named for Ralph Wells, son of J. W. Wells, of Menominee, a lumberman who operated in the area; the village and its station on the E. & L.S. Railroad were named Ralph, but its post office, opened on Jan. 17, 1901, with Wallace M. Taylor as its first postmaster, was named Bryden, but it too was renamed Ralph on June 6, 1904 [David Coon; GSM 1903; PO Archives].

**RAMONA,** Newaygo County: the West Michigan Lumber Company, under the direction of company president and general manager E. B. Wright, built a sawmill here in Lincoln Township in 1881; being beside Diamond Lake, the settlement was given a post office of that name on Dec. 22, 1881, with James L. Alexander as its first postmaster; on April 14, 1895, the office was renamed Diamondloch; the office was closed on June 25, 1895, but was restored on Jan. 11, 1898, with Manassas D. Schmucker as its postmaster; it was given a station named Diamond Loch on the Chicago & Western Michigan (now Pere Marquette) Railroad; in 1904, Dr. Pechuman, of Chicago, who owned a home here, and William Bigelow, a resort owner in the area, renamed it Ramona, because it reminded them of a beautiful scene in Helen Hunt Jackson's novel, Ramona, and the post office was so renamed on June 7, 1904 [Harry L. Spooner; GSM 1889-1931; PO Archives].

**RAMONA PARK,** Emmet County: this settlement in Little Traverse Township had a station on the Pennsylvania Railroad in 1926 [GSM 1927].

**RAMSAY,** Gogebic County: this village on the Black River began as the site of the sawmill of Hubbard & Weed, of Menominee, in 1884; the mill burned in 1889, but the operations of the Castile Mining Company had begun in 1886; it was given a post office as Irondale on Nov. 24, 1886, with Irving Lucia as its first postmaster; on June 29, 1888, it was renamed Ramsay, it is believed, for an official of the Chicago & Northwestern Railroad, which built a station here; the post office was closed on Sept. 14, 1901, but has been restored since June 19, 1903 [F. L. Brighenti, PM; Mich Hist 6:337 1922; PO Archives].

**RANDALL,** Saginaw County: this village began with the opening of a post office at Porter's Station, on the Saginaw Valley & St. Louis Railroad, at its crossing of Swan Creek, in Richland Township, on March 2, 1868, with Thomas A. Porter as its first postmaster; the post office, named Randall, operated until Dec. 10, 1890 [GSM 1879; PO Archives].

**RANDALL BEACH,** Oakland County: a settlement on Lake Orion, in Orion Township, a mile from the village of Lake Orion, in 1926 [GSM 1927].

**RANDOLPH,** Osceola County: Orrin W. Newell became the first postmaster of this rural post office on Jan. 22, 1889, the office operating until Nov. 18, 1889 [PO Archives].

**RANDVILLE,** Dickinson County: the settlement formed around the Groveland Mine, operated by the Groveland Mining Company; a station on the Milwaukee & Northern Railroad in 1880; Horace W. Bent became its first postmaster on March 28, 1891, the office operating until March 31, 1932; it was in Iron County until Dickinson was organized in 1891 [Sawyer; GSM 1893; PO Archives].

**RANKIN,** Genesee County: the hamlet was first called Mundy Centre from its location in the township, which had been named for Lieutenant-Governor Edward S. Mundy; it was given a post office as Rankin on Feb. 8, 1881, with Ira F. Wright as its first postmaster, the office operating until Nov. 14, 1905 [Doris Hidde; PO Archives].

**RANN'S MILL,** Shiawassee County: this settlement in Perry Township grew around the sawmill and the grist mill of B. F. Rann & Company; Benjamin F. Rann became its first postmaster on June 17, 1875, the office operating until Dec. 13, 1890 [GSM 1877; PO Archives].

**RANSOM,** Calhoun County. See Calos.

**RANSOM,** Hillsdale County: a village, founded in 1840, in Rowland Township, which had been named for pioneer settler Rowland Bird; it was given a post office as North Rowland, with William Burnham becoming its first postmaster on April 17, 1848; on Sept. 5, 1848, it was renamed Ransom, honoring Epaphroditus Ransom, governor of Michigan, 1848-50; in 1849, the citizens got an act passed changing the name to Bird, but in 1850, another act was passed restoring the name of Ransom; the post office operated until Aug. 31, 1936 [Albert N. Brown; Reynolds; PO Archives].

**RANSOM,** Keweenaw County: Leander Ransom, superintendent of the Isle Royale & Ohio Mining Company, laid out a village here on Rock Harbor in 1846, and several good buildings were erected; but instead of becoming a village it became the site of Daisy Farm [Dustin].

**RANSOM,** Marquette County: a station on the M. & S.E. Railroad in 1910 [GSM 1911].

**RANSOM CREEK,** Benzie County: in 1864, Mr. Beswick built a sawmill on a stream that emptied into Lake Ann; in 1866, this mill was acquired by Lige Ransom and his son, Lige Ransom, Jr., who added a grist mill in 1869; they then bought a tract of pine land bordering on their mill property [MPH 38:305 1912].

**RANSONVILLE,** Chippewa County: it was first settled about 1885 by David J. Ranson and his loggers [Hamilton; Mich Hist 31:314 1947].

**RAPID CITY,** Kalkaska County: when the Chicago & Western Michigan (now Pere Marquette) Railroad came through here in Charlevoix Township in 1891, the station was named Van Buren for landowners Charles E. and Carrie J. Van Buren, who platted and recorded the village as Van Buren in 1892; Mr. Van Buren became its first postmaster on Nov. 22, 1892; its name was changed to Vanburen on Jan. 18, 1895, and changed again to Rapid City, from its location on the Rapid River, on April 30, 1898 [Stuart Miller; PO Archives].

**RAPID RIVER,** Delta County: the village was named after the Rapid River which has a series of rapids for miles from its mouth to its head waters; it was first named Rapid Siding by the Minneapolis, St. Paul & Sault Ste. Marie Railroad officials, but its name was changed when the village was platted and recorded by Mr. Hibbard in 1887; Hibbard & Wright owned and operated a sawmill and a grocery store, and their employees bought the first lots; Perry G. Wright became the first postmaster on March 3, 1888; as the village grew, added land was platted by W. H. Cole and August Schram [PM; PO Archives].

**RAPID RIVER**, Kalkaska County. See Rugg.

**RAPIDS**, Menominee County: William D. Bigger became the first postmaster of this rural post office in Wallace Township on March 4, 1884, the office operating until Nov. 5, 1887 [GSM 1885; PO Archives].

**RAPINVILLE**, Mackinac County: this rural post office in Garfield Township was opened on July 28, 1886, and was named for farmer Edmund A. Rapin who became its first postmaster; the office operated until Aug. 15, 1906 [GSM 1887-1907; PO Archives].

**RAPSON**, Huron County: this village in Verona Township was named for storekeeper Isaac Rapson who became its first postmaster on Dec. 23, 1885; the office was closed on Nov. 18, 1896, but was restored from April 12, 1897, to Aug. 14, 1905; its station on a branch of the Pere Marquette Railroad was first called Rapson's Siding [GSM 1887-95; PO Archives].

**RAPSON'S CROSSING**, Huron County: John D. Parent was appointed the first postmaster of this rural post office on May 23, 1892, but the office was never in operation and was discontinued on June 20, 1895; see Rapson for the name (PO Archives].

**RASMUS**, Crawford County: lumberman Rasmus Hanson gave the land for Camp Hanson (now Camp Grayling) on the shores of Lake Margrethe (named for his wife); in 1914, the Michigan Central Railroad, on its run from Grayling to Camp Hanson, built a siding here, and for its shipments to and from the camp named it Rasmus, which in reality stood for Michigan National Guard, Camp Hanson, Grayling, Mich.; although on some maps, Rasmus has never been a village [Arthur R. Thayer].

**RATHBONE**, Gratiot County: the village began as a trading point at the center of Lafayette Township; storekeeper Eugene M. Becker became its first postmaster on Oct. 14, 1891, the office operating until Dec. 14, 1904 [Tucker; PO Archives].

**RATTLE RUN**, St. Clair County: it was first settled by 1860; James D. Frink became its first postmaster on July 17, 1876, with the spelling changed to Rattlerun on Oct. 23, 1895, until the office was closed on Dec. 29, 1907; now a hamlet; it was named after the creek just east of it, which was so named because on quiet nights the water running over its pebbly bed made a rattling sound [Arthur St. Pierre; PO Archives].

**RATVILLE**, Shiawassee County. See Hazelton.

**RATZ**, Livingston County: a flag station on the Detroit, Lansing & Northern Railroad, in Genoa Township, from 1882 to 1884; John Schoenhals became its first postmaster on March 3, 1882, the office operating until Feb. 26, 1883 [GSM 1885; PO Archives].

**RAVENNA,** Muskegon County: E. B. Bostwick was the first settler in the area, building a sawmill in 1844; the village site was first settled by Benjamin Smith in 1847, followed later that year by William Rogers, Thomas D. Smith, James Rollinson, and Hiram Wilkinson; the township, formed in 1848, was named by its surveyor, who came from Ravenna, Ohio, and the village took its name; sawmill owner James M. Smith became its first postmaster on Feb. 9, 1848; incorporated as a village in 1922; it was in Ottawa County until Muskegon was organized in 1859 [Ralph B. Rogers, g.s. of Wm. Rogers; Page; PO Archives].

**RAWSONVILLE,** Wayne County: it is on the line between Wayne and Washtenaw Counties; Henry Snow became the first settler here about 1800, and the place became known as Snow's Landing; Ambline Rawson arrived with his father in 1825; the village was platted as Michigan City by Mathew Woods, Amasah Rawson and Abraham Voorhies, and recorded on Jan. 7, 1836, but it was given a post office as Rawsonville on Nov. 14, 1838; the office was closed on Oct. 25, 1895, but was restored from Nov. 20, 1895, to Feb. 28, 1902 [Mich Hist 28:120 1944; County plat liber; PO Archives].

**RAY,** Macomb County: this rural post office in the center of Ray Township was opened on May 1, 1827, with Reuben R. Smith as its first postmaster, the office operating until June 25, 1868; see Ray Center for the name [GSM 1873-1907; PO Archives].

**RAY CENTER,** Macomb County: the first land purchase in the area was made by Reuben R. Smith in 1824, followed by Joseph Chubb, Nathaniel Thompson, and Josiah Lee, all later that year; the township was organized in 1827 and named by Noah Webster as Rhea, after the Latin name of a river in Europe, but was changed to Ray; though located in the southern part of the township, its post office opened on Feb. 13, 1846, with Wilson W. Millar as its first postmaster, was named Ray Center; the office was closed on March 22, 1872, but was restored from June 10, 1872, to July 31, 1906 [Eldredge; PO Archives].

**RAYMOND,** Charlevoix County: Hiram Madlem became the first postmaster of this rural post office on Jan. 24, 1891, the office operating until Jan. 25, 1892 [PO Archives].

**RAYNOLD,** Montcalm County. See Reynolds.

**REA,** Monroe County: it was given a depot on the Michigan & Ohio Railroad, with E. L. Moore as station agent in 1886, and a post office, with Charles C. Hughitt as its first postmaster, on March 2, 1886, the office operating until Oct. 2, 1906 [GSM 1887; PO Archives].

**READING,** Hillsdale County: it was formed by a group in the township who chose the site and called it Basswood Corners from a clump of seven basswood trees near its four corners; but it was given a post office as Reading on Dec. 14, 1840, with Ralph Bailey as its first postmaster; it was platted by David Prouty and Thomas Fuller in 1852, the year the Turner & Young sawmill was built; the railroad came through in 1869 and gave it a station; it was named after its township which had been named after Reading, Penna.; incorporated as a village in 1873 and as a city in 1934 [Vivian L. Moore; PO Archives].

**READINGVILLE,** Washtenaw County. See Oakville, Monroe County.

**READMOND,** Emmet County: Isaac Colburn became the first postmaster of this rural post office, named after its township, on Feb. 19, 1886, the office operating until July 31, 1908 [GSM 1887; PO Archives].

**READY,** Saginaw County: a station on the Cincinnati, Saginaw & Mackinaw Railroad; storekeeper Jesse W. Fry became its first postmaster on Feb. 17, 1898, the office operating until Jan. 31, 1901 [GSM 1899; PO Archives].

**REDAN,** Saginaw County: Hiram Whitney became the first postmaster of this rural post office in the northeastern part of the county on May 15, 1872, the office operating until Feb. 6, 1874 [GSM 1873; PO Archives].

**RED BRIDGE,** Ingham County. See Meridian.

**REDDING'S MILLS,** Berrien County. See Dayton.

**REDFIELD,** Cass County: Messrs. Shaffer and Beardsley built a sawmill here on Christian River, in Jefferson Township, in 1833-34; they sold out to George Redfield in 1837 and he added a grist mill in 1867; the village, also called Redfield's Mills, was given a post office as Redfield on Feb. 23, 1876, with Samuel Akin as its first postmaster, the office operating until Sept. 30, 1901 [Schoetzow; Mathews; PO Archives].

**REDFORD,** Wayne County: its name was derived from Rouge Ford, it having been a favorite crossing place over the River Rouge by the Indians on their trips to Detroit to receive presents from British officers; Azarias Bell became the first white settler in 1818; the settlement was given a post office as North Pekin on Jan. 5, 1833, with David Gable as its first postmaster; the office was renamed Redford on May 11, 1833, and operated until Sept. 16, 1906; when it was restored, it was named Sand Hill, but again renamed Redford on Oct. 1, 1906; from the estate of Nathaniel A. Armstrong, it was platted and recorded as Redford on Jan. 22, 1858; a large portion of Redford Township, including the village of Redford, was annexed by the city of Detroit in 1926 [GSM 1838; Burton; County plat liber; PO Archives].

**REDFORD CENTER,** Wayne County. See Bell Branch.

**RED JACKET,** Houghton County: E. J. Hurlbut built the first house here in 1856, a log boarding house; he sank a shaft nearby for the Red Jacket Mining Company in 1867; he abandoned the mine but reserved the village site and named it, as he had the mine, after the Indian chief, Red Jacket; although incorporated as a village in 1875, it was not given a post office until May 26, 1886, with John W. Howard as its first postmaster; the office was closed on Oct. 11, 1887, but was restored on March 26, 1888;

in 1892, the Red Jacket and Calumet post offices were consolidated under the name Calumet, and in 1929, Red Jacket was annexed to and its name changed to Calumet [Andreas; GSM 1893; PO Archives].

**RED KEG,** Midland County. See Averill.

**REDMAN,** Huron County: Henry B. Gillard and Ronald McDonald became the first settlers here in Bloomfield Township in 1871; the hamlet was named for storekeeper Rudolph W. Redman who became its first postmaster on June 18, 1887, the office operating until Aug. 14, 1905 [Hey; Gwinn; PO Archives].

**RED OAK,** Oscoda County: a station on the Au Sable & Northwestern Railroad; Albert A. Morton became its first postmaster on Aug. 27, 1888 [Mich Manual 1899; PO Archives].

**REDRIDGE,** Houghton County: the stamp mill of the Atlantic Mining Company was built here on the Lake Superior Shore in Hancock Township in 1895-96, and was connected with its mine, at Atlantic Mine, by the 12-mile (9 main, 3 branch) Atlantic Railroad, owned by the company; the manager of the company store, Albert Everett became the first postmaster, with the office named Redridge, on Nov. 2, 1895; the mine was discontinued in 1911 but the post office operated until July 31, 1957 [Florence Gregorich; PO Archives].

**RED ROCK,** Houghton County: this settlement on Keweenaw Bay, in Torch Lake Township, formed around the stone quarry of the Kerber-Jacobs Redstone Company, with its superintendent, William J. Fales, becoming its first postmaster on Aug. 15, 1893; the office operated until Nov. 28, 1898 [GSM 1895-99; PO Archives].

**RED RUN,** Macomb County: Miss Cynthia M. Cole became the first postmaster of this rural post office on July 22, 1857, succeeded by Henry Mitchell on Nov. 6, 1858, the office operating until Sept. 13, 1860 [PO Archives].

**REDRUTH,** Baraga County: a station on the Marquette, Houghton & Ontonagon Railroad; George McDonald became its first postmaster on July 8, 1886; the office was closed on March 29, 1887, but was restored on Oct. 4, 1889 [GSM 1887-89; PO Archives].

**RED STAR,** Sanilac County: Peter Weaver became the first postmaster of this rural post office, 7 miles from Marlette, on Oct. 20, 1899, the office operating until June 30, 1906 [GSM 1901-07; PO Archives].

**REDSTONE,** Midland County: Alfred March became the first postmaster of this rural post office, 20 miles southwest of Midland, on Nov. 30, 1895, the office operating until Dec. 14, 1904 [PO Archives].

**REED,** Oceana County. See Ferry.

**REED CITY,** Osceola County: it was founded by Willis M. Slosson, Frederick H. Todd, William A. Higbee, and James M. Reed, for whom it was named; popularly but never officially called Tunshla (meaning unknown) and later as Todd's Slashings (meaning lumbered-off land belonging to Mr. Todd); it was first platted as Reed City in 1870; Simpson Traut became its first postmaster on Dec. 8, 1871, the year the Grand Rapids & Indiana Railroad came through and built a station here; incorporated as a village in 1872 (it was re-incorporated in 1875 when the first act was found invalid by the courts); incorporated as a city in 1932 ]Harry E. Bone; Chapman; PO Archives].

**REEDER**, Missaukee County. See Lake City.

**REEDS**, Kent County: this station on the Toledo, Saginaw & Muskegon Railroad, in the northwest corner of the county, was given a post office on May 3, 1888, with John Bowers as its first postmaster, the office operating until Jan. 15, 1903 [GSM 1919; PO Archives].

**REEDSBORO**, Alger County: a station on the Detroit, Mackinaw & Marquette Railroad in 1884; lumberman Archibald Gibbs became its first postmaster on March 29, 1886, the office operating until only Feb. 16, 1887 [GSM 1887; PO Archives].

**REEDS' LAKE**, Kent County: the hamlet was named for the brothers, Porter, Lewis, and Ezra Reed, farmers, who settled beside the lake in 1834; a station on the Grand Trunk Railroad [Paul F. Kempter].

**REEDSVILLE**, Muskegon County. See North Muskegon.

**REEMAN**, Newaygo County: this village in Sheridan Township was founded by Jarrad McQueen in 1865; in 1894, Frank Reed built a flour mill and John Brinkman built a general store here, and the town was named from a combination of their names; Mr. Brinkman became its first postmaster on April 9, 1897; a station on the Chicago & Western Michigan (now Pere Marquette) Railroad [GSM 1899; PO Archives].

**REESE**, Tuscola County: in 1865, Robert K. Rogers bought land of Jesse Hoyt for actual settlement here, but Mrs. Louisa Woodruff and her son, Daniel, built and occupied the first house, with Mr. Rogers building his the next year; Mr. A. W. Gates, a stage proprietor, got the town a post office and a plank road, and it was named Gates, with Mr. Rogers becoming its first postmaster on Nov. 13, 1871; G. W. Reese, as superintendent, got the Detroit & Bay City Railroad through here in 1873, and the station was named for him in 1874 as was its post office, on April 30, 1874, and the town became known as Reese; incorporated as a village in 1887 [Howard D. Barcalow; PO Archives].

**REEVES STATION**, Monroe County. See Azalia.

**REMICK**, Clare County: in 1876, a settlement in Surrey Township around the sawmill of Andre Alexander and a station on the Pere Marquette Railroad [GSM 1877].

**REMICK**, Isabella County: the railroad station here, opened by 1878, was called Remick's; it was given a post office as Remick on May 6, 1879, with James A. Remick as its first postmaster, the office operating until Feb. 21, 1887 [GSM 1879; PO Archives].

**REMINGTON,** Montmorency County. See Big Rock.

**REMUS,** Mecosta County: it was first located three miles west of its present site where there was a sawmill and several other buildings, and first called Bingen; it was moved to its present site in 1869 to be on the line of the Detroit, Lansing & Northern Railroad which had just come through the county; Christian W. Wernette became the first postmaster of Bingen on July 20, 1877, with the office renamed Remus on March 15, 1880; it was named for William John Remus who had surveyed the area and was a landowner in it [Mark A. Wernette, PM; PO Archives].

**RENO,** Ottawa County: this station on the Grand Rapids & Indiana Railroad was given a post office on Jan. 14, 1887, with George M. Huntley as its first postmaster [GSM 1887; PO Archives].

**RENOE,** Lake County: a station on the Pere Marquette Railroad, in Elk Township; George W. McShane became its first postmaster on Dec. 30, 1874; the office was closed on Jan. 9, 1877, but was restored from Nov. 7, 1878, to April 21, 1879 [GSM 1877; PO Archives].

**RENTON,** Calhoun County: a station on a branch of the Grand Trunk Railroad, six miles west of Battle Creek, in 1882 [GSM 1883].

**RENWICK,** Washtenaw County. See Salem.

**REPUBLIC,** Marquette County: it was founded in 1871 by English-born Peter Pascoe and named from the mine which he opened in 1872 and managed for the Republic Iron Mining Company; James O. St. Clair became its first postmaster on Sept. 2, 1873; platted as Iron City in 1874, an addition was platted by George C. Cummings for the Republic company in 1879; a station on the Chicago & Northwestern Railroad [Andrease; PO Archives].

**RESCUE,** Huron County: farmer John Carroll became the first postmaster of this rural post office in Grant Township on Aug. 9, 1888; the office was closed on March 31, 1903, but was restored from June 10, 1903, to Aug. 14, 1905 [GSM 1891-1907; PO Archives].

**RESERVE,** St. Joseph County: Heman Huntley became the first postmaster of this hamlet on March 11, 1850, the office operating until Sept. 13, 1860 [GSM 1860; PO Archives].

**REVERE,** Bay County: Joseph Sullivan became the first postmaster of this rural post office in Beaver Township, on April 14, 1880, the office operating until Feb. 2, 1885 [GSM 1881; PO Archives].

**REW,** Clinton County: grocer John Austin became the first postmaster of this rural post office on Feb. 8, 1888, the office operating until March 31, 1903 [GSM 1889; PO Archives].

**REXFORD,** Chippewa County: a station on the Duluth, South Shore

& Atlantic Railroad in 1898; see Rexton for the name [Mich Manual 1899].

**REXTON,** Mackinac County: the headquarters for the D. N. McLeod Lumber Company and its white pine operations were located here; Neil McAulay became its first postmaster on Aug. 16, 1901; Canadian bankers financed the building of the railroad through this locality and the village is said to have been named in honor of the king of England; its post office operated until Sept. 7, 1961 [Mich Hist:30:59 1946; PO Archives].

**REYNOLDS,** Montcalm County: Harry R. Stevens owned the land here on Tamarack Creek, in Reynolds Township, and planned the village in 1869; he became its first postmaster, with the office named Raynold, on Jan. 27, 1870, followed by Jerome R. Reynolds in 1871; Mr. Stevens and his associates were apparently succeeding when a mortgage, of which they had been unaware, clouded the title to their land, and the venture collapsed, and its post office was closed on March 26, 1875; Reynolds Township was given another post office, named Reynold, with Frederick Dietrich as its first postmaster, on April 7, 1884, the office operating until Dec. 5, 1889 [Schenck; GSM 1873; PO Archives].

**RHODES,** Gladwin County: a station on the Michigan Central Railroad; the village was founded by and named for Murray Bentley Rhodes, a lumberman, who became its first postmaster on Dec. 21, 1889 [PM; GSM 1891].

**RIBBLE ROAD,** Huron County: a station on the Saginaw, Tuscola & Huron Railroad in 1884; given a post office named Ribble, on June 27, 1890, with storekeeper Matthew J. Borland as its first postmaster, the office operating until Aug. 30, 1902 [GSM 1891-1903; PO Archives].

**RICE CREEK,** Calhoun County: this settlement in Lee Township was begun by Amos Hadden, from Oswego, N.Y., who bought government land here and settled on it in 1835, his deed having been signed by President Martin Van Buren; William W. Farrand became its first postmaster on Jan. 11, 1841; the office was closed on Nov. 30, 1857, but was restored from June 27, 1884, to Dec. 30, 1905; it was named after the stream running through it [MPH 26:54 1895; Gardner; PO Archives].

**RICE'S,** Clare County: a station on a branch of the Pere Marquette Railroad in 1886 [GSM 1887].

**RICE'S,** Oakland County: the settlement was first called Fairbanks; besides Zeba Rice's fanning mill factory, it had a tavern, a hattery, an ashery, a blacksmith shop, etc.; but the future of the village was doomed by its failure to get Washington to put it on a mail route about 1830 [MPH 18:662 1891].

**RICH,** Lapeer County: the first settlers in the town were Thurston Wells and Jacob Blue in 1854 or early 1855; the brothers Asa and Leighton Richards built their grist mill in the south part of the town in 1856; the town, when erected in 1858, was named for Charles Rich, clerk of the board of supervisors [Page].

**RICHARDSBURG,** Dickinson County: this settlement around the Indiana Mine was named for mine manager G. A. Richards; Sol Beauparlant became its first postmaster on May 29, 1917; the office was later closed but was restored on Aug. 25, 1925, with Lydia M. Anderson as its postmaster, succeeded by Helen V. Anderson on Sept. 4, 1925 [GSM 1919-25; PO Archives].

**RICHFIELD,** Washtenaw County. See Sharon.

**RICHFIELD CENTER,** Genesee County: the first settler here was William Draper in 1825; Rial Irish came in 1836, and he and his family cut a road through the wilderness for 20 miles, which is still called Irish Road; the settlement was first called Maxfield for Captain Maxfield who settled here about 1840 and built a tavern in 1859; it was in Rich Township, Lapeer County, when given a post office as Richfield on Aug. 24, 1841, with Willard Tucker as its first postmaster; the office was closed on Dec. 7, 1843, but was restored from May 1, 1844, to Nov. 15, 1905; in 1855, V. Maxfield and E. E. Goodrich built a sawmill which, with the homes of its workers and a store, formed the original village [Elizabeth C. Ronan; PO Archives].

**RICHLAND,** Kalamazoo County: Richland Township, organized in 1832, was named by Simeon Mills; from its proximity to Gull Lake, the area was called Gull Prairie and the village, platted by Willard and Sylvester Mills in 1833, Gull Corners; adjacent to it, in Feb., 1831, Colonel Isaac Barnes, from Medina, Ohio, was given a post office which he had named Geloster, for his three sons, GEorge, CarLOS, and LesTER, and he and James Porter had the village platted by Carlos Barnes in 1832; on June 30, 1840, its post office was moved to Gull Corners and renamed Richland, after its township; incorporated as a village in 1871 [Mich Hist 32:31 1948; Durant; PO Archives].

**RICHLAND,** Saginaw County: Lemuel Cone purchased land here in 1854 and became the first settler in 1857; when the township was organized in 1862, he named it [Mills].

**RICHLAND,** Tuscola County: about 1859, Horace Parsell and Elisha P. Randall platted 40 acres on the banks of the Cass River, in Almer Township, and named it Richland; but there was another Richland post office in Michigan at the time, and so this one was given a post office as Burnside, honoring Union general, Ambrose E. Burnside; Mr. Randall became its first postmaster on May 31, 1862; the village did not materialize and its post office was transferred to Tuscola Centre on April 25, 1866 [Page; PO Archives].

**RICHLAND JUNCTION,** Kalamazoo County: a hamlet at the intersection of the Chicago, Kalamazoo & Saginaw and the Grand Rapids & Indiana Railroads, one of which is still active, while the other ends at Richland [PM, Richland].

**RICHMOND**, Allegan County. See New Richmond.

**RICHMOND**, Macomb County: the settlement was first called Ridgeway from its high ridge or Ridge Road; it was renamed Lenox after its township which had been organized in 1837; with Mason Harris as its first postmaster, it was given a post office on April 6, 1848; in 1879, it annexed Beebe's Corners, named for Erastus Beebe who had taken up government land here in 1835, and it merged with and became called Richmond which in 1838 had been named after the township, which in turn had been named after Richmond, Ontario County, N.Y., by Philip Cudworth, who became the first postmaster on Aug. 20, 1840; it was incorporated as a village in 1879 and is in both Lenox and Richmond Townships [Leeson; GSM 1860; PO Archives].

**RICHMOND**, Mecosta County: Benjamin F. Gooch became the first settler in the area in 1855; the township organizing meeting was held in the home of Delos A. Blodgett in 1861; he was elected the first supervisor of the township and had it given the maiden name of his mother, Susan Richmond [Chapman].

**RICHMOND'S CORNERS**, Ionia County: this post office in Sebewa Township was opened on July 14, 1857, with Samuel Bretz as its first postmaster; the office was renamed Lake City on Aug. 18, 1858, closed on Jan. 16, 1860, restored on Feb. 27, 1871, renamed Rosina on Jan. 25, 1877, closed on Nov. 5, 1894, and restored again from Jan. 7, 1895, to April 30, 1904 [Schenck; PO Archives].

**RICHMONDVILLE**, Sanilac County: its first building was a store built by Luce, Mason & Company in 1860; Benjamin F. Luce became its first postmaster on June 1, 1860, the office operating until June 30, 1906 [Chapman; PO Archives].

**RICHVILLE**, Tuscola County: the village was founded in 1851 by Lutheran Pastor Loehe who organized and led a group here; they called it Frankenhilf, combining Franconia, a district of Bavaria, and hilf, the German for assistance; railroad conductors found difficulty with the name and called it Richville, from its being fine farmland; John C. Edelman became the first postmaster on June 23, 1862, the year the name was changed to Richville [E. George Moser, PM].

**RIDER'S**, Washtenaw County. See Salem.

**RIDGE**, Alger County: this small cordwood and farming settlement, with a school, is about six miles east of Au Train, and was first settled about 1890 [John Boogren].

**RIDGE**, Marquette County: the village center for surrounding farms, some of them in Delta County, and most of them Finnish [Mich Hist 31:331 1947].

**RIDGE ROAD**, Clinton County: feed mill owner Lucius Clark became the first postmaster of this rural post office in Duplain Township on April 18, 1898, the office operating until July 31, 1900 [GSM 1899; PO Archives].

**RIDGE ROAD,** Saginaw County: Josiah F. Coy became the first postmaster of this rural post office on Nov. 30, 1861, the office operating until May 27, 1864 [PO Archives].

**RIDGEVILLE,** Gladwin County: this, the first post office in the county, was opened on May 15, 1872, with William Wilson as its first postmaster, the office operating until Dec. 9, 1873; the place is now known as the Ridge [Ritchie; PO Archives].

**RIDGEVILLE,** Lenawee County: Charles I. Quick became the first postmaster of this rural post office in Fairfield Township on Dec. 9, 1898, the office operating until Nov. 29, 1902 [GSM 1899; PO Archives].

**RIDGEWAY,** Lenawee County: an old Indian path through here was over a ridge on either side of which was a valley; later, the white man used the same path and called it the ridge way; Coonrod Lamberson built the first house here in 1826 and he named the town which followed, Ridgeway; Stephen V. Miller became its first postmaster on July 26, 1834; another early settler was the father of J. D. Arner who became its postmaster in the 1880s [Naomi Dowling; PO Archives].

**RIDGEWAY,** Macomb County. See Richmond.

**RIDGEWAY,** St. Clair County: a station on the Grand Trunk Railroad, 21 miles from Port Huron, in 1864 [GSM 1865].

**RIENZA,** Mecosta County: William K. Gibbs became the first postmaster of this lumber settlement in Sheridan Township on Feb. 10, 1870, the office operating until April 13, 1874 [GSM 1875; PO Archives].

**RIETZ HILL,** Manistee County. See Oak Hill.

**RIFLE RIVER MILLS,** Arenac County. See Omer.

**RIGA,** Lenawee County: John Knight took up the first land claim here in 1844, and when the Lake Shore & Southern Michigan Railroad came through it was given a depot as Knight's Station; the Rev. Kroenke had the name changed to that of the town of his college roommate in Germany and it was given a post office as Riga on Feb. 12, 1851, with Roswell W. Knight as its first postmaster [Ann Breitner, PM; GSM 1860; PO Archives].

**RIGGSVILLE,** Cheboygan County: it was founded in 1860 by the Riggs brothers and named for them; Robert K. Horning became its first postmaster on March 1, 1880 [Myrton M. Riggs; PO Archives].

**RILEY,** Clinton County: Atwell Simmons became the first settler in the area in 1836; Riley Township was organized in 1841 with Mr. Simmons as its first supervisor; Jonathan Owen became its first postmaster on Sept. 5, 1851, the office operating until March 31, 1903; the village was also called North Riley; see Riley Center for the name [Ellis; PO Archives].

**RILEY CENTER**, St. Clair County: Riley Township was organized in 1841 and named for John Riley, a half-breed Chippewa Indian whose father had bought land here in 1836 and gave John a life lease on it at a rental of six cents a year; Martin Ellenwood became the first postmaster of this village on the Belle River on June 7, 1867, the office operating until Sept. 30, 1933 [Jenks; PO Archives].

**RILEY'S CORNERS**, Calhoun County. See Pine Creek.

**RING**, Gratiot County: this lumber settlement in eastern Wheeler Township was named after a local mill owner; Jabez Phelps became its first postmaster on May 3, 1882, the office operating until Oct. 30, 1883; its station on the Saginaw Valley & St. Louis Railroad was named Ring & Rust Mill [Tucker; GSM 1883-85; PO Archives].

**RIPLEY**, Houghton County: this settlement in Franklin Township began as a ferry landing in 1846; the Quincy Copper Mining Company was organized in 1848 and later built its smelter here; it was given a station on the Mineral Range Railroad and on Feb. 23, 1886, a post office, with James Manley as its first postmaster; the office was closed on Feb. 14, 1888, though the Quincy did not close down its shafts until Sept., 1931 [Mich Hist 41:219 1957; GSM 1889; PO Archives].

**RITCHIE**, Alcona County: a station on the Detroit & Mackinaw Railroad; 31 miles south of Alpena; Betsie Willoughby became its first postmaster on Dec. 28, 1892, the office operating until March 15, 1904 [GSM 1895-1905; PO Archives].

**RIVERBANK**, Osceola County: a station on the Manistee & Grand Rapids Railroad, on the banks of the Pine River, in Leroy Township; the settlement developed around the sawmill and general store of Clarence A. Warren who became its first postmaster on April 1, 1904 [GSM 1905; PO Archives].

**RIVER BEND**, Clinton County: a village with a railroad station, in Eagle Township; Levi Partlow became its first postmaster on Feb. 8, 1871, the office operating until Sept. 30, 1891; it was named from the formation of the Grand River here in the southwest corner of the county [GSM 1879; PO Archives].

**RIVERDALE**, Gratiot County: a station on the Detroit, Lansing & Northern Railroad, in Seville Township; it was founded in 1874 by Arthur G. Newton who first platted the village in 1875 and became its first postmaster on March 10, 1876; from its location on the Pine River, he named it Riverside, but there was another Riverside post office in Michigan and this one was named Riverdale [Tucker; PO Archives].

**RIVER RAISIN**, Washtenaw County: Solomon Brown became the first postmaster of this hamlet in Bridgewater Township on May 7, 1864, the office operating until Feb. 28, 1902; see Raisinville for the name [GSM 1873; PO Archives].

**RIVER ROUGE**, Wayne County: in the late 1700s, French families

(Visger, Navarre, Cicotte, Riopelle, Campau, Labadie, and others) from Detroit bought land from the Indians just below the River Rouge (in French red river, named from its reddish muddy color, so tinted by its clay banks) and began to farm; an 1808 census showed 30 families here, but as succeeding generations divided and re-divided their property, land holdings grew smaller as the population grew larger; it was given a post office on Feb. 19, 1891; incorporated as a village, with Henry Visger as its first president, in 1899; incorporated as a city in 1922; the Ford plant boomed it into an industrial city [Roy A. Berger].

**RIVERSIDE,** Berrien County: a station on the Pere Marquette Railroad, in Hagar Township; Charles Sellers became its first postmaster on March 1, 1872; the village was named from its nearness to the Paw Paw River [Pen Phil 12:3 Sept. 1961; Fox].

**RIVERSIDE,** Missaukee County: the sawmill of Moses Burket and his son Isaac was located here in 1880; the community which grew up around it was named after its township [Stout].

**RIVERSIDE,** Wayne County: an incorporated village in Springwells Township in 1872, it was annexed by the city of Detroit in 1886 [GSM 1873-87].

**RIVER SIDING,** Dickinson County: this spur on the Chicago & Northwestern Railroad was named from its nearness to the Menominee River and was opened in 1882 [Mich Manual 1899].

**RIVERTON,** Mason County: its station on the Mason & Oceana Railroad was first named Harley's, but it was given a post office named Riverton, after its township, on Aug. 25, 1865, with John Satzgaber as its first postmaster; the office was closed on June 23, 1879, but was restored from March 1, 1880, to Sept. 21, 1882, and from Aug. 3, 1888, to Oct. 14, 1903; the place was also called Willson's Farm for John W. Willson and his brother who were farmers and coopers here; John became the postmaster about 1878 [GSM 1879; PO Archives].

**RIVERVIEW,** Wayne County: it began in 1906 as a station on the Detroit, Monroe & Toledo Railroad and from its location a mile and a half from Wyandotte was first called Wyandotte Heights; its being by the Detroit River accounts for its having been renamed Riverview; incorporated as a village in 1922 and as a city in 1938 [Burton].

**RIVES JUNCTION,** Jackson County: this village in Rives Township was founded by Samuel Prescott and Henry Fifield in 1834; it was given a post office as West Rives on June 15, 1839, with Mr. Prescott the first postmaster keeping the office in his home on the west side of the Michigan Central Railroad tracks; the town was moved to the east side of the tracks and renamed Eaton Rapids Junction on March 12, 1866, and then Rives Junction on May 7, 1866 [Isabel Churchill, PM; PO Archives].

**RIVIERE AUX ECORCES,** Wayne County. See Ecorse.

**RIVIERE AUX SIGNES,** Monroe County. See Newport.

**RIX,** Ionia County: Joseph W. Sprague became the first postmaster of this hamlet in Keene Township on May 1, 1851, the office operating until April 24, 1868; named for Rix Robinson, pioneer Indian trader [Schenck; Branch; PO Archives].

**RIX,** Kalamazoo County: Ernest E. Annabel became the first postmaster of this rural post office in Texas Township on Dec. 20, 1897, succeeded by grocer Helen C. Gunn in 1898, the office operating until May 29, 1901; named for the pioneer Rix family; Carrie and Zoe Rix taught the school here at this time [GSM 1899; PO Archives].

**ROARING BROOK,** Emmet County: this resort community on Little Traverse Bay was given a station on the Grand Rapids & Indiana Railroad about 1882 [GSM 1895].

**ROBBINS,** Ontonagon County: this lumber settlement in Haight Township formed around the mill of the Robbins Lumber Company, of Rhinelander, Wis., and Franklin S. Robbins became its first postmaster on Oct. 24, 1891; given a station on the Chicago & Northwestern Railroad in 1892; its post office was closed on Aug. 3, 1898, but was restored from Dec. 18, 1902, to June 30, 1911 [Charles Willman; PO Archives].

**ROBERTS LANDING,** St. Clair County: it was named for its first settler, who came here in 1830; members of the second generation of his family, living here in 1860, included W. C. and W. S. Roberts, general storekeepers, and Samuel Roberts who became its first postmaster on April 29, 1869; its post office was closed on Dec. 15, 1895, but it still retains its tradition as a stopping off place for fishermen and hunters [GSM 1873; Federal; PO Archives].

**ROBINSON,** Houghton County. See Chassell.

**ROBINSON,** Ottawa County: it was first settled by Ira, John, Lucas and Rodney Robinson, brothers of early Indian trader, Rix Robinson, in 1835; the first town meeting was held in the home of Ira Robinson in 1856; John W. Barnard became the first postmaster on June 15, 1857, the office operating until 1892 [Page; PO Archives].

**ROCHESTER,** Oakland County: it was first settled in 1817 by James Graham and his family, from Mount Clemens; in 1818, John Hersey made the first official purchase of land here; most of the early settlers were from western New York State and the town was named after Rochester, N.Y.; Governor Lewis Cass, with Austin E. Wing and Charles Larned, of Detroit, surveyed the area and laid out the first plat of the village in 1826; Morris Jackson, Jr., became its first postmaster on Jan. 12, 1827, succeeded by George N. Shaw in 1828; incorporated as a village in 1869 [Alice D. Serrell; Seeley; PO Archives].

**ROCHESTER COLONY,** Clinton County. See Duplain.

**ROCK,** Delta County: when the Chicago & Northwestern Railroad line from Escanaba to Negaunee was completed in 1865, some of the construction workers settled here, hence Rock dates its founding as 1865;

Congress had granted the line land on each side of its road, so it was from the railroad that J. R. Steele bought the townsite in 1866, and built his home here; near the depot, George English built the first store in 1866; from March 28, 1879, to April 30, 1883, the village was called Malton Spur and its post office Malton, with Mrs. Henrietta Crawford as its first postmaster, while Henry Crawford ran its general store; its depot was named Maple Ridge, after the township, and so was the village for some years; but there was another Maple Ridge post office in Michigan, so this one, when it requested a new post office was given one named Rock, the name suggested by John Niequest when he became its first postmaster on June 16, 1886; the name described the terrain, for glacial drift had to be removed to make the fields arable here [Francis Trombly; PM; Delta Reporter, Sept. 1, 1965; GSM 1887; PO Archives].

**ROCK ELM,** Charlevoix County: Hiram B. Hipp became the first postmaster of this rural post office on the south arm of Pine Lake (now Lake Charlevoix), in Eveline Township, on July 3, 1876, the office operating until Dec. 9, 1886 [GSM 1887; PO Archives].

**ROCKERY,** Antrim County: Lemuel Brewer became the first postmaster of this rural post office in Jordan Township on June 13, 1882; the office was closed on Jan. 6, 1891, but was restored on April 20, 1908 [GSM 1883; PO Archives].

**ROCK FALLS,** Huron County: in 1838, two lumbermen, John and Allan Daggett, began operations here on Lake Huron, in Sand Beach Township, and the settlement which followed was given a post office on June 25, 1867, with George W. Jenks as its first postmaster, the office operating until Nov. 2, 1875 [MPH 39:353 1915; PO Archives].

**ROCKFORD,** Kent County: this village in Algoma Township was first settled by Smith Lapham, from Washtenaw County, in 1843, and he became the first postmaster of Laphamsville on April 5, 1848; the village was platted as Laphamville in 1856, replatted and renamed Rockford in 1865, and its post office was renamed Rockford on Aug. 24, 1866; incorporated as a village by the supervisors in 1866 and by the legislature as a city in 1935 [Dillenback; PO Archives].

**ROCK HARBOR,** Keweenaw County: storekeeper Kneut Neutson became the first postmaster of this settlement on Lake Superior, in Houghton Township, with the name of the office spelled Rockharbor, on March 2, 1911; the office was changed to Isle Royale National Park on June 15, 1959 [GSM 1913; PO Archives].

**ROCKLAND,** Montcalm County: a flag station on a branch of the Detroit, Lansing & Northern Railroad in 1886 [GSM 1887].

**ROCKLAND,** Ontonagon County: the Rockland Mine opened in 1847, and the Rockland post office opened on Jan. 6, 1853, with James B. Townsend as its first postmaster; the office was closed on Sept. 20, 1860, but on Dec. 7, 1863, the National post office was changed to Rockland; Rosendale was laid out by the Minnesota Mining Company in 1858, and

Williamsburg was platted by William Shepard and William Davey and named for themselves; also in 1858, James Cooper platted Webster; these three adjacent plats were consolidated into the village of Rockland in 1864 [Lloyd Preiss, PM; GSM 1860].

**ROCK RIVER**, Alger County: this station on the Detroit & Mackinaw Railroad, at the Rock River charcoal kilns, was named Rock River Kilns when opened in 1882; it was given a post office as Rock River on Feb. 20, 1886, with John H. Johnson as its first postmaster; the office was closed on May 25, 1898, but was restored from Oct. 29, 1898, to June 15, 1906; various locations along the Rock River have been given this name; the river is rocky in places and flows over limestone beds at many points [Charles A. Simon; GSM 1887; PO Archives].

**ROCKVIEW**, Chippewa County: Robert Foster became the first postmaster of this rural post office, five miles from Pickford, on Sept. 26, 1904, the office operating until Oct. 31, 1913 [GSM 1907-15; PO Archives].

**ROCKWOOD**, Wayne County: the settlement here in Brownstown Township dates from about 1834; it was given a post office as Huron Station on July 11, 1861, with William A. Chamberlin as its first postmaster; it was renamed Rockwood on May 1, 1872; incorporated as a village in 1926 [Myron Fountain; PO Archives].

**ROCKY POINT**, Delta County. See Sanders' Point.

**RODINGEN**, Wexford County: this rural post office in Cherry Grove Township was named for Fred Rodingen who became its first postmaster on Aug. 13, 1884, the office operating until Feb. 1, 1887 [GSM 1885-89; PO Archives].

**RODNEY**, Mecosta County: a station on the Detroit, Grand Rapids & Western Railroad; the village was founded in 1879 and named for Rodney Hood, partner in the lumber firm of Hood & Gale; Burton L. Gale became its first postmaster on June 24, 1880 [M. Thompson, PM].

**ROE LAKE**, Alcoma County: a station on the Detroit & Mackinaw Railroad, 28 miles south of Alpena, in 1894 [GSM 1895].

**ROGERS**, Iron County: the Rogers-Brown Mining Company developed the Rogers Mine about 1912 and built homes for the miners and their families; the village is also referred to as the Rogers Location or simply as the Rogers [Eugene Moore].

**ROGERS**, Otsego County: a station on the Michigan Central Railroad, near Vanderbilt, in 1912 [GSM 1913].

**ROGERS**, Tuscola County. See Juniata.

**ROGERS CITY**, Presque Isle County: in the winter of 1868-69, William E. Rogers, Albert Molitor and Frederick Denny Larke came to the area to lumber; Mr. Molitor built a cabin, a dock and a mill on the shore, just to the north, on Lake Huron, and that was the start of Rogers City; it was named for William E. Rogers, owner of the land on which the village was laid out by his partner, Albert Molitor; it was given a post office as Rogers' Mills on Sept. 23, 1870, with Mr. Molitor as its first postmaster; the name was changed to Rogers City on Jan. 19, 1872, then to Rogers on Jan. 22, 1895, and then back again to Rogers City on Jan. 25, 1928; incorporated as a village in 1877 and as a city in 1944 [William H. Whiteley; PO Archives].

**ROGERSVILLE**, Genesee County: Laban Rogers settled here in western Richfield Township in 1846 and his brother Alvah in 1848, and from them the village that developed around the Pere Marquette Railroad station, which was built here by local subscription in 1873, was named; S. J. Rogers became its first postmaster on March 28, 1873; the office was transferred to and renamed Whitesburg on Nov. 16, 1895, but on June 12, 1897, it was returned to Rogersville; R. D., S. J., and C. W. Rogers built their grain elevator storehouse here in 1877 [Ellis; PO Archives].

**ROLF SETTLEMENT**, Ingham County: the first of the Rolf brothers (Ira, Benjamin, Ephraim, Nathan, Hazen, and Manessah) settled here in 1836; in some records the name of the family and their settlement is spelled Rolfe [Foster; Durant].

**ROLLIN**, Lenawee County: the land on which the village stands was first purchased by Addison J. Comstock, of Adrian, in 1833; on March 16, 1835, William Beal, whom Mr. Comstock had employed to manage his sawmill here, became the first postmaster; Azel Hooker opened the first store, also in 1835; it was named after the township which Deacon Matthew Bennett had named for his friend, Rev. David Rollin [Whitney; Dowling].

**ROLLO**, Iosco County: Enos Gray became the first postmaster of this rural post office on Nov. 9, 1868, the office operating until Oct. 31, 1870 [PO Archives].

**ROLLO**, Tuscola County. See Silverwood.

**ROME**, Lapeer County: about 1839, a Lapeer merchant named Evans platted a village on the hills of Hadley Township and named it Rome after its fancied similarity of location; he built a store but that was the extent of the development of what came to be called the Deserted City [Page].

**ROME**, Oakland County: a hamlet in 1864 [GSM 1865].

**ROME CENTER**, Lenawee County: it was first settled by John B. Schureman, a New Yorker, in 1832; David Smith named the township Junius, but Lyman Baker, who had settled here in 1833, got the legislature to change it to Rome; and this village in the center of the township took its name; its post office, opened on May 2, 1836, with Mr. Schureman as its first postmaster, was named simply Rome, and it operated until Dec. 31, 1904 [Naomi Dowling; Bonner; PO Archives].

**ROMEO**, Macomb County: Silas Scott cleared the first land here in 1821 but Ashael Bailey from Connecticut became the first permanent settler in January of 1822; in the fall of 1822, Job Hoxie and his family arrived, and it became known as the Hoxie Settlement and was so designated on Farmer's map of 1828; it was given a post office as Indian Village, with Gideon Gates as its first postmaster, on April 18, 1827, but changed to Romeo, at the suggestion of Mrs. Laura Taylor, on Nov. 11, 1830; it was first platted by J. B. Hollister in 1830; incorporated as a village in 1838 [Eldredge; PO Archives].

**ROMULUS,** Wayne County: it was first settled by the family of Samuel McMath, of Romulus, N.Y., in 1827; he had purchased from the government, and improved, the land, but died before he could bring his family himself; the settlement was given a post office on Sept. 9, 1835; the village was platted from the estate of Lansing B. Misner and recorded on April 4, 1871; incorporated as a city in 1965 [MPH 14:483 1889; PO Archives; County plat liber].

**RONALD,** Ionia County: George Younger and Joshua Shepard became the first settlers here in 1837; upon organization of the town in 1845 it was named by state representative A. L. Roof after the hero in a novel he was reading; Freedom Gates became its first postmaster on Feb. 21, 1850, the office operating until April 19, 1853 [Schenck; Branch].

**RONALD CENTRE,** Ionia County: this rural post office, named from its location in the township, was opened on Feb. 16, 1851, with Ralph Ely as its first postmaster, and operated until March 17, 1870; see Ronald for the name [Schenck].

**RONDO,** Cheboygan County: this station on a branch of the Michigan Central Railroad was given a post office on Sept. 13, 1882, with grocer Charles H. Hoffman as its first postmaster [GSM 1883; PO Archives].

**ROOSEVELT,** Saginaw County: Theodore Roosevelt succeeded to the Presidency on Sept. 14, 1901, and this rural post office was opened on Sept. 26, 1901, with Warren W. Cross as its first postmaster; the office operated until June 3, 1902 [GSM 1903; PO Archives].

**ROOSEVELT PARK,** Muskegon County: it was founded and named by Messrs. Campbell, Wyant, and Cannon; incorporated as a city in 1946 [Andrew Bremer, Jr.].

**ROOT RIVER,** Milwaukee County: when Asher B. Saxton became its first postmaster on Jan. 25, 1836, it was in Michigan Territory; it was renamed Racine on April 12, 1836, and is now in Wisconsin [PO Archives].

**ROOTS,** Jackson County: a station on a branch of the Grand Trunk Railroad, in Henrietta Township, it was given a post office as Tanner, named for farmer Harvey C. Tanner, who became its first postmaster on April 14, 1884; its name was changed to Roots on Sept. 11, 1885, and to Valley Villa on Dec. 20, 1885, but this was rescinded on March 1, 1890, and the Roots post office operated until Nov. 14, 1904 [GSM 1887-1905; PO Archives].

**ROOTVILLE**, Antrim County: James M. Wadsworth became the first postmaster of this settlement in Helena Township on Sept. 30, 1867, the office operating until Feb. 3, 1879 [GSM 1881; PO Archives].

**ROPER'S** Cass County: a station on the Grand Trunk Railroad, five miles east of Cassopolis, in 1878 [GSM 1879].

**ROPES GOLD MINE**, Marquette County: it was the largest in the state from 1883 to 1897; its buildings and trestlework were abandoned when the lode was no longer profitable, but they still stand [Federal].

**ROSCOMMON**, Roscommon County: it was founded in 1845 by George C. Robinson, of Detroit, and was known as the Robinson recorded plat; it was renamed after the county, which had been named after a county in Ireland; Alfred Bennett became its first postmaster on Jan. 9, 1873; it has been the county seat since 1875; incorporated as a village in 1882 [Co. Bd. of Ed.].

**ROSE**, Oakland County. See Rose Center.

**ROSEBURG**, Sanilac County: John Saunders and William Lawson became the first settlers in the area in 1854; Peter Thibodeau became the first supervisor when Fremont Township was organized in 1857; its village was also known as Branagan's Corners for storekeeper John Branagan who became its first postmaster, with the office named Roseburgh, on Dec. 8, 1876; the spelling was changed to Roseburg on Aug. 9, 1893 [Chapman; PO Archives].

**ROSEBUSH**, Isabella County: it was settled by 1844, for Cornelius Bogan had a general store here then at what was called Halfway, it being by tote road midway between Mount Pleasant and Clare; James L. Bush platted the village in 1868 and gave the Ann Arbor Railroad land for a depot if the station would be named for his wife, Rose Bush; in 1873, Elias B. Calkins platted an addition, named it Calkinsville, and was given a post office of that name on July 9, 1873; so the freight came to Rosebush and the mail to Calkinsville, the post office was renamed Rosebush on July 15, 1889, changed back to Calkinsville on June 20, 1890, but changed back permanently to Rosebush on Feb. 19, 1903 [Faith Johnson, PM, GSM 1875; PO Archives].

**ROSEBUSH RANCH**, Iron County. See Triangle Ranch.

**ROSE CENTER**, Oakland County: the first settler in the area was Daniel Danielson in 1835; and on the village site were John A. Wendell and David Gage, in 1836; Mr. Wendell operated Buckhorn Tavern and the place was also known as Buckhorn; Mr. Wendell became the first supervisor when Rose Township was organized in 1837 and the first postmaster of Rose on Oct. 17, 1837 (he held the latter position until his death in 1858, and was succeeded by his son, Everett); the post office was renamed Rose Center on Nov. 6, 1914, and operated until Dec. 31, 1949; the village was platted around the Pere Marquette Railroad depot; another settlement in the township was called Rose Corners [Mrs. Donald E. Adams; Seeley; Durant; PO Archives].

**ROSE CITY,** Ogemaw County: the first homesteader, Hiram Hodge, built a hotel, but did not remain; the second, Allan S. Rose, who came with his father and two brothers from New York State in 1875, built a general store with a post office in it, and he became its first postmaster on Sept. 8, 1875; with M. S. French, a West Branch banker, he formed the French & Rose Lumber Company, and in 1892 got the first railroad through to handle their lumber shipments; the settlement and post office, both named Churchill, were moved a half mile east and renamed Rose City on July 23, 1892; incorporated as a city in 1905 [M. E. Gifford; Pen Phil 7:4 March 1957; PO Archives].

**ROSE CORNERS,** Washtenaw County: Joseph O. Gilbert plowed the first land here in 1831 on land which became the David G. Rose farm, and Mr. Gilbert became the first postmaster of its stage line post office [Beakes].

**ROSEDALE,** Chippewa County: Richard and Hannah Kemp settled here in 1883; he became its first postmaster on June 13, 1883, and she, his wife, named the place from the numerous wild roses which bloomed here [Myrtle Elliott; PO Archives].

**ROSEDALE GARDENS,** Wayne County: this small residential community on US-12 was 13 miles west of Detroit when founded in 1930 [GSM 1931].

**ROSE LAKE,** Osceola County: town clerk Edward C. Cusick became the first postmaster of this settlement in Rose Lake Township on June 21, 1899, the office operating until Aug. 15, 1907 [GSM 1901; PO Archives].

**ROSE LAKE,** Washtenaw County: Moses Y. Hood became the first postmaster of this rural post office on Aug. 30, 1849, succeeded by Daniel D. Sloan on Dec. 20, 1849 [PO Archives].

**ROSELAWN,** Ontonagon County: on Aug. 19, 1893, the Roselawn post office was transferred to and renamed Paulding; the new Roselawn post office was opened on June 1, 1908, with James Bishop as its first postmaster [PO Archives].

**ROSENDALE,** Ontonagon County. See Rockland.

**ROSEVILLE,** Macomb County: it was in Wayne County when tavern-keeper William C. Rose became its first postmaster on Sept. 21, 1836; the community developed largely through an influx of Irish and German settlers about 1843; it was a part of Erin Township until incorporated as a village in 1925; incorporated as a city in 1957 [PM; GSM 1860; PO Archives].

**ROSEVILLE,** Oceana County. See Whiskey Creek.

**ROSINA,** Ionia County. See Richmond Corners.

**ROSS,** Kent County: it began as a depot on the Grand Rapids & Indiana Railroad, in Byron Township, and was first named Ross Station; the village was platted by William Thornton for William Ross in 1871 and was given a post office named Ross on June 22, 1871, with Daniel Ross as its first postmaster [Chapman; GSM 1873; PO Archives].

**ROSS CENTRE,** Kalamazoo County: Ross Township was organized and named by the legislature in 1839; here in it, John Van Vleck, from Saratoga, N.Y., bought land and built a tavern in 1843, and he became the first postmaster on March 13, 1844; the office was changed to Yorkville on April 9, 1845 [Durant; PO Archives].

**ROTHBURY,** Oceana County: in 1865, Nelson Green located here in Grant Township; when the Chicago & Northwestern Railroad took a right-of-way across his land, they named the depot Greenwood Station; it was given a post office as Malta on Jan. 19, 1876, with Clark S. Parks as its first postmaster, there being at the time another Greenwood post office in Michigan; the office was closed on Aug. 27, 1877, but was restored as Rothbury on Sept. 22, 1879, with Charles D. Arnold as postmaster, and the village took the same name [Royal; Page; GSM 1879; PO Archives].

**ROUGEMERE,** Wayne County: a station on the Detroit, Lansing & Northern Railroad, near the River Rouge, five miles west of Detroit, in 1894 [Farmer; GSM 1895].

**ROUND LAKE,** Branch County: this settlement in Noble Township, near the Indiana line, was given a post office on March 8, 1856, with Moses S. Bowdish as its first postmaster, the office operating until Jan. 29, 1873 [GSM 1860; PO Archives].

**ROUND LAKE,** Emmet County. See Larks Lake.

**ROUND LAKE,** Missaukee County. See Jennings.

**ROUND LAKE,** Wexford County: William H. Stewart became the first postmaster of this lumber settlement in Haring Township on May 26, 1882, the office operating until Dec. 28, 1887 [GSM 1883-89; PO Archives].

**ROUSSEAU,** Ontonagon County: a station on the Chicago, Minneapolis & St. Paul Railroad and a post office, both named Rubicon; the clerk of its township of Bohemia, Bert L. Hubbell, became its first postmaster on Oct. 7, 1892; it was renamed in the 1920s for Edward Rousseau, for 26 continuous years supervisor of the same township [Charles Willman; GSM 1893; PO Archives].

**ROWENA,** Bay County: Simon B. Sutherland became the first postmaster of this rural post office on Jan. 16, 1873, the office operating until June 1, 1874 [PO Archives].

**ROWENA,** Gladwin County: a railroad station in the northeast corner of the county, opened by 1872 and closed by 1898 [GSM 1873-99].

**ROWLAND,** Hillsdale County. See Amboy.

**ROWLAND,** Isabella County: this sawmill settlement was given a post office on Feb. 26, 1868, with its name derived from its township of

Rolland; its first postmaster was William Peterson and the office operated until April 29, 1905 [GSM 1873-1907; PO Archives].

**ROW SETTLEMENT,** Washtenaw County: Henry, Conrad, and Gilbert Row, brothers, emigrated here in Sharon Township, coming from Amenia, Duchess County, N.Y., in 1831; they were later joined by their two other brothers, Nicholas and John [Mich Hist 40:62 1956].

**ROXAND,** Eaton County: Andrew Nickle, a native of Ireland, made the first government land purchase here in 1837, but while he went to get his family, Orrin Rowland and Henry Clark became the first actual settlers; William Crother lived here with Roxana, believed to be his wife; her son-in-law had Crother sued for bigamy and won; while her lawyer, Edward Bradley, was a state senator, the townspeople had him petition that the town be named Roxana; the enrolling clerk made the final "a" look more like a "d" and the name became Roxand; but its post office, opened on Dec. 31, 1849, with John Ewing as its first postmaster, was spelled Roxana; the office operated until March 31, 1903; the village was also called Needmore and is on some maps as such [MPH 39:378 1899; PO Archives].

**ROY,** Alcona County: this station on the Detroit, Bay City & Alpena Railroad was named Handy, but on March 23, 1886, it was given a post office named Roy; Francis A. McLachlan was its first postmaster and the office operated until June 23, 1898 [GSM 1887-99; PO Archives].

**ROY,** Missaukee County. See Star City.

**ROYAL OAK,** Oakland County: while inspecting the locality in 1818, Governor Lewis Cass camped under a huge oak tree and recalled the story of the Royal Oak in Scotland under which the Pretender to the throne hid to escape his pursuers, and thus he named the place; William Thurber made the first land entry and became the first settler in the town in 1819; James Lockwood became the first postmaster on April 6, 1826; Sherman Stevens bought 120 acres in 1826 and made the first plat, which he recorded in 1838; incorporated as a village in 1891 and as a city in 1921 [Mich Hist 13:492 1929; Hudson; PO Archives].

**ROYALTON,** Berrien County: the fist settlers in the area were John Pike and his family, from Fort Royal, Beaufort County, South Carolina, and Jehiel Enos, all in 1832; it was platted by Major Timothy S. Smith in 1834; Major Smith became its first postmaster on Feb. 8, 1833; the office was closed on April 13, 1842, but was restored from Nov. 6, 1843, to Dec. 7, 1848, and from Feb. 1, 1865, to June 6, 1870, and finally from June 24, 1874, to Sept. 14, 1905; now a hamlet [Fox; GSM 1879; PO Archives].

**ROYCE,** Oscoda County: William Deyarmond became the first postmaster of this rural post office in Comins Township on Jan. 10, 1881, the office operating until Oct. 27, 1890 [PO Archives].

**ROYSTON,** Montmorency County: storekeeper Charles H. Godfrey became the first postmaster of this rural post office, 7 miles from Hillman, on March 22, 1902 [PO Archives].

**RUBICON,** Huron County: it was named by William D. Ludington who became the first supervisor when the township was organized in 1859 [Chapman].

**RUBICON,** Ontonagon County. See Rousseau.

**RUBY,** St. Clair County: sawmill owner John Beard became the first postmaster of this settlement on the Black River, in Clyde Township, on Sept. 30, 1854, the office operating until Jan. 31, 1907 [GSM 1860; PO Archives].

**RUDYARD,** Chippewa County: this village in Pickford Township was called Pine River when founded in 1883; but there were several communities named Pine River in Michigan, so in 1890, at the suggestion of Fred Underwood (then manager of the Soo Line and later, president of the Erie Railroad), the name was changed to honor the English author, Rudyard Kipling, when it was given a depot; Joseph Glendenning became its first postmaster on Jan. 12, 1891 [Hamilton; PO Archives].

**RUGG,** Kalkaska County: this village, founded in 1867, was first named Rapid River, after its township, and was given a post office of that name on Nov. 8, 1871, with Henry N. Hill as its first postmaster, the office operating until Jan. 14, 1874; on Jan. 30, 1885, it was given a post office named Mossback, with John W. Morley as its first postmaster; mossback was the name given during the Civil War to men who hid themselves in swamps and elsewhere to avoid conscription into the southern army, the fancy being that they would stay hidden till the moss grew on their backs; the name was later applied to extreme conservatives in politics; on Oct. 3, 1898, the Mossback post office was renamed Rugg, honoring pioneer settlers Roland F. and Ward Rugg; the office operated until Dec. 31, 1906 [GSM 1873-99; Lincoln Lib.; PO Archives].

**RUMELY,** Alger County: it was named for Mr. Rumely, from Ohio, who settled here about 1873; given a station on the Munising Railroad about 1890, and a post office on Sept. 24, 1906, with Cyrille Valind as its first postmaster; the office was later closed, but was restored from Dec. 16, 1947, to Aug. 31, 1959 [John Boogren; PO Archives].

**RURAL VALE,** Lapeer County: Gustavus A. Griffin became the first postmaster of this rural post office in Metamora Township on July 23, 1847; the office was closed on Oct. 1, 1857, but was restored from March 19, 1868, to June 4, 1879 [PO Archives].

**RUSE,** Marquette County: a station on the M. & S.E. Railroad, in Skandia Township; Samuel McFarlane became its first postmaster on July 12, 1917 [GSM 1919; PO Archives].

**RUSH,** Shiawassee County: it was first settled by Ransom White in 1839, Avery Thomas in 1842, and Henry Rush and his family in 1843; when organized in 1850, the town was named for the moderator of the first town meeting, Henry Rush, with Avery Thomas as the first supervisor; Lewis Hart became its first postmaster on Jan. 6, 1851, with the office changed to West Haven on July 22, 1857 [Campbell; Ellis; PO Archives].

**RUSHTON**, Livingston County: this stationon the Grand Trunk Railroad was named for Rush Clark who became its first postmaster on June 9, 1884, the office operating until June 29, 1935 [Mich Manual 1899; PO Archives].

**RUSK**, Ottawa County: a settlement around the sawmill of J. F. Fox & Company, in Allendale Township; Charles D. Fox became its first postmaster on Feb. 24, 1892, the office operating until Sept. 31, 1907 [GSM 1893; PO Archives].

**RUSSELL**, Isabella County: a station on the Toledo, Ann Arbor & Northern Michigan Railroad; railroad agent James J. Kirkpatrick became the first postmaster of this sawmill settlement on June 25, 1890; it was named for Edwin Russell who settled in the township in 1868 [Chapman; GSM 1891; PO Archives].

**RUSSELL SETTLEMENT**, Ionia County. See Bonanza.

**RUSSELL'S MILLS**, Lake County: a settlement in Chase Township around the sawmill of A. J. Summerville & Company, with A. J. Summerville the first railroad agent at this station on the Pere Marquette Railroad; H. C. Russell became its first postmaster on May 6, 1879, the office operating until Jan. 26, 1881 [GSM 1881-83; PO Archives].

**RUSSELL'S MILLS**, Montcalm County. See Trufant.

**RUST**, Mecosta County: a station on the Grand Rapids & Indiana Railroad, 7 miles south of Big Rapids, in 1874, serving largely the Ring & Rust sawmill [GSM 1875].

**RUST**, Montmorency County: Erma L. Pearsall became the first postmaster of this rural post office, named after its township, on Oct. 21, 1903; the office was closed on July 14, 1906, but was restored, with Jeremiah H. Cohoon, as its postmaster, on Jan. 19, 1923, and operated until July 8, 1930 [GSM 1907; PO Archives].

**RUSTFORD**, Mecosta County: in 1870, the Detroit, Lansing & Northern Railroad opened and named their station here by the Little Muskegon River, in Deerfield Township; Truman W. Seidmore became its first postmaster on June 23, 1874, the office operating until Sept. 30, 1901 [Chapman; PO Archives].

**RUSTIC**, Clinton County: Levi J. Calkins became the first postmaster of this rural post office on Nov. 21, 1882, the office operating until May 9, 1883 [PO Archives].

**RUTH**, Huron County: in 1855, John Hunsanger, a native of Hadhomor, Nassau, Germany, took up land here in Sheridan Township; in 1856, several families from Baden joined him, and in the early 1860s, another group arrived from Westphalia; this the area became known as the

German Settlement; it was also called Adams Corners for landowner August H. Adams; but when the village was given a post office on Oct. 12, 1880, with Mr. Adams as its first postmaster, it was named Ruth, for Michael Ruth who had given the property for the depot when the railroad came through [Benedict A. Hunsanger, PM; PO Archives].

**RUTHARDT'S SIDING,** Grand Traverse County. See Cedar Run.

**RUTLAND CENTRE,** Barry County: the stage route from Kalamazoo to Grand Rapids passed the home of Ira Shipman, in Rutland Township; on July 15, 1862, a post office was opened in his home with him as the first postmaster of Rutland Centre, but within less than a week afterwards the stage route was changed, and the post office was closed on Oct. 8, 1862; its name was suggested by W. W. Ralph, after Rutland, Vermont [Johnson; PO Archives].

**RYAN,** Saginaw County: storekeeper Michael Moore became the first postmaster of this rural post office in Jonesfield Township on Dec. 31, 1898, the office operating until Sept. 14, 1903 [GSM 1901-05; PO Archives].

**RYERSON,** Muskegon County. See Lakeside.

**RYNO,** Oscoda County: farmer Alexander K. Patullo became the first postmaster of this rural post office, by the Au Sable River, in Comins Township, on Aug. 16, 1880, with the office named Harmon; on Jan. 9, 1888, it was renamed Ryno for storekeeper and then postmaster Charles E. Ryno, the office operating until Dec. 30, 1899 [GSM 1881-89; PO Archives].

**SABLE BRIDGE,** Mason County: a sawmill settlement with a general store, by the Great Sable River, in Victor Township, in 1876 [GSM 1877].

**SAC BAY,** Delta County: the first settlement on the east shore of Bay de Noc, its records go back to 1853; Aaron Olmstead built the first house here on Burnt Bluff Point, in Fairbanks Township; Schulter & Wilson built the first store in 1860; Donald A. Wells provided postal service in his store until the post office was opened in Fayette in 1870 [David S. Coon; GSM 1877; PO Archives].

**SACKET'S,** Macomb County: this rural post office was named for Lemuel Sacket who became its first postmaster on March 27, 1833, the office operating until July 3, 1856 [PO Archives].

**SADDLE BAG SIDING,** Kent County: a station on the Detroit, Grand Haven & Milwaukee Railroad in 1878 [GSM 1879].

**SADDLE LAKE,** Van Buren County: Hay & Wing built a sawmill and a general store here by Saddle Lake, in Columbia Township, and the railroad gave them a station for shipping their timber; Thomas R. Molley became the first postmaster on Aug. 7, 1874; the office was closed on Sept. 21, 1874, but was restored from Oct. 13, 1874, to May 8, 1876 [GSM 1875; PO Archives].

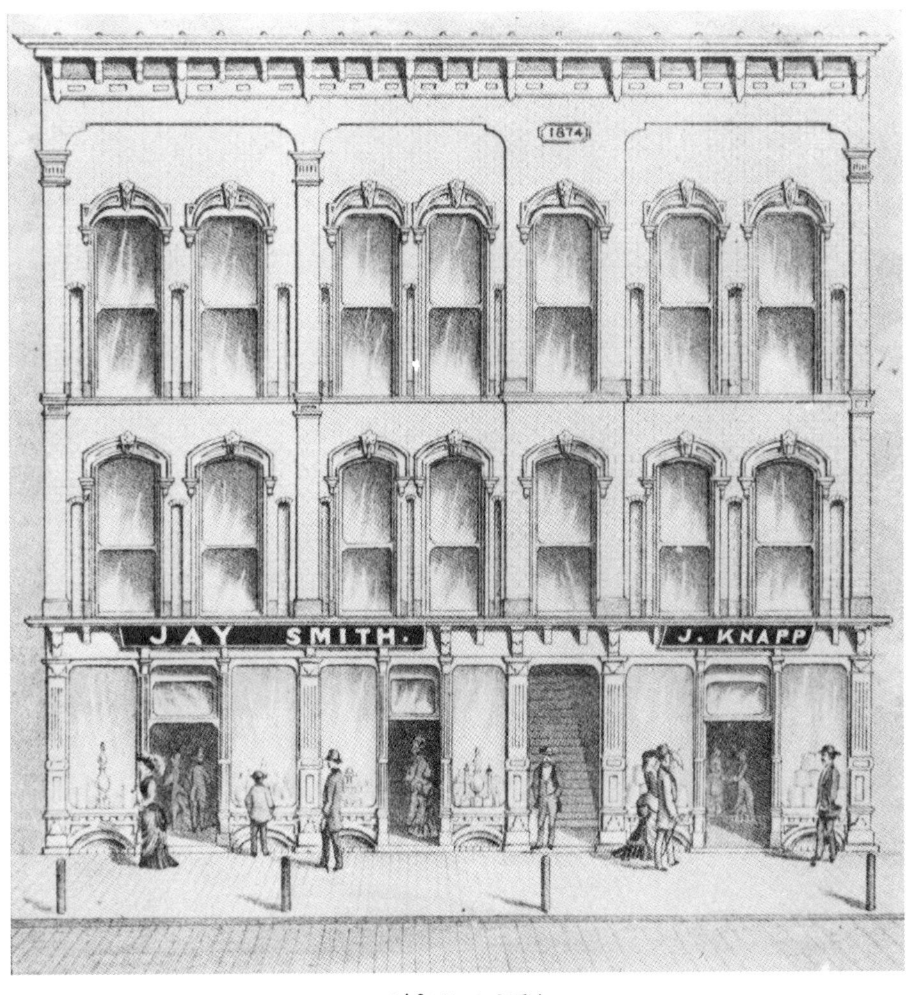


SAGINAW CITY
Jay Smith – Dealer in Drugs, Medicines, Paints, Pure Wines and Liquors for Medicinal Use.

SAGINAW CITY
St. Andrews Academy & Church

**SAGANAW**, Saginaw County. See Saginaw.

**SAGANING**, Arenac County: it was an Indian settlement until about 1871 when they began to move away and white families began to come in; this village on the Saganing River, in Standish Township, was given a station on the Mackinaw division of the Michigan Central Railroad; Samuel R. Hoobler became its first postmaster on July 26, 1876; the office was closed on July 29, 1878, but was restored on Dec. 16, 1885, but then was transferred to and renamed Worth on Nov. 2, 1886; the Saganing post office was re-established from Feb. 6, 1897, to March 14, 1914 [Page; PO Archives].

**SAGE**, Chippewa County: a station on the Detroit, Mackinaw & Marquette Railroad in 1882 [GSM 1883].

**SAGE**, Ogemaw County: Burton J. Corwin became the first postmaster of this rural post office in Cummings Township on Feb. 28, 1898 [GSM 1899].

**SAGER'S LANDING**, Cheboygan County. See Burt Lake.

**SAGERVILLE**, Shiawassee County: Rollin Pond became the first postmaster of this rural post office in Bennington Township on Dec. 14, 1891; the office was established as Sageville, but its spelling was changed to Sagerville on the same day, Dec. 14, 1891; the office operated until Jan. 15, 1901 [GSM 1893; PO Archives].

**SAGE'S MILL**, Cass County. See Adamsville.

**SAGINAW**, Keweenaw County: a copper mining location on Isle Royale; worked from 1875 to 1879 [Stevens].

**SAGINAW**, Saginaw County: Louis Campau built a trading post here in 1816 and platted the Town of Sagina in 1823; Lewis Cass' treaty with the Indians secured the region for the U.S. in 1819, and Fort Saginaw was built in 1822; Colonel David Standard became the first postmaster of Saganaw (later, Saginaw) on Oct. 10, 1831; Harvey Williams built a sawmill here for Gardner Williams in 1834; in 1836, Norman Little, as agent for Alfred M. Hoyt, of New York City, bought the military reservation and his plat included the Campau Sagina plat of 1823 and the Dexter plat of 1835; the panic of 1837 nearly ended his Saginaw City, but he secured fresh capital in 1850 and began building East Saginaw across the river; East Saginaw was incorporated as a village in 1855 and as a city in 1857, consolidated with South Saginaw in 1873, and with Saginaw City in 1889; the East Saginaw post office was opened on Sept. 15, 1851, with Alfred M. Hoyt as its first postmaster; the office was renamed Saginaw East Side (or Saginaw E.S.) on March 17, 1892, and to Saginaw on June 24, 1898; the Saginaw West Side post office operated from March 17, 1892, to Jan. 8, 1932; Saginawe or Saugenah, place of the Sauks, gave to this entire river valley the name Saginaw [MPH 28:481 1898; Mich Hist 15:325 1931, 30:476 1946; PO Archives].

**SAGINAW JUNCTION**, St. Clair County. See Zion.

**SAGINAW MINE,** Marquette County: the name of the Marquette, Houghton & Ontonagon Railroad station here in 1874 was Saginaw, and it was 18 miles west of Marquette [GSM 1879].

**SAGINAW WEST SIDE,** Saginaw County. See Saginaw.

**SAGOLA,** Dickinson County: about 1885, five Chicago men formed the Sagola Lumber Company to log off the pine timber here; there were still Indians in the area and the firm took its name from the Indian word for welcome, and also gave the town the name; it was in Iron County when William S. Laing became its first postmaster on Oct. 9, 1889, the office being transferred to Dickinson County on Oct. 1, 1891, with Diedrick C. Wittenberg as postmaster [Mrs. Elaine Fruik; PO Archives].

**SAILE,** Manistee County: a settlement around the wooden bowl plant of the Chapman Sargent Company, near Arcadia, in 1918 [GSM 1919].

**SAILOR,** Cass County. See Kessington.

**SAILORS ENCAMPMENT ISLAND,** Chippewa County: it was so named because a British vessel was frozen in and wintered here in 1817; it is present-day Neebish Island [GSM 1838].

**SAINT ANTHONY,** Monroe County: a settlement around St. Anthony Catholic church, between Temperance and Ottawa Lake, in 1920 [GSM 1921].

**SAINT ANTHONY,** Wayne County: St. Anthony Catholic church was founded in 1857 and the community of German families around it referred to the area as St. Anthony's; it was given a post office as St. Anthony on Feb. 1, 1875, with Anthony Sellman as its first postmaster, but the office operated until only Nov. 19, 1875; the area is now well within the city limits of Detroit [GSM 1877; PO Archives].

**SAINT CHARLES,** Saginaw County: in 1852, Hiram Davis built the first log cabin here and Charles S. Kimberly the first store; the village was platted by J. B. Parks for Mr. Kimberly, its proprietor; Alonzo Carpenter became its first postmaster on Jan. 21, 1854; incorporated as a village in 1869; Charles Kimberly was a fastidious gentleman and the lumberjacks dubbed him St. Charles, so when it came to naming the village, that name was adopted [Mills; Leeson; PO Archives].

**SAINT CLAIR,** St. Clair County: in 1818, James Fulton became the sole owner of the land here and platted the village, naming it St. Clair, after the lake adjacent to it; the county was created on March 28, 1820, and his village was named the county seat; he met with financial difficulties and in 1824 sold out to Thomas Palmer and David C. McKinistry, of Detroit, who replatted it and renamed it Palmer; on Feb. 14, 1826, with Mark Hopkins as its first postmaster, it was given a post office named St. Clair, and the office retained that name all the time that the village bore the name of Palmer; on April 7, 1846, the legislature restored the name St. Clair to the village; incorporated as a village in 1850 and as a city in 1858;

the lake was first named St. Clare by LaSalle who entered it on Aug. 12, 1679, the feast day of Ste. Clare, and the spelling was later changed to St. Clair for General Arthur St. Clair, the first American governor of the Northwest Territory [Jenks; Schultz; MPH 39:207; PO Archives].

**SAINT CLAIR FLATS**, St. Clair County: it was named from the low, flat level of the Lake St. Clair shore here at the mouth of the St. Clair River which was marsh land filled in with sand from lake dredging, and developed into a settlement in 1895-96; it is now a part of Harsens Island [GSM 1899].

**SAINT CLAIR HEIGHTS**, Wayne County: it was named for the St. Clair family, landowners here; Thomas L. Bennett became its first postmaster on June 14, 1897, succeeded by grocer Henry F. Hiller in 1900; it then adjoined the eastern city limits of Detroit, but is in the present-day area of Hurlbut and Jefferson Avenues, having been annexed by Detroit in 1918 [Burton; GSM 1901; PO Archives].

**SAINT CLAIR SHORES**, Macomb County: the area began being settled about 1779 by the French spreading out from Detroit (pioneer families included Couchez, Frazho, Maison, Trombley, Fresard, Vernier); it was first named L'Anse Cruise (deep bay) from its location; it was renamed when incorporated as a village, with Daniel N. Davis as its first president, in 1925; the name was suggested by Conrad Hess from its location on the shores of Lake St. Clair; Russell W. Swhier became its first postmaster on Feb. 15, 1927; incorporated as a city in 1950 [Virginia MacHarg; PO Archives].

**SAINT CLAIR SPRINGS**, St. Clair County: this post office, now within the corporate limits of the city of St. Clair, was opened on Sept. 26, 1884, with Asa L. Blanchard as its first postmaster, the office operating until Nov. 15, 1902; named from its area, which included the St. Clair Mineral Springs [GSM 1889-1903; PO Archives].

**SAINT COLLINS**, Ontonagon County: a siding on the Duluth, South Shore & Atlantic Railroad; it served as a mail distributing point until the post office was opened at Bruce Crossing on March 5, 1888 [Kenneth Priestley].

**SAINT DOMINIC'S INDIAN MISSION**, Van Buren County: when their land was taxed in Cass County, Chief Simon Pokagon led some 300 of his Pottawattomi here in 1856; about 30 remain; the cemetery behind the settlement contains 1,700 graves [Federal].

**SAINT ELMO**, Midland County: a settlement around the J. C. Perry sawmill, with John Sniter becoming its first postmaster on May 22, 1884, the office operating until Sept. 30, 1904; St. Elmo, by Augusta Evans Wilson (1835-1909), was one of the most popular novels of the period [GSM 1895-1905; PO Archives].

**SAINT GEORGE'S ISLAND**, Chippewa County. See Sugar Island.

**SAINT HELEN**, Roscommon County: a station on the Mackinaw division of the Michigan Central Railroad, by St. Helen's Lake, in Richfield Township, in 1872; the village was founded in 1872 and owned by the Henry L. Stevens & Company lumber firm; Mrs. Louise Tebo became its first postmaster on Feb. 16, 1874; the office was closed on Dec. 6, 1876, but was restored, with William L. Marsh as postmaster, and operated from May 22, 1878, to April 29, 1879; with Henry L. Stevens, Jr., as postmaster, it was restored again on June 7, 1880, and operated until Nov. 5, 1898, but was restored again from Jan. 27, 1903 [GSM 1873; PO Archives].

**SAINT HELENA ISLAND,** Mackinac County: it was on Charlevoix's map of 1733 as Isle Ste. Helene; its present name appears on Lanman's map of 1841; its harbor provided a fishing village from Indian times; at the time of its greatest prosperity, just before the Civil War, it was owned by Wilson Newton and A. P. Newton, brothers and commercial fishermen; believed to have been named by the French for St. Helena, finder of the cross of Christ and wife of the Emperor Constantine [Mich Hist 10:411 1926].

**SAINT IGNACE,** Mackinac County: here in 1671, the French Jesuit, Jacques Marquette, founded the mission of St. Ignace, naming it for St. Ignatius Loyola, the founder of the Jesuits; it was settlers first called it Mackinac and it is on Farmer's old maps as Ancient Fort Mackinac; Francis LaPointe owned and occupied land here before 1812, later selling to the Dousman family which in turn, in 1857, sold it to the brothers David, Patrick, and Michael Murray; Peter W. Hombach became its first postmaster on Nov. 3, 1874; incorporated as a village in 1882 and as a city in 1883; the site of old Fort de Buade, q.v. [MPH 18:624 1891; Mich Hist 42:257 1958].

**SAINT JACQUES,** Delta County: locally it is pronounced St. Jakes; the village began with the erection of kilns here on the Duluth, South Shore & Atlantic Railroad line in 1891; William Howe became its first postmaster on Jan. 11, 1893; the office was closed on Sept. 18, 1895, but on June 22, 1904, the Sturgeon River post office was transferred to and renamed St. Jacques, which was by then at a second location; the office operated until July 31, 1955 [David S. Coon; GSM 1905; PO Archives].

**SAINT JAMES,** Charlevoix County: the village is on Beaver Island, which James Jesse Strang took over for his Mormon (Church of the Latter Day Saints) colony in 1847; it was given a post office named Beaver Island, Michilimackinac County, on Jan. 13, 1849, with Charles R. Wright as its first postmaster; Mr. Strang named the village St. James, after himself, and its post office was renamed St. James, Emmet County, on Oct. 10, 1854; he was the only king to be crowned in the U.S., July 8, 1850; after his murder, by disgruntled followers, in 1856, the colony began to disintegrate; its post office was closed on March 6, 1868, but was restored, with Mr. Wright again its postmaster, on Dec. 19, 1868; the Mormons left the island in 1895, and the village is now a resort town; in the 1870s, it was also called Beaver Harbor [MPH 32:176 1902; PO Archives].

**SAINT JOHNS,** Clinton County: in 1853, a party of four state officials examined the proposed line of the Detroit & Milwaukee Railroad to select land along the right-of-way for purposes of speculation; one of them, John Swegles, exercised his authority to make the purchase of their choice, and he cleared the land and laid out the village; it was named for him, with Rev. C. A. Lamb, a Baptist minister, adding the Saint; the Bingham post office was renamed St. Johns, with George W. Estes as postmaster, on Feb. 6, 1855; it was made the county seat when the railroad came through in 1857; incorporated as a village in 1857 and as a city in 1904 [Elizabeth Millman; PO Archives].

**SAINT JOSEPH,** Berrien County: while waiting here for Tonty to join him in 1679, LaSalle built Fort Miami (it was in Miami Indian territory), to keep his restless men occupied; when he moved southward after a month, he left no one here, for he did not intend to (and never did) return; about 1780, William Burnett built a trading post here; in 1827, it was a settlement called Saranac, after a Great Lakes ship; Calvin Britain settled here in 1829, and in 1831 platted the village as Newburyport, some say after the first vessel to ascend the St. Joseph River, others say after Newburyport, Mass., whence some of the early settlers had come; Mr. Britain became the first postmaster of Saranac in March, 1829, with the name changed to St. Joseph on July 24, 1832; in 1833, the legislature changed the name of the village to St. Joseph (it is on the St. Joseph River, named by the French missionaries); incorporated as a village in 1834 and as a city in 1891 [Paré; Mich Hist 19:190 1935, 39:119 1955; PO Archives].

**SAINT JOSEPH,** St. Joseph County. See Three Rivers.

**SAINT JOSEPH SUR LA BAIE,** Monroe County. See Erie.

**SAINT JOSEPH'S,** Lenawee County: Thomas H. Edwards became the first postmaster of this territorial post office on Dec. 4, 1828, while Lenawee included Cass, Van Buren, St. Joseph, Berrien, and other counties; on Feb. 1, 1830, the office was changed to Edwardsburg [Cole].

**SAINT LAWRENCE,** Marquette County: a station on the Chicago & Northwestern Railroad, three miles west of Ishpeming, in 1883 [Mich Manual 1899].

**SAINT LOUIS,** Gratiot County: Joseph F. Clapp selected a sawmill site on the Pine River and built his cabin here in 1853; Mr. Clapp, with Dr. Abram M. Crawford, had L. D. Preston plat the village in 1855, and named it Pine River; Mr. Clapp became the first postmaster on Nov. 16, 1855; Edward T. Cheesman and Gilbert E. Pratt platted and recorded the adjacent village of St. Louis in 1859; the two villages were consolidated as St. Louis in 1865; incorporated as a village in 1868 and as a city in 1891; General Charles Gratiot, after whom the county was named, was a native of St. Louis, Missouri [Adeline E. Phillips, PM; PO Archives].

**SAINT MARTIN ISLAND,** Delta County: it was discovered and named by Pere Jacques Marquette; he found Indians here, living by fishing;

white fishermen visited it by 1830 but Philemon Thompson and Aaron Olmstead, with their families, became the first settlers in 1845; St. Martin, Gull, Pouty, and Big Summer Islands comprised Winona Township, the water township of Delta County [Andreas].

**SAINT MARTIN ISLANDS,** Mackinac County: Father Claude Allouez, marooned on a smaller island, because of a storm, in 1699, named it for the saint of the day, Nov. 11th; as another St. Martin's day occurs the following day, he named the larger island also St. Martin; since then they have also been called Plaster Islands or Burnt Islands [Emerson R. Smith].

**SAINT MARY,** Chippewa County. See Sault Ste. Marie.

**SAINT MARY'S,** St. Clair County: William I. Parkinson became the first postmaster of this rural post office on Nov. 23, 1866, the office operating until June 8, 1868 [PO Archives].

**SAINT NICHOLAS,** Delta County: following the transient lumbering operations in the area, the place was first settled in 1912 by Mr. and Mrs. Alphonse Heirman who named it after their native village in Belgium; other emigrants from that country followed and it became a Belgian community; never having had a post office, in the early days its mail was brought to the Heirman home for distribution; it is now on an R.F.D. route [Joseph L. Heirman].

**SAINT PAUL,** Van Buren County: Samuel C. Paul became the first postmaster of this rural post office on July 26, 1856, the office operating until April 14, 1860 [PO Archives].

**SALEM,** Macomb County: Leonard Lee became the first postmaster of this rural post office in Feb., 1832, the office operating until March 18, 1842 [PO Archives].

**SALEM,** Washtenaw County: John and Joseph Dickinson became the first settlers here in 1825; George Renwick became the first supervisor in 1832, and Ira Rider the first postmaster on June 4, 1831, with the office named Rider's for him; when George Renwick became the postmaster on May 29, 1841, the office was renamed Renwick for him; the office became Salem on Jan. 28, 1846, but was closed on Dec. 10, 1875; the Summit post office was moved here and renamed Salem on Dec. 15, 1876; the village was named after its township which had been named for Salem, N.Y., from near which many of its pioneers came; originally, the name Salem was that of an ancient Semitic deity [Chapman; Beakes; PO Archives].

**SALEM CENTER,** Allegan County. See Burnips.

**SALINA,** Saginaw County: Aaron K. Penney located here in 1848; he sold out to William Gallagher who, after the discovery of salt here in 1860, laid out the village and named it; to avoid confusion with the post office of Saline, when given a post office on May 13, 1863, with Aaron Linton as its first postmaster, the office was named Spaulding, after its township; the office was renamed South Saginaw on Oct. 20, 1866, but was closed on Aug. 7, 1884; incorporated as the village of South Saginaw in 1866, it became consolidated with the city of Saginaw in 1873 [Mills; PO Archives].

**SALINE,** Washtenaw County: in 1824, Orange Risdon, chief surveyor of the military road from Detroit to Chicago, bought 160 acres here; a few families came in 1826; Mr. Risdon returned from his surveying in 1827, platted the village in 1832, and named it after the Saline River running through it; the river had been so named because of the salt springs in it; Jacob Whitney became its first postmaster on June 28, 1827; incorporated as a village in 1866 and as a city in 1931 [Bessie E. Collins; Mich Hist 38:437 1954; PO Archives].

**SALISBURY,** Marquette County: an iron mine of the Iron Cliffs Company, and its community, dating from about 1872, and located near Ishpeming [Hatcher; Lemmer].

**SALLING,** Otsego County: with the coming through here of a branch line of the Jackson, Lansing & Saginaw Railroad, the village of Bagley (named after an early surveyor of the area) was platted and recorded in 1874; on Oct. 16, 1899, it was given a post office as Salling, for a member of the Salling, Hanson Lumber Company, which was active in this area then; company manager Lewis Jenson was its first postmaster, and the office operating until Jan. 15, 1912; it is not now a village but a part of Bagley Township [Herbert A. Hutchins; PO Archives].

**SALOME,** Oakland County. See Mount Pleasant.

**SALT RIVER,** Isabella County. See Shepherd.

**SALT RIVER,** Shiawassee County: a hamlet in 1864 [GSM 1865].

**SALT RIVER SIDING,** Midland County: a station on the Pere Marquette Railroad, between Sanford and North Bradley, in 1882 [GSM 1883].

**SALT WELLS,** Wayne County: a station on the Wabash Railroad, in Springwells Township, then 7 miles southwest of Detroit, opened about 1882 [Mich Manual 1899].

**SALZBURGH,** Bay County. See West Bay City.

**SAMARIA,** Monroe County: when the Ann Arbor Railroad came through here about 1872, the station, and later the village, was named for Samuel and Mary Weeks, both musically talented, whose home was a gathering place for the young; Sam, a storekeeper, became its first postmaster on Jan. 17, 1879 [Mary Porter, PM].

**SAMMON'S LANDING,** Oceana County. See Little Point Sable.

**SANBORN,** St. Clair County: a station on the Grand Trunk Railroad, 12 miles west of Port Huron, in 1882 [GSM 1883].

**SAND BAY,** Mackinaw County: this lumber settlement on Bois Blanc

Island developed around the sawmill and general store of the E. H. Stafford Manufacturing Company; Mrs. Altha Vohlers became its first postmaster on Nov. 12, 1909 [GSM 1911; PO Archives].

**SAND BEACH,** Huron County. See Harbor Beach.

**SAND CREEK,** Lenawee County: the government granted the land here in Madison Township to Joshua and Rebecca Thurber in 1820; the Wabash Railroad made it a station in 1881; it was given a post office as Thurber, after its first settlers, on Sept. 27, 1881, with merchant William Lafayette Briggs as its first postmaster; the name was changed to Sand Creek on March 5, 1891, to Sandcreek on June 11, 1894, and back to Sand Creek in 1957; it was named after the creek running past it [Dallas R. Ries, PM; PO Archives].

**SAND CREEK,** Ottawa County. See Tallmadge.

**SANDERS' POINT,** Delta County: it was named for John Sanders who located a commercial fishery and boarding house on this promontory into Green Bay; it was given a post office as Sanders' Fishery, with E. P. Royce as its first postmaster, in 1878 (it would seem to have been a mail distributing location rather than a government post office); it was located in Ford River Township and was also called Rocky Point [GSM 1877-79; PO Archives].

**SAND HILL,** Wayne County: it was first settled about 1820; it was given a station on the Detroit, Lansing & Northern Railroad and on Aug. 16, 1880, a post office, with John Parks as its first postmaster; the name of the office was changed to Willmarth on June 5, 1882, back to Sand Hill on June 15, 1882, and finally to Redford on Oct. 1, 1906; the hamlets of Redford Center (which was also called Bell Branch) and Sand Hill combined to form the village of Redford in 1906, and it in turn was annexed by the city of Detroit in 1926 [Burton; GSM 1881; PO Archives].

**SAND LAKE,** Kent County: the first trains of the Grand Rapids & Indiana Railroad to come through here in 1869 brought milling machinery to harvest the white pine in the area; and among the first to do so was Robert L. Salisbury who was named the postmaster on Jan. 31, 1870 and who, with Fred C. Whitmore, purchased land, platted, recorded and named the village in 1871; it was named from its location by a shoal lake; incorporated as a village in 1878; a small part of the village lies in Montcalm County [Beuna Bailey; PO Archives].

**SAND RIVER,** Marquette County: the village began as a station on the Detroit, Mackinaw & Marquette Railroad in 1882; when given a post office on March 14, 1891, with Charles A. Hazen as its first postmaster, it was in Alger County; the office was transferred to Marquette County on Sept. 12, 1908 (it is on the line between the two counties); the office was closed on Dec. 31, 1911, but was restored on Dec. 10, 1912; it was named from its location by the Sand River [GSM 1883; PO Archives].

**SANDS,** Marquette County: this village in Chocolay Township was named for Louis Sands who emigrated from Sweden in 1853 and became a lumberman, banker, etc.; William E. Lathrop became its first postmaster on Jan. 23, 1878, the office operating until Feb., 1955; the village is about a mile north of its Chicago & Northwestern Railroad depot called Sands Station [Bald; GSM 1879; PO Archives].

**SANDSTONE,** Jackson County: in 1832, James Valentine located with Chester Wall here on Sandstone Creek, named from the large deposit of sandstone along it; Benjamin J. Mather became the first postmaster of Sandstone on April 30, 1833; Dr. D. K. Akers located 160 acres of land in Sandstone Township and platted the village of Barry, named for William T. Barry, President Andrew Jackson's postmaster general, and on Feb. 13, 1834, the post office was renamed Barry; but with the collapse of its Bank of Sandstone in 1838, the village of Barry began to decay, and on Jan. 4, 1880, its post office was changed back to Sandstone; the office operated until Oct. 31, 1904 [MPH 35:510 1907; Pen Phil 8:6 April 1958; DeLand; PO Archives].

**SANDSTOWN,** Missaukee County: it was founded in 1890 by Charles Sands and named for him [R. Bruce Bacon].

**SANDUSKY,** Sanilac County: it was founded in 1870 by Wildman Mills and named after his home town of Sandusky, Ohio; Oscar Mills became its first postmaster on Jan. 25, 1879; incorporated as a village in 1885; from its location in the county, it was renamed Sanilac Center on Feb. 19, 1889, but changed back to Sandusky on July 24, 1905, when it was incorporated as a city [Harry C. Smith; PO Archives].

**SANDY,** Mecosta County: this rural post office was in Montcalm County when John C. Williams became its first postmaster on June 20, 1890, but it was transferred to Mecosta County on July 8, 1903, and operated until Jan. 31, 1908 [PO Archives].

**SANDY BEACH,** Cass County: a resort colony located on the north shore of Diamond Lake; the Michigan Central Railroad came through here in 1871 and gave it a station; it was platted and recorded by Mary Sillaber in 1906 [Glover].

**SANDY POINT,** Delta County. See Escanaba.

**SANFORD,** Ingham County. See Okemos.

**SANFORD,** Midland County: in 1864, Charles S. Sanford, from Madison County, N.Y., acquired 213 acres here in Jerome Township; he platted the village in 1870; Jay F. Hamilton became the first postmaster of Sanfordville on June 23, 1871, with its name shortened to Sanford on July 13, 1871; the Pere Marquette Railroad came through the same year and built a station here [Kathryn Cummins; Chapman; PO Archives].

**SANILAC CENTER,** Sanilac County. See Sandusky.

**SANILAC MILLS,** Sanilac County: Darius Cole and Isaac Lenty built a sawmill here in 1844 and the settlement which followed was given a post office on March 11, 1850, with Mr. Lenty as its first postmaster; the office operated until Dec. 3, 1860; the settlement was also known as Pine Hill and was given a post office of that name on May 10, 1866, with Henry Wahly as its first postmaster, this office operating until Sept. 16, 1881 [Mich 33:167 1949; PO Archives].

**SANS SOUCI,** St. Clair County: this shipping and trading center on Harsens Island was given a post office on April 24, 1900, as Sans Souci, with the name changed to Harsens Island on Dec. 31, 1960; Sans Souci was named by its first postmaster, William LaCroix who had large holdings here, and the name meaning in French without care, would seem to refer to the serenity of the surroundings [Hon. Edward T. Kane; PO Archives].

**SANTIAGO,** Arenac County: this lumber settlement on the Au Gres River, in Turner Township, was given a post office on May 26, 1899, with Ella McEwen as its first postmaster; it was named after Santiago de Cuba where the American army had won a major victory in the Spanish-American War, in 1898; now a ghost town [Alfred Campbell; PO Archives].

**SARANAC,** Berrien County. See St. Joseph.

**SARANAC,** Ionia County: Judge Jefferson Morrison bought government land here in 1836; he sold part of it to Dwight & Hutchinson, of Detroit, and they platted the village; Cyprian S. Hooker became its first postmaster on March 14, 1839; the office was closed on June 24, 1841, but on Feb. 12, 1859, the Boston post office was transferred to and renamed Saranac; incorporated as a village in 1869; it was named after the New York resort town to attract settlers from that state [Schenck; Atwell; PO Archives].

**SARATOGA,** Washtenaw County: it was platted in 1836 for its proprietor, G. R. Lillibridge, of Detroit, at the south end of Portage Lake, one of the twenty lakes in its township, and named after the resort town in New York to attract settlers from that state; Edwin Forrest, the great tragedian, is said to have paid $30,000 for half of this paper city's 250 lots [Beakes].

**SARGENT,** Wayne County: Wayne County officials in Dec., 1796, divided the county into four townships: St. Clair, Hamtramck, Detroit, and Sargent; it was named for Winthrop Sargent, then secretary of the Territory of Michigan, but the name was dropped in later redistricting [Dunbar].

**SATTERLEE'S MILLS,** Mecosta County: this village was named for Ethan Satterlee who built the first grist mill and sawmill here on the Little Muskegon River, in Deerfield Township, in 1860; John T. Van Kewren became its first postmaster on Jan. 5, 1867, the office operating until March 31, 1874 [Chapman; PO Archives].

**SAUBLE,** Lake County: a station on the Manistee & Grand Rapids Railroad, in Elk Township, in 1898; storekeeper Charles B. Ross became its first postmaster on March 10, 1910 [GSM 1911; PO Archives].

**SAUGATUCK,** Allegan County: William Gay Butler and family, from Hartford, Conn., settled here in 1830; he platted the village in 1833 and had it recorded as Kalamazoo, it being by the Kalamazoo River; in 1836, the legislature gave that name to the town since bearing it, and to this village the name of Newark, after its township; Rensselaer R. Crosby became the first postmaster of Newark on May 2, 1835, succeeded by Mr. Butler on April 4, 1838; Stephen A. Morrison, who became the third postmaster on Jan. 18, 1842, got it given its old Indian name of Saugatuck, Pottawattomi for river's mouth, for near here the Kalamazoo River empties into Lake Michigan; in 1868, both village and township were renamed Saugatuck; incorporated as a village in 1868 [William Simmons; PO Archives].

**SAULT SAINTE MARIE,** Chippewa County: this, the first European settlement to be made in what is now Michigan, was named by the French Jesuits, Isaac Jogues and Charles Raymbault, in 1641, from its being on the heights overlooking the rapids (in French, sault) and in honor of the Virgin Mary; Jacques Marquette built a mission here in 1668; in 1750, Louis XIV granted 214,000 acres at the Sault (including all of Sault Ste. Marie) to Louis le Gardeur, Sieur de Repentigny who in 1783 became Michigan's only Revolutionary War soldier, refusing allegiance to George III; John Johnston, Henry Rowe School Schoolcraft's father-in-law, became the first British settler in 1793; Governor Lewis Cass raised the Stars and Stripes over Sault Ste. Marie in 1820; first called Le Sault de Sainte Marie, it was shortened when Henry B. Griswold became its first postmaster on Sept. 11, 1823; incorporated as the village of St. Mary in 1849, but the act creating it was annuled in 1851; re-incorporated as Sault Ste. Marie in 1879; incorporated as a city in 1887 (Paré; MPH 32:305 1902; Dunbar; PO Archives].

**SAUNDERS,** Iron County. See Scott Lake.

**SAVILLA,** Barry County: Henry Gerty became the first postmaster of this rural post office on Dec. 7, 1880, the office operating until June 14, 1881 [PO Archives].

**SAWAQUATO BEACH,** Mackinac County. See Curtis.

**SAWYER,** Berrien County: the Chicago & Western Michigan (now Pere Marquette) Railroad built a station here called Troy; it was renamed in 1854 in honor of Silas Sawyer who had a mill nearby; James H. Spaulding became the first postmaster on May 19, 1870 [Fox; PO Archives].

**SAWYER AFB,** Marquette County. See K. I. Sawyer.

**SAWYERVILLE,** Osceola County: Albert E. Sawyer, in company with J. E. Kellogg, bought 3,000 acres of timberland in this county in 1871 and here in Rose Lake Township opened the largest steam sawmill in the county in 1874, cutting up to twelve million feet annually; a hamlet grew up around it [Chapman].

**SCALES PRAIRIE**, Barry County: it was named for Robert Scales who emigrated here in Thornapple Township from Kentucky about 1835 [Mich Hist 33:220 1949].

**SCAMMON**, Chippewa County: this settlement on the south coast of Drummond Island developed around the mill of the Island Cedar Company; company superintendent Clark A. Watson became its first postmaster on Feb. 19, 1884, the office operating until Nov. 15, 1894 [GSM 1885; PO Archives].

**SCAMMON'S COVE**, Chippewa County. See Johnswood.

**SCHAFFER**, Delta County: this village in Bark River Township was founded in 1878 by Henry W. Coburn and Charles M. Schaffer, of Marquette, who operated an iron furnace here; it was named for and by Mr. Schaffer; Mr. Coburn became its first postmaster on Oct. 13, 1887; the office was closed on Feb. 28, 1912, but has been restored since July 30, 1914 [PM; GSM 1889; PO Archives].

**SCHLESSER**, Chippewa County: this hamlet in Detour Township was named for storekeeper John Schlesser who became its first postmaster on April 29, 1892, the office operating until June 30, 1902 [GSM 1893-1903; PO Archives].

**SCHOMBERG**, Leelanau County: a station on the M. & N.E. Railroad, in Centerville Township; John B. Decker became its first postmaster on May 18, 1904, the office operating until Oct. 31, 1934 [GSM 1905; PO Archives].

**SCHOOLCRAFT**, Houghton County. See Centennial.

**SCHOOLCRAFT**, Kalamazoo County: the village was founded and platted by Lucius Lyon, a surveyor; he recorded the plat in 1831 and named it for his friend Henry Rowe Schoolcraft, Michigan's Indian agent; it was given a post office as Prairie Ronde on June 28, 1830, with George Brown as its first postmaster, being renamed Schoolcraft on June 8, 1832; incorporated as a village in 1866 [Charles F. Crawford, PM; Mich Hist 31:30 1947].

**SCHWARZBURG**, Wayne County: about 1825, General John E. Schwarz, of Detroit, built a dam and a little mill here and soon as settlement formed and took his name, but nearby Perrinsville lured away its inhabitants and Schwarzburg is now extinct (Mich Hist 26:319 summer 1942].

**SCIO**, Washtenaw County: in 1835, Samuel W. Foster bought a mill site here on the Huron River; the village was platted by Dr. Cyril Nichols, a Vermonter; Matthew F. Gregory became its first postmaster on Sept. 9, 1835; the office was transferred to and renamed Delhi Mills on Feb. 3, 1871, but the Scio post office was re-established on Sept. 26, 1871; Scio was named after its township, but since the early township records were destroyed by fire it is not known why it was named with the Latin word for I know [Chapman: Beakes; PO Archives].

**SCIOTA**, Shiawassee County: this hamlet formed about 1846 around Mitchell Blood's tavern on the Grand River Road and was named after its township [Ellis].

**SCIPIO**, Hillsdale County: on Jan. 1, 1834, there were but 300 acres of land entered in the present Scipio, divided in ownership between William H. Nelson, Dexter Olds, Silas W. Benson, and Nathaniel Bacon; the township was organized in 1836 at the house of William Porter, and Stillman Ralph was elected its first supervisor; Silas Benson became the first postmaster on June 17, 1836; the office was closed on Feb. 3, 1842, but was restored from Feb. 16, 1892, to Dec. 14, 1903 [Reynolds; Pen Phil 7:3 Jan 1957; PO Archives].

**SCIPIO CENTRE**, Hillsdale County. See Mosherville.

**SCOFIELD**, Monroe County: this village in Exeter Township was settled in 1872; it was named for businessman and lumberman Silas A. Scofield, of the firm of Scofield & Rice, and he became the station agent for the Chicago & Canada Southern Railroad here; Robert Van Vleek became the first postmaster on Jan. 20, 1874, the office operating until Sept. 15, 1935 [Bonner; GSM 1879; PO Archives].

**SCOTDALE**, Berrien County: a station on the Buchanan branch of the Pere Marquette Railroad, in Royalton Township [Fox].

**SCOTT LAKE**, Iron County: after a local pioneer family, this station on the Chicago & Northwestern Railroad, built about 1883, was named Saunders Spur, and later just Saunders; it became the site of the C. Hatterberg Lumber Company veneer mill in 1889; on June 13, 1889, it was given a post office as Saunders, with Robert Barclay as its first postmaster; it is now a farming community [Jack Hill, Sr.; PO Archives].

**SCOTTS**, Kalamazoo County: land here was deeded by the government to Dan Wheeler in 1835; Samuel Scott settled here in 1847 and it became known as Scotts Crossing, and later as Scotts; it was given a post office as Scotts on Feb. 19, 1872, with Servetus Bathrick as its first postmaster, succeeded by William DeLano on Dec. 10, 1872; Mr. Bathrick platted the village in 1874 [Ida L. Orosz, PM; PO Archives].

**SCOTT'S POINT**, Mackinac County: this village with a landing on the north shore of Lake Michigan was given a post office as Orrville on March 25, 1880, with John Blanchard as its first postmaster; the office operated until Oct. 21, 1897; it is believed to have been named for Orrville Scott [Emerson Smith; GSM 1881; PO Archives].

**SCOTTSVILLE**, Macomb County: Urial Day became the first postmaster of this rural post office on March 19, 1852, the office operating until April 27, 1859 [PO Archives].

**SCOTTVILLE**, Mason County: the Pere Marquette Railroad came through here in 1874 and the town which formed was called Mason Center, from its location in the county; James Sweetland built a sawmill here in 1878; he sold it to Hiram E. Scott and Mr. Crowley in 1879, and they added a store and homes and called it Sweetland; it was given a post office of that name on June 20, 1879, with Chauncey W. Rickerd as its first postmaster; Mr. Scott and Charles Blaine platted the village in 1882 and named it Scottville, and the post office was so renamed on Sept. 12, 1882; incorporated as a village in 1889 and as a city in 1907 [Ruth Van der Molen; Federal; PO Archives].

**SCRANTON**, Ottawa County. See Eastmanville.

**SCRANTON MINE**, Ontonagon County: Austin Corser discovered silver here just north of the Little Iron River in 1855, waited until 1872 when the land became open to homesteading to announce his find, and then sold his land to a group of Pennsylvania capitalists who proceeded to develop the Scranton Mine; it operated until 1876 [Jamison].

**SCUDDERVILLE**, Kent County: this village on Rush Creek, with a station on the Lake Shore and Michigan Southern Railroad, was named for Henry W. Scudder, local landowner; from its location in Byron Township, it was given a post office as North Byron on Oct. 7, 1862, with Peter G. Foote as its first postmaster; the office was closed on Dec. 16, 1879, but was restored from March 17, 1894, to Sept. 30, 1903 [Dillenback; GSM 1873; PO Archives].

**SEABROOK**, Luce County: David Terry became the first postmaster of this rural post office, 8 miles southwest of McMillan, the office operating until Jan. 8, 1884; it was in Mackinac County until Luce was organized [GSM 1885; PO Archives].

**SEARS**, Osceola County: Messrs. Barker and Pratt began the first business here in 1869; the village, first called Orient, after its township, was renamed for an early surveyor for the Flint & Pere Marquette Railroad, which came through here in 1870; Nelson Ferguson became its first postmaster on Dec. 8, 1871 [Norris L. Miller, PM; Chapman].

**SEBASTOPOL**, Ottawa County: the allied armies of Turks, French, and English conducted a memorable siege of the Russian city of Sebastopol (or Sevastopol) in the Crimean War of 1854-55; whence likely came the name of this rural post office, opened on March 17, 1855, with Alexander Ullson as its first postmaster, the office operating until Dec. 5, 1859 [GSM 1860; PO Archives].

**SEBEWA**, Ionia County: the first permanent settlements in the area were made by John F. Terrill, Charles W. Ingalls, and John Brown, in 1838; Sebewa Township was organized in 1845 and named by Rufus Goddard after Sebewa Creek, meaning little river; Benjamin D. Weld became the first postmaster on Jan. 24, 1851; Pierce J. Cook, as agent for Elizabeth Cornell, of New Jersey, platted and named the village Cornell in 1867, and the post office was changed to Cornell on July 8, 1880; but the name of Sebewa was restored from Feb. 16, 1881, until the office was closed on Nov. 15, 1913, and the village is still known as Sebewa [Schenck; Branch; PO Archives].

**SEBEWAING,** Huron County: the Rev. John F. J. Auch, a Lutheran minister from Ann Arbor, seeking good farmland for a settlement, and aiming also to do missionary work among the Indians, brought his group here in 1845; it was in Tuscola County when Allen Brewer became its first postmaster on July 23, 1857, and was first spelled Sibbewaing; it became a part of Huron County in 1859; incorporated as a village in 1879; the name is Indian for crooked creek, such as flows nearby [Norman C. Hensel; PO Archives].

**SECILLIA,** Calhoun County. See East Leroy.

**SECORD,** Gladwin County: a Canadian, Marcel Secord, became the first white settler in the county in 1861; he built his lodge at Dick's Fork (named for Mr. Dixon who owned the land); in 1864, he entered a homestead, cleared the land and built a log house; the place was known as Secord and he provided meals and lodging for the early lumbermen of the area (in the county are Secord Township, since 1912, and Secord Dam); hereabouts, nine miles from Gladwin, a rural post office named Secord was opened on Feb. 5, 1908, with Herman Ripke as its first postmaster [Emma Klamer; GSM 1911; PO Archives].

**SECORD'S,** Wayne County: a flag station on the Michigan Central Railroad, in Canton Township, in 1872 [GSM 1873].

**SEDAN,** Charlevoix County: Frederick Goodman became the first postmaster of this settlement on May 31, 1878, the office operating until Feb. 1, 1883; a famous battle in the Franco-Prussian War took place at Sedan on Sept. 2, 1870 [GSM 1883; PO Archives].

**SEDGWICK,** Lenawee County: Mary Bettis was appointed the first postmaster of this rural post office on Feb. 2, 1899, but declined, and Jacob Rosenstiel became its first postmaster on April 22, 1899 [PO Archives].

**SEE WHY,** Chippewa County: a station on the Duluth, South Shore & Atlantic Railroad; the settlement formed around the sawmill and general store of C.Y. (Cornelius Y.) Bennett for whom it was named and who became its first postmaster on May 10, 1912 [Hamilton; GSM 1913; PO Archives].

**SEGWUN,** Kent County: H. B. Alden platted and recorded this village, south of the Grand River, on the line of the Detroit, Grand Haven & Milwaukee Railroad, for Henry O. Chesbro, on Oct. 26, 1863; but it has since become a part of the city of Lowell [Chapman].

**SEIDLER CORNERS,** Bay County: this hamlet was founded in 1902 by Henry Seidler who had a general store, blacksmith shop and saloon here; he added a school in 1905 [M. S. Causley, Jr.].

**SEITZVILLE,** Saginaw County: a station on the Saginaw, Tuscola & Huron Railroad, in 1882 [GSM 1883].

**SELFRIDGE AIR FORCE BASE,** Macomb County: this the first

military air base in Michigan was established in 1917; it was named for Lieut. Thomas E. Selfridge, the first American soldier killed in an airplane crash (Orville Wright was injured in the accident) in 1908 [Dunbar].

**SELKIRK**, Ogemaw County: William O. Neil became the first postmaster of this sawmill settlement in Churchill Township on Sept. 22, 1887, the office operating until May 31, 1955 [GSM 1889; PO Archives].

**SELKIRK RESERVATION**, Allegan County: it was first called the Griswold Mission; in 1839, Rev. James Selkirk began his 38 years of labor here in Wayland Township, on land secured from the government for civilizing and educating some 650 landless and homeless local Indians; it was under the care of the Episcopal Church and had some government aid, but did not succeed [MPH 32:381 1902].

**SELLECK'S CORNERS**, Macomb County: an 1859 map located the settlement of Armada Corners in Armada Township, but it later became better known as Selleck's Corners after "Uncle" John Selleck, popular local tavern keeper [Eldredge].

**SENECA**, Lenawee County: the first settlers in the township, Archibald Brower and Roswell J. Hayward, arrived in 1833; the township was organized in 1836, with Elias J. Baldwin as its first supervisor, and was named after Seneca County, N.Y., whence many of the early settlers had come; the village, named after its township, was given a post office on Sept. 16, 1847, with James B. Foot as its first postmaster; the office was closed on Nov. 15, 1861, but was restored from Dec. 16, 1862, to Dec. 18, 1883, and since Feb. 12, 1884 [H. L. Latchaw, PM; Bonner; PO Archives].

**SENEY**, Schoolcraft County: when the Alger, Smith Company began logging in the vicinity about 1882, Seney came into being; it was named for George R. Seney, of New York, a director of the first railroad from St. Ignace to Marquette; John F. Chisholm became its first postmaster on Dec. 28, 1882; "the most notorious town in the lumbering era . . . it was a rough place" [Martin; Dunbar; PO Archives].

**SENTER**, Houghton County: a station on the Copper Range Railroad, in Portage Township; the settlement formed around the plant of the E.I. du Pont de Nemours Powder Company; Thomas M. Nichols became its first postmaster on April 30, 1910 [GSM 1911; PO Archives].

**SEOLA**, Monroe County: a station on the Toledo & Ann Arbor Railroad, in Ida Township, in 1878 [GSM 1879].

**SERRADELLA**, Iosco County. See Cedarmere.

**SETHTON**, Gratiot County: it began as a trading point in New Haven Township, and was named for Seth Gardner who became its first postmaster on June 14, 1882; the office was closed on Oct. 6, 1885, but was restored from Aug. 3, 1887, to Dec. 14, 1904 [PO Archives; Tucker].

**SEUL CHOIX**, Schoolcraft County: the name of a harbor and a point on Lake Michigan, meaning in French, only choice [Sawyer].

**SEVASTOPOL,** Eaton County. See West Windsor.

**SEVILLE,** Gratiot County: it was first settled by John D. Mallory in 1855, followed by Henry Boyd later the same year; the township was organized in 1856, with Carlisle Weeks as its first supervisor; given a station on the C., S. & C. (now Pere Marquette) Railroad; William G. Faulkner became its first postmaster on Oct. 20, 1875, serving until the office was closed on Jan. 8, 1884 [Tucker; Chapman].

**SEYMOUR LAKE,** Oakland County: in 1836, John B. Seymour, a New Yorker, took up land on the south shore of the lake which has since borne his name; farmer William J. Sherwood became the first postmaster of this office in Brandon Township on March 4, 1878, the office operating until June 24, 1901; now a resort community [Seeley; GSM 1879; PO Archives].

**SHABBONA,** Sanilac County: Robert Wilson became the first settler here in 1864 and the first supervisor when Evergreen Township was organized in 1872; from its location in the township, the village was called Evergreen Center, but when it was given a post office as Shabbona, it took the same name; George H. Jones became its first postmaster on March 21, 1884 [Chapman; PO Archives].

**SHACKSBORO,** Ingham County. See Podunk.

**SHADYSIDE,** Hillsdale County: this resort village on Bird Lake, in Jefferson Township, was given a post office named Acorn on Jan. 22, 1896, with Francis M. Van Orsdale as its first postmaster; with storekeeper M. E. Cromer as postmaster, the office was renamed Shadyside on July 21, 1897, and it operated until Sept. 15, 1903 [GSM 1897-1905; PO Archives].

**SHAFTSBURG,** Shiawassee County: this station on the Grand Trunk Railroad, in Woodhull Township, was founded on land bought in 1846 by John P. Shaft, for whom it was named; he platted the village and built its first hotel; Newton Bacon, dry goods merchant, became the first postmaster of Shaftsburgh on Jan. 19, 1880, with the spelling changed to Shaftsburg on May 25, 1891 [Ellis; PO Archives].

**SHAKESPEARE,** Cass County: it was platted and recorded by Jonathan Brown and Elias B. Sherman, at the Long Rapids of the Dowagiac River, in 1836; although many of its more than a thousand lots were sold, no building was ever built, and it remained a paper village [Glover; Fox].

**SHALDA'S CORNERS,** Leelanau County: Joseph Shalda settled in North Unity in the 1850s and when that community was destroyed by fire about 1871, he and his family and others settled here on present M-22 [Dickinson].

**SHANGHAI CORNERS,** Berrien County. See Pipestone.

**SHANTY PLAINS,** Montcalm County: this settlement in Fair Plains

Township was named from the many frail dwellings first built here, before 1850; its early settlers were transient and left no record of names or dates; it was also the site of a school for several terms [Schenck].

**SHANTYVILLE,** Newaygo County. See Lake.

**SHARON,** Kalkaska County: farmer George Johnson became the first postmaster of this rural post office in Springfield Township on March 11, 1891 [GSM 1893].

**SHARON,** Ontonagon County: a 160-acre copper mining location, two miles west of Norwich; the Sharon Mine opened in 1852 [Stevens].

**SHARON,** Washtenaw County: Lewis C. Kellam and Daniel C. Luce located the first land in the area in 1830, but Ira Anabil, Amos Bullard, and John Bessey became the first actual settlers in 1831; the settlement was known as Peppergrass until the township was organized in 1834 and named after Sharon, Connecticut; the Richfield post office, opened in Feb., 1832, with Joseph O. Gilbert as its first postmaster, was changed to Sharon, with Oliver Kellogg as postmaster, on Jan. 15, 1836, the office operating until July 15, 1855 [MPH 2:522 1877, 4:397 1881; GSM 1839; PO Archives].

**SHARON PLAIN,** Washtenaw County: John Feather became the first postmaster of this rural post office, named after its township, on June 24, 1867, the office operating until only Sept. 18, 1867; see Sharon for the name [PO Archives].

**SHARONVILLE,** Washtenaw County: this rural post office in Sharon Township was opened on Dec. 14, 1891, with Couch C. Dorr as its first postmaster, the office operating until Sept. 15, 1899; see Sharon for the name [PO Archives].

**SHARPSVILLE,** Lapeer County: although this village in Burnside Township was founded in 1874, it was not given a post office until Feb. 17, 1892, when John McRae became its first postmaster; originally a rural post office in Sanilac County, it was transferred to Lapeer County on Dec. 14, 1893, with storekeeper John H. Pringle as its postmaster; the office operated until Jan. 14, 1904 [GSM 1875-1905; PO Archives].

**SHATTUCKVILLE,** Saginaw County: this settlement on Thorn Creek, in Saginaw Township, was named for flour mill owner Samuel N. Shattuck, who served as its first and only postmaster, from March 6, 1877, to Nov. 20, 1878 [GSM 1879; PO Archives].

**SHAVEHEAD,** Cass County: William W. Rice became the first postmaster of this rural post office in Porter Township on July 13, 1858; the office was closed on June 26, 1865, but was restored from Oct. 30, 1865, to June 25, 1872, and from Nov. 10, 1879, to Feb. 5, 1888; it was named for Chief Shave Head (as were also Shavehead Lake and Shavehead Prairie), who with his band occupied the area from about 1775-1830 [Fox; MPH 28:162 1897; PO Archives].

**SHAW,** Newaygo County: Edward G. Hulse became the first postmaster of this settlement in Beaver Township, five miles from Bitely, on July 30, 1897, the office operating until Aug. 16, 1909 [GSM 1913; PO Archives].

**SHAW,** Presque Isle County. See Onaway.

**SHAYTOWN,** Eaton County: a station on the Grand Rapids division of the Michigan Central Railroad, in Sunfield Township; storekeeper Albert C. Jarvis became the first postmaster of the settlement on Feb. 11, 1880; the office was closed on Jan. 20, 1894, but was restored from Jan. 25, 1898, to Feb. 14, 1901 [Durant; GSM 1881; PO Archives].

**SHEARER,** Arenac County: a station on the Detroit, Bay City & Alpena Railroad; storekeeper Edwin F. Alexander became the first postmaster of this sawmill settlement on May 22, 1889, the office operating until Sept. 1, 1898 [GSM 1891; PO Archives].

**SHEBAHYONK,** Huron County: a Sebewaing and Chippewa Indian village, near the village of Sebewaing; they bought the land here from the government in 1847, but sold it and emigrated in 1856 [Chapman].

**SHEFFIELD,** Kent County: a station on the Toledo, Saginaw & Muskegon Railroad in 1888, with S. D. Saunders as its railroad agent; Charles Sipple became its first postmaster on March 6, 1891, and this post office in Cortland Township operated until April 30, 1906 [GSM 1893; PO Archives].

**SHELBY,** Macomb County: William Smith became the first postmaster of this settlement on May 3, 1824; the office was transferred to and renamed Utica on June 17, 1836, but on the same day, the Shelby post office was re-established, with Tobias Rice as the postmaster, and the office operated until Feb. 17, 1842; it was given a station on a branch of the Grand Trunk Railroad; see Shelby, Oceana County, for the name [Pen Phil 9:4 June 1958; PO Archives].

**SHELBY,** Oceana County: it was first called Churchill's Corners for Walter H. Churchill who became its first postmaster on Feb. 28, 1866, but the office was named Shelby; to connect the town with the railroad, which came through in 1872, S. A. Browne, Orrin Deming, and Alexander Pittenger platted it; they named it Barnett after a brakeman who, in return, agreed to pay recording fees, but reneged; in 1873, Martin L. Sweet and Andreas Bevier made an adjacent plat and recorded it as Shelby; both plats were incorporated as the village of Shelby in 1885; General Isaac Shelby, with his Kentucky Rangers, helped recapture Detroit from the British in the War of 1812 [Royal; Hartwick; PO Archives].

**SHELBYVILLE,** Allegan County: the village began as a station on the Grand Rapids & Indiana Railroad in 1870, and was named for the first station agent, Mr. Shelby; but there was then another Shelby post office in Michigan, so when this village was given a post office on May 2, 1872, with Leonard M. Doxy as its first postmaster, the "ville" was added [Esther W. Hettinger; PO Archives].

**SHELDON,** Wayne County: this hamlet was also known as Sheldon's

Corners after Perry Sheldon who, with David Cady and Childs Downer, became the first settlers here in 1825; the township was erected in 1834 and named Canton (merely to avoid duplication, two other Wayne County townships were also given Chinese names: Nankin and Pekin); a station on the Michigan Central Railroad and a post office, named Canton, from Jan. 24, 1852, to March 17, 1857; Asa Parrish was the first postmaster [Burton; GSM 1865-73; PO Archives].

**SHELLDRAKE,** Chippewa County: the village began as a lumbering settlement; George N. Hutton became its first postmaster on April 12, 1895; the office was closed on Sept. 15, 1908, but was restored on Dec. 8, 1911, with Lena M. O'Brien as its postmaster; it was named after the merganser or shelldrake duck, a fish feeder frequenting the shores of Whitefish Bay [Hamilton; PO Archives].

**SHEMACOPINK,** Leelanau County. See Leland.

**SHEPARDSVILLE,** Clinton County: this village on the Detroit & Milwaukee Railroad was platted as Shepard's Station in 1856 by William Shepard, who in that year opened a store here; later he built a grist mill and a sawmill; from its location in Ovid Township, it was given a post office as Ovid Centre on May 14, 1857, with Mr. Shepard as its first postmaster; it was renamed Shepardsville on Jan. 11, 1867; its post office operated until June 15, 1935 [Ellis; Daboll, PO Archives].

**SHEPHERD,** Isabella County: the village was founded by lumberman Isaac N. Shepherd and others; from its location by the Salt River, it was given a post office as Salt River on Aug. 8, 1857, with William R. Robbins as its first postmaster, and he held the office until at least 1873; the village was platted by Elijah Moore in 1866; the railroad came through in 1885 and built its depot on Mr. Shepherd's land, so for a time the station was named Shepherd and the post office Salt River; but on March 8, 1887, the post office was moved to and renamed Shepherd; fire destroyed most of Salt River that year, but present-day Shepherd envelops the old Salt River site; incorporated as a village in 1889 [Ruth C. Lau; PO Archvies].

**SHEPHERD'S CORNERS,** Eaton County: Hiram Shepherd bought a tract of land about two miles east of Charlotte in 1837, then went east for his family, returning with them in 1840; after moving two or three times, he settled for the rest of his life at what became known as Shepherd's Corners [Mich Hist 7:16 1923].

**SHEPHERD'S MILL,** Huron County: a mill settlement in the southern end of the county in 1884 [GSM 1885].

**SHERIDAN,** Barry County. See Morgan.

**SHERIDAN,** Calhoun County: it was first settled in 1831 by Reuben Abbott and his family, from Erie, N.Y.; he built Abbott's Tavern and on May 2, 1834, became the first postmaster, with the office named Kalamazoo; it was changed to Waterburgh on Dec. 23, 1835, and operated until May 19, 1843; Sheridan Township was organized in 1836, and later this village in it took its name; a station on the Michigan Central Railroad [GSM 1838-60; PO ARchives; Everts].

**SHERIDAN,** Huron County: John McIntosh settled here in 1859 and when the township was organized in 1866, he became its first supervisor; it was named for General Philip H. Sheridan [Hey; Gwinn].

**SHERIDAN,** Mecosta County: Edward P. Strong became the first settler here in 1866 and the first supervisor when the township, named for General Philip H. Sheridan, was organized in 1867 [Chapman].

**SHERIDAN,** Montcalm County: Louis Lovell entered land here in 1851; John W. Winsor built the first business, a sawmill; Erastus P. Brown, a shingle-mill owner, became the first postmaster on Oct. 14, 1864; a station on the Toledo, Saginaw & Muskegon Railroad; incorporated as a village in 1877; it was named for General Philip H. Sheridan [Schenck].

**SHERMAN,** Allegan County. See Bravo.

**SHERMAN,** Mason County: this township, organized in 1867, was named for General William T. Sherman, with William Barnhart as its first supervisor [Page].

**SHERMAN,** Muskegon County: Warren A. Sherwood became the first postmaster of this rural post office, named for General William T. Sherman, on March 19, 1866, the office operating until only Nov. 3, 1866 [PO Archives].

**SHERMAN,** St. Joseph County: the first settler in the township (which was named for another pioneer settler, Colonel Benjamin Sherman) was Thomas Cade, Sr., a native of Hull, England, who arrived in 1830 and built his log house and began to farm; when Sturgis was first platted in 1832, it was called Sherman, for it was then in Sherman Township; Philip H. Buck became the first postmaster of Sherman on Aug. 23, 1841, with the office changed to Sturgis on Dec. 29, 1845 [Everts; PO Archives].

**SHERMAN,** Wexford County: Lewis J. Clark opened a store nearby in 1867 and moved into the village-to-be in 1868; it was by the Manistee River and was first called Manistee Bridge; on Feb. 3, 1868, it was given a post office as Sherman, after General William T. Sherman; the first postmaster, John Perry, was succeeded by Mr. Clark in 1869; the village was platted by Sanford Gasser in 1869 and was the first county seat from 1869 to 1881; incorporated as a village in 1887; three fires, the last one in 1912, wiped out its business district [Mich Hist 5:440 1921; Barnes; PO Archives].

**SHERMAN CITY,** Isabella County: the township was organized in 1868 and named for General William T. Sherman; its village, named after it, was given a post office on Feb. 24, 1871, with Amos S. Johnson as its first postmaster, the office operating until Oct. 15, 1913; the village was platted by John Cahoon in 1873 [Chapman; GS, 1873; PO Archives].

**SHERMAN'S MILL,** Benzie County: a lumber settlement with a station on the Manistee & Northwestern Railroad in 1888 [GSM 1895].

**SHERWELL,** Wayne County: this rural post office, opened on June 15, 1899, was named for Walter S. Sherwell, its first postmaster; the office operated until Dec. 31, 1902 [PO Archives].

**SHERWOOD,** Branch County: laid out in 1832 on the farm of E. F. Hazen, it was first called Hazenville; it was given a post office as Durham on March 8, 1833, with Lot Whitcomb as its first postmaster; on June 10, 1839, it was renamed Sherwood in honor of its first settler, Alexander E. Tomlinson, who had come from Sherwood Forest, England; the office was closed on Dec. 4, 1866, but on April 16, 1868, the Newstead post office was transferred to and renamed Sherwood; when the Michigan Central Railroad came through in 1871, it was given a station; incorporated as a village in 1887 [Robert Van Aken; GSM 1860; PO Archives].

**SHERWOOD,** Wayne County: a station on the Detroit & Northwestern Electric Railway, in Greenfield Township, then three miles from Detroit; Julia E. Watch became its first postmaster in 1900 says the Gazeteer 1901, but there is no official record of it [GSM 1901; PO Archives].

**SHERWOOD'S MILLS,** Allegan County: this settlement on Pine Creek near its junction with the Kalamazoo River had two sawmills and a grist mill and was the oldest settlement in the county [GSM 1838].

**SHETLAND,** Leelanau County: farmer Peter Whitney became the first postmaster of this rural post office in Cleveland Township on May 26, 1884, the office operating until Feb. 14, 1905 [GSM 1885; PO Archives].

**SHIAWASSEETOWN,** Shiawassee County: the town, township and county were named from the Indian word for the river that twists about, and the Shiawassee River does; the village originated with Charles Bacon, an adventurer from Ohio, who formed a company to buy and resell land here; the village was platted and recorded in 1836; it was given a post office as Shiawassee on July 12, 1837, with Lemuel Brown as its first postmaster; the office was renamed Shiawassee Town on May 26, 1857, changed to North Newberg on Aug. 4, 1863, and closed on Aug. 26, 1893 [Ellis; PO Archives].

**SHIELDS,** Saginaw County: storekeeper Benjamin W. Sayers became the first postmaster of this rural community in Thomastown Township on Aug. 15, 1894, the office operating until Dec. 15, 1902 [GSM 1895; PO Archives].

**SHILOH,** Ionia County: a station on the Ionia and Stanton branch railroad, in Orleans Township; it was given a post office as Smith's Crossing on Jan. 15, 1877, with Charles Hoyt as its first postmaster; the name was changed to commemorate the American Civil War battle at Shiloh, on Dec. 31, 1877, and the office operated until April 30, 1935 [Schenck; GSM 1879; Branch; PO Archives].

**SHINGLE DIGGINGS,** Berrien County: about 1834, Levi Ballengee bought land here and opened a boarding house for the men building a mill on the Paw Paw River for Griffith & Company of St. Joseph; the company failed and he went into the shingle making business; a thriving settlement grew up but was abandoned after the timber supply was exhausted in 1838 [Mich Hist 43:438 1959].

**SHINGLETON,** Alger County: a station on the Detroit, Mackinaw & Marquette Railroad in 1882, named Jeromeville for David H. Jerome, the first native born governor of Michigan, 1881-83; the site of a shingle mill, it was given a post office as Shingleton, with James M. Carr becoming its first postmaster on Sept. 20, 1887; the office was closed on May 25, 1897, but was restored since Nov. 26, 1891 [Mich Hist 26:75 1942; David S. Coon; GSM 1883; PO Archives].

**SHINGLETOWN,** Saginaw County: a lumber settlement in 1884 [GSM 1885].

**SHIRLAND,** Kalamazoo County: a village in Prairie Ronde Township, platted and recorded in 1831; it may have been named for pioneer settler John Shirley, but he was not one of the five proprietors; it never developed [Durant].

**SHOARDS,** Isabella County: it began as a lumber mill settlement about 1870, but did not survive [Fancher].

**SHOOK'S PRAIRIE,** Branch County. See Butler.

**SHORE ACRES,** Cass County. See Geneva.

**SHOREHAM,** Berrien County: it was founded by William Ducker who had a fine home here and wanted to keep the area residential; incorporated as a village in 1930; its full length was along the Lake Michigan shore and he, being English, liked the "ham" ending, so he named it Shoreham [Juniata V. Cupp].

**SHOREWOOD HILLS,** Berrien County: unincorp. village (including Flower Hills), southwest of Benton Harbor; named from its proximity to Lake Michigan [Columbia Ency.].

**SHOUP,** Oakland County: a station on the Pontiac, Oxford & Northern Railroad, in Addison Township; the settlement formed around the brick making plant of Elwell Ivory; he became its first postmaster on July 21, 1884, the office operating until June 29, 1901 [GSM 1885; PO Archives].

**SHULTZ,** Barry County: a station on the Chicago, Kalamazoo & Saginaw Railroad, in Hope Township; James A. Babcock became its first postmaster on Nov. 24, 1888, succeeded by storekeeper G. H. Otis in 1890, the office operating until July 31, 1933 [GSM 1891; PO Archives].

**SIBBEWAING,** Huron County. See Sebewaing.

**SIBLEY,** Wayne County: limestone was quarried here as early as 1749; about 1823, Solomon Sibley, of Detroit, bought the quarry property; he, and later his sons, developed the mining operations around which the village grew; its station on the Canada Southern Railroad was called Sibley Station; it was given a post office as Sibley on Feb. 27, 1903, with James Bailey, Jr., as its first postmaster; incorporated as a village in 1920; it was annexed by Trenton in 1929, but the name is still used to refer to that section of Trenton [Isabella E. Swan; PO Archives; Burton].

**SIBLEY'S CORNERS**, Oakland County. See Wixon.

**SICKELS**, Gratiot County: William Sickels owned land here in Hamilton Township in 1880 and his wife, Emma C. Sickels became the first postmaster on Feb. 8, 1881, with the office spelled Sickles; she was succeeded in office by Jasper C. Sickels in 1882, the office operating until Dec. 14, 1904; the village was platted and recorded by Thomas H. Harrod for William Sickels and Sheldon L. Wight, proprietors, on Feb. 20, 1882; William (later Judge) Sickels built a grist mill here in 1883 [Chapman: Tucker; PO Archives].

**SIDDONS**, Mason County: William Freeman became the first postmaster of this rural post office by the Sable River, in Grant Township, on Feb. 20, 1882; the office was closed on Feb. 21, 1888, but was restored from April 17, 1888, to July 15, 1902 [PO Archives; GSM 1883].

**SIDNAW**, Houghton County: this village in Duncan Township was founded by lumbering firms harvesting white pine; its first subdivision was platted by Thomas Nester in 1889, followed by Gunlak A. Bergland, and the Michigan Iron & Land Company; a station on the Duluth, South Shore & Atlantic Railroad; storekeeper George Garland became its first postmaster on Dec. 7, 1889; Sidnaw is an Indian word for a small hill by a creek,–property descriptions still bear "addition to Hill Creek" [Walter Beck; GSM 1891; PO Archives].

**SIDNEY**, Genesee County. See Flint.

**SIDNEY**, Montcalm County: Phineas Swift, a New Yorker, became the first regular settler here in 1854; Joshua V. Noah became the first postmaster on Sept. 29, 1862; it was named after its township which was erected in 1857 and named for Sidney, Ohio, whence some of its early settlers had come [Schenck; PO Archives].

**SIEMENS**, Gogebic County: a station, between Bessemer and Ironwood, on the Chicago & Northwestern Railroad, in 1894; it was named for the Siemen brothers, local sawmill owners, as was nearly Siemens Creek [Victor Lemmer].

**SIGEL**, Huron County: when organized in 1863, Sigel Township was named for General Franz Seigel of Civil War fame, but there is no explanation as to why the spelling of the name was changed; the town was given a post office on April 6, 1882, with Major Cowper as its first postmaster, the office operating until July 15, 1903 [PO Archives; Hey].

**SIGMA**, Kalkaska County: a station on the M. & N.E. Railroad and a general store, 10 miles from Kalkaska, in 1910; William T. Kirkby became its first postmaster on May 13, 1914; see Epsilon for its naming [GSM 1911-15; PO Archives].

**SIGSBEE,** Crawford County: this summer resort on the Au Sable River, in Grayling Township, was given a post office on April 26, 1899, with Hugo Schreiber as its first postmaster, the office operating until 1928; it was named for Captain (later Admiral) Charles D. Sigsbee, commander of the battleship Maine when it was blown up in Havana harbor in 1898 [Grace L. Funsch; PO Archives].

**SILOAM,** Iosco County: Emma M. Hitchcock became the first postmaster of this settlement on Jan. 17, 1889 [PO Archives].

**SILVER,** Houghton County: a mining location in Laird Township; saloon keeper Andrew W. Dahlberg became its first postmaster on March 21, 1898 [GSM 1899; PO Archives].

**SILVER CITY,** Ontonagon County: Austin Corser announced his discovery of silver in this locality in 1872, and that year Daniel Beaser platted Silver City; buildings were erected and there was a hotel; but the mine was not profitable and it and the city closed in 1876 [Jamison].

**SILVER CREEK,** Allegan County: a village with a railroad station, in Gun Plain Township; David E. Deming became the first postmaster of Ynouski post office in Kalamazoo County, on May 10, 1844; with John W. Baker as its postmaster, the office was transferred to Silver Creek on May 4, 1854; the office operated here until Dec. 30, 1933 [GSM 1873; PO Archives].

**SILVER CREEK,** Cass County: James McDaniel made the first land purchase here in 1834 and became the first settler in 1835; previously a part of Pokagon, Silver Creek Township was established in 1837; Silver Creek is the outlet of Magician Lake, first called Silver Lake because of its silvery appearance due to its marl bottom; James Allen became the first postmaster on May 10, 1838, with the office renamed Indian Lake on May 18, 1852, but changed back to Silver Creek on Oct. 4, 1852; the office operated until Aug. 22, 1853 [Vanderburg; Mathews; PO Archives].

**SILVER LAKE,** Grand Traverse County: Henry D. Campbell became the first postmaster of this rural post office on March 14, 1864; the office was closed on May 28, 1864, but was transferred to Betsey Lake on Jan. 27, 1868; the Silver Lake post office was re-established on May 25, 1868, and operated until June 13, 1870 [PO Archives].

**SILVER LAKE,** Oakland County: in 1819, Major Oliver Williams, of Detroit, cut his own road through the woods and settled here on the south bank of Silver Lake, in Waterford Township [MPH 10:194 1886].

**SILVER LAKE,** Oceana County: Carrie Mears had some of her land on the northeast shore platted and sold as lots, for a resort community, in 1945 [Royal].

**SILVER LAKE,** Washtenaw County: James W. Hill became the first postmaster of this rural post office on Aug. 15, 1843, the office operating until Sept. 3, 1856 [PO Archives].

**SILVERWOOD**, Tuscola County: when the Pere Marquette Railroad came through here in Dayton Township in 1882, the residents applied for a post office, one suggesting they name the village something easy to remember; thus, on April 13, 1882, they came to get a post office named Easy, with James R. Chapin as its first postmaster; the name was changed to Rollo on March 27, 1890, and on May 2, 1892, from its splendid stand of white pine, Silverwood [Charles Shaver, PM].

**SIMMONS**, Mackinac County: this settlement in Newton Township formed around the mill of the Simmons Lumber Company; Louis Van Valkenburg became its first postmaster on May 20, 1903, the office operating until Feb. 15, 1911 [GSM 1905; PO Archives].

**SIMONS**, Antrim County: a station on the Grand Rapids & Indiana Railroad, in Chestonia Township in 1876; lumberman Walter A. Williams became its first postmaster on Dec. 4, 1886, the office operating until Nov. 21, 1898 [GSM 1887-99; PO Archives].

**SINGAPORE**, Allegan County: in 1837, Oshea Wilder and his sons, from New York, bought a large tract of land near the mouth of the Kalamazoo River from the Barnes family (the patentees) and in 1838 laid out the village, which they named after a famous foreign seaport to attract settlers; the Wilders sold many lots, had a mill built and, in 1839, opened a bank; but the whole venture struggled in vain against failure, though it was not completely abandoned until 1875 [Mich Hist 35:226 1951; Johnson].

**SINGERVILLE**, Keweenaw County: this summer resort post office on Isle Royale was named for Edward T. Singer who became its first postmaster on July 19, 1913 [GSM 1915].

**SINK BROOK**, Allegan County: Willard E. Field became the first postmaster of this rural post office on June 18, 1861; the office was transferred to Rabbit River on July 9, 1864, and was renamed Hamilton on May 19, 1870 [PO Archives].

**SINSINAWA**, Iowa County: George W. Jones became the first postmaster of this post office on Dec. 8, 1834; it was then in Michigan Territory, but is now in Wisconsin [PO Archives].

**SIORITE**, Marquette County: Adolph C. Hubermann became the first postmaster of this rural post office on Oct. 23, 1888, the office operating until July 9, 1890 [PO Archives].

**SIPLON**, Newaygo County: a substation of the Fremont post office, named from its having been located in Herb Siplon's store [PO Archives].

**SISKIWIT**, Keweenaw County: the name of a falls, adjacent islands, a lake, an old mine, an outlet, two rivers (Big and Little Siskiwit), as well as of a village site; the Siskowitt Mining Company operated here near Rock Harbor, on Isle Royale, from 1845 to 1855; on some maps as Siskowit, the name was derived from the Chippewa name for a species of lake trout [Mich Hist 41:1 1957].

**SISSON**, Newaygo County: the settlement was founded by the Sisson

& Lilley Lumber Company (George E. Sisson and Francis Lilley), of Grand Haven, who built a mill here about 1884 [Harry L. Spooner].

**SISSON**, Lenawee County: it was named for Thomas Sisson who bought his land here, six miles northeast of Tecumseh, before 1840; its station on the Lake Shore & Michigan Southern Railroad was called Sisson's, and operated from 1878 to 1908 [Whitney; Mich Hist 38:409 1954].

**SISTER LAKES**, Van Buren County: it was first used as a camping ground by E. Pardee and A. Mykes in 1868; later, several other families camped here in tents too; in 1876, Mr. Pardee bought the land for $100 an acre, cleared off the underbrush, and built a summer resort; Jerome W. Decker became its first postmaster on Sept. 12, 1877, the office operating until April 30, 1957; it was so named because of the two adjacent lakes [Madalyn Bradford; PO Archives].

**SITKA**, Newaygo County: Halby W. Crawford became the first postmaster of this hamlet in Sheridan Township, on Dec. 14, 1868; its naming was evidently influenced by Sitka being in the news as then the capital of Alaska which the U.S. had just purchased from Russia in 1867; the post office was closed on Feb. 2, 1885, but was restored from Dec. 15, 1891, to Oct. 31, 1901 [GSM 1875-1903; PO Archives].

**SIX CORNERS**, Ottawa County: a village in southwestern Chester Township; it had a railroad station and its post office, opened on Feb. 21, 1855, with Albert V. Heyden as its first postmaster, operated until Feb. 4, 1888 [Page; GSM 1877; PO Archives].

**SIX LAKES**, Montcalm County: this village, with a station on the C., S. & C. Railroad, in Belvidere Township, was founded, platted and named by Hiram Clark and Dr. J. B. Daniels in 1876; Alexander M. Hunt became its first postmaster on Dec. 20, 1878; it was named from its proximity to six lakes, now all connected by channels [Schenck].

**SIX MILE CREEK**, Shiawassee County: a hamlet in 1864 [GSM 1865].

**SIXTEEN**, Midland County. See Edenville.

**SKANDIA**, Marquette County: a station on the Munising Railroad; storekeeper Albert H. Peterson became its first postmaster on Dec. 8, 1902; a Scandinavian village, its name means Little Scandinavia [GSM 1905; PO Archives].

**SKANEE**, Baraga County: Captain Walfred Been came here into Huron Bay for shelter from a storm in 1870 and so liked the land that he saw here in Arvon Township that he stayed to found a village, naming it after his home province of Skäne in Sweden; he became its first postmaster on June 23, 1876 [Marvin R. Lindahl, PM].

**SKEELS**, Gladwin County: the first settlers here in Sherman Township were Peter Tressler in 1887 and Simon P. Skeels in 1888, both Civil War veterans; Mr. Skeels opened the first store in 1892; it was in his log house as was the post office of which he became the first postmaster on March 3, 1898, naming it for himself [PO Archives; Ritchie].

**SKINNER,** Bay County. See Auburn.

**SKIPPERVILLE,** Ionia County. See Clarksville.

**SLACHTBURG,** Mason County. See Amber.

**SLAPNECK,** Alger County: John F. Slapneck, of Alleghany, Pa., became a landlooker for a logging outfit in this area in 1881 and this village, named for him, became a whistle stop on the Marquette & Southeastern Railroad; the Slapneck school dates from 1905 [Munising News, June 29, 1906; E. H. Rankin].

**SLATER MISSION,** Barry County. See Prairieville.

**SLAYTON,** Kent County: this village in Grattan Township began with the vinegar factory of E. J. Mason in 1860 and was first named Grant; but there was already a Grant post office in Michigan and this village was renamed for William C. Slayton who became its first postmaster on May 19, 1898, the office operating until July 15, 1902 [Chapman; GSM 1869-1903; PO Archives].

**SLAYTON,** Ogemaw County: this village in Klacking Township was formed around the mill of the Slayton Lumber Company in 1878 and was named for E. T. Slayton, formerly of Lapeer; storekeeper Austin Abbott became its first postmaster on Sept. 22, 1879, the office operating until June 22, 1883 [GSM 1881; PO Archives].

**SLEEPING BEAR POINT,** Leelanau County: legend has it that three bears, a mother and two cubs, were driven from Wisconsin by a forest fire; they swam for the Michigan shore, but the cubs lost their strength and rested while the mother made the shore and lay down exhausted; the cubs became islands and the mother, waiting in sleep for the cubs, became the point of land since known as Sleeping Bear Point; this point is a clump of pine trees and shrubs, clustered together insuch a manner as, by contrast to the whiteness of the sand below, to resemble a black bear in a sleeping posture; the site appears as L'Ours qui Dort, on Jean Baptiste Franquelin's Carte de l'Amerique Septentrionnalle, Quebec, 1688 [Atwell; Clements Lib., U. of Mich.].

**SLIGHTS,** Grand Traverse County: its two-way station on the Grand Rapids & Indiana Railroad was first named Sleights, its post office Slights; this settlement in Blair Township formed around the sawmill of Kelley & Covell; Charles T. Covell became its first postmaster on March 3, 1893, succeeded by Walter N. Kelley on March 23, 1895, and Frank S. Dean on April 23, 1898; the office was changed to Keystone on Dec. 21, 1898 [GSM 1895; PO Archives].

**SLOCUM,** Muskegon County: Giles Bryan Slocum (1808-1884) built a sawmill here on Crockery Creek, in Casnovia Township, about 1865; the settlement was given a post office as Slocum's Grove on July 30, 1867, with Epiphalet Johnson as its first postmaster; Elliott T. Slocum became the postmaster on May 29, 1878, and he platted the village in 1888; its name was shortened to Slocum on June 30, 1894 [Page; GSM 1895; PO Archives].

**SLOCUM JUNCTION,** Wayne County: a station at a junction of the Toledo and Fayette divisions of the Chicago & Canada Southern Railroad, a mile southwest of Trenton, in 1878 [GSM 1879].

**SLOCUM'S GROVE,** Muskegon County. See Slocum.

**SLOCUM'S ISLAND,** Wayne County: it was owned by and named for Giles Bryan Slocum; it remained in the family until 1919 when the heirs of Elizabeth Slocum gave it to the county which developed it into the first Wayne County park, naming it for her, Elizabeth Park; it is linked to the southern tip of Trenton by bridges [Farmer; Federal].

**SLY,** Midland County: Albert A. Anible became the first postmaster of this rural post office on Jan. 22, 1896, the office operating until Oct. 15, 1901 [PO Archives].

**SMATHERS,** Luce County: this rural post office was named for John Smathers who was appointed its first postmaster on Sept. 11, 1906, but it was rescinded on Dec. 6, 1906 [PO Archives].

**SMITH,** St. Clair County. See Allenton.

**SMITH CREEK,** Gladwin County: from about 1883, the Smith brothers operated a sawmill on the banks of the stream which now bears their name, and from which the community derives its name; it got its first school in 1886; later, the district voted to annex to Gladwin, so the school was closed [Ritchie].

**SMITHFIELD,** Jackson County: a rural post office conducted in the tavern of William W. Smith who became the first postmaster on May 7, 1834, the office operating until Feb. 14, 1845 [Mich Hist 43:270 1959].

**SMITH JUNCTION,** Iosco County: a station on a branch of the Detroit & Mackinaw Railroad, a mile east of South Branch, in 1894 [GSM 1895].

**SMITH MINE JUNCTION,** Marquette County: a station on the Chicago & Northwestern Railroad in 1878 [GSM 1879]

**SMITH'S,** Saginaw County: a hamlet two miles northwest of Birch Run in 1880 [GSM 1881].

**SMITH'S,** St. Clair County. See Allenton.

**SMITH'S CORNERS,** Huron County: it began as an Irish and German settlement in 1860 and was first called Bloomfield Heights; it was renamed for a Mr. Smith [Hey].

**SMITH'S CORNERS,** Oceana County: Joseph Walker became the first postmaster of this hamlet in Weare Township on Oct. 29, 1866; the office was closed on Jan. 28, 1879, but was restored from Feb. 27, 1879, to April 10, 1902; it was named for Norman C. Smith who was the supervisor of the township almost continuously from 1861 to 1877 [Royal; Page; PO Archives].

**SMITH'S CORNERS**, St. Clair County. See Allenton.

**SMITH'S CREEK**, St. Clair County: Elisha Smith was a landowner by the stream named for him, and the village took its name; John McSweeney became the first postmaster on Oct. 11, 1861; it was given a station on the Grand Trunk Railroad named Smith's Creek Station in 1865; it was the county seat from 1869 to April, 1871, when it was removed to Port Huron [Jenks; Schultz].

**SMITH'S CROSSING**, Ionia County. See Shiloh.

**SMITH'S CROSSING**, Midland County: a Pere Marquette Railroad station on the line between Midland, Bay and Saginaw Counties, and first called Smithville; it was given a post office of that name on July 3, 1872, with Henry B. Stowits as its first postmaster, the office operating until Nov. 18, 1873; on Feb. 4, 1890, it was given a post office as Smith's Crossing, with Frank L. Coon as its first postmaster, the office operating until July, 1911; but the place is still called Smith's Crossing [Chapman; GSM 1879; PO Archives].

**SMITH'S MILLS**, Lenawee County: a sawmill settlement in 1864 [GSM 1865].

**SMITHVILLE**, Hillsdale County. See Litchfield.

**SMITHVILLE**, Ingham County: somewhere about 1886 a man named Smith raised the dam at Smithville, and in 1890 the mill burned [Adams].

**SMITHVILLE**, Midland County. See Smith's Crossing.

**SMITHVILLE**, Wayne County: this hamlet in eastern Sumpter Township was given a post office as Woodville on April 12, 1852, with Lucius A. Winchester as its first postmaster; it was renamed Smithville on Jan. 18, 1858, but changed to Waltz on Feb. 19, 1872 [Burton; PO Archives].

**SMYRNA**, Ionia County: on March 16, 1848, Dr. Wilber Fisher obtained a rural post office named, at his suggestion, Smyrna; the first settler on the present village site was Calvin Smith in 1853; on Sept. 14, 1853, George W. Dickinson platted and recorded the village as Mount Vernon, after the Virginia estate of George Washington; the village was also known as Mount Vernon Mills, but its post office has remained Smyrna; the county was named after an ancient Greek province and Smyrna was a Grecian city, though now Turkish and called Izmir [Blanche Seeley; Branch; PO Archives].

**SNAY**, Sanilac County: this rural post office was named for storekeeper Charles Snay who became its first postmaster on April 5, 1892, the office operating until June 15, 1901 [GSM 1893-1903; PO Archives].

**SNELL**, Ionia County: this rural post office was named for George

Snell who became its first postmaster on Oct. 10, 1894, the office operating until Jan. 9, 1895 [PO Archives].

**SNOVER**, Sanilac County: Henry Harrison became the first postmaster of this village on May 7, 1895; it was named for Horace G. Snover who represented this district in congress from 1895 to 1898 [Schultz; PO Archives].

**SNOW**, Berrien County: a station in Lake Township on the St. Joseph-Galien branch of the Michigan Central Railroad, opened about 1875 [Fox].

**SNOWFLAKE**, Antrim County: storekeeper William W. Johnson became its first postmaster on May 6, 1879; the office was closed on Oct. 26, 1881, but was restored from Jan. 12, 1882, to Feb. 28, 1901; the settlement, also called Lakeside Farm, was on Intermediate Lake, in Forest Home Township; it was given a station on the Chicago & Western Michigan (now Pere Marquette) Railroad, named Snowflake, in 1891 [Cole; GSM 1881; PO Archives].

**SNOW PRAIRIE**, Branch County: Eleazer Snow came here from New England in 1830 and the place soon became known as Snow Prairie though he sold all his holdings to Moses Olmstead in 1831; from its location in Bethel Township it was given a post office as Bethel Centre on March 1, 1867, with Lorenzo D. Van Volkenburgh as its first postmaster, but it was renamed Snow Prairie on Sept. 19, 1867, and remained so until it was closed on June 15, 1869 [Mich Hist 33:222 1949; Johnson; PO Archives].

**SNOW'S LANDING**, Wayne County. See Rawsonville.

**SNOWTOWN**, Newaygo County: Christopher Culp built a dam and a sawmill here in 1855; in 1857, he sold them to John F. Snow, and henceforth it was called Snowtown, but it did not become a village [Harry L. Spooner].

**SNYDER'S**, Jackson County: this depot and business point in the southern part of Spring Arbor Township since the coming through of the Michigan Central Railroad in 1878 was also called Snyder's Station; it was given a post office as Snyder on Dec. 17, 1884, with Samuel D. Humphrey as its first postmaster; the office was closed on Aug. 2, 1886, but was restored from May 15, 1889, to Oct. 31, 1904; it was named from its being on the land of Louis Snyder, Jr., a pioneer settler [DeLand; PO Archives].

**SNYDER'S MILL**, Delta County: this lumbermill and camp on the Whitefish branch of the Chicago & Northwestern Railroad was named after Harry Snyder, the mill operator [G. T. Springer].

**SNYDERVILLE**, St. Clair County: a hamlet on US-25, 18 miles southwest of Port Huron, in 1926 [GSM 1927].

**SOBIESKI**, Menominee County: it is a small farming community along the Menominee River, together with a few summer cottages; it was first settled by Poles in 1906 and they gave it the name of one of their kings, John Sobieski; its school has been closed but it has a Catholic church, served weekends from Menominee [Mrs. Ethyl Schuyler].

**SOBIESKI**, Presque Isle County: a Polish settlement with a station on the Detroit & Mackinaw Railroad; Anthony Chappa became its first postmaster on March 7, 1910, the office operating until Oct. 31, 1912; it was named for King John Sobieski of Poland [GSM 1911; PO Archives].

**SOCIETY LAKES**, Oakland County: they were named from their proximity to each other; a resort colony southwest of White Lake, dating from 1838 [GSM 1839].

**SODUS**, Berrien County: William H. and David Rector were the first permanent settlers here in 1835-36; in 1859, Sodus became a separate township and David Rector named it after his native town of Sodus, N.Y.; the village took the same name when given a post office on April 13, 1860, with Francis Finnegan as its first postmaster [Coolidge; PO Archives].

**SOLDIERS' HOME**, Kent County: this station on the Grand Rapids & Indiana Railroad was named for and largely served the Michigan Soldiers' Home, established in 1885 and completed in December, 1886, by the Grand River, then three miles north of Grand Rapids, on land donated by that city; Huntley Russell became its first postmaster on March 25, 1892, the office operating until Aug. 14, 1900 [GSM 1895; PO Archives].

**SOLON**, Kent County: it was first settled in 1854 by Mr. Beals and J. M. Rounds; the township was organized in 1857, with Edward Jewell as its first supervisor; the Solon Center school district was organized in 1858 [Dillenback].

**SOLON**, Leelanau County: it was first settled in the 1860s and named by families from Solon, Ohio; William F. Hannaford became its first postmaster on Feb. 13, 1870, the office operating until June 15, 1909; Moses C. Cate, a Civil War veteran and farmer, became the first supervisor of Solon Township in 1872 [Dickinson; Traverse].

**SOMERSET**, Hillsdale County: it was first settled by James D. Van Hoevenburg in 1832; in 1834, he sold his farm to Thomas Gamble who on Sept. 9, 1835, became the first postmaster, with the office named Wheatland after its township; the office was renamed Gambleville on Oct. 17, 1837, when the village was separated from Wheatland Township; in 1841, it was renamed Somerset and removed to Somerset Center; it retained that name when moved back to Gambleville, which was renamed Somerset about 1898; on June 19, 1872, with Oscar D. Brown as postmaster, it was given a post office as Somerset Centre, with the spelling changed to Somerset Center on Nov. 25, 1893; it was named after its township which had been named after Somerset, Niagara County, N.Y. [Pen Phil 7:3 Jan 1957; Howard R. Smith; PO Archives].

**SOMERSET CENTER**, Hillsdale County: Elias Alley built the first home here in 1833; it was named from its being near the center of the settled part of Somerset Township; for its naming and for its postal history see Somerset [Vivian L. Moore].

**SOMERVILLE**, Kent County. See Sparta.

**SONOMA**, Calhoun County: physician John J. Baker became the first postmaster at this station on the Michigan Central Railroad, in Leroy Township, on Jan. 18, 1886, the office operating until Nov. 14, 1903 [GSM 1887-1905; PO Archives].

**SOO JUNCTION**, Luce County: it was named from its location at the junction of the Soo branch and the St. Ignace branch of the old Duluth, South Shore and Atlantic Railroad, now the Soo Line; railroad agent Frank D. Griffin became its first postmaster on Jan. 19, 1891, the office operating until May 30, 1941 [GSM 1893; Kenneth Priestley; PO Archives].

**SOPER**, Wexford County: William Grandholm became the first postmaster of this sawmill settlement in Colfax Township on March 23, 1900, the office operating until Aug. 31, 1901 [GSM 1903; PO Archives].

**SOULETOWN**, Huron County: Charles F. Soule built a sawmill, a grist mill and a general store here on Pinnebog Creek, in Chandler Township, in 1876, and he became the first postmaster, with the office named Soule, on March 1, 1880, the office operating until Nov. 15, 1904 [Hey; PO Archives].

**SOUTH ALBION**, Calhoun County: Daniel Fulton, Jr., became the first postmaster of this hamlet in southern Albion Township on Aug. 29, 1842, the office operating until March 22, 1855; see Albion for the name [GSM 1860; PO Archives].

**SOUTH ALLEN**, Hillsdale County: Allen C. Howe became the first postmaster of this rural post office on June 4, 1883, the office operating until May 29, 1899; see Allen for the name [PO Archives].

**SOUTH ARM**, Charlevoix County: it was named from its location at the tip of the south arm of Pine Lake (now Lake Charlevoix); Soloman G. Isaman located on 80 acres of land here in 1867, built a log house and, about 1873, a general store; he became the first postmaster on Nov. 23, 1874, the office operating until June 30, 1905; South Arm was absorbed by the adjacent city of East Jordan in 1887 [Traverse; PO Archives].

**SOUTH ASSYRIA**, Barry County: the village of Assyria Center was given a post office as South Assyria on June 25, 1850, with Samuel H. Young as its first postmaster; the office was closed on July 24, 1855, but was restored from May 18, 1858, to Feb. 2, 1861; see Assyria for the name [Johnson; PO Archives].

**SOUTH BAY CITY**, Bay County: a station on the Pere Marquette Railroad in 1882 [GSM 1883].

**SOUTH BAYOU**, Mason County: it was first called Weimer for George Weimer, a Civil War captain who came to this area in 1867 and was one of the first Ludington businessmen to invest in resort property; Charles E. Bugg became the first postmaster of Weimer on Aug. 4, 1902, the office operating until May 31, 1904; the place is now known only as the South Bayou on Hamlin Lake [Rose D. Hawley; PO Archives].

**SOUTH BLENDON**, Ottawa County: this mill settlement was given a post office on Feb. 3, 1868, as Ohio Mill, with Charles E. Storrs as its first postmaster; the office was renamed South Blendon on April 9, 1872, and operated until Oct. 15, 1906; see Blendon for the name [Page; PO Archives].

**SOUTH BOARDMAN**, Kalkaska County: the railroad platted the village at the juncture where their line crossed the south branch of the Boardman River; Hamilton Stone bought their plat and with associates began operations in 1874; he built a depot and a hotel; Addison McCoy was another pioneer settler; George W. Briggs became the first postmaster on June 25, 1875; some records refer to it simply as Boardman [Traverse; Powers].

**SOUTH BOSTON**, Ionia County: Riley J. Hess became the first postmaster of this rural post office on Aug. 16, 1849, the office operating until April 23, 1875; see Boston for the name [PO Archives].

**SOUTH BRANCH**, Ogemaw County: the village was founded in 1887 and given a post office named Hunt on Jan. 17, 1889, with Frank Smith as its first postmaster; on Sept. 8, 1893, while Silas Doane was postmaster, it was renamed South Branch, from its location on the south branch of Smith Creek; the spelling was changed to Southbranch on April 14, 1894, but then later back to South Branch; a station on the Detroit & Mackinaw Railroad [PM; GSM 1895; PO Archives].

**SOUTH BUTLER**, Branch County: this settlement was first called Whig Center; from its location in Butler Township, it was given a post office as South Butler on June 10, 1867, with Jackson Pardee as its first postmaster; the office was closed on July 16, 1877, but was restored from Sept. 11, 1877, to Nov. 3, 1905; see Butler for the name [GSM 1891-1907; PO Archives].

**SOUTH CAMDEN**, Hillsdale County: this hamlet in southern Camden Township was given a post office on June 22, 1869, with Thomas E. Cooney as its first postmaster, the office operating until April 30, 1902 [GSM 1919; PO Archives].

**SOUTH CASS**, Ionia County. See Odessa.

**SOUTH CLIMAX**, Kalamazoo County. See West Climax.

**SOUTH EATON**, Eaton County. See Tyler.

**SOUTH FAIRFIELD**, Lenawee County: Rufus Rathbun became the first postmaster of this rural post office in Ogden Township on Feb. 23, 1874, the office operating until Nov. 14, 1903 [GSM 1883-1905; PO Archives].

**SOUTHFIELD**, Oakland County: John Wetmore made the first land entry here in 1821, but the first actual settler was John Daniels in 1823;

from its location in Southfield Township, it was better known as Southfield Centre, but it was given a post office as Southfield on Jan. 15, 1833, with John Thomas as its first postmaster; the post office was located at nearby Crawford Corners, named for Abraham Crawford, large landowner, but the water power afforded by the River Rouge favored the Southfield site, and business as well as post office moved there about 1838; this post office operated until March 15, 1904; Southfield remained a village until the suburban boom; incorporated as a city in 1958; Charles L. Curtis became the first postmaster of its restored post office on Sept. 2, 1959 [Patrick G. Flannery; PO Archives].

**SOUTH FRANKFORT**, Benzie County. See Elberta.

**SOUTHGATE**, Wayne County: the first white settler in the area, Pierre Michel Campau, came in 1795; a part of Ecorse Township, it was a farming community until incorporated as a village in 1955 and as a city in 1958; named from its being the southern entrance gateway to the metropolitan Detroit area [Thomas J. Anderson].

**SOUTH GENOA**, Livingston County: the Genoa post office was changed to South Genoa on March 13, 1863, and operated until March 25, 1867; named from its location in Genoa Township [GSM 1865-67; PO Archives].

**SOUTH GEORGETOWN**, Ottawa County. See Hudsonville.

**SOUTH GRAND BLANC**, Oakland County. See Newark.

**SOUTH GRAND RAPIDS**, Kent County: a station on the Grand Rapids & Indiana Railroad, then three miles from Grand Rapids; storekeeper Noah W. Crocker became its first postmaster on July 24, 1888, the office operating until Dec. 31, 1904 [GSM 1889; PO Archives].

**SOUTH HARRISVILLE**, Alcona County. See Springport.

**SOUTH HAVEN**, Van Buren County: Jay R. Monroe became the first settler here in 1831; Daniel Pierce, to whom he sold the land in 1838, was appointed the first postmaster in 1841, but declined; in 1850, Joseph B. Sturgis, as foreman for Marvin Hannahs, built a sawmill; it passed into the hands of A. S. Dyckman, a prime promotor of the village, which was platted by Thomas C. Sheldon and William A. Booth in 1851; Mr. Sturgis became the first postmaster on May 7, 1852; incorporated as a village in 1869 and as a city in 1902, with Evert S. Dyckman, elder son of A. S. Dyckman, as its first mayor; it was named after its township which was formed in the winter of 1836-37, and was located south of Grand Haven [Rowland; Ellis; PO Archives].

**SOUTH HAVEN LAND SYNDICATE**, Van Buren County: in 1910, they platted a village here along Lake Michigan; the enterprise failed after a few cottages had been erected and the state took it over in 1923; the county added 16 to its 100 acres to form Van Buren State Park [Federal].

**SOUTH HENRIETTA**, Jackson County: a rural post office in southern Henrietta Township with Henry Hurd becoming its first postmaster on Sept. 5, 1851, succeeded by William D. Martin on May 10, 1853, the office operating until Dec. 21, 1866; see Henrietta for the name [PO Archives].

**SOUTH IONIA,** Ionia County: across the Grand River from the city of Ionia, G. W. Arnold surveyed and mapped the hamlet in 1876 [Schenck].

**SOUTH JACKSON,** Jackson County: Hiram Cornell became the first postmaster of this rural post office in Summit Township on June 27, 1837; the office was closed on Oct. 31, 1873, but was restored from Nov. 10, 1873, to May 15, 1902; see Jackson for the name [GSM 1873; PO Archives].

**SOUTH KENT,** Kent County: a branch post office out of Grand Rapids and a geographic expression referring to this area in Kent County; the county was named by Lucius Lyon for eminent attorney James Kent [Paul F. Kempter].

**SOUTH LAKE LINDEN,** Houghton County: this village, a mile south of Lake Linden, in Torch Lake Township, began as the site of the Calumet & Hecla blast furnaces and was given a station on the Hancock and Calumet Railroad; grocer Modest Manseau became its first postmaster on Aug. 21, 1889, but the office was changed to Hubbell on Nov. 19, 1903 [Sawyer; PO Archives].

**SOUTHLAND CENTER,** Wayne County: it began with the J. L. Hudson Company shopping complex, in Taylor Township, north of Eureka Road between Pardee and Rancho Roads, in 1966.

**SOUTHLANDS,** Lenawee County: a station on the T. & W. Electric Railway, near the southeastern border of the county, in 1910 [GSM 1911].

**SOUTH LANSING,** Ingham County: a station on the Lake Shore & Michigan Southern Railroad, then a mile south of Lansing, in 1882 [GSM 1883].

**SOUTH LYON,** Oakland County: the widow Thompson built the first house here in 1832, and her son William kept a store in an addition to it; that part of present South Lyons was called Thompson's Corners; in 1832, the legislature named the township for Lucius Lyon, a member; the village, named from its location in the township, was given a post office on July 13, 1848, with Zeri C. Colvin as its first postmaster; incorporated as a village in 1873 and as a city in 1930 [Thurman S. Bunn; PO Archives; Seeley].

**SOUTH MANISTIQUE,** Schoolcraft County: this lumber settlement on Lake Michigan, in Hiawatha Township, was given a station on the Minneapolis, St. Paul & Sault Ste. Marie Railroad and on March 19, 1883, a post office, with Matthew Gunton as its first postmaster, succeeded by A. C. Hubbell in 1884; see Manistique for the name [GSM 1885; PO Archives].

**SOUTH MANITOU**, Leelanu County. See Manitou.

**SOUTH MILTON**, Antrim County: Edward Wilson became the first postmaster of this rural post office, in southern Milton Township, on Dec. 23, 1889, the office operating until Jan. 14, 1905 [GSM 1907; PO Archives].

**SOUTH MONROE**, Monroe County: unincorp. village, suburb of Monroe [Columbia Ency.].

**SOUTH MONTEREY**, Allegan County: this settlement in southern Monterey Township was given a post office on Feb. 28, 1886, with John M. Granger as its first postmaster, the office operating until March 31, 1903 [GSM 1911; PO Archives].

**SOUTH NANKIN**, Wayne County. See Wayne.

**SOUTH NORWAY**, Dickinson County: this suburb was annexed by the city of Norway in 1891 [Sawyer].

**SOUTH OLIVE**, Ottawa County: the hamlet was named from its location on Olive Township which was organized in 1857 [Lillie].

**SOUTH PARK**, Montcalm County: this summer resort village on the south banks of Baldwin Lake, in Eureka Township, was platted and recorded by M. Cankin for Carpenter C. Merrett and Peter McDermond, proprietors, on Sept. 23, 1895 [Dasef].

**SOUTH PLYMOUTH**, Wayne County. See Denton.

**SOUTH PORTER**, Cass County: this village in southern Porter Township was first settled by William Tibbetts and Daniel Shellhammer in 1829; see Porter for the name [Rogers].

**SOUTH RANGE**, Houghton County: it was founded and platted by the Whealkate Mining Company in 1902, who named it from its location at the south end of the county on land adjoining the Copper Range Mines; it was given a station on the Copper Range Railway and on May 9, 1905, a post office, with William Trevarthen as its first postmaster; incorporated as a village in 1906 [PM; PO Archives].

**SOUTH RILEY**, Clinton County: for speculation, Leland Green bought government land here in 1836; he sold it to Nathan E. Jones, Sr., in 1843; Mr. Jones became the first postmaster on June 19, 1857; the office was closed on April 4, 1867, but was restored from June 3, 1869, to March 31, 1903; it was named from its location in the township, for the naming of which see Riley Center [Ellis; PO Archives].

**SOUTH ROCKWOOD**, Monroe County: it was founded in 1863 by John Strong who named it after Rockwood, Ontario; the post office was opened in his store on July 5, 1877, with Archibald McTaggart as its first postmaster; incorporated as a village in 1955 [S. W. Franke, PM].

**SOUTH ROGERS**, Presque Isle County: a station on the Alpena & Northern Railroad; John Hein became its first postmaster on May 19,

1894, succeeded by Will C. Spens in 1897, the office operating until April 15, 1902; it was named from its location south of Rogers City [Advance; GSM 1895; PO Archives].

**SOUTH SAGINAW**, Saginaw County. See Salina.

**SOUTH SPARTA**, Kent County: Lyman S. Ballard became the first postmaster of this rural post office in southern Sparta Township on Feb. 28, 1856, but the office was changed to Englishville on July 29, 1856 [GSM 1857-60; PO Archives].

**SOUTH SUNFIELD**, Eaton County: James E. Smith became the first postmaster of this rural post office in southern Sunfield Township on Sept. 6, 1858, the office operating until Sept. 11, 1865 [GSM 1865; PO Archives].

**SOUTH WOODSTOCK**, Lenawee County: Neander Darling became the first postmaster of this rural post office in southern Woodstock Township on Sept. 28, 1842, the office operating until Oct. 28, 1846 [PO Archives].

**SOUTH WRIGHT**, Hillsdale County. See Waldron.

**SOVA**, Cheboygan County. See Alverno.

**SPALDING**, Menominee County: this village in Ingallston Township was founded by and named for Jesse Spalding when the Chicago & Northwestern Railroad came through here in 1872; he owned vast timberlands, several sawmills, and was also very influential politically; it was given a post office on Jan. 26, 1874, with Wilmot Armstrong as its first postmaster; the place was also known as Menominee Junction and is now a part of the joint community of Powers-Spalding; Spalding Township in the same county was also named for him [PM; GSM 1875; Escanaba Daily Press, Aug. 26, 1865; PO Archives].

**SPALDING**, Saginaw County. See Spaulding.

**SPARING CREEK**, Oceana County: Henry Mullen became the first postmaster of this rural post office on March 11, 1868, the office operating until March 8, 1871 [PO Archives].

**SPARLINGVILLE**, St. Clair County: George Sparling, a builder and land developer, founded this village about 1923, and it was named for him [Frances Marshall, St. Clair Co. Lib.].

**SPARR**, Otsego County: a station on the Boyne City, Gaylord & Alpena Railroad, in Dover Township; grocer John J. Hanley became its first postmaster on May 5, 1915; it was named for Philip Sparr who settled here in 1873 [William H. Granlund; GSM 1919; PO Archives].

**SPARTA**, Hillsdale County. See Pittsford.

**SPARTA**, Kent County: on Dec. 28, 1848, Gaius P. Stebbins became the first postmaster of Somerville, a rural post office two miles south of present-day Sparta; the settlement itself was called Nashville for Jonathan

P. Nash, founder of the present Sparta village; on Nov. 7, 1850, village and post office were renamed Sparta Center from its location in Sparta Township; on Jan. 13, 1885, it became simply Sparta, but the postmaster continued to use the Sparta Center canceller until at least April 6, 1885; incorporated as a village in 1883 [PO Archives; Pen Phil 10:3 Oct 1959].

**SPAULDING,** Barry County: Charles W. Spaulding located lands here in 1834 and when the township was organized in 1841 it was named for him; in 1843, it was divided and renamed Prairieville and Orangeville [Potter].

**SPAULDING,** Saginaw County: Phineas Spaulding emigrated here from New Hampshire in 1835 and when the township was organized in 1858 it was named for him; Aaron Linton became its first postmaster on May 13, 1863, but it was changed to South Saginaw on Oct. 20, 1866; in some sources as Spalding [Mills; Leeson; PO Archives; Mich Manual 1899, Spalding; Mich Manual 1959, Spaulding].

**SPEAKER,** Sanilac County: August Siche became the first settler in the area in 1856; for storekeeper Andrew Moore the place was first called Moore's Corners; the township was organized in 1858 and named Speaker, and when its village was given a post office on Nov. 8, 1871, with William S. Moore as its first postmaster, it took the same name; the office operated until June 30, 1906 [Chapman; PO Archives].

**SPENCER,** Kalkaska County: a station on the Pere Marquette Railroad, six miles southeast of Kalkaska; Sarah Gregory became its first postmaster on Feb. 17, 1899, the office operating until Nov. 31, 1954 [GSM 1901; PO Archives].

**SPENCER CREEK,** Antrim County. See Alden.

**SPENCER'S MILL,** Iosco County: a sawmill settlement in Plainfield Township in 1876 [GSM 1877].

**SPENCER MILLS,** Kent County: the first regular settlers in the township were Cyrus B. Thomas in 1846 and Henry Stroup in 1848; in 1855, another early settler, Thomas Spencer, built the Spencer Mills, and it was given a post office of that name with him becoming its first postmaster on Oct. 17, 1857; the township, organized as Celsus in 1861, was renamed in his honor; the post office operated until Sept. 30, 1903 [Dillenback; PO Archives].

**SPENSVILLE,** Presque Isle County: it was named for John Spens who built a dock for the lake shipping of lumber here prior to 1896 [Advance].

**SPICER'S CORNERS,** Bay County. See Fisherville.

**SPICERVILLE,** Eaton County: Amos and Pierpont Spicer, Samuel Hamlin and C. C. Darling first settled here in 1835 and as the firm of Spicer, Hamlin & Darling built a sawmill on Spring Brook in 1836; they also platted the village in 1836; William M. Tompkins became its first postmaster on June 3, 1854; the office was closed on April 13, 1857, but was restored from July 8, 1867, to April 29, 1869 [MPH 22:509 1893; PO Archives].

**SPIKE**, Washtenaw County: Charles Cooley became the first postmaster of this rural post office on Feb. 16, 1895, the office operating until March 19, 1896 [GSM 1897; PO Archives].

**SPINK'S CORNERS**, Berrien County: this hamlet in Bainbridge Township was named for landowner and storekeeper E. S. Spink; another merchant, Charles Marshall, became its first postmaster on May 3, 1888, the office operating until June 15, 1907 [GSM 1889; PO Archives].

**SPINNER**, Tuscola County: James McConnell became the first postmaster of this rural post office on May 1, 1873, the office operating until April 8, 1875 [GSM 1877; PO Archives].

**SPINNINGS**, Macomb County: a station on the Detroit & Bay City Railroad in 1878 [GSM 1879].

**SPOONVILLE**, Ottawa County: it was first settled prior to 1857 by John Spoon, who "converted the howling wilderness into smiling fields"; it was given a station on the Chicago & Michigan Lake Shore Railroad in 1870 [MPH 9:332 1886].

**SPOOR**, Oscoda County: Charles N. Smith became the first postmaster of this rural post office in Elmer Township, 5 miles west of Mio, on Nov. 18, 1899, succeeded by Charles V. Kittle in 1900, the office operating until Sept. 14, 1901 [GSM 1901; PO Archives].

**SPRAGUE**, Genesee County: William O. Caldwell became the first postmaster of this rural post office in Munday Township on April 28, 1898, the office operating until Jan. 31, 1901 [GSM 1899-1903; PO Archives].

**SPRATT**, Alpena County: this settlement in Green Township was named for the Spratt family (Thomas G., Melville B., Augustus N., and Frank D.), pioneer lumbermen in the area; Melville B. Spratt became its first postmaster on March 2, 1900, the office operating until Aug. 15, 1934; now a farming community rather than a village [Fred R. Trelfa; PO Archives].

**SPRING ARBOR**, Jackson County: the site of an old Indian village, the present village was founded by Isaac N. Swain about 1838; Lemuel W. Douglass became its first postmaster on May 4, 1839; there is a large spring in the area and both the township and its town were named Spring Arbor [Vera L. Cross; Pen Phil 8:6 April 1958; PO Archives].

**SPRING BROOK**, Gratiot County: William L. Sutherland became the first postmaster of this rural post office in central Fulton Township on Nov. 16, 1855, the office operating until March 9, 1888 [Tucker].

**SPRING BROOK**, Kalamazoo County: a station on the Chicago, Kalamazoo & Saginaw, and the Chicago, Jackson & Western Michigan

Railroads; storekeeper L. G. Baxter became its first postmaster on March 17, 1892, with the spelling changed to Springbrook on April 14, 1895; the office was closed on March 31, 1898, but was restored from May 17, 1898, to Aug. 31, 1906 [GSM 1893-1907; PO Archives].

**SPRING CREEK,** Berrien County: George Drake became the first postmaster of this rural post office, the first post office in Three Oaks Township, on May 13, 1851; the office operated until July 19, 1854 [Fox].

**SPRINGDALE,** Manistee County: this township, erected in 1870, was named from its many ever-flowing springs [Page].

**SPRINGDALE,** Wexford County. See Harrietta.

**SPRINGER SIDING,** Schoolcraft County: it was founded in 1943 by the Soo Line Railroad who named it for a retired engineer (with the Line, 1887-1925), Theodore Daniel Springer, who died at Gladstone in 1931; in 1960, the Line removed the siding track, leaving just a marker [George T. Springer].

**SPRINGFIELD,** Calhoun County: the first platting was done by D. J. Merrill, J. W. Bryce and the Merrill heirs in 1904, and it was first known as Merrill Park; its change of name is attributed to C. W. Post who came here from Springfield, Illinois, it was a part of Battle Creek Township until incorporated as a ctiy in 1952; it was annexed to the city of Battle Creek in 1960 [Corinne J. Wascher].

**SPRINGFIELD,** Oakland County: in 1829, Asahel Fuller, the first settler opened a hotel here on the old Detroit to Saginaw stage line; Giles Bishop became the first postmaster in January, 1832, the office operating until April 24, 1888; Springfield Township was set off in 1837; storekeeper Milton Peters platted a few village lots in 1840; it was named from its abounding in fine springs [Durant; Seeley; PO Archives].

**SPRINGFIELD STATION,** Oakland County: Jonathan B. Billings became the first postmaster at this railroad depot in Springfield Township on Feb. 24, 1857, the office operating until Nov. 29, 1858 [GSM 1860; PO Archives].

**SPRING GROVE,** Allegan County: storekeeper John Sanborn Marr became the first postmaster of this rural post office in Casco Township on Feb. 27, 1878, the office operating until Oct. 31, 1907 [Ensign; PO Archives].

**SPRING HILL,** Wayne County. See Springwells.

**SPRING LAKE,** Ottawa County: Captain Benjamin Hopkins left Canada and built a mill on this point of land in 1837, and it became known as Hopkins Mill; when Thomas W. White and S. C. Hopkins recorded their plat of the village in 1849, they called it Mill Point, and it was given a post office of that name on May 1, 1851, with LeMoyne M. S. Smith as its first postmaster; on May 28, 1867, it was renamed Spring Lake from its location on the shores of Spring Lake; a station on the Detroit, Grand Haven & Milwaukee Railroad; incorporated as a village in 1869; a settlement named Mill Point is just to the south of it [PM; Lillie; PO Archives].

**SPRING MILL**, Alcona County: a hamlet in 1878 [GSM 1879].

**SPRING MILLS**, Kent County: a hamlet in 1859 [GSM 1860].

**SPRING MILLS**, Oakland County: it was founded by Jonas G. Potter and Major F. Lockwood who built a sawmill in this area of springs in 1846; Enos Leek became its first postmaster on Sept. 7, 1857, but the office was transferred to Highland Station on Dec. 23, 1873 [Seeley; Durant; PO Archives].

**SPRINGPORT**, Alcona County: it was first settled by the Holden family whose boat was blown ashore here in 1846, and their son Eugene was the first white child born here, in 1847; its village life began with the store and the mill of Joseph Van Buskirk about 1865; it was first called Sunflower Hill, and for many years it was known as South Harrisville from its being about a mile south of Harrisville; it was renamed from the cold springs gushing from the banks of the bluffs [Dora A. Gauthier; Page].

**SPRINGPORT**, Jackson County: it was founded by John Oyer in 1836 and was first known as Oyer's Corners; it was renamed from the springs in the area and was given a post office as Springport on Dec. 8, 1838, with Augustus F. Gaylord as its first postmaster; when the Lake Shore & Michigan Southern Railroad came through in 1876 it was given a station; incorporated as a village in 1883 [DeLand; Altha Mercer; PO Archives].

**SPRING STATION**, Oceana County: a settlement on Lake Michigan, in the northwest corner of the county, in 1880 [GSM 1881].

**SPRING VALE**, Charlevoix County: the village began as a lumber settlement founded in 1879 by the Cadillac lumbering firm of (Jonathan W.) Cobbs & (George A.) Mitchell; the first postmaster, George Mohorter, appointed on May 6, 1879, kept the office in his general store; the village was torn down in 1925 [Carl Clark; GSM 1881; PO Archives].

**SPRING VALLEY**, Iron County. See Palatka.

**SPRINGVILLE**, Lenawee County: it was first settled in 1832 and named from the many springs and flowing wells in the area; Abram Butterfield became the first postmaster on Jan. 21, 1835, the office operating until Aug. 31, 1905 [George S. May; GSM 1838; PO Archives].

**SPRINGWATER**, Antrim County: George W. Rawson became the first postmaster of this rural post office on Oct. 16, 1901 but it was rescinded on Feb. 17, 1902 [PO Archives].

**SPRINGWELLS**, Wayne County: from the large springs in the area, it was first called Spring Hill; a pioneer settler, Pierre Drouillard, sold his land here to Joseph Gaubielle in 1783; the coming through of the Michigan

Central Railroad in 1837 gave rise to this village in Springwells Township; the village was platted and recorded by Ambrose Riopelle on Dec. 11, 1847; Samuel Ludlow became its first postmaster on Feb. 16, 1855; the office was closed April 4, 1857, restored, but transferred to West End on Feb. 4, 1878; the Springwells post office operated again from July 15, 1910, to July 14, 1917; incorporated as a village in 1921 and as a city in 1923; for industrialist Henry Ford and his son Edsel, it was renamed Fordson in 1925, but it was annexed by the city of Dearborn in 1928 [Mich Hist 32:86 1948; Federal; County plat liber; PO Archives].

**SPRUCE**, Alcona County: sawmill owner Don A. Hecox became the first postmaster of this rural post office in Caledonia Township on May 5, 1898 [GSM 1899].

**SPRUCE**, Dickinson County: a station on the Chicago & Northwestern Railroad, three miles east of Metropolitan, in 1884; the road named many of its stops after trees [Mich Manual 1899].

**SPRUNGTOWN**, Livingston County. See Cohoctah Center.

**SPURR MOUNTAIN**, Baraga County: this settlement around the mines of the Spurr Mountain Iron Company was given a railroad station and on Dec. 30, 1874, a post office, with James McKercher as its first postmaster; the office was closed on Dec. 3, 1887, but was restored on June 4, 1890, with Mary McKercher, as its postmaster, the office operating until June 5, 1896 [GSM 1877-89; PO Archives].

**SQUAWFIELD**, Lenawee County: this village in southwestern Pittsford Township, the home of chief Baw Beese, was the last home of the Indians in the area before the government moved them west in 1839 [Mich Hist 4:405 1920].

**SQUIREVILLE**, Mason County: this rural post office, 7 miles from Pentwater, opened on July 13, 1895, and was named for the Squire family, Emma M. Squire becoming its first postmaster; the office operated until April 30, 1902 [GSM 1897-1903; PO Archives].

**STACK**, Marquette County: a station on the Chicago & Northwestern Railroad, in Turin Township; the settlement formed around the Helena Land & Lumber Company mill and general store; Dennis M. Glavin became its first postmaster on Feb. 26, 1916 [GSM 1917; PO Archives].

**STACY**, Grand Traverse County: this rural post office in Green Lake Township was named for Stacy W. Thompson who became its first postmaster on March 3, 1885, the office operating until Sept. 24, 1890 [GSM 1887-91; PO Archives].

**STAFFORD**, Allegan County: this rural post office was named for Silas Stafford who became its first postmaster on June 15, 1854; he was succeeded by Oziel H. Round on March 20, 1855; the office operated until April 5, 1856 [PO Archives].

**STAFFORD**, Hillsdale County: this rural post office in Wheatland

Township was named for storekeeper Charles E. Stafford who became its first postmaster on July 13, 1897, the office operating until June 15, 1903 [GSM 1899-1905; PO Archives].

**STAFFORD,** Huron County. See Port Hope.

**STAGER,** Iron County: Harvey Mellen, a U.S. land surveyor, discovered iron ore in this district in 1851, but the mining of it did not begin until 1882; in that year the district was opened when the Chicago & Northwestern Railroad reached Iron River, with a spur from Iron River Junction, now Stager; Stager Lake is nearby and the name is understood to refer to stag or deer [Joseph A. Rossi].

**STALWART,** Chippewa County: it was first settled in 1878; in 1881, the community applied for a post office to be named Garfield, after James A. Garfield, then president of the U.S.; but there was already a Garfield post office in Michigan; they then presented the name Arthur, and it was denied for the same reason; it was then suggested that since James A. Garfield and Chester A. Arthur represented the stalwart faction of the Republican party, the village be called Stalwart, and the name was accepted; John J. McKenzie became the first postmaster of this office in Sault Ste. Marie Township on Feb. 15, 1881 [Hamilton; PO Archives].

**STAMBAUGH,** Iron County: the lands embraced by the present city were originally assigned by the U.S. to Elizabeth Slaten in 1855, as the widow of War of 1812 veteran, Joshua Slaten; in 1880, Jay C. Morse sold the site to Escanaba speculators Dr. Louis D. Cyr, Louis Stegmiller, and Richard L. Selden; they had John V. Sydam plat the village in 1882; Mr. Selden became its first postmaster on May 18, 1882; the office was closed on July 6, 1882, but was restored, with Mr. Selden again the postmaster, on July 28, 1882; it was named for John Stambaugh, president of the Todd, Stambaugh Company, of Youngstown, Ohio, who had recently acquired the Iron River (also called Stambaugh) Mine; incorporated as a village in 1890, with Mr. Stambaugh as its first president, and as a city in 1923; it was in Marquette County until Iron was organized in 1885 [Hill; Havighurst; PO Archives].

**STANARD,** Genesee County: this hamlet in Flint Township was founded in 1836 by William N. Stanard and sons, of Genesee County, N.Y. [Wood].

**STANDALE,** Kent County: it was founded by and named for Howard G. Stanton who bought a farm here in 1919 and opened a general store in 1925; this hamlet has been served by the Grand Rapids post office since 1925 [H. Wayne Parker, PM, Grand Rapids].

**STANDISH,** Arenac County: John D. Standish, of Detroit, built a mill here in 1871 and had Peter M. Angus plat the village for it to be on the line of the Michigan Central Railroad, then coming through; before his plat was recorded and while he was away, on Dec. 6, 1872, the name was changed to Granton; at the next session of the legislature he got it changed back to Standish, on April 13, 1874; James S. Gailey became the first postmaster on Jan. 17, 1872; the village, then in Bay County, became a part of Arenac when the latter was organized in July, 1883; incorporated as a village in 1893 and as a city in 1904 [Alfred Campbell; Pen Phil 11:4 Nov 1960; PO Archives].

**STANLEY**, Calhoun County: this rural post office opened in the general store of the Owens Brothers on Jan. 22, 1897, with Sumner Owens as its first postmaster; they were bought out by Nelson Toland and he became the postmaster in 1900; the office operated until May 15, 1903 [GSM 1901; PO Archives].

**STANLEY**, Genesee County: this settlement in Genesee Township was begun in 1835 by Sherman Stanley who, like the man who came with him, Albert T. Stevens, was from Mount Morris, Livingston County, N.Y. [Wood].

**STANNARD**, Ontonagon County: this township was named for William Stannard, of Rockland, the member of the legislature who introduced the bill creating it in 1905 [Jamison].

**STANTON**, Montcalm County: when the people of the county voted to locate the county seat here in 1860, the board bought 40 acres (for $50.00) from Fred Hall, of Ionia, for the site; it was named Fred in his honor, but in 1863 it was renamed for Edwin M. Stanton, secretary of war; the family of Levi Camburn was the first to settle here and he became its first postmaster on March 10, 1862; it was platted in 1865; incorporated as a village in 1869 and as a city in 1881 [L. G. Early, PM].

**STANTON JUNCTION**, Ionia County: a station on the Detroit, Lansing & Northern Railroad in 1878 [GSM 1879].

**STANWOOD**, Mecosta County: the village was settled in 1870 and given a station on the Grand Rapids & Indiana Railroad; the Big Creek post office was transferred here and renamed Stanwood, after the splendid stand of timber in the area, on Oct. 18, 1870; incorporated as a village in 1907 [GSM 1879-1909; PO Archives].

**STAR CITY**, Missaukee County: this settlement in West Branch Township dates from 1872; Chauncey Brace became the first postmaster of Roy on Feb. 27, 1880, with the name changed to Putnam, with Elizabeth Putnam as postmaster, on June 6, 1883, and to Star City on Feb. 13, 1885 [GSM 1887; PO Archives].

**STAR ISLAND**, St. Clair County: hotelman James Slocum became the first postmaster of this summer resort on an island in the St. Clair River on May 27, 1889; the office operated until Dec. 7, 1891 [GSM 1891; PO Archives].

**STARK**, Wayne County: storekeeper John A. McLaughlin became the first postmaster of Livonia Station, a depot on the Pere Marquette Railroad in Livonia Township, on Nov. 14, 1877; for local landowner L. B. Stark, the office was renamed Stark on Nov. 13, 1879, and operated until July 31, 1909 [Burton; PO Archives].

**STARKEVILLE**, Manistee County. See Arcadia.

**STARKEY'S PIER,** Manistee County: this settlement on the shore of Lake Michigan, in Arcadia Township, dates from 1880 [GSM 1881].

**STARK'S CORNERS,** Cass County. See Cushing.

**STARR COMMONWEALTH,** Calhoun County: a publicly supported home for delinquent boys, founded by Floyd Starr in 1913; no penal atmosphere; study, farm work, and play serve to instill pride and self-reliance [Federal].

**STARRVILLE,** St. Clair County: Harrison Butler became the first postmaster of this rural post office in Cottrellville township on Feb. 27, 1880, the office operating until Aug. 15, 1905 [PO Archives].

**STATE LINE,** Branch County: a station on the Fort Wayne, J. & S. Railroad, on the line between Michigan and Indiana, in 1878 [GSM 1879].

**STATE LINE,** Monroe County: a station on the Detroit, Monroe & Toledo Railroad, near the Ohio line, in 1864 [GSM 1865].

**STATE ROAD,** Sanilac County: Andrew J. Wright became the first postmaster of this rural post office on July 7, 1868; the office was transferred to and renamed Deckerville on Jan. 3, 1870 [PO Archives].

**STEAMBURG,** Calhoun County: it was named from its becoming the location in 1856 of the steam sawmill of A. J. Quick and Lucas Payne; it was also known as Quick's Corners; Arthur Moore opened the first store here in Leroy Township in 1870, and other businesses followed [Everts].

**STEAMBURG,** Hillsdale County: it was named from the steam sawmill that Chauncey W. Ferris, a county pioneer, built here in Cambria Township; Wilbur P. Bates became the first postmaster of the settlement around it on Dec. 9, 1896, succeeded by storekeeper J. L. McQueen in 1898, the office operating until May 31, 1902; still a hamlet [Vivian L. Moore; GSM 1903; PO Archives].

**STEAM MILL,** Oakland County. See Mahopac.

**STEARNS,** Lake County: in 1882, Justus Smith Stearns built a sawmill here and went on to become the largest manufacturer of lumber residing in Michigan (125 million feet in 1898) and was elected secretary of state for Michigan in 1899; his settlement here was given a station on the Pere Marquette Railroad in 1884 [GSM 1885; Mich Manual 1899].

**STEARNS,** Midland County: this village on the Chippewa River, in Greendale Township, was first settled in 1868; David J. Look became its first postmaster on Jan. 30, 1882, succeeded by lawyer Henry L. Voorhees later that year, the office operating until Oct. 31, 1912 [GSM 1883-1913; PO Archives].

**STEARNS MILL,** Newaygo County. See Croton.

**STEARNS SIDING,** Lake County. See Wingleton.

**STEBBINSVILLE,** Ionia County. See Collins.

**STEBBINSVILLE,** Oceana County: this rural post office in Greenwood Township was named for Joseph D. Stebbins who became its first postmaster on May 16, 1870, the office operating until May 26, 1874 [PO Archives].

**STEELES LANDING,** Ottawa County. See Lamont.

**STEINER,** Monroe County: a station on the Pere Marquette Railroad, in Frenchtown Township; the village was founded by and named for William Steiner in 1873; lumberman John Kohler became its first postmaster on Sept. 17, 1886 [C. S. McIntyre, 3rd; GSM 1887].

**STELLA,** Gratiot County: Addison Hayden became the first postmaster of this rural post office in southeastern North Star Township (stella is Latin for star), on March 2, 1858; the office was closed on April 14, 1860, but was restored from Jan. 24, 1861, to Aug. 14, 1890 [Tucker; PO Archives].

**STEMM,** Berrien County: this station on the Buchanan branch of the Pere Marquette Railroad, in Oronoko Township, was named for John Stemm who owned a farm nearby; storekeeper John J. Stover became its first postmaster on May 17, 1898, the office operating until Nov. 30, 1907 [Fox; GSM 1899; PO Archives].

**STEPHENS,** Lapeer County: it was platted in 1871 and named for its proprietor, Henry Stephens, of the lumber firm of Stephens, Currier & Townsend; he got the Detroit & Bay City Railroad to build a branch line through it and it became a lumber boom town; Robert Stewart became its first postmaster on Feb. 28, 1872; the office was closed on July 31, 1883, but was restored from July 13, 1886, to April 8, 1887; it was also known as Fish Lake from its location by that body of water; now a ghost town [Page; GSM 1873; PO Archives].

**STEPHENSON,** Marquette County: the Stephenson Mine location of the Cleveland Cliffs Iron Company was developed in 1911 as a residence community for the miners and their families [Sawyer].

**STEPHENSON,** Menominee County: this charcoal and tan bark settlement on the Menominee River was given a station on the Chicago & Northwestern Railroad in 1872 and a post office on July 13, 1874, with Alva F. Burnham as its first postmaster; it was named Wacedah, but on Jan. 10, 1876, it was renamed for Samuel Stephenson, a civic leader who later (1889-1896) became the congressman from this district; incorporated as a village in 1898 [Francis D. Menacher; PO Archives].

**STERLING,** Arenac County: the village began with the sawmill of Norn & Kent in 1871 and was given a station on the Michigan Central Railroad in 1872; William S. Perkins became the first postmaster of Perkins, Bay County, on Jan. 30, 1872, with the name changed for lumberman William C. Sterling, to Sterling, Arenac County, on Jan. 28, 1872; incorporated as a village in 1917 [Alfred Campbell; PO Archives].

**STERLING,** Washtenaw County: this rural post office on the Ann Arbor to Ionia route was opened on Jan. 15, 1836, with Gerardus Noble as its first postmaster, the office operating until August 12, 1845; said to have been named for James Sterling whose sweetheart, Catherine Cuillerier, fearing that her lover might fall victim to the Indian fury, warned him of Chief Pontiac's plot to infiltrate and destroy Detroit in 1763, and he in turn relayed the warning to Major Henry Gladwin; her father, Antoine, was a friend of Pontiac and it is known that the Chief held at least one council in the Cuillerier home; Wacousta is also credited with having given the warning and, of course, both may have [GSM 1838; Blinn; PO Archives].

**STERLING HEIGHTS,** Macomb County: when erected on March 17, 1835, the township was named Jefferson, after the late President; in 1838, it was renamed Sterling, honoring pioneer settler Azariah W. Sterling; on June 1, 1966, the entire township was incorporated as the home rule city of Sterling Heights, effective July 1, 1968; a branch of the Utica post office in 1971 [Leeson; GSM 1860; Mich Manual 1969-1970].

**STETSON,** Oceana County. See Walkerville.

**STEUBEN,** Schoolcraft County: it was founded by the Chicago Lumbering Company which operated sawmills in Manistique from 1860 and located a logging center here in then Harrison Township in 1872; it was named by an official of the firm who had come from Steuben County, N.Y., which in turn had been named for Baron Friedrich Wilhelm von Steuben, inspector general of Washington's army, 1777-1784; a station on the Pere Marquette Railroad; Abraham Hughes became its first postmaster on July 2, 1903; now a summer resort [G. Leslie Bouschor; GSM 1905; PO Archives].

**STEVENS,** Antrim County. See Elk Rapids.

**STEVENSBURGH,** Chippewa County. See Dafter.

**STEVENS LANDING,** Sanilac County. See Birch Beach.

**STEVENSVILLE,** Berrien County: Thomas Stevens, of Niles, a landowner here, donated the right-of-way to the Chicago & Western Michigan (now Pere Marquette) Railroad; he platted the village which George Morrison, who constructed the road, named for him; James Dunham became its first postmaster on May 2, 1872; incorporated as a village in 1893 [Fox; PO Archives].

**STEWART,** Bay County: this summer resort on Saginaw Bay, in Kawkawlin Township was named for resort manager Allie E. Stewart who became its first postmaster on Nov. 21, 1902, the office operating until April 30, 1908 [GSM 1905; PO Archives].

**STICKLEY,** Gogebic County: Albert Stickley, a Grand Rapids furniture maker, built an elaborate summer home on the southwest side of Beaton's Lake about 1911; the Chicago & Northwestern Railroad named the point Stickley where its spur line to Cisco Lake took off from the main line; it was never more than a (now extinct) railroad stopping point [Ivan D. Wright].

**STILES**, Newaygo County: the settlement formed around the Stiles Brothers sawmill; a station on the Chicago & Western Michigan (now Pere Marquette) Railroad; Eppy D. Hazard became its first postmaster on Sept. 13, 1890, the office operating until Dec. 20, 1895 [GSM 1893; PO Archives].

**STIMSON**, Marquette County: a station on the Detroit, Mackinaw & Marquette Railroad, 7 miles west of Marquette, in 1884 [GSM 1885].

**STIMSON**, Mecosta County: Herbert S. Tenney became the first postmaster of this rural post office on Aug. 22, 1889, the office operating until Aug. 15, 1906 [PO Archives].

**STIRLINGVILLE**, Chippewa County: this village in Pickford Township was first called Jolly's Landing; it was renamed for William P. Stirling, storekeeper and steamboat operator, who became its first postmaster on Feb. 29, 1888 [Bayliss; PO Archives].

**STITTSVILLE**, Missaukee County: this rural post office was first named Norwich, after its township, when Orlando C. Gorthy became its first postmaster on March 28, 1879; when John T. Stitt became the postmaster on Feb. 9, 1885, the office was renamed for him; the office was in the Stitt Brothers general store, the stock of goods of which was sold to William J. Becker in January, 1891; the post office operated until Dec. 31, 1932 [Stout; Colyer; PO Archives].

**STOCKBRIDGE**, Ingham County: Heman Lowe became the first settler in the area in 1835; the village was platted by Elijah Smith who named it Pekin after his native town in New York; the plat of Pekin was vacated and that of Stockbridge was made by Silas Beebe who named it after its township; Mr. Beebe became the first postmaster on Oct. 16, 1838; incorporated as a village in 1889 [Foster; PO Archives].

**STOCKING**, Wexford County: this rural post office, opened on Aug. 21, 1883, was named for Erastus P. Stocking who became its first postmaster; the office operated until Feb. 2, 1885 [PO Archives].

**STODDARD**, Lenawee County: storekeeper Harry Winter became the first postmaster of this rural post office in Rome Township on April 17, 1894, the office operating until July 20, 1904 [GSM 1895-1905; PO Archives].

**STONEVILLE**, Marquette County: the village formed around its charcoal kilns and was given a post office on Feb. 10, 1873, with James M. Lawson as its first postmaster; the office was closed on Sept. 29, 1886, but was restored from Jan. 21, 1891, to Jan. 8, 1892, and from Feb. 1, 1892, to March 28, 1895; it was platted by E. M. Spalding for Robert Nelson in 1876; it was named from its being in a stony region, the stone foundations of some of its buildings remain [G. Vance Hiney; Andreas; PO Archives].

**STONINGTON**, Delta County: its lighthouse date from 1865, its settlement, by homesteaders and loggers, from 1872; Hans H. Bonefeld became its first postmaster on July 30, 1897, the office operating until July 31, 1957; it was named from the great bedding of limestone which raises a peninsular table in northern Lake Michigan waters [David S. Coon; PO Archives].

**STONY CREEK,** Ionia County: Archibald Wilcox became the first postmaster of this rural post office on Aug. 2, 1852, the office operating until Nov. 19, 1856 [Schenck].

**STONY CREEK,** Monroe County: the settlement began in the 1830s and was given a post office on July 6, 1840, with Patrick Collins as its first postmaster, the office operating until Jan. 18, 1841 [Wing; PO Archives].

**STONY CREEK,** Oakland County: the first settlement on the north side of Stony Creek, in Avon Township, was made in 1823, by Lemuel Taylor, Sr., and his five sons, from New York State; Nathaniel Millard became its first postmaster on Aug. 16, 1825; the village was platted in 1830 by Mr. Millard, and Elishua and Joshua Taylor, son of Lemuel [Durant; Seeley; PO Archives].

**STONY CREEK,** Washtenaw County: Andrew Muir was the first settler in the area, now Augusta Township; the village was founded by James Miller who came in 1829; the first post office in the township was opened at Paint Creek (q.v.); the first post office named Stony Creek was opened on July 7, 1862, with Calvin H. Stone as its first postmaster, the office operating until July 15, 1905 [Chapman; Beakes; PO Archives].

**STONY ISLAND,** Huron County. See Heisterman Island.

**STONY LAKE,** Oceana County: Arthur B. Butler became the first postmaster of this rural post office near Stony Lake on May 22, 1837, the office operating until Feb. 8, 1854 [PO Archives].

**STONY POINT,** Jackson County: Gardner Tripp began working the sandstone quarry here in Hanover Township in 1840, and the village which followed was named from its industry; the village was platted in 1872; Chancelor P. Hammond became its first postmaster on May 20, 1872, with the spelling changed to Stonypoint on May 3, 1894, and the office operated until April 30, 1902; it was given a railroad depot [Interstate; GSM 1873-79; PO Archives].

**STONY RUN,** Genesee County: when Marston W. Richards became the first postmaster of this rural post office on June 6, 1834, it was in Holly Township, Oakland County; Genesee County was organized on March 8, 1836, and this post office became located in its Grand Blanc Township, with John Stone, Jr., becoming its first postmaster on April 3, 1838; the office was closed on June 3, 1878, but was restored from Dec. 10, 1878, to Oct. 23, 1879 [Pen Phil 10:4 April 1960; Durant; PO Archives].

**STONY RUN SIDING,** Oakland County. See Newark.

**STORMER,** Benzie County: a station on the M. & N.E. and the E. & S.E. Railroads; railroad agent John F. Jenks became its first postmaster on Feb. 3, 1902, the office operating until Jan. 15, 1910 [GSM 1903; PO Archives].

**STOVER**, Antrim County: this settlement in Kearney Township formed around the lumber mill of Stover, Hay & Company in 1875; Edgar W. Rose became its first postmaster on April 28, 1880, the office operating until Dec. 13, 1888 [GSM 1885; PO Archives].

**STOVERVILLE**, Gratiot County. See Sumner.

**STRAITS LAKE**, Oakland County: William Beatty became the first postmaster of this rural post office on the north shore of Upper Straits Lake on April 12, 1837; the office was transferred to and renamed Orchard Lake on March 18, 1873 [Durant; PO Archives].

**STRASBURG**, Monroe County: W. H. Rauch built lime kilns here about 1828; a settlement followed and Eli Hausbarger became its first postmaster on June 24, 1874; the office was closed on July 11, 1876, but was restored on Feb. 12, 1879; it was given a station on the Lake Shore & Michigan Southern Railroad in 1878; named after Strasburg, Germany [Pag. of Historic Monroe; GSM 1879; PO Archives].

**STRATFORD**, Missaukee County: a station on the Chicago & Western Michigan (now Pere Marquette) Railroad, in Norwich Township; railroad agent Emil J. Hans became its first postmaster on March 3, 1898, the office operating until Oct. 27, 1908 [GSM 1899-1909; PO Archives].

**STRATHMOOR**, Wayne County: this community, in what is now the Grand River Avenue and Five Mile Road area in Detroit, was given a post office as Vandeleur on Aug. 5, 1915, with Bertha Storch as its first postmaster; it was renamed Strathmoor on Dec. 23, 1916, and its post office became a station of the Detroit post office in 1920 [GSM 1921; PO Archives; Burton].

**STRICKLAND**, Isabella County: William B. Hildreth became the first postmaster of this lumber settlement in Lincoln Township on June 30, 1870, the office operating until July 30, 1904 [John Cuming; PO Archives].

**STROM**, Gogebic County: Hilda Kruutari became the first postmaster of this settlement on Sept. 25, 1918, the office operating until Feb. 28, 1921; it was named for Alex Strom, county register of deeds, 1911-12 [Victor Lemmer; PO Archives].

**STRONACH**, Manistee County: this village at the head of Lake Manistee was first called Paggeotville; it was renamed when John and Adam Stronach built a sawmill and located their Stronach Lumber Company here in 1841; Adolphus Magnan became its first postmaster on Aug. 9, 1866, the office operating until March 31, 1954; a station on the Pere Marquette Railroad [Mich Hist 26:92 1942; Page; PO Archives].

**STRONGS**, Chippewa County: Mr. Strong loaded logs on the Duluth, South Shore & Atlantic Railroad here and it was called Strongs Siding; in 1899, some fifteen families came to work in a shingle mill here for Eugene A. Turner, of Petoskey; when Mr. Turner became the first postmaster on Oct. 11, 1899, the name Turner was suggested for the office, but he declined and recommended that they just drop the word Siding and call it just Strongs; the post office operated until June 30, 1963 [Minnie L. Walker, ex-PM; PO Archives].

**STRONGVILLE,** Chippewa County: sawmill manager Judson D. Smith became the first postmaster of this settlement in Pickford Township on Sept. 19, 1882, the office operating until Nov. 30, 1912 [GSM 1883; PO Archives].

**STROTHERS' CORNERS,** Ionia County. See Algodon.

**STUART,** Ottawa County. See Grand Haven.

**STUMP,** Muskegon County: Job B. Kinnison became the first postmaster of this lumber settlement, near the mouth of the White River, on March 1, 1880, the office operating until July 25, 1884 [GSM 1881; PO Archives].

**STUMPTOWN,** Montcalm County. See Coral.

**STURGEON,** Baraga County: a station on the Marquette, Houghton & Ontonagon Railroad in 1880 [GSM 1881].

**STURGEON,** Delta County: the Soo Line came through here in Nahma Township and opened a depot in 1887; from its location by the Sturgeon River, it was given a post office named Sturgeon River on July 23, 1891, with railroad agent Charles E. Bersee as its first postmaster; the office was transferred to and renamed St. Jacques on June 22, 1904 [David S. Coon; GSM 1893; PO Archives].

**STURGEON BAY,** Chippewa County: John A. Klise became the first postmaster of this rural post office in Pickford Township, six miles from Rudyard, on Dec. 29, 1897, with the office, which was spelled Sturgeonbay, operating until Nov. 14, 1905 [PO Archives; GSM 1899].

**STURGEON BAY,** Emmet County: Edward Ringler became the first postmaster of this rural post office on March 28, 1908, the office operating until Dec. 15, 1912 [PO Archives].

**STURGEON RIVER,** Delta County. See Sturgeon.

**STURGIS,** St. Joseph County: the first settler in the present township, Judge John Sturgis, from Monroe, Michigan, came in 1827 and built his log cabin in 1828; George Buck built the first house in the present village in 1828; the place was first called Sturgis Prairie, but was platted by Philip H. Buck in 1832 as Sherman, which was then the name of the township, and which had been named for pioneer settler Colonel Benjamin Sherman; an additional plat was made in 1834 by Andrew Backus who, in difference to his daughter's fondness for Sir Walter Scott's novel, called it Ivanhoe; it was given a post office as Sherman on Aug. 23, 1841, with Philip H. Buck as its first postmaster, the office being renamed Sturgis on Dec. 29, 1845; in 1857, the legislature had the entire village replatted under the name of Sturgis; incorporated as a village in 1855 and as a city in 1895 [R. G. Worland; PO Archives].

**STUTSMANVILLE,** Emmet County: it was founded by Joseph S. Stutsman who, with his brothers Abraham and Isaiah, built a sawmill here in 1897 and was sawing timber in 1898, later adding the manufacture of broom handles; for some 44 years, Joseph was a traveling preacher for the Dunkers, now Church of the Brethren; Chris Pontius opened a store here about 1899 and distributed the mail coming by the Cross Village stage [Rhinard R. Stutsman, son of Joseph].

**SUCCESS,** Benzie County: David C. Bryan became the first postmaster of this rural post office on Lake Ann, at the head of the Platte River, in Almira Township, on Dec. 5, 1873, the office operating until Jan. 18, 1877 [GSM 1879; PO Archives].

**SUCCESS,** Charlevoix County: Richard W. Ballensinger became the first postmaster of this rural post office on June 3, 1913 [PO Archives].

**SUCKER CREEK,** Ontonagon County. See Choate.

**SUGAR GROVE,** Mason County: a station on the Pere Marquette Railroad, named in 1870 by the W. A. Genson family from the local maple sugar groves; Stephen Darke became its first postmaster on Oct. 7, 1874, the office operating until Dec. 31, 1901; the place was also known as Clark's Corners for Jacob Clark, a pioneer who signed the application for the erection of its township of Victory [Rose D. Hawley; Page; PO Archives].

**SUGAR ISLAND,** Chippewa County: the British-American dispute over its ownership lasted from 1783 to 1842 when the Webster-Ashburton Treaty placed it in American territory; as a British possession, it had been called St. George's Island; the Indians called it Sisibakwatominiss (Maple Sugar Island), from its abundance of maple sugar trees; it was given a post office as Sugar Island on Jan. 13, 1857 with Michael G. Payment as its first postmaster, the office operating until Nov. 9, 1861; Philetus S. Church was the township supervisor [Bayliss; PO Archives].

**SUGAR RAPIDS,** Gladwin County: Edward L. McGlaughlin became the first postmaster of this rural post office on Aug. 15, 1906, the office operating until Nov. 30, 1912 [PO Archives].

**SULLIVAN,** Muskegon County: among the pioneers here in Fruitport Township was Roswell Knowles who, with his bride, came from New York State early in 1858; a station on the Grand Rapids & Indiana Railroad; the village formed around the mill of the Sullivan Lumber Company and other firms; J. Henry Nash became its first postmaster on March 23, 1887, succeeded by storekeeper Stephen J. Martin in 1888 [MPH 28:78 1897; GSM 1889; PO Archives].

**SUMMERFIELD,** Clare County: this sawmill settlement, named after its township, formed around the mill of William Allen; William Davis became its first postmaster on June 24, 1881, succeeded by Sidney Frary in 1882, the office operating until July 28, 1893 [GSM 1883; PO Archives].

**SUMMERFIELD,** Monroe County. See Petersburg.

**SUMMERTON,** Isabella County: this village on the Salt River, in the northeast corner of Seville Township, lies also in Pine River Township, Gratiot County; Bradley E. Johnson became its first postmaster on July 27, 1870; the office was closed on May 18, 1876, but was restored from April 17, 1882, to Aug. 31, 1905 [Tucker; PO Archives].

**SUMMERVILLE,** Cass County. See Sumnerville.

**SUMMERVILLE,** Montcalm County: a station on a branch of the Detroit, Lansing & Northern Railroad in 1884 [GSM 1885].

**SUMMIT,** Baraga County: a station on the Duluth, South Shore & Atlantic Railroad, opened about 1880, ten miles southeast of L'Anse; named from its location near the highest point in Michigan (elevation 1980); still a hamlet [Andreas].

**SUMMIT,** Grand Traverse County. See Summit City.

**SUMMIT,** Jackson County: named from its having the highest elevations in the county, this township formed the southern half of the old township of Jackson, and was set off in 1857, into a separate township when the city of Jackson was incorporated; among its earliest settlers, outside the city, were Chester Bennett, Jacob Hutchins and Samuel Gates [DeLand].

**SUMMIT,** Washtenaw County: Robert Purdy became the first postmaster of this rural post office in Salem Township, between Pontiac and Ann Arbor, on May 1, 1833; the office was transferred to and renamed Salem on Dec. 15, 1876 [GSM 1838; PO Archives].

**SUMMIT CITY,** Grand Traverse County: this station on the Traverse City Railroad was called Summit but its post office, opened on June 23, 1874, with Joseph A. Swainston as its first postmaster, was named Summit City [Traverse; Sprague; PO Archives].

**SUMMITVILLE,** Lake County: a flag station on the Pere Marquette Railroad, in Chase Township; Samuel G. Randall became its first postmaster on May 2, 1872; on May 6, 1879, the office was changed to Russell's Mills [GSM 1873; PO Archives].

**SUMNER,** Gratiot County: it was first settled in 1854 by George S. Bell and Titus Stover; it was called Belltown for its principal landowner and Stover for its storekeeper; it was platted in December, 1864, by S. S. Hastings and recorded as Estella on Oct. 13, 1868, for George and William Stratton, Thomas Harvey, Lawson S. Ferris, and William Pugsley, proprietors; when organized in 1855, the township had been named for pioneer settler Charles Sumner, and the village was given a post office named Sumner on Oct. 28, 1869, with Morris Tucker as its first postmaster; the village took the same name in 1887 [Tucker; Chapman; PO Archives].

**SUMNERVILLE,** Cass County: in 1835, Isaac Sumner built a sawmill here on the Dowagiac River, in Pokagon Township, and two years later a grist mill; in 1836, he and Junius H. Hatch platted the village; about the same time, Alexander Davis became the first merchant and Peabody Cook proprietor of the first inn; the Pocagon post office, opened in March, 1829, with Samuel Markham as postmaster, was renamed Summerville on July 12, 1837, with the spelling corrected to Sumnerville on March 6, 1899; the office operated until May 31, 1904; the village was originally in Lenawee County [GSM 1838; Glover; PO Archives].

**SUMNERVILLE,** Montcalm County: the village was platted by L. C. Sumner upon his land in 1873; lots were sold and a store built but the superior advantages of nearby Six Lakes for a village site doomed Sumnerville [Schenck].

**SUMPTER,** Wayne County. See West Sumpter.

**SUN,** Newaygo County: settled in 1862, this hamlet in Grant Township was given a post office on May 12, 1884, with James H. Manning as its first postmaster, the office operating until Sept. 30, 1903 [GSM 1885; PO Archives].

**SUNDELL,** Alger County: the M., M. & S. Railroad came through here in Rock River Township in 1908 and the station was named Dorsey; but when Selma Harsila was appointed its first postmaster on Aug. 12, 1922, she sent in her maiden name of Sundell (Swedish) and it was accepted; Jacob J. Harsila ran the general store [Hilia Karppinen; PO Archives].

**SUNFIELD,** Eaton County: Samuel S. Hoyt became the first settler in the area in 1836, but the land on which the present village stands was first bought by speculators; it was given a post office as Sunfield, named after its township, on Feb. 28, 1855, with Samuel W. Grinnell as its first postmaster; the office was closed on July 30, 1872, but has been restored since Sept. 18, 1872; a station on the Detroit, Grand Rapids & Western Railroad; incorporated as a village in 1899 [Ray Freemire, PM; Durant; PO Archives].

**SUNKEN LAKE,** Ogemaw County. See Piper.

**SUNRISE HEIGHTS,** Calhoun County: unincorp. village, suburb of Battle Creek [Columbia Ency.].

**SUOMI,** Marquette County: a Finnish settlement, Suomi being the Finnish name for Finland; it is in Richmond Township and the town clerk, Nattie Holmi, became its first postmaster on Feb. 1, 1908, the office operating until Feb. 14, 1912 [GSM 1909; PO Archives].

**SUPERIOR,** Chippewa County. See Brimley.

**SUPERIOR,** Marquette County: a station on the M. & S.E. Railroad in 1910 [GSM 1911].

**SUPERIOR,** Ottawa County: the village was founded by Cyron Burdick, Elisha Belcher, Caleb Sherman, and lake captain Edward H. Macy; they platted the village on the north shore of Tuscarora or Black River

Lake (now Macatawa Lake) and recorded it as Superior in 1836; it was given a post office as Tuscarora on Aug. 1, 1839, with Captain Macy as its first postmaster; but sand banks blocked its harbor and the village failed in 1840 and its post office was closed on July 24, 1840; the site eventually became the summer resort of Waukazoo, named for Chief Waukazoo [MPH 27:520 1896; Mich Hist 21:264 1937, 23:406 1939; Atwell; PO Archives].

**SUPERIOR,** Washtenaw County: Robert Fleming bought the first land here in 1823 and in that year Eldridge Gee built the first house; John Dix built the next as well as the first sawmill in 1826; the Bank of Superior was established on Jan. 17, 1838; John Brewer became the first postmaster on March 2, 1838, the office operating until June 20, 1862; Henry Kimmel introduced the name [MPH 4:398 1881; PO Archives].

**SURREY,** Clare County: the Wilkins family, who came in 1866, were the second to settle in the county; the area became Surrey Township, named by Mrs. George Hitchcock after Surrey in England [J. C. McNamara].

**SUTTON,** Lenawee County: a station on a branch of the Lake Shore & Michigan Southern Railroad, in Raisin Township, in 1878, named for Townsend I. Sutton who became its first postmaster on Dec. 20, 1883, the office operating until April 15, 1903 [GSM 1885; PO Archives].

**SUTTONS BAY,** Leelanau County: it was founded on a western tributary of Grand Traverse Bay on land formerly owned by Harry C. Sutton, in 1854, and was first called Suttonsburg; it was replatted and renamed Pleasant City for Rev. A. Herbstrit, a Catholic priest, who had bought 6000 acres here about 1860; but his project failed, and the place was renamed Suttons Bay with a post office of that name on Aug. 27, 1861, with Mr. Sutton as its first postmaster; incorporated as a village in 1898 [William Bonek, PM; PO Archives].

**SUTTON'S CORNERS,** Washtenaw County: it was first settled by Benjamin Sutton, from Sussex County, N.J., in 1824; William Allen arrived in 1826 with his wife and brother, Moses [MPH 18:507 1891].

**SUTTON'S CROSSING,** Jackson County. See Munith.

**SWAIN LAKE,** Jackson County: this settlement in Pulaski Township was named for Isaac N. Swain who settled near the lake in 1835; in some records as Swain [Interstate].

**SWAINESVILLE,** Jackson County. See Brooklyn.

**SWAN CREEK,** Allegan County: lumberman Joseph Smith became the first postmaster of this rural post office on Swan Creek, in Pine Plains Township, on June 19, 1878, the office operating until July 7, 1879 [GSM 1879; PO Archives].

**SWAN CREEK,** Monroe County. See Newport.

**SWAN CREEK,** Saginaw County: the township, organized in 1860, was named from the stream running through it; a station on the Michigan

Central Railroad; Charles A. Burke became its first postmaster on July 15, 1869; the office was closed on Oct. 16, 1871, but was restored on Oct. 20, 1892 [Mills; PO Archives].

**SWAN CREEK,** St. Clair County. See Fair Haven.

**SWANSON,** Menominee County: when the Wisconsin & Michigan Railroad came through, Solomon Swanson, supervisor of Holmes Township for 17 years, asked for a spur here, and his name was given to the place from then on; railroad agent Ole Olson became its first postmaster on July 18, 1905 [Evelyn Bergen; PO Archives].

**SWANZY,** Marquette County: it was the site of the iron mines of the Escanaba River Land & Iron Company, in Forsyth Township; given a station on the Chicago & Northwestern Railroad with railroad agent Herman E. Bennett becoming its first postmaster on Oct. 5, 1889, the office operating until Dec. 31, 1905 [GSM 1889-1907; PO Archives].

**SWARTZBURG,** Wayne County: this settlement between Detroit and Plymouth dates from 1825 and was named for its tavern-keeper, General Swartz; in some records also as Swarzeburg and as Swartsburg [MPH 5:244 1884, 18:511 1891].

**SWARTZ CREEK,** Genesee County: the village was founded by German-born Adam Miller, the first settler in the area, in 1836, and was called the Miller Settlement; with Arthur L. Ellsworth as its first postmaster, it was given a post office on Aug. 21, 1843, as Swartz Creek after a small stream nearby (swartz is German for black); the railroad came through in 1876 and called its station Hamilton for William Hamilton, of Flint, a director of the company; but there was another Hamilton in Michigan and, about 1880 it, like the village, took the name of its post office; it was platted in 1877 and incorporated as a village in 1958 [Helen Miller Tague; PO Archives].

**SWEDETOWN,** Houghton County: this settlement, with a station on the Mineral Range Railroad, 3 miles north of Hancock, was built prior to 1899 by the owners of the Quincy Mine whose agents were bringing in Swedish immigrant workers; but the Swedes were either drafted for the Civil War or hired as replacements by men who wished to escape the draft, and the place became a deserted village before its time [Mich Hist 24:94 1940].

**SWEETER,** Muskegon County: Henry H. Ferguson became the first postmaster of this rural post office on May 21, 1902, the office operating until Nov. 30, 1905 [PO Archives].

**SWEETLAND,** Kalamazoo County. See Portage.

**SWEETLAND,** Mason County. See Scottville.

**SWEET'S BRIDGE,** Manistee County. See Conger.

**SWEET'S STATION,** Muskegon County. See Fruitland.

**SWIFT,** Wayne County: it was settled in 1830 and first called Nankin

Center from its location in Nankin Township; it was given a post office as Swift on July 10, 1882, with Edward Lathers as its first postmaster; the office was closed on March 22, 1887, but was restored from Dec. 19, 1895, to Sept. 30, 1902 [GSM 1883; PO Archives].

**SWIFT SIDING,** Mackinac County: it was founded in 1943 by the Soo Line Railroad who named it for Frank Swift, a retired conductor; it did not become a village [George T. Springer].

**SWIZZLETOWN,** Clinton County. See Eureka.

**SYLVAN,** Osceola County: the town was named from its being in a lumbering region when it was organized in 1869; sawmill owner John H. Lanphear was its first supervisor and among its first settlers [Chapman].

**SYLVAN,** Washtenaw County. See Sylvan Center.

**SYLVAN BEACH,** Muskegon County. See Wabaningo.

**SYLVAN CENTER,** Washtenaw County: it was first settled by Cyrus Beckwith in 1830; William Dunham opened the first tavern and in 1838 Elihu Frisbie the first store; named from its location in the township which had been named in 1834 by Edmund E. Conkling, at the suggestion of his wife; it was given a post office as Sylvan on July 8, 1834, with Calvin Hickox as its first postmaster; the office was closed on Aug. 31, 1892, but was restored from March 3, 1893, to June 14, 1902 [Chapman; GSM 1893; PO Archives].

**SYLVAN LAKE,** Oakland County: a station on the Grand Trunk Railroad in 1881; the village was organized by a charter commission in 1921; Naomi A. Hilliker became its first postmaster on May 18, 1922, the office operating until April 30, 1925; incorporated as a village in 1923 and as a city in 1946; named from its location by Sylvan Lake [PO Archives; Leroy Trafton].

**SYLVANUS,** Hillsdale County. See Allen.

**SYLVESTER,** Mecosta County: David Fowler opened the first store here in Hinton Township in 1868; Travis Kelly became the first postmaster on Sept. 3, 1872, the office operating until July 15, 1904; it was named for Sylvester Dresser, a pioneer lumberman in the area [Mich Hist 20:226 1936; Chapman; PO Archives].

**TAFT,** Iosco County: a station on a branch of the Detroit & Mackinaw Railroad, 19 miles northwest of East Tawas, in 1894 [GSM 1894].

**TAHQUAMENON,** Chippewa County: this was the name of the post office (but spelled Taquaminon) first given to the village of Hulbert; the name is retained by a river rising at the conjunction of Luce, Alger, and Schoolcraft Counties and flowing through Chippewa County to Whitefish Bay; its larger falls, nearly 50 feet high, are on the county line of Luce and Chippewa; this is the "rushing Tahquamenaw" of Henry Longfellow's poem Hiawatha; from its copper speckled bed, the Indians gave it their name for dark waters [Sawyer; Emerson Smith].

TECUMSEH
Res.—W. Richard

TITTABAWASSEE TWP.
Res.—H.T. Hawley, M.D.

**TALBOT,** Menominee County: this village in Nadeau Township was founded soon after the Chicago & Northwestern Railroad came through in 1872; it was named for Samuel H. Talbot, a native of Maine, senior member of the lumbering firm of P. S. J. Talbot & Company; Fred W. Sensiba became its first postmaster on Sept. 14, 1883, the office operating until Nov. 14, 1905; its depot and some ten homes were wiped out by fire on May 18, 1906, and it is now a farming community [Ruth M. Thomas; PO Archives].

**TALBOT'S MILLS,** Lenawee County. See Addison.

**TALCOTT,** Charlevoix County. See Walloon Lake.

**TALLMADGE,** Ottawa County: it was first settled by T. B. Woodbury in 1835; the township was organized in the home of Mr. Stoddard in 1838, and named for another pioneer, Mr. Tallmadge; Bethuel Church became its first postmaster on May 13, 1839; the office was closed on Sept. 12, 1882, but was restored from April 16, 1883, to Oct. 31, 1902; the place was also known as Sand Creek [Henry C. Slaughter; Page; PO Archives].

**TALLMAN,** Mason County: the village was founded in 1879 by Horace Butters of the lumber firm of Butters, Peters & Company, his son, Marshall F. Butters, operated its general store; a station on the Pere Marquette Railroad; Marshall F. Butters became its first postmaster on May 31, 1880; the office was closed on Feb. 25, 1887, but was restored from Aug. 27, 1888, to Dec. 14, 1891, and from June 28, 1897, to Oct. 31, 1953; it was named for attorney H. C. Tallman [Page; PO Archives].

**TAMARACK,** Houghton County: the Tamarack Mine of the Tamarack Mining Company was developed by Captain John Daniel who organized the company and sank the first shaft in 1882; a station on the Hancock & Calumet Railroad [Stevens].

**TAMARACK,** Iron County: it was a sput take-off from the Chicago & Northwestern Railroad to the lumbering communities in the area; like several others of these stops, it was named after forest trees [Jack Hill, Sr.].

**TAMARACK,** Montcalm County: Samuel W. Weeks became the first postmaster of this rural post office in Winfield Township on Sept. 22, 1868, the office operating until April 14, 1873; it was named from nearby Tamarack Lake which, upon the north and west shore, was bordered by a growth of tamarack [Schenck].

**TANNER,** Jackson County. See Roots.

**TANNER,** Manistee County: a station on the Manistee & Northwestern Railroad, in Maple Grove Township, named for William W. Tanner who became its first postmaster on Nov. 19, 1889, the office operating until March 30, 1907 [GSM 1891; PO Archives].

**TAPIOLA,** Houghton County: this village in Portage Township was settled by Finns who gave it the Finnish name for abode of the bear; Maria

Nelson became its first postmaster on April 21, 1903; from its location just west of Otter Lake, it was also known as Otter Lake [Wargelin; GSM 1905; PO Archives].

**TAQUAMINON,** Chippewa County. See Tahquamenon.

**TARA'S HALLS,** St. Clair County: an Irish Catholic settlement on the Pine River, in Riley Township; Patrick Kennedy, realtor and builder, became its first postmaster on July 29, 1854, the office operating until Jan. 29, 1863; its name was taken from Thomas Moore's lyric, The harp that once through Tara's halls the soul of music shed, now hangs as mute on Tara's walls as if that soul were fled [GSM 1860; PO Archives].

**TARRY,** Huron County: a station on the Saginaw, Tuscola & Huron Railroad in 1884; it was named for John Tarry who became its first postmaster on March 13, 1891, the office operating until March 15, 1902 [GSM 1893; PO Archives].

**TAWAS BEACH,** Iosco County: it began as a summer resort on Tawas Bay, in Baldwin Township, with a station on the Detroit & Mackinaw Railroad; William Sutherland became its first postmaster on June 12, 1903; it became a part of East Tawas in 1922 [GSM 1905-31; PO Archives].

**TAWAS CITY,** Iosco County: it was founded in 1854 by Oakland County former judge Gideon O. Whittemore when G. O. Whittemore & Company built a sawmill on the site; it was platted in 1855 but not recorded until 1866; township supervisor James O. Whittemore became its first postmaster on Jan. 26, 1856; incorporated as a village in 1885 and as a city in 1895; it was named after the Indian tribe, the Ottawas, others say after Otawas, a local Chippewa chief [Powers; Federal; PO Archives].

**TAYLOR,** Baraga County: a station on the Marquette, Houghton & Ontonagon Railroad, five miles from L'Anse, in 1880; the Taylor Iron Company operated the Taylor Mine, Jay C. Morse, president, and James Pickands, treasurer [Havighurst; GSM 1883].

**TAYLOR,** Wayne County: the first settler in the area was Peter Coan in 1830; Taylor Township was erected in 1847, with Jared Sexton as its first supervisor, and was named for General Zachary Taylor, then fresh from his victories in the Mexican War; given a post office as Taylor Center on Jan. 12, 1863, with Mr. Sexton as its first postmaster, the office operating until Feb. 15, 1914; from then, the town was served by several adjacent post offices until Stanley A. Grendel became the first postmaster of Taylor on Oct. 7, 1958; incorporated as a city in May, 1968 [Burton; GSM 1860; PO Archives].

**TAYLORSVILLE,** Monroe County: this rural post office was named for Amos P. Taylor who became its first postmaster on March 6, 1833; it was changed to North Raisinville on Jan. 20, 1838, and closed on March 19, 1879 [PO Archives].

**TAYLORSVILLE,** Oakland County: Thomas H. Terwilliger became the first postmaster of this rural post office on Sept. 5, 1849, but the office was changed back to Austin on May 11, 1853 [PO Archives].

**TAYMOUTH,** Saginaw County: it was first settled by lumberman James McCormick in 1832; the township was organized as Faymouth in 1842, with the name later changed to Taymouth; it was given a post office as Taymouth on Jan. 18, 1858, with David D. Ross as its first postmaster, the office operating until June 30, 1903 [MPH 27:176 1896; Mills; PO Archives].

**TEAPOT DOME,** Van Buren County: a settlement at the junction of highways M-40 and US-12, four miles south of Paw Paw, in 1930; the name was in the news at the time, it being that of a U.S. oil producing reserve area, near Casper, Wyoming, which Albert F. Fall, secretary of the interior, leased to Harry F. Sinclair without competitive bidding in 1922 and for which he was convicted of bribe-taking in 1929 [GSM 1931; World Ency.].

**TEBO,** Bay County: a station on the Michigan Central Railroad, in Fraser Township, named for Mrs. Emilie Tebo who became its first postmaster on Jan. 6, 1898, the office operating until May 31, 1904 [GSM 1899; PO Archives].

**TECUMSEH,** Lenawee County: it was founded in 1824 by Musgrove Evans, Joseph W. Brown (both Quakers), and Austin E. Wing; in that year, Mr. Evans both platted the village and, on July 29, became its first postmaster; it was the first county seat, 1826-1837; incorporated as a village in 1837 and as a city in 1953; named after the Shawnee chief Tecumseh [Whitney; PO Archives].

**TECUMSEH,** Houghton County: the Tecumseh Copper Company was formed in 1880; the landed estate of the company here consisted of 560 acres [Stevens].

**TEEFT'S,** Saginaw County: a hamlet in 1878 [GSM 1879].

**TEKONSHA,** Calhoun County: Darius Pierce located land here in 1832; he sold it to Timothy Kimball who built a log house and became the first actual settler in 1833; the village was platted by Charles D. Smith, Harris C. Goodrich and Cornelius Wendell in 1836; Mr. Goodrich became the first postmaster of Wirt on Feb. 15, 1836, with the office renamed Tekonsha on June 17, 1836; when the Michigan Central Railroad came through in 1871 it was given a station; incorporated as a village in 1877; it was named for a local Pottawattomi chief, Tekon-quạ-sha [Everts; PO Archives].

**TEMPERANCE,** Monroe County: Lewis Ansted and his wife, Marietta Hayden Ansted (an ardent member of the Women's Christian Temperance Union) owned a 140 acre farm here in Bedford Township and on all deeds to the lots they sold was included the clause that no liquor was to be used, made or sold on the land; this provision was even assented to by the Ann Arbor Railroad when it obtained a right-of-way through the property; Mr. Ansted platted the village about 1884 and successfully petitioned for a post office named Temperance, of which he became the first postmaster on Dec. 8, 1884, serving until 1890; the village is still dry [Hazel K. Sonnichsen; PO Archives].

**TEMPLE,** Clare County: a station on the Toledo, Ann Arbor & Northern Michigan Railroad, in Winterfield Township; the village was founded in 1889 on land given by Mary L. Campbell and for her it was first named Campbell City, a name still carried on all legal documents; hotelman Bert Trall became the first postmaster, with the office named Temple, after Martin Temple, on April 21, 1890, the office operating until Aug. 12, 1966 [Anne Crawford, ex-PM; GSM 1891; PO Archives].

**TEN EYCK,** Wayne County. See Dearborn.

**TERRE COUPE,** Berrien County. See Dayton.

**TERRY STATION,** Bay County. See Linwood.

**TEUCHSAGRONDIE,** Wayne County: in August, 1699, LaSalle and Louis Hennepin, discovered a large village of the Hurons called Teuchsagronde, covering part of the ground where Detroit now stands, and in the New York State archives, Teuchsa Grondie was the name for the present-day site of Detroit [MPH 5:238 1884; Inside 3:42 Dec 1953; Levi Bishop, The Village of Teuchsa Grondi. 1871. Ms. in coll. of Mich. Pioneer Soc., Lansing].

**TEXAS,** Kalamazoo County: it was first settled by William Bishop in 1829, followed by Thomas McLin in 1830; a stage coach post office in 1844, with Oliver C. Hill as its first postmaster, and a government post office on June 23, 1874, with Lewis S. Burdick as postmaster, the office operating until June 29, 1901; named after its township which had been named after the Lone Star State, for the Texas revolt from Mexico was considered as a victory for free men over tyranny; the place was also known as Parson's Corners [MPH 27:568 1896; Durant; PO Archives].

**THAYER,** Gogebic County: a station on the Chicago & Northwestern Railroad, 3 miles east of Gogebic, in 1894 [Mich Manual 1899].

**THAYER,** Oakland County: it was named for John Thayer, from New York, who settled in the area in 1830; John Campbell, a native Scot, came here in Groveland Township in 1834, and he became the first postmaster on July 6, 1880, the office operating until April 30, 1901 [Seeley; GSM 1881; PO Archives].

**THE HEIGHTS,** Roscommon County. See Houghton Lake Heights.

**THELMA,** Antrim County: Charles F. Thomas became the first postmaster of this rural post office on Oct. 21, 1905, the office operating until Oct. 31, 1906 [PO Archives].

**THEODORE,** Dickinson County: when this village was platted for the Lake Superior Ship Canal, Railway & Iron Company by J. A. Van Clive in 1881, it was in Marquette County from which Dickinson was set off in 1891 [Andreas].

**THETFORD,** Genesee County: Grovenor Vinton, a New Yorker, took up the first land and became the first settler in 1835; Nahum M. Wilson named the township after Thetford, Orange County, Vermont, in 1842; its first post office, named Thetford, opened at Fayville, with Corydon E. Fay as its postmaster, on Dec. 26, 1844; it was closed on April 12, 1869, but was restored from July 12, 1898, to Aug. 30, 1902; its second, with Albert B. Calkins as postmaster, opened on Dec. 15, 1855, as East Thetford, but changed to Thetford Centre on Aug. 2, 1861, with Nahum M. Wilson as its postmaster; on June 9, 1873, the office was moved to Henpeck and was again named East Thetford, and it operated until Aug. 30, 1902 [Ellis; PO Archives].

**THOMAS**, Oakland County: in 1873, John Thomas platted 18 acres in northern Oxford Township on the Detroit & Bay City Railroad; businesses soon followed; Homer A. Thomas became the first postmaster on Sept. 29, 1873, the office operating until June 30, 1938 [Durant; PO Archives].

**THOMAS**, Oceana County: John Fortune became the first postmaster of this rural post office on April 9, 1866, with the office changed to Hazel Grove on March 29, 1872 [PO Archives].

**THOMASTON**, Gogebic County: this village in Wakefield Township was founded in 1891 as a semi-terminal for the Duluth, South Shore & Atlantic Railroad; it was a woodsmen and loggers center; Levi W. Dodendorf became its first postmaster on Nov. 7, 1891, the office operating until Aug. 14, 1926; it is believed to have been named for Charles W. Thompson, who became the third postmaster [Gogebic Hist. Soc.; PO Archives].

**THOMASTOWN**, Saginaw County: Thomas McCarty and his father, Edward, entered the first land here in 1830, and built the first log cabin; Thomas Owen, a Welshman, settled here in 1853 and helped organize the township in 1856; Octavius Thompson was the first supervisor [MPH 27:180 1896; Mills].

**THOMPSON**, Iosco County: this township, erected in 1870, was organized by and named for Thomas F. Thompson, its first supervisor; in 1891, it was vacated and attached to Oscoda, but in 1905, it was detatched from Oscoda and attached to Plainfield; its town was named after the township [Otis; Page].

**THOMPSON**, Schoolcraft County: it was named for E. L. Thompson, of Detroit, president of the Delta Lumber Company which had a mill here on Lake Michigan; Alvah B. Mathews became its first postmaster on Dec. 29, 1881, followed by E. T. Slayton, secretary of the company, in 1882 [GSM 1883; PO Archives].

**THOMPSON LAKE**, St. Joseph County: a settlement in Sherman Township, on Thompson Lake, which had been named for Elijah Thompson who settled on its banks about 1840 [Cutler].

**THOMPSON'S CORNERS**, Huron County. See Kilmanagh.

**THOMPSON'S CORNERS**, Oakland County. See South Lyon.

**THOMPSON'S CORNERS**, St. Joseph County: Julius A. Thompson built the first tavern in Burr Oak Township in 1851 [Everts].

**THOMPSONVILLE**, Benzie County: this village on the Betsie River lies in Both Colfax and Weldon Townships; Sumner S. Thompson operated his Thompson Lumber Company to the south of here, but when the railroad came through he moved it here to be on the line and thus began the village named for him; Edgar E. Hunt became its first postmaster on Aug. 15, 1890, succeeded by James H. Winters in 1892; incorporated as a village in 1892 [L. H. Maginity, PM; Powers; PO Archives].

**THORICE**, Chippewa County: this village was named from a combination of the names of its promotors, Charles J. Thoenen and Fred Price; Mr. Thoenen became its first postmaster on Jan. 14, 1905; the office was closed on May 14, 1910, restored on Nov. 19, 1913, with Charles J. Hallmann as postmaster, and changed to Munoskong on Dec. 16, 1926 [Hamilton; PO Archives].

**THORNAPPLE**, Barry County. See Middleville.

**THORNAPPLE**, Eaton County: a station on the Grand River Valley (now Michigan Central) Railroad in 1874, near the Thornapple River whose banks were lined with Thornapple trees [Johnson; Mich Manual 1899].

**THORNTON**, St. Clair County: it was named for William Thornton who bought his land here on the Pine River, in Kimball Township, in 1836; a station on the Port Huron & Northern Michigan Railroad; Stephen V. Thornton became the first postmaster on Oct. 4, 1858; the office was closed on Oct. 14, 1859, but was restored from Nov. 7, 1859, to Jan. 31, 1907 [Andreas; GSM 1873; PO Archives].

**THORNVILLE**, Lapeer County: the settlement was given a post office named Amboy on March 21, 1837, with Joseph S. Gibbins as its first postmaster; he was succeeded by Charles Wright on Dec. 22, 1838; the Steele Brothers built the first store in the township of Metamora here in 1840; Benjamin Thorne, who had come here from Dutchess County, N.Y., in 1839, became the third postmaster on Dec. 3, 1845, and on July 14, 1854, the village and its post office were renamed for him; Samuel Durstine, from Genesee County, N.Y., also came in 1839; its post office operated until June 30, 1905 [MPH 12:403 1888; PO Archives; Page].

**THORP**, Wexford County: Neal D. Ford became the first postmaster of this hamlet in South Branch Township on Aug. 21, 1883 [GSM 1885].

**THREADVILLE**, Genesee County: a settlement on the Thread River, made before 1824, for in that year Flavius Josephus Stanley was a blacksmith here; his eldest daughter, Ann Jeanette, wed the widower John Preston Kellogg, and one of their eleven children was W(ill) K(eith) Kellogg, the Battle Creek cereal magnate [Mich Hist 25:416 1941].

**THREE LAKES**, Baraga County: this old mining settlement was given a station on the Marquette, Houghton & Ontonagon Railroad by 1878; it was named from its location near Ruth, George, and Beaufort Lakes [Martin; GSM 1879].

**THREE OAKS**, Berrien County: it was first settled in 1850 by Henry Chamberlain who named it when it was given a post office on Oct. 6, 1854, and platted it in 1858; Joseph G. Ames was its first postmaster; incorporated as a village in 1867; three white-oak trees growing in a cluster here provided the name [MPH 35:662 1907; Fox; PO Archives].

**THREE RIVERS**, St. Joseph County: it was first platted as Moab by Christopher Shinnaman in 1830; an adjacent plat was made in 1831 by George Buck and Jacob McIntefer and called St. Joseph, which, when it failed in its bid to be the county seat, became farmland; from its location at the confluence of the St. Joseph, Rocky, and Portage Rivers, John H. Bowman named his new plat Three Rivers in Nov., 1836; a month later, George Buck and his associates platted Lockport and named it from their canal and water-power projects; in 1871, the corporation limits of Three Rivers were extended to embrace all these plats; it was given a post office as Bucks on Oct. 10, 1831, with George Buck as its first postmaster, and he was still in office when the name was changed to Lockport on March 8, 1837, but Burroughs Moore was the postmaster when the name became Three Rivers on Feb. 15, 1840; incorporated as a village in 1855 and as a city in 1895 [MPH 38:386 1912; Everts; PO Archives].

**THUMB LAKE**, Charlevoix County: grocer James A. Waggoner became the first postmaster of this lumber settlement in Hudson Township on Sept. 25, 1882; its station on the Boyne City & Southeastern Railroad was called Thumb Lake Junction; named from the shape of the lake it borders on [GSM 1882; PO Archives].

**THUNDER BAY**, Alpena County. See Alpena.

**THURBER**, Lenawee County. See Sand Creek.

**THURMAN**, Eaton County. See Ainger.

**TIETSORT'S CROSSING**, Cass County. See Glenwood.

**TIFFIN**, Lenawee County: Warren Aylsworth became the first postmaster on May 2, 1835, the office operating until only June 5, 1835; in 1837, Lauren Hotchkiss was elected to the state legislature, in 1839, he was ordained a Baptist minister, and in 1840, he built a sawmill here; the settlement which followed became a village named from its location on the Tiffin River, which has since been renamed Bean Creek from the abundance of bean timber which grew on its banks [Hogaboam; PO Archives].

**TIGRIS**, Oceana County: Mrs. Lucy M. Thomas became the first postmaster of this fruit growing settlement in Hart Township in Aug. 22, 1891, the office operating until Jan. 14, 1905; why it was named after the great west Asian river is not known [GSM 1893-1907; PO Archives].

**TILDEN**, Marquette County: an iron mine and its community, named for Samuel Tilden, Democratic nominee for president of the U.S. and the president of the Iron Cliffs Company about 1872; Ebenezer Rowland became its first postmaster on March 16, 1874, the office operating until Feb. 12, 1877 [Hatcher; PO Archives].

**TINKER TOWN**, St. Joseph County. See Howardsville.

**TIOGA**, Alger County: this small settlement in Onota Township formed around the charcoal kilns of Charles H. Schaffer about 1885 [John Boogren].

**TIPTON**, Lenawee County: it was founded by the Rev. Henry Tripp in 1831, organized in 1833, and named Franklin Center after Benjamin Franklin; later, it was renamed Tripp Town, and finally shortened to Tipton; William Camburn became its first postmaster on June 6, 1834 [Thelma Swart, PM].

**TITTABAWASSEE**, Saginaw County: John B. Hughes became the first postmaster of this rural post office on June 4, 1856, the office operating until Oct. 11, 1859 [PO Archives].

**TITTABAWASSEE**, Sanilac County. See Painesville.

**TITUS**, Mecosta County: grocer Christmas Vashaw became the first postmaster of this rural post office in Sheridan Township on Aug. 21, 1897, the office operating until April 15, 1908; probably named for Harold Titus, conservationist and author, a resident of the Grand Traverse area [GSM 1899-1909; PO Archives].

**TITUSVILLE**, Ottawa County: a hamlet near Berlin in 1918 [GSM 1919].

**TOBACCO**, Gladwin County. See Dale.

**TOBIN'S HARBOR**, Keweenaw County: resort manager Edward S. Smith became the first postmaster of this summer resort at the east end of Isle Royale on May 13, 1911, the office operating until Aug. 13, 1938 [GSM 1913; PO Archives].

**TODD HARBOR**, Keweenaw County: this site on the north central part of Isle Royale was the seat of mining operations in 1847-48 [Mich Hist 30:680 1946].

**TOIVOLA**, Houghton County: formerly a logging camp, the village was founded in 1894 by Finns who gave it the Finnish name for the vale of hope; a station on the Copper Range Railroad; Earl N. Drake became its first postmaster on Jan. 19, 1905, succeeded by E. A. Lange in 1906 [Leonard E. Pennanen, PM; Federal; PO Archives].

**TOKIO**, Calhoun County: Carrie I. Ott became the first postmaster of this rural post office, 7 miles from Marshall, on April 24, 1897, the office operating until June 29, 1901 [GSM 1899; PO Archives].

**TOLAND'S PRAIRIE**, Kalamazoo County. See Tolland's Prairie.

**TOLANVILLE**, Washtenaw County. See Milan.

**TOLCOTT**, Charlevoix County. See Walloon Lake.

**TOLEDO BEACH**, Monroe County: Albert C. Van Driesen became the first postmaster of this summer resort on Lake Erie, in LaSalle

Township, on May 29, 1915; a station on the Toledo, O.B. & N. Railroad [GSM 1917; PO Archives].

**TOLLAND'S PRAIRIE**, Kalamazoo County: in some sources as Matthews Prairie and on the Farmer map of 1835 as Fry Prairie; it was first settled by William Tolland, a squatter in 1829, soon followed by N. Matthews, Ralph Tuttle and Sherman Comings; it is also to be found as Toland's Prairie [MPH 5: 256,345 1884; Mich Hist 33:225 1949].

**TOLTEC**, Ontonagon County: a 320-acre copper mining tract; Toltec Consolidated was organized in 1850 and mined from 1851 to 1861, at a loss of about a half million dollars; Toltec was an ancient Mexican Indian civilization whose advanced features included metallurgy [Stevens; Ency. Brit.].

**TOM BENTON**, Eaton County. See Benton.

**TOMPKINS CENTER**, Jackson County: it was first settled by Richard Townley in 1836; Thompkins Township was organized in 1838 and named after the township in New York which had been named by Colonel Robert H. Anderson for Daniel D. Tompkins, a former governor of that state, and which had been the home town of Mr. Townley; it was given a post office as Tompkins on Jan. 22, 1839, with Joseph Wade as its first postmaster, the office operating until Oct. 31, 1904 [Cowles; Daball; PO Archives].

**TOMPKINS CORNERS**, Grand Traverse County. See Hannah.

**TONE**, Chippewa County: this settlement, 4½ miles from Pickford, was given a post office on Aug. 21, 1897, with Thomas Hassett as its first postmaster; the name honored Theodore Wolfe Tone, Irish patriot, admired by the Scottish-Irish settlers here [GSM 1899; Hamilton; PO Archives].

**TONGUISH PLAINS**, Wayne County: an Indian settlement in 1825, named for an Indian chief, more commonly called Toga; later spelled Tonquish [MPH 5:398 1844].

**TONKIN**, Clare County: Alfred Touchette became the first postmaster of this rural post office on Nov. 11, 1891, the office operating until Sept. 15, 1893 [PO Archives].

**TONQUISH**, Oakland County: in 1837, a stage coach post office in Southfield Township; named for a local Indian chief [GSM 1838].

**TONQUISH**, Wayne County: it began as a rural settlement in Nankin Township with farmer Lauren T. Blount becoming its first postmaster on March 9, 1886; the office was closed on March 21, 1895, but was restored from July 30, 1900, to Sept. 30, 1903; gradually the land was subdivided and in 1954 the property of its 21 separate subdivisions was purchased and the first homes opened in 1957; it was given a branch post office in 1961; it was named after Tonquish Creek, which forms the norther border of the village, and which had been named for Indian chief Tonquish [Harriet Gagnon, PO; GSM 1889; PO Archives].

**TOOKER ISLAND**, Keweenaw County: this island off the shores of Isle Royale was named for its former owner, S. C. Tooker, who, with his family, came from California for several summers to occupy his cottage here [Mich Hist 30:680 1946].

**TOPAZ**, Ontonagon County: a station on the Duluth, South Shore & Atlantic Railroad, in Matchwood Township, about 1900; storekeeper Rudolph Stindt became its first postmaster on June 29, 1910; in a mining district, it was named after a semiprecious stone [Charles Willman; GSM 1911].

**TOPINABEE**, Cheboygan County: it was founded in 1881 at the behest of Michigan Central Railroad officials who wanted to see a resort here on Mullett Lake; H. H. Pike, the hotel proprietor who platted the village, named it for the Pottawattomi chief who concluded the treaty giving the white men the site of Fort Dearborn, now Chicago; his name is said to mean Great Bear Heart; Daniel P. Stofer became its first postmaster on April 17, 1882 [Myrtle E. Kennedy; PM; Federal; Page].

**TOQUIN**, Van Buren County: this village in Bangor Township was founded in 1884 in prospect of a branch of the Toledo & South Haven Railroad coming through, and was first called Maplegrove; it did get a station in 1890, and a post office, both named Toquin, with Edwin J. Reed becoming its first postmaster on Jan. 26, 1889, the office operating until Sept. 14, 1905 [Mich Hist 39:152 1955; GSM 1891; PO Archives].

**TORCH LAKE**, Antrim County: Captain John W. Brown built a log house and barn here about 1858, and the settlement which followed became known as Brownstown; he sold out to Wilcox & Newell in 1864; Torch Lake Township (the Indian name was Waswagonink, or lake of torches, from the fishing lights they used on the lake), was organized in 1866, and when Major Cicero Newell became the first postmaster of Torch Lake post office on June 4, 1866, the name Brownstown was dropped; the post office was transferred to and renamed Wilson on March 29, 1872, but the Torch Lake post office was re-established from April 10, 1872, with Ambrose E. Palmer as postmaster, to Aug. 31, 1911 [Traverse; PO Archives].

**TORCH LAKE**, Houghton County. See Lake Linden.

**TORRY**, Cheboygan County. See Wolverine.

**TOTTEN**, Lake County: a station on the Grand Rapids & Indiana Railroad in 1884; this settlement in Ellsworth Township formed around the Totten & Cole planning mill; Edson L. Smith became its first postmaster on Feb. 5, 1885, succeeded by Mrs. Flora Totten in 1886, the office operating until May 16, 1890 [GSM 1887-91; PO Archives].

**TOWER**, Cheboygan County: this village on the Black River, in Forest Township, began as a lumber settlement with a station on the Detroit & Mackinaw Railroad; James A. Kelley became its first postmaster on April 28, 1899; it was named for the daughter of Judge Samuel S. Tower, Ellen May Tower, who died of typhoid fever as an army nurse in the Spanish-American War, in December, 1898; she was the first Michigan woman and one of the first in the U.S. to be given a military burial [Gladys Mason, PM].

**TOWN HOUSE**, Lenawee County. See Townley.

**TOWNLEY**, Lenawee County: a station on the C., J. & M. Railroad, in Rollin Township; storekeeper Chester C. Clark became its first postmaster on Feb. 16, 1892, with the office named Town House, and he was still the postmaster when the office was renamed Townley on March 31, 1902 [GSM 1893-1903; PO Archives].

**TOWNLINE**, Berrien County. See Union Pier.

**TOWN LINE**, Wayne County. See Yew.

**TOWNS**, Branch County: Hattie E. Walworth became the first postmaster of this rural post office in Algansee Township on Nov. 15, 1886, the office operating until Jan. 30, 1904 [PO Archives].

**TRAUNIK**, Alger County: George Nickel homesteaded 160 acres here in Limestone Township about 1895, but the community developed with the coming of Slovene settlers, migrants from the lumber camps, about 1910, first among them Tony Knaus; first known as Buckeye Landing and then as Buckeye Spur, reflecting the activities of the Buckeye Land & Lumber Company in the area; it was renamed by storekeeper Louis Mikulich who became the first postmaster from July 2, 1927, until his death in 1961; it was named for the native Slovene village of many of the settlers, Travnik (meaning meadow), and not to be confused with the Brosnian city of Travnik [Louis F. Mikulich, actg. PM].

**TRAVERSE BAY**, Grand Traverse County. See East Bay.

**TRAVERSE CITY**, Grand Traverse County: French voyageurs found two deep indentations on Michigan's west coast: the larger one they called La Grande Traverse; in 1847, William Boardman, of Napierville, Illinois, bought land on a stream (now Boardman River) winding through the present town; his son Horace became the first white settler when he began logging on his father's land that year; in 1851, Hannah, Lay & Company, of Chicago, bought the Boardman holdings and developed the town; it had been called Wequetong, or Head of the Bay, until Albert T. Lay got it a post office as Traverse City on Feb. 7, 1854, with Dr. David C. Goodale as its first postmaster; incorporated as a village in 1881 and as a city in 1895; Perry Hannah is regarded as the father of Traverse City [MPH 32:64 1902; Sprague; Barnes; PO Archives].

**TRAVERSE CORNERS**, Oakland County: a hamlet in 1864 [GSM 1865].

**TRAVERSE RESORT**, Leelanau County: a station on the Manistee & Northwestern Railroad, four miles northwest of Traverse City, in 1894 [GSM 1895].

**TRAVERSE ROADS**, Newaygo County. See Woodville.

**TRAVIS**, Kalamazoo County: a flag station on the Grand Rapids & Indiana Railroad, 8 miles north of Kalamazoo, in 1878 [GSM 1879].

**TREMAINVILLE**, Monroe County: it is in some records as Tremainesville and as Tremaines Village; it was founded in 1825 by the brothers Isaac (b. 1781) and Calvin (1794-1845) Tremain, from New York State; the Port Lawrence post office was changed to Tremainville on Jan. 7, 1834; in the Michigan-Ohio boundary dispute (called the Toledo War), the site was transferred to Lucas County, Ohio, on March 23, 1835, and is now within the city limits of Toledo; see under Vistula for the terms of the agreement [Treman; Wing; GSM 1838; PO Archives].

**TREMBLE CREEK**, St. Clair County: this settlement was begun by Captain Francois Marsac about 1798, at Tremble Creek, in present Ira Township, on the Ridge Road; the creek was named for Gazet Tremble whose sister married Richard Conner, paymaster to the Indians, and the stream was later renamed Conner's Creek [Eldredge; Andreas].

**TRENARY**, Alger County: a station on the Minneapolis, St. Paul & Sault Ste. Marie Railroad, in Mathias Township; the settlement formed around the Levi D. Trenary sawmill; storekeeper Alanson W. Clark became its first postmaster on Feb. 25, 1903 [GSM 1905; PO Archives].

**TRENT**, Muskegon County: it was first settled by Benjamin Whitney in 1854; he owned a grist mill here and he became the first postmaster of the settlement on July 18, 1867, the office operating until May 15, 1905 [Page; PO Archives].

**TRENTON**, Wayne County: when erected in 1827, Monguagon Township was named by Governor Lewis Cass for a local Pottawattomi chief; its first supervisor, Abram Caleb Truax, laid out the village of Truaxton in 1834; the settlement had been given a post office as Monguago, with Mr. Truax as its first postmaster, on Jan. 2, 1828; the name was changed to Truago on Feb. 3, 1837, and on April 1, 1847, to Trenton, a name derived from the strata of limestone underlying the town; it was platted and recorded as Trenton by George B. Truax and Sophia Slocum in 1850; incorporated as a village in 1855; it annexed the village of Sibley in 1929; incorporated as a city in 1957 [Mich Hist 26:319 1942; Cole; PO Archives].

**TRIANGLE RANCH**, Iron County: it was also called Rosebush Ranch for Judson Rosebush, of Appleton, Wisconsin, who founded it as an experimental cattle ranch in 1920; the project was given up during the depression of the 1930s [Jack Hill, Sr.].

**TRIMOUNTAIN**, Houghton County: this village in Adams Township was founded by the Trimountain Mining Company in 1899; Charles S. McLachlan became its first postmaster on March 29, 1900; it was named from the three nearby mountain peaks [Josephine V. Gelsten, PM].

**TRIPP TOWN**, Lenawee County. See Tipton.

**TRIST**, Jackson County: this settlement in Waterloo Township dates from 1840; the village later developed around the grist mill of Jacob Faisst; storekeeper John Siegrist became its first postmaster on Dec. 19, 1889, the office operating until Dec. 31, 1901 [DeLand; GSM 1891-1903; PO Archives].

**TROMBLEY,** Oakland County: Owen Murphy became the first postmaster of this rural post office on Oct. 4, 1880; the office was closed on Feb. 14, 1881, restored on July 14, 1884, and transferred to and renamed Leonard on Dec. 22, 1884 [PO Archives].

**TROMBLY,** Chippewa County: Mrs. Armilda A. Griffin became the first postmaster of this settlement on Munuscong Lake on March 22, 1910 [GSM 1911].

**TROMBLY,** Delta County: the settlement began in 1879 with the arrival of six Trombly brothers from New York State; they had been persuaded to migrate to Michigan by their brother Frank, who had been here previously [David S. Coon; Delta Reporter, Sept. 1, 1965].

**TROSTVILLE,** Saginaw County. See Frankentrost.

**TROUT CREEK,** Ontonagon County: a station on the Duluth, South Shore & Atlantic Railroad, named after the stream beside it; Anton Marski became the first postmaster on Dec. 18, 1888 [GSM 1889; PO Archives].

**TROUTDALE,** Charlevoix County: this settlement on Bear (now Walloon) Lake was given a post office on Sept. 11, 1879, with Cornelius A. Burnam as its first postmaster, the office operating until Aug. 17, 1881 [PO Archives].

**TROUT LAKE,** Chippewa County: it was settled in 1881 at the junction of two railroads and became a trading center for the Stickney, Charles Johnson, and other lumber camps in the area; Charles Coffey became its first postmaster on Dec. 11, 1888, with the office still operating [Federal; PO Archves].

**TROWBRIDGE,** Allegan County: Leander S. Prouty became the first settler here in 1835; in the morning of the day he settled in his new home, he went to Ostego to wed Harriet Cannon, and they started on their wedding trip in a canoe for their home in Trowbridge the same day; when the town was organized in 1842, he became the first justice of the peace; Stanley C. Foster became the first postmaster on Jan. 15, 1862, but the office was closed on Oct. 8, 1863; named for Charles C. Trowbridge, a Detroiter with local financial interests, being proprietor of the village of Allegan, just to the north [MPH 17:560 1890; Thomas; PO Archives].

**TROWBRIDGE,** Cheboygan County: a station on the Mackinaw division of the Michigan Central Railroad; Henry H. Trowbridge became its first postmaster on June 26, 1882, the office operating until Nov. 30, 1912 [GSM 1883; Blinn; PO Archives].

**TROWBRIDGE,** Ingham County: this railroad transfer point for travelers to Chicago was named Chicago Junction by the railroad officials about 1878, who later renamed it for a prominent railroad family of Detroit [Foster].

**TROY**, Berrien County. See New Troy.

**TROY**, Oakland County: Johnson Niles, from Otsego County, N.Y., purchased the first land here in 1821 and became the first settler in 1822 as well as the first postmaster on Dec. 27, 1826; in 1838, he platted the village and recorded it as Hastings, honoring Eurotas P. Hastings, then president of the Michigan Bank; it was also called Troy Corners; named after its township which had been named after Troy, N.Y., many of the early settlers having come from that area; incorporated as the city of Troy in 1955 [Seeley; J. Lawson Lockhart; PO Archives].

**TRUAGO**, Wayne County. See Trenton.

**TRUAX**, Wayne County. See Trenton.

**TRUFANT**, Montcalm County: Emery Trufant entered the first land here in Maple Valley Township and built a sawmill in 1871; Edwin Russell who built a mill and the place became known as Russell's Mills; Mr. Trufant sold his mill to Joseph B. Hileman and Jacob Hessler, partners, who laid out the village in 1874, and recorded it on March 10, 1875, naming it for the first settler; Mr. Hileman became the first postmaster on Dec. 11, 1871 [Mich Hist 11:684 1927; Schenck].

**TRUITT'S**, Cass County: a station on the Chicago & Western Michigan (now Pere Marquette) Railroad, near the Indiana line, in 1884; grocer James W. Smith became its first postmaster on July 26, 1897, the office operating until June 29, 1901 [GSM 1899; PO Archives].

**TRUMBULL'S**, Jackson County: a station on the Michigan Central Railroad, six miles west of Jackson, in 1878 [GSM 1879].

**TRYON'S CORNERS**, Berrien County: it was named for William H. Tryon, pioneer fruit farmer and storekeeper here in Royalton Township; A. J. Dispennet is said to have become its first postmaster in 1874, but there is no official record of it [Ellis; PO Archives].

**TULA**, Gogebic County: a station on the Duluth, South Shore & Atlantic Railroad, in Wakefield Township; the settlement formed around the Tula Lumber Company mill; Josiah W. Lane became its first postmaster on Feb. 5, 1907, succeeded by company manager A. J. DeVries in 1910, the office operating until 1916; Tula is also a village some 20 miles south of Moscow, Russia [Victor Lemmer; GSM 1911; PO Archives].

**TURIN**, Marquette County: on official documents and on some maps it was designated as Turin, after its township; locally it was called Macfarland's Hill and now simply Macfarland; located largely on the Macfarland farm, the log cabin in which Walter Macfarland was born in 1872, still stands at the edge of the village; it was given a post office as Turin on Feb. 27, 1883, with John R. Berringer as its first postmaster, the office operating until May 31, 1954 [Delta Reporter, Sept. 1, 1965; Rev. Charels J. Reinhart; PO Archives].

**TURNER,** Arenac County: a station on the Detroit & Mackinaw Railroad; the village was founded by and named for Joseph Turner, of Saginaw; John H. Larkin became its first postmaster on Dec. 21, 1885; the office was closed on March 5, 1888, but has been restored since Dec. 15, 1891; incorporated as a village in 1915 [Fred W. Whitehosue; PO Archives].

**TURNERSPORT,** Manistee County. See Pierport.

**TURTLE,** Iosco County· Robert Wilkins became the first postmaster of this rural post office, five miles from Turner, on Feb. 15,1901, the office operating until March 31, 1908 [GSM 1903; PO Archives].

**TURTLE LAKE,** Benzie County: William W. Eaton became the first postmaster of this rural post office in Inland Township on March 12, 1890, the office operating until April 14, 1904 [MPH 31:145 1901; PO Archives].

**TUSCARORA,** Cheboygan County. See Burt Lake.

**TUSCARORA,** Ottawa County. See Superior.

**TUSCOLA,** Livingston County. See Cohoctah Center.

**TUSCOLA,** Tuscola County: the first land purchase in the county for purpose of immediate improvement was made by Dennis Harrison in 1835; Tuscola Township was organized in 1840; Colonel John H. Richardson and his brother, Dr. Paschal Richardson, came in 1848; it was given a post office as Worth, Saginaw County, on March 6, 1848, with Ebenezer Davis as its first postmaster, changed to Tuscola on Jan. 8, 1875; this sawmill village on the Cass River was platted in 1850; its post office operated until Jan. 5, 1962; the name Tuscola is said to have been invented by and suggested by Henry R. Schoolcraft [J. A. Gallery; PO Archives].

**TUSCOLA CENTER,** Tuscola County. See Caro.

**TUSTIN,** Osceola County: in 1872, William J. Townsend became the first settler, Daniel McGovern opened the first store, and the Grand Rapids & Indiana (now Pennsylvania) Railroad, which had sent Dr. J. P. Tustin, a medical missionary, to Sweden to recruit laborers, settled their colony of some 300 persons here in Burdell Township, giving them forty acres of land; the colony was called New Bleking, but the village was named for Dr. Tustin (as later were Tustin, Wis., and Tustin, Calif.); it was given a post office as Tustin on April 10, 1872, with Mr. Townsend as its first postmaster; incorporated as a village in 1893 [Richard Beauleaux; Chapman; PO Archives].

**TWECOMA,** Gogebic County: a station on the Chicago & Northwestern Railroad, in Wakefield Township; Samuel Hill became the first postmaster of this mining settlement on Aug. 12, 1918, the office operating until May 31, 1926 [GSM 1919-27; PO Archives].

**TWELVE CORNERS,** Berrien County: Eddy E. McKee became the first postmaster of this hamlet, then five miles northeast of Benton Harbor, on May 12, 1891, the office operating until Feb. 28, 1905 [GSM 1893-1907; PO Archives].

**TWELVE MILE SIDING,** Mason County: a station on the Pere Marquette Railroad, in Branch Township, in 1880 [GSM 1881].

**TWINING**, Arenac County: the first store here in Dalton Township was built by Mr. Odell; he sold out to lumberman Frederick L. Twining for whom the station was named when the Detroit & Mackinaw Railroad came through in 1894 and he became the first postmaster on July 28, 1897; incorporated as a village in 1903 [Frank Black; PO Archives].

**TWIN LAKE**, Muskegon County: this village in Dalton Township was founded by Archibald B. Buel, Daniel Buzzell and his son George H. Buzzell about 1866; at that time the water level was high and there were two lakes here, hence the name (now it has dropped and there are four); Warren F. Odion became the first postmaster on May 1, 1873, the year Mr. Buell platted the village [John J. McLaughlin, PM].

**TWIN LAKES**, Houghton County: the settlement was named from its nearness to Lake Gerald and Lake Roland, and is sometimes called Lake Roland.

**TWIN MOUNTAIN**, Grand Traverse County: a station on the Manistee & Northwestern Railroad, in 1888 [GSM 1895].

**TWO HEART**, Luce County: it was named from its location on the Two Hearted River where it empties into Lake Superior; the Gazateer 1838 called it "the Double Hearted (or Twin) River"; old lumbermen called it Two Heart River; it is now a sportmen's camp [Mich Hist 31:318 1947].

**TWO RIVERS**, Isabella County: this village in Deerfield Township was named from its location near the confluence of Walker Creek and the Chippewa River; James C. Caldwell, of Fremont, opened a hotel here in 1882 and the place was given a post office as Caldwell on Aug. 26, 1884, with him as its first postmaster, the office operating until Nov. 30, 1906 [Fancher; PO Archives].

**TYLER**, Eaton County: with the office named South Eaton, David B. Bradford became the first postmaster of this rural post office on March 25, 1839; John Tyler became the tenth president of the U.S. on April 4, 1841, and this post office was renamed for him on Dec. 10, 1841, the office operating until Dec. 3, 1845 [Strange; PO Archives].

**TYLERVILLE**, Hillsdale County. See Mosherville.

**TYNER**, Saginaw County: storekeeper Hamilton Winter became the first postmaster of this rural post office in Brant Township on May 4, 1881, succeeded by another storekeeper, George W. Wilson, in 1884, the office operating until Sept. 23, 1887 [GSM 1883-89; PO Archives].

**TYOGA**, Alger County: a station on the Duluth, South Shore & Atlantic Railroad, in Onota Township; the settlement formed around the mill and general store of the Tyoga Lumber Company; John W. Bailey became its first postmaster on Feb. 15, 1906, the office operating until July 31, 1907 [GSM 1907; PO Archives].

**TYRE**, Sanilac County: this village on the Cass River in Austin Township was founded by Alex Soule, John Getty, and others, in 1857; the first store was a log building put up by Richard Collins; Mr. Getty became the first postmaster on Oct. 7, 1863; the office was closed on Sept. 14, 1881, but was restored from Nov. 25, 1881, to July 31, 1964; a station on the Pere Marquette Railroad; the Soule family named it after Biblical Tyre becaue of its stony terrane [Chapman; PO Archives].

**TYRONE**, Kent County: it was first settled in 1849 by Mrs. Louisa Scott and family, who went in to board men working on the state road; Tyrone Township was organized in 1855, with Uriah Chubb as its first supervisor [Dillenback].

**TYRONE**, Livingston County: the first settlers in the area were George Cornell, in 1834, followed by his brothers, Isaac and Henry; the town was organized in 1837-38, and named by Jonathan L. Wolverton after Tyrone, Schuyler County, N.Y.; Jirah Hillman became the first postmaster on May 6, 1839, the office operating until April 30, 1900; Norman Hodges started an adjacent village which failed, but the locality of it is still known as Hodgeburg [Ellis; PO Archives].

**TYRRELL**, Oscoda County: this rural post office in Big Creek Township was named for Carlos M. Terrell who became its first postmaster on Jan. 21, 1888, the office operating until Aug. 31, 1901 [Grace L. Funsch].

**UBLY**, Huron County: Alfred Pagett opened the first store here in 1865 and the settlement became known as Pagett's Corners; he renamed it Ubley after his native town in England, but the depot sign misspelled it Ubly, and it has so remained; he became the first postmaster on April 14, 1880; the office was closed on Sept. 14, 1881, but with him again its postmaster, it was restored on April 19, 1882, and is still operating; the village was platted and promoted by D. H. Pierce; incorporated as a village in 1896 [Hey; PO Archives].

**ULA**, Kent County: Dubois Conklin became the first postmaster of this rural post office in Alpine Township on Sept. 7, 1886, the office operating until Sept. 30, 1902 [PO Archives].

**UMATILLA**, Wexford County: Marilla D. Johnson became the first postmaster of this rural post office in Boone Township on July 3, 1876, the office operating until July 20, 1877 [PO Archives].

**UNADILLA**, Livingston County: the village was known locally as Milan, but there was already a Milan post office in Michigan and this one was given a post office as Unadilla, named after its township, on June 25, 1834, with Elnathan Noble as its first postmaster; the village was platted for Mary Wynans and Alexander Pyper by John Farnsworth in 1837, but the plat was abandoned; its post office operated until July 14, 1906 [Ellis; PO Archives].

**UNDERWOOD**, Montcalm County: this sawmill settlement in Reynolds Township was named for lumberman J. P. Underwood; Archibald McCrimmon became its first postmaster on March 29, 1882, the office operating until June 11, 1884 [GSM 1883; PO Archives].

**UNDINE**, Charlevoix County: farmer Charles H. Whitford became the first postmaster of this lumber settlement on the north shore of Pine Lake (now Lake Charlevoix), in Yates Township, on Jan. 15, 1880, the office operating until March 16, 1896; the name is famous in mythology and literature [GSM 1881-97; PO Archives].

**UNDINE**, Hillsdale County: Joseph U. Dolph became the first postmaster of this rural post office on April 26, 1862; the office was closed, but was restored from March 16, 1864, to Dec. 4, 1865 [PO Archives].

**UNGERS**, Lake County: a station on the Pere Marquette Railroad, in Lake Township; hotelman Richard D. Kibbe became its first postmaster on May 15, 1898 [GSM 1899].

**UNION**, Cass County: Jonas Hartman, who came from Union County, Pa., opened a general store here in 1831; George Meacham became the first postmaster on Aug. 23, 1841; the village was moved a short distance in 1853 to its present site, presumably to get on the Detroit-Chicago road, now US-12; its post office was closed on Oct. 19, 1859, but was restored from May 29, 1860, to Jan. 15, 1914 [Mrs. L. L. Vanderburg; Glover; PO Archives].

**UNION CHURCH**, Muskegon County: in 1882, the Lake Harbor Union Society was organized to build for religious and benevolent purposes here in Norton Township [Page].

**UNION CITY**, Branch County: the area was first surveyed by Robert Clark in 1826; Isaiah W. Bennett bought the first government land here in 1831; Justus Goodwin bought 600 acres from Mr. Bennett in 1833, built a mill race, etc., and was named the first postmaster of Goodwinville on Nov. 9, 1834; he sold 322 acres to E. W. Morgan who platted and recorded the townsite as Union City in 1835; the post office was so renamed on Jan. 23, 1840; incorporated as a village in 1866; both Union City and its Township of Union may have been so named because the Coldwater and the St. Joseph Rivers unite here [Ward W. Baker, PM; GSM 1860; PO Archives].

**UNION CORNERS**, Oakland County: a hamlet in 1864 [GSM 1865].

**UNION DISTRICT**, Washtenaw County: Ansyl Ford became the first postmaster of this rural post office on May 28, 1836, the office operating until Sept. 26, 1859 [PO Archives].

**UNION HOME**, Clinton County: George L. Miller became the first postmaster here on March 13, 1863, with the office in Chauncey Morton's tavern at what came to be called McMaster's Corners; the office was closed on Oct. 13, 1864, but was restored from Feb. 27, 1871, to March 31, 1903 [Ellis; PO Archives].

**UNION LAKE**, Oakland County: it was first settled by Irish immigrants in 1834, and its first church (St. Patrick's) dates from 1860; it was named after Union Lake which is just southeast of it; this rural and resort community in White Lake Township was given a post office on Jan. 19, 1961, with Francis J. Donohue as its first postmaster [Mich Cath Sept. 2, 1965; PO Archives].

**UNION PIER** Berrien County: it was first called Townline from its location on the line between Chickaming and New Buffalo Townships; the business union of C. H. Goodwin and John F. Gowdy, and the six McCartan brothers building a sawmill and a pier gave the village its name as well as its impetus; George Vandy became its first postmaster on May 17, 1870 [Fox; PO Archives].

**UNIONVILLE**, Lenawee County. See Dover.

**UNIONVILLE**, Tuscola County: Horace C. Marvin came here with his family in 1854 and built the first home; he opened a general store and became the first postmaster on Oct. 19, 1861, holding the office until at least 1868; he named the village after his native Union, Ohio; another pioneer and the town surveyor, John Staley, Jr., was postmaster by 1873; a station on the Saginaw, Tuscola & Huron Railroad; incorporated as a village in 1879 [Blinn; Cole; PO Archives];

**UNIVERSITY CENTER**, Bay County: the area was given a post office on July 16, 1961; so named because it was designated for institutions of higher education; Delta College was opened here in Sept. 1961 and Saginaw Valley College in Sept. 1964 [V. M. Kush].

**UNO**, Delta County: a Garden Township summer resort with its manager, Amherst H. Dickinson, becoming its first postmaster on April 15, 1898 [GSM 1899].

**UP RIVER**, Manistee County. See Brown.

**UPSLA**, Bay County: grocer J. P. Hellman became the first postmaster of this rural post office in Williams Township on July 1, 1899, the office operating until Dec. 31, 1904 [GSM 1901-07; PO Archives].

**UPTON**, Clare County: George W. Jones became the first postmaster of this hamlet on the Muskegon River, in Summerfield Township, on Oct. 24, 1877, the office operating until Dec. 30, 1899 [GSM 1879; PO Archives].

**UPTON SETTLEMENT**, Lenawee County: it was named for Nathaniel Upton who, with Dexter Smith and George W. Moore, made the first land purchase and settled here in 1834 [Hogaboam].

**UPTON WORKS**, St. Clair County: a station on the Grand Trunk and the Port Huron and Northwestern Railroads near the Upton Manufacturing Company plant; Frank Upton became its first postmaster on Dec. 4, 1885 [GSM 1887].

**URANIA**, Washtenaw County: Peter Cook, station agent for the

Toledo & Ann Arbor Railroad here in York Township, in 1878, became its first postmaster on Jan. 10, 1879, the office operating until Jan. 31, 1914 [GSM 1879; PO Archives].

**URBAN**, Sanilac County: this rural post office in Moore Township was first named Davis Corners for Simon P. Davis who became its first postmaster on Feb. 18, 1876; the office was renamed Urban on Dec. 26, 1883, and operated until June 30, 1906 [GSM 1885; PO Archives].

**URBANDALE**, Calhoun County: founded by Senator James Henry in 1901, its population in 1926 was 1,450; it is now a part of the city of Battle Creek [Mich Hist 15:194 1931].

**UTICA**, Macomb County: it was first settled in 1817 by Nathaniel Squires and his wife, Jemima; the settlement was first known as Macdougalville until Joseph Stead in 1829 platted and recorded it as Harlow, after an English town; in 1833, at the suggestion of Gurdon C. Leech, it was renamed after Utica, N.Y., many of its early settlers having come from that area; William Smith became its first postmaster on June 17, 1836; incorporated as a village in 1838 and as a city in 1936 [MPH 17:426 1890; Eldredge].

**VALENTINE**, Montmorency County: this station, six miles north of Atlanta, on a branch of the Detroit & Mackinaw Railroad was near Valentine Lake and was named Valentine Lake, but its post office, opened on Dec. 11, 1894, with James O'Connor as its first postmaster, was named Valentine; the office operated until March 15, 1907 [GSM 1895; PO Archives].

**VALERIA**, Genesee County: Andrew N. Felt became the first postmaster of this rural post office on Nov. 2, 1855, the office operating until Nov. 21, 1860 [PO Archives].

**VALLEY CENTER**, Sanilac County: it was named from its location in Maple Valley Township; Frank LaCass became its first settler in 1854, Hiram Stienhoff the second, and the third was John H. Beckett; Mr. Beckett became the first supervisor when the town was organized in 1857, holding the post until 1872; Franklin Allen became the first postmaster on Feb. 18, 1876; the post office was named Becket (one t) until it was renamed Valley Center on Jan. 25, 1882; it operated until Dec. 3, 1940 [Chapman; GSM 1883; PO Archives].

**VALLEY VILLA**, Jackson County. See Roots.

**VALPARAISO**, Berrien County: a now extinct hamlet across the river from Berrien Springs; on Farmer's map of 1853; the name is French for vale of paradise [Fox].

**VAN**, Emmet County: the village was first named Egleston after its township, which has since been renamed; it was given a post office as Egleston on March 15, 1898, with Albert E. Van Every as its first postmaster, the office being renamed Van on Oct. 29, 1898, for the Van Every Brothers, local lumbermen; the office operated until Jan. 14, 1933;

VANBUREN TWP.
Farm Res.– P. Brown

VANBUREN TWP.
Farm Res.– D.A. Featherly

its station on the Grand Rapids & Indiana Railroad was named Van Every's [GSM 1899; PO Archives].

**VAN BUREN,** Kalkaska County. See Rapid City.

**VAN BUREN,** Wayne County: Van Buren Township was erected in 1835 and renamed for Martin Van Buren, the vice president of the U.S.; its village on the Huron River was given a post office as West Huron on May 7, 1834, with Scott Vining as its first postmaster, and took the name of the new township on June 2, 1835; the office was moved to and renamed Rawsonville on Nov. 14, 1838 [Burton; GSM 1860; PO Archives].

**VAN BUREN CENTRE,** Van Buren County: Moody Emerson first squatted here on the north shore of Prospect Lake, in Lawrence Township, but John D. Freeman bought the first land, became the first settler, and in 1826 platted an 80-acre village which he hoped would become the county seat; it had plenty of streets and lots but no houses; in 1839, it was owned by H. N. Phelps, Robert Christie and Charles Chadwick and was on the assessment rolls in the county records; but it failed to appear on any later documents [Ellis].

**VAN BUREN STATE PARK,** Van Buren County. See South Haven Land Syndicate.

**VANDALIA,** Cass County: Stephen Bogue and Charles P. Ball built a grist mill here in Penn Township in 1848-49, and in 1851 laid out the village; Theron J. Wilcox became its first postmaster on July 8, 1850, and Asa Kingsbury its first merchant; the Michigan Central Railroad came through in 1871 and gave it a station; incorporated as a village in 1875; believed to have been named after Vandalia, N.Y. [Fox; Mathews; PO Archives; Glover].

**VAN DECAR,** Isabella County: a Nottawa Township settlement formed in 1880 and named for storekeeper Levi B. Van Decar who became its first postmaster on May 17, 1880, the office operating until Nov. 30, 1905 [GSM 1881; PO Archives].

**VANDELEUR,** Wayne County. See Strathmoor.

**VANDERBILT,** Otsego County: it was settled about 1875 on land owned by the Vanderbilt family of New York, and when the Michigan Central Railroad came through in 1880, this village in Corwith Township was given their name; physician Henry C. Peckham became its first postmaster on June 24, 1880; incorporated as a village in 1901 [Erma G. Malka; PO Archives].

**VANDERCOOK LAKE,** Jackson County: a settlement, four miles south of Jackson, on Vandercook Lake, which had been named for pioneer settler Henry H. Vandercook [GSM 1925].

**VANDERVEST,** Menominee County: Louis Lemieux became the first postmaster of this rural post office on Oct. 12, 1892, the office operating until June 27, 1893 [GSM 1893; PO Archives].

**VAN DYKE**, Macomb County: this village on M-53, adjoining the north end of Detroit, was named from its chief thoroughfare, Van Dyke Road, which begins in Detroit and was named in 1885 for James A. Van Dyke, then mayor of that city; it was platted in 1917 by local landowner Walter C. Piper who named its streets after then Michigan-made cars: Ford, Dodge, Packard, Cadillac, Hudson, etc.; merchant Christopher J. Bristow became its first postmaster on March 25, 1925, the office operating until Aug. 1, 1957 [Burton; Federal; PO Archives].

**VAN EVERY'S**, Emmet County. See Van.

**VAN FOSSENVILLE**, Jackson County. See Concord.

**VAN HORN'S**, Jackson County: it was named for William Van Horn who settled here in Blackman Township about 1850; it was given a station on the Grand Rapids division of the Michigan Central Railroad in 1878 called Van Horn's Crossing [Interstate; GSM 1879].

**VAN NESS'S MILLS**, Monroe County. See Dundee.

**VAN'S HARBOR**, Delta County: this settlement in Garden Township formed around the lumber mill and general store of Van Winkle & Montague in 1881; it was named for Lewis Van Winkle who became the first postmaster on March 12, 1890, the office operating until March 31, 1914 [Mich Hist 12:390 1928; GSM 1891; PO Archives].

**VAN TOWN**, Ingham County: it was named for the Van Buren family who resided on its four corners; given a post office as Vantown on Dec. 12, 1898, with Willis Jackson as its first postmaster, the office operating until Sept. 14, 1901 [Foster; PO Archives].

**VAN WINKLE**, Delta County: a station on the Minneapolis, St. Paul & Sault Ste. Marie Railroad, 12 miles north or Van's Harbor and named for the same man, Lewis Van Winkle (some say he himself spelled his name Van Winkel); Frederick M. Olmstead became its first post master on Sept. 21, 1891, the office operating until May 3, 1894 [Priestley; GSM 1893; PO Archives].

**VANZILE**, Houghton County. See Kitchi.

**VARNA**, Genesee County. See Clio.

**VARNEY**, Huron County: a station on the Pere Marquette Railroad; Alexander M. Johnson became its first postmaster on Feb. 1, 1899, the office operating until Aug. 14, 1905 [GSM 1901; PO Archives].

**VASSAR**, Tuscola County: it was founded by Townsend North and James M. Edmunds in 1849 and named by Mr. North for Matthew Vassar (the uncle of Mr. Edmunds' wife), founder of Vassar College, Poughkeepsie, N.Y., who loaned money to get the village started; Dr. William Johnson became its first postmaster on Sept. 26, 1851; incorporated as a village in 1871 and as a city in 1944 [Kenneth H. Priestley].

**VAUGHNVILLE**, Keweenaw County: Joel A. Vaughn got a patent to some eight acres here in 1849, platted it and named it for himself; after his death in 1862, the property was resold and the hamlet dwindled [Benedict].

**VEENVLIETS**, Saginaw County: a depot on the Michigan Central Railroad, it was also called Veenvliet Station, 5 miles northwest of Vassar; see Blumfield Center for the name [GSM 1895].

**VELZY**, Kent County: Sidney Stark became the first postmaster of this sawmill settlement on March 12, 1890, the office operating until Aug. 31, 1901 [GSM 1891-1903; PO Archives].

**VENICE**, Cass County: it was platted and named by Orlando Crane in 1836, but no lots were sold or buildings erected and it became part of the city of Dowagiac and was replatted; from its marshiness, it was probably named after Venice, Italy [Fox].

**VENICE**, Shiawassee County: this village on the Shiawassee River was named after its township; Charles Wilkinson became its first postmaster on Feb. 19, 1851; the office was closed on July 29, 1852, but was restored from Feb. 2, 1881, to Aug. 14, 1894 [GSM 1861-95; PO Archives].

**VENTURA**, Ottawa County: G. W. Jocelyn operated the general store in this village in Holland Township; the place was also known as Davisville but was given a post office as Ventura on July 30, 1862, with Abraham H. Stansbury as its first postmaster, the office operating until Nov. 14, 1902 [Page; GSM 1879-1903; PO Archives].

**VERGENNES**, Kent County: Vergennes Township was first settled in 1836 by Sylvester Hodges, from New York State, and organized in 1838, with Rodney Robinson as its first supervisor; Noble H. Finney became its first postmaster on Aug. 12, 1837; the office was closed on Nov. 1, 1837, but was restored from Oct. 9, 1848, to April 4, 1871; the Alton post office was transferred to and renamed Vergennes on June 11, 1900, and operated until Dec. 31, 1909 [Dillenback; GSM 1873; PO Archives].

**VERMILAC**, Baraga County: a station on the Duluth, South Shore & Atlantic Railroad, 10 miles west of Nestoria, opened in 1871 [Mich Manual 1899].

**VERMILION**, Chippewa County: farmer William H. Clarke became the first postmaster of this rural post office on the Lake Michigan shore, in Whitefish Township, on May 23, 1896, with the office first spelled Vermillion but changed to Vermilion on June 27, 1896 [GSM 1897; PO Archives].

**VERMONTVILLE**, Eaton County: as a circuit preacher in Michigan in 1835, Rev. Sylvester Cochrane decided to settle a Congregationalist colony here; that winter, back in Vermont, he organized the colony and drew up its compact; they came, bought their land, and settled on it in 1836; the town was organized in 1837 with Oren Dickinson as its first supervisor; Dr. Dewey H. Robinson became its first postmaster on June 13, 1840; incorporated as a village in 1871 [MPH 28:197 1897; Williams].

**VERNCROFT**, Roscommon County: Carrie C. Thomas became the first postmaster of this rural post office in the southwest corner of the county on Sept. 26, 1914 [GSM 1919; PO Archives].

**VERNE,** Saginaw County: a station on the Cincinnati, Saginaw & Mackinaw Railroad; Dexter B. Crosby became its first postmaster on Jan. 7, 1884, the office operating until May 15, 1901 [PO Archives].

**VERNON,** Shiawassee County: it was first settled in 1833 by Henry Leach, of Detroit, followed soon by a squatter named Lathrop, and Jacob Wilkinson, the first permanent settler; James Ratan became its first postmaster on Sept. 6, 1842; the Detroit & Milwaukee Railroad came through in 1856 and made it a station; the village was first platted in 1856 but not recorded until 1866; Milo Harrington opened the first store in 1857; incorporated as a village in 1871, with Russell E. Bell, a former D. & M. engineer as its first president; named after its township which was evidently named for George Washington's home, Mount Vernon [Ellis; Campbell; GSM 1860].

**VERNON CENTER,** Isabella County: this village on the Little Tobacco Creek was platted as Vernon City in 1870 by John L. Markey; it was named after its township which had been named by a settler from Vernon, Shiawassee County [Gancher].

**VERNON CENTER,** Shiawassee County. See Durand.

**VERONA,** Calhoun County: General Ezra Convis, a member and speaker of the state legislature, bought the land here in Emmett Township in 1835 and platted the village in 1836; he was making it a worthy rival of nearby Battle Creek until its enterprise and activity seemed to expire with him in 1836; John Stewart became its first postmaster on July 11, 1838, the office operating until Nov. 21, 1844 [Everts; PO Archives].

**VERONA,** Gogebic County: in 1899, the Pickands Mather Company formed the Menominee Exploration, which became the Verona Mining Company with its Caspian, Bengal, and Buck-group mines, which produced more than 20 million tons of ore before they closed; Verona was given a post office on June 7, 1906, with Isaac A. Burdeau as its first postmaster, the office operating until Dec. 31, 1953 [GSM 1907; Havighurst; PO Archives].

**VERONA,** Huron County: it was first settled by Thomas Philp in 1954, and he and Andrew McAllister founded the village in 1858, naming it after Shakespeare's Verona; Jeremiah Ludington built a sawmill, a grist mill and a shingle mill here in 1866, and the place was given a post office named Verona Mills on July 37, 1868, with Mr. Ludington as its first postmaster; the village is also known as Verona Hills [Hey; PO Archives].

**VERONA PARK,** Calhoun County: unincorp. village, suburb of Battle Creek [Columbia Ency.].

**VESPER,** Menominee County: a station on the Chicago & Northwestern Railroad, in Meyer Township; storekeeper Edwin Johnson became its first postmaster on Jan. 12, 1904, the office operating until March 16, 1912 [GSM 1905; PO Archives].

**VESTABURG,** Montcalm County: the first settler in the area was Charles Deaner in 1860; the village was founded by George W. O'Donnell in 1874, and he named it for his wife, Vesta Burgess O'Donnell; he platted the village in 1875 and became its first postmaster on Sept. 14, 1875; the office was closed on Nov. 30, 1877, but has been restored since Jan. 2, 1878; its railroad station also dates from 1875 [Elsie C. Throop, PM; PO Archives].

**VEVAY,** Ingham County: Charles Thayer, of Ann Arbor, made the first land purchase here in 1835; it was named after its township which, when organized in 1838, was believed to have been named after Vevay Township, Switzerland County, Indiana, which was named after Vevay, a resort town in Switzerland; Thomas H. Rogers became its first postmaster on Jan. 22, 1842, the office operating until only May 11, 1842 [Foster; PO Archives].

**VICKERYVILLE,** Montcalm County: it was founded and platted in 1856 by John Vickery as Vickery Corners; from its location in Bloomer Township it was given a post office as West Bloomer on March 2, 1857, with Benjamin S. Carey as its first postmaster; with Lora C. Jenks as postmaster, it was renamed Vickeryville on Nov. 22, 1869; the office operated until July 31, 1953 [Schenck; PO Archives].

**VICKSBURG,** Kalamazoo County: Brady Township was organized in 1829 and named for General Hugh Brady, commander of the U.S. forces at Detroit; John Vickers came here about 1830 and platted the village of Vicksburg about 1836; it was included in the Brady plat made after Vicker's death in 1849; it was given a post office as Brady on Feb. 3, 1837, with Israel R. Brown as its first postmaster; the office was changed to Holland on June 16, 1843, to Lincoln on Jan. 27, 1849, with the Brady post office re-established the same day, Jan. 27, 1849, and renamed Vicksburgh on Dec. 12, 1871; a station on the Grand Rapids & Indiana Railroad in 1867; incorporated as the village of Brady on Oct. 19, 1871, on the same day the resolution was amended to change the name to Vicksburg [Mabel W. Hawkins; PO Archives].

**VICKSBURG,** St. Clair County. See Marysville.

**VICTOR,** Clinton County: Welcome J. Partello became the first settler here in 1836; in that year, Robert G. McKee located land here and settled on it in 1837; when organized in 1843, the town was named by William J. Upton and Daniel H. Blood, who had come here from Victor, N.Y.; Hugh Haggerty became its first postmaster on July 13, 1848, the office operating until Jan. 31, 1902 [Ellis; PO Archives].

**VICTORIA,** Ontonagon County: in the 80 houses of this village on the Ontanagon River, in Rockland Township, lived the workers in the nearby mines; Charles R. Everett became its first postmaster on Sept. 16, 1899; the Victoria Mine was closed in 1921, and the village was abandoned, but the post office, serving the area, operated until Dec. 14, 1935; some of the principal mines in the area were financed by British investors, and this one was named for Queen Victoria; the name remains in nearby Victoria Dam, built in 1931 [GSM 1901; Federal; PO Archives].

**VICTORSVILLE**, Lenawee County: storekeeper William H. Marshall became the first postmaster of this rural post office, four miles from Blissfield, on June 25, 1890; the office operating until Sept. 30, 1901 [GSM 1891; PO Archives].

**VICTORY CORNERS**, Mason County: N.L. Bird built the first house here in 1862 on land he was homesteading; it was the site of the first school in the township, 1866; Victory Township was formed in 1868 and named to commemorate the Union victory in the Civil War, and this settlement in it took its name; it was given a post office as Victory on May 21, 1868, with Silas Slaught as its first postmaster; the office was closed on March 5, 1879, but was restored from May 6, 1879, to Oct. 31, 1900 [Rose D. Hawley; Ellsworth; PO Archives].

**VIENNA**, Genesee County. See Pine Run.

**VIENNA**, Macomb County. See Meade.

**VIENNA**, Monroe County: a station on a branch of the Michigan Central Railroad, 1½ miles from Erie, in 1882 [GSM 1895].

**VIENNA**, Montmorency County: this sawmill settlement in Albert Township was given a station on a branch of the Michigan Central Railroad as Vienna Junction and a post office as Vienna, with storekeeper Edward J. Putnam as its first postmaster on Feb. 23, 1887, the office operating until Dec. 31, 1913 [Page; PO Archives].

**VINCENT**, Menominee County: this rural post office was opened on June 12, 1883, and named for Nelson B. Vincent its first postmaster, the office operating until April 8, 1886 [PO Archives].

**VINCENT**, Presque Isle County. See Posen.

**VINCENT**, St. Clair County: Hiram Manning became the first postmaster of this rural post office on the Black River in Clyde Township on June 10, 1868, the office operating until July 14, 1876 [GSM 1877; PO Archives].

**VINE**, Iosco County: John D. Bullock became the first postmaster of this sawmill settlement on Oct. 20, 1881. succeeded by grocer Richard Tompkins in 1882, the office operating until July 8, 1905 [GSM 1883-1905; PO Archives].

**VINELAND**, Berrien County: a station on the St. Joseph-Galien branch of the Michigan Central Railroad, in Lincoln Township, in 1890; Albert S. Roe became its first postmaster on Dec. 14, 1891, succeeded by storekeeper G. P. Beardsley in 1892; the office operated until Oct. 15, 1907; named from its being in a grape growing region [Fox; GSM 1893; PO Archives].

**VIOLA**, Mackinac County. See Corinne.

**VIOLA**, Wexford County: Thomas C. Thornton became the first postmaster of this rural post office in Colfax Township on Feb; 12, 1879, the office operating until Jan. 21, 1881 [GSM 1883; PO Archives].

**VIRGINIA CORNERS**, Kalamazoo County: it was first settled in 1830 by Basil Harrison who, though born in Maryland, had resided in Virginia [Mich Hist 19:194 1935].

**VISTULA**, Monroe County: a land company bought this site and platted the village in 1832 and the Michigan Territorial Legislative Council authorized a road to be built from the settlement, also in 1832; Theodore Bissell became its first postmaster on Jan. 8, 1834, the office operating until only Jan. 9, 1835; when the Michigan-Ohio boundary dispute (called the Toledo War) was settled in 1836, it became a part of Lucas County, Ohio, and is now within the city limits of Toledo; the terms of the federal government were that if Michigan would accept the Harris Line, which favored Ohio, instead of the Fulton Line, which favored Michigan, in return for Michigan being given the Upper Peninsula, then Congress would also act favorably on Michigan's request for statehood; Michigan accepted [Hogaboam; Dunbar; Pen Phil 12:5 Feb 1962; PO Archives].

**VOGEL CENTRE**, Missaukee County: it was named for John Vogel, Netherlands-born American Civil War veteran who became the first settler here in Clam Lake Township in 1869; in his store its post office was opened on Feb. 25, 1879, with Arie de Jong as its first postmaster, the office operating until May 31, 1914 [Mich Hist 30:456 1946; PO Archives].

**VOLINIA**, Cass County: when the township was organized in 1833, Josephus Gard named it Volhynia, after a province in Poland, and believed to have been given in honor of General Thaddeus Kosciusko, the Polish patriot who came to help the colonies in our Revolutionary War; the name was soon reduced to Volenia and then to Volinia; it was given a post office as Volinia on May 8, 1834, with Mr. Gard as its first postmaster; the village was platted and recorded in 1836 by Levi Lawrence, David Hopkins, Obed Bunker and John Shaw; its post office was closed on March 6, 1838, but was restored from April 11, 1840, to Dec. 11, 1851, when it was transferred to and renamed Pickett's Corners; the Volinia post office was again restored from Jan. 13, 1863, to Oct. 31, 1902 [Mrs. L. L. Vanderburg; MPH 27:509 1986; Glover; PO Archives].

**VOLINIA POST OFFICE**, Cass County. See Huyckstown.

**VOLNEY**, Newaygo County: a country store with a post office of which Jesse P. Delong became the first postmaster on Aug. 31, 1880; among the names sent in were Viola and Olney, but there were already Michigan post offices with those names, so the department put the V from Viola in front of Olney and made the name Volney, which was accepted; this post office in Beaver Township operated until Aug. 16, 1909 [Mich Hist 30:532 1946; Harry L. Spooner; PO Archives].

**VREELANDT**, Wayne County. See Flat Rock.

**VRIESLAND**, Ottawa County: it was founded in 1847 by Dutch settlers under the leadership of Rev. Maarten Anne Ypma; John V. Van Winkoop became its first postmaster on Aug. 3, 1866; a station on the Chicago & Western Michigan (now Pere Marquette) Railroad; named after the province of Friesland in the Netherlands [Willard C. Wichers; PO Archives].

**VULCAN**, Dickinson County: in this area in 1872, Dr. Nelson P. Hulst began exploration for the Milwaukee Iron Company and developed the famous Vulcan Mine; the village which in turn developed from it was founded by Lewis Whitehead in 1877; Milton C. Belknap became its first postmaster on Oct. 31, 1877; a station on the Chicago & Northwestern Railroad; it was in Menominee County until Dickinson was organized in 1891; Vulcan was the Greek god for metal working [William J. Marinelli, PM].

**WABANINGO**, Muskegon County: this resort community on Lake Michigan was settled before 1883 and its organization began in 1895; it was first called Sylvan Beach but was given a post office as Wabaningo, the name of a local Ottawa chief, on April 20, 1897, with John Nequist as its first postmaster; the office was closed in 1939, restored in 1944, and made a branch of the Whitehall post office under the name Wabaningo Station in 1954 [David A. Forbes; PO Archives].

**WABIK**, Marquette County: a station on the Peninsular division of the Chicago & Northwestern Railroad, a mile west of Champion, in 1890; it served a mining region and its name was derived from pewabic, the Chippewa word for any mineralized formation [Mich Manual 1899].

**WACEDAH**, Menominee County. See Stephenson.

**WACOUSTA**, Clinton County: the first settlers in the area were Calvin Marvin and his three grown sons, in 1835; Calvin (better known as Deacon) Marvin became the first supervisor of the township (Watertown, named after Watertown, N.Y.) in 1837; in that year, the Waterloo Joint Stock Company was organized to plat the village, which they named Watertown after its township, and to sell the lots therein; the venture failed and the land was sold at auction; Messrs. Hunter and Silsbee bought the mill property in 1839, and with them the village began; it was given a post office as Wacousta on May 13, 1839, with Charles Hubbell as the first postmaster appointed, but he declined and Walter Hubbell accepted the post on July 16, 1839; the office was closed on Nov. 12, 1856, but was restored from Dec. 1, 1856, to March 31, 1903, and from July 29, 1903, to Sept. 30, 1937; it is said to have been named for the Indian maiden who, in the Conspiracy of Pontiac in 1763, had warned Major Henry Gladwin, commander of the fort at Detroit, of the intended surprise attack on the fort, and thus thwarted the plot [MPH 5:328 1884; Mich Hist 16:387 Fall 1932; PO Archives].

**WADE**, Clare County: William A. Thompson became the first postmaster of this rural post office in Sheridan Township on April 7, 1879, the office operating until March 7, 1883 [PO Archives; GSM 1881].

WALKER TWP.
Res.- G.M. Edison

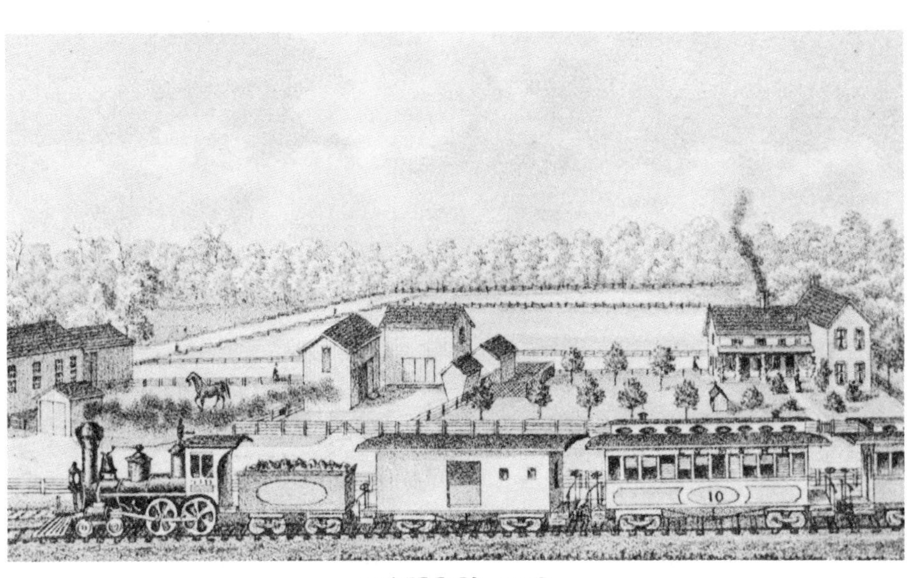


WHITEFORD TWP.
Res. & Blacksmith Shop - A. Bordeaux

**WADHAMS,** St. Clair County: in 1825, Detroit interests, led by Robert Smart, a Scot, built a mill here on the Black River in Kimball Township, but named the place Clyde Mills, after a river in Scotland (the Gazeteer 1838 calls it simply Clyde); he sold out to Ralph Wadhams, by whose name the village came to be known; Mr. Wadhams was the first and only postmaster of Clyde Mills, March 16, 1835, to Dec. 17, 1872; with grocer Ivory H. Wakefield as its first postmaster, the village was given a post office as Wadhams on June 8, 1886; the office was closed on Oct. 26, 1887, but was restored from Feb. 19, 1890, to Oct. 11, 1905 [Jenks; GSM 1838-1907; PO Archives].

**WADSWORTH,** Huron County: a station on the Port Huron & Northwestern Railroad in 1884; storekeeper James R. Frank became its first postmaster on July 21, 1885, the office operating until Aug. 14, 1905 [GSM 1885; PO Archives].

**WAGAR,** Oceana County: this rural post office, 19 miles from Hart, was named for Arthur K. Wagar who became its first postmaster on March 13, 1901, the office operating until April 14, 1904 [GSM 1905; PO Archives].

**WAGAR'S,** Montcalm County: a station on the Stanton branch of the Detroit, Lansing & Northern Railroad in 1878 [GSM 1879].

**WAGARVILLE,** Gladwin County: it was founded about 1879 and named for Wellington and Will Wagar, brothers, who lived here; it was the first village in Galdwin Township and a thriving one, due largely to its fine creamery; overcome by fire in 1922, the village was soon rebuilt and still exists [Ritchie].

**WAHJAMEGA,** Tuscola County: William A. Heartt, a lumberman, came here in 1852, located in 1853, became the first postmaster on Aug. 8, 1857, and platted the village; the name was coined from the initials of the three partners who operated the sawmill here: William A. Heartt, James A. Montgomery and Edgar George Avery; its post office was closed on May 31, 1905, but was restored from Dec. 2, 1914, to Aug. 31, 1940; the village was absorbed when the original Michigan Farm Colony, now Caro State Hospital, was founded here [J. A. Gallery; PO Archives].

**WAH ME MEE,** Emmet County: Charles E. Field was appointed the first postmaster of this rural post office on April 25, 1899, but declined, and the office, never in operation, was discontinued on Feb. 14, 1901 [PO Archives].

**WAHWAHSOO,** Otsego County: resort proprietor Mary E. Quick became the first postmaster of this summer resort on Otsego Lake, in Bagley Township, on July 16, 1913; a station on the Michigan Central Railroad [GSM 1915; PO Archives].

**WAINOLA,** Ontonagon County: this village in Greenland Township was first settled by Finns who gave it the name of Wainola, or home of Waino, a legendary name for the Finnish family; storekeeper Johannes

(John) Malila became its first postmaster on March 4, 1914, the office operating until Oct. 31, 1939 [Wargelin; GSM 1915; PO Archives].

**WAISKA,** Chippewa County: the name of a bay where Lake Superior narrows into the St. Mary's River, as well as of a river and a settlement; on some maps as Waiskey, it was named for Waishkai, chief of a local Chippewa tribe [Federal; Hamilton].

**WAIT,** Lapeer County: this rural post office in Rich Township was named for storekeeper and first postmaster, John W. Wait, on April 28, 1899, the office operating until 1904 [GSM 1901-05; PO Archives].

**WAKEFIELD,** Gogebic County: the first settler came in 1884; George M. Wakefield, one of the fee owners of the Brotherton Mine in the area, surveyed and platted the village in 1885-86, and it was named for him; James W. Bedell became its first postmaster June 12, 1886; a station on the Chicago & Northwestern Railroad; it was in Ontonagon County until Gogebic was organized in 1887; incorporated as a village by the supervisors in 1887 and by the state in 1893 and as a city in 1919 [Margaret Williams; PO Archives].

**WAKELEE,** Cass County: it was first laid out in 1871 by Levi Garwood who named it for C. Wakelee, first treasurer of the Peninsular (now Grand Trunk) Railroad, which built a depot here; Benjamin F. Higgins became the first postmaster on Jan. 30, 1872, the office operating until Nov. 20, 1939; its depot too is closed [Mrs. L. L. Vanderburg; Rogers; PO Archives].

**WAKEMAN,** St. Joseph County: the township was organized in 1843 and named for Hiram Wakeman, one of its largest landowners; it was renamed Mendon in 1844 [Cutler].

**WAKESHMA,** Kalamazoo County: Joseph Hamenway became the first postmaster of this rural post office, named after its township, on March 10, 1852; the office was closed on Aug. 30, 1855, but was restored from Jan. 12, 1858, to June 11, 1875 [PO Archives].

**WAKESHMA CENTRE,** Kalamazoo County. See Fulton.

**WALBURG,** Alpena County: Louis List became the first postmaster of this rural post office in Wilson Township on Feb. 18, 1902, succeeded by Anna Binchus in 1902, the office operating until Oct. 31, 1905 [GSM 1903-07; PO Archives].

**WALDENBURG,** Macomb County: it began as the site of a sawmill but an influx of German settlers in the 1830s turned it into a farming community with a church, school, stores, etc.; it was named after Waldenburg, Germany; the Macomb post office was moved here on March 29, 1860, as Waldenburgh, changed to Waldenburg on Aug. 10, 1893, and closed on Sept. 15, 1906 [Eldredge; PO Archives].

**WALDRON,** Hilldsale County: Russell Coman was the first white settler in the area, coming from New York State in 1835; the settlers in 1837 sent in the name Coman for their town, but through an error the name given was Canaan; it was renamed Wright in 1844, and from its location in the township, the village was called South Wright and was given a post office of that name on Nov. 2, 1855, with Joel S. Hubbard as its first postmaster; in 1877, the north part of the village was platted and named for Henry Waldron, of Hillsdale, who represented this district in congress; its post office was so renamed on May 21, 1877; incorporated as a village in 1905 [Hogaboam; Lela Spray; PO Archives].

**WALES**, St. Clair County: Wales Township was organized in 1841, with Clark S. Cusick as its first supervisor, and this village in it took its name; inn-keeper Benton Bartlett became its first postmaster on May 1, 1851, succeeded on his death by his widow Angelina [Andreas; PO Archives].

**WALHALIA**, Mason County: originally an Indian village; its first white settlement was named Merritt; when the Pere Marquette Railroad came through its station here was named Manistee Junction and it was given a post office of that name on Jan. 10, 1891, with Charles H. Bates as its first postmaster; it was renamed on Feb. 8, 1905, by an admirer of Wagner's opera Die Valkyrie, Walhalla meaning the banquet hall of the gods [Rose D. Hawley; PO Archives].

**WALKER**, Kent County: it was first settled by Canadians, the Samuel White and the Jesse Smith families, both in 1836; Walker Township was organized in 1838, and this village in it was named after it; with Solomon Wright as its first postmaster, it was given a post office as Indian Creek, after its principal stream, on Dec. 30, 1847; when the Detroit, Grand Haven & Milwaukee Railroad came through in 1856 it was given a station; with Horace Austin as postmaster, its post office was renamed Walker on July 14, 1884, North Grand Rapids on April 16, 1891, and closed on Aug. 29, 1894 [MPH 27:505,571 1896; Dillenback; PO Archives].

**WALKER'S CORNERS**, Ogemaw County: Kort Blakeley operated a store here in Edwards Township by 1884; nearby Chapman Lake was named for the head of the Chapman Lumber Company, the first in the area [Ritchie].

**WALKER'S JUNCTION**, Lenawee County. See Cambridge Junction.

**WALKER'S MILLS**, Livingston County: the post office at Hamburg was changed to Walker's Mills on Aug. 10, 1861, but was closed on April 5, 1862 [PO Archives].

**WALKER'S POINT**, Mackinac County: George French became the first postmaster of this rural post office on Bois Blanc Island, in Lake Huron, on Feb. 21, 1899, succeeded by Fannie K. Hamilton in 1900; the office was later closed but was restored on May 1, 1916, with Silas Miller as postmaster [GSM 1901; PO Archives].

**WALKERVILLE**, Oceana County: this village in Leavitt Township was founded, platted, and named Walkerville by Fayette Walker in 1883 on land he owned; it was given a post office named Stetson on Nov. 2, 1883, after Alvin C. Stetson, its first postmaster; it became the terminal station of the 27-mile Mason & Oceana Railroad in 1886; on May 13, 1898, it was renamed Walkerville; incorporated as a village in 1908 [Archie Holbrook; Hartwick; PO Archives].

**WALKEY,** Benzie County: Jane E. Phillips became the first postmaster of this rural post office on Jan. 8, 1891, the office operating until only Nov. 11, 1891 [PO Archives].

**WALKUP,** Newaygo County. See West Troy.

**WALLACE,** Menominee County: early in 1870, the Chicago & Northwestern Railroad gave a grant of land to Mellen Smith if he would cut its timber and ship it by rail; he led in organizing the township, which was named Mellen for him; when the railroad came through, the agent assigned to the depot was Wallace Sutherland; it was called Wallace's Siding and later just Wallace; it was given a post office as Wallace with Mellen Smith as its first postmaster on Jan. 30, 1877 [Norbert Hanson, actg. PM].

**WALLACEVILLE,** Wayne County: this settlement on the River Rouge, in Dearborn Township, was named for local sawmill owner John B. Wallace; he became its first postmaster on Oct. 28, 1862, the office operating until July 31, 1901 [GSM 1873; PO Archives].

**WALLED LAKE,** Oakland County: Walter B. Hewitt took up government land here in 1825 and Bela Armstrong in 1826; Jesse Tuttle came from Pennsylvania in 1830, built his home, and in 1831, platted the village; William Tenney became its first postmaster on Jan. 12, 1833; incorporated as a city in 1954; places along the shore of its square mile lake (Walled Lake) had the appearance of having been walled, either by man or by a drift deposit or by the action of water and ice, and this is believed to have caused its naming [Parthena Philp].

**WALLETT'S,** Washtenaw County: Nehemiah P. Parsons became the first postmaster of this rural post office on June 4, 1834, the office operating until Jan. 23, 1840 [PO Archives].

**WALLIN,** Benzie County: a station on the Chicago & Western Michigan (now Pere Marquette) Railroad; lumber inspector William D. Truxbury became the first postmaster of this lumber settlement on Feb. 17, 1893 [GSM 1895; PO Archives].

**WALLOON,** Charlevoix County: William Hoagland became the first postmaster of this rural post office on May 9, 1883, the office operating until May 7, 1884; see Walloon Lake for the name [PO Archives].

**WALLOON LAKE,** Charlevoix County: in 1872, John Jones, Jr., and his sons Clarence and Elliot, homesteaded in this area; they also cut ties for the Grand Rapids & Indiana Railroad which came through here in 1874, and the stop was named Melrose for Mel Rose, an early local surveyor; the township was named Melrose but the townspeople applied for a post office named Bear Lake, but there already a Bear Lake post office in Michigan, and they were given one named Tolcott on Oct. 19, 1897, with Frank Jones as its first postmaster; the office was renamed Talcott on March 4, 1899, and Walloon Lake on Sept. 22, 1900; J. R. Haas, a local butcher, suggested the name which he had seen on an old railroad map; the railroad people were curious as to how it had got there, and they found that years before a group of Walloons from Belgium, had settled at the north end of Bear (now Walloon) Lake, but that now no trace of them remained [Elver Carroll, PM; PO Archives].

**WALNUT**, Oakland County: Esther H. Haskins became the first postmaster of this rural post office on July 24, 1891, the office operating until Oct. 5, 1900 [PO Archives].

**WALSH**, Schoolcraft County: this station on the Detroit, Mackinaw & Marquette Railroad was opened for loading logs in 1886; it was given a post office as Eklund, for Nels A. Eklund, who became its first postmaster on July 1, 1927; the office was renamed Walsh, for a local lumberman, on Aug. 16, 1927, and operated until June 30, 1933 [Fred H. Hahne; GSM 1887; PO Archives].

**WALSH**, Washtenaw County: this rural post office in Northfield Township was named for farmer William Walsh who became its first postmaster on July 18, 1881, the office operating until Jan. 13, 1885 [GSM 1883; PO Archives].

**WALTON**, Eaton County: land entries by speculators were made here in present Walton Township as early as 1832, but Captain James W. Hickok became the first actual settler in 1836, and the first postmaster of its post office, named East Bellevue, on Aug. 24, 1838; the township was organized in 1839 and the second settler, Parley P. Shumway was elected its first supervisor; the post office was renamed Walton on Dec. 31, 1840, and operated until Aug. 17, 1849 [MPH 3:405 1881; Durant; PO Archives].

**WALTON**, Grand Traverse County: it began in 1873 as a junction of the Grand Rapids & Indiana and the Traverse City Railroads, and was called Walton Junction; A. F. Phillips, a section foreman with the former road, built the first house and later ran the first hotel here; given a post office as Walton on Feb. 14, 1873, with James L. Gibbs as its first postmaster; the village receded with the end of the lumber boom [Traverse; PO Archives].

**WALTZ**, Wayne County: St. John's Ev. Lutheran church here dates from 1845; the Pere Marquette Railroad opened its station here in Huron Township in 1872; the village was platted by and named for Josiah Waltz in 1872; its post office operated from Feb. 19, 1872, to Sept. 27, 1873, and from June 23, 1874, with William D. Millspaugh as postmaster [Mich Hist 42:127 1958; Carlisle; PO Archives].

**WALWORTH**, Lenawee County: this rural post office, 7 miles east of Adrian, was named for Eugene D. Walworth who became its first postmaster on Sept. 30, 1893, the office operating until Sept. 15, 1900 [GSM 1895; PO Archives].

**WAMPLER'S LAKE,** Jackson County: it was named for Joseph Wampler, one of the three original surveyors of the area in 1824 (the other two were Robert Clark and Henry Park); this resort community now lies largely within the W. J. Hayes State Park [DeLand].

**WANICOTT,** Sanilac County: John Galbraith became the first postmaster of this rural post office on Dec. 13, 1855; the office was closed on Feb. 1, 1858, but was restored from Oct. 8, 1860, to July 13, 1864 [PO Archives].

**WANSTEN,** Muskegon County: a settlement on Holton Road, northeast of North Muskegon, with a contract postal station [A. Marks, NMPO].

**WARD,** Saginaw County: this station on the Detroit, Grand Rapids & Western and the Saginaw Valley & St. Louis (now Pere Marquette) Railroads, 9 miles west of Saginaw, was opened by 1884, and was called Graham's or Graham Station; it was given a post office named Ward on Jan. 20, 1898, the office operating until Oct. 31, 1902 [GSM 1885; PO Archives].

**WARD'S,** Alger County: a station on the Detroit & Mackinaw Railroad in 1882; it was in Schoolcraft County until Alger was organized in 1885 [GSM 1883-87].

**WARD'S LANDING,** St. Clair County. See Marine City.

**WARNER,** Monroe County: a station on a branch of the Lake Shore & Michigan Southern Railroad, a mile north of Monroe, in 1882 [GSM 1883].

**WARNERVILLE,** Livingston County. See Green Oak Centre.

**WARREN,** Macomb County: its settlement preceded the township which was formed in 1837 as Hickory, renamed Alba in 1838, and Warren in 1839; George W. Corey became its first postmaster on March 19, 1840; the office was closed on Dec. 20, 1841, but was restored, with Mr. Corey again its postmaster, on Jan. 27, 1849; incorporated as a village in 1893, and as a city, including all the charter township of Warren, in 1955; the village was also known as Cottageville, but never officially; named for General Joseph Warren (1741-1775), who fell at the Battle of Bunker Hill [Gerald L. Neill; GSM 1879; PO Archives].

**WARREN CITY,** Ottawa County: it was platted in 1836 and recorded in 1837; the commissioners designated it as the county seat in 1840, but it never served as such; now a ghost town [Lillie].

**WARRENDALE,** Wayne County: this settlement was located at the then (1924) western city limits of Detroit; named after its chief thoroughfare, Warren Avenue, which was opened in Detroit in 1869 and named for General Joseph Warren, Revolutionary War hero [Farmer; GSM 1925].

**WARRENVILLE,** Chippewa County. See De Tour.

**WARREN WOODS,** Berrien County: a tract of 300 acres in Chickaming Township, 200 of which are primeval forest; named for Mr. and Mrs. Edward K. Warren who gave the tract for a park and natural laboratory; they also gave the 300 acre tract called Warren Dunes, in Lake Township, having a mile and a quarter of lake frontage; both are maintained free to the public by the Edward K. Warren Foundation of Three Oaks [Fox].

**WARSAW**, Lenawee County: although this settlement dates from about 1878, it was not given a post office until Sept. 8, 1892, when Frank Bugbee became its first postmaster; the office operated until June 15, 1895 [GSM 1879; PO Archives].

**WARSAW**, Macomb County: it was platted by Leander Tromble about the depot grounds of the new Grand Trunk Railroad in 1862; incorporated as a village, but it became, "as it properly should," a part of Mount Clemens [Eldredge].

**WASAS**, Ontanogon County: Finns emigrated to the area as miners as early as 1870; as the mines became depleted and the forests denuded, most of them remained to farm; a community of them formed this village which they named after a province in Finland [Harri Virjo; Jamison].

**WASEPI**, St. Joseph County: it was platted and recorded in 1874; Darius C. Gee, one of the original proprietors, became the first postmaster on May 18, 1875; the village grew from its location at the crossing of the Michigan Central and the Grand Rapids & Indiana Railroads; named after a local band of Indians known as the Nottawa-seepe [Everts].

**WASHINGTON**, Macomb County: Asahel Bailey made the first government land purchase in the area in 1821, followed by Gideon Gates, George Wilson, and John Bennett, all later that year; the town was named after the township which was organized in 1837 and named for the Father of Our Country; Otis Lamb became the first postmaster on Sept. 10, 1826 [Eldredge; PO Archives].

**WASHINGTON**, Sanilac County: John Jones, hunter and trapper, was the first settler in the area, followed by Jonathan Lee and George Mitchell in 1850; a schoolhouse was built in 1852 and George Pack built the first sawmill in 1857; named from its township, which was organized in 1855, with Mr. Jones as its first supervisor [Chapman].

**WASHINGTON HARBOR**, Keweenaw County. See Johns.

**WASHINGTON HEIGHTS**, Calhoun County: it was annexed by the city of Battle Creek in 1927 [Mich Manual].

**WATERBURGH**, Calhoun County. See Sheridan.

**WATERFORD**, Berrien County. See Watervliet.

**WATERFORD**, Oakland County: Alpheus Williams and Captain Archibald Phillips became the first settlers here in 1819; the name of the township and thence the village was proposed about 1825 by Shubael Atherton, due to its large area of water surface; Thomas J. Drake became the first postmaster on Feb. 4, 1835; the post office was transferred to and renamed Drayton Plains on Aug. 24, 1858, but the Waterford post office was re-established on Nov. 13, 1858, and has continued to date [Mrs. Donald E. Adams; PO Archives].

**WATERFORD,** Wayne County: this village in Northville Township was platted by Dyer Ramsdell and recorded on March 17, 1837; it did not survive but its name is retained by nearby Waterford Lake [County plat liber].

**WATERFORD CENTRE,** Oakland County: a station on the Detroit, Grand Haven & Milwaukee Railroad; the Elizabeth Lake post office, opened on May 2, 1835, with William Terry as its first postmaster, was transferred to Waterford Centre on July 13, 1841, and operated here until May 7, 1858; named from its location in its township [GSM 1860; PO Archives].

**WATERHOUSE CORNERS,** Branch County. See Kinderhook.

**WATERLOO,** Jackson County: Hiram Putnam became the first settler here in 1834; the township, organized in 1836, was first named East Portage; sawmill owner Patrick Hubbard became the first postmaster on July 24, 1837, and he had the township and its post office renamed after the famous battle [Interstate; PO Archives].

**WATERS,** Otsego County: the village began as a sawmill settlement at the north end of Bradford Lake in 1873; it was given a post office as Bradford Lake on July 18, 1876, with Charles H. Davis as its first postmaster; it was renamed Waters on Dec. 21, 1885, being in the area of many lakes; it was also given a railroad station by 1876 [GSM 1877; William H. Granlund; Mich Hist 32:332 1948].

**WATERSMEET,** Gogebic County: the Milwaukee, Lake Shore & Western Railroad extended its line from here to the iron ore range fifty miles west in 1884; Sereno M. Streeter became the first postmaster of the first post office in the county here on Jan. 14, 1884; the Indians referred to the site as a place where the waters meet, the waters being the middle branch of the Ontonagon River and Duck Creek; it was in Ontonagon County until Gogebic was organized in 1887 [Curtis Heyman, PM].

**WATERSVILLE,** Genesee County: a hamlet in 1864 [GSM 1865].

**WATERTOWN,** Clinton County: Ezra Billings became the first postmaster of this rural post office on Feb. 9, 1841, the office operating until April 13, 1842 [PO Archives].

**WATERTOWN,** Sanilac County: Edward Cash became the first settler in the area in 1851; the first school was built in 1867; John Gimmel built the first sawmill in 1882 and William Tomelson the first store in 1883; David L. Soule became its first postmaster on Jan. 30, 1895, the office operating until Feb. 28, 1905 [Chapman; PO Archives].

**WATERTOWN,** Tuscola County. See Markell.

**WATERVALE,** Benzie County: farmer John Hunt became the first postmaster of Herring Lake on Feb. 14, 1890, with the office renamed Watervale on Sept. 28, 1892; the office was closed on Oct. 21, 1895, but was restored from Dec. 27, 1895, to March 1, 1898 [GSM 1891; PO Archives].

**WATERVILLE,** Ionia County: in 1836, Robert Hilton, of Grand Rapids, made large land purchases here on Lake Creek, in Boston Township, including a mill site, and platted a village which he named Waterville; James H. Hoag opened the mill as well as a store in 1838, and was made postmaster on April 5, 1838; but the village did not prosper and its post office was moved to Saranac on March 14, 1839 [Schenck; Branch; PO Archives].

**WATERVLIET,** Berrien County: it was started when Sumner and Wheeler built a sawmill here in 1833; Isaac Moffatt opened the first store in 1836; Smith and Merrick platted the village, probably in 1838; Isaac N. Swain became its first postmaster on March 21, 1848; it was named after Watervleit, N.Y., by its founders who came from that state; the name is supposed to mean Waterford, and by that name it appears on Farmer's map of 1853 and in the Gazeteer of 1860; incorporated as a village in 1891 and as a city in 1924 [Fox; PO Archives].

**WATKINS,** Washtenaw County: a station on the D., H. & S.W. Railroad, in Manchester Township, in 1878 [GSM 1879].

**WATKINS' STATION,** Jackson County: the father of L. D. Watkins bought land here in Norvell Township in 1833 and came with his wife and family from Keene, N.H., to settle on it in 1834; the D., H. & I. Railroad depot on their Fairview Farm was named Watkins' Station [MPH 22:262 1893].

**WATROUS,** Huron County: a flag station on the Pontiac, Oxford & Northern Railroad in 1884 [GSM 1885].

**WATROUSVILLE,** Tuscola County: in 1851, Patrick McGlone became the first settler here, opening an inn, and the place became known as McGlone Corners; Aaron Watrous came with a crew to begin lumbering on the Cass River in 1852, and built his mill here in 1853; he platted the village and on Dec. 11, 1855, became the first postmaster of Watrousville; the office operated until Sept. 14, 1935 [Page; PO Archives].

**WATSON,** Allegan County: Eli Watson, from Jefferson Coutny, N.Y., bought land here in 1836 and settled on it in 1837, and the township when organized was named for him; its village was given a post office on June 30, 1869, with Artemus W. Beals as its first postmaster; the office was closed on March 13, 1872, but on Oct. 4, 1881, the Watson Corners post office was transferred to and renamed Watson, and it operated until Oct. 31, 1905; its station on the C., J. & M. Railroad was called Fisk [Johnson; GSM 1873; PO Archives].

**WATSON,** Marquette County: a mail distributing point in the general store of the Watson Store Company, prior to 1918 [GSM 1919].

**WATSON CORNERS,** Allegan County: Carson E. Clapp became the first postmaster of this hamlet on May 25, 1876, the office operating here until Oct. 4, 1881; see Watson for the name [PO Archives].

**WATTON,** Baraga County: a station on the Duluth, South Shore & Atlantic Railroad, in Covington Township; this Finnish village was founded by August Kotila in 1903; Miriam Kotila became its first postmaster on March 23, 1912 [GSM 1913; PO Archives].

**WAUCEDAH,** Dickinson County: it began as an iron mining settlement named Breen after the mine discovered in 1866 and opened in 1871 by Thomas and Bently Breen; a station on the Chicago & Northwestern Railroad; David R. Gifford became the first postmaster of Waucedah, Indian for over there, on June 26, 1877, the office operating until April 15, 1942 [Sawyer; GSM 1881; PO Archives].

**WAUKAZOO,** Ottawa County. See Superior.

**WAUKAZOOVILLE,** Leelanau County: it was founded by Rev. George N. Smith in 1849; James McLaughlin and his son-in-law, William H. Case, built the first house in 1849; they had been sent here as missionaries by the Waukazoo band of Ottawas at Old Wing; the settlement was annexed by Northport in 1852 [Northport PM].

**WAVERLY,** Clinton County. See Eagle.

**WAVERLY,** Van Buren County: Reuben Myers became the first settler here in 1837 and was joined by his brother, Merwin Myers, in 1839; the township was set off in 1842 and named by F. C. Annable, then a member of the legislature, in honor of Sir Walter Scott; Dr. Stephen L. Babbitt became its first postmaster on Feb. 16, 1852, the office operating until May 13, 1886 [Ellis; PO Archives].

**WAWATAM BEACH,** Cheboygan County: it was the site of Fort Michilimackinac, 1812-1781; a mile and a half from Mackinaw City, it was developed as a resort by Vine Harding in 1906 [GSM 1907].

**WAYLAND,** Allegan County: Colonel Isaac Barnes and his sons built a sawmill here in the winter of 1836-37; the settlement was given a post office as Wayland on May 10, 1844, with George Barnes as its first postmaster; it was named after its township which had been named after Wayland, N.Y.; three and a half miles east, Nelson Chambers had founded Chambers' Corners in 1838; when the Kalamazoo & Grand Rapids Plank Road came through in 1854, the post office was transferred to Chambers' Corners but retained the name Wayland; Isaac Kellogg platted the village and recorded it as Lomax City in 1861, but it was incorporated as the village of Wayland in 1858 [Mich Hist 16:387 1932; Mrs. Milo Farnsworth; PO Archives; GSM 1860].

**WAYLAND CENTRE,** Allegan County. See Bradley.

**WAYNE,** Cass County: the township was organized in 1835 and named by Cornelius Higgins for General Anthony Wayne; Justus Gage became its first and only postmaster, from July 30, 1842, to Jan. 13, 1849 [Mathews; Fox; PO Archives].

**WAYNE**, Wayne County: the English surrendered the Northwest Territory (including almost all of Michigan) to General Anthony Wayne, as American general in command, on July 11, 1796; the county was created and named for him on Aug. 15, 1796; this site in it was first settled by George M. Johnson in 1824, who built a log house for the entertainment of travelers; the village was platted as Derby's Corners by Ezra Derby in 1835; from its location in Nankin Township, it was given a post office as South Nankin on April 22, 1835, with William D. Wescott as its first postmaster; it was renamed Wayne on Dec. 11, 1851; incorporated as a village in 1869 and as a city in 1960 [GSM 1838; Burton; PO Archives].

**WAYNE'S MILL**, Alger County. See Onota.

**WEADOCK**, Cheboygan County: it was founded as a sawmill settlement in Monroe Township about 1894; lawyer Herbert F. Baker became its first postmaster on Dec. 3, 1895; it was named for congressman Thomas A. E. Weadock, who had been an attorney for lumbering firms in the area; now farmland [Monica Porter; PO Archives].

**WEARE**, Oceana County: Dr. Daniel G. Weare settled here in 1855 and when the township was organized in 1860, it was named for him; Andrew L. Carr became its first postmaster on June 24, 1869; the office was closed on May 17, 1879, but with grocer E. M. Graves as postmaster, it was restored on Nov. 15, 1897, and operated until April 10, 1902 [Royal; Hartwick; PO Archives].

**WEARESVILLE**, Gladwin County: William S. Tubbs became the first postmaster of this rural post office on March 4, 1895, the office operating until June 3, 1896 [PO Archives].

**WEAVER**, Mecosta County: lumberman Sylvester Dresser became the first postmaster of this rural post office on March 3, 1893, the office operating until Feb. 28, 1905 [PO Archives].

**WEAVERSVILLE**, Newaygo County. See Fremont.

**WEBBERS**, Ionia County: a station on the Detroit, Grand Rapids & Western Railroad opened in 1869 [Mich Manual 1899].

**WEBBERSVILLE**, Ingham County: it was first settled by Ephraim Meech in 1837; on Feb. 12, 1840, with Caleb Carr as its first postmaster, it was given a post office as Phelpstown (it was then in Phelps Township, named for David Phelps, in whose home the first town meeting was held); on Jan. 28, 1850, it was renamed LeRoy, with Perry Henderson as postmaster (named after LeRoy, N.Y., the former home of Orren Dana, the first township clerk; others say for Daniel LeRoy, the first attorney general of Michigan); on Nov. 17, 1862, the LeRoy post office was closed; on Feb. 27, 1867, the village was moved a mile and renamed for postmaster Hubert P. Webber, there being another LeRoy post office in Michigan by that time; incorporated as a village in 1883 [Foster; Adams; PO Archives].

**WEBSTER**, Ontonagon County. See Rockland.

**WEBSTER**, Washtenaw County: Thomas Alexander became the first settler in the area in May, 1826; Luther Boyden and Israel Anus arrived later that year; when the township was formed in 1833, Munnis Kenny suggested the name of Daniel Webster; Moses Kingsley became the first postmaster on May 11, 1833; the office was changed to Walsh on July 18, 1881, and closed on Jan. 13, 1885; but the Webster post office was re-established on April 13, 1882, and operated until Aug. 30, 1900 [MPH 13:546 1889; Chapman; PO Archives].

**WEEKS**, Lapeer County: storekeeper Robert A. Butler became the first postmaster of this rural post office in Burnside Township on Sept. 6, 1899, the office operating until March 31, 1904 [PO Archives].

**WEESAW**, Berrien County. See New Troy.

**WEIDMAN**, Isabella County: John S. Weidman built a lumber mill here about a decade before he, his wife Maggie, and the surveyor E. F. Guild platted and recorded the village in 1894; grover Horace H. Parsons became its first postmaster on Sept. 26, 1894; a station on the Detroit, Grand Rapids & Western Railroad [PM; Fancher].

**WEIMER**, Mason County. See South Bayou.

**WEINSBURG**, Washtenaw County: a German Luthern farming settlement in Scio Township; school teacher John Schneider became its first postmaster on Jan. 30, 1890, the office operating until May 15, 1901 [GSM 1891; PO Archives].

**WELCH**, Mackinac County. See Garnet.

**WELCH**, Ogemaw County: a flag station on the Mackinaw division of the Michigan Central Railroad, 5 miles south of West Branch, in 1878 [GSM 1879].

**WELDON**, Benzie County: the first settler in the town was Arthur T. Case in 1863, later a member of the state legislature; the town was organized in 1868; lumberman Henry G. Waite became its first postmaster on June 20, 1879, the office operating until Sept. 30, 1903; the village was named after its township [MPH 28:116 1897; PO Archives].

**WELDON CREEK**, Mason County: it was the site of an old Indian reservation; John Wells opened his store here on Indian Creek in Eden Township in 1875; given a station on the Pere Marquette Railroad with John J. Gilding as station agent and he became the first postmaster on May 14, 1875, with the office named Weldon Creek; it operated until April 18, 1892 [GSM 1879; PO Archives].

**WELLINGTON**, Crawford County: although this post office in Beaver Creek Township had eight postmasters from Thaddeus E. Hastings on Dec. 6, 1881, until the office was closed in 1918, it was more of a post office than a village; Wellington Batterson was a county official, and the name may have been given for him [Grace L. Funsch].

**WELLINGTON**, Gogebic County: a station on the Chicago & Northwestern Railroad in 1894; since this line was completed with British capital, it is likely British as were Gladstone, Brampton, etc., and named for the Duke of Wellington [Mich Manual 1899].

**WELLS**, Arenac County: a station on the Michigan Central Railroad, in Moffitt Township, in 1872; the hamlet had a school and on Sept. 29, 1881, the Culver post office was transferred here and renamed Wells; it was named for N. M. Wells, then assistant engineer on location for the railroad [Page; GSM 1879; PO Archives].

**WELLS**, Delta County: in 1847, Jefferson Sinclair and Daniel Wells, Jr., acquired the Billings and Richards sawmill (the first in the Upper Peninsula, built in 1840) and the Joseph Smith mill (built in 1844), and operated as Sinclair & Wells; they were joined by Nelson and Harrison Ludington in 1850-51, and the N. Ludington Company was organized; Isaac Stephenson became a stockholder in 1858, and in 1888, the firm was re-organized as the I. Stephenson Company and built a sawmill at the mouth of the Escanaba River where the village of Wells was located; George T. Burns became its first postmaster on Nov. 20, 1884; it was named for Daniel Wells, Jr. [Charles J. McCauley, PM, 1923-48].

**WELLS**, Lenawee County. See Wellsville.

**WELLS**, Tuscola County: Joseph Wells became its first postmaster in 1857; when the township was organized in 1858 it was named for him, and he was elected the first treasurer in 1859 [Page].

**WELLSBURG**, Chippewa County: a station on the Duluth, South Shore & Atlantic Railroad, opened in 1872; Edward J. Guck became its first postmaster on Feb. 4, 1889, the office operating until Nov. 30, 1909 [GSM 1891; PO Archives].

**WELLSFIELD**, Lenawee County. See Wellsville.

**WELLS' SETTLEMENT**, Macomb County. See Memphis.

**WELLSTON**, Manistee County: a station on the Chicago & Western Michigan (now Pere Marquette) Railroad in 1885; the village was founded by the Swigart Land Company and named for Adelmer J. Wells who became its first postmaster on June 30, 1892; the office was transferred to and renamed Dublin on April 18, 1898, but was returned to Wellston, with William A. Martin as postmaster, on Sept. 22, 1908 [Frank M. Fortelka, PM].

**WELLSVILLE**, Lenawee County: this village in Palmyra Township was named for Allen G. Wells who became its first postmaster on March 8, 1859; the office was closed on Oct. 12, 1877, but was restored from Nov. 6, 1877, to July 14, 1904; given a station on the Lake Shore & Michigan Southern Railroad in 1878; in some records as Wells and as Wellsfield [GSM 1865; PO Archives].

**WELSH**, Benzie County: Richard T. Reilly became the first postmaster of this rural post office on Aug. 19, 1891, the office operating until only Nov. 24, 1891 [PO Archives].

**WENATCHEE,** Berrien County: a station on the Buchanan branch of the Pere Marquette Railroad, in Buchanan Township, prior to 1919 [Fox].

**WENDIGO,** Keweenaw County. See Windigo Mine.

**WENONA,** Bay County. See West Bay City.

**WENONA BEACH,** Bay County: Wenona was the mother of Hiawatha in Henry Longfellow's poem; the name was popular in this area, having been given to a village just to the south which became West Bay City in 1877; Wenona Beach on Saginaw Bay, in Bangor Township, was developed about 1892 by Spencer O. Fisher in connection with his West Bay City electric street railway [Butterfield].

**WENSTREN'S CORNERS,** Jackson County: this hamlet in Henrietta Township was named for John Wenstren who settled here in 1836 [Interstate].

**WEQUETONSING,** Emmet County: a Presbyterian committee met at Elkhart, Indiana, and accepted the offer of 80 acres here on Little Traverse Bay made to them in 1877; they used it for what they called the Presbyterian Resort, the name later changed to Wequetonsing, which was the Indian name for Little Traverse Bay; the original Indian name for this place was Wababikang; a station on a branch of the Grand Rapids & Indiana Railroad in 1882; Josiah R. Laforce became its first postmaster on May 13, 1886; the office was closed on Sept. 29, 1886, but was restored, with Mr. Laforce again the postmaster, on May 27, 1887, and operated until June 6, 1957 [Mrs. G. W. Leece; PO Archives].

**WESLEY,** Mason County: grocer Lewis W. Rose became the first postmaster of this hamlet in Summit Township on Nov. 1, 1895, the office operating until June 30, 1902; since its only church was Methodist, it was evidently named for the founder of Methodism, John Wesley [GSM 1899-1903; PO Archives].

**WEST BAY CITY,** Bay County: Joseph Trombley bought 2000 acres here in 1843 and platted 25 of them into a village in 1851; mill owner and later state senator Thomas Whitney named it Bangor after his birthplace in Maine; but there was already a Bangor post office in Michigan, so when merchant William F. Benson became the first postmaster here on May 18, 1864, the office was named Banks in honor of General Nathaniel P. Banks; the office was closed on May 1, 1866, but was restored from Nov. 17, 1870, to Feb. 27, 1891; Banks was incorporated as a village in 1871; adjacent to it, in 1862, Dr. Daniel Hughes Fitzhugh platted a village which he called Salzburgh after a salt mine and resort in Austria and because of the salt making begun here at the time; George Staudacher became the first postmaster of Salzburgh on March 19, 1869, with the name shortened to Salzburg on Dec. 2, 1893, the office operating until Oct. 20, 1894; just to the north of it, in 1863, Henry W. Sage, of Sage, McGaw & Company, built a mill, homes, etc., and platted a village called Lake City; but there was another Lake City in Michigan, and the wives of Messrs. Sage and McGraw renamed it Wenona after the mother of Hiawatha in Henry Longfellow's poem; George H. Bates became its first postmaster on Feb. 14, 1865; incorporated as a village by the supervisors in 1866 and by the legislature in 1867; in 1877, the legislature consolidated Wenona, Salzburgh, and Banks into the city of West Bay City, which in 1905 was annexed by the city of Bay City [Butterfield; Page; PO Archives].

**WEST BENTON,** Eaton County: David Verplank became the first postmaster of this rural post office on Jan. 12, 1855, the office operating until Oct. 19, 1860; see Benton for the name [PO Archives].

**WEST BERLIN,** St. Clair County: John Whitcomb became the first postmaster of this rural post office in western Berlin Township on Oct. 12, 1850, the office operating until June 5, 1860 [PO Archives].

**WEST BLOOMER,** Montcalm County. See Vickeryville.

**WEST BLOOMFIELD,** Oakland County: Nathaniel J. Daniels became the first postmaster of Marion post office in West Bloomfield Township on March 8, 1833; on March 31, 1834, it was renamed West Bloomfield and moved to the public house of Mr. Rundel; the office operated until Nov. 23, 1865 [Durant; PO Archives].

**WEST BRANCH,** Ogemaw County: when the railroad came through here in 1871, a store and a hotel were built and the town was named from its location on the west branch of the Rifle River; Zenas H. Wright became its first postmaster on Nov. 17, 1873; incorporated as a village in 1885 and as a city in 1905 [Ami W. Davis; PO Archives].

**WEST CAMPBELL,** Ionia County: storekeeper Isaac Gibson became the first postmaster of this rural post office in western Campbell Township on Dec. 16, 1867, the office operating until Aug. 30, 1902; see Campbell for the name [Schenck; PO Archives].

**WEST CARLISLE,** Kent County: its station on the Grand Rapids & Indiana Railroad was named Carlisle but its post office, opened on March 18, 1884, with Frank B. Foote as its first postmaster, was named West Carlisle; the office operated until Sept. 15, 1910 [GSM 1895; PO Archives].

**WEST CASCO,** Allegan County. See Casco.

**WESTCHESTER,** Oakland County: the Garland Construction Company purchased the J. A. Mercer farm in 1853, platted it, and named it Westchester Village; incorporated as the village of Westchester in 1957; the name has no local significance [Chad M. Ritchie].

**WEST CLIMAX,** Kalamazoo County: Joel A. Gardner became the first postmaster of this rural post office in western Climax Township on May 11, 1842; the office was changed to South Climax on April 5, 1870, and operated until Sept. 7, 1881; see Climax for the name [GSM 1860; PO Archives].

**WEST DELHI,** Ingham County: Thomas Treat became the first postmaster of this rural post office in western Delhi Township on Jan. 10, 1856, the office operating until Jan. 5, 1867; see Delhi for the name [Foster; PO Archives].

**WEST DETROIT,** Wayne County: this place, then three miles from Detroit, began as a station on the Grand Trunk Railroad and was called Grand Trunk Junction; the Michigan Central car shops were located here in 1873 and many employees built their homes nearby; it was given a post office as Detroit Junction on June 23, 1874, with August R. Sink as its first postmaster; it was renamed West Detroit on Jan. 14, 1887, but closed on Aug. 10, 1889, when it was annexed by the city of Detroit [Farmer, GSM 1865-87; PO Archives].

**WEST END,** Wayne County: a station on the Michigan Central Railroad, in Springwells Township, two miles west of Detroit; its post office operated from Feb. 4, 1878, to Jan. 31, 1906 [GSM 1881-1907; PO Archives].

**WEST ERIE,** Monroe County. See Lambertville.

**WEST FARMINGTON,** Oakland County: a post office opened on Feb. 27, 1828, in what was then the western part of Farmington Township, but is now in Novi Township; John Gould, the first postmaster, conducted the office in his home, and it operated until Aug. 16, 1848 [Durant; PO Archives].

**WESTFIELD,** Kalamazoo County: James S. Cowgill became the first postmaster of this rural post office on May 14, 1839; the office was changed to Prairie Ronde on Jan. 31, 1846, and operated until June 17, 1862 [PO Archives].

**WEST GENEVA,** Van Buren County. See Lacota.

**WEST GREENBUSH,** Alcona County: a station on the Detroit & Mackinaw Railroad, some 5 miles southwest of Greenbush, in 1894 [GSM 1895].

**WEST GUN LAKE,** Allegan County: a hamlet near Bradley, in 1920; see Gun Lake, Barry County, for the name [GSM 1921].

**WEST HARRISVILLE,** Alcona County. See Lincoln.

**WEST HAVEN,** Shiawassee County: Horace Hart and his four sons, from Monroe County, Mich., became the first settlers in the area in 1836; the founders of the village were E. E. White and D. M. Estey in 1868-69; it was given a post office as Rush, named after pioneer settler Henry Rush, on Jan. 6, 1851, with Lewis Hart as its first postmaster; it was changed to West Haven, from its location in New Haven Township, on July 22, 1857, with the spelling changed to Westhaven on April 28, 1894, the office operating until Oct. 31, 1901 [Ellis; PO Archives].

**WEST HAVEN CENTRE,** Gratiot County: Joseph Wiles became the first postmaster of this rural post office on Sept. 26, 1863, the office operating until Dec. 14, 1904 [PO Archives].

**WEST HIGHLAND,** Oakland County. See Highland.

**WEST HOLT,** Ingham County: Samuel J. Haley became the first postmaster of this rural post office in Delhi Township on June 21, 1899, the office operating until Sept. 29, 1900; named from its being west of the village of Holt; see Holt for the name [PO Archives; Adams].

**WEST HOUGHTON,** Houghton County: the Montezuma Company bought 200 acres here as a copper mining location about 1850, but very little mining was done; the Sheldon-Douglass Estate, of Houghton, which owned the surface, platted the village which became known as West Houghton, they selling quite a number of lots [Stevens].

**WEST HURON,** Wayne County. See Van Buren.

**WESTLAND,** Wayne County: the area, in Nankin Township, around the J. L. Hudson Company shopping complex named Westland Center, from its location west of Detroit; incorporated as a city in 1966, with Thomas Brown as its first mayor [Detroit Free Press, April 26, 1966].

**WEST LEROY,** Calhoun County: Ira Case bought the first land here in 1935, but David C. Fish became the first permanent settler in 1836; his wife suggested the name in honor of their first-born son, LeRoy Fish, when the township was set off in 1837; a marsh through it caused the two sections to be called East Leroy and West Leroy; Truman S. Cole became the first postmaster of West Leroy on Jan. 26, 1852, the office operating until Sept. 30, 1903; the marsh has since been redeemed [Everts; PO Archives].

**WEST MARION,** Livingston County: Sylvester Rounds became the first postmaster of this rural post office on Feb. 2, 1848, the office operating until July 5, 1849; see Marion for the name [PO Archives].

**WEST MILAN,** Monroe County. See Cone.

**WEST MILLBROOK,** Mecosta County: Nelson A. Ellis became the first postmaster of this rural post office in western Millbrook Township on April 24, 1883, the office operating until Oct. 31, 1905 [GSM 1907; PO Archives].

**WESTMINSTER,** Grand Traverse County: this station on the Traverse City Railroad was the site of the lumber mill of the (Henry H. and Levi J.) Hadley Brothers Company, completed in 1883 [Traverse].

**WEST NECK,** Kalamazoo County: Friend C. Bird became the first postmaster of this rural post office on May 1, 1851, the office operating until Oct. 12, 1852 [PO Archives].

**WEST NOVI,** Oakland County: this settlement was given a post office as Hickville after Daniel Hickok, who became its first postmaster on June 20, 1839; it was renamed West Novi on Oct. 27, 1854; see Novi for the name [GSM 1860; PO Archives].

**WEST OGDEN,** Lenawee County: Benjamin L. Hicks became the first postmaster of this rural post office in Ogden Township on Oct. 11, 1843, the office operating until Jan. 11, 1878 [PO Archives].

**WEST OLIVE,** Ottawa County: this village on the west side of Olive Township was platted by R. M. Paget in 1870 and given a post office on Nov. 8, 1870, with John P. Hanchett as its first postmaster; it was given a station on the Chicago & Western Michigan (now Pere Marquette) Railroad by 1884 [Anne M. Palich, PM].

**WESTON,** Lenawee County: Ezra Cole was the first settler here in Fairfield Township in 1835; the village, first known as Oakford, was given a post office of that name on July 27, 1854, with Northright Knapp as its first postmaster; on June 15, 1869, it was renamed for Edward Payson Weston, a professional pedestrian; a station on the Lake Shore & Michigan Southern Railroad [Irene M. Robinson, PM].

**WESTON,** Van Buren County: Horace Stimson became the first postmaster of this rural post office on Sept. 25, 1837; the office was transferred to and renamed Lawrence on April 17, 1844 [PO Archives].

**WESTPHALIA,** Clinton County: on Aug. 26, 1836, Rev. Anton Kopp and a large number of farmers from Westphalia, Germany, sailed from Breman and landed in New York five weeks later; they pressed on to Detroit and then to Ionia where, in the recently opened land office, they could buy the most for their slender means; they had come as a unit and they bought as a unit the lands on which their descendants live today; shoemaker Anton Dunnebacker built the first house in 1849; Rev. George Godez became the first postmaster on Sept. 5, 1851; Joseph Platte built the first store in 1852, and in 1854, John A. Fedewa put in a stock of goods; incorporated as a village in 1883 [Paré; Daboll].

**WEST POINT,** Schoolcraft County: a station on the Minneapolis, St. Paul & Sault Ste. Marie Railroad in 1888, named from its being on the west border of the county [Mich Manual 1899].

**WEST PORTAGE,** Jackson County. See Henrietta.

**WEST PRESQU'ILE,** Ontonagon County: Austin Corser became the first postmaster of this rural post office on Aug. 19, 1847, the office operating until Oct. 25, 1848 [PO Archives].

**WEST RAISINVILLE,** Monroe County. See Raisinville.

**WEST RIVES,** Jackson County. See Rives Junction.

**WEST ROCK,** Delta County: the building of the railroad brought the first settlers to the area in 1865; later, Thomas Kaminen built the first home here and paved the way for other Finnish families to come and settle; named from its being west of Rock [Delta Reporter].

**WEST SEBEWA,** Ionia County: a post office in western Sebewa Township opened on April 14, 1871, with Nathaniel Steward as its first postmaster, succeeded by Andrew C. Steward on Nov. 14, 1871, the office operating until April 30, 1904; see Sebewa for the name [Schenck; PO Archives].

**WEST SHERMAN,** St. Joseph County: Jairus Parker became the first postmaster of this rural post office on May 6, 1839, the office operating until May 1, 1844; see Sherman for the name [PO Archives].

**WEST SHERMAN,** Wexford County. See Claggettville.

**WEST'S LANDING,** Oscoda County: it was named for Jasper West who owned a 100-acre farm here in (then) Grove Township in 1879 [Mich Hist 42:161 1958].

**WEST'S MILLS,** Saginaw County: a settlement around the sawmill of (A. J.) West & Lewis, in Jonesville Township; George Docket became its first postmaster on June 23, 1874, the office operating until Oct. 20, 1881; its railroad station was named Meridian [GSM 1883; PO Archives].

**WEST SUMMIT,** Wexford County: Hanson S. Carrier became the first postmaster at this railroad station on April 10, 1872, the office operating until Feb. 6, 1874 [GSM 1873-75; PO Archives].

**WEST SUMPTER,** Wayne County: it was named for General Thomas Sumter, Revolutionary War hero, but through an engrossing clerk's error the name was misspelled and has since remained so in the township and the town which was established by an act of the legislature in 1835; John A. Craft became its first postmaster on March 24, 1874, the office operating until Feb. 28, 1902 [Burton; GSM 1860; PO Archives].

**WEST TROY,** Newaygo County: storekeeper Winfield S. Brewer became the first postmaster of Walkup on Feb. 20, 1882; the office was renamed West Troy from its location in Troy Township on Aug. 9, 1882, and operated until May 29, 1893 [GSM 1883; PO Archives].

**WESTVILLE,** Montcalm County: Hiram Weller became the first settler here in 1853; although when erected in 1864, the township was (and still is) spelled Douglass, it was named for Stephen A. Douglas, the Democratic presidential candidate of 1860; Eli M. Mallet became the first postmaster of its village on May 2, 1872, succeeded by Jesse H. Jordan on Feb. 24, 1873; the village was named, platted and recorded by Daniel West, a New Yorker, who owned 120 acres, mostly here in Douglass Township; its post office operated until Oct. 31, 1907 [Dasef; Schenck; PO Archives].

**WEST WATSON,** Allegan County. See Abronia.

**WEST WINDSOR,** Eaton County: Thomas J. Sloan, from Oneida County, N.Y., became one of the first settlers in 1844; George P. Carman became its first postmaster on Oct. 1, 1849; E. D. Davison built a steam sawmill here in 1856 and his brother-in-law, A. R. Williams, opened the first store; its post office operated until June 15, 1905; the village was nicknamed Sevastopol at the time of the Crimean War; see Windsor for the name [Durant; PO Archives].

**WESTWOOD,** Kalkaska County: James Campbell, a native of London, Canada, bought land in Rapid River Township, opened a general store near here in 1873, moving the business here when the Grand Rapids & Indiana

Railroad came through and built a station; the depot was first named Havana but the place was given a post office as Westwood on Nov. 12, 1873, with Mr. Campbell as its first postmaster; in partnership with William Duncan, C. Graham and C. M. Hall, he built a sawmill here in 1877; its post office operated until April 30, 1914 [Traverse; GSM 1875; PO Archives].

**WESTWOOD**, Oakland County. See Beverly Hills.

**WETMORE**, Alger County: this village in Munising Township began as a small, mostly Indian, settlement called Floeter, and was given a post office of that name on July 2, 1883, with Francois X. Brusette as its first postmaster; the office was closed on July 28, 1884, but was restored on Dec. 26, 1884, with William Floeter as its postmaster; it was closed again on June 1, 1888, but was restored again on Oc. 23, 1888; it was renamed Munising (the present Munising was then known as Old Munising) on Oct. 23, 1889; a station on the Duluth, South Shore & Atlantic Railroad; William L. Wetmore had come here to cut off hardwood for charcoal about 1871, and he built kilns and a general store; when he retired about 1894, the village was renamed for him, and when its post office was restored on Dec. 3, 1895, it too was renamed for him; it was in Schoolcraft County until Alger was organized on March 17, 1885 [Mrs. Ruth R. Jansen, PM; PO Archives].

**WET PRAIRIE**, Calhoun County: John E. Westlake entered the first land here in northern Burlington Township in 1834; later David Coddington bought the land; in 1836, he sold it to Abram Kimble who on May 5, 1838, became the first postmaster, with the office named Abscota, the office operating until March 29, 1900 [Everts; PO Archives].

**WETZELL**, Antrim County: this settlement in Mancelona Township formed around the mill of the Wetzell Turning Works and took its name; a station on the Grand Rapids & Indiana Railroad; James C. McMahon became its first postmaster on Nov. 8, 1881, the office operating until April 30, 1910 [GSM 1885; PO Archives].

**WEXFORD**, Wexford County: it was founded by John Lennington, a general storekeeper; William Masters became its first postmaster on Feb. 17, 1865; the place was also known as Hanover; nearly destroyed by fire in 1909, it was partly rebuilt but gradually became a ghost town [Barnes; GSM 1873; PO Archives].

**WHEAL KATE**, Houghton County: a 240-acre copper mining tract, on which was located the little mountain of Wheal Kate and which took its Cornish name; some exploratory work was done on the lands in the 1860s [Stevens].

**WHEATFIELD**, Calhoun County: Estes Rich built the first log house here in Emmet Township in 1831, followed by Benjamin and Henry L. Dwinell, of Auburn, N.Y.; they, with Robert Wheaton, built a bridge of poles across the Kalamazoo River here in 1835; it was given a depot on the Michigan Central Railroad named White's Station for Charles H. White, owner of the local flour mill and cheese factory, and he became the first postmaster on Dec. 29, 1870; from its being in a wheat growing region, it was renamed Wheatfield on June 2, 1881, the office operating until Dec. 17, 1896 [PO Archives; Gardner; GSM 1873].

**WHEATFIELD,** Ingham County: David Gorsline became the first white settler in the area in 1836; in 1841, he had the name of the town changed from Brutus to that of his native Wheatfield, Niagara County, N.Y., a fitting name, for it was a fine wheat-growing region; Simon P. Hendrick became its first postmaster on Sept. 5, 1851, the office operating until Dec. 15, 1855 [Foster; Durant; PO Archives].

**WHEATLAND,** Hillsdale County: it was first settled by Edmund B. Brown in 1834 and tavern-keeper Eli Eastman in 1835; Wheatland Township was organized in 1835; Thomas Gamble became the first postmaster on Sept. 9, 1835, with the office named Wheatland, but changed to Gambleville, after the postmaster, on Oct. 17, 1837; it was renamed Somerset on June 8, 1841; the Wheatland Centre post office was renamed Wheatland on Feb. 3, 1882, operating until March 31, 1903; it was in a wheat growing region [Pen Phil 7:3 Jan 1959; Reynolds; PO Archives].

**WHEATLAND,** Ionia County. See Orleans.

**WHEATLAND,** Mecosta County: William Schiedel became the first settler in 1860 and Jacob Schiedel the first supervisor when Wheatland Township was organized in 1862 [Chapman].

**WHEATLAND,** Wexford County: Jonathan Wheat became the first postmaster of this rural post office named for him on March 4, 1872, the office operating until Dec. 4, 1878 [GSM 1875; PO Archives].

**WHEATLAND CENTRE,** Hillsdale County: Aaron Van Vleet became the first postmaster of this rural post office in Wheatland Township on May 11, 1838, with the office changed to Wheatland on Feb. 3, 1882 [GSM 1860; PO Archives].

**WHEATLEY,** Gladwin County: Benjamin J. Wheatley had a general store here in Grout Township and on Nov. 15, 1897 he became the first postmaster, naming the office for himself, the office operating until Jan. 31, 1914 [Mrs. O. J. MacMurray; PO Archives].

**WHEELER,** Allegan County: this rural post office was named for Chester C. Wheeler who became its first postmaster on Sept. 8, 1856, the office operating until Dec. 23, 1857 [GSM 1860; PO Archives].

**WHEELER,** Gratiot County: it was founded by Albert P. Foland in 1862, who moved his general store a quarter of a mile north to be near the Pere Marquette Railroad when it came through here in 1872; Daniel D. Brooks became its first postmaster on May 28, 1869, followed by Mr. Foland in 1870; it was first platted by S. S. Hastings for Charles J. and Mary M. Allen in 1876; it was named by and for James B. Wheeler, a pioneer settler of 1859 and the first supervisor of the township in 1862 [Tucker; PO Archives].

**WHEELER'S CORNERS,** Genesee County: this hamlet, ten miles from Flint, was settled prior to 1890, and was named for Elmer G. Wheeler, landowner and justice of the peace [GSM 1891].

**WHEELERVILLE,** Shiawassee County: this rural post office was named for Humphrey Wheeler who became its first postmaster on Aug. 3, 1857, the office operating until Dec., 1865 [PO Archives].

**WHIG CENTER,** Branch County. See South Butler.

**WHIGVILLE,** Genesee County. See Gibsonville.

**WHIGVILLE,** Lapeer County: in the winter of 1837-38, quite a colony from some of the southern counties located in the southwest part of Dryden Township, among them James Allen and James Deming and Uriah Townsend; they were mostly Whigs, hence the name given to the locality and retained in nearby Whigville Lakes; the settlement was given a post office as Whigville on July 8, 1850, with Stephen Grinnell as its first postmaster, the office operating until July 3, 1856 [Page; PO Archives].

**WHIPPLE,** Grand Traverse County: Miss Jessie R. Williams became the first postmaster of this rural post office on April 17, 1888, the office operating until Nov. 18, 1889 [PO Archives].

**WHISKEY CREEK,** Oceana County: the area was first settled in 1849; A. S. Anderson handled the mail distribution in 1856; it was the first county seat until 1865; George Stewart, who lived in a house-store over a creek, laid in a stock of one barrel of whiskey in the fall, sold three barrels that winter, and had two left in the spring, and as some people believed the creek had something to do with it, they named the stream Whiskey Creek [Royal; Page].

**WHITE,** Delta County. See Woodlawn.

**WHITE,** Hillsdale County: this settlement on the St. Joseph River, in Amboy Township, was named for sawmill owner Benjamin White; Samuel Jacobus became its first postmaster on Feb. 2, 1872, the office operating until Dec. 14, 1903 [GSM 1873; PO Archives].

**WHITE,** Houghton County: a mine location; Frank G. White was agent for the Phoenix Consolidated Copper Company in the 1800s [Stevens].

**WHITE CITY,** Gogebic County: this privately owned resort on Lake Gogebic was founded on the Chicago & Northwestern Railroad and named for one of their conductors who was also a road contractor in Chicago [Victor Lemmer].

**WHITE CLOUD,** Newaygo County: it was founded by Sextus N. Wilcox and Lester C. Morgan who built a lumber camp here in Everett Township in 1871; also known as Morgantown and as Morganville, it was given a railroad depot as Morgan Station in 1873, and a post office of the same name on July 22, 1873, with Mr. Morgan as its first postmaster; it was renamed White Cloud on March 26, 1877; Fred Ramsey became president when the village was incorporated in 1879; incorporated as a city in 1950 [S. E. Douglass, D.O.; PO Archives].

**WHITEDALE,** Schoolcraft County. See Gulliver.

**WHITE DOG CORNERS,** Ingham County: the first meeting for organizing Wheatfield Township in 1841 was held in the home of William Tompkins; the place was named by pioneer settler George Hay whose white dog was killed by a falling tree and buried with some ceremony [Durant].

**WHITE FEATHER,** Bay County: a station on the Mackinaw division of the Michigan Central Railroad, in Pinconning Township; James Lomas built a mill here by a stream which the Indians had named White Feather River, in 1874, and C. Ives built a shingle mill at about the same time; Charles Powell became the first postmaster of the settlement on Aug. 14, 1874; the office was closed on March 16, 1875, but was restored from May 25, 1875, to June 27, 1878, and from Nov. 10, 1879, to June 14, 1881; both mills burned and were not rebuilt [Page; PO Archives].

**WHITE FISH,** Schoolcraft County: a station on the Detroit & Mackinaw Railroad in 1882 [GSM 1883].

**WHITEFISH LAKE,** Montcalm County: this resort village on the east shore of Whitefish Lake was platted and recorded for H. E. and T. Campbell, on Oct. 4, 1906, and again for James A. and Mary A. Skinner, on Aug. 14, 1907; both plats were made by J. F. Daoust [Dasef].

**WHITEFISH POINT,** Chippewa County: it was founded about 1871 as a supply landing for lumber camps and as a commercial fishery; Sylvester P. Mason became its first postmaster on Sept. 24, 1877; named from the abundance of whitefish here [Mrs. Albert Hutton; GSM 1881; PO Archives].

**WHITEFORD,** Monroe County: James White was the clerk of the meeting which organized Whiteford Township in 1834, at which meeting David White was elected the first supervisor; Aaron B. Watkins became the first postmaster on June 2, 1835; with James White as postmaster, the office was transferred to Lucas County, Ohio, Sept. 19, 1835 [Mich Hist 38:408 1954; Wing; PO Archives].

**WHITEFORD CENTRE,** Monroe County: in his diary covering his journey from Philadelphia to Tecumseh in 1840, Elwood Comfort refers to Whiteford Centre as a "smart village"; Hiram Wakeley became its first postmaster on June 26, 1867, the office operating until Sept. 30, 1905; see Whiteford for the name [Mich Hist 38:408 1954; Wing; PO Archives].

**WHITEHALL,** Muskegon County: mill owner Charles Mears and businessman Giles B. Slocum platted the village and named it Mears in 1859; Albert (brother of Charles) Mears became its first postmaster on June 23, 1862; it was renamed Whitehall, from its being by White Lake, on April 1, 1867; incorporated as a village in 1867 and as a city in 1942 [City Mgr.; Mich Hist 30:534 1946].

**WHITE LAKE,** Oakland County: the township was named from its largest lake, whose waters are clear and beautiful; the area was first settled by Harley Olmsted, from Monroe County, N.Y., in 1830; the first houses on the village site were built by Jesse Seeley and Cornelius G. Wyckoff in 1833; it was given a post office as White Lake on June 17, 1836, with Marfield Ludlow as its first postmaster; it was renamed Mayville on June 10, 1840; the Plainville post office was changed to White Lake on May 29, 1841, and operated until Jan. 31, 1910 [Durant; Seeley; PO Archives].

**WHITE LAKE CENTRE,** Oakland County. See Oxbow Lake.

**WHITE OAK,** Ingham County: it was first settled by Daniel Dutcher, from Montgomery County, N.Y., in 1835, followed by a group of 36 pioneer settlers the next year; John E. Clements became the first postmaster on July 20, 1848, the office operating until Nov. 15, 1902; named after its township which had been named from the predominent tree of the locality [Foster; Durant; PO Archives].

**WHITE OAK,** Van Buren County: a station on the Michigan Central Railroad in 1864 [GSM 1865].

**WHITE OAK SPRINGS,** Iowa County: when Hugh E. Colter became its first postmaster on Jan. 26, 1836, it was in Michigan Territory, but is now in Wisconsin [PO Archives].

**WHITE PIGEON,** St. Joseph County: it was first settled by John Winchell, from Wayne County, Mich., in 1827; Colonel Asahel Savery, tavern-keeper, became the first postmaster of the county's first post office, called Millville, in 1828; this stage post office was succeeded by a government post office named White Pigeon Prairie on Feb. 16, 1833, with Alfred Allen as its first postmaster; the name was shortened to White Pigeon on Jan. 21, 1835; the village was platted and recorded by Robert Clark, Jr., for Niles F. Smith, Neal McGaffrey (both of whom settled here in 1828-29) and Colonel Savery, in 1830, and incorporated in 1837; named for "Wahbememe, Chief White Pigeon, who about 1830 gave his life to save the settlement" [Alba Columba Club marker, 1909; MPH 18:513 1891; Cutler; PO Archives].

**WHITE PINE,** Ontonagon County: a station on the Chicago, Minneapolis & St. Paul Railroad, in Carp Lake Township; Thomas H. Wilcox, a mining engineer, found mass copper in the Mineral River and formed the White Pine Copper Company to mine it, with himself as superintendent; its settlement was given a post office as White Pine Mine on June 7, 1915, with Axel G. Johnson as its first postmaster; the mine closed about 1920, but in 1946, W. E. (Tex) Romig developed a process to recover copper from the ore by flotation and the mine was re-opened; its post office, renamed simply White Pine, was restored on Feb. 1, 1954, with Clarence Broemer as its first postmaster [C. A. Broemer; GSM 1917; PO Archives].

**WHITE RIVER,** Muskegon County: Charles Mears made the first settlement here at the mouth of the White River in 1836; it was given a post office on Jan. 29, 1858, with Sylvester J. B. Watson as its first postmaster, the office operating until Jan. 2, 1879 [Page; PO Archives].

**WHITE RIVER,** Oceana County: the first settler here on the White River in Greenwood Township was Henry D. Clark in 1854; he was followed by Alfred A. Caine who became the first postmaster on March 17, 1855 [Hartwick; MPH 22:237 1893; PO Archives].

**WHITE ROCK,** Huron County: the site marks the boundary of the Treaty of Detroit, 1807, whereby the southeastern part of the state was ceded to Michigan by the Indians; Edward Petit, the first white settler in the county, opened a trading post on present-day Shebeon Creek in 1829 and later moved it here; found on some early maps as White Rock City, it was boomed as such by promotors in 1835-36, while it was still a wilderness; it was sufficiently settled to be given a post office on Feb. 5, 1859; William Van Camp was its first postmaster and the office, named White Rock, operated until April 30, 1907; a large white boulder in Lake Huron marked the entrance to the place and gave it its name [MPH 3:200 1881; Chapman; PO Archives].

**WHITESBURG,** Genesee County: this village in Thetford Township was named for Clark White, prominent pioneer settler; Isaac O. Rogers built a grist mill here in 1852; Alanson Dickinson became the first postmaster on March 16, 1866; the office was moved to and renamed Rogersville on March 28, 1873; it was moved to and renamed Whitesburg on Nov. 16, 1895, but back again to Rogersville on June 12, 1897; the village was platted and recorded by Carlos P. Wilson about 1870; its station on the Pere Marquette Railroad was named Rogers [Ellis; GSM 1897; PO Archives].

**WHITE'S JUNCTION,** Charlevoix County: a station on the Boyne City & Southeastern Railroad, a mile northwest of Boyne Falls; its settlement, called White's Camp, formed around the White Lumber Company mill about 1894 [GSM 1899].

**WHITE'S LAKE,** Jackson County: this settlement in Henrietta Township was named for R. R. White who settled near the lake named for him, in 1836 [Interstate].

**WHITE'S STATION,** Calhoun County. See Wheatfield.

**WHITESVILLE,** Lapeer County. See Lapeer.

**WHITE SWAN,** Kent County: John Davis became the first postmaster of this rural post office in the northeast part of the county on Dec. 21, 1853; the office was closed on April 14, 1860, but was restored from Feb. 15, 1864, to April 14, 1870, and from Oct. 10, 1870, to May 20, 1878 [GSM 1881; PO Archives].

**WHITETOWN,** Hillsdale County. See Austin.

**WHITEVILLE,** Isabella County: this rural post office was named for storekeeper Omer L. White who became its first postmaster on Jan. 2, 1884, the office operating until Feb. 25, 1902 [GSM 1885; PO Archives].

**WHITE WATER,** Grand Traverse County: Oscar Eaton became the first postmaster of this rural post office on July 16, 1857; the office was changed to Acme on June 10, 1869 [PO Archives].

**WHITEWOOD,** Berrien County: William H. Merrifield became the first postmaster of this rural post office on Nov. 11, 1862, the office operating until Dec. 27, 1864 [PO Archives].

**WHITEWOOD,** Wayne County. See Highland Park.

**WHITING,** Lapeer County: Ontario-born Lysander R. Whiting settled here in North Branch Township in 1857 and operated a steam sawmill in section 56; the settlement was given a post office on Feb. 20, 1882, with storekeeper David Holm as its first postmaster; the post office was transferred to and renamed King's Mill on Dec. 4, 1883, but on Jan. 14, 1884, the Whiting post office was re-established, with Mr. Whiting as its postmaster, the office operating until Dec. 31, 1902 [Page; PO Archives].

**WHITING,** Van Buren County: Cornelius Osterhout became the first postmaster of this rural post office on Sept. 25, 1837, the office operating until Sept. 20, 1838 [PO Archives].

**WHITMAN,** Marquette County: a station on the L. S. & I. and the M. & S.E. Railroads in 1910 [GSM 1911].

**WHITMANVILLE,** Cass County. See LaGrange.

**WHITMORE LAKE,** Washtenaw County: Jonathan F. Stratton, a surveyor, and Luke H. Whitmore, who lived near Ann Arbor, were land looking when they camped here soon after 1825; Mr. Stratton suggested the name of the lake and it was placed on the maps with that name; Mr. Whitmore became a local landowner and the first county treasurer in 1829; on June 9, 1834, George W. Dexter became the first postmaster of the village which formed by the lake; it was first called Northfield after the township, but was changed to Whitmore Lake on Dec. 27, 1854 [Clare Rorabacher; PO Archives].

**WHITNEY,** Arenac County: the settlement formed around the Whitney lumber mill at which the first town meeting was held in 1880 [Page].

**WHITNEY,** Menominee County: it was founded about 1878 and named for Charles Whitney, a land surveyor for the Pittsburgh & Lake Superior Iron Company; this village in Harris Township was given a station on the Chicago & Northwestern Railroad and on Oct. 30, 1883, a post office, with John C. Kirkpatrick as its first postmaster; the office operated until June 30, 1939 [Ruth M. Thomas; PO Archives].

**WHITNEY BEACH,** Gladwin County: the aftermath of the lumber boom saw the development of resort areas along the river in Hay Township, and this was one of the first, owned and operated by Arthur Whitney, formerly a hunter and trapper from Highwood [Ritchie].

**WHITNEYVILLE,** Kent County: it was named for Peter Whitney, of

Ohio, who in 1841 moved with his family onto this site in Cascade Township. the township was organized in 1848 and was given a post office on Feb. 8, 1849, with William C. White as its first postmaster; the office was closed on Aug. 27, 1868, but was restored from Oct. 23, 1877, to July 31, 1909 [Dillenback; Mich Hist 17:147 1933; PO Archives].

**WHITTAKER,** Washtenaw County: Frank Whittaker opened a general store here about 1860 and the village was named for him; given a station on the Wabash Railroad in 1880 and a post office on Jan. 9, 1882, with William H. Bishop as its first postmaster [Frances Sikorski, PM; PO Archives].

**WHITTEMORE,** Iosco County: David Belleknap was the first settler; the village was founded in 1879 and named by a group of its citizens for Frank Whittemore; Robert H. Martin became its first postmaster on April 13, 1880; incorporated as a city in 1907 [Henry K. Hasty].

**WICKWARE,** Sanilac County: the first permanent settler in present Greenleaf Township was Stephen Greenman in 1858, followed by Alexander Nichol in 1859; Hugh Jordan built the first sawmill in 1879; it was named for Alfred Wickware who became the first postmaster on Oct. 31, 1882, the office operating until June 30, 1906 [Chapman; PO Archives].

**WILBER,** Iosco County: the township was erected in 1878 and named for Loran Wilber, the pioneer settler in whose house the organizing meeting was held; its village formed around the sawmill of A. J. Rodman; Alice J. Abbott became its first postmaster on July 19, 1890, the office operating until May 31, 1932 [Page; GSM 1891; PO Archives].

**WILBER,** Sanilac County: the first settler in the area was Theodore Laurel in 1853; John Pace opened the first store; its depot on the Port Huron & Northwestern Railroad was named Wilber Station in 1881 [Chapman].

**WILBUR LAKE,** Jackson County: this settlement in Pulaski Township was named for John Wilbur who settled near the lake in 1835; its post office, named simply Wilbur, was opened on April 15, 1884, with Jediah D. Cook as its first postmaster, and it operated until April 19, 1887 [Interstate; GSM 1889; PO Archives].

**WILCOX,** Newaygo County. See Willcox.

**WILDER'S PRAIRIE,** Calhoun County. See Eckford.

**WILDERVILLE,** Calhoun County: it was named for Oshea Wilder, a surveyor who came here from New York State in 1831; its station on the C., J. & M. Railroad was named Wilder's; George H. Soule became the first postmaster of Wilderville on Jan. 8, 1887, the office operating until June 30, 1899 [Roy Lord; GSM 1887; PO Archives].

**WILD FOWL PORT,** Huron County. See Bay Port.

**WILDWOOD,** Cheboygan County: the hamlet of Mentor Corners in

Mentor Township was given a post office as Mentor on April 14, 1882, with John D. Burket as its first postmaster; with Samuel L. Keyes as postmaster, it was renamed Wildwood on Oct. 6, 1884 [PO Archives; GSM 1883].

**WILEY**, Mason County: this station on the narrow gauge Mason & Oceana Railroad was named Wiley's in 1886; it was given a post office as Wiley on Sept. 8, 1888, with John F. Genter as its first postmaster; the office operated until Oct. 14, 1903 [PO Archives; GSM 1889].

**WILKINSON**, Berrien County. See Lakeside.

**WILLARD**, Bay County: it was named for Levi Willard in whose home the first Beaver Township elections were held in 1867, John Peter Ittner became the first postmaster of this rural post office on Feb. 26, 1885, the office operating until Dec. 31, 1907 [Gansser; GSM 1887; PO Archives].

**WILLCOX**, Newaygo County: storekeeper Miron M. Deake became the first postmaster of this rural post office in Dayton Township on May 28, 1898, the office operating until Oct. 31, 1903; in some records as Wilcox [GSM 1899; PO Archives].

**WILLETS**, Monroe County. See Willits.

**WILLIAM MITCHELL STATE PARK**, Wexford County: it was named for William W. Mitchell (nephew of George A. Mitchell, founder of the city of Cadillac) who, with Jonathan W. Cobbs, as Cobbs & Mitchell, operated a number of sawmills in the area in the 1890s [Mich Hist 25:238 1941].

**WILLIAMS**, Bay County: it was first settled in 1854 by John Gaffney, Charles Bradford, and George W. Smock; John C. Rowden, who came in 1855, became its first postmaster on Aug. 26, 1868, succeeded by Spencer O. Fisher on March 26, 1872, the office operating until April 10, 1874; named after its township [Gansser; PO Archives].

**WILLIAMS**, Kalamazoo County: it was founded by the Chester A. Williams family who had a grist mill here; Elijah Post became its first postmaster on May 29, 1878, succeeded by Mr. Williams, the office operating until Dec. 30, 1933; a station on the Michigan Central Railroad in 1882; now a hamlet [Durant; PO Archives].

**WILLIAMS**, Midland County: a hamlet in 1878 [GSM 1879].

**WILLIAMSBURG**, Grand Traverse County: three families from Monroe County, N.Y., moved here in 1856; the settlement became known as Mill Creek from the stream beside it; about 1860, with the coming of the railroad, the town was moved some quarter of a mile south (on present M-72) and renamed Williamsburg; it was given a post office as Dunbar on March 29, 1867, named for Eber J. Dunbar, its first postmaster; it was renamed Williamsburgh on June 18, 1869, shortened to Williamsburg on June 23, 1894 [PO Archives; Barnes; GSM 1879].

**WILLIAMSBURG,** Mackinac County: this settlement on Mackinac Island which had its heyday at the peak of the northwest fur trade in the 1880s, was restored as an historic site in the 1940s [Mich Hist 25:412 1941]

**WILLIAMSBURG,** Ontonagon County. See Rockland.

**WILLIAMS ISLAND,** Alger County: just west and south of Grand Island; it was named for Vermont-born Indian trader Abraham Williams who became the first white settler here in 1840; it became a part of Alger County in 1885 [Mich Hist 22:282 1938].

**WILLIAMS LAKE,** Oakland County: it was named for Ferdinand Williams who built his log cabin on its shores in 1829; his father, John R. Williams, was a figure in Detroit history and John R. street was named for him [Ripley].

**WILLIAMS' LANDING,** Alger County: this site on Grand Island was named for the same man as was Williams Island, Abraham Williams, who established a trading post here in 1840 [Hatcher].

**WILLIAMSPORT,** Clinton County. See Eureka.

**WILLIAMSPORT,** Manistee County: it began about 1871 with the building of the new channel to see which the tug Williams, of Manistee, ran an excursion from Manistee (it was the first craft to use the channel), and from this the people named the place Williamsport; its mill burned down within a year of erection; Mr. Shanks had a boarding house here and ran the ferry across the channel; it never became a village [Virginia Stroemel].

**WILLIAMSTON,** Ingham County: at one time it was called Cedar from its location by the Cedar River; Hiram and Joseph Putnam, from Jackson County, Mich. became the first settlers on the village site in 1834; O. B. Williams arrived from Batavia, N.Y., in 1839, and in 1840, he and his brother, James M. Williams, bought land from the Putnams, built a dam and a sawmill in 1840, a grist mill in 1842, and in 1845 made the first plat of the village which was named for them; James M. Williams became the first postmaster on May 10, 1842, with the office named Williamstown, but changed to Williamston on Dec. 2, 1884; incorporated as a village in 1871, with James N. Williams as its first president, and as a city in 1944 [MPH 18:448 1891; Max M. Graham; PO Archives; Durant].

**WILLIAMSVILLE,** Cass County: on July 5, 1849, storekeeper Josiah Williams, as proprietor, filed the first plat of this village in the southeast corner of North Porter Township, naming it after himself; Sylvester M. Barrett became its first postmaster on July 13, 1858, the office operating until Feb. 14, 1903 [Glover; Fox; PO Archives].

**WILLIAMSVILLE,** Livingston County: Amos Williams, his son, Samuel Williams, and his son-in-law, Garry Briggs, became the first settlers in the area in 1833, and they built a sawmill in 1834; the village was platted and named Unadilla, after its township, by Darwin N. Edson and the heirs of Curtis Noble; it was later renamed for its first settlers [Ellis].

**WILLIS,** Washtenaw County: it was first called Potter for Willis L. Potter, a farmer who owned most of the land on which his village in Augusta Township was built; the village owes its existence to the coming through of the Grand Trunk Railroad in 1880; it was given a post office as Newcomb on Sept. 27, 1881, but changed to the first name of Mr. Potter on Dec. 15, 1887 [Beakes; 1889; PO Archives].

**WILLITS,** Monroe County: a station on the Toledo & Ann Arbor Railroad, in Bedford Township; Harriet M. Lord became its first postmaster on Nov. 8, 1880, the office operating until Sept. 23, 1887; in some records as Willets [GSM 1881; PO Archives].

**WILLMARTH,** Wayne County. See Sand Hill.

**WILLOW,** Wayne County: this station on the Pere Marquette Railroad was opened about 1872; it had a post office from July 13, 1892, to May 31, 1915 [PO Archives].

**WILLOW CREEK,** Huron County. See Huron City.

**WILLOW RUN,** Washtenaw County: it was the site of the Willow Run Airport when the federal government began in 1942 to build a hundred million dollar bomber plant, operated by Ford until June 30, 1945; Willow Village, founded in 1943, was the government's housing project for Willow Run workers and their families; it was given a post office in 1943; the site is now a part of Ypsilanti Township and still includes an airport; named from the Willow Run, a small stream running through the region and a tributary to the Huron River [Mich Hist 41:248 1957].

**WILLSON'S FARM,** Mason County. See Riverton.

**WILLVILLE,** Lake County: this hamlet in Eden Township was settled in 1873; Stephen E. Dickens became its first postmaster on Jan. 17, 1877, the office operating until April 20, 1883; it was also known as Eden [GSM 1885; PO Archives].

**WILLWALK,** Chippewa County: this settlement on Sugar Island was named for William Walker, pioneer storekeeper here, who became its first postmaster on Feb. 27, 1917 [GSM 1919; Hamilton. PO Archives].

**WILMOT,** Tuscola County: Oscar Watson first bought government land here in 1868; a station on the Pontiac, Oxford & Northern Railroad; it was platted in 1883; a storekeeper Ozro G. McComb became its first postmaster on Nov. 26, 1883, the office operating until March 31, 1943; it was named for John F. Wilmot [Rev. Raymond Pilarski; GSM 1885; PO Archives].

**WILSON,** Alpena County: it began with a sawmill about 1865; Wilson Township was organized in 1871 and this settlement took its name; the Chicago & Northwestern Railroad came through and opened a station here in 1873 [David S. Coon; Fred R. Trelfa].

**WILSON,** Antrim County. See Eastport.

**WILSON**, Lake County. See Luther.

**WILSON**, Menominee County: the Chicago & Northwestern Railroad came through Spalding Township in 1872-73, and to serve the charcoal kilns here the road built a depot called Ferry Switch; a school was built in 1881-82; the village was given a post office as Myra on Feb. 24, 1881, with storekeeper Daniel McIntyre as its first postmaster; on Nov. 1, 1881, the name was changed for Frank D. Wilson who had built a large sawmill here and he became the postmaster on Nov. 7, 1881; the depot operated until 1950 [Ora E. Corriveau, PM].

**WILSON'S**, Berrien County: James H. Wilson built his sawmill here in Mill Creek in 1835; with the coming through of the Michigan Central Railroad in 1849, the place was given his name; it was also called Wilson's Side Track [GSM 1865; Noggle].

**WILSON'S**, Jackson County: a station on the Fort Wayne & Jackson Railroad, six miles southwest of Jackson, in 1880 [GSM 1881].

**WILSON'S POINT**, Chippewa County: it was named for Captain Thomas Wilson, a lumberman, who here on Sugar Island obtained ship's knees for boats; he founded the Wilson Boat Line [Hamilton].

**WILWIN**, Mackinac County: a station on the Duluth, South Shore & Atlantic Railroad, in Hendrick's Township; Frank Chesbrough built a sawmill here in 1915 and his lumber company platted the village in 1916; it was named for the founder's two sons, Will and Erwin; Alfred King was appointed its first postmaster on Oct. 9, 1916, but declined, and storekeeper Seward M. Shaw took the office on July 11, 1917, and it operated until 1927; now a ghost town [William J. Chesbrough].

**WINCHESTER**, Mecosta County: a station on the Detroit, Grand Rapids & Western Railroad, 3 miles south of Barryton, in 1898 [Mich Manual 1899].

**WINCHESTER**, Monroe County: a settlement on Lake Erie at the mouth of Otter Creek; it is believed to have been named for General James Winchester who, with his Kentucky militia, protected the settlers of this area in the War of 1812 [GSM 1860].

**WINDE**, Delta County. See Beaver.

**WINDIGO MINE**, Keweenaw County: the site of the unsuccessful operations of the Wendigo Copper Company on Isle Royale, 1890-92, and now the site of Windigo Inn; both Wendigo and Windigo are variations of Weendigo, the name of a mythical, cannibal people, much feared by the local Indians [Mich Hist 9:412 1925; Dustin].

**WINDOM**, Lenawee County: this settlement in Rollin Township formed around the mill of F. H. Whitaker & Company; Amanda M. Whitaker became its first postmaster on May 29, 1891, the office operating until April 30, 1902 [GSM 1893; PO Archives].

**WINDSOR**, Eaton County: it was first settled by Orange Towslee in

1837, followed later the same year by Oramel D., John D., and William P. Skinner, from Windsor, Vermont, and when the town was organized in 1842, with John D. Skinner as its first supervisor, they had it named Windsor; Oramel D. Skinner became its first postmaster on Oct. 1, 1894 [MPH 39:387 1899; Durant; PO Archives].

**WINDSOR,** Osceola County: it was founded by Mr. Windsor in 1870.

**WINDSOR,** Otsego County. See Elmira.

**WINEGARS,** Gladwin County: this village in Hay Township was named for W. S. Winegar, a landowner here from at least 1888, for the Entry Book, April 9, 1888, records a contract: "Thaddeus A. Smith vs. Stillwell, Lefaiver and Winegar"; a station on the Michigan Central Railroad; storekeeper Marguerite W. Hull became its first postmaster on Nov. 18, 1919, the office operating until March 8, 1957 [Else M. Kelly; PO Archives].

**WINFIELD,** Ingham County. See Kinneyville.

**WINFIELD,** Monroe County. See Dundee.

**WING LAKE,** Oakland County: it was named for Austin Wing, a member of the party which surveyed the area in 1818 and set the limits of its Waterford Township, which was organized in 1834 [Ripley].

**WINGLETON,** Lake County: Eber Brock Ward, president of the Pere Marquette, decided to run his railroad across the county in 1873; his wife's sister wed Justus S. Stearns, and Mr. Ward set him up in business; the Stearns Lumber Company located here and its railroad stop was called Stearns Siding; it was given a post office as Wingleton, named for G. LaForest Wing, another local lumberman, on June 28, 1882, with his mill manager, William F. Dermont, as its first postmaster; the office was closed on Feb. 19, 1892, but was restored on May 26, 1892, with railroad agent Charles H. Bates as its postmaster [Judkins; GSM 1883; PO Archives].

**WING'S JUNCTION,** Osceola County: a station on the Pere Marquette Railroad, 4 miles east of Hersey, in 1882, named for lumberman G. LaForest Wing [GSM 1883].

**WINN,** Isabella County: this village in Fremont Township was named for Mr. Winn; Franklin J. Williams became its first postmaster on Dec. 19, 1867, the office operating until Nov. 1, 1881; storekeeper William Wiley Dush, platted the village as Dushville and it was given a post office of that name on Jan. 26, 1882, with him as its postmaster, but the name Winn was restored to the village and to its post office on Jan. 14, 1898 [Fancher; PO Archives; Vada Green, PM].

**WINONA** Houghton County: the Winona Copper Mining Company was organized in 1864; the Winona Copper Company was organized in 1898 and took over its lands; this mining community was given a post office on April 5, 1899, with George McElveen as its first postmaster [Stevens; PO Archives].

**WINSOR,** Huron County: it was first settled by G. U. Bean, Richard Winsor, after whom the township was named when organized in 1880, and John T. Linson was its first supervisor [Gwinn].

**WINTERFIELD,** Clare County: Orson N. Earl became the first postmaster of this settlement, named after its township, on Oct. 24, 1877, the office operating until Jan. 15, 1906 [GSM 1881; PO Archives].

**WINTERS,** Alger County: this settlement in Rock River Township was named for John D. Winters who became its first postmaster on Sept. 20, 1889 [PO Archives].

**WINTHROP MINE,** Marquette County: this mine was opened in 1870 by A. B. Meeker, A. G. Clark and H. J. Colewell, who later organized the Winthrop Iron Company; a station on the Marquette, Houghton & Ontonagon Railroad; since Boston capitalists operated in this area, it may have been named for Governor Winthrop [Andreas; Mich Manual].

**WIOTA,** Iowa County: when William S. Hamilton became its first postmaster on March 23, 1835, it was in Michigan Territory, but is now in Wisconsin [PO Archives].

**WIOTA,** Isabella County: Joel Drake became the first postmaster of this rural post office near the northwest corner of Coe Township on Aug. 8, 1857, the office operating until March 14, 1871 [Fancher; PO Archives].

**WIRT,** Calhoun County. See Tekonska.

**WISE,** Isabella County: a station on the Pere Marquette Railroad; the settlement formed around the sawmill of John H. Freeney and was first known as Freeney's Mill; Wise Township, organized in 1872, was named for pioneer settler George W. Wise, and this village when given a post office on July 9, 1884, with Mr. Freeney as its first postmaster, took its name; the office was closed on Jan. 29, 1892, but was restored, with storekeeper J. B. Loomis as postmaster, on Jan. 9, 1893, and operated until Nov. 30, 1906 [John Cumming; GSM 1885; PO Archives].

**WISNER,** Tuscola County: land entries were made here by Joshua Terry in 1853, by Green Bird in 1854, and by Isaiah Jester in 1855; Moses Wisner was inaugurated as governor of Michigan on Jan. 5, 1859, and this township, organized in 1861, was named for him; Henry H. Gilbert became its first postmaster on Dec. 11, 1871, the office operating until May 31, 1905 [Page; PO Archives].

**WITBECK,** Marquette County. See Witch Lake.

**WITCH LAKE,** Marquette County: this village on Witch Lake began with a station on the Chicago, Milwaukee & St. Paul Railroad named Witbeck and it was given a post office of the same name on Nov. 27, 1888, with Jarvis S. Hayward as its first postmaster; the office was closed on July 9, 1890, but was restored from Feb. 8, 1893, to Dec. 30, 1899, and from

June 21, 1905; it was renamed Witch Lake on May 28, 1910 [GSM 1895-1911; PO Archives].

**WITHEY,** Houghton County: this village in Duncan Township began as a station on the M. & N. Railroad named Frost Junction; it formed around the mill and general store of the Farnham Lumber Company and was given a post office as Farnham on Aug. 17, 1889, with Frank H. Farnham as its first postmaster; the office was renamed Withey on Dec. 15, 1891, and operated until May 7, 1897 [GSM 1891-95; PO Archives].

**WITHINGTON,** Jackson County: a settlement around the William H. Wenstren flour mill in Leoni Township; S. Edwin St. John became its first postmaster on July 28, 1890, the office operating until May 3, 1900 [GSM 1891-1907; PO Archives].

**WITTMUND,** Menominee County. See Nathan.

**WIXOM,** Oakland County: it was first settled by Lewis Norton in 1830, Alonzo Sibley in 1831, and Abijah Wixom in 1832, and was first called Sibley's Corners; it was platted and renamed by Willard C. Wixom, son of Abijah, in 1871; John W. Knox became its first postmaster on April 10, 1872; incorporated as a village in 1957 and as a city in 1958 [Pearl S. Willis].

**WOLCOTT'S CORNERS,** Oakland County. See North Farmington.

**WOLF CREEK,** Lenawee County: this settlement on Wolf Creek, in Rome Township, was given a post office on May 2, 1835, with Lyman W. Baker as its first postmaster; the office was closed on Nov. 20, 1866, but was restored from Jan. 15, 1892, to Dec. 31, 1902 [GSM 1838; PO Archives].

**WOLF'S PRAIRIE,** Berrien County. See Berrien Springs.

**WOLFTON,** Huron County: this rural post office was named for storekeeper William Wolf who became its first postmaster on Sept. 14, 1891, the office operating until March 15, 1904 [GSM 1893; PO Archives].

**WOLVERINE,** Cheboygan County: a station on the Michigan Central Railroad; it was platted as Torrey in 1881 by John N. Sanborne on land owned by Daniel McKillop; it was given a post office named Wolverine on Jan. 3, 1881, with George D. Richards as its first postmaster; incorporated as a village in 1903; named after the state animal, the wolverine, which name goes back to at least 1835 [Mich Hist 12:593 1928; Powers; PO Archives].

**WOLVERINE,** Houghton County: the Wolverine Mine of the Wolverine Copper Company, organized by eastern capitalists, was opened by local men in 1882; it held sixth place as a producer among Lake Superior copper mines by 1899 [Stevens].

**WOLVERINE LAKE,** Oakland County: Dr. Howard Stuart and Mr. L. A. Green conceived the idea of promoting a dam that would flood the lowlands and swamps between a chain of small lakes here and so create one large lake; work was begun on the dam in 1918 and the gate was closed in March, 1923; in Nov., 1923, the residents petitioned the county supervisors to name it Wolverine Lake, after the state animal, the wolverine; incorporated as a village in 1954 [Parthena Philp].

**WOOD**, Lenawee County: a station on the branch of the Lake Shore & Michigan Southern Railroad, on the line between Lenawee and Monroe Counties, in 1882 [GSM 1885].

**WOOD**, Oscoda County: this rural post office in Elmer Township was named for Marcus J. Wood who became its first postmaster on July 6, 1905, the office operating until Jan. 15, 1914 [GSM 1907; PO Archives].

**WOOD**, Van Buren County: Maude A. Curtis became the first postmaster of this rural post office on Dec. 22, 1892, the office operating until Oct. 4, 1893 [PO Archives].

**WOODBRIDGE**, Hillsdale County. See Cambria.

**WOODBRIDGE**, Lenawee County: farmer DeWitt C. Turner became the first postmaster of this rural post office in Woodstock Township on Oct. 8, 1879, the office operating until Aug. 8, 1887 [GSM 1881-89; PO Archives].

**WOODBRIDGE**, Livingston County. See Parkers Corners.

**WOODBURN**, Oceana County: this settlement in Crystal Township formed around the mill and general store of the Pentwater Lumber Company; Charles W. Brown became its first postmaster on April 14, 1880, the office operating until Jan. 15, 1899 [PO Archives; GSM 1883].

**WOODBURY**, Eaton County: it was founded with the coming through of the Chicago, Kalamazoo & Saginaw Railroad in 1889, and was named for one of its officials; Charles A. Lapo became its first postmaster on Nov. 18, 1889, the office operating until Nov. 15, 1933; now a hamlet [Agnes H. Fisher; PO Archives].

**WOODBURY**, Wayne County. See Gibraltar.

**WOOD CREEK FARMS**, Oakland County: it was developed as a subdivision by George Wellington, of Franklin, Michigan, in 1937; he named it after a beautiful New England estate; incorporated as a village in 1957 [Alice C. Billiu].

**WOODHAVEN**, Wayne County: this six square-mile area in Brownstown Township was incorporated as a village in 1961; its chief developers were Roy Short and the first village president, Edward Sedlock; its eastern boundary is Trenton [Mich Manual; Detroit News, Sept. 19, 1965, 14D].

**WOODHULL**, Shiawassee County: it was named for Josephus Woodhull who with his two sons, John and Josephus, became the first settlers here in 1836; town organization began in 1838, with John Woodhull as the first supervisor; David J. Tower became the first postmaster on Jan. 14,

1850; the office was closed on Nov. 12, 1857, but was restored from Dec. 15, 1856, to Aug. 1, 1870, and from Nov. 19, 1874, until it was changed to Shaftsburgh on Jan. 19, 1880 [MPH 1:318 1875; Campbell; PO Archives].

**WOODIN'S MILLS,** Isabella County. See Horr.

**WOOD LAKE,** Montcalm County. See Hiram.

**WOODLAND,** Barry County: it was first settled by Charles and Jonathan Galloway (brothers) and Samuel S. Haight, in 1837; on Jan. 27, 1848, Nehemiah Lovewell became the first postmaster of Woodland, named from its location amid dense woods; given a station on the Chicago, Kalamazoo & Saginaw Railroad in 1889; incorporated as a village in 1892 [Johnson; Potter; PO Archives].

**WOODLAND BEACH,** Monroe County: unincorp. village, northeast of Monroe, named from its location on Lake Erie [Columbia Ency.].

**WOODLAND PARK,** Newaygo County: Negro realtors Marion E. Arthur, of Cleveland, and Alvin E. Wright, of Chicago, platted this all-colored resort town on the shores of Woodland Lake in 1923 [Harry L. Spooner].

**WOODLAWN,** Berrien County: Philip B. Andrews became the first postmaster of this rural post office on Nov. 11, 1862, the office operating until Dec. 13, 1866 [PO Archives].

**WOODLAWN,** Delta County: this village in Cornell Township began as a settlement around a co-operative sawmill and was first called White; it was given a station on the S.E. & L.S. Railroad and on March 23, 1905, a post office named Woodlawn, with railroad agent Martin Johnson as its first postmaster [David S. Coon; GSM 1907; PO Archives].

**WOODMAN,** Tuscola County: a station on the Saginaw, Tuscola & Huron Railroad, in a timber region, in 1884 [GSM 1885].

**WOODMERE,** Wayne County: a station on the Canada Southern and the Lake Shore & Michigan Southern Railroads in 1878, then six miles southwest of Detroit; Michael F. Ruolo became its first postmaster on July 17, 1884, the office operating until May 31, 1901, when the area was absorbed by Detroit; the name is retained locally by its burial ground, still named Woodmere Cemetery [GSM 1879; Burton; PO Archives].

**WOODRUFF'S GROVE,** Washtenaw County: it was first settled in 1823 by Benjamin Woodruff who came here with a group from Ohio; John Bryan became its first postmaster on May 9, 1825, the office operating until Jan. 20, 1828; it was adjacent to Ypsilanti and was in Wayne County until Washtenaw was organized in 1829 [Chapman; PO Archives].

**WOOD'S CORNERS,** Hillsdale County. See Lickley's Corners.

**WOOD'S CORNERS,** Ionia County: Jesse Wood, from Washtenaw County, first settled here in Orleans Township in 1841; travel over the town-line road moved John Lansing to build a tavern in 1865; the next year, Daniel Bennett also opened a tavern and on April 15, 1869, his son, Jefferson E. Bennett became the first postmaster; a railroad station by 1876; its post office operated until May 15, 1905 [Dillenback; Schenck; PO Archives].

**WOOD'S MILL,** Montcalm County: a station on the Stanton branch of the Detroit, Lansing & Northern Railroad, serving a lumber settlement, in 1878 [GSM 1879].

**WOOD SPUR,** Ontonagon County: the settlement began as a siding on the Ontonagon & Brule River (later, part of the Chicago, Milwaukee & St. Paul) Railroad, opened in 1882 [Jamison].

**WOOD STATION,** Lenawee County: a depot on the Erie & Kalamazoo Railroad, in Riga Township, 3 miles east of Knight's Station (now Riga), founded in 1853 by Roswell W. Knight who built side tracks and sheds here to furnish wood for the railroad [Bonner].

**WOODSTOCK,** Lenawee County. See Cement City.

**WOODVILLE,** Bay County: a settlement with a station on the Gladwin branch of the Michigan Central Railroad, in Mount Forest Township, in 1894 [Gansser].

**WOODVILLE,** Ionia County: having tried unsuccessfully to found a village of his own named Woodville, E. L. Morse moved his stock of goods two miles west to Pewamo and opened his store there in 1857 [Branch].

**WOODVILLE,** Jackson County: in 1830, Jonathan Wood began to farm in Blackman Township; the settlement which followed took his name; it became a coal mining settlement and was given a signal station on the Michigan Central Railroad in 1886 [John Daball].

**WOODVILLE,** Newaygo County: this settlement in Everett Township was founded by the West Michigan Lumber Company at the head of the Pere Marquette River; its depot on a branch of the Chicago & Western Michigan (now Pere Marquette) Railroad was first named Traverse Roads; the Home post office was transferred here on April 20, 1874, and renamed Woodville from the abundant pine wood in the area [H. L. Spooner; Pen Phil 8:3 April 1958; PO Archives].

**WOODVILLE,** Wayne County. See Smithville.

**WOODWARD'S MILLS,** Washtenaw County. See Milan.

**WOODWARDVILLE,** Wayne County. See Highland Park.

**WOOLMITH,** Monroe County: a hamlet a mile from Scofield in 1894 [GSM 1895].

**WOOSTER,** Newaygo County: a sawmill settlement in Sherman Township; its flag station on a branch of the Chicago & Northwestern Railroad was named Worcester (pronounced Wooster), in 1882; it was given a post office as Wooster Hill on Nov. 14, 1882, with William Moll as its first postmaster; the office was closed on Oct. 22, 1891, but was restored as Wooster on May 11, 1895, with storekeeper Cornelius Mast as its postmaster [GSM 1883-97; PO Archives].

**WORCESTER**, Marquette County. See Marquette.

**WORCESTER**, Newaygo County. See Wooster.

**WORDEN**, Washtenaw County: the Peebles family (John, Reuben, and David) settled here in Salem Township in 1831, and the place was given a stage post office as Peebles Corners in 1838; E. S. Worden owned 156 acres in the area and this place, now a village, was given a post office as Worden on March 7, 1882, with Silas Pratt as its first postmaster, the office operating until Jan. 31, 1902; a station on the Toledo, Ann Arbor & Northern Michigan Railroad [J. Gordon McDonald; MPH 27:505 1896; PO Archives].

**WORDEN'S MILLS**, Montcalm County: it was named for mill owner Ananias Worden; to get the workers' trade, William Potter opened a general store here in 1847, probably the first store in Montcalm Township [Dasef].

**WORMWOOD**, Grand Traverse County: farmer George Cook became the first postmaster of this rural post office in Grant Township on June 20, 1879, with the office named Cayton; it was renamed Wormwood on Feb. 24, 1880, and operated until June 16, 1884 [Page; PO Archives].

**WORTH**, Arenac County: a station on the Mackinaw division of the Michigan Central Railroad, in Standish Township, in 1872; the village was founded by N. B., Elemar E., and Fred W. Bradley in 1884; it had a post office from Nov. 2, 1886, to Dec. 31, 1908 [Alfred Campbell; PO Archives].

**WORTH**, Saginaw County. See Tuscola.

**WRIGHT**, Hillsdale County: the Russell Coman family came here in 1835 and the Samuel Coman family in 1836; in the winter of 1837-38, the townspeople petitioned for organization as a township under the name of Coman, but through manipulation, the name sent to the legislature was Canaan; the legislature changed its name from Canaan to Wright in 1844 [Hogaboam].

**WRIGHT**, Ottawa County: Tallmadge Township was organized in 1838; from it Wright Township was separated by an act of the legislature in 1847; the village was named after its township which had been named for the Wright family which owned section 20; Leonard Roberts became its first postmaster on Feb. 9, 1848; the office was closed on June 25, 1864, but was restored from Oct. 22, 1877, to Dec. 14, 1903 [Page; PO Archives].

**WRIGHT'S**, Midland County: in 1852, this site in northern Lincoln Township became the headquarters of (Eben) Wright & Ketcham's lumber firm, most of the buildings belonging to it; given a post office as Wright's Bridge on June 23, 1871, with Lot Holmes as its first postmaster, the office operating until Oct. 26, 1891 [Chapman; PO Archives].

**WRIGHT'S**, Ogemaw County: a hamlet in the southwest corner of the county in 1880 [GSM 1881].

**WRIGHTVILLE**, Livingston County: Millie J. Carpenter became the first postmaster of this rural post office on Nov. 19, 1898, the office operating until May 15, 1900 [PO Archives].

**WURTSMITH AIR FORCE BASE**, Iosco County: it was proposed by the USAF in 1923 and tested in 1925; it was a Selfridge Field gunnery camp, named Camp Skeel, until World War II; it was renamed Oscoda Air Field and made independent of Selfridge in 1944, but made a subsidiary of Selfridge again in 1945; it was made an independent base again in 1951; it was renamed in 1953 in honor of Major General Paul B. Wurtsmith, a Michigan World War II hero, till then the only flying general to win the Distinguished Service Medal in combat [Major A. D. Rally, USAF].

**WYANDOTTE**, Wayne County: in 1818, after a government survey, land down the Detroit River was auctioned off, with Major John Biddle acquiring 2,200 acres of it; a stock company bought the Biddle farm in 1854, developing it into a village which they named after the Indian tribe which had once had a village here; it was platted and, on Dec. 1854, recorded by the Eureka Iron Company which then had a blast furnace here; William Sichles became its first postmaster on Feb. 14, 1855; incorporated as a city in 1867 (its thoroughfare is Biddle Avenue); it annexed the village of Ford City in 1923 [Burton; County plat liber; PO Archives].

**WYANDOTTE HEIGHTS**, Wayne County. See Riverview.

**WYLIE**, Grand Traverse County: it came into being with the Wylie Cooperage Company about 1888; its station on the Manistee & Northwestern Railroad was named Wylie's; it became a ghost town about 1915 when the source of the raw elm logs was depleted; originally about a mile south of Interlochen, part of its townsite is now in that village [GSM 1891; Traverse].

**WYLIE**, Mason County: it was founded in 1887 and named for a local resident, Lemuel Wylie; it was formed because it was an irregular corner of Riverton and Eden Townships and was too far for the children in the area to walk to school; the school built here, called the Wylie School, closed in 1939 [John D. Campion, Jr.].

**WYMAN**, Montcalm County: this village in Home Township was founded by O. W. Avery in 1879 and first platted as Averyville; Harvey P. Wyman became the first postmaster on June 20, 1879; the office, named Averyville, was changed to Wyman on Aug. 12, 1880; both men were lumbermen; a station on the Detroit, Lansing & Northern Railroad; its post office operated until Dec. 31, 1944 [Schenck; PO Archives].

**WYOMING**, Jackson County: Robert Jackson became the first postmaster of this village, six miles from Jackson, on June 19, 1839, the office operating until May 25, 1852 [PO Archives; GSM 1860].

**WYOMING,** Kent County: there was a village of Wyoming in Kent County by 1859; the present city was formed from Wyoming Township in 1948; incorporated as a city in 1958, and given a post office in 1960 [Edward Von Solkema; GSM 1860].

**WYOMING,** Keweenaw County: it was platted in 1862 on the site of a stamping mill and the old Wyoming Mine; for some time it was known as Hilltown for Samuel W. Hill, a prominent local mining man; it was called Helltown by the miners from its saloons and the brawls coming out of them [Frances S. Rozich; Federal].

**YAGERV,** Monroe County: Charles Wilson became the first postmaster in 1895 [Blinn].

**YALE,** Gogebic County: it was the site of the Yale Mine and its workmen's settlement, but is now within the city limits of Bessemer; its name reflects the eastern financing of the mine [Victor Lemmer].

**YALE,** St. Clair County: this village on Mill Creek was founded in 1851 by Nathan White as Brockway Center, named after its township; Orrin P. Chamberlin became its first postmaster on May 11, 1865; it was platted in 1865; at the suggestion of B. R. Noble and honoring Yale University, it was renamed Yale on June 24, 1889; incorporated as a village in 1895 and as a city in 1905 [Jenks; PO Archives].

**YALMAR,** Marquette County: it was settled shortly after the Civil War and was named for Hjalmar Bahrman, whose family still operates the farm; the Hj is pronounced Y; Charles Wilson became the first postmaster on Feb. 6, 1895, the office operating until Feb. 27, 1933; it is on some maps incorrectly spelled Yalmer [Ernest H. Rankin; PO Archives].

**YANKEE POINT,** St. Clair County. See Marine City.

**YANKEE SPRINGS,** Barry County: it was first settled by Calvin Lewis, a New Yorker, in 1836; he built an inn which his brother, William "Yankee Bill" Lewis, bought from him and made celebrated as Yankee Springs House until 1855 when traffic was diverted from it by a new road; William Lewis became the first postmaster, with the office spelled Yankee Spring, on Nov. 4, 1837, succeeded by Seth Lewis on July 24, 1840, the office operating until July 31, 1905; his nickname and a spring behind his hotel gave the place its name; in 1936, the federal government bought the tract and in 1943 deeded it to Michigan which now operates it as Yankee Springs State Recreation Area [MPH 26:302 1895; Johnson; PO Archives].

**YARGERVILLE,** Monroe County: this village in LaSalle Township was settled around the grist mill, the sawmill and the general store of Richard W. Yarger, and was named for him; he became the first postmaster on Jan. 30, 1890, the office operating until Oct. 15, 1906 [GSM 1891; PO Archives].

**YATES,** Manistee County: Robert Knowles became the first postmaster of this rural post office on June 9, 1884; the office was transferred to and renamed Lemon Lake on April 21, 1902 [PO Archives].

YPSILANTI
Res.- D.B.Green

YORK TWP.
Milan House - L. Burnham, Proprietor

**YATES**, Oakland County: a station on a branch of the Michigan Central Railroad, two miles from Rochester, in 1886 [GSM 1887].

**YELLOW JACKET**, Houghton County: an old mining location, named by the mining company [Victor Lemmer].

**YEREX CORNERS**, Lapeer County: this lumber settlement on a branch of Mill Creek, in Goodland Township, operated until at least 1882 [Page].

**YEW**, Wayne County: Henry Pierson became the first postmaster of this post office at Town Line railroad station in the northeast part of the county, with the office named Brown's Corners, June 25, 1866; it was renamed Yew on Nov. 6, 1866; the office was closed on Oct. 20, 1875, but was restored from Jan. 4, 1876, to July 31, 1902; the yew is a flowering tree; the site is now within the city limits of Detroit [GSM 1887; Burton; PO Archives].

**YNOUSKI**, Kalamazoo County. See Silver Creek.

**YORK**, Branch County. See Bronson.

**YORK**, Washtenaw County. See Mooreville.

**YORK'S**, Sanilac County: a station on the Port Huron & Northwestern Railroad in 1882 [GSM 1883].

**YORKVILLE**, Kalamazoo County: it was first settled in 1833 by Tillotson Barnes who came from Oneida County, N.Y., which also had a town of Yorkville; the Rose Centre post office was transferred to and renamed Yorkville on April 9, 1845, the office operating until July 31, 1939; a station on the Detroit, Toledo & Milwaukee Railroad [Durant; PO Archives].

**YOUNGS**, Alger County: this station on the Manistique Railway was named McDonald but its post office, opened on May 5, 1899, was named for Frank Youngs, its first postmaster; the office, 14 miles south of Grand Marais, operated until May 15, 1901 [PO Archives; GSM 1903].

**YOUNGS**, Dickinson County: Henry M. Lowry became the first postmaster of this rural post office on March 21, 1911, the office operating until June 30, 1912 [PO Archives].

**YOUNGS**, Menominee County: Albert Heath was appointed the first postmaster of this rural post office on March 29, 1907, but it was rescinded on June 25, 1907 [PO Archives].

**YOUNG'S PRAIRIE**, Cass County: it was named by Nathan Young after himself when the surveying party, with which he was connected, was running out the land here in 1827; it was first settled by squatters in 1828; George Jones and John Rinehart, and the four sons of each, commenced to make farms here in present Penn Township in 1829 [Mich Hist 33:231 1949; Rogers].

**YPSILANTI**, Washtenaw County: it was the site of the Indian trading post of Gabriel Godfroy from 1809 to 1820; John Steward settled here in 1824 and with Judge Augustus Brevoort Woodward, of Detroit, platted the village, which they and Mr. Harwood recorded on April 21, 1825; at a meeting held to decide upon a permanent name, Judge Woodward suggested that of the Greek war of independence hero, General Demetrius Ypsilanti; Isaac Powers became the first postmaster on Feb. 13, 1826; it was in Wayne County until Washtenaw was organized in 1829; incorporated as a village in 1832 and as a city in 1858 [Chapman; Wayne County plat liber; PO Archives].

**YUBA,** Grand Traverse County: David R. Curtis first settled here in East Bay Township in 1852; William H. Fife became the first postmaster on Feb. 16, 1865, the office operating until June 15, 1904 [Traverse; PO Archives].

**YUMA,** Wexford County: the village began with the moving of the Jenny coal kilns and chemical plant from Harrietta to this point in Springville Township which had been given a station on the Toledo, Ann Arbor & Northern Michigan Railroad in 1888; the village was platted in 1893 and Rollin H. Jenny became its first postmaster on Jan. 3, 1893, the office operating until May 26, 1961 [Powers; Wheeler; PO Archives].

**ZEBA,** Baraga County: Rev. Frederic Baraga founded an Indian mission here in 1831 but moved across the Keweenaw Bay to Assinins in 1843; the settlement which eventually formed here was given a post office on Sept. 3, 1910, with Mary E. Spruce as its first postmaster; the office was closed on June 30, 1912, but was restored from April 16, 1913, with William Tollefson as the postmaster, until Nov. 30, 1933; its name is Indian for little river, and it is largely an Indian settlement [Mich Hist 6:315 1922; GSM 1913; Federal; PO Archives].

**ZEELAND,** Ottawa County: it was founded in 1847 by Rev. Cornelius Vander Meulen, Jannes Vander Luyster, Jan Steketes and Christian de Herder; James Walker became its first postmaster on June 5, 1848; a station on the Chicago & Western Michigan (now Pere Marquette) Railroad; the village was platted and recorded in 1849; its post office was closed on May 11, 1850, but has been restored since June 14, 1854; incorporated as a village in 1875 and as a city in 1907; named after the Netherlands province whence the colonists came [Mich Hist 12:85 1928; Lillie; PO Archives].

**ZEISER BAY,** Menominee County: the site of the sawmill of Hayward Brothers; named for local lumberman Charles Zeiser [Sawyer].

**ZILWAUKIE,** Saginaw County: Daniel and Soloman Johnson, of New York City, built a steam sawmill here in 1848; Zilwaukie Township was established in 1854; the plat of Zilwaukie village was recorded in 1855, but its local government was always vested in the township; the Johnsons so named it to lure German immigrant workers here, hoping they would confuse the name with Milwaukee; Albert C. Jones became its first postmaster on Sept. 16, 1861; the office was closed on June 23, 1852, but was restored from Sept. 1, 1852, to May 14, 1910, when it became a branch of the Saginaw post office; the Gazeeter 1860 and the post office spell it Zilwaukee, the centennial history Zilwaukie [Rev. Eugene A. Forbes; GSM 1860; PO Archives].

**ZION**, St. Clair County: its station on the Pere Marquette Railroad was first named Saginaw Junction and was in Grant Township; it was given a post office as Zion on Jan. 26, 1885, with William M. Wilson as its first postmaster, succeeded by storekeeper Alexander W. Atkins in 1886, the office operating until May 15, 1903 [GSM 1887; PO Archives].

**ZUG ISLAND**, Wayne County: Samuel Zug, a penniless bookkeeper from Pennsylvania, came here in 1836, and earned his fortune making furniture; in 1859, he turned to real estate, bought 325 acres of marsh at the mouth of the Rouge River for a mansion; about then someone else cut the canal that made his property an island; the swamp was too much for him, so he moved out, selling it for $300,000 as an industrial dumping ground; it was cleared for the Detroit International Fair and Exhibition in 1889; it is now steel mill property; Sam, who became Wayne County auditor, died in 1896 [Farmer; Free Press].

**ZUTPHEN**, Ottawa County: this Dutch settlement was named after a town in the Netherlands; storekeeper Johannes (John) Glupker became its first postmaster on June 16, 1882, the office operating until Oct. 15, 1906 [W. C. Wichers; GSM 1883; PO Archives].

## DOCUMENTATION

Bibliography; Sources; Acknowledgments

Adams, Mrs. Franc L. Pioneer History of Ingham County. Lansing: Wynkoop, Hallenbeck, Crawford Co. 1923. Designated as Vol. 1, but there is no record of succeeding volumes.

Advance. Presque Isle County Advance, Rogers City. 50th Anniv. ed., June, 1928. Covers the county history year by year. Bound facsimile copy in Burton HC-DPL.

Andreas. History of St Clair County. Chicago: A. T. Andreas & Co. 1883.

Andreas, A. T., Prop. History of the Upper Peninsula of Michigan. Chicago: Western Historical Co. 1883.

Atwell, Willis. Do You Know: an Illustrated History of Michigan. Grand Rapids: Booth Newspapers. 1937.

Bald, F. Clever. Michigan in Four Centuries. New York: Harper. 1954, rev. and enl. 1961.

Ball, Adele. Early History of Owosso. Owosso: Bentley Foundation, 1969.

Barnes, Al. Vinegar Pie and Other Tales of the Grand Traverse Region. Detroit: Wayne State Univ. Press. 1959.

Bayliss, Joseph E. and Estelle L., in collab. with Milo S. Quaife. River of Destiny: the St. Marys. Detroit: Wayne State Univ. Press. 1955. Devoted mostly to Chippewa County.

Beakes, Samuel W. Past and Present of Washtenaw County. Chicago: S. J. Clarke. 1906. The first 534 of its 823 pages are biographical.

Beeson, Lewis, ed. This is Michigan: a Sketch of These Times and Times Gone. Lansing: Michigan Historical Commn. 1949.

Benedict, C. Harry. Red Metal: the Calumet & Hecla Story. Ann Arbor: Univ. of Michigan Press. 1952. A copper mining history.

Blois, John T. See Gazeteer of the State of Michigan.

Bonner, Richard T., ed. Memoirs of Lenawee County. 2v Madison: Western Historical Assn. 1909.

Branch, Rev. E. E., editor-in-chief. History of Ionia County. 2v Indianapolis: B. F. Bowen & Co. 1916.

Bulkley, John McClelland. History of Monroe County. 2v Chicago: Lewis Pub. Co. 1913. v2 is entirely biographical.

Burton, Clarence M. and M. Agnes, editors. History of Wayne County and the City of Detroit. 4v Chicago-Detroit: S. J. Clarke Pub. Co. 1930. v3-4 are biographical.

Burton HC-DPL: Burton Historical Collections, initiated and endowed by Clarence M. Burton, and housed in its own quarters in the main Detroit Public Library. An expert staff makes accessible its unique treasury of Michigan history in particular,–printed volumes, typescripts, documents, records, manuscripts, etc.

Butterfield, George E. Bay County, Past and Present. Bay City: C. & J. Gregory. 1918. Bay City: Board of Education. Centennial ed., rev. and enl. 1957.

Campbell, George T., et al. The Past and Present of Shiawassee County. 2v Lansing: Michigan Historical Pub. Assn. n.d. (ca. 1905).

Carlisle, Fred. Chronology of Notable Events in the History of the Northwest Territory and Wayne County. Detroit: Gulley, Bornman & Co. 1890.

Catlin, George B. The Story of Detroit. Detroit: Detroit News. 1923.

Chapin, Henry H. See Gazeteer.

Chapman. History of Kent County. Chicago: Charles S. Chapman & Co. 1881.

Chapman. History of Washtenaw County. Chicago: Charles S. Chapman & Co. 1881. Committees in each township supplied the data.

Chapman. Portrait and Biographical Album of Gratiot County; also Containing a Complete History of the County. Chicago: Chapman Bros. 1884.

Chapman. Portrait and Biographical Album of Huron County; also Containing a Complete History of the County. Chicago: Chapman Bros. 1884.

Chapman. Portrait and Biographical Album of Isabella County; also Containing a Complete History of the County. Chicago: Chapman Bros. 1884.

Chapman. Portrait and Biographical Album of Midland County; also Containing a Complete History of the County. Chicago: Chapman Bros. 1884.

Chapman. Portrait and Biographical Album of Mecosta County; also Containing a Complete History of the County. Chicago: Chapman Bros. 1883.

Chapman. Portrait and Biographical Album of Osceola County; also Containing a Complete History of the County. Chicago: Chapman Bros. 1884.

Chapman. Portrait and Biographical Album of Sanilac County; also Containing a Complete History of the County. Chicago: Chapman Bros. 1884.

Chauncey, Albert E. Berrien County: a 19th Century Story. Benton Harbor: Burch Printers. 1955.

Christensen, Robert S. The Halfway-East Detroit Story. n.p. 1962.

Cole, Maurice F. Michigan Postal Markings. Ferndale: Author. 1955.

Collin, Rev. Henry P. A 20th Century History and Biographical Record of Branch County. Chicago: Lewis Pub. Co. 1906.

Coolidge, Judge Orville W. A 20th Century History of Berrien County. Chicago: Lewis Pub. Co. 1906.

Cowles, Albert E. Past and Present of the City of Lansing and Ingham County. Lansing: Michigan Historical Pub. Assn. 1906.

Crandell, Alger Buell. Thumb of Laughter. Sanilac: Sanilac Club. 1961. The charter members of the Sanilac County Historical Society present an account of their childhood days in the county.

Cunningham, Wilbur M. Land of Four Flags. Grand Rapids: Eerdman. 1961. Deals chiefly with early Berrien County history.

Cutler, Harry G. History of St. Joseph County. 2v Chicago: Lewis Pub. Co. n.d. Daboll, Sharman B. Past and Present of Clinton County. Chicago: S. J. Clarke Pub. Co. 1906.

Darling, Birt. City in a Forest: the Story of Lansing. New York: Stratford House. 1950.

Dasef, John W. History of Montcalm County. 2v Indianapolis: B. F. Bowen & Co. 1916.

DeLand, Colonel Charles V. History of Jackson County. Indianapolis: B. F. Bowen & Co. 1903.

Dickinson, Julia Terry. The Story of Leelanau [County]. Omena: Solle's Book Shop. 1951.

Dillenback, J. D. History and Directory of Ionia County. Grand Rapids: J. D. Dillenback. 1872.

Dillenback, J. D., and Leavitt. History and Directory of Kent County. Grand Rapids: J. D. Dillenback. 1870.

Dondineau, Arthur, and Leah A. Spencer. Our State of Michigan. New York: Macmillan Co. 1925.

Downhour, Gloria. A Study of Place Names in Isabella County. Mt. Pleasant: Central Michigan Univ. 1962. Typewritten monograph.

DuMonde, Neva. Thumb Diggings. Lexington: Author. 1962. A popular history of Sanilac County.

Dunbar, Willis Frederick. Michigan: a History of the Wolverine State. Grand Rapids: Eerdmans. 1965.

Durant, Samuel W. History of Ingham and Eaton Counties. Philadelphia: D. W. Ensign & Co. 1880.

Durant, Samuel W. History of Kalamazoo County. Philadelphia: Everts & Abbott. 1880. Separate index volume (139 p.) abstracted and typed by Ruth (Mrs. C. A.) Robbins Monteith for L. H. Stone chapter, D.A.R., Kalamazoo. n.d.

Durant, Samuel W. History of Oakland County. Philadelphia: L. H. Everts & Co. 1877.

Dustin, Fred. Isle Royale Place Names. Mich Hist 30:680-722 1946. Includes lakes, coves, etc.

Dustin, Fred. Some Indian Place Names Around Saginaw. Mich Hist 12:729-739 1928.

Eldredge, Robert F. Past and Present of Macomb County. Chicago: S. J. Clarke Pub. Co. 1905.

Ellis, Franklin. History of Berrien and Van Buren Counties. Philadelphia: D. W. Ensign & Co. 1880.

Ellis, Franklin. History of Genesee County. Philadelphia: Everts & Abbott. 1879.

Ellis, Franklin. History of Livingston County. Philadelphia: Everts & Abbott. 1880.

Ellis, Franklin. History of Shiawassee and Clinton Counties. Philadelphia: D. W. Ensign & Co. 1880.

Elsworth, R. H. Wayside Notes on Mason County. 2v 1898-1905. Scrapbooks formed from his column in the Ludington Record-Appeal; bound copy in Burton HC-DPL.

Ensign. History of Allegan and Barry Counties. Philadelphia: D. W. Ensign & Co. 1880.

Everts, L. H. History of Calhoun County. Philadelphia: L. H. Everts & Co. 1877. No author given; Preface signed by the Publishers.

Everts, L. H. History of St. Joseph County. Philadelphia: L. H. Everts & Co. 1877.

Fancher, Isaac A. Past and Present of Isabella County. Indianapolis: Bowen. 1911. Separate volume Index, comp. by Mrs. Myrta Wilsey Burwash. n.p., n.d.

Farmer, Silas. History of Detroit and Wayne County and Early Michigan. 3v New York: Munsell & Co. 3rd ed., rev. and enl. 1890.

Fasquelle, Ethel R. When Michigan Was Young: the Story of its Beginnings, Early Legends and Folklore. Grand Rapids: Eerdmans. 1950.

Federal Writers' Project. Michigan: a Guide to the Wolverine State, by the Writers' Program of Michigan's WPA. New York: Oxford Univ. Press. 1941, 3rd ed. 1946. Final supervision of the work by Harold Titus.

Fisher, David, and Frank Little, eds. Compendium of History and Biography of Kalamazoo County. Chicago: A. W. Bowen & Co. 1906.

Florer, Warren W. Early Michigan Settlements. Ann Arbor: Author. 1941. Limited to German immigrants; designated as Vol. 1, but there is no record of succeeding volumes.

Foster, Theodore G. Place Names in Ingham County. Mich Hist 26:480-517 1942.

Fox, George R. Place Names of Berrien County. Mich Hist 8:6-35 1924.

Fox, George R. Place Names of Cass County. Mich Hist 27:463-491 1943.

Fox, Truman B. History of Saginaw County. E. Saginaw: Enterprise Print. Reprint: Mount Pleasant: Clarke Historical Library of Central Michigan Univ. 1962.

Fuller, George W., ed. Historic Michigan. 2v n.p.: National Hist. Assn. 1924. Selected almost entirely from the publications of the Michigan Pioneer and Historical Society and the Michigan Historical Commission.

Gagnieur, William F., S. J. Indian Place Names in the Upper Peninsula, and Their Interpretation. Mich Hist 2:526-555 1918, 9:109-111 1925.

Gansser, Augustus H. History of Bay County. Chicago: Richmond & Arnold. 1905.

Gardner, Washington. History of Calhoun County. 2v Chicago: Lewis Pub. Co. 1913.

Gates, William B., Jr. Michigan Copper and Boston Dollars. Cambridge: Harvard Univ. Press. 1951. Almost exclusively economic.

Gillard, Kathleen I. Our Michigan Heritage. New York: Pageant Press. 1955.

Glover, Lowell H. A 20th Century History of Cass County. Chicago: Lewis Pub. Co. 1906.

Goodrich, Calvin. The First Michigan Frontier. Ann Arbor: Univ. of Michigan Press. 1940. History of and folkways in the French and British periods.

Gregorich, Joseph. Contributions of the Slovenes to the Chippewa and Ottawa Indian Missions. Mich Hist: 168-187 spring 1941.

GSM: Gazeteer of the State of Michigan. Published irregularly by various publishers in Detroit from 1838. From 1873, it was titled Michigan State Gazeteer. Edited by John T. Blois, 1838-1840, George W. Hawes, 1860-1866, Henry H. Chapin, 1867-1869, Montague T. Platt, 1870-1871, J. E. Scripps and R(alph) L. Polk, 1873-1874, R. L. Polk & Co., 1875-1932, when it was discontinued.

Gwinn, Florence McKinnon. Pioneer History of Huron County. Bad Axe: Huron County Pioneer & Historical Society (of which the author was then secretary). 1922.

Hagman, Arthur, ed. Oakland County Book of History. Pontiac: Oakland County Sesqui-Centennial Committee. 1970.

Hamilton, Mrs. W. E. Place Names of Chippewa County. Sault Ste. Marie: Evening News, Oct. 25, 1938. Rev. and enl. in Mich Hist 27:638-643 1943.

Hartwick, L. M., and L. H. Tuller. Oceana County: Pioneers and Businessmen of Today; History, Biography, Statistics, etc. Pentwater: News Steam Print. 1890. Its historical content is largely quoted from Page, q.v.

Hatcher, Harlan. A Century of Iron and Men. Indianapolis: Bobbs-Merrill. 1950. This history, chiefly of the Cleveland-Cliffs Iron Company, includes accounts of company towns. The author, vice-president of Ohio State Univ. in 1950, became president of the Univ. of Michigan the following year.

Havighurst, Walter. Vein of Iron: the Pickands Mather Story. Cleveland: World Pub. Co. 1958.

Hawes, George W. See Gazeteer.

Hey, Chet, and Norman Eckstein. Huron County Centennial History, 1859-1959. Bad Axe: Hey. 1959.

Hill, Jack. History of Iron County. Iron River: Reporter Pub. Co. 1955.

Hogaboam, James J. The Bean Creek Valley: Incidents of its Early Settlement. Hudson: J. M. Scarritt. 1876. A pioneer history of Lenawee and Hillsdale Counties.

Hudson Co., J. L., comp. A Souvenir of Michigan's Centennial Year containing 36 historical articles. (Cover title: Michigan Pioneers: the first 100 years of Statehood, 1837-1937). Detroit: J. L. Hudson Co. 1937.

Ingalls, E. S. Centennial History of Menominee County. Menominee: Herald Power Presses. 1876.

Inside Michigan. qtly v1-9. Ann Arbor: Inside Michigan Pub. Co. 1951-1959.

Interstate. History of Jackson County. Chicago: Inter-State Pub. Co. 1881.

Jamison, James K. By Cross and Anchor: the Story of Frederic Baraga on Lake Superior. Paterson: St. Anthony Guild Press. 1946.

Jamison, James K. This Ontonagon Country. Ontonagon: Herald. 1939, 3rd ed. 1948.

Jenks, William Lee. St. Clair County: Its History and Its People. 2v Chicago: Lewis Pub. Co. v2 is entirely biographical.

Johnson, Crisfield. History of Barry and Allegan Counties. Philadelphia: D. W. Ensign & Co. 1880.

Johnson, Crisfield. History of Branch County, with Biographical Sketches. Philadelphia: Everts & Abbott. 1879.

Johnson, William W. Indian Names in the County of Mackinac. MPH 12:375-381 1888. Covers rivers, islands, lakes, etc., not communities.

Judkins, LaVerne M. Going Farther: a Treatise on Lake County. Ludington. 1962.

Kelton, Dwight H. Mackinac County: Ancient Names of Rivers, Lakes, etc. MPH 6:349-351 1883.

Knapp, John I., and Richard I. Bonner. Illustrated History and Biographical Record of Lenawee County. Adrian: Times Prington Co. 1903.

Konwiser, Harry M., ed. U.S. Stampless Cover Catalog. Verona, N.J.: S. G. Rich. 3rd ed. 1942.

Kuusisto, Mrs. W. E. Early History of Gogebic County. 18 p. 1952. Written for Michigan State Library, Lansing.

Leeson. History of Macomb County. Chicago: M. A. Leeson & Co. 1882. Mr. Leeson signed the Writers' Preface.

Leeson, M. A. History of Saginaw County. Chicago: Charles C. Chapman & Co. 1881.

Lemmer, Victor F. History of Gogebic County. The WPA wrote the book, but it was never published; Mr. Lemmer secured carbon copies of the material and edited it; the Michigan State Library typed the manuscript, to be published in three volumes, of which Volume Two, the first to be published, appeared in 1954.

Lewis, Ferris E. Michigan Yesterday and Today. Hillsdale: Hillsdale Educational Publishers. 1956; 5th ed. (4th rev.) 1965. An extensive revision of his My State, which see next.

Lewis, Ferris E. My State and its Story. Hillsdale: Hillsdale School Supply Co. 1937, 4th ed. 1949.

Lillie, Leo C. Historic Grand Haven and Ottawa County. Grand Rapids: A. P. Johnson. 1931. Printed for the author.

MHM: Michigan History Magazine, volume 1, 1917. Published quarterly by the Michigan Historical Commission, Lansing. With vol. 31, no. 1, March 1947, it was retitled Michigan History. Edited by George N. Fuller, 1917-1946, by Lewis Beeson, 1946- .

MPH: Michigan Pioneer and Historical Collections, Lansing. 40 vols., 1876-1929. This annual of the MP&H Society was succeeded by Michigan Historical Collections (irregular) and Michigan History Magazine (quarterly), q.v. above.

Martin, John B. Call it North Country: the Story of Upper Michigan. New York: Alfred A. Knopf. 1944.

Mathews, Alfred. History of Cass County. Chicago: Waterman, Watkins & Co. 1882.

May, George S. A Pictorial History of Michigan: The Early Years. 1967. The Later Years. 1969. Grand Rapids: Eerdmans.

Michigan Almanac, 1962 (first annual). Lansing: Republican State Central Committee.

Michigan Heritage. quarterly, 1959- . Kalamazoo: Kalamazoo Valley Genealogical Society.

Michigan History (mag.). See MHM.

Michigan Manual. Published annually by the State, Lansing.

Michigan State Gazeteer. See GSM.

Mills, James Cooke. History of Saginaw County. 2v Saginaw: Seemann & Peters. 1918.

Moore, Charles. History of Michigan. Chicago: Lewis Pub. Co. 1915.

Moore, Vivian Lyon. Deaths, Hillsdale County. v1, 1829-1867; v2, after 1867. Typewritten, bound, in Burton HC-DPL.

Moore, Vivian Lyon. Hillsdale County Lineages. 2v, typewritten, bound, in Burton HC-DPL.

Moore, Vivian Lyon. Sketches of Old Hillsdale: Genealogical and Historical. 5v, typewritten, bound, in Burton HC-DPL.

Murdoch, Angus. Boom Copper: the Story of the First U.S. Mining Boom. New York: Macmillan Co. 1943. Devoted mostly to Keweenaw and Houghton Counties.

Newton, Stanley. The Story of Sault Ste. Marie and Chippewa County. Sault Ste. Marie: Sault News Printing Co. 1923.

Noggle, Frank D. Historical Sketch of the Galien Woods Area. n.p., n.d. Offset, unbound copy in State Library, Lansing. Pioneer term for the hardwood forest which in the early days covered southwestern Berrien County.

Nute, Grace L. Lake Superior. Indianapolis: Bobbs-Merrill. 1944.

Oliver, David D. Centennial History of Alpena County, from 1837 to 1876. Alpena: Argus Printing House. ca. 1892, t.p. 1903. It covers just 39 years and deals almost exclusively with the city of Alpena.

Otis, Edna M. Their Yesterdays: Au Sable and Oscoda, 1848-1948. n.p., 1948. First published serially in the Oscoda County Gazette as Stories on Au Sable and Oscoda Townships.

Page. History of Bay County. Chicago: H. R. Page & Co. 1883. It also covers Arenac County, which was set off from Bay about the time this book was ready for press.

Page. History of the Lake Huron Shore. Chicagp: H. R. Page & Co. 1883. Includes Bay, Iosco, Alpena, and Alcona Counties, all of which were then sparsely settled.

Page. History of Lapeer County. Chicago: H. R. Page & Co. 1884.

Page. History of Manistee, Mason, and Oceana Counties. Chicago: H. R. Page & Co. 1882.

Page. History of Muskegon County. Chicago: H. R. Page & Co. 1882. Our copy bound with Page's Ottawa County, but with separate title page, index, etc.

Page. History of Ottawa County. Chicago: H. R. Page & Co. 1882.

Page. History of Tuscola and Bay Counties. Chicago: H. R. Page & Co. 1883.

Page. The Traverse Region. See Traverse.

Paré, George William. The Catholic Church in Detroit, 1701-1888. Detroit: Gabriel Richard Press. 1951. Covers the state from 1701 to 1857, when the Diocese of Marquette was created, followed by the Diocese of Grand Rapids in 1882.

Peckham, Howard. Pontiac and the Indian Uprising. Chicago. rev. ed. 1961.

Pen Phil: The Peninsular Philatelist. v1, no. 1, 1950. Official organ of the Peninsular State Philatelic Society; issued irregularly from the addresses of the various editors.

Pieters, Aleida J. Dutch Settlement in Michigan. Grand Rapids: Eerdmans. 1923.

PO Archives: United States Post Office Records; from the beginning to 1930 housed in the National Archives & Records Service, Office of Civil Archives, and from 1930, in the Post Office Department, Division of Postmasters, Post Office Changes, and Rural Appointments; we used transcript in Michigan State Library, Lansing, to Aug. 6, 1917, and from then to date in Washington quarters.

Potter, William W. History of Barry County. Grand Rapids: Reed-Tandler Co. 1912.

Powers, Perry F. History of Northern Michigan. 3v Chicago: Lewis Pub. Co. 1912. Vols. 2-3 comprise biographies.

Quaife, Milo M., and Sidney Glazer. Michigan, from Primitive Wilderness to Industrial Commonwealth. New York: Prentice-Hall. 1948.

Quaife, Milo M. Condensed Historical Sketches of Each of Michigan's Counties. Detroit: J. L. Hudson Co. 1940. First published serially in the Detroit Free Press from August, 1940.

Qualey, Carlton C. Pioneer Scandinavian Settlement in Michigan. Mich Hist 24:435-450 1940.

Reynolds, Eldon G., ed. Compendium of History and Biography of Hillsdale County. Chicago: A. W. Bowen & Co. 1903.

Ripley, Paul E. Lakeland's Paradise: the Story of Waterford Township for Children. Pontiac: Waterford Township Board of Education. 1961.

Ritchie, Bernice Walker. The Gladwin County First Settler Centennial, 1861-1961: a History of Gladwin County. Gladwin. 1961.

Robinson, George. History of Cheboygan and Mackinac Counties. Detroit. 1873.

Rogers, Howard S. History of Cass County, from 1825 to 1875. Cassopolis: W. H. Mansfield. 1875.

Rowland, Oran W. History of Van Buren County. 2v Chicago: Lewis Pub. Co. Vol. 2 is biographical.

Russell, Curran N. and Donna D. Baer. The Lumbermen's Legacy. Manistee: Manistee County Historical Society. 1954. Largely pictorial.

Sawyer, Alvah L. History of the Northern Peninsula. 3v Chicago: Lewis Pub. Co. 1911. Vols. 2-3 are biographical.

Schenck, John S. History of Ionia and Montcalm Counties. Philadelphia: D. W. Ensign & Co. 1881.

Schoetzow, Mae R. A Brief History of Cass County. Marcellus: Marcellus News. 1935.

Schultz, Gerard. A History of Michigan's Thumb. Elkton, Mich.: Author. 1964; rev. ed. A New History of Michigan's Thumb. Elkton, Mich.: Author. 1969.

Seeley, Thaddeus. History of Oakland County. 2v Chicago: Lewis Pub. Co. 1912.

Severance, Henry O. Michigan Trailmakers. Ann Arbor: George Wahr. 1930.

Silliman, Sue I. St. Joseph [County] in Homespun: a Centennial Souvenir. Three Rivers: Three Rivers Pub. Co. 1931.

Sprague, Elvin L., and Mrs. George N. Smith. History of Grand Traverse and Leelanau Counties. n.p.: B. F. Bowen, 1903.

Stannard, Mae E., and Beatrice Plumb Hunzicker. Glimpses of Huron Shore in Early

Days. Harrisville: Alcona County Review. 1926. In the early days the counties of Alcona, Alpena, and Iosco were referred to as the Huron Shore Region.

Stevens, Horace J. The Copper Handbook. Houghton: Author. annual, 1900-1912.

Stout, George S. Story of a Year in Missaukee County. Lake City: The Independent. 1891.

Strange, Daniel. Pioneer History of Eaton County, 1833-1866. Charlotte: Charlotte Republican. 1923.

Sugars, William P. Tales of a Forgotten Village. n.p. 1953. Printed in Ypsilanti for the author.

Swineford, A. P. Mineral Resources of the Upper Peninsula. Marquette. 1876.

Thomas, Dr. Henry F. A 20th Century History of Allegan County. Chicago: Lewis Pub. Co. 1907.

Traverse. The Traverse Region: Grand Traverse, Cheboygan, Emmet, Charlevoix, Leelanau, Antrim, Benzie, Kalkaska, and Wexford Counties. Chicago: H. R. Page & Co. 1884.

Treman, E. M. History of the Tremaine Family in America. 2v Ithaca, N.Y. 1901. Cf. vol. 1, p. 87.

Tucker, Willard D. Gratiot County. Saginaw: Seeman & Peters. 1913.

Turrell, Archie M. Some Place Names of Hillsdale County. Mich Hist 6:573-582 1922.

Wargelin, John. The Finns in Michigan. Mich Hist 24:179-203 spring 1940.

Warren (Edward K.) Foundation. The Region of Three Oaks. 1939. Covers Berrien County (Michigan) and northern Indiana.

Wheeler, John H. History of Wexford County. n.p.: B. F. Bowen. 1903.

Whitney, W. A., and R. I. Bonner. History and Biographical Record of Lenawee County. 2v Adrian: Willard Stearns. 1879-1880.

Williams, Rev. Wolcott B. Past and Present of Eaton County. Lansing: Mich. Historical Publishing Assn. n.d. (about 1900).

Wing, Talcott E., ed. History of Monroe County. New York: Munsell & Co. 1890.

Wood, Edwin O. Historic Mackinac. 2v New York: Macmillan. 1918.

Wood, Edwin O. History of Genesee County. 2v Indianapolis: Federal Publishing Co. 1916.

Mrs. Donald E. Adams, Michigan Historical Commission; Fannie Adams, township clerk, Beverly Hills; Miriam Altman, Mount Clemens Public Library; Elaine Ammerman, Krause Memorial Library, Rockford; Wendell H. Anderson, Eaton County Board of Education; Leslie Archer, Berrien County Historical Society.

Allen Babcock, village president, Elberta; James M. Babcock, Burton Historical Collection; Blaine E. Bacon, city clerk, Otsego; Lawrence M. Bailey, controller, Lincoln Park; Howard D. Barcalow, village clerk, Reese; Carl Bates, Clinton County Board of Education; Louis F. Battjes, city clerk, East Grant Rapids; Robert H. Beal, deputy superintendent of schools, Macomb County; Dr. Louis Beeson, Historical Society of Michigan; Evelyn Bergen, Spies Public Library, Menominee; Roy A. Berger, city clerk, River Rouge; Ashton Berst, retired city manager, Pleasant Ridge; Willis O. Best, village clerk, Prescott; Alice C. Billiu, village clerk, Wood Creek Farms; Richard Bivins, city clerk, Belding; Gladys F. Blakely, Saginaw Public Library; Thomas W. Blinn, postal historian, Belding; Kenyon Boyer, Marquette County Historical Society; Madelyn M. Bradford, Van Buren County Library; William P. Bradish, city manager Crystal Falls; Andrew Bremer, Jr., city clerk, Roosevelt Park; Prentiss M. Brown, Michigan Historical Commission; Thurman S. Bunn, city clerk, South Lyon; H. D. Burpee, Hastings Banner; W. A. Butler, Holland Evening Sentinel.

Margaret M. Caffall, Lapeer Public Library; Alfred Campbell, Arenac County Board of Education; Lewis D. Capen, Mecosta County Historical Society; Genevieve M. Casey, state librarian; Monroe S. Causley, Jr., Bay City Public Library; Sister M. Claudia, I.H.M., Marygrove College Library; Yvonne Coates, assistant village clerk, Orchard Lake; Betty Cochran, Midland Daily News; David C. Colyer, postal historian, Birmingham; George Cook, Netherlands Pioneer and Historical Foundation, Holland; David S. Coon, Delta County Historical Society; William Creger, Midland County superintendent of schools; Mary J. Crowther, Dorsch Memorial Library, Monroe; John Cumming, Central Michigan University-Clarke Historical Library; Kathryn Cummins, Midland County Historical Association; Juniata V. Cupp, village clerk, Shoreham.

John Daball, Jackson Public Library; Rudolph J. Dalpra, editor, Diamond Drill, Crystals Falls; Ami W. Davis, city clerk, West Branch; M. H. Dean, Alma Record; Leon J. Deur, Newaygo County Board of Education; James Doherty, Petoskey News Review; Margaret A. Downey, Wayne County Library; Irene Dudley, Burton Historical Collection; Clinton Dunathan, Delta County Historical Society.

Myrtle Elliott, Chippewa County Historical Society; Thomas Farrell, State Highway Department; Lucille L. Filley, Cass County Library; Jule Fosbender, Tecumseh Public Library; Donald L. Frazier, Adrian Telegram.

J. A. Gallery, Tuscola County Advertiser; Naomi Gibbing, Utica Public Library; Madeleine Gibson, Michigan College of Mining Library; Bernard Hamlin Glenn, Fowlerville Board of Library Commissioners; William H. Granlund, Otsego County Board of Education; Amos R. Green, Berrien County Historical Society; Lucille M. Griffith, village clerk, Perry; Isaac E. Grove, Monroe County Board of Education.

Glen Hammond, city clerk, Evart; Nellie Hansen, Alcona County Historical Association; Faye Hanson, DeWitt Public Library; Bruce C. Harding, Michigan Historical Commission; Dorothy G. Harris, Friends' Historical Society of Swarthmore College; Henry K. Hasty, city clerk, Whittemore; Rose D. Hawley, Mason County Historical Society; Betty A. Hayes, village clerk, Morrice; Mrs. William Heal, village clerk, Burlington; Neil Hercules, Gaylord Herald Times; Hazel Hayes, Herrick Public Library, Holland; Esther Warner Hettinger, Allegan County Historical Society; Doris Hidde, Flint Public Library; Ina Hight, Howell Carnegie Library; Mrs. Carol Hills, Brighton City Library; G. Vance Hiney, Marquette County superintendent of schools; John L. Holmes, Sturgis Public Library; Roberta Houston, Branch County Library; Effa J. Hunter, city clerk, Beaverton; Herbert A. Hutchins, Historical Society of Michigan.

Edith (Mrs. G. C.) Jamsen, Michigan State Library; Alex Jozik, Jr., postal historian, Detroit; Geneva Kebler, Michigan Historical Commission; Clare Keeler, village clerk, North Branch; Mrs. Else M. Kelly, Gladwin County Library; Paul F. Kempter, Grand Rapids Public Library; Lawrence Key, Coleman Tribune; Florence Kirtland, Monroe County Historical Society; Robert S. Kramp, UP branch, Michigan State Library; Lawrence P. Kress, city clerk, Ferndale; Amalia M. Kropp, Leelanau Historical Society. Victor F. Lemmer, past president, Historical Society of Michigan; Dorothy M. Lents, city clerk, Madison Heights; Dallas Lincoln, village clerk, Lakeview; Esther (Mrs. E. B.) Loughlin, Michigan State Library; Mrs. S. L. Loupee, Cass County Historical Society; Margaret Lovett, Allegan County Historical Society; Genevieve Ludlow, village clerk, Quincy.

Erna McBrian, city clerk, Manton; B. Courtney, Traverse City Public Library; Mrs. M. F. McGuirk, Bad Axe Public Library; Virginia MacHarg, St. Clair Shores Public Library; Mrs. Georgia McKinley, Fenton Historical Society; Ann W. McLay, Port Huron Public Library; Erma G. Malka, village clerk, Vanderbilt; Marie Marsh, New Baltimore Public Library; George S. May, Michigan Historical Commission; Edna Medbery, city clerk, Montague; Mrs. Harold Millman, Bement Public Library, St. Johns; Beatrice Moorman, village clerk, Barryton; Mrs. J. E. Moss, Historical Society of Michigan.

Ann Noonan, Grand Rapids Public Library; Myrta Null, village treasurer, Montgomery; L. Clarke Oldenburg, trustee, Schoolcraft College; Dorothy Olmstead, Genesee County Library; John Pahl, Allegan County Historical Society; Eileen Patterson, Burton Historical Collection; Fannie Pell, city clerk, Plainwell; John W. Peterson, Benzie County Patriot; Mrs. V. Peterson, Otsego County Board of Education; Robert Poloski, village clerk, Posen; Daniel Porter, Berrien County Historical Society; Linda Potts, Frankfort Public Library; Marvin Preston, postal historian, Ferndale; Kenneth H. Priestley, postal historian, Vassar; Richard Puffer, village clerk, Climax; Frances L. Pyle, Ann Arbor Public Library.

Mrs. Olive Raduchel, Houghton Public Library; Ernest H. Rankin, Marquette County Historical Society; Lee D. Reasoner, township clerk, Bath; Ruth Rhody, deputy village clerk, Flat Rock; Phil Richards, Alpena News; Myrton M. Riggs, Cheboygan Daily Tribune; Lydia Ripatte, Missaukee County Historical Society; Charles A. Robinson, Charlevoix County Board of Education; Jeannette Roberts, Lenawee County Library; Elizabeth C. Ronan, Genesee County Historical Society; Joseph A. Rossi, county clerk, Iron County; Rex R. Royal, Oceana Herald; Gladys Rubingh, village clerk, Pierson. F. X. Scannell, Michigan State Library; Howard C. Schultz, city clerk, Douglas; Mary Schutte, village clerk, Ahmeek; Mrs. Ethyl Schuyler, Menominee; Alice D. Serrell, Heritage Committee for Michigan; Leland Service, Tuscola County Advertiser; Ethelyn Sexton, Olivet College Library; Louise Shaw, city clerk, Oak Park; Mrs. Hollis Shelton, Monroe Evening News; Emerson R. Smith, Michimimackinac Historical Society; Rhea J. Smith, Mecosta County Historical Society; William K. Smith, Genesee County Library; George Southworth, Burton Historical Collection; Harry L. Spooner, Newaygo County Board of Education; Bernice Cox Springer, Burton Historical Collection; John Stafford, Gratiot County Herald; Theodore F. Stafford, postal historian, Kalamazoo; Clio M. Stinson, Montcalm County Board of Education; Virginia S. Stroemel, Manistee County Historical Society; Charles A. Symon, Munising News.

Helen M. Tague, city clerk, Swartz Creek; James R. Ticknor, Marine City Historical Association; Ruth M. Thomas, Menominee County Library; Viola E. Toben, city clerk, Berkley; Thomas Tobey, State Highway Department; Donald Toepfer, Kalamazoo Public Library; Lyle A. Torrant, Jackson County superintendent of schools; Fred R. Trelfa, Alpena News; Ethel K. Turner, village clerk, Lake Linden.

Philip H. Van Antwerp, Detroit councilman; Paul Van den Branden, city clerk, Centerline; Berenice (Mrs. L. L.) Vanderburg, Cass County Historical Society; Ruth H. Van Der Molen, Mason County Library; Carolyn Vander Weele, city clerk, Parchment; Eileen B. Van Horn, city clerk, Keego Harbor; Edward Van Solkema, city clerk, Wyoming.

Henry L. Wagner, city manager, Kingsford; Beth Ward, Dowagiac Public Library; Corinne J. Wascher, Willard Library, Battle Creek; William H. Whiteley, Presque Isle County Advance; Eleanor G. Whitney, Benton Harbor Public Library; Willard C. Wichers, Michigan Historical Commission; Margaret Williams, city clerk, Wakefield; Pearl S. Willis, city clerk, Wixom; Hon. Charles Willman, Ontonagon County Historical Society; Sylvia Wixson, Aitken Memorial Library, Croswell; Otto Woelke, village clerk, Pigeon; M. Louisa Wolcott, Missaukee County Historical Society; R. G. Worland, city clerk, Sturgis; Jean Worth, Escanaba Daily Press.

W. T. Yake, Detroit & Mackinaw Railway; Harriet J. Young, Carnegie Public Library, Charlotte; Bernard J. Youngblood, Wayne County register of deeds.